This Is America's Story

WIDELY ACCLAIMED CLASSIC IN A *NEW* EDITION

This is the history your students will enjoy learning.

Students become engrossed in ▶ **the narrative right from the start...** The writing is simple, forceful, and always to the point. Rich details about people from every walk of life give this account an unmatched vitality. See also pages 41, 103, 390, 472.

CHAPTER **4**

English Settlers Start Colonies in North America

1607–1733

1600	1650	1700

Puritans settle Boston
Dutch settle New Amsterdam
Pilgrims settle Plymouth
English settle Jamestown

English settle Georgia
Pennsylvania settled by Quakers
English capture New Amsterdam

What this chapter is about —

In September, 1620, a small group of brave men and women set sail from Plymouth, England. They were headed for North America in a tiny vessel called the *Mayflower*. The journey they undertook proved to be a hard one. Half-

96

way across the Atlantic the ship began to leak. The passengers were worried too when storms drove the ship far north of its course.

When they finally spotted the North American shoreline, the passengers were exhausted but relieved. Most waited in the *Mayflower* while some of

◀ Late in 1620 the *Mayflower* brought the Pilgrims to North America. There they started a colony and called it Plymouth.

their group searched the coast for a place to go ashore. During the month of waiting one of the women, Susannah White, gave birth to a baby boy. At last the search party located a suitable place for a settlement, one that they called Plymouth. After three months at sea, the newcomers could now start to build homes. They could begin their new lives in America.

Even before the group landed at Plymouth, another English settlement had been made far to the south in what is now Virginia. In the years that followed, still other groups landed along the coast of North America. These peo-

ple came to the new land [for] different reasons. Most of th[em were Eng]lish men and women, thou[gh there were] also people from other cou[ntries. From] the various settlements sta[rted by these] people grew colonies, wh[ich later] developed into the Unit[ed States of] America. In this chapter [you will read] about the early beginnings [of our coun]try. As you read the stor[y of the Eng]lish colonies, look for ans[wers to these] questions:

1. Why and how did peo[ple go to the] English colonies?
2. How did the first succe[ssful English] colony get its start?
3. How were the New E[ngland colo]nies started?
4. What Southern Co[lonies were] started?
5. How were the Mid[dle Colonies] started?

1 Why and How Did People Go to the English Colonies?

You remember that while Spain was building its huge colonial empire, England was still a small and weak country. England's growing strength was shown, however, when English ships defeated the Spanish Armada. By the early 1600's, English people began to take an interest in starting colonies of their own in North America.

At that time, the only way to cross the ocean was in small sailing ships. These were usually crowded and uncomfortable, and they were at the mercy of the wind and weather. It might take months to make the crossing, or the ships might be lost in the Atlantic gales and never reach their destination. Moreover, North America was little known. Why, then, were English

men and women willing to undergo the hardships that lay ahead of them if they became colonists?

Of course, some of them went to North America in a spirit of adventure just as the Spaniards did, hoping to find gold. But most of the English colonists had other reasons. Let us see what they were.

THE SETTLERS SEEK FREEDOM

America means freedom to earn a better living. There were several reasons why English men and women were ready to leave England for America. For one thing, most of the English people had once been farmers. They had rented land from wealthy landowners

◀ **Students learn systematically from the clear, chronological organization....** History builds from event to event, from cause to result. Unit and chapter introductions set the scene, section headings pose questions that focus the reading, and paragraph headings provide an outline of major topics. See also pages 72-73, 424-425, 516-517.

97

Skills to Practice (cont.)

to Fort Kaskaskia? **(c)** What forts did they capture after their victory at Kaskaskia?

Questions to Think About

1. Why did it take great courage for the members of the Continental Congress to vote for the Declaration of Independence?
2. Read again what Abigail Adams said about the Patriot cause on page 198. Why did she think the Patriots would not be "conquered" even if they were "defeated"? Explain in your own words what she meant.
3. Look back at the account of Nathan Hale on page 202. What do his words and actions tell us about his character?
4. American persistence, French aid, and British mistakes were major factors in the outcome of the Revolutionary War. Explain the importance of each.

Linking Past and Present

The Liberty Bell. The chief attraction in Independence Hall in Philadelphia is the grand old Liberty Bell. Although the Bell is chipped and cracked, you can see on it the date when it was made (1753) and the names of its makers. Around the base you can still read this inscription from the Bible: "Proclaim liberty throughout all the land unto all the inhabitants thereof." The Liberty Bell pealed out the birth of our nation in 1776 and later our victory in the Revolutionary War. Through the years it tolled in solemn tones to announce the deaths of beloved American patriots. In 1835 the Bell rang for the last time — it had cracked badly. On June 6, 1944, however, Americans heard its voice again, this time over a nation-wide radio broadcast. The Bell was struck with a rubber mallet to celebrate the landing of Allied troops on the coast of France during World War II.

The message of Valley Forge. Every year thousands of Americans visit places made famous during the Revolutionary War, places which remind us that our freedom was dearly bought. One spot a visitor never forgets is Valley Forge, Pennsylvania, where the Continental Army spent the winter of 1777–1778. The old camp grounds have been restored and look much as they did over 200 years ago. You see the crude log huts that gave poor shelter to Washington's ragged, hungry soldiers. Beyond are the grounds where, in spite of cold and snow, Baron von Steuben drilled the troops in preparation for the spring campaign. You see the houses where Washington, Lafayette, and other officers stayed. As you remember that desperate winter when the American cause seemed lost, you realize that Valley Forge is more than an old camp ground. It is a reminder of the spirit that rose above hardship and fear of defeat to win the independence we enjoy today.

The Stars and Stripes. Our flag is almost as old as the nation itself. For more than 200 years, it has flown over the land of the free. The design for our nation's first flag was voted upon by the Continental Congress on June 14, 1777. (We now celebrate that day each year as Flag Day.) It was agreed that this flag should have thirteen stripes — one for each state — alternating red and white, and thirteen white stars on a blue field.

For a while, a new stripe and a new star were added whenever a state joined the Union. But it soon became clear that this would spoil the beauty of the flag. So in 1818 the number of stripes was reduced to thirteen, but a star continued to be added for each new state. Our flag grew with our nation until in 1912 it had 48 stars. The number of stars remained the same until 1959, when Alaska and Hawaii were admitted to the Union. Today the flag proudly displays 50 stars on its field of blue.

212

◀ **Students learn how America's past enriches its present and future...** Lively vignettes at the end of each chapter link symbols, settings, and people of the past to present-day America. See also pages 66, 184, 266.

Students approach each period ▶ of history with a solid understanding of its place in time... Clear, concise unit and chapter introductions and time lines give students a preview of each historical era and place it in the broad scope of history. See also pages 186, 268, 374.

CHAPTER **3**

Spain Establishes a Great Empire

1500–1780

Balboa reaches Pacific Ocean

Spain conquers Mexico

Coronado explores Southwest

Spanish settle St. Augustine

Santa Fe settled

Spanish build mission at San Diego

What this chapter is about —

A gallant ship bearing the white-and-gold banner of Spain is heading eastward across the Atlantic. Its fore and aft decks are high above the water, and its sails are brightly decorated with paintings. High up in the crow's-nest a sailor looks anxiously in all directions for swift-sailing pirate ships. For this is a treasure galleon of the Spanish fleet, carrying riches to Spain. Piled in the hold are heavy bars of gold and silver, boxes of pearls and emeralds, chests of gold and silver ornaments. What a prize for a bold pirate!

72

This is the textbook that accommodates a variety of learning styles.

Students see history unfold on ▶ eighty-seven brilliant maps... An in-depth, full-color map program makes America's story more graphic, more exciting, more meaningful for all your students. See also pages 108, 205, 591.

FRENCH EXPLORERS PENETRATE NORTH AMERICA

Though Frobisher made two more voyages to the same region, he failed in his search for a Northwest Passage.

Champlain explores the Great Lakes region. Although explorer after explorer returned to Europe without having found a short cut to Asia, others were always ready to continue the search. Each hoped to succeed where others had failed. One of these was a French explorer named Samuel de Champlain (sham-PLAIN). Champlain came to America for the first time in 1603. For years he roamed the coasts and the forests, the rivers and the lakes of America.

Champlain explored the Atlantic coast all the way from the mouth of the St. Lawrence River to the southern part of what is now Massachusetts. He

MAP STUDY
The routes of three explorers for France are shown here. (a) Which explorer came to America first? (See the small inset map.) (b) How far up the St. Lawrence did Cartier travel? (c) What lakes did Champlain explore?

sailed up the St. Lawrence and started the town of Quebec, the first permanent French settlement in America. Continuing up the river to what is now Montreal, he turned south and pushed on to the southern end of a beautiful lake that has been named Lake Champlain in his honor. On a later trip Champlain traveled still farther inland, moving north and west from the St. Lawrence. He made his way along other rivers into the northern part of Lake Huron. From there he swung down to Lake Ontario

59

People in America's Story

GEORGE WASHINGTON

As commander of the Continental Army, chairman of the Constitutional Convention, and the first President of the United States, George Washington won a lasting place in American history as "Father of His Country."

Defense of the Virginia frontier was entrusted to young Colonel Washington during the French and Indian War.

Martha Custis (far right), shown with her two grandchildren, married the future President in 1759.

Washington rallied the hard-pressed American troops through the early years of the Revolution, including the grim winter at Valley Forge. In the painting below, Washington watches his troops pass in review.

199

◀ Students meet history makers face to face... The fascinating personalities of American history greet your students from portraits, prints, drawings, and photographs. To these revealing records of our ancestors, captions have been added with just enough description to complete the picture. Period art is used to give students authentic glimpses of our past. See also pages 114, 277, 413, 486.

GAINING SKILL

Reading Bar Graphs

How many people did our country have when the Constitution went into effect in 1789? Nobody knew at the time. To find out, the government in 1790 appointed 217 people to take a **census** (SEN-sus) — a count of the population. Throughout the thirteen states the census-takers went from door to door, asking how many people lived in each household. Every ten years since then, the government has taken a census.

Suppose you wanted to find out how the population of the nation grew in the thirty years following the first census. If you looked up census figures in a reference book, here is what you would find:

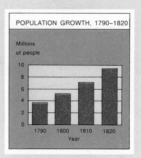

POPULATION GROWTH, 1790–1820

Millions of people

Year	Population
1790	3,929,214
1800	5,308,483
1810	7,239,881
1820	9,638,453

Information presented in this form (listed in columns) is called a **table.**

Another way of showing population figures is a **graph.** A graph is a drawing that helps you see the meaning of figures quickly and easily. The graph you see on this page is called a bar graph, since it uses columns or bars.

To read a graph, you need to know what the parts of the graph are and how they fit together. First, look at the title. It tells you what kind of information is given. Next, look at the horizontal axis — the information shown along the bottom of the graph. Third, look at the vertical axis — the numbers listed along the left side of the graph.

Notice that the numbers increase by equal amounts and are regularly spaced. In other words, if a bar stood for 4 million people, it would be exactly twice as tall as a bar that stood for 2 million people.

Now answer the following questions.
1. What kind of information is given in the graph? (Look at the title.)
2. For what years is the information given?
3. About how many people did the nation have in the first year shown on the graph?
4. Compare the bars for the [...] years shown. Between th[...] the nation's population (a[...] ble or **(b)** more than doub[...]
5. Compare the graph with [...] this page. Which of the t[...] more exact information? [...] you *see* the information n[...]

This is the program that teaches students the skills needed to study history.

◀ **Students learn to use historical data...** Lessons teach the use of maps, graphs, time lines, source material, and reference books. These skills are reinforced in map and graph captions, Chapter Check Ups, and end-of-unit activities. See also pages 67, 117, 369, 423.

CHECK UP ON CHAPTER 4

Words to Know

1. Pilgrim
2. charter
3. proprietor
4. tolerance
5. Puritan
6. Quaker
7. plantation
8. representative government
9. indentured servant
10. religious freedom
11. trading company
12. proprietary colony

Places to Locate

1. Jamestown
2. Plymouth
3. Boston
4. Providence
5. New Haven
6. Savannah
7. Charleston
8. New York (city)
9. Philadelphia
10. Delaware River
11. Connecticut River
12. Hartford

Facts to Remember

1. How did each of the following take part in the settling of an English colony? Name the colony and tell why the person was important. **(a)** John Smith **(b)** Roger Williams **(c)** Anne Hutchinson **(d)** James Oglethorpe **(e)** William Penn
2. **(a)** To what English colony did Africans first come? **(b)** Why were the Africans made slaves?
3. **(a)** What three colonies led the way in establishing freedom of religion?

(b) Explain why religious freedom was emphasized in each of those colonies.

Skills to Practice

1. Make a time line for the period 1600 to 1650. Mark off ten-year periods on the line. Then place the following dates on it: 1607, 1619, 1620, 1630, and 1649. Alongside each date write a phrase that tells why it was important. (*Example:* 1607, Jamestown started.)
2. Look at the map on page 108. **(a)** What group of colonies is shown in the inset map (the smaller map)? **(b)** What do the arrows on this map show? (Note that the arrows lead away from Massachusetts.) **(c)** What towns were started along the Connecticut River? **(d)** Were those towns southwest or southeast of Boston?

Questions to Think About

1. **(a)** Why were the first settlements in North America located near mouths of rivers or bays? **(b)** Why did people who left the earlier settlements often settle near rivers?
2. What freedoms that we cherish today had their beginnings in the English colonies?

115

Students find meaning in the ▶ American experience... This is the thoughtful American history that takes students beyond facts. Recall questions conclude every section. Chapter Check Ups review information, vocabulary, and skills, and provide discussion topics that strengthen students' understanding of history. See also pages 232-233, 265, 635, 638-639.

This Is America's Story...
Student Book
Teacher's Edition
Teacher's Key
Resource Book
Activity Book
Tests

TEACHER'S EDITION

This Is America's Story

WILDER   LUDLUM   BROWN

prepared by Susan A. Roberts

HOUGHTON MIFFLIN COMPANY   BOSTON

Atlanta   Dallas   Geneva, Ill.   Hopewell, N.J.   Palo Alto   Toronto

To the Teacher

The purpose of this Teacher's Edition is to help you use *This Is America's Story* to best advantage in planning and teaching your American history course. The Teacher's Edition consists of two parts: (1) this opening section of 72 pages (see table of contents on the facing page), and (2) the complete student textbook with teacher's annotations printed in color.

You will find the following supplementary publications also of great value:

1. The *Teacher's Key* provides answers for all study material in the student textbook and for exercises and tests in the *Resource Book* (and in the *Activity Book* and the *Tests* booklet).

2. The *Resource Book* provides black-line masters of activity sheets for all 32 chapters, of tests for chapters and units, and of a midterm and a final examination.

3. The *Activity Book* provides, in the form of a student booklet, all the activity sheets from the *Resource Book*.

4. The *Tests* provides, in booklet form, all chapter and unit tests and the midterm and final examinations from the *Resource Book*.

The Teacher's Edition was written by Susan A. Roberts. Dr. Roberts teaches history in Del Norte High School, Albuquerque, New Mexico. She also wrote the *Resource Book*.

Student's Edition ISBN: 0-395-31145-4

Teacher's Edition ISBN: 0-395-31765-7

Contents *Teacher's Edition*

Teaching Suggestions

Complete student's text with annotations
(See table of contents on pages 5–13.)

Teaching *This Is America's Story*

You are about to introduce your students to a great adventure — following the dramatic story of America from pre-Columbian times to the present. You will want your students to learn about the people and events that have shaped their country and made it a land of opportunity and a leader among the nations of the world. You will also want your students to learn to appreciate the foundations of our society and to understand the responsibilities of citizens in a free nation. This textbook is designed to help you and your students achieve those goals.

OBJECTIVES OF THE TEXTBOOK

This Is America's Story has been planned to meet three broad objectives: (1) to tell America's story in an interesting and understandable way, (2) to develop study skills, and (3) to build an appreciation of our nation's heritage.

Telling America's Story. The narrative of this textbook has been planned to provide a comprehensive chronological account of American history. Unit 1 of *This Is America's Story* begins with background information about the first Americans and about developments in Europe that led to exploration and colonization. Unit 2 covers the founding of colonies in America by the English, French, and Spanish and describes the development of ways of living in those three colonial empires. The events that led the English colonists to break away from Great Britain and to fight for their independence are told in Unit 3. That unit also presents the struggle of people in Canada and Latin America to gain greater self-determination. Unit 4 emphasizes the birth and growth of the United States as a republic under the Constitution. The structure and processes of our constitutional system of government are explained, and the story of how our young nation gained the respect of other countries is told. In Unit 5 the textbook describes important changes in the development of different sections of the United States in the first half of the nineteenth century. The story of the expansion of the United States across the continent begins

Unit 6. That unit then explores our nation's division and reunion during the era of the Civil War. The narrative goes on in Unit 7 to examine the shaping of modern America following the Civil War. Changes that resulted from powerful postwar forces and which had far-reaching impact on people's lives are the focus of Unit 8. In Unit 9 students will read about the expansion of American interests and territories beyond the North American continent and the emergence of the United States as a world leader. Finally, Unit 10 tells the nation's story since 1920.

Logical organization is an important characteristic of the narrative of *This Is America's Story*. Students will find that the pattern of organization, visible throughout the narrative, will guide their reading and study. Unit previews, unit and chapter time lines, chapter introductions concluded by guide questions, section and chapter check ups, and unit reviews provide a clear-cut structure for students to follow. Section, column, and paragraph headings, moreover, provide immediate guidance for specific reading assignments.

Effective learning cannot take place if students have to struggle with a textbook written in language beyond their comprehension. Special care has been taken to ensure that students can both read and comprehend *This Is America's Story*. The narrative is written in language that is straightforward and appropriate to the student level of experience. Since vocabulary development is also vital to students' mastery of content, boldface type is used in *This Is America's Story* to highlight the first appearance in the narrative of key words. Difficult or unfamiliar words are defined or explained within the text narrative. For review, these words are listed in "Words to Know" at the end of each chapter. Key words and terms are also listed and defined in the Glossary (pages 719–723).

Personalization is a device often used in the narrative to present material that otherwise might prove difficult for students to grasp. Students will learn about life in the Spanish colonies, for example, from a series of imaginary letters written by "Philip Andrews," a fifteen-year-old visitor to New Spain in the early 1700's (pages 86–90). Another example is the personalized discussion of the business cycle on pages 501–504. This account explains such concepts as *boom, depression,* and *monopoly* by telling how economic developments affected the business of an imaginary furniture manufacturer and his employees in the 1890's. Note, too, the dramatic fashion in which the break between the North and the South in the 1850's is told in Chapter 19 (pages 412–417).

Since the use of illustration also adds meaning to historical content, the pictures in *This Is America's Story* provide an effective teaching resource. Pictures such as those on pages 90, 138–139, and 204 help to capture students' interest and provide additional insights into events of the past. When the stages of an event or the factors involved in understanding an important issue need special clarification, a graphic treatment is provided. See, for example, the drawings that explain "Why English Settlers Went to America" (pages 98–99) and "What the Different Sections Wanted" (pages 350–351). Maps, graphs, and charts throughout *This Is America's Story* also contribute to students' understanding.

Because the narrative is interesting and understandable, and because maps, pictures, graphs, and charts are effectively coordinated with the narrative, *This Is America's Story* can be successfully used in classes with a variety of learning styles. Teachers will find many suggestions in the *Teacher's Edition* for using the textbook to meet the needs of different students. These suggestions appear on pages T14–T57 and also in the annotations on student pages in the *Teacher's Edition*.

Developing Study Skills. The second broad objective of *This Is America's Story* is to help students develop study skills. Students will find in this textbook many opportunities to learn and practice important skills.

As a prelude to skill development, students need to find out how to use the textbook they will be studying in their American history course. As a tool for helping students get acquainted with the textbook, teachers can use the pages called "How This Book Tells America's Story" (pages 16–19). Discussing this section with students early in the course will prepare them to make full use of the textbook's many features in pursuing their study.

For actual instruction in specific skills, the textbook provides a "Gaining Skill" lesson at the end of each chapter. (You will see the titles of these lessons in the table of contents of the student book, pages 5–13. Also see the chart on page T11.) Each of these lessons teaches a specific skill, by leading students through a series of steps that define the skill and then by providing opportunities to practice it.

The skills introduced in these "Gaining Skill" lessons are many and varied. Students will learn the use of maps, graphs and other charts, time lines, pictures, source material, and reference books. Study skills, such as using the library, preparing for reports, and studying for tests, are included as well. Additional opportunities for practice and reinforcement then appear throughout the book. Maps, charts, and graphs closely correlated to the narrative provide practice in using such materials. Captions for maps and graphs ask questions that reinforce students' skills. Unit and chapter time lines help to develop students' understanding of chronology. Students also learn to "read" pictures — that is, to look at pictures and think about the information or understanding to be derived from them.

Reading source material is still another study skill developed in *This Is America's Story*. A number of carefully selected passages from source material appear throughout the narrative, thus acquainting students with the value of first-hand materials in the study of history.

In every Chapter Check Up, students will find a set of exercises called "Skills to Practice" which calls for them to use skills they have learned in previous chapters. In the list of "Things to Do" at the end of each unit, students will find activities that also involve the use of various skills. Still additional opportunities for skill reinforcement are provided in the *Resource Book*. (See page T13.)

The following chart identifies the specific skills taught in the "Gaining Skill" lessons and shows where additional practice is provided throughout the textbook.

Skill Development in *This Is America's Story*

The chart below shows how this textbook's skill program is organized. The first column of page numbers identifies the "Gaining Skill" lessons where skills are introduced. The final column shows where opportunities for additional practice are provided. Even further opportunity for skill practice is provided in the activity pages of the *Resource Book*.

	Skill	*Introduced*	*Additional practice*
Maps	Using the grid system	47	55, 67
	Locating places	67	*
	Tracing routes and finding directions	95	*
	Using scale	231	284, 310, 710
	Reading special purpose maps	313, 423, 531	472, 596
Graphs, charts, and tables	Reading diagrams	167	174, 254, 257, 328, 343
	Reading bar graphs	267	307, 317, 481, 538, 701
	Reading circle graphs	329	426, 704
	Reading pictographs	403	421, 567
	Reading line graphs	499	519, 646, 711
	Reading tables	555	667
	Reading flow charts	599	677
Chronology	Building a sense of time	117	134, 284, 452, 636, 710
	Reading time lines	213	230, 312, 368, 498
Pictures	Reading pictures	135	*
	Using historic photographs	477	498, 502, 544, 554, 565
	Reading political cartoons	637	554, 565, 639, 649
Primary and secondary sources	Using primary sources	185	211, 249, 328, 402
	Finding points of view in primary sources	251	475, 636, 637, 649
	Comparing primary and secondary sources	345	367
	Comparing points of view	515	637
	Distinguishing fact from opinion	577	617, 682
	Evaluating information	617	666
Research and study	Using reference books	149	166, 265, 713
	Using the library	285	287, 533, 579, 639, 713
	Preparing reports	369	371, 533, 579, 639, 713
	Studying for tests	453	455, 533, 579, 639, 713
	Exploring local history	683	713

*Additional practice is provided throughout the textbook.

Building Appreciation of the Nation's Heritage. In order to accomplish the third broad goal — building in students an appreciation and understanding of their nation, *This Is America's Story* focuses on the values and ideals, rights and obligations, and laws and institutions that Americans have established and cherished through the years. In this book students will read about American ideals which developed in colonial times and found expression in the Declaration of Independence and the Constitution. The narrative honors the achievements of the American people as they established homes, farms, industries, transportation systems, towns, and cities across the continent, thus contributing to the growth and development of modern America. The narrative also seeks to present balanced accounts of events that became special concerns of the nation. It points out, for example, the inhumanity of slavery while helping students understand why slavery existed, and presents in honest terms the conflict that developed between cultures as white settlers took over Indian lands.

This goal of developing student awareness of traditional American values is given special emphasis as the students begin their study of the textbook. An introductory section called "This Is America" (beginning on page 20) focuses on the United States as a "land of promise" (page 21) and a "land of progress" (page 22). Similarly a closing section called "America Faces the Future" (pages 714–717) reminds students of their nation's traditions, ideals, and institutions and encourages them to think about their role as future citizens.

The teaching of American history traditionally highlights the memory of men and women who made significant contributions to our heritage. *This Is America's Story* maintains that tradition. Individuals and their stories fill the pages of the textbook, thus bringing the account to life in the minds of young readers. Moreover, in the series of pictorial features called "People in America's Story" (listed on page 15), major figures in American history are given special recognition. Individuals who have served in the nation's highest office also are highlighted in the pictorial features called "Our Presidents" (listed on page 15). Patriotic landmarks and symbols are dealt with as well, especially in the "Linking Past and Present" features at the ends of chapters. Among the landmarks and symbols told about in "Linking Past and Present" are Jamestown, Slater's mill, Andrew Jackson's home, great cities of the West, places where Abraham Lincoln lived, the national parks, the Tomb of the Unknown Soldier, the Liberty Bell, the Statue of Liberty, the flag, and the *Arizona* monument at Pearl Harbor.

Helping students develop a confidence in their nation's future is yet another aspect of this third objective of *This Is America's Story*. As a way of achieving that goal, the textbook focuses on what the United States has meant to its citizens. In the early chapters students learn why people left Europe to seek a new life in America. Thus, students become aware of the fact that from its very beginnings America has been regarded as a land of opportunity. Continuing their study, students learn about the promise of equality in the Declaration of Independence and the guarantee of individual rights in the Constitution. Further study reveals how America has continued to attract newcomers and how more groups within the nation's population — black Americans, Hispanic Americans, Indians, Asian Americans, and women — have attained their rights and made use of new opportunities. Students can feel proud that the United States is a nation where freedom, liberty, and individual rights are cherished and protected.

Confidence in the nation's future as a world leader is also developed in the text. In Chapter 13 students find out how the young United States gained the respect of other nations of the world. The increased involvement of the nation in world affairs during the twentieth century is given substantial treatment in Units 9 and 10. The narrative tells students about their country's participation in two world wars, one to "make the world safe for democracy" and one to preserve freedom in a world threatened by totalitarian dictatorships. The Marshall Plan, which students read about in Chapter 31, is an example of United States foreign policy in which students can take pride. By studying the lessons of American foreign relations, students can feel confident that the United States will continue to be a nation dedicated to the preservation of freedom within the community of nations.

In such ways, *This Is America's Story* carries out its three broad objectives. By providing thorough coverage of content along with a program for skill development, the textbook enables students to succeed. In addition, the textbook promotes an appreciation of the American heritage, an understanding of how the United States became what it is today, and a confidence in the nation's future.

ADDITIONAL AIDS

The authors and publisher of *This Is America's Story* have sought to make this book an effective classroom tool for busy teachers. To facilitate classroom management and to add to the teaching value of *This Is America's Story,* a number of additional aids are offered as part of the total program.

Teacher's Edition. The purpose of this *Teacher's Edition* is to help you use *This Is America's Story* most effectively in planning and teaching your American history course. The *Teacher's Edition* (1) includes this 72-page guide which you are now reading and (2) provides teacher's annotations on the student pages.

Teachers will find many valuable suggestions in the chapter strategy pages (T14–T57) of the 72-page guide. Chapter objectives are provided at the beginning of the strategy section for each chapter (see page T15, for example). Unit preview ideas and chapter "getting started" and "wrap-up" strategies are included as well. One or more classroom strategies are then provided for each section of the chapter. In these strategies teachers will find a great variety of learning activities — suggestions for class discussions and debates, topics for student research and reports, picture projects, bulletin board displays, chart and list-making, additional map work, and more.

Similarly the annotations on the student pages in this *Teacher's Edition* provide a wealth of teaching ideas. Some annotations suggest guide questions for class discussion of specific topics or provide additional information and insights. Some annotations provide reminders of especially useful parts of the book. Others suggest activities or areas for additional student research. Annotations also indicate to teach-ers those spots in the text where related strategies appear in these front pages of the *Teacher's Edition.*

Book and audiovisual lists, arranged by units, appear on pages T58–T71 of the *Teacher's Edition.* For each unit, the bibliography includes (1) a list of titles valuable for the teacher's background information and (2) a list of books suitable for students. Both nonfiction and fiction titles are included in the student lists. The audiovisual list suggests films and filmstrips appropriate for use with each of the ten units.

Teacher's Key. The separate booklet called the *Teacher's Key* provides answers for all study questions in *This Is America's Story* and also for exercises and tests in the *Resource Book* (and in the *Activity Book* and the *Tests* booklet).

Resource Book. An especially important aid for teachers using *This Is America's Story* is the collection of black-line masters called the *Resource Book.* The Resource Book provides three kinds of material: (1) In the activity pages, teachers will find a variety of exercises and activities for all 32 chapters of the textbook. Both content review and skill practice are provided for in the activity pages. In addition, the final page of each chapter of the *Resource Book* offers directions for a project different from conventional workbook exercises. These project activities are especially useful in providing opportunities for every student to experience success.

(2) A full set of black-line test masters are also included in the *Resource Book.* Tests are provided for all 32 chapters and 10 units of *This Is America's Story.* A midterm examination (covering the narrative up through the reconstruction period) and a final examination are included as well. Test items have objective answers and are focused on understanding of content.

(3) Finally, the key pages of the *Resource Book* offer full answers to exercises on the activity pages and in the tests, as well as suggestions for classroom management of project activities. A chart correlating chapter objectives and test items is provided.

Activity Book and *Tests.* For those teachers who prefer to use student booklets, the pages of the *Resource Book* are available in two separate publications: the *Activity Book* and the *Tests* booklet.

UNIT 1   Preview

Have students read the title of Unit 1 on page 24. Ask: What areas of the world will be studied in this unit? (Europe, Asia, and the American continents.) What brought people from these areas together? (The search for an ocean route to Asia.) Now direct student attention to the unit time line. Point out that this time line shows how Europeans gradually extended their geographic knowledge of the world through exploration. Tell students that the pictures on pages 24 and 25 tell the story of European exploration in another way. During the 1300's Crusaders brought Europeans into contact with parts of the Middle East. Tools of navigation, like the compass and map pictured on page 25, enabled Columbus and others to make their long ocean voyages. Now have students read the introduction on page 25. Discuss what the title of Unit 1, the time line, the pictures, and the introduction all contribute to the story of European exploration.

CHAPTER 1   (pages 26–47)
Explorers Find the American Continents

STUDENT OBJECTIVES

After completing their study of Chapter 1, students will be able to:

1. Identify changes that led to European exploration.
2. Explain why western Europeans were interested in finding new routes to Asia.
3. Tell how Portugal discovered an all-water route to the East.
4. Explain why Columbus sailed west, and evaluate the importance of Columbus's voyage.

TEACHING STRATEGIES

Getting Started. Have students open their textbooks to page 26 and give them five minutes to preview the material in this chapter. Point out the numbered section titles (pages 27, 35, and 40). Ask students to look for the headings *within* each section. At the end of the five minutes have them close their books. Then either outline the chapter as a class, writing student responses on the board, or have each student write an outline to hand in. This teaching strategy may help identify students with reading problems.

An alternative way to open the chapter is to have students look at the opening picture and the time line on page 26. How does the picture tie in with the class's preview discussion of Unit 1? And how does the chapter time line compare with the unit time line?

SECTION 1 (PAGES 27–35)

Student Reports. Give students an opportunity to learn more about the lives of medieval serfs. Make the assignment flexible, based, if you wish, on *one* of these suggestions: Have students (1) write a one-week diary of entries that reflect the day-to-day life of a serf (even though serfs could not, of course, read or write); (2) draw or make a model of a manor, serf's cottage, typical furniture in a cottage, or clothing of that period; (3) do outside reading and report back to the class on the obligations of both serfs and nobles; (4) do outside reading and report to the class on how a serf could become free.

Map Study. Students will understand this chapter better if they refer to the maps that accompany the narrative. Help the class review map-reading skills by teaching the skill lesson, "Reading Maps: Using the Grid System" (page 47).

Using Text Headings. After they have read Section 1 (pages 27–35), have students begin with the boldfaced heading "The Crusades help to increase trade" on page 30 and reread the remaining headings through the rest of the section. Help students see that these headings present a sequence of events. Ask students to use the headings to identify the changes that led to European exploration. This exercise demonstrates to students that the textbook's headings present main ideas and will be helpful to them in their reading.

SECTION 2 (PAGES 35–39)

Class Discussion. Divide students into groups of five and have each student take one of the following parts: a ship captain, a student of navigation, a map maker, a traveler, or a shipbuilder at Prince Henry's school of navigation (page 36). Give the groups fifteen minutes to discuss what contributions each might have made in helping the sailors and ships of Portugal become the finest of those times. Then discuss as a class how Prince Henry and his school of navigation enabled Portugal to establish its water route to India (page 38).

Bulletin Board. Take students to the school library and have them locate information on the achievements of the West African kingdoms of the 1400's. Whatever material students find, pictorial or narrative, should be used to put together a bulletin board display. The display could include written reports, maps, drawings, and time lines.

SECTION 3 (PAGES 40–45)

Identifying Points of View. Several European monarchs turned down the chance to sponsor Columbus's voyage before Queen Isabella agreed to finance his trip. Tell this to students and have them read the textbook account (pages 40–41). Afterwards, have them write three paragraphs on Columbus and his plan to sail west. The paragraphs are to present three different views: one favorable, one unfavorable, and a third which balances both points of view. (You may prefer to have students work on this activity in groups and include drawings of maps to bolster the viewpoints expressed in their paragraphs.)

Student Reports. Have students use their textbooks and library sources to prepare written reports on Christopher Columbus. Tell them to cover these topics in their reports: (1) details about the early life of Columbus, (2) the difficul-ties he had preparing for his first voyage, (3) facts about his voyages to the Americas, (4) details of his later life. Refer students to the feature on Columbus (page 44). Remind students to include appropriate maps and drawings in their reports.

Chapter Wrap Up. After students have studied the chapter, you might have them repeat the outline exercise presented in "Getting Started" and compare their final outlines with their initial efforts.

Evaluation. Review Chapter 1 by using the Chapter Check Up (pages 45–46).

See the *Resource Book* for activity sheets (pages 3–6) and test (pages 135–136).

CHAPTER 2 (pages 48–67)
Europeans Learn More About America

STUDENT OBJECTIVES
After completing their study of Chapter 2, students will be able to:

1. Describe the ways of life of three Indian groups in North America at the time of the earliest European explorations.
2. Identify European explorers who tried to find short cuts to Asia through America.
3. Explain the significance of Magellan's voyage.
4. Describe the routes of early explorers in the interior of North America.
5. List the European countries that claimed land in North America about 1700 and locate those claims on a map.

TEACHING STRATEGIES

Getting Started. Much of the material in this chapter centers on map study. As an introduction to geographic names, distribute outline maps of North America. (See *Resource Book.*) Without allowing the use of resource material, ask students to label Canada, the United States, and Mexico and then to draw in (where necessary) and label the following: Atlantic Ocean, Caribbean Sea, Pacific Ocean, Mississippi River, Rocky Mountains, St. Lawrence River, Lake Ontario, Hudson Bay, Lake Superior, Lake Michigan, Lake Erie, Lake Huron, and the Gulf of Mexico.

After the students have finished their maps, have the class read the chapter introduction (pages 48–49). Tell them that the explorers of North America found the places students labeled on their maps. Then have students turn to the map on page 37 and hold a class discussion on how little Europeans knew about the world before their explorations of North and South America. Keep the students' maps for future reference. You may want to tie this map study into the chapter skill lesson, "Reading Maps: Locating Places" (page 67).

SECTION 1 (PAGES 49–52)

Comparison. After students have read Section 1, ask them to compare and contrast Iroquois, Cheyenne, and Hopi ways of life. Using the following categories to guide the discussion, write students' responses on the board: region where each group lived, kind of land, dwellings, sources of food, role of women, ceremonial life, relations with neighbors. Ask if there were more similarities or more differences among the three groups. Remind students that Europeans in the period of exploration assumed that all Indians were members of a single group, but that today we know that there were many different groups.

Chart-Making. Have students make a chart of lasting contributions of the Indians. Have them start with the contributions mentioned in the paragraph on page 52; also point out the material on foods from "Linking Past and Present" (page 66). Other possibilities for student research are irrigation and handcrafts.

SECTION 2 (PAGES 52–56)

Class Discussion. Have students read the boldfaced heads on page 53 ("Columbus fails to find Asia" and "Cabot also fails to find Asia"). Point out that Columbus has been credited with finding America and that Cabot reached the northern coast of North America. Ask: What is a *failure?* What is a *success?* Why did people in the 1400's consider these individuals to be failures? Why has it taken later events to show that the voyages of these two men were achievements, not failures? Discuss how the perspective of history can change the interpretation of particular events.

Debate. Divide the class into two groups and have them debate this question: Who made the more important contribution to the Age of Discovery, Columbus or Magellan? At the end of the debate, have the class evaluate the achievements of both explorers.

SECTION 3 (PAGES 56–63)

Map Study. As the students read the section, they should trace the route of each explorer on the text maps, paying special attention to geographic names and locations.

Student Research. After students have read Section 3, ask: What was the first permanent French settlement established in America? (Quebec, page 59.) Who started it? (Champlain.) Tell students the following were also established by the French: Biloxi, Mississippi; Mobile, Alabama; Baton Rouge, Louisiana; and Detroit, Michigan. Have students use library sources to answer the following questions about *one* of these cities: (1) When was it started? (2) Who established it? (3) How many people live there today? (4) What makes the city unique?

SECTION 4 (PAGES 63–65)

Class Discussion. Help students become aware that during the period of time covered in this chapter (from Columbus's later voyages to La Salle's journey to the mouth of the Missis-sippi River), European geographic knowledge greatly expanded (page 63). Discuss this great advance in European understanding. Ask students how the new interest in learning discussed in Chapter 1 related to this growth of knowledge. What other events covered in Chapters 1 and 2 contributed to expanded knowledge? Can students think of any other advance in learning, science, or technology that happened as quickly or had as great an impact? (Students might mention electricity, airplanes, atomic energy, space travel, electronics.)

Finding Criteria. Have the class set up criteria for the rule of "finders, keepers" as it might apply to the nations of the world today. Is there any land remaining on earth that is available for finding and claiming? Ask if nations have claimed land in Antarctica, for example. (They have.) Can nations lay claim to parts of the oceans? (Yes. Nations can claim *territorial waters.*)

Chapter Wrap Up. Repeat the "Getting Started" strategy. Have students, again with no outside aids, locate places on a blank map of North America. Return their first maps and let them see how much they have learned about geographic locations in North America.

Evaluation. Review Chapter 2 by using the Chapter Check Up (pages 65–66).

See the *Resource Book* for activity sheets (pages 7–10) and test (pages 137–138).

Concluding Unit 1. See unit summary, review, and activities on pages 68–69. See *Resource Book,* pages 139–140, for unit test.

UNIT 2   Preview

Have students read the title of Unit 2 and look at the time line and pictures on pages 70-71. Remind students that a good story answers five important questions: Who? What? When? Where? and Why? Ask: What part of the story does the unit title tell? (*Who* was involved, *what* they were doing, and *where* the activity was taking place.) Say Pizarro and Cartier (shown in two of the pictures) were among the Europeans who came to the Americas. Then ask what part of the story the time line tells. (*When* the process of colonization and empire-building took place.) Have students read the unit introduction on page 71. Ask students to identify *why* some Europeans came to the Americas. (English settlers came to find new opportunities and a freer way of life.)

CHAPTER 3   (pages 72–95)
Spain Establishes a Great Empire

STUDENT OBJECTIVES
After completing their study of Chapter 3, students will be able to:

1. Use maps to identify the extent of the Spanish Empire.
2. List three conquistadors and describe their conquests.
3. Describe how different groups of people lived in Spanish American colonies.
4. Explain how England and other nations threatened Spain's power.

TEACHING STRATEGIES

Getting Started. On the board, write the phrase "When Spain moves, the whole world trembles" (page 85). Discuss what this phrase means. Next have students read the introduction to Chapter 3 (pages 72–73). Ask them how the information on these pages further explains the meaning of the phrase. Finally, discuss how other nations might have felt about Spain. How might other nations have chosen to attack Spain's power? Tell students that they will discover specific answers to these questions as they read Chapter 3.

SECTION 1 (PAGES 73–85)

Comparison. Have students compare and contrast the explorations and conquests of Balboa, Pizarro, and Cortés. Ask these questions: With what part of North or South America was each involved? Who had the support of the Spanish government? Who did not? What did each achieve? In what ways does the term *conquistador* fit all three? What was the signifi-

cance of their exploits? (For answers have students refer to pages 83 and 85.) Use this strategy either for in-class discussion or as a written assignment.

Reading for a Purpose. Have students gather additional information about the Incas and Aztecs. You may want to ask students to add Inca and Aztec accomplishments to the chart of Indian contributions they made while studying Chapter 2 (page T15). Discuss with the class how the Incas and Aztecs compare to the Iroquois, Cheyenne, and Hopi.

Map Study. Introduce the skill lesson, "Reading Maps: Tracing Routes and Finding Directions" (page 95). Then reinforce the skill lesson with the following strategy. Assign students one of these explorers: Coronado, Ponce de León, Cabeza de Vaca, Estevanico, or de Soto. On a map have students trace the route taken by their explorer. Then have students write three or four questions relating to direction. You could also have students construct maps showing the routes of the explorers.

SECTION 2 (PAGES 86–90)

Class Discussion. Have students find the boldfaced term in Section 2. (The term is *viceroy*, page 86.) Tell students to use the glossary to find the meaning of the term. Then point out that the term can also mean "representative of a sovereign or king." Ask: In what ways did Spanish viceroys *represent* Spanish monarchs? (See pages 86–87.)

Student Research. Remind students that Mexico City was the capital of New Spain and the largest, most splendid city in Spanish America (pages 88–89). Then have students use their textbooks and library sources to find out these details about Mexico City: (1) Mexico City is built upon the site of what famous Aztec city? (Tenochtitlán.) (2) The city lies within what geographic feature? (Valley of Mexico.) (3) What did the Spanish build in 1629 to control floods in Mexico City? (A huge canal that drained rain water and a near-by lake.) (4) For how long did Spain control Mexico City? (Three hundred years.) (5) In the 1980's, Mexico City was the largest metropolitan area in which hemisphere? (Western Hemisphere.)

Chart-Making. Have students make a list of some of the lasting influences of Spanish America. Refer them specifically to the material in "Linking Past and Present" (page 94).

SECTION 3 (PAGES 91–93)

Identifying Viewpoints. Point out that observers view events differently. Ask: How would the English have viewed Drake's exploits? How would the Spanish have viewed his exploits? Students can practice looking at events from different perspectives. Tell them to write three short newspaper articles about Drake's adventures, one for an English newspaper, one for a Spanish newspaper, and one for the newspaper of a country not involved in the conflict between Spain and England. Discuss the criteria for a balanced account.

Group Work. Point out to students that the events surrounding the defeat of the Spanish Armada have the elements of an adventure story: action, suspense, and conflict. Divide the class into groups. Have each group illustrate the events in this story. (Students could illustrate the following: Spanish ships leaving the coast of Spain, English and Spanish ships clash-ing in the English Channel, fire ships and storms aiding English efforts.) Have groups write captions beneath the illustrations and a paragraph that summarizes the significance of the battle.

Chapter Wrap Up. Remind students of their discussion of Spain's power (see strategy on page T17). Ask students to list ways that Spain's power was evident. Discuss the events that enabled other European nations to gain a foothold in the Americas.

Evaluation. Review Chapter 3 by using the Chapter Check Up (pages 93–94).

See the *Resource Book* for activity sheets (pages 11–14) and test (pages 141–142).

CHAPTER 4 (pages 96–117)
English Settlers Start Colonies in North America

STUDENT OBJECTIVES
After completing their study of Chapter 4, students will be able to:

1. List reasons that led people to go to the English colonies.
2. Describe how Jamestown got its start.
3. Explain how the New England Colonies were started.
4. Explain how the Southern Colonies were started.
5. Explain how the Middle Colonies were started.
6. Identify important leaders in the colonies.

TEACHING STRATEGIES

Getting Started. Tell the class to plan a colony. The colony must be open to all people and all settlers are to be given land. Discuss the factors that could cause a colony to fail. Then divide the class into groups. Have the groups answer the following questions: Where should the colony be located? Who will settle in the colony? How is the colony going to be financed? What rules and regulations will be necessary for people living in the colony? Have each group share its plan with the rest of the class. This strategy will help to emphasize the kinds of questions the English settlers dealt with when they made their plans to colonize North America.

SECTION 1 (PAGES 97–101)

Class Discussion. Point out that America meant freedom to many English colonists in the early 1600's. Have students help you identify what kinds of freedom were sought. (See pages 98–99.) Ask: Why could poor people expect to be able to own land in America? How would distance from England increase the likelihood of religious freedom? Of self-government? Point out that the colonists brought with them more than just clothing, tools, supplies, and so forth. They brought *ideas* and *hopes*. Discuss how their ideas and hopes have contributed to our American heritage.

Identifying Main Ideas. Help students identify the main ideas of Section 1. Ask: How were colonies financed? What groups of people settled the colonies? How was slavery started in the colonies?

SECTION 2 (PAGES 101–104)

Class Discussion. Discuss why the colony of Jamestown eventually proved successful. List the reasons that students suggest on the board. (The colony was sponsored by a company; John Smith was a strong leader; new settlers and provisions arrived from England; colonists found a product they could trade with England.)

Chronological Order. Introduce the skill lesson, "Building a Sense of Time" (page 117). Then have students extract the dates in Section 2 (1607, 1609, 1619), list why they are significant, and arrange them in chronological order. (Remind students that some dates may be significant for more than one reason.) Ask: In what century did these events occur? (The events occurred in the 1600's, or the seventeenth century.)

SECTION 3 (PAGES 105–110)

Comparison. Have students compare the Pilgrims with the Puritans. Categories for comparison might include their religion, their treatment in England, their arrangements for coming to America, the number who came, the location of their colony, their livelihood in America, and the growth of their colony.

Class Discussion. Discuss how religious freedom developed in the English colonies. Help students to understand how lack of religious freedom in England led Puritans to migrate to Massachusetts Bay and how religious intolerance in Massachusetts Bay led to the starting of Rhode Island. Tell students to note how other colonies contributed to the development of freedom of religion. (Toleration Act, page 110.) After they have read this chapter, students could list in chronological order the steps that led to freedom of religion.

SECTION 4 (PAGES 110–112)

Bulletin Board. Have students put together a bulletin board display featuring various aspects of colonial life in the 1700's. The display could include: (1) drawings of colonial houses (such as the ones pictured on page 110); (2) lists of materials used to make colonial houses (for example, logs, reeds, and bricks); (3) pictures and definitions of colonial furnishings (for example, tinderboxes, trenchers, highboys, canopies, and rocking chairs); (4) descriptions of colonial clothing (for example, cocked hats, panniers); (5) lists of favorite colonial foods (for example, johnnycake, corn pone, hominy). Tell students to add to the display as they study the next chapter.

Class Discussion. Discuss southern agriculture. Ask: What important crops did Southerners grow? How did southern agriculture lead to the purchase of more and more slaves by planta-

tion owners? What country bought raw materials from the Southern Colonies? At the end of class, have students help you summarize the main points of the discussion on the board.

SECTION 5 (PAGES 112–115)

Student Research. Have students turn to the picture of William Penn on page 114. Then have them use their textbooks and library sources to answer the following questions: (1) When was Penn born? (October 14, 1644.) (2) Where did Penn become interested in the Quaker religion? (In Ireland, managing his father's estates.) (3) How many times was Penn imprisoned for his religious beliefs? (Three times.) (4) When did Penn first see his colony? (In 1682.) When did Penn die, and where? (He died in England in 1718.)

Outside Reading. Have students examine the elements that made the colony of Pennsylvania prosper. Ask students to report on one of the following: the types of settlers that were attracted to the colony; the plans Penn drew up for Philadelphia; the way land was distributed to the colonists; the government of the colony; the relationship of the Indians to the colonists. Students will need to do outside reading in order to prepare their written or oral reports.

Chapter Wrap Up. Discuss the elements of successful colonization by focusing on one of the colonies.

Evaluation. Review Chapter 4 by using the Chapter Check Up (pages 115–116).

See the *Resource Book* for activity sheets (pages 15–18) and test (pages 143–144).

CHAPTER 5   (pages 118–135)
How Did People Live in the English Colonies?

STUDENT OBJECTIVES

After completing their study of Chapter 5, students will be able to:

1. Use a map to show how mountains, rivers, and harbors affected the development of the colonies.
2. List ways in which the colonists made their living.
3. Identify products that were produced in the New England, Middle, and Southern colonies.
4. Compare attitudes toward religion and education in the New England, Middle, and Southern colonies.
5. List challenges that settlers on the frontier faced.

TEACHING STRATEGIES

Getting Started. Help students understand how geographical conditions can affect the development of a colony. Ask: Why would farming become important to an area that had rich soil and a warm climate? Why would trading and fishing develop in an area with many large harbors? Why might settlements be located along rivers? Why might mountains cause the colonies to remain isolated from one another? Tell students to study the map on page 130, noting the location of mountainous areas, rivers, and harbors.

As they read Chapter 5, tell students to note how geographical conditions affected the colonists in different areas.

SECTION 1 (PAGES 119–123)

Chart-Making. Have students set up a chart that will help them compare ways of living in different English colonies. Make four columns across the chart, labeling the columns *New England Colonies, Southern Colonies, Middle Colonies,* and *frontier region.* Down the left-hand side of the chart, have them use the following headings: *ways of earning a living, homes, furniture, food, clothes, religion, education,* and *use of leisure time.* Students should fill in the appropriate information for the New England colonies as they study Section 1. The remainder of the chart should be completed as students progress through the chapter.

SECTION 2 (PAGES 124–127)

Reading Pictures. Tell the class that pictures can be sources of factual information and ask students to sharpen their picture-reading skills. Teach the skill lesson "Reading Pictures" (page 135). Then have students turn to the pictures that illustrate this chapter. Discuss what the pictures indicate about life in the colonies. Then divide the class into groups and assign each group a picture. Tell each group to compose five questions that deal with the subject matter of its picture. Remind students to include questions based on the picture captions. You may want the members of each group to write answers for their questions.

SECTION 3 (PAGES 127–128)

Classroom Discussion. Discuss trade in the Middle Colonies. Ask: What products did the colonists trade? With whom did they trade? What seaports grew into important trading centers, and why? Then have students apply the same discussion questions to the New England and Southern Colonies.

SECTION 4 (PAGES 129–133)

Comparison. Ask students to identify the advantages and disadvantages of life on the frontier. Set up two columns on the board, one to be headed *advantages* and the other, *disadvantages.* Students should help you list information in the correct column. Discuss whether the advantages outweighed the disadvantages.

Classroom Discussion. Discuss the contributions of women in colonial society. Have students review the references to colonial women in this chapter. Then have them decide to what extent women took part in various aspects of colonial life. Ask: How did a woman's life in colonial times differ from a woman's life today?

Bulletin Board. Remind students that information can be presented both in words and in pictures. Have students turn to page 132 and reread the section headed "What kinds of houses and furniture were used on the frontier?" Ask students to make drawings of the items described. Then ask them to write appropriate captions for their drawings. Have students construct a bulletin board based on the theme of frontier living. Students could illustrate essential tools such as axes and plows.

Chapter Wrap Up. Have students write several paragraphs summarizing what life was like in the English colonies. Remind students to use only the main ideas of the chapter in their paragraphs.

Evaluation. Review Chapter 5 by using the Chapter Check Up (pages 133–134).

See the *Resource Book* for activity sheets (pages 19–22) and test (pages 145–146).

CHAPTER 6   (pages 136–149)
France Gains, Then Loses, a Huge Empire in North America

STUDENT OBJECTIVES

After completing their study of Chapter 6, students will be able to:

1. Describe what New France was like in the 1700's.
2. Explain how New France differed from the English colonies.
3. List reasons for the rivalry between the French and the English.
4. Describe how a struggle in North America developed between France and England.
5. State the significance of the French and Indian Wars.

TEACHING STRATEGIES

Getting Started. Discuss with students how nations gain and lose territory. Point out that nations may gain land by the following methods: claiming territory not already claimed by someone else, buying territory from another nation, taking territory by force, or having territory ceded by other nations. After the discussion, have students open their books to the map in Chapter 2 (page 64) that shows European claims in North America around 1700. Ask: If the English wanted to expand inland from the Atlantic coast, what European nation would they confront? Tell students to keep their answer to this question in mind as they read Chapter 6.

SECTION 1 (PAGES 137–140)

Class Discussion. Discuss why English settlers came to the colonies. (They wanted land, self-government, freedom of religion, economic opportunities, and a chance to "start over.") Then ask students to list reasons that explain why the French came to America. (Refer students to pages 138–139.) Ask: Why would English settlers come into conflict with the Indians? (The English system of colonization resulted in a conflict over land.)

Comparison. Ask students to compare New France with the Spanish colonies (see Chapter 3). Tell students that their points of comparison should include (1) what the countries wanted from their colonies, (2) the groups of people who went to the colonies, (3) colonial government, (4) ownership of land, and (5) religion. Discuss with students why New France and the Spanish colonies had more resemblance to each other than to the English colonies.

List-Making. As they read Chapter 6, have students list the lasting effects of French settle-ment in North America. Students could use reference books to complete their lists. If the class needs practice in selecting appropriate reference materials, you may want to introduce the skill lesson, "Using Reference Books" (page 149), as part of this assignment.

SECTION 2 (PAGES 140–142)

Finding Key Words and Phrases. Ask students to head one page in their notebooks *England* and another, *France*. Then have them turn to pages 141 and 142 and review English and French strengths and weaknesses in their North American struggle. Under the appropriate heading, list a key word or phrase that identifies each strength or weakness of each country.

SECTION 3 (PAGES 142–147)

Class Discussion. Write the following state-ment on the board: "I am sure that I can save this country, and that nobody else can." Tell students that this is what William Pitt (page 145) said when he came to power. Ask: How did Pitt influence the outcome of the war? Discuss the influence one person can have on historical events.

Class Discussion. Discuss what makes an event historically significant. Tell students that all the historical events they study are impor-tant but that some are more important than others because of their impact on the times in which they occur and on the future. Ask stu-dents to list the historically significant events they have already studied (for example, the voy-age of Columbus and England's defeat of the Spanish Armada). Then discuss with students the historical significance of Great Britain's vic-tory in the French and Indian War.

Chapter Wrap Up. Have students study the map on page 146. Then have them compare it with the map on page 64 (see "Getting Started"). Discuss how the peace treaty of 1763 altered European claims in North America. Ask: Who lost land? Who gained land?

Evaluation. Review Chapter 6 by using the Chapter Check Up (pages 147–148).

See the *Resource Book* for activity sheets (pages 23–26) and test (pages 147–148).

Concluding Unit 2. See unit summary, re-view, and activities on pages 150–151. See *Resource Book,* pages 149–150, for unit test.

UNIT 3 Preview

Direct student attention to the title of Unit 3 on page 152. ("New Nations Are Born as American Colonists Shake Off European Rule.") Ask: What is the theme of this unit? Have students examine the time line and pictures on pages 152-153. How do these elements highlight events that led to the independence of the colonies? Then ask students to read the introduction on page 153. What colonies in North and South America became independent or gained control of their own affairs? (The thirteen English colonies, the Spanish colonies, and Canada.)

CHAPTER 7 (pages 154–167)
How Were the English Colonists Governed?

STUDENT OBJECTIVES
After completing their study of Chapter 7, students will be able to:

1. Identify the rights that English colonists brought with them to America.
2. Describe the kind of government that developed in the English colonies.
3. Explain how disagreement over trade developed between Britain and the colonies.

TEACHING STRATEGIES

Getting Started. Review with students what they have learned in previous chapters about European colonies in North America. Ask the following questions: Where were Spanish, French, and English colonies located? In which group of colonies did colonists have the greatest freedom? Ask students to give examples of the kinds of freedom that English colonists had.

Now have students read the chapter introduction (pages 154–155). Ask: What freedoms do Americans have today? What are the origins of those freedoms? As they study Chapter 7, tell students to note carefully the development of freedom in the colonies.

SECTION 1 (PAGES 155–158)

Using Study Guide Questions. Tell students that questions can often serve as study guides for textbook material. Point out that the heads within Section 1 can be phrased as questions and used as study guides. (For example, "The English people limit royal power" would become "How did the English people limit royal power?") Ask students to list the heads in Section 1 and rephrase them as questions. Have students write answers to their study guide questions. Ask students to concentrate on writing skills as they complete their answers. Remind students to use the answers to their study guides when they review the material in this section.

Class Discussion. Discuss the development of freedom in the colonies. Be sure students understand how geographic isolation contributed to that development. Ask students to explain how lack of interest on the part of British officials further stimulated the growth of freedom in the colonies. Point out that several groups within the colonial population were still not free. Ask students to name those groups (pages 157–158).

SECTION 2 (PAGES 158–160)

Comparison. Have students use Section 2 to compare and contrast colonial governments. Ask students to list the similarities of colonial governments. Then have them identify differences among these governments. You may want students to construct a chart in their notebooks that shows the similarities and differences of colonial governments.

SECTION 3 (PAGES 160–165)

Class Discussion. Ask students to state in their own words what the fundamental question between Britain and the colonies was. (Do colonies exist for the benefit of the parent country?) Have students list the reasons Britain used to justify its control of colonial trade, manufacturing, and government. Then ask students to explain what the colonists felt their obligations to Britain were. Have students compare and weigh the two viewpoints. Be sure students understand that in a conflict such as this, both sides usually have legitimate reasons for the viewpoints they support.

Debate. Divide the class in half. One side is to argue that the colonies existed for the benefit of Britain and that the trade laws were both reasonable and necessary. The other side should argue that the colonies existed for their own benefit and that the laws were unfair restrictions of colonial trade and manufacturing. At the end of class, summarize the main points of both sides on the board.

Chapter Wrap Up. Review the rights that the colonists had established by 1763. Ask: Which rights had their origins in Britain? Which rights had developed in the colonies? Review the regulatory measures Parliament had passed. Ask students to predict how the colonists would react if tighter controls were imposed by Britain.

Evaluation. Review Chapter 7 by using the Chapter Check Up (pages 165–166).

See the *Resource Book* for activity sheets (pages 27–30) and test (pages 151–152).

CHAPTER 8   (pages 168–185)
The American Colonists Resist Strict Control by Britain

STUDENT OBJECTIVES
After completing their study of Chapter 8, students will be able to:

1. Identify ways in which the British government tried to tighten its control over the American colonies.
2. Describe how the colonists reacted to stricter control by Britain.
3. Identify Patriot leaders.
4. List ways in which the colonies began to unite.
5. State the significance of the fighting at Lexington and Concord.

TEACHING STRATEGIES

Getting Started. Read aloud the two news announcements on pages 168–169. Ask students why these events were historically significant. (They showed that the disagreement between the colonies and Britain had reached the point of armed conflict.) Point out that the announcements came from two different colonies, one in New England and one in the South. Ask: What had caused relations between the British government and the colonies to go wrong? Tell students that this chapter describes the events that led to the breakdown of the relationship between Britain and the colonies.

SECTION 1 (PAGES 169–171)

Student Research. Have students examine the picture of Pontiac on page 171. Then have them use their textbooks and library sources to answer the following questions: (1) About when do historians believe Pontiac was born? (Around 1720.) (2) Scholars are unsure of the location of Pontiac's birthplace. Near what present-day cities may he have been born? (Either near Defiance, Ohio, or Detroit, Michigan.) (3) Pontiac became the leader of what Indian tribes? (The Chippewa, Potawatomi, and Ottawa Indians.) (4) When did Pontiac die? (1769.)

Class Discussion. Discuss the reasoning that led to the establishment of Grenville's program. Then ask students to examine this program from different perspectives. Have them consider how each of the following might have felt about specific parts of the program: (1) a British landowner reacting to Grenville's plan for raising money to pay off debts and to run the empire, (2) a pioneer living west of the Allegheny Mountains reacting to the Proclamation of 1763, (3) an American merchant or shipowner reacting to the strict enforcement of the Navigation

Acts, (4) a colonial lawyer or newspaper editor reacting to the Stamp Act. At the end of class, summarize the main points of the discussion.

SECTION 2 (PAGES 171–178)

Class Discussion. Discuss the concept "no taxation without representation." Ask: Who did the colonists believe had the right to establish taxes? Then help students list the protest actions taken by the colonists against the Stamp Act. Discuss which actions were most effective and why. Tell students that, as they read further in this chapter, they should note which of the actions the colonists repeated.

Chart-Making. Have the class examine the Townshend Acts (page 173). Ask: What rights did these acts threaten? Tell students to rule two columns on a blank page in their notebooks. In one column, students should list the rights that were in jeopardy. In the other column, students should explain why the colonists objected to the threatened loss of each right.

Class Discussion. Have students skim the pages from the boldfaced heading "New Laws Stir New Protests in the Colonies" (page 173) to the end of the section (page 178). Point out that these pages describe colonial reaction to British policies during the 1760's and early 1770's. Have students list the methods colonists used to show their displeasure. (The list should include: public protests, letters, boycotts, the Boston Massacre, the Boston Tea Party.) Then discuss the effectiveness of colonial protests. Ask: Which were peaceful means of protest? Did all colonists support these methods of protest? (No. Refer students to the last paragraph in Section 2, page 178.)

SECTION 3 (PAGES 178–183)

Debate. Divide the class into two groups. Both groups are to represent colonists who attended the First Continental Congress. The debate should focus on ways in which the colonists might have protected their rights and, at the same time, settled their differences with Britain. One group is to represent the position of delegates like Patrick Henry and Samuel Adams. This group will argue that firm steps should be taken against Britain. The other group should argue that the colonists ought to move carefully. Give groups a class period to prepare their arguments.

Student Reports. Have students prepare written or oral reports on the lives of such Patriots as Patrick Henry, Samuel Adams, John Hancock, and Paul Revere. Tell students to use these questions in organizing their reports: (1) When was the individual born, and where? (2) What is known about the individual's early life? (3) When or how did the individual become involved in the movement for independence?

(4) When did the individual die? (5) What was the individual's greatest contribution to our American heritage? Tell students to illustrate their reports with pictures and drawings.

Class Discussion. Discuss the historical significance of the battles of Lexington and Concord. Center the discussion around these questions: What did it mean to the colonists and to the British that their troops had met in open conflict? How did this violence differ from the Boston Massacre (page 174)? Why are the battles considered the beginning of the Revolutionary War? What did Ralph Waldo Emerson mean when he called the fighting at Concord "the shot heard around the world"? Discuss what the monuments described in "Linking Past and Present" (page 184) tell us about the historical importance of Lexington and Concord.

Chapter Wrap Up. Remind students that this chapter has been an account of the events leading up to the outbreak of war between the colonies and Britain. Tell students that it is important for them to understand the sequence of these events. List the important events on the board and ask students to arrange them in chronological order. (You may want students to construct a time line.) Be sure students are able to explain the significance of each event.

Evaluation. Review Chapter 8 by using the Chapter Check Up (pages 183–184).

See the *Resource Book* for activity sheets (pages 31–34) and test (pages 153–154).

CHAPTER 9 (pages 186–213)
The Thirteen English Colonies Win Their Independence

STUDENT OBJECTIVES
After completing their study of Chapter 9, students will be able to:

1. Name events that led the colonies to declare their independence from Britain.
2. List the strengths and weaknesses of the Americans in the Revolution.
3. Identify significant battles in the Revolutionary War.
4. Describe the terms of the treaty that ended the American Revolution.

TEACHING STRATEGIES

Getting Started. Ask students to consider how the waging of a war would be affected by the following: (1) places where battles are fought, (2) training and equipment of an army or navy, (3) amount of money available for supplies, (4) public support of the war. Tell students that in this chapter, they will examine how factors such as these influenced the outcome of the American Revolution.

SECTION 1 (PAGES 187–192)

Bulletin Board. Ask students to put together a bulletin board display reflecting Patriot attitudes toward independence. Students could write news accounts of the events described in Section 1 and editorials based on the ideas expressed in *Common Sense* and the Declaration of Independence (pages 190 and 193–195). The bulletin board display could also include drawings and cartoons, appropriate maps and diagrams, and brief reports about the people mentioned in Section 1.

Class Discussion. Tell students that the phrase "the point of no return" is often used by historians when they examine events leading up to conflicts. Discuss what the phrase means. (Students will probably suggest such meanings as (1) the time when people can no longer solve disagreements peacefully, or (2) the point where conflict becomes inevitable.) Then have students apply the phrase to events in the colonies during the 1760's and 1770's. Ask: Did the colonists try to find peaceful ways of mending the breach with England? Was it "too late" for peace after the Boston Massacre? The Boston Tea Party? The Battle of Bunker Hill? How did British policies in 1775 and 1776 affect Americans? Discuss why the colonists were finally willing to step outside of the established government and declare their independence.

Reading a Primary Source. In discussing the account of the Declaration of Independence (page 191), you may want to have students look ahead to the actual document (pages 193–195). Since the Declaration is difficult for students to read, they will need guidance if they are to study it in detail. Follow these steps if you want the class to examine the Declaration of Independence: (1) Outline the Declaration on the board, and point out that it is divided into three parts: (a) the Preamble, (b) the list of grievances against George III, (c) the actual declaration of independence. (2) Read the document aloud. (3) Have student groups paraphrase portions of the document. Note that the annotations which accompany the document contain additional teaching hints.

Class Discussion. Point out that not all colonists were eager for a break with Britain. Mention that John Adams himself said one third of the colonists were Patriots, one third were Loyalists, and one third were indifferent. Ask students to consider how Patriots, Loyalists, and indifferent colonists would react to the Declaration of Independence. This strategy should help students to understand how deeply split the American colonists were on the question of independence.

Chart-Making. Have students set up a chart showing factors that affected the outcome of the American Revolution. Have students rule four columns labeled as follows: (1) British strengths, (2) British weaknesses, (3) American strengths, (4) American weaknesses. Mention that the heads in Section 2 will help students locate appropriate details for their charts. You may want students to list the boldface headings that fall between pages 196–198. (There are nine.)

Student Reports. Remind students that Americans received help from several liberty-loving Europeans during the Revolution (page 197). Ask: What well-known foreign soldiers fought in the war? (Marquis de Lafayette, Baron de Kalb, Baron von Steuben, Casimir Pulaski, Thaddeus Kosciusko.) Have students prepare written or oral reports on the lives of these soldiers. Tell them to use these topics in organizing their reports: (1) early life of the individual, (2) contributions to American victory in the Revolution, (3) later life of the individual. You may want students to find out how these soldiers have been honored by Americans then and now. Suggest that students use library sources to locate this information.

Map Study. Have students locate these important battles of the Revolution on the maps in their books: (1) Bunker Hill, (2) Fort Ticonderoga, (3) Dorchester Heights, (4) Long Island, (5) Trenton and Princeton, (6) Oriskany, (7) Saratoga, (8) Monmouth, (9) Kings Mountain, (10) Cowpens, (11) Vincennes, (12) Yorktown. In each case students should know where the battle was fought (the state), which side won, and why the battle is considered significant.

Time Line. Stress the chronology of events during the Revolution by having students construct a time line that shows the dates mentioned in Chapter 9. Be sure that students' time lines run from April, 1775 to October, 1781.

Reading Pictures. Have students examine the picture and caption on page 207. Ask: What is the subject of the picture? (Frontiersmen being recruited into the army.) Have students describe the "battle gear" of these Revolutionary soldiers. Then have students examine the pictures of British troops on pages 186 and 202. Ask: Which army was better equipped for battle? You may want to discuss why American troops, who lacked many supplies, were able to win the war.

Chapter Wrap Up. Discuss the lasting impact of the Revolution on American history. Then point out that the American Revolution also had an impact on other countries. Have students look at the title of Chapter 10. Ask: What other parts of the Western Hemisphere were affected by the American Revolution? (Latin America and Canada.)

Evaluation. Review Chapter 9 by using the Chapter Check Up (pages 211–212).

See the *Resource Book* for activity sheets (pages 35–38) and test (pages 155–156).

CHAPTER 10 (pages 214–231)
The Spirit of Independence Affects Canada and Latin America

STUDENT OBJECTIVES

After completing their study of Chapter 10, students will be able to:

1. Identify ways in which Canada was affected by the American Revolution.
2. Tell how the Spanish colonies gained their independence.
3. Name outstanding leaders of the revolutions in the Latin American colonies.
4. Tell how the revolution in Brazil differed from those in the Spanish colonies.

TEACHING STRATEGIES

Getting Started. Tell students to imagine that both radio and television existed in 1783. Then ask them to consider what might have been reported in a news broadcast announcing American independence. List the points students suggest on the board. Then ask the class to consider how the peoples living in Canada and Latin America might have reacted to the news of the American Revolution. Discuss the fears that Britain, Portugal, and Spain might have had concerning their colonies. Discuss what parent countries and colonists might have learned from the American experience. (Both would have learned that it was possible for colonies to win their independence.)

SECTION 1 (PAGES 215–218)

Class Discussion. After the class has read Section 1, divide students into three groups. One group should present the viewpoint of the French Canadians who wished to keep their French ways of living. A second group should present the viewpoint of English-speaking Canadians who wanted more rights and self-government. A third group should represent Britain and explain how its government attempted to please both French and British Canadians. At the end of class, summarize the main points.

SECTION 2 (PAGES 219–221)

Comparison. Have students study Lord Durham's report on conditions in Canada (page 220). Then have them compare the recommendations he made with the way Britain treated the American colonies. Discuss these questions: What might Britain have done to hold on to its American colonies? Since its experiences in the American Revolution, what had Britain learned about managing colonies?

SECTION 3 (PAGES 221–227)

Map Study. Review the achievements of Bolívar and San Martín. Then introduce the skill lesson, "Reading Maps: Using Scale" (page 231). Have students turn to the map of South America on page 225 and tell them to do the following: (1) Trace the route followed by Bolívar in freeing northern South America from Spain's control. (2) Use the scale to determine the approximate distance covered by Bolívar's army. (3) Trace the route followed by San Martín in freeing most of southern South America. (4) Use the scale to determine the approximate distance covered by San Martín's army. (5) Trace Bolívar's southward route to Peru and the Battle of Ayacucho. Use the scale to determine the approximate distance Bolívar covered.

Bulletin Board. Have groups of students participate in a bulletin board project that will feature our American neighbors as they are today. Each group should choose a single country and use the library to find out about that country's people, geography, government, economy, and relations with the United States. Have groups collect pictures of the country, its people, and products. Students could prepare reports, posters, maps, charts, and diagrams.

SECTION 4 (PAGES 227–229)

Reading for a Purpose. Have students use library sources and the textbook to find answers to these questions: (1) Why was Brazil claimed by the Portuguese and not the Spanish? (The Line of Demarcation gave the eastern part of Latin America to Portugal.) (2) How did Brazil get its name? (The Portuguese named the country *Brazil* after a red dye obtained from the brazilwood trees that grew there.) (3) What was Brazil's first important export? (Sugar.) (4) Why did the Portuguese royal family come to live in Brazil in 1808? (France invaded Portugal in 1807.) (5) When did Brazil become a republic? (November 15, 1889.)

Chapter Wrap Up. Have students make a chart comparing the changes that occurred in Canada, Spanish America, and Brazil during the 1800's. The categories for comparison should include (1) government prior to the revolution, (2) date(s) of revolution, (3) description of the revolution (violent or peaceful), (4) status after the revolution (dependent or independent), (5) type of government after the revolution, (6) difficulties faced after the revolution.

Evaluation. Review Chapter 10 by using the Chapter Check Up (pages 229–230).

See the *Resource Book* for activity sheets (pages 39–42) and test (pages 157–158).

Concluding Unit 3. See unit summary, review, and activities on pages 232–233. See *Resource Book,* pages 159–160, for unit test.

Have students read the title of Unit 4 on page 234. ("The United States Is Established on a Firm Basis.") Point out that people and events contributed to the success of the nation. Have students look at the pictures of George Washington on pages 234–235. Ask: In what two capacities did Washington serve the nation? (He served as a general and as the first President.) Point out to students the inscription on the portrait of Washington (page 234). Mention that those words indicate the degree of respect and affection felt toward Washington by the people of his time. Then ask students to examine the time line on page 234. Tell students that the events highlighted there show that the nation was growing and becoming stronger. Have students read the introduction on page 235. Ask them to identify important steps taken by the people of the United States. (Adopting the Constitution, putting the government on a firm financial basis, building a permanent capital, adding new territory to the nation.) Mention that when the United States had met challenges at home, it was able to give attention to challenges abroad. Point out that in this unit students will learn how the United States became a "nation among nations."

CHAPTER 11   (pages 236–251)
The Thirteen States Create a Firm Union Under the Constitution

STUDENT OBJECTIVES
After completing their study of Chapter 11, students will be able to:

1. Explain why the states had difficulty working together after the Revolution.
2. Identify the weaknesses of the Articles of Confederation.
3. Tell where the Constitutional Convention was held and name key delegates to the convention.
4. List compromises agreed to by the delegates and explain what these compromises achieved.
5. List arguments that were used for and against the adoption of the Constitution.

TEACHING STRATEGIES
Getting Started. Ask the class to suggest symbols of our country: the flag, the bald eagle, the Liberty Bell, the Statue of Liberty. Discuss what these symbols mean. Point out that the symbols represent the country as a whole. Then read aloud the Pledge of Allegiance (page 248).

Ask: To what do citizens pledge their allegiance? (The flag, the republic.) Tell students that in this chapter they will learn how our nation's government was planned and established.

SECTION 1 (PAGES 237–241)

Vocabulary Study. Remind students that boldfaced words in the text identify special terms. Ask students to list the boldfaced terms in this chapter and to use the glossary at the back of the book to find the meaning of each. Point out that two of the terms are proper nouns (House of Representatives and Senate) and should be capitalized. Mention that *constitution* is capitalized when it refers to the specific document. Have students write sentences that clearly show the meaning of the terms.

Identifying Similarities. Guide students in identifying the common elements of the early state constitutions (page 237): (1) separation of powers among three branches of government, (2) legislatures with greater powers than either executives or judiciaries, (3) bills of rights and (4) limitations on voting. When students have finished reading Chapter 11, ask them to compare the Articles and the Constitution to these state constitutions.

Class Discussion. Have students reread the paragraph under the boldfaced heading "What was the new government like?" (page 238). Ask: Why were many Americans wary of powerful governments? Ask students to recall events from the 1760's and 1770's. (Students should refer to events in Chapters 8 and 9.) Discuss how the Articles of Confederation reflected the experiences Americans had undergone as colonists.

Class Discussion. Discuss the Articles of Confederation. Have students look up the term *confederation* in a dictionary. (The term means a league of nations, independent nations or states joined under a central authority that is usually confined to defense and foreign relations.) Ask students if the word *confederation* accurately describes the type of government the United States had under the Articles. Discuss why Americans chose to make the state governments strong.

SECTION 2 (PAGES 242–249)

Comparison. Have the class compare the Virginia Plan with the New Jersey Plan (page 244). Be sure students understand the major differences between the plans. Ask: Which plan favored a central government that was stronger than the state governments? Which plan based representation on state population? Which states favored each plan, and why? Point out that the debate between the delegates was finally settled by the Great Compromise (page

245). Have students summarize the main points of the Great Compromise.

Bulletin Board. Have students put together a bulletin board display highlighting the Constitutional Convention. Students could (1) prepare illustrated reports on Philadelphia, (2) write reports about the lives of key participants, (3) draw pictures of the event and the delegates, (4) construct a poster featuring the Preamble to the Constitution. Encourage the class to use library resources.

Class Discussion. Have students reread Benjamin Franklin's statement on page 246. "I have often and often in the course of this session looked at that [half-sun] without being able to tell whether it was rising or setting. But now at length I have the happiness to know that it is a rising, and not a setting sun." Ask: To what session was Franklin referring? (Constitutional Convention.) Point out that Franklin was using a metaphor when he likened the new nation to a half-sun. By comparing the United States to a *rising* sun, what did Franklin indicate about the nation's future? (That the nation would grow and become strong.) Discuss the events in this period that set the nation on its path to success. (For example, the adoption of the Constitution by the states.)

Reading Primary Sources. Teach the skill lesson, "Finding Points of View in Primary Sources" (page 251). Then have students examine Jefferson's letter (page 247) for point of view. Mention that this letter identifies what Jefferson thought were the strengths and weaknesses of the Constitution proposed by the Constitutional Convention. Ask students to help you list the strengths and weaknesses on the board. Have students identify the element Jefferson wanted to add to the document. (Bill of Rights)

Chapter Wrap Up. Emphasize the debt of gratitude Americans owe to the delegates of the Constitutional Convention. Have students use the chapter to help you list on the board advantages we have today as a result of the achievements of the Constitutional Convention.

Evaluation. Review Chapter 11 by using the Chapter Check Up (pages 249–250).

See the *Resource Book* for activity sheets (pages 43–46) and test (pages 161–162).

CHAPTER 12 (pages 252–267)
The New Government Is Successfully Launched

STUDENT OBJECTIVES
After completing their study of Chapter 12, students will be able to:

1. Identify the three branches of the federal government and tell what the function of each is.
2. List rights that are protected by the Constitution.
3. Identify the head of each department in the first presidential Cabinet.
4. List the points of Hamilton's financial plan.
5. Explain why the first political parties were formed.

TEACHING STRATEGIES

Getting Started. Call attention to the oath taken by Washington when he was sworn in as President (pages 252–253). Point out that the President pledged to uphold the Constitution. As they read Chapter 12, have students note how the Constitution has given our government a firm basis.

SECTION 1 (PAGES 253–258)

Class Discussion. Have students help you list on the board the powers of the federal government and the state governments. Draw two columns, one for federal powers and one for state powers. Students can use the chart on page 254 to extract a list of federal powers. The list under "state powers" will be the powers not granted to the federal government (such as the power to regulate education, to license, to punish criminals). Point out that federal and state governments share some powers.

Making a Diagram. Remind students that diagrams are a good way to show the relationship between different parts of government. Review the skill lesson from Chapter 7, "Reading Diagrams" (page 167). Then have students construct a diagram of the federal government showing the legislative, executive, and judicial branches. Students should use the diagram on page 257 as a model for their diagrams. As a part of this strategy, go over the meaning of these terms: *separation of powers, veto, checks and balances, judicial review.*

Class Discussion. Have students reread the summary paragraph on page 257. Ask: What is meant by the statement that our Constitution is "a living document"? Have students suggest ways our nation has changed since the founders drafted the Constitution. (Student suggestions will probably include: (1) the United States is bigger, (2) more people live in the United States today, (3) the government is more powerful, (4) there are many more cities and towns, (5) ways of living have changed.) Discuss the various problems that could have occurred if our founders had not foreseen the need for a "living" plan of government. Remind students that on page 255 they learned some of the ways in which the Constitution changes to meet new situations. (For example, through interpretation and the amendment process.)

SECTION 2 (PAGES 258–262)

Class Discussion. As an oral or written assignment, have students answer the questions that follow the boldface heading "The new government is set up" (page 258). In answering these questions, students will establish a basis for examining the Washington administration. Then tell students that some historians call Washington "the only indispensable person in American history." Discuss why Washington deserves such a high ranking.

Identifying Main Ideas. Give students an opportunity to study Hamilton's financial plan. Have them read pages 260–261 to find the main points of his plan: (1) The federal government was to assume the states' debts. (2) The federal government was to set up a Bank of the United States. (3) The federal government was to raise money by passing tariff laws. Tell students to explain *how* each part of Hamilton's plan was put into effect, and *why*. At the end of class, list the main points of Hamilton's financial plan on the board.

Student Reports. Have students use their textbooks and library sources to prepare written or oral reports about Alexander Hamilton. (Be sure students refer to the pictures and caption on page 261.) Have students use the following questions in organizing their reports: (1) When was Hamilton born, and where? (2) What is known about his early life? (3) What were his contributions to the new nation? (4) How did he die, and when? At the end of the assignment, you may want to discuss how Hamilton's influ-

ence is still evident in the United States today. (Our government's policies include some of his suggestions: for example, government bonds, protective tariffs, and taxation.)

SECTION 3 (PAGES 262–265)

Comparison. Have students help you list on the board some of the differences between the nation's first two political parties. Categories for comparison might include (1) party leaders, (2) groups of people most likely to support each party (for example, poor people or wealthy people, farmers or merchants), (3) each party's position on the strength of the central government, (4) each party's position on the relationship between state and central governments.

Outside Reading. Have students prepare oral or written reports about one of the following: (1) the election of 1800, (2) *Marbury v. Madison,* (3) the Democratic-Republican Party, (4) the Federalist Party. Refer students to the skill lesson in Chapter 6, "Using Reference Books" (page 149), and tell them to use the information from the lesson in selecting appropriate reference books for research on their topics.

Bulletin Board. Have students put together a bulletin board display of the first five Presidents. Refer students to the feature on page 264. Then tell students to draw or show pictures of these men, write brief reports of their lives, and highlight their achievements.

Chapter Wrap Up. Focus on the successful launching of the new government. Ask students to explain how the following strengthened the new government: (1) paying the national debt, (2) putting down the Whiskey Rebellion, (3) establishing the principle of judicial review.

Evaluation. Review Chapter 12 by using the Chapter Check Up (pages 265–266).

See the *Resource Book* for activity sheets (pages 47–50) and test (pages 163–164).

CHAPTER 13   (pages 268–285)
The United States Gains the Respect of Other Nations

STUDENT OBJECTIVES

After completing their study of Chapter 13, students will be able to:

1. Identify problems the United States had with Britain and France during the first years of American independence.
2. Explain how President Jefferson was able to double the size of the United States.
3. List reasons why the United States decided to go to war with Britain.
4. State the effects of the War of 1812.
5. Identify the main points of the Monroe Doctrine.

TEACHING STRATEGIES

Getting Started. Point out that, in order to be strong, a new nation must gain the respect of other nations. Discuss what the characteristics of a strong nation might be. (For example, ability to defend itself, ability to protect the rights of its citizens.) Tell students to note in Chapter 13 how the United States proved to the rest of the world that it was worthy of respect.

SECTION 1 (PAGES 269–273)

Class Discussion. Have students read Section 1, referring them specifically to the summary of events in Europe (pages 269–271). Tell students that the stage was set for conflicts to break out which could have involved the United States. Ask: What nations were at war in Europe? Why did many Americans feel that the United States owed support to France? What country would the United States have had to fight if Americans had supported France? Focus student attention on Washington's advice and the policy of neutrality that was adopted (page 270). Then discuss how world affairs can influence the course of a nation's history. Have students summarize the main points of the discussion.

SECTION 2 (PAGES 273–275)

Outside Reading. Introduce the skill lesson "Using the Library" (page 285), emphasizing the differences between author, title, and subject cards. Then send students to the library to find out more about the treaty that kept New Orleans open to Americans before 1802. (Pinckney Treaty.) Remind students to use the card catalog in locating appropriate books. Tell students to write a report that answers the following questions: (1) When was the Pinckney Treaty signed? (1795.) (2) What countries signed it? (Spain and the United States.) (3) What were the terms of the treaty? (Americans could use the Mississippi River and the port of New Orleans for three years; the boundary between the United States and West Florida was fixed at 31°N.)

Map Study. Review compass directions with students. (See the skill lesson in Chapter 2, "Reading Maps: Locating Places," page 67.) Have students study the map showing the Louisiana Purchase and answer the questions in the caption (page 274). Then ask: What river formed the eastern boundary of the Louisiana Purchase? (Mississippi.) What mountains formed part of the western boundary? (Rocky Mountains.) Discuss why Jefferson considered the buying of the Louisiana Purchase to be a "great achievement" (page 275).

SECTION 3 (PAGES 275–282)

Identifying Causes and Effects. Point out that wars usually have more than one cause. Then have students help you list reasons that explain why the United States went to war against Britain in 1812 (page 276). Point out the heading on page 278: "The War of 1812 Has No Winner" and discuss why the nations involved ended the war. Then have students identify the effects of the war (pages 281–282). You might want to have students make a two-column chart that summarizes causes and effects of the War of 1812.

SECTION 4 (PAGES 282–283)

Class Discussion. Summarize the main points of the Monroe Doctrine (page 283). Then have students consider how each of the following would probably have reacted to the Monroe Doctrine: (1) an American who wanted the United States to gain the respect of other countries, (2) Latin Americans who feared European interference in their countries, (3) a Spanish or French official who hoped to regain lost lands in the Americas, (4) Russian officials who wanted to establish settlements in the Western Hemisphere.

Chapter Wrap Up. Review the characteristics that make a nation strong and gain it the respect of other nations (see "Getting Started"). Then discuss how the United States had become "a nation among nations." Ask the class to help you list the achievements of the United States during the period discussed in Chapter 13.

Evaluation. Review Chapter 13 by using the Chapter Check Up (pages 283–284).

See the *Resource Book* for activity sheets (pages 53–56) and test (pages 165–166).

Concluding Unit 4. See unit summary, review, and activities on pages 286–287. See *Resource Book,* pages 167–168, for unit test.

UNIT 5 Preview

Have students read the title of Unit 5 on page 288. ("The American Way of Living Changes as the Different Sections Develop.") Then tell students that from time to time certain individuals, discoveries, inventions, events, or acts of legislation have had a profound impact on the American way of life. Point out that this period of American history includes a number of such "landmark" developments. Have students study the time line and pictures on pages 288–289. Show them that the time line and pictures highlight laws, inventions, individuals, and events which changed the way Americans lived. Then ask students to read the introduction on page 289. Ask: Did the sections of the United States develop in the same way? Have students identify characteristics of the Northeast, South, and land west of the Appalachians.

CHAPTER 14 (pages 290–313)
The Northeast Becomes the Center of Trade and Manufacturing

STUDENT OBJECTIVES

After completing their study of Chapter 14, students will be able to:

1. List reasons why the Northeast became the center of commerce and manufacturing.
2. Tell how tariffs, inventions, and the factory system spurred the development of manufacturing.
3. List effects of the Industrial Revolution on American ways of life.
4. Identify changes in travel and communication that brought the American people closer together by the mid-1800's.

TEACHING STRATEGIES

Getting Started. Have the class study the pictures that illustrate Chapter 14. Remind students to pay particular attention to captions. Set up three columns on the board. In one column list the page numbers where the pictures appear. In another, have students identify the subject of each picture. For the third column, ask students to suggest additional information that can be drawn from the captions. Ask students to suggest what life was like in the Northeast by this time. Then assign Chapter 14 for student reading.

SECTION 1 (PAGES 291–300)

Class Discussion. Ask students to read the section under the boldfaced heading "New markets are found in Europe" (page 294). Ask:

What was the situation that prompted President Jefferson to send warships to the Mediterranean Sea? (Pirates were raiding American trading ships.) Tell students that the pirates had been operating in Mediterranean waters since the mid-1500's. Americans had been paying sums of money for protection to the Barbary States since 1795. Discuss why America's refusal to pay such protection money indicated that the nation had grown stronger.

Student Reports. Ask students to look at the picture of the clipper ship on page 295. Then have them use their textbooks and library sources to answer the following questions: (1) What made a clipper ship different from other sailing ships? (Clipper ships had narrower hulls and carried larger sails on taller masts.) (2) Who designed the first clipper ship? (John W. Griffiths.) (3) What was that ship's name and when was it launched? (It was named *The Rainbow* and it was launched in 1845.) (4) Who was the most famous builder of clipper ships? (Donald McKay.) (5) Where did that individual build most of his ships? (In Boston, Massachusetts.)

Using Headings to Review. After they have read Section 1, have students reread and list the boldfaced headings that fall within the subsection entitled "Manufacturing Becomes Important" (pages 296–298). Discuss how these present a sequence of events that explains how manufacturing developed in the Northeast. Then ask these questions: In what country did the Industrial Revolution begin? (Britain.) How did textile manufacturing spread to the United States? (Slater built textile machines from memory and set up mills.) What was manufactured in the New England and middle states? (Textiles, articles made from iron.) What American invention made factory-produced clothing cheaper? (Sewing machine.) Tell students to use headings to help them review other parts of Chapter 14.

Identifying Point of View. Have students reread the explanation of protective tariffs and look at the drawings (pages 298–299). Then have the class identify the arguments for and against the protective tariff law of 1816 (page 300). This strategy will help students see how different groups of Americans had different needs. At the end of class, list on the board the groups who supported the tariff (for example, manufacturers) and the groups who did not (for example, southern producers of raw materials, shipowners).

SECTION 2 (PAGES 300–302)

Class Discussion. Draw two columns on the board. Label one *Before the Factory System* and the other, *After the Factory System*. Then have students reread the section under "The factory system brings important changes in the worker's life" (page 301). Ask: Where were goods made before the factory system? Who owned the tools used to make goods after the factory system? How were wages and hours decided before and after the factory system? Have students help you fill in the columns on the board.

SECTION 3 (PAGES 302–311)

Map Study. Point out that not all maps show the same information. Then ask students to suggest different kinds of information they have seen on maps. (For example, cities, state boundaries, or roads.) Teach the skill lesson, "Reading Maps: Population Density" (page 313). Ask: What does the map in the skill lesson show? (Population density in the United States by 1850.) Then have students turn to the maps on pages 303, 305, and 310 and discuss what each shows. (Early roads, canals, and railroads.) Ask: Did the Northeast or the South have a better transportation system? (Northeast.) What two sections of the country were brought closer together by the growth of transportation? (Northeast and West.)

Bulletin Board. Ask students to put together a bulletin board display highlighting the changes made in travel and communication during the period of this chapter. Have students draw pictures and diagrams of inventions; write brief reports on the lives of the inventors; construct poster-sized maps showing new transportation routes; and write reports on the National Road, the Erie Canal, the *Clermont,* and the *Tom Thumb.*

Chapter Wrap Up. Put a list on the board of key words and key people from this chapter. (For example, Industrial Revolution, tariff, Samuel Morse, Elias Howe.) Ask students to explain how each was related to the development of trade and manufacturing in the Northeast.

Evaluation. Review Chapter 14 by using the Chapter Check Up (pages 311–312).

See the *Resource Book* for activity sheets (pages 57–60) and test (pages 169–170).

CHAPTER 15 (pages 314–329)
Cotton Becomes King in the South

STUDENT OBJECTIVES
After completing their study of Chapter 15, students will be able to:

1. Identify cotton as the South's leading crop by the mid-1800's.
2. Explain how the cotton gin led to increased production of cotton.
3. Describe how plantation families, small farmers, and slaves lived in the mid-1800's.
4. List ways in which the North and South had grown apart by 1850.

TEACHING STRATEGIES

Getting Started. Show students pictures (pages 314, 320–321, and 323) that illustrate the development of the South as an agricultural area. Ask students to identify the subject of each picture and list students' comments on the board. Then discuss how these pictures differ from the ones students examined in "Getting Started" for Chapter 14. (Students should notice that the Northeast was industrial; the South, agricultural.) Tell students to note, as they read Chapter 15, factors which contributed to the development of agriculture in the South.

SECTION 1 (PAGES 315–319)

Class Discussion. Have students consider the significance of the invention of the cotton gin. Discuss whether cotton would have become the South's chief crop had the cotton gin not been invented. Have students study the illustration showing how the cotton gin worked (page 316). Point out what a simple machine it was and how easy it would have been for people to have copied it. Then have students read Eli Whitney's letter to his father (pages 315–316). Ask: Is it likely that somebody else would have invented a cotton gin if Whitney had not? Finally, have students compare the significance of this invention with other inventions they have studied. (For example, the compass, the sewing machine, the steamboat, the railroad, and the telegraph.)

Map Study. Have students study the map entitled "The South Expands" (page 319) and ask them to locate the cotton-growing areas. Discuss the geographical conditions which must be present for cotton to grow. (Short winters; long, hot summers; a high yearly rainfall.) Have students construct maps that show the cotton-growing states before 1860.

Graph Study. Have students turn to the graph on page 317 and answer the question in the accompanying caption. Then ask: (1) What kind of graph is shown on page 317? (A bar graph.) (2) What is the title of the graph? ("The American Cotton Boom.") (3) How many millions of bales of cotton were being produced by 1840? (About 1.5 million bales.) (4) Between 1800 and 1860, cotton production had increased by about how many millions of bales? (About 3.75 million.) (5) During which decade did cotton production increase the most? (During the 1850's.)

Student Research. Have students turn to pages 318–319 and identify several important southern ports. (Mobile, New Orleans, Charleston, and Savannah.) Then have students use their textbooks and library sources to answer the following questions: (1) In what states are the ports located? (2) What is the latitude and longitude of each port? (3) When was each city established? (4) How many people live in each city today? Remind students to use almanacs and atlases in finding answers.

SECTION 2 (PAGES 319–323)

Comparison. Have students compare the lives of plantation families, slaves, and small farmers. Tell students to use these categories for comparison: (1) homes, (2) daily activities, (3) education, (4) legal status, (5) property. Discuss why plantation families became the leaders of the South.

Bulletin Board. Tell students that pages 319–320 describe how cotton was grown and picked before 1860. Then have students read in "Linking Past and Present" how machines have changed cotton harvesting methods (page 328). Ask students to put together a bulletin board display featuring cotton cultivation in the United States today. (Students will need to do outside reading.) Students could draw pictures of the cotton plant, write reports that describe the steps involved in cotton cultivation, list pests and diseases cotton plants are subject to, draw pictures of the machines used in cotton agriculture, and list products made from the cotton plant.

SECTION 3 (PAGES 324–327)

Class Discussion. Have students reread the white Southerners' defenses of slavery (pages 325–326). Then discuss reasons that explain why Southerners were reluctant to end slavery. Point out that some Southerners claimed the slaves were better off than workers in the northern factories. Review working conditions under the factory system (pages 301–302). Ask students to identify the differences between northern workers and slaves.

Chart-Making. Set up a chart that summarizes the differences between the North and the South (pages 326–327). Use these categories for comparison: (1) major products, (2) industrial or agricultural, (3) kind of labor. Then discuss this question: What reasons explain why the North and South had developed differently? Have students write a summary of the class discussion.

Chapter Wrap Up. Review how various groups of Southerners lived before 1860 and discuss the effect of cotton on the South. Have students consider these questions: As long as cotton was king, was it likely that the white Southerners would insist on the right to own slaves? Would the South seek to expand its cotton-growing areas and, at the same time, slavery? Tell students to note, in the coming chapters, how Americans dealt with the questions of slavery and expansion.

Evaluation. Review Chapter 15 by using the Chapter Check Up (pages 327–328).

See the *Resource Book* for activity sheets (pages 61–64) and test (pages 171–172).

CHAPTER 16 (pages 330–345)
Pioneers Push the Frontier Westward

STUDENT OBJECTIVES
After completing their study of Chapter 16, students will be able to:

1. Explain why the term *the West* applied to different areas at different times.
2. Identify groups of people who led the way in settling the region between the Appalachian Mountains and the Mississippi River.
3. Identify the main points of the Ordinances of 1785 and 1787.
4. List the states that were added to the Union between 1792 and 1850.
5. Identify characteristics of frontier life that promoted belief in equality.

TEACHING STRATEGIES

Getting Started. Before they open their texts to Chapter 16, ask students to draw what they consider to be symbols of the pioneers. (Students will probably draw log cabins, long rifles, raccoon-skin caps, Conestoga wagons, etc.) Tell students that this chapter is an account of the settlement of territory between the Appalachian Mountains and the Mississippi River. Have students note in their reading how the symbols they drew came to be a part of our American heritage.

SECTION 1 (PAGES 331–333)

Student Reports. Tell students to write several diary entries of the experiences one of the following would probably have had: (1) a long hunter, (2) a backwoods settler, (3) a pioneer farmer. Have students compare their diary entries at the end of this assignment. Also discuss how persons in the East might have reacted to the experiences students described in the diaries.

Map Study. Have students turn to the physical map of the United States in the atlas at the back of the book. Ask students to trace the outline of the United States and locate and label (1) the Ohio River Valley — the West in the late 1700's, and (2) the Mississippi River Valley — the West in the early 1800's. Have students draw in and label the Appalachian Mountains and the Mississippi River. Also have them shade in the Old Southwest and the Northwest Territory. Then ask students to help you list on the board the states that were carved out of these two areas.

SECTION 2 (PAGES 333–336)

Class Discussion. Ask the class to consider the difficulties faced by Congress as settlers poured into the new territories on the frontier. Have students discuss these questions: How could land be fairly divided and sold? What rights should settlers have? Should new states have equality with the original thirteen states? Then have students turn in their texts to the account of the Ordinance of 1785 and the Northwest Ordinance (pages 334 and 336). Ask students to help you list on the board the main points of these laws. Then discuss how these laws provided wisely for the division of land in the territories and for territorial government.

Student Research. Ask students to pick a state that was first a territory. Assign students to find out (1) when the state became a territory of the United States, (2) something about its history as a territory, and (3) when the state actually achieved statehood. Ask: Was the state ever considered part of a frontier region, and when? Help students construct time lines that show important dates in the history of the state.

SECTION 3 (PAGES 336–339)

Oral Reports. Have each student present a report in a program modeled after an educational television production. The title of the program could be "The West During the First Half Century of the New Republic." The program could include reports on these topics: travel to the West, the growth of towns, the clash between Indians and pioneers, and the admission of new states. Encourage students to illustrate their reports with pictures and maps.

SECTION 4 (PAGES 339–343)

Class Discussion. Discuss ways in which pioneer living encouraged the attitude of equality. First ask the class to list challenges all settlers faced (for example, sickness, danger, isolation). Discuss how facing the same problems did away with social-class differences. Remind students that because of their belief in democracy, Westerners were eager to participate in government. Have students skim pages 342–343. Then ask: What requests did the representatives from the frontier make of Congress? (Cheaper land, government funding of transportation routes.) How did the requests become laws?

Chapter Wrap Up. Have students reread the chapter introduction on pages 330–331. Point out the guide questions at the end of the introduction. Have students help you list answers to the questions on the board. Then have students summarize the main points of the chapter.

Evaluation. Review Chapter 16 by using the Chapter Check Up (pages 343–344).

See the *Resource Book* for activity sheets (pages 65–68) and test (pages 173–174).

The Nation Undergoes Change During the Jackson Years

STUDENT OBJECTIVES

After completing their study of Chapter 17, students will be able to:

1. List reasons why Jackson became a popular hero.
2. Identify Jackson's policies toward the second national bank, the tariff, and Indian removal.
3. List changes that gave more Americans a larger share in the government by the mid-1800's.
4. List ways in which reformers tried to improve life in America.
5. Identify the political parties of the mid-1800's.
6. Name the Presidents that served between 1825 and 1845.

TEACHING STRATEGIES

Getting Started. Ask students to consider these questions: Do people shape events or do events create opportunities for some individuals to emerge as leaders? How could a person become the symbol for a period of history? Discuss students' answers. Tell students that this chapter is an account of the changes that took place during the years Andrew Jackson was President. Mention that some people call the years of his presidency the "Age of Jackson," or the "Jacksonian Era." Ask students to keep this discussion in mind as they read Chapter 17.

SECTION 1 (PAGES 347–349)

Classifying. Have students reread pages 348–349. Tell the class that these pages summarize reasons which explain why Jackson was a popular leader. Point out that these reasons fall into two categories: (1) personal characteristics, (2) events in which he had been involved. Ask students to list the reasons under appropriate headings. Tell students to add to the list as they complete this chapter.

Student Reports. Teach the skill lesson, "Preparing Reports" (page 369). Then have students write a report on either the election of 1824 or the election of 1828. Tell them to use the questions that follow as the basis of an outline for their reports: (1) Who were the candidates? (2) What were the campaigns like? (3) What effect did the House of Representatives have on the outcome of the election? (4) What influence did other politicians have on the outcome of the election?

SECTION 2 (PAGES 349–355)

Comparing Points of View. Discuss Jackson's use of presidential authority in (1) the appointment of government officials, (2) the nullification crisis, (3) the renewal of the Charter for the Bank of the United States, and (4) the removal of Indians. Tell students that other Presidents have had these concepts of presidential authority: (1) that only *Congress* has ultimate authority because it directly represents the will of the people, (2) that the President can do anything not actually forbidden by the Constitution or a law, (3) that a President only has the powers specifically stated in the Constitution or a law. Ask: With which point of view would Jackson probably have agreed? (The second.) Then discuss how presidential authority is affected by (1) the system of checks and balances (page 256), (2) separation of powers (page 256).

Class Discussion. Discuss the nullification crisis of 1832-1833, focusing on Calhoun's theory of nullification and on the issue of secession. Have students use the glossary to define the terms *nullify* and *secede*. Then discuss what Jackson meant when he said, "To say that any state may at pleasure secede from the Union is to say that the United States is not a nation" (page 351).

SECTION 3 (PAGES 355–357)

Class Discussion. Discuss the extension of voting rights during this period. Point out that, by the mid-1800's, all white men aged 21 or older and black men in five New England states could vote. Ask students to name the groups of people who still could not vote. Mention that today nearly every person over the age of 18 is eligible to vote.

Citizenship Training. Tell students that pages 355–357 describe how American citizens increased their participation in government. Ask students to find the section called "America Faces the Future," following the last chapter of the book. There they will read about the contributions each individual can make to our country today. Review with students the rights they possess as Americans. Then point out that responsibilities go hand-in-hand with rights. Have students help you list on the board ways in which they can contribute to our country.

SECTION 4 (PAGES 357–363)

Student Reports. Have students write a report on one of the reform issues of this period: prison reform, improved treatment of the mentally ill, expanded opportunities for the disabled, temperance and the problem of alcoholism, or women's rights. So that students will be able to organize the material for their reports, reinforce the skills presented in the lesson on page 369.

Chart-Making. Have students make a chart that shows differences between the Democratic Party and the Whig Party. Categories for comparison might include: (1) party leaders, (2) attitude toward strong federal government, (3) attitude toward the tariff, and (4) section(s) of the country where each party was strongest. Have students find out who the two successful Whig presidential candidates were in 1840 and 1848 (Harrison and Taylor).

Bulletin Board. Have students put together a bulletin board display that highlights the Jacksonian Era. Students could write reports on leaders and reformers, make drawings that illustrate different viewpoints toward issues such as the tariff, post quotations from selected American literature, and prepare posters showing how Americans had gained a larger share in government than before.

Chapter Wrap Up. Discuss again how Jackson was a symbol for his age. Ask: How was Jackson responsible for such changes as increased voting rights? Review the other reforms that came about in the mid-1800's. Discuss why emphasis on public education was important for the development of our nation. Ask: How can educated citizens contribute to their country?

Evaluation. Review Chapter 17 by using the Chapter Check Up (pages 367–368).

See the *Resource Book* for activity sheets (pages 69–72) and test (pages 175–176).

Concluding Unit 5. See unit summary, review, and activities on pages 370–371. See *Resource Book,* pages 177–178, for unit test.

UNIT 6   Preview

Have students read the title of Unit 6 on page 372. ("The Nation Expands and Is Torn by War.") Ask: What two stories are linked together in the unit title? (The story of expansion and the story of a war.) Say that as new territories were added to the United States, a dispute arose over slavery. This dispute eventually culminated in the Civil War. Mention that the picture on page 372 tells more about expansion. Point out that many settlers traveled to new territories in wagon trains such as the one pictured. Then have students examine the time line on page 372. Ask: When was the Civil War fought? (Between 1861 and 1865.) Have students read the introduction on page 373. Ask students to identify the two opposing sides in the war. (The North and South.) Point out the pictures of Union troops on 372–373 and Fort Sumter on 373 (note the Confederate flag over the fort). Finally, tell students that a great American led the nation through this difficult period of history. He has been honored by a monument in Washington. (See the picture, page 373.) Ask: What is the name of that leader? (Abraham Lincoln.)

CHAPTER 18   (pages 374–403)
The United States Gains More Land and Reaches from Sea to Sea

STUDENT OBJECTIVES
After completing their study of Chapter 18, students will be able to:

1. Use maps to show the routes taken by Lewis and Clark and Pike as they explored territory west of the Mississippi.
2. Summarize how the United States acquired the Louisiana Purchase, Florida, Texas, the Southwest, California, and Oregon.
3. Identify reasons that explain why the United States and Mexico went to war in 1846 and list results of that war.
4. List effects of the California gold rush.

TEACHING STRATEGIES

Getting Started. Introduce Chapter 18 by having students turn to the map entitled "The United States in 1853" (page 388). Have students study the map to see how the United States gained more land and in time reached from sea to sea. Discuss why Americans would have been eager to expand, and read aloud the quotation in the chapter introduction. Tell students to notice, as they read Chapter 18, the ways in which the United States gained territory.

SECTION 1 (PAGES 375–378)

Map Study. On an outline map of the United States, have students trace the routes of exploration followed by Lewis and Clark and by Pike. Tell students to mark one point of interest on each route. Then ask the students to write or tape a descriptive paragraph about the points of interest they have chosen. (Points of interest could be geographical features, plants and animals of the region, Indians of the region, climate, and so on.) Students will need to do some outside reading to complete this assignment.

Student Reports. Ask students to study the settlement of the portion of the Louisiana Territory described in this section. Have them choose to do one of the following: (1) advertise land west of the Mississippi River by drawing a poster designed to attract new settlers, (2) write a letter to a relative who lives along the Atlantic coast, describing life as a prairie farmer, (3) write a letter to a relative back east, describing life in one of the new towns that began to appear west of the Mississippi, or (4) write about or draw a picture of the experiences of a pioneer family. You can repeat this assignment when students study the settling of Texas, California, and Oregon.

SECTION 2 (PAGES 378–380)

Class Discussion. Refer students to the map on page 379. Point out that Florida, owned by Spain, was bordered by territory owned by the United States. Discuss difficulties Spain would have in controlling territory far from home. Tell students that, in fact, Spain was unable to defend its claim to Florida. Ask: What country claimed the Gulf coast? (See map on page 379.) Then assign Section 2 for reading. Ask students to explain why Spain was willing to sell Florida. What were the terms of the Adams-Onís Treaty? (See page 380.)

SECTION 3 (PAGES 380–389)

Class Discussion. Discuss why some historical events seem to inspire people. Point out that the gallant stand of Texans at the Alamo caught public attention. Then ask students to evaluate the impact of the Alamo siege on the outcome of the fight for independence in Texas. Discuss the significance of the cry "Remember the Alamo!"

Reading for a Purpose. Take students to the library to find more information about American reaction to the war with Mexico. Tell them to look for answers to these specific questions: (1) What reasons for war with Mexico did Polk give to Congress? (2) What were the arguments against a war with Mexico? (3) In which sections of the country did many people oppose the war, and why? (4) Which sections of the country favored a war, and why? Have students prepare written answers.

SECTION 4 (PAGES 389–396)

Class Discussion. Have students read Sutter's account of the discovery of gold (pages 390–391). Then discuss the California gold rush. Ask: Who were the forty-niners? What routes did they take to reach California? What was life like in the mining camps? How did the gold rush hasten the admission of California to the Union?

SECTION 5 (PAGES 397–401)

Comparison. After students have read Section 5, ask them to compare the claims of the United States and of Britain to Oregon. Tell students to use these categories for comparison: (1) early explorers, (2) trade, (3) settlers. Remind students of the "finders keepers" rule discussed earlier (see T16). Ask: What makes a claim valid — that *explorers* from a country claim new territory, or that *settlers* from a country go to live there? Have students summarize the main points of the agreement which settled the controversy over Oregon (page 401).

Chapter Wrap Up. Review the maps in this chapter, focusing on the areas that were added to the United States during the 1800's. Bring in a copy of "America the Beautiful" and have students read the words of the song. Point out the references in that song to the various parts of our country and to the fact that it stretches "from sea to shining sea." Discuss if there was now "land enough" for the "young American buffalo."

Evaluation. Review Chapter 18 by using the Chapter Check Up (pages 401–402).

See the *Resource Book* for activity sheets (pages 73–76) and test (pages 179–180).

CHAPTER 19 (pages 404–423)
The North and the South Break Apart

STUDENT OBJECTIVES

After completing their study of Chapter 19, students will be able to:

1. Identify the main points of the Missouri Compromise.
2. State northern and southern attitudes toward states' rights.
3. Identify the main points of the Compromise of 1850.
4. List events of the 1850's which led the North and South closer to conflict.
5. Explain why Southerners viewed Lincoln's election in 1860 as a threat.
6. Tell how the Civil War began at Fort Sumter in 1861.

TEACHING STRATEGIES

Getting Started. Review with students the differences between the North and the South by the early 1800's. Then discuss the expansion of Americans into the territories added to the United States from the Louisiana Purchase (1803) to the Gadsden Purchase (1853). Ask: How would this expansion heighten the controversy over slavery? Would Southerners be able to take slaves into the territories? What could happen if the North tried to block the spread of slavery into the territories? Could the disagreements between the two sections become so intense that they could not be resolved peacefully? Tell students to keep these questions in mind as they read Chapter 19.

SECTION 1 (PAGES 405–411)

Class Discussion. Discuss Thomas Jefferson's reaction to the dispute that arose over the question of slavery in Missouri. Refer students to Jefferson's statement (page 406). Ask: With the continued expansion of the United States, could the question of slavery in the territories be laid to rest? Then discuss the terms of the Missouri Compromise and the way in which this compromise temporarily relieved the South and satisfied the North. Finally, point out that *Congress* had decided how the question of slavery in the territories would be dealt with (page 406). Ask: How might Southerners perceive this legislation as a threat? (Congress might, at some point, decide to legislate on the rights of slaveholders in the states where slavery was already established.)

Comparison. Have students compare what the North and South each gained from the Compromise of 1850. Ask students to decide which provisions favored which side. Discuss whether the compromise favored both sides equally.

Review other compromises that had been worked out since the Revolutionary War. (Great Compromise, page 245; compromise over the tariff in 1833, page 351; Missouri Compromise, page 406.) Why was each of these compromises significant? (Resolved differences and promoted unity.)

SECTION 2 (PAGES 411–417)

Outside Reading. Discuss the power of the written word. Then tell students to find out more about *Uncle Tom's Cabin*. Have students answer these questions: (1) Who was Harriet Beecher Stowe? (2) In what forms did *Uncle Tom's Cabin* appear? (3) How popular was *Uncle Tom's Cabin*? (4) What was the story about? After students have answered those questions, ask them to read Lincoln's statement on page 412. Discuss the influence of *Uncle Tom's Cabin* on the American public in the 1850's.

Comparison. Have students write or tape two short news stories, one that might have appeared in a northern newspaper and one that might have appeared in a southern newspaper. The stories should be about one of the following: (1) the Underground Railroad, (2) the violence in the territory of Kansas, (3) the birth of the Republican Party, (4) the Supreme Court's decision in the Dred Scott case, or (5) John Brown's raid at Harpers Ferry. This strategy will help students realize not only the different attitudes of Northerners and Southerners, but also the intensity of feeling involved.

SECTION 3 (PAGES 417–421)

Class Discussion. Teach the skill lesson, "Reading Maps: Election Results" (page 423). Then discuss the historical significance of the election of 1860. Ask these questions: Why did the Democratic Party split? How did this split affect the outcome of the election of 1860? Why did the South see the election of a Republican President as a threat to its way of life? Was it "too late" for peace after secession had begun? Why would a civil war be a tragic war? Have students summarize the main points of the discussion.

Bulletin Board. Have students put together a bulletin board display highlighting Abraham Lincoln. They should first look at the picture feature on Lincoln (page 442) and then decide on possible elements of the display. The display should include written reports on the life of Lincoln, reports on the members of his family, a list of public offices he held, quotations from his famous speeches, drawings that feature different aspects of his life (for example, as a rail splitter and as a lawyer), maps showing places where he lived, and human-interest stories about events in his life. As they read the next chapter, students should add to the bulletin board display.

Identifying Key Events. Ask students to skim Section 3 and then ask them to list the events that led to the breakdown of the union between the North and the South. Go over the list of events with students, beginning with the election of Lincoln in 1860 and ending with the bombardment at Fort Sumter in 1861. Then ask students to construct time lines showing the events. At the conclusion of the assignment, discuss with students the different ways in which key events in history can be presented.

(For example, narrative, table, time line, list, and so on.) Discuss how devices such as time lines and lists can be effective.

Chapter Wrap Up. Write on the board, "The Civil War could not have been avoided." Ask students to react to this statement in a class discussion. Students should consider the compromises that had been made to avoid war, as well as the events which finally culminated in the outbreak of war.

Evaluation. Review Chapter 19 by using the Chapter Check Up (pages 421–422).

See the *Resource Book* for activity sheets (pages 77–80) and test (pages 181–182).

CHAPTER 20   (pages 424–453)
The North and the South Fight a War and Are Reunited

STUDENT OBJECTIVES
After completing their study of Chapter 20, students will be able to:

1. List the advantages that each side had in the Civil War.
2. Explain how Union strategies brought victory after four years of fighting.
3. List ways in which the war affected people in the North and in the South.
4. Identify the main points of Lincoln's plan to unite the nation and explain how his assassination kept the plan from being carried out.
5. Explain how the Emancipation Proclamation and the Thirteenth Amendment gave slaves their freedom.
6. List the steps Congress took to reconstruct the South.
7. Describe the changes in the South after the Civil War.

TEACHING STRATEGIES

Getting Started. Have students turn to the map called "The States Choose Sides" (page 427). Tell students to study the map and to review what they have already learned about the different sections of the country (Chapters 14 and 15). Then ask: Which side had the largest population? Which side had the industries that could supply the tools of war? What would each side have to accomplish in order to win the war? Tell students they will find the answers to these questions in this chapter.

SECTION 1 (PAGES 425–427)

Comparison. Divide the class into two groups. Have one group list the advantages of the North at the beginning of the Civil War and the other group, the advantages of the South (pages 426–427). Each group should select the advantages they feel were most likely to influence the outcome of the war. Then have the groups compare the strengths of the North and the South. Discuss whether one side had a greater number of important advantages than the other side.

SECTION 2 (PAGES 428–439)

Class Discussion. Point out the boldfaced term *strategy* on page 428 and have students use the glossary to find its meaning. Mention that in a war, both sides adopt strategies they think will result in victory. Have students help you list on the board the strategies of the North and the South (pages 428 and 430). Refer students to the maps (pages 430, 434, and 438) to illustrate how northern strategies were designed to "divide and conquer." Ask: How did the capture of the Mississippi cut the South in two? How did the blockade of southern ports strangle southern shipping? Why was the battle at Gettysburg the turning point of the war? How did General Sherman divide the southeast? Have students prepare written answers for these questions.

Writing Reports. Review the skill lesson for Chapter 17, "Preparing Reports" (page 369). Then give students an opportunity to make a closer study of one of the Civil War battles mentioned in Chapter 20. Tell students to select a battle and to focus on the following: (1) the location of the battle, (2) the leaders for each side, (3) details about the fighting, (4) the outcome of the battle, and (5) the significance of the battle. Ask students to determine how the one battle they select fits into the overall strategy of the North or the South. Encourage students to make maps and drawings to illustrate their reports.

SECTION 3 (PAGES 439–441)

Comparison. Ask the class to compare and contrast the effects of the war on the lives of people in the North and the South. Tell students that their points of comparison should include the following: (1) the work force, (2) supplying the army, (3) transportation, (4) hardships and shortages at home, and (5) the raising of money to pay for the costs of the war. Then have each student make a chart based on the class discussion.

SECTION 4 (PAGES 441–443)

Class Discussion. Read this statement aloud to the class: "Next to the defeat of the Confederacy, the heaviest blow that fell upon the South was the assassination of Lincoln" (page 443). Discuss what Jefferson Davis meant by those words. Then have students skim Section 4 to find evidence that supports Davis's statement. (Lincoln's plan to rebuild the Union.) Summarize the main points of Lincoln's plan on the board. Finally, tell students to keep Davis's statement in mind as they read in Section 5 about the plans made by Congress to reconstruct the South. Have students evaluate this statement again after they have studied Section 5.

SECTION 5 (PAGES 444–451)

Class Discussion. Have students turn to page 444 and read the material presented under the boldfaced heading "Problems must be solved." On the board, list the problems identified by the text. Then have students skim Section 5 to see how Congress tried to solve each of these problems. Summarize the main points of Congress's plan on the board. Point out that reconstruction can be looked at in many ways. Ask: What groups of people benefited from reconstruction? Ask students to describe how southern whites regained control of local governments and how reconstruction affected southern politics. Finally, ask students to describe how industry and transportation changed in the South after the war (pages 450–451).

Chapter Wrap Up. Teach the skill lesson, "Studying for Tests" (page 453). Tell students to keep their answers to the questions that accompany the lesson and to use them in their review of Chapter 20. Then remind students of Lincoln's statement when he took the oath of office for his first term. Lincoln had said, "Suppose you go to war, you cannot fight always; and when, after much loss on both sides, and no gain on either, you cease fighting, the [same] old questions . . . are again upon you" (page 420). Discuss this statement as it applies to the Civil War and to the period of reconstruction after the war.

Evaluation. Review Chapter 20 by using the Chapter Check Up (pages 451–452).

See the *Resource Book* for activity sheets (pages 81–84) and test (pages 183–184).

Concluding Unit 6. See unit summary, review, and activities on pages 454–455. See *Resource Book*, pages 185–186, for unit test.

Preparing for the Midterm Examination. If you plan to give a midterm examination, you might remind students to prepare by reviewing the Chapter Check Ups. Also tell them to study the Summary of Important Ideas at the ends of the first six units and to reread the Unit Reviews. Let students know how many and what kinds of questions will be on the midterm examination. You may want to tell them what themes in American history will receive the greatest emphasis.

A midterm examination is provided in the *Resource Book,* pages 187–190.

UNIT 7 Preview

Ask students to suggest words and phrases that describe the United States today (for example, *industrial*). Then have the class read the introduction (page 457) and study the unit-opening pictures and time line (pages 456–457). Ask students to list factors which contributed to the shaping of modern America. Tell students that Unit 7 is an account of the events which helped to create the United States we are familiar with today.

CHAPTER 21 (pages 458–477)
The Last Frontier in the West Is Settled

STUDENT OBJECTIVES

After completing their study of Chapter 21, students will be able to:

1. Explain how the Homestead Act of 1862 and the transcontinental railroad made it possible for large numbers of settlers to move West.
2. List ways in which white settlements upset the Indian way of living on the Great Plains.
3. Identify the changes in the late 1800's in the federal government's policy toward the Indians.
4. Explain how miners, ranchers, and farmers hastened the settlement of the last frontier.

TEACHING STRATEGIES

Getting Started. Have students read the first sentence of Section 3 (page 468). ("In 1890, a United States government report announced that the frontier had disappeared.") Remind the class of the movement of pioneers toward the frontier throughout America's history. Have students recall the pioneer way of life that they studied in Chapter 16. Ask: Would the disappearance of the frontier mean that adventurous pioneers could no longer make a fresh start? Would it mean the end of the pioneer way of life? Discuss the significance of the frontier. Then tell students that in Chapter 21 they will find out where the frontier was in the late 1800's and what happened to it.

SECTION 1 (PAGES 459–462)

Reading for a Purpose. Have students use library sources to find out more about the Homestead Act of 1862. Tell students to look for answers to these questions: What groups of people were eager to take advantage of this law? (Civil War veterans, blacks, adventurous people.) Who actually got most of the land? (Speculators and large railroad companies.) When did the

United States government end the policy of homesteading begun in 1862? (1974.) Ask students to prepare written answers to these questions.

Class Discussion. Remind students of the difficulties faced by the forty-niners as they tried to reach the gold fields in California (pages 392–393). Ask: What had made coast-to-coast travel less difficult by 1862? (Transcontinental railroad.) Have students look at the map on page 460 and note the route taken by the transcontinental railroad. Ask: By 1884, what other railroads had reached the Pacific coast? (Northern Pacific, Southern Pacific, Santa Fe.) Then discuss the effect of the transcontinental railroads on the settlement of the West.

SECTION 2 (PAGES 462–468)

Using Primary Sources. Review what students have already learned about written primary sources and point out that historic photographs are primary sources as well. Teach the skill lesson, "Using Historic Photographs" (page 477). Then have students read the account written by an Indian chief in 1805 (pages 462–463) and the statement by Chief Joseph (page 466). What difficulties, faced by Indians, did these chiefs identify? Have students turn to the feature on page 465 and look at the photograph of Chief Joseph's surrender. Ask: What information can be drawn from the photograph? (Indian efforts to resist the advance of white settlements were unsuccessful. Tribes were forced to surrender.) Discuss how documents and photographs can increase our understanding of the American past.

Identifying Main Points. Have students skim Section 2. Ask them to identify the main points of these policies: the removal of eastern Indians to western lands, settling Indians on reservations, the Dawes Act of 1887, and the Indian Reorganization Act of 1934. Discuss why the government tried different policies. You might have students look ahead to Chapter 26 and read about American Indians in recent decades. (See pages 562–563.)

SECTION 3 (PAGES 468–475)

Bulletin Board. Have students put together a bulletin board display featuring cattle ranching on the western plains in the late 1800's and early 1900's. The display could include songs about cattle ranching (for example, "Home on the Range"), pictures of the equipment used by cowboys, reports on the activities involved (for example, roping and branding cattle), and maps of the states where cattle ranching was important.

Student Reports. Have each student prepare a written report on one of the following groups of people: cattle ranchers, sheep farmers, homesteaders, or prospectors. The reports should include (1) where the people settled, (2) how they made a living, (3) what challenges they faced, (4) what part they played in settling the last frontier. Encourage students to illustrate their reports with maps and drawings.

Chapter Wrap Up. Remind students of the westward movement of pioneers from colonial days to 1890. Then have them reread the last paragraph of the chapter (page 475). Ask: What groups of people helped to settle the last frontier? How did the closing of the frontier affect the American way of life? What brought the East and West closer together? Point out that although the frontier has vanished, other "frontiers" still remain for Americans to explore. Ask students to suggest what these might be. (For example, space, the ocean beds, scientific research.)

Evaluation. Review Chapter 21 by using the Chapter Check Up (pages 475-476).

See the *Resource Book* for activity sheets (pages 85-88) and test (pages 191-192).

CHAPTER 22 (pages 478-499)
The United States Becomes a Great Industrial Nation

STUDENT OBJECTIVES
After completing their study of Chapter 22, students will be able to:

1. Identify factors that made it possible for the United States to develop as an industrial nation.
2. List new methods of manufacturing that led to the mass production of goods.
3. Describe changes that took place in retail selling in the late 1800's.
4. Explain how the incorporation of business aided the development of industries.
5. List ways in which new forms of communication and transportation affected people's lives.
6. Identify outstanding business leaders of the late 1800's.

TEACHING STRATEGIES

Getting Started. Have students consider what they would do in the following situation: a bicycle, given as a birthday present, has a broken pedal which cannot be fixed. (Students will probably suggest replacing the defective part.) Point out that it was not always possible for people to replace parts of equipment simply and cheaply. Mention that great changes in the way things are made, shipped, and sold had to take place before it became possible for defective parts to be replaced quickly. Remind students of the Industrial Revolution (page 296). Mention that this chapter describes later developments in industry. Tell students that the boldfaced terms in this chapter indicate the changes in industry that occurred during the late 1800's. Have students list those terms and use the glossary to find their meanings.

SECTION 1 (PAGES 479-482)

Student Reports. Have students skim Section 1 and identify the factors that made the United States a leading industrial nation. (Abundant natural resources, plentiful labor supply, inventions.) Point out to the students that money is also necessary to develop industry. In the late 1800's Europeans invested their money in American industry (page 481). Have students find out how Europeans were persuaded to invest in America and bring that information to class in the form of: (1) a brochure, (2) a drawing, (3) a speech, (4) a poster, (5) an advertisement. At the end of the assignment, discuss the effect foreign investments had on the development of American industry (page 481).

Student Research. Have students look at the picture of Thomas Edison on page 482. Then have them use their textbooks and library sources to answer the following questions: (1) Where was Edison born, and when? (He was born in 1847 at Milan, Ohio.) (2) How long did his formal education last, and why? (He went to school for only three months. His mother removed him from school when the teacher punished him for asking "too many" questions.) (3) What disability did Edison overcome? (He was partially deaf.) (4) How many inventions did he patent in his lifetime? (He patented 1,093.) (5) What was the name of his workshop, and where was it located? (His workshop was in Menlo Park, near Plainfield, New Jersey.) (6) In 1929 Edison's workshop was moved by Henry Ford to what new location? (Dearborn, Michigan.) (7) When did Edison die? (In 1931.) (8) What were some of his great achievements? (Answers could include any of the inventions mentioned on page 482.)

SECTION 2 (PAGES 483-486)

Comparison. Have students look closely at the subsection entitled "American Industry

Creates a Market for Its Products" (pages 484–485). Ask students to help you list on the board the new methods of selling that emerged in the late 1800's. Have students compare those stores with the kinds of stores that are common in our society today. In what ways are the stores similar? In what ways are they different? Discuss how retailing has changed over the last hundred years.

SECTION 3 (PAGES 486–493)

Class Discussion. After students have read Section 3, discuss how ways of living were affected by each of the following: telegraph and cable, telephones, radios, railroads, automobiles, and airplanes. Then discuss how these changes in communication and transportation aided the growth of industry. Have students summarize the main points of the discussion.

SECTION 4 (PAGES 493–497)

Chart-Making. Have students make a chart comparing James J. Hill, Andrew Carnegie, and John D. Rockefeller. Categories for comparison might include their backgrounds, how they got their start in business, and their business successes. Discuss how "captains of industry" contributed to the nation's development.

Learning About Careers. Chapter 22 introduces students to a wide variety of careers. After students have read all four sections, have them go back through the chapter and list the kinds of occupations that are mentioned (for example, factory work, retailing, and occupations related to transportation and communication). Then have students put together a bulletin board display featuring a variety of careers. The display could include (1) reports that describe certain occupations, (2) pictures of people involved in different types of work, (3) lists of skills required in specific occupations. You might want students to read "Thinking About Careers" in the reference material at the back of the book.

Chapter Wrap Up. Review the boldfaced terms introduced in this chapter. Have students explain how these terms related to changes in American industries during the 1800's. Ask students to recall ways in which communication and transportation networks changed. Then discuss how these changes affected the status of the United States as a "nation among nations." (The United States became the leading industrial power.)

Evaluation. Review Chapter 22 by using the Chapter Check Up (pages 497–498).

See the *Resource Book* for activity sheets (pages 89–92) and test (pages 193–194).

CHAPTER 23 (pages 500–515)
Business and Industry Face New Problems

STUDENT OBJECTIVES

After completing their study of Chapter 23, students will be able to:

1. List ways in which businesses and industries were affected by rapid industrialization during the late 1800's.
2. Identify labor organizations that were formed during the late 1800's.
3. List ways in which federal and state governments began to regulate business and industry.

TEACHING STRATEGIES

Getting Started. Introduce this chapter by bringing to class one or more news stories relating to business or industry. These might be articles on employment, the economic cycle, industrial use of natural resources, working conditions, or labor union activities. Pass the news stories around the class. Make the point that some of the challenges faced by business and labor today are similar to the ones brought about by rapid industrialization in the late 1800's and early 1900's. Then assign Chapter 23 for reading.

SECTION 1 (PAGES 501–505)

Class Discussion. Have students read Section 1. Then discuss the factors involved in economic booms and depressions (page 503). Draw two spirals on the board. Label one *boom* and the other, *depression*. Then ask students to help you list the characteristics of booms and depressions on the board beside the appropriate spiral. (*Boom*: business expansion, increased use of resources, high wages, rising prices, and high risk/profit investments. *Depression*: decreasing demand, decreasing production, decreasing employment, business failures, human suffering.) Discuss the relationship between booms and depressions.

Comparison. Teach the skill lesson, "Comparing Points of View" (page 515). Then have students compare and contrast the positive and negative features of monopolies. Tell students to list the benefits of monopolies. What advantages do large business organizations have? Have them identify problems caused by monopolies. Ask students to make two drawings or posters: one showing the positive features of monopolies; the other showing the negative features of monopolies. Tell students that later in this chapter they will learn what steps the federal government took to regulate monopolies (pages 512–513).

SECTION 2 (PAGES 506–511)

Chart-Making. Have students prepare a chart that compares and contrasts the Knights of Labor, the American Federation of Labor, and the Congress of Industrial Organizations. Tell them to use the following categories for comparison: early leaders, groups included, workers' goals, and the methods used by workers to accomplish goals. At the end of the assignment, discuss why some organizations were successful while others were not.

Reading for a Purpose. Ask students to reread the subsection entitled "Labor Unions Try to Win Better Working Conditions" (pages 510–511). Then tell them to answer specific questions about the railroad strike and the Haymarket riot. Ask these questions: (1) When did the event take place, and where? (2) What had the workers been asking for? (3) What was the outcome of the event?

SECTION 3 (PAGES 512–513)

Class Discussion. Discuss the significance of the antitrust legislation passed by Congress in the late 1800's and early 1900's. (Sherman Antitrust Act, page 512; Interstate Commerce Act, page 513; Clayton Act, page 512.) Point out that these laws were passed by Congress because the public was demanding government regulation of business and railroad abuses. Ask: When was each law passed? What were the laws designed to do? Were they successful? Why, or why not? Remind students that some monopolies were to be permitted. Discuss why this was so. Tell students that these laws were important because they established a precedent: that the federal government had the power to regulate private businesses in order to protect the public.

Chapter Wrap Up. Have students reread the chapter introduction (pages 500-501). Review the effects of rapid industrialization on American ways of living. Have students categorize these effects as *positive* or *negative*. Then ask students to explain how each of the following contributed to improvement of working conditions in the late 1800's and early 1900's: (1) labor organizations, (2) employers, (3) state and federal governments.

Evaluation. Review Chapter 23 by using the Chapter Check Up (pages 513–514).

See the *Resource Book* for activity sheets (pages 93–96) and test (pages 195–196).

New Forces Affect American Farming

STUDENT OBJECTIVES
After completing their study of Chapter 24, students will be able to:

1. Identify improvements in farm machinery during the late 1800's and early 1900's.
2. List methods that made farming on dry lands possible.
3. Identify problems faced by farmers in the late 1800's and early 1900's.
4. Explain how such organizations as the Grange helped farmers solve some of their problems.
5. List ways in which the state and federal governments aided farmers in the late 1800's and early 1900's.
6. Identify political parties supported by farmers in the 1890's.

TEACHING STRATEGIES

Getting Started. Read the chapter introduction aloud. Direct students' attention to William Jennings Bryan's statement about farming. Ask: What did Bryan mean by his declaration that "the great cities rest upon our broad and fertile prairies"? Remind students that farming has always been an important aspect of American life. Point out that Chapter 24 tells how farming changed during the late 1800's and early 1900's. Then assign Section 1 for reading.

SECTION 1 (PAGES 517–521)

Student Reports. Discuss how new machines and farming methods affected farmers in the late 1800's and early 1900's. Point out that farming had become a way of earning a living. Then tell students to describe the changes in farming in one of these forms: (1) a news story, (2) a diary entry, (3) a letter to a relative in a city. Students' reports could include drawings and descriptions of the new machines and methods, lists of problems brought about by the changes in farming, and a description of the feelings farmers may have had about the changes that had occurred.

Student Research. Have students look at the picture on page 521. Ask: Why were dams such as this one built in the late 1800's and early 1900's? (To provide water for the irrigation of large agricultural areas.) Then ask students to use their books and library sources to find answers to these questions about irrigation: (1) In what three types of climate is irrigation used? (In desert regions, in areas with seasonal rainfall, in areas that experience frequent droughts.) (2) What irrigation methods are used in the United States? (Sprinkler irrigation, trickle irrigation, surface irrigation, and subirrigation.) (3) What group of people first used irrigation in the United States? (The Hopi Indians of Arizona and New Mexico.) (4) What group of people first used modern methods of irrigation in the United States? When? Where? (The Mormons, in the 1840's, in the Salt Lake Valley of Utah.)

Bulletin Board. Ask students to put together a bulletin board display featuring farming methods and farm machinery of the late 1800's and early 1900's. The display could include written reports on such methods as dry farming and irrigation, and drawings or pictures of the following machines: reapers, threshers, planters, seeders, and combines. At the end of the assignment, discuss with students how changes in farming during the late 1800's and early 1900's compared to changes in business and industry (Chapters 22 and 23).

SECTION 2 (PAGES 522–524)

Class Discussion. Have students look up the boldfaced term *supply and demand* in the glossary at the back of the book. Then discuss the effect of the rule of supply and demand on American farmers in the late 1800's. Ask: How did the rule of supply and demand affect the price of farm land, the cost of transporting crops to market, and crop prices in years of large production? What could farmers have done to make the rule of supply and demand work *for* them instead of *against* them? How does this rule work in our society today? Finally, discuss the cause-and-effect relationship implied in the rule of supply and demand.

Class Discussion. Ask students to help you list on the board the problems faced by farmers in the late 1800's and early 1900's. (Debt and high interest payments, high railroad rates, falling prices, and worn-out land.) Ask: What were some of the causes of these problems? Why did farmers try to solve these problems by growing even larger crops? Point out that increasing production set off another chain of problems for farmers. Remind students of the spiral effect of the booms and depressions they examined in Chapter 23. Have students draw a spiral that shows the problems faced by farmers.

SECTION 3 (PAGES 524–529)

Student Reports. Review the skill lesson for Chapter 17, "Preparing Reports" (page 369). Then have students write a report on one of the following: (1) the kinds of courses offered by the agricultural or land grant college nearest your community, (2) the kinds of services provided by the Department of Agriculture in your state.

Comparison. After students have read Section 3, have them identify ways in which the

Grange and the government came to the aid of farmers in the late 1800's and early 1900's. Then have the class compare the advantages of social organization (the Grange) with political organization (political parties). What were the disadvantages of each? Have students set up charts that show the advantages and disadvantages of both social and political organizations.

Comparing Point of View. Tell students that the trend of farming as a business (pages 519–520) still continues. Today such farming organizations are called *agribusinesses.* Mention that agribusinesses can afford to charge lower prices for their products than small farmers. Discuss the difficulties that owners of small and middle-sized farms would have in competing with agribusinesses. Then tell students to draw two pictures that express point of view: (1) the attitude of a worker in an agribusiness toward the price of farm products, and (2) the attitude of a small farmer toward the price of farm products. (Students can use the drawing on pages 298–299 as a model for this assignment.)

Chapter Wrap Up. Direct student attention to the guide questions at the end of the introduction to Chapter 24 (page 517). Then have students help you summarize the main points of the chapter. On the board set up three columns and label them as follows: (1) new methods and machinery, (2) farmers' concerns, and (3) efforts to solve problems. At the end of class, ask students to evaluate the importance of farming in our nation today.

Evaluation. Review Chapter 24 by using the Chapter Check Up (pages 529–530).

See the *Resource Book* for activity sheets (pages 97–100) and test (pages 197–198).

Concluding Unit 7. See unit summary, review, and activities on pages 532–533. See *Resource Book,* pages 199–200, for unit test.

UNIT 8   Preview

Have students look at the opening pages of Unit 8 (pages 534–535). Ask: What is the title of Unit 8? ("New Conditions Bring Changes in American Life.") Remind students of the changes in business, industry, and technology that they studied in the last unit. Then have students read the introduction. Point out that nations are made up of people. Tell students that in Unit 8 they will see how Americans were affected by new conditions. Finally, have students focus on the time line and pictures. Ask: What inventions changed the way people lived?

CHAPTER 25   (pages 536–555)
Industrialization Changes Life in Cities and on Farms

STUDENT OBJECTIVES

After completing their study of Chapter 25, students will be able to:

1. Identify major groups of immigrants who came to the United States between the mid-1800's and the mid-1900's.
2. List reasons why the growth of industry encouraged immigration.
3. Identify reasons why cities grew rapidly in the century after the Civil War.
4. List ways in which cities changed between the mid-1800's and mid-1900's.
5. Identify people who worked to improve conditions in American cities during the late 1800's.
6. List ways in which farms and small towns changed after the Civil War.

TEACHING STRATEGIES

Getting Started. Bring to class some pictures that show various aspects of life in present-day America. Ask students to identify the subject matter of each picture. Discuss what things they see that are characteristics of America today but would *not* have been true a century ago. Remind students of the changes in industry and farming that they studied in Unit 7. Ask students to consider what it must have been like to have been born in the late 1800's and to have lived through so many major changes. How might an individual feel about rapid changes in technology? Then have students read about Civil War veteran Albert Woolson in the introduction to this chapter (pages 536–537). Have students list other changes Civil War veterans would have seen if they had lived to present times. (For example, computer technology and space exploration.) After students have completed their list of recent changes, assign Section 1 for reading.

SECTION 1 (PAGES 537–543)

Class Discussion. Tell students that on the base of the Statue of Liberty, a gift of the French people to the United States in 1876, is the following inscription: ". . . Give me your tired, your poor, your huddled masses yearning to breathe free . . ." Then refer students to the words of American poet William C. Bryant (page 537). Discuss with students what the United States meant to immigrants. Have students recall what America meant to English colonists (pages 97–99). Ask: Why did immigrants continue to come to the United States in the late 1800's and early 1900's? Why might people today want to immigrate to the United States?

Using Graphs. Have students turn to the graph on page 538. Ask: What is the title of the graph? ("Immigration, 1820–1980.") What is the horizontal label? (Millions of people.) What information is shown vertically? (Decades between 1820 and 1980.) Have students answer the questions in the graph caption. Then have them skim Section 1 to find answers to these questions: (1) Between 1820 and 1850, from where did the largest number of immigrants come? (Ireland.) (2) From where did the largest number of immigrants come between 1850 and 1890? (Germany.) (3) When did the sources of immigration shift to southern and eastern Europe? (From 1890 to the 1920's.)

SECTION 2 (PAGES 543–546)

Bulletin Board. Have students work in groups to put together projects for a bulletin board display. The display should feature the growth of cities from the Civil War to present times. Each group should work on a different project. Have them choose from the following: (1) collecting pictures of cities and writing captions for those pictures, (2) drawing pictures that show typical stages in the growth of cities (see number 4 in "Things To Do" on page 579), (3) making tables that show how the population of selected cities has changed over the last century, (4) constructing posters that show the reasons why cities and urban areas have grown in the last century, and (5) drawing maps of the United States that show the ten largest cities in 1880 and 1980. (See the table on page 555 and the map on page 545.)

SECTION 3 (PAGES 546–551)

Community Study. Have students find out more about the community in which they live. Write the following questions on the board and have students copy them on a sheet of paper. Ask students to prepare written answers to the questions. (1) Is their community a suburb of a large metropolitan area? If so, what area? (2) What public services are provided in their community? (3) Does their community have tall buildings? Where? (4) What distinguishing features does their community have? (5) Did the community exist a century ago? If so, how has the population changed?

SECTION 4 (PAGES 551–553)

Class Discussion. Discuss the changes in life on farms and in small towns described in this section. Summarize the changes on the board. Then ask students to explain how each of the following affected ways of living in rural areas: electricity, automobiles, radio, television, and the telephone. Ask: How have these developments made it possible for people living in rural and urban areas to see and hear the same things?

Chapter Wrap Up. Use either of the following strategies to conclude Chapter 25:

(1) Review the boldfaced terms in the chapter. Ask students to explain what each term has to do with the arrival of people from other lands and the growth of cities. Discuss how terms such as *suburb, metropolitan area,* and *megalopolis* are important in much of present-day America.

(2) Point out that Chapter 25 tells how many Americans moved from rural areas to urban areas. Ask: How did this shift in population affect the size of cities? What did people hope to find in the cities? Mention that on page 705 students will read about the recent shift of people to small farms and towns. Discuss the advantages and disadvantages of rural and urban living.

Evaluation. Review Chapter 25 by using the Chapter Check Up (pages 553–554).

See the *Resource Book* for activity sheets (pages 101–104) and test (pages 201–202).

CHAPTER 26 (pages 556–577)
America Provides More Opportunities for More People

STUDENT OBJECTIVES
After completing their study of Chapter 26, students will be able to:

1. Identify the largest minority groups in the United States and tell how each has overcome obstacles and made use of new opportunities.
2. Describe ways in which women gained greater opportunities in the century after the Civil War.
3. Explain how educational opportunities expanded in the late 1800's.
4. Identify important forms of leisure-time activity in American life.
5. Identify important individuals in American literature, art, and music of the past century.

TEACHING STRATEGIES

Getting Started. Tell students that they can learn about history from a number of different perspectives. Remind them that they have learned about history by studying events in the order in which they occurred. Point out that they can also study themes in history. Have students read the introduction on pages 556–557. Ask: What are some themes in American history? (The search for opportunities, growth and change.) Point out that this chapter tells

how certain changes increased opportunities for many Americans. Then assign Section 1 for reading.

SECTION 1 (PAGES 557–563)

Class Discussion. Direct students to Thomas Jefferson's statement on page 558. Ask: How are the rights of both the majority and minority groups protected in our country? (Bill of Rights.) Have students turn to the Bill of Rights at the back of the book. Ask them to help you list on the board the rights that are protected by those ten amendments. (For example, the right to choose one's religion, the right of free speech.) Discuss how the following further protect citizens' rights: (1) the system of checks and balances (page 257), (2) separation of powers (page 256), (3) the jury system (page 156). Tell students that in later sections of this chapter they will learn how court decisions and laws concerning voting practices have extended the rights of many Americans. Then have students prepare written summaries of the class discussion.

Bulletin Board. Have students put together a bulletin board display that features individuals from various minority groups who have made contributions to the nation either in the past or in recent times. Students will need to use library sources. The display could include (1) written reports on the lives of the individuals, (2) pictures of the individuals, (3) posters highlighting specific achievements, (4) newspaper clippings or magazine articles. Tell students that the individuals they select may be persons who have been successful in government, science, industry, music, literature, art, entertainment, or other fields of work.

SECTION 2 (PAGES 563–567)

Class Discussion. Discuss how opportunities have increased for women during the past century. Remind students of the changes in industry, business, and technology they have studied in recent chapters. Then discuss how those changes affected the lives of women. Ask: What new jobs were created because of these changes? Why were women attracted to these jobs? Point out that wider opportunities in education have made it possible for women to enter professions once closed to them. Have students help you make a list of those professions on the board. Then discuss how opportunities for women have been affected by their right to vote.

Writing Reports. Have students write reports on some aspect of the women's suffrage movement. The reports could deal with: (1) leaders of the movement, (2) methods used by women to reach their goals, (3) the success of the movement in various states, (4) the effect of World War I, or (5) the passage of the Nineteenth Amendment. To complete this assignment, students may need to do outside reading.

SECTION 3 (PAGES 568–575)

Class Discussion. Discuss the importance of education in American society today. Ask: How does education increase an individual's opportunities? How do educated people contribute to our nation? How does the public education system make it possible for the great majority of young people to attend school?

Student Research. Remind students that since the late 1800's, vacations have become a part of American life (page 571). Ask students to find out about national parks in the United States that are favorite vacation spots. Have students turn to the map of national parks (page 591) and to "Linking Past and Present" (page 598). Then put a list of national parks on the board (for example, Grand Canyon, Yellowstone, Yosemite). Ask students to make posters that feature selected national parks. Posters could include: (1) drawings or pictures of scenic spots, (2) something about the history of the park, (3) a list of interesting facts about the park, and (4) a map of the state (or states) in which the park is located.

Chart-Making. Have students skim Section 3 and make a list of the individuals mentioned there. Then have students set up four columns labeled *recreation*, *literature*, *art*, and *music*. Tell students to classify the individuals according to the field in which they made their contributions.

Class Discussion. Bring to class examples of works mentioned in Section 3. You may want to choose a particular theme — American poets, American artists, or American musicians. Discuss how writers, poets, musicians, and those individuals in the field of entertainment contribute to our understanding of the American past. Ask: How do the achievements of such people enrich our lives?

Chapter Wrap Up. Tell students that many people call the United States the "Land of Opportunity." Ask: How were opportunities increased for many Americans during the 1900's? (For example, Supreme Court decisions, amendments to the Constitution.) How are the lives of the people mentioned in this chapter evidence that America is a land of opportunity? (They have had the opportunity to make important contributions to society.) Then have students help you list on the board opportunities they now have or will have as adults.

Evaluation. Review Chapter 26 by using the Chapter Check Up (pages 575–576).

See the *Resource Book* for activity sheets (pages 105–108) and test (pages 203–204).

Concluding Unit 8. See unit summary, review, and activities on pages 578–579. See *Resource Book,* pages 205–206, for unit test.

UNIT 9   Preview

Ask students to read the title of Unit 9. Then tell them that the introduction (page 581) gives information about the increased involvement of the United States in world affairs during the late 1800's and early 1900's. Have students study the time line and pictures (pages 580–581). Ask: With what parts of the world did Americans become involved?

CHAPTER 27   (pages 582–599)
American Leaders Face New Issues

STUDENT OBJECTIVES

After completing their study of Chapter 27, students will be able to:

1. Identify the Presidents from 1869 to 1921.
2. Identify the territories added to the United States in the late 1860's.
3. List reform laws passed during Theodore Roosevelt's administration.
4. List reform laws passed during Woodrow Wilson's administration.

TEACHING STRATEGIES

Getting Started. Ask students to help you list on the board the Presidents who served between the 1860's and the 1920's. (See "Our Presidents," pages 587–588.) Mention that the years an individual serves as President are called that person's *administration*. Tell students that the different administrations have characteristics that make them stand apart from one another. Discuss what these characteristics might be. (For example, laws that were passed, reforms carried out, personality of a President, policies toward other countries.) Tell students to note, as they read Chapter 27, the characteristics of each administration.

SECTION 1 (PAGES 583–589)

Comparison. Have students compare the purchase of Alaska with the Louisiana Purchase (page 275) by answering the following questions: (1) What reasons did the United States have for making the purchase? (2) What country sold the territory to the United States? (3) Why was that country willing to sell the territory? (4) What was the reaction of the American people to the purchase? (5) What was known about the territory at the time of the purchase?

SECTION 2 (PAGES 590–594)

Bulletin Board. Have students put together a bulletin board display featuring Theodore Roose-

velt. The display could include: (1) pictures and drawings of Roosevelt at different times in his life, (2) pictures and drawings of the members of his family, (3) brief reports on his early life, (4) lists of his achievements as an adult, (5) clippings and articles about him.

Class Discussion. Bring to class several cans of soup (or their labels) and pass them around. Tell students to make a list of the ingredients that are identified on the labels. Ask: Why is it important for people to know what is in the food they are eating? Point out that companies today must list the ingredients of food products they sell for people to use. Have students read the section under the heading "Protection from harmful products" on page 593. Ask: Why must companies label foods and other products honestly? (Because of the Pure Food and Drug Act.) Under whose administration was this important law passed? (Theodore Roosevelt's administration.) Then discuss what Roosevelt meant when he said, "No man may poison the people for his private profit."

SECTION 3 (PAGES 595–597)

Student Reports. Have students write reports on the life of Woodrow Wilson. Tell students to use these questions as guides for their reports: (1) When was Wilson born, and where? (2) What are some facts about his early life? (3) When did he become the president of Princeton University? The governor of New Jersey? (4) What were some of his achievements as President of the United States? Remind students to prepare outlines and to illustrate their reports.

Class Discussion. Tell students that Presidents build on the achievements of those who precede them. Point out that Woodrow Wilson continued the reforms set in motion by Theodore Roosevelt. Have students skim Sections 2 and 3 and make a list of the reforms supported by both Presidents. Discuss how Roosevelt's "square deal" (page 592) and Wilson's "New Freedom" were linked.

Chapter Wrap Up. Review Chapter 27 by playing a game of "Clues" with students about the Presidents mentioned in the chapter. Have students take several minutes to review details about the Presidents. (Remind them of the feature "Our Presidents," pages 587–588.) Then have them close their books. Students should be prepared to identify the Presidents from the clues that you provide. Use such clues as "I am thinking of the Democrat from New York" (Cleveland) or "During this President's administration Congress passed the Pure Food and Drug Act" (Theodore Roosevelt). You will find it helpful to prepare a written list of clues before class.

Evaluation. Review Chapter 27 by using the Chapter Check Up (pages 597–598).

See the *Resource Book* for activity sheets (pages 109–112) and test (pages 207–208).

CHAPTER 28   (pages 600–617)
The United States Gains Possessions Overseas

STUDENT OBJECTIVES
After completing their study of Chapter 28, students will be able to:

1. Explain how the search for new markets affected American foreign policy during the late 1800's and early 1900's.
2. Explain how American involvement in Hawaii led to its acquisition by the United States and ultimately to statehood.
3. List territories acquired by the United States as a result of war with Spain in 1898.
4. Describe the governments set up by the United States in the Philippines, Puerto Rico, and Cuba.
5. Locate the Panama Canal on a map.
6. Identify other Pacific and Caribbean islands acquired by the United States in the late 1800's and early 1900's.

TEACHING STRATEGIES

Getting Started. Tell students that from the time the first colonists came to America, people had always been able to expand into new territories and to acquire more land. Have students note that after 1848 the United States stretched from the Atlantic to the Pacific Ocean. Point out that this chapter tells how the United States acquired additional possessions. Discuss what overseas possessions could mean to the United States. (Supplies of raw materials, markets for farm and manufactured products, investment opportunities, coaling stations and naval bases, and the respect of other nations.)

SECTION 1 (PAGES 601–602)

Class Discussion. After students have read Section 1 of this chapter, ask them to identify the main incentive for American expansion during the late 1800's and early 1900's. (Trade.) In discussing why Americans needed new markets for their trade, remind students of these facts: (1) Between 1860 and 1890 agricultural and industrial productivity had increased. (2) American farms and factories were producing a surplus of consumer goods. (3) American business leaders were looking for investment opportunities in other countries. Then have students explain how the search for new markets influenced United States foreign policy.

SECTION 2 (PAGES 602–608)

Answering Research Questions. Have students use their texts and library sources to answer these questions about the war between Spain and the United States: (1) Between what

months in 1898 did the war take place? (April and August.) (2) What individual, later to become President, took part in the war? (Theodore Roosevelt.) (3) How did certain newspapers affect the public's attitude toward the war? (Their emotional and exaggerated accounts of Spanish misrule in Cuba made many Americans demand United States intervention.) (4) What areas did the United States acquire as a result of the war? (Guam, Puerto Rico, and the Philippines.)

SECTION 3 (PAGES 608–611)

Class Discussion. Point out that the "march of the flag" (page 609) outside American borders meant that the United States had increased its responsibilities as well as its territories. Ask: For what new territories was the United States now responsible? Have students skim Section 3 and help you list on the board the problems that were faced in each of those areas at the time of acquisition. Discuss how the United States government tried to solve these problems.

SECTION 4 (PAGES 611–614)

Reading Pictures. Have students turn to the picture on page 613 and ask these questions: (1) What is the subject of the picture? (Digging the Panama Canal.) (2) What kind of equipment was used to dig the canal? (Cranes, huge earth-moving machines.) Point out that the land around the canal site appears mountainous and rugged in the picture. Discuss the problems this would have caused engineers. Then have students read the caption. What details about the Panama Canal does it add?

SECTION 5 (PAGES 614–615)

Chart-Making. Ask students to help you list on the board the possessions added to the United States during the late 1800's and early 1900's. Then have students make charts classifying these possessions under the following headings: (1) Pacific Ocean, (2) Caribbean Sea. Tell students that the charts will help them locate these islands on the maps on pages 605 and 612.

Chapter Wrap Up. Point out the cause-and-effect relationships that are evident in this chapter. Ask: How did the need for new markets awaken American interest in world affairs? How did business investments and trade opportunities overseas lead to changes in American foreign policy? How did the United States acquire new possessions? Emphasize that a theme of this chapter is the increased involvement of the United States in world affairs.

Evaluation. Review Chapter 28 by using the Chapter Check Up (pages 615–616).

See the *Resource Book* for activity sheets (pages 113–118) and test (pages 209–210).

CHAPTER 29 (pages 618–637)
The United States Plays a Larger Part in World Affairs

STUDENT OBJECTIVES
After completing their study of Chapter 29, students will be able to:

1. Identify reasons for United States involvement in Asia and Latin America during the late 1800's and early 1900's.
2. Identify changes in foreign policy that occurred after 1898.
3. List reasons why the United States became involved in World War I.
4. Identify the major points of President Wilson's peace plan.
5. List the major provisions of the Versailles Treaty.

TEACHING STRATEGIES

Getting Started. Ask students to read the chapter introduction (pages 618–619). Then discuss the factors that would cause a country to change its policies toward other countries. (For example, trade, war.) Point out that Chapter 29 tells how events outside the borders of the United States affected Americans. Tell students that at the end of Chapter 29 you will ask them to discuss whether it is possible for nations not to be affected by world affairs.

SECTION 1 (PAGES 619–626)

Student Research. Mention that Perry first visited Japan in 1853. Then have students use their textbooks and library sources to answer these questions about Perry's second visit to Japan in 1854: (1) What kind of treaty did Perry arrange with the Japanese government? (A trade treaty.) (2) Who was President at this time? (Franklin Pierce.) (3) How did Perry publicize his visit when he returned home in 1856? (He published his records in a report entitled *Narrative of the Expedition of an American Squadron to the China Seas and Japan.*)

Class Discussion. Point out to students that foreign policies are often given a name. Remind them of President Monroe's statement of policy concerning Latin America (pages 282–283). Ask: What was that policy called? (Monroe Doctrine.) Have students skim Section 1 to find the name given to the foreign policy formulated by John Hay in 1899. (Open Door Policy.) Ask: What did America hope to achieve in Asia as a result of this policy? (See page 621.) Then discuss how the Open Door Policy in Asia and a broader interpretation of the Monroe Doctrine in Latin America increased American involvement overseas.

SECTION 2 (PAGES 627–632)

Class Discussion. Discuss Wilson's decision to go to war with Germany. Have students read Wilson's message to Congress (page 630). Ask: What did he fear would result from war? What reasons did he give for going to war? Mention that later in the message, Wilson stated Americans would need to dedicate their "lives and . . . fortunes" in order to win the war. Have students skim the text under the heading "The United States plays a valiant part in World War I" (page 630). Discuss the ways in which Americans mobilized for war. (For example, factories, shipyards, and farmers increased production.)

Student Projects. Ask students to do one of the following projects: (1) Report on the sinking of the *Lusitania.* (2) Reproduce a World War I propaganda poster. (3) Present to the class a sampling of World War I songs. (4) Report on famous American soldiers or officers who fought in the war (for example, General Pershing or Sergeant Alvin York). (5) Report on or collect pictures of the new kinds of warfare (for example, tanks, airplanes, trench warfare). (6) Draw and color poster-sized maps of the countries involved in the war.

SECTION 3 (PAGES 632–635)

Class Discussion. Direct student attention to Wilson's summary of United States aims in World War I (page 633). Then have students summarize the main points of Wilson's plan for peace. Discuss how his Fourteen Points were designed to "make the world safe for democracy." Then ask these questions: (1) Which part of his plan did President Wilson refuse to give up? (Peace-keeping association of nations.) (2) What was this association to be called? (The League of Nation.) (3) How was the League to be organized? (page 633) (4) What were the goals of the League? (page 634) (5) What measures could the League take against warring member nations? (page 634) Discuss why the League was unable to fulfill its mission.

Chapter Wrap Up. Remind students that at the beginning of the twentieth century, American foreign policies involved the United States deeply in world affairs. Point out that by 1920 many Americans were urging the government to adopt a policy of isolation. Discuss the factors which brought about this shift in public opinion. Discuss why a leading nation, such as the United States, could not remain uninvolved in world affairs.

Evaluation. Review Chapter 29 by using the Chapter Check Up (pages 635–636).

See the *Resource Book* for activity sheets (pages 117–120) and test (pages 211–212).

Concluding Unit 9. See unit summary, review, and activities on pages 638–639. See *Resource Book,* pages 213–214, for unit test.

UNIT 10 Preview

Point out that the unit introduction identifies the years since 1920 as a "time of remarkable experiences." Have students skim the introduction and list experiences they will expect to learn more about in Unit 10 (war, economic trouble, challenges at home and abroad, recent changes in the way Americans live). Then have the students study the pictures on pages 640 and 641. Discuss how these pictures are related to the themes to be covered in Unit 10.

CHAPTER 30   (pages 642–667)
Our Country Faces Problems at Home and Abroad

STUDENT OBJECTIVES
After completing their study of Chapter 30, students will be able to:

1. Identify the chief events of the administrations of Presidents Harding, Coolidge, and Hoover.
2. List programs established by the government during the New Deal.
3. Identify events in Europe and Asia that led to the outbreak of World War II.
4. Describe the event that caused the United States to enter World War II.
5. List the steps taken by the United States to win the war.
6. Explain how the war affected the lives of Americans.

TEACHING STRATEGIES

Getting Started. Mention that Chapter 30 is arranged chronologically (You may need to review the meaning of the term *chronological*.) Sections 1 and 2 deal with events that occurred during the administrations of Presidents Harding, Coolidge, Hoover, and Roosevelt. Section 3 is an account of the events which led to the beginning of World War II. Section 4 describes how the United States and its allies won World War II. You may want students to skim Chapter 30, noting the events and people discussed in this period of history, before they begin their study of Section 1.

SECTION 1 (PAGES 643–645)

Class Discussion. Have students skim Section 1 and then ask: What was the national mood by the time of the 1920 election? (To "get back to normal.") Discuss why the mood of Americans had changed. Ask: Why did Americans want to withdraw from world affairs? What had happened to the spirit of reform at home? Was it possible for the United States to avoid involvement in world affairs? Tell students to keep their answers to these questions in mind as they study this chapter.

Bulletin Board. Have students put together a bulletin board display that features aspects of American life during the Great Depression. The display could include: (1) lists of popular songs and movies, (2) stories about acts of unselfishness and heroism, (3) collections of pictures that show the impact of the Depression on the lives of Americans, and (4) newspaper and magazine accounts of hardships. You may want to refer to the list of books in the bibliography for Unit 10 on pages T63–T64.

SECTION 2 (PAGES 645–650)

Student Reports. Tell students to prepare written reports on the life of Franklin D. Roosevelt. Refer students to the feature on Roosevelt (page 647) and help them make a list of topics their reports will cover. These topics could include: (1) when and where Roosevelt was born, (2) facts about his childhood, (3) his education, (4) the political posts he held prior to his election as President, (5) details about his illness in 1921 and his triumph over disability, (6) the part played in his career by Eleanor Roosevelt, and (7) his actions and policies as President. Remind students to use library sources, prepare outlines, and illustrate their reports.

Class Discussion. Have students skim pages 646–649 and identify significant steps taken during Roosevelt's early years in office. (Students should identify such measures as the laws to aid farmers, the CCC program, the Wagner Act, the Social Security Act, the TVA.) Ask: What did Roosevelt hope to accomplish by this legislation? (He hoped to end the Depression.) What was the total program called? (The New Deal.) Point out that the New Deal legislation increased the power and cost of the federal government. You may want to discuss how legislation passed several decades ago can still influence the lives of Americans.

SECTION 3 (PAGES 651–656)

Class Discussion. After students have read Section 3 and Section 4 up to page 659, discuss how world events drew the United States into World War II. Ask these questions: Why had disarmament failed? What land-hungry nations were seizing other countries? What governments in the 1930's were hostile to individual freedom and national self-determination? Why did the policy of appeasement fail to prevent war? How did the attack on Poland finally begin World War II? Why did Americans sympathize with the Allied nations? What event caused the United States to declare war on the Axis Powers?

Class Discussion. Have students identify ways Americans turned their efforts toward victory (pages 659–661). Ask: Men between what ages were called into military service? (18 to 45.) Who replaced workers that had left for the armed services? (Disabled persons and women.) How did farmers contribute? (Increased production.) How was money raised to pay for the war? (Higher taxes, war bonds.) What system was devised to make food supplies and scarce commodities available to those who needed them? (Rationing.) Discuss the "unusual jobs" (page 661) people did during the war. How did these efforts contribute to victory? (Released supplies and men for overseas fighting.) Emphasize the scope of the war, the enormous cost, and the millions of individuals — military and civilian — involved.

Student Reports. Have students prepare written or oral reports on *one* of the following: (1) the attack on Pearl Harbor, (2) the relocation of Japanese Americans, (3) D-Day (June 6, 1944), (4) new types of weapons and methods of warfare, (5) the bombing of Hiroshima and Nagasaki, or (6) the Holocaust.

Chapter Wrap Up. Point out to students that the people living in the United States during the 1930's and early 1940's underwent two significant experiences: (1) the Great Depression; (2) World War II. Ask students to consider what it must have been like to grow up during those times. Then emphasize the debt of gratitude we owe to all Americans who brought the nation through those troubled years.

Evaluation. Review Chapter 30 by using the Chapter Check Up (pages 665–666).

See the *Resource Book* for activity sheets (pages 121–124) and test (pages 215–216).

CHAPTER 31   (pages 668–683)
The Postwar Years Bring Change

STUDENT OBJECTIVES
After completing their study of Chapter 31, students will be able to:

1. List ways in which the government assisted veterans after World War II.
2. List problems faced by President Truman during his years in office.
3. Name the leaders of the two opposing groups of nations that emerged during the cold war.
4. List events that threatened world peace during the Truman and Eisenhower administrations.
5. Identify changes that took place in the United States during President Eisenhower's years in office.

TEACHING STRATEGIES

Getting Started. Direct student attention to the title of Chapter 31 ("The Postwar Years Bring Change"). Explain the difference between *pre*war and *post*war years. Then remind students of significant prewar events. (See Chapter 30.) Point out that by August, 1945, peace was at hand. Ask students to suggest what the expectations of many Americans must have been for the postwar years. (Students' answers will probably include the following suggestions: Americans would want to buy things that had been unavailable during depression and war years; Americans would want to relax and enjoy years of peace; Americans would expect other countries to do their part in keeping the peace.) Would American hopes for the postwar years be dashed? Tell students that Chapter 31 is an account of national and worldwide events during the Truman and Eisenhower administrations. Emphasize that at the end of Chapter 31 you will ask students to measure the outcome of the postwar years against American expectations in 1945.

SECTION 1 (PAGES 669–671)

Student Reports. Have students use their textbooks and library sources to prepare written or oral reports on the life of Harry S. Truman. Tell them to answer these questions in their reports: (1) When was Truman born, and where? (2) Why was he unable to enter the Military Academy at West Point? (3) What jobs did he hold before he entered politics? (4) Whom did he marry? (5) What political offices did he hold before becoming President in 1945? (6) What were significant events that took place while he was President? (7) When did he die and where was he buried?

Class Discussion. Tell students that wars have a disruptive effect on the lives of individuals. Point out that many Americans had interrupted their careers or education when World War II began in order to serve in the armed services. Ask students to suggest other ways in which Americans were affected by World War II. (For example, family members were separated and many families suffered the loss of members killed in action.)

SECTION 2 (PAGES 671–676)

Class Discussion. Have students look up the term *cold war* in the glossary at the back of the book. Explain that this term had first been used in the 1930's to describe the way in which Nazi Germany conquered other nations without actually declaring war and launching a military attack. In the mid-1940's the term was popularized and applied to the uneasy peace that existed after World War II. Discuss what a "cold" war would be like. What would turn a "cold" war into a "hot" one? Then ask students to skim Section 2 and identify characteristics or developments of the cold war period. (For example, two opposing groups of nations led by superpowers, trouble spots threatening to engulf the world in war, discord within the Security Council of the United Nations, Communist take-over of Eastern Europe and other areas.) Discuss what the issue of self-determination had to do with the events that occurred during the cold war.

Class Discussion. Remind students that by the end of World War I, many Americans were reluctant to play an active role in world affairs. Ask: What was that attitude called? (Isolationism, page 635.) Point out that by the mid-1940's the United States had emerged as a leading world power. Discuss how the following actions indicated that Americans had accepted this role of world leadership: (1) joining the UN, (2) establishing the Marshall Plan, (3) signing the Rio Pact, (4) participating in NATO, and (5) sending troops to Korea.

SECTION 3 (PAGES 676–679)

Bulletin Board. Have students put together a bulletin board display featuring American achievements in space. The display could include: (1) pictures and drawings of various spacecraft (for example, rockets, planetary and interplanetary probes, space shuttles); (2) reports on significant "firsts" (for example, first manned space flight, first landing on the moon);

(3) reports on people involved (for example, astronauts, scientists, engineers); (4) pictures of space centers (for example, the Johnson Space Center in Texas, Cape Canaveral in Florida, and Edwards Air Force Base in California); (5) clippings and pictures from newspapers and magazines; (6) lists of space-travel terms; (7) stories of eyewitness accounts.

SECTION 4 (PAGES 679–681)

Class Discussion. Discuss the ways in which black Americans sought to overcome discrimination during the 1950's. Begin by reading the first section of the Fourteenth Amendment. (See back of book.) Ask: What does the Fourteenth Amendment guarantee? (Equal protection for all citizens.) Remind students that the Fourteenth Amendment became a part of the Constitution after the Civil War and was specifically intended to protect blacks (page 445). Then discuss the significance of the following: (1) the Supreme Court's ruling in the Brown case, (2) the black boycott of buses in Montgomery, Alabama, and (3) the spread of boycotts against other segregated public services. Point out that Martin Luther King, Jr., rose to prominence at this time. Ask: How did he urge blacks to seek equal treatment? (Without the use of force or violence.) Tell students that Chapter 32 will complete the account of the civil rights movement that began in the 1950's. Have students look at pages 685–686.

Chapter Wrap Up. Remind students that they were to consider how the postwar years measured up to American expectations in 1945. Ask: Was the desire for prosperity realized? What effect did the cold war have on hopes for world peace? Then discuss the ways in which the United States demonstrated its willingness to promote world peace.

Evaluation. Review Chapter 31 by using the Chapter Check Up (pages 681–682).

See the *Resource Book* for activity sheets (pages 125–128) and test (pages 217–218).

CHAPTER 32 (pages 684–711)
Americans Face the Challenge of a Modern World

STUDENT OBJECTIVES

After completing their study of Chapter 32, students will be able to:

1. State the national and international challenges faced by Presidents Kennedy and Johnson.
2. Identify changes in American foreign policy during President Nixon's years in office.
3. Describe changes in American ways of living since 1960.
4. Identify challenges faced by President Carter in the late 1970's.
5. Name important developments of President Reagan's administration.

TEACHING STRATEGIES

Getting Started. Write this statement on the board: "Today's news is tomorrow's history." Ask students to explain that statement. Then ask them to help you identify the factors that make up "history." (For example, dates, people, important events, causes and effects, and so on.) Point out that it is often easier to interpret the history of times long past than the history of recent decades. Discuss why this might be so. Tell students that, although it may be too early to see the whole picture of events occurring several months or even several years ago, it *is* possible to note the continuation of American themes. Discuss how recent history is built upon the events and ideas of past years. In what ways do Americans still follow the blueprint laid down by the founders of our nation? Ask students to make a list of themes in American history. Tell them that they will use this list to review Chapter 32 and the text.

SECTION 1 (PAGES 685–692)

Class Discussion. Tell students that the goals of a President are often summed up in a phrase. Remind students of Theodore Roosevelt's "square deal" (page 592), Woodrow Wilson's "New Freedom" (page 595), Franklin Roosevelt's "New Deal" (page 646), and Harry Truman's "Fair Deal" (page 671). Review what these Presidents wanted to accomplish. Then tell students that certain phrases came to be applied to the Kennedy and Johnson administrations. President Kennedy's programs were called the "New Frontier" (page 685). How did they constitute a "new" frontier? The measures passed by Congress during Johnson's administration were part of his plan for a "War on Poverty" (page 687). Have students list these

measures. Ask: How would passage of these measures be a "war" on poverty? Discuss the theme that is apparent in the administrations of all these Presidents. (The effort to extend greater opportunities to all Americans.)

Class Discussion. Explain the term *cornerstone* to the class. Then discuss how the Monroe Doctrine has been a cornerstone of American foreign policy in Latin America. Remind students of the main ideas expressed in the Monroe Doctrine (pages 282–283). Then discuss the missile crisis in Cuba in 1962 (page 690). Ask: What countries were involved in the dispute? How were the Soviet Union's actions in Cuba a threat to the principles outlined in the Monroe Doctrine? How was a war avoided?

SECTION 2 (PAGES 693–701)

Class Discussion. Point out that energy consumption has become a major concern over the past two decades. Have students skim the section under the heading "The nation faces a shortage of oil" (pages 696–697). Ask: What event made Americans aware of the dangers in dependency on other countries for resources such as oil? What did President Nixon and Congress do to help Americans cut down on the amount of energy used? Have students help you list on the board the other forms of energy which are being developed to meet the nation's needs. (You may want students to clip pictures and articles on these sources of energy.) Then discuss ways in which Americans can make wise use of all sources of energy available to them.

Bulletin Board. Go over the meaning of the term *bicentennial* with students. Then have them put together a bulletin board display featuring bicentennial themes. The display could include: (1) descriptions of celebrations during 1976, (2) reports on the lives of famous Americans, (3) timelines showing significant events in American history, (4) collections of items for a "time capsule" to be opened a century from now, (5) charts showing the Presidents and their years in office (see the list of Presidents on page 762), and (6) lists and pictures of great American achievements.

SECTION 3 (PAGES 701–709)

Class Discussion. Have students read the section under the boldfaced heading "Modern Advances Affect Ways of Living" (pages 701–705). Then tell students that they will spend a class period discussing the impact of technological changes on American life. Ask: What changes had the greatest impact on transportation and communication?

Studying Different Presidencies. Mention that one way to study presidencies is to see how different administrations address challenges that arise in two areas: (1) overseas, and (2) at home. Remind students that they have already learned the meaning of the term *foreign policy* (page 601). Tell students that a President's *domestic policy* is the approach taken to meet challenges at home. Have students skim the section under the boldfaced heading "Our Recent Presidents" (pages 705–709). Then ask students to help you list on the board the foreign and domestic policies of recent Presidents.

Chapter Wrap Up. Point out to students that they have studied several centuries of American history in just a few months. Remind them of some of the continuing themes in American history. (For example, the desire for freedom, the spirit of exploration.) Mention that, although ways of living have changed, those themes have remained constant throughout American history. Ask: How have these themes been apparent in recent decades? Point out that the civil rights movement of the 1960's was a continuation of the American quest for freedom; space exploration has been a continuation of the spirit that led settlers westward across the continent. Then have students reread the chapter introduction on pages 684–685. Discuss what changes our nation's founders would see if they were present in our country today.

Evaluation. Review Chapter 32 by using the Chapter Check Up (pages 709–710).

See the *Resource Book* for activity sheets (pages 129–132) and test (pages 219–220).

Concluding Unit 10. See unit summary, review, and activities on pages 712–713. See *Resource Book,* pages 221–222, for unit test.

Preparing for the Final Examination. If you plan to give a final examination for the course, remind students to prepare by reviewing the Chapter Check Ups. Also tell them to study the Summary of Important Ideas at the ends of all ten units and to reread the Unit Reviews. Let students know how many and what kinds of questions will be on the final examination. You may want to tell them what themes in American history will receive the greatest emphasis.

A final examination for the course is provided in the *Resource Book,* pages 223–226.

America Faces the Future
(pages 714–717)

TEACHING STRATEGY

Class Discussion. Have students reread the closing paragraph on page 717. Ask: Who did Benjamin Franklin feel was responsible for "keeping the republic"? (Each one of us.) Have students skim pages 716–717 and suggest ways in which individuals can be responsible citizens. (For example, keeping informed of national and international events, discussing current issues, voting in local and national elections, and so on.) You may want to write these responsibilities on the board or post them on the bulletin board. Conclude the class discussion by emphasizing the importance of liberty and self-government in our American heritage.

Reference Section

TEACHING STRATEGIES

Thinking About Careers (page 718). Remind students that how they earn their living as adults can be of great benefit to the future of the United States. Then have them put together a bulletin board display featuring careers that contribute to the well-being of our country. The display could include: (1) pictures showing people at work, (2) stories about individuals who have contributed through their careers, (3) descriptions of particular careers, and (4) posters and advertisements designed to attract individuals to certain careers.

Constitution (pages 730–758). You may want students to complete the activity pages calling for study of the Constitution (see pages 51–52 of the *Resource Book*). You may also want to review strategies from Chapter 11 that refer to the Constitution (see pages T27–T28).

The States (page 759) and Flags of the Nation and the States (pages 760–761). Have students use the information on these pages to put together a bulletin board display featuring the fifty states. The display could include: (1) poster-sized drawings of the state flags, (2) maps showing state capitals, (3) a list of states arranged by size of population, and (4) a time line showing the entry of states to the Union. (You may want to suggest that students arrange the time line by decades.)

The Presidents (page 762). Write this statement on the board: "The Vice-President is only a heartbeat away from the most powerful office in the world." Discuss what the statement means. Then have students use their textbooks and library sources to list the Vice-Presidents that have served since 1789. You may also want students to answer the following questions: (1) What official duty does the Constitution give the Vice-President? (To preside over the United States Senate.) (2) What amendment spells out the procedures to be followed in case of presidential disability and provides for a procedure to fill a vacancy in the vice-presidency? (The Twenty-Fifth Amendment.) (3) By 1980, how many Vice-Presidents had become President either by succession or election? (Thirteen.)

Bibliography

This bibliography includes standard titles which will be found in many libraries as well as books published in recent years. The publishers of the original hard-cover editions are cited. Many of these books are also available in paperback editions.

UNIT 1
EUROPE SEEKS AN OCEAN ROUTE TO ASIA AND FINDS THE AMERICAN CONTINENTS

FOR TEACHERS
American Heritage Pictorial Atlas of United States History. American Heritage.
Brebner, John B. *The Explorers of North America, 1592–1806.* Doubleday.
Catton, Bruce and William B. *The Bold and Magnificent Dream: America's Founding Years, 1492–1815.* Doubleday.
Claiborne, Robert. *The First Americans.* Time-Life Books.
Driver, Harold E. *Indians of North America.* University of Chicago Press.
Hordern, Nicholas; Simon Dresener; and Martin Hillman. *The Conquest of North America.* Doubleday.
Josephy, Alvin M., Jr. *The Indian Heritage of America.* Knopf.
Morison, Samuel Eliot. *Admiral of the Ocean Sea.* Little, Brown. A biography of Columbus.
Morison, Samuel Eliot. *The European Discovery of America: The Northern Voyages.* Oxford University Press.

FOR STUDENTS
Baity, Elizabeth C. *Americans Before Columbus.* Viking.
Bakeless, Katherine and John. *They Saw America First.* Lippincott.
Baker, Betty. *Settlers and Strangers: Native Americans of the Desert Southwest and History As They Saw It.* Macmillan.
Berger, Josef, and Lawrence C. Wroth. *Discoverers of the New World.* American Heritage Junior Library.
Berry, Erick. *Leif the Lucky, Discoverer of America.* Garrard.
Chu, Daniel, and Elliott Skinner. *A Glorious Age in Africa.* Doubleday.
Foster, Genevieve. *Year of Columbus, 1492.* Scribner. Events throughout the world at the time of Columbus's great voyage.
Gridley, Marion E. *Indian Tribes of America.* Rand McNally.

Keating, Bern. *Famous American Explorers.* Rand McNally.
Lavine, Sigmund A. *The Games the Indians Played.* Dodd, Mead.
Madden, James F. *The Wonderful World of Maps.* Hammond. An easy introduction to maps and concepts such as distance and direction.
Meredith, Robert K., and E. Brooks Smith, eds. *The Quest of Columbus.* Little, Brown.

UNIT 2
EUROPEANS START COLONIES AND BUILD EMPIRES IN THE AMERICAS

FOR TEACHERS
American Heritage History of the Indian Wars. American Heritage.
American Heritage History of the Thirteen Colonies. American Heritage.
Bolton, Herbert E. *Bolton and the Spanish Borderlands.* John F. Bannon, ed. University of Oklahoma Press.
Boorstin, Daniel J. *The Americans, Vol. 1: The Colonial Experience.* Random.
Bridenbaugh, Carl. *Cities in Revolt: Urban Life in America, 1743–1776.* Oxford University Press.
Bridenbaugh, Carl. *Cities in the Wilderness: The First Century of Urban Life in America, 1625–1742.* Oxford University Press.
Chidsey, Donald B. *The French and Indian War.* Crown.
Hofstadter, Richard. *America at 1750: A Social Portrait.* Knopf.
Horgan, Paul. *Conquistadors in North American History.* Farrar, Straus.
Morgan, Edmund S. *The Puritan Dilemma: The Story of John Winthrop.* Little, Brown.
Spruill, Julia C. *Women's Life and Work in the Southern Colonies.* Russell & Russell.
Tannenbaum, Edward R. *New France.* University of Chicago Press.
Ver Steeg, Clarence L. *The Formative Years: 1607–1763.* Hill & Wang.

FOR STUDENTS
Alderman, Clifford L. *Rum, Slaves and Molasses: The Story of New England's Triangular Trade.* Macmillan.
Alderman, Clifford L. *The Story of the Thirteen Colonies.* Random.
Barth, Edna. *Turkeys, Pilgrims, and Indian Corn: The Story of the Thanksgiving Symbols.* Clarion.

Bulla, Clyde, and Michael Syson. *Conquista!* Crowell. Story about the encounter of exploring Spaniards and western Indians.

Clapp, Patricia. *Constance: A Story of Early Plymouth.* Lothrop.

Fox, Paula. *The Slave Dancer.* Bradbury. Story of a kidnapped boy forced to play his fife on a slave ship to dance the slaves for exercise.

Kurtz, Henry Ira. *Captain John Smith.* Watts.

Loeb, Robert H., Jr. *Meet the Real Pilgrims: Everyday Life on Plimoth Plantation in 1627.* Doubleday.

O'Dell, Scott. *The King's Fifth.* Houghton. Story of a teen-ager's adventures on an expedition to the legendary Seven Cities of Gold.

O'Dell, Scott. *Sing Down the Moon.* Houghton. Story of the forced migration of the Navahos from their homeland.

Russell, Francis. *The French and Indian Wars.* American Heritage Junior Library.

Speare, Elizabeth G. *Life in Colonial America.* Random.

Speare, Elizabeth G. *The Witch of Blackbird Pond.* Houghton. Story of a young girl's rebellion against her Puritan surroundings.

Waterhouse, E. B. *Serra, California Conquistador.* Parker & Son.

Wilson, Forrest. *Build Your Own Early American Village.* Pantheon. Tells how to construct a colonial village.

Wright, Louis B. *Everyday Life in Colonial America.* Putnam.

UNIT 3
NEW NATIONS ARE BORN AS AMERICAN COLONISTS SHAKE OFF EUROPEAN RULE

FOR TEACHERS

Alden, John R. *History of the American Revolution.* Knopf.

Alden, John R. *The South in the Revolution, 1763–1789.* Louisiana State University Press.

American Heritage Book of the Revolution. American Heritage.

Crane, Verner W. *Benjamin Franklin and a Rising People.* Little, Brown.

Dann, John C., ed. *The Revolution Remembered: Eyewitness Accounts of the War for Independence.* University of Chicago Press.

Dorson, Richard M., ed. *America Rebels: Narratives of the Patriots.* Pantheon.

Gipson, Lawrence H. *The Coming of the Revolution: 1763–1775.* Harper.

Lynch, John. *The Spanish American Revolutions, 1808–1862.* Norton.

Miller, John C. *Origins of the American Revolution.* Stanford University Press.

Nye, Russell B. *Cultural Life of the New Nation: 1776–1830.* Harper.

Peckham, Howard H. *The War for Independence: A Military History.* University of Chicago Press.

Wills, Garry. *Inventing America: Jefferson's Declaration of Independence.* Doubleday.

FOR STUDENTS

Alderman, Clifford L. *Samuel Adams: Son of Liberty.* Holt, Rinehart.

Asimov, Isaac. *The Birth of the United States: 1763–1816.* Houghton.

Bakeless, John E. and Katherine L. *Signers of the Declaration.* Houghton.

Collier, James L. and Christopher. *My Brother Sam Is Dead.* Scholastic. Story set during the Revolutionary War.

Commager, Henry Steele. *Great Declaration.* Bobbs.

Davis, Burke. *Black Heroes of the American Revolution.* Harcourt.

De Pauw, Linda Grant. *Founding Mothers: Women of America in the Revolutionary Era.* Houghton.

Dupuy, Trevor N. *Military History of Revolutionary War Land Battles.* Watts.

Dupuy, Trevor N. *Military History of Revolutionary War Naval Battles.* Watts.

Fast, Howard. *The Hessian.* Morrow. Story of a young Hessian soldier who finds refuge in a Connecticut village during the Revolution.

Ferguson, Linda W. *Canada.* Scribner. Canadian history from Indian times to present.

Forbes, Esther. *Johnny Tremain.* Houghton. Story of a young Boston silversmith who becomes involved in the Patriot cause.

Fritz, Jean. *Traitor: The Case of Benedict Arnold.* Putnam.

Fritz, Jean. *What's the Big Idea, Ben Franklin?* Coward. A biography.

Latham, Frank B. *The Trial of John Peter Zenger, August 1735: An Early Fight for America's Freedom of the Press.* Watts.

Leckie, Robert. *The World Turned Upside Down: The Story of the American Revolution.* Putnam.

Montross, Lynn. *Washington and the Revolution.* Houghton.

Phelan, Mary Kay. *The Story of the Boston Massacre.* Crowell.

Reeder, Red. *Bold Leaders of the American Revolution.* Little, Brown.

UNIT 4
THE UNITED STATES IS ESTABLISHED ON A FIRM BASIS

FOR TEACHERS

American Heritage History of the Congress of the United States. American Heritage.

Billington, Ray A. *Westward Expansion.* Macmillan.

Boorstin, Daniel J. *The Americans, Vol 2: The National Experience.* Random.

Corwin, Edward S. *The Constitution and What It Means Today.* Princeton University Press.

Dangerfield, George. *The Era of Good Feelings.* Harcourt.

Fribourg, Marjorie. *U. S. Congress: Men Who Steered Its Course, 1787–1867.* Macrae.

Glusker, Irwin, and R. M. Ketchum. *American Testament: Fifty Great Documents of American History.* American Heritage.

Hofstadter, Richard. *The American Political Tradition and the Men Who Made It.* Knopf.

Horsman, Reginald. *The War of 1812.* Knopf.

Miller, John C. *The Federalist Era, 1789–1801.* Harper.

Perkins, Dexter. *A History of the Monroe Doctrine.* Little, Brown.

Rossiter, Clinton. *American Presidency.* Harcourt.

Schachner, Nathan. *Founding Fathers.* Barnes.

Smelser, Marshall. *Democratic Republic, 1801–1815.* Harper.

Whitney, David C. *The American Presidents.* Doubleday. Presidencies from Washington to Carter.

FOR STUDENTS

Barry, James P. *The Louisiana Purchase, April 1803.* Watts.

Brown, Dee. *Andrew Jackson and the Battle of New Orleans.* Putnam.

Cabral, Olga. *So Proudly She Sailed: Tales of Old Ironsides.* Houghton. Stories of life aboard the *Constitution* on peaceful days as well as during exciting battles.

Hayman, LeRoy. *What You Should Know About the U.S. Constitution and the Men Who Wrote It.* Scholastic.

Johnson, Gerald W. *The Congress.* Morrow.

Judson, Clara I. *George Washington, Leader of the People.* Follett.

Lawson, Don. *War of 1812: America's Second War for Independence.* Abelard.

Lewis, Anthony. *The Supreme Court and How It Works.* Random.

McConnell, Jane and Burt. *Presidents of the United States.* Crowell.

Sheean, Vincent. *Thomas Jefferson: Father of Democracy.* Random.

Smith, Irene. *Washington, D. C.* Rand McNally.

Vaughan, Harold. *The Monroe Doctrine, 1823: A Landmark in American Foreign Policy.* Watts.

UNIT 5
THE AMERICAN WAY OF LIVING CHANGES AS THE DIFFERENT SECTIONS DEVELOP

FOR TEACHERS

American Heritage History of Railroads in America. American Heritage.

American Heritage History of Seafaring America. American Heritage.

Clark, Thomas D. *Frontier America: The Story of the Westward Movement.* Scribner.

Cohn, David L. *The Life and Times of King Cotton.* Oxford University Press.

De Tocqueville, Alexis. *Democracy in America.* Various editions.

Filler, Louis. *The Crusade Against Slavery, 1830–1860.* Harper.

Franklin, John Hope. *The Militant South, 1800–1861.* Harvard University Press.

Genovese, Eugene D. *Roll, Jordan, Roll: The World the Slaves Made.* Random.

Green, Constance M. *Eli Whitney and the Birth of American Technology.* Little, Brown.

Nye, Russel B. *William Lloyd Garrison and the Humanitarian Reformers.* Little, Brown.

Remini, Robert V., ed. *The Age of Andrew Jackson.* University of South Carolina Press.

Schlesinger, Arthur M., Jr. *The Age of Jackson.* Little, Brown.

Spann, Edward K. *The New Metropolis: New York City, 1840–1857.* Columbia University Press.

Stampp, Kenneth M. *The Peculiar Institution.* Knopf. A study of slavery.

Taylor, George Rogers. *The Transportation Revolution, 1815–1860.* Harper.

Ware, Norman. *Industrial Worker, 1840–1860.* Peter Smith.

FOR STUDENTS

Andrist, Ralph K. *Steamboats on the Mississippi.* American Heritage Junior Library.

Bakeless, John. *Adventures of Lewis and Clark.* Houghton.

Coit, Margaret L. *Andrew Jackson.* Houghton.

Fisher, Leonard. *The Factories.* Holiday. About the early New England factories.

Fleischmann, Glen H. *Cherokee Removal 1838: An Entire Indian Nation Is Forced Out of Its Homeland.* Watts.

Lindstrom, Aletha Jane. *Sojourner Truth: Slave, Abolitionist, Fighter for Women's Rights.* Messner.

Meltzer, Milton. *Hunted Like a Wolf: The Story of the Seminole War.* Farrar, Straus.

Meltzer, Milton. *In Their Own Words: A History of the American Negro, 1619–1865.* Crowell.

Meltzer, Milton. *A Light in the Dark: The Life of Samuel Gridley Howe.* Crowell.

Meltzer, Milton. *Underground Man.* Bradbury. Story of a northern farm boy who became an abolitionist.

Steele, William O. *Old Wilderness Road: An American Journey.* Harcourt.

Syme, Ronald. *Osceola: Seminole Leader.* Morrow.

Wright, Louis B. *Everyday Life on the American Frontier.* Putnam.

UNIT 6
THE NATION EXPANDS
AND IS TORN BY WAR

FOR TEACHERS

American Heritage Picture History of the Civil War. Doubleday.

Billington, Ray A. *Westward Expansion.* Macmillan.

Craven, Avery O. *The Coming of the Civil War.* University of Chicago Press.

Davis, Burke. *Our Incredible Civil War.* Holt, Rinehart.

Fehrenbacher, Don E. *Manifest Destiny and the Coming of the Civil War, 1840–1861.* AHM Publishing.

Flood, Charles Bracelen. *Lee: The Last Years.* Houghton.

Franklin, John Hope. *Reconstruction After the Civil War.* University of Chicago Press.

Kirwan, Albert D., ed. *Confederacy: A Social and Political History in Documents.* Meridian.

Lewis, Meriwether, and William Clark. *Journals of Lewis and Clark: A New Selection.* John Bakeless, ed. New American Library.

McFeely, William S. *Grant: A Biography.* Norton.

Mitchell, Joseph B. *Decisive Battles of the Civil War.* Putnam.

Oates, Stephen B. *With Malice Toward None.* Harper. A biography of Lincoln.

Singletary, Otis A. *The Mexican War.* University of Chicago Press.

Stampp, Kenneth M. *Era of Reconstruction, 1865–1877.* Knopf.

Thomas, Benjamin P. *Abraham Lincoln: A Biography.* Knopf.

Thomas, Emory M. *The Confederate Nation, 1861–1865.* Harper.

Williams, T. Harry. *Lincoln and His Generals.* Knopf.

Woodward, C. Vann, ed. *Mary Chesnut's Civil War.* Yale University Press. A famous Civil War diary.

Woodward, C. Vann. *Origins of the New South, 1877–1913.* Louisiana State University Press.

FOR STUDENTS

Andrist, Ralph K., and Archibald Hanna. *The California Gold Rush.* American Heritage Junior Library.

Bakeless, Katherine and John. *Confederate Spy Stories.* Lippincott.

Barry, James P. *Bloody Kansas, 1854–1865: Guerrilla Warfare Delays Peaceful American Settlement.* Watts.

Bishop, Jim. *The Day Lincoln Was Shot.* Harper.

Davis, Burke. *Mr. Lincoln's Whiskers.* Coward. Based on the true story of a girl's letter to President Lincoln.

Downey, Fairfax, and Paul M. Angle. *Texas and the War with Mexico.* American Heritage Junior Library.

Green, Margaret. *President of the Confederacy, Jefferson Davis.* Messner.

Hunt, Irene. *Across Five Aprils.* Grossett. Story of the agonies of one family during the Civil War.

Latham, Frank B. *Abraham Lincoln.* Watts.

Latham, Frank B. *Dred Scott Decision, March 6, 1857: Slavery and the Supreme Court's Self-Inflicted Wound.* Watts.

Latham, Frank B. *Lincoln and the Emancipation Proclamation: The Document That Turned the Civil War into a Fight for Freedom.* Watts.

Levitin, Sonia. *The No-Return Trail.* Harcourt. A true story about a young pioneer who traveled by wagon train to California in 1841.

O'Dell, Scott. *The 290.* Houghton. Story of a ship built secretly for the Confederate navy.

Scott, John Anthony. *Woman Against Slavery: The Story of Harriet Beecher Stowe.* Crowell.

Skold, Betty Westrom. *Sacagawea.* Dillon.

Werstein, Irving. *This Wounded Land: The Era of Reconstruction: 1865–1877.* Delacorte.

UNIT 7
MODERN AMERICA TAKES SHAPE

FOR TEACHERS

American Heritage History of American Business and Industry. American Heritage.

American Heritage History of the Automobile in America. American Heritage.

American Heritage History of the Great West. American Heritage.

Atherton, Lewis. *The Cattle Kings.* University of Nebraska Press.

Billington, Ray A. *Westward Expansion.* Macmillan.

Brooks, Thomas R. *Toil and Trouble: A History of American Labor.* Delacorte.

Brown, Dee. *Bury My Heart at Wounded Knee: An Indian History of the American West.* Holt, Rinehart.

Cochran, Thomas C., and William Miller. *The Age of Enterprise: A Social History of Industrial America.* Macmillan.

Conrat, Maisie and Richard. *The American Farm: A Photographic History.* California Historical Society and Houghton.

Ginger, Ray. *Age of Excess: The United States from 1877 to 1914.* Macmillan.

Hicks, John D. *The Populist Revolt: A History of the Farmers' Alliance and the People's Party.* University of Nebraska Press.

Kramer, Mark. *Three Farms: Making Milk, Meat and Money from the American Soil.* Atlantic-Little, Brown.

Paul, Rodman W. *Mining Frontiers of the Far West, 1848–1880.* Holt, Rinehart.

Stratton, Joanne L. *Pioneer Women: Voices from the Kansas Frontier.* Simon & Schuster.

Webb, Walter P. *The Great Plains.* Grosset.

Wertime, Theodore A. *The Coming of the Age of Steel.* University of Chicago Press.

FOR STUDENTS

Brown, Dee. *Lonesome Whistle: The Story of the First Transcontinental Railroad.* Holt.

Cousins, Margaret. *The Story of Thomas Alva Edison.* Random.

Fanning, Leonard M. *Fathers of Industries.* Lippincott.

Garst, Shannon. *Amelia Earhart: Heroine of the Skies.* Messner.

Garst, Shannon. *Chief Joseph of the Nez Perces.* Messner.

Hayes, Wilma P. *Eli Whitney: Founder of Modern Industry.* Watts.

Kurland, Gerald. *John D. Rockefeller: Nineteenth Century Industrialist and Oil Baron.* SamHar Press.

Latham, Frank B. *The Transcontinental Railroad, 1862–1869: A Great Engineering Feat Links America Coast to Coast.* Watts.

McGaa, Ed. *Red Cloud: The Story of an American Indian.* Dillon. Biography of a Sioux chief.

Meltzer, Milton. *Bread and Roses: The Struggle of American Labor, 1865–1911.* Knopf.

Reynolds, Quentin. *The Wright Brothers: Pioneers of American Aviation.* Random.

Seidman, Laurence. *Once in the Saddle.* New American Library. Cowboy life on the frontier from 1866 to 1896.

Simon, Charlie May. *The Andrew Carnegie Story.* Dutton.

Straight, Treva Adams. *The Price of Free Land.* Lippincott. A true story of homesteading in western Nebraska.

Walker, Robert H. *Everyday Life in the Age of Enterprise, 1865–1900.* Putnam.

Wilder, Laura Ingalls. *The Little House Books,* 9 vols. Harper.

Wulffson, Don L. *Extraordinary Stories Behind the Invention of Ordinary Things.* Lothrop.

UNIT 8
NEW CONDITIONS BRING CHANGES IN AMERICAN LIFE

FOR TEACHERS

Banks, Ann. *First-Person America.* Knopf. A collection of actual interviews that reveal what life was like in America in the early twentieth century.

Flexner, Eleanor. *Century of Struggle: The Woman's Rights Movement in the United States.* Harvard University Press.

Franklin, John Hope. *From Slavery to Freedom: A History of Negro Americans.* Knopf.

Green, Constance W. *The Rise of Urban America.* Harper.

Handlin, Oscar. *The Uprooted.* Little, Brown.

Harding, Vincent. *There is a River: The Black Struggle for Freedom in America.* Harcourt.

Higham, John. *Strangers in the Land.* Atheneum.

Houston, Jeanne Wakatsuki and James D. *Farewell to Manzanar.* Houghton. The story of a Japanese American family during World War II.

Josephy, Alvin M. *Red Power: The American Indians' Fight for Freedom.* American Heritage.

Lingeman, Richard. *Small Town America: A Narrative History, 1620 to the Present.* Putnam.

McMurray, Linda O. *George Washington Carver: Scientist and Symbol.* Oxford University Press.

Meier, Matt S., and Feliciano Rivera. *The Chicanos: A History of Mexican Americans.* Hill and Wang.

Schlesinger, Arthur M. *Rise of the City: 1878–1898.* Macmillan.

Wertheimer, Barbara M. *We Were There: The Story of Working Women in America.* Pantheon.

Woodward, C. Vann. *The Strange Career of Jim Crow.* Oxford University Press. Study of segregation during the late nineteenth century.

FOR STUDENTS

Bales, Carol Ann. *Tales of the Elders: A Memory Book of Men and Women Who Came to America as Immigrants, 1900–1930.* Follett.

Blue, Rose. *We Are Chicano.* Watts. A twelve-year-old boy explains his ethnic heritage.

Coolidge, Olivia. *Women's Rights: The Suffrage Movement in America, 1848–1920.* Dutton.

Dahl, Borghild. *Karen.* Dutton. Story of a Norwegian girl who came to the United States in 1870 and settled in the Dakota Territory.

Giblin, James Cross. *The Skyscraper Book.* Crowell.

Gonzalez, Gloria. *Gaucho.* Knopf. Story of a Puerto Rican boy growing up in New York City.

Greenleaf, Barbara Kaye. *America Fever: The Story of American Immigration.* Four Winds.

Huthmacher, J. Joseph. *A Nation of Newcomers: Ethnic Minorities in American History.* Dial.

Latham, Frank B. *The Rise and Fall of Jim Crow: The Long Struggle Against the Supreme Court's Separate-But-Equal Ruling.* Watts.

Meltzer, Milton. *In Their Own Words: A History of the American Negro, 1865–1916.* Crowell.

Schwartz, Alvin. *Old Cities and New Towns: The Changing Face of the Nation.* Dutton.

Stearns, Monroe. *Mark Twain.* Watts.

Sung, Betty Lee. *An Album of Chinese Americans.* Watts.

Taylor, Mildred. *Roll of Thunder, Hear My Cry.* Dial. Story of black pride and black heritage.

Turner, Mary, ed. *We, Too, Belong: An Anthology About Minorities in America.* Dell.

Webb, Robert N. *America Is Also Irish.* Putnam. About Irish immigration and Irish contributions to America.

White, Florence M. *First Woman in Congress: Jeannette Rankin.* Messner.

UNIT 9
THE UNITED STATES WIDENS ITS HORIZONS

FOR TEACHERS

Allen, Frederick L. *The Big Change: America Transforms Itself, 1900–1950.* Harper. Informal history of changes in American life.

American Heritage History of World War I. American Heritage.

Beale, Howard K. *Theodore Roosevelt and the Rise of America to World Power.* Johns Hopkins University Press.

Bemis, Samuel F. *Short History of American Foreign Policy and Diplomacy.* Holt, Rinehart.

Darracott, Joseph. *The First World War in Posters.* Dover.

Filler, Louis, ed. *The President Speaks: From William McKinley to Lyndon B. Johnson.* Putnam.

Freidel, Frank. *The Splendid Little War.* Little, Brown. A history of the Spanish-American War.

Hofstadter, Richard. *Age of Reform: From Bryan to F.D.R.* Knopf.

LaFeber, Walter. *The New Empire: An Interpretation of American Expansion, 1860–1898.* Cornell University Press.

Link, Arthur S. *Woodrow Wilson and the Progressive Era, 1910–1917.* Harper.

May, Ernest R. *Coming of War, 1917.* Rand McNally.

McCullough, David. *The Path Between the Seas: The Creation of the Panama Canal 1870–1914.* Simon & Schuster.

Mowry, George E. *The Era of Theodore Roosevelt: 1900–1912.* Harper.

Natural Wonders of America: An American Heritage Guide. American Heritage.

Tabrah, Ruth M. *Hawaii: A History.* Norton.

FOR STUDENTS

Garraty, John A. *Theodore Roosevelt, the Strenuous Life.* American Heritage Junior Library.

Jantzen, Steven. *Hurrah for Peace, Hooray for War: The United States in World War I.* Knopf.

Lawson, Don, ed. *Great Air Battles: World Wars I and II.* Lothrop.

Lawson, Don. *The United States in World War One: Story of John J. Pershing and the American Expeditionary Forces.* Abelard.

May, Ernest R. *The Progressive Era, 1901–1917.* Silver.

Ortiz, Victoria. *The Land and People of Cuba.* Lippincott.

Peare, Catherine O. *The Woodrow Wilson Story: An Idealist in Politics.* Crowell.

Werstein, Irving. *Turning Point for America: The Story of the Spanish-American War.* Messner.

UNIT 10
THE UNITED STATES BECOMES A WORLD LEADER

FOR TEACHERS

Allen, Frederick Lewis. *Only Yesterday: An Informal History of the 1920's.* Harper.

Allen, Frederick Lewis. *Since Yesterday: The 1930's in America.* Harper.

American Heritage History of the Twenties and Thirties. American Heritage.

American Heritage Picture History of World War II. American Heritage.

Davis, Kenneth S. *Eisenhower: American Hero.* American Heritage.

Donovan, Robert J. *Conflict and Crisis: The Presidency of Harry S. Truman, 1945–1948.* Norton.

Goldman, Eric F. *The Crucial Decade and After: America, 1945–1960.* Random.

Kessner, Thomas, and Betty Caroli. *Today's Immigrants, Their Stories.* Oxford University Press.

Leuchtenburg, William E. *Franklin D. Roosevelt and the New Deal, 1932–1940.* Harper.

Manchester, William. *Portrait of a President: John F. Kennedy in Profile.* Little, Brown.

Miller, Douglas T., and Marion Nowak. *The Fifties: The Way We Really Were.* Doubleday.

Raines, Howell. *My Soul Is Rested: Movement Days in the Deep South Remembered.* Putnam. A study of the civil rights movement.

Shannon, David A. *Between the Wars: America, 1919–1941.* Houghton.

FOR STUDENTS

American Heritage Picture History of World War II. Simon & Schuster.

Berger, Melvin. *Computers in Your Life.* Crowell.

Bliven, Bruce, Jr. *The Story of D-Day: June 6, 1944.* Random.

Coy, Harold. *The First Book of Presidents.* Watts. From Washington to Carter.

Frank, Anne. *Anne Frank: The Diary of a Young Girl.* Doubleday. True story of a Jewish family's fate in Nazi-occupied Amsterdam.

Hoopes, Roy. *The Changing Vice-Presidency.* Crowell. Biographical sketches of all the Vice-Presidents.

Hunt, Irene. *No Promises in the Wind.* Follett. A story of the Depression.

Johnson, Gerald W. *The Presidency.* Morrow. An explanation of what Presidents do.

Katz, William Loren. *An Album of the Great Depression.* Watts. Heavily illustrated.

Lawson, Don. *The United States in the Korean War: Defending Freedom's Frontier.* Abelard.

Lawson, Don. *The United States in World War II: Crusade for World Freedom.* Abelard.

Lawson, Ted W. *Thirty Seconds Over Tokyo.* Random.

Leuchtenburg, William E. *Age of Change, from 1945.* Silver.

Lindop, Edmund. *Dazzling Twenties.* Watts.

May, Ernest R. *Boom and Bust, 1917–1932.* Silver.

Meltzer, Milton. *Brother, Can You Spare a Dime? The Great Depression, 1929–1933.* Knopf.

Meltzer, Milton. *In Their Own Words: A History of the American Negro, 1916–1966.* Crowell.

Meltzer, Milton. *Never to Forget: The Jews of the Holocaust.* Harper.

Rutland, Jonathan. *Exploring the World of Robots.* Watts.

Wilson, Beth P. *Giants for Justice: Bethune, Randolph, and King.* Harcourt. Biographies of three influential black leaders.

Zisfein, Melvin B. *Flight: A Panorama of Aviation.* Knopf.

Audiovisual Aids

Sir Francis Drake: The Rise of English Sea Power. 30 mins., b/w. Encyclopaedia Britannica. Tells the story of Sir Francis Drake and discusses the beginning of English sea power.

Spain in the New World: Colonial Life in Mexico. 13 mins., color. Encyclopaedia Britannica. Describes colonial Mexico and presents the views of different Spanish colonists.

Spanish Influences in the United States (2nd edition). 13 mins., color. Coronet Films. Presents an overview of the influence of Spanish culture on the United States.

William Penn and the Quakers (The Pennsylvania Colony). 11 mins., color. Coronet Films. Discusses the founding and development of Pennsylvania.

FILMSTRIPS

Colonial America (set of 5). McGraw-Hill. Shows the varied ways of living in the colonies.

Story of the Pilgrims (set of 2). Society for Visual Education. Depicts the English background of the Pilgrims, their voyage to America, and the first year of their settlement.

The Voyageur, Beaver Pelts and the Fur Trade (series). Midwest Visuals. Follows the early French fur traders through Canada to America's Midwest.

UNIT 3
NEW NATIONS ARE BORN AS AMERICAN COLONISTS SHAKE OFF EUROPEAN RULE

FILMS

American Revolution: The Background Period (revised). 10 mins., color. Coronet Films. Discusses political, social, and economic conditions prior to the Revolution.

American Revolution: The Impossible War. 25 mins., color. Learning Corporation of America. Dramatizes the American Revolution.

American Revolution: The War Years (revised). 10 mins., color. Coronet Films. Points out the major phases of the American Revolution.

Benjamin Franklin. 25 mins., color. National Audio Visual Center. Presents highlights in Franklin's life.

Canada's History: Colony to Commonwealth. 16 mins., color. Coronet Films. Describes Canada's cultural traditions and history.

Dawn of the American Revolution: A Lexington Family. 16 mins., color. Coronet Films. Shows the mood in the colonies before the Revolution and the causes of the conflict.

Deborah Sampson: A Woman in the Revolution. 21 mins., color. BFA Educational Media. Tells about the life of Deborah Sampson and her role as a soldier in the Revolutionary War.

Declaration of Independence by the Colonies. 20 mins., color. Encyclopaedia Britannica. Summarizes grievances of the colonists and episodes that led to the Declaration of Independence.

Mexico's History. 16 mins., color. Coronet Films. Reviews the history of Mexico, focusing on the Spanish conquest, the revolt against Spain, the Juarez revolt, and the social revolution of 1910.

Thomas Jefferson. 28 mins., color. Handel Film Corporation. Presents the many facets of Jefferson's life and accomplishments.

Thomas Paine. 13 mins., color. Encyclopaedia Britannica. Portrays in animation the life of the revolutionary journalist.

Valley Forge: The Battle for Survival. 16 mins., color. Handel Film Corporation. Depicts Washington's meeting with his staff at Valley Forge in 1777 and explains why the colonists fought the Revolutionary War.

Yorktown. 14 mins., color. Perspective. Recreates the siege and surrender of the British at Yorktown in 1781.

You Are There: Paul Revere's Ride. 22 mins., color. BFA Educational Media. Dramatizes the events connected with Revere's famous ride.

FILMSTRIPS

Benjamin Franklin: Symbol of the American Revolution (set of 2). Guidance Associates. Reviews Franklin's life.

Declaration of Independence. Q-ED Productions. Describes events that led to the split with Britain and explains the meaning of the Declaration of Independence.

The Revolution (set of 5). McGraw-Hill. Surveys the Revolutionary War era, including events that precipitated the war, the war itself, and its immediate aftermath.

UNIT 4
THE UNITED STATES IS ESTABLISHED ON A FIRM BASIS

FILMS

American Revolution: The Postwar Period (revised). 11 mins., color. Coronet Films. Describes the weaknesses of the Articles of Confederation and the steps that led to the writing of the Constitution.

Art of Diplomacy: In the Beginning. 14 mins., color. Screen News Digest. Blends paintings and motion pictures to document foreign policy from the Declaration of Independence to the Monroe Doctrine.

Bill of Rights in Action Series (10 films, 21–23 mins. each), color. BFA Educational Media. Dramatizes modern-day situations that test the meaning of our constitutional rights on issues of capital punishment, due process of law, equal opportunity, freedom of religion, freedom of speech, juvenile law, the right of privacy, the guarantee against self-incrimination, trial by jury, and women's rights.

Bill of Rights of the United States. 20 mins., color. Encyclopaedia Britannica. Explains the first ten amendments to the Constitution.

Constitution of the United States. 22 mins., color. Encyclopaedia Britannica. Describes the writing of the Constitution and explains that this document is the foundation of the United States government.

Elections in the United States. 19 mins., color. BFA Educational Media. Acquaints students with the mechanics of voting and with the rights of both voters and candidates.

George Washington. 26 mins., color. Journal Films. Traces the development of the qualities that made Washington the outstanding leader of the nation's early years.

James Madison. 25 mins., color. Journal Films. Shows how Madison's ideals and actions helped to build a free society.

Louisiana Purchase: Key to a Continent. 16 mins., b/w. Encyclopaedia Britannica. Traces events that led to the acquisition of the Louisiana Territory.

President of the United States: Too Much Power. 25 mins., color. Encyclopaedia Britannica. Examines the powers of the President and the constitutional limitations on presidential powers.

United States Congress: Of, By, and For the People. 26 mins., color. Encyclopaedia Britannica. Presents a historical perspective of the establishment of Congress and its role in government.

United States Supreme Court: Guardian of the Constitution. 24 mins., color. Encyclopaedia Britannica. Highlights the history and landmark cases of the Supreme Court.

War of 1812. 14 mins., color. Coronet Films. Explains the causes and the ultimate results of the War of 1812.

Washington, D.C.: Capital City U.S.A. 22 mins., color. Encyclopaedia Britannica. Points out many of the sights, sounds, and activities of the capital city.

FILMSTRIPS

American Political Party System (set of 4). Eye Gate House. Shows the development of American political parties and the part they have played in the nation's history.

George Washington: What Was He Really Like? Multi-Media Productions. Analyzes the personal characteristics and leadership qualities of Washington.

Origins of the Constitution: The Struggle for Consensus (set of 3). Prentice-Hall Media. Examines the formulation of the Constitution.

People's Choice. Guidance Associates. Explains the unique features and problems of the electoral college.

Story of the Star Spangled Banner. Society for Visual Education. Presents our national anthem and the circumstances under which Francis Scott Key wrote it.

This Honorable Court: Supreme Court of the United States (set of 2). Guidance Associates. Explores the Supreme Court and some of its major decisions.

Washington, D.C. (set of 5). Encyclopaedia Britannica. Points out the beauty and historical significance of the nation's capital.

UNIT 5
THE AMERICAN WAY OF LIVING CHANGES AS THE DIFFERENT SECTIONS DEVELOP

FILMS

America: The Land. 24 mins., color. Xerox. Uses letters, diaries, town records, and other sources to recreate the lives of pioneers who made their way through the Cumberland Gap.

Andrew Jackson. 26 mins., color. Journal Films. Portrays important events in the life of Jackson, including his presidency.

Frontier Experience. 25 mins., color. Learning Corporation of America. Depicts the hardships of pioneers who lived on the frontier.

Industrial Revolution: Beginnings in the United States. 23 mins., color. Encyclopaedia Britannica. Describes industrial progress from the first thread mill in 1791 to the expansion of the railroads.

Inventions in America's Growth (1750–1850). 10 mins., color. Coronet Films. Discusses the contributions of inventions to the growth of America prior to 1850.

The Jackson Years: The New Americans. 27 mins., color. Learning Corporation of America. Pictures the era of the "People's President."

Plantation South. 17 mins., color. Encyclopaedia Britannica. Traces the plantation system from its beginnings in Virginia to its spread into the deep South.

Saga of the Erie Canal. 11 mins., color. Coronet Films. Recreates the period during which the Erie Canal was constructed.

Slavery and Slave Resistance. 24 mins., color. Coronet Films. Tells how blacks endured and resisted slavery.

Transportation Revolution: The Story of America's Growth. 19 mins., color. Learning Corporation of America. Explains how changing modes of transportation affected ways of life.

Westward Movement I: Settlers of the Old Northwest Territory. 15 mins., color. Encyclopaedia Britannica. Traces the beginning of the westward movement, with emphasis on the migration of settlers to the Northwest Territory shortly after the Revolutionary War.

FILMSTRIPS

Colonial Times to Civil War (set of 6). Learning Corporation of America. Surveys important technological changes that affected agriculture, industry, transportation, and communication.

Pioneer Community (set of 6). Coronet Instructional Media. Gives an authentic view of the homes, tools, shops, and craft workers of a pioneer village in the early 1800's.

Social Reform Movements — A Series. Educational Audio Visual. Examines the origins and nature of reform movements in America.

**UNIT 6
THE NATION EXPANDS
AND IS TORN BY WAR**

FILMS

Abraham Lincoln. 26 mins., color. Journal Films. Tells the story of this great leader's part in the dramatic events of the mid-1800's.

Background of the Civil War. 21 mins., color. BFA Educational Media. Analyzes the differences between the North and the South and the events that led to the outbreak of war.

Civil War: Promise of Reconstruction. 28 mins., color. Learning Corporation of America. Examines the Union government's Port Royal experiment, which foreshadowed Reconstruction efforts to aid freed slaves.

Gettysburg: 1863. 19 mins., color. Centron. Explains and illustrates the strategy, tactics, and importance of the Battle of Gettysburg.

Journals of Lewis and Clark. 27 mins., color. Encyclopaedia Britannica. Recreates stages of the Lewis and Clark expedition as told in the journals of the explorers themselves.

Meet Mr. Lincoln. 27 mins., b/w. Films Incorporated. Uses still pictures to record Lincoln's presidential years, showing him as his contemporaries saw him.

Oregon Trail. 25 mins., b/w. Encyclopaedia Britannica. Depicts the hardships of the pioneers who traveled westward across the continent in Conestoga wagons.

Pony Express in America's Growth. 11 mins., color. Coronet Films. Shows the need for better communication between the East and the West and reenacts Pony Express rides.

Struggle for Vicksburg. 19 mins., color. Centron. Explains the significance of control of Vicksburg during the Civil War and the strategy that led to its fall.

True Story of the Civil War. 33 mins., b/w. McGraw-Hill. Uses Brady photographs to tell the story of the Civil War, describing its causes, battles, and leaders.

Westward Movement II: Settlement of the Mississippi Valley. 16 mins., color. Encyclopaedia Britannica. Discusses the mass migration of settlers west of the Mississippi following the Louisiana Purchase.

Westward Movement IV: Texas and the Mexican War. 18 mins., color. Encyclopaedia Britannica. Reviews the fight for Texas independence and the war with Mexico.

Westward Movement V: The Gold Rush. 24 mins., color. Encyclopaedia Britannica. Stresses the impact of the gold rush era.

Years of Reconstruction, 1865–1877. 25 mins., color. McGraw-Hill. Deals with the bitterness of the Reconstruction Era and the failure to reach a reasonable peace.

You Are There: Harriet Tubman and the Underground Railroad. 21 mins., color. BFA Educational Media. Focuses on the Fugitive Slave Law and follows one of Harriet Tubman's trips leading slaves out of the South.

FILMSTRIPS

Civil War (set of 5). McGraw-Hill. Covers the events that resulted in war, the war itself, and its immediate aftermath.

Civil War and Reconstruction (set of 6). Encyclopaedia Britannica. Presents causes of the Civil War, battle scenes, and the struggle between Andrew Johnson and Congress for control of Reconstruction.

Legacy of the Civil War (set of 4). Eye Gate House. Shows the rise of southern nationalism, the Civil War as a revolution, Reconstruction, and the effects of the Civil War on civil rights issues today.

Lewis and Clark Adventures (set of 2). Multi-Media Productions. Follows the Lewis and Clark expedition.

UNIT 7
MODERN AMERICA TAKES SHAPE

FILMS

American Indian, Part 2: How the West was Won — and Honor Lost. 25 mins., color. McGraw-Hill. Covers the forced exodus of the Sioux from their land and the final wars, ending in the defeat of Geronimo in 1886.

American Indian, Part 3: The Lament of the Reservation. 24 mins., color. McGraw-Hill. Discusses the living conditions of the 600,000 Indians on barren reservations.

Ghost Towns of the Westward March. 18 mins., color. Alfred Higgins Productions. Shows ghost towns that once played a vital role in westward expansion.

Growth of Farming in America: 1865–1900. 13 mins., b/w. Coronet Films.

Interior West: The Land Nobody Wanted. 20 mins., color. Encyclopaedia Britannica. Explains how irrigation and modern technology have made it possible to create farmlands and build cities in desert lands.

Inventions in America's Growth II (1850–1910). 11 mins., color. Coronet Films. Uses photographs and models to show the impact of inventions on American life.

Kitty Hawk to Paris: The Heroic Years. 29 mins., color. Learning Corporation of America. Traces the development of aviation.

Power and Wheels: The Automobile in Modern Life. 17 mins., color. Encyclopaedia Britannica. Traces the history of the automobile and its influence on American culture through the eyes of two visitors from outer space.

Railroad Builders. 14 mins., color. Encyclopaedia Britannica. Surveys the building of the first transcontinental railroad and the contributions of railroad builders to westward expansion.

Rise of Labor. 30 mins., color. Encyclopaedia Britannica. Traces the history of the American labor movement.

Small Business Keeps America Working. 28 mins., color. Chamber of Commerce. Uses the stories of small business owners to present the spirit of the free enterprise system.

FILMSTRIPS

Agribusiness (set of 2). Prentice-Hall Media. Describes the transformation of American farming into a business.

America Comes of Age: Industrial America (set of 3). Prentice-Hall Media. Surveys the growth of industry.

America Comes of Age: Politics and People (set of 3). Prentice-Hall Media. Focuses on the politics and people of this period.

America Comes of Age: Railroads West (set of 3). Prentice-Hall Media. Describes the building of western railroads and their effects on American society.

American Inventions: Key to Mass Production (set of 2). Multi-Media Productions. Examines how American industry developed mass production techniques.

Civil War to World War I (set of 6). Learning Corporation of America. Traces the inventions and technology that shaped America from the Civil War to World War I.

Growth of the Labor Movement (set of 2). Guidance Associates. Surveys the history of the labor movement.

Settling the West (set of 6). Coronet Instructional Media. Shows people who explored and settled the West.

UNIT 8
NEW CONDITIONS BRING
CHANGES IN AMERICAN LIFE

FILMS

Amazing Grace. 52 mins., color. Pyramid. Takes a searching look at the vitality of the American experience in song.

American Experience: Becoming an American. 22 mins., color. BFA Educational Media. Presents Italian American, Chinese American, and Mexican American families as they experience the process of assimilation and change that immigrants undergo.

An American Farmer. 15 mins., color. Screen News Digest. Shows the challenges and rewards of a modern farmer.

American Indian Speaks. 23 mins., color. Encyclopaedia Britannica. Documents the Indian people and the Indian heritage.

American Parade, We the Women. 30 mins., color. BFA Educational Media. Examines the role of women throughout American history.

Black History: Lost, Stolen, or Strayed (Parts 1 and 2). Each 27 mins., color. BFA Educational Media. Studies the contributions of black Americans to the development of the United States.

Golden Door — Immigrants. 16 mins., color. Hearst Metrotone News. Tells the story of America's immigrant heritage and its influence on the nation's development.

Immigrant Experience: The Long, Long Journey. 28 mins., color. Learning Corporation of America. Focuses on the dreams and problems of new immigrants by telling about a family of Polish Americans.

Mark Twain's America. 54 mins., b/w. McGraw-Hill. Describes how Mark Twain saw America.

Mexican-American Speaks: Heritage in Bronze. 20 mins., color. Encyclopaedia Britannica. Examines the history and cultural heritage of Hispanic Americans in the Southwest.

Rise of the American City. 32 mins., color. Encyclopaedia Britannica. Surveys the growth of American cities and discusses how people who moved to the cities played a part in that growth.

Siu Mei Wong: Who Shall I Be? 17 mins., color. Learning Corporation of America. Tells the story of a Chinese American ballet student.

FILMSTRIPS

American Immigrants: Europe on the Move. Multi-Media Productions. Concentrates on Americans of European origin, from their life in Europe to their adjustment to life in America.

Japanese Americans: An Inside Look (set of 2). Multi-Media Productions. Relates the story of the Japanese Americans.

Leading American Negroes (set of 6). Society for Visual Education. Presents biographies of outstanding black Americans and their contributions to American culture.

Living on a Farm (set of 6). Coronet Instructional Media. Tells about life on different types of modern farms.

Story of America's People (set of 10). Eye Gate House. Discusses the cultural contributions of Americans of various ancestries.

Women in American History — A Series. Educational Activities. Presents a variety of women's activities and achievements.

UNIT 9
THE UNITED STATES
WIDENS ITS HORIZONS

FILMS

America's Wonderlands: National Parks. 52 mins., color. National Geographic. Includes scenes of national parks throughout the United States.

1898. 54 mins., color. McGraw-Hill. Reviews American history in the second half of the 19th century, covers the Spanish-American War, and talks about Theodore Roosevelt as a symbol of the new age.

Great War. 52 mins., b/w. McGraw-Hill. Describes the outbreak and progress of World War I, the role of the United States in that war, and the impact of the war on the American people.

Hawaii — The Fiftieth State. 17 mins., color. Encyclopaedia Britannica. Presents the geography and history of the islands and shows scenes of Honolulu and of sugar and pineapple plantations.

Imperialism and European Expansion. 14 mins., color. Coronet Films. Discusses causes and effects of the imperial expansion of 1875–1914 in Africa, Asia, and the islands of the Pacific.

Panama Canal: Gateway to the World. 14 mins., color. Encyclopaedia Britannica. Explains the history of the building of the canal and its importance to the United States and to the world.

The Philippines: Island Republic. 16 mins., color. McGraw-Hill. Describes the Philippines, its cultural background, and the role of the United States in the republic's development.

Puerto Rico: The Caribbean Americans. 16 mins., color. International Film Bureau. Presents the island's history and way of life through the experiences of a young Puerto Rican.

Teddy Roosevelt: The Right Man at the Right Time. 28 mins., color. Learning Corporation of America. Traces important events in Roosevelt's presidency and his part in bringing about reforms.

White House, Past and Present. 13 mins., color. Coronet Films. Tours the White House, describing the Presidents who have helped shape its history.

World War I: A Documentary on the Role of the U.S.A. 28 mins., b/w. Encyclopaedia Britannica. Discusses the entry of the United States into World War I, its part in the Allied victory, and Wilson's role at the peace conference.

FILMSTRIPS

Muckrakers and Reformers. Multi-Media Productions. Deals with the muckraking journalists and reformers of the Progressive Era (1900–1915).

Woodrow Wilson: Idealism and American Democracy (set of 2). Guidance Associates. Presents Wilson's ideas about democracy and his fight for the League of Nations.

World War I to Tomorrow (set of 6). Learning Corporation of America. Shows how reliance on technology and natural resources has changed American life since World War I.

UNIT 10
THE UNITED STATES BECOMES A WORLD LEADER

FILMS

American Parade: FDR, the Man Who Changed America. 30 mins., color. BFA Educational Media. Shows Roosevelt's charisma and traces the steps by which he expanded federal responsibilities.

American People in World War II. 25 mins., color. McGraw-Hill. Looks at the American home front in World War II.

Energy — The American Experience. National Audio Visual Center. 29 mins., color. Shows the development of various energy sources parallel with the growth of American industry.

Focus on Korea. 20 mins., b/w. Hearst Metrotone News. Focuses on the troubled history of the Republic of Korea and on the Korean War.

Golden Twenties. 68 mins., b/w. McGraw-Hill. Recalls fashions, personalities, and events that characterized the 1920's.

I Am a Soldier. 51 mins., color. McGraw-Hill. Follows the story of a United States Army company in Vietnam.

Life in the Thirties. 52 mins., b/w. McGraw-Hill. Recreates the devastating effects of the Great Depression and focuses on the leadership of Franklin D. Roosevelt.

Marxism: The Theory That Split a World. 26 mins., color. Learning Corporation of America. Examines communism and its effects on the world.

Ten Seconds That Shook the World. 50 mins., b/w. Metromedia. Tells the story of the atomic bomb's development, from the Manhattan Project to Hiroshima.

Truman and the Cold War. 16 mins., b/w. Learning Corporation of America. Discusses Truman's role in aiding countries whose freedom was imperiled by the Soviet Union.

World War II: Background and Causes. 17 mins., b/w. Coronet Films. Relates problems left unsettled by the Treaty of Versailles to events that led to World War II.

World War II: 1939–1941. 16 mins., b/w. Coronet Films. Traces the war from the invasion of Poland to the bombing of Pearl Harbor.

World War II: 1942–1945. 17 mins., b/w. Coronet Films. Traces the war from the entry of the United States to the Allied victory.

FILMSTRIPS

Great Depression (set of 2). Eye Gate House. Traces the history of the Great Depression and shows how it changed the attitudes of people for years to come.

The 1960's: Decade of Hope and Despair (set of 2). Guidance Associates. Discusses American society during the 1960's.

The United States Flag (set of 2). Society for Visual Education. Relates the history and proper display of the American flag.

United States: A World Leader (set of 6). Encyclopaedia Britannica. Describes events that swept the United States into World War II and the nation's role in postwar world affairs.

World War II (set of 5). McGraw-Hill. Presents photographs, songs, and voices from World War II.

This Is America's Story

FIFTH EDITION

This Is America's Story

FIFTH EDITION

Howard B. Wilder
Robert P. Ludlum
Harriett McCune Brown

HOUGHTON MIFFLIN COMPANY   BOSTON

Atlanta   Dallas   Geneva, Ill.   Hopewell, N.J.   Palo Alto   Toronto

ABOUT THE AUTHORS

Howard B. Wilder served for many years as a teacher of history and as Head of the Social Studies Department at Melrose High School, Melrose, Massachusetts.

Robert P. Ludlum is the former President of Anne Arundel Community College, Maryland. He also served as Dean of the College of Arts and Sciences at Adelphi University and taught political science and history at Hofstra University and at Texas A & M University.

Harriett McCune Brown taught history for many years in the junior high school grades in Los Angeles, California.

Cover: The first Stars and Stripes superimposed over the present-day flag of the United States. *Frontispiece:* Ceremonies marking the dedication of the Statue of Liberty, October 28, 1886.

Printed in the U.S.A.

Student's Edition ISBN: 0-395-31145-4

Teacher's Edition ISBN: 0-395-31765-7

George Washington, shortly after
the Battle of Yorktown

Contents

Columbus's first landing in America

Minutemen at the Battle of
Bunker Hill

The *Constitution* and Bunker Hill Monument

The Alamo

UNIT **6**

The Nation Expands and Is Torn by War   **372**

The Lincoln Memorial

UNIT **7**
Modern America Takes Shape   456

Steam engine

World War I recruiting poster

12

The National Mall,
Washington, D.C.

Maps

Graphs and Charts

People in America's Story

Our Presidents

Documents

How This Book Tells America's Story

As you read this book, you will find out how America began and how it grew into the nation we know today. One way to tell the story would be to list all the events that took place year by year since America's beginnings. You would find it very difficult, however, to study American history in this fashion. Even more important, trying to memorize a list of events is not a good way to study history. You would not be able to tell what the really important events were and why they were important. You would also have a hard time seeing how certain events were connected with others.

To help you follow America's story. To make our country's history meaningful, the authors of *This Is America's Story* organized the book into 10 units and 32 chapters. If you look at the Table of Contents (pages 5–13), you will see that the title of each unit deals with an important development in America's story. Unit 1, for example, tells how Europeans first came to the Western Hemisphere (*Europe Seeks an Ocean Route to Asia and Finds the American Continents*).

Every unit begins with a two-page *introduction,* like the one (reduced in size) shown below. The pictures in each unit introduction will help you form an idea of what you will be reading about. In the unit introduction shown below, for example, you see a map and a compass of the kind used by explorers of long ago. You also see Columbus and his crew stepping onto the island where they landed in 1492 after crossing the Atlantic Ocean.

Under the pictures you see a time line that picks out important events of the unit. You also see a short paragraph that introduces you to the unit. Whenever you start a new unit in this book, take time to look at the pictures, the time line, and the unit introduction. Together they will help you know what to expect in the chapters of that unit.

Look again at the Table of Contents. You will find that each unit has two or more

Unit introduction

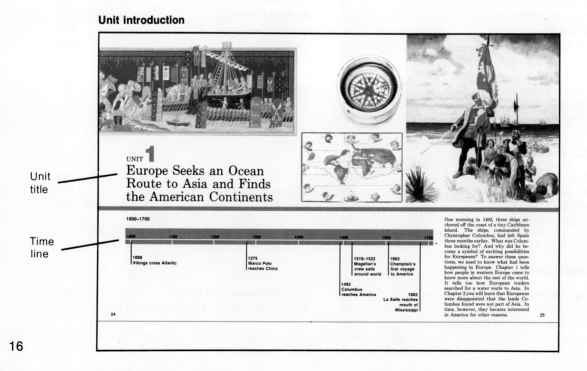

Unit title

Time line

chapters. The chapters of each unit tell part of the unit's story. In Unit 1, for example, Chapter 1 tells how explorers found the American continents, while Chapter 2 tells how Europeans added to their knowledge of America. At the beginning of each chapter you will find an interesting picture. It might be said to "preview" the chapter since it shows a scene that is connected with the story told in the chapter. On the first page of Chapter 2 (shown below) you see a meeting of French explorers and American Indians. How does the picture tie in with the subject of the chapter? (Look at the chapter title.) How does the picture introduce you to the kinds of people who play important parts in the events of the chapter? (Look at the clothes, the housing, and the kinds of weapons the people used.)

To guide you in reading a chapter. As you begin reading each chapter, you will see the words "What this chapter is about." Following those words is the chapter introduction, which ends with numbered *guide questions.* The guide questions list the important ideas that will be discussed in the chapter.

To help you locate the answers to the guide questions, the chapter is divided into two or more *sections.* The titles of these sections are exactly the same as the guide questions. (See the examples below.) Throughout the chapters you will find two other kinds of headings that will guide your reading: *column headings,* to indicate general topics, and *paragraph headings.*

If you read the unit and chapter introductions and make use of the different kinds of headings, you will find it easy to follow America's story as it is told in this book.

To help you understand and remember. *Study questions* are another helpful part of *This Is America's Story.* To understand what you are reading, you need to stop now and then to remember what you have read and to ask yourself what it means. The study questions will help you do that.

As you finish reading each section of a chapter, you will find a list of numbered questions called *Check Up.* Answering these questions is a good way of helping you check your memory of what you have just read.

Beginning of Chapter 2

At the end of each chapter, you will find a different set of study questions. Use the *Chapter Check Up* questions to review the entire chapter. As in the sample below, you will find five groups of questions: (1) Words to Know; (2) Places to Locate; (3) Facts to Remember; (4) Skills to Practice; (5) Questions to Think About.

Following the Chapter Check Up, you will find special features called *Linking Past and Present*. These features tell you how the past affects the lives of Americans today. On page 66, for example, you will read how foods that we enjoy today were first grown by American Indians. On page 250 you will learn that the names of many of our fifty states come from American Indian words or from words used by French and Spanish explorers. A *Linking Past and Present* feature on page 616 tells how our Naval Academy was started.

To build your skills. As you read *This Is America's Story,* you will have the chance not only to find out about your country's past but also to develop skills that are important in reading any history book. At the end of each chapter you will find a page

called *Gaining Skill.* (See the example on the next page.) On these pages you will learn how to do many useful things — how to read maps and graphs, how to list events in order, and how to get information from pictures. Developing these skills will help you learn faster and will make your study of history more interesting.

To locate the places you read about. Maps are important in studying America's story. As you read about explorers sailing across oceans and pioneers following trails through mountain passes, look at the maps that go along with the story. On page 59, for example, the book tells you about the first French explorers of North America. Notice that the map on that page shows where they explored and what routes they took. On pages 14–15 you will find a list of all the maps in this book.

To review the unit as a whole. The end of a unit is a good place to stop and review what you have read in all the chapters of the unit. To help you do that, each unit ends with two special pages. (See an example on pages 68–69.) These pages have three parts: (1) The *Summary of Important*

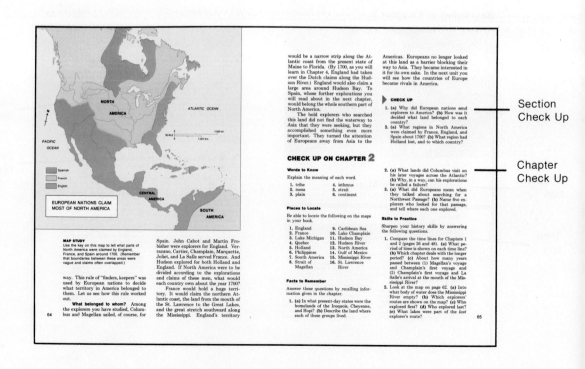

Section Check Up

Chapter Check Up

Ideas brings together the important events and ideas of the whole unit. (2) The *Unit Review* provides questions that will help you think back over those events and ideas. (3) The list called *Things to Do* suggests extra ways of using what you have learned.

To locate information. You will learn a great deal about America's story as you go through this book. At times you will want to know where to find extra information. The reference section at the back of the book is valuable for that purpose. (1) In the *Glossary* you will find the meanings of words that are important in the study of American history. You will also find pronunciations for difficult words. (2) The *Atlas* is a set of three useful maps: a world map, a map of the states and their capital cities, and a map showing our nation's physical features. (3) In Chapter 11 you will find out how the Constitution of the United States came to be written. At the back of the book you will find the complete *Constitution* with notes to help you read it. Blue tabs near the top of each page will help you locate the Constitution easily. (4) The page called *The States* provides special informa-

tion about our nation's fifty states. (5) You will find pictures of all the state flags and of several flags that have flown over the United States on the pages called *Flags of the Nation and the States*. (6) Another chart, *The Presidents,* lists our nation's Chief Executives. (7) In the list of *Important Dates in American History* you will find significant events listed in the order in which they happened. (8) Finally, learn to use the *Index* at the back of the book. The Index will not only help you locate information on a particular subject, but will help you find pictures, maps, and graphs as well. On the first page of the Index, you will find suggestions on how to use it.

To get the most out of your reading of *This Is America's Story*, remember to use all the various aids described above. Now, before you begin your study of the first unit, turn to the next page and read the introduction to *This Is America's Story*. Called *This Is America,* the introduction gives you interesting facts about our country and tells how expanding freedom and opportunity have enabled Americans to build a great nation.

A skill page

Linking
Past
and
Present

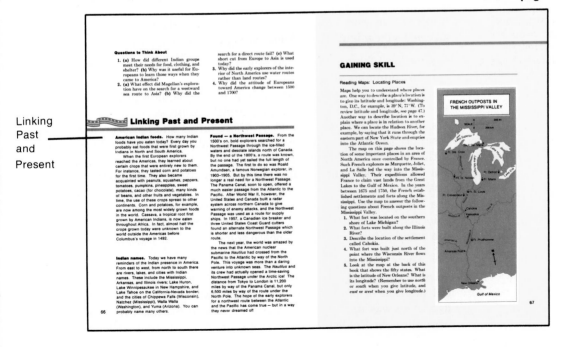

This Is America

One of America's greatest resources is its rich farmland. This picture shows a farm in Iowa.

Suppose you were asked to describe America. Here are a few of the answers you might give. America is . . .

- a nation of more than 230 million people whose ancestors came from countries all over the world.
- a vast country of three and a half million square miles.
- a land blessed with abundant natural resources.
- a leader in trade and industry, whose farms and factories not only supply the needs of its own people but also send food and goods to the peoples of other lands.
- a republic, governed under the oldest written constitution in the world.
- a country in which important officers of the national, state, and local governments are chosen by, and are responsible to, its citizens.
- a world power which seeks peace and stands ready to defend liberty.

These statements give us a picture of America today. But they do not explain why and how the United States has grown to its present position of power and leadership. Two hundred and fifty years ago there was no nation named the "United States." Instead there were thirteen English colonies along the Atlantic coast, French colonies in the Great Lakes region and Mississippi Valley, and Spanish colonies in the Southwest. In addition, people who were called Indians inhabited the thick forests, rolling prairies, and vast plains of North America. How has it been possible for our nation as we know it today to develop?

AMERICA: LAND OF PROMISE

"The driving force behind our [nation's] progress," President Truman once said, "is our faith in our democratic institutions. That faith is embodied in the promise of equal rights and equal opportunities which the founders of our Republic proclaimed to their countrymen and to the whole world." It was the search for freedom and opportunities that led people to leave Europe in the 1600's and brave the dangers of the Atlantic to settle in America. These settlers had their individual reasons for leaving Europe. But all had one thing in common — they had a dream of a new and better life.

Early Americans who settled in the English colonies had become accustomed to certain rights that had been won from the rulers of England. Building new homes amid the hardships of an unfamiliar land strengthened their love of freedom. When stricter regulations by the British government threatened these rights, the colonists drew up the Declaration of Independence. In this statement, Americans proclaimed that all people were entitled to certain rights. To preserve these rights, the colonists fought for independence from British rule. Then, to protect their hard-won freedom, they established a government that would be controlled by the people.

Some of our nation's most beautiful scenery lies along California's Pacific coast, near Monterey.

The promise of freedom and greater opportunities was largely responsible for the expansion of the United States into the vast region that lay beyond the thirteen original states. Year after year restless Americans moved westward in search of fresh opportunities, while newcomers left Europe to start life over in America. In a series of giant strides the United States acquired new territories which gave our nation the boundaries it has today. When states were carved out of those territories, the people of the new states possessed the same rights of self-government as did people in the older, eastern states.

AMERICA: LAND OF PROGRESS

As territories were settled and new states were created, the American way of life began to change. Canals and railroads were built to transport the growing numbers of people and the goods they needed. Factories equipped with new machines produced an increasing variety of goods. Towns grew into cities, and in time the larger cities were surrounded by suburbs where people who worked in the cities lived. By the early 1900's the United States had become a mighty industrial power with the highest standard of living in the world.

Many things contributed to the nation's economic growth. Among them were a wealth of natural resources, the creativity of inventors and scientists, and the boldness of far-sighted business leaders. But this economic development also owed much to the people who ran the machines, worked in the mines, farmed the soil, and built the railroads that transported farm produce and manufactured goods to market. America's greatest resource has always been its people.

We should remember that the United States is a nation of immigrants. From the beginning of this country's history, people have come to its shores from other parts of the world. The earliest settlers had to clear land, build homes, plant crops, and depend on their wits to survive in a place where much was strange to them. Some of the American colonists were indentured servants, who had to labor sev-

Denver, the capital of Colorado, is the largest city of the Rocky Mountain region.

eral years in payment for their passage across the ocean. During the 1600's and 1700's many people from Africa were brought to America and forced into a life of slavery.

Throughout the 1800's and early 1900's millions of immigrants came to the United States, many of them with no other possessions than what they could carry in a few bundles. Their labor and loyalty proved a valuable human resource to their adopted land. Most of the immigrants were Europeans, but others came from elsewhere in the Americas and from Asia and Africa.

Progress toward a better life implies the fulfillment of the promise of equal rights and liberties contained in the Declaration of Independence. To safeguard these liberties, the Bill of Rights was added to the United States Constitution. Later amendments to the Constitution, laws passed by Congress, and decisions of the Supreme Court have also protected individual rights and liberties.

As the United States has grown, the American ideal of freedom has taken on wider meaning. It includes the right of the individual to choose a job, to run a business, to travel, and to live where he or she pleases. It also implies the goal of our system of public education — to prepare young Americans to live useful and satisfying lives. Such rights and opportunities do not exist in all countries, nor were they available to all American people in the past. An important part of the story you will read in this book is how the ideal of freedom came to apply to all people in this country.

You are now about to read America's story. You will learn how our country was started and how it grew to be a great nation. You will also study the lives of outstanding men and women. But remember that it was the hard work, courage, loyalty, and dreams of many people from different lands that have built our republic. As in the past, Americans today can find inspiration and new understanding from learning about the history of this land of freedom.

Presidents George Washington, Thomas Jefferson, Theodore Roosevelt, and Abraham Lincoln are honored at Mount Rushmore National Memorial in South Dakota.

Above: a Crusader ship from the 1300's. *Next page:* an Italian compass from the 1500's; Columbus landing on San Salvador in 1492; a map showing Magellan's route, drawn in the mid-1500's.

Europe Seeks an Ocean Route to Asia and Finds the American Continents

1000–1700

See p. T14 for a unit preview strategy. See pp. T58–T71 for lists of useful books and audiovisual aids.

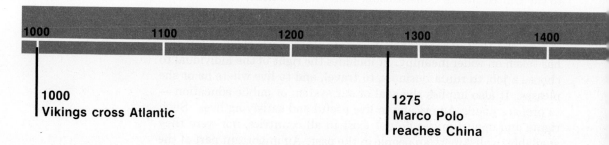

1000	1100	1200	1300	1400

1000
Vikings cross Atlantic

1275
Marco Polo reaches China

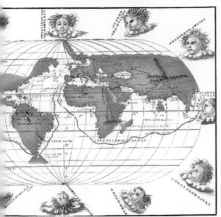

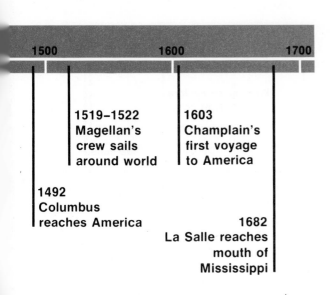

1519–1522
Magellan's
crew sails
around world

1603
Champlain's
first voyage
to America

1492
Columbus
reaches America

1682
La Salle reaches
mouth of
Mississippi

1500   1600   1700

One morning in 1492, three ships anchored off the coast of a tiny Caribbean island. The ships, commanded by Christopher Columbus, had left Spain three months earlier. What was Columbus looking for? And why did he become a symbol of exciting possibilities for Europeans? To answer these questions, we need to know what had been happening in Europe. Chapter 1 tells how people in western Europe came to know more about the rest of the world. It tells too how European traders searched for a water route to Asia. In Chapter 2 you will learn that Europeans were disappointed that the lands Columbus found were not part of Asia. In time, however, they became interested in America for other reasons.

Vocabulary preview: latitude, longitude, monopoly, grid, equator, prime meridian

Explorers Find the American Continents

1000–1500   See pp. T14–T15 for chapter teaching strategies.

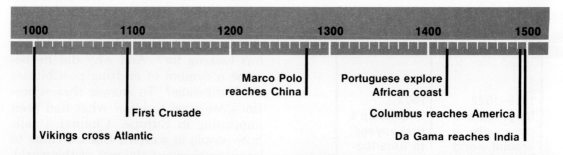

1000	1100	1200	1300	1400	1500

Marco Polo reaches China

Portuguese explore African coast

First Crusade

Columbus reaches America

Vikings cross Atlantic

Da Gama reaches India

What this chapter is about —

The history of our country might be compared to the steps in a long, long walk — a long march from the past to the present. Many people have taken part in this march of history, and we ourselves are taking the step that marks the present. What the future steps may be, we cannot know. But, looking back at the steps taken in the past and at the people who took them, we may learn how to direct our own steps better in the future.

American history had its beginnings on the continents of Asia, Europe,

26

and Africa. In this chapter, we will first look back at Europe. We will turn back to a time when castles along the European coast looked out upon the unknown sea. You will learn how Europeans took the first step in the long march — how they ventured out onto the sea and discovered what seemed to be a new world. In this chapter you will find answers to the following questions:

1. How did changes in Europe lead to geographical discoveries?
2. How did European explorers seek and find a water route to Asia?
3. Why did Columbus sail westward, and what did he accomplish?

1 How Did Changes in Europe Lead to Geographical Discoveries?

HOW PEOPLE LIVED IN WESTERN EUROPE ABOUT THE YEAR 1000

In western Europe about the year 1000, during a period called the Middle Ages (about A.D. 500–1400), each little neighborhood lived by itself. It was almost as if the villages were separate islands. The people of one village hardly knew what happened in villages only a few miles away. To understand the life of most of the people, suppose that you were living in Europe about that time. What would your life be like?

Your home and its furniture are very simple. You and your father and mother and brothers and sisters live in a cottage built of wood. It has no windows. The roof of the cottage is of thatch, that is, a thick covering of straw or reeds or leaves. The hard-packed earth is the floor. There are just two openings in the cottage. One is the door, and one is a hole in the roof to let out the smoke from the fire. Unfortunately, the hole also lets in the rain. There is no chimney and no oven or stove. In summer your meals are cooked out-of-doors over an open fire.

There is little furniture in your cottage, and what there is, is rough. A box with a straw mattress on it is the bed. The table is made of boards laid on trestles. (A trestle is like a sawhorse.) There are some three-legged stools and a chest. Your food is cooked in an iron pot and eaten from dishes made of baked and hardened clay. You have no lamps or even candles. Lack of light doesn't matter, however, because nobody in the family can read, and everyone goes to bed at sundown and gets up at sunrise.

Your food and clothing have little variety. Your mother has spun the yarn, woven the cloth, and made the clothing that you and other members of your family wear. Most of it is of wool or coarse linen.

Your meals are simple and consist of the same things over and over again — mostly bread and a little meat. You eat few vegetables and fruits. You have a little salt but no pepper or any other spices. You use no sugar, and if your food is sweetened at all, it is with honey or occasionally with fruit juices.

You live on a manor. Your cottage is one of a dozen or more that stand together by the side of a winding, unpaved road. The cottages form a village belonging to a noble, whose large

27

● See p. T14 for a strategy suggesting that students gather additional information on serfs.

house is nearby. The village and the farms around it are called a manor, and the noble who owns it is called the lord of the manor. Your family and the other people on the manor work for the noble as serfs. They have to farm his land part of the time, help build and repair his roads and bridges, and serve him in other ways.

Your parents and the other serfs, in fact, are not much better off than slaves. They may not be sold, as slaves can be, but they have to remain on the manor — they are "bound to the soil," as the saying goes. If a new lord takes over the land, they must serve him. Serfs cannot own their land outright, nor are they allowed to go elsewhere to find land of their own or to find other jobs. They may not even leave the manor without the lord's permission.

The manor is nearly self-sufficient. We have seen how you and your family and your neighbors live on the manor. But is there any connection between your manor and others? The truth is that your manor has very little to do with others. It is almost self-sufficient. By *self-sufficient* we mean it can get along by itself, without receiving many products from the outside world and without making many things to sell or trade. The food eaten on the ★ manor is grown on it. The manor has its own blacksmith shop and its own mill where all the grain is ground. From the hides of animals raised on the manor some serfs make shoes for the people and saddles and harness for the horses. Other serfs dye wool from the manor's own sheep and make it into cloth. The blacksmith and the wheelwright (wheel maker) make the wagons and farm tools and keep them in repair. Only a few products, such as salt, iron, and millstones, need to be brought into the manor from outside.

"But aren't there any towns?" you ask. Yes, there are towns, but most of the people live in the countryside. Towns are for trade, and the people of the villages rarely go to them. As we have seen, the manors are almost self-sufficient. Most people in the Middle Ages have little need for towns.

Serfs grew all the food on a European manor and made their own tools, shoes, and clothes. Almost nothing came from outside the manor.

You have just learned what life was like in western Europe about the year 1000. Gradually this life began to change.

WHY LIFE IN WESTERN EUROPE BEGAN TO CHANGE

In the early Middle Ages, people in western Europe had little to do with other parts of the world. Indeed, as we have seen, each manor to a large extent lived by itself. To be sure, lords of different manors sometimes fought each other or banded together under some more powerful lord to make war on his enemies. Such wars gave Europeans some knowledge of what was going on outside their tiny villages. Later, Europeans

★ Ask students if communities in the United States today are self-sufficient.

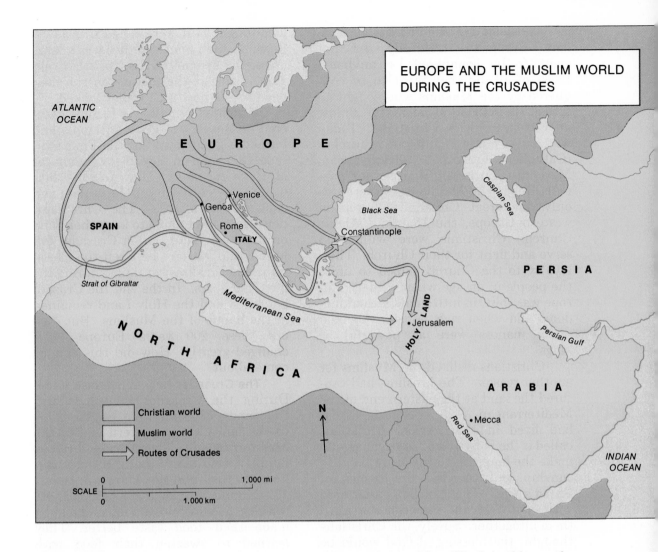

EUROPE AND THE MUSLIM WORLD
DURING THE CRUSADES

ATLANTIC
OCEAN

E U R O P E

Venice
Genoa
SPAIN
Rome
ITALY

Black Sea

Constantinople

Caspian Sea

P E R S I A

Strait of Gibraltar

Mediterranean Sea

N O R T H   A F R I C A

HOLY LAND

Jerusalem

Persian Gulf

N

A R A B I A

Red Sea

Mecca

INDIAN
OCEAN

Christian world

Muslim world

Routes of Crusades

0   1,000 mi
SCALE
0   1,000 km

MAP STUDY   See Teacher's Key.
This map shows how the Muslims extended their
power from Arabia into Africa and Europe.
(a) What sea lies between Europe and Africa?
(b) In what part of Europe did the Muslims
conquer land? (c) How are the routes of the
Crusaders shown on the map?

began to take a greater interest in more
distant parts of the world. This came
about because of wars between Europeans and people who lived in countries to
the south and southeast of Europe. As a
result of these wars, life in Europe
began to change. Let us see how this
happened.

    The Muslims invade Europe. About
the year 600 a new religion, called Islam,

grew up in Arabia. (Find Arabia on the
map above.) Islam is based on the
teachings of a great religious leader
named Mohammed. Followers of Islam
are called Muslims. The Muslims in
Arabia began a great war of conquest.
Soon their armies occupied all of North
Africa and crossed the Strait of Gibraltar into Spain. For centuries the Muslims pushed hard against the Christians
in Europe, trying always to gain more
territory. The map above shows how
much land the Muslims conquered.
Thinking of all these conquests, the
people of Europe wondered, "What is to
become of us if the Muslims force their
way even farther into Europe?"

29

Christians are angered by the Muslims. Europeans naturally did not want to be conquered by anybody. Least of all did they want to be conquered by the Muslims who sought to spread the religion of Islam, for almost all Europeans were Christians. Today we have many Christian churches (Catholic, Episcopal, Presbyterian, Methodist, Lutheran, Baptist, and others). But in the Middle Ages there was only one great Christian Church in western Europe, the Roman Catholic Church. Christians were willing to serve and fight for their Church. Their loyalty to the Church helped to unite the people in an age when western Europe was split up into small, weak kingdoms and when rich nobles who held many manors were as powerful as kings.

Christians disliked the Muslims for another reason. The Muslims had captured the land at the eastern end of the Mediterranean Sea. Because Christ had lived in that region, Christians called it the Holy Land. Many hoped to make the long trip to the Holy Land to worship and to visit the scenes of Christ's life. The Muslims interfered with such visits and sometimes stopped them altogether. Surely, the Christians thought, the blessing of God would be given to the people who helped recapture the Holy Land.

Christians make war against the Muslims. In 1095 the Pope, head of the Roman Catholic Church, held a great meeting. He urged the Christians to make war on the Muslims and to recover the Holy Land. Filled with enthusiasm by the Pope's words, knights by the thousands put on their armor and seized swords, battle-axes, lances, and shields. Eager for battle, the knights mounted their war horses and rode off to capture the Holy Land. This expedition was called a Crusade (meaning "taking the cross") and the knights

who fought in it were called Crusaders. Sewn on each man's clothes was a large cross, the symbol of the Christian religion. Look at the picture on the next page to see how a Crusader looked.

Knights from all over Europe gathered at the city of Constantinople and formed a great army for the First Crusade. (See map on page 29 for the routes of the Crusades.) They fought their way to the Holy City of Jerusalem and captured it in 1099. The Christians, however, were unable to keep their hold on the Holy Land. Other Crusades followed, and warfare between the Christians and Muslims continued during the next 200 years. In the end the Crusaders failed and the Holy Land remained in the hands of the Muslims. But during these 200 years Europe itself changed greatly. How did this change come about?

The Crusades help to increase trade. During the Crusades thousands and thousands of people went from Europe to the lands at the eastern end of the Mediterranean. There they became familiar with many useful articles and luxuries they had not known at home. They found that such spices as pepper, ● nutmeg, cloves, cinnamon, and ginger made their food taste better. They learned to sweeten their food with sugar. They learned to use soap and to take baths more often. They admired the precious stones — diamonds, rubies, emeralds, and sapphires — that they saw there. They also found medicines to heal the sick, dyes (like indigo) to color cloth, and fragrant perfumes. In the Eastern lands they discovered many things — glassware and china, swords and armor and other metal products, silks and other fabrics, rugs and wall hangings — that were better than anything in Europe.

All these articles helped to make life more pleasant and more comfortable. When the Crusaders returned

30

● Point out that spices were also used to preserve food. Have students list ways in which food is preserved today. Were any of those ways available to people in the Middle Ages?

Crosses were sewn on the Crusaders' clothes to show the goal of their journey—the capturing of the Holy City of Jerusalem. One knight in this picture is ready for battle, with helmet and shield.

home, they told their neighbors and families about these luxuries. Naturally Europeans wanted such good things for themselves. They soon learned they could buy these luxuries from Italian merchants.

Italian merchants carry Eastern goods to Europe. Even before the Crusades, certain Italian cities, like Venice and Genoa, had been carrying on some trade with the eastern Mediterranean. During and after the Crusades, when Europeans began to demand Eastern products, Italian merchants were glad to supply these goods. Trade increased rapidly. Italian ships, called galleys, began to go more and more often to the ports of the eastern Mediterranean. There they exchanged

woolen cloth, leather, and tin for the spices, silks, and jewels wanted by Europeans.

The galleys of the Italian merchants not only sailed the Mediterranean but also went into the Atlantic and carried goods to seaports along the west coast of Europe. Other merchants then carried these goods by river and by land far into the interior. It therefore became necessary to improve the roads, which up to this time had been little used. Also, wherever the merchants went, they needed marketplaces in which to trade their goods. Around these marketplaces towns grew up. As time passed and trade increased, the towns grew into cities. Life in western Europe had indeed begun to change.

31

● Discuss why trading centers grow into towns and cities.

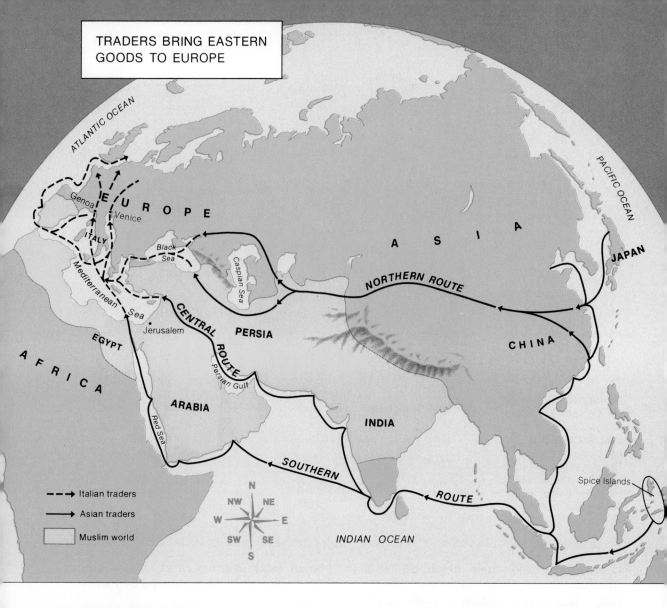

ATLANTIC OCEAN

PACIFIC OCEAN

Genoa
E U R O P E
Venice
ITALY
Black Sea
Caspian Sea
A S I A
JAPAN
NORTHERN ROUTE
Mediterranean
Sea
Jerusalem
CENTRAL ROUTE
PERSIA
CHINA
EGYPT
AFRICA
Persian Gulf
ARABIA
Red Sea
INDIA
SOUTHERN
Spice Islands
ROUTE
- - - ▶ Italian traders
——▶ Asian traders
☐ Muslim world
N
NW NE
W E
SW SE
S
INDIAN OCEAN

MAP STUDY   See Teacher's Key.
Marco Polo followed the trade routes shown here on his journeys to and from Asia. Notice that the Muslim world lay across the routes, between Europe and Asia. Why were Asian goods called "Eastern"? To answer, look at the compass on the map.

TRAVELERS' TALES AWAKEN EUROPEAN INTEREST IN ASIA

While these changes were taking place, travelers began to go from Europe to visit the unfamiliar lands of Asia: Persia, the Spice Islands,[1] India, and

China. (Find these lands on the map above.) The travelers came back with exciting stories that made Europeans eager to know still more about these lands. The most famous of these travelers was named Marco Polo.

Marco Polo tells about the wonders of Asia.   Marco Polo's home was in Italy, in the city of Venice. When he was only seventeen years old, he set out with his father and his uncle on an overland journey to Asia. Marco Polo was gone for 24 years, from the year 1271 to 1295. During that time he traveled over a great part of Asia, even seeing the Pacific Ocean. So remote were his travels that he visited some places

[1]Today Persia is known as Iran. The Spice Islands are part of the East Indies and belong to Indonesia.

32

not seen again by Europeans for 600 years.

Marco Polo saw and heard about many wonders. He reported that once he saw a city so large that to go all around it a person would have to walk a hundred miles. Later he saw one even larger. (Travelers of all times have sometimes exaggerated their experiences to make a better story. Marco Polo exaggerated here and there, but his story still had much truth in it.) Marco Polo marveled at seeing the Chinese people burning coal. He didn't know what it was, so he described it as "a kind of black stone, which is dug out of the mountains and burns like wood."

Marco Polo found that the people of Asia wove the finest carpets in the world. They made splendid silk cloth. They had spices of all kinds, ebony and other fine woods, gold and silver, pearls and precious stones, fine harness for horses, and excellent weapons for soldiers. Their cities were so rich and had so much trade that a single one of them was visited by thousands of boats each year.

The ruler over China and much of the rest of Asia was called the Great Khan. Europeans could not imagine, said Marco Polo, how rich and powerful this ruler was. One of his many palaces was so large that the wall enclosing it was one mile long on each side. In the palace itself there was a dining hall where 6,000 people could eat at one time. In his wars the Khan used armies larger than Europeans had ever known. One of his armies was ten times as big as all the armies Europe had sent on the First Crusade.

Here in Marco Polo's own words is a description of the Khan's marvelous system of communication:

From the city of Kanbalu there are many roads leading to the different provinces, and . . . upon every great high road, at the distance of twenty-five or thirty miles . . . there are stations. . . . At each station four hundred good horses are kept in constant readiness, in order that all messengers going and coming upon the business of the grand khan, and all ambassadors, may have relays, and, leaving their jaded [exhausted] horses, be supplied with fresh ones. . . . In consequence, . . . ambassadors to the court, and the royal messengers, go and return through every province . . . of the empire with the greatest convenience and facility; in all which the grand khan exhibits a superiority over every other emperor, king, or human being.

In the intermediate space between the post-houses, there are small villages settled at the distance of every three miles. . . . In these are stationed the foot messengers, likewise employed in the service of his majesty. They wear [belts] round their waists, to which several small bells are attached, in order that their coming may be perceived at a distance; and as they run only three miles, that is, from one of these foot-stations to another . . . the noise serves to give notice of their approach, and preparation is accordingly made by a fresh courier to proceed . . . instantly upon the arrival of the former. . . .

Marco Polo's stories make people want to visit Asia. The wonders just described are only a few of those Marco Polo heard of and saw. After he returned to Europe, a book was written about his adventures. Those who could read spread the news. Throughout Europe people talked about the stories the ★ book contained. When they learned that Eastern goods cost only a fraction of what the Italian merchants charged, people began to ask, "Why can't other Europeans go to Asia, as Marco Polo has done, and find out more about it? Why can't we find a way there and get some of the riches of China by exchanging our goods for theirs?"

★ Have students identify the points in Marco Polo's stories that made Europeans interested in Asia.

INVENTIONS AND IMPROVEMENTS MAKE LONG OCEAN VOYAGES POSSIBLE

About the time that Europeans were talking about finding a way to distant parts of Asia, changes were taking place in Europe that would make that very thing possible. As you know, people in western Europe did little traveling or trading before the Crusades. They also did very little reading or writing. Interest in learning was concentrated chiefly among priests and leaders of the Church, who conducted schools and preserved what few books there were. These books were written in Latin, which few people could read, and contained only knowledge of past centuries. Very little new knowledge was added. But as Europeans began to take an interest in trade and travel, more people began to read and write and study. People became interested in the learning of the ancient Greeks and Romans, which had been forgotten for hundreds of years. Europeans also heard about or developed certain inventions that made it easier to sail ships out of sight of land.

New instruments aid sailors. For one thing, people in Europe learned about the compass. To us a compass is a common article, but it was new to the Europeans of that time. First they learned to magnetize an iron needle so that it always pointed north. Next they learned to put the needle in a little box above a card on which north and the other directions were marked. Later they had a compass similar to the ones we have today.

A captain who had a compass could tell in which direction his boat was sailing. But a captain needed to know not only in what direction he was going but where he was. For this purpose, instruments called the cross-staff and the astrolabe (AS-troh-layb) were used. With their aid a captain could tell, by looking at certain stars, how far north or south of the equator he was. In this manner he was able to figure out his **latitude.** Then clocks came into use, and careful tables of times and distances were made. By looking at the stars again, and by using these tables and a clock, a captain could tell how far east or west he was. Thus he knew his **longitude.** To know the latitude and longitude of a place locates it exactly on earth's surface. Of course, sailing still depended largely on the captain's skill. But these instruments, as you can see, made sailing much safer than it had been and made long ocean voyages possible.

The maps and charts that sailors began to make were another help. With new and better maps to aid them, captains were more willing to sail out of ● sight of land.

A new method of printing is invented. For hundreds of years only one copy of a book could be made at a time. It had to be copied slowly by hand, letter by letter. About the middle of the 1400's, a new method of printing was invented. The new method used ★ what we call movable type. For each letter of the alphabet there were sets of tiny separate letters that could be put together to form words. By the use of crude printing presses, a number of

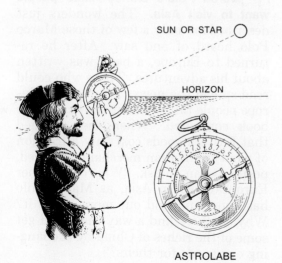

SUN OR STAR ◯

HORIZON

34   ASTROLABE

EARLY PRINTING PRESS

books could then be printed from the same type.

The invention of printing did more than any other thing to spread stories of new lands throughout Europe. After 1450, when travelers journeyed into new lands or on unknown seas, they could write accounts of their trips and make maps to show the routes they had followed. Then these could be printed for the use of all travelers. In this way, the invention of printing encouraged travel and exploration.

▶ **CHECK UP**   See Teacher's Key.

1. **(a)** Describe life on a manor about the year 1000. **(b)** Were towns important in Europe during the early Middle Ages? Why?
2. **(a)** Who were the Muslims? **(b)** What was their religion? **(c)** Why did the Muslims become enemies of the Christians in Europe?
3. **(a)** What were the Crusades? **(b)** How did they affect trade between Europe and lands east of the Mediterranean? **(c)** How did Eastern goods reach Europe?
4. How did travelers' tales and the invention of printing increase interest in Asia?
5. **(a)** What inventions made long sea voyages possible? **(b)** How did each invention help sailors?

2 How Did European Explorers Seek and Find a Water Route to Asia?

ITALIAN CITIES CONTROL TRADE WITH ASIA

As we have seen, the people of Europe had become accustomed to using Eastern products — spices, sugar, perfumes, silks, and the like. These goods were brought to them by Italian traders. By the 1400's, Italian cities (especially Venice and Genoa) had begun to trade with Asian lands and were making huge profits. The Italian merchants did not actually journey to Asia themselves. Arabian traders traveled to the distant lands and returned with goods that they sold to the Italians. Let us see what important routes these Arab traders followed as they traveled between Asia and ports in the Mediterranean.

Trade with the far lands of Asia follows three routes. Look at the map on page 32 and, as you read, trace the three routes the traders used. (1) The northern route was a long and difficult one. It led from China westward across the wide plains of Asia (a journey of half a year or more), then across the Black Sea to the Mediterranean Sea. (2) The central route went both by sea and by land. Arabian vessels carried wares northward along the western coast of India and into the Persian Gulf. Then caravans took the goods overland to the seaports of the eastern Mediterranean.

35

● To eliminate the Italian merchants as middlemen, other Europeans had to trade directly with Asia. How would direct trade affect prices? (They would fall.)

★ See p. T14 for a strategy that will help students think about these advances in navigation.

(3) The southern route was mostly a water route from China to India, then across to Arabia and on into the Red Sea. From there it was only a short distance by land to the seaports of Egypt where Italian merchants picked up the goods.

Remember that no matter where these routes ended, Italian merchants were on hand to buy the goods from Arab traders. Because the cities of Italy were nearer the East and because the Italians had been given special privileges by the Muslims, the merchants from other countries of Europe did not have a chance to share in this profitable trade. In other words, the Italian cities had what we call a **monopoly** of the Eastern trade.

Other Europeans are jealous of the Italians. You can imagine how jealous of the Italian cities the other seafaring countries of Europe were. They looked at the trade routes controlled by the Italians. They saw Italian purses growing fat while their own stayed thin. Europeans had some goods that they traded to the Italians in exchange for Eastern luxuries. But their goods were not as valuable as the Eastern goods, so they had to make up the difference by paying gold and silver to the Italian merchants. Countries cannot keep on buying more than they sell, any more than people can keep on spending more than they earn.

There was another reason, too, why the countries of Europe resented the Italian monopoly of trade. During the early Middle Ages the nobles were almost as powerful as the kings and queens and the people had no feeling of loyalty to their country. This condition had gradually changed. Monarchs had slowly overcome the lords and were becoming the heads of strong, united countries. For the first time the people of France and England, Portugal and Spain, knew what it meant to feel proud of their countries. They wanted their

countries to become wealthy and powerful, and they knew that trade with Asia would help to make them so. The kings and queens too were eager to become rich. They stood ready to furnish ships and money and to send daring sailors to find the way to distant lands.

Europeans seek new routes to Asia. It is small wonder, then, that sailors of these new nations began to dream of finding other routes to India and China. They said, "Venice and Genoa control the well-known routes to Asia. Why not look for a new way by water so that we can have our share of Eastern riches?" Indeed, what could stop them? They now had instruments ★ to make sailing safer. They had maps and charts to guide them. And what is more, they had dreams of adventure and fame and wealth. Such dreams lead people to press onward in spite of failures and hardships.

PORTUGUESE SAILORS REACH INDIA BY WATER

Prince Henry of Portugal encourages exploration. The small country of Portugal was the first to find a water route to Asia. Much of the credit for this discovery belongs to a member of the Portuguese royal family, Prince Henry. Prince Henry's great interest was the sea. By exploring the west coast of Africa, he hoped to spread Christianity and to build up a profitable trade for his country in gold and ivory. But perhaps Prince Henry also had hopes that by venturing farther and farther into the unknown sea along the African coast, the Portuguese might find an all-water route to Asia.

To help carry out these ambitions, Prince Henry built a school for sailors at the southwestern tip of Europe. Here he gathered ship captains, students of navigation (the science of sailing ships), makers of maps and instruments, travelers, and shipbuilders. Soon the sailors

● Introduce the concept of *nationalism*. Simply defined, nationalism means "intense pride in one's country."

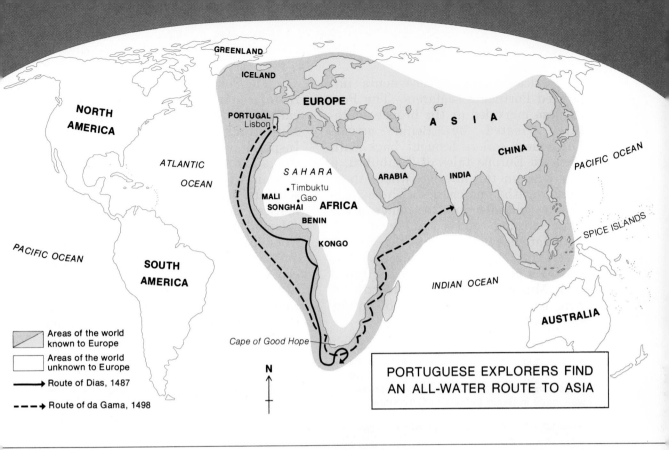

PORTUGUESE EXPLORERS FIND AN ALL-WATER ROUTE TO ASIA

Areas of the world known to Europe
Areas of the world unknown to Europe
→ Route of Dias, 1487
---→ Route of da Gama, 1498

MAP STUDY   See Teacher's Key.
Before the 1490's Europeans knew nothing about the areas shown in white on this map of the world. (a) What continents were completely unknown to Europeans before the 1490's? (b) What continent did da Gama sail around to get to India?

and ships of Portugal became the finest of those times. Prince Henry himself became known as "the Navigator."

Portuguese sailors explore the western coast of Africa.   Prince Henry began to send ships along the west coast of Africa to explore and to trade. He commanded each captain to build a six-foot stone tower on the coast marking the farthest point he had reached. No Europeans at that time, of course, realized how huge the continent of Africa is. It took great courage, therefore, to sail ships ever southward along what seemed a never-ending coast. Many sailors believed the terrible tales they had heard about the unknown seas — that there were whirlpools waiting to

pull ships into the depths of the ocean, that evil monsters were lurking below the surface to destroy those who dared sail the unknown waters. Because of these stories sailors would often turn back from the "Great Sea of ● Darkness," as they called it. But Prince Henry commanded the captains to keep on, and stone towers were built farther and farther south on the coast of western Africa.

The Portuguese learn about West ★ African kingdoms.   As they sailed along the western coast of Africa, Portuguese sailors might have felt they were leaving civilization behind them. But in Africa they learned about vast and rich kingdoms ruled by powerful emperors. At one time the Mali kingdom had been so large that people sometimes said it took a year to travel from one end of it to the other. Other rich African kingdoms included Songhai (SONG-hy), Benin (beh-NEEN), and Kongo. (See the map on this page.)   **37**

● Have students identify the probable location of the "Great Sea of Darkness" (see map on this page).

★ See p. T14 for a strategy that involves students in a bulletin board project.

Africa's many achievements impressed Portugal's seafarers. The Portuguese marveled at the bronze sculptures created by Benin artists. Portuguese sailors brought back with them to Europe tales of Timbuktu, a city deep in the interior, where there were wealthy merchants. These merchants sent gold from the mines of the Mali kingdom and cotton grown by Mali farmers north across the Sahara desert in long camel caravans. The travelers in the camel caravans traded with Muslim merchants in North Africa, exchanging gold and cotton for salt, cloth, and copper.

After Portugal made contact with Benin in the late 1400's, trade developed between the two kingdoms. The beautiful ivory carving below was made in Benin for sale to Europeans.

The Portuguese learned that centuries of commerce between the West Africans and Muslims had brought the Muslim religion to much of the region. Inspired by their new religion, these rulers had built great universities. One was in the city of Timbuktu where scholars studied religion and mathematics. Many African rulers built splendid mosques (Muslim houses of worship) as well, including an enormous one made of brick in the Songhai city of Gao.

In time, the Portuguese found Africans who were glad to trade with them. By the mid-1400's Portugal had built up a rich trade along the African coast and had exchanged ambassadors with the kingdoms of Benin and Kongo. At first the Portuguese traded mostly for gold. Later, they began to trade for slaves.

India is reached at last. After Prince Henry's death in 1460, Portuguese captains continued to explore the coast of Africa. Late in 1487, Bartholomew Dias (DEE-ahs) sailed his ship around the southern tip. When he was quite sure that the way was now clear to sail on to India, he hastened back with the news. The king of Portugal joyfully named the southern end of Africa the Cape of Good Hope. Several years later, in 1498, another Portuguese explorer proved that Dias was right. Vasco da Gama (duh GAM-uh) sailed around the Cape of Good Hope and headed north along the eastern coast of Africa. Then, pointing the prow of his ship eastward, he crossed the Indian Ocean to India. There he set up a stone tower to mark the end of the search for a water route to Asia. Then he sailed for home with a shipload of spices, silks, and jewels as proof that he had indeed reached India.

Portuguese explorers make the known world larger. Before Prince Henry's ships began their voyages of exploration, Europeans knew little about the world. (Look at the map on page 37.) But the Portuguese explorers

38

● Have students look at the map on p. 37. Portugal had begun exploration about 1420. How long did it take to find a water route to Asia? (78 years)

Before Europeans knew much about the world, sailors believed that sea monsters were a danger of travel in distant waters.

added a great deal to European knowledge of geography. As the captains returned from their trips, the map makers would add more information to their maps. These maps gave the people of Europe a much better idea of what the world was like.

PORTUGAL CONTROLS THE ALL-WATER ROUTE TO INDIA

Portugal grows rich from its Eastern trade. The Portuguese understood at once the value of the all-water route to India that da Gama found. He had brought back a cargo worth 60 times what his voyage had cost! If you could buy for a dollar something that you could sell for 60 dollars, you would be pleased. The king of Portugal, the ship captains, and the merchants felt just that way about it. They increased the number of ships sailing to Asia. Also, they set up trading posts in India and sent soldiers to guard the posts. Portugal was now the sole master of the new all-water route to India.

The Italian cities lose their trade to Portugal. In the early 1500's, Lisbon, capital of Portugal, became the most important port in Europe. Sailors thronged the streets and taverns, while ship captains and merchants sat in quiet rooms and made plans for future voyages. Heavily laden vessels from India sailed into Lisbon's harbor. They carried valuable Eastern goods — precious stones, spices, cloth. The ships of other nations were waiting to transport these goods to other ports of Europe. As you know, the Italian cities of Venice and Genoa had long been Europe's leading ports. Because water transportation was cheaper, Portuguese merchants were now able to sell Eastern goods at lower prices than the Italian merchants. That is why Lisbon became the leader in the rich Eastern trade that had once been the monopoly of the Italian cities.

▶ **CHECK UP**   See Teacher's Key.

1. By what routes did early traders bring goods from distant Asian lands?
2. **(a)** What European cities controlled trade with Asia? **(b)** Why were other Europeans jealous of these cities?
3. Why were the people of western Europe interested in trading with Asia?
4. **(a)** Who was Prince Henry the Navigator? **(b)** What use did Portugal make of its new knowledge about the African kingdoms? **(c)** How did Portugal find an all-water route to India? **(d)** What were the results of this discovery?

3 Why Did Columbus Sail Westward, and What Did He Accomplish?

Even before da Gama reached India, the voyages of earlier Portuguese ship captains had led Europeans to wonder about other routes to Asia. After all, a water route controlled by the Portuguese would be no better for the other nations of Europe than the old routes controlled by the Italian cities. Some people had a daring new idea: Why not try to find a water route to Asia and its riches by sailing *westward*?

The Vikings come to North America. Today we know that about the year 1000, people called Vikings from northern Europe had sailed west from Europe and found land across the Atlantic. Their boats, called "long ships," were small, only 70 feet or so long and about 18 feet wide, and the crowded passengers were exposed to the rough waters of the north Atlantic. The Vikings knew how to sail their boats skillfully, and they became known as the best shipbuilders and sailors in Europe.

The Vikings traveled far and wide, reaching Russia to the east and finding Iceland and Greenland to the west. They eventually came to North America, where they made settlements. These settlements were not large, although almost 180 men and women, probably taking with them some cattle, are known to have gone along on one voyage to North America.

It is not certain how far inland into North America the Vikings went. Viking legends, called sagas, told of a fertile, grape-growing land called Vinland, where Viking men and women had settlements. Vinland must have been North America. We know today there was a Viking settlement in what is now Newfoundland. The Vikings may even have reached the Hudson River or beyond, possibly going hundreds of miles inland. The Vikings stayed in their settlements for several years, but they lost interest in the new lands. Very few other Europeans in the late 1400's ever heard about their voyages and the lands they had found.

Columbus plans to sail westward to Asia. One man was sure that he could reach Asia by sailing west instead of east. He had almost certainly never heard about the Viking explorations or Vinland. But Christopher Columbus was a dreamer who had the courage to try to make his dreams come true. Columbus had grown up in the Italian port of Genoa. He loved the sea and had become a sailor when he was fourteen years old. When he was not actually on shipboard, he made maps and charts for a living. He studied the charts of others, read the reports of new voyages, and talked with other sailors. Slowly his great dream about sailing westward to Asia changed from a dream into a definite plan.

Columbus thought his plan would be easier to carry out than it really was. Because he planned to sail into unknown seas, he had to guess what he would find, and he guessed wrong. He knew that the world was round, but he thought it was much smaller than it is. Also, he thought that Asia was much larger than it is. Naturally, therefore, he thought that the distance he would have to sail westward from Europe to reach Asia was much *shorter* than it is. As the first globe on page 43 shows, Columbus knew nothing of the two continents that would block his way to Asia.

Columbus prepares for his voyage. Columbus was sure that it would

● Ask students why the Vikings don't get credit for discovering America.

★ Use the map (p. 43) to help students explore in greater depth Columbus's perception of the world.

The Vikings were the first Europeans to sail to North America. One expedition to eastern Canada was led by a Viking named Leif Ericson.

be easier and cheaper to reach Asia by sailing westward than by sailing all the way around Africa as the Portuguese were trying to do. But Columbus was not a rich man. He could not buy ships, pay for supplies for a long voyage, or hire crews. He needed help to carry out his bold plan.

As we have learned, the rulers of Europe were eager for greater wealth and had already helped some ship captains to make important voyages. So Columbus turned to the monarchs of Spain and Portugal for help. But for years no one would listen to his story, and Columbus became discouraged. He almost gave up hope of ever being able to try out his plan. Finally he persuaded King Ferdinand and Queen Isabella of Spain to give him ships and money to prepare for the westward voyage to Asia.

At last everything was ready and the time to set sail arrived. It was early in the morning of Friday, August 3, 1492. In the harbor of the Spanish village of Palos, Columbus stood on the deck of a small ship, the *Santa Maria*, giving orders to the crew of 40 men. The *Santa Maria* sailed slowly from the harbor and put out to sea. Two other ships, the *Niña* (NEE-nyah) and the *Pinta*, each with some 25 men on board, also sailed under Columbus's command. For years Columbus had dreamed of this day and planned for it. Now he and his companions were going to try to reach Asia by sailing westward into unknown seas.

Columbus finds another world. It was a long and difficult voyage. The men grew fearful as day after day the

41

See p. T15 for a strategy that suggests how students might examine Columbus's proposed voyage from three different perspectives.

ships slid westward through unknown waters. This was the dreadful Great Sea of Darkness, where monsters supposedly lay in wait. Columbus restlessly walked the deck, keeping watch on everything — the wind, the sails, the weather, the men. He kept a record of each day's progress. Soon he had to keep two records. One, which he kept for himself, gave the true distance they had come from Spain. The other, which he let the crew see, showed the distance covered each day as much less than it really was. He did this to keep the men from worrying about being so far from home. But at last, ten weeks after the little port of Palos had dropped from sight behind them, they saw sure signs of land. We can imagine how triumphant Columbus must have felt. We can do even more; we can read his own story of his triumph. It appears in *The Journal of Christopher Columbus*, written as though it were happening to other people, which was the custom of the time. Here is part of it:

WEDNESDAY, 10TH OF OCTOBER — The course was W.S.W. [west of southwest], and they went at the rate of 10 miles an hour, occasionally 12 miles, and sometimes 7. During the day and night they made 59 leagues,[2] counted [for the sailors' sake] as no more than 44. Here the people could endure no longer. They complained of the length of the voyage. But the Admiral [as Columbus referred to himself] cheered them up in the best way he could, giving them good hopes of the advantages they might gain from it.

THURSDAY, 11TH OF OCTOBER — The course was W.S.W., and there was [a rougher] sea than there had been during the whole of the voyage. They saw sandpipers and a green reed near the ship. Those on the *Pinta* saw a cane and a pole, . . . a sand-plant, and a small board. The crew of the caravel *Niña* also saw signs of land. . . . Everyone breathed afresh and rejoiced at these signs.

After sunset the Admiral returned to his original west course, and they went along at the rate of 12 miles an hour. . . . As the caravel *Pinta* was a better sailor, and went ahead of the Admiral, she found the land, and made the signals ordered by the Admiral. The land was first seen by a sailor named Rodrigo de Triana. But the Admiral, at ten in the previous night . . . , saw a light, though it was so uncertain that he could not affirm it was land. . . . The Admiral asked . . . the men to keep a good look-out . . . , and to watch well for land; and to him who should first cry out that he saw land, he would give a silk doublet [jacket], besides the other rewards promised by the Sovereigns [Ferdinand and Isabella], which was 10,000 [gold coins] to him who should first see it. At two hours after midnight the land was sighted at a distance of two leagues.

FRIDAY, 12TH OF OCTOBER — The vessels were hove to [stopped], waiting for daylight; and on Friday they arrived at a small island . . . called, in the language of the Indians, Guanahani [gwah-nah-HAH-nee]. Presently they saw . . . people. The Admiral went on shore in the armed boat, and Martin Alonzo Pinzon, and Vincente Yanez, his brother, who was captain of the *Niña*. The Admiral took the royal standard, and the captains went with two banners of the green cross, . . . with an F and a Y [for Ferdinand and Ysabel] and a crown over each letter. . . . Having landed, they saw trees very green, and much water, and fruits of [various] kinds. The Admiral called to the two captains, and to the others who leaped on shore . . . and said that they should bear faithful testimony that he . . . had taken . . . possession of the said island for the King and for the Queen.

42 [2]A league was about 3 miles.

● Explain that historians call Columbus's journal a *primary source*. What value is there in reading Columbus's own story of his voyage?

COLUMBUS REACHES AMERICA

Columbus believed that the globe was smaller than it really is (left) and that Asia stretched farther around it. If he sailed west about 3,200 miles, he thought, he would reach Japan.

But the globe is bigger than Columbus thought (below) and America lies between Europe and Asia. So Columbus discovered America instead of a new route to Asia.

If America had not existed, Columbus would have had to sail about three times as far as he had expected to reach Japan.

MAP STUDY The globe at the top of this page shows how Columbus thought he could sail across the Atlantic Ocean from Europe to Asia. The other globe shows the actual world. What land blocked Columbus's way?

43

See Teacher's Key.

People in America's Story

CHRISTOPHER COLUMBUS

Born in Genoa, Christopher Columbus was one of the greatest navigators of all time. His landing in the West Indies led to lasting contact between Europe and the Americas.

Above you see Columbus's own drawing of the *Santa Maria*.

A westward route to Asia was the daring plan Columbus proposed to Ferdinand and Isabella of Spain. After many delays, they gave him three ships, and he set off. When Columbus sighted land, he found something even more important than a new route to Asia. He had found America. On his return to Europe he was greeted with enthusiasm. Artists painted his portrait (above) and Queen Isabella received him at court (right).

Why was Columbus's voyage important? On October 12, 1492, Columbus had landed on an island called Guanahani, which he named San Salvador. This island lies in the Bahama Islands, southeast of Florida. Still seeking the mainland of Asia, Columbus sailed along the coasts of two other islands, Cuba and Hispaniola (his-pahn-YOH-lah), before returning to Spain. Because he thought these islands were part of the East Indies off the eastern coast of Asia, he called them "the Indies." Today, as a result of Columbus's mistake, this group of islands is called the West Indies and the original people of the American continents are called Indians.

What had Columbus accomplished? He had not reached Asia; he had not discovered a new route to India and other Asian lands. But what he did do was even more important. Although he did not know it at the time, Columbus had landed in America.

▶ **CHECK UP** See Teacher's Key.

1. Why were some European countries interested in a westward route to Asia?
2. **(a)** Why did Columbus think he could reach Asia by sailing westward? **(b)** Why did he fail?
3. Why was Columbus's voyage important?

CHECK UP ON CHAPTER 1

See Teacher's Key.

Words to Know

The following words are important in understanding Chapter 1. Can you explain the meaning of each word?

1. serf	**7.** Islam
2. manor	**8.** Crusade
3. monopoly	**9.** Holy Land
4. longitude	**10.** trade route
5. navigation	**11.** latitude
6. Muslim	**12.** self-sufficient

Places to Locate

If you know the location of the places mentioned in the chapter, the story will have more meaning for you. Be able to locate the following places on the maps in your book.

1. Africa	**12.** Venice
2. Asia	**13.** Spain
3. Europe	**14.** Cape of Good Hope
4. China	**15.** Spice Islands
5. India	**16.** Indian Ocean
6. Benin	**17.** Black Sea
7. Mali	**18.** Red Sea
8. Kongo	**19.** Persian Gulf
9. Genoa	**20.** Atlantic Ocean
10. Lisbon	**21.** Pacific Ocean
11. Portugal	**22.** Mediterranean Sea

Facts to Remember

Recalling the facts about a subject offers a chance to review what you have read. Check your mastery of the facts by answering the following questions about important people and events.

1. **(a)** Where did Marco Polo's travels take him? **(b)** What effect did the news of his travels have on other Europeans?
2. **(a)** Who was Prince Henry the Navigator? **(b)** What did he do to encourage the exploration of unknown regions?
3. **(a)** What countries did Portuguese explorers find as they sailed south along West Africa? **(b)** What impressed the Portuguese about the people with whom they came into contact?
4. **(a)** Why did Columbus need the help of European rulers before he could carry out his plan to sail west? **(b)** Who finally agreed to help him?

Skills to Practice

Practicing such skills as using time lines and maps will make your study of history easier and more interesting. Sharpen your skills by answering the following questions.

1. Look at the time line at the beginning of this chapter (page 26). **(a)** What is the time span (the overall time period) of the chapter? **(b)** What is the first year printed on the time line? **(c)** Did the First Crusade take place before or after that date? **(d)** What is the last date printed on the time line? **(e)** Did Columbus reach America before or after that date?
2. Look at the map on page 32. **(a)** What was the importance of the routes shown on that map? **(b)** Name two bodies of water that were part of the central route and two bodies of water that were part of the southern route. **(c)** What part of a trip from Europe to the Spice Islands would have been the same whether you took the central or the southern route?

Questions to Think About

The study of history teaches us to understand and apply what we have learned. Use the knowledge gained in this chapter to answer the following questions. Be sure to give reasons for your answers.

1. **(a)** What are some advantages that a country has when it is self-sufficient? **(b)** What are some disadvantages?
2. What connection did the Crusades have with Europe's discovery of America?
3. **(a)** Would you give Prince Henry or da Gama the credit for discovering a new route to Asia? Give reasons. **(b)** Do Venice and Genoa deserve any credit for this discovery?
4. Columbus called the people he found in 1492 "Indians." **(a)** Why did he give them this name? **(b)** Why are they still called Indians?

Linking Past and Present

One reason for studying history is that it helps us to understand the world in which we live today. For the past is not dead; it is linked to the present in many ways. This feature of your textbook, "Linking Past and Present," appears at the ends of chapters. In it you will find interesting bits of information which show that events and people of times past have left their mark on the American people and the nation of the present day.

Why America, not Columbia? How does it happen that the two great continents of North and South America are not named for Christopher Columbus? The reason lies in the past. One of the many explorers who followed Columbus to America was an Italian called Amerigo Vespucci (veh-SPYOO-chih). Vespucci's account of his voyages across the Atlantic greatly impressed a famous German map maker. This map maker began to put the name *Terra America* ("land of Americus") on his maps. Because many sailors and explorers used these maps, "America" soon became an accepted name.

In the 1700's and 1800's, however, poets and other writers often referred to our nation as "Columbia," after Columbus, of course. Columbia became a poetic or literary name for America. For example, you may be familiar with the old patriotic song "Columbia, the Gem of the Ocean."

Columbus is not forgotten. Although the Americas were not named for Columbus, people in the Western Hemisphere use his name in other ways. Most of our 50 states have a city, town, or county named after Columbus — such as Columbus, Ohio, and Columbia, South Carolina. Our nation's capital is located in the District of Columbia. Columbia University in New York City bears his name, and the great river of our Pacific Northwest is called the Columbia. One of the republics of South America is named Colombia. And two cities in Panama are Cristóbal and Colón — Spanish for "Christopher" and "Columbus."

● Columbus is also honored by a holiday. Do students know the date of that holiday? (October 12)

For answers see Teacher's Key.

Have students use the atlas maps at the back of the book to practice finding the latitude and longitude of specific locations.

GAINING SKILL

Reading Maps: Using the Grid System

On many maps and globes, you can see a set of crisscross lines, called a **grid.** Map makers draw those lines to help people locate places. The lines that run from north to south are called longitude lines, or meridians. Lines drawn from east to west are called latitude lines, or parallels.

Two lines in this grid system are especially important. The latitude line that is halfway between the poles is called the **equator.** Find that line on the map below. Notice that it is numbered 0° (which is read as "zero degrees"). All other latitude lines are numbered to tell how many degrees north or south of the equator they are. The half of the world north of the equator is called the Northern Hemisphere. The half of the world south of the equator is the Southern Hemisphere.

Another important line is a longitude line running through Great Britain. That line is called the **prime meridian,** and it is 0° ("zero degrees") longitude. All other longitude lines are numbered to tell how many degrees east or west of the prime meridian they are. The prime meridian divides the Eastern Hemisphere from the Western Hemisphere.

Use the map on this page to answer these questions.

1. Is the United States in the Northern or the Southern Hemisphere?
2. In what ocean does the equator cross the prime meridian?
3. On what continent would you find each of the following locations?
   20°S, 140°E
   20°S, 60°W
   60°N, 120°W
   40°N, 80°E
   0°, 20°E
   80°S, 120°E

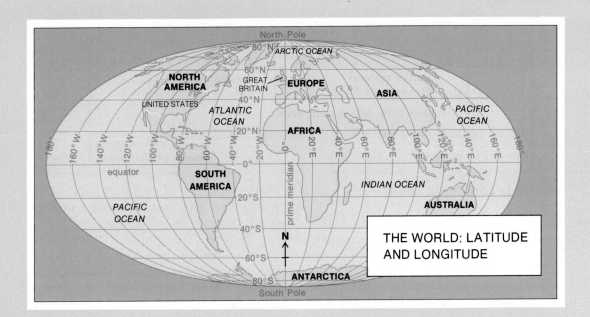

THE WORLD: LATITUDE AND LONGITUDE

CHAPTER **2**   *Vocabulary preview: plain, mesa, isthmus*

Europeans Learn More About America

1492–1700   See pp. T15–T16 for chapter teaching strategies.

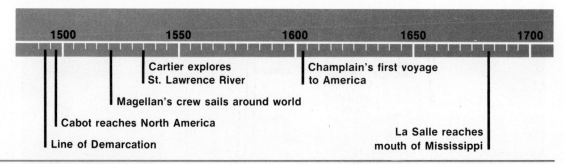

| 1500 | 1550 | 1600 | 1650 | 1700 |

Cartier explores St. Lawrence River

Champlain's first voyage to America

Magellan's crew sails around world

Cabot reaches North America

La Salle reaches mouth of Mississippi

Line of Demarcation

What this chapter is about —

Across empty spaces on old maps the words *Terra Incognita* often appear. These Latin words mean "unknown land" or "unexplored country." The map makers wrote *Terra Incognita* on the maps to show that they did not know what the unexplored parts of the world were like and therefore could not draw those areas accurately.

Before Christopher Columbus began the voyage described at the end of the last chapter, the map makers might have written *Terra Incognita* over a large portion of the world. Europeans

48

Ask students to think of English words derived from the Latin *terra* (for example, *territory, subterranean, extraterrestrial*). Have students look up these words.

◀ The travels of La Salle and other daring explorers taught Europeans much about the land and people of North America.

not Asia, what was it? Who were its inhabitants? What promise, if any, did this land offer Europeans?

In this chapter you will learn who the original people of North America were and how Europeans found out more about the land across the Atlantic. As you read, you will find answers to the following questions:

1. Who were the first Americans, and how did they live?
2. How did explorers find a great barrier blocking the way to Asia?
3. What explorers sought short cuts to Asia through America?
4. How did the search for short cuts to Asia open up America?

1 Who Were the First Americans, and How Did They Live?

When the European explorers came to America, there were people living in what is now the United States. To these people, this region of the world was not *Terra Incognita*. It was their homeland! They traveled its rivers, climbed its mountains, and farmed its land.

Who were these first Americans? ● Today we use one word, *Indians,* for all the people who lived in America before the Europeans came. (The term *Native Americans* is sometimes used too.) Most historians believe that long ago the ancestors of these people came from Asia to North America. They think that there was land between the continents where now there is sea, and that people made their way across this land as they hunted wandering herds of animals.

The Indians who lived in America were divided into many different tribes. A tribe was a large group of people speaking the same language and sharing a way of life. By the time the first European explorers arrived in America, there were hundreds of Indian tribes. These tribes were as different from one another as were the people of England and Italy, for example. To get an idea of what Indian life was like around the year 1500, you will read about tribes who made their homes in the eastern forests, the grassy plains, and the dry lands of the Southwest.

The Iroquois live in the eastern woodlands. In the forests of what is now northern New York State lived the Iroquois (EAR-uh-kwoy). Their bark-covered "long houses" were several hundred feet long and had space for ten to twenty families. The long houses also contained large rooms for meetings and religious services. The Iroquois lived in villages of several hundred people each. To protect the villages, they built high fences, or palisades, of logs driven upright into the ground. The villages made such a grand appearance that Europeans called them "castles."

Like many other tribes, the Iroquois were farmers. They grew corn, beans, and squash in the fields outside their villages. They also gathered fruit ★

49

★ Have students locate the Iroquois, Cheyenne, and Hopi on the map, p. 50.

and nuts in the forests and used hooks, spears, and nets to catch fish. To add to their food supply and to get furs and skins for clothing, they hunted deer and other animals.

There were several tribes of Iroquois — among them the Mohawk, Seneca, Onondaga, Oneida, and Cayuga. Women had an important place in these tribes. They were viewed as the heads of the families and chose the sachems (SAY-chumz), or chiefs, who led the tribes.

The Iroquois traded with one another, exchanging furs, tools, and other goods. They used seashells as wampum, or money. Disputes over trade some-

times led to war. Battles were fought with bows and arrows and tomahawks.

The Cheyenne live on the Great Plains. A tribe with a different way of life from the Iroquois was the Cheyenne (shy-AN). The Cheyenne lived in a part of North America called the Great Plains. (A **plain** is flat or rolling land with very few trees.) Herds of buffalo roamed the vast, grassy lands that stretched from the Mississippi River to the Rocky Mountains and from Canada to Mexico. The Cheyenne were just one of many Indian tribes living in this area. They spent winters in villages near rivers and streams, living in dome-shaped "earth lodges" made from logs covered with dirt and brush. In the spring Cheyenne women planted beans, corn, and squash near these villages. Then during the summer, hunting parties went out to hunt the buffalo. The hunters lived in tepees. These cone-shaped tents made of skins could be easily moved from place to place.

● **MAP STUDY**   See Teacher's Key.

On this map you see where important Indian tribes lived when Europeans first came to America. (Many tribes later moved to different areas.) Indian tribes in each of the large regions shown here had similar ways of living.
(a) In which region did the Iroquois live?
(b) The Cheyenne? (c) The Hopi?

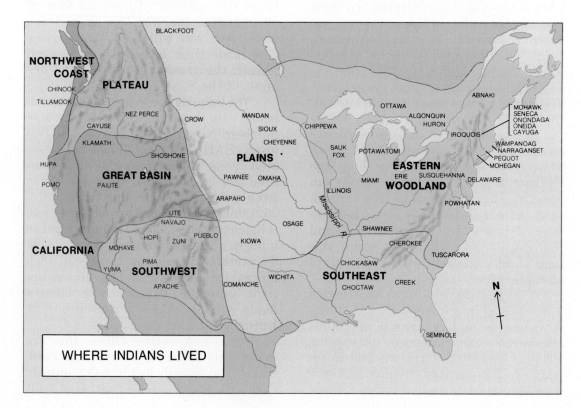

WHERE INDIANS LIVED

● Indians who lived in what is now southern Texas were part of the northern Mexico culture region.

Many North American Indians had tribal councils. Members of the council settled disagreements and made important decisions affecting the life of the tribe as a whole.

Hunting the buffalo was not easy. The Cheyenne traveled on foot, carrying their supplies on platforms mounted on two poles and pulled by dogs. When a hunting party drew near a herd of buffalo, the men of the tribe joined together to stampede the animals over a cliff or corner them in a narrow place. Then they killed the shaggy beasts with bows and arrows. The buffalo provided meat, skins for clothing, and bones to use as hoes or other tools.

The Cheyenne fought many wars to protect their hunting grounds. They did not try to kill as many of their enemies as possible, however. In fact, a Cheyenne fighter would make a special effort to touch an enemy in battle and get away without being harmed. A fighter who succeeded in this goal won honor and respect.

Cheyenne ways of living were tied to their religious beliefs. Every summer the chiefs brought the people together for a religious ceremony called the Sun Dance. In this ceremony, which lasted for several days, the people asked the Great Spirit to make them successful farmers, hunters, and fighters.

The Hopi dwell in the Southwest. To the Southwest, in what is now Arizona, were the dwellings of the Hopi (HOH-pih). Their ways of living were not like those of either the Iroquois or the Cheyenne. The Hopi lived in a land where very little rain fell. Water was scarce, and they had to make good use of every drop of moisture. The Hopi farmers even planted their fields so the crops could catch the morning dew. Although the Hopi occasionally hunted with bows and arrows and spears, farming supplied most of their needs. Among their crops were corn, cotton, and tobacco. Hopi men developed great skill in the weaving of cloth, and the women made pottery and baskets, which are still much admired and copied today.

Hopi homes were very different from those of Indians who lived on the Plains or in the forests. The Hopi made their homes of stone and of sun-dried clay called adobe (ah-DOH-bee). The dwellings were large, two or more stories high, and were built against cliffs or on high **mesas** (steep hills with flat tops). Each building was divided into space for a number of families. The homes had no

51

● Point out that the Cheyenne used every part of the buffalo. See item 6 in "Things To Do" (p. 69).

★ See p. T15 for a strategy calling for students to make a chart comparing the Iroquois, Cheyenne, and Hopi.

ground-level doors or windows. The Hopi used ladders to enter their homes through the roof. These ladders could be removed to keep outsiders away.

Religion was important to the Hopi people. In elaborate religious ceremonies the Hopi showed reverence for the universal Spirit who, they believed, ruled people and nature. They performed snake dances that lasted for days as one way of asking for the Spirit's blessing. The Hopi were peaceful people who fought only if their homes were threatened. Murder was unknown, and stealing was rare.

● **Indian and European ways of life affect each other.** You have now learned how some Indian tribes lived before Europeans came to North America. Their ways of life were different from those in Europe, Asia, and Africa because for thousands of years there was little or no contact between North America and the other continents. Then, over several hundred years, European explorers and settlers came into contact with the Indians. They introduced them to new things that brought change to their way of life. For example, before the Europeans came, dogs had been the only work animal known to the Cheyenne. Then the Europeans brought horses to America. No longer did the Cheyenne follow the time-honored pattern of spring plantings, summer hunts, and autumn harvests. They gave up farming and rode their swift ponies to chase the buffalo.

One disastrous result of contact with Europeans was that Indians caught diseases never before known in America. Smallpox, measles, and tuberculosis spread rapidly among the Indians, causing terrible suffering and thousands of deaths. You will read more about the effects of European settlement on the first Americans in later chapters.

Did Indian life have an impact on ★ the European settlers as well? It did indeed. Indians taught Europeans how to find their way along trails through the forests and how to survive in what was to the explorers and settlers a new land. They taught the settlers how to grow American food crops and how to make medicines from American plants. Many Indian words — *moccasin, tobacco, chipmunk, wampum,* and *powwow* — became a part of the English language. Today we still use such Indian inventions as canoes, ponchos and parkas, hammocks, and snowshoes.

▶ **CHECK UP**   See Teacher's Key.

1. **(a)** Describe the homes of the Iroquois, Cheyenne, and Hopi. **(b)** How did the people of each of these Indian groups get their food?
2. What were the attitudes of the Iroquois, Cheyenne, and Hopi toward war and peace?
3. **(a)** How did contact with Europeans affect the Indians? **(b)** How did Europeans learn from the Indians?

2 How Did Explorers Find a Great Barrier Blocking the Way to Asia?

As you read in Chapter 1, Christopher Columbus and his crew were the first Europeans to make contact with the Indians in the late 1400's. Many people in Spain had looked on Columbus as a foolish adventurer when he set sail from Palos in 1492. But when he returned the next year saying that he had reached "the Indies," he was hailed as a hero. Europeans thought he had found a di-

★ See p. T16 for a strategy that calls for students to list Indian contributions.

● **MAP STUDY**
Columbus continued
his search for Asia in
later voyages to the
Caribbean area. (a) On
which of his voyages
did he reach the
northern coast of
South America?
(b) From what country
did John Cabot sail,
and what part of
America did he see?

See Teacher's Key.

● Because of the global
projection, a scale that
would be accurate for all
areas is not possible on
this map. Help students
use other maps to
calculate the distance
from Spain to the West
Indies.

ASIA

North Pole

GREENLAND

ICELAND

ENGLAND

EUROPE

CABOT
2ND VOYAGE 1498

CABOT
1ST VOYAGE 1497

LABRADOR

NEWFOUNDLAND

NORTH
AMERICA

SPAIN

ATLANTIC OCEAN

San Salvador I.

Cuba

Hispaniola

Puerto Rico

Jamaica

COLUMBUS 2ND VOYAGE 1493

COLUMBUS 4TH VOYAGE 1502

COLUMBUS 3RD VOYAGE 1498

Caribbean Sea

N

CENTRAL
AMERICA

PANAMA

SOUTH AMERICA

COLUMBUS

rect water route to Asia. Ferdinand and
Isabella gave him the grand title of "Admiral of the Ocean Sea." The story of
★ his discovery was printed and read in
many countries. Columbus himself,
however, was not content with discovering islands. He wished to find Asia and
claim its rich trade for Spain.

Columbus fails to find Asia. Late in
1493 Columbus sailed westward again.
This time he commanded seventeen vessels, instead of the small expedition of
three ships that he had on his first voyage. Twice more, in later years, Columbus led fleets across the Atlantic. On
these various journeys he landed at
Puerto Rico, Hispaniola, Jamaica,
Cuba, and other islands of the Caribbean Sea. (Look at the map on this
page.) Although Columbus never saw

the mainland of North America, he
sailed along the coasts of South America and of Central America. He never
found what he was seeking — the riches
of India. Yet he would not admit that
the land he saw was not part of Asia. In
his heart, however, he must have suspected the truth, because on his second
voyage he made his men swear that they
were sure they had reached Asia. If Columbus himself had felt no doubts,
would he have thought it necessary to
demand such an oath? Columbus died
in 1506 without knowing he would become famous for finding America.

Cabot also fails to find Asia. The
success of Columbus's first voyage led
other explorers to sail westward. In
1497, a captain named John Cabot set
out from an English port in a small ship

53

★ Discuss how Europeans would have responded if Columbus had returned to Spain
saying, "I have discovered an unknown land."

with a crew of only eighteen men. Cabot was an Italian navigator who had lived many years in London and now sailed under the English flag. Like Columbus, Cabot believed he could reach Asia by sailing west.

Sailing farther north than Columbus had done, Cabot crossed the Atlantic in two months. He came to the ● northern coast of what we know as North America. Cruising along this coast, Cabot felt sure that he had reached Asia, but he did not find the rich cities he expected. Soon his supplies ran low, and he had to return to England. Cabot tried again the next year to reach Asia. Not only did he fail to find it, but we are not sure that he ever returned from the trip. Although Cabot had actually reached North America, this achievement meant little at the time, for he had not gained Asia's wealth.

Europeans continue their search for Asia. If Columbus and Cabot did not realize the truth about the lands they had reached, others soon did. Daring ship captains sailing under the flag of Spain were busy exploring the coasts of South America, Central America, and Florida. You will read later, in Chapter 3, that one adventurous Spaniard, Balboa, even crossed the Isthmus (ISS-mus) of Panama and found an ocean on the other side. (An **isthmus** is a narrow strip of land that connects two larger masses of land.) Before long, explorers had covered much of the new territory without finding any proof that it was part of Asia. They knew that Cabot had failed to find Asia farther north. They began to realize that these lands were not part of Asia either.

At first Europeans were not interested in America for its own sake. This may seem strange to you unless you remember that they were eager to find a westward route to the riches of India and China. To them the continents were only a barrier blocking the path to Asia. For many years explorers tried to find a passageway through or around the American continents.

Magellan finds a way around the world. Ferdinand Magellan, a Portuguese captain, was one of these explorers. He undertook a voyage that was to prove Columbus's idea had been right — that Asia could be reached by sailing westward. Because he was not popular in his own country of Portugal, Magellan went to Spain with a plan for reaching India by finding a passage through the land Columbus had found. The king of Spain gave him permission to try.

In the fall of 1519, Magellan sailed from Spain with 5 ships and some 240 men. The ships sailed across the rough Atlantic and then turned south along the coast of South America. As they sailed southward, the weather grew steadily colder and more bitter. Then for six weeks the ships fought through the narrow, bleak, and stormy strait ★ near the tip of the continent. (Today this strait is called the Strait of Magellan. Follow Magellan's travels on the map on the next page.) At last Magellan and his men came out into a wide sea so calm and quiet that they named it *Pacific*, a word that means "peaceful."

For four and a half dreary months they sailed across the Pacific Ocean. Hunger, thirst, and disease tortured the men until finally they reached the Philippine Islands. From there Magellan's men cruised south to the Spice Islands, where they picked up a load of cloves. Then, in a long sweep, they sailed around southern Africa and back to Spain. Every kind of disaster happened to the expedition — storms, hunger, sickness, death, mutiny, desertion. But at last, in 1522, the men who remained alive anchored once more in a Spanish harbor. Their shipload of valuable spices more than paid for the cost of the expedition.

★ Have students look up the term *strait* in a dictionary.

VOYAGE OF MAGELLAN AND HIS CREW

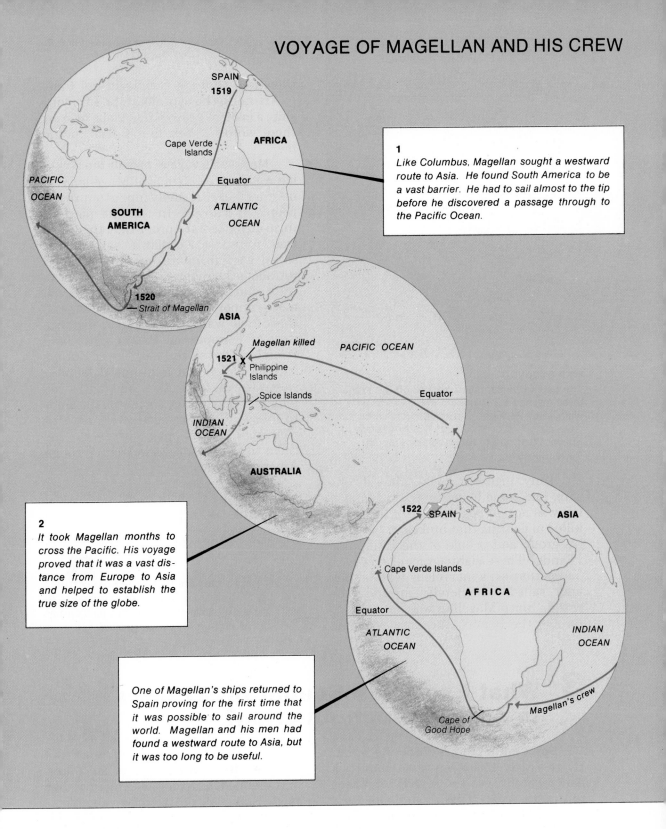

SPAIN
1519

Cape Verde
Islands

AFRICA

PACIFIC
OCEAN

Equator

ATLANTIC
OCEAN

SOUTH
AMERICA

1520
Strait of Magellan

1

Like Columbus, Magellan sought a westward route to Asia. He found South America to be a vast barrier. He had to sail almost to the tip before he discovered a passage through to the Pacific Ocean.

ASIA

Magellan killed

PACIFIC OCEAN

1521 X

Philippine
Islands

Spice Islands

Equator

INDIAN
OCEAN

AUSTRALIA

1522   SPAIN

ASIA

Cape Verde Islands

AFRICA

Equator

ATLANTIC
OCEAN

INDIAN
OCEAN

Magellan's crew

Cape of
Good Hope

2

It took Magellan months to cross the Pacific. His voyage proved that it was a vast distance from Europe to Asia and helped to establish the true size of the globe.

One of Magellan's ships returned to Spain proving for the first time that it was possible to sail around the world. Magellan and his men had found a westward route to Asia, but it was too long to be useful.

MAP STUDY   Above are three different views of the world. Starting with the top view, trace the route of Magellan's crew around the world and back to Spain. How many times did the expedition cross the equator?

55

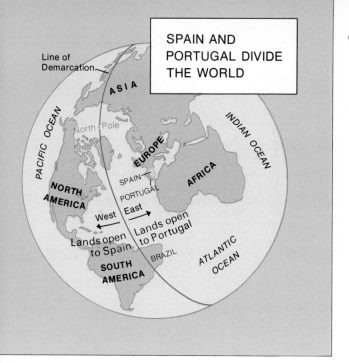

SPAIN AND
PORTUGAL DIVIDE
THE WORLD

MAP STUDY   See Teacher's Key.
The Line of Demarcation marked off the areas
to be claimed by Spain and the areas to be
claimed by Portugal. Note that this division
gave almost all of North and South America to
Spain. What part of South America could
Portugal claim?

Only eighteen men, aboard one
ship, had come home to Spain. Magellan was not among them. He had been
killed in fighting that broke out between
his group and people of the Philippine
Islands. These eighteen men, however,
had performed a marvelous feat — they
had sailed completely around the
world. Since Magellan was not alive to
receive the honors, the king of Spain

● See p. T16 for a strategy asking students to compare
the achievements of Columbus and Magellan.

presented to Juan Sebastián del Cano
(CAH-noh), the captain of the surviving
ship, a coat-of-arms with a globe bearing
these words: "You first sailed around
me."

**Magellan's voyage reveals the size of ●
the world.**   The voyage of Magellan and
his crew was extremely important to the
people of Europe. In the first place, it
furnished absolute proof that the world
was round. Magellan's sailors had
sailed west from Europe and, without
retracing their course, had come back to
their starting point. What was even
more important, the voyage showed
that Asia was an enormous distance
west of Europe and that a great land
stretched across the path from Europe
to Asia. Magellan had indeed found a
westward route to Asia, but it was too
long and dangerous for merchant ships
to follow. Yet Europeans were not discouraged. Magellan's discovery led
them to search for a short cut through
America to Asia.

▶ **CHECK UP**   See Teacher's Key.

1. Why did Columbus make more than
   one voyage west across the Atlantic?
2. **(a)** What led Cabot to sail westward?
   (b) How successful was his expedition?
3. **(a)** What was Magellan's purpose in
   sailing westward? **(b)** What two things
   did Magellan's voyage prove?

3 What Explorers Sought Short Cuts to Asia Through America?

Spain and Portugal divide the world.
By the early 1500's only two countries
had profited from the search for water
routes to Asia. These countries were
Spain and Portugal. As you know, Portugal was growing rich from trade with
India and would not allow any other
countries to share that trade. Portugal

also claimed the land its explorers had
discovered in Africa. Spain had found
and claimed territory in America that
might someday prove to be valuable.

After Columbus had claimed for
Spain what he thought to be Asia, it
looked as though Spain and Portugal
might be rivals for the same lands. The

56

Spanish and Portuguese rulers had therefore asked the Pope to decide which new lands should belong to each of them. In 1493 the Pope drew an imaginary line through the Atlantic Ocean and extending around the world through the North and South Poles. Portugal was to have the lands east of this line; Spain, the lands that lay west of it. This Line of Demarcation, as it came to be called, was shifted farther west by a treaty between Spain and Portugal the next year. As the map on page 56 shows, Spain claimed most of North and South America, while Portugal claimed Africa, India, and large areas in the rest of Asia.

England, France, and Holland seek a share in the trade with Asia. What about the other countries of Europe, such as England, France, and Holland? They had no share in the profitable trade. These other countries, watching Portugal grow rich from its Eastern trade, wanted to get a share of that trade for themselves. They asked, "Can't we find another route to Asia and thus get ahead of Portugal as Portugal has gotten ahead of the Italian cities?"

One question led to another. Magellan's route to Asia around the American continents was, as we have seen, too long and too difficult to be valuable for trade. "Can't we find a better, shorter path?" many Europeans asked. "Perhaps there is a *northwest* passage that would give us a good, direct route to Asia." Knowing little of what we now call North America, they believed they might find a waterway *through* it. For over a hundred years, daring explorers sent out by France, Holland, and England sailed along the Atlantic coast seeking a Northwest Passage, which they never found. Let us follow some of these sailors on their explorations.

Verrazano searches the coast. Among the first to seek a route through America was Verrazano (vehr-rah-ZAH-noh). Although he was an Ital-

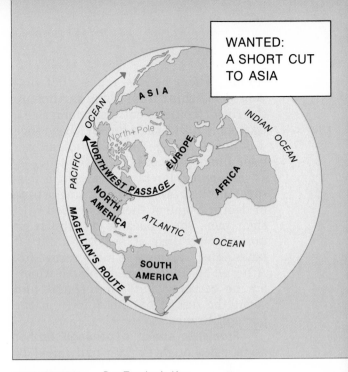

WANTED: A SHORT CUT TO ASIA

MAP STUDY   See Teacher's Key.
This map shows why Europeans searched for a Northwest Passage to Asia. (a) Which line shows an imaginary Northwest Passage? (b) Was the route that Magellan followed to Asia longer or shorter than the imaginary northwest route?

ian by birth, his most important voyage was made under the flag of France. This voyage took place in 1524, just two years after Magellan's sailors completed their famous trip around the world. Verrazano sailed westward to look for a passage to Asia. As the map on page 59 shows, he followed the coast of North America from what is now North Carolina as far north as Newfoundland. But he found no passage through the land and returned disappointed to France.

Cartier explores the St. Lawrence River. Some ten years later another explorer for France, Jacques Cartier (car-TYAY), followed Verrazano to America. Cartier discovered and explored the St. Lawrence River. Three or four times he crossed from France to the St. Lawrence, seeking a passage to Asia. He sailed up and down the river and spent winters in camps on its banks. He found an Indian village far inland where the city of Montreal now

57

stands. There he saw rapids that prevented his ships from going farther up the river. To his great disappointment, Cartier realized that the St. Lawrence was not a passage to Asia, but only a river (map, page 59).

Many explorers who sought a passage through America met misfortune or death. Some of them quarreled with their men, some became unpopular at home, some died at sea or in far-off lands. But Cartier was more fortunate. After all his adventures in North America he returned safe and sound and spent the rest of his life quietly in the ports of France.

Frobisher seeks a passage farther north. Although Cartier had failed to reach Asia by sailing up the St. Lawrence River, Europeans still thought there must be a passage somewhere. An English captain named Martin Frobisher decided to search farther north. In June 1576, he set sail from England with three small vessels. They had hardly left the English coast when one of the three ships was lost in a storm. The crew of the second ship became afraid and soon deserted to return home. But Frobisher kept on his course. He went far to the north, touching Greenland and rounding its southern tip. At last he came to the stretch of water we now call Frobisher Bay. Unable to make his way against the ice, he was forced to turn back (map, page 60).

Jacques Cartier questions Indians on the shores of the St. Lawrence about a Northwest Passage to the Pacific. Note the basket of American vegetables—corn and squash.

★ You may want to have students turn to "Reading Maps: Locating Places" (p. 67). The skill lesson shows another map relating to French exploration.

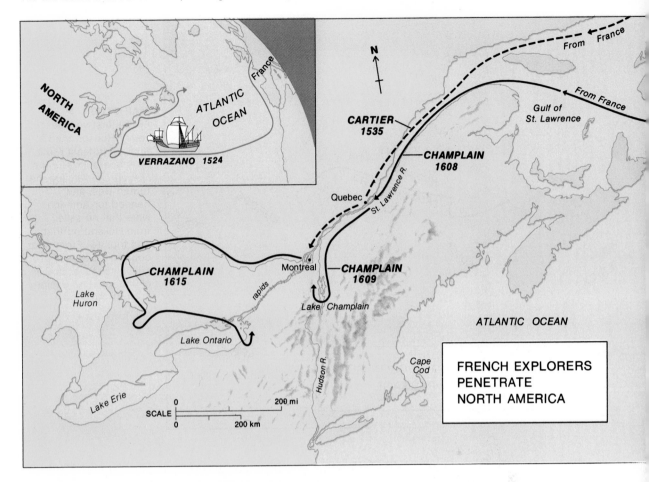

FRENCH EXPLORERS
PENETRATE
NORTH AMERICA

Though Frobisher made two more voyages to the same region, he failed in his search for a Northwest Passage.

Champlain explores the Great Lakes region. Although explorer after explorer returned to Europe without having found a short cut to Asia, others were always ready to continue the search. Each hoped to succeed where others had failed. One of these was a French explorer named Samuel de Champlain (sham-PLAIN). Champlain came to America for the first time in 1603. For years he roamed the coasts and the forests, the rivers and the lakes of America.

Champlain explored the Atlantic coast all the way from the mouth of the St. Lawrence River to the southern part of what is now Massachusetts. He

MAP STUDY See Teacher's Key.
The routes of three explorers for France are shown here. (a) Which explorer came to America first? (See the small inset map.) (b) How far up the St. Lawrence did Cartier travel? (c) What lakes did Champlain explore?

sailed up the St. Lawrence and started the town of Quebec, the first permanent French settlement in America. Continuing up the river to what is now Montreal, he turned south and pushed on to the southern end of a beautiful lake that has been named Lake Champlain in his honor. On a later trip Champlain traveled still farther inland, moving north and west from the St. Lawrence. He made his way along other rivers into the northern part of Lake Huron. From there he swung down to Lake Ontario

● Champlain is sometimes called "the Father of New France." Ask students to explain why.

● Refer students to "Linking Past and Present" (p. 66), where they can read the outcome of the search for a Northwest Passage.

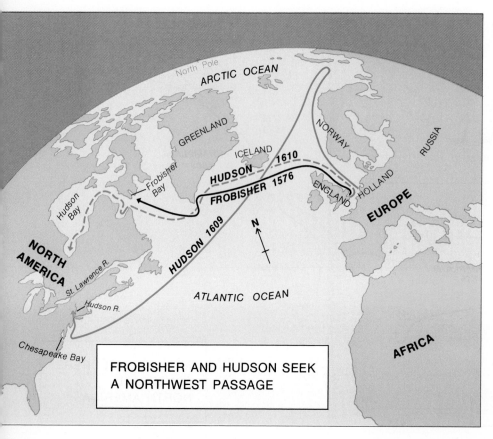

FROBISHER AND HUDSON SEEK
A NORTHWEST PASSAGE

MAP STUDY ●
On his first voyage Henry Hudson tried to find a northeast route to Asia around Europe. Discouraged by ice, he turned west and headed for America. Note that he sailed from Holland on that first trip. (a) From what country did he sail in 1610? (b) What bodies of water did he explore in North America?

See Teacher's Key.

and then back to Quebec. To follow his explorations, look at the map on page 59. It took a bold and energetic man to travel such distances in an unknown wilderness.

Champlain learned, and taught others, much about the geography of North America. When he died in 1635, map makers could draw plainly and exactly great areas of North America that had been unknown to Europeans before Champlain's explorations. But Champlain had found no short cut to Asia.

Henry Hudson finds a river. Another mariner who tried to find a passage to Asia was an Englishman named Henry Hudson. Hudson was employed by Dutch merchants to try to find a route to China. In the year 1609 he set out in a small ship named the *Half Moon*. At first he tried to reach Asia by sailing north of Europe, but his little ship ran

into dangerous ice and snow. Hudson then turned and set his course westward across the Atlantic. He reached North America and traveled south along the coast as far as Chesapeake Bay. But Hudson soon found he could not reach China by way of this bay. Sailing northward again, he came upon the broad river that now bears his name. ★ He passed through the large bays at the mouth of the river. His hopes must have risen as he sailed between the beautiful wooded banks. But the river narrowed, and Hudson finally realized that this was not a strait through America but only a river.

Henry Hudson discovers a great bay. Hudson's next voyage brought not only failure but death. In 1610 he set out again, this time under the banner of his own country, England. In the small ship *Discovery*, he headed west once

60

★ Ask if students know what major American city, settled by the Dutch, is located on the Hudson River. (New York City)

more on a voyage from which he was never to return. This time, like Frobisher, he turned far north. He and his crew fought their way through an ice-blocked strait and there, before their eyes, a great body of clear water stretched to the south and west.

All summer long, Hudson and his crew sailed the waters of this huge bay, seeking a passage to Asia. When winter came, the group had to camp on the frozen shores of the bay. By spring only a small amount of food was left. The crew had suffered so many hardships that most of the men could take no more. They forced Hudson, with his young son and a few loyal men, into a boat and set it adrift. Henry Hudson was never heard of again. Only four members of the crew managed to make their way back to England. Today the name Hudson Bay reminds us of the brave explorer who perished in its icy waters without finding the passageway he sought. (The map on page 60 shows Hudson's explorations.)

Contacts with Indians along the Mississippi River were a valuable source of information for Father Marquette.

Marquette and Joliet explore the Mississippi. Daring captains like Verrazano and Frobisher, as you have read, touched only the edges of North America. Other explorers, such as Cartier and Champlain, made their way up rivers that were natural pathways, pushing deeper and ever deeper into the interior. In time, still other adventurous explorers spread in many directions through the wilderness of the interior, hoping to find an easy way through North America.

Following Champlain's death, some French explorers pushed far beyond the town of Quebec to Lake Superior. They were accompanied by priests who preached to the Indians. One of those priests was Father Jacques Marquette (mar-KET). From the Indians he heard tales of a "great water" that emptied into an even greater one. This, he thought, must be the short cut to Asia that so many had been seeking.

In 1673, with an explorer named Louis Joliet (JOH-lih-ET), Father Marquette set out to find this short cut. Marquette and Joliet and five companions left Lake Michigan in two bark canoes. (Look at the map on page 62 to

THE FRENCH EXPLORE THE MISSISSIPPI

● Have students look up the term *portage*, used on this map, in a dictionary.

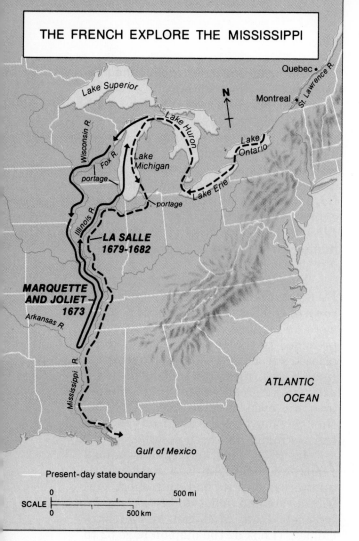

MARQUETTE AND JOLIET 1673

LA SALLE 1679-1682

Quebec

Montreal

Lake Superior

Lake Huron

Lake Michigan

Lake Ontario

Lake Erie

St. Lawrence R.

Wisconsin R.

Fox R.

portage

portage

Illinois R.

Arkansas R.

Mississippi R.

ATLANTIC OCEAN

Gulf of Mexico

Present-day state boundary

SCALE

0 ——— 500 mi

0 ——— 500 km

● **MAP STUDY**   See Teacher's Key.
Here you see the routes of Frenchmen who explored the Mississippi River and thus opened up a water route into the interior of North America. (a) Which of these explorers reached the mouth of the Mississippi River? (b) How are the boundaries of present-day states shown on the map?

trace their route.) They paddled up the Fox River, carried their canoes across to the Wisconsin River, and floated down to the Mississippi. Here at last, they believed, was the great passage to Asia. But after they had paddled a long distance down the Mississippi, to the mouth of the Arkansas River, they knew they had not found the long-sought passage. The Mississippi, they realized, flowed southward. It emptied into the Gulf of Mexico, not into a sea

route to Asia. It would not lead them to Asia. Sadly they turned back and returned to Lake Michigan, this time by way of the Illinois River.

La Salle reaches the mouth of the Mississippi. When Joliet was returning to Quebec to report on his journey, he met an expedition headed by another Frenchman. This man was Robert Cavelier, Sieur de La Salle (luh SAL). La Salle had given up the easy life of a noble to explore the wilds of North America. You can imagine that he listened eagerly to the story of how Joliet and Marquette had found the "great water." La Salle's ambition was to obtain for France the rich fur trade of the Great Lakes and the upper Mississippi. In the years that followed, he dreamed of an even greater plan. Why not find the mouth of the Mississippi and claim ★ for France the vast interior of North America?

It was several years before La Salle was ready to set out on his search for the mouth of the Mississippi. His first attempt was not successful. After terrible sufferings he had to return to a fort that he had built on Lake Ontario. But La Salle refused to give up. He and his men set out again, even though it was winter. This time everything went well. They traveled by canoe across Lake Erie, Lake Huron, and Lake Michigan. At the southern end of Lake Michigan they set out on foot for the

BUILDING A BIRCH-BARK CANOE

★ Ask if students know what major American city, settled by the French, is located at the mouth of the Mississippi River. (New Orleans)

Illinois River, dragging their canoes on sleds that they had built. In canoes again, they paddled down the Illinois. Ice floated in the Mississippi when they reached it, but the weather grew warmer as they went south. At last, in April, 1682, they reached the Gulf of Mexico. (Trace La Salle's journey on the map on page 62.) La Salle claimed for the French king the huge river valley from the Great Lakes to the Gulf of Mexico.

La Salle met an untimely death. In a later expedition he was murdered by his own men because of the hardships they had been forced to endure. But La Salle's travels had important results. Now the French had found a route, mostly by water, that cut North America in two. They also could claim as their territory the enormous stretches of land covered by their explorers.

▶ **CHECK UP**   See Teacher's Key.

1. **(a)** How did Spain and Portugal come to claim all the newly discovered lands? **(b)** How did England, France, and Holland feel about this arrangement? Why?
2. How did the following find out that the rivers they explored were not short cuts to Asia? **(a)** Cartier (St. Lawrence) **(b)** Hudson (Hudson) **(c)** Marquette and Joliet (Mississippi)
3. **(a)** Why did La Salle want to explore the Mississippi Valley? **(b)** What route did he follow?

4 How Did the Search for Short Cuts to Asia Open Up America?

Geographic knowledge of America grows. Europeans wished at first that America did not exist. Because they wanted to reach Asia, they searched for a short and easy route through or around America. We have seen that they did not succeed. But their explorations resulted in a great deal of new and accurate geographical information. Each explorer drew maps and wrote reports of what he had seen.

La Salle reached the mouth of the Mississippi just 190 years after Columbus reached San Salvador. During that time, knowledge of geography had been increased tremendously. You can see this by looking at just two maps. The first one, on page 37, shows how little Europeans knew about the world before their explorations began. The other is the map on page 64, showing what was known about North and Central America in 1700. Comparing these maps, you can see how much was learned in the search for a short cut to Asia.

Explorers make land claims. Besides their desire to find a short cut to Asia, explorers had another reason for braving hardships and dangers. They wanted to make their countries more powerful by claiming land in America. Of course, in making their claims none of the European countries paid attention to the fact that Indians had occupied the land for generations.

It became the rule of exploration that land belonged to the European country whose explorers were the first to see it. For example, when Cartier discovered the St. Lawrence River, he took possession of all the nearby country in the name of his king, Francis I of France. He put up a marker to warn all who passed by that the land was French. Explorers sent out by other countries claimed land in the same

63

● See p. T16 for a strategy that examines this tremendous increase in geographic knowledge.

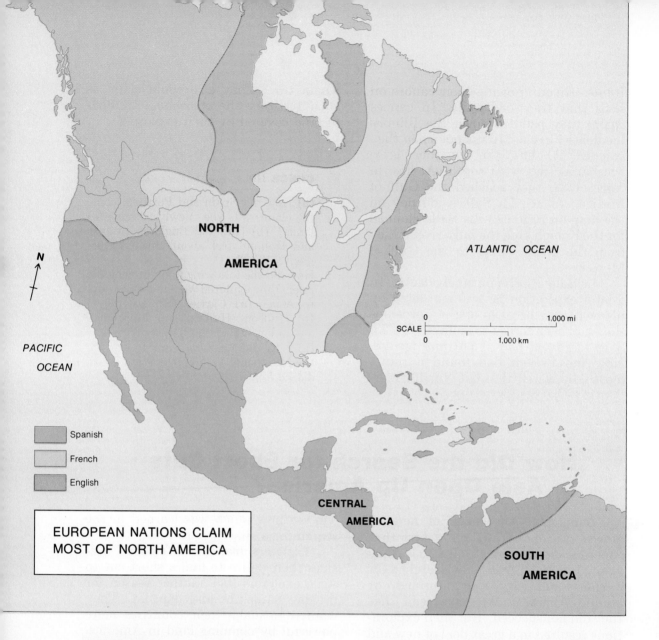

NORTH

AMERICA

ATLANTIC OCEAN

PACIFIC

OCEAN

SCALE
0   1,000 mi
0   1,000 km

Spanish

French

English

CENTRAL

AMERICA

SOUTH

AMERICA

**EUROPEAN NATIONS CLAIM
MOST OF NORTH AMERICA**

MAP STUDY
Use the key on this map to tell what parts of
North America were claimed by England,
France, and Spain around 1700. (Remember
that boundaries between these areas were
vague and claims often overlapped.)

● way. This rule of "finders, keepers" was
used by European nations to decide
what territory in America belonged to
them. Let us see how this rule worked
out.

      What belonged to whom? Among
the explorers you have studied, Columbus and Magellan sailed, of course, for

Spain. John Cabot and Martin Frobisher were explorers for England. Verrazano, Cartier, Champlain, Marquette,
Joliet, and La Salle served France. And
Hudson explored for both Holland and
England. If North America were to be
divided according to the explorations
and claims of these men, what would
each country own about the year 1700?

      France would hold a huge terri-
tory. It would claim the northern Atlantic coast, the land from the mouth of
the St. Lawrence to the Great Lakes,
and the great stretch southward along
the Mississippi. England's territory

64

● See p. T16 for a strategy that deals with this rule of
"finders, keepers."

would be a narrow strip along the Atlantic coast from the present state of Maine to Florida. (By 1700, as you will learn in Chapter 4, England had taken over the Dutch claims along the Hudson River.) England would also claim a large area around Hudson Bay. To Spain, whose further explorations you will read about in the next chapter, would belong the whole southern part of North America.

The bold explorers who searched this land did not find the waterway to Asia that they were seeking, but they accomplished something even more important. They turned the attention of Europeans away from Asia to the Americas. Europeans no longer looked ● at this land as a barrier blocking their way to Asia. They became interested in it for its own sake. In the next unit you will see how the countries of Europe became rivals in America.

▶ **CHECK UP**   See Teacher's Key.

1. **(a)** Why did European nations send explorers to America? **(b)** How was it decided what land belonged to each country?
2. **(a)** What regions in North America were claimed by France, England, and Spain about 1700? **(b)** What region had Holland lost, and to which country?

CHECK UP ON CHAPTER 2

See Teacher's Key.

Words to Know

Explain the meaning of each word.

1. tribe
2. mesa
3. plain
4. isthmus
5. strait
6. continent

Places to Locate

Be able to locate the following on the maps in your book.

1. England
2. France
3. Lake Michigan
4. Quebec
5. Holland
6. Philippines
7. South America
8. Strait of Magellan
9. Caribbean Sea
10. Lake Champlain
11. Hudson Bay
12. Hudson River
13. North America
14. Gulf of Mexico
15. Mississippi River
16. St. Lawrence River

Facts to Remember

Answer these questions by recalling information given in the chapter.

1. **(a)** In what present-day states were the homelands of the Iroquois, Cheyenne, and Hopi? **(b)** Describe the land where each of these groups lived.

2. **(a)** What lands did Columbus visit on his later voyages across the Atlantic? **(b)** Why, in a way, can his explorations be called a failure?
3. **(a)** What did Europeans mean when they talked about searching for a Northwest Passage? **(b)** Name five explorers who looked for that passage, and tell where each one explored.

Skills to Practice

Sharpen your history skills by answering the following questions.

1. Compare the time lines for Chapters 1 and 2 (pages 26 and 48). **(a)** What period of time is shown on each time line? **(b)** Which chapter deals with the longer period? **(c)** About how many years passed between (1) Magellan's voyage and Champlain's first voyage and (2) Champlain's first voyage and La Salle's arrival at the mouth of the Mississippi River?
2. Look at the map on page 62. **(a)** Into what body of water does the Mississippi River empty? **(b)** Which explorers' routes are shown on the map? **(c)** Who explored first? **(d)** Who explored last? **(e)** What lakes were part of the *last* explorer's route?

65

Questions to Think About

1. **(a)** How did different Indian groups meet their needs for food, clothing, and shelter? **(b)** Why was it useful for Europeans to learn those ways when they came to America?
2. **(a)** What effect did Magellan's exploration have on the search for a westward sea route to Asia? **(b)** Why did the search for a direct route fail? **(c)** What short cut from Europe to Asia is used today?
3. Why did the early explorers of the interior of North America use water routes rather than land routes?
4. Why did the attitude of Europeans toward America change between 1500 and 1700?

Linking Past and Present

● **American Indian foods.** How many Indian foods have you eaten today? Every day you probably eat foods that were first grown by Indians in North and South America.

When the first European explorers reached the Americas, they learned about certain crops that were entirely new to them. For instance, they tasted corn and potatoes for the first time. They also became acquainted with peanuts, squashes, peppers, tomatoes, pumpkins, pineapples, sweet potatoes, cacao (for chocolate), many kinds of beans, and other fruits and vegetables. In time, the use of these crops spread to other continents. Corn and potatoes, for example, are now among the most widely grown foods in the world. Cassava, a tropical root first grown by American Indians, is now eaten throughout Africa. In fact, almost half the crops grown today were unknown to the world outside the Americas before Columbus's voyage in 1492.

★ **Indian names.** Today we have many reminders of the Indian presence in America. From east to west, from north to south there are rivers, lakes, and cities with Indian names. These include the Mississippi, Arkansas, and Illinois rivers; Lake Huron, Lake Winnipesaukee in New Hampshire, and Lake Tahoe on the California-Nevada border; and the cities of Chippewa Falls (Wisconsin), Natchez (Mississippi), Walla Walla (Washington), and Yuma (Arizona). You can probably name many others.

Found — a Northwest Passage. From the 1500's on, bold explorers searched for a Northwest Passage through the ice-filled waters and desolate islands north of Canada. By the end of the 1800's, a route was known, but no one had yet sailed the full length of the passage. The first to do so was Roald Amundsen, a famous Norwegian explorer, in 1903–1905. But by this time there was no longer a real need for a Northwest Passage. The Panama Canal, soon to open, offered a much easier passage from the Atlantic to the Pacific. After World War II, however, the United States and Canada built a radar system across northern Canada to give warning of enemy attacks, and the Northwest Passage was used as a route for supply ships. In 1957, a Canadian ice breaker and three United States Coast Guard cutters found an alternate Northwest Passage which is shorter and less dangerous than the older route.

The next year, the world was amazed by the news that the American nuclear submarine *Nautilus* had crossed from the Pacific to the Atlantic by way of the North Pole. This voyage was more than a daring venture into unknown seas. The *Nautilus* and its crew had actually opened a time-saving Northwest Passage *under* the Arctic ice! The distance from Tokyo to London is 11,200 miles by way of the Panama Canal, but only 6,500 miles by way of the route under the North Pole. The hope of the early explorers for a northwest route between the Atlantic and the Pacific has come true — but in a way they never dreamed of!

66

For answers see Teacher's Key.

Have students develop similar questions and ask them of one another. Questions might be based on the map on page 59.

GAINING SKILL

Reading Maps: Locating Places

Maps help you to understand where places are. One way to describe a place's location is to give its latitude and longitude: Washington, D.C., for example, is 39°N, 77°W. (To review latitude and longitude, see page 47.) Another way to describe location is to explain where a place is in relation to another place. We can locate the Hudson River, for example, by saying that it runs through the eastern part of New York State and empties into the Atlantic Ocean.

The map on this page shows the location of some important places in an area of North America once controlled by France. Such French explorers as Marquette, Joliet, and La Salle led the way into the Mississippi Valley. Their expeditions allowed France to claim vast lands from the Great Lakes to the Gulf of Mexico. In the years between 1675 and 1750, the French established settlements and forts along the Mississippi. Use the map to answer the following questions about French outposts in the Mississippi Valley.

1. What fort was located on the southern shore of Lake Michigan?
2. What forts were built along the Illinois River?
3. Describe the location of the settlement called Cahokia.
4. What fort was built just north of the point where the Wisconsin River flows into the Mississippi?
5. Look at the map at the back of this book that shows the fifty states. What is the latitude of New Orleans? What is its longitude? (Remember to use *north* or *south* when you give latitude, and *east* or *west* when you give longitude.)

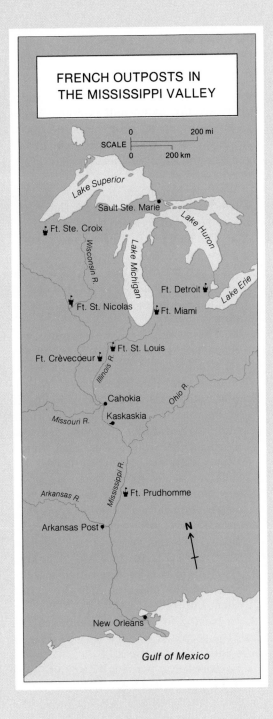

FRENCH OUTPOSTS IN THE MISSISSIPPI VALLEY

UNDERSTANDING UNIT 1

SUMMARY OF IMPORTANT IDEAS

Unit 1 has told the story of how countries of western Europe found and explored America. To help you keep in mind the major ideas in this unit, we have included the following summary in outline form:

1. Western European countries, seeking new routes to the East, found the continents of North and South America.

   a. The demand in Europe for Eastern goods increased after the Crusades. The high prices of these goods and the desire to share in the rich trade caused countries in western Europe to look for new routes.

   b. The search for a water route was made easier by important inventions (the compass and astrolabe) and better maps. The Portuguese carefully explored the coast of Africa. Finally, da Gama rounded the Cape of Good Hope and reached India in 1498. Because Portugal controlled this new route, other European countries looked for different routes to the East.

   c. Columbus, believing that Asia was larger and the earth smaller than they actually are, persuaded the rulers of Spain to sponsor an expedition to seek a westward route to the East. Thinking that the islands he discovered in 1492 were off the coast of Asia, he called them the Indies.

2. In looking for westward routes to the East, the people of western Europe learned more about the Americas.

   a. Europeans eventually found hundreds of tribes of Indians living throughout the North American continent. Although the tribes had many similar religious and social beliefs, methods of hunting and gathering and farming made one tribe different from the next.

   b. Magellan's expedition (1519–1522) showed that other continents lay across the westward route to the East. Because Magellan's route was too long for trade, France, England, and Holland sent explorers to look for short cuts to Asia.

   c. These explorations opened up North America. The French explored along the St. Lawrence, the Great Lakes, and the Mississippi. The English explored to the north of present-day Canada, and the Dutch along the Hudson River.

   d. European explorers greatly increased general knowledge of the Americas. Spain, France, and England — each claiming the lands they explored — divided the North American continent among themselves.

UNIT REVIEW   See Teacher's Key.

1. **(a)** Why did people living in Europe in the year 1000 take little interest in the outside world? **(b)** Why did the demand for Eastern goods in western Europe increase after the Crusades?

2. **(a)** Why were Spain and Portugal interested in a new route to the East? **(b)** Why did the great geographic discoveries take place when they did?

3. **(a)** In what ways were the Iroquois, Cheyenne, and Hopi alike? **(b)** In what ways were they different from one another?

68

4. (a) Why did the search for new routes to the East continue after Portugal's discovery of an all-water route to India? (b) What countries took a leading part in this search? (c) In what directions was the search made? (d) With what success?

5. (a) Why did Portugal and Spain ask the Pope to help settle their claims to newly discovered lands? (b) How might such a question be settled today?

6. (a) What became the basis for claims to American colonies? (b) What areas were claimed by Spain, England, France, and Holland?

THINGS TO DO

The activities suggested below will help you remember what you have already learned. Those marked with an asterisk (*) are suggested for the whole class. There are other activities for people who like to write, for instance, or to speak, draw, or read.

*1. Start a game called "Can You Identify?" to help you learn the dates, events, and persons mentioned in the chapters in this unit. Get a supply of large cards. Print the name or event in large letters on one side; on the other side print a brief identification. Example: *da Gama* (on one side); *Portuguese explorer who sailed east to India* (on the other side). Choose teams and see which team can identify most.

*2. Make a chart of the explorers you read about in Chapter 2, using these headings: Name, Date, Country for Which He Sailed, and Results of Voyage.

3. Make a picture map showing the voyages of Dias and da Gama. Draw in the monsters and whirlpools in the Great Sea of Darkness, Prince Henry's school, the stone towers on the African coast, and so on.

4. Look up Joaquin Miller's poem *Columbus*. Read it to the class.

5. Imagine that you were an Indian boy or girl who saw Columbus land on Guanahani. Write the story as that person would have told it. Or write a newspaper account of one of these events: (a) Marco Polo tells Europeans about his visit to China, (b) da Gama reaches India, (c) Columbus tells the Spanish rulers about his discovery, (d) Magellan's crew returns to Spain, (e) La Salle reaches the Gulf of Mexico, (f) Hudson discovers a great bay.

6. The buffalo was the Plains Indians' major natural resource. Look in an encyclopedia or a book on Indian life to find out what became of the buffalo herds and why. Report to the class on what you find out.

7. On page 59 you read that Lake Champlain was named after the French explorer Samuel de Champlain. Look at a map of the United States and see how many other features (cities, rivers, and lakes) you can find that are named after explorers. Make a list of those features.

8. Report to the class on the life of one of these explorers: Marquette, Joliet, La Salle, Cartier, Champlain, Magellan, Cabot.

9. Have you read a story or seen a television program or motion picture about the Crusades, early trade with Asia, or explorations in America? Tell the class about the story.

Left to right: Pizarro; the *Golden Hind*; Jamestown in 1625; and Cartier arriving at Gaspé Peninsula in Canada.

UNIT **2**

Europeans Start Colonies and Build Empires in the Americas

1500–1800

See p. T17 for a unit preview strategy. See pp. T58–T71 for lists of useful books and audiovisual aids.

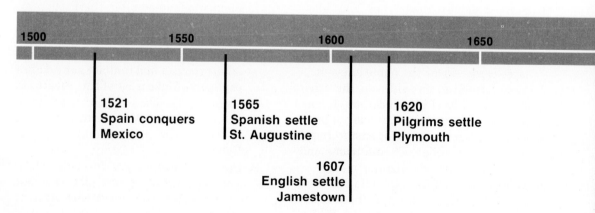

1500	1550	1600	1650

1521
Spain conquers
Mexico

1565
Spanish settle
St. Augustine

1620
Pilgrims settle
Plymouth

1607
English settle
Jamestown

70

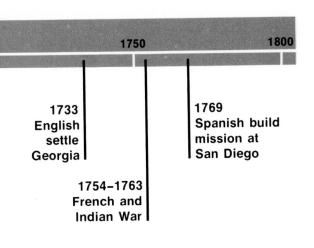

1750

1800

1733
English
settle
Georgia

1769
Spanish build
mission at
San Diego

1754–1763
French and
Indian War

Unit 1 told the story of European explorers who traveled long distances to find out more about the American continents. In Unit 2 you will learn how ever-increasing numbers of Europeans came to the Americas. Chapter 3, for example, tells how Spain established a mighty empire in the Western Hemisphere. In Chapter 4 you will learn about the beginnings and growth of English colonies in America. Most English settlers came to America in search of new opportunities and a freer way of life. Chapter 5 describes ways of living in the English colonies. Finally Chapter 6 tells about the French colonies in America and how France and England fought a war that determined the future of North America.

CHAPTER **3**

Vocabulary preview: conquistador, mission, viceroy

Spain Establishes a Great Empire

1500–1780   See pp. T17–T18 for chapter teaching strategies.

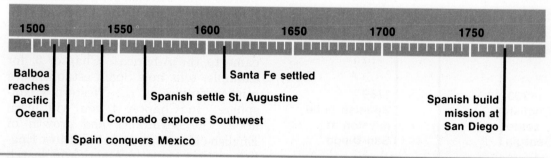

| 1500 | 1550 | 1600 | 1650 | 1700 | 1750 |

Balboa reaches Pacific Ocean

Spain conquers Mexico

Coronado explores Southwest

Spanish settle St. Augustine

Santa Fe settled

Spanish build mission at San Diego

What this chapter is about —

A gallant ship bearing the white-and-gold banner of Spain is heading eastward across the Atlantic. Its fore and aft decks are high above the water, and its sails are brightly decorated with paintings. High up in the crow's-nest a sailor looks anxiously in all directions for swift-sailing pirate ships. For this is a treasure galleon of the Spanish fleet, carrying riches to Spain. Piled in the hold are heavy bars of gold and silver, boxes of pearls and emeralds, chests of gold and silver ornaments. What a prize for a bold pirate!

72

● Students may need to look up *fore, aft, crow's-nest,* and *galleon.*

◀ Spain was the first European country to build a mighty empire in the Americas. After conquering Mexico, Spanish forces headed north, spreading power by building forts and churches, like this one at El Paso, in what is now Texas.

Are these the riches of India? Have the Spaniards at last found a passage to Asia? No, this ship with its precious load has come from Spain's colonies in America. And it is carrying only a fraction of the wealth that is transported every year to Spain from its colonies.

In this chapter you will learn how a great Spanish empire was established in the Western Hemisphere and how Spain grew rich and became the envy of other European nations. You will find out what life in Spanish America was like. As you read, look for answers to these questions:

1. How did Spanish explorers build a mighty empire?
2. What was life like in Spanish America?
3. How did England and other nations threaten Spain's power?

1 How Did Spanish Explorers Build a Mighty Empire?

Spain takes the lead in exploration. Columbus, you remember, discovered several islands in the Caribbean Sea — Cuba, Hispaniola, and others. Though he found little gold, he was so sure he had discovered islands off the coast of Asia that Spain sent over ships with men and women to start settlements. Soon more and more settlers came to take up land and develop large farms. Bold adventurers and penniless soldiers also flocked to Cuba and Hispaniola in the hope of making their fortunes. But little gold was ever found on the islands. The only way to become wealthy was to farm the rich soil or to raise cattle, and this was too slow for people who dreamed of great riches. So from these Caribbean settlements adventurers set out to explore the mainland.

The American lands attract many Spaniards. Many Spaniards were eager to leave Europe behind. In those days, young men of the upper class in Spain, as well as many others, chose soldiering as a career. In the early 1500's, however, Spain's armies were not always at war, and these soldiers wanted adventure and riches. The American lands, unknown and unexplored by Europeans, beckoned to them. What brave *caballero* (cah-bah-YAY-roh), or gentleman of Spain, wouldn't risk his life for fame and fortune?

We must also remember that the Spanish people were deeply religious, and believed it their duty to convert people to Christianity. Thus, many Spaniards saw a chance not only to gain riches but also to save souls. So from Spain came courageous priests, stout-hearted soldiers, and dashing caballeros — in search of converts for their Church, gold for their monarch, or wealth for themselves.

Tales could be told about many of these Spanish explorers, sometimes called **conquistadors** (kohn-keess-tah-DOHRS), or conquerors. But we will describe in detail the adventures of only three. You will probably recognize their names: Balboa, Pizarro, and Cortés.

BALBOA DISCOVERS THE PACIFIC

The first of these Spanish explorers was Vasco Nuñez de Balboa, a tall and

73

● See p. T17 for a strategy that centers on Balboa, Pizarro, and Cortés.

Balboa, standing on a peak on the Isthmus of Panama, was the first European to see the shining Pacific Ocean from the shores of America. He claimed for Spain the Pacific and all the lands it touched.

haughty man and an excellent swordsman. He owned a farm in Hispaniola but was restless and unhappy there, for the love of adventure was in his blood. Balboa heard tales from the Indians about a land rich in gold. This land (which we now know was Peru) could be reached by sea from the other side of the
● Isthmus of Panama. Balboa seized upon this chance to make a name for himself. He wrote a letter to King Ferdinand of Spain, describing the land and asking for help. Here is part of his
★ letter:

In the mountains [of Peru] there are certain *caciques* [chiefs] who have great quantities of gold in their houses. It is said . . . that all the rivers of these mountains contain gold; and that they have very large lumps in great abun-

dance . . . and the Indians say that the other sea [Pacific] is at a distance of three days' journey. . . . They say that the people of the other coast are very good and well-mannered; and I am told that the other sea is very good for canoe navigation, for . . . it is always smooth and never rough like the sea on this side. . . . They say that there are many large pearls and that the caciques have baskets of them. . . . It is a most astonishing thing and without equal, that our Lord has made you the lord of this land.

What a shrewd letter! Notice that Balboa actually knew very little about this land, since almost every sentence began with "they say" or "it is said." The king apparently noticed this fact, for in spite of the compliment at the end of the letter, he refused aid. If Balboa wished to go to Peru, he had to go on his own.

Balboa crosses the Isthmus of Panama. On a September day in 1513 Balboa, with a large group of Spaniards and

74

Indians, set out from a small settlement on the Caribbean side of the Isthmus. The Spaniards were armed with crossbows, swords, and firearms. You can see on the map, page 77, that the distance to be covered was not great. But there were many hardships to be overcome. The tropical forest was alive with stinging insects and poisonous snakes. Resentful Indians threatened the Spaniards' lives. And the tangled vines and swamps of the forest slowed their march to a mile or two a day.

At length Balboa and his men came to high mountains that their Indian guides told them overlooked the "other sea" to the south. As they neared the summit of the mountains, Balboa ordered his men to wait. He climbed the last steep distance alone. There before him, as far as his eye could see, stretched a vast, shimmering sea. Eagerly he beckoned to his men to join him so that they could see the great water. They were the first Europeans to look on the Pacific Ocean from the shores of America.

Balboa claims the Pacific Ocean for Spain. Four days later they reached the waters of the Pacific. With the banner of Spain fluttering in the breeze and his drawn sword in his hand, Balboa stepped into the waves and claimed the sea and all the lands that bordered it for his royal master. Balboa named his discovery the South Sea because it lay directly south of the place where he had started his march (map, page 77). It was not until after Magellan's voyage that the sea was called Pacific, the name we use today.

Balboa returned with news of his discovery. He made plans to set sail on the South Sea to search for gold. But a new governor had been appointed in Panama. The governor and other Spaniards were jealous of Balboa and prevented him from carrying out his plan to find the land of gold that he had described to the king. The unfortunate Balboa was finally accused of treason and was killed.

PIZARRO CONQUERS PERU

After Balboa's death, Spaniards began to hear more about the land he had hoped to conquer. This land, which we now call Peru, was the empire of the Inca Indians. These Indians worshiped ★ the sun and believed that their rulers were children of the sun. These Indians were skilled farmers who knew how to irrigate lands that were too dry for crops. They wove fine cloth and made beautiful articles of pottery and metal. What was more important to the gold-hungry Spaniards, the Incas were said to wear golden shoes and to eat from golden dishes. Here, indeed, was a land worth finding.

Pizarro reaches the land of the Incas. The man who determined to conquer Peru was Francisco Pizarro (pih-ZAHR-oh). He had crossed the Isthmus with Balboa and was an old hand at exploration. Pizarro was not a nobleman like Balboa. His family was a humble one, and he had never learned to read or write. He was a harsh man, but he made a good explorer because he could endure hardships and disappointments without becoming discouraged.

Pizarro knew that he would have great difficulty in conquering the Inca ruler, who lived high in the Andes Mountains. So Pizarro spent several years enlisting men and getting ready for his great venture. He landed safely on the coast of Peru, where he remained for some time sizing up the situation. At last, in the autumn of 1532, Pizarro set out for the Inca cities with a band of only about 180 Spaniards. Pizarro, however, was counting on firearms and horses to overcome the much greater numbers of the Incas. He and his men struggled up the steep mountainsides, leading their horses after them, and came at last to the city of Caxamarca

75

● Mention that *pacific* means "peaceful."

(kah-hah-MAHR-kah), where the Inca ruler awaited them.

Pizarro imprisons the Inca ruler and gains a royal ransom. The ruler, Atahualpa (ah-tah-WAHL-pah), with thousands of his subjects gathered about him, sat on a throne of gold in the great square. We may well imagine that he did not fear this small band of white men with their weapons, for he had never before seen a gun. The Spaniards tried to persuade Atahualpa to become a Christian and a subject of the king of Spain. A priest talked to him through an interpreter, telling him about the Christian religion and urging him to accept the Christian God. Atahualpa listened, but was not impressed. He pointed to the sun and said, "My god still lives in the heavens and looks down upon his children." Then he threw to the ground the Bible that the priest had offered him. This angered the religious Spaniards, and Pizarro gave the signal to fire. While the Inca ruler looked on in horror from his golden throne, the Spaniards massacred thousands of his subjects. Pizarro took Atahualpa prisoner.

When the royal prisoner saw how eager the Spaniards were for gold, he made a bargain with Pizarro for his freedom. Atahualpa touched the wall of a small room as high above his head as he could reach. He promised to fill the room with gold to that height if his captors would release him. Pizarro agreed, and during the days that followed, a steady stream of Indians entered the room with gold objects from palaces and temples. At last the room was filled. This was indeed a royal ransom. Atahualpa had carried out his side of the bargain, but Pizarro had no intention of keeping his promise. For him the bargain was simply an easy way to get the Inca gold. Later on, he found an excuse

The Incas built the city of Machu Picchu high in the Andes Mountains. The remains of the city can still be seen today.

MAP STUDY
Use the key to find
where the Aztecs,
Mayas, and Incas
lived. These were the
main Indian peoples
found by the early
Spanish conquerors in
America. From what
islands did Cortés and
Balboa set out on their
explorations?

See Teacher's Key.

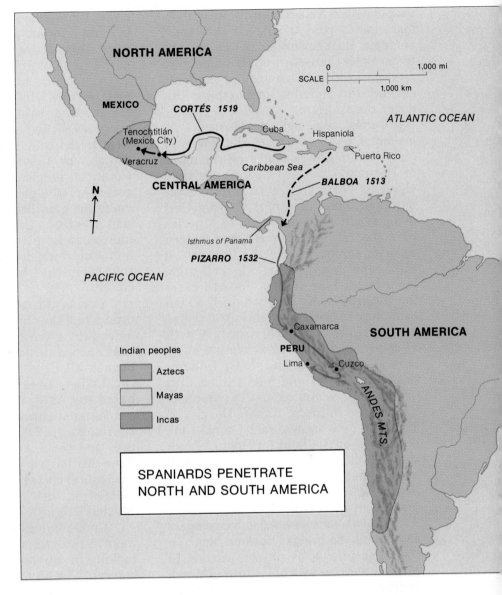

NORTH AMERICA

SCALE

0   1,000 mi

0   1,000 km

ATLANTIC OCEAN

MEXICO

CORTÉS 1519

Cuba

Hispaniola

Tenochtitlán
(Mexico City)

Puerto Rico

Veracruz

Caribbean Sea

BALBOA 1513

N

CENTRAL AMERICA

Isthmus of Panama

PIZARRO 1532

PACIFIC OCEAN

Indian peoples

Aztecs

Mayas

Incas

Caxamarca

SOUTH AMERICA

PERU

Lima

Cuzco

ANDES MTS.

SPANIARDS PENETRATE
NORTH AND SOUTH AMERICA

to kill Atahualpa, who was strangled to death by the Spaniards.

Pizarro meets a violent death. It was not long before Pizarro conquered other cities, and soon he controlled the whole Inca empire (see map above). He founded the Spanish city of Lima (LEE-muh), which grew to be one of the most important cities of South America. Pizarro's harsh treatment of the Indians led to many revolts and endless fighting. There also was much jealousy and plotting among the Spaniards

themselves. Pizarro died as violently as he had lived, for he was finally assassinated by his own countrymen.

CORTÉS CONQUERS MEXICO

The Spanish also heard tales of other rich lands. Sailors who had touched the coast of the mainland opposite Cuba brought back stories of a great land to the north and west (Mexico) where much treasure was to be found. This land, they said, was ruled by a powerful people called Aztecs. All the neighboring Indians paid tribute to the Aztec emperor. The governor of Cuba decided to check on these stories. He planned to send an expedition to explore the land, convert the Indians, and perhaps discover the treasure.

Cortés sets out for Mexico. As leader of the expedition, the governor chose an ambitious soldier by the name of Hernando Cortés. Cortés was then about 33 years old. Born into a noble but poor Spanish family, he had left home at nineteen and sailed to America to make his fortune. He had helped Spanish forces subdue the Indians in Cuba and later became a well-to-do landowner. Like Balboa, he was eager for adventure. He gladly agreed to become leader of the expedition.

Cortés left Cuba early in 1519 with 11 ships, 600 men, several priests, a few horses and cannon, and many Indians. (Turn to page 77 and follow his course on the map as you read.) The Spanish fleet landed in Mexico where the city of Veracruz now stands, and Cortés took possession of the land for Spain. From the inhabitants of that region he heard more about the Aztecs and their emperor, who was called Moctezuma (mahk-teh-ZOO-muh).[1]

Cortés meets with Aztec messengers and "burns his bridges" behind him. In the meantime, swift runners carried to
● Moctezuma news of white-skinned, bearded strangers who rode on great beasts and had weapons that made sounds like thunder. The Aztecs had a legend about a "fair god" who once ruled their land. Hundreds of years before, he had departed in a great canoe, promising that he would one day return to them. Was it possible, wondered Moctezuma, that the leader of these strange beings was their ancient god? Moctezuma dared take no chances, so

he sent messengers with words of greeting and dazzling gifts. Among the gifts were two plates as large as wagon wheels, one of gold and one of silver.

Cortés was more eager than ever to meet a ruler who owned such treasure. He made a bold decision. He would overpower this emperor and win his wealth and lands for Spain, and also, of course, for Cortés and his men. He would no longer take orders from the governor of Cuba, but instead would make his own decisions. Cortés wisely sent a letter to the Spanish king, telling ★ him what he planned to do. Then he announced his decision to his men and told them that he was starting a new colony.

Cortés was a leader who inspired others to follow him, and his men gladly agreed to his daring plan. To make sure that no men turned fainthearted, Cortés burned all his ships! He learned that the Indian tribes along the coast, who hated the Aztec rule, would be glad to join him in fighting against Moctezuma. In August, 1519, the little band of white men and their Indian allies set out for Tenochtitlán (tay-nohch-tee-TLAHN), the capital city of the Aztecs, which was located in the mountains of central Mexico.

Cortés arrives at Tenochtitlán. Two months later the weary Spaniards stood looking in amazement upon the Aztec capital. The city was built on islands in a large but shallow lake, and was connected with the mainland by three raised roads, or causeways. Crisscrossing the city were many canals that served as streets, and brightly colored canoes darted back and forth. Alongside these canals were footpaths. Most of the buildings were dazzling white. Great temples to Aztec gods towered above the city.

The Spaniards were met by Moctezuma, ruler of the Aztecs. A tall and dignified man, dressed in blue and gold, he was carried on a couch borne by his

---

[1]Though this ruler is often called "Montezuma," the spelling "Moctezuma" is more accurate.

★ Why was it wise for Cortés to write the king? Have students look for further information about Cortés's relationship with the governor of Cuba (p. 79).

The Aztec city of Tenochtitlán is shown here. Drawn by a modern artist, this picture is based on the descriptions of the Spanish conquerors. The gold that the Spaniards sought was made by the Aztecs into beautiful jewelry (left).

subjects. When he alighted, a carpet was put down to protect his golden sandals from the earth. On all sides important Aztec officials stood without daring to raise their eyes in the presence of their ruler. Moctezuma and Cortés gravely exchanged gifts, and the Spaniards slowly entered the city.

Although he feared the strangers, Moctezuma treated them as honored guests. They lived for some months in the city, storing up gold and treasure by trade with the Indians. The Aztecs did not appear to be hostile, but Cortés realized that his small band was greatly outnumbered.

The Spaniards fight their way out of Tenochtitlán. Then Cortés received news that the governor of Cuba had sent an expedition to Mexico to take him prisoner. With some of his followers, Cortés left the city and returned to the coast. There he captured the leader of the expedition. By describing the

treasure that would be theirs when the Aztecs were conquered, Cortés persuaded the others to join him. Returning to Tenochtitlán with his recruits, Cortés discovered that in his absence fighting had broken out between the Spaniards and the Aztecs. When they found that Spaniards could be killed, the Aztecs realized that the white strangers were not gods and had turned on them in fury.

After several days of bitter fighting, Cortés decided that he and his men had to get out of the city. Even their cannon and arms were no match for thousands of Aztec warriors. Loaded down with gold and jewels, the Spaniards tried to steal away in the darkness of night, but their flight was discovered. A fierce battle followed. Many Spaniards plunged into the lake and drowned; hundreds of others were killed by Aztec knives and arrows. Cortés and those of his men who escaped had suffered a terrible defeat. It is said that Cortés sat under a tree outside the city and wept over the loss of 450 of his valiant men.

Tenochtitlán finally surrenders to Cortés. Cortés knew that he had to continue his attempt to conquer Tenochtitlán and the Aztecs. He had to succeed or he could never return to Cuba — unless he wished to be hanged for treason. But it was not until 1521 that the city finally surrendered. Cortés then tore down the capital of the Aztecs and built in its place a Spanish city that he called Mexico City. Christian churches soon replaced the temples of the Aztecs.

Cortés continues his conquests. Cortés did not stop with the conquest of the Aztecs. As commander of the Spanish forces in Mexico, he sent expeditions throughout the Aztec empire and into Central America. Some of these expeditions he himself led. Cortés seized the gold and silver mines and other wealth that he found and forced the Indians to work for the Spaniards.

SPAIN EXPANDS FAR BEYOND MEXICO

So far you have learned about Balboa, Pizarro, and Cortés. There were, of course, many other famous explorers who claimed for Spain the regions they explored while searching for fame and treasure. Some of these explorers moved northward and eastward into what is now New Mexico, Texas, Florida, and California.

The Spanish search for "cities of gold." Stories had long been told about the "seven cities of gold," in what is now New Mexico. The streets of these cities, it was said, were paved with gold, and people ate from gold and silver plates. Francisco Coronado (kor-uh-NAH-doh) led an expedition to locate these rich cities and to capture their wealth for the Spanish empire. He assembled 225 horsemen, more than 60 other soldiers, and 1,000 slaves. With them the explorers took horses, oxen, cows, sheep, pigs,

80

Long before Europeans came to America, the Indians had developed their own customs and skills. The great Pueblo at Taos, New Mexico, is an adobe apartment house in which Indians have lived for hundreds of years. Early pueblos were described as "cities of gold," a legend that lured Spaniards into the land north of Mexico.

★ See p. T17 for a strategy dealing with the routes taken by Spanish explorers. Also see "Reading Maps: Tracing Routes and Finding Directions" (p. 95).

Coronado's expedition marched hundreds of miles in search of the "cities of gold."

and mules carrying supplies. They set out in 1540 and did not return until two years later. They explored Arizona, New Mexico, and Texas, and went as far north as present-day Kansas.

Coronado reported that he reached a region that "is the best I have ever seen for producing all the products of Spain, for besides the land itself being very fat and black and being very well watered by rivulets and springs and rivers, I found prunes like those of Spain and nuts and very good sweet grapes and mulberries." But Coronado's group found no gold. The "seven cities" turned out to be small Indian villages where life was hard and where there were no riches. Coronado later learned from his Indian guides that the stories about the cities of gold were not true.

About 50 years later an explorer named Juan de Oñate (hwahn day ohn-YAH-tay) led a group of soldiers and settlers into New Mexico and took over an Indian town that he renamed San Juan. Santa Fe was settled soon after. Oñate, too, was disappointed not to find ● the cities of gold, which many Spaniards still believed to exist. During these years the Spanish began to settle Texas and established San Antonio and a number of smaller outposts.

The Spanish learn more about North America. Other Spanish explorers increased Spain's knowledge about parts of North America. Ponce de León (POHN-say day lay-OHN) discovered Florida while searching for a "fountain of youth." He never found such a fountain, and little came of his expedition. But other Spaniards did make a settlement at St. Augustine, Florida, in 1565. It is the oldest city in the United States. Because Florida lacked gold and silver and farming was difficult, the Spanish did not send many settlers to the area.

Another Spaniard, Cabeza de Vaca (kah-BAY-sah day VAH-kah), wandered for years through Mexico and what is now the state of Texas. De Vaca had a companion named Estevanico

81

(ays-tay-vah-NEE-koh). An African, Estevanico had been taken to North America as a slave. At one point he led a Spanish expedition into territory that is now the American Southwest.

Yet another explorer, Hernando de Soto, was the first European to see the Mississippi River. He reached it about 140 years before La Salle (p. 63). The Spanish made no effort to colonize the area, so La Salle was able to claim it for France later on.

The Spanish explore California. Not many years after Cortés had conquered Mexico City, Spanish ships sailed up the Gulf of California. Later the vessels went north along the west coast of Lower California. (Lower California is a long peninsula in northwestern Mexico. Find it on the map on page 85.) On one voyage the Spaniards discovered a fine harbor that they named San Diego.

For a long time the Spaniards centered their attention on Lower California. There they built **missions** for the conversion of the Indians. (A mission was a frontier settlement founded by the Spanish. It usually included a church, a village, a fort, and farmland.) In 1769, however, a large group of settlers and monks led by Father Junípero Serra (hoo-NEE-pay-roh SEHR-ah) decided to go farther north. The travelers arrived successfully at San Diego, where they built a mission. Then they pushed on and started a second mission at Monterey. (Life on a mission is described on page 90.)

The Spanish build many missions and forts in California. The Spanish moved farther and farther north, establishing their missions and *presidios*

Bold adventurers left Spain to seek wealth in America. Spanish priests came to America in search of converts to their religion. Guides such as Estevanico (bottom, right) led expeditions into unknown areas.

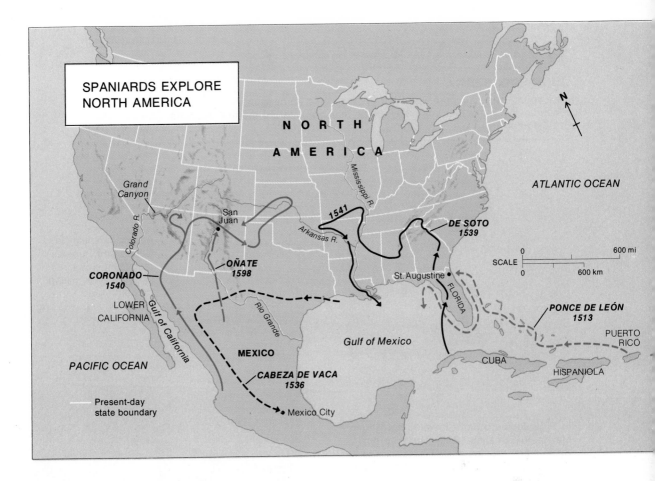

SPANIARDS EXPLORE
NORTH AMERICA

MAP STUDY   See Teacher's Key.
On this map the boundaries of present-day
states help you follow the travels of five Spanish
explorers in North America. (Remember that the
states did not actually exist at that time.)
(a) Which explorers started out by heading
north from Mexico? (b) Which ones explored
Florida?

(forts) at various locations in California. At first the settlements were tiny.
Only a few priests and a handful of soldiers lived in each one. Later, as Indians were converted to Christianity, the
settlements grew larger.

Among the missionaries, Father
Serra was one of the most industrious
and successful. After helping start the
mission at San Diego, he quickly established missions at San Antonio de
Padua, San Gabriel, and San Luis
Obispo. After a few years he founded

four more. They were at San Francisco,
San Juan Capistrano, Santa Clara, and
San Buenaventura. Father Serra visited all the missions several times,
traveling on muleback or horseback to
check on the missionaries' work. He
brought thousands of people into the
Catholic Church with his exciting sermons and his example of dedication and
hard work. Throughout his life, he
urged fair treatment for the Indians as
he preached and worked among them.

SPAIN GAINS WEALTH AND POWER FROM ITS EMPIRE

Spain's new empire is immense.
Spanish explorers, priests, and settlers
had carved out a vast empire. It included all of South America (except

83

Have students research other important Spanish
missionaries; for example, Eusebio Francisco Kino.

People in America's Story

Tell students that California is represented by a statue of Serra in the Statuary Hall in the United States Capitol.

JUNÍPERO SERRA

As a young man, Junípero Serra left Spain to take up missionary work in America. We remember him today as the man who started the first missions in California.

At missions like San Carlos (left), priests taught Indians such skills as flour milling, carpentry and woodworking, weaving, and metalworking.

In 1769 Junípero Serra traveled north from Mexico to San Diego Bay. There he built Spain's first mission in California. In the years that followed, he and other priests started 21 missions along the California coast. Some missions, such as San Antonio de Padua (right), can still be seen today.

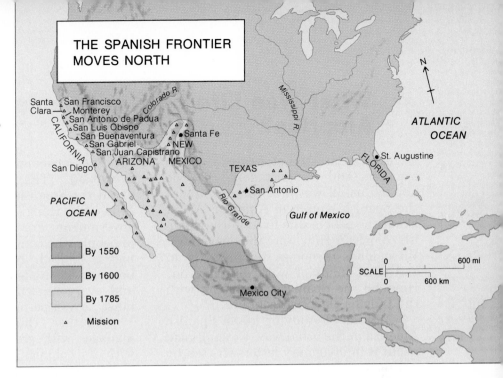

THE SPANISH FRONTIER MOVES NORTH

MAP STUDY
Spanish settlers gradually followed the missions northward into what is now the United States. Use the key to see how far the frontier reached by 1550, by 1600, and by 1785. In what present-day western states were missions started?

See Teacher's Key.

By 1550
By 1600
By 1785
▲ Mission

Brazil, which Portugal claimed), all of Central America, and Mexico. It also included Florida, the coast around the Gulf of Mexico, the southwestern part of what is now the United States, and all the islands of the West Indies. (The map on page 87 shows the mighty empire of Spain.)

This enormous area was divided into two parts: (1) As shown on the map, the part called New Spain included Mexico and the West Indies. (2) The name Peru was given to Spanish possessions in South America except for Venezuela.

Spain becomes the richest and most powerful nation in Europe. The Spaniards stripped the Aztec and the Inca empires of stored-up wealth. Then they forced the Indians to dig still more gold and silver from the mines of Mexico and Peru. During the 1500's the riches of its American empire made Spain the wealthiest country in Europe.

Wealth means power. Spain's new-found wealth made it, for a time, Europe's most powerful nation. Spain was able to build strong colonies in America and to send soldiers to protect them. A huge navy guarded Spain's great fleet of merchant ships against attack.

Spain's power reached its height in the latter half of the 1500's. Philip II, an earnest Catholic, ruled over a vast empire in Europe and America. His power was increased still further because the Pope looked to Philip to make Christians of the Indians in Spain's great realm and to defend the cause of the Catholic Church everywhere. When people thought of Philip's wealth and power, they said, "When Spain moves, the whole world trembles."

▶ **CHECK UP** *See Teacher's Key.*

1. For what reasons did Spaniards come to the Americas?
2. **(a)** How did Balboa add to Spain's claims? **(b)** What peoples and lands did Cortés and Pizarro conquer for Spain? **(c)** What were the results of these conquests?
3. What other explorers carved out new colonies for Spain? Tell where in each case.
4. What effect did its American empire have on Spain?

85

● See p. T17 for strategies that examine the extent of Spanish power and the lasting influence of the Spanish in the Americas.

2 What Was Life Like in Spanish America?

Exciting as are the stories of Spanish explorers and conquistadors, they do not tell us all we want to know about the Spanish empire in America. What about the people who lived in the Spanish colonies? How were they governed? What kinds of homes did they live in and what kinds of work did they do? How did the Spaniards get along with the Indians they had conquered?

Instead of studying life in Spanish America in the usual way, we shall read about it in imaginary letters written by a fifteen-year-old boy called Philip Andrews. Let us suppose that Philip, son of an English father and a Spanish mother, went to New Spain in the early 1700's to visit his mother's relatives. Although there was no real Philip Andrews, these letters give a true picture of life in the Spanish colonies. Imagine that the letters were found long after Philip wrote them and that the finder put in the headings. As you read, remember that a boy in the 1700's wrote more formal letters, even to his parents, than would young people today.

THE SPANISH GOVERNMENT CONTROLS THE SPANISH COLONISTS

ON SHIPBOARD, BOUND FOR NEW SPAIN

Dear Mother and Father,

What good luck I have had — and at the very beginning of my trip, too! One of my fellow passengers on the ship is a Spanish official. In talking with him I have learned a great deal about the Spanish colonies even before reaching them. So in this first letter I can give you a general idea of New Spain and its government, even though I have not yet arrived there.

The government controls almost everything. The most striking thing about the Spanish colonies is how carefully everything is controlled by the government. For example, the number of people who come to the Spanish colonies is limited. No one but Catholics born in Spain itself may settle there, and everyone who enters New Spain must have a permit to do so.

Another thing the government manages with great care is the trade with its colonies. Only Spanish merchants, using Spanish vessels, can trade with New Spain. Every spring a great fleet of heavily guarded merchant ships sails to Veracruz from Spain. The ships are loaded with manufactured goods, such as cloth, shoes, and tools. These Spanish goods are traded for corn, cattle, hides, and other products of New Spain.

The people in the colonies do not like the way trade is regulated by Spain. They have to buy what they need from the merchants at Veracruz. The colonists must also sell what they make or grow to the same merchants. The colonists have nothing to say about the prices of the goods they buy or the goods they sell. And they are not allowed to grow anything produced in Spain because if they did, Spanish merchants would not be able to sell their own products in the colonies. What the colonists want is to be free to trade with other countries.

Another example of control is the way New Spain is governed. The king of Spain appoints a colonial governor, called a **viceroy.** This official has great power while the people have no real share in the government. The viceroy and his assistants control the lives of

● Have students use the letters (pp. 86–90) to list ways Spain regulated the lives of its colonists.

● Compare the lives of the Indians to serfs (p. 28).

the people, issuing all sorts of regulations. As you can see, the people of New Spain are far from free to do as they like.

Your affectionate son,
PHILIP

THE SPANIARDS AND THE INDIANS

ON SHIPBOARD

Dear Mother and Father,

I have been talking again with my friend, the Spanish official. One question I asked him was how the Spaniards get along with the Indians. He says that when the Spanish conquerors first reached America, they cared nothing for the Indians. They killed the Indians and drove them away from their homes. The Spanish government, however, did not approve of mistreating the Indians. In order to protect them and to help Christianize them, the government established a new system back in the 1500's.

The Indians work for the Spaniards. When a Spanish captain had conquered a region, the land and the Indians on it were divided among him and his followers. The Spaniards were supposed to see that the Indians were treated kindly, converted to Christianity, and allowed plots of land to farm for themselves. In return, the Indians were supposed to work on the estates or in the mines of the owners for a small sum. When I asked my friend how this plan worked out, he shook his head and said that the Spanish landowners paid little attention to laws issued in far-off Spain. As far as I can tell, the Indians were no better off than serfs living in Europe in the Middle Ages. They were not allowed to leave the land and were forced to work the fields for the owners for no pay at all. They were often shamefully overworked and sometimes almost starved. My friend says that Spanish priests

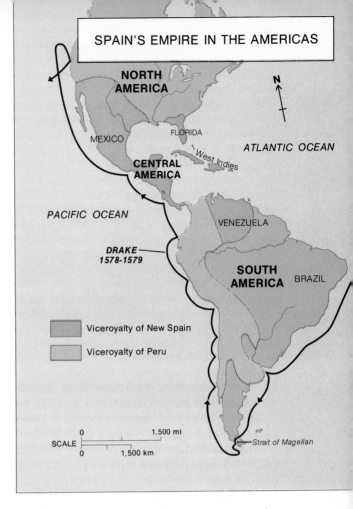

SPAIN'S EMPIRE IN THE AMERICAS

NORTH AMERICA

MEXICO
FLORIDA
ATLANTIC OCEAN
West Indies
CENTRAL AMERICA
PACIFIC OCEAN
VENEZUELA
DRAKE 1578-1579
SOUTH AMERICA
BRAZIL

Viceroyalty of New Spain
Viceroyalty of Peru

SCALE
0   1,500 mi
0   1,500 km

Strait of Magellan

N

MAP STUDY   See Teacher's Key.
New Spain and Peru were the two large divisions (viceroyalties) of the Spanish empire in America. Note that the division called Peru was much larger than the present-day country of that name. What areas were part of New Spain?

tried to make the lot of the Indians easier but found it difficult to help them.

The Indians become Christians. A priest who is returning to New Spain tells me that the Spaniards have tried all along to make Christians of the Indians. Spanish priests have always preached to the Indians, and they have built churches throughout New Spain. In distant territories they have also made settlements called missions. In these missions the priests care for the ★ Indians and educate them as well as teach them religion. When I reach New Spain, I will try to visit a mission.

87

★ Compare the treatment of Indians who lived around estates or mines to the treatment of those who lived near missions.

Taxco, an important silver-mining center, shows the kind of town built by the Spanish in America.

We are not far from New Spain now, and in my next letter I should be able to tell you some things I have learned first-hand. We expect to land at Veracruz and go from there to Mexico City. I am looking forward to seeing many new and interesting things when we finally arrive there.

Your affectionate son,
PHILIP

LIFE IN MEXICO CITY

IN MEXICO CITY

Dear Mother and Father,
Since I last wrote you I have reached New Spain! In this letter I shall tell you what Mexico City is like.

Mexico City is the largest and richest city in New Spain, and it is also one of the most beautiful. Part of it is surrounded by a shallow lake, so that goods for the great marketplace in the center of the city may travel by water as well as by land. The city is built around a large central plaza or public square where the cathedral and viceroy's palace stand. There are also wide, well-paved roads running through the city at

right angles. Where necessary, earth and stones have been thrown into the lake, and roads have been built on top of this filled-in land. Most of the houses here are two stories high with iron balconies across the front. Each house is built around an open-air courtyard where the members of the family can sit without being seen by their neighbors or passers-by in the street.

Mexico City is the capital of New Spain. This city is different from the others in New Spain, for it is the capital. The highest officer, the viceroy, lives here. As the representative of the king of Spain, he is head of the government and has many duties and responsibilities. The viceroy appoints other government officers who also live in the city. Actually, Mexico City is like the capital of Spain itself but on a smaller scale, and the viceroy and his attendants are similar to the king and his court.

Another sign that Mexico City is the capital is the great cathedral. This beautiful church is said to be the largest in the Western Hemisphere. The cathedral is the church of the archbishop of New Spain, who is the highest Catholic official in the province. The presence of the archbishop draws many officers of

88

● As they read along, have students note some of the features that made Mexico City famous. (roads, marketplace, cathedral, university)

the Church to Mexico City, just as the viceroy attracts government officers. In addition to the cathedral, there is also the University of Mexico. This university and the one in Lima, Peru, were both started in 1551. They are the two oldest universities in New Spain. There are many other less important churches and schools, too.

Mexico City is known for its splendor and ceremony. Great parades are held in honor of important events, such as the arrival of a new viceroy or the departure of an old one. Frequently there are solemn religious processions. At other times festive parties are given by the rich at their expensive homes in or near the city. These men and women dress in elegant silks and wear costly jewels. But thousands and thousands of poor people do not share in this wealth and luxury. They do all the hard work and live in miserable one-room huts on the edge of the city.

There are five main groups in New Spain. I think you would be interested in the groups of people who live in New Spain: (1) The Spaniards born in Spain hold the most important positions in the Church and the government. (2) The Spaniards look down on the *Creoles* (pronounced KREE-ohls in English, cray-OH-lace in Spanish), who are of Spanish ancestry but were born in New Spain. Many of the landowners, merchants, and businessmen are Creoles. (3) Then there is a large group of *mestizos* (mes-TEE-sohz), who are part Spanish and part Indian. They work as laborers and skilled craftsmen in the cities, and many of them are miserably poor. (4) The Indians make up another large group. As I have told you before, many unfortunate Indians are forced to work in the fields and the mines. (5) Black slaves from Africa do much hard labor on the large farming estates and at ports like Veracruz. Blacks and Indians have the lowest rank in New Spain.

In a short time I expect to take a trip into other parts of New Spain to see what life is like away from the capital. During my journey I plan to visit Uncle Pedro and Aunt Rosita.

Your affectionate son,
PHILIP

THE HACIENDAS AND THE MISSIONS

IN NORTHERN NEW SPAIN

Dear Mother and Father,
I left Mexico City some time ago and began a trip on horseback through the country. I have seen how people live in many parts of New Spain. I want to tell you especially about two important ways of living in order to give you a clearer idea of the Spanish colonies.

A visit to a hacienda. First of all, I'll tell you about what are called the *haciendas* (hah-sih-EN-duhz). These are large estates or ranches owned by rich people. Haciendas are found throughout the country, and I have stopped at many of them. If I describe the one owned by Uncle Pedro, you will get a good picture of them all.

Uncle Pedro's house is built around a courtyard, as are those in Mexico City. Near the house itself is a church where the family and the Indians worship. There are stables for horses, and not far away are many huts occupied by the Indian peasants, who do all the hard tasks on the hacienda. At the house they cook and clean and serve. They also take care of the crops and of the huge herds of cattle that are the chief part of their master's wealth.

Uncle Pedro, like the masters of all the haciendas, is a splendid horseman and spends many hours every day in the saddle. He rides for pleasure and also to keep an eye on the work being done on the hacienda. Aunt Rosita runs the household and teaches the children how to behave. The life of the family is comfortable but not exciting. Their time is

89

● See p. T18 for a strategy that will help to expand students' knowledge of these groups of people.

Cattle first came to America in Spanish ships. This painting shows how they were unloaded. The Spaniards also brought horses to America. Many horses ran wild or were captured by Indians.

spent in entertaining visitors (like me!) and in visiting their friends. All who pass by are welcome at the hacienda for as long as they want to stay. The family amuses the guests with dances, riding, and occasionally a bullfight.

A visit to a mission. I stayed at many haciendas besides Uncle Pedro's as I traveled northward from Mexico City. Life on the haciendas is peaceful and easygoing. It is even more peaceful in the missions, which I visited next. These missions belong to the Catholic Church. They are found far from the older Spanish settlements. The priests who started the missions devoted their lives to teaching the Indians. These priests often endured severe hardships and great suffering for their religion. They have converted the nearby Indians to Christianity and hold church services for them in the missions. Hundreds of Christian Indians live around a mission. They take care of the crops and tend the cattle and do the other necessary work. At most of the missions, under the direction of the priests, the Indians have spent years and years

in building churches of great beauty. These churches have heavy walls and high towers and are gorgeously decorated inside. The woodwork is delicately carved, and many churches have religious scenes painted on the walls.

Close by the churches are schools and workshops. The Indians pass back and forth — to work, to worship, and to learn. Over all gleams the brilliant sunshine; now and then the bell tolls in the tower of the church. You cannot imagine a scene more peaceful and orderly than this one.

Soon I will be coming home, and how glad I shall be to see you! I hope that my letters have reached you safely, and that they have given you a good idea of what I have seen of the life of the people in New Spain.

Your affectionate son,
PHILIP

———

This ends Philip's letters. They tell about life in New Spain and, in fact, throughout Spain's American colonies. If Philip had visited Peru, he would have discovered some differences in the way the people lived there, but his letters in general would have been much the same.

▶ **CHECK UP**   See Teacher's Key.

1. **(a)** In what ways did Spain regulate life in its American colonies? **(b)** What groups of people especially profited from these regulations?
2. **(a)** How did the Spanish government try to protect the Indians? **(b)** Why were the government's plans not always successful?
3. **(a)** Describe Mexico City in the days of Spanish control. **(b)** What groups of people lived in New Spain?
4. **(a)** Describe life on the haciendas. **(b)** What was the purpose of the missions? **(c)** Describe the life of the Indians who lived around the missions.

90

● Tell students that there is an old Spanish expression *mi casa es su casa,* which means "my house is your house."

3 How Did England and Other Nations Threaten Spain's Power?

You have learned how Spain built up a huge empire in the Americas and became the leading power in Europe. How do you suppose other European powers felt about Spain's important position in the world? As you may guess, they resented and feared the power of Spain. They were also jealous of Spain for having so many wealthy colonies. They believed that Spain had no more right to the riches of the new lands than they themselves had. In fact, when the king of France heard of the Line of Demarcation dividing the newly found lands between Spain and Portugal (page 56), he
● scornfully asked, "Who can show me the will of Father Adam leaving all the world to Spain and Portugal?" Naturally England, France, and Holland were eager to lessen the power of Spain.

EUROPEAN NATIONS DEFY SPAIN

Spain loses trade and treasure. One way for other nations to strike at Spain was to carry on a secret trade with its colonies. Even though Spanish regulations forbade such trade, non-Spanish traders would make agreements to deliver goods in the seaport towns. They would anchor off the coast and land their merchandise at night in small boats. This illegal trade took much wealth from the pockets of Spanish merchants.

Another way to strike at Spain was by actually attacking its merchant and treasure ships. In the 1500's, armed ships from France, Holland, and England roamed the seas. They captured Spanish ships and plundered rich towns along the coasts of Spanish America. The treasure and other booty snatched by these raiders cannot be valued exactly but must have been worth millions

of dollars. Later on, raiding sea rovers even helped themselves to Spanish territory. French pirates took over the western end of Hispaniola and attacked Spanish trade in the Caribbean. English pirates established themselves on the coast of Central America. Dutch pirates took over an island off the coast of what is now Venezuela.

The sea dogs of England nip at Spain. The English were the most successful in striking at Spain. When Columbus found America, England was not a powerful country. Wars between rival noble families had left England weak. Under the capable rule of Queen Elizabeth I (1558–1603), however, England rapidly grew stronger. Because England was an island, the English had learned to be good sailors and skillful shipbuilders. This fact made it easier for them to prey on Spanish shipping. The captains of the English vessels that swooped down on the ships of Spain came to be known as "sea dogs."

Francis Drake angers the king of Spain. The most famous of all the sea dogs was Francis Drake. Brought up in a town on the English coast, he had learned the ways of the sea before he was ten years old. Drake felt a bitter hatred for the Spaniards. For many years he proved his boldness and skill by capturing Spanish vessels and attacking ★ Spanish towns. Once he and his men landed on the Isthmus of Panama and coolly seized a Spanish mule-train bearing costly treasure. After this the Spaniards called him "Drake the Dragon," and the king of Spain offered a huge sum of money to anyone who could kill him.

In 1577 Drake left England in his ship, the *Golden Hind*, on a dangerous expedition. The Spaniards had never

★ See p. T18 for a strategy that suggests having students look at Drake's exploits
from three perspectives.

In 1580 Francis Drake triumphantly returned home with a shipload of gold and silver taken from Spanish vessels. Queen Elizabeth showed her approval by boarding the *Golden Hind* and making Drake a knight.

been attacked in their "Spanish lake," as they boastingly called the South Sea (Pacific Ocean). Why not follow Magellan's route to the Pacific and surprise the Spaniards? Drake crossed the Atlantic and, after sixteen days of difficult sailing, succeeded in passing through the Strait of Magellan. Then he sped north along the western coast of South America, capturing unsuspecting ships and frightening the people in the coast towns. His greatest prize was the Spanish treasure ship known as the "Glory of the South Sea." Taking the ship completely by surprise, Drake seized precious stones, chests full of gold pieces, and tons of pure silver. At last the *Golden Hind* was loaded with priceless treasure.

How could he return home? With all of Spanish America hostile toward him, Drake decided that the longest way round was indeed the shortest way home. He continued north along the coast of California (map, page 87), crossed the Pacific, and sailed around Africa to England. His expedition was

the second to sail around the world. Drake's voyage was also important for other reasons. Not only had he brought home treasure that was worth millions, but he had proved that the South Sea was no more a Spanish lake than it was an English one. When he arrived home, he was given a great welcome. Queen Elizabeth, standing on the deck of the *Golden Hind*, rewarded him by making him a knight — Sir Francis Drake.

SPAIN STRIKES BACK BUT IS DEFEATED

Philip of Spain prepares to attack England. King Philip of Spain was furious over the attacks of the sea dogs on his ships and his people. Drake's latest success was too much for a king of Spain to endure. He notified the queen of England that Drake was nothing but a pirate and ought to be hanged. But Philip of Spain had a deeper reason for being angry at England. Several European countries, of which England was

92

Trace Drake's voyage around the world. Use the map on p. 87.

See p. T18 for a strategy dealing with the clash between Spain and England.

★ Discuss the significance of the defeat of the Spanish Armada.

one of the most important, had broken away from the Roman Catholic Church earlier in the 1500's. As the most powerful Catholic ruler in Europe, Philip decided that the time had come to crush England. He gathered a fleet of 130 war vessels, put on board 19,000 soldiers and 8,000 sailors, and sent them to attack England. This great expedition was called the Invincible Armada, which means "unconquerable fleet."

The Spanish Armada is defeated. When the Armada reached the English Channel, it was met by about 150 English vessels. Among the commanders of the English fleet were Sir Francis Drake and Martin Frobisher, the explorer. The English ships could move about faster and shoot better than those of the Spaniards. They darted back and forth around the ships of the Armada, firing quickly and sailing away before the heavy enemy ships could return their fire. The English also launched fire ships and let them drift among the Spanish vessels.

For days the battle raged, but finally the Spaniards fled up the English Channel with the English in pursuit.

Then nature came to England's aid. A fierce gale blew up, and many of the enemy ships that had survived the battle were driven ashore or swamped. The rest of the Armada was hopelessly scattered. Proud Spain had suffered a terrible defeat. It lost a third of its ships and thousands of men.

After the defeat of the Armada in 1588, Spain's power began to decline. For almost a century Spain had been the strongest nation in Europe, but England had proved to the world that Spain could be beaten. Other countries could now make settlements in parts of North and South America not controlled by Spain, without fear of interference. In the next chapter, for example, you will learn how the English started colonies in North America.

▶ **CHECK UP**   See Teacher's Key.

1. **(a)** Why were other nations jealous of Spain? **(b)** How did they strike at Spain's power?
2. How did England win a great naval victory over Spain?

CHECK UP ON CHAPTER 3   See Teacher's Key.

Words to Know

1. Aztecs
2. Incas
3. sea dog
4. conquistador
5. caballero
6. mission
7. mestizo
8. hacienda
9. viceroy

Places to Locate

1. Mexico
2. Peru
3. Andes
4. Cuba
5. West Indies
6. Santa Fe
7. Lower California
8. San Diego
9. Caribbean Sea
10. San Antonio
11. St. Augustine
12. Isthmus of Panama

Facts to Remember

1. Where did each of the following people explore? In each case tell why their explorations were important. **(a)** Balboa **(b)** Pizarro **(c)** Cortés **(d)** Coronado **(e)** Ponce de León **(f)** Estevanico **(g)** De Soto
2. **(a)** What lands were included in what the Spanish called New Spain? **(b)** In what ways did the Spanish government control life in New Spain? **(c)** How were the Indian people of New Spain affected by Spanish control?
3. **(a)** Why were Spain and England enemies in the 1500's? **(b)** What was the Spanish Armada?

93

Skills to Practice

1. Arrange the following events in the order in which they happened. Start with the earliest event.
   a. St. Augustine is settled.
   b. The Spanish conquer Mexico.
   c. Father Serra starts missions in California.
   d. The Spanish conquer Peru.
2. Look at the map on page 85. **(a)** Name two towns or cities where missions were established. **(b)** In what present-day states are they located? **(c)** How does the map use colors to show the spread of Spanish settlement?

Questions to Think About

1. What made it possible for Cortés and Pizarro, with only small forces of men, to conquer the huge Indian empires in Mexico and Peru?
2. In 1588 the Spanish Armada was met by English ships in the English Channel. Why was the outcome of the battle between the Spanish and English fleets so important?
3. Why did the Spanish continue to search so long for the "seven cities of gold"? Why would it have been hard for them to admit that the cities probably did not exist?

 # Linking Past and Present

Spanish names live on. The Spaniards who came to North America left lasting evidence of their explorations in Florida and the Southwest. We find towns and cities, mountains and rivers, and states with Spanish names. Florida, for instance, was named by Ponce de León. Because it was Easter time when he reached the new land, he named it "Florida" after the Spanish name for Easter — *Pascua florida*. A famous site within Florida is also connected with Ponce de León. Cape Canaveral, home of the John F. Kennedy Space Center, was named after a Spanish town in the region Ponce came from — Canaveral de León.

As for the name "California," the story goes that in the 1500's people in Europe believed there was an island called "California" which was rich with gold and jewels. When ship captains returned to Mexico from exploring our southwest coast, they described the land in glowing terms to Cortés. He remarked, "Yes, this must truly be the island of California." And so, in spite of the geographical error, the land was named. The states of Colorado, Nevada, and Montana also have Spanish names.

Many towns and cities in our Southwest date back to Spanish days. Santa Fe ("Holy Faith"), San Antonio ("Saint Anthony"), and El Paso ("the pass") were founded by the Spaniards. Most of the missions founded in California have become towns and cities and still keep their Spanish names. In 1781 the Spaniards started a town which they called *Nuestra Señora Reina de Los Angeles* ("Our Lady the Queen of the Angels"). That Spanish town has become one of the largest cities in the United States. Its long Spanish name has been shortened to Los Angeles.

Many geographical names in the Southwest are also Spanish: Sierra Nevada ("snowy mountain ridge"); Colorado ("red") River; Rio Grande ("great river"). Spanish words, too, have made their way into the English language. You probably know the meaning of such Spanish words as *plaza, corral, rodeo, patio, siesta, adobe, avocado.*

Our oldest city. The oldest city in the United States was settled not by England but by Spain. St. Augustine, Florida, was more than forty years old when the first English settlers came to Jamestown, Virginia. Started in 1565 to protect the land Ponce de León had discovered, St. Augustine was laid out like a city of Spain with a plaza or square in the center. A Spanish fort begun in the 1630's is still standing today. Other Spanish landmarks also remain — the cathedral, the ancient schoolhouse, and the oldest house of any kind in the United States. St. Augustine today is a resort city and a shipping center.

● Have students check the meanings of these words in a dictionary.

Bring road maps to class and have students plan routes between specific places. Ask them to use directional terms to describe their routes.

GAINING SKILL

Reading Maps: Tracing Routes and Finding Directions

A map allows you to find out how to get from one place to another. It can be used to plan the route for a long vacation trip. It can also be used to follow the routes of explorers and conquerors of centuries ago.

To understand routes you first need to know how to find directions. Many maps have a symbol such as an arrow to show you which way is north. Once you know that, you can figure out where east, west, and south are. Sometimes you may also need to use the words for intermediate directions: northeast, southeast, northwest, and southwest.

On pages 78–80, you read how Cortés landed in Mexico at a place the Spanish named Veracruz and how he went on to de-feat the Aztecs. The map below tells the same story in a different way. Use the information on the map to answer the following questions.

1. From what city in Cuba did Cortés begin his voyage? What bodies of water did he cross? In what direction did he sail?
2. What peninsula did the Spanish sail around? In what directions did they go to round that peninsula?
3. After landing at Veracruz, in what direction did the Spanish forces travel as they made their way to Cempoala?
4. After leaving Cempoala what Aztec towns did Cortés pass through on his way to Tenochtitlán?

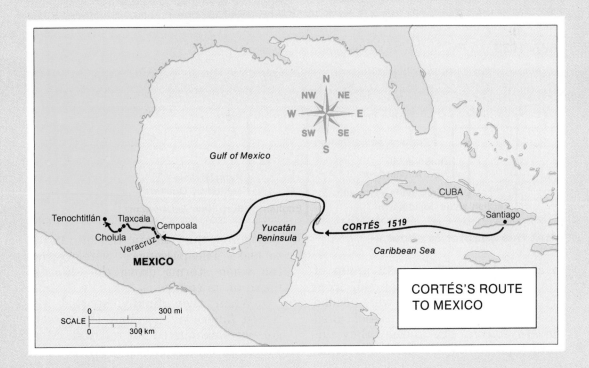

CORTÉS'S ROUTE TO MEXICO

Vocabulary preview: charter, proprietor, indentured servant, representative government, proprietary colony, plantation, chronological, century, decade

English Settlers Start Colonies in North America

1607–1733   See pp. T18–T19 for chapter teaching strategies.

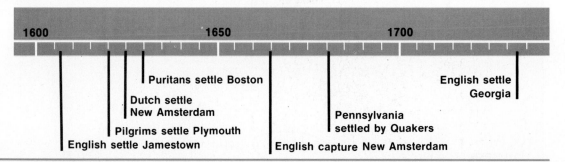

1600   1650   1700

Puritans settle Boston

Dutch settle New Amsterdam

Pilgrims settle Plymouth

English settle Jamestown

English settle Georgia

Pennsylvania settled by Quakers

English capture New Amsterdam

What this chapter is about —

In September, 1620, a small group of brave men and women set sail from Plymouth, England. They were headed for North America in a tiny vessel called the *Mayflower*. The journey they undertook proved to be a hard one. Half-way across the Atlantic the ship began to leak. The passengers were worried too when storms drove the ship far north of its course.

When they finally spotted the North American shoreline, the passengers were exhausted but relieved. Most waited in the *Mayflower* while some of

96

● Have students research some of the hardships connected with ocean voyages of that time. (for example, spoiled food, lack of water, illness, storms, crowding)

● See p. T18 for a strategy that asks students to explore the factors involved in planning colonies.

◀ Late in 1620 the *Mayflower* brought the Pilgrims to North America. There they started a colony and called it Plymouth.

their group searched the coast for a place to go ashore. During the month of waiting one of the women, Susannah White, gave birth to a baby boy. At last the search party located a suitable place for a settlement, one that they called Plymouth. After three months at sea, the newcomers could now start to build homes. They could begin their new lives in America.

Even before the group landed at Plymouth, another English settlement had been made far to the south in what is now Virginia. In the years that followed, still other groups landed along the coast of North America. These peo-ple came to the new land for many different reasons. Most of them were English men and women, though there were also people from other countries. Out of the various settlements started by these people grew colonies, which, in turn, developed into the United States of America. In this chapter you will read about the early beginnings of our country. As you read the story of the English colonies, look for answers to these questions:

1. Why and how did people go to the English colonies?
2. How did the first successful English colony get its start?
3. How were the New England Colonies started?
4. What Southern Colonies were started?
5. How were the Middle Colonies started?

1 Why and How Did People Go to the English Colonies?

You remember that while Spain was building its huge colonial empire, England was still a small and weak country. England's growing strength was shown, however, when English ships defeated the Spanish Armada. By the early 1600's, English people began to take an interest in starting colonies of their own in North America.

At that time, the only way to cross the ocean was in small sailing ships. These were usually crowded and uncomfortable, and they were at the mercy of the wind and weather. It might take months to make the crossing, or the ships might be lost in the Atlantic gales and never reach their destination. Moreover, North America was little known. Why, then, were English men and women willing to undergo the hardships that lay ahead of them if they became colonists?

Of course, some of them went to North America in a spirit of adventure just as the Spaniards did, hoping to find gold. But most of the English colonists had other reasons. Let us see what they were.

THE SETTLERS SEEK FREEDOM

America means freedom to earn a better living. There were several reasons ★ why English men and women were ready to leave England for America. For one thing, most of the English people had once been farmers. They had rented land from wealthy landowners

97

★ See p. T18 for strategies that ask students to examine reasons for English colonization.

Why English Settlers Went to America

"You can't farm my land any longer. I can make more money raising sheep."

"You go to the same church the king goes to, or you'll go to jail!"

and raised crops. But there came a time when the landowners could make more money by raising sheep and selling the wool to be made into clothing. So the landowners fenced off much of the farmland and made it into pastures for sheep. Only a few persons were needed to tend the large flocks that grazed on the land where formerly many people had lived and worked.

For this reason large numbers of unfortunate people were not only homeless but jobless as well. They wandered about looking for work. Many were forced to steal or beg for food. The government in England treated such wanderers very harshly. But America offered these people a chance to make a better living.

America means greater freedom to own land. In England in the early 1600's, there were many people who could never hope to own land. Land belonged chiefly to the upper classes and was handed down to the oldest son, so that younger sons had no land of their own. But in America there was

so much land that even poor people could become landowners.

America means freedom of religion. There was still another reason why people left England. In Europe in the 1600's rulers usually controlled the religion of their subjects. People were not free to worship as they wished. In England, for example, the people were supposed to accept the monarch as the head of the Church of England. They were expected to attend the services of this church, agree to its teachings, and give money for its support.

Many English people did not like these religious restrictions. Devout Catholics could not accept the teachings of the Church of England, which differed from those of the Catholic Church. They also believed it wrong to accept anyone but the Pope in Rome as the rightful head of the Church. On the other hand, there were people who felt that the Church of England was too much like the Catholic Church. These people wanted either to make more changes in the Church of England or to

"The king will do all the governing from now on. He doesn't want any complaints from you!"

"In America there are acres of land, just for the taking — gold, too, and furs! Just sign here for your passage!"

separate from it entirely and set up their own church organizations. But all who did not obey the religious laws of England, no matter what the reason, were likely to be severely punished. Many English men and women wished to go far away, to America, and there be free to worship as they pleased.

America means freedom to share in government. Although the people in England during the 1600's had more rights than those in many lands, they were not satisfied with their government. King James I (who followed Queen Elizabeth) and his son Charles I believed that God had given to kings the right to govern their kingdoms. James and Charles thought that their subjects should accept without question whatever the king felt was good for them. Many English people believed they were losing their rights under such a government. If they went to colonies in America, might they not regain the right to share in their government? They were willing to trade the comforts of their old homes for freedom in a new land.

COLONIES ARE STARTED

Suppose you were an English person of the 1600's and you wanted to settle in America for one of the reasons just described. How could you get there? You would have to get in touch with people who were interested in starting colonies.

Trading companies finance colonies. No matter what your personal reason for going to America might be, most of the people who wanted to establish colonies were interested in making money. You remember how rich the Portuguese merchants had grown from their trade with India. English merchants wanted colonies in America for the same reason — they hoped to grow rich by starting colonies and trading with them. But not many individual merchants had enough money to fit out ships and to stand the losses if their ships sank. So groups of merchants formed trading companies. Each merchant paid in a share of the money needed, and each expected to receive a share of the profits.

99

A charter must be obtained. Besides money for ships and supplies, two other things were necessary before a colony could be started. These were (1) permission to settle in a certain region; and (2) the right to set up a government there. Permission to settle and to establish a government was granted by the Crown (monarch) in a document, or paper,
● called a **charter.** Usually charters were given to trading companies. Sometimes, however, they were given to rich nobles who were friends of the monarch. Nobles who started colonies were called **proprietors.** Both proprietors and trading companies needed men and women willing to make the long, dangerous voyage to colonies in America. So, if you wanted to settle in America, you would find it necessary to seek out a proprietor or a trading company and make the necessary arrangements.

Poor people can go to America. If you had some money, as many colonists did, you would be expected to pay for your passage and for your supplies. But if you had no money, you could still get to the colonies, provided you were willing to give up your freedom for a few years. You could make a bargain with the ship's captain for your passage. He would transport you without cost and would collect the price of your passage from someone in the colony who wanted to buy your services. You would then have to work for this person during a certain period of time — from four to seven years. You would be called an **indentured servant.** When you had ★ served out your time, you could then take up land of your own. Giving four to seven years of one's life for passage money to cross the Atlantic may seem to us like a hard bargain, but thousands of people seized the opportunity to

People from Africa were taken to Virginia and sold to the English settlers, as servants at first and then as slaves.

★ Ask students to compare the obligations of indentured servants with those of medieval serfs (p. 28).

come to the English colonies as indentured servants.

Slavery is introduced in the English colonies. There was one group of people who came to America against their will. These were Africans, the first of whom were brought to Virginia in the early 1600's as indentured servants. Like other indentured servants, the first Africans in the English colonies could gain their freedom in four to seven years. But before long an important change took place. White colonists began to treat Africans as slaves and required them to work in bondage for life.

Most of the men and women who were sent to America as slaves came from the western coast of Africa (page 37). Slavery had long existed in West Africa, but it was different from the slavery that was to develop in America. For one thing, slaves in Africa could often win their freedom. And usually they were thought of as family members.

As colonies were established in America, Europeans began to buy African slaves and ship them across the Atlantic. As the slave trade grew, it became very cruel. Thousands, and then millions, of people were taken from their villages in Africa, marched to the coast, and sold into slavery. Then they were loaded onto ships for the long ocean voyage to America. To carry as many people as they could, ship captains crowded the men and women into tiny spaces. The people were held in chains so they could not resist or escape by jumping overboard. So much did the Africans want freedom that many preferred drowning in the sea to slavery. Those Africans who survived the ocean crossing were sent to work on the islands of the Caribbean. Others were sent to colonies in North or South America.

You can tell from this account of how Africans came to America that their situation was very different from that of the English people who decided of their own will to come to the new land. Nevertheless, black people were to play an important part in the settling and development of the English colonies.

Now that we have seen what kinds of people became colonists and what arrangements had to be made to get colonies started, let us turn to the story of how the first English colonies actually got under way.

▶ **CHECK UP**   See Teacher's Key.

1. For what reasons did English people settle in America?
2. **(a)** What was a trading company? **(b)** What things were needed in order to start a colony?
3. What was the difference between an indentured servant and a slave?

2 How Did the First Successful English Colony Get Its Start?

Starting a settlement in a new and distant land, as you can well imagine, was far from easy. Indeed, the first attempts of English people to start a colony in America met with failure.

Sir Walter Raleigh's attempt to start a colony fails. In the latter part of the 1500's, at a time when the English sea dogs were swooping down on Spanish treasure ships, there lived an adventur-

● Students may want to use the world map in the atlas (see back of book) to list present-day countries along the west coast of Africa.

Jamestown was England's first successful colony in North America. This picture shows how it probably looked in 1607.

ous Englishman named Sir Walter Raleigh. Raleigh persuaded Queen Elizabeth to let him try to establish a colony in America. He sent out an expedition that explored the coast of what is now North Carolina and found good soil and favorable climate. To this general region the name of Virginia was given.

Although Raleigh spent a large sum of money, his efforts to start a colony in America ended in failure. A group of colonists sent out to the island of Roanoke, off the Carolina coast, mysteriously disappeared. When a ship from England visited Roanoke some years later, it found no sign of the colony; the fort was deserted and the people had vanished. To this day no one knows exactly what happened to the lost colony of Roanoke. After this failure, twenty years passed before another attempt was made to start an English colony.

Jamestown is started. On a day ★ late in April, 1607, three little ships sailed into the mouth of Chesapeake Bay. The men aboard them had spent many long and dreary days crossing the Atlantic. But relief filled their hearts as they drew near the shores that were clad in the soft green of spring. Near the southern end of the bay they found the mouth of a wide river. Guiding their

102

● Mention that the first child born in an English colony was Virginia Dare, born in Roanoke, 1587.

★ Have students locate Jamestown (map, p. 108).

● See p. T18 for a strategy that calls for students to list reasons that explain Jamestown's success.

vessels slowly up this river, they finally chose a pleasant spot to go ashore. There they set to work to build a village.

These men who arrived in America in 1607 were colonists sent out by the London Company. The London Company had been formed to develop trade in North America. It had a charter from King James I to make settlements along the coast of what are now the states of Virginia and North Carolina. In honor of James I, the colonists named the river the James and their village Jamestown. (See map, page 108.)

Life is difficult in Jamestown. Hardships and dangers awaited these colonists in the unknown wilderness. They fell sick from drinking the river water and from the dread fever carried by mosquitoes from nearby swamps. They feared the Indians, who had many villages in the area and were ruled by a strong chief. And they were weakened by lack of food. Even though food was scarce, quite a few of the colonists foolishly spent their time digging for gold instead of planting crops. Many of the men were unused to hard work and considered themselves too good to labor with their hands. For food, therefore, the colonists depended on wild fowl and animals, the scanty supplies that might come from England, and what corn they could obtain from the Indians. By autumn of the first year barely a third of the men who had first set foot at Jamestown were still alive.

John Smith becomes the leader. Very likely the little settlement would have perished completely in those early years but for the efforts of one man, Captain John Smith. It was Captain Smith who saw to it that defenses were built against Indian attacks. He was firm in his dealings with the Indians and thus forced them to be cautious about attacking the new colony. Smith also insisted that the men work, that they plant corn for food and not spend their time digging for gold. He established

the policy of "no work, no food." In September, 1609, however, Captain Smith was badly burned by an explosion of gunpowder. He went back to England to receive treatment for his burns and to escape some violent quarrels with other colonists. He never returned to Virginia.

Jamestown is saved. ● Dark days fell on Jamestown after the departure of Captain John Smith. There was so little food in the winter of 1609–1610 that the colonists later called it the "starving time." When spring came, the 60 men who remained alive were ready to give up and go back to England. But just as they reached the mouth of the river, they met ships bringing supplies and more colonists. Greatly encouraged, they returned to the settlement. Jamestown was saved from failure.

Through the leadership of Captain John Smith, the Jamestown settlement was able to survive its first difficult years.

103

Ætatis suæ 21. A.° 1616.

Some Indians became friendly with the Virginia colonists. Pocahontas, the daughter of an Indian chief, married John Rolfe, one of the Jamestown settlers. She sailed with him to England, where this portrait was painted in 1616.

The colony grows stronger. Fortunately, the bitter struggle of these early years at Jamestown was not repeated. More settlers came from England, among them men who were skilled in carpentry and other useful trades. The early settlers at Jamestown had been men and boys, but in 1619 a shipload of women settlers came over from England. Now the men were able to marry and establish homes.

One of the early settlers, named John Rolfe, learned from the Indians how to produce fine tobacco. This plant was unknown to Europeans until they learned about it from the American Indians. Smoking soon became popular in England, so the Jamestown colonists found it easy to sell all the tobacco they could grow. The colony at last began to prosper. Workers were needed to grow

tobacco, and many white indentured servants were imported. About this time, a Dutch ship brought twenty people from Africa to Jamestown to work in the tobacco fields. As you read earlier, these Africans were indentured servants, not slaves. Small farms gave way to much larger ones. The colony now spread far beyond the limits of Jamestown and became known as Virginia.

The settlers are given a voice in their government. Jamestown began as a colony of the London Company, and for some time it was ruled by men selected by the company. In 1619, however, the Virginia settlers were allowed to choose their own representatives to help make laws for the colony. This group of representatives was called the House of Burgesses. The colonists now had a voice in their government.

People who choose the men and women to make their laws are said to have **representative government.** The establishment of the House of Burgesses in 1619 is important because it helped plant the idea of representative government, or self-government, in the colonies of England.

———

Jamestown was the first successful English settlement in what is now the United States. During the next hundred years or so, twelve other English colonies were established on the Atlantic coast. So that the story of their early years will be clearer, we will divide these colonies into three groups: (1) the New England Colonies; (2) the Southern Colonies; (3) the Middle Colonies. ★

▶ **CHECK UP** See Teacher's Key.

1. **(a)** Why was life hard for the early settlers of Jamestown? **(b)** How did conditions improve?
2. How did the Jamestown colonists obtain a share in their government?

104

3 How Were the New England Colonies Started?

SETTLEMENTS ARE MADE IN MASSACHUSETTS

At the same time that the first settlers were landing at Jamestown, another group of English people moved to the city of Leyden in Holland. These were men and women who at home had wished to separate from the Church of England and worship as they saw fit. For this reason, they were called Separatists. Because they had been persecuted in England, they fled to Holland. But they were not happy there. The language, customs, and people of Holland seemed strange to them. These English wanderers, or Pilgrims, as they later came to be called, did not want their children to forget English ways. Also, the Separatists were farmers who did not like working in a city. They decided to seek new homes in America.

The Pilgrims go to America. Some of the Pilgrims returned to England to make plans for their new venture. They were joined by other Separatists who wished to leave England. Because they were poor people, they had to get help. One of the trading companies agreed to furnish a ship and supplies. In return, the Pilgrims agreed to work for seven years as servants of the company. Everything they produced was to go to the company except supplies that they needed for their own use.

As you read on page 96, the *Mayflower* and its 102 passengers finally came to anchor in a harbor in what is now Massachusetts in November, 1620. The charter of the Pilgrims gave them permission to settle on land owned by the London Company in Virginia. But the land they had reached was outside the region owned by the company. What were they to do?

The Pilgrims plan a government. Before they went ashore from the *Mayflower*, some of the men gathered in the ship's cabin to discuss their problem. Because their charter did not hold good in their new location, they decided to make their own plans for managing their affairs. After thinking about the kind of life they wanted to lead, they drew up an agreement in which they said:

> In the name of God, Amen. We whose names are underwritten, . . . having undertaken . . . a voyage to plant the first colony in the northern parts of Virginia, do . . . solemnly [agree] to enact . . . such just and equal laws . . . from time to time, as shall be thought [best] for the general good of the Colony, unto which we promise all . . . obedience.

This important agreement is known as the Mayflower Compact. Later on, a governor was chosen and laws were made. When the settlement grew larger, the people elected representatives to an assembly. Here, as in Jamestown, the beginnings of self-government appeared early in the life of an English colony.

The Pilgrims settle in Plymouth. The Pilgrims landed on the bleak shore and gave the name of Plymouth to their settlement. The dangers and discomforts they faced were described by one of their leaders in these words:

> They had now no friends to welcome them, nor inns to entertain or refresh their weatherbeaten bodies, no houses or much less towns to repair to, to seek for succor [help]. . . . And for the season, it was winter, and they that know the winters of that country know them to be sharp and violent and subject to

● Help students to understand that the *Mayflower Compact* was like a contract, binding all who signed it to its terms.

cruel and fierce storms, dangerous to travel to known places, much more to search an unknown coast. Besides, what could they see but a hideous and desolate wilderness . . . ?

During the next few months, over half the little band perished of cold, hunger, and disease. When spring came, however, the remaining Pilgrims decided to stay in this new land rather than return to England. In spite of hardships, they had freedom to worship as they chose and to govern themselves.

Indians help the Plymouth settlers. Life in Plymouth became more bearable as the months passed. The Wampanoag Indians, who occupied the land where the Pilgrims settled, grew friendly with the newcomers. Squanto, an Indian from another tribe, also befriended the settlers. Squanto taught the Pilgrims how to plant corn and catch fish. Without Squanto's help and the friendship of the Wampanoags, Plymouth Colony probably would not have survived.

In the fall of 1621, the colonists held a great feast. Some settlers brought back plump turkeys from a hunting trip. Others caught cod in the bay or prepared berries and corn bread. Still others made a huge salad from wild vegetables. Ninety Indians arrived at the settlement with slain deer. The Pilgrims and the Indians ate a splendid meal together to celebrate their friendship and survival. They called the meal ● the feast of Thanksgiving, and it became their tradition to hold such a feast every fall.

As time passed, the Plymouth colony grew stronger, though it never became very large. Under Governor William Bradford the Pilgrims finally settled their debts with the London merchants and obtained the rights to the land they lived on.

★ **The Puritans establish Massachusetts Bay Colony.** Plymouth Colony soon had a neighbor. This was the Massachusetts Bay Colony, which was started by English people who also sought religious freedom in America. These people were called Puritans because they wanted to change or "purify" the Church of England. Like the Separatists, they were persecuted by the English government for their religious beliefs. Most of these Puritans were well-to-do, middle-class English people. Some already belonged to a trading company called the Massachusetts Bay Company, which had been granted land and a charter by the king. They decided they would cross the Atlantic Ocean and start a colony in Massachusetts.

The Puritans arrive in Boston. In the spring of 1630, eleven vessels filled with colonists left England for Massachusetts. A Puritan leader named John Winthrop was the governor of the colony. There was no trouble getting colonists, for at that time the Puritans were being persecuted more severely than ever in England. Before the summer was over, 2,000 men, women, and children had settled in Boston or nearby.

Although many more colonists arrived in the next ten years, the Puritans had a constant struggle to make a living on the rocky soil of New England. The winters were cruelly cold, and large numbers of people died of disease. But the Puritans were courageous people, and they had able leaders. Before long, mills were built to grind grain and saw lumber, and a few shops were started to make much-needed household articles. The colonists began to carry on a lively trade with England, exchanging furs, fish, and lumber for goods they needed.

The Puritans refuse religious freedom to others. Strange though it may seem to us, the Puritans who had come to Massachusetts to worship in their own way were not willing to allow others the same freedom. Persons who were not Puritans were allowed to live in the Bay Colony if they obeyed Puritan rules, but

★ See p. T19 for a strategy that calls for students to compare the Pilgrims with the Puritans.

● See p. T19 for a strategy dealing with the development of religious freedom in the English colonies.

they could have no share in the government. They had to pay taxes to support the church, but they were not permitted to criticize it. As you can see, there was no real religious freedom among the Puritans. The idea of respecting the religion of others, or religious tolerance, was unheard of in early Boston.

Massachusetts Bay and Plymouth unite. Massachusetts Bay Colony, which began with a larger number of people than Plymouth, grew more rapidly than its neighbor. In 1691 the two colonies united under the name of Massachusetts.

The Pilgrims came to America to worship in freedom and to govern themselves. Here you see a famous painting of the Pilgrims on their way to church.

OTHER COLONIES ARE SETTLED IN NEW ENGLAND

Rhode Island is started. Soon after the Bay Colony was started, a young minister named Roger Williams began to preach ideas that displeased the Puritan leaders. He said that the white people had no right to the land they had cleared and settled unless they bought it from the Indians. He also insisted that every person had the right to worship God as he or she saw fit.

The Puritan leaders were so angered by these ideas that they decided to send Roger Williams back to England. Learning of their plans, Williams fled from Massachusetts Bay Colony early in 1636. He was aided by the Indians, who looked on him as their friend.

107

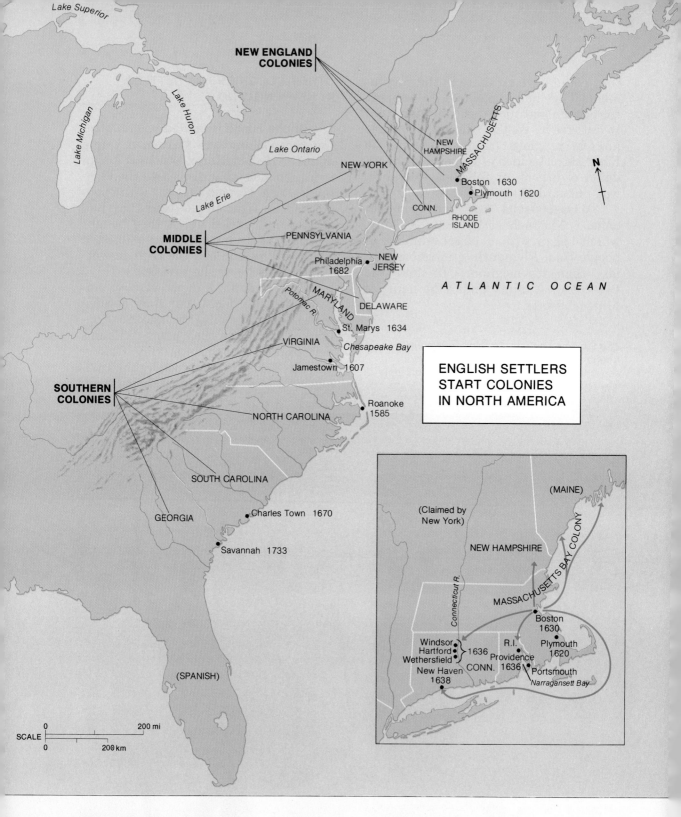

Lake Superior

Lake Michigan

Lake Huron

Lake Ontario

Lake Erie

NEW ENGLAND COLONIES

NEW HAMPSHIRE

MASSACHUSETTS

• Boston 1630
• Plymouth 1620

CONN.

RHODE ISLAND

N

NEW YORK

MIDDLE COLONIES

PENNSYLVANIA

Philadelphia 1682

NEW JERSEY

DELAWARE

MARYLAND

Potomac R.

St. Marys 1634

Chesapeake Bay

VIRGINIA

Jamestown 1607

ATLANTIC OCEAN

Roanoke 1585

SOUTHERN COLONIES

NORTH CAROLINA

SOUTH CAROLINA

GEORGIA

Charles Town 1670

Savannah 1733

(SPANISH)

ENGLISH SETTLERS START COLONIES IN NORTH AMERICA

(MAINE)

(Claimed by New York)

NEW HAMPSHIRE

MASSACHUSETTS BAY COLONY

Connecticut R.

Windsor
Hartford
Wethersfield

1636

New Haven 1638

R.I.

Providence

CONN. 1636

Boston 1630

Plymouth 1620

Portsmouth

Narragansett Bay

SCALE

0   200 mi

0   200 km

MAP STUDY The thirteen English colonies stretched along the Atlantic coast. Notice that people from Massachusetts helped to settle the other New England colonies (see small map). (a) What were the four New England Colonies? (b) Name the Middle Colonies. (c) Name the Southern Colonies.

See Teacher's Key.

Anne Hutchinson angered the Puritan leaders of Massachusetts by challenging their teachings. She was brought to trial (above) and was then forced to leave the colony.

He moved southward from one Indian village to another until he reached the shores of Narragansett Bay. There he settled, with five friends, at the place where the city of Providence now stands. Other settlers also made their homes nearby, and in time Roger Williams's colony became known as Rhode Island.

Another person who fled to Rhode Island was a Puritan named Anne Hutchinson. The Puritan ministers in Massachusetts had always believed that people should follow strict rules of behavior. Anne Hutchinson challenged this by stating that each human being had direct, personal contact with God, without the need of church or ministers. She discussed her ideas in religious meetings in her home, and so angered the Puritan ministers that they forced her from the Massachusetts colony in 1637. Anne Hutchinson and some of her followers fled to the colony of Rhode Island, where they established the town of Portsmouth.

The Rhode Islanders did not agree among themselves on many questions, but they did hold fast to one idea — that each person had the right to worship God in his or her own way. For the first time, religious freedom was permitted by the people of an American colony. Gradually, the idea of freedom of religion, like the idea of self-government, came to be accepted in the remaining English colonies.

Colonists from Massachusetts settle Connecticut and New Hampshire. The Rhode Islanders were not the only people who left Massachusetts Bay Colony. A pastor of the Bay Colony, Thomas Hooker, had a number of followers who wanted to worship in their own way. They also thought they could find better land for farming. In the same year that Roger Williams began his settlement at Providence (1636), Hooker and his followers left Massachusetts. Taking their cattle and whatever belongings they could carry, they pushed westward through the wilderness until they reached the broad Connecticut River. Hooker's group and other colonists from Massachusetts built villages at Hartford, Windsor, and Wethersfield. Still another group, seeking to follow its own ideas of worship, started a trading center at New Haven. After many years the different settlements in this region united to form a single colony. That colony was known as Connecticut.

Meanwhile, small settlements had been made north of the Bay Colony by people from England. Adventurous settlers from Massachusetts Bay joined with these groups from England to make the beginnings of the colony of New Hampshire. (Find Connecticut, Rhode Island, and New Hampshire on the map, page 108.)

109

● Ask students to write reports on the lives of Roger Williams and Anne Hutchinson.

★ Point out that Rhode Island and Connecticut didn't get charters from the king until the early 1660's.

► **CHECK UP**   See Teacher's Key.

1. **(a)** Why did the Pilgrims decide to go to America? **(b)** What help did they get? **(c)** What steps did the Pilgrims take to form a government for their colony?

2. **(a)** How was Massachusetts Bay Colony started? **(b)** Why did it grow rapidly?

3. **(a)** What other colonies were started by people from Massachusetts? **(b)** Why were these colonies established?

4 What Southern Colonies Were Started?

The settlement of one southern colony, Virginia, was described earlier in this chapter. Other southern colonies soon followed.

As we have learned, the rulers of England sometimes granted large tracts of land to nobles, who became known as owners or proprietors of this land. The proprietors rarely came to America themselves, but they held control of the land granted to them. They in turn could establish colonies and give out sections of land to settlers. Colonies established in this way on land owned by proprietors were known as **proprietary colonies.** The earliest of these proprietary colonies to be settled was Maryland.

Maryland offers religious toleration. Two shiploads of colonists landed in 1634 near the mouth of the Potomac (puh-TOH-muk) River. Here they started a settlement called St. Mary's. These people had been sent out from England to establish a colony on land given by the king to Lord Baltimore. Baltimore was a devout Catholic. He hoped not only to gain some profit from the colony but also to provide a refuge where Catholics might worship as they wished. This did not mean, however, that only Catholics could make their homes in the colony.

Many settlers soon flocked to Maryland, as Lord Baltimore's colony came to be called. For the most part, Maryland was a colony of farmers. Wealthier people and those who would bring other settlers to Maryland obtained large estates. Less fortunate people were able to purchase small farms. In addition to paying for their land, all paid a tax to the proprietor.

In time, the Catholics in the colony were outnumbered by the people of other religious beliefs. In 1649, at the urging of the proprietor, a law called the Toleration Act was passed. This act said that no one who was a Christian should be persecuted because of his or her beliefs. Under the Toleration Act both Catholics and Protestants were free to worship in their own ways. The Toleration Act of Maryland was another important step toward religious freedom in the colonies.

COLONIAL HOUSES

EARLY BARK WIGWAM   LOG HOUSE   SALT-BOX HOUSE   DUTCH HOUSE

● See p. T19 for a strategy that asks students to discuss agriculture in the Southern Colonies.

Proprietors settle the Carolinas.
South of Maryland was Virginia, and south of Virginia lay a vast stretch of land which Charles II, king of England, had given to a group of nobles. They called the region Carolina after the Latin name for Charles, *Carolus*. In 1670, a group sent out by these proprietors started a settlement which they called Charles Town (later Charleston). Even before this date, people from Virginia had made their way into the northern part of Carolina.

In time, the colony broke up into two parts. North Carolina included the settlements started by Virginians. South Carolina included Charles Town and other nearby settlements. (Look at the map on page 108.) South Carolina, especially, grew rapidly. The fertile soil and warm climate encouraged tobacco raising. Later on, rice also became an important crop. The fine harbor of Charles Town made it easy to trade with England.

Georgia is started by James Oglethorpe. Between South Carolina and Spanish Florida lay a large tract of land which was not colonized for a long time. Finally, a man named James Oglethorpe made a settlement on this land. There were two main reasons for establishing a colony here: (1) The English were anxious to prevent Spain from extending its settlements north from Florida. Establishing an English colony south of the Carolinas would help to keep the Spaniards out. (2) Oglethorpe was much interested in the unfortunate people who were sent to English prisons simply because they had committed some trifling crime. Oglethorpe hoped to give these prisoners, who were cruelly treated, a new start in life. He and a number of other men obtained permission from the king to make settlements in this region.

It was not until 1733 that Oglethorpe brought about a hundred settlers from England. They started a village which they called Savannah. The colony itself was named Georgia after George II, who was then king of England. Many people from the British Isles settled in Georgia, as well as people from other countries in Europe, such as Italy and Austria. A group of Portuguese Jews settled in Georgia too. Over the years the colony grew slowly but steadily. Like the Carolinas, Georgia became chiefly a colony of large farms.

Slavery spreads throughout the Southern Colonies. As the Southern Colonies grew, **plantations** were established in Virginia, South Carolina, and Maryland. These plantations were large farms where tobacco, rice, or other crops were grown for trade with England. Often the owners of the plantations could not find enough people to work in their fields. As a result, they began to buy more and more African slaves.

Why did the colonists enslave black Africans? There were two main reasons.

(1) For one thing, the colonists wanted workers on their farms who would not run away. Indentured servants from Europe often ran away and moved to another colony. And even if indentured servants did not run away, after a certain period of years they became free to leave and work for themselves. Enslaved Africans, on the other hand, had a harder time running away. Because their skin color set them apart from Europeans, it was fairly easy to capture a runaway slave.

(2) Most colonists believed that people with a different appearance and religion were not entitled to the same rights as Europeans. Therefore Europeans found it easy to justify buying African slaves.

Slavery existed throughout the English colonies. New England merchants, for example, bought slaves as personal servants. But since the farms of New England were small and did not

111

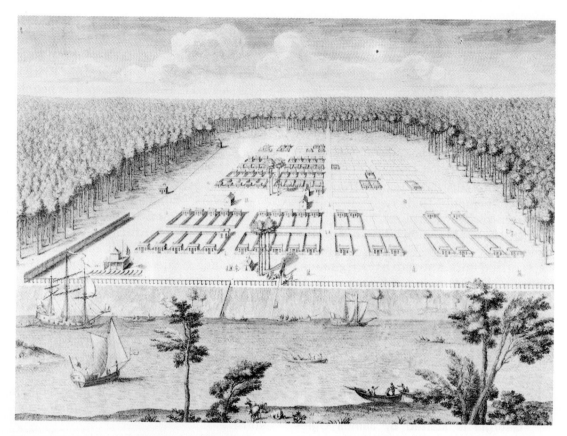

Savannah, Georgia, was started in 1733. The colonists had to cut down trees and clear stumps before the rows of houses could be built.

require many workers, slavery did not take a strong hold in that region. It thrived in the South, however, where more and more slaves were brought to America from Africa to work on the large plantations.

▶ **CHECK UP**   See Teacher's Key.

1. **(a)** Why was the Maryland colony started? **(b)** How was religious freedom established there?
2. How were the Carolinas settled and developed?
3. For what two main reasons was Georgia started?
4. Why did slavery spread in the Southern Colonies?

5 How Were the Middle Colonies Started?

Between New England and the Southern Colonies there grew up another group of settlements, known as the Middle Colonies. Not all of these started as English settlements. If you look at the map on page 113, you will see that New York and the Hudson River region were originally settled by the Dutch. Perhaps you remember that Henry Hudson discovered this river while he was sailing

● See p. T19 for a strategy that asks students to examine evidence of the Dutch heritage in America.

for the Dutch and that he claimed that region for Holland. (See pages 60–61 to review Hudson's explorations.)

The Dutch establish New Netherland. In the early 1620's, the Dutch started a settlement, called New Amsterdam, on the island of Manhattan. The Dutch also occupied the entire Hudson River valley, and their settlements extended from New Amsterdam to Fort Orange, where Albany, New York, is today. Large estates along the Hudson were given by the Dutch to all landlords, or patroons, who brought 50 settlers with them to work the land. Smaller plots of land were given free to others who wished to do their own farming. The whole colony was called New Netherland. In time the Dutch spread their control south to the Delaware River. There they took over some settlements that had been made earlier by Sweden. Fur trading with the Indians was the most important business of the Dutch, and New Netherland soon became a prosperous colony.

New York and New Jersey take the place of New Netherland. The Dutch colony of New Netherland greatly troubled the English. By looking at the map on this page you can see how completely New Netherland (New York) separated the New England colonies from the English settlements to the south. So long as New Netherland belonged to the Dutch, the English colonies could not be joined. Then too, the English cast ★ envious eyes on the splendid harbor at New Amsterdam, with its thriving trade. Bitter feeling between England and Holland in Europe gave the English an excuse to attack New Netherland.

In 1664 an English fleet appeared in the harbor of New Amsterdam. The Dutch colony was governed at that time by Peter Stuyvesant (STY-vuh-sant), a peppery old man with a wooden leg. Stuyvesant was eager to offer battle, but the people of New Amsterdam re-

fused to back him up. So, in spite of his fussing and fuming, the settlement surrendered without striking a blow, and New Netherland became an English possession. The Duke of York, the brother of the king of England, was made proprietor of the former Dutch territory, and the colony was renamed New York in his honor. The town of New Amsterdam became New York also. The land east of the Delaware River was granted by the duke to two English nobles, who gave their colony the name of New Jersey.

MAP STUDY   See Teacher's Key.
The Dutch and Swedes made the first settlements in what later became New York, New Jersey, and Delaware. The Dutch took over the Swedish colonies in 1655, but the English seized all the Dutch lands in 1664. (a) What towns did the Dutch start? (b) What town did the Swedes settle?

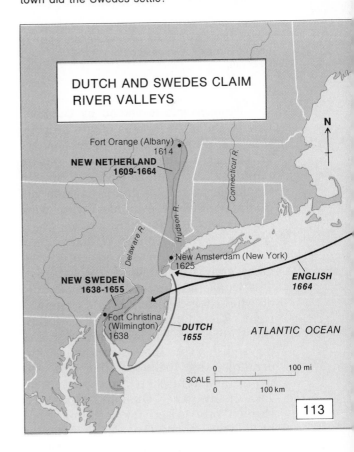

DUTCH AND SWEDES CLAIM RIVER VALLEYS

Fort Orange (Albany) 1614
NEW NETHERLAND 1609-1664
Connecticut R.
Delaware R.
Hudson R.
New Amsterdam (New York) 1625
ENGLISH 1664
NEW SWEDEN 1638-1655
Fort Christina (Wilmington) 1638
DUTCH 1655
ATLANTIC OCEAN
N
SCALE 0 — 100 mi
0 — 100 km

113

★ Have students discuss why a good harbor would be valuable to a colony.

William Penn, an English Quaker, established Pennsylvania as a place where Quakers and people of other religions could worship in freedom.

Pennsylvania is settled by Quakers. One of the most famous of the proprietors was William Penn. His father was an admiral in the British navy and an important man in England. Through his father young William became acquainted with the nobles who were making settlements in America.

As a young man, William Penn joined one of the most persecuted religious groups in England, the Quakers. The Quakers believed that they should do what their consciences told them was right. They not only refused to follow the Church of England but in many ways disobeyed the government. For example, they believed that war was wrong and refused to take part in it. Like many other Quakers, Penn was thrown into prison for teaching what he believed to be the truth. After he was released, he was anxious to start a colony where Quakers would not be persecuted.

It happened that the king owed Penn's father a large sum of money. When his father died, Penn told the king he was willing to take a grant of land in America in payment of the debt. The king agreed to Penn's suggestion. No doubt he was very pleased to pay his debt in land and at the same time get many Quakers to leave England. The king gave the name of Pennsylvania (or "Penn's woodlands") to the region west of the Delaware River between the present states of New York and Maryland.

Penn's colony becomes prosperous. William Penn arrived in Pennsylvania with a group of settlers in 1682. They laid out the capital city according to Penn's plans and named it Philadelphia, which means "City of Brotherly Love." Penn believed in religious freedom and welcomed people of all faiths to his colony. Large numbers of Quakers and English people of other religions flocked to Pennsylvania. People from other lands also settled in the colony. Among them were thrifty and hard-working Germans who had been treated harshly in their own country. These Germans came to be known as Pennsylvania Dutch.[1]

Penn was a wise and kind proprietor who treated his colonists fairly and expected honest work from them. The colonists found that land in Pennsylvania was cheap and easy to get. They had little fear of Indian attacks because Penn made friends with the neighboring Indians and treated them honestly. For these reasons, Pennsylvania grew rapidly and became a successful colony. By ★ the late 1700's, Philadelphia had become the largest and busiest city in the thirteen English colonies.

[1]In the German language, the word for "German" is *Deutsch* (doytch), which the English settlers mispronounced as "Dutch."

114

★ See p. T19 for a strategy that will help students to identify factors that made Pennsylvania successful.

Delaware becomes a separate colony. Unfortunately, Penn's first grant of land did not include any coastline. Penn was able to obtain from the Duke of York the land now known as Delaware. This land, which had first been controlled by the Swedes, then by the Dutch, and finally by the Duke of York, became a part of Pennsylvania. A number of years later it was made into a separate colony under the name of Delaware.

Thus ends the story of how the thirteen English colonies were established. Our next chapter will show how people lived in these English colonies.

See Teacher's Key.

 CHECK UP

1. **(a)** Where did the Dutch settle in North America? **(b)** Why did the English object? **(c)** What happened to the Dutch colony?
2. **(a)** Who established and settled Pennsylvania? **(b)** Why did it become a successful colony? **(c)** How were New Jersey and Delaware settled and how did they become English colonies?

CHECK UP ON CHAPTER 4

See Teacher's Key.

Words to Know

1. Pilgrim
2. charter
3. proprietor
4. tolerance
5. Puritan
6. Quaker
7. plantation
8. representative government
9. indentured servant
10. religious freedom
11. trading company
12. proprietary colony

Places to Locate

1. Jamestown
2. Plymouth
3. Boston
4. Providence
5. New Haven
6. Savannah
7. Charleston
8. New York (city)
9. Philadelphia
10. Delaware River
11. Connecticut River
12. Hartford

Facts to Remember

1. How did each of the following take part in the settling of an English colony? Name the colony and tell why the person was important. **(a)** John Smith **(b)** Roger Williams **(c)** Anne Hutchinson **(d)** James Oglethorpe **(e)** William Penn
2. **(a)** To what English colony did Africans first come? **(b)** Why were the Africans made slaves?
3. **(a)** What three colonies led the way in establishing freedom of religion? **(b)** Explain why religious freedom was emphasized in each of those colonies.

Skills to Practice

1. Make a time line for the period 1600 to 1650. Mark off ten-year periods on the line. Then place the following dates on it: 1607, 1619, 1620, 1630, and 1649. Alongside each date write a phrase that tells why it was important. (*Example*: 1607, Jamestown started.)
2. Look at the map on page 108. **(a)** What group of colonies is shown in the inset map (the smaller map)? **(b)** What do the arrows on this map show? (Note that the arrows lead away from Massachusetts.) **(c)** What towns were started along the Connecticut River? **(d)** Were those towns southwest or southeast of Boston?

Questions to Think About

1. **(a)** Why were the first settlements in North America located near mouths of rivers or bays? **(b)** Why did people who left the earlier settlements often settle near rivers?
2. What freedoms that we cherish today had their beginnings in the English colonies?

115

3. The Southern Colonies had many large plantations while farms in New England tended to be small. How did that difference affect the spread of slavery?

4. Compare the attitude toward religious freedom in colonial Massachusetts and in colonial Pennsylvania. Which colony offered more religious freedom—Massachusetts or Pennsylvania? Explain your answer.

Linking Past and Present

Jamestown comes to life again. Visitors to Jamestown, the first English town in America, find themselves stepping back into the 1600's. Riding at anchor in the James River are full-sized models of the three tiny ships that brought the English settlers to Virginia. The old village has been rebuilt, and ladies and gentlemen in clothing of the 1600's stroll through the streets.

Visitors can step into thatch-roofed houses like those in early Jamestown and see in the museum the tools, weapons, and dishes used by the settlers. They can look at the old church tower, the foundation of the first government building, and the gravestones in the old graveyard.

Jamestown did not have a long life. After Williamsburg became the capital of Virginia in 1699, the little town was gradually abandoned. As years went by, the marshy peninsula became an island in the James River, and the town fell into ruins. But in 1956 Virginia celebrated the 350th anniversary of Jamestown by rebuilding the old town one-half mile from the original site. Now this valuable part of our American heritage lives again and will be preserved for us and for future Americans.

Mayflower II. In 1957, the *Mayflower* sailed into Plymouth Harbor once more. *Mayflower II* was sent to America as a gift of the British people. Made of sturdy oak, the new *Mayflower* had been carefully built as much like the old Pilgrim ship as possible. The captain and the crew of about 50 were experienced in handling sailing ships; all were eager for the adventure. Except for a radio and navigation instruments which were required by law, the ship was fitted out like the original. Quarters were small; there was no refrigeration. The food put aboard for the crew was similar to what the Pilgrims ate — dried and salted meat, ship's biscuit, and cheese — although some canned goods were added.

On April 20, *Mayflower II* set sail from Plymouth, England, for Plymouth, Massachusetts. People on both sides of the Atlantic waited eagerly for news of the gallant little ship and its crew. When the *Mayflower* finally appeared near Cape Cod, it was greeted by ships and aircraft of all kinds. Fifty-four days after setting sail, the *Mayflower* arrived in Plymouth Harbor. Captain and crew, dressed like Pilgrims, were rowed ashore. A great crowd cheered as they watched this "landing of the Pilgrims." *Mayflower II* is now permanently docked at Plymouth, a symbol of the courage and endurance of these early settlers of America.

The Dutch left their mark. Even though Holland held territory in North America for only a short time, we have many reminders today of the early Dutch settlers. Santa Claus, for instance, was introduced into this country by the Dutch colonists. They also introduced the game of bowling. The Dutch Reformed Church, now called the Reformed Church in America, has thousands of members today. In many parts of America people live in modern Dutch colonial houses, patterned after the old Dutch homes. These houses have sloping roofs and often a "Dutch door" — that is, a door with separate upper and lower halves. They may also have a "stoop," or porch, with two seats cozily facing each other. In some villages along the Hudson River, old stone houses built by the Dutch 300 years ago are still standing.

116

Some students may want to research the clothing of the 1600's. Have them draw pictures of the styles and display their drawings on the bulletin board.

For answers see Teacher's Key.

Have students put in chronological order important events that have taken place in your community or region.

GAINING SKILL

Building a Sense of Time

As you read this book, you will be studying events that took place over nearly a thousand years of history — from the Viking voyages to modern times. To talk about such a long span of time, people need to have some system for arranging events. History books usually present events in **chronological** order; that is, they start with the earliest events and end with the most recent ones. Chronological order is order based on time.

It is not always possible to present the whole story of America's history in chronological order. For example, in Chapter 2 you read about the French explorers who traveled down the Mississippi. Some of those expeditions took place in the 1670's and 1680's, long after the settling of the first English colonies described in this chapter. But it would be confusing to interrupt the story of the English colonists to tell what the French were doing a thousand miles farther west. Thus, a history book may also group events together by topic or subject.

How can you learn the order of important events? First, of course, you should notice dates as you read. Dates are important in your study of history. They are needed to (1) tell when important events took place, (2) keep events in the right order, and (3) estimate the number of years from the beginning to the end of a historical period.

There are special terms that make learning dates easier. One important term is **century.** A century is a period of one hundred years. Most of the colonies discussed in this chapter were started within a single century, the 1600's.

You may have heard people say that we live in the twentieth century. That term is another way of saying the 1900's. The table below shows the system for numbering centuries.

Years	Century
1 - 100	First century
101 - 200	Second century
201 - 300	Third century
301 - 400	Fourth century

Thus, following this system the 1800's are the nineteenth century and the 1900's are the twentieth century.

Sometimes we need to know more than the century in which an important event occurred. For that reason events are often grouped in **decades** (DEK-aydz). A decade is a period of ten years. The 1630's, for example, were a decade. (Read 1630's as "sixteen thirties.")

1. On a separate sheet of paper arrange the following events in chronological order.
   a. The Puritans settle Boston.
   b. England gains control of New Netherland.
   c. Jamestown is settled.
   d. English colonists establish Charles Town.
   e. The House of Burgesses is established.
   f. The Pilgrims settle at Plymouth.
2. In which of these colonies were settlements started during the decade of the 1630's? **(a)** Connecticut **(b)** Maryland **(c)** Georgia **(d)** South Carolina
3. How many decades are there in a century?

117

How Did People Live in the English Colonies?

1607–1775 See p. T20 for chapter teaching strategies.

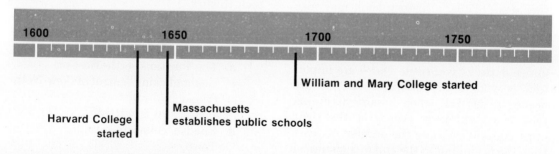

1600   1650   1700   1750

William and Mary College started

Massachusetts
establishes public schools

Harvard College
started

What this chapter is about —

In Adam's fall
We sinned all.

Thy life to mend
This Book attend.

The Cat doth play,
And after slay.

A Dog will bite
A thief at night.

An Eagle's flight
Is out of sight.

◀ By the 1750's, when this picture of Bethlehem, Pennsylvania, was painted, prosperous farm communities were found in all the colonies.

The verses you see at the bottom of page 118 are from an old schoolbook that was called the *New England Primer*. If you had been a colonist in New England in the 1700's, you would probably have learned to read and spell from this primer. As you can see, schoolbooks of colonial days were not much like ours today. In fact, life in the colonies was different from life today in many ways.

In order to understand what life was like in the English colonies, what do we need to know? Certainly we ought to know what kinds of houses the colonists lived in, how they earned their living, what clothes they wore, and what food they ate. We should also know about their schools, their religions, and their amusements. This chapter will tell you about such things, and it will also point out how ways of living differed throughout the colonies. Consider these questions as you read:

1. How did the colonists live in New England?
2. What was life like in the Southern Colonies?
3. What was life like in the Middle Colonies?
4. How did people live in the frontier region?

1 How Did the Colonists Live in New England?

In different parts of the world today, ways of living are affected by **geographical conditions.** By geographical conditions we mean such things as temperature, rainfall, soil, the land surface, and so on. For example, we should not expect the Eskimos of the cold Arctic to live as the people of hot central Africa do. In somewhat the same way, people's ways of living differed in the thirteen colonies. Of course, geographical conditions in the English colonies did not differ as much as do conditions in the Arctic and central Africa. But they varied enough to influence the lives of the colonists.

Geographical conditions in New England and the South are different. If you look at the map on page 130, you will see that inland from the Atlantic coast a line of hills and mountains extends from the northeast to the southwest. You will also notice that these hills and mountains are much closer to the coast in the North than in the South. As a result, the Southern Colonies had much more flat coastal land for farming than did the colonies in the North. Also, in the North the soil is rocky, and farmers had to work harder to grow crops. Then, too, the winters in the North are longer and colder than they are in the South. Farming at first was very important in all the colonies. Because of the different geographical conditions, however, farming remained important much longer in the Southern Colonies than in ★ the Northern Colonies.

Now look again at the map. See how many rivers lead from inland areas to the coast, like threads worked into a piece of cloth. These rivers were the highways of the colonies, because good roads did not exist. At the mouths of many of the rivers, especially in the North, were good harbors. Because of these good harbors, trade and shipping became important in the North.

● Refer students to "Linking Past and Present" (p. 134) for information that explains how New England got its name.

Keeping these geographical conditions in mind, let us examine the life of the English colonies. The easiest way to do this will be to study closely one of the sections — New England — and then to compare the others with it.

New Englanders make their living in various ways. In spite of poor soil and long, hard winters, many New Englanders were farmers. (You must remember that in colonial days it was difficult to transport food long distances, so each section of the colonies had to grow its own.) Some people, however, made their living by fishing in the ocean off the New England coast. They caught so many fish that they could not sell them all at home. Therefore, they built ships large enough to carry the fish to sell in the other colonies, in Europe, and in the West Indies. These ships brought back goods received in exchange for the fish. Many New Englanders also took part in the slave trade, transporting slaves from Africa to the Americas.

All this trade called for workers to build ships and to make their fittings (such as sails, rope, and anchors). Other workers began to make articles needed on land. In this way New England became a region of fishermen, sailors, merchants, and skilled workers as well as farmers.

Many New England workers learned their trades by serving as **apprentices.** An apprentice was a young person who learned a trade from a skilled worker — for example, a sailmaker, a carpenter, or a blacksmith. Apprentices worked for their masters for several years and lived with their masters' families. They received low wages while they were learning and a little money and some clothes when they finished their apprenticeship. By that time they had learned their trade and could work for themselves.

What was the colonial New England home like? New Englanders lived in the seaports and in small villages surrounded by farms. Their houses were plain and strongly built. If you had entered one of these houses, you would have found yourself in a small hall. To

This picture shows how skilled colonial workers poured hot metal into a mold to make brass tools and housewares.

120

one side would be the kitchen, which also served as a dining room and living room. On the other side of the hall would be a bedroom, and there would be another bedroom upstairs. The huge fireplace in the kitchen could hold logs so big that two persons were needed to put them in place. Here all the cooking was done in kettles hung over the fire or placed on the coals. The furniture was simple and homemade, and there were not many dishes or eating utensils.

Food in New England was good, and there was plenty of it. For meat, families raised cattle, pigs, and chickens and shot wild animals in the forest. Almost every family had a garden and grew many of the same kinds of vegetables we eat today. Of course there were no refrigerators and foods could not be canned as they are now. Colonial women pickled and dried vegetables and fruits for use in winter.

The family's clothes were made at home. Women spun wool from their own sheep into thread and then wove it into cloth. Skins were tanned for shoes and for harness and for men's clothing. In winter the men wore leather breeches and heavy coats. Women wore woolen dresses and, for outdoors, cloaks or capes with hoods. Boys and girls wore the same kinds of clothes as grownups. People who could afford it had Sunday clothes of fine cloth from England, but there were few ribbons, ruffles, or bright colors.

In the seaports one might see larger houses belonging to rich merchants and shipowners. These houses had expensive furniture made by skilled cabinet-makers, and the family lived in large comfortable rooms. But we must remember that all colonial houses lacked the comforts we take for granted today. They had no gas, no electricity, no central heating, no bathrooms, no running water, no telephones or television sets, no window screens, and few rugs.

The kitchen was the most important room in a colonial home. What activities took place in a kitchen like this one?

Religion is important in colonial New England. In the heart of every New England village stood its church, for the New Englanders were deeply religious. Many of them were Puritans. They were conscientious people who believed that they had to lead lives of righteousness. God was just, they believed, but He would surely punish evildoers. To the Puritans many things were evil and life was serious. They disapproved of light-hearted amusements such as dancing and playing games. The church was the center of their social life, and before or after services on Sunday everyone met friends and heard the news. The Puritan ministers were stern, God-fearing men. They had great influence among the people and were consulted on every question.

121

Skilled workers were among the leading citizens of colonial towns and cities. One of the most famous was Boston silversmith Paul Revere. This painting shows Revere holding a silver teapot—an example of his fine work.

Sundays were important days in Puritan Massachusetts. Everybody was required by law to attend church services. The people listened to long sermons both morning and afternoon. Prayers alone often lasted three quarters of an hour. The churches were unheated, and the hard benches were uncomfortable. The men sat in one part of the church, and the women and girls in another. The boys usually sat together in the balcony, and if there was any noise, the offenders were punished in front of the whole congregation. No one could work or travel on Sundays. People were expected to read the Bible and think about religion.

Not all New Englanders were Puritans, of course. In Chapter 4 you read how Roger Williams and Anne Hutchinson started settlements in Rhode Island, a colony that was open to settlers of different beliefs. The rules for behav-

122

ior on Sunday were less strict in Rhode Island than in Puritan Massachusetts.

Punishments are severe in colonial New England. The Puritans tried to make the colonists lead righteous lives by passing many strict laws. They expected these laws to be obeyed. If the laws were broken, people were punished in ways that we would consider very cruel today. There were fifteen crimes that carried the punishment of death. There were also severe punishments for less serious crimes.

Certain kinds of punishment were widely used in colonial days. People who lied might have to sit with their hands and legs fastened in a board called the stocks. Or they might have to stand on a platform with their head and hands locked in a wooden board called a pillory. There was a whipping post, also, where people accused of wrongdoing were tied up and given a certain number of lashes on the back with a whip. A man or woman sentenced to the ducking stool was tied to a chair at the end of a long pole and ducked into a pool of water. The stocks, the pillory, and the whipping post often stood in front of the church where passers-by could jeer or even throw things at the unfortunate lawbreakers.

Of course, we must remember that these punishments were also common in England in those days. It is not surprising that the stern Puritans believed strict punishment was the only way to keep people from breaking the laws.

New Englanders believe in education. Because it was very important for every Puritan to be able to read the Bible, more children in New England were sent to school than in any other section. In fact, as early as 1647, Massachusetts passed a law requiring all villages with a certain number of families to provide schools. Reading and writing and arithmetic were about the only subjects taught. Children did not learn

Students will read more about Paul Revere at the end of Chapter 8.

much more than you learn in the first few grades of school, but what they learned they learned thoroughly. Hornbooks taught them the ABC's. A hornbook was a wooden frame holding a piece of paper protected by a thin covering. Textbooks were difficult and rather dull. Books like the primer mentioned on page 119 taught religion and correct behavior along with reading. Teachers were strict. Children who misbehaved in school would be whipped.

In larger communities, there were more advanced schools called Latin grammar schools that boys, but not girls, attended. And in 1636, only six years after the colony itself was established, Massachusetts had a college. A minister named John Harvard gave all of his books and half of his money to start it. Other people contributed what they could. Today Harvard College is the oldest institution of higher learning in the United States. In the early days, however, it was not much like our idea of a college, for its chief purpose was to prepare young men to be ministers. Since only men could become ministers, no young women attended Harvard.

Reading matter increases as New England grows. Everybody has to work hard just to make a living in a newly settled country. There is little spare time for reading. It is not surprising, therefore, that for many years the colonists had few books, newspapers, or magazines. But after 1700 the greatest hardships were over and more reading matter appeared. Because New Englanders were so interested in religion, some of the first books were collections of sermons. Almanacs were an especially popular form of reading material. In them people could find useful information about crops, the weather, health hints, and so on. Almanacs were often the only reading matter in country districts. As the colonies grew older, people liked to read about their early history. And as the colonies grew larger, people read newspapers to find out what was happening outside their own settlements. But colonial newspapers were very different from those of today. They came out only once a week and were quite short. The news that colonial newspapers contained was days and even weeks old.

Ways of living in New England differed from those in the other colonies. Now that we know what life in New England was like, we can compare it with life in the Southern and Middle Colonies and on the frontier.

A HORNBOOK

CHECK UP See Teacher's Key.

1. Explain how the geography of a region can affect the life of the people.
2. In what ways did New Englanders make their living?
3. Describe a colonial New England home.
4. **(a)** In what ways did religion affect life in New England? **(b)** How was education provided for?

123

2 What Was Life Like in the Southern Colonies?

Southern climate and soil encourage the growth of plantations. The life of the South was very different from that of New England. The South even looked different. Although there were many small farms and villages in the South, the fertile plains of the region were also covered with plantations. In fact, the Southern Colonies are often called the "plantation colonies."

The people who settled in the South did not find a harsh climate or unfriendly soil to discourage them from farming, as did New Englanders. Instead, southern farmers found rich soil which easily produced valuable crops. Tobacco was the first and most important product. Later, rice and indigo (used in making dyes) were grown in South Carolina and Georgia. Such crops brought high prices, and farmers wanted to raise as much as they could. Because these crops wore out the soil, farmers wanted to let some land lie idle each year to recover its fertility. For these reasons, successful farmers bought more and more land. In this way large plantations were established.

No plantation owner could farm the land without help, because the plantations sometimes covered several hundred and even several thousand acres. The owners, as you have already read, got the workers they needed by purchasing African slaves. Slavery, therefore, became widespread in the South, especially after 1700.

Plantations require many workers. As you read in Chapter 4, African slaves were usually transported to the islands of the Caribbean and then sent to colonies in the Americas. Those who were sent to southern plantations quickly found that their new owners controlled every part of their lives. They were forced to depend on their owners for practically everything — their cabins, their food, their clothes, their tools.

Most slaves were made to work in the fields. On some large plantations, however, specially trained workers were needed. Slaves then learned trades that required much skill. The following description of such a plantation was written by the daughter of the owner:

My father had among his slaves carpenters, coopers, sawyers, blacksmiths, curriers, shoemakers, spinners, weavers and knitters. . . . His carpenters and sawyers built and kept in repair all the dwelling houses, barns, stables, plows, harrows, gates, etc., on the plantations. . . . His coopers made the hogsheads the tobacco was [packed] in. . . . The tanners and curriers . . . tanned and dressed the skins . . . and the shoemakers made them into shoes for the [slaves]. . . . The blacksmith did all the iron work required by the establishment, as making and repairing plows, harrows, teeth chains, bolts, etc., etc. The spinners, weavers, and knitters made all the coarse cloths and stockings used by the [slaves], and some of finer texture worn by the white family. . . .

My father kept no steward or clerk about him. He kept his own books and superintended, with the assistance of a trusty slave or two, and occasionally of some of his sons, all the operations at or about the house. . . .

Slaves lead hard lives. Of course, not all plantations were as large as the one described above, nor were all slaves taught trades. Most of the slaves were field hands, whose work was supervised by **overseers.** For any violation of the owners' rules, overseers punished the slaves, usually by whipping them.

124

Large farms called plantations were found throughout the Southern Colonies. This plantation, in South Carolina, was called Rice Hope.

Slaves could be sold whenever the owner wanted. The mother of a slave family might be sold to a new owner, while her children and husband had to stay with the old owner. In this way, the slave system cruelly broke up families, and there was little the enslaved people could do about it.

Black men and women did not, of course, accept slavery willingly. In many ways they sought freedom. Family life was so important that some slaves risked punishment to slip off and visit relatives on nearby plantations. Others ran away to escape unfair treatment and strict rules. But runaway slaves were usually caught and returned to their owners for severe punishment.

Not all black people are slaves. About one of every ten black persons in the colonies was free. Of the free blacks, most had been granted their freedom as a reward for loyal service. A few had earned money by doing extra work and had bought their freedom. Free blacks usually lived in the towns and cities of the Southern and Middle Colonies.

There they earned a living as servants or as skilled workers.

Commerce grows in the South. Southern planters (owners of plantations) found it profitable to raise huge crops of tobacco and other products, which they sold to England. With the profits from these crops, they bought in England many things for their personal use, such as fine furniture and clothing. In this way a thriving trade grew up between the plantation owners and the merchants of England. Such seaports as Charleston, South Carolina, and Savannah, Georgia, became the centers of this trade.

Life on a southern plantation is different from life in New England. Instead of dwelling close together in villages as did the New Englanders, most southern colonists lived far apart on their plantations. The best location for a plantation

125

● Have students locate Charleston and Savannah on a map (p. 126).

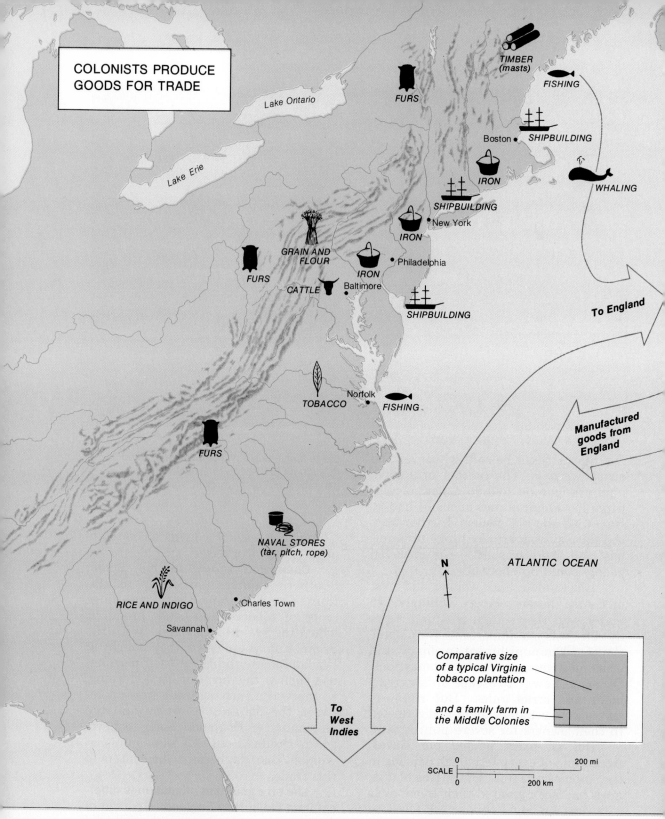

COLONISTS PRODUCE
GOODS FOR TRADE

Lake Ontario

Lake Erie

TIMBER
(masts)

FISHING

FURS

SHIPBUILDING
Boston •

IRON

WHALING

SHIPBUILDING

GRAIN AND
FLOUR

IRON
• New York

FURS

IRON
• Philadelphia

CATTLE
Baltimore •

SHIPBUILDING

To England

TOBACCO

Norfolk •
FISHING

Manufactured
goods from
England

FURS

NAVAL STORES
(tar, pitch, rope)

N

ATLANTIC OCEAN

RICE AND INDIGO
• Charles Town

Savannah •

To
West
Indies

Comparative size
of a typical Virginia
tobacco plantation

and a family farm in
the Middle Colonies

0   200 mi
SCALE
0   200 km

MAP STUDY While farming was the most important way of earning a
living in all the colonies, goods were also produced for trade. (a) What
were the chief products of the New England Colonies? (b) Of the Middle
Colonies? (c) Of the Southern Colonies?

See Teacher's Key.

was on a river so that the tobacco or other crops could be loaded onto a ship from the planter's own wharf. Near the river stood the owner's house, which was often large and grand in appearance. The kitchen was usually a separate building so that heat from the fires would not add to the discomfort of the owner's family during the warm summers. From the big house on the river the owner rode out to direct the work on the plantation.

The South and New England also differ in education and religion. In regions where ways of living were so very different, you might also expect to find differences in education and religion. Each snug New England village could have its own school, but the southern plantations were so widely scattered that children had to be taught at home. Or, in some cases, teachers from England taught the children from several plantations. The children of slaves and indentured servants, however, had little chance to get an education. Few of them learned to read and write.

The sons of some rich planters were sent to college in England. But others went to the College of William and Mary in Virginia. This college, founded in 1693, was the second in the English colonies. As in New England, young women in the South were not expected to go to college.

Just as education differed in the two sections, so did religion. Most of the southern planters belonged to the Church of England rather than to a strict Puritan church, like the one in Massachusetts. Although the Southerners went to church on Sunday, religion did not influence their lives as ● much as it did the lives of people in New England. Nor were ministers as powerful in the South as they were in New England. Punishments were severe, but people were not punished for small misdeeds.

▶ **CHECK UP**   See Teacher's Key.

1. **(a)** Why did large plantations develop in the South? **(b)** What part did slaves play in plantation life?
2. **(a)** How did the South differ from New England in home life? **(b)** In commerce? **(c)** In education? **(d)** In religion?

3 What Was Life Like in the Middle Colonies?

Between New England and the South lay the Middle Colonies. This section was not exactly like either of the others. Not only was it located between them on the map, but its way of life was midway between the other two.

The soil and climate of the Middle Colonies, for example, were better for crops than those of New England but not quite so good as those of the South. In manufacturing and commerce, the ★ Middle Colonies ranked next to New England. Their trade was carried on in two big seaports: New York at the mouth of the Hudson River, and Philadelphia near the mouth of the Delaware River. Farm products were exported, along with timber and fur. In fact, the Middle Colonies produced so much wheat and corn that they were called the "bread colonies." Grain was exported as far away as the English colonies in the West Indies.

The Middle Colonies were a mixture in other ways. There were not only big estates like the southern plantations

127

★ See p. T20 for a strategy that asks students to examine trade in the Middle Colonies.

This painting, by the American artist Edward Hicks, shows a prosperous Quaker farm in colonial Pennsylvania. What were some of the chores that people did on this farm? What kinds of animals were raised?

but also many small farms and farm villages like those in New England. There was no single main religion, like that of the Puritans in Massachusetts. The Middle Colonies had Quakers, Catholics, and people of other religions. In fact, as you have learned, the idea of religious freedom was established from the beginning in Pennsylvania. There were more schools in the Middle Colonies than in the South, but not so many as in New England.

Even the people in the Middle Colonies were more of a mixture than in either of the other two sections. Colonists from many countries settled in the Middle Colonies. They included thousands of Germans and Scotch-Irish (Scottish people who had lived for a time in Ireland). There were also French, Irish, Scots, Swedes, and, of course, the Dutch.

▶ **CHECK UP** See Teacher's Key.

1. In what ways was life in the Middle Colonies a mixture of both northern and southern ways of living?
2. What kinds of people settled in the Middle Colonies?

128

4 How Did People Live in the Frontier Region?

So far, we have been reading about life in the colonies which lay along the Atlantic seaboard. To the west of these settlements was another region, called the **frontier.** If we are to get a true picture of life in the English colonies in the 1700's, we should know something about this western region.

Why did people move to the frontier? The frontier was the farthest edge of the land where colonists had settled. In the western forests, back-breaking labor was necessary to provide food and shelter. Why, then, did men and women leave safe and settled communities to move to the frontier?

Here are some of the reasons: (1) As we know, there are always people who love adventure. The frontier attracted them, even though they faced dangers and hardships. (2) There were others who disliked settled communities where they were told what to do and what not to do. These people wanted to live alone. They went west to be free to live in their own way. (3) In the streams and forests of the West were animals whose furs could be sold for a good price in the East. Some people, therefore, went to the frontier region to be trappers and fur traders. (4) Still others moved west because land was cheap there. Cheap land attracted people who did not have enough money to buy land near their old homes along the coast. Indentured servants, for example, often moved to the frontier to begin new lives for themselves after they had served their time and become free. (5) Lastly, many people who found life unpleasant in Europe journeyed directly to the frontier where they could live and worship as they pleased without interference. The Scotch-Irish, in particular, passed through the Middle Colonies and settled in large numbers on the frontier.

How did the pioneers move westward? When pioneers went west, they followed the easiest routes inland. They tried to find routes that had no steep ups and downs. (The old rule of the woods is, "Never go over anything you can go around; never step on anything you can step over.") The best routes of all were the rivers. On rivers the pioneers could travel by canoe or raft or boat rather than having to cut a path through the forest. Next best were the valleys and the gaps in the hills. The map on page 130 shows the main routes that the settlers followed.

Some of the pioneers made their way up the Connecticut River. Others went up the Hudson to the Mohawk River and west on that stream. Others followed the Susquehanna River. Still others went up the Potomac, and then up the Shenandoah River. From there they pushed into the great Valley of Virginia, which lay between the Blue Ridge Mountains on the east and the Allegheny Mountains on the west. The land along these routes was quite well ★ occupied by 1760, as the map on page 130 shows.

Just before the American Revolution broke out in 1775, pioneers began to pass through the gaps in the Allegheny Mountains to the land sloping slowly down to the Mississippi River. They traveled in groups, some by water, some by land. They went on foot and on horseback, their household goods strapped to the backs of pack horses. When they reached a spot where they wished to settle, they stopped. As pioneers moved steadily westward, the frontier — the farthest edge of settlement — moved westward also.

Frontier life is dangerous. Pioneers faced many dangers. For one thing, they were nearest to the French lands

129

★ Have students trace these routes on the map (p. 130).

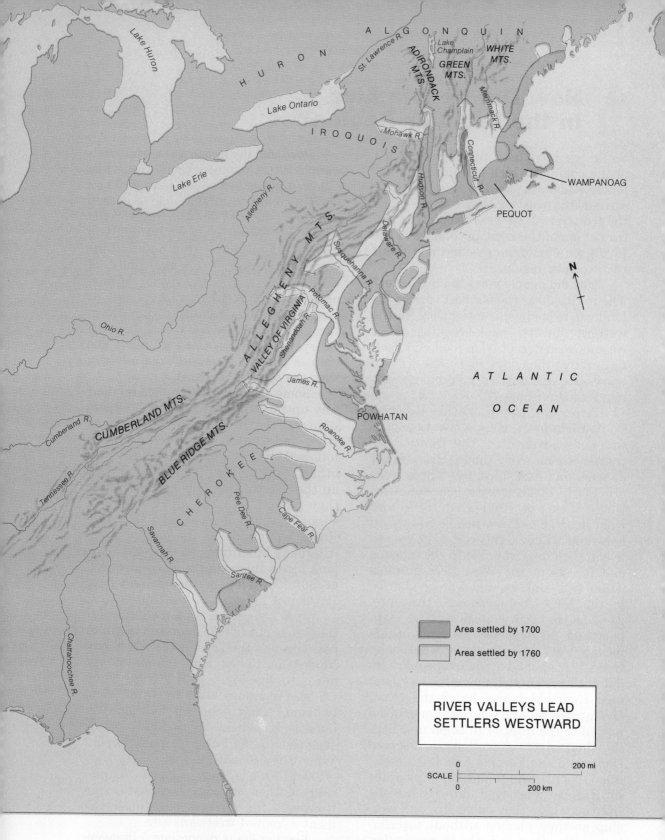

Lake Huron

Lake Ontario

Lake Erie

HURON   ALGONQUIN

St. Lawrence R.

Lake Champlain

GREEN MTS.

WHITE MTS.

ADIRONDACK MTS.

Mohawk R.

Merrimack R.

IROQUOIS

Connecticut R.

Hudson R.

WAMPANOAG

PEQUOT

Allegheny R.

Delaware R.

N

Susquehanna R.

ALLEGHENY MTS.

Ohio R.

Potomac R.

Shenandoah R.

VALLEY OF VIRGINIA

James R.

ATLANTIC

OCEAN

Cumberland R.

CUMBERLAND MTS.

BLUE RIDGE MTS.

Roanoke R.

POWHATAN

Tennessee R.

CHEROKEE

Pee Dee R.

Cape Fear R.

Savannah R.

Santee R.

Chattahoochee R.

Area settled by 1700

Area settled by 1760

**RIVER VALLEYS LEAD
SETTLERS WESTWARD**

SCALE

0   200 mi

0   200 km

MAP STUDY Early settlers followed the river valleys inland from the
Atlantic coast. The colored areas on this map show what regions they had
settled by 1700 and by 1760. What rivers did the settlers follow westward?

130

Dense forests covered much of the frontier region. Settlers who moved to the frontier cut down trees to build log cabins. Then they cleared land for farming.

in Canada and the Ohio River Valley. If a war broke out, they would be the first to be attacked. Another danger came from the clash between the settlers' way of life and that of the Indians. The Indians depended on game that they hunted. They saw the pioneers taking over more and more land, cutting down the forests where the animals lived. The Indians tried to stop this threat to their lands. Often they attacked the lonely settlements of the newcomers.

To protect themselves, the pioneers usually fortified their settlements. They drove pointed logs into the ground to make a high fence called a stockade. At the corners of the stockade they built two-story cabins, called block-houses, from which they could keep watch. They kept food and water and ammunition inside the stockade for use during attacks. Bold pioneers who built their cabins and cleared their farms outside the stockade took refuge inside when danger appeared.

At most times, the settlement served as a trading post where the pioneers bargained with the Indians for furs. Some, however, preferred to trap the wild animals themselves instead of getting the furs from the Indians. These trappers were absent from the settlement most of the time and used it only as headquarters — a place to buy what they needed and to sell the skins of the animals they caught.

After cutting trees and building cabins, pioneers planted their crops. Tree stumps often remained in the fields for years, making plowing a problem.

What kinds of houses and furniture were used on the frontier? The pioneers lived in the wilderness, far from the older settlements. They had to make or grow whatever they needed. A pioneer's cabin was likely to be small, perhaps twelve feet wide and fourteen feet long. It was built of logs a foot or more across, which were fitted together at the corners. The spaces between the logs were plastered with sticky clay. The roof was made of long shingles. The door consisted of heavy logs split in two, called puncheons. The curved sides of the puncheons formed the outer part of the door; on the inside the flat sides were crisscrossed by strong timbers. The window was made by cutting out a section of one or two logs. A huge fireplace occupied nearly all of one end of the cabin. Across the inside of the fireplace was fastened a pole, called a lug pole, from which hung a chain to support the kettle.

Most of the furniture was homemade, for furniture was usually too heavy to carry to the frontier. Beds were made of dogwood poles with woven elm bark or hickory slats. Stools were built by fitting three legs into the curved portion of a puncheon. The legs might be cut to slightly different lengths so that the stool would stand firmly on the uneven floor. Several puncheons laid flat side up on a rough frame formed a table. To build a cupboard, the pioneer laid boards across wooden pegs that had been driven into the log walls of the cabin.

Frontier food and clothes are simple. A good number of the pioneers were unmarried men. But many were married couples who wanted to start new homes for themselves and their children. In the wilderness there were wild animals that the pioneer families could shoot or trap for food. There were birds also, and the streams were full of fish and turtles. After trees were cut down and fields were cleared in the forest, the pioneers could start growing corn, wheat, and vegetables. Then, too, pioneer families might have a cow or two, a few pigs, and some chickens. In the 1700's, some frontier farmers began to raise cattle.

The clothes of the pioneers, like their furniture, were homemade. The hides of animals were often used for this purpose. The deerskin shirt and the coonskin cap were two sure marks of the frontiersman. But the frontier women made most of the clothes worn by their families. These clothes were called

132

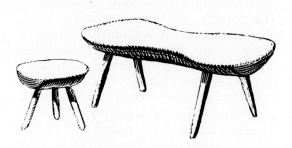

FRONTIER FURNITURE

See p. T20 for a strategy calling for students to draw pictures illustrating life on the frontier.

homespun because the women sewed them from a plain cloth made of yarn spun at home.

———

This description has shown you that ways of living differed in the various sections of the colonies. The differences were strengthened by the fact that people in one section had little to do with people in other sections. Indeed, travel was so difficult that many colonists were born and lived and died without going outside their own colonies. The colonists thought of themselves as Virginians, Pennsylvanians, or New Yorkers, rather than as Americans.

Yet we must remember that, in spite of differences, all the sections were alike in certain ways. All the colonies — New England, Middle, and Southern — were colonies of England. All had governments that were much alike. Most of the colonists spoke English, and this common language helped to bind them together. But what drew the English colonies most closely together were their common problems — the need to make a living far from Europe, to cut down the forests and make farms, and to adapt to new ways of life. It was because of their likenesses and common problems that the thirteen colonies were able at a later time to unite into one country.

▶ **CHECK UP**   See Teacher's Key.

1. For what reasons did people move to the frontier?
2. **(a)** By what kinds of routes did the pioneers move westward? **(b)** How did the pioneers protect themselves from dangers?
3. What were houses, furniture, food, and clothing like on the frontier?

CHECK UP ON CHAPTER 5   See Teacher's Key.

Words to Know

1. almanac
2. frontier
3. pioneer
4. planter
5. wharf
6. indigo
7. homespun
8. geographical conditions
9. apprentice
10. stockade
11. overseer

Places to Locate

1. Potomac River
2. Mohawk River
3. Shenandoah River
4. Allegheny Mountains
5. Blue Ridge Mountains
6. Susquehanna River

Facts to Remember

1. How did differences in geographical conditions affect ways of farming and the kinds of crops grown in the northern and southern colonies?

2. **(a)** How were young people taught to read and write in the three groups of colonies? **(b)** What groups of children had little chance of learning to read and write?
3. What were some of the likenesses and common problems of the thirteen colonies?

Skills to Practice

1. Name the colony in which each of the following cities was located: Boston, Philadelphia, Savannah, Norfolk, Charleston, and Baltimore. (If you need to, use the maps on pages 108 and 126.)
2. Study the maps on pages 108 and 130. Then name a river that settlers may have used to travel to the frontier in each of the following colonies: New

Skills to Practice (cont.)

York, Pennsylvania, Virginia, North Carolina, and Georgia.

3. The years from 1501 to 1600 are called the sixteenth century. Look at the time line on page 118. **(a)** What period of time is covered by Chapter 5? **(b)** That period spreads over two centuries. Name those centuries.

4. On page 124 a colonial woman describes her father's plantation. Read the description and make a list of the occupations she names. If there are any you do not know, look them up in a dictionary.

Questions to Think About

1. Did life in a New England village or on a southern plantation more nearly resemble life on a European manor in the Middle Ages? Explain.

2. How did a school in colonial times differ from your school today?

3. What qualities do you think a typical frontier settler would probably have had? Why?

4. Are people today more or less dependent on geographical conditions than people were 300 years ago? Why? In answering, consider transportation, houses, farming, sources of power, etc.

Linking Past and Present

● **Colonial Williamsburg.** A visit to Williamsburg, Virginia, is a chance to see how people lived in the English colonies before the Revolutionary War. This famous town was the capital of Virginia from 1699 to 1779. After the capital was moved to Richmond, Williamsburg declined in importance and became a quiet little town. Then in the 1930's, John D. Rockefeller, Jr., arranged to have it rebuilt as it was in the 1700's.

Today the main streets look much as they did some 200 years ago. The houses have been furnished as they were in colonial days. Even the gardens are planted with the favorite shrubs and flowers of the colonists. You see the stately Capitol, flying the British flag as of old; the beautiful palace, once home of the royal governors; and even the jail, where the jailer waits to show you around. Shops of colonial times display their wares; you see the wig-maker's shop, the bake shop, the blacksmith shop. To carry out the spirit of colonial days, the guides who take you around wear clothes in the style of the 1700's.

John Smith named New England. Most people know that John Smith was a leader of the Jamestown colony, but few realize that

this remarkable Englishman explored the North Atlantic coast and gave New England its name. In 1614, after he had returned to Europe from Virginia, Smith set out with two ships on a trading expedition to America. Reaching the coast of what is now Maine, Smith explored the shore as far south as Cape Cod. He made an excellent map of that region which he called "New England," giving names to many rivers and bays. The Charles River, flowing into Massachusetts Bay, was named after Prince Charles, who later became king of England. Farther down the coast, Smith found an excellent harbor that he called "Plimouth." When the Pilgrims sailed to North America six years later, they had with them a copy of Smith's map. After some searching, they found "Plimouth" and started a colony there.

After Smith returned to England with a cargo of fish and furs, he wrote a book called "A Description of New England," which included his map. This book and later books that Smith wrote gave valuable information about New England and Virginia. The Pilgrims, the Puritans, and later colonists used Smith's books and maps. The name given by John Smith — New England — has lasted to this day, along with other names such as Plymouth, Charles River, and Cape Ann.

● Have students prepare brochures and posters designed to attract tourists to Williamsburg.

For answers see Teacher's Key.

Have students practice reading pictures throughout the text. Be sure to emphasize the importance of captions.

GAINING SKILL

Reading Pictures

The pictures in this book can tell you many things about America's story if you look at them carefully and think about them. Sometimes pictures are better than words, because pictures can *show* you how people lived in past times. Pictures can give you information about the houses people lived in, the tools they used, and the clothes they wore.

The picture on this page shows Baltimore, Maryland, as it looked in 1752. Study the picture and then answer the following questions.

1. On the basis of the picture, list three ways in which the people of this settlement made their living.
2. Describe the landscape beyond the edges of the town. Suppose that new residents wanted to build more houses to enlarge the town. What task would they have had to undertake first?
3. Compare this picture with the one of Jamestown on page 102. In which settlement did the residents seem to fear being attacked? What evidence led to your answer?
4. In what settlement, Baltimore or Jamestown, do you think life was more comfortable? Give reasons for your answer.
5. What are some important ways in which life in early Baltimore probably differed from life on the frontier, as shown on pages 131 and 132?
6. Compare this picture with the one of Charleston on page 164. Which town appears to be the busier seaport?

135

CHAPTER **6**   *Vocabulary preview: allies, treaty*

France Gains, Then Loses, a Huge Empire in North America

1600–1763   See p. T21 for chapter teaching strategies.

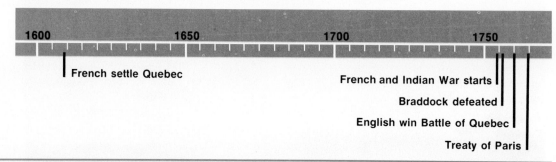

1600   1650   1700   1750

| French settle Quebec

French and Indian War starts |
Braddock defeated |
English win Battle of Quebec |
Treaty of Paris |

What this chapter is about —

Summer sunlight flashed from swords, musket barrels, and gold lace as 23 canoes and barges touched the wooded riverbank. A party of officials, soldiers, and Indians stepped ashore and, after some shouting of orders, lined up facing a great oak tree. A French military officer took his place beneath the tree. As he gazed down the Ohio River, the French officer may have felt that he had before him the whole of western North America. With a flourish, he removed his plumed hat and read a short proclamation. Workers then nailed a metal

◀ The city of Quebec, overlooking the St. Lawrence River, was the capital of France's huge North American empire.

plate to the tree and buried another at its foot as a lawyer recorded the event on an official document. With that, the whole party returned to the boats, oars and paddles broke the peaceful surface of the river, and all headed eastward in the direction from which they had come.

On the tree now could be seen the royal arms of France, while the plate beneath it proclaimed that the Ohio River, "all the streams that fall into it, and all the lands on both sides of those streams" belonged to the kings of France, "by right of arms" and countless treaties. It was dated July 29, 1749.

What was the purpose of this elaborate ceremony? You will learn the answer in this chapter. You will also read how France in the end lost its colonies, leaving England supreme in North America. But first you will get acquainted with New France itself. To help you understand the chapter, we will answer the following questions:

1. What was New France like in the 1700's?
2. Why did the French and the English come to blows in North America?
3. What were the results of the French and Indian wars?

1 What Was New France Like in the 1700's?

We have read how Spain and England started settlements in the Western Hemisphere and how those settlements grew into prosperous colonies. Now we are ready to learn the story of France's American colonies. France, you remember, claimed a vast territory in North America. Called New France, it sprawled across much of what is now Canada and stretched far down the Mississippi to the Gulf of Mexico. (The map on page 64 shows the size of New France. Notice how large it was, compared with the territory of the English colonies along the Atlantic coast.)

The population and settlements of New France are small. While English colonists were busy making settlements along the Atlantic coast of North America, French adventurers were still exploring the interior. As a result, although the French territory in North America was huge, only a few settlements had been made. Indeed, the little settlements along the St. Lawrence seemed lost amid the vast forests that covered the land. By 1750 there were only about 80,000 French settlers in all of New France. At the same time, the English colonies had over 1,500,000 ★ people.

Quebec and Montreal were the only towns of any size. Quebec, built upon rocky bluffs high above the St. Lawrence River, was the first French town in New France. Settled about the same time as Jamestown, Quebec had only a hundred colonists at the end of its first twenty years. Even after that, it grew very slowly. Montreal had its beginning as a fur-trading post in an Indian town. The other French settlements were mostly tiny forts along the St. Lawrence, the Great Lakes, and the Mississippi River. These were held by a few soldiers and were used as fur-trading

137

● Ask students to find two American Indian inventions in this picture (snowshoes and the canoe).

● Europeans first heard about Niagara Falls from the French missionary priest shown in this painting. Father Hennepin, who explored with La Salle, described the falls in a book he wrote about his travels.

posts. Thus, while the English colonists had been busy building towns and clearing farms, the French had spent much more of their time in exploring and fur trading.

★ **The people and government of New France differ from the English colonies.** In several ways the people in the settlements of New France were not like the English colonists. As we know, English people came to North America to seek a better life for themselves and their families. Most of them were energetic and self-reliant people who wanted to succeed in their new homes. Many of the French, on the other hand, were officials and soldiers. They came to America because their government wanted to build up the colony of New France. A large number of these officials and soldiers were unmarried men who were not especially interested in settling down for good.

Unlike the English colonists, the French colonists did not take part in their government. There was, in fact, no self-government in the French settlements. New France was ruled by a governor appointed by the king of France. The colonists had nothing to say about making the laws or spending the money for the colony. As for religion, all the settlers of New France were members of the Catholic Church. France was a Catholic country, and all settlers in its colonies were required to follow that religion.

Fur trading is important in New France. Most of the people of New France did not live in the towns. Many of them were fur traders who paddled their canoes up the waterways of the

★ See p. T21 for strategies that ask students to compare French, Spanish, and English colonies.

interior to collect furs from the Indians. These furs were carried back to Quebec or Montreal and shipped to Europe, where they brought high prices. This profitable trade in furs had an effect on the growth of New France. The fur traders were not interested in building settlements and developing the country as the English colonists were.

There were farmers in New France, too. But much of the farmland along the St. Lawrence and along the coast was granted by the French king to important French people, in the form of huge estates. The farmers living on the land had to work for the owners most of the time, much as the serfs of the Middle Ages worked for the lord of the manor (page 28). This was not like the system in the English colonies, where everyone who had the price could own land. It is no wonder that many French colonists preferred the free and profitable life of the fur trader to the life of the farmer.

French missionaries work among the Indians. The French were interested in winning the Indians to Christianity. Like the Spanish, they sent priests to their American colonies. Father Marquette, who helped Joliet explore the Mississippi (page 61), was a French missionary. The missionaries endured severe hardships, traveling endless miles in canoes and on foot to reach Indians who lived far from the French settlements. Even while the priests lived among the Indians, their lives were full of danger. During the long winters they not only faced starvation but almost froze to death in their crude huts. Some priests were even killed by Indians.

Nevertheless, the courageous missionaries gained for the French the friendship of several Indian tribes.

● **The influence of New France remains to this day.** Although France later lost its territory in North America, French customs and language and religion have lasted to this day. In Canada, English *and* French are the official languages; money and stamps are printed in both languages. In the province of Quebec, a majority of the people speak only French and that is the language used in most schools. Many French-style buildings are seen in Quebec, and the spires of Catholic churches rise above the villages of the province. There are so many descendants of the French settlers in Quebec, and they have kept so many of their French customs, that modern visitors might think it was still a French land.

▶ **CHECK UP**   See Teacher's Key.

1. **(a)** How did New France differ from the English colonies in population? **(b)** In size? **(c)** In government?
2. In what ways did the people in New France earn a living?
3. What reminders of France can be found in present-day Quebec?

2 Why Did the French and the English Come to Blows in North America?

Have you ever thrown a rock into a quiet pool and watched the ripples spread out in ever-widening circles? In much the same way, an event in history may have effects that are felt in some far-distant spot. In the 1600's and the 1700's, for example, wars broke out in Europe between France and England, and the ripples caused by those wars spread across the Atlantic to their colonies. Let us see how this came about.

France and England become rivals.
★ From 1643 to 1715, France was ruled by King Louis XIV. Louis XIV was absolute master of France. He was an ambitious king, and under his leadership France became powerful. He even had plans to bring other parts of Europe under his control. Louis was also interested in strengthening the colony of New France in order to increase French power and prosperity. Such ambitions worried the English. "If Louis extends his power," they thought, "he will endanger our trade and our colonies, and perhaps threaten the British Isles themselves." Fear of French power during Louis XIV's reign and afterward caused England to fight a series of four wars with France. The wars began in 1689 and ended in 1763. Of course, the two countries were not actually at war during all these years, but they were watching each other closely even when they were not fighting.

When France and England were at war, it was only natural that the French and English colonists in America should go to war, too. The colonists were determined not only to protect the land they had already won in America but also to gain more territory. The English colonists, in particular, wanted more room to the west for their settlements to grow. Thus, the stage was set for war between New France and the colonies of England. Just as we often try to pick the winner before a football game by comparing the two teams, let us consider the strong points of each side in the struggle between the French and English colonies.

★ Some students may want to use reference materials to read more about this monarch. See "Using Reference Books" (p. 149).

Frontier settlements were in danger during the wars between France and England. In 1704, the French and Indians attacked Deerfield, Massachusetts.

What advantages did France have over the English in America? France had several advantages over the English:

(1) France, as you already know, controlled more land in North America than did England.

(2) This vast area was ruled by a single powerful government, while each of the thirteen English colonies had a separate government. The French governor did not have to ask thirteen separate colonial legislatures for money. He was in a position where he could issue orders to the people of New France, who had to obey them. During a war, therefore, New France was organized in such a way that the French could act quickly.

(3) The French government in Europe did not depend on the colonists in New France to do much fighting. The government sent soldiers and ships to protect them. This meant that the French were well prepared when the wars began.

(4) Finally, the French had strong **allies** (friends) among such Indian tribes as the Hurons and the Algonquins (al-GONG-kwinz). From the days of the early explorers the French had kept on friendly terms with these Indians and had traded freely with them. French missionaries had lived among them. When war came, the French could count on aid from these people.

What advantages did the English colonies have? The English colonies had their strong points too:

(1) There were many more settlers in the English colonies than there were in New France.

(2) The English colonists were not scattered over a wide area but lived in a smaller and more thickly settled region. For this reason the English colonies could be defended more easily.

(3) Most of the English settlers had come to America to establish homes. Because they had families and land to defend, they had more reason to fight than did many of the wandering French fur traders.

(4) Finally, the English colonies also had Indian allies. They were the Iroquois, whose tribes were the best fighters in the eastern part of North America. The Iroquois and the French had been enemies since the days when

141

● See p. T21 for a strategy that asks students to compare the strengths and weaknesses of the English and French in their North American struggle.

Champlain (page 59) and his companions went with some Indians to the shores of the lake which bears his name. There they met a party of Iroquois men who were old enemies of the Indians in Champlain's group. Fighting broke out. The whites, with their superior weapons, overcame the Iroquois and killed a number of them. At a later time the French and the Iroquois also came to blows over the fur trade in the Great Lakes region. When the French and the English were at war, therefore, the Iroquois aided the English.

▶ **CHECK UP**   See Teacher's Key.

1. Why did France and England fight in North America?
2. **(a)** What advantages did France have in the wars with England in North America? **(b)** What advantages did England have?

3 What Were the Results of the French and Indian Wars?

As we have said, whenever England and France went to war in Europe, their colonists went to war in America. In America the first three wars were named for the monarch who happened to be ruling England or Britain[1] at the time. They were King William's War, Queen Anne's War, and King George's War.

Neither side wins in the first three wars. These first three wars between the colonists accomplished very little. The French, with their Indian allies, made frequent attacks on English settlements. The English struck back by attacking the chief forts of the French in America — Quebec on the St. Lawrence River, and the great fortress of Louisbourg on Cape Breton Island. (Find these forts on the map on page 143.) They failed to capture Quebec, and although they succeeded in capturing Louisbourg, they had to surrender it when peace was made. France did recognize England's claims to Nova Scotia (Acadia) and Newfoundland. But these three wars made no important change in the English and French possessions in America, and neither side won a clear-cut victory. Though hard-fought, the wars in America were overshadowed by the bigger wars in Europe.

Both Britain and France claim the Ohio Valley. The fourth war, called the French and Indian War, started in North America. It began because both the French and the British wished to control the rich lands along the Ohio River. The French wanted to build a line of forts and trading posts that would connect their settlements on the lower Mississippi River with the rest of New France. Such a plan would not only strengthen their empire but would also keep English people from settling in the Ohio River Valley.

The British, however, were unwilling to let France have this land without a struggle. They did not want to be limited to a narrow strip of land along the Atlantic seaboard. More English settlers were arriving each year. Much of the land along the coast was already cleared and occupied, and more and more settlers were eager to push westward. About this time a group of Virginia colonists formed a company to set-

---

[1]In 1707 the countries of England and Scotland were joined in a single kingdom called Great Britain. So the name *Britain* is commonly used for the kingdom after that date.

Be sure students read about the Acadians in "Linking Past and Present" (p. 148).

tle the lands in the Ohio River Valley. The king granted 200,000 acres of land to the Ohio Land Company, as it was called.

The French begin to fortify the disputed territory. When the governor of New France learned of this grant in 1749, he sent an expedition to the Ohio country. As the expedition traveled down the Ohio River, it left lead plates as land markers to claim the region for France (page 136). The French also warned the Indians to have nothing to do with the English. Shortly afterwards, the French began to build forts on Lake Erie and at points southward toward the Ohio River. (The map on this page shows the location of some of the forts.)

The British try to drive the French out of the Ohio Valley. The British, in turn, became alarmed at the French advance into the Ohio region. In the fall of 1753 a messenger was sent through the wil-

derness to the forts that the French had built in the disputed region. The messenger was George Washington, who at that time was just 21 years old. He carried a letter from the governor of Virginia to the French commander of the forts. This letter warned the French to leave the territory because it belonged to Great Britain. Over difficult trails, through snow and rain, young Washington made his way to deliver his message. But the French commander refused to heed the warning, and Washington started back. On his return trip he narrowly escaped death when he slipped off a raft and nearly drowned.

The next year Washington returned to the Ohio country, this time with a small group of soldiers. They had been sent out to seize Fort Duquesne (doo-CANE), a French fort at the fork where two streams join to form the Ohio River. (See map below.) But Washington and his men were outnumbered.

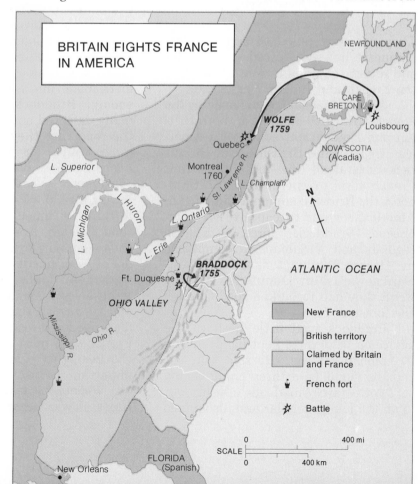

BRITAIN FIGHTS FRANCE IN AMERICA

MAP STUDY
(a) What route did Wolfe follow in his campaign against Quebec? (b) Near what important rivers and lakes did the French have forts? (c) Who claimed Florida at this time?

See Teacher's Key.

143

General Braddock's soldiers, marching in long regular lines, were easy targets for a surprise attack by French and Indian forces.

They not only failed to capture Fort Duquesne but were forced to surrender and return to Virginia. With this clash the French and Indian War began.

General Braddock is defeated by the French. To carry on the war, both Britain and France sent soldiers to America. In 1755, the British decided to attack several of the most important French forts. General Edward Braddock, the British commander-in-chief in America, set out to capture Fort Duquesne. Braddock's force of English regulars and Virginians, accompanied by George Washington, moved westward toward Fort Duquesne. As they went, they had to build a road through the forest.

Braddock paid little heed to the advice on wilderness fighting given him by colonial soldiers. He said that the Indians might be a threatening enemy to "your raw American militia, but upon the King's regular and disciplined troops . . . it is impossible they should make any impression." But Braddock's overconfidence had tragic results. As the British troops advanced through the wilderness in long columns, a force of French and Indians took them by surprise. The red coats of the British soldiers made fine targets for the hidden enemy. Braddock's brave troops were badly defeated and had to retreat. But the road that they had built became a main route for pioneers who later pushed their way westward.

French successes continue. Following Braddock's defeat, French good fortune continued. The British failed to send enough troops to America, and their commanders (like General Braddock) were not used to fighting in the wilderness. The American colonies themselves were slow to work together and to furnish the money and the soldiers needed for victory. As a result, the French won most of the battles during the next two years, capturing several important British forts.

William Pitt takes a hand. The fortunes of war began to change in 1758.

144

● See p. T21 for a strategy that asks students to consider the extent to which one person can influence historical events.

The man most responsible for this change was not a soldier but a leader of the British government. His name was William Pitt. Pitt persuaded the colonies to furnish more troops and money. He inspired the British to fight harder. Pitt also sent younger and more vigorous commanders to America. Now it was Britain's turn to win victory after victory. The great French fort at Louisbourg (page 142) was again attacked by a large British army and forced to surrender. The English were also able to capture several forts along the western frontier. Among them was Fort Duquesne, which the English renamed Fort Pitt in honor of William Pitt. From that small fort has grown the modern city of Pittsburgh, a great industrial center.

Two gallant generals face each other at Quebec. The battle that was to decide the outcome of the war took place at Quebec, four years after Braddock's defeat. The British forces were under the command of General James Wolfe.

New Englanders captured Louisbourg in 1745 (below). Returned to France three years later, the fortress was finally taken by Britain in 1758.

Wolfe was an able leader who had taken part in the capture of Louisbourg. In the early summer of 1759, a British fleet, carrying thousands of soldiers under Wolfe's command, sailed up the broad St. Lawrence and anchored below the city of Quebec. It was impossible, however, to attack this French stronghold directly. Located on a high cliff, Quebec was protected by strong walls and many cannon.

General Louis Montcalm, the French leader, had vowed to defend Quebec or die. He knew that it would be difficult for the French to defend Quebec for any length of time. Although Montcalm had more soldiers than Wolfe, many of them were untrained. The city was short of food, and no help could be expected from France while the English navy controlled the St. Lawrence. Montcalm's only hope was to hold Quebec until winter, when ice on the river would force the English fleet to withdraw.

The Battle of Quebec decides the fate of New France. Meanwhile, from across the river, Wolfe's cannon were bombarding the city but doing little damage. Because winter was approaching, Wolfe decided on a daring move.

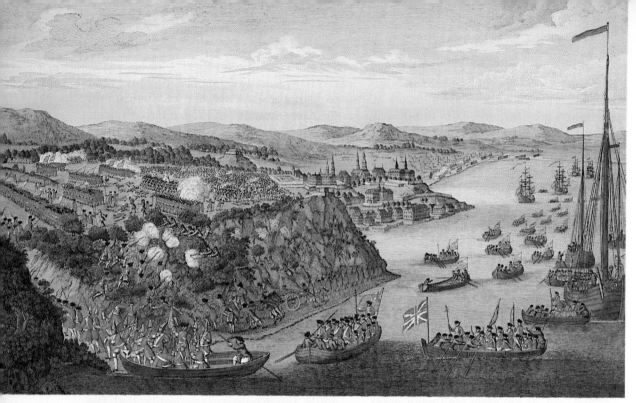

British forces captured Quebec by climbing the steep cliffs along the St. Lawrence and surprising the city's French defenders.

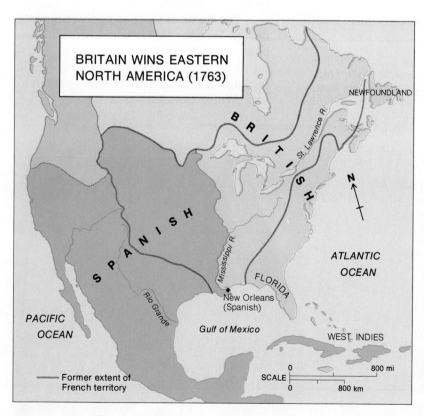

BRITAIN WINS EASTERN NORTH AMERICA (1763)

NEWFOUNDLAND

B R I T I S H

St. Lawrence R.

SPANISH

Mississippi R.

Rio Grande

New Orleans (Spanish)

FLORIDA

ATLANTIC OCEAN

PACIFIC OCEAN

Gulf of Mexico

WEST INDIES

N

— Former extent of French territory

SCALE

0   800 mi

0   800 km

See Teacher's Key.

MAP STUDY
Three years after the Battle of Quebec, France and Britain signed the Treaty of Paris. By the terms of the treaty, Britain won control over all eastern North America. (a) What happened to Florida as a result of the treaty? (b) Who became owner of New Orleans?

146

One night a thin line of British soldiers struggled up the cliffs at a point left undefended by the French. The next morning the French were amazed to see the British forces forming their lines on a broad plain outside the city walls. Montcalm ordered his troops to attack the enemy. Although the French fought bravely, they were no match for the well-trained English regulars. General Montcalm was fatally wounded. As he lay dying, he said, "I am glad that I need not live to see the surrender of Quebec." General Wolfe also received a fatal wound. When he learned that the enemy was retreating, his last words were: "Now I can die in peace."

British troops entered Quebec, pulled down the French flag, and raised the British flag. The Battle of Quebec has been called one of the greatest battles in the world's history. It is important because it decided whether North America would be chiefly French or British. The British easily captured Montreal, putting an end to the fighting in North America. Meanwhile, the war continued in other parts of the world, with the British winning victory after victory. In 1763 the conflict was finally ended by a treaty called the Peace of Paris. (A **treaty** is a formal agreement between two or more countries.)

France gives up all claims in North America. The peace treaty of 1763 was a humiliating blow to the proud French nation. Great Britain took from France all of its territory east of the Mississippi River except New Orleans. As the map (page 146) shows you, this vast territory included the settlements in what we now call Canada as well as the region south of the Great Lakes. Spain, which had sided with France in the war, had to give Florida to England. To make up for this loss, France gave Spain the city of New Orleans and the French claims west of the Mississippi River. Except for two small islands near Newfoundland and some islands in the Caribbean Sea, France lost all its North American possessions.

 CHECK UP   See Teacher's Key.

1. **(a)** What were the names of the first three wars between the French and English in North America? **(b)** What was the outcome of these first three wars?
2. **(a)** What dispute led to the outbreak of the French and Indian War? **(b)** Why did France win most of the battles in the early years?
3. **(a)** Why did Britain begin to win? **(b)** What battle decided the outcome of the war?
4. What were the terms of the peace treaty?

CHECK UP ON CHAPTER 6   See Teacher's Key.

Words to Know

1. province
2. missionary
3. treaty
4. New France
5. allies
6. Peace of Paris

Places to Locate

1. Louisbourg
2. Quebec (city)
3. Montreal
4. New Orleans
5. Ohio River
6. St. Lawrence River

Facts to Remember

1. **(a)** What Indian groups were allies of France in the French and Indian War? **(b)** What Indians were allies of the British?
2. **(a)** What part did George Washington play in the French and Indian War? **(b)** Why was General Braddock's force defeated in the campaign to take Fort Duquesne?

147

See p. T21 for a strategy that calls for students to discuss the nature of historically significant events.

Facts to Remember (cont.)

3. **(a)** Who were the two generals who were killed in the Battle of Quebec? **(b)** Tell which side each fought for.

Skills to Practice

1. Look at the painting of Father Hennepin's arrival at Niagara Falls on pages 138–139. **(a)** Describe the landscape. **(b)** Describe the clothing of the French explorers and their Indian companions.
2. **(a)** According to the map on page 64, what three European nations had land claims in North America about 1700? **(b)** Which European nations still had land claims in North America after the French and Indian War? (See the map on page 146.) **(c)** Explain the change that had taken place.

Questions to Think About

1. **(a)** Why was the outcome of the French and Indian War important to Great Britain? **(b)** To France? **(c)** To us today?
2. It has been said that the French fur trade was one reason for France's losing its North American territory. Explain why this may have been so.
3. Britain and its colonists in America did not agree on how much each had contributed to defeating the French. Can you see why? Explain.

Linking Past and Present

French customs in the land of Louis. French influence remains strong in Louisiana, which was named for King Louis XIV of France. French people settled the region, and their descendants still carry on many colorful customs of their ancestors. Perhaps you have heard about the famous Mardi gras (MAR-dih GRAH) in Louisiana's largest city, New Orleans. Mardi gras is a French carnival which takes place the last few days before Lent. The city is filled with merry-makers in every kind of costume, dancing and parading in the streets and watching the spectacular floats. Then, at midnight before the first day of Lent, Mardi gras ends.

Because of its past, Louisiana is the only state where laws are patterned after French rather than English law. It is also the only state which is divided into parishes instead of counties. The parishes were originally districts of the Catholic Church. When Louisiana became a state, these districts took the place of counties, but continued to be called parishes.

French names in America. Many place names in our country remind us that France once controlled a large chunk of North America. As you have learned, Lake Champlain, on the border between New York and Vermont, is named for the famous "Father of New France." Vermont itself is a French name meaning "green mountain." French names are also found in the states of the upper Mississippi Valley. In Wisconsin are such cities as Prairie du Chien ("dog's prairie" — after the little prairie dogs found in that region), Fond du Lac ("end of the lake"), Eau Claire ("clear water"), and La Crosse ("the crossing"). The Illinois cities of Joliet and La Salle are named for two famous French explorers. St. Louis, Missouri, named for a French saint and king, was founded by the French as a fur-trading post.

Acadians. Many people in Louisiana today are called "Cajuns." The "Cajuns" are French-speaking people whose ancestors were among the first settlers of Canada. In 1755 the British forced a large number of French settlers to leave Nova Scotia and find homes elsewhere. About 4,000 of the Acadians, as they were called, made their way to Louisiana. Their descendants still live there, speaking a French dialect which has been greatly influenced through the years by contact with English, Spanish, and other languages.

148

GAINING SKILL

Using Reference Books

Reference books help people find answers to questions. Many different kinds of factual information are contained in reference books. But to find the information you want, you must choose the right book.

Suppose you wanted to find someone's telephone number. Where would you look? Although you may never have thought of it, a telephone directory is a reference book. To find the number you want, you must know that the directory is organized alphabetically by the last names of the people who are listed.

Other reference books can be as easy to use as the telephone directory. You just need to choose the right book for the facts you want and know how that book is organized. Four kinds of reference books that people often use are listed here:

DICTIONARY. A book that lists words alphabetically and gives their definitions and pronunciations (and often their origins).

ATLAS. A book of maps that may also give information about products, population, and climate.

ENCYCLOPEDIA. A large book or a set of books containing articles on a great many subjects, arranged in alphabetical order.

ALMANAC. A book of facts, published once a year. Gives up-to-date information on many subjects, especially people, places, events, and statistics.

What kind of reference book would you use to answer each of the following questions? (Some answers might be found in more than one reference book.)

1. Who was the king of France in 1749, when French explorers claimed the Ohio River Valley?
2. What rivers join to form the Ohio River?
3. How far is Quebec from Montreal?
4. What part did George Washington play in the French and Indian War?
5. In the quotation from General Braddock on page 144, what does the word *militia* mean?
6. What is the address of the Canadian Embassy in Washington, D.C.?
7. What Canadian provinces border the United States?
8. How is the government of modern Canada organized?
9. What are some words that have the same meaning as *prosperous*?
10. What are the most recent population figures for each of the Canadian provinces?
11. In what wars since 1763 have Great Britain and France been allies instead of enemies?
12. What states were eventually formed from the land between the Appalachian Mountains and the Mississippi River?
13. Who are your state's senators and representatives in Congress today?

149

UNDERSTANDING UNIT 2

Unit 2 has told how European nations settled colonies and developed empires in North and South America.

1. Spain established a great American empire.

a. In Mexico and Peru, Cortés and Pizarro conquered Indian empires possessing great wealth; other Spaniards roamed far and wide in search of riches. Spanish priests came to the colonies with the hope of converting Indians to Christianity.

b. Within a century Spain acquired Florida and the southwestern part of the present-day United States, Mexico, the West Indies, and all of Central and South America (except Brazil).

c. Spain permitted only Spanish Catholics to settle in its colonies, regulated colonial trade for its own benefit, and denied the colonists a share in the government. Spaniards held high positions in the Church and the government and looked down on the Creoles and mestizos. Large churches and universities were built in Spanish America before the English colonies were settled.

d. Wealth from its colonies helped make Spain powerful and aroused the fear and envy of England, France, and Holland. Eager to reduce Spanish power and to share in the colonial wealth, they struck at Spain.

2. England, France, and Holland also established colonies in the Americas.

a. English settlers who came to America sought freedom to make a better living, to obtain land, to worship as they pleased, and to share in the government. Geographic conditions help to explain why different ways of living developed. Some of the English colonies offered less freedom than others, but colonists often left older settlements to start new settlements where they could live as they wished. Wherever they lived, the English colonists had some things in common — a form of government in which the colonists had a voice, the English language, and the problem of earning a living 3,000 miles from the home country. The Dutch colony of New Netherland was annexed by the English in 1664.

b. One group of colonists came to America against their will. These were black people who were forced into bondage in Africa, transported across the Atlantic, and sold to American colonists who needed workers to farm large plantations. Though at first the Africans in the English colonies were treated like indentured servants, their situation soon became that of lifetime slavery.

c. The French claimed a vast territory which included most of present-day Canada and the land drained by the Mississippi. The small population made a living in the fur trade and by agriculture. The French government strictly regulated life in New France. French priests were active missionaries among the Indians.

d. Rivalry between France and England in Europe led to wars which extended to North America. The English colonists, feeling themselves hemmed in by the French, had reasons of their own for fighting. Defeated in the French and Indian War, France surrendered Canada and the land east of the Mississippi to England and gave French territory west of that river to Spain. Nevertheless, the French language and French ways of living have survived to this day in parts of the Western Hemisphere.

UNIT REVIEW

1. (a) What kinds of people helped to establish Spain's American empire? (b) Why was each group interested in going to the colonies?
2. How did the discovery of great riches in Mexico and Peru affect (a) the Indians, (b) the spread of Spanish exploration and colonization, and (c) Spain's position as a world power? (d) How did Spanish exploration and settlement spread north into what is now the United States?
3. (a) Why did English settlers come to America? (b) How did English efforts at colonization differ from those of Spain and France?
4. (a) To what extent were geographic conditions responsible for differences in ways of living in New England, the Middle Colonies, and the South? (b) Why was life on the frontier different from life along the seaboard?
5. Compare Spanish, English, and French colonies in the Americas about 1750. Take into account (a) size, (b) government, (c) chief ways of making a living, and (d) relations with Indians.
6. (a) Why did colonial wars break out between the French and the English in North America? (b) What advantages did each side possess? (c) Why did the English win? (d) How did the English victory affect the future of North America?

THINGS TO DO

Projects marked with an asterisk (*) are for the whole class.

*1. Make a chart showing the thirteen English colonies. Arrange them under the section (New England, Middle Colonies, Southern Colonies) to which they belonged. Use these headings for your chart: Name of Colony, Date, Who Started It, Reasons for Starting It.
*2. Make more cards for your game, "Can You Identify?" (page 69), using the names, terms, and dates found in Chapters 3, 4, 5, and 6.
3. Write or tape entries in an imaginary diary kept by a boy or girl who went with (a) Jamestown settlers in 1607, (b) Pilgrims in 1620, (c) Puritans in 1630, (d) Spanish settlers in a California mission in 1775.
4. Find pictures showing the clothes or the homes of French, English, Spanish, or Dutch colonists. Show the pictures to the class.
5. Look for books in the library about (a) the Spanish conquest of Mexico or Peru; (b) the Spanish settlement of Arizona, New Mexico, or California; or (c) the French and Indian War. Choose an interesting part of the book and tell the class about it.
6. Find out about one of the following people and prepare a report: Francis Drake, Estevanico, Eusebio Kino, Pocahontas, Ponce de León, Squanto, Phillis Wheatley, Roger Williams.

Left to right: Patriots raising Liberty Pole; "Spirit of '76"; Liberty Bell; Washington crossing the Delaware

UNIT **3**

New Nations Are Born as American Colonists Shake Off European Rule

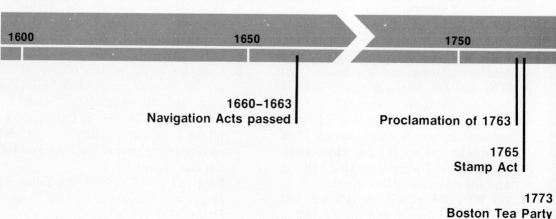

1600–1850

See p. T22 for a unit preview strategy. See pp. T58–T71 for lists of useful books and audiovisual aids.

1600   1650   1750

1660–1663
Navigation Acts passed

Proclamation of 1763

1765
Stamp Act

1773
Boston Tea Party

1775–1783
American Revolution

152

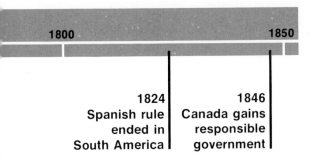

1800   1850

1824
Spanish rule
ended in
South America

1846
Canada gains
responsible
government

Unit 3 tells the story of how colonists in North and South America cut many of the ties that bound them to Europe. The first three chapters of this unit tell what happened to the thirteen English colonies. Chapter 7 describes the relations between the colonies and Great Britain. In Chapter 8 you will see how stricter regulations by the British government caused growing resistance among the colonists. Chapter 9 tells about the war in which the thirteen colonies won their independence. The final chapter of the unit describes what happened somewhat later in other parts of the Western Hemisphere. You will read how the Spanish colonies won their independence, and how Canada gained control of its own affairs.

153

How Were the English Colonists Governed?

1607–1763   See p. T22 for chapter teaching strategies.

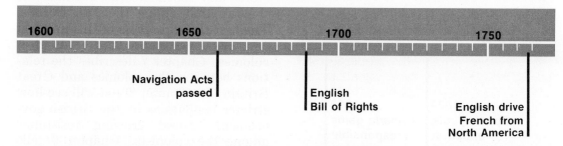

1600   1650   1700   1750

**Navigation Acts
passed**

**English
Bill of Rights**

**English drive
French from
North America**

What this chapter is about —

Have you ever stopped to think what rights you have because you are an American? Imagine, for example, that you and your family are starting off for church. There is no law in the United States that says what church you must attend. You have the right to decide how and where you worship. In other words, freedom of religion is one of your rights as an American. Or suppose that your parents do not like a law that has been proposed by Congress. If they wish, they may criticize the action of Congress when talking with their

154

Representative government got its start in America when the Virginia House of Burgesses held its first meeting in 1619.

friends. They may write letters to newspapers telling what they think. Or they may even hire a hall and make a public protest if they want to. These are examples of freedom of speech, which is a right very precious to Americans. Perhaps you can think of other rights that we enjoy.

How did we get these rights? Some of them developed in America. Others, as we will discover in this chapter, were brought to the colonies by English settlers who cherished them dearly. We will learn about the governments under which the colonists lived. We will find that each colony made its own laws. We will also learn how England regulated the trade of the colonies, and how England and the colonies disagreed about colonial government and trade regulations. As you read, keep in mind these questions:

1. What rights did the English colonists bring to America?
2. What kind of government grew up in the English colonies?
3. Why did England and its colonies disagree over colonial affairs?

1 What Rights Did the English Colonists Bring to America?

Colonists of Spain, France, and England lead different lives. Let us pay a visit to three widely scattered places in North America about the year 1750. The first place is Mexico City, in New Spain. As we learned in Chapter 3, the colonists here have little freedom. Although they are loyal Spaniards and good Catholics, they have no part in the government of New Spain or of Mexico City. That is all controlled by the viceroy. The colonists are not free to criticize the government or the king. Even their business affairs are very strictly controlled by the government.

We go now to a farming area in the St. Lawrence Valley of New France. The lives of the people here are not very free either. Like the Spanish colonists, the settlers of New France are loyal to the Catholic Church and to their king, but they have no share in the government. The king's representatives have almost complete power over the inhabitants of New France. Many of the colonists have no land of their own. They live on the estates of powerful landowners. The settlers are allowed to keep a share of the crops they raise, but they must perform many duties for the landowners. The people even have to accept the owners' advice on such matters as getting married.

The last stop in our journey is at the home of Sarah and Jonathan Blake in the colony of Massachusetts. Sarah and Jonathan came from England to make a better living. Their life in America is much freer than that of the Spanish and French colonists. They own their own house and farm, which they are free to manage as they wish. And Jonathan has a right to share in the government of the colony. Like other men

155

● See p. T22 for a strategy that asks students to review the similarities and differences of Spanish, French, and English colonies.

with property, he may vote for representatives to serve in the **legislature** for the whole colony. This legislature decides many important questions, including the taxes that each colonist must pay. The colonists also have certain other rights. For example, persons cannot be punished for crimes unless they have been found guilty by a group of fellow citizens called a **jury.**

Why is it that the English colonists possess more freedom than French and Spanish colonists? They owe much to their English ancestors, who loved freedom and insisted on having certain rights. Let us see how this came about.

The English people limit royal power. At the time North and South America were being settled, England, France, and Spain all had monarchs. But, while the monarchs of France and Spain had become all-powerful in their countries, the people of England had from time to time limited the power of their rulers. In fact, whenever a monarch tried to interfere with certain rights that English citizens considered their own, the people protested. Three of these protests play a part in our story. They were important steps in the struggle to limit the power of English monarchs and to increase the rights of the English people.

(1) The first of these steps was taken long ago, in the year 1215. At that time England was ruled by a tyrant named King John, who wished to govern just as he pleased. But a group of nobles forced him to set his seal to a document, or official paper, called *Magna Charta* (KAR-tuh), a Latin term that means "Great Charter." In Magna Charta, King John had to accept certain limits upon his power. He agreed that nobles and freemen (landholders) should not be punished at the whim of the king, but must be judged by a jury under the laws of the land. The king also had to agree to consult a Great Council of nobles and church officers on many matters. To be sure, the nobles were looking after themselves when they forced King John to accept this document. In time, however, the rights promised in Magna Charta came to apply to all the people.

(2) Another ruler who was forced to heed the people's wishes was Charles I. King Charles, who was king when the Puritans left England (page 106), was determined to rule as he saw fit. He paid little attention to Parliament, the body of English lawmakers made up of nobles and representatives of the people. He also collected taxes without Parliament's consent. The protests against these highhanded acts became so loud that Charles was obliged to agree to a statement called the Petition of Right. This stated that the people should not be taxed without the consent of Parliament. When Charles failed to keep his written promise, an uprising in England cost him his throne and his life.

(3) Still another English king, James II, trampled on the rights of the Parliament and the people. In 1689, after James II had been forced to flee from England, a document called the Bill of Rights was drawn up. No English ruler since then has seriously interfered with the rights listed in this document.

English rights are transplanted to America. By accepting these important papers — Magna Charta, the Petition of ★ Right, and the English Bill of Rights — English monarchs admitted that their people possessed important rights. For example, individuals had the right to a fair trial by a jury and to bring complaints to the attention of the king or queen. They also had a right to elect representatives to the law-making body. In England, that was Parliament, which had the power to pass laws and to decide what taxes were to be paid.

These rights are important to us because the English colonists who settled in America claimed similar rights.

156

The right to trial by jury is just one of the freedoms that English colonists claimed and which are part of the American heritage today.

In the early charters giving permission to start colonies in North America, the Crown (the king or queen) declared that the settlers were to have the same "liberties . . . as if they had been abiding and born within this our realm of England." That is why colonists in New England enjoyed more freedom than those in New Spain or New France. We will see in the next chapter that these rights meant so much to the English colonists that they were willing to fight to protect them.

The spirit of freedom grows in America. English colonists in America not only had all the rights of English citizens, but they enjoyed even greater freedom than did people in England. It is not hard to understand why this was true. For one thing, the settlement of the English colonies, as you know, was carried out chiefly by trading companies or by proprietors. In the early days, the English rulers were only mildly interested in what was going on in the colonies. They were too busy with affairs in England to worry much about the struggling settlements across the sea. This lack of interest on the part of the English government permitted the colonists to enjoy great freedom in managing their own affairs.

We must remember, too, that 3,000 miles of ocean separated the colonies and England. It took weeks or even months for orders to be sent across the ocean to the colonies. Naturally this gave the colonies more freedom to govern themselves. Also America itself, with its plentiful land and new opportunities, encouraged this feeling of freedom. People believed that by overcoming the dangers of the wilderness and building up settlements, they had earned a right to say how they should be governed.

It would be wrong, however, to think that people in the English colonies were entirely free. The colonists lacked certain rights that Americans today take for granted. It was dangerous, for example, to criticize the Crown or its officers too loudly. Many colonists, including women, slaves, and indentured servants, were not allowed to vote. Settlers in some colonies had

157

● See p. T22 for a strategy that asks students to examine factors that contributed to the growth of freedom in America.

● See p. T22 for a strategy that calls for students to use guide questions in reviewing Section 1.

less freedom than those in others. Furthermore, the rights of Indians were generally ignored. Nevertheless, by 1750 government throughout the English colonies allowed greater freedom than could be found elsewhere in the Americas or in most parts of Europe. In the next section we will see what this gov-
● ernment was like.

▶ **CHECK UP**   See Teacher's Key.

1. Name the three important steps in the struggle of the English people to increase their rights and limit the power of the English monarchy.
2. Why did the English colonists have greater freedom than people in England?

2 What Kind of Government Grew Up in the English Colonies?

Imagine that we have come from Europe to visit the Massachusetts colony about the year 1750. Suppose, too, that we have a letter of introduction to Jonathan Blake from his brother in England. When we knock at the door of the Blakes' cottage and present our letter, Sarah and Jonathan greet us courteously. They ask us to sit down on stools and benches before the dancing flames in their huge fireplace. When we question them about the government of the English colonies, Jonathan replies in words like these:

★ **Colonial governments are much alike.** "The government of one colony may differ slightly from the government of another, but in all colonies conditions are much the same. A colonial government is really like the government in Britain, only on a smaller scale. In each colony there is a governor in charge, just as the king is the head of the government in Britain. Each colony also has its own legislature. The legislature is like the British Parliament. In addition, there are courts to try cases in each colony, just as there are courts in Britain. But these colonial governments do not have the last word in their affairs. They have to take orders from Britain. For example, Parliament may pass laws that the colonies in America

have to obey. Then, too, laws passed by the legislature of a colony may be set aside by Britain. This is not often done, however. Our colonial governments really have a good deal of power in carrying on the affairs of the colonies."

Colonial governors are chosen in various ways. "The governors of the different colonies do not inherit their positions as the ruler of Britain does," says Jonathan. "Nor are they all chosen in the same way. In Rhode Island and Connecticut, the governors are elected by the legislators. This gives the people of these colonies a good deal more power than the citizens of other colonies enjoy. In three other colonies — Maryland, Pennsylvania, and Delaware — the governor is chosen by the proprietor of the colony. In these cases, however, the governor selected by the proprietor must be approved by the king.

"You may be wondering about the eight remaining colonies: Massachusetts, New Hampshire, New York, New Jersey, Virginia, North and South Carolina, and Georgia. Most of these colonies were founded by trading companies or proprietors, who at the start had the power to appoint governors. But for one reason or another, the king has taken over the government of all these colo-

158

★ See p. T22 for a strategy that asks students to examine colonial governments.

● Mention that in Britain, representatives did not have to live in the area that they represented in Parliament.

nies. Their governors are now appointed by the king and are responsible to him. So, you see, the colonists do not have a great deal to say about choosing their governors."

The voters choose the lawmakers. "Our governors are very important and powerful people," Jonathan goes on, "but they share the work of government with the legislatures. Most legislatures have two branches or houses — an upper house and a lower house which is often called an assembly. The upper house is small. Its members are appointed by the governor rather than elected, and it is not as important as the lower house. The lower house is made up of representatives elected by the voters. Each town or county in the colony is allowed to send one or more representatives to this lower branch. So the people, through their representatives, do have a voice in the passing of laws and the voting of taxes."

At this point, Sarah speaks up. "Not everybody, of course, has the right to vote for those representatives to the legislature," she says. "Women cannot vote. Nor are all the men who have reached the age of 21 allowed to vote, either. Usually only those who are free men and who own a certain amount of land or other property are given this right. In some places, property owners must also belong to a certain church in order to vote. Here in Massachusetts Bay Colony, in earlier times, only members of the Puritan Church were allowed to vote."

The colonists manage their local governments. "I hope," says Jonathan, "that we have given you a clear picture of the government of our colonies. But no doubt you also want to know how each neighborhood or locality is governed. Well, here in New England each town takes care of its own affairs. **Town meetings** are held from time to time. In these meetings all the voters of the village or town can take part because the town is small. The voters can voice their opinions, vote for local officers, and decide what to do about local affairs. As you can see, the town meeting allows a great deal of self-government.

In colonial Boston, town meetings were held at Faneuil Hall, still a meeting place today.

"Of course I have never traveled very far from home, but I am told that in the Southern Colonies they do not have town meetings. Because of the large plantations, the people are scattered over the countryside and there are fewer settlements. So their local government is carried on by counties, each county covering a large area. The business of the county is in the hands of a sheriff and several justices of the peace. These officials are appointed by the governor, not elected by the voters. In the Middle Colonies, there is a mixture of town and county government."

Conflicts often arise in colonial government. "Of course," Jonathan continues, "although we colonists get along pretty well, we do have disputes and quarrels. Sometimes a governor wants to have his own way regardless of the wishes of the people. But the legislature of each colony has the right to vote on tax laws, and in most colonies it votes the governor's salary. So the governor cannot afford to be too highhanded.

"Then, too, the people do not always agree among themselves. There may be disagreements between the people who live in large towns and those who live on farms. Or arguments may come up between people who live in the settled regions along the seacoast and those who live on the frontier. Disputes also develop between those who are well-to-do and those who are not. But, on the whole, our form of government works very well. I think we are fortunate to have as great a part in ruling ourselves as we have."

————

The Blakes' story makes it plain that by 1750 the English colonists had come a long way on the road to self-government. Though not everyone had a share in the government, many did. People who possess such precious rights do not willingly give them up. As we will see, the colonists fought for these rights and handed them down to later generations of Americans. Thus, we have received a priceless heritage that must not be taken for granted and that all Americans should be able to enjoy.

▶ **CHECK UP**   See Teacher's Key.

1. In what ways were the governments of the English colonies alike?
2. In what ways did the government in Britain have control over the colonial governments?
3. **(a)** How were the governors of the various colonies selected? **(b)** How were the members of the legislatures chosen? **(c)** Who had the right to vote in the colonies?

3 Why Did England and Its Colonies Disagree Over Colonial Affairs?

Although English colonists had rights and some voice in their government, they were subject to control by the homeland. In fact, English officials had very definite ideas about colonies and how they should be run. What were these ideas and how did the colonists feel about them?

ENGLAND SAYS THAT COLONIES EXIST FOR THE GOOD OF ENGLAND

People in England believed that the colonies existed for the benefit of the English homeland. After all, they reasoned, the colonies had been started by England. The colonists enjoyed certain

● See p. T22 for a strategy that calls for students to debate the pros and cons of British trade policies.

rights, including some self-government, only because England allowed it. Also, England provided armies and ships to help protect the colonies from the Indians and the French. The feeling in England, therefore, was that the colonies owed much to the homeland and should be willing to obey laws and regulations that would benefit England.

Trade means wealth for England. What did England want of the colonies? England expected them to add to its wealth. To be sure, no gold or silver mines, such as those that enriched Spain, had been discovered. There was another way, however, by which the colonies could bring riches to England. This was through trade. For example, the colonies produced plentiful supplies of certain goods that England wanted. Among them were tobacco, indigo, rice, and materials for building ships. On the other hand, the colonists needed many articles manufactured in England — clothes, hats, kettles, weapons, dishes, and tools.

Whale hunting was dangerous but provided a living for New England colonists. Many things could be made from whale products. Especially valuable was whale oil, which the colonists used in lamps to light their homes.

For a number of reasons, England wanted its American colonies to sell most of their raw materials to the homeland and in turn buy from England most of the manufactured products the colonists needed. Manufacturing articles for the colonies would bring employment to many people in England as well as profits to manufacturers. There would also be good profits for shipbuilders, shipowners, and merchants if goods passing to and from the colonies were carried in English vessels or in vessels built in the English colonies. But how, thought people in England, can we keep so profitable a trade for ourselves alone?

England passes laws to control colonial trade. In order to protect England's trade with its colonies, Parliament had from time to time passed laws known as Navigation Acts. Two of the most important of these were passed by Parliament in the 1660's. The Navigation Acts included the following regulations:

(1) The colonists were required to export certain of their products only to England or to other English colonies. At first only a few products — such as sugar, tobacco, and indigo — had to be sold to England. As time went on, however, more articles produced by the colonists were added to the list.

Ironworking was practiced by the colonists as early as the 1600's. This picture shows a scene at the Saugus ironworks in Massachusetts.

(2) All goods coming to the colonies from other countries had first to pass through England. For example, if a cargo of tea were sent from China to Philadelphia, it had to be taken to England first. There it could be taxed by the government and then shipped on to Philadelphia.

(3) All goods going to or coming from the colonies were to be carried by ships built in England or in the colonies. Three fourths of the crews of these vessels, said the Navigation Acts, had to be English.

England controls colonial manufacturing. In early days the settlers had little time or opportunity to manufacture goods. As the colonies became larger and more settled, some manufacturing began. Goods were not made in factories, as they would be today, but by people in their homes. In time, colonial manufacturing grew until it threatened to hurt the sale of goods made in England. So Parliament passed other acts to make sure that articles made in the colonies would not interfere with the sale of English goods. Colonists might

make their own clothes or hats, for example, but they could not manufacture clothes or hats to sell in other colonies or in other countries. Colonists might also manufacture iron, but were not allowed to make it into finished articles.

The colonists did not suffer as much from these laws controlling trade and manufacturing as you might expect. Because certain articles had to be sold to England, the colonists were sure of a good market for these goods. Colonial shipbuilding and shipping increased because goods were supposed to be carried in English or colonial vessels. It is true, too, that England's colonial regulations were far less strict than those of Spain. Nevertheless, England felt free to regulate colonial trade and manufacturing with little thought for the wishes of the colonists.

THE COLONISTS SAY THAT THE COLONIES EXIST FOR THEIR OWN BENEFIT

The settlers in America did not agree that the purpose of the colonies was to make England wealthy. In fact, they did not believe they owed the homeland anything. The colonists remembered that in crossing the ocean to settle in

162

HOW THE NAVIGATION ACTS REGULATED TRADE

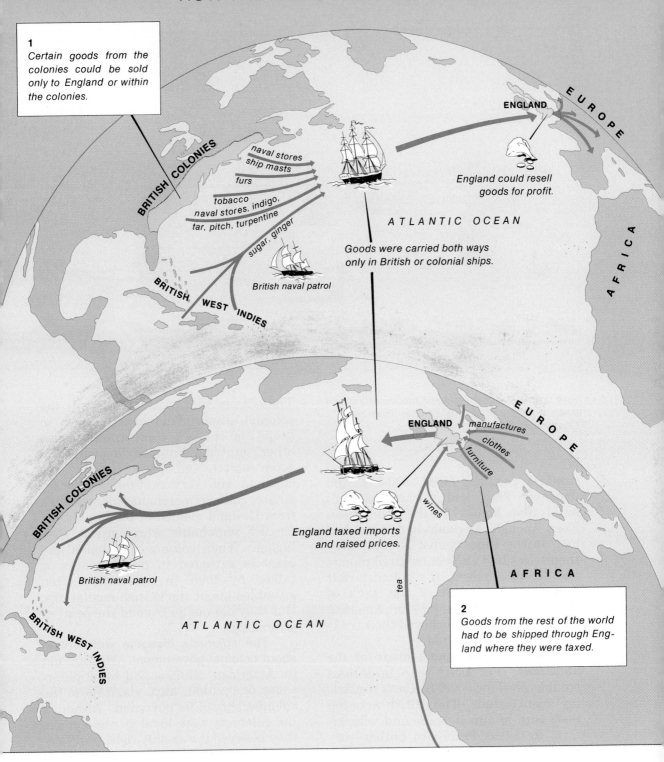

1 Certain goods from the colonies could be sold only to England or within the colonies.

BRITISH COLONIES

naval stores
ship masts
furs
tobacco
naval stores, indigo,
tar, pitch, turpentine
sugar, ginger

BRITISH WEST INDIES

British naval patrol

ENGLAND

EUROPE

England could resell goods for profit.

ATLANTIC OCEAN

AFRICA

Goods were carried both ways only in British or colonial ships.

ENGLAND   manufactures
clothes
furniture

EUROPE

BRITISH COLONIES

British naval patrol

England taxed imports and raised prices.

wines

tea

AFRICA

BRITISH WEST INDIES

ATLANTIC OCEAN

2 Goods from the rest of the world had to be shipped through England where they were taxed.

MAP STUDY These maps show how Britain tried to limit the amount of trade its colonies could carry on directly with the rest of the world. (a) How did Britain control the export of colonial goods to foreign countries? (b) How did Britain regulate the colonies' *imports* of goods from other countries?

163

How does this picture suggest the importance of trade in the life of colonial Charles Town (now Charleston), South Carolina?

America, they had faced hardships and dangers. They had worked hard to build new homes in the wilderness. Even though England had furnished help in the wars against France, they themselves had also contributed money and troops. Indeed, the colonists felt they had done most of the work of building the new empire in America. For this reason they believed their trade should not be regulated.

The colonists ignore many of the trade laws. For many years no serious trouble developed over the laws regulating colonial trade. The British were too busy with affairs at home and with efforts to defeat France to bother very much about enforcing these laws. Although some officers were appointed to enforce the Navigation Acts, many of them never crossed the Atlantic to carry out their duties in the colonies.

The officers who were stationed at the colonial seaports did not try hard to keep the settlers from trading with other countries. So smuggling (shipping goods secretly and against the law) was common and very profitable. For instance, colonial merchants smuggled tea from Holland instead of buying it from English merchants whose prices were higher. When colonial merchants and planters gathered in public places or talked by their firesides, they often grumbled about the British regulations. But they did not go beyond the point of grumbling.

The colonists disagree with Britain about colonial government. Britain and its American colonies had some differences of opinion, also, about how the colonies should be governed. Although the colonists were loyal to the Crown, they believed it was only right that they should be allowed to manage their own affairs. The spirit of freedom was strong in America; and England, after all, was far away. The colonists felt that people in Britain, including the king and his

164

Remind students that Britain and France had fought four wars in rivalry for American colonies (p. 140).

advisers, knew little about conditions in America. The king and Parliament, on the other hand, thought otherwise. They believed that Great Britain possessed wide powers of government over its settlements in America. One government officer spoke of the colonies as "these American children, planted by our care, nourished up by our indulgence [kindness] to a degree of strength . . . , and protected by our arms."

Before 1763, however, Great Britain did not often insist upon using its powers of government. To be sure, from time to time a charter was taken away from a colony or proprietor. And the British government continued to claim the right to tax the colonists and to set ● aside laws passed in the colonies. But these powers were not often used.

———

To sum up, the colonists in 1763 did ★ not entirely accept Britain's right to control their government and their trade, but there had been no open conflict. It is easy to see, however, that any move by Britain to enforce the trade laws or govern more strictly in the colonies was likely to lead to trouble.

▶ **CHECK UP**   See Teacher's Key.

1. **(a)** Why did people in England believe that the colonies existed for the benefit of England? **(b)** Why did the English colonists feel that they owed England nothing?
2. **(a)** What were the provisions of the Navigation Acts? **(b)** What was the attitude of the colonists toward the laws regulating colonial trade?
3. How did the colonists and the British leaders disagree on the way the colonies should be governed?

CHECK UP ON CHAPTER 7

See Teacher's Key.

Words to Know

1. smuggle
2. county
3. legislature
4. jury
5. trial
6. petition
7. town meeting
8. representative
9. regulate
10. Parliament
11. justice of the peace

Facts to Remember

1. **(a)** What was Magna Charta? **(b)** How did that document limit the power of English kings and queens?
2. **(a)** What was the Petition of Right? **(b)** What was the English Bill of Rights? **(c)** How did each of those documents further limit royal power in England?
3. **(a)** Why did England try to regulate colonial trade? **(b)** Explain why the English colonists actually suffered little from England's regulation of their trade and manufacturing before the year 1763.

165

1. Name the *best* kind of reference book to use in looking for answers to the following questions:
   a. What does *petition* mean?
   b. What was the Petition of Right that King Charles I of England was forced to accept?
   c. Who are the present-day governors of the states that were the original thirteen colonies?
   d. How far is it from Bristol, England, to Philadelphia, Pennsylvania?
2. Look at the map on page 163. **(a)** What kinds of goods came to the colonies by way of England? **(b)** What goods could the colonists sell only within the colonies or to England? **(c)** How does the map help to make clear the effect of the Navigation Acts?

Questions to Think About

1. Why are the great documents of *English* freedom (page 156) mentioned in an *American* history textbook?
2. **(a)** What kinds of questions did the New England colonists settle at their town meetings? **(b)** Were town meetings an example of representative government? Explain.
3. What freedoms do Americans have today that the people of the English colonies did not have?
4. Why did the English colonies escape the strict regulation imposed on the Spanish and French colonies?

Linking Past and Present

The town meeting. Many New England towns still hold town meetings, just as they did in colonial days. At certain times, all the voters gather to discuss and then to vote directly on any problems that have to do with running the town's affairs. This is democracy in its simplest form, for every voter has a direct voice in how things are run. The voters hear how the town's money is being spent, and if anything is going on that they don't like, they are free to say so.

Of course, this kind of government is not possible in all communities. The town meeting system never got started in the Southern Colonies or in the frontier region because people in those areas lived too far apart to get together for meetings. Also, in most cities there are so many voters that town meetings are not practical. Instead, citizens elect some city officials, and others are appointed.

Freedom of the press. Freedom of the press (the right to print one's opinions without restriction) has always been important to Americans. In the 1730's, an immigrant from Germany named John Peter Zenger published the New York *Weekly Journal.* Zenger printed a series of articles criticizing the policies and actions of the royal governor of New York. For one thing, the governor had interfered in the election of a representative to the colonial assembly. Although the governor's candidate had lost anyway, Zenger's paper did not hesitate to expose the governor's unfair action. In further issues, the paper told about other ways in which the governor had used his power unfairly, and it called upon the people of the colony to defend their liberties. Finally, Zenger was arrested, and four issues of his newspaper were burned in front of the City Hall. His wife, Catherine, went on publishing the *Weekly Journal.*

At his trial, Zenger was defended by Andrew Hamilton, a well-known lawyer from the neighboring colony of Pennsylvania. Hamilton argued that the publisher had printed the truth about the governor. He went on to say that a citizen had the right to criticize an unjust government. Although the judge made known his feeling that Zenger was guilty, the jury took only a few minutes to return a verdict of "not guilty." The courageous publisher was set free. Zenger's trial was an important landmark in establishing the freedom of the press in America.

GAINING SKILL

Reading Diagrams

In this chapter you have read how the governments of the English colonies were organized. One way to show how something is organized is to draw a **diagram.** A diagram can make clear how each part of an organization is related to the other parts.

The diagrams on this page show two different kinds of colonial governments. Use the diagrams and the information in the chapter to answer these questions.

1. In Diagram A, how is the governor chosen?
2. In Diagram A, what part of the government do the colonists have the power to choose?
3. How are the members of the upper house of the legislature chosen in this system?
4. From your reading, name three colonies that had governments similiar to the one shown in Diagram A.
5. How is the governor chosen in the system shown in Diagram B?
6. Under which system — A or B — do the colonists have greater power?
7. Remember that some of the English colonies were controlled by proprietors. Which system — A or B — is similar to the government of a proprietary colony?

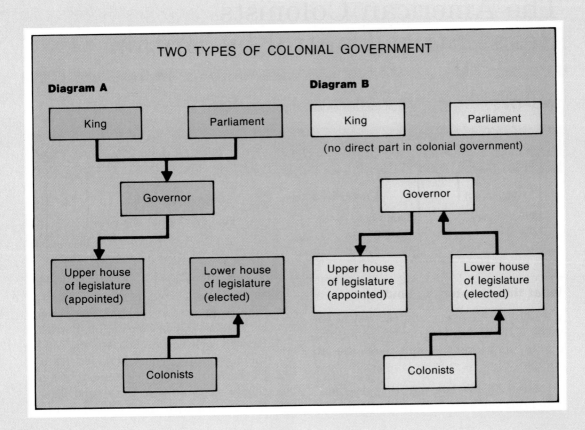

TWO TYPES OF COLONIAL GOVERNMENT

Diagram A

| King | Parliament |

Governor

Upper house of legislature (appointed)

Lower house of legislature (elected)

Colonists

Diagram B

| King | Parliament |

(no direct part in colonial government)

Governor

Upper house of legislature (appointed)

Lower house of legislature (elected)

Colonists

CHAPTER 8

Vocabulary preview: boycott, repeal, writs of assistance, duty, primary source

The American Colonists Resist Strict Control by Britain

1763–1775 See pp. T23–T24 for chapter teaching strategies.

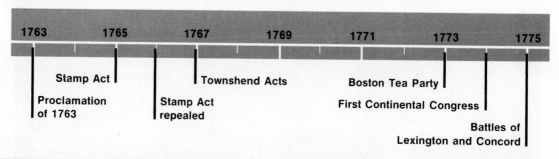

1763	1765	1767	1769	1771	1773	1775

Stamp Act

Proclamation of 1763

Townshend Acts

Stamp Act repealed

Boston Tea Party

First Continental Congress

Battles of Lexington and Concord

What this chapter is about —

If radio or television had existed in the year 1775, these two news announcements might have come over the air suddenly:

(March 23) We interrupt this program to bring you a special news bulletin. A Virginia leader today advised Americans to prepare for war. In a speech before the Virginia Convention, Patrick Henry, well-known statesman, said there is no longer any hope for peace. Declaring that Americans must fight if they wish to be free, Henry ended his fiery speech with these defiant words:

"I know not what course others may take; but as for me, give me liberty, or give me death!"

(April 19) The top news story of the moment comes from Boston. Fighting broke out today between American colonists and soldiers of the British army. A column of his Majesty's soldiers, marching to Concord, Massachusetts, to destroy war supplies, clashed with colonists assembled at Lexington. Shots were fired and several colonists were killed. Heavy fighting later took place at Concord Bridge.

Fighting between Great Britain and its American colonists! Only twelve years before, at the end of the French and Indian War in 1763, no one would have guessed that this would happen. Something must have gone seriously wrong to provoke such defiant words and violent acts. In this chapter we will learn about events between 1763 and 1775 that led to fighting between Britain and the American colonies. To understand the course of events, we will seek answers to these questions:

1. How did Britain try to tighten control over the American colonies?
2. How did the American colonists react to stricter control by Britain?
3. What happened when Britain punished the colonists for their resistance?

1 How Did Britain Try to Tighten Control Over the American Colonies?

Britain considers new plans for its colonies. If we had been present at a meeting of the king's ministers (as the members of the king's cabinet were called) in London at the close of the French and Indian War in 1763, we might have heard George Grenville, the prime minister, address his companions in words like these:

"Gentlemen, a great war has just ended. After long and hard fighting we have defeated our powerful enemy, France. Victory has brought us a vast territory in America. Today Britain is the proud ruler of the greatest empire in the world.

"All this is very satisfying. But our victory has also brought problems. Now that we have gained additional territories in America, we must decide how they shall be governed. We will need to send an army to keep order in these new ● lands of ours.

"Governing our American colonies and keeping an army there is going to be very expensive. In the war just ended, we already have spent a great deal. We have had to borrow money, and the only way we can repay this debt is by increasing taxes. But landowners here in Britain are even now groaning about the heavy taxes they are required to pay. I do not want to tax the British people any more than is necessary. I am convinced, moreover, that the colonies can contribute some of the money we need. And there is good reason why they should. If we have to keep an army in America, won't the colonists benefit more from it than British taxpayers?"

Grenville didn't actually say these words, but we may be sure that they tell

● Britain's territory now extended to the Mississippi. Ask: With the French threat ended, why was an army in this territory necessary? (conflict between settlers and Indians)

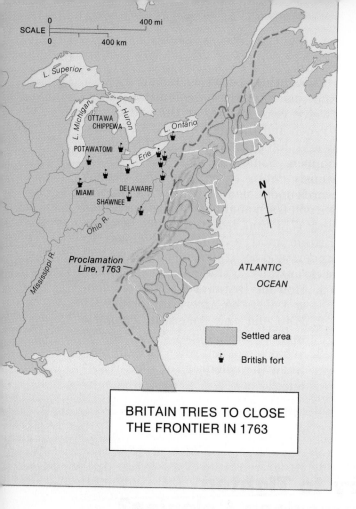

SCALE

BRITAIN TRIES TO CLOSE
THE FRONTIER IN 1763

MAP STUDY   See Teacher's Key.
In 1763 the British government ordered colonial settlers *not* to go west of the line shown on this map. What important Indian tribes lived in the Ohio region?

what he was thinking. From his point of view Grenville's reasoning was sound. He and the other members of the British government were convinced that the colonies should be governed more efficiently and contribute more money to pay expenses. And while Grenville was working out a plan to strengthen British power in America, news arrived which made him more certain than ever that he was right.

Pontiac's War convinces Grenville he is right. You remember that pioneers had been settling in the region west of the Allegheny Mountains (map, page 130). This fact angered the Indians who had called this land home long before the arrival of the settlers. In the spring of 1763, several Indian tribes united in a plan to force the white settlers out of their territory.

The leader of the Indians was an Ottawa chief named Pontiac. He persuaded the Shawnee, Delaware, Chippewa, and other tribes of the Great Lakes area to attack British forts and settlements in the Ohio region. At first the attacks were successful. Most of the forts were captured and many settlers were killed and their homes burned. Later, however, more British forces were sent to help the pioneers, and Pontiac was defeated.

Pontiac's War, Grenville said, showed that it was necessary to have an army in America to keep control over the Indians. He also decided there would be less trouble if the white settlers and the Indians were kept apart and settlement of the Ohio region were delayed.

Grenville puts into effect a new program for the colonies. Grenville and the British government took steps to tighten their control over the American colonies:

(1) *The Proclamation of 1763.* In 1763 the British government issued a proclamation stating that no settlements were to be made west of the Allegheny Mountains except by special permission. If any settlements were there already, the settlers were supposed "to remove themselves." All trade with the Indians would be closely controlled by the British government. To guard the frontier, about 10,000 British soldiers would be stationed in the American colonies.

(2) *Strict enforcement of the Navigation Acts.* Grenville also called for strict enforcement of the Navigation Acts. He realized that if smuggling could be stopped, greater profits would flow into the pockets of British merchants and manufacturers. More taxes

● See p. T23 for a strategy that calls for students to examine Grenville's program from different perspectives.

In 1763 Chief Pontiac led Indians in a plan to destroy frontier settlements in the Ohio Valley. The Indians captured most of the British forts in the region before their defeat.

on goods would also be collected. To carry out Grenville's idea, new officers ● were sent to America with strict orders to search for smugglers and to punish lawbreakers.

(3) *The Stamp Act.* To raise more money in the colonies, Parliament, at Grenville's suggestion, passed the Stamp Act in 1765. Under this law stamps sold by the British government had to be placed on a great many articles, such as legal papers, newspapers, almanacs, calendars, and playing cards. Some of the stamps cost only a few cents, but others were quite expensive.

The British leaders felt that the Stamp Act and other laws were fair. They little dreamed what a storm would be stirred up in the colonies.

▶ **CHECK UP**   See Teacher's Key.

1. **(a)** Why did Grenville think the American colonies should contribute more money for defense and other government expenses? **(b)** How did Pontiac's War convince Grenville that he was right?
2. What were the three parts of Grenville's program?

2 How Did the American Colonists React to Stricter Control by Britain?

Grenville's program angers the colonists. Each part of Grenville's program was disliked by one group or another in the colonies. The settlers in the Ohio region, for example, were angry over the ★ Proclamation of 1763. After the defeat of the French in the French and Indian War, they had expected to be free to settle this region. They wanted no meddling by a faraway government in what they considered their own affairs. So they defied the Proclamation of 1763 and continued to settle wherever they

pleased. As for the colonial merchants and shipowners, they did not want to have the Navigation Acts enforced, because smuggling had brought them large profits.

THE COLONISTS TAKE ACTION AGAINST THE STAMP ACT

Taxation without representation is opposed. The greatest excitement was caused by the Stamp Act. In Britain most people agreed with Grenville that

171

News of the Stamp Act spread throughout the colonies. In this picture, colonists are reading about the new tax they will have to pay.

us in any shape without our having a legal representative where they are laid, are we not reduced from . . . free subjects to slaves?"

Many other colonists protested loudly against the Stamp Act and against "taxation without representation." In the Virginia House of Burgesses, young Patrick Henry, a member from the frontier region, rose to speak against the act. Though not yet 30 years old, Patrick Henry spoke with great force and power. He declared that it was the right of the colonists to vote their own taxes. Stirred by Henry's speech, the House of Burgesses condemned the Stamp Act. News of this bold action spread to other colonies and caused heated discussion.

The Stamp Act Congress protests. Later in the year (1765), a Stamp Act Congress met in New York. Delegates came from nine of the colonies. A formal protest was drawn up and sent to Parliament. In this protest the delegates expressed their loyalty to Britain. They declared, however, that the right to tax the colonists belonged not to Parliament but to the assemblies of the people in the colonies.

Colonial groups take action. In various colonies people banded together in groups called "Sons of Liberty" and "Daughters of Liberty" to protect their rights. Feeling ran high against officials who had been appointed to distribute the hated stamps. In Boston a mob strung up a dummy of Andrew Oliver, who had been appointed to sell the stamps there. Crowds also destroyed Oliver's office and wrecked the home of a prominent British official. Stamp sellers in other colonies were also threatened, and many of them resigned their positions. Steps were taken to destroy the stamps and to prevent their being landed in America.

A colonial boycott brings repeal of the hated Stamp Act. The colonists pro-

the colonies should be taxed to help pay for the army in America and for other colonial expenses. The stamp tax seemed to the British a fair way to do this. The colonists, however, took a very different point of view. Americans believed that taxes should be voted by colonial legislatures whose members were chosen by the colonists themselves. They opposed taxation by Parliament because the colonists were not represented in that body. If Parliament could vote a stamp tax without their consent, what other articles might be taxed in the future? "Why not our lands?" questioned Samuel Adams of Boston. "Why not the produce of our lands, and everything we possess or make use of? . . . If taxes are laid upon

172

tested against the Stamp Act in still another way. Many colonists refused to buy goods from England. It was this **boycott,** or refusal to buy British goods, that had the greatest effect in England. The king's ministers were not much troubled by the Sons and Daughters of Liberty or the protests of the Stamp Act Congress. But when trade with the American colonies dropped off sharply, British merchants and manufacturers began to complain.

In 1766, Parliament **repealed** (removed) the Stamp Act. At the same time, however, Parliament declared
● that it still had a right to tax the colonies if it pleased, even though the colonies did not send representatives to Parliament. But the people in America paid little attention. All that mattered to them was that the hated Stamp Act had been repealed. Throughout the colonies there was great rejoicing. Bells rang, crowds shouted, and people proclaimed their loyalty to Britain.

NEW LAWS STIR NEW PROTESTS IN THE COLONIES

The British government should have learned a lesson from its experience with the Stamp Act. The American colonists had made it clear that they would resist any interference with what they considered their rights. But King George III and his ministers did not like having their plans blocked by a group of colonists across the Atlantic Ocean. In addition, the British government still felt it was necessary to raise money in America to help pay the cost of governing and protecting the colonies.

The Townshend Acts anger the colonists. Within a year after the repeal of the Stamp Act, Parliament passed new laws to control the colonies. These laws became known as the Townshend Acts because they were proposed by Charles Townshend (TOWN-zend), a minister of the king. He was unfriendly to the colonists, and his attitude was, "Let the Americans dare disobey these acts, and we will see who is master."

Every one of the Townshend Acts angered the colonists. What were these acts, and why did the colonists object to them?

(1) Once again the Navigation Acts were to be strictly enforced. So that the British might look for smuggled goods, officers were to use general search warrants called **writs of assistance.** These writs (legal papers) would allow them to enter and search any house or building. The colonists were outraged when they learned that their homes could be searched by any officer who had a writ of assistance.

(2) The Townshend Acts placed **duties,** or taxes, on a number of goods imported into the colonies. The list included such articles as lead, paper, paint, glass, and tea. The purpose of these duties was to raise money. The colonists were angry because this law seemed to tax them without their consent.

(3) The money raised from the duties was to be used to pay British officials in America, including the governors of royal colonies. The colonists objected to this plan, because it took away the right of their assemblies to control the salaries of colonial officials.

(4) Still another law forbade the New York Assembly to meet. This law was intended to punish the Assembly for not voting money to support British soldiers stationed in the colony. If such a thing could happen in New York, thought the colonists, might not all the colonies soon lose their assemblies?

The colonists resist the Townshend ★ **Acts.** A new storm of protest broke out in the colonies. Wherever people gathered, they spoke angrily against the Townshend Acts. Led by Samuel

173

★ See p. T23 for a strategy that asks students to examine the rights that were threatened by the Townshend Acts.

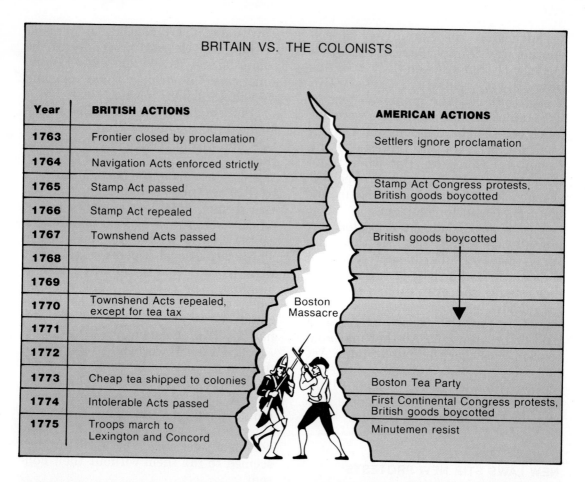

BRITAIN VS. THE COLONISTS

Year	BRITISH ACTIONS	AMERICAN ACTIONS
1763	Frontier closed by proclamation	Settlers ignore proclamation
1764	Navigation Acts enforced strictly	
1765	Stamp Act passed	Stamp Act Congress protests, British goods boycotted
1766	Stamp Act repealed	
1767	Townshend Acts passed	British goods boycotted
1768		
1769		
1770	Townshend Acts repealed, except for tea tax	
1771		
1772		
1773	Cheap tea shipped to colonies	Boston Tea Party
1774	Intolerable Acts passed	First Continental Congress protests, British goods boycotted
1775	Troops march to Lexington and Concord	Minutemen resist

Boston Massacre

British attempts to control the colonists, and the colonists' protests against those attempts, resulted in a widening split between Britain and the Americans.

Adams, the Massachusetts legislature sent to the other colonies a letter urging all to work together against these latest acts of Parliament. As in the case of the Stamp Act, however, Americans were not content with words alone. They started boycotting British goods on a large scale. Merchants agreed among themselves not to import goods from Britain, nor to buy and sell goods brought from Britain by others. As a result, trade between Britain and the colonies again dropped off sharply.

The Boston Massacre strengthens opposition. In Boston, feelings ran es-pecially high. Soldiers who had been sent there to maintain order only made matters worse. The British wore bright scarlet uniforms, and the Bostonians taunted them by calling them "red-coats" and "lobsterbacks." On a snowy night in March, 1770, when a fire alarm had brought many people into the streets, a crowd of boys began throwing snowballs at a sentry. Other soldiers hurried to the sentry's aid. Soon a threatening crowd gathered. Some of the soldiers fired into the crowd, killing several citizens, among them a black sailor named Crispus Attucks. This incident became known as the Boston Massacre. The people of Boston were outraged when they learned about the shooting. Their anger was so great that the British troops had to withdraw to a fort in Boston harbor.

People in America's Story

Mention that Franklin experimented with electricity. He proved lightning is electricity by flying a kite in a thunderstorm. The lightning struck the kite and traveled down a wire where it produced a spark. Have students find out the practical results of his research (lightning rod).

BENJAMIN FRANKLIN

Statesman, author, printer, and inventor, Benjamin Franklin is remembered today as one of the outstanding leaders of our nation's early years.

Spokesman for the colonies was a natural role for Franklin because of his bold mind and his reputation abroad. Franklin presented American protests against the Stamp Act to Parliament in 1766 (above). When the Stamp Act was repealed a short time later, Franklin received much of the credit.

The Continental Congress chose Franklin as Postmaster General in 1775. He soon had mail service in operation from Maine to Georgia.

The picture to the right shows Franklin sitting next to an efficient heating stove, one of his many inventions. He is reading *Poor Richard's Almanac,* which he published every year from 1733 to 1758. The almanac became famous for its wise sayings.

News of the Boston Massacre swept through the colonies. There is no telling what might have happened if Parliament had not decided, at that very time, to repeal the Townshend duties. The duties were taken off, not so much because the colonists had protested as because the boycott was hurting English merchants and manufacturers. But in repealing the Townshend Acts, Parliament kept the threepenny tax on tea to show that it had the right to tax the colonists.

Tea causes more trouble. For a time after the repeal of the Townshend Acts in 1770, there was fairly good feeling between the colonies and Britain. But suddenly, in 1773, the British government took an unwise step that led once ● more to trouble. It allowed the British East India Company (a company that carried on trade with Asia) to send tea directly to America. In other words, its ships did not have to stop first in England and pay the usual heavy tax. This arrangement made it possible for the East India Company to sell its tea in America at a very low price. But the colonists still had to pay a tax on tea.

Although the colonists would be getting tea at a bargain price, they were not pleased. They asked suspiciously, "Is this a trick to make us forget that we have to pay a tax on tea?" American merchants also became alarmed. Those who had been selling tea smuggled from Holland could not meet the low price offered by the East India Company. These merchants feared that in the long run their business would be ruined.

Boston holds a tea party. Merchants and patriotic colonists made up their minds that the British East India Company should not be allowed to sell tea in the colonies. When ships carrying the tea reached some American ports, the tea was unloaded and locked up in storehouses. In other ports the ships were turned away. In many places, women organized boycotts of tea.

Crispus Attucks, a black sailor, was one of the victims of the Boston Massacre. This picture shows the American view of what happened.

The Boston Tea Party was staged by the colonists as a protest against "taxation without representation." Men disguised as Indians boarded ships in Boston Harbor and destroyed thousands of dollars worth of tea.

At Boston, where feeling was especially strong, trouble broke out. One night in 1773, a party of men dressed up as Indians boarded the tea ships in Boston Harbor. Let us hear the story of the Boston Tea Party as told by a man who was there:

It was now evening, and I immediately dressed myself in the costume of an Indian, equipped with a small hatchet . . . and a club. . . . [After painting] my face and hands with coal dust in the shop of a blacksmith, I [went] to Griffins Wharf, where the ships lay that contained the tea. When I first appeared in the street, after being thus disguised, I fell in with many who were dressed, equipped, and painted as I was, and [we] marched in order to the place of our destination [and boarded the ships]. . . .

We then were ordered by our commander to open the hatches, and take out all the chests of tea and throw them overboard, and we immediately proceeded to execute his orders; first cutting and splitting the chests with our tomahawks, so as thoroughly to expose them to the effects of the water.

In about three hours from the time we went on board, we had thus broken and thrown overboard every tea chest to be found in the ship, while those in the other ships were disposing of the tea in the same way, at the same time. We were surrounded by British armed ships, but no attempt was made to resist us. We then quietly returned to our several [homes], without having any conversation with each other, or taking any measures to discover who were our associates. . . .

As news of the Boston Tea Party spread through the colonies, there was much excitement. Many colonists rejoiced at the bold action of the citizens of Boston. They agreed with the following jingle by an American poet:

When a certain great king, whose
    initial is G,
Shall force stamps upon paper, and
    folks to drink tea;

177

● Ask: Is this story a primary source? (Refer students to "Gaining Skill: Using Primary Sources," p. 185.)

When these folks burn his tea and
  stamp paper, like stubble,
You may guess that this king is then
  coming to trouble.

But other colonists were upset. They
felt that the colonists had a right to protest against unjust laws but not to take
the law into their own hands. They did
not believe it was right to use violence
and to destroy property.

CHECK UP   See Teacher's Key.

1. What did the colonists mean by "no
   taxation without representation"?
2. **(a)** In what ways did the colonists protest against the Stamp Act? **(b)** What
   was the result?
3. **(a)** What were the Townshend Acts?
   (b) How did the colonists resist them?
4. Why did colonists in Boston decide to
   hold a "Tea Party"?

3   What Happened When Britain Punished the Colonists for Their Resistance?

**Laws planned to punish Massachu-
setts anger the colonists.** When news of
the Boston Tea Party reached Britain,
most people there agreed that the colonists had gone too far. George III and
his ministers were angry and felt that
the unruly colonists had to be taught a
lesson. For this reason several laws
were passed in 1774 to punish Massachusetts. One of these laws closed the
port of Boston. Its people could not
trade with the outside world until the
owners of the tea had been paid for their
loss. Another law took away from Massachusetts many rights of self-government. More troops were sent to Boston,
and their commander, General Thomas
Gage, was appointed governor of Massachusetts.

To the colonists these laws seemed
so harsh that they called them the Intolerable Acts. (*Intolerable* means un-
bearable.) When news of the Intolerable Acts spread to other colonies, people
felt sorry for Massachusetts and angry
at the British government. Food and
supplies poured into Boston from other
colonies. The Virginia House of Burgesses proclaimed a day of prayer and
fasting as a protest against the Intolerable Acts.

**Patriots throughout the colonies work
together.** You may wonder how it was
that the other colonies heard about
Massachusetts' punishment and responded so quickly. The colonists who
resisted strict control by the British
came to be known as Patriots. Even
before the Intolerable Acts, Patriots in
all the colonies had found a way to work
together. Samuel Adams had suggested
that a committee be formed in Boston
to write letters to, or "correspond" with,
citizens of other towns. They would tell
what was happening or what they believed should be done to protect their
rights. Similar committees were soon
formed by Patriots in many Massachusetts towns and in other colonies. These
groups became known as Committees of
Correspondence. The committees in
the various colonies began to correspond with each other. By the time
the Intolerable Acts were passed, there
were Committees of Correspondence
throughout the colonies.

**The First Continental Congress
meets.** Because of what was happening
to Massachusetts, the colonists decided
to hold a meeting to discuss how they
could (1) protect their rights and (2) settle their differences with Britain. In
September, 1774, over 50 delegates, representing 12 of the colonies, assembled
in Carpenters' Hall, Philadelphia. This
meeting has become known as the First

178

● Mention that the people of Boston were expected to provide housing for the British
troops. Discuss how colonists would react.

To show their anger at the British government's plans to punish Massachusetts, colonists pulled down statues of King George III.

Continental Congress. (People in the English colonies on the continent of North America were commonly called Continentals by the British.)

The delegates to the First Continental Congress thought of themselves as English, and they wanted to defend their rights as English subjects. They all felt that such laws as the Stamp Act, the Townshend Acts, and the Intolerable Acts were unfair to the colonies. But they were not agreed on what action to take. Some of the bolder men, including Patrick Henry and Samuel Adams, thought that firm steps should be taken. They believed that George III and Parliament should be shown that the colonists' rights must be respected. Other delegates advised the colonists to move carefully. They did not wish to anger Britain any further or to endanger American trade. Hardly any of the delegates thought of separating from Britain.

Before returning to their homes, the delegates to the First Continental Congress agreed that Massachusetts should not obey the Intolerable Acts and if necessary should resist those laws with force. The Congress drew up a paper addressed to the king protesting the Intolerable Acts as "unjust" and "cruel." The Congress also protested against being taxed without representation. In addition, the Congress proposed a plan to boycott British goods throughout the colonies. Each town was urged to form a committee to publish the names of those who failed to cooperate in this plan. Finally, the delegates arranged for another Continental Congress to meet in May, 1775, if relations between the colonists and Britain were no better by that time.

The colonies prepare to fight. In the past, the protests of the colonies and their boycotts of British goods had brought results. The Stamp Act had been repealed, and the Townshend Acts had been abandoned. This time, however, the British government stood firm. Either the colonies must give in or they must fight. Which should it be? As the year 1774 drew to a close and 1775 began, more and more colonists came to believe that they must fight.

179

● See p. T23 for a strategy that asks students to examine the views of delegates at the First Continental Congress.

Groups of men all over the colonies began to meet for military drill. Massachusetts defied its governor, General Gage, and started to organize an army.

Most of the colonists still did not expect to break away from Great Britain. They thought that firm resistance to the laws they disliked, and perhaps a little fighting, would bring the British government to its senses. Then the hated laws would be changed, and the Americans would go on as before — as loyal colonists of Great Britain. Yet could they? Rising before a body of fellow-Virginians on March 23, 1775, the fiery Patrick Henry cried:

Gentlemen may cry, peace, peace — but there is no peace. The war is actually begun! The next gale that sweeps from the north will bring to our ears the clash of resounding arms! Our brethren are already in the field! Why stand we here idle? What is it that gentlemen wish? What would they have? Is life so dear, or peace so sweet, as to be purchased at the price of chains and slavery? Forbid it, Almighty God! I know not what course others may take; but as for me, give me liberty, or give me death!

The British act. The British could not remain idle while the people of Massachusetts defied the government by gathering arms and ammunition. In April, General Gage planned to send a force of soldiers to the town of Concord, some eighteen miles from Boston, to destroy war supplies that the Patriots

Patrick Henry, a bold leader in the defense of American rights, became well-known throughout the colonies for his powerful speeches.

"The British are coming!" Hearing a galloping horse, a farmer leans out his window to hear Paul Revere shout the famous warning. Soon many farmers like this one were dressed, armed, and ready to meet the British soldiers.

had collected there. He hoped also to capture the Patriot leaders, Samuel Adams and John Hancock, who were staying in the town of Lexington between Boston and Concord. On the night of April 18, Gage ordered his men to set out from Boston for Lexington and Concord.

Paul Revere warns the Patriots. The Patriots, however, were on the watch. Their soldiers were called minutemen because they could assemble quickly from their homes. Ready to ride into the country and alert the minutemen were Paul Revere, a silversmith of Boston, and a companion named William Dawes. A poet named Longfellow later wrote these verses about Paul Revere:

He said to his friend, "If the British march
By land or sea from the town tonight,
Hang a lantern aloft in the belfry arch
Of the North Church tower as a signal light,
One, if by land, and two, if by sea;
And I on the opposite shore will be,
Ready to ride and spread the alarm
Through every Middlesex village and farm,
For the country folk to be up and to arm.

The friend kept watch in Boston and learned that the redcoats were preparing to march. The poet goes on:

Meanwhile, impatient to mount and ride,
Booted and spurred, with a heavy stride
On the opposite shore walked Paul Revere.

181

● Find a copy of "Paul Revere's Ride" and read it to the class. Ask: Why is the poem *not* a primary source?

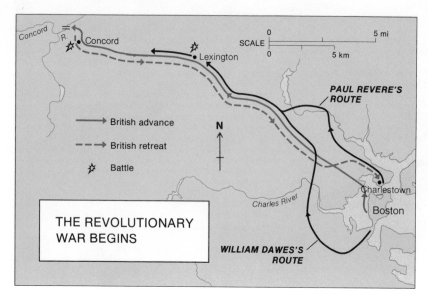

MAP STUDY
Warned by Revere and Dawes, colonial minutemen gathered to meet the British troops. (a) What route did Paul Revere take? (b) At what towns outside Boston did fighting take place? (Look for battle symbols.) (c) Where did the British turn back?

See Teacher's Key.

And lo! as he looks, on the belfry's
  height
A glimmer, and then a gleam of light!
He springs to the saddle, the bridle he
  turns,
But lingers and gazes, till full on his
  sight
A second lamp in the belfry burns!

So through the night rode Paul
  Revere;
And so through the night went his
  cry of alarm
To every Middlesex village and farm.

The poet does not tell us so, but Paul Revere was captured by the Brit-ish after he had reached Lexington and had warned Adams and Hancock. Nei-ther Revere nor Dawes reached Con-cord, but a third messenger succeeded. ● He warned the farmers along the way to Concord and gave the alarm in the town. (See the map on this page.)

A shot is "heard round the world." When the British soldiers reached Lex-ington in the early morning of April 19, 1775, they found a band of determined minutemen barring their way. Shots were fired. Eight of the Patriots were killed and ten more were wounded. Then the British marched on to Con-cord six miles away. There they burned the courthouse and destroyed military

AMERICANS AND BRITISH CLASH AT LEXINGTON

● The third messenger's name was Samuel Prescott.

supplies collected by the colonists. At a bridge on the edge of town, the British met another group of determined minutemen, and several volleys were fired by each side. But the fighting was not over. As the British soldiers marched back to Boston, other Patriots seized guns and took their positions along the road. From behind stone walls and trees the Americans fired on the British. Before the redcoats reached Boston, nearly 300 were killed, wounded, or missing.

What would happen next? Blood had been shed on both sides. Possibly the colonists still could have gone back to resisting unjust laws with written protests and fiery speeches. But the colonists did not put down their arms. Instead, they went on to defend their rights and create a new nation. For this reason, another poet (Ralph Waldo Emerson) said of the fighting at Concord:

> By the rude bridge that arched the
> flood,
> Their flag to April's breeze unfurled,
> Here once the embattled farmers
> stood,
> And fired the shot heard round the
> world.

▶ **CHECK UP**   See Teacher's Key.

1. **(a)** What were the Intolerable Acts? **(b)** Why were they passed?
2. **(a)** Why did the First Continental Congress meet? **(b)** What actions did the delegates take?
3. What led to fighting at Lexington and Concord?

CHECK UP ON CHAPTER 8

See Teacher's Key.

Words to Know

1. boycott
2. patriot
3. minuteman
4. redcoat
5. delegate
6. repeal
7. correspond
8. duty
9. proclamation
10. intolerable
11. writs of assistance

Places to Locate

1. Concord
2. Boston
3. Lexington

Facts to Remember

1. **(a)** What was the Proclamation of 1763? **(b)** Why did the British government issue this proclamation? **(c)** How did the colonists feel about it?
2. The American colonists showed their resistance to British control in various ways. Tell how each of the following played a part in those events: **(a)** Patrick Henry, **(b)** Samuel Adams, **(c)** Crispus Attucks, **(d)** the Sons and Daughters of Liberty, **(e)** Paul Revere.

Skills to Practice

1. Compare the maps on pages 130 and 170. **(a)** Find the Proclamation Line of 1763. What natural feature of the land did that line follow? **(b)** In 1763 did most English settlers live east or west of the Proclamation Line?
2. Look at the chart on page 174. **(a)** How did the colonists protest the closing of the frontier? **(b)** How did they protest the Townshend Acts? **(c)** What laws did the British pass as a result of the Boston Tea Party?
3. Read the story of the Boston Tea Party on page 177. What words can you find in the story that show that the colonists had planned their actions?

Questions to Think About

1. **(a)** Why did British leaders fail to understand the American colonists? **(b)** Why were the colonists unable to see Britain's side of the quarrel?
2. If Britain had treated the colonists more wisely, would they have been con-

183

● See p. T24 for a strategy that asks students to examine the historical significance of the fighting at Lexington and Concord.

tent to remain under British control? Give reasons for your answer.

3. Did the repeal of the Stamp Act mean that Parliament had changed its attitude on the question of taxing the colonists? Explain.

4. Tell in your own words what Patrick Henry said in his March 23, 1775, speech (page 180).

5. Americans today pay taxes to their government. Do they object as strenuously as the English colonists in America objected to paying taxes voted by Parliament? Explain.

 # Linking Past and Present

Reminders of the minutemen. On the village green at Lexington, Massachusetts, a great boulder marks the spot where the minutemen assembled against the British regulars on April 19, 1775. On the boulder are engraved these words, believed to have been spoken by the minuteman leader, Captain John Parker:

> Stand your ground.
> Don't fire unless fired upon.
> But if they mean to have a war
> Let it begin here.

Beyond Lexington, in the town of Concord, is the spot where the minutemen "fired the shot heard round the world." Here, a large bronze figure of a minuteman, rifle in hand, stands beside his plow. The old wooden bridge "that arched the flood" is long since gone; but an exact copy of it now crosses the Concord River. Our country has honored these early Patriots with the Minuteman National Historical Park, which includes many historic spots on the Lexington-Concord road.

It is interesting to know that two British redcoats killed in the clash at Concord were buried nearby. A stone marks their resting place, and each year flowers are placed on the grave.

Yankee Doodle. Americans were being called Yankees as far back as the 1760's, when the Americans and the British fought together in the French and Indian War. The redcoats in their fine uniforms used to poke fun at the untrained colonial soldiers, calling them "Yankee Doodles." (A "doodle" was a fool.) An English army doctor wrote some new verses to an old tune, ridiculing the Yankee Doodles. But the joke backfired. The Americans liked the catchy tune and, in spite of the redcoats' laughter, were soon singing "Yankee Doodle" as a marching song. "Yankee Doodle" continued to be popular in America long after the Revolution, and is still well known today.

The nickname Yankee has lasted also. In the war between the North and South, Northerners were called Yankees. During the two World Wars, American troops — northern or southern — were called Yanks by the Europeans. And today in Mexico and other parts of Latin America, we are referred to as "Yanquis." So a name given in fun more than 200 years ago has become a common word today.

Paul Revere. In a busy downtown part of Boston stands a house that was already old when Paul Revere bought it in 1770. He lived in it for 30 years. It is the only house built in the 1600's that still stands in a large American city. The windows have small panes in diamond shape, joined by lead frames, and the second floor juts out over the first. Paul Revere was a skilled metal worker, who could make anything from beautiful silver bowls and tea sets to large bronze church bells. Pieces of his silverwork are treasured today; and the bells that he made are still rung in the steeples of many New England churches.

● You may want the class to prepare a bulletin board display that features other famous songs, such as "America the Beautiful," "America," and "This Is My Country."

GAINING SKILL

Using Primary Sources

One of the Patriot leaders at the First Continental Congress was John Adams of Boston. During the Congress, Adams wrote regularly to his wife Abigail, who was managing their farm near Boston. In return, Abigail Adams kept her husband informed of events in the Boston area.

Letters such as those of John and Abigail Adams are called **primary sources.** The most common kind of primary source is a document that was written at the same time as the events it described. Letters, diaries, cargo lists, and tax records are all primary sources. Pictures drawn by someone who actually saw an event are also primary sources.

Two special kinds of punctuation are sometimes used when primary sources are printed in a book. A set of dots like this . . . is called an ellipsis (ih-LIP-sus). When you see an ellipsis, it means that some words have been left out. Sometimes you may see a word enclosed in brackets like these [   ]. Such a word is not part of the primary source; it has been added to replace an unfamiliar word or to give the reader extra information.

Read the passage from Abigail Adams's letter. Then answer the questions.

Braintree [Massachusetts]
14 September, 1774

The Governor is making all kinds of warlike preparations, such as mounting cannon upon Beacon Hill, digging intrenchments. . . . The people are much alarmed. . . .

In consequence of the [gun] powder being taken from Charlestown [a town near Boston], a general alarm spread through many towns and was caught pretty soon here. . . . About eight o'clock Sunday evening there passed by here about two hundred men, preceded by a horsecart, and marched down to the powder-house, from whence they took the powder, and carried it into the other parish and there [hid] it. I opened the window upon their return. They passed without any noise, not a word among them till they came against this house, when some of them, [seeing] me, asked me if I wanted any powder. I replied, No, since it was in so good hands. The reason they gave for taking it was that we had so many Tories [people loyal to Britain] here, they dared not trust us with it. . . . This town appears as [excited] as you can well imagine, and, if necessary, would soon be in arms. Not a Tory but hides his head. The church parson [a Tory] thought they were coming after him and ran up [to his attic]; they say another jumped out of his window and hid among the corn, whilst a third crept under his board fence. . . .

1. What preparations was the royal governor making for war?
2. Why might the British have taken the gunpowder that the Patriots were storing in Charlestown?
3. What group took the gunpowder from Braintree — the Patriots or the British?
4. What seems to be the mood of the people? What clues in the letter help you answer that question?
5. To which event was Abigail Adams an eyewitness? When was she merely reporting what others had told her? What phrase gives you a clue?

185

CHAPTER **9**   *Vocabulary preview:* revolution, privateer

The Thirteen English Colonies Win Their Independence

1775–1783   See pp. T24–T25 for chapter teaching strategies.

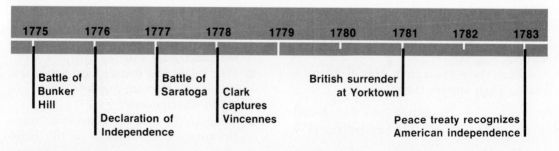

1775	1776	1777	1778	1779	1780	1781	1782	1783

Battle of
Bunker
Hill

Declaration of
Independence

Battle of
Saratoga

Clark
captures
Vincennes

British surrender
at Yorktown

Peace treaty recognizes
American independence

What this chapter is about —

Serious and honest people do not overthrow one government and set up another unless they believe their rights and liberties can be maintained in no other way. For this reason many of the American colonists hesitated to break away from the rule of Great Britain. One of them, Thomas Jefferson, said: "Prudence, indeed, will dictate that Governments long established should not be changed for light and [passing] causes."

Yet British soldiers and American Patriots had died in the fighting at Lex-

186

● Remind students that colonists still thought of themselves as English citizens. They
believed the rights they were defending were the rights of all English citizens.

ington and Concord on April 19, 1775. An open break between the colonies and Great Britain had taken place. Should the Patriots throw off the British government once and for all? Or should they try to heal the break and continue to live as subjects of King George?

These were burning questions in 1775.

In this chapter we will learn how the colonists made their decision. We will also study the war which was fought to win our independence. To help us in our study, we will look for answers to the following questions:

1. Why did the thirteen colonies decide to declare their independence?
2. What strengths and weaknesses did Americans have in the Revolution?
3. How did the thirteen colonies win their independence?

1 Why Did the Thirteen Colonies Decide to Declare Their Independence?

GREAT BRITAIN AND THE COLONIES DRIFT FURTHER APART

News of the fighting at Lexington and Concord spread quickly through the colonies. Meanwhile, the British troops of General Gage remained in Boston while Patriot recruits gathered in the towns surrounding the city. The Patriots had guns but no uniforms. They had little training, but they did have the courage to face the king's soldiers.

The colonists fight bravely in the Battle of Bunker Hill. During the night of June 16, 1775, a force of 1,200 Americans climbed Bunker Hill and Breed's Hill overlooking the city of Boston. (Look at the map on page 188.) If they could hold these hills, the Patriots might force the English troops to leave Boston. When the morning light came, the startled British found that the Americans had taken up their position on Breed's Hill. It is interesting that while the Patriots received orders to seize Bunker Hill, they fortified nearby Breed's Hill instead. So, although the battle was fought on Breed's Hill, Americans have always called it the Battle of Bunker Hill.

General Gage sent a group of redcoats to drive off or capture the bold Americans. While the citizens of Boston watched from their housetops, the lines of British soldiers advanced in perfect order toward the summit of the hill. Twice they nearly reached the top, only to be driven back by the sharpshooting Americans. The hillside was covered with the dead and dying. But the Patriots were running short of powder. When the redcoats attacked a third time, the Americans were forced to withdraw from the hill. The British were fond of boasting that their regular troops were the finest in the world. Yet in the Battle of Bunker Hill, Patriot farmers stood up to the regulars and caused more than twice as many losses as they suffered themselves.

Colonial troops force the British to leave Boston. During the months following the Battle of Bunker Hill, the Patriot forces surrounded Boston but were unable to drive the British out of the city. Then, early in 1776, 59 cap-

187

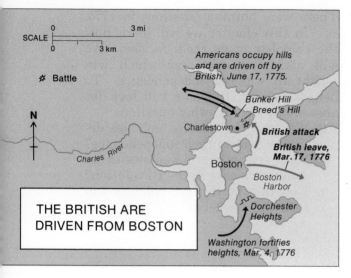

THE BRITISH ARE
DRIVEN FROM BOSTON

SCALE

0   3 mi

0   3 km

✵ Battle

N

Charles River

Americans occupy hills
and are driven off by
British, June 17, 1775.

Bunker Hill
Breed's Hill

Charlestown

British attack

British leave,
Mar. 17, 1776

Boston

Boston
Harbor

Dorchester
Heights

Washington fortifies
heights, Mar. 4, 1776

MAP STUDY   See Teacher's Key.
This map shows what happened in Boston in
1776. British troops (red lines) drove Patriot
forces from heights in Charlestown. How did
the Americans (black lines) force the British to
leave Boston?

tured cannon that had been dragged
overland from Fort Ticonderoga in
northeastern New York reached the
Patriots outside Boston. The Patriots
planned to place these cannon on Dorchester Heights, another hill overlooking the city and harbor. On a night
early in March, 1776, the Patriots succeeded in occupying Dorchester
Heights. General Howe, the new British commander, decided that he could
no longer hold Boston. On March 17,
1776, the British troops embarked on
ships in the harbor and sailed away to
Halifax, Nova Scotia. The Patriots entered Boston and held it from then on.
There were no more major battles in
New England during the Revolutionary
War. (A **revolution** is a change or upheaval in society. The war that Americans fought to win their independence
has several names: the Revolutionary

After capturing Fort
Ticonderoga, Patriots
dragged cannon to
Boston. The cannon
were used to fortify
Dorchester Heights,
overlooking the city.

War, the American Revolution, and the War of Independence.)

Blows are struck elsewhere. In the months between the fighting at Lexington (April, 1775) and the capture of Boston (March, 1776), the colonists struck other blows. A group of Patriots led by Ethan Allen seized Fort Ticonderoga (from which the cannon were later taken to Boston) and the British fort at Crown Point, also in northeastern New York. Encouraged by these victories, two American expeditions invaded Canada. The Americans seized Montreal, but they failed to take Quebec. In the end, both expeditions withdrew. Far to the south, in the Carolinas, more fighting took place. At Moore's Creek, North Carolina, Patriots defeated a group of colonists who had taken the side of the British. Also, a British attack on Charleston, South Carolina, was successfully turned back. The map on page 190 shows where these battles took place.

THE COLONIES DECLARE THEMSELVES INDEPENDENT

The attitude of the British government becomes stricter. Between the spring of 1775 and the spring of 1776, as we have seen, the colonists had taken up arms. Even so, most of them still hoped to remain British subjects. They believed that their willingness to shed blood would show King George III and his ministers how bitterly they opposed strict control by Great Britain. As a result, the colonists (and many people in England too) hoped that the British government would change its attitude. But, instead of adopting a milder attitude toward America, the king decided to be even more firm. He agreed with the British general at Boston, who wrote that the colonists "will be lions whilst we are lambs, but if we take the resolute part [firm stand] they will undoubtedly prove very meek."

The statue of a minuteman at Concord, Massachusetts, honors all Patriots who fought in the American Revolution.

Stricter laws were adopted, which greatly hurt the trade and industry of the colonies. The king refused to listen to the grievances of his American subjects, and proclaimed them to be rebels. What is more, he hired German soldiers, called Hessians, to serve in his armies in America. This act greatly angered the colonists. It was bad enough to have British redcoats swaggering up and down their streets. It was still worse for the country to be occupied by hired soldiers speaking a foreign language. Many Americans were forced to admit that there was little hope for fair treatment from Great Britain.

Colonial leaders call for independence. Must the colonies, then, throw off the government of Great Britain and become independent? A few leaders thought so — and said so. One of these was Samuel Adams. For years he had

189

★ See p. T24 for a strategy that calls for students to construct a bulletin board highlighting Patriot attitudes toward independence.

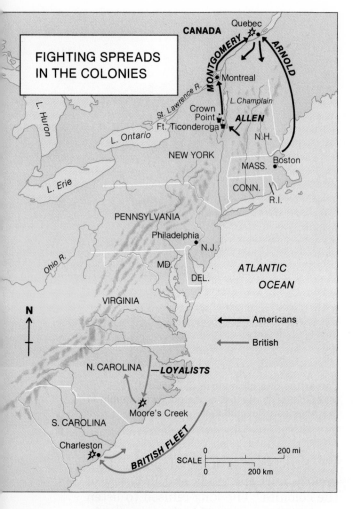

FIGHTING SPREADS
IN THE COLONIES

← Americans

← British

—LOYALISTS

BRITISH FLEET

SCALE
0   200 mi
0   200 km

MAP STUDY   See Teacher's Key.
After seizing Fort Ticonderoga, Americans
invaded Canada but were turned back. In what
states did the Patriots defeat early British efforts
to win control of the South?

been protesting against such measures
as the Stamp Act, the Townshend Acts,
and the Intolerable Acts. He was convinced that the colonies had to break
away from Britain. Such views made
Sam Adams unpopular with many
Americans and caused the British to
regard him as a dangerous person. But
he continued to urge bold action.
Adams had not been disturbed when he
learned that the British were on their
way to Lexington to capture him. In-

stead he had exclaimed: "What a glorious morning this is!" Even after the
fighting at Lexington and Concord some
Americans still tried to find a way to
patch up their differences with Britain,
but Adams came out more strongly
than ever in favor of independence.

The most stirring arguments in
favor of independence came from the
pen of Thomas Paine. Tom Paine, who
had recently come to America from
England, wrote a pamphlet called *Common Sense.* In it he called on Americans to break away from Great Britain.
This, wrote Paine, was the common-
sense thing to do. Why should a huge
continent be tied to a little island thousands of miles away? Why should the
colonists submit to laws that hurt their
trade and industry? Why should American colonists go on pledging loyalty to a
king who cared nothing for them, and
who had sent armies to oppress them?
"Everything that is right or reasonable," declared Tom Paine, "pleads for
separation."

Paine's pamphlet, which appeared
early in 1776, sold quickly. By their firesides and in public places, Americans
throughout the colonies talked about
the ideas so forcefully expressed by
Paine. Many who had been opposed to
independence, or who had been uncertain, now felt they wanted the colonies
to become independent.

**The Second Continental Congress
takes a bold step toward independence.**
As you read in Chapter 8, the First Continental Congress had arranged for the
meeting of another Congress if ill feeling
between Great Britain and the colonies
continued. In 1775, shortly after the
battles at Lexington and Concord, the
Second Continental Congress began its
sessions in Philadelphia. Among its
members were most of the important
colonial leaders.

At first, the majority of the delegates in Congress hoped to come to
terms with King George and his govern-

ment. As the months passed, however, the chances of a peaceful settlement grew dimmer. To more and more Americans, independence seemed the only answer. Finally, the Congress yielded to this growing demand for independence. Early in June, 1776, Richard Henry Lee of Virginia rose to his feet. He said he had been directed by his colony to present a motion. As the delegates listened, he read it: "Resolved, that these United Colonies are, and of right ought to be, free and independent states."

You can imagine the excitement in Congress in the days that followed. Delegates gathered in little groups to discuss independence and the all-important motion of Richard Henry Lee. Meanwhile, a committee was appointed to draw up a Declaration of Independence. The member of the committee who did most of the writing of the Declaration was Thomas Jefferson. This tall, 33-year-old Virginian had a rare gift for expressing his thoughts in clear, inspiring words. Soon he had prepared a Declaration for the Congress to consider.

The Declaration of Independence is adopted. Jefferson's Declaration did two important things:

(1) It expressed a bold new idea of the rights of the people. Before this time most people had believed that whatever rights they had were granted to them by the government under which they lived. But Jefferson believed that people are entitled to certain rights that cannot be taken from them by any government. In the Declaration he expressed this belief in ringing words:

> We hold these truths to be self-evident, that all men[1] are created equal, that they are endowed by their Creator with certain unalienable Rights, that among these are Life, Liberty and the pursuit of Happiness.

---
[1]*Men* is used here to mean all human beings.

Jefferson went on to say that the purpose of a government is "to secure these rights," and governments must have "the consent of the governed." Whenever a government does not protect these rights or have the consent of the governed, "it is the Right of the People to alter or to abolish it." Then the people should set up a new government, in such a form as to bring about "their Safety and Happiness."

(2) Secondly, the Declaration of Independence broke all ties with Britain. The colonies had suffered patiently, wrote Jefferson, under the harsh British laws. Now "it is their right, it is their duty, to throw off such Government. . . . We, therefore, the Representatives of the United States of America, in General Congress, Assembled, . . . do . . . solemnly . . . declare, That these United Colonies are, and of Right ought to be Free and Independent States." Jefferson ended the Declaration with these dramatic words:

> And for the support of this Declaration, with a firm reliance on the protection of divine Providence, we . . . pledge to each other our Lives, our Fortunes and our sacred Honor.

The Declaration of Independence was signed in bold handwriting by John Hancock, President of the Congress, so that, as he said, "George the Third might read it without his spectacles." Later the other delegates added their signatures.

You will find the complete text of the Declaration of Independence on ★ pages 193–195. This famous document is a vitally important part of our heritage. It should be read carefully and thoughtfully by all Americans.

A new nation is born. After a few days of discussion, Congress adopted the Declaration of Independence on July 4, 1776. After long months of uncertainty the fateful step had been taken. No longer were the Americans

★ See p. T25 for a strategy that helps students to read and understand the Declaration of Independence.

The Declaration of Independence was approved by the members of the Second Continental Congress on July 4, 1776. The delegates heeded the advice of Benjamin Franklin (seated in the center) who said, "We must all hang together or assuredly we shall all hang separately."

fighting as British subjects for their rights in the British Empire. Now they were citizens of a new nation. No longer would they refer to the "United Colonies." Now they spoke proudly of the *United States of America!*

▶ **CHECK UP**   See Teacher's Key.

1. **(a)** How did the Patriots capture Boston? **(b)** Where else had fighting taken place between the Patriots and the British troops?
2. **(a)** How did the British king try to stop the rebellion? **(b)** Why did many colonists begin to favor independence?
3. **(a)** What steps did the Second Continental Congress take to separate from Great Britain? **(b)** What were the two most important ideas of the Declaration of Independence?

•2 What Strengths and Weaknesses Did Americans Have in the Revolution?

As news of the Declaration of Independence spread through the states, people received it with mixed feelings. Despite their happiness they wondered: What will happen now? How can the United States succeed against the power of Great Britain? It was one thing for the Congress to declare the United States free and independent; it was another thing to win independence. What chance had thirteen small states against the army and navy of Great Britain—the most powerful nation in the world?

192

The Declaration of Independence

When in the Course of human events, it becomes necessary for one people to dissolve the political bands which have connected them with another, and to assume among the powers of the earth, the separate and equal station to which the Laws of Nature and of Nature's God entitle them, a decent respect to the opinions of mankind requires that they should declare the causes which impel them to the separation.*

The Right of the People to Control Their Government

We hold these truths to be self-evident, that all men are created equal, that they are endowed by their Creator with certain unalienable Rights, that among these are Life, Liberty and the pursuit of Happiness. That to secure these rights, Governments are instituted among Men, deriving their just powers from the consent of the governed, That whenever any Form of Government becomes destructive of these ends, it is the Right of the People to alter or to abolish it, and to institute new Government, laying its foundation on such principles and organizing its powers in such form, as to them shall seem most likely to effect their Safety and Happiness. Prudence, indeed, will dictate that Governments long established should not be changed for light and transient causes; and accordingly all experience hath shown, that mankind are more disposed to suffer, while evils are sufferable, than to right themselves by abolishing the forms to which they are accustomed. But when a long train of abuses and usurpations, pursuing invariably the same Object evinces a design to reduce them under absolute Despotism, it is their right, it is their duty, to throw off such Government, and to provide new Guards for their future security. Such has been the patient sufferance of these Colonies; and such is now the necessity which constrains them to alter their former Systems of Government. The history of the present King of Great Britain is a history of repeated injuries and usurpations, all having in direct object the establishment of an absolute Tyranny over these States. To prove this, let Facts be submitted to a candid world.

★ Tyrannical Acts of the British King

He has refused his Assent to Laws, the most wholesome and necessary for the public good.

He has forbidden his Governors to pass Laws of immediate and pressing importance, unless suspended in their operation till his Assent should be obtained; and when so suspended, he has utterly neglected to attend to them.

He has refused to pass other Laws for the accommodation of large districts of people, unless those people would relinquish the right of Representation in the Legislature, a right inestimable to them and formidable to tyrants only.

He has called together legislative bodies at places unusual, uncomfortable, and distant from the depository of their Public Records, for the sole purpose of fatiguing them into compliance with his measures.

*In punctuation and capitalization the text of the Declaration follows accepted sources.

★ Discuss events that probably led Jefferson to list each of these grievances. Refer to previous chapters if necessary.

He has dissolved Representative Houses repeatedly, for opposing with manly firmness his invasions on the rights of the people.

He has refused for a long time, after such dissolutions, to cause others to be elected; whereby the Legislative powers, incapable of Annihilation, have returned to the People at large for their exercise; the State remaining in the mean time exposed to all the dangers of invasion from without, and convulsions within.

He has endeavoured to prevent the population of these States; for that purpose obstructing the Laws for Naturalization of Foreigners; refusing to pass others to encourage their migrations hither, and raising the conditions of new Appropriations of Lands.

He has obstructed the Administration of Justice, by refusing his Assent to Laws for establishing Judiciary powers.

He has made Judges dependent on his Will alone, for the tenure of their offices, and the amount and payment of their salaries.

He has erected a multitude of New Offices, and sent hither swarms of Officers to harass our People, and eat out their substance.

He has kept among us, in times of peace, Standing Armies without the Consent of our legislatures.

He has affected to render the military independent of and superior to the Civil power.

He has combined with others to subject us to a jurisdiction foreign to our constitution, and unacknowledged by our laws; giving his Assent to their Acts of pretended Legislation:

● For quartering large bodies of armed troops among us:

For protecting them, by a mock Trial, from Punishment for any Murders which they should commit on the Inhabitants of these States:

For cutting off our Trade with all parts of the world:

For imposing Taxes on us without our Consent:

For depriving us in many cases, of the benefits of Trial by Jury:

For transporting us beyond Seas to be tried for pretended offences:

For abolishing the free System of English Laws in a neighbouring Province, establishing therein an Arbitrary government, and enlarging its Boundaries so as to render it at once an example and fit instrument for introducing the same absolute rule into these Colonies:

For taking away our Charters, abolishing our most valuable Laws, and altering fundamentally the Forms of our Governments:

For suspending our own Legislatures, and declaring themselves invested with power to legislate for us in all cases whatsoever.

He has abdicated Government here, by declaring us out of his Protection and waging War against us.

He has plundered our seas, ravaged our Coasts, burnt our towns, and destroyed the lives of our people.

He is at this time transporting large Armies of foreign Mercenaries to
★ compleat the works of death, desolation and tyranny, already begun with

circumstances of Cruelty & perfidy scarcely paralleled in the most barba-
rous ages, and totally unworthy the Head of a civilized nation.

He has constrained our fellow Citizens taken Captive on the high Seas
to bear Arms against their Country, to become the executioners of their
friends and Brethren, or to fall themselves by their Hands.

He has excited domestic insurrections amongst us, and has endeavoured to bring on the inhabitants of our frontiers, the merciless Indian
Savages, whose known rule of warfare, is an undistinguished destruction
of all ages, sexes and conditions.

● *Efforts of the Colonies to Avoid Separation*

In every stage of these Oppressions We have Petitioned for Redress in the
most humble terms: Our repeated Petitions have been answered only by
repeated injury. A Prince, whose character is thus marked by every act
which may define a Tyrant, is unfit to be the ruler of a free people.

Nor have We been wanting in attentions to our British brethren. We
have warned them from time to time of attempts by their legislature to
extend an unwarrantable jurisdiction over us. We have reminded them of
the circumstances of our emigration and settlement here. We have appealed to their native justice and magnanimity, and we have conjured them
by the ties of our common kindred to disavow these usurpations, which,
would inevitably interrupt our connections and correspondence. They too
have been deaf to the voice of justice and of consanguinity. We must,
therefore, acquiesce in the necessity, which denounces our Separation,
and hold them, as we hold the rest of mankind, Enemies in War, in Peace
Friends.

The Colonies Are Declared Free and Independent

We, therefore, the Representatives of the United States of America, in General Congress, Assembled, appealing to the Supreme Judge of the world
for the rectitude of our intentions, do, in the Name, and by Authority of the
good People of these Colonies, solemnly publish and declare, That these
United Colonies are, and of Right ought to be Free and Independent
States; that they are Absolved from all Allegiance to the British Crown, and
that all political connection between them and the State of Great Britain, is
and ought to be totally dissolved; and that as Free and Independent States,
they have full Power to Levy War, conclude Peace, contract Alliances, establish Commerce, and to do all other Acts and Things which Independent
States may of right do. And for the support of this Declaration, with a firm
reliance on the protection of divine Providence, we mutually pledge to each
other our Lives, our Fortunes and our sacred Honor.

195

★ Stress that because they believed British rule to be unjust, the writers of this
document felt they owed no allegiance to George III.

● See p. T25 for a strategy that asks students to examine the viewpoints of Patriots, Loyalists, and indifferent colonists.

WHAT WERE THE WEAKNESSES OF THE UNITED STATES?

The Patriot forces lack training and organization. Against Britain's armies of well-trained regulars, the Patriots seemed ill-matched. For one thing, the soldiers of the Continental Army had little experience in military tactics and fighting in open battle. Their training had been limited largely to frontier warfare against the Indians and the French. Their officers, too, had little experience compared to British officers. What is more, the Continental Army was loosely organized. Patriots had joined up, not because they had been ordered to do so, but of their own free will. Such volunteers felt free to return to their homes whenever their short terms of service were finished. As a result, the leaders of the army could hardly tell from day to day how many troops were under their command. Also, the colonies had no real navy. Against the strongest navy in the world the Americans could send not one first-class fighting ship.

The Patriots lack equipment and money. In order to carry on a war, the Patriots needed equipment and supplies — muskets and cannon, bullets and powder, uniforms and food. Unfortunately, the Second Continental Congress had little money to buy these things. Nor did Congress have the power to tax the people. It could only ask the states to give money, and the sums received were disappointingly small. Congress also tried to buy supplies with paper money that it printed in large quantities. But people did not like to take this money in payment for goods. Paper money is not worth much unless it can be exchanged for gold and silver, or unless the government that issues it is strong. The Continental Congress had little gold or silver, and it was a new and weak government. As the war dragged on, Continental paper money bought less and less. "Not worth a continental" became a way of saying that something was worthless.

Loyalists oppose the Patriots. The leaders of the Revolution not only had to fight the forces of the king; they also had to face enemies within their own villages and towns. Even after the Declaration of Independence had been signed, a large number of people, perhaps as many as a third of the colonists, remained loyal to the king. These people were known as Loyalists or Tories. ● Some Loyalists merely refused to help the Patriot cause. Others gave food and shelter to the king's armies or actually joined the British forces. Although the Loyalists thought they were doing right, the Patriots naturally regarded them as traitors. Sometimes Loyalists were "tarred and feathered" or forced to leave town. Patriots attacked their homes and destroyed or seized their property.

WHAT WERE THE STRENGTHS OF THE UNITED STATES?

In spite of all their handicaps, the Patriots managed to fight on year after year and finally to defeat the British. ★

The Patriots fight for a cause they believe in. The Continental soldiers lacked training and supplies, but at least they were fighting in their own country. Accustomed to outdoor life, they knew how to use firearms and how to make the most of scarce supplies. The officers and soldiers who had fought against the French and Indians had learned the value of alertness and self-reliance. And they were fighting for a noble cause — freedom and the safety of their homes and families. The British armies, on the other hand, were filled with soldiers who had been forced into service. Far from their homelands across the ocean, the British and Hessian soldiers naturally did not fight with the same spirit as the Americans.

196

The Patriots profit from British blunders. The mistakes that the British generals made also helped the Patriots' cause. Many of these generals had been appointed because they had wealthy and powerful friends in the home government. They looked with contempt on the poorly trained colonial troops and doubted that such soldiers would fight very hard or very long. Like the members of an overconfident athletic team, the British commanders grew careless. Instead of striking swift, hard blows at the Continental Army, they pursued it in a leisurely way. The British officers made blunders and allowed almost certain victory to slip through their fingers.

The Patriots receive foreign aid. The Patriots were helped by liberty-loving Europeans who hastened to this country to serve in the Continental Army. Among these volunteers was the Marquis de Lafayette. This dashing young French nobleman defied the orders of the king of France in order to come to America to fight for freedom. With Lafayette came the Baron de Kalb, who gave his life for American independence. Other important foreign soldiers joined our forces. They included the Baron von Steuben (who had fought under the great military leader, King Frederick of Prussia) and two Polish officers and lovers of liberty, Casimir Pulaski (poo-LAH-ski) and Thaddeus Kosciusko (kos-ee-US-koh). Americans were grateful for the help of these Europeans whose love of freedom inspired them to fight for the American cause.

Even more important was the assistance given the United States by foreign governments. At the start of the fighting, American representatives were sent to France in the hope of getting help. Because France was an old enemy of Great Britain, Congress reasoned that the French government might seize the chance to strike at the British by aiding America. Benjamin Franklin, America's wise and able statesman, worked long and hard to gain the help of France. When it appeared that the Americans had some chance of defeating the British, the French king agreed to help the Patriots. A treaty was signed making France and the United States military allies. France agreed to send money, supplies, soldiers, and ships to the Americans.

When France became our ally, Great Britain declared war on France. Then, other European nations were drawn into the struggle. The British declared war on Holland when Dutch bankers lent money to the American colonists. France persuaded its ally, Spain, to enter the war against Great Britain. During the later years of the war, Spanish as well as French ships kept the British navy busy. The Spanish army also gave important aid to the American cause. In 1779–1780 General Bernardo de Galvez, the Spanish governor of Louisiana, captured the British strongholds of Natchez and Baton Rouge in the lower Mississippi Valley and then went on to take Mobile. (See map, page 205.) These victories extended Spain's empire in North America. They also deprived the British of their ability to threaten the Americans from the southwest.

George Washington proves an excellent leader. ● An important reason for our country's victory was the leadership of George Washington. In the spring of 1775, the Second Continental Congress named Washington to be commander-in-chief of the Continental Army. Congress could hardly have made a better choice. Born in Virginia on February 22, 1732, the son of a well-to-do planter, Washington had had a good deal of military experience. As we learned in Chapter 6, Washington had led forces against the French and Indians. He also had experience in government affairs and had served in the First Continental Congress.

Abigail Adams, like other women of the time, served the Patriot cause by managing the family farm during the absence of her husband.

Tall, broad-shouldered, and dignified, Washington was a natural leader. His bravery and calm manner inspired officers and soldiers alike. He refused to give up in the face of shrinking armies, lack of money and supplies, and unfair criticism. Through the darkest days of the war, Washington steadily fought on. Many fainthearted Patriots were encouraged by the strength of their commander.

● **Women aid the Patriot cause.** An important British general once said that even if he could defeat all the men in America, he would still have to face all the women. American women were strong backers of the Patriot cause. As Abigail Adams, wife of Massachusetts Patriot John Adams, wrote, "If we should be defeated, I think we shall not be conquered. Let us learn by defeat the power of becoming unbeatable."

In the years before fighting actually broke out, colonial women took part in boycotts against British goods. They also formed organizations called Daughters of Liberty (page 172) to protest British taxes. Some women, such as Mercy Otis Warren of Massachusetts, wrote pamphlets calling on the colonists to resist British policies.

During the war years trade with Britain was cut off, forcing women to provide most of the clothing needed in America. Sewing bees became patriotic events where women turned out homemade clothes. Other women collected medical supplies for the troops, or lead for use in manufacturing bullets. Some women did their part by running farms and businesses while their sons and husbands were at war. Serving with the American army was still another way in which women helped out. They performed as doctors, nurses, guides, spies, cooks, and seamstresses.

A few women also became soldiers. Early in the war a former indentured servant named Deborah Sampson disguised herself as a man and joined the Continental Army. Sampson fought until she was wounded in a battle outside Philadelphia. Another woman, Margaret Corbin, took over her husband's cannon after he was killed in a battle in New York in 1776. She helped defend against the British until she herself received serious wounds.

Black Americans support the cause of independence. In every major battle of the Revolution, black Americans fought with the white Patriots. Black minutemen faced the British at Lexington and Concord. One of them, Peter Salem, also fought in the Battle of Bunker Hill and was hailed as a hero for his part in the conflict. Later, at the Battle of Yorktown, an observer wrote that "three-quarters of the Rhode Island

People in America's Story

GEORGE WASHINGTON

As commander of the Continental Army, chairman of the Constitutional Convention, and the first President of the United States, George Washington won a lasting place in American history as "Father of His Country."

Defense of the Virginia frontier was entrusted to young Colonel Washington during the French and Indian War.

Martha Custis (far right), shown with her two grandchildren, married the future President in 1759.

Washington rallied the hard-pressed American troops through the early years of the Revolution, including the grim winter at Valley Forge. In the painting below, Washington watches his troops pass in review.

Black and white soldiers fought side by side in every important battle of the American Revolution. This picture shows Peter Salem, a hero at the Battle of Bunker Hill.

regiment consists of [black men], and that regiment is the . . . best under arms, and the most precise in its maneuvers."

In the early years of the fighting, American slaveholders had tried to keep blacks out of the Continental Army. But when the British offered freedom to any slaves willing to fight on their side, the American army began to accept black soldiers. In all, nearly 5,000 blacks, both free and slave, fought beside white Americans during the Revolution.

Partly as a result of the patriotic service of black soldiers, some states began to pass laws limiting slavery and the slave trade. In 1780 Pennsylvania became the first state to pass a law gradually abolishing slaveholding.

The Patriots face a hard struggle. The courage of the Continental soldiers, Washington's leadership, the patriotic spirit of women and blacks, and help from foreign countries — all these made possible America's victory in the Revolutionary War. But the struggle was not easy, nor was success certain at any time. Month after month the Patriots were called on to meet disappointment, to endure hardship, and to fight desperately. These were, as Tom Paine wrote, "the times that try men's souls." But even when the future seemed almost hopeless, as it did on many occasions during the long seven-year struggle, the Patriots refused to admit defeat.

▶ **CHECK UP** See Teacher's Key.

1. **(a)** What were the weaknesses of the Patriots in the War of Independence? **(b)** What were their strengths?
2. **(a)** What were the British weaknesses during the American War of Independence? **(b)** What were their strengths?

3 How Did the Thirteen Colonies Win Their Independence?

● As you read about the Revolutionary War, remember that the soldiers who fought and died on the battlefields were ordinary people who had left their work and shouldered their rifles to face the trained British armies. Back in their homes — in towns, on farms and plantations, and in log cabins along the frontier — families eagerly waited for news of what was happening. There was no radio or television to give up-to-the-minute reports. Days, sometimes weeks, passed before word of battles reached people at home. For reports of

200

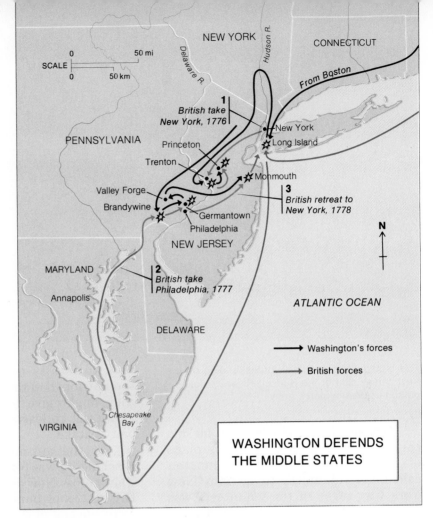

MAP STUDY
Sea power enabled the British to take New York, then Philadelphia. But Washington kept up the fight until the British held only New York City in the Middle States. What major battles (marked by symbols) are shown here?

See Teacher's Key.

NEW YORK

CONNECTICUT

From Boston

Delaware R.

Hudson R.

SCALE
0   50 mi
0   50 km

PENNSYLVANIA

1
British take New York, 1776

New York

Long Island

Princeton

Trenton

Monmouth

Valley Forge

3
British retreat to New York, 1778

Brandywine

Germantown

Philadelphia

NEW JERSEY

N

MARYLAND

2
British take Philadelphia, 1777

Annapolis

DELAWARE

ATLANTIC OCEAN

→ Washington's forces

→ British forces

Chesapeake Bay

VIRGINIA

WASHINGTON DEFENDS
THE MIDDLE STATES

the war, they had to depend on soldiers passing by, a peddler on the road, a letter, or an old newspaper. People eagerly shared these scraps of information with their neighbors. There must have been times during the dark days of the war, when the outcome seemed very doubtful.

THE MIDDLE STATES BECOME A BATTLEGROUND

The early fighting, as we have seen, broke out around Boston (page 187). Later, New York became the center of the fighting. There were two chief reasons why this was so: (1) The city of New York had the finest harbor along the coast. The British needed to control it if they were to keep their army supplied. (2) By holding the line of the

Hudson River and Lake Champlain to the north, the British could keep New England cut off from the rest of the colonies. With the colonies divided, the British would find it easier to conquer first one section and then another.

The British take New York City. Hoping to prevent the British from seizing New York, Washington moved his forces from Boston to Long Island. (See map on this page.) There they were attacked late in the summer of 1776 by the British forces from Halifax under General Howe. The Americans were badly defeated. Under cover of darkness and fog, however, the American army managed to escape to the north of New York City. The British took over the city, where they were given a royal welcome by wealthy Loyalists. They controlled New York until the end of the war.

This painting shows British forces landing on the New Jersey side of the Hudson River in their pursuit of Washington's army.

Nathan Hale gives his life for his country. Wishing to learn of the plans of the British, General Washington called for volunteers to go into New York City. One of the volunteers was 21-year-old Captain Nathan Hale. Before the war he had been a schoolteacher in Connecticut. Washington chose Nathan Hale for the dangerous task of finding out about the British plans. In disguise Hale made his way into New York City but was captured by the British and hanged as a spy. As Nathan Hale faced death, his last words were: "I only regret that I have but one life to lose for my country."

Washington retreats into New Jersey. More bad fortune followed the loss of New York. Washington lost 2,600 of his best soldiers and large supplies of ammunition and guns when the British captured two American forts on the Hudson River. Perhaps the British forces could have ended the Revolution by immediately attacking Washington's discouraged troops. But General Howe did not wish to destroy the Patriot army because he hoped to win the Americans back to loyalty to Britain. Now that the Patriots had tasted defeat, he hoped they might give in. This, as General Howe was to learn to his sorrow, was a bad mistake.

In the autumn of 1776, General Washington was forced to retreat southward across New Jersey. Howe and the British troops pursued him slowly. Toward the end of the year, the Continental forces crossed the Delaware River into Pennsylvania. (See Washington's route on the map on page 201.) These were discouraging days for the American commander-in-chief. Many of his soldiers had lost hope and had returned to their farms and their jobs. He had expected to find additional troops in New Jersey, but not even a hundred men appeared. At the same time that Washington moved into Pennsylvania, approaching British troops caused Congress to flee from its meeting place in Philadelphia. The American cause seemed hopeless. It is said that some of the British generals were so sure the war was almost over that they sent their belongings to their ships to be ready to sail for home.

Victories at Trenton and Princeton cheer the Patriots. Washington, however, refused to give up hope. He de-

● Tell students that the Continental Congress reassembled in York, Pennsylvania.

cided on a bold move. In the bitter cold of Christmas night, 1776, he and his army turned and recrossed the Delaware River. At Trenton, New Jersey, they found 1,400 Hessian soldiers who had been celebrating the holiday. Washington's men took them by surprise and captured a thousand prisoners. Then Washington moved back a few miles. Lord Cornwallis, sent in a hurry to capture Washington, thought he had "the old fox" in a tight place. Once again, however, the American leader showed his skill and daring. Leaving campfires burning brightly to deceive the British, Washington and his soldiers quietly moved away in the darkness. The next morning Cornwallis was awakened by the dull boom of distant cannon. It was Washington's army attacking three regiments of British soldiers at nearby Princeton. Washington soundly defeated these enemies too.

The daring victories at Trenton and Princeton gave new courage to the Patriots. Although their cause was far from won, Americans could face the future with more hope.

The British plan to crush the Americans. In 1777 the British commanders made plans to cut off New England by seizing control of the Hudson Valley. An army from Canada, under General John Burgoyne (Gentleman Johnny, as the British called him), was to march south by way of Lake Champlain to Albany. There it was to be met by General Howe's forces from New York City. A third army was to march from Fort Oswego on Lake Ontario eastward across New York State to join the other two armies in Albany.

The plan was a good one, but it did not work. The army from Fort Oswego never reached Albany. It was met on the way by American troops at Oriskany (or-ISS-kuh-nih) in one of the bloodiest battles of the war. After the fighting at Oriskany, the British retreated to Oswego. As for General Howe, instead of sending troops to aid Burgoyne, he ordered the army in New York City to board a fleet bound for Chesapeake Bay. After landing, Howe and the army marched north toward Philadelphia.

Saratoga is a turning point in the war. Burgoyne, left on his own, marched south and captured Fort Ticonderoga. But the farther the British advanced, the greater their troubles became. Angry New Yorkers and New Englanders cut down trees to block their way. They also burned crops and drove off cattle, leaving the countryside bare of supplies. In the face of such obstacles Burgoyne and his men advanced slowly. When the General sent 700 Hessians eastward to get supplies, Patriots surrounded and defeated them near Bennington, in the present state of Vermont. At length Burgoyne clashed with American forces near Saratoga, New York (map, page 205). The British were defeated. Greatly outnumbered, and with no chance of receiving help, General Burgoyne surrendered his whole army on October 17, 1777.

Burgoyne's surrender was a turning point in the war. It was the American victory at the Battle of Saratoga and the capture of Burgoyne and his men that persuaded the French king to give aid to the American cause (page 197). Without this aid the Patriots might have had too little money and too few supplies to keep their armies in the field.

Washington winters at Valley Forge. Now let us return to General Howe, who, with his army, had turned toward Philadelphia. Washington tried to stop him at Brandywine and Germantown but was defeated in both battles. Howe succeeded in capturing Philadelphia (map, page 201).

General Howe and his men spent the winter of 1777–1778 in Philadelphia. For them it was a jolly and comfortable time. They had warm homes to shelter them and plenty to eat. There was a constant round of dances and parties.

Molly Hays won fame for her heroism at the Battle of Monmouth. Her fellow soldiers gave her the nickname Molly Pitcher.

But this winter, so pleasant for Howe's men, proved a nightmare for the Continental Army.

Washington and his troops set up camp nearby at Valley Forge. Food was scarce. Rough log huts were all the shelter the soldiers had against the wintry winds and drifting snow. Their ragged clothing gave them little protection against the bitter cold. Many soldiers did not have shoes, and few had blankets to keep them warm during the long winter nights. The Continental money was worth so little that farmers would not take it in exchange for food. They preferred to sell their pigs and cattle to the British for gold or silver. Under such conditions some of the Continental soldiers became discouraged and returned home; many others fell sick. But Washington knew the value of the victory at Saratoga, and he moved calmly and encouragingly among his cold and hungry troops. The German Baron von Steuben drilled the Patriot forces all winter to get them ready for more fighting in the spring.

Fighting ends in the middle states. In mid-June, 1778, the British abandoned Philadelphia and began a march across New Jersey toward New York City. Washington pursued the British troops and would almost certainly have defeated them at Monmouth, New Jersey, except for the action of an American officer, General Charles Lee. Instead of following Washington's orders to attack, Lee ordered his men to retreat!

In this battle Mary Hays became one of the most famous fighters in the Revolution. In the sweltering heat she carried pitchers of water to thirsty soldiers until her husband was wounded. Then, while caring for her husband, she took up his gun and joined in the fighting. The soldiers gave Mary Hays the nickname Molly Pitcher, and General Washington later made her a sergeant in the Continental Army.

In spite of the Americans' resistance, the British reached New York, where Washington kept them bottled up until the end of the war. No other

● Be sure students read about the restoration of Valley Forge in "Linking Past and Present" (p. 212).

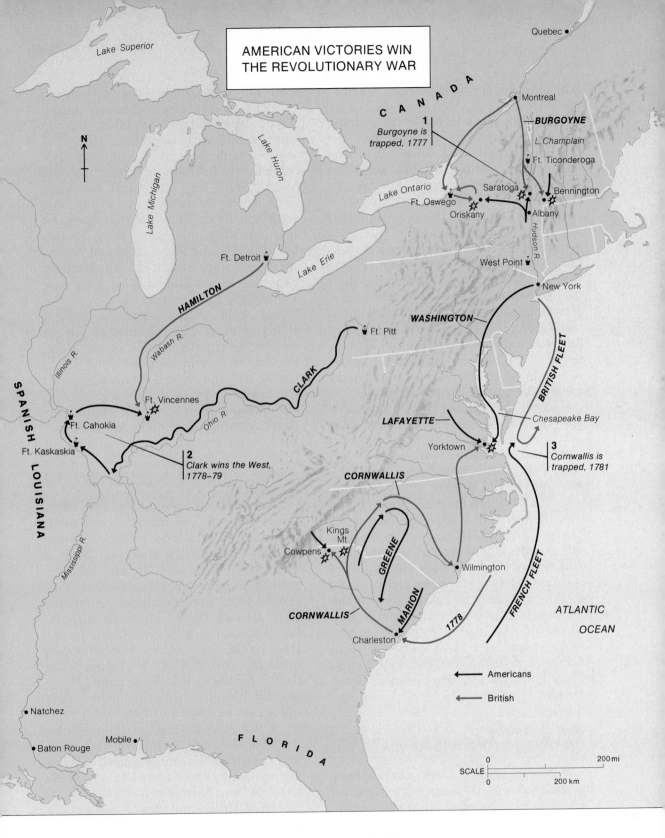

AMERICAN VICTORIES WIN THE REVOLUTIONARY WAR

Quebec

Lake Superior

CANADA

Montreal

BURGOYNE

1
Burgoyne is trapped, 1777

L. Champlain

Ft. Ticonderoga

Lake Ontario

Saratoga

Bennington

Lake Huron

Lake Michigan

N

Ft. Oswego

Oriskany

Albany

Hudson R.

Ft. Detroit

Lake Erie

West Point

HAMILTON

New York

Wabash R.

Ft. Pitt

WASHINGTON

BRITISH FLEET

Illinois R.

CLARK

Ft. Vincennes

Ohio R.

LAFAYETTE

Chesapeake Bay

SPANISH

Ft. Cahokia

Yorktown

3
Cornwallis is trapped, 1781

Ft. Kaskaskia

2
Clark wins the West, 1778–79

LOUISIANA

CORNWALLIS

Mississippi R.

Kings Mt.

GREENE

Cowpens

Wilmington

CORNWALLIS

MARION

1778

FRENCH FLEET

ATLANTIC OCEAN

Charleston

Natchez

Americans

British

Baton Rouge

Mobile

FLORIDA

SCALE

0   200 mi

0   200 km

MAP STUDY Three significant American victories brought about the defeat of the British. (a) Where were these victories and in what order did they take place? (b) What country's fleet helped trap Cornwallis at Yorktown?

205

See Teacher's Key.

important battles took place in the middle states.

A traitor plans to betray his country. One event occurred, however, that was a serious blow to the American cause. Among the Patriot leaders who had fought brilliantly early in the war was Benedict Arnold. He had attacked Quebec at the start of the war and had taken a leading part in the Battle of Saratoga that led to Burgoyne's surrender. Arnold was an ambitious man who felt that he deserved more credit than he had received for his services to the Patriot cause. But he had been criticized and court-martialed for misusing his powers as military governor of Philadelphia. Moreover, Arnold had fallen deeply in debt. His need for money and his wounded pride tempted him to enter the pay of the British. He not only gave the British military secrets but persuaded Washington to place him in command of the fort at West Point, New York. Arnold planned to turn the fort over to the British.

The plot to surrender West Point was discovered in 1780 by the capture of Major André (AHN-dray), the English officer with whom Arnold was dealing. André was executed as a spy, but Arnold managed to reach the British lines in safety. During the remainder of the war he fought under the British flag. Years later he died in England, an unhappy man. His name came to mean "traitor" in his native land, and he was looked on with contempt even in Great Britain.

WAR IS WAGED ON THE FRONTIER AND AT SEA

George Rogers Clark attacks forts in the West. At the same time that the war was being carried on in the middle states, fighting had also been taking place in the frontier region to the west. (See the map on page 205.) Here the British were aided by their Indian al-

lies. The Indians knew they would lose more by an American victory than they would if the British triumphed. We can imagine one of them saying, "If the Patriots win the war, they will push their settlements farther and farther into the West. Soon our lands will be taken over. If the British win, we will be able to go on living as we always have, at least for a little longer." With British backing, Indian forces attacked settlements not only west of the Appalachian Mountains but also in New York and Pennsylvania.

A bold young Virginian named George Rogers Clark decided to put an end to the British activity in the West. He obtained permission from the governor of Virginia to lead an expedition to the frontier. In 1778, he led a force of two hundred men down the Ohio River. Clark surprised and captured the British frontier forts in the present state of Illinois. Vincennes (vin-SENZ), in what is now Indiana, also came under his control.

Clark gains control in the West. Colonel Henry Hamilton, the British commander at Fort Detroit, was alarmed by Clark's success. With a force of British and Indian soldiers, Hamilton recaptured the fort at Vincennes from the handful of Americans Clark had left there. Although the British commander expected Clark to attack, he thought nothing would happen until the spring of 1779. Instead, the daring American led a little band of men against Vincennes in midwinter. Wading across swamps and flooded lands in icy water that reached to their waists, the frontiersmen surprised Hamilton and captured Vincennes again. Clark's victories gave the Americans a hold on the vast area between the Great Lakes, the Ohio River, and the Mississippi.

American privateers prey on enemy shipping. Meanwhile, Americans were waging war on sea as well as on land. From the harbors of New England, fish-

The victories of George Rogers Clark over the British in the West helped establish the American claims to land west of the Appalachians. Clark's little army was made up of volunteer frontiersmen, such as the recruits shown in the painting above.

ing vessels and merchant ships that had been fitted out with guns and crews sailed forth to seize enemy shipping. These **privateers,** as they were called, captured many British merchant vessels and brought them to port. The cargo of a captured ship was sold and the money divided among the crew of the privateer. Later in the war, as British men-of-war kept a close watch along the coast for privateers, fewer American ships dared to venture out.

The Americans build a navy. When they were colonists of Britain, the Americans, of course, had no navy; they had always depended for protection on the British fleet. Now this powerful fleet was fighting against the Americans, not for them. Early in the war Congress had begun to build a navy. John Paul Jones, a Scottish sailor who had settled in Virginia a few years before the war, advised Congress to build small, speedy ships. During the whole Revolutionary War, however, there were only about 40 ships in the United States Navy. Before the end of the war all but six of these were either captured or sunk by their crews to prevent the enemy from taking them.

John Paul Jones wins respect for the American navy. Our navy, although small, gave a good account of itself. The most famous sea fight of the Revolution took place in 1779 between a British vessel and a ship built in France and commanded by John Paul Jones. Jones had been cruising along the British coast with his vessel, the *Bonhomme Richard* (buh-NAWM ree-SHAR), and three other ships. Meeting a fleet of merchant ships guarded by two British warships, he attacked the larger enemy warship, called the *Serapis.*

During the bloody three-hour battle, the *Bonhomme Richard* suffered great damage and was leaking badly. Jones ran his ship so close to the *Serapis* that their cannon almost touched. The British commander called out, "Have you lowered your flag?" In words that have become famous, Jones replied, "I have not yet begun to fight," and went on shooting. Soon the decks of the *Bonhomme Richard* were littered with dead and wounded men. But the *Serapis* also had been badly damaged. When its mainmast fell, the British commander surrendered to Jones.

John Paul Jones had shown that Americans could fight on sea as well as on land. Although he spent most of his later life in Europe, his body was brought back to the United States after his death. He now lies in an honored grave at the Naval Academy in Annapolis.

THE WAR IN THE SOUTH BRINGS VICTORY

The British change their plans. After three years of fighting, the British faced a difficult problem. Several campaigns in the middle states had brought them no nearer to defeating the Patriots than they had been in 1775. When France entered the war in 1778, the British had to face the power of that country as well. Expecting to gain the help of large numbers of Loyalists, they shifted the war to the southern states. From the close of 1778 to the end of the war, nearly all the fighting took place in the South.

British and American forces battle in the South. At first it seemed that the British had made a wise decision. They won victories that gave them control of Georgia and most of South Carolina. Only a few roving bands of Patriots courageously kept up the fight. Led by daring leaders such as Francis Marion (nicknamed "the Swamp Fox"), these bands hid in swamps and ventured forth from time to time to pounce on small British forces.

At last, the Americans were able to check the British in the South. Late in 1780, the British leader, General Cornwallis, set out to conquer North Carolina. Part of his army, however, was defeated by frontier fighters at Kings Mountain on the border of North and South Carolina. Then, Washington sent one of his ablest generals, Nathanael Greene, to lead the Patriot troops in the South. The Americans won an important victory at Cowpens in South Carolina but were pursued far into North Carolina by the main British army. Because supplies were hard to get, Cornwallis was forced to give up his hold on North Carolina. He then withdrew his army to the coast. (See the map on page 205 for the war in the South.)

The Patriots' cause looks hopeless. Even though Cornwallis had been prevented from taking North Carolina, the Americans were becoming discouraged over the course of the war. Washington, as you know, had been using most of his troops to keep the British bottled up in New York. It was now the spring of 1781. The Patriots had been fighting for six long years and victory still seemed far away. Volunteers were restless at being kept in the army, and food and supplies were always scarce. Even Washington was becoming discouraged and feared the end was near. But then Cornwallis made a move that gave Washington his chance to strike a crushing blow at the British.

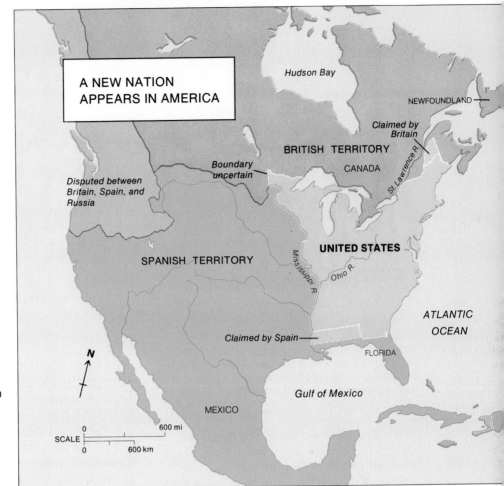

A NEW NATION
APPEARS IN AMERICA

Hudson Bay

NEWFOUNDLAND

Claimed by
Britain

BRITISH TERRITORY

CANADA

Boundary
uncertain

St. Lawrence R.

Disputed between
Britain, Spain, and
Russia

UNITED STATES

SPANISH TERRITORY

Mississippi R.

Ohio R.

ATLANTIC
OCEAN

Claimed by Spain

FLORIDA

N

Claimed by Spain

Gulf of Mexico

MEXICO

SCALE 0 ——— 600 mi
       0 ——— 600 km

See Teacher's Key.

MAP STUDY
The peace treaty of
1783 left the
boundaries of the
United States uncertain
in three places.
(a) Where were those
places? (b) What
natural waterways did
the nation's northern
and western
boundaries follow?

Cornwallis is caught in a trap. Lord
Cornwallis had marched his men northward into Virginia, which was defended
only by a small American force under
Lafayette. "That boy cannot escape
me," Cornwallis boasted scornfully.
But "that boy," Lafayette, whose forces
were not strong enough to meet the
British, managed to slip away. Cornwallis then began to fortify Yorktown,
which was located on a peninsula extending into Chesapeake Bay. At this
base he expected supplies and more
troops to come by sea from New York.
● This was a fatal mistake. A large
French fleet from the West Indies closed
the entrance to Chesapeake Bay, and a
British fleet sent to relieve Cornwallis
was driven off.

Washington, meanwhile, had made
a bold move. Leaving New York, he
joined his army with several thousand
French soldiers and raced to Virginia. A
force of about 16,000 American and
French troops closed in on Cornwallis at
Yorktown.

Cornwallis surrenders. Although
the British fought desperately, they
knew their cause was hopeless. Surrounded on all sides, Cornwallis and his
entire army surrendered to the Americans and French on October 19, 1781.
On the next page you will read what an
eyewitness said happened on that day: 209

● Have students locate Yorktown on the map on p. 205. Discuss why Cornwallis's
choice of Yorktown as a base was indeed a "fatal mistake."

Celebrations were held at Yorktown in 1981 to mark the two-hundredth anniversary of the Patriot victory over Lord Cornwallis.

● At about twelve o'clock, the combined army [Americans and French] was arranged and drawn up in two lines, extending more than a mile in length. The Americans were drawn up in a line on the right side of the road, and the French occupied the left. At the head of the former the great American commander [Washington] . . . took his station, attended by his aides. At the head of the latter was posted the excellent Count Rochambeau and his [staff]. The French troops, in complete uniform, displayed a martial and noble appearance; their band of music . . . produced while marching . . . a most enchanting effect. The Americans, though not all in uniform, nor their dress so neat, yet exhibited an erect soldierly air, and every [face] beamed with satisfaction and joy.

Between the two victorious armies the British troops marched out to surren-der, their bands playing "The World Turned Upside Down." The victory at Yorktown meant the end of the fight for independence.

Great rejoicing followed the surrender of Cornwallis. Bonfires sent their flames high into the sky, bells rang, and prayers were said in thanksgiving. Independence had been won at last.

American independence is recognized. Although the actual fighting in America was over in 1781, the peace treaty was not signed until 1783. By this treaty Great Britain recognized the United States as an independent nation. The new nation's territory was to stretch from Canada to Florida, and from the Atlantic Ocean to the Mississippi River. The river itself, however, was to be open to the trade of both Great Britain and the United States. Americans were to be permitted to fish off Newfoundland and the mouth of the St. Lawrence River. In a separate treaty Great Britain returned Florida to Spain. To see how North America looked in 1783, look at the map on page 209.

● Ask: Why is this report a primary source? (It was written by an eyewitness.)

King George III said sourly that, considering the "knavery" of the Americans, perhaps it might "not in the end be an evil" that they had left the British Empire. As for the Americans, the opinions of George III no longer mattered. They had won their freedom and had created a new nation.

▶ **CHECK UP**   See Teacher's Key.

1. **(a)** Why were the early days of fighting discouraging to the Patriots? **(b)** How did Washington keep the Patriot cause alive?
2. **(a)** How did the British plan to end the war in 1777? **(b)** Why did the plan fail? **(c)** Why was the Battle of Saratoga important?
3. **(a)** How did George Rogers Clark win control of the West for the Americans? **(b)** How successful were the Americans in fighting at sea?
4. **(a)** Why did the British shift the war to the South? **(b)** Where did battles take place there? **(c)** How was Cornwallis trapped at Yorktown?
5. What were the terms of the peace treaty ending the war?

CHECK UP ON CHAPTER 9   See Teacher's Key.

Words to Know

1. abolish
2. recruit
3. Loyalist
4. Hessian
5. privateer
6. volunteer
7. revolution
8. declaration

Places to Locate

1. Oriskany
2. Saratoga
3. Trenton
4. Princeton
5. Yorktown
6. Vincennes
7. Cowpens
8. Hudson River
9. Ticonderoga
10. Delaware River
11. New York City
12. Philadelphia
13. Kings Mountain
14. Chesapeake Bay

Facts to Remember

1. **(a)** What did Thomas Paine urge Americans to do in *Common Sense*? **(b)** What effect did this pamphlet have on American opinion?
2. **(a)** Why did the members of the Second Continental Congress decide to declare independence from Britain? **(b)** What two main important ideas did Thomas Jefferson express in writing the Declaration of Independence?
3. **(a)** Describe the weaknesses of the American Patriots in fighting the Revolutionary War. **(b)** Describe their strengths.
4. What was the importance of each of the following battles? **(a)** Bunker Hill **(b)** Saratoga **(c)** Vincennes **(d)** Yorktown
5. Tell how each of the following contributed to the American victory: **(a)** Nathan Hale, **(b)** George Washington, **(c)** Lafayette, **(d)** Peter Salem, **(e)** Molly Pitcher, **(f)** John Paul Jones.

Skills to Practice

1. Look back through this chapter (pages 186–211) and identify the page on which each of the following primary sources appears:
   a. A passage from Thomas Paine's *Common Sense*.
   b. A description of Cornwallis's surrender at Yorktown.
   c. A British general's claim that the colonists would be meek if the British government would be firm.
   d. Samuel Adams's description of the day of the Battle of Lexington as glorious.
   e. John Paul Jones's reply to a challenge from a British ship captain.
   f. The complete words of the Declaration of Independence.
2. Look at the map on page 205. **(a)** From what fort did George Rogers Clark's expedition leave? **(b)** What rivers did he and his men follow as they marched

to Fort Kaskaskia? **(c)** What forts did they capture after their victory at Kaskaskia?

Questions to Think About

1. Why did it take great courage for the members of the Continental Congress to vote for the Declaration of Independence?
2. Read again what Abigail Adams said about the Patriot cause on page 198. Why did she think the Patriots would not be "conquered" even if they were "defeated"? Explain in your own words what she meant.
3. Look back at the account of Nathan Hale on page 202. What do his words and actions tell us about his character?
4. American persistence, French aid, and British mistakes were major factors in the outcome of the Revolutionary War. Explain the importance of each.

Linking Past and Present

The Liberty Bell. The chief attraction in Independence Hall in Philadelphia is the grand old Liberty Bell. Although the Bell is chipped and cracked, you can see on it the date when it was made (1753) and the names of its makers. Around the base you can still read this inscription from the Bible: "Proclaim liberty throughout all the land unto all the inhabitants thereof." The Liberty Bell pealed out the birth of our nation in 1776 and later our victory in the Revolutionary War. Through the years it tolled in solemn tones to announce the deaths of beloved American patriots. In 1835 the Bell rang for the last time — it had cracked badly. On June 6, 1944, however, Americans heard its voice again, this time over a nation-wide radio broadcast. The Bell was struck with a rubber mallet to celebrate the landing of Allied troops on the coast of France during World War II.

The message of Valley Forge. Every year thousands of Americans visit places made famous during the Revolutionary War, places which remind us that our freedom was dearly bought. One spot a visitor never forgets is Valley Forge, Pennsylvania, where the Continental Army spent the winter of 1777–1778. The old camp grounds have been restored and look much as they did over 200 years ago. You see the crude log huts that gave poor shelter to Washington's ragged, hungry soldiers. Beyond are the grounds where, in spite of cold and snow, Baron von Steuben drilled the troops in preparation for the spring campaign. You see the houses where Washington, Lafayette, and other officers stayed. As you remember that desperate winter when the American cause seemed lost, you realize that Valley Forge is more than an old camp ground. It is a reminder of the spirit that rose above hardship and fear of defeat to win the independence we enjoy today.

The Stars and Stripes. Our flag is almost ● as old as the nation itself. For more than 200 years, it has flown over the land of the free. The design for our nation's first flag was voted upon by the Continental Congress on June 14, 1777. (We now celebrate that day each year as Flag Day.) It was agreed that this flag should have thirteen stripes — one for each state — alternating red and white, and thirteen white stars on a blue field.

For a while, a new stripe and a new star were added whenever a state joined the Union. But it soon became clear that this would spoil the beauty of the flag. So in 1818 the number of stripes was reduced to thirteen, but a star continued to be added for each new state. Our flag grew with our nation until in 1912 it had 48 stars. The number of stars remained the same until 1959, when Alaska and Hawaii were admitted to the Union. Today the flag proudly displays 50 stars on its field of blue.

● Have students put together a bulletin board display highlighting the history of the American flag.

Give students a list of events from the period before the Revolutionary War. Have students look up the dates, arrange the events in chronological order, and make a time line.

GAINING SKILL

Reading Time Lines

When you look back over a period of time — the past week, a vacation, or a school year — certain events stand out in your mind as important. The same is true in the history of our country. Though a great many events make up the story of America's past, some events stand out among all the rest. Such events might include an important battle, the election of a new President, or a discovery.

One quick way to look at important events is to place them on a time line. In this book, time lines appear at the start of each unit and chapter. They show major events arranged in chronological order.

Look at the time line on this page. Use the information on the time line to answer the questions in the next column.

1. What is the first date marked on the time line? What is the last date shown?
2. In what year was Benedict Arnold's treason discovered?
3. When did a treaty bring the War of Independence to an end?
4. Which took place first — the Battle of Trenton or the Battle of Saratoga?
5. Did the Americans form an alliance with the French before or after the Battle of Saratoga?
6. The following events are not shown on the time line. Find the place on the time line where each belongs.

1775   Battle of Bunker Hill
1779   George Rogers Clark recaptures Vincennes
1780   Battle of Cowpens

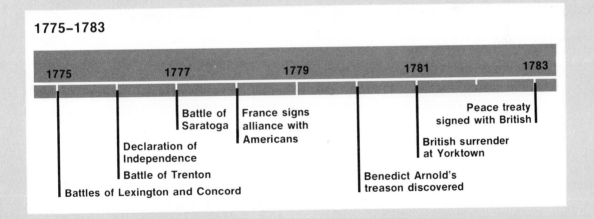

1775–1783

1775   1777   1779   1781   1783

Battle of Saratoga
France signs alliance with Americans
Peace treaty signed with British
Declaration of Independence
British surrender at Yorktown
Battle of Trenton
Benedict Arnold's treason discovered
Battles of Lexington and Concord

CHAPTER **10** *Vocabulary preview:* responsible government, scale

The Spirit of Independence Affects Canada and Latin America

1763–1850 See p. T26 for chapter teaching strategies.

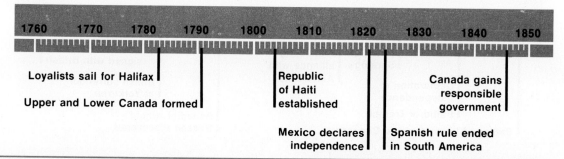

| 1760 | 1770 | 1780 | 1790 | 1800 | 1810 | 1820 | 1830 | 1840 | 1850 |

Loyalists sail for Halifax

Upper and Lower Canada formed

Republic of Haiti established

Mexico declares independence

Spanish rule ended in South America

Canada gains responsible government

What this chapter is about —

"I swear before . . . the God of my fathers, I swear by my honor and by my native land, that I will give no rest to my arm or repose to my soul until I have broken the chains that oppress us. . . ."

The man who spoke these solemn words was not an English colonist speaking in support of the American Revolution, but a patriot from Spanish Venezuela in South America. As we will see in this chapter, the revolution of the thirteen British colonies was only one of several explosions that shook the West-

214

● Be sure students understand the term *Western Hemisphere.*

After the United States won its independence from Great Britain, other colonies in the Western Hemisphere began to shake off European rule. Simón Bolívar was a leader in the struggle against Spanish colonial rule. He is often called "the George Washington of South America."

ern Hemisphere. As a result of these explosions, other new nations were born in the Americas. By 1825, Spain's colonies had cut the ties that bound them to their parent country. Brazil was no longer a colony of Portugal but an independent nation. Of all the European countries that had carved out empires in America, only Great Britain still held an important colony — Canada. Yet even Canada, which did not fight a war for independence, followed a path which led it finally to self-government.

It is important for us as Americans to know something about the neighbors who share the Western Hemisphere with us. This chapter will tell what happened in Canada and in Latin America after the American Revolution. To follow the important points in the story, look for answers to the following questions as you read:

1. How was Canada affected by the American Revolution?
2. How did Canada win self-government by a peaceful revolution?
3. How did the Spanish colonies gain their independence?
4. How did Brazil become independent?

1 How Was Canada Affected by the American Revolution?

Before we can understand how Canada was affected by the American Revolution, we must first turn back to the year 1763. That was the year, you remember, when Great Britain and France signed a peace treaty that gave the British all the territory of New France.

The British government tries to gain the loyalty of New France. "What is to become of us now?" This was a question the French people in North America were asking in 1763. "Will our new rulers force us to stop speaking our own language and prevent us from going to our own church?" Although the terms of surrender gave the French settlers the right to keep their language and religion, there were many fears that this agreement would not be carried out. The French colonists also wondered: "Will the lands on which we have built our homes be taken from us and given to English people?"

The French colonists learned to their relief that the British government had no thought of forcing them to adopt English customs and speech. As we know, the thirteen British colonies at this time were beginning to talk of liberty and of defending their rights. Great Britain realized that if the French settlers felt wronged, they might listen gladly to this dangerous talk among the British colonists to the south. So Great Britain continued much the same kind of government as the French colonists were accustomed to. These colonists were also promised the right to worship in the Roman Catholic Church and to keep their lands. By fair treatment Great Britain hoped to win the trust and loyalty of the French Canadians.

The American invasion of Canada fails. Great Britain was quite right in thinking that the trouble in the thirteen

215

● Discuss why French settlers demanded the right to keep their language and religion.

Loyalists left their old homes in the thirteen colonies rather than stay where they were not wanted. This painting shows a Loyalist family in flight, hoping to find safety in British Canada.

colonies might have an effect on Canada.[1] Soon after fighting had broken out between the American colonies and
• the British government, Ethan Allen and a force known as the Green Mountain Boys made a surprise attack. As you read on page 189, they captured the British forts of Crown Point and Ticonderoga on Lake Champlain. Ethan Allen's bold capture of these two forts opened the way to Canada. Knowing that Great Britain would use Canada as a base from which to attack the colo-

_____

[1]Because you are familiar with the name *Canada*, we are using that term instead of *British North America*, which is a more accurate term for this period of Canadian history. Actually, the entire region was not called Canada until 1867.

216

nies, the Continental Congress decided to act quickly. American forces were sent to invade Canada. They seized and held Montreal for several months, but were unable to take the capital at Quebec. When British reinforcements came up the St. Lawrence, the American troops retreated from Canada.

The American colonies fail to get aid from the French in Canada. The American Patriots knew that the French Canadians had no great love for the British. So the Continental Congress sent a committee to Montreal to try to secure help for the American colonies from the French Canadians. The committee included Benjamin Franklin, famous for his powers of persuasion. But the citizens of Montreal had no great love for the Americans, either. In fact, the people of Montreal simply had no interest in joining in the movement for independence. The committee failed in its mission, and all hope of getting aid from Canada faded.

From this time on, the two large British possessions in North America went separate ways. The thirteen colonies won their independence, while Canada continued to be a possession of Great Britain.

Many American Loyalists sail to Nova Scotia. Although Canada did not unite with the American colonies, it was greatly affected by the American Revolution. You have already learned that not everyone in the thirteen colonies was in favor of independence. Probably one third of the colonists were Loyalists, who sided with Great Britain. After the war the bitter feeling against the Loyalists remained. Some of them returned to England, but many wished to stay in North America. Why not go to the British possessions to the north? The British government in Canada was ready to welcome the Loyalists and to make arrangements for transporting them. They were promised free land with which to start a new life.

• Have students find out more about Ethan Allen (p. 189) and prepare written or oral reports.

Thousands of Loyalists found refuge in Canada. Conditions were often hard at first, with some families having to live in tents.

After the treaty of peace was signed in 1783, a flood of Loyalists boarded ships in New York City, eager to go to their new homes. There were well-dressed aristocrats who took with them such possessions as they had managed to save. There were also black people who were the slaves of well-to-do Loyalists. And there were also merchants, doctors, lawyers, soldiers, farmers, and people who worked at various trades.

Thirty thousand of these homeless people set sail for Halifax, Nova Scotia. After landing, the Loyalists spread out to build settlements and to clear farmland in Nova Scotia. Some went to New Brunswick, directly north of what is now Maine, and to nearby Prince Edward Island. Soon Nova Scotia and the surrounding territory became a strong British colony.

Other Loyalists reach Canada by land. During the Revolution, many Loyalists had moved into Canada from the western sections of the colonies. After the war, as many as 10,000 crossed the border from New York State into Canada. Most of these people settled north of Lake Ontario and along the upper St. Lawrence, west of Montreal. This territory was part of what had been the old French province of Quebec. The new settlers were given land and tools by the government, and soon log cabins and little villages sprang up in the wilderness.

English-speaking people form the beginnings of British Canada. New France, you will remember, had never been thickly populated. At the time it passed into the hands of the British, its population numbered only about 80,000. The thousands of Loyalists who moved from the United States brought about a great change in the population. The French were no longer in a majority except in the eastern part of old Quebec. Moreover, English-speaking people continued to arrive in Canada in large numbers. Many Americans along the frontier pushed into the Great Lakes region in the early 1800's. People came in large numbers from the British Isles • too. In all of these ways, the number of English-speaking Canadians increased.

English-speaking Canadians demand and receive more rights. The American Revolution had another effect on our

• Explain that the British Isles include Northern Ireland, Scotland, Wales, England, and several small islands.

neighbor to the north. The Loyalists who moved to Quebec were not satisfied to live under the laws made to govern the French Canadians. They wanted a government in which they would be represented as they had been in the American colonies. The French Canadians, on the other hand, who lived in the older (eastern) part of Quebec, wished to remain French and keep their French customs. How was Great Britain to please both the British and French Canadians?

In 1791 it was decided to divide old Quebec into the two provinces of Upper and Lower Canada. (See map below.) Upper Canada was the western part of old Quebec where many Loyalists had settled. Lower Canada was the eastern part of Quebec where the French were in the majority. Each province was to have its own government, headed by a governor appointed by Great Britain.

Each governor, in turn, was to choose leading citizens to serve on his council. There was also to be an assembly elected by the voters in each province. The British people in Upper Canada were pleased with this arrangement. At the same time, Great Britain hoped that the French people of Lower Canada would gradually learn to like the British system of government.

▶ **CHECK UP**   See Teacher's Key.

1. What did the British do to gain the loyalty of the French in Canada after 1763?
2. In what parts of Canada did Loyalists from the American colonies settle?
3. **(a)** Why were the British people in Canada dissatisfied? **(b)** Why was Quebec divided into two provinces? **(c)** How were the two provinces to be governed?

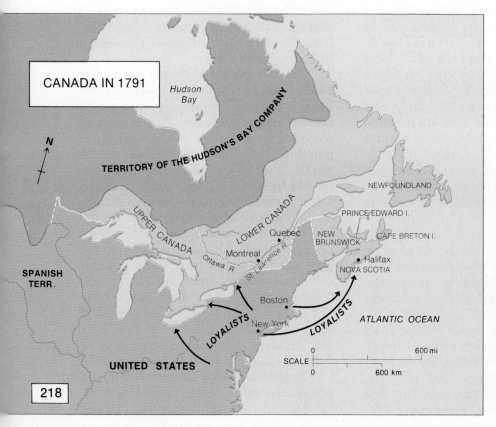

CANADA IN 1791

See Teacher's Key.

MAP STUDY
In 1791 two new provinces, Upper and Lower Canada, were formed out of the province of Quebec. Note that New Brunswick, Nova Scotia, Newfoundland, and Prince Edward Island were separate colonies. What fur-trading company controlled most of northern Canada?

2 How Did Canada Win Self-Government by a Peaceful Revolution?

It was not long before Canadians began to find fault with their new government, and a quarrel with Great Britain followed. In fact, during the 1800's this quarrel led to a great change in Canada's government. Revolutions need not be bloody wars; they may be brought about peacefully. In this section we will see how a peaceful revolution brought self-government to the Canadians.

The British plan of government keeps a tight rein on Canada. The governments set up in Upper and Lower Canada did not give people the same rights of self-government that had existed in the American colonies. Those in authority in Great Britain realized that serious mistakes had led to the loss of the thirteen colonies. They were determined that the same thing should not happen in Canada. For one thing, they agreed that Parliament should not tax a British colony.

But the British leaders also thought, "We lost the American colonies not only because we taxed them but also because we gave them too much freedom in handling their own affairs. We must 'tighten the reins' on our remaining colony in America so that there will be no chance for another revolt. We will allow the people to elect assemblies and give them power to raise their own taxes to run the government. But the assemblies will not have full power to make laws. A governor sent from England, and his council, will really control the government of each province. In this way the Canadian people will not get ideas about liberty and self-government."

Canadians demand reforms in their government. The Canadians of each province soon realized that the governor and his council held the real power over the government. These men paid little attention to the wishes of the assembly. They ran the government for the good of Great Britain, rather than for the good of Canada. In other words, the government of the provinces was not *responsible* to the people of Canada. More and more people began to demand what they called **responsible government.** They wanted their elected assemblies to have the real power to govern the provinces. They also wanted more freedom from Britain in managing their affairs.

In Lower Canada, where the British and the French lived side by side, the feeling against the governor and his council was especially bitter. The French people feared that the British government was trying to make them accept the English language and customs. This they would never do. They were French and intended to remain so. Because the French had a majority in the assembly, they even refused to vote taxes to run the government if they disliked the governor's plans. Some fiery leaders urged revolt.

In Upper Canada the quarrel was not between the English-speaking and the French-speaking groups. Instead, it was between those who wanted responsible government and the wealthy people who controlled the government and meant to keep on doing so. As the quarrel grew more bitter, reform leaders urged the people to rebel if their demands were not granted. There was much talk of independence. In 1837 things came to a head. Riots and fighting broke out, but were soon stopped by government troops.

Lord Durham recommends changes in the Canadian government. The British government was shocked by the riots

Government troops were called out in 1837 to stop riots against British rule in Canada. Canadian bitterness over British control led to the appointment of Lord Durham to study the situation.

and the bitter feeling that caused them. Wise leaders in England said, "Our present policy in Canada has failed. We must do something different or we may lose the Canadian provinces as we did the American colonies." Accordingly, England sent Lord Durham, a wise and able statesman, to study conditions in Canada and recommend what should be done.

Lord Durham's report proved a turning point in Britain's attitude, not only toward Canada but also toward its colonies all over the world. He warned Great Britain to give up the idea that colonies existed for the good of the parent country. He said that the elected representatives of the people (the assembly) must be given more power. The only way to keep the Canadian provinces in the British Empire, Lord Durham believed, was to give Canadians the same rights that people in England enjoyed — in other words, responsible government. He also suggested that the two Canadas be united again under one government.

Canada receives responsible government. Soon after Lord Durham made his report, Upper and Lower Canada were once more joined in a single province under one governor. But it was several years before Britain was ready to give Canada responsible government. Finally, in 1846, responsible government was introduced in Canada. The governor appointed to the council representatives from the party that controlled the elected assembly. This council now determined the policies of the government. Thus the Canadians gained control of their affairs except for such matters as defense, trade with other nations, and the making of treaties. Britain still had control over these matters.

Responsible government in Canada had been brought about without a war. As soon as the Canadians had won their demands, all talk of independence died down. Great Britain had shown its faith in the ability of the Canadians to govern themselves.

220

See p. T26 for a strategy that asks students to compare British policies in Canada and in the American colonies.

▶ **CHECK UP**   See Teacher's Key.

1. **(a)** Why did the assemblies elected by the people of Upper and Lower Canada have little power? **(b)** Why did the Canadian people want responsible gov-

ernment? **(c)** What events in 1837 brought the matter to a head?

2. **(a)** What changes in the Canadian government did Lord Durham recommend? **(b)** How was the plan for responsible government carried out?

3 How Did the Spanish Colonies Gain Their Independence?

In the early part of the 1800's, even before Canada won responsible government, stirring events were taking place in Spain's Latin American[2] colonies. Uprisings against Spanish rule broke out in one colony after another. The revolt of the Spanish colonies reminds us in some ways of the revolt of the English colonies. Both had grievances against the country that ruled them because of taxes and trade regulations. Both fought bloody battles to win independence.

Several differences, however, made the winning of independence much more difficult for the Spanish colonies than for the English colonies. (1) The thirteen English colonies occupied a narrow strip of land along the seacoast. But the territory of the Spanish colonies stretched across most of South America, Central America, Mexico, and part of the present United States. (2) In many parts of Spanish America, great mountain ranges and tropical forests separated the settlements. This made it difficult to send messages and to move armies from one place to another. (3) Another difference was in government. The English colonists cherished certain rights and had a good deal of self-gov-

ernment. But in the Spanish colonies, the people were under the iron rule of the Spanish king and had no chance to try self-government. When we consider that they won their independence in spite of these difficulties, we realize what a remarkable achievement it was.

THE COLONIES OF SPAIN HAVE REASON FOR REVOLT

What grievances did the Spanish colonists have? Chapter 3 told how strictly Spain controlled the trade of its colonies. As time went on, people who wanted to make money through trade grew more and more bitter about these regulations. But probably the most serious complaint of the colonists arose among the Creoles (Spanish people born in the Americas). The Creoles held few if any of the important public offices in their own colonies. Instead, positions in the Church and government were nearly always given to people who had been born in Spain. The Spaniards looked down on the Creoles as inferiors. It is easy to understand why Creoles resented this attitude.

There were other grievances also. Many of the colonists believed that the time had come for them to have a voice in how they were governed. To Spain such ideas seemed dangerous, and the Spanish government tried hard to prevent them from spreading in the colonies. Colonists could only buy books or papers that had been approved by the

---

[2]Latin America is the large area reaching from the southern border of the United States to the tip of South America. As you know, most of that region was colonized by people who spoke Spanish or Portuguese. Because both those languages developed from Latin, the name *Latin America* came into use.

221

★ Discuss whether it is possible to keep ideas like these from spreading.

Spanish authorities. No printed information about the American Revolution could be circulated in the Spanish colonies. In fact, no Spanish colonists were allowed to visit the United States without special permission. It was feared they would bring back ideas of independence.

The American and French Revolutions influence the Spanish colonies. In spite of these strict rules, people in the Spanish colonies did find out that the English colonies had actually won their independence. They also heard exciting stories of a great revolution that had swept France, beginning in 1789. During the French Revolution, the French people threw off the rule of the king and the nobles and set up a republic. This

news was eagerly discussed in the Spanish colonies. If other people could break the chains that bound them, why could not the Spanish colonists do the same? Young Creoles who returned from study in Europe began to work enthusiastically for independence. In many parts of the colonies secret societies were organized to plan a revolution against Spain. Then, in the early 1800's, Spain became entangled in European wars. It was too busy to pay much attention to its colonies in America, and the colonists chose this time to revolt.

Haiti wins its independence. Actually, the first revolution against colonial rule took place not in the Spanish colonies but in the French colony of Haiti (HAY-tee) on the island of Hispaniola. Centuries earlier Columbus had started a settlement on Hispaniola. After a time, French settlers moved onto the western end of the island and it became a French colony. The French started large coffee and sugar plantations there, and brought in slaves to do the heavy labor. The slaves, who made up a vast majority of the population, were cruelly treated, and in 1791 they rose in revolt. Under the brilliant leadership of Toussaint L'Ouverture (too-SAN loo-ver-TYOOR), a former plantation slave, they defeated the French and set up a republic. Although French troops were sent to reconquer the island, heavy fighting and deadly yellow fever forced them to leave. In 1804, some years before the Spanish colonies on the mainland won their freedom, Haiti became the first Latin American nation to gain independence.

MEXICO GAINS ITS INDEPENDENCE

The long struggle for Mexican independence is begun by Father Hidalgo. ★ *"Viva la Independencia!* Long live Independence!"* These stirring words were uttered in 1810 by Father Miguel Hidalgo (hih-DAL-goh), a parish priest

Toussaint L'Ouverture, born a slave in Haiti, led that country's struggle for independence from France. He declared the slaves free and drew up a constitution providing for self-government.

222

Mexico City's great cathedral, begun by the Spanish in 1573, glows under artificial lighting at night. The streaks of light in front of the cathedral were traced by headlights of automobiles passing by while this time-exposure photograph was being shot.

in the Mexican village of Dolores. Hidalgo had devoted his life to helping and teaching the Indians of Mexico, whose life under Spanish rule was full of hardships. He had made secret plans for a revolt. Independence, Father Hidalgo hoped, would bring about better conditions for all the people of Mexico.

The "Cry of Dolores," as Hidalgo's slogan is called, started his Indian followers on the path of revolution. Although at first they captured several towns, the Indians were no match for the Spanish troops who were sent to stop them. Hidalgo was defeated, taken prisoner, and executed. His head was carried through the streets in an iron cage as a warning of what would happen to those who dared to revolt against Spain.

The revolution did not end with Hidalgo's death. Thousands of his followers continued to fight under new leaders. Many mestizos (people who were part Indian and part Spanish) joined the revolt. Through long, discouraging years they carried on their fight, making surprise attacks on different towns and then retreating into the hills.

The Creoles take over the movement for independence. By themselves the Indians and mestizos of Mexico might never have won the fight for independence. But the Creoles, who had been watching the unequal struggle between the rebels and Spaniards, saw a chance to use the revolution to gain control of Mexico. They planned to join the rebels and, when independence was won, take over the government for themselves.

An ambitious young Creole officer named Agustín de Iturbide (ee-toor-BEE-day) was the leader in this plan. He tricked the Indian leaders into accepting his aid. Together the Creole and Indian forces captured Mexico City and forced the Spaniards to leave. Iturbide and his soldiers declared Mexico's independence in 1821.

Mexico and Central America win independence. Iturbide was not interested in ideas of liberty; he wanted con-

223

● See p. T26 for a strategy that asks students to use maps in studying the revolutions led by Bolívar and San Martín.

trol of Mexico for himself and other Creoles. So the revolution, which was begun to help the Indians, ended with Iturbide being crowned emperor of Mexico! Many Creoles did not like the idea of an emperor, and after a year Iturbide was forced out. But the Indians were little better off than before. The Republic of Mexico was at last established in 1824, after fourteen years of fighting. About the same time the Spanish provinces in what is now Central America also declared their independence.

● BOLÍVAR AND SAN MARTÍN FREE SOUTH AMERICA

While Mexico was carrying on its revolution against Spain, much had been happening in South America. The story of its independence is the story of three great leaders — Miranda, Bolívar, and San Martín. As you read about what they did, refer to the map on page 225.

Miranda is the father of the revolution in Venezuela. Francisco Miranda (mee-RAHN-duh), who was born in Venezuela, spent most of his life working for the cause of freedom in South America. For a time he lived in Europe. There he went from one European government to another, trying to get help for the independence movement. After the United States gained its freedom, he also appealed to our government for help. Miranda organized patriotic societies for young Creoles who had gone to Europe to be educated. His fiery speeches led many young men to take up the cause of independence.

Miranda was no longer young when he returned to Venezuela in 1810 to lead a revolution against Spain. As the white-haired old man rode through the streets of Caracas (kuh-RAH-kus), capital of Venezuela, the people cheered wildly. But a year later, a frightful earthquake destroyed Caracas and ended the revolution for the time being. Miranda was captured by the Spanish and put in prison, where he died.

Bolívar becomes leader of the Venezuelan revolution. There now appears in our story one of the most remarkable men in the pages of history. Young Simón Bolívar (boh-LEE-vahr) will live forever in the memory and in the hearts of South Americans. As a symbol of liberty, he means as much to the people of South America as George Washington does to us.

Bolívar was the son of a wealthy and powerful Creole family in Caracas. Like many young Creoles, Bolívar was trained as a soldier. He married a beautiful Spanish woman, but their happiness was cut short by her tragic death not long afterward. Feeling that he had little left to live for, Bolívar went to Europe. There he met Miranda, and was inspired by the old patriot's enthusiasm. Bolívar decided to devote the rest of his life to freeing his homeland. It was Bolívar who took the oath mentioned at the beginning of this chapter. He was the man who became the leader of the Venezuelan rebels after Miranda's death.

Bolívar wins independence for northern South America. Bolívar had little trouble in recruiting a revolutionary army to fight the Spaniards. He was the kind of person who made people eager to follow his leadership. Bolívar collected an army of 2,100 men, many of them tough cowboys of the Venezuelan plains. When he found the Spanish troops in Venezuela too strong for him, Bolívar decided on a daring move. He led his soldiers on a difficult march over the high Andes Mountains into neighboring Colombia. In a surprise attack he defeated the Spanish forces there.

Bolívar now felt strong enough to return and strike at the Spanish troops in Venezuela. In 1821, he won an important battle in the western part of that country. Soon all of northern South

★ Have students note the use of *patriot* with a small "p" to describe Miranda. Remind the class that the leaders of the American Revolution were called *Patriots*.

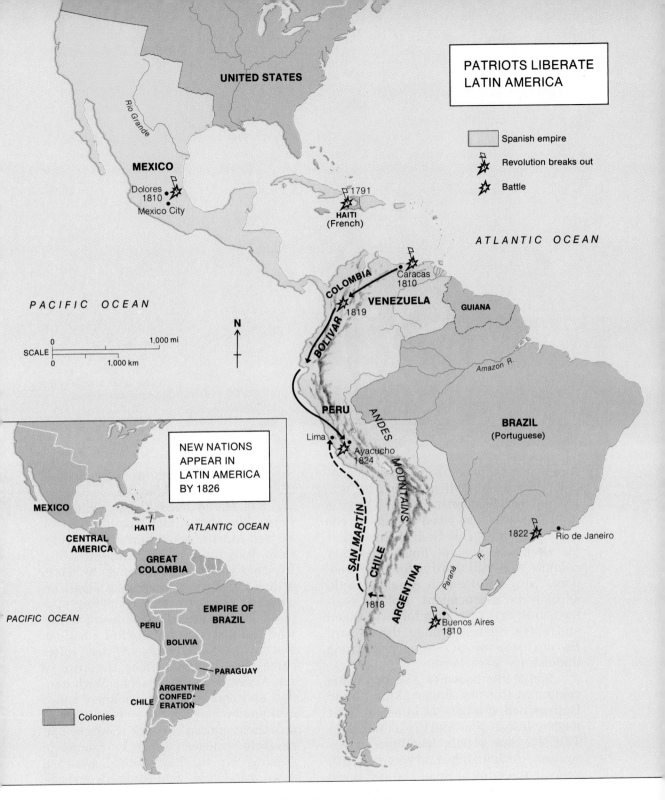

PATRIOTS LIBERATE
LATIN AMERICA

UNITED STATES

Rio Grande

MEXICO

Dolores
1810
Mexico City

1791

HAITI
(French)

Spanish empire

Revolution breaks out

Battle

ATLANTIC OCEAN

PACIFIC OCEAN

COLOMBIA

Caracas
1810

VENEZUELA

GUIANA

N

SCALE
0   1,000 mi
0   1,000 km

BOLÍVAR

1819

Amazon R.

PERU

Lima

Ayacucho
1824

ANDES

MOUNTAINS

BRAZIL
(Portuguese)

NEW NATIONS
APPEAR IN
LATIN AMERICA
BY 1826

MEXICO

CENTRAL
AMERICA

HAITI

ATLANTIC OCEAN

GREAT
COLOMBIA

SAN MARTÍN

CHILE

1822

Rio de Janeiro

PACIFIC OCEAN

PERU

EMPIRE OF
BRAZIL

BOLIVIA

PARAGUAY

ARGENTINE
CONFED-
ERATION

Paraná
R.

ARGENTINA

1818

Buenos Aires
1810

CHILE

Colonies

MAP STUDY   Revolutions against colonial rule broke out in widely
separated parts of Latin America at different times. Only after years of
fighting did the campaigns of leaders like Bolívar and San Martín win final
independence from Spain. (Haiti won independence from France, and Brazil
from Portugal.) (a) How can you tell on this map where important outbreaks
took place? (b) What does the inset map show?

225

See Teacher's Key.

San Martín of Argentina, a brilliant military leader, freed Chile after crossing the Andes Mountains.

America was freed from Spain's control. Wherever Bolívar went, he was greeted with wild enthusiasm. The title of "Liberator" was given to him by the grateful people. But Bolívar knew that his work was not yet finished. Other colonies were still fighting for their freedom. No part of South America could actually be independent, Bolívar realized, until every Spanish fort was taken and every Spanish soldier driven out. His next step was to conquer the strong Spanish forces in Peru.

San Martín becomes a leader in the south. In this new undertaking Simon Bolívar had the help of another great leader, José de San Martín (sahn mahr-TEEN). San Martín was born in Argentina. Although he had spent twenty years in the army of Spain, he still loved his native land. Soon after a revolt in Argentina drove out the Spanish government (1810), San Martín sailed home to join the rebel forces. Although his own country had freed itself, San Martín, like Bolívar, realized that the

Spanish forces had to be defeated throughout South America.

San Martín frees Chile. Chile and Peru were still under Spain's control. So San Martín asked himself this question: Why not cross the Andes to Chile, free that country, and then go by sea to attack Peru? San Martín set about organizing an army and collecting supplies. He was joined by Chilean patriots who had fled from home after a bad defeat by the Spaniards. At last, after three years of preparations, the Army of the Andes began its march. With cannon and equipment, the soldiers toiled over snowy heights. They took sleds to pull their cannon through the snow and movable bridges to cross mountain streams. Up, up they climbed, and then down into Chile. San Martín's surprise attack was successful, and in 1818 all Chile was freed from Spanish control.

San Martín enters Peru. After defeating the Spanish troops in Chile, San Martín undertook the second part of his plan. In 1821, he and his army landed on the coast north of the city of Lima, capital of Peru. While the Spanish forces moved farther inland, San Martín entered Lima. The people of the city greeted him with joy. Shortly afterward, the independence of Peru was proclaimed. But San Martín knew that the strong Spanish forces remaining in Peru had to be defeated if freedom was really to be won. He also knew that he did not have enough men to defeat the Spaniards.

San Martín resigns in favor of Bolívar. Meanwhile, Bolívar was advancing southward with his army. When San Martín heard this, he made arrangements to meet Bolívar to discuss plans for the final defeat of the Spanish forces. No one knows exactly what happened at this meeting. Both men wanted independence for all of South America. But Bolívar was an ambitious man who sought fame and glory. San Martín, on the other hand, had no ambition to become famous. Bolívar must have persuaded San Martín to leave his army in Peru and allow Bolívar to complete the conquest. At any rate, on the eve of victory San Martín, who had accomplished so much for the cause of independence, left Peru. He later went to Europe, where he spent the rest of his life.

Spanish control in South America comes to an end. With the two armies united under his command, Bolívar swept on to victory. In 1824 he defeated the last strong Spanish forces in the Battle of Ayacucho (ah-yah-KOO- ● choh). This victory not only freed Peru but won independence for all of Spanish South America. At last the dreams of Miranda, Bolívar, San Martín, and all the thousands of other patriots had come true.

After winning independence, the former Spanish colonies became free republics with governments patterned after that of the United States. These new republics, however, faced many difficulties. Their people had no experience in governing themselves, as had the ★ people of the thirteen English colonies. For the next hundred years and more, the people of the Latin American republics were to suffer wars and revolutions, and to have little voice in running their governments.

▶ **CHECK UP**   See Teacher's Key.

1. What complaints did the Spanish colonies have against Spain?
2. How did the revolutions in the thirteen English colonies and in France affect the Spanish colonies?
3. **(a)** What was the first Latin American colony to win its independence? **(b)** Why did the people in that colony rise in revolt?
4. How did Mexico win its independence?
5. **(a)** What parts of South America were freed by Bolívar? **(b)** By San Martín? **(c)** How was a final defeat of the Spanish forces in South America brought about?

4 How Did Brazil Become Independent?

We have yet to tell the story of Brazil, the largest of the Latin American countries. Unlike the rest of South America, Brazil was discovered and settled by the Portuguese. Even today Brazilians speak Portuguese instead of Spanish.

The Portuguese claim and colonize Brazil. A Portuguese sea captain named Pedro Cabral (kuh-BRAHL) set out from Portugal in 1500 to follow da Gama's route to India. A storm blew his little fleet so far to the west that he

227

● See p. T26 for a strategy asking students to use library sources and the text in answering questions about Brazil.

reached the bulge of South America nearest to Africa. Since the land lay east of the Line of Demarcation (see map, page 56), he claimed it for Portugal. At that time, Portugal was much more interested in its rich trade with India, but a few settlements were made in Brazil.

The Portuguese soon discovered that the fertile soil of Brazil would grow sugar cane. This news brought many settlers, and it was not long before great plantations were producing sugar for most of Europe. The coastal parts of Brazil did not have as many Indians as Mexico or Peru. So the Brazilian plantation owners bought large numbers of African slaves to grow the cane. Brazil was governed by a royal governor and was divided into several districts, each one headed by a Portuguese nobleman.

In the early 1800's there were about three million people in Brazil. The capital city, Rio de Janeiro (REE-oh duh zhuh-NAIR-oh), had about 100,000 inhabitants, and there were several towns along the coast. Both gold and diamonds were mined in Brazil. But for the most part the life of the people centered about the plantations, with their miles of sugar cane, their sugar mills, and workers' huts.

Brazil becomes the home of the king of Portugal. The story of how Brazil became independent is not one of long and bloody struggle like that of the

Early Portuguese settlers started large plantations in Brazil. Some plantation families led prosperous lives, as shown in this picture, a painting on wall tiles.

Spanish colonies. In 1808, the people of Brazil learned that the royal family of Portugal was coming to live in their capital city because of wars which were then raging in Europe. These wars forced John, the Portuguese ruler, and hundreds of Portuguese nobles to seek refuge across the sea.

At first, the colonists of Brazil were pleased and honored to have the royal family and the nobles in their midst. It was not long, however, before ill feeling broke out between the Portuguese and the Brazilians. The Portuguese, used to the splendor of a European court, looked down on the people of Brazil. The Brazilians, in turn, resented the fact that King John gave important government positions to people from Portugal. Soon, the Brazilians began to talk about independence.

Dom Pedro refuses to leave Brazil. When the wars in Europe were over, the king returned to Portugal with his court. He left his young son, Pedro, to rule Brazil in his place. Dom Pedro was a handsome and headstrong prince, much loved by the Brazilians because of his interest in their country. When he was ordered by the government of Portugal to return to Europe, he angrily refused.

Brazil becomes independent of Portugal. The Portuguese government said it would not accept Dom Pedro's decision to remain in Brazil. When this news reached Dom Pedro, he declared: "It is time! Independence or death!" The ● people of Brazil cheered this defiance of Portugal. In 1822, Pedro was crowned Pedro I, Emperor of Brazil. By the end of the next year all Portuguese troops had been forced out, and Portugal had no choice but to agree to the independence of Brazil.

Pedro I was followed by his son Pedro II, a man respected and admired by everyone. During the fifty years of his reign he accomplished many things for his people. Brazil then became a republic.

Thus ends our story of how the spirit of freedom which began in the thirteen English colonies affected Canada and Latin America. ★

▶ **CHECK UP**   See Teacher's Key.

1. How did Brazil become a Portuguese colony?
2. What ways of living developed in Brazil?
3. How did Brazil win independence?

CHECK UP ON CHAPTER 10   See Teacher's Key.

Words to Know

1. Creoles
2. council
3. liberator
4. mestizo
5. responsible government

Places to Locate

1. Mexico
2. Brazil
3. Haiti
4. Halifax
5. Caracas
6. Argentina
7. Venezuela
8. Colombia
9. Nova Scotia
10. New Brunswick

Places to Locate (cont.)

11. Chile
12. Peru
13. Andes
14. Rio de Janeiro
15. Central America

Facts to Remember

1. **(a)** Who was Father Hidalgo? **(b)** How were he and the "Cry of Dolores" important in Mexico's history? **(c)** How did Mexico finally get its independence?

229

Facts to Remember (cont.)

2. **(a)** From what country did Haiti get its independence? **(b)** Who was the main leader of that struggle?
3. **(a)** In what ways did Lord Durham say the government of Canada should be changed? **(b)** What was the result?
4. Tell how each of the following played a part in the struggle for independence in the South American countries: **(a)** Miranda, **(b)** Bolívar, **(c)** San Martín.
5. In what ways was Brazil's winning of independence different from the independence movement in the rest of South America?

Skills to Practice

1. Look at the time line on page 214. **(a)** Over what period of time did the events of Chapter 10 happen? **(b)** What were the dates of each of the events shown on the time line?
2. Using the map on page 218, describe the parts of Canada to which Loyalists from the thirteen American colonies moved.
3. Look at the map on page 225. **(a)** List the dates and places where revolutions broke out in Latin America. **(b)** From what three European nations did Latin Americans win independence? **(c)** In what country was the Battle of Ayacucho fought?

Questions to Think About

1. Why did Canada's peaceful revolution take so much longer than the American Revolution?
2. Spain tried to keep ideas of independence out of its colonies. Is it possible for a government to do that for any length of time? Give reasons for your answer.
3. Compare the difficulties faced by Simón Bolívar and José de San Martín in winning independence for the Spanish colonies of South America with the difficulties faced by George Washington in the fight for independence in North America.

Linking Past and Present

Mexican independence day. If you are ever in Mexico City in the middle of September, you can join the Mexican people in a celebration like our own Fourth of July. In the Zócalo, the great plaza before the National Palace, thousands of people gather in a happy, noisy fiesta on the night of September 15. Then, just at midnight, the President of Mexico steps out onto a balcony of the palace. The noise dies down. Presently, a bell over the main entrance of the palace begins to ring. It is Mexico's "Liberty Bell," brought from Father Hidalgo's church in Dolores.

Now the President steps to the front of the balcony and cries out, "Viva la Independencia!" The crowd roars back, "Viva!" Skyrockets burst overhead, fireworks explode, and Mexico begins its celebration of independence, which lasts all through the next day.

National birds. As you probably know, an eagle with outstretched wings is a symbol of the United States. You may not know that the eagle is an important symbol for Mexicans as well. When Mexico won its independence from Spain in 1821, it adopted a green, white, and red flag. In the center of the flag was an emblem showing an eagle holding a big snake in its beak. This emblem had its origin in the ancient history of Mexico, when the Aztec Indians were a poor, wandering tribe. According to legend, the Aztecs once came to the shore of a lake where they saw a huge eagle perched on a cactus, gripping a snake. Since the eagle and the snake were both sacred to the Aztecs, they decided that here was a good spot to build a village. They named their village Tenochtitlán ("village of the eagle"). That village became their capital and grew into Mexico City.

230

● Have students look up national symbols of other countries mentioned in this chapter. (For example, the maple leaf is a symbol of Canada.)

For answers see Teacher's Key.

Have students apply the first question in this exercise to other maps in the textbook, including those in the atlas.

GAINING SKILL

Reading Maps: Using Scale

Maps come in many different sizes. A map of the United States can be big enough to cover a wall. Or, it can be smaller than a page in a book. Yet common sense tells you that the size of the United States has not changed. It is only the maps that are different. Map makers would tell you that the two maps use different **scales**. A map's scale is distance in miles or kilometers shown on the map as either inches or centimeters.

You can use the scale on a map to find many things. For example, you can find the distance between two points, the length of a river, or the width of a lake. Since all the places on one map have the same scale, you can also compare the size of two areas — two parks, for example — that are shown on that map.

The map on this page shows Canada as it is today. Use the map and its scale to answer the questions in the next column.

1. How many miles does an inch stand for on this map?
2. Lay a piece of paper on the map and mark off the distance from Edmonton to Winnipeg. Then compare that distance to the scale. How far apart are those two Canadian cities?
3. The United States and the province of Manitoba share a common border. How long is that border?
4. What is the distance from the southeast corner of the Yukon Territory to Victoria?
5. How far is Victoria from Ottawa?
6. Which province is larger, Newfoundland or New Brunswick?
7. Which Canadian province or territory has the largest area?
8. Why would it be wrong to compare the area of Lake Superior on this map with that of Lake Ontario as shown on the map on page 170?

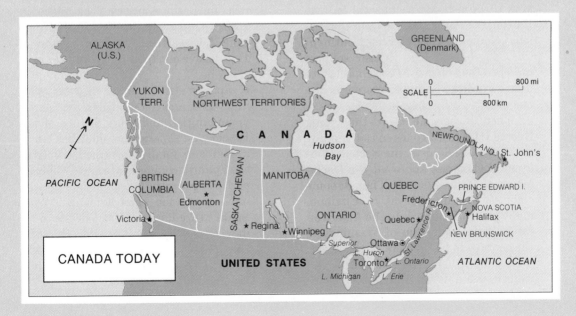

CANADA TODAY

UNDERSTANDING UNIT 3

SUMMARY OF IMPORTANT IDEAS

In Unit 3 you have read about the birth of new nations in the Western Hemisphere.

1. When the English Parliament after 1763 tried to control the American colonies more strictly, the colonists resisted and won their independence (1783).

a. The colonists claimed the rights of English people, and in America they enjoyed even greater freedom than men and women who lived in England.

b. The British Parliament felt justified in taxing the colonists. The colonists objected to "taxation without representation" and to stricter government control (use of writs of assistance, for example). They boycotted British goods in order to secure repeal of the hated laws. Because Parliament passed harsh laws to punish Massachusetts for the Boston Tea Party, leaders from the various colonies met in the First Continental Congress. When British soldiers marched to Concord, Massachusetts, to destroy military supplies stored by the colonists, fighting began.

c. When it became clear that King George III refused to listen to the grievances of the colonists, the Second Continental Congress approved the Declaration of Independence. Though some colonists remained loyal to England, many gave full support to the American cause. The leadership of Washington, the courage of his soldiers, the patriotic service of other American men and women, valuable aid from foreign coun-tries, the advantage of fighting on familiar ground, and British mistakes helped the thirteen colonies win their independence.

2. While Canada remained in the British Empire, the colonies of Spain, France, and Portugal followed the example of the United States and became independent.

a. The Loyalists who fled to Canada from the thirteen American colonies demanded greater rights to govern themselves. Through the governors and their councils, however, the British Parliament retained its power in Canada until 1846, when responsible government was introduced. A council appointed from the elected assembly now controlled the government. So, although Canada did not break away from the British Empire, the Canadians obtained a form of government that was responsible to them.

b. The first rebellion against colonial rule in Latin America took place in Haiti. Under the leadership of Toussaint L'Ouverture, the black people of Haiti drove out the French and set up a republic.

c. Spain's strict control over its colonies, the Creoles' resentment of lack of opportunities, and the influence of the French and American revolutions led to unrest and finally to armed revolt in the Spanish colonies. Miranda, Bolívar, and San Martín were leaders in the movement for independence from Spain. In addition, Brazil declared its independence from Portugal. By 1825, the Spanish and Portuguese colonies in North, Central, and South America had become independent states.

1. **(a)** How did the British government and the colonists differ in their views on the proper relationship of the home country and the colonies? **(b)** Did the same differences exist in the case of Spain and the Spanish colonies? Explain.

2. **(a)** Why did the colonists object to the Stamp Act and the use of writs of assistance? **(b)** Why did Parliament pass these acts? **(c)** How did the colonists go about persuading Parliament to repeal laws they did not like?

3. What were the advantages **(a)** of the thirteen colonies and **(b)** of Britain in the Revolutionary War? **(c)** Why did the colonists win the war?

4. **(a)** What main points were stated in the Declaration of Independence? **(b)** Why is it one of the world's great documents?

5. **(a)** Where were the first battles of the American Revolution fought? **(b)** What American victory led to an important alliance with France? **(c)** What battle ended the fighting in the Revolutionary War?

6. **(a)** What was the first colony in Latin America to revolt against European rule? **(b)** Who was the leader of that revolt?

7. **(a)** What stand did Canada take during the American Revolution? Why? **(b)** What does the term *responsible government* mean? **(c)** How did Canada achieve responsible government?

8. **(a)** Why did the Spanish colonies revolt when they did? **(b)** Who were the great leaders in this revolt? **(c)** How did Brazil break away from Portugal?

THINGS TO DO

The projects marked with an asterisk (*) are for the whole class to do.

*1. Add to your card game names, terms, and dates from Chapters 7, 8, 9, and 10. You now have enough cards for the class to hold a lively drill.

*2. Make a chart in the form of a ladder called "Steps That Led to the Revolution." Starting with the bottom rung of the ladder, place in their correct order the chief events from 1763 to 1776 that led to the Revolution. You should have eight or ten events.

*3. Learn the Declaration of Independence (page 193) from the beginning to the sentence ending "to effect their Safety and Happiness."

4. Draw a cartoon illustrating the feeling of the colonists about one of the following: the Stamp Act, the Proclamation of 1763, or the Intolerable Acts.

5. Select eight or ten important leaders from Revolutionary days and prepare a "clues" program for the class. Give one clue at a time to see how soon your classmates can identify the person being described.

6. Imagine that you had fought on the Patriot side in one of the famous battles of the Revolution. Write an account of what happened.

7. Form a committee to find out more about how the Latin American countries won their independence. Each member of the committee might choose one Latin American country and use the library to find out how that country achieved independence. Report your findings to the class.

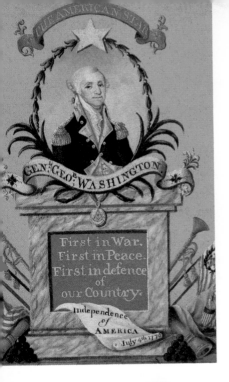

Left to right: President Washington; raising the flag at New Orleans; salute to President Washington in New York harbor.

The United States Is Established on a Firm Basis

1770–1825

See p. T27 for a unit preview strategy. See pp. T57–T72 for lists of useful books and audiovisual aids.

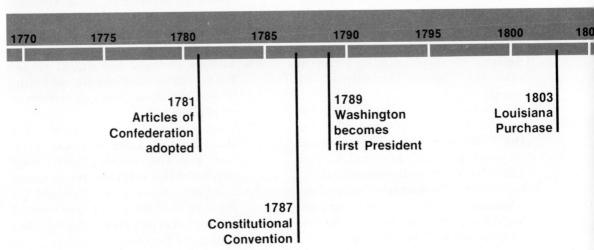

| 1770 | 1775 | 1780 | 1785 | 1790 | 1795 | 1800 | 180 |

1781
Articles of Confederation adopted

1789
Washington becomes first President

1803
Louisiana Purchase

1787
Constitutional Convention

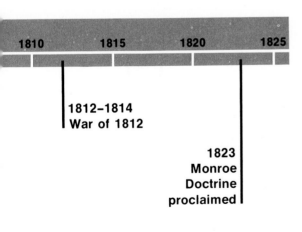

1810   1815   1820   1825

1812–1814
War of 1812

1823
Monroe
Doctrine
proclaimed

In Unit 3 you learned how the United States became free and independent. In this unit you will find out how the young nation overcame the difficult problems that it faced. Chapter 11 tells of the troubled times that followed the American Revolution and how our Constitution drew the thirteen states together in a firm union. Chapter 12 explains how the government of our new republic got off to a strong start. Two important steps it took were to put the United States on a sound financial basis and to build a permanent capital. In Chapter 13 you will find out why the United States fought a second war with Great Britain and how our country doubled in size and won a place for itself among the nations of the world.

Vocabulary preview: constitution, convention, population, compromise, House of Representatives, Senate, elector, federal system, federal government, ratify

The Thirteen States Create a Firm Union Under the Constitution

1775–1789   See pp. T27–T28 for chapter teaching strategies.

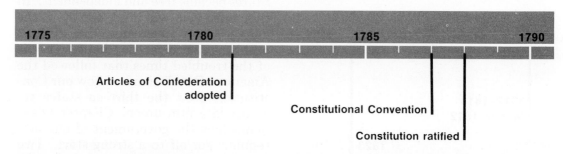

| 1775 | 1780 | 1785 | 1790 |

Articles of Confederation adopted

Constitutional Convention

Constitution ratified

What this chapter is about —

All our lives we act according to rules. We obey family rules at home, school rules in school, traffic rules when we walk or ride on the street. When we play football or basketball or baseball, we are expected to follow the rules of the game. If it were not for rules, groups of people could not live together peacefully, work together efficiently, or play together in harmony.

A nation, too, must have rules or agreements for running its affairs. These rules are part of its system of government. When the United States de-

236

clared its independence, however, there were no rules for running its government; in fact, there was no government for the thirteen states as a whole. During the Revolutionary War, the Continental Congress did manage the affairs of the union of states. But the states did not want this Congress to have much power and often ignored its requests.

After the war, a group of American leaders met to take on the difficult task of planning a new government for the whole nation. These men succeeded in drawing up a remarkable plan which has lasted, with few changes, to the present day. This plan is called the Constitution. In this chapter you will learn how the Constitution was drawn up. As you read, look for answers to these questions:

1. How was the United States governed after the Revolutionary War?
2. How did the Constitution become the foundation of our government?

1 How Was the United States Governed After the Revolutionary War?

Our government under the Constitution did not start until 1789, several years after the United States was born. In the first years of our nation's life, the states were not as firmly united as they are now. They had to learn by experience that a strong union was necessary if the United States were to become a successful nation. In order to understand how our Constitution came to be written, we need to know what kind of government the United States had in the years just after it won independence from Britain. This story takes us back to the days before the Revolutionary War.

The colonies become states. In 1775 and 1776, as British rule in the colonies began to crumble, Americans started setting up new governments. In each state a written plan of government, or **constitution,** was drawn up.

The constitutions in each of the thirteen states had much in common.

All the states provided for three branches of government: a legislature (to make laws), a governor (to enforce the laws), and a system of courts (to explain the laws and apply them in particular cases). The legislatures were generally given the greatest powers, including the right to keep tight control over taxation. Each of the state constitutions also had a bill of rights, describing the ways in which an individual's liberties would be protected. The bills of rights provided for freedom of speech, freedom of the press, and freedom of religion. They also granted people the right to a fair trial, protected them against searches of their homes, and forbade various injustices. Finally, the states limited the right to vote to free men. In most cases only those men who owned property or paid taxes were allowed to vote.

Americans have limited experience in working together. Thomas Jefferson

237

● See p. T27 for a strategy that calls for students to examine the meaning of boldfaced terms.

★ See p. T27 for a strategy that asks students to identify similarities in the state constitutions.

had written, in the Declaration of Independence, of "the United States of America." The new states, however, were not firmly united. People in the states did not even think of themselves as Americans, but as Virginians, Rhode Islanders, and so on.

The Americans, to be sure, had some things in common. Most of them followed English ways of life, and most spoke the same language. In the past it had been natural for them to draw closer together in time of danger. Yet even common dangers had failed to bring about any real union among the colonies.

When the French and Indian War broke out, for instance, the colonies had talked about uniting to defend themselves against the French and Indians. In 1754, representatives from most of the colonies met in Albany, New York, to consider a plan for common defense. A council was to be elected which would have power to make treaties with the Indian tribes, build forts, and raise armies to protect all the colonies. Although ● the Albany Plan of Union, as it was called, offered advantages, the colonies failed to adopt it. Each colony wanted complete control of its own affairs and refused to share that responsibility with the representatives of any other colony. The American colonies were not yet willing to work together in a common cause.

Only when Britain tightened its control of the colonies (Chapter 8) did the colonists begin to work together to protect their rights. As you know, they sent representatives to the First and Second Continental Congresses. The Second Continental Congress met for the first time in May, 1775, and continued to hold meetings until March, 1781. It was this Congress which declared independence and managed the affairs of the United States during the Revolutionary War. The Continental Congress directed the war effort, raised what

money it could, and made the alliance with France. But no real powers were given to it by the people or the states. It was an emergency government, held together by the common desire to win the war.

The Articles of Confederation are adopted. Meanwhile, the states realized that a regular government was needed for the nation, and the members of Congress worked out a plan for such a government. The states were to be joined in a union known as the Confederation. The plan for this union was called the Articles of Confederation.

When the new plan was sent to the states for approval, it ran into trouble. At that time, about half the states had claims to large areas of land west of the ★ Appalachian Mountains (map, next page). Naturally those states wanted to keep their western lands, but the states that had *no* western claims did not agree. They were afraid of remaining forever small and weak in comparison with their large neighbors. They believed that the western lands should be turned over to the new national government, and they refused to accept the Articles of Confederation until this was done. Finally the states claiming western lands agreed to give up their claims, and the Articles were approved. Because of this delay, the new government was not established until 1781. By then, as you know, the War of Independence was almost over.

What was the new government like? The government of the Confederation was not like our national government today. There was no President with power to carry out the laws and no Supreme Court to settle important disputes. To run the nation's business there was a Congress made up of representatives from each state. Whether large or small, each state had only one vote. And nine states had to agree on any decision before the Confederation could act.

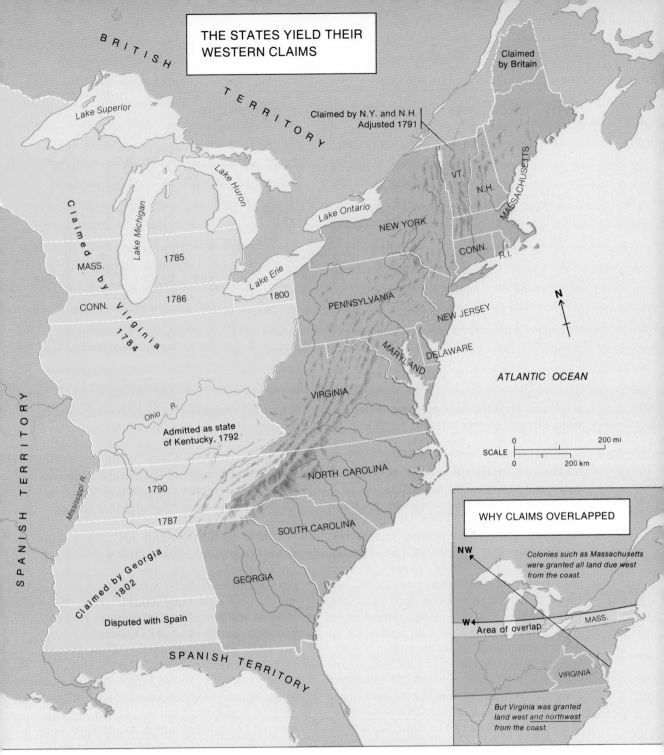

THE STATES YIELD THEIR WESTERN CLAIMS

B R I T I S H   T E R R I T O R Y

Lake Superior

Claimed by Britain

Claimed by N.Y. and N.H.
Adjusted 1791

Lake Huron

Lake Michigan

1785

Claimed by Virginia

Claimed by Conn.

MASS.

CONN.

1784

1786

Lake Ontario

Lake Erie

1800

VT.

N.H.

MASSACHUSETTS

NEW YORK

CONN.

R.I.

PENNSYLVANIA

NEW JERSEY

MARYLAND

DELAWARE

N

ATLANTIC OCEAN

Ohio R.

Admitted as state
of Kentucky, 1792

VIRGINIA

SCALE

0 — 200 mi

0 — 200 km

Mississippi R.

1790

1787

NORTH CAROLINA

SOUTH CAROLINA

S P A N I S H   T E R R I T O R Y

Claimed by Georgia
1802

GEORGIA

Disputed with Spain

S P A N I S H   T E R R I T O R Y

WHY CLAIMS OVERLAPPED

NW

Colonies such as Massachusetts
were granted all land due west
from the coast.

W

Area of overlap

MASS.

VIRGINIA

But Virginia was granted
land west and northwest
from the coast.

MAP STUDY The dates on the map tell when eastern states gave up their claims to western lands (shown by broken lines). Why had the claims of some states overlapped? (See inset.)

See Teacher's Key.

The new government under the Articles of Confederation could (1) wage war and make peace and organize an army and navy when needed; (2) control the relations of the United States with other nations; (3) regulate trade

239

Why Americans Criticized the Confederation

"We asked the states for money to pay these bills months ago, but I don't know if we'll ever get it."

"It's not fair! He got his kettles from another state where the tax on foreign-made goods is lower than ours."

with the Indians and oversee other Indian affairs; (4) arrange for carrying the mail; (5) borrow money to pay necessary expenses; and (6) ask each of the states to contribute money to pay the expenses of the Confederation.

The Confederation proves to be a weak government. When the new government came into power, it did not work well. For one thing, the country was upset after long years of war. Farming and business had been neglected, prices were high, and food and goods were scarce. These conditions would have added to the problems of any government. But the main trouble was that the Articles of Confederation did not give the central government enough power. Americans had just fought a war because the British Parliament had insisted on its right to tax the colonists and to regulate their trade. Now the states were afraid to turn over these rights even to a central government of their own.

Among the many weaknesses of the Articles of Confederation, these were the most important:

(1) Congress was not given the right to tax. It could not force citizens to pay taxes; it had to *ask* the state governments for money. Usually the states did not pay as much as they were asked to pay. The result was that Congress never had enough money, and the government was always in debt.

(2) Congress did not have the power to regulate trade that was carried on between states. The merchants in each state naturally wanted to make as much profit as they could. They persuaded their state governments to keep out the products of other states by taxing such products heavily. New Jersey farmers who took their vegetables to New York City, for example, had to pay a tax not only on the vegetables but also on the boats that carried them. If this sort of thing continued, trade between the states would have been sharply cut down. Yet Congress lacked the power to deal with such problems.

(3) Still another weakness of the Confederation was that it had no satisfactory way of settling quarrels among the states. For example, Pennsylvania

See p. T27 for a strategy that asks students to examine the relationship between the states and the central government under the Articles of Confederation.

"If I have to pay a tax on every load of vegetables I bring across the state line, I'll go out of business!"

"I claim I've got a right to fish over there, but there's no court where I can take you to prove it."

and Connecticut almost started fighting over a piece of land claimed by both states. Yet Congress had no power to set up United States courts to settle arguments of this kind.

The states see a need for changing the government. Considering the weaknesses of the Articles of Confederation and the confusion which naturally follows a war, it is not surprising that many Americans were dissatisfied. People tended to blame the government for any problem that turned up. By 1785 the affairs of the United States were in such trouble that Americans realized something had to be done. Unless a stronger union were established, they feared there would soon be no nation at all.

At this very time Virginia and Maryland were arguing about navigation rights on the Potomac River and Chesapeake Bay. In 1785, representatives from the two states met and agreed on regulations for boats sailing these waters. This success led them to think it would be a good idea if other states could join them and agree on a plan for regulating trade.

A meeting is called to improve the government. Maryland and Virginia asked the other states to send representatives to discuss this problem at a meeting to be held at Annapolis, Maryland, a year later. Only five of the thirteen states sent representatives. These citizens talked about the problems of the Confederation. They decided to see if the government could be improved. They invited all of the states to send representatives to still another meeting, or **convention,** to be held in Philadelphia. This time twelve of the thirteen states accepted. Rhode Island was the only state that refused to send delegates to the meeting.

▶ **CHECK UP** See Teacher's Key.

1. What attempts at union had been made before the Articles of Confederation were adopted?
2. What powers did the central government have under the Articles of Confederation?
3. What were the weaknesses of that government?

241

● Have students note that this convention was called to *improve* the Articles, not to draft a new document.

2 How Did the Constitution Become the Foundation of Our Government?

A CONSTITUTIONAL CONVENTION MEETS IN PHILADELPHIA

● Early in June, 1787, about 30 men sat in a small room on the first floor of the State House in Philadelphia where the Declaration of Independence had been signed. In spite of the summer heat, the doors and windows were closed because the men wanted to keep secret what went on in their meetings. Loose dirt had been shoveled onto the street outside so that they would not be disturbed by the noise of passing carriages and wagons. All the men were dressed in the style of the times: knee breeches with silver buckles just below the knee, silk stockings, low shoes, long waistcoats, and open coats extending almost to their knees.

George Washington is elected chairman. Near one end of the room was a raised platform upon which stood a large chair with a gilded half-sun carved on its high back. In this chair sat a man well over six feet tall and weighing more than 210 pounds. This man was George Washington, who had been the choice of all for chairman of the meeting. Fifty-five years old at the time of this meeting, George Washington was dignified, serious, and thoughtful. As commander of the army which had won their independence, he was respected by everybody in the United States. His election as chairman was both natural and wise. Although he did not take much part in the discussions that followed, the members paid close attention when he did speak.

Able men attend the Convention. All together, 55 men attended the Philadelphia Convention. These men were well known in their states. In a day when there were few colleges, many of the men nevertheless were well educated.

Most of them had been leaders in the Revolution, and most of them lived in the older villages and cities near the coast.

As Washington glanced about the room, he recognized the faces of many friends and acquaintances. One of these people was a fellow Virginian, much younger than himself, upon whom Washington depended a great deal. This was *James Madison,* a short, slender man, 35 years of age. He spoke quietly and modestly, but the members listened carefully to his words, because Madison knew a great deal about government. For one thing, he had studied the governments of many countries. He had also served as a member of the governments of Virginia and of the United States, both during and after the Revolution. The careful notes taken by Madison give us a great deal of information about what went on in the meetings of the Convention.

Benjamin Franklin, wise, humorous, and at 81 the oldest member present at the meeting, also played a useful part. Franklin had first entered Philadelphia one cold Sunday morning many years before, when he was only seventeen years old. He was a poor apprentice then and had just run away from his master in Boston. His clothes were dirty from traveling, and his pockets were "stuffed out with shirts and stockings." He had walked the streets of Philadelphia munching a "great puffy roll" and carrying two others under his arms.

Much had happened to the runaway apprentice since that day long ago. He had tried many things and had succeeded at all of them. He had been a writer, a publisher of a newspaper, and an inventor. He had also served as an official of the United States at home

242

● See p. T28 for a strategy that calls for students to put together a bulletin board display highlighting the Constitutional Convention.

Debate over a constitution for the United States began early in June, 1787, at Philadelphia's Independence Hall (right, above).

and as its representative abroad. In 1787, he was "president" (governor) of Pennsylvania. During the meetings he moved around the room, giving good advice, calming members when they disagreed, and cheering everybody with a wise comment or a funny remark.

Gouverneur Morris, born in New York, attended the meeting as a representative of Pennsylvania. His body was disabled (for he had a wooden leg and could not use one arm), but his mind was keen and alert. He was an effective writer. His sentences were clear, direct, and graceful. He wrote most of the actual language used in the document describing the new plan of government agreed upon by the Convention.

PLANS FOR A NEW GOVERNMENT ARE WORKED OUT

The men who gathered at Philadelphia included many of the wisest citizens of the United States. As we will see, they needed all their experience and wisdom to solve the difficult problems that lay ahead.

The Articles of Confederation are discarded. The states had been invited to send delegates to Philadelphia for one purpose — to improve the Articles of Confederation. Yet the meeting had hardly begun when the men agreed on a bold step. They decided to abandon the ● unsatisfactory Articles of Confederation and draw up an entirely *new* plan of government. Because this meeting voted to write a constitution, it has been called the Constitutional Convention.

"But," asked the members of the Convention, "if we are going to have a

243

● Discuss whether this bold step helps to explain why the meetings were held in secret.

new government instead of patching up the old one, what kind of Constitution shall we write?" Gouverneur Morris supplied the answer to this question. He said that the Constitutional Convention must plan a national government strong enough to work successfully, yet *not* so strong that it would break down the authority of the states. Such a plan would not be easy to work out. If the states turned over too much power to the central government, they might be seriously weakened. On the other hand, if the states did not give up enough power to make the United States strong, the central government would not work much better than the Confederation.

Virginia proposes a plan for a strong government. Soon after the meetings began, some of the members suggested a plan to the Convention. It was called the *Virginia Plan* because it had the support of the Virginia representatives. According to this plan, the government of the United States was to be made up of three parts: (1) a Congress to make the laws; (2) a separate branch of the government, headed by a President, to enforce these laws; and (3) United States courts to see that justice was done under the laws. Under the Virginia Plan, Congress was to be divided into two houses. The members of the first house were to be elected by the people directly. Such states as Delaware might have only one representative because of their small populations. (**Population** means the number of people.) States with large populations, like Virginia, would probably have ten or more representatives. The members of the second house were to be elected by the first house.

Here was a plan that would set up a central government based upon the people. It would make the government of the United States much stronger and the state governments weaker.

New Jersey offers a plan for a weaker government. A number of the members of the Constitutional Convention did not like the Virginia Plan. Some said, "We cannot be sure that the voters will elect capable representatives to Congress. The state governments, not the people, should choose the representatives." Others said, "The Virginia Plan will take too much power from the states. They will be too weak and the national government too strong." The members from the smaller states added still another objection: "The large states with greater populations will have so many representatives in Congress that the small states will have little to say about the passing of laws."

A delegate from the small state of New Jersey offered another plan to the Convention. In the *New Jersey Plan,* each state (regardless of its size) would send the same number of representatives to Congress. This plan would make certain that the states would remain strong, and that the small states would have the same number of votes as the large ones. But a number of delegates objected to the New Jersey Plan because (1) the representatives would be chosen by the state governments, not the people; and (2) the people in the large states would not be represented fairly. In other words, the large states would have no more votes in Congress than the small states.

THE CONSTITUTION IS WRITTEN

An agreement is reached. For many days the Convention discussed these two plans. The large states naturally wanted the Virginia Plan; the small states favored the New Jersey Plan. This was the most important disagreement that the Convention had to deal with. If the Constitutional Convention were to succeed, an agreement had to be reached. When people disagree, it helps

244

See p. T28 for a strategy that asks students to compare both plans of government.

The Constitution was signed on September 17, 1787. In this picture the artist showed every signer. George Washington is standing at the right, and Benjamin Franklin is seated (center).

if each side will give way a little. This way of settling a problem is called a **compromise.** The delegates at the Convention were determined to work out a compromise. One man told the Convention he would rather "bury his bones" in Philadelphia than go home without making a strong union.

Finally, each side did give way a little, and a compromise was reached. It was agreed that Congress should have two houses: the **House of Representatives** and the **Senate.** In the House of Representatives, a state would be represented according to population. Of course this would give the large states more representatives than the small states. But in the Senate the states would be equal, each having two sena-

tors and two votes. Equal representation in the Senate would protect the small states, since every law had to be approved by both houses. And the arrangements for the House and the Senate meant that both the people and the states would be represented. (See Article I, Sections 2c and 3a of the Constitution.)

When this plan, called the Great Compromise, was agreed upon, the representatives of all the states were willing to work together to finish writing the Constitution.

Many other compromises are made. All summer long the members of the Convention worked on the new plan of government. As other difficult problems came up, they, too, were settled by compromises. Here are a few of them:

(1) By the terms of the Great Compromise, the number of representatives that each state would have in the House was to depend on the number of people living in the state. But southern states

245

Have students read Article I, Sections 2c and 3a (see text of Constitution at the back of the book).

had many more slaves than the northern states. How should slaves be counted? If each slave were counted separately, the number of southern votes in the House would have been greatly increased. A compromise was reached on this question. It was agreed to count five slaves as three instead of five persons. (See the Constitution, Article I, Section 2c.)

(2) The members disagreed on another important question: Should Congress have the power to control trade with foreign countries? The northern states, where many people made a living by shipping, wanted Congress, not the states, to regulate foreign trade. But the southern states bought many things from Europe. They were afraid that Congress might tax those goods, thus adding to the cost of the things they bought. The South also feared the slave trade might be stopped by Congress. So another compromise was made. Congress was given the power to regulate commerce with foreign countries and between the states, but it could not stop the slave trade for the next twenty years.

(3) Still another serious question was raised: how should the President be elected? The Constitution made the President a very important official. If Congress had the power to elect Presidents, it would in effect have the power to tell that official what to do. On the other hand, there were members of the Convention who did not trust the judgment of the people in selecting a President. So another compromise was made. The President and Vice-President were to be chosen by a group of citizens called **electors.** Each state would select as many electors as it had senators and representatives. If no candidate for President had the votes of more than half the electors, the House of Representatives would decide between the candidates. (See the Constitution, Article II, Section 1b.)

Still other compromises were made as the members of the Convention worked out the new plan of government. The members discussed each problem until they felt they had solved it. Whenever tempers rose during the discussion, Benjamin Franklin would tell a story. He told one about a Frenchwoman, who, in an argument with her sister, said, "I don't know how it happens, Sister, but I meet with nobody but myself that's always in the right!" In good humor once more, the members would return to their work.

The Convention's work is completed. At last the Constitution was written, and its members were ready to go home. Although nobody was completely satisfied, the members believed they had written the best Constitution possible. The new central government would be stronger than the old, because it had been given important powers that the Confederation government did not have. These powers included the right to tax and to control trade among the states. At the same time the states still had enough powers to control their local affairs. This kind of government, in which separate states are united under a strong government, is called a **federal system.** (The word *federal* itself applies to the central government, as in **federal government.**)

Would the new central government be strong enough to be successful? Or would it be too strong? Only time would tell.

Before the meeting broke up, Franklin rose and pointed to the half-sun on Washington's chair. "I have often and often in the course of this session," he said, "looked at that [half-sun] without being able to tell whether it was rising or setting. But now at length I have the happiness to know that it is a rising and not a setting sun." With their work completed, on September 17, 1787, the members said good-bye and left Philadelphia for their homes.

246

SHALL THE CONSTITUTION BE ACCEPTED?

Let the people choose. The members of the Constitutional Convention had worked long and hard to write what they believed to be a good plan of government. But the only way they could find out how their fellow citizens felt was to send the Constitution to the states for approval. In each state the voters elected representatives to decide whether or not to **ratify,** or accept, the new federal government. Meanwhile, throughout the country — in homes, in

Americans throughout the country read the Constitution to see what the new government would be like. Here young Daniel Webster, who later became a famous senator, reads the Constitution.

meeting places, and on street corners — the Constitution was talked about. Some Americans strongly favored the new government; others opposed it.

Some Americans feared a strong government. Those Americans who opposed the Constitution feared it would set up too strong a central government. They could not forget that, only a few short years before, they had fought a long war to protect their precious liberties against the tyranny of a strong British government. Now they saw that the Constitution proposed a government that would be able to tax the people and to force the people to obey laws. Those who disliked the Constitution asked: "What is to prevent this new strong government from taking away our rights?"

Jefferson suggests a Bill of Rights. These fears were well expressed by Thomas Jefferson, who, you remember, had written the Declaration of Independence. Jefferson had not attended the Constitutional Convention because he had been sent to represent the United States in France. When he received a copy of the Constitution, he found much that he approved of, but he also found important weaknesses. He expressed his views as follows in a letter to ● James Madison:

> I like the organization of the government into legislative, judiciary and executive [branches]. I like the power given the [Congress] to levy taxes, and . . . I approve of the greater House being chosen by the people directly. . . . I will now tell you what I do not like. First, [there is no] bill of rights, providing clearly . . . for freedom of religion, freedom of the press, protection against standing armies, . . . and trials by jury in all matters [that may be tried] by the laws of the land. . . . Let me add that a bill of rights is what the people are entitled to against every government on earth. . . .

247

● See p. T28 for a strategy that asks students to use this letter to identify what Jefferson thought were the strengths and weaknesses of the Constitution.

The Pledge of Allegiance

I pledge allegiance to the flag of the United States of America and to the Republic for which it stands, one nation under God, indivisible, with liberty and justice for all.

Most young people have repeated this Pledge many times in school. When they say the Pledge, they are promising to be loyal to the American Flag and to the United States. In addition, they are saying that our country is a united nation in which every American is entitled to liberty and justice.

The Pledge of Allegiance was written in 1892 by a man named Francis Bellamy. It made its first public appearance in a magazine for which Bellamy worked, *The Youth's Companion.* Many Americans, reading the Pledge, felt that it expressed in a few words the deep feeling of loyalty which they felt toward their country. Today the Pledge has become a traditional part of American school life.

Friends of the Constitution campaign for its adoption. In answer to objections like Jefferson's, the friends of the Constitution said that the rights of the people would be perfectly safe. They also pointed out that no laws could be passed by Congress without the consent of the people's representatives in the House. They explained the ways in which the new union would be better than the Confederation.

Those who favored the Constitution spoke at meetings in the various states. They also explained the new union in articles printed in newspapers and in pamphlets. The most famous of these articles was a series called *The Federalist,* written by James Madison, Alexander Hamilton, and John Jay. These articles gave a clear explanation of the Constitution and presented strong arguments for ratifying it.

The Constitution wins approval. Slowly those who approved the Constitution gained support. Delaware ratified the Constitution first, then Pennsylvania. So did New Jersey, Georgia, Connecticut, Massachusetts, Maryland, South Carolina, and New Hampshire. This made nine states, and it had been agreed that if nine states accepted the Constitution, it should become the new government.

In some of these states, however, the Constitution had won by only a small number of votes. Its friends had been compelled to promise that they would work for the addition of a bill of rights to protect the liberties of the people. Two important states, Virginia and New York, still had not accepted the Constitution. In Virginia, Patrick Henry, the fiery speaker of Revolutionary days, worked against accepting the Constitution. He feared the great power given the federal government. Yet without Virginia the new government would lack the support of the largest state. And without New York the nation would be separated into two parts.

At last Virginia accepted the Constitution by the close vote of 89 to 79. In New York the Constitution won by the votes of only three representatives. (The remaining two states, North Carolina and Rhode Island, did not ratify the Constitution until nearly two years after the other states had agreed to the new government.)

● Have students prepare written or oral reports about *The Federalist.*

The Congress of the Confederation arranged that the new government should begin in the spring of 1789. The states were asked to hold elections for the new President and members of the new Congress. A new and stronger union was to be tried at last.

No American can read the story of our Constitution without realizing what a debt of gratitude we owe to the wise men who wrote it. In giving the United States its Constitution, these men laid the foundation of our nation. This remarkable document has not only given us a strong and stable government but has also protected the liberties which we hold dear. (You will find the complete Constitution at the back of this book, as well as notes to help you read it with greater understanding.)

▶ **CHECK UP**

1. Who were some of the outstanding men present at the Constitutional Convention?
2. **(a)** What was the Virginia Plan? **(b)** The New Jersey Plan? **(c)** How was the disagreement between large and small states settled?
3. What other important compromises were adopted by the Convention?
4. **(a)** Why did some citizens oppose the Constitution? **(b)** What did Jefferson think should be added to it? Why?

CHECK UP ON CHAPTER 11

Words to Know

1. elector
2. population
3. compromise
4. ratify
5. federal system
6. constitution
7. convention
8. House of Representatives
9. Senate
10. federal government

Facts to Remember

1. In what ways were the constitutions adopted by the state governments alike?
2. Identify each of the following: **(a)** Albany Plan of Union, **(b)** Second Continental Congress, **(c)** Articles of Confederation.
3. How did each of the following play a part in the Constitutional Convention? **(a)** George Washington **(b)** James Madison **(c)** Benjamin Franklin **(d)** Gouverneur Morris
4. **(a)** Explain the disagreement between large and small states over the method of choosing representatives in Congress. **(b)** How was the disagreement settled?
5. **(a)** What was *The Federalist*? **(b)** How did it help to win the people's approval of the Constitution?

Skills to Practice

1. Look at the map on page 239. **(a)** Which states claimed western lands? **(b)** Which state claimed the most land? **(c)** Which state claimed land that was also claimed by Spain? **(d)** What was the approximate east-west distance of Massachusetts's western land claim? **(e)** How did that compare with the east-west distance of Connecticut's land claim?
2. The pictures on pages 240–241 illustrate three weaknesses for which the government under the Articles of Confederation was criticized. Following are three of those weaknesses. Which of the weaknesses is illustrated by each picture? **(a)** Congress had no power to tax. **(b)** Congress had no power to regulate trade. **(c)** Congress had no power to settle arguments between the states.
3. Read Thomas Jefferson's letter to James Madison on page 247. What rights did Jefferson think should be included in a bill of rights?

Questions to Think About

1. Should the Articles of Confederation have been blamed for all the problems faced by the United States following the Revolution? Why or why not?
2. The Constitution has been called a "bundle of compromises." What does that mean?
3. Some people, who were opponents of the strong government outlined in the Constitution, made the following argument. They pointed out that the American people had just fought a long and difficult war to win freedom from another strong government. How would you have answered their argument?

 # Linking Past and Present

● **Names of the states.** When our Constitution was adopted, there were only thirteen states in the Union. Now, as you know, there are fifty states. Have you ever wondered where some of the states got their names?

Many of the states are named after Indian tribes or have names taken from Indian languages. *Alibama* was the name of an Indian tribe living in what is now Alabama. Missouri was the name given to the river by the Indians. It meant "muddy water." In the language of the Sioux Indians, Dakota meant "alliance of friends." Kentucky is taken from an Indian name meaning "tomorrow" or "Land of Tomorrow." Ohio was an Iroquois name which meant "great." In another Indian language, *michi* meant "great" and *gama* meant "water." Thus we have Michigan, the name first given to the lake and then to the state. Connecticut comes from the Indian word *quonecktacut,* meaning "long river" or "river of pines."

There are other Indian names. Arkansas was the Algonquin name for the Quapaw Indians. Illinois is an Indian word believed to mean "river of men." Iowa means "sleepy ones," a word applied to a Sioux tribe by other Indians. Kansas, meaning "people of the South Wind," was the name of another Sioux tribe. Massachusetts was an Algonquin name for "the place near the big little hills." Minnesota, in Sioux language, meant "sky-colored water." Nebraska signified "flat river." Mexico was the name of an Aztec war god whose name is carried on in our state of New Mexico. Oklahoma takes its name from a Choctaw word that means "red people." Tennessee was the Indian name for the chief town of the Cherokees, on what is now the Little Tennessee River. Texas received its name from an Indian word meaning "friends" or "allies." Utah comes directly from the name of the Ute Indians. Wisconsin, spelled in different ways, meant "meeting of the rivers," while Wyoming meant "mountains and valleys."

Some of our states, as you have read (pages 94 and 148), were named by Spanish or French explorers — states like Florida, California, and Louisiana. Montana is a Spanish word that means "mountainous" while Nevada means "snow-clad."

Several states were named by the early settlers or proprietors in memory of places in Europe or in honor of kings or queens or nobles. Maryland was named in honor of Queen Henrietta Maria, wife of King Charles I of England. New Jersey took its name from the island of Jersey off the coast of England, and New Hampshire was named by its settlers in memory of the English county of Hampshire. Delaware gets its name from Lord De La Warr, an English governor of Virginia who came to America in 1610.

Two men in our own history are also honored. The state of Washington was named in memory of George Washington, and the District of Columbia recalls Christopher Columbus. The smallest state once had the largest name! It was called "The State of Rhode Island and Providence Plantations." Because it was so awkward, the name was shortened to "Rhode Island," for the island of Rhodes located in the Mediterranean.

As for the two newest states, Alaska is an Eskimo word meaning "great land," and Hawaii probably comes from a Polynesian word meaning "homeland."

250

● Have students review the spelling of the state names. Then hold a spelling-bee.

Use the primary sources quoted in earlier chapters to give students additional practice in identifying points of view.

GAINING SKILL

Finding Points of View in Primary Sources

You have already learned that a primary source is first-hand information about events that happened in the past (page 185). A primary source will often reveal the feelings, opinions, or views of people who took part in those events. The following primary source is part of a speech Benjamin Franklin gave in 1787 at the Constitutional Convention. Read the speech to discover Franklin's opinion of the Constitution.

> I confess that there are several parts of this constitution which I do not at present approve, but I am not sure I shall never approve them: For having lived long, I have experienced many instances of [having] to change opinions . . . which I once thought right, but found to be otherwise. . . . The older I grow, the more apt I am to doubt my own judgment, and to pay more respect to the judgment of others. . . .
>
> I agree to this Constitution with all its faults, if they are such; because I think a general Government necessary for us. . . . I doubt too whether any other Convention we can obtain, may be able to make a better Constitution. . . . Thus I consent, Sir, to this Constitution because I expect no better, and because I am not sure, that it is not the best. The opinions I have had of its errors, I sacrifice to the public good. I have never whispered a syllable of them abroad. Within these walls they were born, and here they shall die. If every one of us . . . were to report the objections he has had to it . . . we might prevent its being [approved], and thereby lose all [its] great advantages. . . . I hope therefore that . . . we shall act heartily and unanimously in recommending this Constitution.

1. Does Franklin support or oppose the Constitution? What is his opinion about its overall quality?
2. Some delegates wanted to hold a second convention to try to improve the Constitution. What was Franklin's point of view on that subject?
3. Franklin does not list any specific features of the Constitution that he disagrees with. What reason does he give for not doing so?
4. Eventually all but three of the delegates signed the Constitution. What would Franklin have probably thought about that? (In answering, consider the last sentence in his speech.)

251

CHAPTER **12**

The New Government Is Successfully Launched

1789–1825   See pp. T28–T29 for chapter teaching strategies.

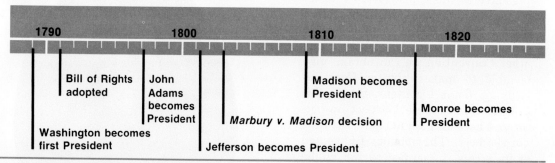

1790   1800   1810   1820

Bill of Rights adopted

John Adams becomes President

Madison becomes President

Monroe becomes President

Washington becomes first President

Marbury v. Madison decision

Jefferson becomes President

What this chapter is about —

It was noon on Thursday, April 30, 1789. A large crowd had gathered on Wall Street in New York City. Onto the balcony of Federal Hall stepped George Washington. He wore a dark brown suit with knee breeches, white silk stockings, and shoes with silver buckles. A sword hung at his side.

Catching sight of the tall, dignified figure on the balcony, the people below applauded loudly. George Washington placed his hand on a large Bible and slowly spoke the following words: "I do solemnly swear that I will faithfully

252

execute the office of President of the United States and will, to the best of my ability, preserve, protect, and defend the Constitution of the United States." As he finished, the crowd broke into shouts of "God bless our Washington! Long live our beloved President!" Washington turned and went inside to speak to the members of the new Congress.

Thus in 1789 our country began to govern itself under the new Constitution. The Articles of Confederation had been tried and found unsatisfactory;

now the new Constitution was to be tried. We Americans today know that the Constitution is strong and lasting, but the people who lived in 1789 did not know how it would work out. Would the new government under the Constitution be any better than the Confederation? Would it last longer? Everywhere thoughtful Americans were wondering about these questions.

In this chapter we will find out more about the new government under the Constitution. We will answer the following questions:

1. What kind of government did the Constitution establish?
2. How did the new government settle certain important problems?
3. How did political parties get started?

1 What Kind of Government Did the Constitution Establish?

We the people of the United States, in order to form a more perfect union, establish justice, insure domestic tranquillity, provide for the common defense, promote the general welfare, and secure the blessings of liberty to ourselves and our posterity, do ordain and establish this Constitution for the United States of America.

These now famous words, which every American should know, form the introduction or preamble (PREE-am-bul) to the Constitution of the United States of America. "We the people . . . establish this Constitution. . . ." What a long way Americans had traveled along the road of self-government! In a day when almost every country in the world accepted the rule of kings and queens, the makers of our Constitution had created a government based on the right of the people to rule. At a time

when laws in other countries were issued in the name of a monarch, Americans had accepted as their highest law a constitution in the name of the people.

Our central government has important powers. Those who planned the new government hoped that it would bring a "more perfect union" and "insure domestic tranquillity" (maintain order). In Chapter 11 we learned that the Confederation had done neither of these because it was weak. But the makers of the Constitution gave the new central government important powers that the Confederation had lacked. (For the most important powers, see the chart on page 254.)

Certain powers are left to the states. If the Constitution created a strong central government, what powers, then, were left to the states? The members of the Constitutional Convention were careful to divide the powers so that the

253

★ This excerpt was paraphrased from *Letters from a Pennsylvania Farmer* by John Dickinson.

states would not be swallowed up by the United States government. They gave the United States control over all matters that concerned the Union or *all* the states. (See Article I, Section 8, of the Constitution for a list of powers granted to the federal government.) On the other hand, each of the states was left free to control affairs that did not affect the other states. As a matter of fact, the Constitution leaves to each state all powers not definitely given to the United States.

Let us see how this division of powers worked out. Because war concerns all the states, the United States government was given the power to declare war. This was clearly stated in the Constitution. But each state has the power to make its own laws for punishing crimes like murder or theft, since these laws affect chiefly the people within the state where a crime takes place. You will not find this power of the states

mentioned in the Constitution, but it belongs to the states since it is not definitely given to the federal government.

Americans want the rights of the people protected. The new government was strong. But was it too strong? Americans love freedom and still today do not want government to put limits on their liberties. So Americans look closely at the power of their government. Of freedom and government, one wise American said:

> Who are the free people? Not those whose government is reasonable and just, but those whose government is so checked and controlled that it cannot be anything but reasonable and just.

The original Constitution did contain a few statements guaranteeing some rights to the people. Even so, you remember, Thomas Jefferson and other Americans feared that the new government might interfere with the rights of the people. They thought the Constitution should be changed to prevent the government from ever interfering with the rights they felt to be so important to individuals.

The Constitution gave the national government powers that it had not been granted under the Articles of Confederation. Compare the lists.

WHAT THE CONFEDERATION GOVERNMENT COULD DO	WHAT THE GOVERNMENT UNDER THE CONSTITUTION CAN DO	
1 Declare war and make peace, and organize an army and navy.	1 Declare war and make peace, and organize an army and navy. Also, when necessary, call on state militia.	5 Tax the people directly.
2 Control the relations of the United States with other nations and with Indians.	2 Control the relations of the United States with other nations and with Indians.	6 Coin all money and regulate its value.
3 Regulate trade with the Indians.	3 Regulate trade with the Indians, trade between states, and trade with foreign nations.	7 Organize a system of courts.
4 Borrow money to pay expenses.	4 Borrow money to pay expenses.	8 Govern the capital city of the United States and territory not yet made into states.
5 Ask the states to raise money to pay government expenses.		9 Do anything else, not definitely stated, that is necessary to carry out any of the powers that are mentioned.

● See p. T28 for a strategy that asks students to list the powers belonging to the federal government and those belonging to the states.

Each of the states limited voting rights. Just one state, New Jersey, allowed women to vote. In 1807, however, New Jersey changed its law and took the vote away from women.

The Bill of Rights guards our liberties. In 1791, ten **amendments** (additions) were added to the Constitution. These amendments are called the Bill of Rights because they state the rights of the American people under their government. The words are somewhat difficult for anyone but a lawyer to understand fully, but they mean a great deal. Because there is a Bill of Rights in our Constitution, you are not in danger of losing your freedom.

Here are a few of the rights people in America enjoy: (1) Americans may hold any religious beliefs and may worship as they see fit. (2) Americans may meet together in peaceful groups and may freely ask the government to change laws they believe are wrong. (3) Americans may speak or write their opinions freely and may criticize the government. (4) An American charged with a serious crime may claim the right to be tried by a jury in a court of law.

(5) Private houses may not be entered and searched by officers of the law except for good reason.

Turn to the Constitution at the back of this book and read the entire Bill of Rights. We Americans must never forget how many of our personal liberties we owe to the Bill of Rights and the rights which are guaranteed in other parts of the Constitution.

The Constitution can be amended. One section of the Constitution (Article V) explains how it can be changed or **amended.** There is more than one method. But the most common way has been for an amendment to be proposed by Congress and approved by the legislatures in three fourths of the states. Our Constitution was so wisely planned that few amendments have been added in almost two centuries.

Interpretation and custom also affect the government. Besides amendments, there are other ways in which the federal government has adapted to changing conditions.

(1) In settling cases, the Supreme Court sometimes has to decide just what the words in the Constitution 255

mean. The Constitution states, for instance, that Congress may make any laws "which shall be necessary and proper" for carrying out its specific powers. The Supreme Court has interpreted this to mean that Congress can use added powers if they are necessary to carry out powers stated in the Constitution. By giving the "necessary and proper" phrase a broad meaning, the Court has enabled the national government to grow more powerful.

(2) Certain customs or ways of doing things have grown up over the years. Although these customs are not provided for in the Constitution, they are just as closely followed as if they were. The two-party political system is an example of such a custom. Another one is the President's **Cabinet.** The Constitution provides for the appointment of heads of departments under the President. But it says nothing about their acting together as a group to advise the President, nor does it use the word *Cabinet.* Yet, even though the Constitution is silent on political parties and the Cabinet, each has become an important part of our government.

The government has three branches. So far we have been speaking of the government in general terms. "The government," we have said, "can do this. It cannot do that." Actually, the United States government is organized into three separate parts, or branches (diagram, next page). Each branch has its own special duties. One branch makes the laws. It is the **legislative** branch, or Congress, and consists of the House of Representatives and the Senate. The second branch puts the laws into effect and sees that they are obeyed. It is the **executive** branch and is headed by the President. The third branch decides cases growing out of the breaking of laws, and also decides whether the laws themselves violate the Constitution. This **judicial** branch consists of the Supreme Court and other federal courts. To divide the government in this way into separate branches, each with its own powers, is called **separation of powers.**

Why are powers separated? Why did the members of the Constitutional Convention divide the federal government so carefully into three separate branches? The reason is that they wanted to prevent tyranny, that is, the cruel or unjust use of power. They believed that if wide powers are given to one official, or even just a few officials, those powers are likely to be misused. For example, government officials could easily become tyrants if they had the power not only to *make* the rules but also to arrest and punish anybody accused of breaking the rules. But in our system of government, a group of elected citizens makes the laws; other officials arrest people who are believed to have broken laws; and a third group of citizens judges whether arrested people really have broken the laws. In this way, the chance for tyranny is much reduced.

Each branch has power to check the others. Even though they had divided the government into three branches, the members of the Constitutional Convention were not sure they had gone far enough. One branch of the government still might do the wrong thing. To prevent this, the Constitution provides that one branch may check another. For example, if Congress passes an unwise law, the President can disapprove or **veto** it. This prevents Congress from becoming too strong. Or if Congress believes the President has chosen the wrong person to help him enforce the laws, the Senate may refuse to approve that person's appointment. The President will then have to choose someone else. Also, the Supreme Court may check Congress and the President by deciding the meaning of a law in case of a dispute. It can even declare a law **unconstitutional** (contrary to the Consti-

See p. T28 for a strategy calling for students to construct a diagram of the federal government.

THE THREE BRANCHES OF THE UNITED STATES GOVERNMENT

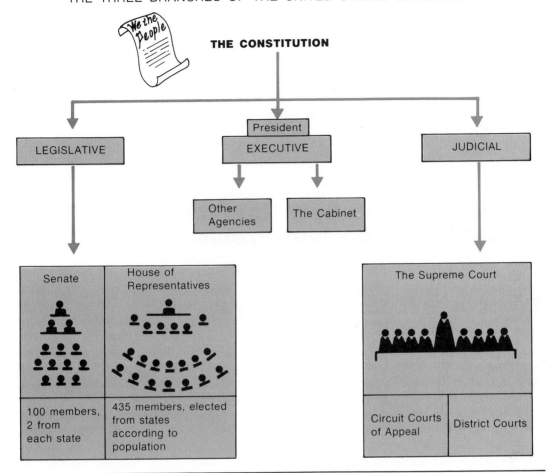

The Constitution provides for separation of powers among three branches of government. What are those three branches?

tution) so that it is no longer a law. Limiting power by having one branch of government check the others is called a system of **checks and balances.** The Constitutional Convention believed this system would make it difficult for any one branch to become too powerful.

———

You have been given only a general idea of what our government under the Constitution is like. What is most im-

portant to realize is that our Constitution is a *living* document, one capable of meeting new conditions. In the years since it was put into operation, the United States has grown tremendously in size, population, and power. To keep pace with these changes, the national government has expanded enormously. In fact, if the members of the Constitutional Convention could visit our capital city today, they would be completely bewildered to see the many activities carried out by the government. Yet the Constitution was so skillfully drawn up that the plan of government it provides serves us as well today as it did the people of two hundred years ago.

Discuss how the Constitution guarantees that no branch of government will have absolute power.

▶ **CHECK UP**   See Teacher's Key.

1. **(a)** What important powers does the national government have under the Constitution which it did *not* have under the Articles of Confederation? **(b)** How did the Constitution divide government powers between the states and the national government?
2. **(a)** What part of the Constitution protects the rights of the people? **(b)** What are some of the rights guaranteed by the Constitution?
3. How can the Constitution be amended?
4. **(a)** What are the three branches of the federal government? **(b)** What are the duties of each branch?
5. **(a)** How can the President check the actions of Congress? **(b)** How can Congress check the President? **(c)** How can the Supreme Court check the President or Congress?

2   How Did the New Government Settle Certain Important Problems?

The day set for the new government to take over was March 4, 1789. On that day, however, only a few of the newly elected members of Congress had arrived in New York City, the temporary capital. At that time travel (by horse, stagecoach, or ship) was slow. Congress met at last in the early part of April.

As you know, George Washington, the most famous and best-loved man in the United States, had been elected President. John Adams of Massachusetts, a prominent leader in the Revolution, became Vice-President. Washington was notified by Congress of his election and journeyed to New York from his home at Mount Vernon in Virginia. It was not until April 30 that he was inaugurated (sworn in) as President of the United States in the ceremony described at the beginning of this chapter.

The new government is set up. Although the Constitution outlined the general plan and the powers of each branch, all the details of government had to be worked out by the new Congress and the President. For instance, how was the government to raise money for its expenses? The Constitution called for a Supreme Court and other courts. How many should there be?

How many judges should be chosen for the Supreme Court? Who would be the best people for those important positions? The President could not handle all the executive affairs of the government alone. What departments should be created to help him? These were only a few of the problems facing the ● new government.

A great deal was accomplished in the first few years. In 1789, Congress passed a law establishing the Supreme Court and other federal courts. The Supreme Court was to have a Chief Justice and five Associate Justices,[1] to be chosen by the President and approved by the Senate. John Jay, a well-known statesman and lawyer from New York, was made Chief Justice. Congress also created several departments to help manage government affairs.

Washington chooses a Cabinet. One of the departments created by Congress was the Department of State. This department was to have charge of our relations with foreign countries. At the head of this department, as Secretary of State, Washington placed the brilliant

---

[1]The number of judges on the Supreme Court has changed several times. At present there are nine, including the Chief Justice. ★

★ Tell students that decisions in the Supreme Court are reached by majority vote. An odd number of judges makes a tie vote unlikely.

George Washington chose a Cabinet to help him run the government. This picture shows (from left to right) Cabinet members Edmund Randolph, Henry Knox (seated), Alexander Hamilton, and Thomas Jefferson meeting with President Washington.

Thomas Jefferson. A trusted old soldier of the Revolution named Henry Knox was made the head of the War Department. It was his job as Secretary of War to manage the army and handle all military affairs. Alexander Hamilton was appointed to the difficult position of Secretary of the Treasury. He was head of the Treasury Department and was responsible for raising money and handling the finances of the government. In addition, Washington appointed Edmund Randolph as Attorney General. Randolph's job was to advise the government on legal matters.

Washington not only depended on these four men to run their departments but also turned to them for advice in solving the problems of his government. In time they became known as the President's Cabinet. Through the years new departments have been created, so today the Cabinet is much larger.

The new government faces financial problems. The first serious problem the new government faced had to do with money matters. The United States owed a great deal of money. During the Revolutionary War the Continental Congress, having little money, had been forced to borrow to meet its expenses. The government of the Confederation, as we have learned, did not have much money either. By 1789, the sums that had been borrowed had not been repaid.

A government, like a person, cannot succeed if it fails to pay its debts. It loses the faith and respect of its citizens and of other nations. If the new government was to be a success, then, it would have to find ways to pay the money it owed.

Hamilton was well suited for the job of putting government finances in order. The man who would have charge of raising money and paying the government debts was Alexander Hamilton, Secretary of the Treasury. Hamilton had been born in the West Indies but moved to New York City when he was fifteen years old. He attended college there and then fought on the Patriot side dur-

259

● Have students find out the names of the persons in the Cabinet today and report back to class.

ing the American Revolution. Hamilton was so capable that he became a member of George Washington's military staff. After the war he became a lawyer. He was a member of the Constitutional Convention and believed firmly in a strong central government. As a matter of fact, by writing most of the essays in *The Federalist*, he helped bring about the adoption of the Constitution. Hamilton was 32 years old when he became Secretary of the Treasury. Hard-working, intelligent, and shrewd about money matters, he was well fitted for the task.

Hamilton tackles the problem of the nation's debts. Hamilton found that he had to deal with not one but many debts. The United States had borrowed money both in Europe and from its own citizens. The separate states had borrowed, too. When a government borrows, it gives the lender a promise to repay the loan at a certain time. This promise is called a bond. To persuade people to lend the money, the government offers to pay an extra amount each year for the loan of each dollar. This extra payment is called interest.

In the uncertain years after the Revolution many people had serious doubts that the United States would pay its debts. For this reason the bonds which had been issued had fallen sharply in value. Hamilton wanted to combine the national and state debts into one large debt and to issue new bonds for the full value of all the money that was owed. These bonds could then be paid off in an orderly way, and the honor of the nation would be upheld.
● Congress voted to accept this plan.

Hamilton makes a bargain. There were some congressmen, however, who did not want to include the debts of the different states in this plan. "Why should the United States help pay what the *separate states* have borrowed?" they asked. Hamilton replied that the reason the states had borrowed was to

help win independence for the country as a whole. Therefore, he felt, the national government should pay these state debts. But some states, like Virginia, had already paid off their debts. These states, mostly in the South, objected to this part of Hamilton's plan.

It happened that at this same time Congress was debating where to establish the nation's permanent capital. The southern states were eager to have the capital in the South, so Hamilton made a bargain. He suggested that if the southern congressmen would vote for taking over the state debts, he would use his influence to get the capital located in the South. His offer was accepted. Congress voted to take over the state debts, and it was agreed to locate the new capital on the banks of the Potomac River between Maryland and Virginia. That is how Washington, in the District of Columbia, became the capital of the United States. For ten ★ years, however, until the new city could be built, Philadelphia was our country's capital.

Hamilton proposes a bank. Another part of Hamilton's program was to set up a Bank of the United States. The government would help manage the bank and keep its money there. The bank would lend money to the government and issue paper money. Hamilton believed that Congress could establish the bank under its power to borrow money and regulate the money system. The bank would make the government stronger. Congress agreed and the bank was established.

Hamilton suggests a new tax. Where was the government to get the money it needed to pay its bills? Soon after Congress was established, it had passed a law placing a tax on goods brought into the United States from other countries. This kind of tax is called a **tariff.** For example, nails brought into the country were taxed 1 cent a pound; molasses from the West

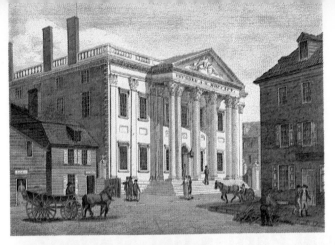

Indies, 2½ cents a gallon. There were also taxes on imported tea, coffee, sugar, paper, shoes, and so on.

Because the tariff failed to raise enough money, Hamilton recommended a tax on goods manufactured and sold *within* the country. At Hamilton's suggestion, Congress taxed all whiskey made and sold in the United States.

A rebellion against the whiskey tax fails. The farmers who lived far back from the coast strongly objected to Hamilton's plan for a tax on whiskey, because it hit them directly. These farmers raised corn. There were no railroads or highways in those days, and corn was too bulky to ship to distant markets. Therefore, the farmers made their corn into whiskey. The whiskey took up less space and was much easier to take to market. Of course, the farmers did not like to be taxed for making their whiskey. In western Pennsylvania in 1794, they angrily refused to pay the

tax, and carried on what was called the Whiskey Rebellion. But President Washington knew that no government is worthy of the name unless its laws are obeyed. The whiskey tax was a law, and the Pennsylvania farmers were disobeying it. President Washington raised an army of 15,000 soldiers and forced the Pennsylvanians to pay the tax.

The government is well established. In 1795, Hamilton left his place as Secretary of the Treasury and became a lawyer again. He could be proud of what he had accomplished. His plans had solved the money problems of the new government. Americans had begun to trust the government, and this, in turn, helped to make it successful. The new government had earned respect by arranging to pay back the money it owed. And by putting down the Whiskey Rebellion, it had shown that its laws must be obeyed. In brief, the new government was firmly established.

261

"Linking Past and Present" (p. 266) explains how our currency came to be based on the decimal system.

1. Who were the members of Washington's first Cabinet?
2. (a) What serious financial problems did the new government face? (b) How did Hamilton plan to put the government's financial affairs in order? (c) Why was the Bank of the United States established?
3. (a) What two kinds of taxes did the government use to raise money? (b) Why did farmers in Pennsylvania carry on the Whiskey Rebellion?

3 How Did Political Parties Get Started?

Hamilton's plans lead to political parties. As we have seen, Hamilton's plans were accepted by Congress and put into effect. Not all the people of the United States, however, believed the plans were wise. An American who disliked the plans might have said something like this: "What good to me is Hamilton's new system of repaying the debts of the United States? Of course, it is fine for those who own the bonds. But only wealthy people own them. My neighbors and I own none. I have nothing to do, either, with Hamilton's bank. As for his taxes, the tax on whiskey hurts a poor farmer like me. Worst of all, Hamilton's plans may make the government too strong. What will prevent it from being tyrannical just as the British government was before the Revolution?"

Many people held much the same views. Some were poor farmers and workers in cities. Others, who were well-to-do, were not troubled by the paying of debts and taxes but feared that the United States government might become too powerful. They wanted the states to be stronger and the power of the United States to be limited. One of those who shared these feelings was Thomas Jefferson. In fact, Jefferson became the leader of the people who opposed Hamilton's program.

When people who hold similar views unite to influence the government, we say that they have formed a political party. Thomas Jefferson's followers came to be known as the Democratic-Republican Party.[2] Those who supported Hamilton's ideas formed what was called the Federalist Party.

Political parties develop during Washington's administration. The Federalist and Republican parties began during Washington's first term as President. George Washington himself did not join either party (although his sympathies lay with the Federalists). He was so respected by the American people, however, that both Jefferson and Hamilton asked him to serve a second term. Washington was elected a second time in 1792. During his second term in office, the Federalist Party became powerful.

When the election of 1796 drew near, Washington felt that two terms as President were enough for one person, and he announced that he did not want a third term. He started the custom, which continued until the time of President Franklin D. Roosevelt, that no person should serve more than two terms as President. (This custom was later made law by the Twenty-Second Amendment to the Constitution.) When Washington left the presidency, he went back to Virginia to live on his beloved plantation, Mount Vernon. There he died about two years later, at the age of 67.

---

[2]The name of Jefferson's party was soon shortened to Republican. It should not be confused with the Republican Party of today. It really was the ancestor of the present Democratic Party.

● See p. T29 for a strategy calling for students to compare the two political parties.

John Adams, Federalist, is elected President. As Washington's second term as President drew to a close, bitter rivalry arose between the Federalists and the Republicans over the presidential election. By a narrow margin the Federalist candidate, John Adams of Massachusetts, was elected second President of the United States. Adams had had much experience in the service of his country and had served as Vice-President during both of Washington's terms as President. He was a man of ability and absolute honesty, never swerving from what he believed to be right.

Honest and capable as he was, John Adams was not a popular President. People found him cold, even rude at times, and in general hard to get along with. What is more, during the excitement of a quarrel with France, the Federalists in Congress adopted some very harsh laws. One of these, called the Sedition Act, limited the right of the people to criticize the President and Congress. The Republicans charged that this law interfered with the right of free speech. As a result, both John Adams and the Federalist Party became unpopular, and Adams was defeated in the election of 1800.

John Marshall establishes judicial review. Just before he left office, President Adams appointed John Marshall as Chief Justice of the United States. A Virginian, Marshall had fought in the Revolutionary War, and had later served as a member of Congress and as Secretary of State.

During his 34 years as Chief Justice, Marshall did much to shape the whole form of our government. One of his most important decisions came early in his service on the Supreme Court, in a case called *Marbury v. Madison* (1803). In this famous case he declared an act of Congress to be unconstitutional. As you read on page 256, that meant that the act was not in agreement with the Constitution and therefore could not be allowed to go into effect. Marshall stated that "the Constitution is superior to any ordinary act of the legislature, and the Constitution, and not such ordinary act, must govern. . . ." In other words, the Constitution is, as it says itself, "the supreme law of the land."

The power of the United States courts to declare acts of Congress and the state legislatures unconstitutional is known as **judicial review.** This power has been used by the courts ever since Marshall's day.

Thomas Jefferson, Republican, becomes President. ★ Thomas Jefferson, leader of the Democratic-Republicans, was elected in 1800 to take the place of John Adams as President. Born in Virginia on April 13, 1743, Thomas Jefferson was a graduate of the College of William and Mary. Jefferson had an active and searching mind and read widely throughout his life. Almost every subject — architecture, art, science, religion, government — interested him. He was an inventor, an architect, a musician, and a writer. Over six feet two in height, he was a commanding figure in any group.

Although Thomas Jefferson was a wealthy man who had enjoyed every advantage, he dressed plainly and disliked ceremony or show. Instead of riding in a fine carriage to his inauguration, he walked. Jefferson believed that the future of the country depended on its development as a nation of small farmers. He placed great trust in the sound judgment of the people as a whole and believed that education was important for every citizen in a democracy. It was he who wrote in the Declaration of Independence that "all men are created equal" and that they are entitled to "life, liberty, and the pursuit of happiness."

When he became President, Jefferson, like Washington and John Adams before him, had had much experience.

263

See p. T29 for a strategy that calls for students to put together a bulletin board display featuring the first five Presidents.

Our Presidents

GEORGE WASHINGTON   1789–1797

From Virginia. Commander of the Continental Army during the Revolutionary War and chairman of the Constitutional Convention, Washington was a natural choice for first President. He took the oath of office in New York City, the nation's temporary capital. "The Father of His Country" served two terms. Climaxing a lifetime of public service, Washington devoted all his strength and wisdom to launching the new government.

JOHN ADAMS   1797–1801

Federalist from Massachusetts. Our second President was the first to live in the White House in the new capital at Washington. Adams, who had been Washington's Vice-President, was the only President whose son also became Chief Executive. He and Thomas Jefferson both died on July 4, 1826, the fiftieth anniversary of the Declaration of Independence, which Adams had helped Jefferson to write.

THOMAS JEFFERSON   1801–1809

Democratic-Republican from Virginia. Chief author of the Declaration of Independence, this tall, sandy-haired man was our most versatile Chief Executive — musician, architect, inventor, and educator, as well as statesman. He doubled the size of the country with the Louisiana Purchase in 1803, the greatest peacetime acquisition of land in the history of our nation. One of Jefferson's proudest accomplishments was having founded the University of Virginia.

JAMES MADISON   1809–1817

Democratic-Republican from Virginia. The "Father of the Constitution," Madison also drafted the first ten Amendments. Though frail and soft-spoken, he faced enemy gunfire while in office when the British attacked Washington, D.C., during the War of 1812. He was the first President whose inaugural costume was completely American-made. Madison's wife, Dolley, became famous as a gracious White House hostess.

JAMES MONROE   1817–1825

Democratic-Republican from Virginia. Monroe was a soldier, lawyer, member of the Continental Congress, and Secretary of State under Madison. His presidency was called "the Era of Good Feelings," and he was elected to a second term almost without opposition. He warned that European interference would not be welcome in the Western Hemisphere, a statement that became known as the Monroe Doctrine.

He had been a member of the legislature of Virginia, a member of the Second Continental Congress, and governor of Virginia. He had represented the United States in Europe. Jefferson had also been Secretary of State under Washington and Vice-President under Adams. As President he served two terms, from 1801 to 1809.

The Federalist Party disappears. During Jefferson's administrations the Republican Party grew stronger. The Democratic-Republicans elected the next two Presidents — James Madison, who served from 1809 to 1817, and James Monroe, who was President from 1817 to 1825. Meanwhile, the Federalist Party became weaker and weaker. Finally, in Monroe's first term, that party disappeared, and Monroe was re-elected without opposition. Because there was only one political party, the years of Monroe's presidency are called the Era of Good Feelings.

▶ **CHECK UP** See Teacher's Key.

1. **(a)** How did political parties develop during Washington's presidency? **(b)** What were these parties called, and what did each party stand for?
2. **(a)** Who were the first five Presidents? **(b)** To what party, if any, did each belong?

CHECK UP ON CHAPTER 12 See Teacher's Key.

Words to Know

1. amendment
2. legislative
3. executive
4. judicial
5. Cabinet
6. tariff
7. amend
8. veto
9. separation of powers
10. judicial review
11. unconstitutional
12. checks and balances

Facts to Remember

1. **(a)** Why was the Bill of Rights added to the Constitution? **(b)** How does the Bill of Rights protect Americans?
2. **(a)** What are the three branches of the United States government? **(b)** What officials carry out the duties of each branch? **(c)** What does *separation of powers* mean?
3. **(a)** What departments were created by Congress to assist President Washington? **(b)** Who was appointed the head of each department?
4. **(a)** What financial problems did the new government face? **(b)** What plans were made to solve those problems?
5. **(a)** Who followed George Washington as President? **(b)** Who became the third President?

Skills to Practice

1. Name the *best* kind of reference book to use in looking for answers to the questions below. Choose your answers from this list: *almanac, atlas, dictionary, encyclopedia.*
   a. How many different cities served as the capital of the United States before Washington, D.C., was built?
   b. What departments are there in the President's Cabinet today?
   c. What is the area of the District of Columbia?
   d. What is the difference between the words *legislative, legislature,* and *legislator*?
2. Arrange the following events in the order in which they happened. Start with the earliest event.
   a. Hamilton recommends a plan to deal with the nation's debts.
   b. Jefferson is elected President.
   c. Washington appoints the members of the first Cabinet.
   d. The Constitution is ratified and goes into effect.
   e. Washington is inaugurated the first time.

Questions to Think About

1. What are some of the rights listed in the Bill of Rights? Why do citizens also have responsibilities that go along with those rights?
2. Why is it that a Constitution drawn up many years ago meets so well the needs of our country today?
3. Although the parties themselves have changed, our country has always had two major political parties since the early 1800's. **(a)** What are the advantages of a two-party system of government? **(b)** Why have new political parties developed throughout our country's history?

 # Linking Past and Present

Our national capital. Most cities grow gradually, according to the needs of their citizens and the nature of their land. But our national capital, Washington, D.C., grew up more or less according to a plan that was laid down in the early days of our nation. You can still see many signs of the planning today, even though the city has grown much larger than its founders ever dreamed it would.

George Washington had the foresight to choose Pierre Charles L'Enfant (lahn-FAHN), a French artist and engineer, to design the capital. In his work L'Enfant was assisted by Benjamin Banneker, a black astronomer, mathematician, publisher of almanacs, and surveyor.

L'Enfant planned a city "magnificent enough to grace a great nation." He wanted a city of grandeur, with plenty of open spaces. On a hill overlooking the Potomac he placed the Capitol, where Congress meets today. A mile away would be the President's house, the beautiful White House we all know so well. To the east of the Capitol Building, L'Enfant planned a monument to honor George Washington. Between the two would be a broad park. That is the beautiful Mall that you can see today, with the Capitol at one end and the Washington Monument, with its reflecting pool, at the other.

L'Enfant also laid out, between the Capitol and the White House, the broad thoroughfare we know as Pennsylvania Avenue. He also planned other wide avenues to run through the city, radiating like the spokes of a wheel from various circles and plazas. Many of these were actually built and may be seen today, usually with fine statues or other memorials. They give the city a feeling of space and openness.

Although L'Enfant's plans were followed in a general way, they were too expensive for a new nation to work out quickly. But in time, most of the buildings and monuments envisioned by the planners were finished. Today Washington, D.C. is considered to be one of our nation's most beautiful cities.

Our money system. The next time you do any figuring with money, give thanks to Thomas Jefferson for our simple decimal system. During and after the Revolution, people had money troubles because there was no single money system. Thirteen states as well as Congress issued money. People also used foreign coins.

In 1789, the only coins being made in the United States were large copper pennies, called Franklin pennies. When Alexander Hamilton became Secretary of the Treasury, he urged Congress to establish a mint for making coins. Thomas Jefferson recommended that the new money be based on the decimal system, or a system of tens. Ten cents were to make one dime, ten dimes one dollar. The dollar was to be the unit of currency, so that money would be figured in dollars or decimal fractions of dollars. By using the decimal point, cents could be written as hundredths of a dollar, as $4.25 or $.09. Such numbers are easy to add, subtract, multiply, or divide.

Congress accepted the recommendations of Hamilton and Jefferson, and in 1792 the first coins were minted. Later, the government also issued nickels, quarters (of a dollar), and half dollars.

266

GAINING SKILL

Have students look at the graph on page 307. Ask: What does this graph show? (population growth, 1820–1860) Have students use the information in that graph and on this page to construct a bar graph showing population growth for the period 1790–1860.

Reading Bar Graphs

How many people did our country have when the Constitution went into effect in 1789? Nobody knew at the time. To find out, the government in 1790 appointed 217 people to take a **census** (SEN-sus) — a count of the population. Throughout the thirteen states the census-takers went from door to door, asking how many people lived in each household. Every ten years since then, the government has taken a census.

Suppose you wanted to find out how the population of the nation grew in the thirty years following the first census. If you looked up census figures in a reference book, here is what you would find:

Year	Population
1790	3,929,214
1800	5,308,483
1810	7,239,881
1820	9,638,453

Information presented in this form (listed in columns) is called a **table.**

Another way of showing population figures is a **graph.** A graph is a drawing that helps you see the meaning of figures quickly and easily. The graph you see on this page is called a bar graph, since it uses columns or bars.

To read a graph, you need to know what the parts of the graph are and how they fit together. First, look at the title. It tells you what kind of information is given. Next, look at the horizontal axis — the information shown along the bottom of the graph. Third, look at the vertical axis — the numbers listed along the left side of the graph.

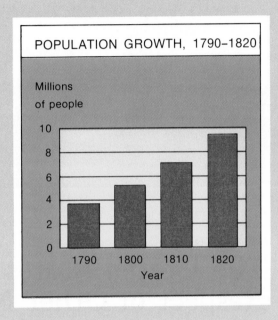

POPULATION GROWTH, 1790–1820

Notice that the numbers increase by equal amounts and are regularly spaced. In other words, if a bar stood for 4 million people, it would be exactly twice as tall as a bar that stood for 2 million people.

Now answer the following questions.

1. What kind of information is given in the graph? (Look at the title.)
2. For what years is the information given?
3. About how many people did the nation have in the first year shown on the graph?
4. Compare the bars for the first and last years shown. Between those years did the nation's population **(a)** almost double or **(b)** more than double?
5. Compare the graph with the table on this page. Which of the two gives you more exact information? Which helps you *see* the information more quickly?

267

CHAPTER 13

Vocabulary preview: neutral, impress, embargo, militia, blockade

The United States Gains the Respect of Other Nations

1789–1823   See p. T30 for chapter teaching strategies.

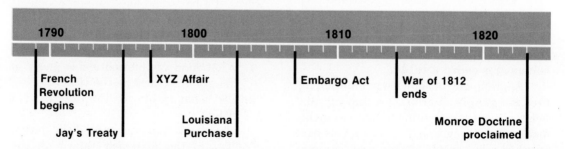

| 1790 | 1800 | 1810 | 1820 |

French
Revolution
begins

XYZ Affair

Embargo Act

War of 1812
ends

Louisiana
Purchase

Monroe Doctrine
proclaimed

Jay's Treaty

What this chapter is about —

Nations do not live by themselves any more than people do. The border of one nation is also its neighbor's border. Nations trade with one another. The citizens of one country travel in many other countries. In a hundred ways the affairs of one nation are linked with those of the other countries of the world. Just as people must learn to live with others, so nations must wisely manage their relations with other countries. But every nation also wants to be strong enough to be respected by other countries.

In 1812 the United States and Great Britain again went to war. In one battle the *Constitution,* better known as *Old Ironsides,* defeated the *Guerrière,* a British warship.

You read in Chapters 11 and 12 how the United States managed its affairs at home during its first years of independence. In this chapter you will see how the United States found a place for itself among the nations of the world. You will also read how, despite its efforts to remain at peace, the United States was drawn into a second war with Great Britain.

As you read, look for answers to these questions:
1. What problems did the United States have with Great Britain and France?
2. How did our country gain a vast territory beyond the Mississippi?
3. Why did the United States go to war with Great Britain a second time?
4. How did President Monroe warn Europe against interfering in the Americas?

1 What Problems Did the United States Have with Great Britain and France?

The United States in 1789 was a weak nation. Although we think of our country as strong and powerful, we need to remember that in 1789 this was not true. At that time the United States covered a large amount of land, but in other ways it was small and weak. The nation had fewer than four million people. The regular American army consisted of only 672 officers and soldiers. There was no navy. Also, the United States was just beginning a new kind of government, and no one knew how it would work out. In 1789 few countries allowed their people as much voice in the government as the people of the United States had under the Constitution.

In addition, our young nation was hemmed in on three sides by territory belonging to powerful European countries. As the map on page 209 shows, the territory of Great Britain stretched like a fence all along our northern boundary. To the west and south we were hemmed in by Spanish territory. The United States and Great Britain were not good friends, because the American Revolution had left bitter feelings on both sides. The United States and Spain were not friendly either. In fact, the best friend the United States had at that time was France. As you remember, France and the United States became allies during the American Revolution, and the French gave valuable help to the Patriots.

The French Revolution leads to war in Europe. Americans would have been pleased if they had been left alone, in a peaceful world, to try out their new government and to build their nation. But this was not to be. Once more, as in the French and Indian wars (page 142), events in Europe changed the course of America's history. Less than three months after George Washington became the nation's first President, the great revolution which we mentioned in Chapter 10 began in France. For hundreds of years the French people had had little liberty. Their monarchs had

269

● Mention that, under the treaty, France would have been within its rights to ask the United States for military assistance.

ruled them with a strong hand and had not allowed them to take an active part in their government. The nobles, who enjoyed many privileges, had also treated the people unfairly. Now the French people were determined to make a change. In 1789 they began a revolution which lasted for years.

The French Revolution was different from the American Revolution in a very important way. The purpose of the American Revolution had been to win freedom from another country. The French Revolution was a revolt by the people of France against the government of France. This revolution greatly alarmed the ruling classes of other countries in Europe. What was to prevent this uprising from spreading to their countries? If this should happen, their governments might be overthrown as France's had been. Such fears led two European countries — Austria and Prussia — to go to war with France. This was the beginning of a series of wars which in time involved most of the countries of Europe. These wars lasted, almost without a pause, until 1815.

The United States remains neutral. What was the United States to do about ● its treaty of alliance with France? Many Americans, among them Thomas Jefferson, were glad to see the French people get rid of their king and govern themselves. These Americans were grateful for the help France had given in the American Revolution. They felt that the United States owed help to France in return. On the other hand, could the United States afford to be drawn into a European war? Great Britain had joined in the wars against France. If we helped France, the United States might have to fight Great Britain again.

George Washington felt very strongly that Europe's quarrels were not our concern. We were far from Europe, he said, and should be putting our efforts into organizing our government

and building a strong and prosperous nation. Matters were made worse by "Citizen" Edmond Genêt (zhuh-NAY), the ambassador sent by the new French republic to the United States. In his efforts to gain aid for France, Genêt set out to win the sympathy of the American people.

Worried and uncertain what to do about France, President Washington asked the advice of Hamilton, Jefferson, and the rest of his Cabinet. Hamilton and Jefferson clashed over this matter as they did on so many subjects. But both these men agreed that the United States should stay out of the European war. Even Jefferson, despite his sympathy for the French republic, realized that the United States was too weak to wage war out of friendship for France. So President Washington signed an official paper declaring that the United States would be "friendly and impartial" to both sides in the war. In other words, the United States would try to remain **neutral.**   ★

It was all very well for the United States to declare that it would be neutral in the European war. But it is difficult for a nation to stay neutral. Warring countries protest if they believe that a neutral nation acts in any way to harm them or help their enemies. When the United States declared that as a neutral nation it had the right to trade with any of the warring nations, trouble began.

THE UNITED STATES HAS TROUBLE WITH GREAT BRITAIN

The British seize American ships and sailors. The chief threat to America's neutrality came from Great Britain, which had the world's most powerful navy. Britain did not intend to let the United States aid the French by shipping needed goods to France. The British navy, therefore, set out to stop such trade. The following story tells what

270

happened time and again a short distance off the eastern coast of the United States:

"The sails of an American schooner flash in the sun as it skims south before a fair wind. Its hold is filled with a cargo to be traded in the French islands of the West Indies. Suddenly the lookout spies a British frigate on the horizon. Quickly the British ship overtakes the schooner and forces it to stop. A boat is lowered from the British warship and a scarlet-coated officer is rowed to the schooner. He clambers aboard, followed by some of his men. He demands the right to inspect the cargo and to see the crew. After a glance at the cargo he declares that the schooner is breaking Britain's rules of the sea and seizes the schooner. He also claims that some members of the crew are English sailors who are needed in the British navy. He leaves some of his men on board to help sail the schooner to the nearest British port and takes back to his ship the sailors he said were English. They will be **impressed** into (forced to serve in) the Royal Navy."

The impressment of crew members for the Royal Navy was a common practice in those days. Sailors were badly needed for British warships, and British officers were not too much concerned if the men they seized were actually American citizens. They insisted that anyone who was born an Englishman always remained an Englishman, and took the attitude "What are you going to do about it?"

The British maintain forts on the American border. The actions of the British on the high seas made Americans furious. But the United States had still another complaint against Great Britain. British soldiers continued to occupy forts along the northwestern boundary of the United States. The map on page 209 shows where this boundary was. The British kept soldiers in these forts because, for one

British naval officers took American sailors off American ships and forced them to serve in the Royal Navy. Such actions angered citizens of the young republic.

Americans began to build a navy when war with France seemed likely. Here we see how ships of that time were built. Workers carried lumber up the scaffolding as they built the hull of the *Philadelphia*.

thing, Americans had not paid certain debts they had owed to English merchants since before the Revolutionary War. The British also held the forts because they wanted the fur trade profits.

John Jay makes a treaty and prevents a war. In spite of these difficulties with the British, President Washington worked to maintain peace. He did not want the weak young nation to fight a dangerous war. So in 1794 he sent John Jay (who was Chief Justice of the Supreme Court) to England to seek an agreement with the British government. Washington hoped such an agreement would put an end to the trouble between the two countries. Jay did obtain an agreement, which is called Jay's Treaty. Among other things, the treaty stated that the British should turn over the forts along the Great Lakes to the United States. But the British did not promise to stop searching American ships and impressing American sailors.

Many Americans disliked Jay's Treaty because the British did not promise to stop interfering with American ships. President Washington, however, was certain that the treaty would prevent war between Great Britain and the United States. The treaty was approved in 1795, and Washington's judgment proved correct. The danger of war between the two countries was removed for the time being.

TROUBLE BREWS WITH FRANCE

Soon after Jay's Treaty with Great Britain had been signed, serious trouble began between the United States and France. Jay's Treaty itself was partly to blame. The treaty, many people in France believed, showed that the United States was becoming more friendly with Great Britain. The French decided that American ships should not be allowed to carry goods which might reach the enemies of France. Following the example set by Great Britain, French ships began to capture American ships. In a short time more than 300 American vessels had been seized by the French.

272

The XYZ Affair angers Americans.
War with Great Britain had been avoided by sending John Jay to arrange a treaty. Now John Adams, who had become President in 1797, took a similar step to avoid war with France. He sent three men to France to try to make a treaty. At the beginning of their talks, the French representatives demanded the payment of a large amount of money before they would even talk about a treaty. The Americans proudly refused to pay what they felt was a bribe. They wrote to President Adams to tell him what had happened. In their letters, however, they did not use the real names of the French representatives, calling them simply X, Y, and Z. Hence this event is known as the XYZ Affair.

The United States fights an undeclared war with France. The people of the United States became angry when they heard about the XYZ Affair. "Millions for defense," they cried, "but not one cent for tribute!" The situation was so tense that fighting broke out at sea. Though the American navy had very few ships, these vessels attacked French vessels, and armed American ships of all kinds captured French ships whenever they could. Our government also began to recruit an army. Despite the fight-ing, the United States and France were not officially at war, since Congress never declared that a state of war existed.

France and the United States reach an agreement. While the feeling against France was at its height, President Adams learned that the French government wanted to end the conflict. At once he sent representatives to France, and in 1800 an agreement was signed. This agreement ended the treaty of alliance we had had with France since 1778 ● (page 197). It also cleared the way for the ships of both nations to sail the ocean in peace. The unofficial war with France ended.

▶ **CHECK UP**   See Teacher's Key.

1. Why did the United States want to remain neutral in the wars between France and Britain?
2. **(a)** What rights did this country want as a neutral nation? **(b)** How did Britain interfere with those rights?
3. **(a)** In what ways did Jay's Treaty provide a satisfactory settlement of the dispute with Britain? **(b)** How was it *not* satisfactory?
4. **(a)** What events led to our undeclared war with France? **(b)** How was the dispute ended?

2 How Did Our Country Gain a Vast Territory Beyond the Mississippi?

One piece of good fortune stands out in the early relations of our country with European nations. The story has to do with the pioneers who had moved into the territory west of the Appalachian Mountains. As we know, western settlers for the most part earned their living by trapping and farming. But it is not enough to trap animals or to grow a crop of corn. To earn a living, trappers and farmers must be able to *sell* their furs or crops in a market where people will pay well for such items. In the 1700's and early 1800's the settlers of the West had no roads over which to haul their produce to market. The easiest way to move their goods was to load them onto flatboats or rafts. These could be floated down streams to the Ohio River, and from the Ohio down the

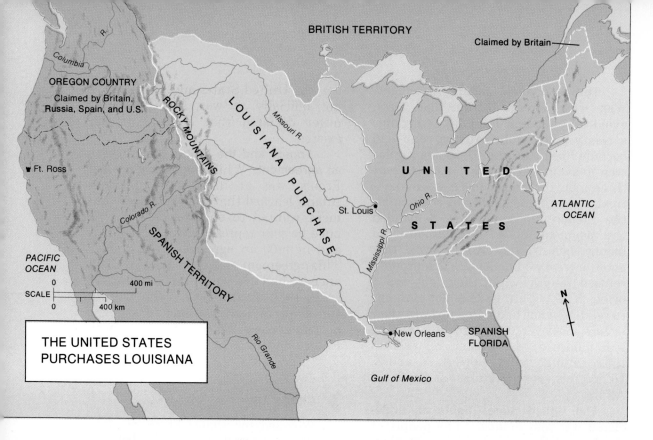

BRITISH TERRITORY

Claimed by Britain

OREGON COUNTRY

Claimed by Britain, Russia, Spain, and U.S.

ROCKY MOUNTAINS

LOUISIANA PURCHASE

Columbia R.

Missouri R.

▼ Ft. Ross

Colorado R.

SPANISH TERRITORY

PACIFIC OCEAN

SCALE

| 0 | 400 mi |
| 0 | 400 km |

UNITED STATES

St. Louis

Ohio R.

Mississippi R.

ATLANTIC OCEAN

N

THE UNITED STATES PURCHASES LOUISIANA

Rio Grande

• New Orleans

SPANISH FLORIDA

Gulf of Mexico

MAP STUDY   See Teacher's Key.
(a) In 1803 what countries owned territory north and south of the United States? (b) What countries claimed the area to the northwest of the Louisiana Purchase?

Mississippi to New Orleans. There the goods could be shipped away by sea.

The Mississippi River and New Orleans are important to the West.   Because it was a water highway, the Mississippi River was important to the United States. But the United States did not control the Mississippi. The river was the boundary between the United States and the vast Spanish territory to the west. (See map, page 209.) Nor did we own New Orleans, which also belonged to Spain. Spanish officials allowed Americans to reload their goods on ocean-going boats in New Orleans, but the Americans were never sure how long they would be able to do that. If the Spanish withdrew permission, the western settlers would have no way of getting their goods to market.

New Orleans becomes French.   In 1802 the Westerners saw their fears realized. Permission to use the port of New Orleans was withdrawn. Even before this happened, President Jefferson had learned to his surprise that New Orleans no longer belonged to Spain. By a secret treaty, France had obtained from Spain not only New Orleans but also the vast territory of Louisiana, which lay west of the Mississippi River.

France at that time was governed by Napoleon, a great soldier who seemed likely to conquer all of Europe. Napoleon had plans to establish a French empire in America. Suppose he were to undertake wars of conquest in North America as he had in Europe? President Jefferson clearly saw the danger. He wrote to Robert Livingstone, the American representative in France:

The [transfer] of Louisiana . . . by Spain to France works most sorely on the United States. . . . There is on the globe one single spot, the possessor of which is our natural and habitual enemy. It is New Orleans, through which the produce of three-eighths of our territory must pass to market, and

● See p. T30 for a strategy that calls for students to do outside reading on the Pinckney Treaty between the United States and Spain.

[this western territory] will [soon] yield more than half of our whole produce and contain more than half of our inhabitants. . . . The day that France takes possession of New Orleans . . . we must [depend on] the British fleet and nation.

In this statement Jefferson pointed out that the Americans might have to join forces with the British and fight Napoleon to keep the French out of New Orleans. But Jefferson did not want to have to depend on the British. Nor did he want to fight if he could help it. "If only," thought Jefferson, "if only I could *buy* New Orleans, then I could satisfy the Westerners and also avoid the danger of war with France." So Jefferson suggested to France that it sell New Orleans to the United States.

Jefferson acquires Louisiana. Jefferson's suggestion was made just when Napoleon was about to get into another war. Napoleon wanted to be free to fight in Europe without worrying about territory in America, and he needed money to pay for the war. Also, the slave revolt in Haiti (page 222) had spoiled his plans for a colonial empire in North America. So he offered to sell not only the city of New Orleans but the whole of Louisiana! The price was set at $15 million, and in 1803 the United States took possession of Louisiana.

Flatboats carried animals, farm goods, and passengers down the western rivers. River travel, cheaper and easier than land transportation, was important to Westerners.

The map on page 274 gives a clear idea of the importance of the Louisiana Purchase. Not only had it brought full control of the Mississippi River to the American government, but it had also doubled the size of the United States. Jefferson called the purchase of Louisiana "a great achievement," and so it was. In the Louisiana Territory there would be space for millions of Americans.

▶ **CHECK UP**   See Teacher's Key.

1. Why were the Mississippi River and New Orleans important to the United States?
2. How was Jefferson able to buy all of Louisiana?

3 Why Did the United States Go to War with Great Britain a Second Time?

BRITAIN AND AMERICA FIGHT AGAIN

In 1803 a new war broke out between Napoleon and Great Britain. Once more each side tried to prevent American ships from carrying supplies to the enemy. Once more the British navy stopped American vessels and impressed men from their crews. France also captured American vessels when it could, although the French did not seize American sailors. Once again Americans wondered, "What should the United States do?"

275

● See p. T30 for a strategy that asks students to examine the significance of the Louisiana Purchase.

Jefferson tries to avoid war. This time it was Thomas Jefferson who as President was expected to answer the question. Jefferson hated war because of its destruction of life and property. But how could he force Britain and France to respect the rights of American ships at sea without fighting? Jefferson believed there was a way. "The European nations," he thought, "badly need American goods. They also need to make profits by selling some of their goods in the United States. If we threaten to stop trading with Great Britain and France, these countries will agree to let our ships alone."

To carry out his idea, Jefferson planned (1) to refuse to buy European goods and (2) to place an **embargo** on American shipping. In other words, he ordered an end to foreign trade. The Embargo Act, passed in 1807, forbade American vessels to leave for any foreign ports.

Jefferson's plan was tried in several forms, both by him and by James Madison, who became President in 1809. Though intended to hurt France and Great Britain, Jefferson's plan in fact nearly ruined American merchants and shipowners. When the embargo made it unlawful for their vessels to sail the seas, some of the merchants ignored the law and sailed anyway. So, in spite of the Embargo Act, France and Great Britain continued to seize American ships.

The United States moves closer to war with Britain. So far as interference with our shipping was concerned, we had almost as much reason to go to war with France as with Great Britain. But feeling ran stronger against Britain. The people of the American West and South believed that the British encouraged the Indians of those regions to make war. The Indians, however, felt that the United States had robbed them of their lands by unfair treaties. In 1811 a great Shawnee leader named Tecum-seh (teh-KUM-suh) tried to unite the Indians north of the Ohio River in an effort to halt further American expansion (page 338). There were rumors that the British in Canada had furnished Tecumseh and his forces with supplies and guns. As a result, bitter feeling against the British spread, especially among Westerners.

Many settlers in the West and South also wanted the United States to add to its territory. They looked north to Canada, which was British, and south to Florida, which belonged to Spain. At this time Spain and Great Britain were allies. If Americans should fight Britain, thought the settlers, the United States might be able to conquer both Canada and Florida.

A group of young men in Congress at that time were keenly interested in developing the West. Among them were Henry Clay of Kentucky and John C. ★ Calhoun of South Carolina. They talked so much about going to war that they earned the nickname "War Hawks." When these War Hawks told why they wanted war, they spoke not only about British violations of American rights on the seas but also about capturing Canada and Florida.

The United States, though unprepared, goes to war with Britain. Pushed on by the War Hawks, Congress declared war on Britain in June, 1812, while Madison was President. The United States was not prepared to fight. Its army and navy were pitifully small. There were fewer than 7,000 men in the army and few good officers. To the regular army might be added the soldiers supplied by the states, called **militia** (muh-LISH-uh). There were not enough militia, however, and they were seldom well trained. Also, the United States had only sixteen ships in its navy when the war began, and Congress voted no funds to enlarge the navy. Congress did not even vote enough money to carry on the war.

People in America's Story

Tell students that Jefferson was born in 1743. He married Martha Wayles Skelton in 1772. Jefferson's wife died in 1782 and he reared their two daughters, Martha and Mary, himself.

THOMAS JEFFERSON

Best remembered as the author of the Declaration of Independence, Thomas Jefferson is also known for his achievements as President, diplomat, architect, inventor, and political thinker.

Words became splendid weapons in the American Revolution when Jefferson wrote the Declaration of Independence. Stating his own deep belief in human liberty, he set up ideals for all the American Patriots.

Like Franklin, Jefferson believed that knowledge is power. On his estate at Monticello (below), he not only tried out his own inventions but experimented with new plants and ideas from Europe.

American sailors row Oliver Hazard Perry to a new ship after escaping from a sinking vessel during the Battle of Lake Erie in 1813.

The war is unpopular in New England. Not only was the United States poorly prepared. Many Americans actually opposed going to war. The war was especially unpopular in New England. The people of this section wanted to send their merchant ships to sea in spite of the danger of British capture. Even if only a few ships escaped capture, the goods they carried sold at such high prices that the merchants made large profits. The New Englanders had disliked Jefferson's embargo because of its interference with their trade. When war came, the British fleet blockaded the Atlantic coast. (A **blockade** is the use of naval forces to cut off shipping along a coastal area.)

As the war continued, New Englanders became more and more dissatisfied. Finally, late in 1814, a meeting was held at Hartford, Connecticut. The Hartford Convention, as it is called, protested the government's war policy and declared that if Congress violated the Constitution, the states could take steps to protect their rights. The war ended, however, before the Hartford Convention put its words into action.

THE WAR OF 1812 HAS NO WINNER

The United States started a war against Britain without a big army or navy, without enough money, and without the wholehearted support of all the people. How did the nation fare under so many handicaps?

Neither side captures territory in the war on land. Soon after the war started, American attacks were launched against Canada. In 1813, American soldiers set on fire the government buildings in what was then the Canadian capital city, York (now called Toronto). But the fighting along the Canadian border was not successful. Although the Americans attempted several invasions between 1812 and 1814, they did not conquer Canada. On the other hand, the British never successfully invaded the northern United States.

In 1814, the British did raid our Atlantic coast and burn some towns. In August of that year, they even sailed up Chesapeake Bay and seized the city of

278

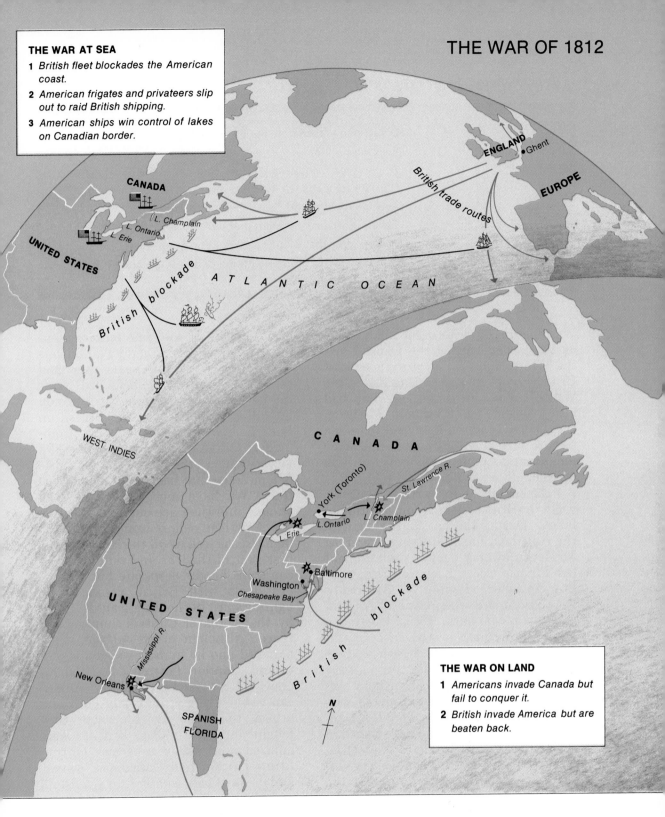

THE WAR AT SEA

1 *British fleet blockades the American coast.*
2 *American frigates and privateers slip out to raid British shipping.*
3 *American ships win control of lakes on Canadian border.*

ENGLAND
• Ghent

EUROPE

CANADA

L. Champlain

L. Ontario

L. Erie

UNITED STATES

British trade routes

British blockade

ATLANTIC OCEAN

WEST INDIES

C A N A D A

York (Toronto)

St. Lawrence R.

L. Ontario

L. Champlain

L. Erie

Baltimore

Washington

Chesapeake Bay

U N I T E D S T A T E S

Mississippi R.

New Orleans

British blockade

SPANISH FLORIDA

N

THE WAR ON LAND

1 *Americans invade Canada but fail to conquer it.*
2 *British invade America but are beaten back.*

MAP STUDY Overwhelming seapower enabled the British to put pressure on America by a blockade and to attack at widely separated points. (a) What American cities did the British attack after sailing up Chesapeake Bay? (b) At what city west of Florida did Americans win a victory?

279

● Have students recite or sing other verses of our
national anthem.

● *The Star-Spangled Banner*

O say! can you see, by the dawn's early light,

What so proudly we hail'd at the twilight's last gleaming,

Whose broad stripes and bright stars, thro' the perilous fight,

O'er the ramparts we watch'd were so gallantly streaming?

And the rockets' red glare, the bombs bursting in air,

Gave proof thro' the night that our flag was still there.

O, say, does that Star-Spangled Banner yet wave

O'er the land of the free and the home of the brave?

Washington. In revenge for the burning of York, they burned the Capitol and the White House. The story goes that British troops, before setting fire to the White House, ate a dinner that had been cooked for President Madison. But Dolley Madison managed to save a picture of George Washington and some important documents before the British arrived.

Americans felt better, however, when a British attack on Baltimore failed. During the battle, the sight of the American flag still flying over Fort McHenry after a heavy bombardment
★ led Francis Scott Key to write "The Star-Spangled Banner." Americans were also proud when General Andrew Jackson in January, 1815, defeated a British army at New Orleans. In this battle more than 2,000 British soldiers were killed and wounded. Only a very few of the Tennessee and Kentucky volunteers, free blacks, and Indians who made up Jackson's army were lost. Actually, a peace treaty had been signed in Europe before the battle of New Orleans took place. But the slow sailing vessels of that time had not brought the news of peace soon enough.

Americans win some victories at sea. United States warships gave a
280 good account of themselves. Though army officers of the time lacked training, American sailors and naval officers knew their jobs. For years they had sailed the seas and defended their rights. American fleets, hastily built on inland waters, defeated the British on Lake Erie and Lake Champlain. Commodore Oliver Hazard Perry reported a victory against the British on Lake Erie in a message that has never been forgotten. "We have met the enemy," he wrote, "and they are ours."

American sailors won glory on the high seas as well as on the lakes. In the first year of the war, individual American ships fought desperate but victorious duels with British vessels. The fighting spirit of the Americans is shown by the words of Captain James Lawrence. Although his vessel was badly battered and he himself was dying of a wound, Captain Lawrence ordered his crew, "Don't give up the ship!" American vessels were often better built and armed than the British ships they fought against. The British were amazed at our victories because for centuries Britain had "ruled the waves" and its navy had usually won against all enemies.

As the war continued, however, the larger British fleet drove most of the American vessels into port and kept

★ Students can read more about Francis Scott Key and "The Star-Spangled Banner" in
"Linking Past and Present" (p. 284).

● See p. T30 for a strategy that asks students to examine the causes and effects of the War of 1812.

them there. It is true that armed American merchant vessels, or privateers, captured large numbers of English trading ships. But sea victories alone could not win the war.

Both sides gladly end the war. In 1814, the great wars which had raged in Europe for more than 20 years were coming to an end. Great Britain was tired of fighting and wanted peace in America as well as Europe. Because the United States had failed to capture Canada and wanted to resume normal trade, Americans also were glad to make peace. So a treaty ending the war was signed at the city of Ghent, in Belgium, on Christmas Eve, 1814. By the Treaty of Ghent everything was restored to what it had been before the war. Nothing was said about the impressment of sailors or the seizure of ships, which had

been reasons for declaring war. But, with the European wars over, the need for impressment had ended.

THE WAR OF 1812 HAS IMPORTANT EFFECTS

The war brings about a united and stronger nation. At first glance you might suppose that the war had no important results in the United States, but that is not so. Although the treaty changed nothing, the war itself did have important results:

(1) The war helped to create a national spirit — that is, a pride and confidence in the strength of the nation. In the years immediately after the War of 1812, the people of New England, the South, and the West forgot many of their differences in their pride in being Americans. They turned their backs on Europe and devoted themselves to building a greater and more powerful United States.

After the failure of the British attack on Fort McHenry (below), Francis Scott Key wrote "The Star-Spangled Banner."

(2) The war helped to build up manufacturing in this country. Before the war, most manufactured articles used by Americans were imported from other countries. Trade in these articles was almost ended by Jefferson's embargo and by the dangers of wartime shipping. Unable to get manufactured goods from abroad, people in the United States began themselves to manufacture many of the things they needed.

(3) The War of 1812 produced new leaders. Two outstanding generals in the war — Andrew Jackson and William Henry Harrison — later became Presidents. Other men who played important parts in the war continued to be leaders for many years.

The war affects the attitude of other nations toward the United States. The War of 1812 also had effects outside our boundaries:

(1) The people of Canada had taken no part in the troubles between the United States and Great Britain. You can imagine how Canadians felt when they learned that their neighbor to the south wanted to seize their territory. A feeling of bitterness against Americans developed in Canada. That feeling lasted for many years.

(2) As a result of the war, European nations developed greater respect for the United States. Our country had shown, for a second time, that it was willing to fight if necessary. In the future, Europe would be more ready to let the United States control its own affairs.

▶ **CHECK UP**   See Teacher's Key.

1. **(a)** How did Jefferson try to keep the United States out of the European war? **(b)** Why did his plans fail?
2. **(a)** What sections of the country favored war with Great Britain in 1812? Why? **(b)** Which section opposed it? Why?
3. **(a)** What were some important results of the war? **(b)** In what way was the war a failure?

4 How Did President Monroe Warn Europe Against Interfering in the Americas?

The United States faces European threats to the Americas. Several years after the War of 1812, our country took a bold step which showed that it was becoming a strong nation. By the early 1820's, as you read in Chapter 10, the Latin American colonies of Spain and Portugal had won their freedom. It was well known that the king of Spain wanted to regain his colonies and was trying to get the help of other European powers. Great Britain was opposed to such a plan. It wanted the new nations of Latin America to remain independent so that they could carry on trade with anyone they wished, including Britain.

The United States, naturally, was sympathetic toward the new countries which, like itself, had won independence. In addition, the United States did not want to see Spain or any other European nation seize territory in the Western Hemisphere. That seemed a possibility not only in Latin America but in other parts of the Americas. At that time, for example, Russia owned Alaska and had started to settle farther south. In 1811 Russians had built Fort Ross, just north of San Francisco.

The Monroe Doctrine is proclaimed. The United States government decided to make its position clear. In a message

Fort Ross was a Russian trading post near San Francisco. One goal of the Monroe Doctrine was to halt the building of such settlements.

to Congress in 1823, President Monroe declared that (1) the United States would consider it an unfriendly act if European nations interfered with any of the new governments in the Americas; (2) the United States would oppose the establishment of any new colonies in this hemisphere; (3) the United States on its part would not meddle in European affairs.

In other words, Monroe warned Europe, "The Western Hemisphere is not your concern. Keep out of it and we will keep out of Europe's business." The United States was able to take this firm stand because it knew that Great Britain, with its strong navy, also wanted European nations to keep their hands off America. Monroe's official statement, which became known as the
● Monroe Doctrine, was one of the most important steps ever taken by our government. For years the Monroe Doctrine was the foundation of our relations with European countries.

———

This chapter has told the story of how our young nation took its place among other nations. The United States had protected itself — by treaty and by war. It had doubled its territory. It had even felt strong enough to warn all the nations of Europe: "Stay away from the Western Hemisphere!"

▶ **CHECK UP**   See Teacher's Key.

1. **(a)** Why did President Monroe issue the Monroe Doctrine? **(b)** What important statements did it contain?
2. What was Great Britain's attitude toward the Latin American republics? Why?

CHECK UP ON CHAPTER 13   See Teacher's Key.

Words to Know

1. neutral
2. embargo
3. militia
4. tribute
5. impress
6. blockade

Places to Locate

1. New Orleans
2. Lake Erie
3. Washington, D.C.
4. Louisiana Purchase

Facts to Remember

1. **(a)** What agreement was made between the United States and Great Britain in Jay's Treaty? **(b)** Why were some Americans not satisfied with the treaty?
2. **(a)** Tell what happened in the XYZ Affair. **(b)** Why did it lead to fighting between the United States and France?

283

● See p. T30 for a strategy that asks students to consider how various individuals would probably have reacted to the Monroe Doctrine.

Facts to Remember (cont.)

3. (a) Who sold Louisiana to the United States? (b) Why was the Louisiana Purchase important?
4. How did each of the following play a part in the War of 1812? (a) Francis Scott Key (b) Andrew Jackson (c) Oliver Hazard Perry (d) James Lawrence

Skills to Practice

1. (a) Was the area of the Louisiana Purchase larger or smaller than the area of the present-day state of Louisiana? (See the maps on pages 274 and 319.) (b) What river formed the eastern boundary of the Louisiana Purchase? (c) What city is located at the mouth of that river?
2. Arrange the following events in the order in which they happened. Start with the earliest event.
   a. The Embargo Act is passed.
   b. Jay's Treaty is signed.
   c. The War of 1812 ends.
   d. Louisiana is purchased.
3. Tell who was President at the time each of the events listed above took place.

Questions to Think About

1. Explain why some people thought the decision to declare war on Britain in 1812 was not a good one.
2. George Washington believed that the United States should not get mixed up in European affairs. So did President James Monroe. Is it possible for our country today to follow the same policy? Explain your answer.
3. The British believed that the United States, in declaring war on their country, was helping Napoleon. Why?
4. Some historians have said that Napoleon helped to make the United States a great power. Explain what they mean.

Linking Past and Present

The Star-Spangled Banner. All Americans know the stirring music of our national anthem. The story of how it came to be written goes back to the War of 1812. In September, 1814, a British fleet in Chesapeake Bay was trying to capture Baltimore, Maryland. The British planned to bombard Fort McHenry, which guarded the city. About this time, a young American lawyer named Francis Scott Key boarded a British ship to ask for the release of a friend who was being held prisoner. The release was granted, but the two men were forced to remain aboard because the bombardment of Fort McHenry was about to begin.

As the shells began to pour into the fort, Key anxiously watched the Stars and Stripes over the fort. The flag was still there "at the twilight's last gleaming," but would it survive the "perilous fight"? Next morning, in the "dawn's early light," Key saw with joy that "our flag was still there." The British had failed to take Fort McHenry! Key wrote the first verse of his song on the ship, and then completed it after he was released. The words were set to music, and the inspiring song soon became popular. But it wasn't until over a hundred years later, on March 3, 1931, that Congress made "The Star-Spangled Banner" our national anthem.

The Library of Congress. One of the largest libraries in the world is located in Washington, D.C. The Library of Congress holds more than 20 million books and pamphlets, far more than when it was rebuilt after the War of 1812.

When the British burned the Capitol in 1814, the library used by the members of Congress at that time also went up in smoke. Congress immediately began buying books to build up a new library. In 1815 it bought Thomas Jefferson's private collection of 6,000 books. Since then, the Library of Congress has continued to grow. Every working day, about 7,000 books arrive to be stored there. And in addition to its books, the Library of Congress now has millions of manuscripts, maps, photographs, motion pictures, recordings, newspapers, and posters.

● Mention that the Library of Congress contains some 80 million items today.

GAINING SKILL

Using the Library

In studying history you sometimes need to use books, magazines, or newspapers in the library. You can easily find the information you want if you know how the library is organized.

Reference books are usually kept together in one part of the library. Books of fiction (those that tell stories) are kept in another area and are arranged alphabetically by the author's last name. Biographies are arranged alphabetically by the name of the person who is the subject of the book. All other books are classified by subject and have numbers that indicate the topic of each book. Your teacher or librarian can explain how books are classified and numbered on the library shelves.

The quickest way to find a particular book is to use the library's card catalog. The card catalog is a set of drawers filled with cards. All the cards are arranged al-phabetically. Every book in the library has an author card and a title card in the card catalog. Many books also have subject cards. Subject cards are useful when you want to find several books on a certain topic.

When you find the card for a book you want to read, write down the number found in the upper left corner of the card. That is the classification number or call number. It tells where the book is kept on the shelves.

Examples of catalog cards are shown on this page. Look at them carefully. Then answer the questions.

1. What information is given on the top line of the title card? On the top line of the author card? Of the subject card?
2. When was this book published? Where was it published?
3. How many pages does the book have?
4. What is the book's call number?

Tecumseh

E
99
.S35
T32   Schraff, Anne E.
          Tecumseh, by Anne Schraff. Minneapolis:
       Dillon Press, 1979. 56 p., ill.

          1. Tecumseh, Shawnee chief, 1768–1813.
          2. Shawnee Indians—Biography.   3. Indians
       of North America—Biography.

TITLE CARD

E
99
.S35
T32   Schraff, Anne E.
          Tecumseh, by Anne Schraff. Minneapolis:
       Dillon Press, 1979. 56 p., ill.

          1. Tecumseh, Shawnee chief, 1768–1813.
          2. Shawnee Indians—Biography.   3. Indians
       of North America—Biography.

AUTHOR CARD

          INDIANS OF NORTH AMERICA—BIOGRAPHY
E
99
.S35
T32   Schraff, Anne E.
          Tecumseh, by Anne Schraff. Minneapolis:
       Dillon Press, 1979. 56 p., ill.

          1. Tecumseh, Shawnee chief, 1768–1813.
          2. Shawnee Indians—Biography.   3. Indians
       of North America—Biography.

SUBJECT CARD

UNDERSTANDING UNIT 4

Unit 4 has told about the adoption of the Constitution and the progress made by the United States in its early years.

1. Our country lacked an effective government until the Constitution was adopted.

a. At the outbreak of the Revolutionary War there was no United States but only thirteen American colonies. The Second Continental Congress served as an emergency government. In 1781, the states adopted the Articles of Confederation. Under the Articles, the central government had the power to wage war and make peace, to control relations with foreign countries, and to borrow money. But Congress did not have the right to levy taxes or control commerce between the states. The weaknesses of this government led to a demand for a stronger union.

b. The Constitutional Convention met in Philadelphia in 1787. The delegates worked out a plan of government which included many important compromises. The new government went into effect when nine states approved the new Constitution. The contest was close in most states because many Americans feared a strong government. Under the Constitution, Congress could levy taxes and regulate commerce between the states. Federal courts were provided. Powers not given to the United States by the Constitution were left to the states. Separating powers among the executive, legislative, and judicial branches enabled each branch of the government to check the others.

c. In 1789, with the inauguration of Washington as President, the new government began. Alexander Hamilton developed a financial plan to pay the national and state debts, to raise money through tariffs and taxes, and to establish a national bank. The government gained respect for its laws by putting down the Whiskey Rebellion. Differences over how strong the federal government should be led to the formation of political parties.

2. The United States in time won the respect of other nations.

a. In 1789, a revolution broke out in France. When other European countries went to war against France, the United States, though an ally of France, declared its neutrality. During wars which lasted until 1815, both France and Great Britain seized American shipping and in other ways interfered with American rights. The United States protested to both countries, boycotted European goods, and placed embargoes on shipping.

b. Influenced in part by the hope of gaining additional territory, the United States went to war with Great Britain in 1812. This war aroused a new national spirit in the United States and built up American manufacturing. Earlier (1803), the United States had bought Louisiana from Napoleon. Thus, the national territory was doubled, and the country gained control of the Mississippi.

c. During the early 1800's, the Spanish and Portuguese colonies (from Mexico southward) declared their independence. By 1825 all had ceased to be colonies. The United States sympathized with these countries in their struggle for independence; and Great Britain, for commercial and other reasons, wanted the new countries to remain independent. To safeguard the Western Hemisphere from European interference, President Monroe announced the Monroe Doctrine.

UNIT REVIEW   See Teacher's Key.

1. **(a)** How was our country governed during the early years of the Revolutionary War? **(b)** Under the Articles of Confederation? **(c)** What were the weaknesses of these governments? **(d)** Why was a convention called in Philadelphia in 1787? **(e)** What were the chief compromises in the Constitution?

2. **(a)** What powers were written into the Constitution to strengthen the new government? **(b)** Why were the following ideas included in the Constitution? (1) Division of powers between the state and national governments. (2) Separation of powers between branches of the central government.

3. **(a)** What is the Bill of Rights? **(b)** Why was it added to the Constitution?

4. **(a)** What was Hamilton's financial plan? **(b)** How did it cause political parties to be formed? **(c)** How did his plan add to the nation's strength?

5. **(a)** Why did the United States go to war with Britain in 1812? **(b)** What were the results?

6. **(a)** How was the United States able to purchase all of Louisiana in 1803? **(b)** Why was this purchase important?

7. **(a)** Why were both the United States and Great Britain opposed to the restoring of Spanish rule in the colonies which had revolted from Spain? **(b)** What were the provisions of the Monroe Doctrine?

THINGS TO DO

Items marked with an asterisk (*) are for the whole class.

*1. Make cards for the new names, words, and dates you have learned about in Unit 4. Hold a "spell down" with the cards to see who can identify the greatest number.

*2. Learn the Preamble to the Constitution printed in the back of your book. Look up the meaning of any words you do not know.

*3. On an outline map show how the territory of the United States had expanded by 1803. Use one color for the territory granted to the United States in the Treaty of 1783; use a different color for the Louisiana Territory.

4. Write an imaginary conversation between: **(a)** a Federalist and a Republican in 1800; **(b)** a member of the Constitutional Convention from New Jersey and one from Virginia; **(c)** a New England merchant and a War Hawk in 1812.

5. Choose a committee to give a program on "The American Navy in the War of 1812." Your committee will want to consult books in your school or public libraries for details. Prepare talks on the following battles: **(a)** Captain Perry and the battle of Lake Erie; **(b)** the battle of Lake Champlain; **(c)** the battle between the *Constitution* and the *Guerrière*; **(d)** the British attack on Baltimore (Fort McHenry).

6. Write a newspaper article, such as might have appeared at the time, on one of the following subjects: **(a)** adoption of the Constitution; **(b)** inauguration of Washington; **(c)** purchase of Louisiana; **(d)** the declaration of war in 1812; **(e)** Monroe's presenting of the Monroe Doctrine to Congress.

Left to right: railroad in the Northeast; farm in Illinois; Andrew Jackson; cotton bales on New Orleans dock.

The American Way of Living Changes as the Different Sections Develop

1770–1860

See p. T31 for a unit preview strategy. See pp. T58–T71 for lists of useful books and audiovisual aids.

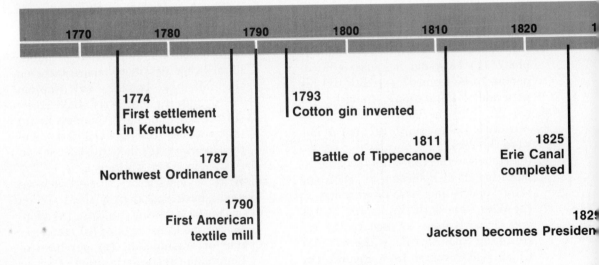

1770   1780   1790   1800   1810   1820   1

1774
First settlement
in Kentucky

1793
Cotton gin invented

1787
Northwest Ordinance

1811
Battle of Tippecanoe

1825
Erie Canal
completed

1790
First American
textile mill

1829
Jackson becomes Presiden

288

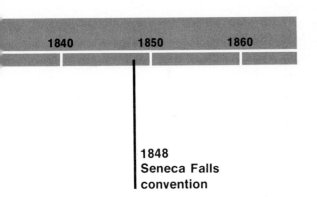

1840   1850   1860

1848
Seneca Falls
convention

If George Washington could have visited the United States in the 1840's, he would have been amazed at the changes that had taken place since his lifetime (1732–1799). In this unit you will find out what some of those changes were. Chapter 14, for example, tells how the Northeast became the shipping and manufacturing center of the nation. In Chapter 15 you will learn how the South became a great cotton-growing section and how slavery became firmly established. Chapter 16 tells how Americans settled in the land beyond the Appalachians. In Chapter 17 you will find out how Americans gained a greater voice in government and started reforms to improve the quality of life.

Vocabulary preview: Industrial Revolution, factory system, labor union, turnpike, population density

The Northeast Becomes the Center of Trade and Manufacturing

1780–1860   See pp. T31–T32 for chapter teaching strategies.

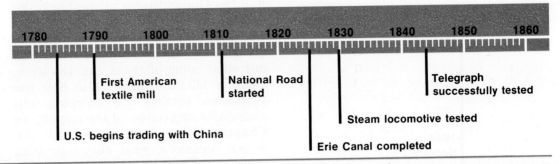

1780	1790	1800	1810	1820	1830	1840	1850	1860	

First American textile mill

National Road started

Telegraph successfully tested

Steam locomotive tested

U.S. begins trading with China

Erie Canal completed

What this chapter is about —

If you looked at a newspaper printed ten years ago, you might find that some of the events reported in headlines on the front page seem to have little importance today. On the other hand, something that got little attention in the newspaper — an invention, a scientific discovery, or the starting of a new kind of business — may turn out to have had far-reaching effects on people's lives.

In the early 1800's, certain changes were taking place in the Northeast. Although people did not realize it at the time, these changes would greatly affect

290

life in this country. One was a tremendous increase in shipping and trade. The swift clipper ships, their sails spread to catch the wind, carried American trade all over the world. Other important changes were the result of new inventions. In this chapter you will learn how, by the 1850's, these changes had helped to make the Northeast the center of trade and manufacturing. You will also learn how inventions changed travel and communication. In this chapter we will answer the following questions:

1. How did trade and manufacturing grow in the Northeast?
2. How did machines change ways of living in America?
3. What changes were made in travel and communication?

1 How Did Trade and Manufacturing Grow in the Northeast?

COMMERCE GROWS

Imagine that you could turn the clock back and visit Boston harbor in the 1840's. All along the waterfront many kinds of ships are tied up. Though some of these vessels carry foreign flags, most of them fly the Stars and Stripes of the United States. Here is a fleet of fishing boats unloading cargoes of cod caught off the Grand Banks of Newfoundland. Alongside is a packet ship, which carries goods and passengers to Europe. Beyond it is a freighter, built to carry bulky cargoes such as grain or lumber. Nearby, with towering masts and the sharp, slender lines that suggest great speed, is a clipper ship, pride of the merchant fleet. Next to the clipper is a whaler, just returned from a two-year voyage to the Pacific. The scene is one of busy activity. Shouting fills the air as sweating workers load and unload cargoes. And as they work, the sailors talk of the ports and people they have seen in their travels to faraway lands around the world.

Other harbors of the Northeast,[1] such as New York or Salem, Massachusetts, were also humming with activity in the 1840's. The Atlantic ports had not always been so busy, however. What had been happening to American shipping and trade in the years after the Revolution?

American shipping suffers after the Revolution. As you read in Chapter 5, New Englanders had begun in colonial days to build and sail ships and to carry on trade. In fact, one of the reasons for the Revolution was that England had tightened its control over American trade (pages 170, 173). During the Revolutionary War, however, many Yankee ships had been captured or sunk by the British navy. A number of sailors had lost their lives, and others had given up a life of seafaring to join the pioneers going west. In addition to losing ships

---

[1]We are using the term *Northeast* rather than *New England* because the Middle Atlantic states of New York, Pennsylvania, and New Jersey were also affected by the growth of commerce.

291

and sailors, American merchants lost most of their overseas markets. After the United States broke away from England, many of the ports of the British Empire were closed to Yankee ships. Especially serious to American merchants was the loss of trade with the West Indies. Americans had made large profits in this trade before the Revolution. For all these reasons American ● trade and shipping declined in the late 1700's.

Americans open trade with China. But energetic American merchants and sea captains refused to be defeated. "If we can't trade in British ports," they said, "we will find new places to trade. Why not send ships across the Pacific to China and other parts of East Asia?" In 1784 a ship called the *Empress of China* set sail from New York, bound for China. A year later, it returned with silks and tea from the Chinese city of Canton. About the same time, the *Grand Turk* left Salem, Massachusetts, and headed for Asia.

At first, Americans did not know what cargoes would bring the highest profits in Asian ports. But Captain Robert Gray, skipper of the *Columbia* out of Boston, spent a winter off the coast of Oregon. From there he sailed westward to China. He found he could get a good price in Chinese ports for the furs that he had bought from the Oregon Indians. Captain Gray then returned from China to the east coast of the United States by sailing west around Africa and across the Atlantic. He was the first American to sail around the world. (The map on the next page shows his route.)

After Gray's return, more and more ships heading for China first stopped along the west coast of North America. There they traded with the Indians, exchanging knives, needles, kettles, and other useful articles for furs. The furs in turn were carried to China to be exchanged for Asian goods.

Merchants trade with California. Another place to which Yankee ships sailed in ever-increasing numbers was California, still under Spanish rule in the early 1800's. At first the Americans sought the skins of sea otters, which were abundant along the coast. Then they began stopping at California's harbors to get supplies and make repairs. Spain tried to keep these foreign vessels out of California, but when Mexico broke away from Spanish rule in 1821, the ports were opened to all ships. There soon grew up a busy trade in cattle and hides with Mexican ranchers in California.

Richard Henry Dana, a young man from Massachusetts, worked for two years on one of the ships that traded in California. He later wrote a book about ★ the California trade. Here is his description of the goods carried by one American ship that traded for hides at San Francisco:

> Our cargo was an assorted one; that is, it consisted of everything under the sun. We had spirits of all kinds (sold by the cask), teas, coffee, sugar, spices, raisins, molasses, hardware, crockery-ware, tin-ware, cutlery, clothing of all kinds, boots and shoes . . . , calicoes and cottons . . . , crapes, silks; also shawls, scarfs, necklaces, jewelry, and combs for the women; furniture; and, in fact, everything that can be imagined. . . .

Richard Dana correctly foresaw the future of San Francisco. As he was leaving it, he wrote:

> If California ever becomes a prosperous country, this bay will be the center of its prosperity. The abundance of wood and water; the extreme fertility of its shores; the excellence of its climate, which is as near to being perfect as any in the world; and its facilities for navigation, affording the best anchoring-grounds in the whole western coast of America — all fit it for a place of great importance.

AMERICAN SHIPS TRADE WITH THE WORLD

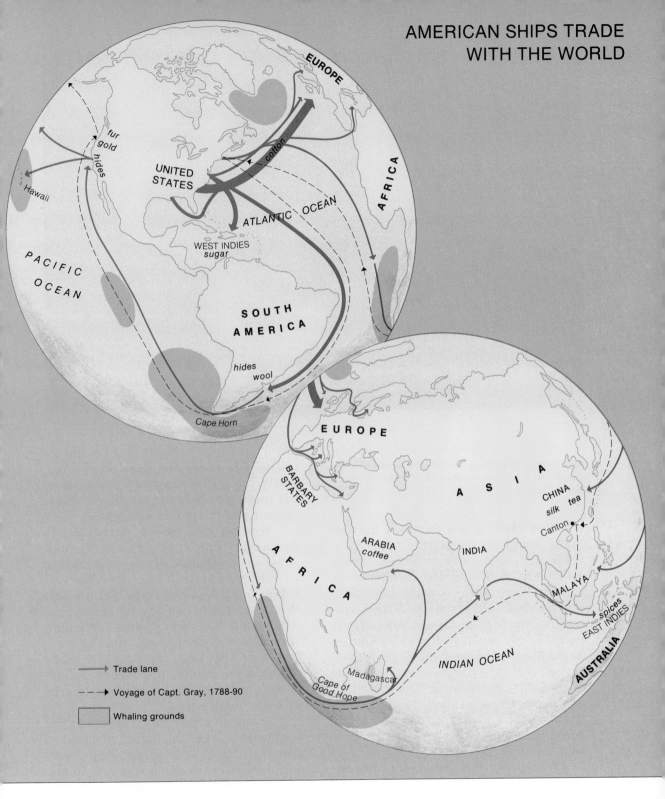

EUROPE

fur
gold
hides

UNITED
STATES

Hawaii

cotton

AFRICA

PACIFIC
OCEAN

ATLANTIC OCEAN

WEST INDIES
sugar

SOUTH
AMERICA

hides
wool

Cape Horn

EUROPE

BARBARY
STATES

ASIA

CHINA
silk tea

Canton

ARABIA
coffee

INDIA

AFRICA

MALAYA

spices
EAST INDIES

AUSTRALIA

Madagascar

INDIAN OCEAN

Cape of
Good Hope

→ Trade lane

- - → Voyage of Capt. Gray, 1788-90

☐ Whaling grounds

MAP STUDY   Here you see the major trade routes of American merchants in the early
1800's. (a) Compare the width of the trade lanes shown on the maps.
Which would you say was larger, American trade with Europe or with Asia?
(b) What was the chief product sought by American traders in the West
Indies? (c) In the East Indies?

293

In 1801 the United States sent warships to fight the Barbary pirates. In one battle the Americans set fire to a captured vessel at Tripoli, stronghold of the pirates.

New markets are found in Europe. Soon American merchants opened up trade with still more countries. Some sailed into the Baltic Sea, seeking to establish trade with Russia, Denmark, and Sweden. Others steered their vessels into the Mediterranean Sea to trade with the cities which dotted its shores. The Mediterranean trade, however, turned out to be dangerous. The rulers of several countries on the northern coast of Africa (called the Barbary States) seized merchant ships. The captured sailors were thrown into prison or sold into slavery.

For years the American government, like the governments of European countries, tried to bribe the pirates into letting their ships alone, but with little success. Finally, President Jefferson decided to teach the Barbary pirates a lesson. In 1801, the United States sent a naval squadron to make war on the pirates. The American fleet fought valiantly, but still it was many years before our trading ships could sail the Mediterranean Sea in complete safety.

Whaling and fishing increase. At the same time that more and more American merchant ships were trading with Europe and China, larger fleets of fishing and whaling ships put to sea. Whale oil was in demand for lamps, and whalebone had many uses. Whaling was hard and dangerous, and the voyages were very long. Two or three years might pass before the weary sailors caught sight of the familiar landmarks of their home ports.

American sailors bring wealth to the Northeast. The far-flung voyages of American merchant ships, fishing vessels, and whalers made shipping in the Northeast even more important than it had been before the Revolution. Shipping centers such as New York, Boston, and Salem hummed with activity. The harbor warehouses stored merchandise imported from all over the world.

Young men scarcely out of their teens became captains of merchant ships, made great fortunes, and retired before middle age.

American shipping is hurt by the War of 1812. You read in Chapter 13 how President Jefferson's embargo interfered with American shipping in 1807. The War of 1812 also kept American merchant vessels off the high seas. As trade came to an end, warehouses overflowed with goods, sailors lost their jobs, and ships rotted in the ports. A traveler reported that the streets along the New York waterfront were deserted and that grass had begun to grow on the wharves.

Once the War of 1812 was over, however, people of the Northeast turned again to the sea to seek their fortunes. Yankee ships and sailors soon were to be found on all the seas and in many distant ports. Packet ships began making scheduled trips with passengers and freight between American and European ports.

In the mid-1800's Americans developed fast new ships, called *clippers* for the way they "clipped off" the miles. The clipper *Hurricane* is shown here with sails fully set.

Clipper ships set speed records. In the 1840's, New England shipbuilders brought out a new kind of ship designed for speed. These clipper ships were especially useful in the China trade. They carried great towering sails and covered long distances at record speed. The clipper ships became the pride of American sailors and the envy of the world.

The most famous clippers were designed by Donald McKay of Boston. His *Flying Cloud* made the trip from New York around Cape Horn (the tip of South America) to San Francisco in 89 days. Sailing before a strong wind, it covered as much as 375 miles in a day.

In the era of clipper ships (1840–1860), American shipping reached a peak. But the days of the clipper ships were numbered. Already, ocean-going steamboats had appeared. The British perfected these ships and began to make them of iron. Americans, however, retained their faith in the speedy wooden clippers and looked with scorn on the steamboats with their squat lines and ugly smokestacks. But the day was not far distant when the wooden sailing ships would have to give way to the new rulers of the sea.

MANUFACTURING BECOMES IMPORTANT

● Along with its flourishing shipping and trade, the Northeast became the manufacturing center of the United States. This would hardly have been possible if an important step in human history had not taken place in England in the late 1700's. This change was the large-scale use of machines to produce goods. The effects of this change were so important that it became known as the **Industrial Revolution.** The Industrial Revolution has had a greater and longer-lasting effect on people's lives than all the wars ever fought.

English inventors lead the way for the Industrial Revolution. The Industrial Revolution began when new machines for spinning thread and weaving cloth were invented. Before the middle of the 1700's, almost every home had its spinning wheel (for making thread) and its hand loom (for weaving cloth). But the spinning wheel was slow; it took a spinner many hours to make enough thread to weave a piece of cloth. In the 1760's, an Englishman named James Hargreaves built a machine called a spinning jenny (possibly named after his wife). This machine, which replaced the spinning wheel, could spin eight threads instead of one. With later improvements, it could spin 80 threads at one time.

In a few years another Englishman, Edmund Cartwright, invented a loom (a weaving machine) that was run by water power. With this loom a weaver could work much faster and make wider cloth than with the old hand loom. Constant improvements were made in spinning machines and power looms. Later, steam as well as water power was used to drive the machines.

The first factories are started. Before these machines were invented, all spinning and weaving had been done in people's homes. But the new machines were expensive, and families could not afford to own them. Also, the machines had to be located near streams so that they could be driven by a water wheel. Richard Arkwright is often given the credit for establishing the first factory. He put several spinning machines together in one building and hired men and women to run them. Soon other factories were built, and England began turning out large quantities of manufactured cotton cloth. Because these factories made woven fabrics (called textiles), they were known as textile factories.

Samuel Slater introduces the new machines in America. England jealously guarded its new textile machines and tried to keep other countries from using them. A law was passed making it a crime for anyone to take a machine, or even the plans of one, out of the British Isles. But no law can control what people carry in their heads. In 1789, an Englishman named Samuel Slater settled in Pawtucket, Rhode Island. Slater had worked in English factories, and he was sure he remembered the textile machines well enough to build them himself. He was right. Within a year he had built from memory a spinning machine that could spin 72 threads at once. Slater set up spinning mills in ★ Rhode Island and Massachusetts. After Slater had shown the way, many other cotton mills were started in New England.

Manufacturing increases during the War of 1812. The Industrial Revolution was slow in getting started in the United States. The chief reason was that Americans were used to getting manufactured goods from Great Britain and other European countries in exchange for raw materials like grain, lumber, and cotton. As we know, however, President Jefferson's embargo, and later the War of 1812, interfered with American trade. During the war Americans were cut off almost entirely from British goods.

296

★ Have students read "Linking Past and Present" (p. 312) to find out about the museum on the site of one of Slater's mills.

Samuel Slater started the first American textile mill at Pawtucket, Rhode Island. Typical of early factories, it was built near a good source of water power.

But the Americans were self-reliant people, and they said, "If we can't get manufactured goods from England, why not start factories and make those things ourselves?" This is just what they did. New factories sprang up in many places. In 1814, Francis Lowell opened a textile factory in Waltham, Massachusetts. It was the first factory in which all the steps needed to make raw cotton into finished cloth took place under one roof. Factories began to produce not only cotton, woolen, and linen fabrics but also a great variety of articles made out of leather, iron, and felt. This method of bringing workers together to produce goods by machinery in factories is called the **factory system.**

New England and the middle states lead in manufacturing. Most of the early American factories, especially the textile mills, were located in New England.

There were several reasons. (1) New England had swift-running rivers that supplied the needed water power. (2) Because New England fields were rocky and hard to farm, many people were willing to leave their farms and work in the new factories. (3) New England had plenty of ships to carry the factory products to other sections of the United States and to other countries.

The factories established in the middle states (New York, Pennsylvania, and New Jersey) manufactured many articles made of iron. In Pennsylvania there were deposits of iron ore which had been used even in colonial times. In the 1800's, the variety of iron goods made in this country began to increase — iron rims for wooden wagon wheels, guns, stoves, axes, and other tools. The South and the West were much slower in starting manufacturing. In the early 1800's, those regions had few factories.

297

● Discuss whether these reasons still influence the location of factories. Have students suggest other factors affecting the location of industries.

Why Southerners Liked Free Trade

Southerner: "This is a nice deal for us. The English buy our cotton and we can get anything we want from the English factories — cheap!"

Northerner: "Those English manufacturers have a head start. Their goods are so cheap that they'll put us out of business before we can get going!"

Textile mills built in Lowell, Massachusetts, were among the first to make use of the factory system. Most of the workers in these early factories were young women, who left small towns and farms to take jobs in the mills. The young women, called "Lowell girls," lived in boarding houses that were run by the company. To attract hard-working young women from respectable families, the companies enforced strict rules in the mills. A traveler who visited Lowell wrote:

I happened to arrive at the first factory just as the dinner hour was over, and the girls were returning to their work. . . . They were all well dressed . . . and that phrase necessarily includes extreme cleanliness. They had serviceable bonnets, good warm cloaks, and shawls. The rooms in which they worked were as well ordered as themselves. In the windows of some, there were green plants which were trained to shade the glass; in all, there was as much fresh air, cleanliness, and comfort, as the nature of the occupation would possibly admit of. . . .

Howe invents the sewing machine. The invention of new machines helped speed the growth of manufacturing in the United States. The textile industry, for example, badly needed a machine that would sew cloth. Several inventors had tried to make such a machine, but Elias Howe was the first to succeed. Howe had been born on a New England farm. Like all farmers of that time, he had learned to repair and even to make many kinds of tools. He had also worked in a factory where he became familiar with machinery. Howe knew that if he could invent a workable sewing machine, he would make his fortune. He worked hard and suffered many disappointments as one attempt after another ended in failure.

At last, in 1845, Howe perfected a sewing machine which was run by a hand-turned wheel. Howe's machine not only lightened the work of people who made their own clothes but was widely used in clothing factories. Garments made on the sewing machine could be produced and sold much more cheaply than clothing that was sewn by hand.

298

Why Northerners Wanted Tariffs

Southerner: "We don't manufacture much in the South. Now everything we need costs more. And if we don't buy from the English, maybe they won't buy our cotton."

Northerner: "Now we can compete with the English! The tariff gives us a chance to show what we can do and to build up America!"

THE GOVERNMENT ENCOURAGES MANUFACTURERS

Cheap British goods threaten American manufacturers. Manufacturing increased rapidly during the War of 1812. But American factory owners found themselves in trouble after the war. When trade was once more possible, British merchants shipped large quantities of goods to their former customers in America. The British goods were cheap in price (1) because the factories that made them were larger and more efficient than American factories and (2) because English manufacturers wanted to get rid of large quantities of goods that had piled up during the war. As a result, the United States was flooded with British goods which sold at lower prices than American-made goods. Many people naturally bought the cheaper British goods.

Factory owners in the United States were alarmed. Orders were falling off, factories were shutting down, and ruin seemed certain for the new industries. The factory owners sought help from the government. They asked for a tariff — that is, a tax on imported goods. The factory owners believed that a tariff would protect them from the less expensive English goods.

How does a protective tariff work? Suppose Mr. Jones in your town owns a shoe factory. Of course, he wants to make money. But to be sure of a profit, he must sell his shoes for a price higher than the cost of the materials and labor used in making them. In other words, if it costs Mr. Jones $6 to make a pair of shoes, he would want to sell them for at least $7 a pair. But suppose that Mrs. Smith in a nearby town also manufactures shoes. Perhaps her factory is more efficient or for some reason she can hire workers for lower wages. At any rate, Mrs. Smith is able to make shoes of the same style and quality for $5 a pair. Then, Mrs. Smith can afford to sell her shoes for only $6 a pair and still make the same profit as Mr. Jones. Naturally people will buy the less expensive shoes, and Mr. Jones will have a hard time selling his shoes. But if $1 could somehow be added to the price of Mrs. Smith's shoes, she and Mr. Jones would compete on even terms.

299

● See p. T31 for a strategy that calls for students to examine the protective tariff and the reactions of different groups to it.

By substituting "the United States" for Mr. Jones and "Great Britain" for Mrs. Smith, we can understand the situation after the War of 1812. If a protective tariff were placed on goods brought into this country, English-made products would cost the buyer as much as the same things made in the United States. To sell their goods on even terms with the British, American manufacturers therefore wanted a tariff on foreign goods.

Tariffs are established on foreign goods. The American manufacturers asked Congress for help, and in 1816 a tariff law was passed. It placed taxes, called duties, on many imported articles. This tariff was of great help to American factory owners.

But there was another side to the tariff question. Many Americans did
● not want a tariff on imports. They knew that if Great Britain could not sell manufactured goods in the United States, the British were not so likely to buy American food and raw materials. This meant that our trade with Britain would suffer. For this reason, the tariff of 1816 was a blow to shipowners, and they spoke angrily against it. So also did the Southerners who wanted to sell tobacco and cotton to Britain. Many other people also protested, since every

person who bought manufactured articles would have to pay the higher prices of American goods.

Manufacturing continued to grow rapidly in New England and the middle states. So also did the demand for higher tariff duties and for tariff protection on more kinds of goods. In 1824 and again in 1828, Congress passed ★ higher tariff laws.

▶ **CHECK UP**   See Teacher's Key.

1. **(a)** What happened to American shipping during and just after the Revolution? **(b)** Explain how and where American merchants and sea captains found new markets.
2. **(a)** How did the War of 1812 hurt shipping? **(b)** Why were the clipper ships important?
3. **(a)** Explain the term *Industrial Revolution.* **(b)** What inventions in England paved the way for the Industrial Revolution? **(c)** How were the new machines introduced into the United States?
4. **(a)** How did the War of 1812 affect manufacturing in the United States? **(b)** Why were many of the early factories located in New England?
5. **(a)** Why did factory owners ask for a tariff on imported manufactured goods? **(b)** How would a tariff help them?

2 How Did Machines Change Ways of Living in America?

Working conditions in the early factories are poor. We should remember that early factories were nothing like our modern factories with their huge complicated machines, thousands of workers, and long assembly lines. The early factories were usually large wooden buildings, without good lighting or ventilation. They were cold in the winter and hot in the summer. They

had none of the conveniences and safety features found in factories today. There were no restrooms or cafeterias, and they were not designed to protect workers from injury.

Not only men and women but also children worked in these factories. In fact, children as young as seven or eight were hired. The eight-hour day was unheard of at that time. Workers were

300

The machines used in this New England textile mill of the early 1800's were run by water power.

on the job from sunrise to sunset, standing at the machines for twelve to fifteen hours a day. In spite of the long hours, workers made very little money. Men were paid perhaps five dollars a week, women about two dollars for the same work, and children often only a dollar a week.

The workers were not as unhappy over these conditions as we might expect. Most of them came from nearby farms where they had been used to hard work and long hours, and where children were expected to help with the work. Although factory wages were low, the prices of things that people needed to buy were also low. Nor did the workers have to stay in the factories to make a living. In fact, many of the young men and women workers expected to get their own farms after they married. And some felt they could always head for the West, where there were plenty of opportunities to make a new start. The only trouble was that

the West got farther and farther away, and it took more and more money to start a new life there.

The factory system brings important ●
changes in the worker's life. As time went on, it became clear that the factory system was having an effect on American life. In earlier days, when goods had been made in the homes, most people had worked for themselves. They had owned their own tools and could work whatever hours they wished. Furthermore, workers took pride in what they produced with their own hands and brains. With the coming of factories, however, workers lost much of their freedom as well as the pleasure they had taken in their work. The machines and the tools they used were no longer theirs. The articles they made did not belong to them but to their employer. If they wanted to keep their jobs, they had to work the number of hours set by the employer and to accept the wages that were offered.

Early labor unions try to improve conditions. Although it is true that American workers were better off than those in other lands, their lot was far from

301

● See p. T32 for a strategy that asks students to examine the effects of the factory system on workers.

easy. More and more people were coming to America from other countries, which meant that factory owners had no trouble in getting workers. Wages were kept low because if one worker quit, there were plenty of other workers to take his or her place.

Hoping to improve working conditions, a few groups of workers banded together to form **labor unions.** The unions were made up of skilled craftworkers. Their chief object was to win shorter hours and better wages. Workers also demanded greater opportunities for free education for their children. A number of unions started up during the 1830's, but they were not successful. It was not until after the Civil War that strong labor unions were started.

The factory system leads to the growth of cities. Another change brought about by the use of machines was the growth of cities. As more factories were started, more and more people left the farms and moved to factory towns. After 1820 large numbers of the workers who came from Europe settled in these towns. Towns that were conveniently located along canals or railroad lines became centers for transporting goods. The number of stores and shops increased, and banks and warehouses were established. Before long, many factory towns became busy cities.

During the Revolutionary War there had been only five towns of over 8,000 people in the United States. In 1840, there were 44 towns of over 8,000; by 1860, there were 141. These figures show that cities grew rapidly in size and number. But we should remember that the majority of Americans still lived on farms or in villages.

City dwellers enjoy new comforts. The growth of industry brought new conveniences to Americans, especially to those living in cities. In many homes, candles were replaced by oil-burning lamps. Stoves took the place of fireplaces for cooking and heating. The floors of many rooms were covered with carpets. In the kitchen, tinware was now used in place of heavy iron and copper pots and pans. More and more comfortable furniture was to be found in most homes. The larger cities used gas for lighting streets and built water systems to replace wells and springs.

▶ **CHECK UP**   See Teacher's Key.

1. **(a)** Describe working conditions in early factories. **(b)** What changes did the factory system bring about in workers' lives?
2. How did the factory system affect cities?

3 What Changes Were Made in Travel and Communication?

While the Northeast was developing into a manufacturing and trading section, other important changes were taking place throughout the nation. One change was in transportation. Roads and canals were built to connect the eastern part of the country with the western section. New inventions made it easier for farmers to get their goods to

market and for manufacturers to sell their products where they were needed.

ROADS AND CANALS INCREASE TRADE AND TRAVEL

Do you remember that the first Congress under the Constitution, which was supposed to meet on March 4, 1789, did

● See p. T32 for a strategy that calls for students to examine the purpose of various maps.

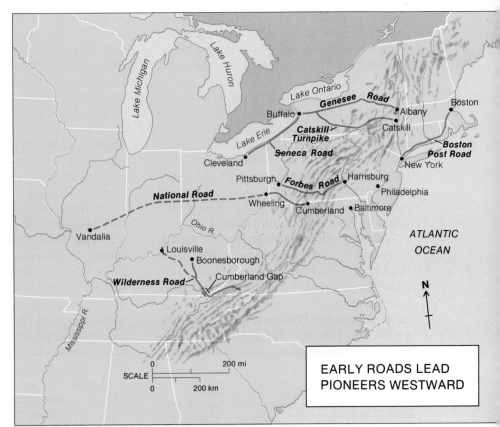

See Teacher's Key.

● MAP STUDY
Broken lines show the extension of the National Road and the Louisville branch of the Wilderness Road.
(a) Why didn't the Wilderness Road run in a straight line from Virginia to Kentucky?
(b) What two roads connected eastern cities with Lake Erie?

EARLY ROADS LEAD PIONEERS WESTWARD

not open until a month later (page 258)? Poor roads throughout the country were the main reason for the delay. Roads were unpaved, and many of them had deep holes, choking dust, or oozing mud. Carriages bumped and swayed over these rough roads. In fact, between some towns it just was not possible to travel by carriage. Many people went on horseback.

The National Road connects East and West. As time went on and larger numbers of people moved westward, better and faster transportation was needed. A great forward step was taken in 1811. The United States government pro-
★ vided funds for the construction of the Cumberland Road, also called the National Road. The surface of the National Road was made of crushed rock. At first the road ran from Cumberland, Maryland, to Wheeling on the Ohio

River. (See map, this page.) Other stretches were later added. In time the National Road reached Vandalia, Illinois, not far from the Mississippi River, and it became the main overland route to the West. Over the road traveled many wagons, coaches, riders on horseback, herds of cattle, pack horses, and people on foot. The merchants of Pennsylvania and Maryland made good profits by selling food and other things to travelers using the National Road.

Turnpikes are built. Many people, especially Westerners, thought the states should build more new roads. But the state governments had little money, so private companies began to build them. The new roads had much better surfaces than colonial roads. Over them rolled stagecoaches and canvas-covered Conestoga wagons. These wagons were used to carry freight or to

303

★ Discuss how government funding for this road was evidence of a strong national government.

transport families and their belongings to new homes in the West. Often a line of coaches and wagons would be interrupted by herds of sheep or cattle being driven to market. At certain points along the roads travelers were halted at toll gates, where they had to pay a toll or tax. The toll money helped to pay the companies for the cost of building and keeping up the roads. At first the toll gate was only a pole, or pike, set across the road and raised or turned aside to let travelers pass. The roads came to be called **turnpikes.**

Canals furnish cheap water routes. Travel by water was also becoming more important. Lakes and rivers had been used for transportation since the days when Indians had glided over the water in their canoes. But water travel had its problems. For one thing, long distances often separated rivers and lakes. And

some bodies of water had rapids or waterfalls. To make water travel more practical, canals were dug around rapids or to connect lakes and rivers. By using the canals people could travel many miles by water. (The map on the next page shows where some important canals were located.) Travel by canal, although slow, was much cheaper than over roads. Canal boats were usually pulled by horses or mules driven along the canal bank. So many canals were built from 1825 to 1850 that this period has been called the Canal Era.

The Erie Canal was an important route. Governor DeWitt Clinton of ● New York realized what canal trade would mean to New York City. It was largely because of his dreams and determination that the Erie Canal was built. Completed in 1825 after eight years of hard work, the canal was 40 feet wide and 363 miles long. It ran through the Mohawk River valley in New York State, connecting Albany with Lake Erie. The Erie Canal made possible an all-water route from the harbor of New

Canal-building boomed in the early 1800's, linking the eastern seaboard with Lake Erie and the Old Northwest. In this picture a boat pulled by a team of horses glides along a canal.

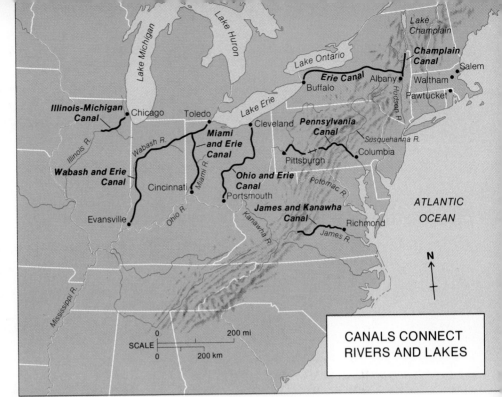

CANALS CONNECT RIVERS AND LAKES

See Teacher's Key.

MAP STUDY
Boats were pulled on rails over hills between the two sections of the Pennsylvania Canal. (a) Which canals provided a connection between the Atlantic Ocean and inland rivers or lakes? (b) Which linked the Great Lakes with the Ohio River?

York City to the Great Lakes. Boats could go north up the Hudson River to Albany and then west on the canal to Buffalo on Lake Erie.

When the canal was opened, Clinton traveled on a canal boat from Buffalo to New York City. It was a ten-day trip. He poured water carried from Lake Erie into the Atlantic Ocean to celebrate the joining of these waters by the canal.

The Erie Canal rapidly became the busiest and most important route between the West and the Atlantic seaboard. Before the canal was built, the cost of moving goods between Buffalo and New York City had been about $100 a ton. The canal immediately reduced the cost to about $10 a ton. In addition, goods could be transported three times as fast. New York City, already the largest city in the United States, grew even more rapidly because of the canal trade. Products from the Great Lakes region could be shipped by water all the way to New York and from there to other ports along the Atlantic coast or to Europe. In turn, manufactured goods from the eastern states and Europe were shipped to the West by means of the canal.

THE STEAM ENGINE MARKS A NEW ERA

In the early 1800's a new kind of power caused a revolution in transportation and greatly changed ways of living in the United States. This power was steam. People had known for some time that steam could be put to work. A Scotsman named James Watt had invented the first practical steam engine in the last half of the 1700's. Factory owners in Great Britain and in America began to use the steam engine to run machines. Not only was it more efficient than water power, but steam-driven machinery could be set up anywhere. There was plenty of coal and wood in the United States to use as fuel for steam engines. It was only natural for inventors to ask the question, "Why not use steam to move boats or wagons?"

305

Boats powered by steam made water transportation faster and cheaper. Races between steamboats on the Mississippi became a popular custom.

John Fitch fails to develop a successful steamboat. One person interested in steam power was John Fitch, a Connecticut clockmaker who had moved to Philadelphia. He knew that a boat with a steam engine would not have to depend on the wind or on oars. In 1787, he launched on the Delaware River a crude vessel driven by steam. Later, Fitch built another steamboat that made trips between Philadelphia and Trenton. But he lacked the money to develop a really successful steamboat.

Robert Fulton builds the first successful steamboat. Another American, named Robert Fulton, gets the credit for making the steamboat a success. Born in Pennsylvania, Fulton had little education but became an artist and earned his living by selling pictures. At the age of 21, he went to Europe, where he soon became more interested in machines and inventions than in painting. He began to experiment with the idea of putting a steam engine in a boat. After patient planning and much hard work, Fulton at last launched a steamboat in 1803. The boat sank. Undiscouraged, Fulton built another. Although this one floated and even moved under its own power, it was very slow. Fulton returned to the United States and started work on still another steamboat.

Early in 1807, Fulton's new steamboat was nearly completed in a shipyard on the East River in New York City. People who had watched it being built laughed at the inventor and called his boat "Fulton's Folly." But Fulton kept on with his work. On a day in August, the *Clermont,* as the boat was called, set out on a trial trip up the Hudson. Smoke and sparks poured from its smokestack, the engines clattered noisily, paddle wheels splashed at the sides. But the boat moved steadily up the river and made the trip to Albany and back — a distance of about 300 miles — in 62 hours. After this journey had been completed, Robert Fulton wrote:

The power of propelling boats by steam is now fully proved. The morning I left

● Discuss what Fulton meant by this statement.

New York there were not perhaps 30 persons in the city who believed that the boat would ever move one mile per hour or be of the least [use]; and, while we were putting off from the wharf, which was crowded with spectators, I heard a number of sarcastic remarks. This is the way ignorant men compliment [inventors].

The steamboat proves valuable. No longer was the steamboat called "Fulton's Folly." New and improved steamboats were quickly built. In fact, in a few years steamboats loaded with goods and passengers were puffing up and down many rivers. Steamboat travel in those early days, however, had many dangers. Hidden rocks, floating logs, swift currents, and exploding boilers often caused accidents. Sometimes the boats caught fire from sparks that flew out of their smokestacks. Then passengers and crew worked together to put out the blaze. And there was danger of collision when rival steamboats raced each other.

In spite of these dangers, steamboat travel steadily increased. Steamboats on the Great Lakes brought many settlers to the West and carried goods to

and from that region. By the late 1830's, the steamboat also had been tried successfully on the ocean. But, as we read earlier, Americans clung to their swift sailing vessels and allowed ★ the British to get ahead of them in this new form of ocean transportation.

Steam railroads are begun. While the steamboat was being developed, other inventors were trying to use the steam engine to improve travel on land. One of the earliest was an American named Oliver Evans. Evans was so certain that railroads could be built that he made this prediction in 1812:

The time will come when people will travel in stages moved by steam engines from one city to another as fast as birds fly — fifteen to twenty miles an hour.... A carriage will set out from Washington in the morning, and the passengers will breakfast at Baltimore, dine in Philadelphia, and sup at New York the same day.

To accomplish this, two sets of railways will be laid ... nearly level ... made of wood or iron, on smooth paths of broken stone or gravel, with a rail to guide the carriages so that they may pass each other in different directions

See Teacher's Key.

GRAPH STUDY
The population of the United States more than tripled between 1820 and 1860. About how many people were there in 1820? In 1860? By about how many millions did the population grow between 1820 and 1860?

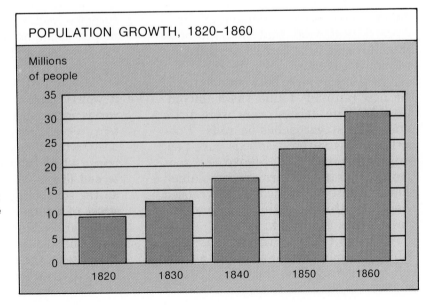

POPULATION GROWTH, 1820–1860

Millions of people

(Bar graph showing population in millions for years 1820, 1830, 1840, 1850, 1860 with vertical scale 0 to 35.)

307

★ Discuss the advantages steamboats had over ships powered by wind.

and travel by night as well as by day, and the passengers will sleep in these stages as comfortably as they do now in steam stage-boats.

● Although Evans's ideas seem very sensible to us today, most people of his time scoffed at them. But rails (wooden at first and later covered with strips of iron) had already been laid for short distances. Over these rails carriages were drawn by horses.

An Englishman named George Stephenson invented the first successful steam-driven locomotive. Then in 1830, the *Tom Thumb,* a locomotive built by Peter Cooper, made a successful trial run out of Baltimore, Maryland. This run was made on the Baltimore and Ohio road, a "railroad" on which coaches had been pulled by horses. On one occasion the *Tom Thumb* raced a horse-drawn coach. The locomotive passed the horse and was ahead when it broke down. The horse won!

What were the early trains like? The early railroad trains seem like toys when compared with modern trains. The engines were crude open wagons and burned wood instead of coal. Many people refused to trust the new invention. They not only considered the steam locomotives dangerous but claimed that God had not intended human beings to be carried so swiftly by mechanical means.

People who were bold enough to try the new railroads found them uncomfortable. The earliest cars were little more than stagecoaches on rails. Poor springs and uneven roadbeds gave passengers a bad jolting. Smoke and soot blew in their faces. Farmers complained that the noise of the locomotives caused their hens to stop laying eggs and the cows to lose their milk!

Charles Dickens, the famous English writer, had this to say about a train ride during his visit to the United States in 1842:

A typical railroad station in the mid-1800's was a center of bustling activity whenever a train steamed in to unload or take on passengers.

The train calls at stations in the woods, where the wild impossibility of anybody having the smallest reason to get out is only to be equaled by the apparently desperate hopelessness of there being anybody to get in. It rushes across the turnpike road, where there is no gate, no policeman, no signal: nothing but a rough wooden arch, on which is painted "WHEN THE BELL RINGS, LOOK OUT FOR THE LOCOMOTIVE." On it whirls headlong, dives through the woods again, emerges in the light, clatters over frail arches, rumbles upon the heavy ground, shoots beneath a wooden bridge which intercepts the light for a second like a wink, suddenly awakens all the slumbering echoes in the main street of a large town, and dashes on haphazard, pell-mell, neck-or-nothing, down the middle of the road. . . . On, on, on tears the mad dragon of an engine with its train of cars; scattering in all directions a shower of burning

308

sparks from its wood fire; screeching, hissing, yelling, panting; until at last the thirsty monster stops beneath a covered way to drink [to take on water], the people cluster round, and you have time to breathe again.

Railroads grow rapidly. The early locomotives and coaches were constantly improved, and railroads spread rapidly. In 1830, there were about 30 miles of railroad track in the United States. Ten years later, there were 2,800 miles; in 1850, about 9,000 miles. The early railroads ran short distances and usually connected two cities. But three great railroad systems — the Baltimore and Ohio, the Pennsylvania, and the New York Central — were begun in this early period. The map on page 310 shows where the railroad lines were built. Most of the lines ran east and west. For many years, there were few railroads connecting the North and the South.

Why were railroads important? Of all the new methods of transportation that developed in the early 1800's, the railroads proved to be the most important. Factories in the Northeast wanted markets for their manufactured goods. The railways made it easy for factories to ship goods to the western farmers who needed them. In turn, the railroads carried the products of the West to eastern markets. All this could be done more swiftly than by road or canal. The railroads also provided transportation between points where water travel was impossible. By making it easier for people to travel and for products to be shipped back and forth, the railroads helped to bind the West and the Northeast more closely together.

A NEW INVENTION REVOLUTIONIZES COMMUNICATION

A means of rapid communication is needed. Although methods of transportation improved greatly in the early 1800's, people still had no fast way of sending messages. To communicate with someone at a distance, it was necessary to send a letter or go see the per-

309

See p. T32 for a strategy calling for students to make a chart comparing the advantages and disadvantages of roads, canals, and railroads.

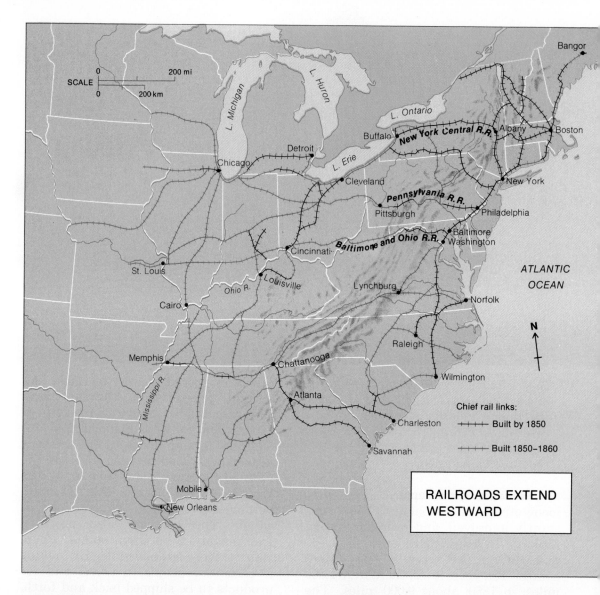

RAILROADS EXTEND WESTWARD

Chief rail links:
++++ Built by 1850
++++ Built 1850–1860

MAP STUDY See Teacher's Key.
(a) At what cities did several railroad lines meet? (b) About how long was the railroad from Chicago to New Orleans? (c) How might a traveler have gone from Cleveland to Baltimore?

son. As settlers moved farther westward, it became even more important to be able to communicate quickly over great distances. Then, too, the railroads needed some way of sending fast messages. Early railroads had only a single track. It was very difficult to control train traffic when messages could not be sent ahead of the trains from station to station.

Morse invents the telegraph. Samuel F. B. Morse discovered a way to fill this need. Like Robert Fulton, Morse was a successful artist who also had a keen interest in science. He was particularly interested in electricity. Morse believed that he could send messages through a wire by the power of electricity. He began a series of experiments to prove his idea.

By 1837 Morse was greatly encouraged. He had succeeded in inventing the instrument now called the telegraph. This instrument could send signals through copper wire. To make use of the signals, Morse invented the Morse Code, a system of dots and dashes representing the letters of the alphabet. But to prove that his invention was really useful, he had to raise money to build a telegraph line that could send signals over long distances.

Morse and his friends tried for years to get members of Congress to take an interest in the plan. During this time Morse was so poor that he could hardly support his family; often he went hungry himself. Finally, Congress voted money for his project. A telegraph line was built from Washington to Baltimore, a distance of about 40 miles.

The telegraph is successful. In May, 1844, Morse in Washington prepared to send a message over the telegraph to friends in Baltimore. "What hath God wrought!" he tapped out on the telegraph key. The message was received clearly at the other end of the line and sent back to him correctly. The telegraph was a success.

The need for the telegraph had been so great that lines were rapidly built. The lines soon connected all the larger cities along the east coast. The telegraph made it possible to put out newspapers containing the day's news from all over the nation. Private and business messages could be sent speedily; railroads dispatched their trains ● more efficiently. Morse's telegraph had done much to bring people closer together.

▶ **CHECK UP**   See Teacher's Key.

1. **(a)** What was the National Road? **(b)** Why was it important? **(c)** What were turnpikes?
2. **(a)** Why were many canals built? **(b)** For what reasons was the Erie Canal so important?
3. **(a)** How was the first successful steamboat developed? **(b)** Why were steamboats important? **(c)** What were early trains like? **(d)** How did railroads help the growth of the nation?
4. **(a)** How was the telegraph developed? **(b)** Why was it important?

CHECK UP ON CHAPTER 14   See Teacher's Key.

Words to Know

1. textile
2. tariff
3. power loom
4. telegraph
5. turnpike
6. invention
7. toll
8. factory system
9. communicate
10. spinning jenny
11. labor union
12. manufacture
13. Industrial Revolution

Places to Locate

1. Cape Horn
2. Wheeling
3. Vandalia
4. National Road
5. Erie Canal
6. Lake Erie
7. Hudson River
8. New York (City)

Facts to Remember

1. **(a)** What parts of the world did American merchant ships trade with in the early 1800's? **(b)** What kinds of goods were traded?
2. **(a)** What was the Industrial Revolution? **(b)** What kinds of inventions helped that movement get under way? **(c)** Why were many factories built in New England? **(d)** What effect did factory work have on workers' lives?
3. **(a)** What advantages did canal transportation have over travel by river and road? **(b)** What effect did the Erie Canal have on New York City?

311

● See p. T32 for a strategy in which students make a bulletin board display showing changes in travel and communication.

Facts to Remember (cont.)

4. Tell what each of the following persons invented and why the invention was important: **(a)** Elias Howe, **(b)** Robert Fulton, **(c)** Samuel F. B. Morse.
5. **(a)** When were the first railroads built in the United States? **(b)** Why did railroads become important?

Skills to Practice

1. Make a large copy of the Unit 5 time line (pages 288–289). Add to your time line, in correct position, the additional events shown on the chapter time line on page 290. Also add the following events: Independence is won; the Constitution is adopted; the War of 1812 begins.
2. Look at the map on page 293. **(a)** How is the route of Captain Robert Gray shown on the map? **(b)** On his way from Boston to China, did Captain Gray sail around Cape Horn or the Cape of Good Hope? **(c)** What large island near the east coast of Africa did he pass? **(d)** For what goods did he exchange furs in China?
3. Look at the map on page 303. What cities were connected by each of the following roads? **(a)** Genesee Road **(b)** Forbes Road **(c)** Boston Post Road

Questions to Think About

1. How have working conditions improved since the days of the early factories?
2. Skilled workers often opposed the use of new machines to produce goods. Why?
3. The population of New Orleans grew from 46,000 in 1830 to 130,000 in 1850. One reason for this rapid growth was the building of railroads in the eastern United States. Explain.
4. The wars fought between Britain and France in the late 1700's and early 1800's speeded the industrial development of both Britain and the United States. Why?

 # Linking Past and Present

Carrying the mail. When we mail a letter anywhere in the United States today, we know that it will reach its destination within a few days. In colonial days, mail service was much more uncertain. Important letters were sent by post-riders on horseback, who had a regular route from one city to another. For ordinary mail, people would ask someone going in the right direction to carry a letter. It would be passed along in this way until it reached the person to whom it was addressed. During the Revolution, the Continental Congress established a post office department, and Benjamin Franklin was appointed its head. Later, under the Constitution, Congress made use of its power "to establish post offices and post roads" and set up the Post Office Department.

The post office grew slowly. In the early 1800's, a letter sent from Maine to Georgia took 20 days to get there! As railroads spread across the country, mail service improved. The first regular air mail service began in 1918 when United States Army pilots began to fly mail between New York, Philadelphia, and Washington, D.C. Today long-distance mail is carried by airplanes that cross the country in a few hours.

Slater's mill. Samuel Slater's first textile mill was destroyed by a flood in 1807, but his second mill, built in 1793, can still be seen in Pawtucket, Rhode Island. A museum has been set up in the old mill as a memorial to Slater. Some original pieces of the machinery that he built from memory are on display, and exhibits tell Slater's story and show how cloth was made in the past. You can see, for example, how spinning and weaving were done by hand before power-driven machines were invented. You can also watch flax plants being broken down into long fibers and spun into linen yarn. The sights at the old Slater Mill remind us how the American textile industry developed from the machines of two centuries ago.

312

● Mention that railway cars first began to carry mail in 1864.

Have students turn to the population map in Chapter 21. Discuss how population density in the United States changed between 1850 and 1890.

GAINING SKILL

Reading Maps: Population Density

In the early 1800's, American trade and industry developed rapidly. In those years roads, canals, and railroads reached new areas. The population of the United States grew fast too. All of these changes affected the settlement of our country.

The map on this page shows **population density** in 1850. Density is a word used to describe how many people live in a specific area. If many people live in one place, we say it has high population density. If only a few people live in an area, we say it has low population density. In the map below, population density is measured by the number of people per square mile.

Use the map to answer the following questions.

1. Look at the key. What color is used to show 2 to 18 people per square mile? More than 90 people?
2. What part of the state of Maine had fewer than 2 people per square mile in 1850?
3. How would you describe Florida's population density in 1850?
4. What parts of the United States had the highest population density in 1850?
5. By 1850 what present-day states west of the Mississippi had areas with more than 18 people per square mile?

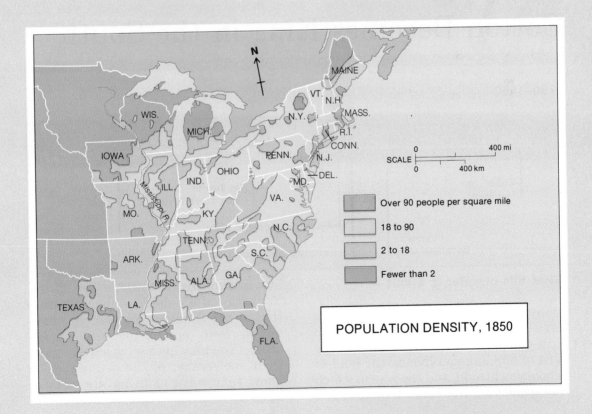

Over 90 people per square mile

18 to 90

2 to 18

Fewer than 2

POPULATION DENSITY, 1850

Cotton Becomes King in the South

1790–1860   See pp. T32-T33 for chapter teaching strategies.

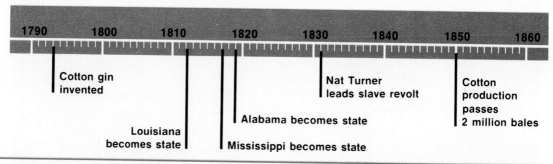

| 1790 | 1800 | 1810 | 1820 | 1830 | 1840 | 1850 | 1860 |

Cotton gin
invented

Louisiana
becomes state

Alabama becomes state

Mississippi becomes state

Nat Turner
leads slave revolt

Cotton
production
passes
2 million bales

What this chapter is about —

Many of you who read this book live in large cities. That fact has much to do with the way you live. It affects the type of building you live in, the kind of school you attend, and the way in which you spend your free time. Others of you live in suburbs or towns or on farms. Your way of life differs somewhat from that of city dwellers. Some of you have moved from one community to another. You may even have lived in more than one section of the country. You know that ways of living are not the same all over the United States.

314

◀ By 1860 cotton had become the leading crop of the South. Large numbers of slaves worked the cotton fields.

In the mid-1800's, differences in ways of living in different sections of the country were much greater than they are today. The Northeast, as we saw in Chapter 14, had become a manufacturing, shipping, and trading center. The South continued, as it was in colonial times, to be chiefly a farming region. By 1860, cotton had outdistanced all other farm products and become the South's chief crop.

This chapter tells how "cotton became king." We will learn how cotton growing changed ways of living in the South and made slavery seem so important. We will answer the following questions:

1. How did the cotton gin make cotton the leading crop in the South?
2. How did the people of the South live in the years before 1860?
3. How did different ways of living tend to divide the North and South?

1 How Did the Cotton Gin Make Cotton the Leading Crop in the South?

From the days of the first settlers, the
● South had been a farming region. By the year 1790, it had changed very little since colonial times. Slaves still did the work on the large plantations and in the planters' homes. Large crops of indigo, tobacco, and rice were still being grown and exported. Although some cotton was grown, it was not as profitable as the other crops. The cotton bolls (pods) contained seeds and fibers that were hard to separate. Until the seeds were taken out, the cotton fiber could not be used for making cloth. The seeds had to be picked out by hand; it took a worker a whole day to clean a pound of cotton fiber.

Eli Whitney invents the cotton gin.
Plantation owners had long wanted a machine to clean cotton faster and more easily than it could be done by hand. A man named Eli Whitney invented a machine to do this job. Even as a boy, Whitney had shown a keen interest in mechanical things. He is said to have taken his father's watch apart and put it together again so cleverly that he was

not discovered. After studying at Yale College, Eli Whitney decided to become a teacher. He received an offer to teach in a Carolina school. But before going to the school, he visited the Georgia plantation of Catherine Greene. What happened then is best told by Whitney himself in a letter to his father: ★

During this time I heard much said of the extreme difficulty of ginning cotton, that is, separating it from its seeds. There were a number of very respectable gentlemen at Mrs. Greene's who all agreed that if a machine could be invented which would clean cotton [rapidly], it would be a great thing both to the country and to the inventor.

I . . . happened to be thinking on the subject and struck out a plan of a machine in my mind. . . . In about ten days I made a little model, for which I was offered, if I would give up all right and title to it, a hundred guineas [about $500]. I concluded to [give up] my school and turn my attention to perfecting the machine.

315

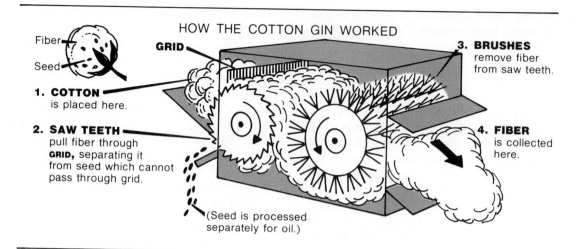

HOW THE COTTON GIN WORKED

Fiber
Seed

GRID

3. BRUSHES remove fiber from saw teeth.

1. COTTON is placed here.

2. SAW TEETH pull fiber through **GRID**, separating it from seed which cannot pass through grid.

4. FIBER is collected here.

(Seed is processed separately for oil.)

Eli Whitney (right) invented the cotton gin to separate fibers from seeds. Whitney's cotton gin helped make the United States the largest cotton producer in the world. (The word *gin* is short for "engine.")

I made one before I came away which required the labor of one man to turn it and with which one man will clean ten times as much cotton as he can in any other way before known and also cleanse it much better than in the usual [way]. This machine may be turned by water or with a horse, with the greatest of ease, and one man and a horse will do more than fifty men with the old machines. It makes the labor fifty times less, without throwing any class of people out of business.

Whitney made his first cotton gin in 1793. His invention brought him little money, however, and a great deal of trouble. In order to have the sole right to build and sell his invention, an inventor must get a **patent** from the government. Whitney took out a patent on his cotton gin, but because the idea of the invention was simple, others copied it and built cotton gins from which he received no profit. It took Whitney several years to prove that he alone had the right to build and sell cotton gins.

The South grows more cotton. Although Whitney gained little profit from the cotton gin, his invention was a history-making event. As you read in Chapter 14, new machines for spinning thread were being used in the Northeast and in England. More and more cotton was needed to keep these machines busy. With the cotton gin, the South could grow and sell much more cotton than ever before.

316

See p. T32 for a teaching strategy that asks students to consider the historical significance of the cotton gin.

Southerners quickly realized that Eli Whitney's invention gave them a chance to make a good profit. Farmers and plantation owners stopped growing the crops they had been raising and planted cotton instead. They also bought more land in order to raise more cotton. But the soil in parts of the Old South (Virginia, Maryland, and North Carolina) proved unsatisfactory for cotton growing. The best soil for cotton was in South Carolina and Georgia. Even the good cotton lands were often spoiled, however, because planters were too eager to make quick profits. Growing cotton on the same land year after year wore out the soil. Instead of trying to keep the soil in good condition by changing crops or using fertilizer, many cotton growers tried to raise as much cotton as possible and then move on to new lands.

Southerners seek better land for cotton. To the southwest of the older settled South lay vast stretches of fertile land covered with thick forests. The rivers that flowed through this region could be used to float cargoes of cotton to towns on the Gulf of Mexico. From these towns the cotton could be shipped to Europe.

During the fifty years following the invention of the cotton gin, great numbers of people pushed south and west ★ into these unfarmed lands. Some of these people were plantation families from Virginia and the Carolinas. Along with them went large numbers of black people who, as slaves, had to go where their owners took them. Other settlers in the new lands were white farmers from the foothills and backwoods of the Old South. Few of them owned slaves or had much wealth, but hoped by hard work to become owners of plantations.

The newcomers staked out farms and then cleared the dense underbrush and timber from the land. Often settlers were so eager to start planting cotton that they did not cut down the taller trees. Instead, the trees were left standing but were killed by "girdling" — that is, by removing a ring of bark near the ground. To fill the growing need for workers, many more slaves were sold to these new cotton planters

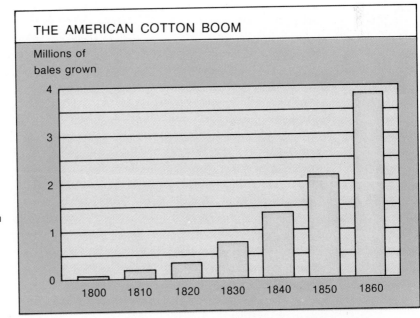

THE AMERICAN COTTON BOOM

See Teacher's Key.

GRAPH STUDY
After the cotton gin came into use, the amount of cotton grown in the United States boomed, nearly doubling from decade to decade. By 1860 about how many bales of cotton were being grown?

317

★ See p. T32 for a strategy calling for students to examine southern expansion.

● of the "lower South" by the plantation owners who stayed in Virginia and the Carolinas. (Congress had passed a law in 1808 saying that slaves could no longer be brought into the United States. But by that time the natural growth of the slave population kept the number increasing. There was no law to forbid buying and selling slaves *within* the United States.) In time, stately homes and broad fields of growing cotton replaced the endless stretches of thick forest. Some of the more adventurous people even took up lands in the region of Texas far beyond the Mississippi.

Cotton is King. By the 1840's, a wide belt of land extending southwest from the Carolinas had been settled. Its most important product, in fact the

leading product of the entire South, was cotton. To be sure, large quantities of tobacco were still grown in the older states of Virginia and the Carolinas. Sizable crops of rice were also raised in South Carolina and Georgia, and sugar cane grew in Louisiana. But cotton was more important than all other southern products. In 1790, just before the invention of the cotton gin, the United States had produced about 4,000 bales of cotton, each bale weighing 500 pounds. By 1850, the output of cotton had climbed to over two million bales. Most of it was grown in the newly settled lands that became known as the Cotton Kingdom. (See the map on the next page.)

Slowly but surely the cotton states grew in importance. Their population increased faster than that of the older southern states. Louisiana (1812), Mississippi (1817), and Alabama (1819) became states of the Union. The ports of ★ Mobile and New Orleans became more important centers of trade than

As the population of the South grew larger, people began to move beyond the Mississippi to Texas. This picture shows that by 1840 Austin, Texas, was a thriving settlement. What were most of the houses made of?

Charleston and Savannah. Because there were few factories or mines or centers of industry in the South, most Southerners thought their prosperity depended on the raising of cotton. That is why they said, "Cotton is King."

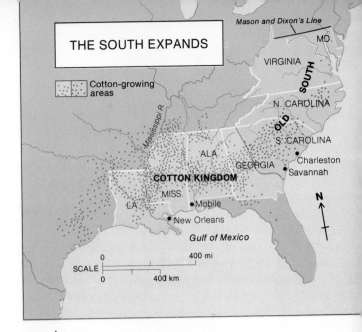

THE SOUTH EXPANDS

Cotton-growing areas

Mason and Dixon's Line
MD.
VIRGINIA
SOUTH
N. CAROLINA
OLD
S. CAROLINA
Mississippi R.
ALA.
GEORGIA
Charleston
Savannah
COTTON KINGDOM
MISS.
LA.
Mobile
New Orleans
Gulf of Mexico
N
SCALE
0   400 mi
0   400 km

MAP STUDY   See Teacher's Key.
(a) What states were part of the Old South?
(b) Name the states that were part of the Cotton Kingdom.

▶ **CHECK UP**   See Teacher's Key.

1. **(a)** Why did the South grow much more cotton after the invention of the cotton gin? **(b)** What changes in ways of farming resulted?
2. **(a)** Why did the cotton planters need more land? **(b)** Where did they find it? **(c)** What three southern states had been added to the Union by 1819?
3. What was meant by the saying "Cotton is King"?

2 How Did the People of the South Live in the Years Before 1860?

Plantation owners were the leaders of the South. As the South devoted itself more and more to the raising of cotton, a small group of planters became rich and powerful. Cotton could be grown most profitably on large plantations worked by slaves. (This system of growing one crop on large tracts of land with slave labor is called the **plantation system.**) But slaves cost money. In the 1850's the price of a field hand — a slave who worked in the fields — was from $1,200 to $2,000.

By 1860, only about one white family out of four in the South owned slaves. In fact, out of a white population of over 6 million, fewer than 10,000 people owned 50 or more slaves. These owners of many slaves and large plantations made the greatest profits and controlled most of the wealth of the South. The plantation families were the leaders of their neighborhoods and of the South

as a whole. Plantation owners also spoke for the South in Congress.

How were the plantations managed? All cotton plantations were managed in much the same way. At the end of the short southern winter the land was plowed — and the cotton was planted. Through the long summer the plants had to be carefully tended day by day, to keep out weeds and to prevent damage by insects. In early autumn the cotton was ready to pick. Then into the fields would go the pickers, with long bags slung over their shoulders. Bending low in back-breaking labor, the men, women, and children would pluck the cotton from the plants and push it into the bags. Prizes were often given to the fastest pickers.

A typical plantation covered hundreds of acres and required the work of fifty to a hundred slaves. Each morning the field hands gathered at a central

319

New Orleans became a leading port for the Cotton Kingdom. Here river steamers unload cotton bales for shipment to textile mills in New England and Great Britain.

place. The owner or overseer directed them where to go and what to do that day. After the orders were given, the slaves scattered to their places of work. All day long, through the seasons of plowing and planting and harvesting, the field hands labored under the eye of the owner or the overseer.

When at last the cotton was picked, it was taken to the cotton gin. The larger plantations had their own cotton gins, worked in the early days by horses or water power, and later by steam. The gins removed the seeds from the fiber. The clean cotton then was packed into big bales, five or six feet long and two or three feet wide. If the plantation was located on a river, the bales were piled on a wharf ready to be loaded on steamboats. From other plantations the bales were hauled in wagons to the riverbank.

The bales were shipped down the rivers to ports such as Mobile in Alabama and New Orleans in Louisiana.

From there they were shipped to the factories of the Northeast or to Great Britain. The machines in these factories made the cotton into yarn and the yarn into cloth.

What was the life of the plantation family? The plantation owner's family usually lived in a large, comfortable house surrounded by spreading trees and graveled walks. Many of these houses had tall porches with roofs supported by huge white pillars. The porches not only shaded the houses from the intense summer sun but also gave them a grand appearance. Inside the houses were large rooms with high ceilings and tall windows.

The owner supervised the affairs of the plantation. He or she taught and directed the slaves in their work and gave instructions to the overseer if one was employed. Plantation owners included both men and women, though most were men. The owner's wife not only directed the house servants and managed the affairs of the home, but gave the slaves what medical care they received. Sons of the owner took little part in running the plantation until they had finished college. Daughters

320

● See p. T32 for a strategy that asks students to put together a bulletin board display featuring cotton cultivation and products today.

learned from their mothers how to supervise the work of the plantation household.

How did the slaves live? All the hard work on the plantation was done by the slaves. The field hands worked from early in the morning until nightfall. The more fortunate of the slaves were house servants. On a large plantation each member of the owner's family had his or her own slave as a personal servant. A few slaves worked as carpenters and blacksmiths or took care of the horses. The great majority, however, were field hands.

The homes of the slaves were located not far from the owner's house. The slaves lived in log cabins, chinked with mud. The cabins generally contained only a single room, often without windows. At one end was a big fireplace which furnished heat in cold or rainy weather, and over which the slave fami-

ly's food was cooked. The furniture was rough and there was little of it. The slaves' food was simple. It consisted largely of pork, corn meal, and molasses, provided each week by the plantation owner, and perhaps some vegetables grown by the slaves in their own garden plots. A few pieces of cheap clothing made on the plantation were expected to last the slaves a whole year.

The people held in slavery lived a hard life. The laws governing their behavior, often called **slave codes,** were ● strict. Slaves could not leave the plantation, for instance, or travel in groups, or hold meetings. It was illegal to teach an enslaved person to read, though small numbers of blacks managed to learn anyway.

Some plantation owners treated their slaves kindly. But many were cruel, whipping the slaves if they misbehaved or ran away. The greatest fear of slaves, however, was not that they would be beaten but that they and their families would be sold. When members of a family were sold to different owners, they usually never saw one another again.

The owners of large cotton, rice, and sugar plantations built splendid homes. White columns gave a plantation house the stately look of a Greek temple and also provided a shady porch.

Many slaves rebel. Because of their lack of freedom, the slaves were not willing workers. They showed this in various ways. Most slaves simply did not work any harder than they had to, or they stole food or clothes from their owners. Sometimes the burdens of slave life became too great to bear. Many slaves who reached the point of despair tried to run away. At other times desperate slaves would rise in rebellion.

One of the bloodiest of these revolts was led by Nat Turner in Virginia. Turner had taught himself to read and write. He came to believe that he had a divine mission to slay white people. In 1831 Turner collected a band of slaves, and together they killed 57 white people before being captured by state and federal troops. More than a hundred blacks — many of them innocent of any connection with the uprising — were killed during the panic that spread among the white people. Other major slave uprisings in the early 1800's were led by Gabriel Prosser in Virginia and Denmark Vesey in South Carolina.

One successful revolt took place on board a ship. In 1841 over a hundred slaves were being carried from Virginia to Louisiana on a slave-trading ship called the *Creole*. Led by a black named Madison Washington, the slaves seized control of the ship and sailed it to a port in the British West Indies. The United States demanded that the slaves be returned, but they never were.

Probably as many as two hundred slave uprisings took place during the years that slavery existed in this country. Few of them won freedom for any of the slaves, but they showed that blacks did not humbly accept their enslavement.

Some Southerners live in cities. In the North the growth of manufacturing had attracted many people from rural areas and from Europe to the cities. But cotton producing was far more important to the South than manufacturing. For that reason, cities in the South tended to be smaller than those in the North. Of the ten biggest cities in the country in 1860, only two — Baltimore

Some blacks tried to escape slavery. They hoped to find safety in the North or in Canada. But if they were caught, they faced severe punishment.

322

Students will read about the underground railroad in Chapter 19.

Most white Southerners lived on small farms and worked their own land. Proud and hardworking, they raised such crops as corn, wheat, and potatoes for food.

and New Orleans — were located in the South.

In the southern cities and towns there were white doctors, lawyers, merchants and skilled workers. There were also many free blacks. By 1860 some 260,000 free blacks lived in the South. Most had moved to cities in search of greater opportunities. In the cities they could own property, hold jobs, and keep their wages. A handful became successful in business. But for most free blacks life was hard. They could not vote or get an education. And they were not allowed to compete for jobs on an equal basis with white workers.

The small farmers are the largest group in the South. The people who lived on plantations or in cities made up only part of the southern population. The largest group in the South was made up of white people who owned and worked small farms. These farms were located in the less fertile areas of the South, often on land that was being cleared or that had been abandoned by the big planters. Some farming was also

done by people known as mountain whites. They were descendants of sturdy pioneers who had pushed their way through the forests to settle in the valleys of the Appalachian Mountains.

In contrast to the plantation owners, the small farmers had to work with their own hands for a living. Their homes were small and simply furnished. Some owned a slave or two, but on most small farms the work was done by the members of the family. Besides cotton, they raised food crops, especially corn. The year's crop of cotton on each farm amounted to only a few bales. But if the small farmers worked hard and were lucky enough to have good crops for a season or two, they might make enough money to buy more land. They hoped that someday they too might own broad cotton fields and numerous slaves.

▶ **CHECK UP**   See Teacher's Key.

1. **(a)** What was the plantation system? **(b)** Why were the plantation owners the leaders in the South?
2. **(a)** How did the plantation slaves live? **(b)** How did slave codes affect the lives of the slaves?
3. How did the small farmers of the South live?

323

● See p. T32 for a strategy that asks students to compare the ways in which plantation owners, slaves, and small farmers lived.

3 How Did Different Ways of Living Tend to Divide the North and South?

When the United States became independent near the end of the 1700's, there were some differences between the North and the South. These differences, however, were not very great. At that time, in both the North and South most people made their living by farming. There were few cities, and the South had about as many towns and cities as the North. Not much manufacturing was carried on in either North or South.

Different ways of living and thinking develop. As the years rolled by, the differences between the North and the South became steadily greater. In the North more and more attention was paid to manufacturing, trade, and business. More cities grew up in the North. Most of the nation's railroads were built there too. But the South, as we have just seen, continued to be chiefly a land of farms and plantations. Cotton became king, and the growing and selling of cotton was the most important way of making a living in the South.

People whose lives are different often think differently as well. They are likely to see things in different ways. If ● a tariff law was to be passed, for instance, a Northerner might say: "This tariff will keep out foreign goods and help me sell my goods at a higher price." But a Southerner might say: "This tariff won't help me get better prices for the cotton and other crops I sell. Instead, it will just raise the prices of tools, clothes, and other things I buy from England."

The northern states free their slaves. Another difference between the North and the South was their thinking about slavery. When black people had first come to the colonies, they had been bought by white settlers in the North as well as in the South. As time went on, the slave labor system seemed to work better on plantations than on small farms or in factories. And most farms in the North were small. Therefore, the northern states found it easy to give up slavery.

One by one, in the years after the Revolutionary War, the northern states passed laws to end slavery, and black people in those states won their freedom. These blacks were known as freedmen and freedwomen. By the early part of the 1800's, slavery had disappeared from all the states north of Maryland. (In colonial times the boundary between Pennsylvania and Maryland had been surveyed by two men named Mason and Dixon. This line, called Mason and Dixon's Line, came to be the boundary between slave and free states.)

In the 1700's some Southerners question slavery. In colonial times and for some time after, many white Southerners did not favor slavery, even though they used slave labor. Slaves were expensive to own. They had to be fed and clothed, even in years when crops sold for low prices. Some white Southerners also questioned whether it was right for any human being to own another. George Washington hoped the day would come when slavery would no longer exist. He made arrangements to have his own slaves freed at the time of ★ his death. Men like Patrick Henry and Thomas Jefferson had doubts about slavery, since it did not agree with ideas of freedom expressed in the Declaration of Independence.

If slavery was wrong or not always profitable, why was it not given up in

★ Tell students that the act of freeing a slave is called *emancipation.*

One of the worst fears of slaves was that their families would be broken up. At slave auctions family members could be sold to different buyers. Here a family waits to be sold at a slave market.

the South? For one thing, freeing slaves would have been very expensive for their owners. To set the slaves free, said the owners, would be giving up property that was very valuable. And what would happen to the blacks once they were freed? Most had little education or training to help them earn a living on their own. Freedom would raise many problems for them as well as for the white people.

The cotton gin establishes slavery firmly in the South. Eli Whitney's invention of the cotton gin in 1793 did much to discourage the thought of ending slavery in the South. Cotton raising became profitable, and most Southerners believed that large quantities of cotton could not be grown without the work of slaves. As more and more land

was given over to cotton, the demand for slaves increased. By 1840, there were many more slaves in the South than before the invention of the cotton gin. Yet the price of the average slave had more than doubled. In short, the more important the cotton crops and plantations became to white Southerners, the more important slavery became to them also. No longer did southern whites talk about slavery as an evil which in time might disappear.

White Southerners defend slavery. Many people in the South were upset by the words and acts of Northerners who criticized slavery. These Northerners believed it was wrong for any person to own another human being. The most outspoken of them wanted slavery **abolished,** or ended, at once. Later chapters will tell more about the **abolitionists,** as they were called.

The more slavery was attacked by the abolitionists, the more vigorously white Southerners defended it. Southerners especially resented criticism from

325

● See p. T33 for a strategy that asks students to examine southern defenses of slavery before 1860.

people who lived in a different part of the country.

●   Some white southern leaders wrote books and made speeches claiming that slavery was a good thing. They declared that the Bible mentioned slavery and that it was perfectly natural for one human being to own another. John C. Calhoun, one of the best-known statesmen of the South, said there had "never yet existed a wealthy and civilized society in which one portion of the community did not in fact live on the labor of the other." Southern church leaders had once doubted whether slavery ought to continue. As cotton became even more important, however, and as abolitionists criticized the South, south-

ern churches began to defend slavery. Some church organizations which had members both in the North and the South broke into separate branches.

A few white Southerners even argued that slavery was a benefit to black people. They claimed that the slaves were better off on a well-run plantation than in Africa, and that the slaves were happier than many of the white workers in northern factories. They pointed out that the northern factories closed down when there was no work. The factory workers were then out of a job and had no wages. "At least," said Southerners, "the slaves are fed and clothed. And they have no worries about losing their jobs." Little attention was given to the views of black people on these questions.

How far apart would the North and South grow? The North and South, then, developed different ways of living.

Not all white Southerners supported slavery. At this meeting, held in Baltimore in 1845, blacks and whites discussed ways of ending slavery.

● See p. T33 for a strategy that asks students to identify differences between the North and South.

In the North there were more and more factories, trade increased, and cities grew in number and in size. Men and women who came from Europe to make new homes in America preferred to settle in the North where they did not have to compete with slave labor. In the South, cotton was king. White Southerners raised and sold cotton and used their money to buy tools and more land and more slaves. Enslaved blacks had no choice about how they lived. And cotton became the chief export of the United States.

These differences in ways of living influenced the viewpoints of Northerners and Southerners toward slavery. Many Northerners who made their living in business and commerce came to believe that slavery was wrong. White Southerners whose interest was in managing and enlarging cotton plantations came to believe that the slave system was justified. They argued that slaves were better off than northern factory workers who had to work under unhealthy conditions and for very low wages. But Northerners could answer

that factory workers were free to change jobs whenever they chose.

As time went on, differences between these two sections of the country became greater and greater. And as the North and South grew further apart, the argument over slavery became more dangerous and threatening. One Southerner declared that "rather than yield our dearest rights and privileges" — meaning slavery — "we should see the Union scattered to the winds." Would it come to this? Would the cotton-growing South and the industrialized North become so different that they could no longer remain parts of the same country?

▶ **CHECK UP**   See Teacher's Key.

1. Why was slavery ended in northern states?
2. **(a)** How did white Southerners feel about slavery before 1793? Why? **(b)** After 1793? Why?
3. **(a)** On what grounds did abolitionists object to slavery? **(b)** How did white Southerners defend slavery?

CHECK UP ON CHAPTER 15   See Teacher's Key.

Words to Know

1. patent
2. overseer
3. field hand
4. cotton gin

5. abolish
6. abolitionist
7. plantation system
8. slave codes

Places to Locate

1. Alabama
2. Louisiana
3. Mississippi

4. Mobile
5. New Orleans
6. Gulf of Mexico

Facts to Remember

1. **(a)** Why was cotton not an especially profitable crop for southern plantation owners before Eli Whitney invented the cotton gin? **(b)** How did his invention make it worthwhile for planters to grow cotton?
2. **(a)** Explain the meaning of each of these terms: Old South, Lower South, Cotton Kingdom. **(b)** Name the states that were part of each of those regions.
3. **(a)** What was the plantation system? **(b)** Describe a typical plantation — its size, location, the methods of farming, and the kind of people who lived on it.
4. **(a)** What kinds of work did slaves do? **(b)** How were their lives restricted? **(c)** In what ways did they show their feelings about their lack of freedom?
5. How were the lives of southern whites who had to small farms different from the lives of the big plantation owners?

327

★ Discuss what is meant by the statement that "the argument over slavery became more dangerous and threatening."

Skills to Practice

1. Reread Eli Whitney's letter (pages 315–316). **(a)** How did Whitney explain the meaning of the words *ginning cotton*? **(b)** What kind of power did he plan to use to run his machine? **(c)** How did he compare the amount of work that could be done by 50 men *without* his machine and by one man and a horse *with* his machine?
2. Look again at the bar graph on page 317. **(a)** What kind of information does the graph provide? **(b)** In your own words compare the information given for the years 1830 and 1840.
3. Study the picture of the cotton gin on page 316. **(a)** What part of the machine actually separates the seeds from the cotton fibers? **(b)** What use is later made of the seeds? **(c)** Why does the machine have brushes?

Questions to Think About

1. Why did plantation owners buy slaves instead of hiring free workers to grow their cotton?
2. **(a)** Why was slavery not profitable in the North? **(b)** How was that connected with the passage of laws ending slavery in the northern states?
3. Some historians have said that dependence on cotton planting and on slave labor hurt the South and slowed its development. Explain what they mean.
4. Between 1789 and 1850 the North and South seemed to grow more and more different in ways of living and doing things and in ways of thinking. Why?

Linking Past and Present

Cotton today. Cotton growing is no longer the chief occupation in the South, although it is still an important crop. Besides cotton, rice, sugar, and tobacco, which have long been grown in the South, farmers now also grow a large variety of fruits and vegetables and raise cattle as well. Industries such as mining, lumbering, textile manufacturing, and steelmaking have made the South an important industrial region. A good many years ago, cotton growing moved west into Arkansas, Texas, Arizona, and California. Texas and California, in fact, are now the largest cotton-growing states in the nation. Of the old cotton states, only Mississippi is still among the top five cotton-producing states.

A mechanical cotton picker. As you have read, the invention of the cotton gin in 1793 had important results in the development of the South. The cotton gin, by greatly speeding up the process of separating the seed from the fiber, brought about a tremendous increase in cotton growing. In more recent years, another machine has speeded cotton harvesting. This is the mechanical cotton picker. Picking cotton by hand is a slow, exhausting, back-straining job. A person who can pick a bale of cotton in a week is rated as a "good picker," but mechanical pickers can pick 20 or more bales in a day, thus reducing both hard labor and expenses. Almost all the cotton that is grown in the United States today is picked by machine.

Lott Cary. The state of Virginia holds a unique national landmark — the birthplace of a former slave, Lott Cary. The house is found in Central City, a small town not far from the state capital of Richmond.

Lott Cary's life was one of hard work and achievement. Born a slave in 1789, he taught himself to read and write, using the New Testament as a textbook. Hired to work in a tobacco warehouse, he eventually saved enough money to buy freedom for himself and his children. Cary became a Baptist minister, and in 1821 went as a missionary to Liberia, a colony established in Africa for freed slaves. He became a leading figure in Liberia, and was named governor of the colony shortly before his death.

● Have students find Liberia on the world map at the back of the book.

Tell students that during the 1850's the United States produced seven-eighths of the world's cotton supply. Ask students to construct a circle graph showing this information.

GAINING SKILL

Reading Circle Graphs

Population figures show that about 9,685,000 people lived in the southern states in 1850. Of those people, 6,242,000 were white and 3,443,000 were black. Most southern blacks were slaves, but about 238,000 were free.

If you wanted to show these population figures in another way, you could use a circle graph. A circle graph shows how a whole is divided into parts. The different parts of a circle graph can then be compared to see which is the largest, which is the next largest, and so on.

As with all graphs, it is important to read the title on a circle graph to be sure you interpret the information correctly. For example, the graph below shows the population of the South in 1850. If it showed the population of the entire country, the circle would be divided differently. The sections for the black population would be smaller because blacks made up a smaller

share of the national population than they did of the southern population.

Now look below at the second circle graph. Use that graph to answer the following questions.

1. What does the whole circle stand for?
2. Notice that the figures printed on the graph stand for *percentages* and are not the actual number of slaveowners. **(a)** What percentage of slaveholders owned 50 or more slaves? **(b)** What percentage owned from 1 to 9 slaves? **(c)** What percentage owned fewer than 50 slaves?
3. Which was the largest group of slaveholders, according to the graph?
4. By 1860, about one southern white family in four owned slaves. On a separate sheet of paper, draw a circle graph to show that information. Be sure to give your graph a title.

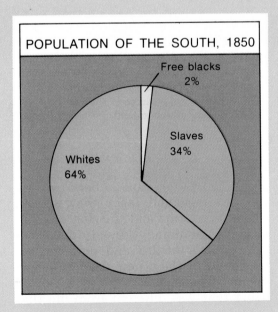

POPULATION OF THE SOUTH, 1850

Free blacks 2%

Slaves 34%

Whites 64%

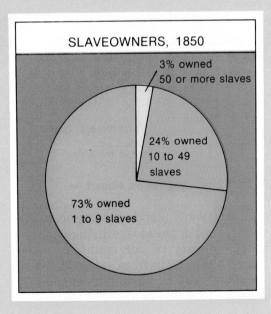

SLAVEOWNERS, 1850

3% owned 50 or more slaves

24% owned 10 to 49 slaves

73% owned 1 to 9 slaves

COURTESY TIME-LIFE BOOKS INC.

CHAPTER **16** *Vocabulary preview:* survey, territory, secondary source

Pioneers Push the Frontier Westward

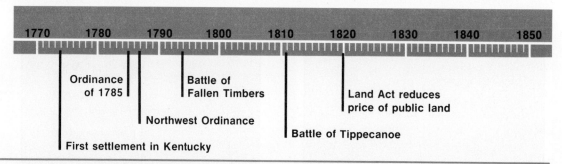

1770–1850 See p. T34 for chapter teaching strategies.

| 1770 | 1780 | 1790 | 1800 | 1810 | 1820 | 1830 | 1840 | 1850 |

Ordinance of 1785

Battle of Fallen Timbers

Land Act reduces price of public land

Northwest Ordinance

Battle of Tippecanoe

First settlement in Kentucky

What this chapter is about —

The westward march of American pioneers is one of the most stirring chapters in the history of our country. Many Americans set out from safe and settled communities in covered wagons in search of a new life in the West. These people left us a valuable heritage. By their courage and labor they started productive farms and thriving communities. In so doing, they also added to the nation's wealth and power. Furthermore, in these new frontier settlements, Americans developed a way of living that was different from life that

330

● Tell students that in this context, *game* means wild animals used for food.

◀ In the late 1700's thousands of pioneers left the settled areas of the original thirteen states and moved into frontier regions west of the Appalachians.

existed in other parts of the country at the time.

We learned in Chapter 5 about the first pioneers who moved west of the Atlantic seaboard. In this chapter we will see how pioneers pushed still far-ther west and started homes in the regions beyond the Appalachian Mountains. As you read, keep in mind the following questions:

1. How did the westward march of pioneers begin?
2. What plan was worked out for governing new territories?
3. How did the West grow in the first half century of the new republic?
4. How did conditions in the West encourage a democratic way of life?

1 How Did the Westward March of Pioneers Begin?

What was the West? Before beginning our story of the westward movement, we need to understand clearly what is meant by "the West." Today, as you know, Americans use different terms to mean different parts of the West. For example, we speak of the Far West (the Pacific coast), the Mountain West (the Rocky Mountain region), and the Southwest (Arizona, New Mexico, and Texas). In 1800, however, people referred only to "the West." They used this term to describe any frontier region or territory that lay between the well-established settlements and the areas where white people had not yet settled. As pioneers moved steadily westward, the frontier moved westward also.

Different groups of pioneers push back the frontier. First to feel the call of the West were the Indian traders or "long hunters." They usually traveled alone into the Indian lands, armed with hunting knives and long rifles (from which probably came the term long hunter). They lived in the open and
● killed game for food. The long hunters were as skilled as the Indians in the ways of the woods. They hunted for furs and traded goods with the Indians for more furs. In the spring they returned to settled areas with their packs of furs. The most famous of these long hunters was Daniel Boone, who spent many years pushing his way into regions little known to white settlers.

After the long hunter came the backwoods settlers. These settlers, like ★ the long hunters, were mostly unmarried men who lived by themselves. The typical backwoodsman built a shelter or a rough log cabin in the forest. He began to cut down trees and to plant crops between tree stumps. But he was only a part-time farmer. The rest of his time he spent hunting or trading with Indians.

Sometimes this backwoodsman sold his land and moved even farther west to begin all over again. Sometimes he stayed and slowly changed his way of living. Either way, the pioneer farmers replaced the backwoodsmen. These farmers, many of whom were married couples starting a new life together, cut down more trees. They put up fences and built houses and barns. They plowed more and more land and planted more crops. As their neighbors did the same thing, the wild animals began to

331

★ See p. T34 for a strategy that asks students to learn how backwoods settlers, long hunters, and pioneer farmers lived.

● See p. T34 for a strategy calling for students to make a map showing the Old Southwest and the Northwest Territory.

disappear, and less trapping and hunting were done in the area they settled. The farmers and their neighbors built a school and a church. A sawmill was set up to cut boards from logs; a gristmill was built to grind the farmers' grain. Soon a storekeeper started a shop nearby. Before long, a village had grown up. In a few years the region was well settled. It was no longer considered "the West." That term now applied to frontier areas still farther west.

The West moves with the frontier. This same process was repeated over and over again as our country expanded. In the early 1600's, any place a few miles back from the Atlantic coast was frontier and would have been called "the West." As pioneers moved inland along the rivers, the West moved also. In the years just before the Revolution, pioneers had begun to make their way through the gaps in the Appalachian Mountains. In the late 1700's, the Ohio River Valley was the West. In the early 1800's, the Mississippi River Valley became the West. Still later the West was the Pacific coast. So, you see, the term "West" was applied to different areas at different periods of our nation's history. In this chapter you will learn how the region between the Appalachian Mountains and the Mississippi River was settled and how it grew.

Americans begin the settlement of the Old Southwest. Even before the Revolutionary War, restless pioneers had begun to push through the Appalachian Mountains to the fertile lands beyond. Most of these pioneers came from Virginia and North Carolina. They settled in what became known as the Old Southwest. This region was south of the Ohio River, between the Appalachian Mountains and the Mississippi River. Look at the map on page 335. You will see that rivers like the Cumberland and the Tennessee rise in the Appalachian Mountains and flow west and north into the Ohio. It was chiefly along these rivers that pioneers first made their way into the valleys west of the Appalachian Mountains.

Settlements are made in Tennessee and Kentucky. The earliest settlement in the Old Southwest was made in what is now eastern Tennessee. Several years before the Revolution (1769), a group of pioneers crossed the mountains from North Carolina. They settled on the Watauga (wah-TAW-guh) River, which flows into the Tennessee River. Soon they were joined by a young Scotch-Irishman named James Robertson, who

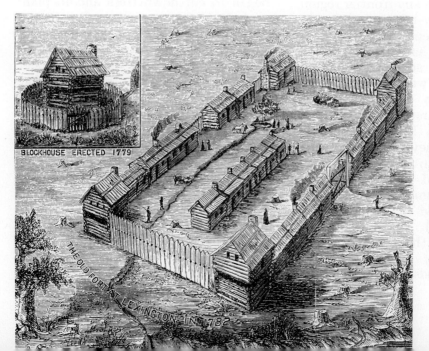

BLOCKHOUSE ERECTED 1779

THE OLD FORT AT LEXINGTON IN 1782

To protect their settlements, the pioneers built stockades or forts. This picture shows the fort at Lexington, Kentucky. In the close-up view, you see the fort's blockhouse, a two-story cabin from which watch could be kept.

332

became a leader of the Watauga settlement. In a few years there were other settlements on nearby rivers. In 1779, James Robertson led a few pioneers into middle Tennessee. They started a town on the Cumberland River and called it Nashville.

The first settlement to be made in what is now Kentucky was the town of Harrodsburg. In 1774 a group of settlers led by James Harrod started this town. ● But Daniel Boone, the famous hunter and scout, was chiefly responsible for opening the way into the bluegrass country of Kentucky. He blazed or marked a trail through the mountains by way of Cumberland Gap and along the Kentucky River. In 1775 he led a band of pioneers over this Wilderness Road to a site on the Kentucky River.

The town they started there was named Boonesborough. A third town, started as the Revolutionary War began, was named Lexington, in honor of the first battle of the war. By the end of the Revolution, the settlements of Harrodsburg, Boonesborough, and Lexington had all become important towns in Kentucky.

▶ **CHECK UP**   See Teacher's Key.

1. What three kinds of pioneers were important in settling the West?
2. **(a)** Where was "the West" in the early 1600's? **(b)** In the late 1700's? **(c)** In the early 1800's?
3. Where and how were early settlements made in Tennessee and Kentucky?

2 What Plan Was Worked Out for Governing New Territories?

The early westward trickle of brave pioneers grew into a steady flow after the Revolutionary War. Times were hard in the East, and adventurous Americans were attracted to the fertile lands beyond the Appalachians.

The spread of western settlements brings problems. As the frontier settlements grew, governing them became a difficult matter. The problem first arose in the Old Southwest, much of which was claimed by Virginia and North Carolina. Long distances and poor traveling conditions made it hard for these two states to govern the regions beyond the mountains. Besides, the frontier settlers showed a spirit of independence. They were not content to remain forever under the control of older ★ eastern states. They wanted to set up governments of their own.

As you read in Chapter 11, the Articles of Confederation were not adopted until the states with western lands agreed to give up their land claims to the central government. The first land to be turned over to the national government lay north of the Ohio River, a region known as the Old Northwest. Thousands of people in the East wanted to settle in the Old Northwest. But they were unwilling to go until they knew how much, if anything, they would have to pay for land. Also, they wanted to know what kind of government they might have there. Congress answered these questions by passing two important laws.

Congress arranges for surveying lands in the Northwest. To start with, the lands of the Northwest needed to be surveyed. (To **survey** means to measure land to determine its exact boundaries.) New settlers naturally would want to know the exact boundaries of their land, and records of the bounda-

333

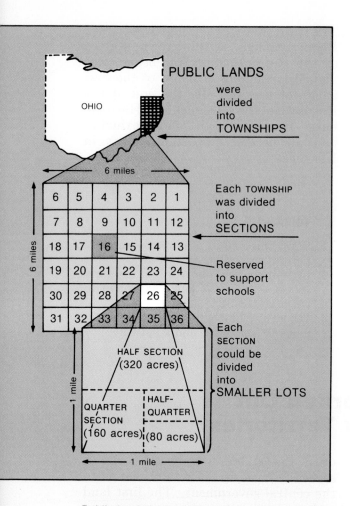

PUBLIC LANDS were divided into TOWNSHIPS

OHIO

6 miles

6 miles

6	5	4	3	2	1
7	8	9	10	11	12
18	17	16	15	14	13
19	20	21	22	23	24
30	29	28	27	26	25
31	32	33	34	35	36

Each TOWNSHIP was divided into SECTIONS

Reserved to support schools

Each SECTION could be divided into SMALLER LOTS

1 mile

HALF SECTION (320 acres)

QUARTER SECTION (160 acres)

HALF-QUARTER (80 acres)

1 mile

Public lands in the new territories were divided in three stages as shown by this diagram. What were those three stages? What was the smallest lot a settler could buy?

to rent or sell to help pay for public schools. (See the diagram on this page.)

The Ordinance of 1785 provides for the sale of land. Laying out townships was only part of the land problem in the Northwest. Should the land be sold or given free to the people who settled it? Congress needed money badly. Under the Ordinance of 1785, Congress decided that the land should be sold at auction *by sections* to the highest bidder. (A section, you remember, contained 640 acres.) The least that would be paid for the land was one dollar an acre.

Although this price seems very low today, dollars were hard to earn in those days. Few people could get together enough money to buy a section of land at $640. The result was that land companies were formed by investors in the East. They bought up the land in the Northwest and offered free transportation to pioneers who would settle there. The land companies planned to divide the land into smaller lots, which could then be sold to settlers at a good profit.

The Northwest Territory is organized. An even more important step was taken by the Congress of the Confederation in 1787. In that year Congress passed a famous law called the Northwest Ordinance. This law set up a ● plan of government for the Northwest Territory, the new name given to the Old Northwest. The word **territory,** as used here, means land that had not yet been made into states.

The Northwest Ordinance provided for three steps which had to be taken before the people of the territory could have self-government.

(1) As long as the number of settlers in the Northwest remained small, its affairs were to be managed by a governor and three judges chosen by Congress.

(2) When the number of adult free men in the territory reached 5,000, they could elect an assembly. (Women did not yet have the vote in any part of the

ries would have to be kept by the government. The system set up by Congress in the Ordinance of 1785 may be familiar to those of you who live in states carved out of the Old Northwest or in states west of the Mississippi. The land was divided into squares six miles across, called townships. Each township was divided into 36 sections, each of which was one square mile in area. Each section contained 640 acres, which could be divided into quarter sections of 160 acres each or into even smaller plots. The sixteenth section of each township was to be given to the people

334

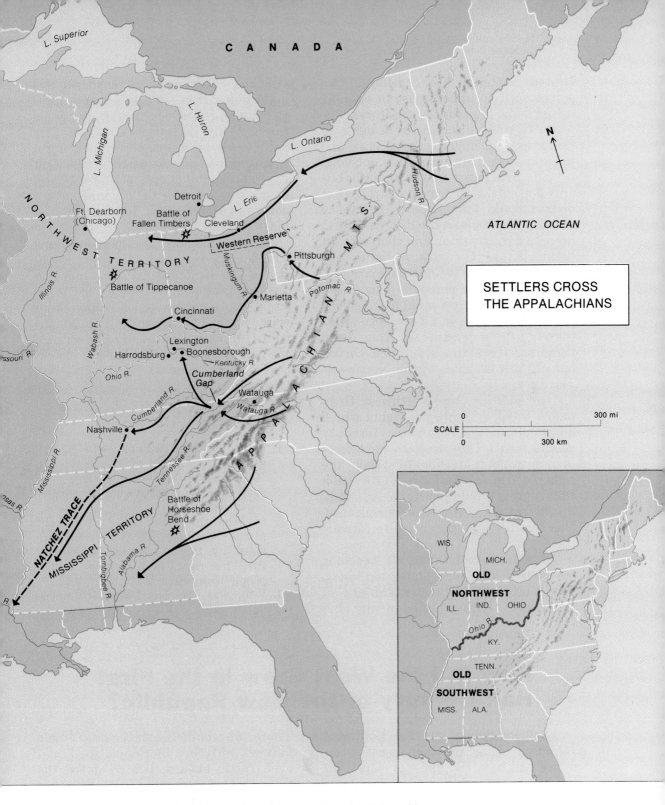

CANADA

L. Superior

L. Huron

L. Michigan

L. Ontario

L. Erie

Hudson R.

ATLANTIC OCEAN

N

NORTHWEST TERRITORY

Detroit

Ft. Dearborn
(Chicago)

Battle of
Fallen Timbers

Cleveland

Western Reserve

Pittsburgh

Battle of Tippecanoe

Marietta

Muskingum R.

Potomac R.

APPALACHIAN MTS.

Illinois R.

Cincinnati

Wabash R.

Lexington

Missouri R.

Harrodsburg

Boonesborough

Kentucky R.

Ohio R.

Cumberland
Gap

Watauga

Cumberland R.

Watauga R.

Nashville

Tennessee R.

NATCHEZ TRACE

MISSISSIPPI TERRITORY

Mississippi R.

Battle of
Horseshoe
Bend

Tombigbee R.

Alabama R.

**SETTLERS CROSS
THE APPALACHIANS**

SCALE

0   300 mi

0   300 km

WIS.

MICH.

**OLD
NORTHWEST**

ILL.   IND.   OHIO

Ohio R.

KY.

TENN.

**OLD
SOUTHWEST**

MISS.   ALA.

MAP STUDY   The arrows in this map show the general routes followed by
the pioneers who moved west. In the battles shown here, United States
forces defeated Indians. (a) What was the dividing line between the Old
Northwest and the Old Southwest? (b) What settlements shown here were in
the Old Northwest? (c) In the Old Southwest?

335

See Teacher's Key.

United States.) This assembly, together with an upper house or council, would make laws for the territory. The territory could also have a delegate in Congress who might suggest laws and make speeches, but who could not vote.

(3) Whenever 60,000 free inhabitants had settled in a given district, that district could take steps to become a state. The people of the district had to prepare a constitution and then request permission of Congress to enter the Union as a state. If Congress approved, the district would enter the Union as a full-fledged state "on equal footing with the original states in all respects whatsoever." It was expected that from
● three to five states would be carved out of the vast lands of the Northwest Territory.

In addition, the Northwest Ordinance listed a number of rights which all people in the Northwest Territory should have. They were to have freedom of worship, freedom of speech, the right to trial by jury, and protection from unreasonable punishments. Public education was to be encouraged. The Northwest Ordinance also forbade
★ slavery in the Northwest Territory.

The Northwest Ordinance becomes the pattern for United States territories. The Northwest Ordinance was one of the wisest laws ever passed by any government. This new law gave settlers important rights. It also set up a form of government which would change as the needs of the settlers changed. The law arranged a simple government for a small group of pioneer settlements. And it promised the people of those settlements that in time they would have a government on equal terms with the older states.

The Northwest Ordinance became a model of government for other territories of the United States. As pioneers opened up new land farther west, territorial governments of the same kind were set up by Congress. The Northwest Ordinance did much to encourage the American dream of liberty and self-government.

▶ **CHECK UP**   See Teacher's Key.

1. **(a)** How did the Ordinance of 1785 provide for the division of land in the Old Northwest? **(b)** How was the land to be sold? **(c)** Why were land companies organized?
2. **(a)** What three steps in the government of the Northwest Territory were provided by the Northwest Ordinance? **(b)** What rights were promised to the people living there?
3. Why was the Northwest Ordinance important?

3 How Did the West Grow in the First Half Century of the New Republic?

Settlers throng into the Northwest Territory. After the Northwest Ordinance had been adopted, pioneers hungry for land flocked by the hundreds into the Northwest Territory. Many of them took the old road that Braddock had cut through western Pennsylvania (page 144). They traveled by horseback or in slow wagon trains to Pittsburgh. There they built big flatboats. Whole families, with their household goods and even cattle aboard, floated down the Ohio. When they came to a place that looked like a good spot to settle, they ran their clumsy rafts ashore.

Towns grow up in the Northwest Territory. In April, 1788, forty-seven settlers floated down the Ohio in a flatboat they

★ Mention that this no-slavery provision made the Ohio River the dividing line between states without slaves and states with slaves.

Soldiers of the United States Army built Fort Dearborn in 1803. By the 1830's the city of Chicago had grown up around it.

had named the *Mayflower*. They stopped where the Muskingum River joins the Ohio and started Marietta, the first town in the Northwest Territory. (See the map on page 335.) These settlers had been sent out by the Ohio Land Company. One of the first things they did was to build a stockade for protection. Other settlers followed, and it was not long before a group of log cabins clustered about the stockade. Within two years Marietta was a village with churches and schools and a population of a thousand.

This story was repeated in other parts of the Northwest Territory. A few months after Marietta was settled, Cincinnati was started farther down the Ohio. By 1790, the town boasted 1,300 inhabitants. Six years later, Moses Cleaveland started the city on Lake Erie that bears his name.[1] In 1803, United States troops built Fort Dearborn on Lake Michigan, where the great city of Chicago now stands.

[1]The name of the city is now spelled Cleveland. Nobody knows for certain just how or why the first "a" was dropped out. One story is that a newspaper owner left it out to shorten the name at the top of his paper.

Indians and pioneers clash in the Northwest. Life was a struggle for the pioneers of the Northwest as they faced such hardships as backbreaking work, freezing winters, and lack of ordinary comforts. But there was an even more serious problem. As we know, there were already many people living in this region. They were the Indians, who called the forests and prairies of the Northwest home. Their way of life was totally different from that of the pioneers. As the pioneers moved into the Northwest and began to claim land, trouble was sure to break out.

Indian leaders had signed treaties by which they were supposed to turn over large tracts of land to the United States government. But the very idea of selling or giving away land was strange to the Indians. They believed that land belonged to all people, not just to one group. Furthermore, they felt that their leaders had often been cheated by the whites. The Indians deeply resented the presence of the pioneers, who drove away the wild animals on which the Indians depended for food. The pioneers in turn resented and feared the Indians.

337

See p. T34 for a strategy calling for students to present oral reports on western settlement during the early 1800's.

At times Indian leaders and United States Army officers met to discuss ways of settling conflicts over land. Such meetings rarely solved the differences between the two sides, and fighting often broke out.

The power of the Indians is broken. When George Washington became President, fighting was already going on between Indians and white settlers in the Northwest. Washington sent two expeditions against the Indians, both of which were defeated. Finally he ordered General Anthony Wayne, a hero of the Revolutionary War, into action. With well-trained troops and friendly Indian guides, Wayne marched into northwest Ohio. On August 20, 1794, Wayne and his men defeated a force of about 2,000 Shawnee, Ottawa, and Chippewa on a field covered with fallen trees. With all hope of holding onto their lands crushed after this Battle of Fallen Timbers, the Indians agreed to sign new treaties.

Wayne's victory brought an uneasy peace for a few years. Before long, however, fighting began again. A Shawnee leader named Tecumseh tried to persuade all the tribes west of the Appalachians to join together to resist the expansion of white settlement. In November, 1811, while Tecumseh was seeking allies among the southern Indians, Governor William Henry Harrison of Indiana Territory moved against the Shawnee. Harrison defeated the Indians in a skirmish near the Tippecanoe River and burned down their village. Two years later, during the War of 1812, Tecumseh was killed. His death put an end to Indian efforts to make a unified stand against white settlement.

New states add stars to the flag of the United States. Soon after George Washington had become President, new states began to come into the Union. The fourteenth state to add its star to

338

● Refer students to p. 276 where they first read about Tecumseh.

the flag was Vermont. Though people today do not think of Vermont as "western," at the time of the Revolution it was part of the frontier. Vermont had set up its own state government at the beginning of the Revolution but it was not officially recognized by Congress until 1791.

Parts of the Old Southwest petitioned for statehood soon afterward. Kentucky became a state in 1792, and Tennessee followed in 1796. The rest of the Old Southwest was later organized into the Mississippi Territory. This was the region settled by southern cotton planters (page 318). Soon there were enough people in the Mississippi Territory to form two states. Mississippi entered the Union in 1817 and Alabama in 1819.

In the Northwest, after the Indian treaties had been signed, the population of the Ohio region grew so fast that in 1803 Ohio became a state. Indiana and Illinois followed in 1816 and 1818. Michigan entered the Union in 1837. When Wisconsin became a state in 1848, five states filled the Northwest Territory. As we will see in later chapters, several other states (Louisiana, Maine, Missouri, Arkansas, Florida, Texas, Iowa, and California) joined the Union in the first half of the 1800's. In little more than half a century the young nation had grown to include 31 states.

The Shawnee chief Tecumseh tried to persuade the Indians west of the Appalachians to unite in defense of their lands. His forces were defeated in 1811 at the Battle of Tippecanoe.

CHECK UP   See Teacher's Key.

1. What towns grew up in the Northwest Territory?
2. **(a)** What was the basic cause of the trouble between settlers and Indians in the Northwest? **(b)** Why was General Wayne sent to the Northwest? **(c)** How did Tecumseh's death affect the Indians of the Northwest?
3. **(a)** What states were made from the Old Southwest? **(b)** From the Old Northwest?

4 How Did Conditions in the West Encourage a Democratic Way of Life?

In the frontier days of the late 1700's and early 1800's, life in the West was very different from life in the older settlements of the East and South.

The pioneer is a new type of American. If we could actually have known some of the people who went west, we would clearly see how Westerners were different from Southerners or Easterners. Let us visit a typical cluster of frontier cabins somewhere along the lower Ohio River soon after 1800. In these frontier cabins live three young pioneer couples.

339

● Have students construct a time line that shows when these states were admitted to the Union.

Before these three couples moved west, their ways of living had been very different. Back home, Robert and Priscilla Adams belonged to wealthy and respected New England families, which from colonial days had made a good living from shipbuilding and trade. John Wagner and his wife Kate had only recently arrived in the United States from Europe. Thomas and Margaret MacKenzie came from the back country of Virginia, where they had made a scanty living by thrift and hard work.

If the three couples had ever met in the East, they probably would not have become friends. But here in the lands beyond the mountains all three faced the same problems and dangers. After staking out their farms, they cleared the land of trees and built homes. They planted and harvested their crops. Because they had been able to bring along only a few household articles by flatboat or wagon, these pioneers depended on their own skill to make most of the things they needed in the home or on the farm. When tasks required the labor of more than one person, neighbor helped neighbor.

It is not surprising that in the new West the Adamses, Wagners, and MacKenzies became close friends. Along the frontier, neighbors never asked, "Who are your parents?" or "How much money do you have?" What counted in the new settlements were strength and bravery, the ability to stand hardship, and the willingness to help one's neighbors.

A pioneer describes life on the frontier. A good way to get a true understanding of the qualities of the frontier people is to read what they themselves said about their life. The description that follows was written by a pioneer in Ohio. This is what he said:

I can hardly realize how greatly things have changed since that period, and what a primitive and simple kind of life prevailed. . . . Houses and barns were built of logs, and were raised by the collection of many neighbors together on one day. . . .

This kind of mutual help of the neighbors was extended to many kinds of work, such as rolling up the logs in a clearing, grubbing out the underbrush, splitting rails, cutting logs for a house, and the like. When a gathering of men for such a purpose took place, there was commonly some sort of mutual job laid out for the women, such as quilting, sewing, or spinning up a lot of thread for some poor neighbor. This would bring together a mixed party and it was usually arranged that after supper there should be a dance or at least plays which would occupy a good part of the night and wind up with the young fellows seeing the girls home in the short hours or, if they went home early, sitting with them by the fire in that kind of interesting chat known as sparking.

PIONEER NEIGHBORS BUILDING LOG HOUSE

● Have students find out more about the tasks described in this passage (for example, raising houses, quilting, and spinning).

Settlers enjoyed getting together at frontier post offices whenever mail arrived. Here, settlers meet at the Tranquility, Tennessee, post office.

An Englishwoman who published a book in 1832 describing her travels through the United States has given us still another account of pioneer life. In the following passage she describes the life of an Ohio pioneer woman:

The house was built of logs, and consisted of two rooms, besides a little shanty or lean-to, that was used as a kitchen. Both rooms were comfortably furnished with good beds, drawers, etc. The farmer's wife, and a young woman who looked like her sister, were spinning, and three little children were playing about. The woman told me that they spun and wove all the cotton and woolen garments of the family, and knit all the stockings; her husband, though not a shoemaker by trade, made all the shoes. She manufactured all the soap and candles they used, and pre-

pared her sugar from the sugar-trees on their farm.

A spirit of equality develops on the ● **frontier.** The simple, rough life of the frontier helped pioneers to develop ideas different from those found in older and more settled parts of the country. First of all, frontier folk believed that every person was as good as the next and should have as good a chance to succeed. Everybody on the frontier had the same kind of house, ate the same kind of food, wore the same kind of clothes, did the same kind of work, and faced the same dangers. It has been said that democracy means, not "I am as good as you are," but "You are as good as I am." That is the way the Westerners felt.

The feeling of equality bred by frontier living caused Westerners to have a firm faith in democratic government. They believed that all white men should share the right to vote and the right to hold government office. It is true that at the time few people thought

341

● See p. T34 for a strategy that asks students to list factors contributing to the development of equality on the frontier.

Not long after moving to the new territories, frontier settlers chose representatives to make local laws. This picture shows a meeting of delegates at Boonesborough in 1775.

of extending those rights to women, blacks, or Indians. But, as we will see, this growing belief in the right of people to vote and hold office began to spread to other parts of the country.

The Westerner develops other qualities. Besides their strong democratic feeling, people on the frontier were usually optimistic. In other words, they looked on the bright side of things. Everywhere they saw signs of the great progress they and their friends had made in starting new lives. They saw that unlimited opportunities lay ahead for those who were willing to work. This made them hopeful, energetic, and cheerful. On the other hand, they were inclined to be loud and boastful about themselves and the West. To the Easterner, the settler from the West seemed rough and ignorant, lacking in manners and education.

The West works for its own interests in Congress. As new states were organized beyond the Appalachian Mountains, the West was able to send its own

representatives to Congress in Washington. These representatives asked Congress to help meet the needs of the West. First, they wanted cheaper land. As you know, western settlers had to pay the government or the land companies for the land they settled on. In 1820 a land law was passed by Congress which partly satisfied the western demand for cheap land. Under the new law a person could buy 80 acres (or one eighth of a section) at $1.25 an acre, or $100 in all. Before this law, a settler had to buy a whole section, which cost at least $640. After 1820, any man who could get together $100 could own a good-sized farm. A woman could buy land if she was a widow or could prove she was the head of a family.

Secondly, western congressmen asked for better transportation. Good transportation was very important to Westerners because they had to get their products to market in order to make a living. But canals and roads were expensive. The western states believed that the national government should share the cost with them. Time and again they asked for aid. In 1811 the national government financed the construction of the National Road,

● Refer to the transportation maps in Chapter 14 (pp. 303, 305, and 310). Ask: What sections of the country benefited most from these networks? (Northeast and West.)

which ran west from Maryland (page 303). After the success of the Erie Canal, several western states also received help in building canals to connect rivers with the Mississippi River and with the Great Lakes.

During the early 1800's, the representatives of the frontier states spoke boldly in Congress about what the Westerners wanted. As a result, congressmen from the East and the South realized that the West had become a new and important section of the United States with interests of its own.

▶ **CHECK UP**   See Teacher's Key.

1. **(a)** What problems and dangers did Westerners face? **(b)** What qualities did Westerners develop?
2. **(a)** What two things did western representatives in Congress ask the government to do for the West? **(b)** How successful were they?

CHECK UP ON CHAPTER 16

See Teacher's Key.

Words to Know

1. ordinance
2. democratic
3. optimistic
4. township
5. section
6. long hunter
7. territory (U.S.)
8. survey

Places to Locate

1. Cleveland
2. Chicago
3. Pittsburgh
4. Ohio River
5. Marietta
6. Cincinnati
7. Tennessee
8. Kentucky
9. Nashville
10. Northwest Territory
11. Tennessee River
12. Cumberland River
13. Muskingum River
14. Watauga River
15. Kentucky River
16. Lexington, Ky.
17. Cumberland Gap
18. Harrodsburg
19. Boonesborough
20. Mississippi Territory

Facts to Remember

1. Describe how each of the following kinds of pioneers lived on the frontier: **(a)** long hunters, **(b)** backwoods settlers, **(c)** pioneer farmers.
2. **(a)** Where was the region called the Old Southwest? **(b)** What part did Daniel Boone play in the settling of that region by white pioneers?
3. **(a)** Where was the region called the Old Northwest? **(b)** What two laws were passed by Congress to help make the development of that region orderly?
4. **(a)** How did Indian people living in the Northwest Territory feel about the arrival of white pioneers? **(b)** What opposing forces fought the Battle of Fallen Timbers? **(c)** What was the result? **(d)** Why was Tecumseh an important Indian leader?
5. What kinds of laws did the representatives of western states try to get passed in Congress? Tell why in each case.

Skills to Practice

1. Use the map on page 335 to complete these statements:
   a. Many people who settled in Mississippi and Alabama followed a trail called the ____?____.
   b. Three towns settled by pioneers in Kentucky were ____?____, ____?____, and ____?____.
   c. The ____?____ River was the dividing line between the Old Northwest and Old Southwest.
   d. States made out of the Old Northwest were ____?____, ____?____, ____?____, ____?____, and ____?____.
   e. States made out of the Old Southwest were ____?____, ____?____, ____?____, and ____?____.
2. Look at the diagram on page 334 showing the division of western lands. Use it to answer these questions: **(a)** How many sections were there in a township? **(b)** How many acres were there in a full section? **(c)** Why is Section 16 shown in a special way?

343

Questions to Think About

1. Do "frontier" conditions exist anywhere in the United States today? Explain.
2. (a) What is the American "West" today? (b) Why has this term not always meant the same thing or applied to the same region?
3. What evidence is there that legislation dealing with the Northwest Territory did not grant women the same rights as men?

 # Linking Past and Present

Boone country. Kentucky has many reminders of Daniel Boone — famous frontiersman, Indian fighter, explorer, and long hunter. The old Wilderness Road, over which he led settlers into Kentucky, still bears the same name but is now a modern highway. All that remains of the settlement at Boonesborough is an old graveyard; but a fort has been rebuilt on the site, along with a Boone museum. Boone Creek, Boone Hill, and Boone County in northern Kentucky remind us that this region was Daniel Boone's "stamping ground." An early settlement at Harrodsburg, which Boone helped to found, has been rebuilt and shows what a pioneer settlement was like. And in Frankfort, Kentucky, the graves of Daniel Boone and his wife, Rebecca, are marked by a tall stone monument.

● **Conestoga wagons and prairie schooners.** A familiar scene in a western movie or television program is the pioneer train of covered wagons lumbering across prairie or desert. One of the earliest types of covered wagon, the Conestoga (KON-ess-TOH-guh), took its name from a valley in southeastern Pennsylvania, not far from Philadelphia. This fertile valley was settled in colonial times by German farmers. To haul their crops to market, they built a special type of wagon with broad, heavy wheels, well-suited for travel over rough and hilly country. The wagon box was curved up at each end to keep the heavy loads from shifting on the hills. The wagon was covered with a large hood of tough homespun cloth to protect passengers and goods from sun, rain, and heat. Conestogas proved so practical that they came to be widely used in the days before the railroads. Thousands of pioneers moving west carried their possessions in Conestoga wagons.

The heavy Conestoga wagons used on eastern roads were not practical for travel west of the Mississippi River. The pioneers who crossed the western prairies and mountains learned to build lighter wagons that could be drawn by two or four horses or oxen. When these canvas-covered wagons rolled across the wide prairies, they reminded people of schooners on the ocean. For this reason they came to be called prairie schooners. A few of the prairie schooners have been preserved in museums . They are vivid reminders of the pioneer days of the West.

Western Reserve. Anyone living in northeastern Ohio knows that this part of the state is often called the Western Reserve. The story of that name takes us far back in American history. When Connecticut gave up its western lands to Congress in 1786, the state kept for itself a large piece of land on the shore of Lake Erie. Part of this Western Reserve, as it was called, was given to citizens of Connecticut who had lost property in the Revolution. Part was sold to a land company.

In 1800 the Western Reserve was added to the Northwest Territory, and in 1803 it became part of the new state of Ohio. Although the region was then divided into several counties, the old name held on. Located in that region today are the important cities of Cleveland, Akron, Sandusky, Ashtabula, and Youngstown. Case Western Reserve University in Cleveland also carries on the old name.

344

● Take students to the library to find out about Conestoga wagons, prairie schooners, and flatboats (p. 336). Have students draw pictures of each.

For answers see Teacher's Key.

Have students turn to the accounts on pp. 340–341.
Ask: Are the accounts primary or secondary sources?
(Primary.) Have students use both accounts to
summarize typical activities of pioneer families.

GAINING SKILL

Comparing Primary and Secondary Sources

If you were writing a history of the Northwest Territory, you would probably need to use primary sources to find your information. You might look at newspapers, town charters, letters written by settlers, or diaries. As you know, primary sources are actual records that have survived from the past.

Another way for you to find information would be to use **secondary sources.** A secondary source is an account of an event written at a later time by someone who was not an eyewitness. This textbook, for example, is a secondary source. The authors were not actually present at the events described in the book. Instead, they got their information from other writings, including both primary sources and secondary sources.

The two accounts on this page help to point out some of the differences between primary and secondary sources. Read them carefully and then answer the questions.

The Ohio Company sent out a small group of settlers in December, 1787, and in the spring of the next year they established the settlement of Marietta at the junction of the Ohio and Muskingum rivers. The Scioto Company brought a company of 600 Frenchmen to the area in 1790. . . . A third group, send out by New Jersey speculator John Cleves Symmes to settle a tract he had purchased from Congress, laid the foundations of Cincinnati in 1788. Eight years later, Moses Cleaveland led a band of pioneers to begin developing the Connecticut Land Company's holdings. . . . Here, on the Ohio lake front, the town of Cleveland was founded.

[Marietta, Ohio]
Thursday, [May] 29th [1788]. This day the axe is laid to the root of the trees. . . . Find the soil very good, but was tormented beyond measure by myriads [swarms] of gnats. They not only bite surprisingly, but get down one's throat. . . .

The Indians are frequently in here, and seem to be on friendly terms. I have shaken hands with many of them. My people [are] employed in clearing land. I have been, this afternoon, sowing garden seeds. . . .

Tuesday, [June] 10th. The people [are] hewing timber for the house, which I am in hopes to raise in eight or ten days. . . .

Thursday, 19th. All hands employed in planting corn and garden seeds. . . .

Friday, [July] 4th. All labor comes to a pause today in memory of the Declaration of Independence. . . .

Monday, 14th. All hands at work on the house. Eat green peas today from my own garden, planted exactly five weeks ago. . . . Things do grow amazingly!

1. Which of the two accounts is the secondary source?
2. Which of these accounts gives you a better picture of day-to-day life? Which gives you more general information about the settlement of Ohio?
3. Is the account of the Battle of Fallen Timbers (page 338) a primary or a secondary source?
4. Compare the primary source on this page with the pioneer's account on page 340. Which was written while events were taking place? Which was written from memory?

345

CHAPTER **17**

Vocabulary preview: spoils system, nullify, secede, secession, republic, democracy, reform, panic

The Nation Undergoes Change During the Jackson Years

1824–1860   See pp. T35–T36 for chapter teaching strategies.

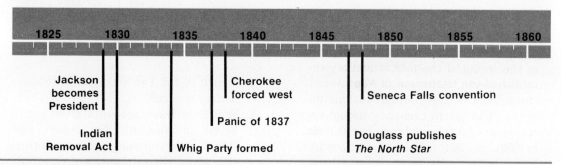

1825   1830   1835   1840   1845   1850   1855   1860

Jackson becomes President

Indian Removal Act

Whig Party formed

Cherokee forced west

Panic of 1837

Seneca Falls convention

Douglass publishes *The North Star*

What this chapter is about —

In the last three chapters you read about important changes in the Northeast, the South, and the new West. But what was taking place in the nation *as a whole,* from the late 1700's until the 1850's?

You already know that in its first years the young nation was placed on a firm foundation and won the respect of other countries. In this chapter you will find that during the first half of the 1800's more Americans had greater opportunities for "life, liberty, and the pursuit of happiness." Democratic

346

◀ In 1829 Andrew Jackson was inaugurated as President. He became the first person from a frontier state to hold that office.

ideas spread throughout the country. As the number of voters increased, more Americans took an interest in election campaigns. Americans also became more concerned with people who were less fortunate than themselves. Many Americans found better opportunities to get an education and to improve their lives.

A number of these changes began or gathered strength during the 1830's.

As a result, they have become linked with the name of Andrew Jackson, who was President at that time. In this chapter we will find answers to these questions:

1. Why did Americans celebrate Andrew Jackson's election as President?
2. What important steps did Jackson take as President?
3. How did more Americans win a larger share in the government?
4. How was the life of the American people improved?
5. What political parties sought to win the presidency?

1 Why did Americans Celebrate Andrew Jackson's Election as President?

As pioneers pushed back the frontier and more western states joined the Union, the democratic ideas of the Westerners influenced the other parts of the country. The man who best represented the rough-and-ready democracy of the frontier was Andrew Jackson of Tennessee. Jackson was the first man
● from a western state to be elected President of the United States. In this section you will read how that came about.

The North, South, and West become rivals. You have read in this unit that the three sections of our country were developing in very different ways. The North was interested in manufacturing and shipping. The South specialized in growing certain crops, particularly cotton, for export. The rapidly growing West wanted cheap land for settlement and good transportation for its products. The special interests of the North, South, and West were often in conflict, and for this reason the three sections became rivals. The members of Con-

gress were usually more concerned with the needs of their own sections than with the interests of the nation as a whole.

President John Quincy Adams spends four unhappy years in the White House. In the election of 1824, each section of the country hoped to elect a President who would favor its own interests. New England supported John Quincy Adams, son of John and Abigail Adams. This candidate had served as Secretary of State under President Monroe. The South supported William Crawford of Georgia. From the West came two "favorite sons," Henry Clay of ★ Kentucky and Andrew Jackson of Tennessee. When the votes were counted, no candidate had won a majority.

In such a case, the Constitution says that the House of Representatives shall choose a President from the three candidates who had won the most votes (Twelfth Amendment). Henry Clay, who had received the fewest votes of the

347

★ Have students look up the term *favorite son*. (A *favorite son* is a presidential candidate nominated by delegates from that person's home state.)

Crowds of enthusiastic supporters gathered at the White House to celebrate the inauguration of President Jackson.

four candidates, asked his supporters to vote for Adams. With this help, Adams was elected President by the House of Representatives.

John Quincy Adams was the only President in the history of our country whose father had also been President. The second President Adams was very capable, with a long record of government service. As Secretary of State under President Monroe, he had made important decisions which greatly affected our country's future. But Adams was a stern man who would not do anything that was against his principles, even if he became unpopular as a result. Congress quarreled with him and opposed him on many issues. His years as President were filled with trouble and disappointment.

Andrew Jackson becomes President. When the House of Representatives chose Adams as President in 1824, Andrew Jackson and his friends were angry. Jackson had received more popular votes than Adams in the regular election. The people who supported

Jackson claimed that he had been robbed of the presidency and that the will of the people had not been carried out. They set to work to make sure that Jackson would be elected the next time. They did their work so well, and President Adams was so unpopular, that Jackson won an easy victory over his rival in 1828.

On March 4, 1829, the city of Washington was filled with excitement. That was the day when Andrew Jackson was to take office. "A monstrous crowd is in the city," commented Senator Daniel Webster of Massachusetts. "I never saw anything like it before. Persons have come five hundred miles to see General Jackson, and they really seem to think that the country is rescued from some dreadful danger." A vast crowd of people watched Jackson take the oath of office on the steps of the Capitol. Afterwards, everyone tried to get close enough to shake the hand of the new President. At a reception in the White House, aristocrats and common folk, "statesmen and stable-boys, fine ladies and washerwomen, white people and black" thronged the house and grounds.

Jackson is the people's idol. What was the reason for the excitement?

348

See p. T35 for a strategy that asks students to write reports about the elections of 1824 and 1828.

● See p. T35 for a strategy calling for students to examine the reasons for Jackson's popularity.

Andrew Jackson was a popular hero, not only in the West but in other parts of the country too. Like many Americans, he had a humble background. Like them he had faced danger, hardship, and poverty. Jackson had been born to Scotch-Irish parents on the Carolina frontier. When he was fourteen years old, he had been taken prisoner by British soldiers during the Revolution. To his dying day he bore the scar of a sword cut received when he refused to shine the boots of a British officer.

When he was a young man, Jackson moved to Tennessee. Although he had little schooling, he practiced law and became a judge in frontier communities. After Tennessee became a state, he was elected to serve as its representative in Congress.

Jackson's Indian campaigns made him a popular hero. In March, 1814, he defeated the Creeks at the Battle of Horseshoe Bend in Alabama (map, page 335), crushing Indian resistance in the Old Southwest. His victory over the British at New Orleans in 1815 (page 280) added to his fame.

Jackson appealed to many people ● not only because of what he had done but also because of the kind of man he was. Bold and courageous, Jackson was a man of action and of strong feelings. As a boy he would never admit he was beaten; as a young man he had fought several duels. Moreover, he never hesitated to stand up for what he thought was right. Jackson had a fiery temper, which was easily aroused against those he thought were his enemies. His quick temper and lack of schooling sometimes led him to make mistakes. But he was honest and hard-working. He was as loyal to his friends as he was bitter toward his enemies. And as President, he was determined to serve well the nation he loved.

▶ **CHECK UP**   See Teacher's Key.

1. **(a)** How did the North, South, and West become rivals? **(b)** What part did this rivalry play in the election of 1824?
2. **(a)** Why was Andrew Jackson a popular hero? **(b)** Why was he able to defeat John Quincy Adams in 1828?

2 What Important Steps Did Jackson Take as President?

★   **Jackson believed in presidential authority.** Andrew Jackson was a born leader who felt it his duty to carry out the will of the people who had elected him. Jackson, therefore, was not slow to tell Congress and the Supreme Court that he, the President, knew what was best for the country. Some of his actions caused bitter feelings, but on the whole he served the nation well.

Jackson extends the spoils system. Soon after Jackson became President, he fired a large number of government officials, mostly postmasters. Many of these officials had held their jobs for years and had expected to hold them for the rest of their lives. But Jackson wanted to appoint people of his own party to take the places of the fired officials. Many of the people who got these jobs had worked hard for Jackson's election. When candidates who are elected to office reward their supporters in this way, they are using what is called the **spoils system.** This name comes from the old saying, "To the victor belong the spoils." (A *victor* is someone who wins, and the word *spoils* means "rewards.")

349

★ See p. T35 for a strategy that asks students to compare several concepts of presidential authority.

● See p. T35 for a strategy calling for students to examine Calhoun's proposals and Jackson's reaction to the nullification crisis.

What the Different Sections Wanted

Westerner: "Fine! That makes land easier to buy, but we need money to develop the West and the eastern bankers don't like to lend it to us. The federal government should help us build roads and bridges."

Northerner: "Well, we don't want *all* our money used to build up the West. By the way, there'll be no slavery in the West, will there? We want no more slave states."

Some earlier Presidents had given government jobs to their supporters, but Jackson was the first President to use the spoils system widely. This was not a good practice. Officials chosen chiefly for their support of a person or a party, rather than for ability, may do poor work.

South Carolina protests against the high tariff. Soon after Jackson became President, a quarrel started over the tariff. You read in Chapter 14 that manufacturers in the Northeast kept demanding higher tariffs in order to get better prices for their manufactured products. But the people of the South manufactured very little. They were mostly farmers and had to buy many manufactured products. So Southerners opposed tariff laws that raised the prices of these products. Nevertheless, tariff laws were passed in 1816, 1824, and 1828.

When the people of South Carolina heard about the tariff of 1828, their state legislature wrote a statement protesting against Congress's passing of the law. This statement was largely the

work of John C. Calhoun. Calhoun was a famous South Carolinian who at that time was Vice-President of the United States. In his protest Calhoun declared ● that, under the Constitution, Congress had no power to pass tariff laws which favored one section or group over another. When Congress went beyond its specific powers to pass a law, said Calhoun, it was the right of any state to **nullify** (NULL-uh-fy) that law (to declare that the law was not in force). The idea that a state could refuse to obey a law of Congress was called nullification.

South Carolina threatens nullification. Calhoun's protest showed how ★ deeply South Carolina felt about the tariff. South Carolina did nothing more, however, until a new protective tariff law was proposed in 1832. Southern members of Congress fought this measure but failed to defeat it. The law was passed. South Carolina now decided to act. A special meeting of delegates was called by the South Carolina legislature, and they nullified the tariff laws of 1828 and 1832. The delegates

★ Point out that Calhoun resigned his vice-presidency as a result of this controversy.

Southerner: "Wait a minute! You can open up the West *if* we can move there with our slaves. But build the roads yourself. We don't want the federal government to get too strong!"

also warned against any steps being taken to force the state to accept the hated tariff laws. If that were done, South Carolina would **secede,** or withdraw, from the United States.

Andrew Jackson's hot temper boiled over when he learned what South Carolina had done. Above everything else he loved the United States. He had fought under its flag; he had sworn to enforce its laws. "If one drop of blood be shed [in South Carolina] in defiance of the laws of the United States," he said, "I will hang the first man of them I can get my hands on to the first tree I can find."

A compromise tariff ends the nullification threat. In a proclamation Jackson used milder language, but he was no less firm. "To say that any state may at pleasure secede from the Union," he wrote, "is to say that the United States is not a nation." Jackson declared that he would enforce the tariff laws, and he called on the people of South Carolina to aid him. Meanwhile, he prepared to send an army to South Carolina to enforce the law.

Fortunately, Henry Clay of Kentucky suggested a compromise tariff. ● Clay's bill provided that the tariff would be gradually lowered over a period of ten years. Congress passed the bill in 1833, and South Carolina withdrew its nullification. Both sides felt they had won a victory: South Carolina, because the tariff had been lowered, and President Jackson, because he had put an end to the threat of secession (suh-SESH-un). (**Secession** is the withdrawal of a state from the Union.) The affair showed, however, that the South would fight to protect its interests. And although Jackson had won his point, the question of secession was to come up again in later years.

Jackson puts an end to the second United States Bank. Meanwhile, President Jackson began an attack on the Bank of the United States. The first Bank of the United States had been started as part of the plans of Alexander Hamilton (page 260). It had been followed by the second Bank of the United States in 1816. By the time Jackson entered the White House, the bank had become wealthy and powerful. For this very reason Jackson distrusted it. He believed that the people who ran such a powerful bank could influence government officials to pass laws friendly to it. He felt it was undemocratic to put such power in the hands of a few wealthy persons. Jackson decided to put an end to the bank.

The second bank had been given a charter to run until 1836. At that time, if the bank were prevented from getting a new charter, it could be put out of business. But in 1832 — four years before the old charter was up — the friends of the bank persuaded Congress to pass a bill giving the bank a new charter. They thought that President Jackson would not dare to take action just before an election. This trick failed. Jackson vetoed the bill by refusing to sign it.

351

Osceola led the Seminole Indians in the fight to keep their Florida homeland (page 354).

When Jackson was triumphantly re-elected in 1832, he felt that the people had shown their approval of his attack on the bank. He was more determined than ever to destroy it. Under Jackson's orders, the Secretary of the Treasury withdrew all the government money deposited in the bank and placed it in certain state banks. These state banks were nicknamed "pet banks." When its charter ran out in 1836, the second Bank of the United States went out of existence. Thus Andrew Jackson was successful in his fight against the bank, just as he had been successful in the quarrel over nullification.

President Jackson supports a harsh Indian policy. Another step taken during Jackson's presidency had tragic results for the eastern Indians. For years, land-hungry white settlers had looked with envy at Indian lands east of the Mississippi. They argued that those lands should be opened to white settlement and that the Indians should be moved to lands in the west. Then, they reasoned, clashes between Indians and white settlers could be avoided, for the land west of the Mississippi would belong to the Indians forever. At that time few people thought that white settlers would ever want to live on the western plains.

Many treaties were signed in the 1820's with Indian tribes. Under those treaties the Indians were paid to give up their lands and move west. Then, in 1830, Congress passed the Indian Removal Law. That law authorized the President to move the eastern tribes to lands west of the Mississippi — by force if need be. Jackson was a strong supporter of Indian removal, believing that both the Indians and white settlers would benefit if the two groups were separated.

● Have students look at the map (p. 354) to see what groups of Indians were moved.

People in America's Story

Tell students that Rachel Jackson died shortly before Andrew Jackson became President. Mrs. Jackson's niece, Emily Donelson, served as hostess of the White House.

ANDREW JACKSON

Our seventh President, Andrew Jackson was a forceful leader who was determined to strengthen the unity of the growing nation.

The first President born in a log cabin, Andrew Jackson's election demonstrated the growing power of new states on the frontier. Crowds greeted Jackson (above) as he traveled to Washington for his inauguration.

This portrait of Rachel, Andrew Jackson's wife, hangs in the Hermitage, the Jackson family home in Tennessee.

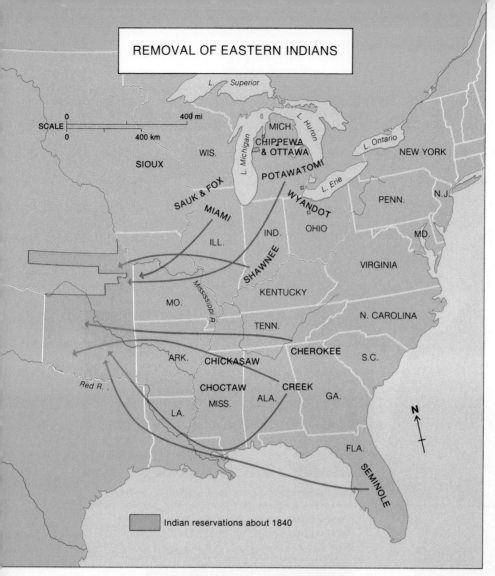

REMOVAL OF EASTERN INDIANS

SCALE

0   400 mi

0   400 km

L. Superior

MICH.

CHIPPEWA & OTTAWA

L. Michigan

L. Huron

L. Ontario

NEW YORK

WIS.

SIOUX

POTAWATOMI

WYANDOT

L. Erie

PENN.

N.J.

SAUK & FOX

MIAMI

IND.

OHIO

MD.

ILL.

SHAWNEE

VIRGINIA

MO.

MISSISSIPPI R.

KENTUCKY

TENN.

N. CAROLINA

ARK.

CHICKASAW

CHEROKEE

S.C.

Red R.

CHOCTAW

MISS.

ALA.

CREEK

GA.

LA.

N

FLA.

SEMINOLE

Indian reservations about 1840

See Teacher's Key.

MAP STUDY
(a) What Indian peoples were forced to move out of southern states? (b) What Indians had to leave the Great Lakes region?

By the mid-1830's the Choctaw, Chickasaw, and Creeks had all moved peacefully, though unhappily, to lands assigned them in the West (map, this page). But other Indians decided to fight. The Sauk and Fox were Indians who lived in Illinois and Wisconsin. In the early 1800's most of the Sauk and Fox people voluntarily gave up their lands to the United States and moved across the Mississippi River. In 1832, however, a Sauk chief named Black Hawk led his people in an attempt to regain their homeland in Illinois. Soldiers of the United States Army and the Illinois militia quickly defeated the Sauk and Fox in what was called the Black Hawk War. The Seminole Indi-

ans, who also fought removal, were able to hold out longer. Led by the courageous Osceola (os-ee-OH-la), the Seminole fought a seven-year war (1835–1842) in Florida before most of them were forced west.

Instead of fighting, the Cherokee Indians of Georgia took their case to the Supreme Court. Living on rich farmland, the Cherokee had adopted many of the ways of white settlers. They had set up a government under their own constitution and had their own newspaper and their own written language, invented by one of their people named Sequoya (sih-QUOY-ah). The Cherokee had tried to get along with their white neighbors, and in 1815 many

354

● See p. T35 for a strategy that asks students to examine the extension of voting rights in the mid-1800's.

Cherokee had fought under Andrew Jackson at the Battle of New Orleans (page 280). But Jackson was determined to force all the Indians west. Even when the Supreme Court ruled in favor of the Cherokee, both he and the Georgia state government continued to put pressure on them to leave Georgia. Finally, in 1838, federal troops rounded up 15,000 Cherokee men, women, and children and forced them to leave their homeland. During the long march west, thousands of people died of disease and starvation. So many people died that the route the Cherokee followed was called the "trail of tears."

▶ **CHECK UP**   See Teacher's Key.

1. **(a)** What was the spoils system? **(b)** Why did President Jackson make use of it?
2. **(a)** Why did the North favor a high tariff? **(b)** Why did the South oppose it?
3. **(a)** What were Calhoun's ideas about nullification? **(b)** What did South Carolina do in protest against the tariff law of 1832? **(c)** How was the tariff quarrel settled?
4. **(a)** Why did Jackson oppose the United States Bank? **(b)** How did he put an end to it?
5. What was Jackson's policy toward the Indians?

3   How Did More Americans Win a Larger Share in the Government?

By the middle of the 1800's the people of the United States had gained a larger share in the government of their republic than they had ever had before. How did this come about?

**Requirements for voting, become ●
more democratic.** First of all, an important change took place in the laws that stated who should have the right to vote. Not every adult was allowed to

---

Republic and Democracy

Perhaps you have heard our government sometimes called a **republic,** sometimes a **democracy.** Neither name appears in the Constitution, but today the United States is both. In a republic supreme power is in the hands of the people who vote. The voters control the government through the representatives and officials they elect. A democracy is a government in which the great majority of the people can vote for candidates of their choice.

Today a number of countries that are ruled by Communists *call* themselves republics or democracies but actually are not. Whether these governments are headed by a single dictator or a small group of powerful leaders, they and not the people make decisions. To call these countries "republics" or "democracies" is to ignore the true meaning of these words.

The United States is a true republic because it is governed by elected officials. It is also a true democracy because the great majority of adult citizens have the right to vote.

★

★ See p. T35 for a strategy that asks students to consider contributions they can make as citizens.

vote in the thirteen original states. Blacks and Indians could not vote, nor could women (except in New Jersey for a few years). Only white men who owned property could vote. (Since land was cheap and easily obtained in our country's early days, this voting requirement was not too difficult for white men to meet.) In frontier communities, however, a spirit of democracy was growing. So, when the first three new states were created — Vermont, Kentucky, and Tennessee — their voting requirements were more democratic. Vermont and Kentucky gave the right to vote to all free white men over 21 years of age. Although Tennessee did not go so far, it allowed more freedom in voting than did the older states of the East.

Later, as other states were formed in the West, they followed the example of Vermont and Kentucky and let all free white men vote. Gradually the older states dropped their property requirements for voting. By 1860, all free white men could vote in all the states. Free black men living in the North, however, still did not have the same rights and opportunities as white men. By 1860, only five states (all the New England states except Connecticut) allowed free black men to vote. And women still could not vote in any state.

Elections become more democratic. Meanwhile, there were changes going on that allowed the voters more control of the government. For example, laws were changed so that certain government officials, formerly appointed, now

As more people gained the right to vote, Election Day became an exciting time. People filled the streets, eager to hear news of election results.

were elected directly by the voters. The method of choosing a President also became more democratic. In early days the members of Congress belonging to each political party nominated the various candidates for President. By 1840, however, presidential candidates were selected by party conventions, as they are today. The conventions were made up of delegates chosen by the voters. Thus, voters had a greater share in deciding which men should run for President. The voters also were allowed to ● elect the presidential electors, who, according to the Constitution, choose the President.

Although changes such as these began soon after the nation was founded, they were hastened by the election of Andrew Jackson as President. Throughout his years in office, Jackson worked hard to give voters a greater share in the government.

▶ **CHECK UP**   See Teacher's Key.

1. **(a)** How had voting requirements changed by 1860? **(b)** What people still could not vote?
2. How did the methods of choosing presidential candidates and electing the President become more democratic?

4   How Was the Life of the American People Improved?

REFORMERS SEEK TO IMPROVE CONDITIONS

It is important in a free nation like ours that people have the right to vote and hold public office. But many Americans, during and after Jackson's administration, were concerned about more than political rights. They thought that people should also have the chance to live useful, happy lives. At this time, more Americans had the opportunity to read, and there were more books, magazines, and newspapers to make them think. They read and thought about many things, but in particular they thought about the statement in the Declaration of Independence about "life, liberty, and the pursuit of happiness" (page 191). Looking around them, they saw their rich, young country with unlimited opportunities for many citizens. Yet they also saw unfortunate people whose lives were full of hardship, obstacles, and unhappiness.

Reformers work to change conditions. A number of men and women decided that something should be done to make life better. When they found conditions that they thought were wrong or unfair, they tried to change or **reform** the situation. These people, called reformers, wrote books and articles telling what they thought was wrong. They held meetings and people came to hear what they had to say. They wrote new laws that were supposed to improve conditions, and they tried to get the laws passed. What were some of the conditions that reformers wanted to change?

Reformers try to abolish slavery. ★ One problem that reformers in the North wanted to do something about was slavery. They argued that it was wrong for one person to own another and they insisted that slavery be abolished. As you read in Chapter 15, these people were called abolitionists.

One of the leading abolitionists was a young New Englander named William Lloyd Garrison. He went to Baltimore, Maryland, to help manage an abolitionist newspaper. He worked hard trying

357

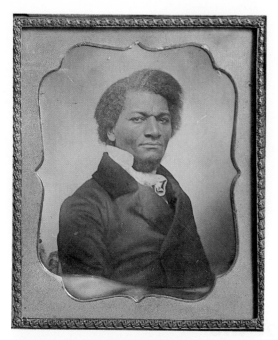

Frederick Douglass, an escaped slave, became one of the nation's best-known abolitionist leaders.

to convince people that slavery was wrong. The newspaper failed, but in the last issue Garrison wrote, "My pen cannot remain idle, nor my voice be suppressed, nor my heart cease to bleed, while two million of my fellow-beings wear the shackles of slavery. . . . "

Garrison returned to Massachusetts, and on January 1, 1831, he published a new newspaper, *The Liberator*. In one issue he declared: "I am in earnest — I will not equivocate — I will not excuse — I will not retreat a single inch — *and I will be heard*." Garrison's fiery words against slavery stirred up bitter feeling in the North as well as the South. But he continued to fight slavery — through his paper, through his friends, and through speeches and meetings.

Two other abolitionist leaders in the 1830's were Sarah and Angelina
● Grimké (GRIM-kay). Their antislavery speeches attracted much attention, especially because the Grimké sisters came from a southern family that owned slaves.

Free blacks work for abolition. Black leaders were among the most effective abolitionists. Many blacks who joined the antislavery cause were slaves who had escaped and made their way to freedom in the North. Frederick Douglass, who had been born a slave in Maryland, was one of these black leaders. When he was eleven years old, he escaped and headed for New York. Douglass became a noted speaker and writer for antislavery groups and published a newspaper called *The North Star*. He continued to work for black rights during and after the Civil War and also supported other reforms, such as voting rights for women. In his later life he served as the United States' representative in Haiti.

William Wells Brown was another black who escaped from slavery and became a famous writer and lecturer. Both Douglass and Brown traveled to England to seek foreign support for the antislavery movement.

Many black women also became abolitionists. Sojourner (SOH-jern-er) Truth was one of the most inspiring speakers at antislavery meetings. Six feet tall, she was an impressive figure. She and Harriet Tubman (page 413) were the best-known of the black women who devoted themselves to the cause of freedom.

Some black abolitionists had never been slaves. One was James Forten, a wealthy Philadelphia manufacturer. Forten had served in the American navy during the Revolutionary War and later made a fortune manufacturing sails. He contributed much money to abolitionist activities and was especially generous to William Lloyd Garrison.

These were only a few of the blacks who were active in the antislavery crusade. As a result of their efforts and those of white people like Garrison and the Grimké sisters, a strong antislavery group was active in the North. The movement against slavery had begun simply as one of many reforms. Before long, however, it stirred up stronger feeling than any other reform movement.

Reformers become interested in criminals. In the early 1800's, people who had committed even minor crimes were sent to prison, where they were cruelly treated. Little effort was made to help them become better citizens and lead useful lives when their prison terms were over. Conditions in the prisons themselves were often very bad. Little effort was made to keep the jails clean, and the prisoners did not receive proper food, medical care, or exercise. Young people who had made only a single mistake were put in the same cells with experienced criminals. Many people came out of prison worse than they had been before they went in.

Sojourner Truth won her freedom in 1827 when New York abolished slavery. She spoke against slavery at many abolitionist meetings.

A number of people became interested in the treatment of prisoners. Chief among them was a Massachusetts woman named Dorothea Dix, who spoke and wrote unceasingly about prison conditions. As a result of her efforts, punishment of prisoners became less brutal. The work begun by Dorothea Dix has continued to this day.

The mentally ill are helped. Dorothea Dix was also determined to improve the conditions under which the mentally ill lived. In those days mental illness was looked upon as a disgrace and the mentally ill were harshly treated. They were usually locked up in institutions and sometimes were even chained to walls. They were poorly fed and received no medical care. Their keepers made fun of them and treated them cruelly.

Dorothea Dix did much to change the treatment of the mentally ill. She traveled across the country, speaking to audiences about the problem. As a result of her efforts, associations were formed to study better methods of treating mental illness, and hospitals were built for the treatment of people suffering from this disability.

Opportunities for the disabled are expanded. Samuel G. Howe was another person who became interested in helping disabled people. He especially wanted to help educate and train blind people, so that they could earn their livings and lead independent lives. In the 1830's Howe raised money to begin this work. He started the Perkins Institute for the Blind in Boston, where thousands of blind people have been taught useful skills. Since that time other organizations have also aided the blind.

Other public-spirited people were concerned with the problems of the deaf. One of these was Thomas H. Gallaudet, who worked out ways to teach children who could not hear. In 1817 he started the first school in the United States for deaf children.

359

Young women had few opportunities for education in the early 1800's. In this picture of an evening school, the students work by candlelight as the teachers (in bonnets) lead the class.

Medicine makes advances. The study of medicine and methods of treating illnesses made progress in this period. A few medical schools had been started in the 1700's, but now more were established. A few admitted women, and in 1849 Elizabeth Blackwell became the first American woman to graduate from a medical school.

Doctors were learning more and more about diseases, and began to depend on the use of vaccination to prevent smallpox. A great boon was the discovery in 1846 by Dr. W. T. G. Morton of Boston that ether could be used as an anesthetic to dull the effects of pain. With ether, a patient could be put to sleep before an operation and feel no pain.

Temperance leaders oppose the use of alcohol. A good deal of attention was also given to the problem of alcoholism. Those who became the victims of liquor often lost their jobs and sometimes committed crimes. They brought disgrace and suffering to their families. Temperance societies were formed to teach people the bad effects of alcohol and to persuade them to stop drinking. Some temperance leaders went further

and tried to get state legislatures to pass laws forbidding the sale of liquor. Maine passed such a law in 1846, and in the next few decades several other states followed its example.

Women ask for their rights. A good many women took an active part in the abolitionist and temperance movements and other reforms. But they found it hard to get people to listen to them. Although more women were taking jobs in factories, most people thought that a woman's place was in the home. They thought that women did not need the same rights and opportunities as men. Women, therefore, had almost no chance to get a good education, and most jobs that required training and education were closed to them. When a woman married, her husband was allowed to manage any property she owned. Moreover, women could not vote. People frowned on women who took an active part in public meetings and expressed their ideas.

As women reformers worked for one reform or another, they became interested in winning more freedom for themselves and for other women. In 1848, a convention for women's rights

● Discuss how women's political rights have changed since the mid-1800's.

was held at Seneca Falls, New York. The meeting was organized by Lucretia Mott and Elizabeth Cady Stanton. The delegates drew up a declaration of rights asking for all the privileges belonging to them as citizens of the United States. Many people thought the Seneca Falls women were wrong to ask for such rights. One newspaper called the meeting "shocking and unnatural." American women did not get equal rights as a result of the convention. But more and more women did begin to take part in activities aimed at gaining more rights and opportunities.

EDUCATION MOVES AHEAD

During and after the time when Andrew Jackson was President, thoughtful people found many conditions that needed to be improved. One of the things they were most concerned about was education. Education is very important in a nation like ours. Since citizens have the opportunity to vote and take part in the government, they should be able to read and write and keep themselves well-informed.

Public education starts slowly. In the early 1800's there were few opportunities for education as we know it today. You will remember that the early colonists set up schools of various kinds. Later, when the Northwest Ordinance was adopted, it stated that knowledge was necessary for good government. It declared that in the Northwest Territory "schools and the means of education shall forever be encouraged." In Virginia, Thomas Jefferson tried to start a system of schools that would help to educate poor children. Jefferson was far ahead of his times in his thoughts about education.

For many reasons, none of these early plans to provide education succeeded very well. In the West, many families were struggling so hard to get started in their new homes that they had little time to think about schooling. In the South, only the children of planters received much education. As you know, public schools had been established in the North. But these schools suffered during the Revolutionary War and the unsettled years which followed.

Parents who could afford it usually sent their children to private schools. In many states the practice in the public schools was to have parents pay a share of the cost of their children's education. Poor children could attend these schools without paying only if their parents were willing to take a "pauper's" oath. This oath required them to admit that they were too poor to pay the cost of educating their children. Most poor people kept their children out of school rather than take the oath.

During the 1830's, people began to demand that schools be paid for by taxation. Workers felt that their sons and daughters should have a chance to get an education. They believed that schooling, like voting, should be available to all.

Free public schools are established. The foremost leader in the fight for better education was Horace Mann. As secretary of the Massachusetts Board of Education, Mann insisted that free public schools should be open to the children of all the people, rich and poor alike. Not everyone agreed with Mann. At first many well-to-do people said, "Why should we be taxed to pay for the education of the poor?" But gradually the idea of schools supported entirely by public taxation was accepted. As part of this trend, school terms were made longer, more subjects were taught, and textbooks were improved. By 1850 elementary schools supported by taxes were common in the northern states.

During these same years, young people were also given more opportunities to go beyond grade-school educa-

361

● Review attitudes toward education in colonial times. (See Chapter 5.)

Rip Van Winkle, by James Fenimore Cooper, is one of America's best-loved stories. Here, Rip returns to his village after sleeping for twenty years.

tion. Boston had established the first high school in 1821, and other northern cities soon followed its example. More colleges were also started. Instead of preparing students to be ministers only, the colleges began to offer such subjects as history and law. In addition, young women began to find it a little easier to carry on their schooling. Education beyond the elementary grades had once been thought unnecessary for women. Seminaries or private schools were now opened for them, and a few colleges accepted women students.

Blacks face obstacles to education. Getting an education was almost impossible for most black Americans in the early 1800's, whether they were slaves or free. Two black men did graduate from New England colleges before the Civil War — John B. Russwurm from Bowdoin in 1826 and Jonathan Gibbs from Dartmouth in 1853. The great majority of blacks, however, had no opportunity for education. A few elementary schools for free blacks were established in northern cities and in Washington, D.C. But neither blacks nor poor whites went to school in the slave states. A handful of plantation owners provided teachers to teach their slaves to read and write even though such instruction was strictly forbidden by state laws.

OPPORTUNITIES FOR READING INCREASE

At the same time that educational opportunities were opening up for some American children, much more was being written for Americans to read.

American authors produce an American literature. American authors began

362

Have students write a report on one of the authors named in this section.

to write about our nation's history and about American life. Since Americans were proud of their country, these books were eagerly read. Some of the earliest were written by Washington Irving and James Fenimore Cooper, both New Yorkers. Irving's *Legend of Sleepy Hollow* and *Rip Van Winkle* not only were interesting stories but showed what life was like in the Hudson Valley. Cooper wrote exciting tales of Indians and frontier life. His best known books were *The Last of the Mohicans* and *The Deerslayer*. A southern writer, William Gilmore Simms of South Carolina, wrote novels about people who lived on the southern frontier.

Edgar Allan Poe, who grew up in Virginia, wrote poems which were both beautiful and sad. People today still read *The Raven* and *Annabel Lee*. Poe is also famous for his mystery stories, like *The Tell-Tale Heart* and *The Gold Bug*.

Many of the best-known writers lived near Boston. One was Henry Wadsworth Longfellow. His poems, such as *Hiawatha, Evangeline, Paul Revere's Ride* (of which a little is quoted in Chapter 8), and *The Courtship of Miles Standish*, delighted readers. John Greenleaf Whittier not only wrote poems, such as *Snow-Bound*, about nature, but also tried to make people aware of the evils of slavery. He was called "the abolitionist poet." Nathaniel Hawthorne wrote about New England life in short stories like *The Great Stone Face* and novels like *The House of the Seven Gables*. Oliver Wendell Holmes was noted for humorous writings in which he poked fun at people and events of his day. Perhaps the most famous of the New England writers was Ralph Waldo Emerson. Emerson was a serious thinker who wrote essays about duty and self-reliance. He believed that every person had the ability to live a worthwhile life, and he had great faith in America.

Inexpensive newspapers are printed. Beginning in the 1830's, Americans were able to keep better informed about what was going on in the world. Earlier newspapers had been expensive and had not sold in large quantities. In 1833, the New York *Sun* started publishing a daily paper that sold on street corners for a penny. This paper was so successful that other newspapers started publishing penny dailies. After the telegraph came into use, news could be sent much more quickly over long distances. Better printing presses were also invented. Because of these changes, the average person was able to buy each day, for a small cost, more news and information than had ever been available to people before.

———

These improvements and reforms ★ showed that the character of the United States was beginning to change. Although Americans were still busy earning a living, they began to have time for other things. They had time to read newspapers and books and they were able to give more thought to education for their children. Americans also began to give more attention to the condition of people who through no fault of their own were denied a full opportunity to get ahead in life.

▶ **CHECK UP**   See Teacher's Key.

1. **(a)** What is a reformer? **(b)** What were some of the conditions that reformers wanted to change?
2. **(a)** Why did people come to believe in free public education? **(b)** How were opportunities for education in the United States improved?
3. **(a)** Who were some of the outstanding American authors in the first half of the 1800's? **(b)** Beginning in the 1830's, how were Americans able to become better informed about what was going on in the world?

★ See p. T36 for a strategy asking students to prepare reports on the reforms of this period.

Our Presidents

JOHN QUINCY ADAMS 1825–1829

National-Republican from Massachusetts. Lawyer, Harvard professor, and an able Secretary of State under Monroe, John Quincy Adams was a short, sharp-witted man like his father, the second President. During his term as President, Adams tried, unsuccessfully, to have Congress approve government promotion of scientific research and education. Defeated for re-election, he served in the House of Representatives until his death in 1848.

ANDREW JACKSON 1829–1837 ●

Democrat from Tennessee. First President to be born in a log cabin, Jackson grew up on the Carolina frontier. He tried teaching school and then became a lawyer, judge, and general. During the War of 1812 he showed such toughness that his troops called him "Old Hickory." A strong-willed President, Jackson was given another nickname — "King Andrew I" — by his opponents. He was the first President to ride on a train.

MARTIN VAN BUREN 1837–1841

Democrat from New York. The first President born an American citizen rather than a British subject, Van Buren was called the "Little Magician" because of his skill in politics. He had been Jackson's Vice-President before being elected to the presidency. Defeated for re-election, because many people blamed him for the Panic of 1837, he later ran for President unsuccessfully as the candidate of the Free Soil Party.

WILLIAM HENRY HARRISON 1841

Whig from Ohio. An Indian fighter and frontier governor, Harrison became famous as the general who defeated the Indians in the Battle of Tippecanoe. Later, he served in Congress and as ambassador to Colombia. Harrison had retired to his farm in Ohio when he was nominated for the presidency by the Whigs. Elected at 68, "Old Tippecanoe" became the first President to die in office.

JOHN TYLER 1841–1845

Whig from Virginia. Tyler had been a Democrat before the Whigs nominated him as Harrison's running mate. First Vice-President to become President through the death of his predecessor, Tyler insisted that he was not just an acting President but should have the full powers of the presidency. Later in life Tyler tried in vain to restore friendship between the North and South. He was serving in the Confederate Congress at the time of his death.

● See p. T36 for a strategy asking students to put together a bulletin board display featuring the Jacksonian Era.

● See p. T36 for a strategy that asks students to construct a chart showing the differences between the Democratic and Whig parties.

5 What Political Parties Sought to Win the Presidency?

Two new political parties develop. At the same time that the changes just described were taking place in American life, there was also a change in political parties. The Federalist Party died out soon after Monroe became President (page 265). For a few years there was only one political party, the Democratic-Republican or Republican. After Monroe left the presidency, however, the Democratic-Republican Party split into two parts. You read on pages 347–348 about the presidential elections of 1824 and 1828. In the 1830's the friends and supporters of Andrew Jackson became known as the Democratic Party. Many of the same kinds of people who had supported Thomas Jefferson were members of the Democratic Party. It came to stand for low tariffs and states' rights (page 407) and opposed a strong federal government. Many Southerners and Westerners belonged to the Democratic Party.

Those who disliked "King Andrew I," as they called Andrew Jackson, formed a political party to oppose him and his beliefs. This party was called at first the National Republican Party but later became known as the Whig Party. It stood chiefly for high tariffs and a strong federal government. Many Whigs had belonged to the Federalist Party in earlier years. The Whig Party was strongest in the East.

Martin Van Buren follows Jackson as President. As Jackson's second term drew to a close, he made clear to the Democrats that he wanted his Vice-President, Martin Van Buren of New York, to follow him as President. The Democrats easily elected Van Buren in 1836.

The nation enjoys a period of prosperity. All sections of the country prospered during the 1830's. In the West there had been an enormous increase in the buying of government land. Many of the buyers did not intend to farm the land. They planned to sell it and make a profit. Such people are known as speculators. To pay for the land, they borrowed paper money issued by the western banks. But many of these banks, called wildcat banks, put out paper money without enough gold or silver to back it up. For a time things went well. As prices of western land rose, big profits were made.

In the South, people planted more and more cotton and thus were able to sell more and more to English factories. This meant greater prosperity for the South. Western farmers sold large amounts of food to the South and became more prosperous. With money to spend, the Southerners and Westerners bought manufactured goods from the East. Factories grew, people had jobs, and businesses of all kinds increased. Even England was affected by the prosperity the American people were enjoying during the 1830's. Americans were buying great quantities of luxuries and other goods from English traders and merchants.

Prosperity ends in a panic. Suddenly, in 1837, the period of prosperity ended and a **panic** followed. Fear and ★ hard times swept the nation as people became alarmed about severe financial problems. One reason for the Panic of 1837 was a step taken by President Jackson shortly before he left office. Jackson announced that all sales of government land in the West had to be paid for in gold or silver (hard cash), not in paper money.

When the land speculators took their paper money to the wildcat banks

365

★ Have students look up the term *panic* in the glossary at the back of the book. Discuss the causes and effects of the Panic of 1837.

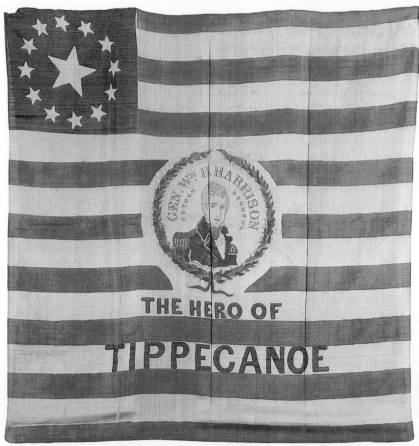

William Henry Harrison, nicknamed "Old Tippecanoe," won the presidential election of 1840.

and asked for hard cash, they could not get it. So the speculators began to sell their land, and land prices dropped sharply. At the same time, people became fearful when they realized that the government had little faith in the paper money issued by the western banks. They rushed to the banks to exchange their paper money for gold and silver. The fear soon spread to the East. Everywhere people demanded hard cash. Because the banks did not have enough gold and silver, they had to close their doors.

Hard times become widespread. English manufacturers and traders failed because they could not collect money owed them by American businesses. American manufacturers went out of business because people could no

longer buy their products. Factories closed; people lost their jobs. Cotton planters also suffered because English manufacturers could no longer buy large quantities of cotton. Western farmers grew poor because people in the South no longer bought as much of their food.

The Whigs elect Harrison and Tyler. Many people blamed the unlucky Martin Van Buren for the Panic of 1837. The Whigs made the most of this. As their candidate for President in 1840, they chose William Henry Harrison of Ohio. For Vice-President they selected John Tyler of Virginia. Harrison, who was 68 years old at this time, had won fame for his victory in 1811 at the Battle of Tippecanoe (page 338). He had also fought bravely and well in the War of

366

1812. The Whigs emphasized Harrison's military record and his nickname of "Old Tippecanoe." Their campaign was an exciting one, with many parades and enthusiastic speeches. "Tippecanoe and Tyler too!" they shouted, and soon their shouts were loud with triumph as they won the election.

William Henry Harrison was the first President elected by the Whig Party. He was also the first President of the United States to die in office. Tired out by the campaign, he died only one month after taking the oath of office. Vice-President John Tyler then became President. But Tyler was not a strong believer in Whig ideas. He had been nominated for Vice-President chiefly to win the votes of Southerners who otherwise might not have voted for Harrison. He had many bitter conflicts with Whig leaders and with Congress.

Quarrels within the Whig Party helped to cause its defeat in 1844, when James K. Polk was elected President. Four years later another Whig President (Zachary Taylor) was elected, but in the 1850's the Whig Party disappeared. The Democratic Party, however, has continued to exist up to the present day.

▶ **CHECK UP**   See Teacher's Key.

1. **(a)** What two new political parties developed while Andrew Jackson was President? **(b)** What did each of those parties stand for?
2. **(a)** Why was there prosperity in the United States during the early 1830's? **(b)** Why did that prosperity end in the Panic of 1837? **(c)** How did the Panic of 1837 affect Martin Van Buren's chances for a second term as President?

CHECK UP ON CHAPTER 17

See Teacher's Key.

Words to Know

1. nullify
2. secede
3. panic
4. reform
5. temperance
6. secession
7. republic
8. democracy
9. spoils system

Facts to Remember

1. Describe President Jackson's policy on each of the following: **(a)** the appointment of government officials, **(b)** the Bank of the United States, **(c)** the ownership of Indian lands.
2. **(a)** In what ways did states limit the right to vote in the early 1800's? **(b)** By 1860 how had voting rights been extended to more people?
3. **(a)** Who were the abolitionists? **(b)** Name four outstanding abolitionist leaders.
4. Tell how each of the following played a part in the reform movements described in this chapter: **(a)** Dorothea Dix, **(b)** Samuel G. Howe, **(c)** Elizabeth Blackwell, **(d)** W. T. G. Morton, **(e)** Elizabeth Cady Stanton, **(f)** Horace Mann.
5. Name a book or story written by each of the following American writers: **(a)** Washington Irving, **(b)** James Fenimore Cooper, **(c)** Edgar Allan Poe, **(d)** Henry Wadsworth Longfellow, **(e)** Nathaniel Hawthorne.
6. Name the Presidents in order from John Quincy Adams through Zachary Taylor. Identify the political party to which each belonged.

Skills to Practice

1. Look back at Daniel Webster's comment on the inauguration of Andrew Jackson (page 348). Is this comment a primary or secondary source? Explain your answer.
2. Copy on a separate sheet of paper the events shown on the four chapter time

Skills to Practice (cont.)

lines in Unit 5 (see pages 290, 314, 330, and 346). Beside each event write its date. Then draw one large time line and place on it all those events in their correct order.

Questions to Think About

1. The people who supported Andrew Jackson gave him the nickname "the people's President." Why did they call him that?

2. What is meant by *nullification*? Why did this issue arise? How did President Jackson's views on nullification differ from those of John C. Calhoun?
3. In the 1830's the nation had very few public schools (schools paid for with money raised by taxation). Why did many Americans demand that public schools be started? Why did others argue against public schools?
4. What were some of the results of the reform movements of the 1830's and 1840's? How did they affect the lives of average Americans?

Linking Past and Present

Andrew Jackson's home. Many visitors to Nashville, Tennessee, go to see the old mansion called the Hermitage. This beautiful house was built by Andrew Jackson for his wife Rachel soon after he returned from the Indian wars in Florida. Today the Hermitage looks much as it did during their lifetime. The white two-storied house has the wide verandas and tall columns of the fine southern homes of that period. Many pieces of Jackson's own furniture are to be found in the spacious rooms. Both Andrew and Rachel Jackson are buried in the beautiful garden of the Hermitage.

Chicago, Illinois. One of the cities that was started in the period you have been reading about was Chicago. The secret of Chicago's growth was its location as a crossroads for trade. Even in Indian times, this location was a crossroads. Joliet, Marquette, and La Salle visited the place where Chicago now stands, for here was a portage between Lake Michigan and the Illinois River, by which they could reach the Mississippi. In about 1775 a black fur trapper from New Orleans named Jean Baptiste Point du Sable built a trading post there. His business did well, and a pioneer settlement soon grew up around the trading post. Fort Dearborn was built in 1803 to protect the settlers. By 1831 there were

about 350 people living nearby. Then, suddenly, the settlement began to grow rapidly. By 1837 there were 5,000 people in Chicago.

The Erie Canal helped Chicago to grow. Manufactured goods from the East could be shipped by water from New York to the Great Lakes and from there around to Chicago. Farmers of the Midwest began to think of Chicago as their chief trading center, a place where they could sell their goods for shipment to the East, and where they could buy the things they needed. Another spurt occurred in 1848, when the Illinois Canal was completed. This connected Chicago directly with the Illinois River and the Mississippi. It was now possible to ship goods from New York City to Chicago, and from there, by way of the Illinois Canal and the Mississippi River, all the way to New Orleans!

The first railroad from the East reached Chicago in 1852. Soon, every important east-west railroad made Chicago one of its terminal points, until Chicago had become one of the greatest rail centers in the world. Warehouses, factories, stores, and banks grew up along the docks and the railroads. Immigrants poured in to find jobs. So you see, Chicago's location at a natural crossroads played an important part in making it one of the largest cities in the United States.

368

For answers see Teacher's Key.

A number of topics for student research can be found in the annotations and teaching strategies (pp. T35–T36) for this chapter. Have students write a report, or prepare an outline for a report.

GAINING SKILL

Preparing Reports

The first step in preparing a history report is to choose a topic. Think about the length of the report and what you will want to say. Then decide on a topic that is the right size. For example, if you are planning to write a two-page report, "The American Revolution" is probably too big a topic. A better choice might be "The Battle of Bunker Hill."

The key to a good report is organization. Suppose you decide to make a report on Henry Clay. You might plan to include information on three main topics:

I. General information about Clay's life
II. Clay and the War of 1812
III. Clay's work as a "compromise maker" in the tariff and slavery disputes

Once you have chosen your topic and planned your organization, you are ready to begin reading books on your subject. As you read, you should also be taking notes. To take useful notes, keep in mind the main topics of your report. Write each note on a separate card, or put the notes for each main division of your report on a separate sheet of paper.

If there is material that you want to quote — such as a passage from one of Clay's famous speeches — copy it exactly. Otherwise, express your ideas in your own words.

When you have finished taking notes, look through them and arrange them in order in each main division. You will find that your notes for each topic will fall into groups. At this point, you can expand your list of main topics into an outline. For example, look at the top of the next column to see how your outline for the first main division in a report on Clay might look.

I. General information about Clay
A. When and where Clay was born
B. Early life
C. Political offices he held
D. Leaders Clay was associated with

The following exercises will give you further help in learning how to prepare a report.

1. Suppose you were writing a report on Andrew Jackson. Rearrange this list to make it an outline of three main topics, with subtopics under each one.

Jackson's early life
His use of the spoils system
His leadership at the Battle of New Orleans
His years as President
His boyhood on the Carolina frontier
His years as a lawyer and judge in Tennessee
His military career
His reaction to South Carolina's threat of secession
His actions as a general in the Indian wars in Florida and Alabama

2. Look back at Section 4 of this chapter (pages 357–363). What are the three main topics within this section? What are the subtopics under each head? Copy the headings in this section in the form of an outline.

In Unit 5 you have read about important changes which had taken place in the United States by 1860.

1. Different ways of living developed in various sections of the country during the first half of the 1800's.

a. Although New England sea captains could not enter British ports after the Revolutionary War, they found new markets and ways of making money. American commerce again suffered before and during the War of 1812, but it increased greatly after 1815. A profitable trade was developed with China and with Spanish ranchers in California. Meanwhile, the use of machinery and the factory system spread from England to America.

b. By present-day standards, wages, hours, and working conditions were unsatisfactory in the early factories. The growth of industry increased the number and size of cities. Many new conveniences and improved transportation and communication were developed.

c. The invention of the cotton gin by Eli Whitney in 1793 led to a great increase in the planting of cotton. When the land in the Old South "wore out," the planters sought new and more fertile land to the southwest.

d. Differences in ways of living in the North and the South led to disagreements. The manufacturing North came to favor protective tariffs, the agricultural South to oppose them. Be-cause of its spreading factory system and its small farms, the North favored free labor; the plantation South depended on slave labor.

e. Opportunities offered by the West (the frontier region between settled areas and the wilderness) attracted thousands of pioneer families. The Ordinance of 1787 provided for a territorial government in the Northwest Territory and also for the admission, in time, of new states in that region. The pattern set by this law was followed in the case of later territories.

f. Different ways of living which had developed in the North, the South, and the West led to political rivalry between the three sections. Andrew Jackson's election as President was hailed as a victory for the West.

2. During his presidency, Andrew Jackson took several important steps.

a. Jackson refused to recognize the right claimed by South Carolina to nullify a protective tariff law.

b. Claiming that it had grown too wealthy and powerful, Jackson decided to put an end to the Bank of the United States. In 1832 he vetoed a bill that would have renewed the bank's charter.

c. A harsh policy of Indian removal was carried out.

d. Unsound trading in western land caused the government to require that payments be made in gold and silver. This was a factor that led to the Panic of 1837.

3. Democratic ideas spread through the country in the first half of the 1800's.

a. By 1840, presidential candidates were selected by delegates to national conventions.

b. During Andrew Jackson's administration, the right to vote was extended to practically all white men.

c. In the 1830's, reformers worked for the abolition of slavery, for women's rights, for temperance, and for the better treatment of prisoners and the mentally ill. Free public schools were established, a new interest in reading and literature developed, and inexpensive newspapers were published. Opportunities for the disabled were also expanded.

UNIT REVIEW   See Teacher's Key.

1. **(a)** Why did commerce and manufacturing develop in New England and the Middle Atlantic states? **(b)** Why did manufacturing become increasingly important during the War of 1812? **(c)** What step was taken to protect American manufacturers after the war? **(d)** How did the increase in industry affect the growth of cities? **(e)** How did it affect communication and transportation? Why?

2. **(a)** Why did the South need more land after 1793? **(b)** Why were the plantation owners the most influential group in the South? **(c)** What other groups lived in the South?

3. **(a)** What stand did the North and the South take on the tariff question? **(b)** On the question of slavery?

4. **(a)** What were the chief needs of the West? **(b)** Why did democratic ideas spread more quickly in the West than in other sections? **(c)** What issues did Andrew Jackson fight for?

5. How did the advance of white pioneers affect the Indians west of the Appalachians?

6. **(a)** Why did a panic develop in 1837? **(b)** What were the results?

7. **(a)** What advances were made in education in the first half of the 1800's? **(b)** Why were Americans able to keep better informed about what was going on in the world? **(c)** What movements were started to improve conditions in the United States?

THINGS TO DO

The items marked with an asterisk (*) are for the whole class.

*1. Start a new set of cards for Unit 5. Include names, terms, and dates found in Chapters 14, 15, 16, and 17.

2. Make a map showing one of the following: **(a)** the Erie Canal and the Hudson River route; **(b)** the National Road; **(c)** the Cotton Kingdom, including the chief cities and rivers used for transportation; **(d)** the Northeast with its chief ports and factory towns.

3. Draw a cartoon to show **(a)** how clipper ship captains felt about the steamship; **(b)** how farmers felt about the early railroads; **(c)** the special interests of the North, South, and West; **(d)** Jackson and the Bank.

4. Write an article as it might have appeared in a newspaper of the times on **(a)** the completion of the Erie Canal; **(b)** the factory built by Samuel Slater; **(c)** the voyage of the *Flying Cloud*; **(d)** the election of John Quincy Adams.

5. Prepare an oral or written report on **(a)** Henry Clay or John C. Calhoun; **(b)** Tecumseh, Osceola, or Sequoya; **(c)** any one of the inventors or writers mentioned in this unit.

6. Write a letter to a friend describing **(a)** your visit to Washington at the time of Jackson's inauguration; **(b)** the race between *Tom Thumb* and the horse; **(c)** your trip to a southern plantation.

Left to right: covered wagons heading west, Union troops, the Lincoln Memorial, Confederate flag over Fort Sumter.

The Nation Expands and Is Torn by War

1800–1880

See p. T36 for a unit preview strategy. See pp. T58–T71 for lists of useful books and audiovisual aids.

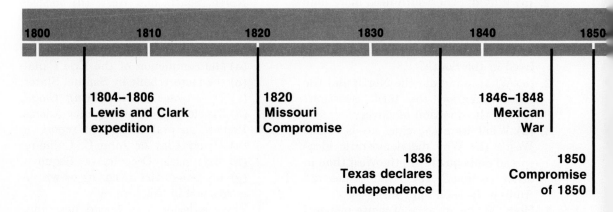

1800	1810	1820	1830	1840	1850

**1804–1806
Lewis and Clark
expedition**

**1820
Missouri
Compromise**

**1846–1848
Mexican
War**

**1836
Texas declares
independence**

**1850
Compromise
of 1850**

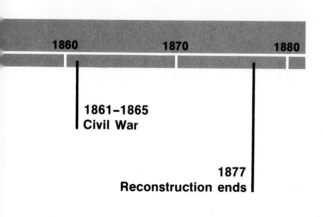

1860   1870   1880

1861–1865
Civil War

1877
Reconstruction ends

The tragic story of the American Civil War will be told in this unit. During that war Americans in the North and South carried different flags and fought against one another. As background for understanding the Civil War, Chapter 18 tells how the United States expanded across the entire continent. Chapter 19 explains how the question of slavery in the new territories brought differences between the North and South to a head. In Chapter 20 you will trace the course of the Civil War and learn about some of the great battles that took place. You will also learn the outcome of the war and read about efforts to solve the problems that it created.

COURTESY TIME-LIFE BOOKS INC.

CHAPTER **18** *Vocabulary preview:* expansionist, annex, forty-niner, vigilante, joint occupation

The United States Gains More Land and Reaches from Sea to Sea

1803–1860   See pp. T36–T37 for chapter teaching strategies.

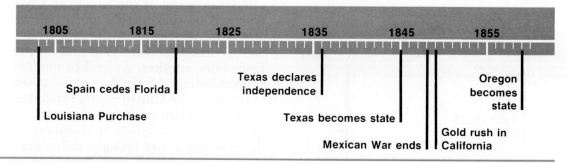

| 1805 | 1815 | 1825 | 1835 | 1845 | 1855 |

Spain cedes Florida

Texas declares independence

Oregon becomes state

Louisiana Purchase

Texas becomes state

Mexican War ends

Gold rush in California

What this chapter is about —

As American pioneers marched steadily westward, they looked eagerly at lands still farther west. They wanted to own that land. One enthusiastic American compared the United States with the buffalo that roamed over the plains:

Make way, I say, for the young American buffalo — he has not yet got land enough; he wants more land as his cool shelter in summer — he wants more land for his beautiful pasture grounds. I tell you, we will give him Oregon for his summer shade, and the region of Texas as his winter pasture. Like all of

374

his race, he wants salt, too. Well, he shall have the use of two oceans — the mighty Pacific and the turbulent Atlantic shall be his. . . .

In 1783 our country stretched from Canada to Florida and from the Atlantic Ocean to the Mississippi River. Twenty years later, as you read in Chapter 13, President Jefferson bought the Louisiana Territory. Although the Louisiana Purchase doubled the size of the United States, Americans were not satisfied. The speaker whose words are quoted here was correct in thinking that the "American buffalo" would not be content with the territory it owned in 1803.

This chapter explains how the United States gained more and more territory, until it reached from the shores of the Atlantic Ocean across the continent to the Pacific. You will find answers to these questions:

1. How was the Louisiana Territory explored and settled?
2. How did the United States acquire Florida?
3. How did our country gain Texas, the Southwest, and California?
4. How did the discovery of gold bring California into the Union?
5. How did the United States gain part of the Oregon Country?

1 How Was the Louisiana Territory Explored and Settled?

What was the Louisiana Territory like in 1803? When Jefferson surprised the country by buying Louisiana from France, Americans knew very little about that vast territory. Louisiana lay between the Mississippi River and the Rocky Mountains; it stretched northward to Canada and southward to the Gulf of Mexico. (See map on page 377.) Here indeed was land for the "American buffalo"! The Great Plains extended westward from the Mississippi, rising gradually to the Rockies. In the upper Mississippi Valley were forests where deer and other game lived. Farther south and west, enormous herds of shaggy buffaloes roamed the plains, feeding on the prairie grass that stretched for hundreds of miles. The broad Missouri River, with its headwaters in the northern Rockies, made its way across those plains to join the Mississippi. And the Mississippi, swollen by the waters of the Missouri, wound in and out through endless acres of land on its way to the Gulf of Mexico.

New Orleans was the only city in the Louisiana Territory. A few thousand French and American settlers lived along the Mississippi in 1803, most of them in villages settled long before by the French. (You remember that the entire river valley had once been a part of New France.) The chief settlements in the Louisiana Purchase were St. Louis and New Orleans. St. Louis was only a small fur-trading town of about 160 log cabins. New Orleans, however, was a thriving city of 10,000 people located a hundred miles from the mouth of the Mississippi.

New Orleans had had a colorful history. Started by the French in 1718, it had been given to Spain with the rest of Louisiana at the end of the French and Indian War (page 147). During the late

375

● Remind students that Jefferson's first intention was to buy just New Orleans (p. 275).

See p. T36 for a strategy that calls for students to trace on an outline map the routes of Lewis and Clark and Pike (p. 377).

1700's, wealthy Spaniards moved to New Orleans and lived there in grand style. Then Louisiana again fell into the hands of the French. Finally it changed owners for the last time when it was bought by the United States in 1803. At that time New Orleans had many people of French and Spanish origin and a large black population, both slave and free. It was the chief port for the products of the Mississippi Valley. Near the city were large plantations of indigo, sugar cane, and cotton.

Lewis and Clark explore the Louisiana Territory. President Jefferson was eager to learn more about this vast land the United States had bought. So he sent a small expedition of soldiers to explore the Louisiana Territory. The leaders were Meriwether Lewis and William Clark (a younger brother of George Rogers Clark of Revolutionary War fame). Another member of the expedition was Clark's slave York. (York was freed at the end of the expedition.)

Setting out from St. Louis in May, 1804, the explorers journeyed up the Missouri through the lands of the Sioux (SOO) Indians. (Find their route on the map, next page.) The Sioux were just

Lewis and Clark's expedition gave Americans valuable information about the Louisiana Territory. Here Sacagawea points the way.

one of the many Indian peoples who lived in the land between the Mississippi and the Rockies. Lewis had been instructed by President Jefferson to tell the Indians that they would find the people of the United States to be their "faithful friends."

Lewis and Clark spent the winter of 1804–1805 among the Mandan Indians in what is now North Dakota. There they had the good fortune to meet an Indian woman named Sacagawea (SAK-uh-juh-WEE-uh). Some years earlier Sacagawea had been captured and taken by force from her own Shoshone tribe far to the west. When Lewis and Clark continued their journey in the spring, she agreed to go along and serve as guide and interpreter.

With Sacagawea's valuable help, the expedition followed the Missouri River into the Rockies. While in the mountains, Sacagawea was able to lead them to her own tribe of Shoshone. Her brother was chief of the tribe and was able to provide Lewis and Clark with badly needed horses and supplies.

After crossing the mountains, the expedition traveled by boat to the Pacific. They made the return trip safely and reached St. Louis in 1806 after a journey of 8,000 miles.

The expedition of Lewis and Clark not only gave the people of the United

376

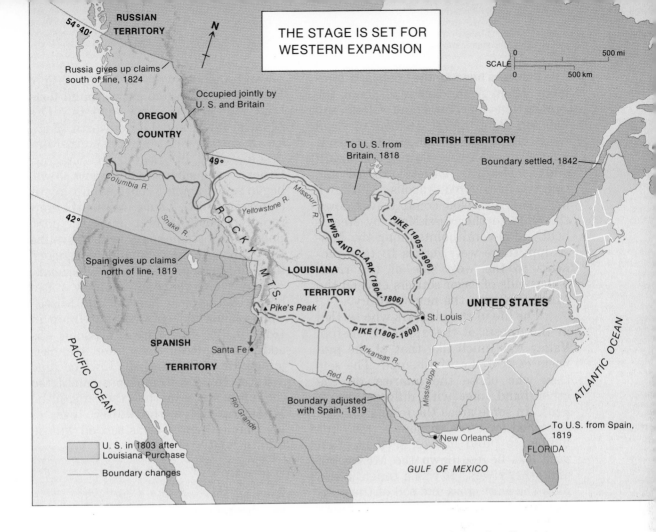

THE STAGE IS SET FOR WESTERN EXPANSION

54°40' RUSSIAN TERRITORY

Russia gives up claims south of line, 1824

Occupied jointly by U. S. and Britain

OREGON COUNTRY

BRITISH TERRITORY

To U. S. from Britain, 1818

Boundary settled, 1842

49°

Columbia R.

Yellowstone R.

Missouri R.

LEWIS AND CLARK (1804-1806)

PIKE (1805-1806)

42°

Snake R.

R O C K Y   M T S

Spain gives up claims north of line, 1819

LOUISIANA

TERRITORY

Pike's Peak

St. Louis

UNITED STATES

PIKE (1806-1808)

SPANISH

Santa Fe

TERRITORY

Arkansas R.

Red R.

Rio Grande

Mississippi R.

PACIFIC OCEAN

ATLANTIC OCEAN

Boundary adjusted with Spain, 1819

To U. S. from Spain, 1819

U. S. in 1803 after Louisiana Purchase

Boundary changes

New Orleans

FLORIDA

GULF OF MEXICO

SCALE

0   500 mi

0   500 km

MAP STUDY   See Teacher's Key.
This map shows how the nation's boundaries changed in the years from 1803 to 1842. (a) What two areas were gained in 1818 and 1819? (b) What nations occupied the Oregon Country?

States information about the new lands; it also paved the way for hunters, traders, and pioneer farmers. The record of Lewis and Clark's journey has been published and may be found in many libraries.

Zebulon Pike explores more of the Louisiana Territory. At about this time an explorer named Zebulon Pike led an expedition north along the Mississippi, in search of its source. Although he did not find it, he learned a great deal about the region of the upper Mississippi. After returning from this exploration, Pike set out again from St. Louis in 1806. This time he headed west. His purpose was to explore the Louisiana Territory south of the route taken by Lewis and Clark. After following the Arkansas River for many weeks, Pike came to the Rockies. Pike's Peak in ● Colorado, which he discovered, is named for this brave explorer.

It was winter when Pike and his men reached the Rockies. Cold and tired, they turned south in search of the Red River. Actually they entered territory along the river called the Rio Grande. This land was not a part of Louisiana but belonged to Spain. As a result, Pike and his men were taken prisoner by Spanish soldiers and were brought before the Spanish governor of the region. Pike was later released. He returned through Spanish territory to American soil with valuable maps and much useful information.

377

● Have students locate Pike's Peak on the map on this page.

Pioneers head for the Louisiana Territory. When Americans read about the explorations of Lewis and Clark and Zebulon Pike, many decided to head west. Some set out in flatboats that floated down rivers flowing westward and southward. Others crossed the country in covered wagons. Within a few years pioneers could travel down the Ohio to the Mississippi by steamboat. At several points along the Mississippi there were ferries to take pioneers to the west side of the river. Thousands of eager settlers crossed the Mississippi into the new territory.

The life of the pioneers who settled in the forests of the upper Mississippi Valley was much like that of the pioneers east of the Mississippi. The settlers who chose the prairies, on the other hand, met with different problems. In some areas the rolling prairies stretched for miles without a tree. For lumber to build houses, settlers often used logs floated down the Mississippi and other rivers. It was a tough job to plow the wiry grass and sod of the prairies, and farmers had to use huge plows pulled by teams of oxen. But once the land was plowed, fine crops of corn and wheat could be raised. In some parts of Missouri and Arkansas, white settlers from the southern states and the slaves they brought with them started cotton plantations.

States are organized west of the Mississippi River. Before long, new towns began to appear west of the Mississippi River. Some of them grew around forts built to protect the settlers. Des Moines, Iowa, and Leavenworth, Kansas, began as forts. Minneapolis, Minnesota, grew up near Fort Snelling. Other towns, such as Davenport, Iowa, began as fur-trading centers built by fur companies. St. Louis, Missouri, grew rapidly as a fur center and river port. Soon many steamboats were traveling the Mississippi, carrying passengers, furs, and farm produce to New Orleans.

In a few years several new states bordered the west bank of the Mississippi. Louisiana entered the Union in 1812. In 1821, the state of Missouri was added, and fifteen years later Arkansas joined the Union. In 1846, Iowa became a state. In 1858, Minnesota completed the row of states on the west bank of the Mississippi. How the western part of Louisiana Territory was settled will be told in a later chapter.

▶ **CHECK UP**   See Teacher's Key.

1. **(a)** What parts of the Louisiana Territory were explored by Lewis and Clark? **(b)** By Pike? **(c)** What were the results of these explorations?
2. How did the life of pioneers west of the Mississippi River compare with pioneer life east of the Mississippi?
3. What states were created in the territory just west of the Mississippi?

2 How Did the United States Acquire Florida?

★ When our country bought Louisiana Territory, neither the French nor the Americans were sure just what its boundaries were. You remember that Jefferson wanted to get control of the mouth of the Mississippi so that Westerners could send their products to market through the port of New Orleans. Spain, however, owned a narrow strip of land along the Gulf of Mexico (called West Florida), as well as the peninsula we now call Florida, which was then

378

★ See p. T36 for a strategy that asks students to write reports about the settlement of the Louisiana Purchase.

THE UNITED STATES
GAINS FLORIDA

SOUTH CAROLINA

GEORGIA

N

MISSISSIPPI   ALABAMA

Mississippi R.

WEST   Mobile   FLORIDA
Pensacola   • St. Augustine

• New Orleans

Ceded by Spain, 1819

EAST
FLORIDA

GULF OF MEXICO

Occupied by U. S. by 1813

SCALE

0   200 mi
0   200 km

See Teacher's Key.

MAP STUDY
Americans claimed that some of West Florida was part of the Louisiana Purchase, but Spain disputed that claim until 1819. What states gained an outlet to the Gulf of Mexico through West Florida?

known as East Florida (map, above). Spain claimed that West Florida extended as far west as New Orleans and the Mississippi River. Jefferson, on the other hand, claimed that the Louisiana Purchase included land *east* of the Mississippi River.

The United States expands into West Florida. The argument went on for years. Finally, when Louisiana became a state in 1812, the American government simply added to it all the territory east of the Mississippi that is now included in that state. Spain was too weak to defend its claim.

The United States, however, wanted to own all of West Florida. Americans were rapidly settling the land to the north of that area, and settlers in Alabama and Mississippi wanted to use the rivers that flowed through Spanish territory to the Gulf of Mexico. The United States offered to buy West Florida, but Spain refused to sell. During the War of 1812, our government occupied more of West Florida. After the war, therefore, the United States was holding a large part of West Florida, although Spain did not admit our right to do so.

Andrew Jackson marches into East Florida. Meanwhile East Florida had become a trouble spot. Runaway slaves from Georgia had been going into East Florida and settling there, safe from American authorities. Furthermore, the Indians of Florida often raided frontier settlements just north of the Spanish border. Although Spain had agreed to hold the Indians in check, it did not have enough troops in Florida to do so. Finally, in 1818, President Monroe ordered General Andrew Jackson to halt the Indian raids.

Jackson obeyed his orders too well. He marched his men into Florida, although he had no right to invade Spanish territory, and he captured two Spanish forts. In fact, what he actually did was invade and conquer East Florida. The American people applauded Jackson. But he had created an embarrassing situation for President Monroe, who had no desire to make an enemy of Spain. The two forts were returned to Spain, and the American forces were withdrawn.

The United States buys Florida. Jackson's invasion of Florida made it clear to Spain that it was unable to de-

379

Saint Augustine, settled in 1565, is the oldest city in the United States. People can still visit the old Spanish fort, which dates from 1672.

fend this territory. Also, Spain had its hands full with the revolutions going on in Mexico and South America (Chapter 10). So, in the Adams-Onís Treaty with the United States in 1819, Spain gave up its claims to both East and West Florida. In return, the United States agreed to pay $5 million to Americans who claimed Spain owed them money. This treaty also defined the boundary between the United States and Spanish territory west of the Mississippi.

Two years later, the treaty went into effect. For the second time since 1783, the United States had acquired new territory.

▶ **CHECK UP** See Teacher's Key.

1. **(a)** How did the United States expand into West Florida? **(b)** Why did Andrew Jackson invade East Florida?
2. How did Florida become part of the United States?

3 How Did Our Country Gain Texas, the Southwest, and California?

In 1821, as you read in Chapter 10, Mexico declared its independence from Spain. The new Republic of Mexico claimed all the land colonized by Spaniards in what is now the southwestern part of the United States. (The map on page 377 shows the location of that land.) But American pioneers were beginning to move into that region, and there were many people who thought it should belong to the United States. They believed that it was the destiny of the United States to extend from the Atlantic Ocean to the Pacific. These land-hungry Americans were called **expansionists,** because they wanted to expand or enlarge the territory of the United States. In 1845, James K. Polk, a strong believer in expansion, entered the White House. During his presidency a huge amount of territory was added to the United States. The story of how this came about is told in the following pages.

380

● See p. T36 for a strategy in which students examine how the United States acquired Florida.

TEXAS BECOMES A NATION, THEN A STATE

Americans settle in Texas. The story begins about 1820 in Texas. This land was thinly settled. A few wealthy Spaniards owned huge estates. There were also several missions, founded by missionary priests, and a few military posts. Most of the inhabitants of Texas, however, were Indians. These included farming peoples such as the Wichita. There were also hunting groups such as the Apache, the Kiowa, and the Comanche.

In 1822, a young man named Stephen F. Austin led a few American families into Texas to make their homes. Two years before, his father had persuaded the Spanish government (which then ruled Texas) to give him a huge tract of land there for American set-

tlers. After his father died, Stephen Austin went ahead with his plan. He arranged with the government of Mexico, which by that time had won its independence from Spain, to bring settlers to Texas. He promised that the colonists would belong to the Catholic faith, would become Mexican citizens, and would obey Mexican laws. Austin was able to offer land to settlers for very little money, and his colony grew rapidly. The land was cultivated, and homes and schools were built.

The Mexican government liked the idea of building up Texas and opened other parts of it for settlement by Americans. A rush for land followed. At one time, a settler could buy 4,000 acres for as little as $30. Many small farmers from the United States bought land, and plantation families from the South moved into Texas with their slaves. Free blacks also settled in Texas, and many of them worked as cowboys. By 1835, there were 30,000 colonists from the United States in Texas. This was a much greater number of settlers than

This picture of a marketplace shows what towns in the American Southwest looked like when that region was still part of Mexico.

Known as the "cradle of Texas liberty," the Alamo was captured by Mexican forces in 1836 (page 384).

Spain had sent in more than three hundred years.

Mexico becomes alarmed. Mexico realized too late that it had been a mistake to allow Americans to settle in its territory. They did not get along well with the government or with the Spanish-speaking people in Texas. The Americans were different in language, religion, and ways of living. Furthermore, they were independent in spirit and disliked many of the Mexican laws. But the Mexican government naturally expected them to obey its laws. It is easy to see that there would be quarrels between the American colonists and the Mexican government. One quarrel was about slavery. Mexico had laws forbidding slavery in its territory, but many

Americans brought their slaves into Texas anyway.

Texans declare their independence. To prevent these disputes from growing more serious, the Mexican government tried to stop more American colonists from entering Texas. This only made the Americans already there angrier. When an ambitious general named Santa Anna seized control in Mexico, matters went from bad to worse. The Americans in Texas resented Santa Anna's harsh rule and finally revolted against Mexico. On March 2, 1836, they declared Texas an independent nation.

Mexico tried to crush the revolt. General Santa Anna led troops into Texas to punish the Americans. The Texans suffered two severe defeats but

382

People in America's Story

Tennessee for three years. His experiences
as an adopted member of that tribe made him
sympathetic to Indian interests.

SAM HOUSTON

A leader in the fight for independence from Mexico, Sam Houston later
served as president of the Republic of Texas and, after Texas became a
state, as its United States senator and governor.

Leaving behind a successful career in Tennessee
politics, Sam Houston moved to Texas in 1829.
There he became a leader among settlers who
disliked Mexican rule. After commanding forces
that defeated the Mexicans in 1836, Houston
helped set up a new republic. The flag of that
republic, shown above, later became the state
flag of Texas.

Houston's greatest
victory against Mexico
was in the Battle of
San Jacinto (right). He
captured Mexican
general Santa Anna,
who agreed to give the
Texans their
independence.

383

won a final and glorious victory. The first defeat was at the Alamo (AL-uh-moh) in the city of San Antonio. The Alamo was an old Spanish mission surrounded by high walls. A force of fewer than 200 Texans, under the command of Colonel William Barrett Travis, barricaded themselves in the mission and were besieged by 3,000 Mexican soldiers under Santa Anna. Most of the defenders were recent arrivals from the United States; others were Mexicans who opposed Santa Anna. In spite of unequal odds, the Texans refused to surrender and held out for thirteen days. When the battle was over, all were dead. "Remember the Alamo" became a Texas battle cry. Soon after the siege of the
● Alamo, Mexican troops surrounded and attacked a Texan force at Goliad. Here again the Texans were greatly outnumbered and were forced to surrender. Santa Anna ordered them all executed, claiming they were traitors to Mexico. His cruelty aroused all Texas.

Texas wins independence. In the battle of San Jacinto (san juh-SIN-toh) on April 21, 1836, the Texans avenged these defeats. A Texan force of 800 men
★ under General Sam Houston surprised a larger Mexican army. Shouting their battle cry, "Remember the Alamo! Remember Goliad!" they killed, wounded, or captured almost all of the enemy force. Santa Anna himself was made prisoner. This victory practically ended the war. The Mexicans were forced to withdraw across the Rio Grande; Texas had won its independence.

In 1836, a flag with a single star proclaimed the Republic of Texas. Sam Houston, once governor of Tennessee, became its first president. The first Congress of the Republic met at Columbia. Later the capital was established at a site on the Colorado River and called Austin, in honor of Stephen F. Austin, the "Father of Texas."

Texas joins the Union. The Texans had no intention of remaining an independent republic for long. They considered themselves Americans, and they wanted to be a part of the United States. Furthermore, they did not feel safe, since Mexico had refused to recognize their independence. So in 1836, Texas petitioned Congress to be **annexed,** or added, to the United States. But many Americans objected to admitting Texas into the Union. Texas, they said, would become a slave state. With its entrance into the Union, slave states would outnumber free states. Another reason for objection was that Mexico still claimed Texas and threatened to go to war if the United States accepted Texas. As a result, the Senate refused to approve the request of Texas for admission into the Union.

For nearly ten years the Lone Star Republic remained independent. By 1845, however, after the election of President Polk, the feeling against admitting Texas was not so strong. In December, 1845, Texas was admitted to the Union. Today Texans call their state the Lone Star State and fly the Lone Star Flag below Old Glory. They are proud of their heroic fight for independence and of the fact that they had once been an independent republic.

THE UNITED STATES AND MEXICO GO TO WAR

Mexico resents the annexation of Texas. The government of Mexico had never recognized the independence of Texas. Also, Santa Anna had informed the United States government that the annexation of Texas would mean war with Mexico. As a result, when Texas joined the United States, Mexico became very angry. To make matters worse, Texas boldly claimed for its southern boundary the Rio Grande. Mexico insisted that the Texas Republic

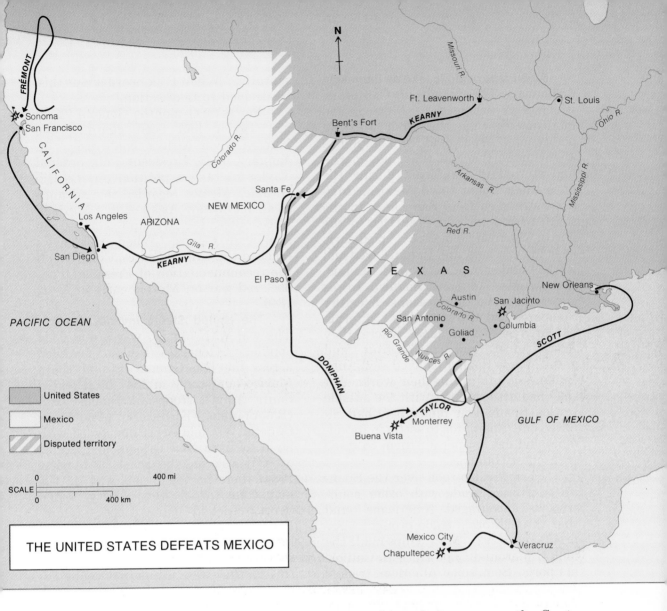

THE UNITED STATES DEFEATS MEXICO

Legend:
- United States
- Mexico
- Disputed territory

SCALE
0 — 400 mi
0 — 400 km

MAP STUDY   See Teacher's Key.
Trace the routes of Kearny, Taylor, and Scott as you read about them in the text. (When Kearny left Santa Fe, he sent part of his army south to join Taylor.) What important battles were fought in Mexico?

had included only the land as far south and west as the Nueces (noo-AY-sehs) River. (See map, above.)

Americans eye New Mexico. The annexation of Texas had another result. Americans who wanted the United States to expand began to look beyond Texas to other lands belonging to Mexico. For years American traders had

been making their way over the Santa Fe (FAY) Trail to the region of New Mexico. Each year a caravan of wagons creaked out of Independence, Missouri, and crawled across the plains of what is now Kansas toward Santa Fe. This town in New Mexico was so far from the sources of Mexican goods that its settlers would buy almost anything that American traders brought. Most of the traders took their profits and returned home, but a few stayed in Santa Fe. Americans began to want this whole region as a territory of the United States.

385

● Point out to students that the land between these two rivers was a disputed area.

Americans begin to take an interest in California. The region of California, which also belonged to Mexico, had more people than the other Mexican possessions. You read in Chapter 3 about the settlements that missionaries had started in California during the days when Spain ruled Mexico. Missions stretched from San Diego in the south to beyond San Francisco in the north. Spanish soldiers occupied forts near the missions, and Indians lived and worked under the direction of the mission priests. In time Spanish towns grew up around the missions. Wealthy Spaniards had also settled in California on large grants of land, where they raised horses and cattle, fruit, and grain. These Spaniards lived well, with Indian servants to do their work. But they had little contact with the outside world. Spain, you remember, had allowed only Spaniards to settle in its colonies and did not permit them to trade with other countries.

When Mexico took over the Spanish territories, trade with other countries was encouraged. Americans found that the California trade brought large profits (page 292). Many ships made the long trip around Cape Horn to California ports. Soon some American traders set up business in California; other Americans became ranchers. By 1846, several hundred Americans lived in California. Like all Americans they preferred to live under their own government, and there was talk about adding California to the United States. In fact, some Americans were willing to go to war to get California as well as New Mexico.

War begins with Mexico. With so much ill feeling between Mexico and the United States, the stage was set for war. In late 1845, President Polk had sent a representative to Mexico City to offer to buy California and New Mexico. But the Mexican government refused even to see the American representative. When Polk heard about this, he decided to take action.

For several months General Zachary Taylor had been guarding the Nueces River with a small army. In January, 1846, President Polk ordered Taylor to take a position on the Rio Grande. Mexico regarded this advance as an act of war. As a result, a Mexican force crossed the river and attacked the American troops. When this news reached the United States, Congress on the recommendation of President Polk declared war on Mexico early in May, 1846.

The United States invades Mexico. The war with Mexico was a one-sided conflict. General Taylor marched across the Rio Grande into northern Mexico, and early in 1847 he defeated Santa Anna's troops at Buena Vista (BWAY-nah VEES-tah). Meanwhile, General Winfield Scott had sailed with an army from New Orleans and landed at Veracruz on the coast of Mexico. From there he fought his way up the mountains toward Mexico City. When Scott reached Chapultepec (chuh-POOL-tuh-peck), an ancient palace and fortress near Mexico City, he demanded its surrender. Among the defenders of this fortress were a hundred young cadets from the national military school. When the commander refused to surrender, the Americans stormed and captured Chapultepec. The Mexican cadets died bravely fighting. They have become heroes of Mexico just as the men who defended the Alamo are heroes of our country. On September 14, 1847, the American troops entered Mexico City itself. The war was practically over.

California and the New Mexico region are conquered. While fighting was going on in Mexico, the United States had seized control of California and New Mexico. This was not difficult since (1) these regions were far from Mexico City and (2) they were defended only

386

See p. T37 for a strategy that helps students examine the causes and results of the war with Mexico.

Chapultepec was a fortress guarding the entrance to Mexico City. In spite of the heroic defense of young Mexican cadets, it was captured by American troops in 1847.

by small groups of Mexican soldiers. This is how it happened.

Soon after the war began, an American force under Colonel Stephen W. Kearny had set out for Santa Fe. After capturing that city without a struggle, part of his small army moved on westward across the desert to California. Meanwhile, Americans who lived in California had already overthrown the Mexican government. Their revolt was called the Bear Flag Revolution because the Americans carried a flag which showed the figure of a grizzly bear. John C. Frémont, a United States Army officer, became a leader of the new Bear Flag Republic proclaimed by the Californians. Colonel Kearny ar-

rived soon after the revolt began. Despite stiff resistance from Mexican settlers near San Diego who opposed the Bear Flag Republic, he was able to take over all of California. The new Bear Flag gave way to the Stars and Stripes, though it survives today as the state flag of California. Thus, early in the Mexican War, the United States gained control over the regions of California and New Mexico.

THE UNITED STATES ACQUIRES THE SOUTHWEST

The war brings a vast territory to the United States. In February, 1848, the Mexican government was forced to make peace. Mexico had to accept the Rio Grande as its border. In so doing, it recognized Texas as belonging to the United States. (Texas at this time included not only the present state of

387

● Have students draw a time line of the war with Mexico, showing events from January, 1846, to February, 1848.

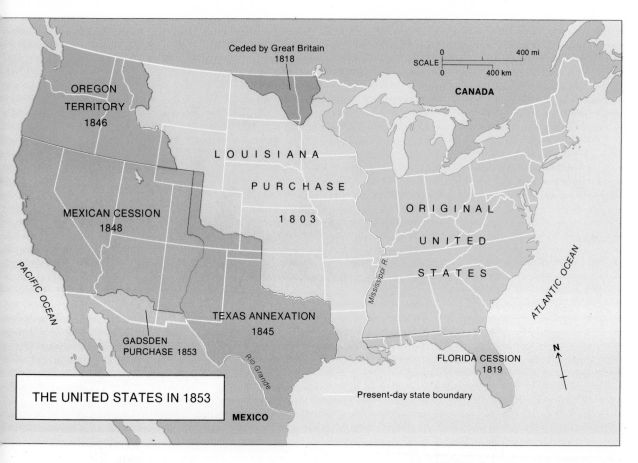

THE UNITED STATES IN 1853

Ceded by Great Britain 1818

OREGON TERRITORY 1846

CANADA

LOUISIANA

PURCHASE

1 8 0 3

ORIGINAL

UNITED

STATES

MEXICAN CESSION 1848

GADSDEN PURCHASE 1853

TEXAS ANNEXATION 1845

PACIFIC OCEAN

Mississippi R.

ATLANTIC OCEAN

Rio Grande

FLORIDA CESSION 1819

N

Present-day state boundary

MEXICO

SCALE
0 — 400 mi
0 — 400 km

MAP STUDY   See Teacher's Key.
By 1848 the United States had acquired territory stretching from the Atlantic to the Pacific. What additional land was acquired in 1853?

Texas but also parts of New Mexico, Colorado, Oklahoma, Wyoming, and Kansas.) As part of the peace treaty, Mexico also had to turn over a huge area called the Mexican Cession. It contained the present states of California, Nevada, Utah, most of Arizona, and parts of New Mexico, Wyoming, and Colorado. The Mexican Cession amounted to almost half of Mexico's territory. In return, the United States agreed to pay Mexico $15,000,000 in cash and also to pay American citizens $3,250,000 which the Mexican government owed them.

Who lived in the Mexican Cession?
When Mexico signed the treaty that

turned over the Mexican Cession to the United States, there were about 75,000 Spanish-speaking people in the region. Mexico insisted that the rights of those people be respected. The United States agreed that the Spanish-speaking people could keep their language, religion, and culture. Their property and political rights would be respected as well.

Other inhabitants in the Mexican Cession included some 250,000 Indians. Many of the tribes in the region had long resisted Spanish and Mexican rule. They were equally determined to protect their way of life from the newly victorious Americans. During the next forty years, the Apache, Comanche, and Navajo fought the United States Army to hold onto their land.

The United States buys more land from Mexico. In 1853, the United States paid Mexico $10 million for a stretch of

● The story of what happened to these and other western tribes will be told in Chapter 21.

Mexican and American troops fought in California as well as in Mexico. This battle took place near Los Angeles.

land in the southern part of what are now New Mexico and Arizona. This area was needed to provide a route for a railroad which the United States wanted to build to the west coast. Since the arrangements were made by an American named James Gadsden, this land was called the Gadsden Purchase. (See the map on page 388.) In a few short years, therefore, the United States had reached its present boundary in the Southwest.

▶ **CHECK UP**   See Teacher's Key.

1. **(a)** Why did Americans begin to settle in Texas after 1822? **(b)** Why did the Texans revolt against Mexico?
2. **(a)** How did Texas become an independent republic? **(b)** Why did some Americans oppose the admission of Texas into the Union?
3. **(a)** How did the annexation of Texas lead to war with Mexico? **(b)** Where did fighting take place in Mexico? **(c)** How did the United States win control of California and New Mexico?
4. **(a)** What were the results of the Mexican War? **(b)** What was the Gadsden Purchase?

4 How Did the Discovery of Gold Bring California into the Union?

The Mexican Cession opened up vast stretches of new land for restless pioneers. But not many American settlers were interested in the dry and mountainous regions that made up much of the Southwest. They did not yet realize the value of these lands for cattle raising. Nor did they know that rich deposits of copper, gold, and silver were located here. The story of California, on the other hand, is quite different. An exciting discovery brought adventurous Americans stampeding into California soon after it became part of the United States.

Gold is discovered in California. Gold had long been mined throughout Spain's colonies. And after Mexico

389

gained its independence from Spain, mining continued in California. But by the time California had been made a United States territory, much richer mines were discovered.

In the 1840's, a man named John Sutter lived in California, not far from where the city of Sacramento stands today. Sutter had spent his youth in Switzerland. Longing to see the world and make his fortune, he had set out for America. In 1839, he had settled in California, where he soon acquired much land. He raised wheat and corn and owned great herds of cattle, horses, and sheep.

On a rainy afternoon early in 1848, he was visited by James Marshall, a man who was building a sawmill for Sutter some miles away. Marshall was breathless with excitement and demanded to see him alone. This is how
● John Sutter described Marshall's visit:

I was surprised to see him. Only the day before I had sent him all the supplies he could possibly need. . . . I could not [understand] the purpose in this unexpected visit. Yet I conducted him from my office to my private rooms — parlor and bedroom — where we shut the door.

"Is the door locked?" said Marshall.

"No," I answered, "but I will lock it if you wish." He was a [strange] fellow and I only supposed he took this way of telling me some secret.

Then he said distinctly: "Are we alone?"

"Surely," I answered.

[Marshall then asked for some scales.]

Shrugging, and thinking to humor him, I went myself and fetched the scales. On my return I failed to lock the door. Then Marshall dug feverishly into his pantaloon pockets and pulled forth a white cotton rag which had something rolled up in it. Just as he was unfolding it to show me the con-

tents, the door was opened by a clerk who was merely passing through on some business and was not aware we were in the room at all.

"There!" screamed Marshall, "did I not tell you we had listeners!"

Quickly he thrust the rag back into his pocket. I [quieted] him, my curiosity aroused. Ordering the surprised clerk to retire, I locked the door.

Then he drew out the rag again. Opening the cloth carefully, he held it before me in his hand. It held what might have been an ounce and a half of gold dust — dust, flakes and grains. The biggest piece was not as large as a

● See p. T37 for a strategy that asks students to discuss the gold rush of 1849 and its effect on the development of California.

pea and varied from that down to less than a pinhead in size.

"I believe it is gold!" whispered Marshall, his eyes wild and restless. "But the people at the mill laughed at me — said I was crazy!" I examined his find closely.

"Yes, it looks like gold," I admitted slowly. "Come let us test it. . . ."

The test showed that Marshall had indeed discovered gold!

Gold seekers rush to California. The news of the discovery of gold could not be kept behind locked doors for long. Quickly it spread through the neighbor-

hood, then through all California. By 1849 it had leaped across the United States and around the world. Adventurous people by the thousands deserted shops, farms, offices, and headed for California. The dream of getting rich from a few weeks of work in the California ● gold fields lured them on. Great crowds of uninvited visitors rushed to John Sutter's land. They camped in his fields, trampled down his crops, stole his horses and cattle. Sacramento was

Prospectors flocked to California after gold was found in 1849. These forty-niners are washing gold out of the soil of a riverbank.

391

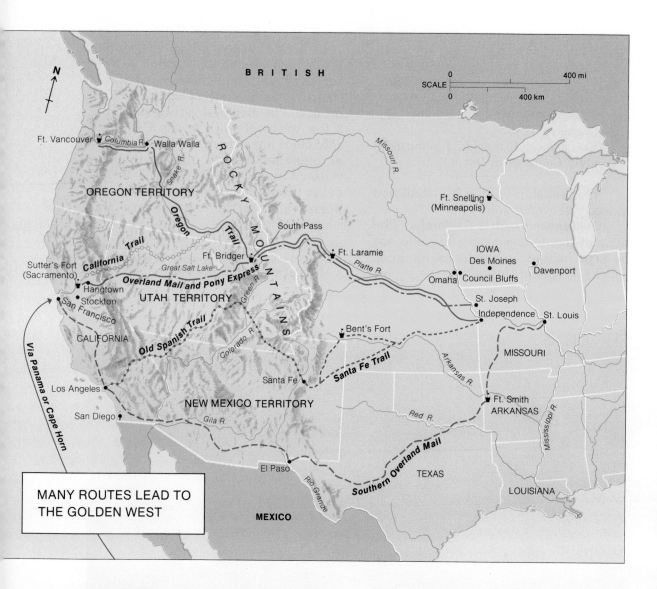

BRITISH

SCALE

Ft. Vancouver • Columbia R. • Walla Walla

OREGON TERRITORY

ROCKY MOUNTAINS

South Pass

Snake R.

Oregon Trail

Missouri R.

Ft. Snelling
(Minneapolis)

California Trail

Sutter's Fort
(Sacramento)
Ft. Bridger
Great Salt Lake

Ft. Laramie
Platte R.

IOWA
Des Moines

Davenport

Overland Mail and Pony Express

Hangtown
Stockton
San Francisco

UTAH TERRITORY

Green R.

Omaha Council Bluffs

St. Joseph

Independence • St. Louis

CALIFORNIA

Old Spanish Trail

Colorado R.

Bent's Fort

Santa Fe Trail

Arkansas R.

MISSOURI

Los Angeles

San Diego

NEW MEXICO TERRITORY

Gila R.

Santa Fe

Red R.

Ft. Smith
ARKANSAS

Mississippi R.

Via Panama or Cape Horn

MANY ROUTES LEAD TO
THE GOLDEN WEST

El Paso

Rio Grande

Southern Overland Mail

TEXAS

LOUISIANA

MEXICO

MAP STUDY   See Teacher's Key.
(a) What states lined the western bank of the
Mississippi River by the mid-1800's? (b) By what
routes could people travel to the west coast?
Tell where each of the routes began and where
each ended.

started on part of Sutter's land. From a
settlement of just four houses in April,
1848, it soon grew to a booming city of
almost 10,000.

The **forty-niners,** as the people
who rushed to California for gold were
called, were not like the ordinary American pioneers. Most were men without

families, adventurers seeking to make a
fortune in gold.

**The forty-niners come by land and
sea.**   The forty-niners had a choice of
several routes to California. Look at the
map on this page and trace the routes as
you read. Independence, Missouri, was
the starting point for the overland travelers. From here they could take the old
trail to Santa Fe and go on across the
deserts of New Mexico, Arizona, and
California. This route took over two
months, and those who followed it suffered from heat and thirst. More of the
forty-niners followed the Oregon Trail

392

(of which we will read later) as far as the Great Salt Lake. Then they struggled on across deserts and mountains to northern California. These adventurous travelers ran the dreadful risk of being caught in the mountains by deep winter snow.

The gold seekers could also go to California by sea. The safest but longest trip was around South America and north to San Francisco. Because this journey took from six to nine months, many of the forty-niners chose a faster route by way of Panama. Ships of every kind, jammed with passengers, sailed from the Atlantic coast of the United States to the east coast of Panama. From there the travelers crossed the Isthmus through jungle and swamp to the Pacific coast. Many died of fever or diseases caused by insect bites. Those who survived boarded ships for San Francisco.

Not all of the people who rushed to California were from the United States. Thousands of Mexicans moved north, attracted by the news of the gold discoveries. In addition, large numbers of people from China came to California to work in the mines.

Life was rough in California in 1849. After reaching California, the gold seekers rushed to the rivers and mountainsides where gold had been found. There they staked out their claims (small plots of land) and started digging gravel and washing it for gold. Life at the mines or diggings was rough. Anyone who moved in on another person's claim was tried by a court of miners and punished. People who stole gold were hanged. Fighting, robbery, and murder were common in the mining camps. The camps often had odd names, such as Hangtown, You-Bet, Red Dog, and Ground Hog Glory. Within ten years about $500 million worth of gold was found in California. Some of the miners who came the first year, when gold was plentiful, became rich. But the latecomers, for all

Black explorers like Jim Beckwourth helped blaze trails through the rugged American West. Beckwourth discovered a way through the Sierra Nevadas that is now called Beckwourth Pass. A hunter, trapper, and scout, he lived for a time with the Crow Indians.

their trouble, were often no better off than they had been back home.

Some people realized that they could make more money by selling food and supplies to the miners than by looking for gold. The miners carried bags of gold dust and paid for goods in ounces of gold instead of with dollars. Prices were much higher than in other parts of the United States. Eggs were 50 cents apiece, onions were a dollar a pound, and bread was 50 cents a loaf.

The miners' chief amusements were gambling, racing, and drinking. It was hard to keep law and order when thousands of gold-seekers were bent on making fortunes by any means possible.

Crime was especially serious in San Francisco. Adventurers from all over the world passed through that city on their way to the diggings. San Francisco grew rapidly as boarding houses, hotels, and saloons were hastily put up to serve the crowds of gold seekers. Gamblers and criminals flocked there to prey on the miners. Murder became an everyday happening. In self-defense, some citizens formed committees to keep order. They called themselves the **vigilantes** (vij-uh-LAN-teez). (To be *vigilant* is to be alert to danger.) Many of the most desperate criminals were arrested, tried, and hanged. Others got out of town before they were caught.

California becomes a state. By the end of 1849, California had grown so tremendously that its people drew up a state constitution. In September, 1850, California was admitted to the Union as a free state. Travel was so slow that it took over a month for Californians to get the news from the eastern part of the country.

By 1860, there were 380,000 people in California, most of them in the northern part of the state. This was four times the population ten years earlier. San Francisco had become an important city with more than 50,000 inhabitants. When gold was no longer plentiful, many mining camps became deserted ghost towns; others, however, developed into flourishing communities. Stockton and Sacramento, located at the entrance to the gold regions, grew rapidly. Hangtown changed its name to Placerville and became a settled community. Los Angeles and San Diego in the south were not affected by the gold rush. They remained small towns for many years.

The Overland stage connects California with the East. California was 2,000 miles away from the eastern part of the United States. Naturally travelers to or from the coast did not want to spend several months on the way. So stagecoach lines were established which ran from cities on the Missouri River to points in California. The most important of these was the Overland Mail. It carried mail and passengers from St. Louis and St. Joseph to San Francisco.

The stagecoaches, called Concord coaches, were pulled by four or six horses and carried as many as nine passengers and three sacks of mail. They traveled day and night, stopping every ten or fifteen miles at wayside stations to change horses. Passengers paid about $200 for the trip, which took from 20 to 25 days. The journey was dangerous. If the coaches hit something or lost a wheel, passengers might be injured or killed in the accident. Another danger came from bandits who waylaid the coaches, especially those carrying gold from the mines. Travelers were robbed and bags of gold stolen by these outlaws. Not content with stealing, they often killed their victims in cold blood.

The Pony Express furnishes fast mail service. The stagecoach, however, was too slow for important mail. In 1860 the famous Pony Express was established for that purpose. It took from eight to twelve days to cover the distance from St. Joseph, Missouri, to Sacramento, California. The riders for the Pony Express were carefully picked. They needed to be strong and brave, for they had to ride over mountain and desert in all kinds of weather and they often had to fight off bandits. The riders wore buckskin suits and carried rifles, knives, or six-shooters. The men rode for stretches of about one hundred miles ● apiece. Each rode at top speed, dashing into a station every ten or fifteen miles to change horses. A rider would throw his saddlebags containing the mail on a fresh horse, mount, and speed on his way in less than two minutes. One of the best Pony Express riders once covered 120 miles in eight hours.

● Ask students to recall Marco Polo's description of the Great Khan's communication system (p. 33). Have students compare that system to the Pony Express.

The writer Mark Twain, traveling west on the Overland stagecoach, described the thrill of seeing a Pony Express rider:

We had had a . . . desire, from the beginning, to see a pony-rider, but somehow or other all that passed us and all that met us managed to streak by in the night, and so we heard only a whiz and a hail, and the swift phantom of the desert was gone before we could get our heads out of the windows. But now we were expecting one along every moment, and would see him in broad daylight. Presently the driver exclaims:

"Here he comes!"

Every neck is stretched further, and every eye strained wider. Away across the endless dead level of the prairie a black speck appears against the sky, and it is plain that it moves. Well, I should think so! In a second or two it becomes a horse and rider, rising and falling, rising and falling — sweeping toward us nearer and nearer — growing

An Overland stage heads west. Few people made the trip for pleasure, since it meant a three-week journey in a lurching, crowded stagecoach.

Pony Express riders carried mail from St. Joseph, Missouri, to Sacramento in eight days. Here a rider dashes off on a fresh horse.

more and more distinct, more and more sharply defined — nearer and still nearer — and the flutter of the hoofs comes faintly to the ear — another instant a whoop and a hurrah from our upper deck, a wave of the rider's hand, but no reply, and man and horse burst past our excited faces, and go winging away. . . .

The Pony Express operated for only a little more than one year. In that short time, however, its riders became glamorous figures in American life. Their heroic deeds have been told in stories and motion pictures. The company that operated the Pony Express went out of business in 1861, about the same time that a telegraph line to San Francisco was completed. Mail continued to go by stagecoach until the first cross-country railroad was completed in 1869. (Locate the routes of the Overland Mail and the Pony Express on the map on page 392.)

▶ **CHECK UP**   See Teacher's Key.

1. **(a)** Where was gold discovered in California? **(b)** By what routes did the gold seekers travel to California? **(c)** What was life like in the gold mining towns?
2. How did the gold rush help California become a state?
3. What kinds of communication and transportation linked California and the East?

● See p. T37 for a strategy that asks students to compare British and American claims to Oregon.

5 How Did the United States Gain Part of the Oregon Country?

Suppose the map on page 388 were a jigsaw puzzle. It would have four pieces representing the steps by which the United States extended its territory west of the Louisiana Purchase until it reached the Pacific Ocean. So far in this chapter you have read about the addition of three of those pieces — the Texas Annexation, the Mexican Cession, and the Gadsden Purchase. The remaining piece is Oregon. How was that piece fitted into the puzzle?

Four nations claim Oregon. All the region between Alaska and California was once called Oregon. This beautiful land had many fur-bearing animals. In the early 1800's Oregon was claimed by four nations.

(1) Spain said it owned Oregon because, when Balboa reached the Pacific Ocean in 1513, he had claimed all the lands it touched for Spain. Also, later Spanish explorers had sailed along the Oregon coast.

(2) Britain claimed Oregon because Sir Francis Drake, in his voyage around the world, had sailed along the coast of Oregon in 1579. Still more important were the British explorations by Captain James Cook and Captain George Vancouver. Captain Cook had explored the coast as far as northern Alaska. Captain Vancouver had discovered Puget Sound and had sailed around Vancouver Island, which was named in his honor.

(3) In the 1700's, Russia laid claim to Oregon. A navigator named Vitus Bering had discovered the strait now named for him and crossed it to claim Alaska for Russia. The Russians established colonies in North America and hunted furs along the coast of Alaska and south to California.

(4) The fourth country to make a bid for Oregon was the United States. ● Captain Robert Gray, who carried furs from Oregon to China (page 292), had sailed up the mouth of the Columbia River. The explorations of Lewis and Clark, who also reached the mouth of the Columbia, strengthened the claim of the United States.

Pioneers faced many dangers on the way to Oregon. This picture and the one on page 396 are both by artist Frederic Remington.

The journey to Oregon took about five months through spring, summer, and fall. When pioneers finally reached their destination, they built settlements like this one at Oregon City.

Rival fur companies compete for furs in Oregon. Early in the 1800's, both British and American traders began to see possibilities for a rich fur trade in Oregon. The British had already built up a large and profitable fur trade in the region around the Great Lakes and Hudson Bay. John Jacob Astor was a leader in the American fur trade. He had come to America from Germany soon after the Revolutionary War. Astor dreamed of establishing a line of trading posts extending west from the Mississippi to the Pacific. Furs could be sent from these posts to a port in Oregon and from there they could be shipped to cities in China.

Astor organized the American Fur Company and hired French-Canadian fur traders to work for him. In 1811, Astor's men made the difficult journey to the Pacific coast. They built a fur-trading post, called Astoria, near the mouth of the Columbia River. No sooner had the American company established its post than it discovered that the British had built a post where Spokane, Washington, is today. For a short time these two companies were rivals for the Oregon fur business. But the War of 1812 ruined Astor's plans. At that time, the Americans sold their holdings to the British.

Britain and the United States share Oregon. After the war, both the United States and Great Britain still had strong claims to Oregon, and neither intended to give them up. In 1818 the two countries agreed, therefore, to the **joint occupation** of Oregon; that is, they decided to own Oregon together. Shortly afterward, both Spain and Russia gave up their claims to Oregon. Spain agreed to claim no land north of the forty-second parallel, while Russia gave up any claims south of the latitude of 54°40'. (See map, next page.) Thus, the United States and Great Britain were free to try to work out their plan of joint occupation in the Oregon Country.

The British settle Oregon first. For about 20 years after 1818, not many Americans went to Oregon. Only a few fur traders and other daring persons from the East were willing to risk the long and dangerous journey across the western plains and mountains. The British, on the other hand, were making good profits from the Oregon fur trade, which was very largely controlled by the Hudson's Bay Company. There was no regular government in Oregon during this period. In Fort Vancouver, John McLoughlin, a Canadian, was employed by the Hudson's Bay Company to act as governor. McLoughlin treated the Indians fairly and welcomed the few Americans who found their way to Oregon. He believed that the people in Oregon should not rely on fur trading for their living but should also raise their own food. Soon there were crops growing in fields around Fort Vancouver, and farms were being started throughout Oregon.

Americans learn about Oregon. News of this Pacific Northwest region did not attract many Americans until the late 1830's. Then the news was spread by missionaries who had gone there to teach Christianity to the Indians. Among these missionaries were Henry and Eliza Spalding and Marcus and Narcissa Whitman. In 1836 they made the dangerous journey to Fort Vancouver, where they were welcomed by John McLoughlin. Narcissa Whitman and Eliza Spalding were the first white women to cross the western mountains into the Pacific Northwest.

The Whitmans started a mission at Walla Walla near the Columbia River. For about eleven years they worked among the Cayuse Indians. The Whitmans were finally killed by the Cayuse in a misunderstanding during a measles epidemic. Before this tragedy, however, they had written enthusiastic letters ★ back East describing the rich farm lands, the climate, the forests, and the salmon fishing in Oregon.

399

● Remind students that the term *parallel* means "line of latitude."

★ Discuss how letters like these would have attracted more settlers to Oregon.

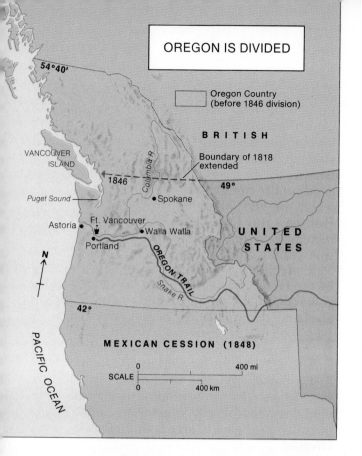

OREGON IS DIVIDED

Oregon Country (before 1846 division)

BRITISH

Boundary of 1818 extended

VANCOUVER ISLAND

Columbia R.

1846

49°

Puget Sound

Spokane

Astoria

Ft. Vancouver

Walla Walla

UNITED STATES

Portland

OREGON TRAIL

Snake R.

42°

MEXICAN CESSION (1848)

SCALE

0 — 400 mi

0 — 400 km

PACIFIC OCEAN

54°40'

N

MAP STUDY See Teacher's Key.
The Oregon dispute was settled by extending the border between Canada and the United States to the Pacific. The part of Oregon that the United States gained was called the Oregon Territory. What were some settlements there?

Americans follow the Oregon Trail.
Reports from the Whitmans and others reached the East soon after the Panic of 1837 broke out. Many people were out of work at that time and feeling discouraged. Soon covered wagons began rolling westward. The route these pioneers followed was the famous Oregon Trail (map, page 392). The pioneers gathered at some town along the Missouri River, such as Independence or St. Joseph or Omaha. Here they banded together in large caravans for protection. When the spring grass was high enough to feed the horses and cattle, they set out on their 2,000-mile journey. Scouts on horseback went far ahead of the wagons to see what lay ahead. For many days the long line of prairie schooners, horses,

400

cattle, and oxen crawled westward from dawn to dusk. Each night the wagons were drawn up in a circle. If all went well, there was time to reach Oregon before snow fell in the Rockies and made the mountains impassable. If anything delayed the pioneers, they knew they would be in serious trouble.

The trail left the Missouri River and followed the Platte River along its north branch into the Rockies. From here the pioneers climbed a steep grade to the South Pass, a broad, level valley that cut through the Rockies. To the west they found the Green River and from there they crossed to the Snake River. The Snake took them north and west to the great Columbia. Oregon at last!

Oregon is divided. By the early 1840's several thousand Americans had made their way to Oregon, where they had become farmers and had started little villages. But these settlers were not satisfied to have Oregon shared by the United States and Great Britain. Like American settlers in Texas and California, they wanted a government of their own and they wanted to be part of the United States. Soon the governments of Great Britain and the United States began to realize that the plan of joint occupation would no longer work.

Many Americans insisted that the United States should claim all of Oregon, just as they called for the annexation of Texas and the whole Southwest. James K. Polk was their champion. When he ran for President in 1844, he strongly supported both causes. Popular slogans like "All of Oregon or none" and "Fifty-four forty or fight" expressed the feelings that people had about Oregon. After his election, President Polk set out to gain Oregon as well as the Southwest.

So many Americans had settled in Oregon that the British fur trade was no longer as profitable as it had been. The

● Point out that the United States was claiming land all the way north to Alaska.

British government, realizing this, was willing to compromise but not to give up all of Oregon. The United States also was willing to compromise. Early in 1846, the quarrel between the United States and Mexico threatened to turn into war (page 386). It would have been unwise for President Polk to risk war with the British at the same time. In June of 1846, therefore, an agreement was reached between the governments of Great Britain and the United States. This agreement divided Oregon between the two countries at the forty-ninth parallel of latitude. The border between Canada and the United States had previously been set at that latitude from the Great Lakes to the Rocky Mountains. The agreement of 1846 simply extended this line to the Pacific Ocean (map, page 400).

The land in the Pacific Northwest below the forty-ninth parallel was organized by Congress as the Oregon Territory. Its population continued to grow, and in 1859 part of the territory was admitted to the Union as the state of
● Oregon. The rest of the territory was then called Washington. Out of it, years later, the states of Washington and Idaho were formed.

In this chapter you have learned (1) how East and West Florida were secured from Spain, (2) how Texas joined the Union, (3) how a war with Mexico added California and the Southwest to the United States, and (4) how the great Pacific Northwest became part of our country. The westward march of American pioneers had begun when "the West" was only a few miles inland from the Atlantic seacoast. Now it had reached the Pacific Ocean. Finally, the United States stretched across North America for 2,800 miles, "from sea to shining sea."

▶ **CHECK UP**   See Teacher's Key.

1. **(a)** What four countries claimed the Oregon Country in the early 1800's? **(b)** What was the basis for the claim of each of these countries? **(c)** How was Oregon governed after 1818?
2. **(a)** Why were the British interested in Oregon? **(b)** Why did Americans begin to settle there? **(c)** By what route did American settlers reach Oregon?
3. How did Great Britain and the United States settle their rival claims to Oregon?

CHECK UP ON CHAPTER 18   See Teacher's Key.

Words to Know

1. annex
2. cession
3. vigilante
4. expansionist
5. forty-niner
6. joint occupation

Places to Locate

1. St. Louis
2. Texas
3. Rio Grande
4. Astoria
5. Santa Fe
6. San Antonio
7. Independence
8. Missouri River
9. Nueces River
10. Platte River
11. Columbia River
12. San Francisco

Facts to Remember

1. **(a)** What was the purpose of the Lewis and Clark expedition? **(b)** Describe the route taken by Lewis and Clark. **(c)** How did Sacagawea help those explorers?
2. **(a)** What did *West Florida* and *East Florida* mean in the early 1800's? **(b)** How did Florida become part of the United States?
3. **(a)** What part did Stephen Austin and Sam Houston each play in the history

401

Facts to Remember (cont.)

of Texas? **(b)** Tell how each of the following was involved in the Mexican War: James K. Polk, Zachary Taylor, Stephen W. Kearny.

4. **(a)** Why did California's population grow so fast in the 1850's? **(b)** How did people travel between California and the eastern states at that time?
5. **(a)** What was the Oregon Trail? **(b)** Tell why people followed that trail and how they traveled.

Skills to Practice

1. Look back through this chapter (pages 374–401) and find two primary sources. Write on your paper the page number where you find each primary source, the person who originally wrote it, and a short description of what the source is about.
2. Look at the map on page 388. Tell what present-day states were either partly or totally carved out of each of the following territorial additions to the United States: **(a)** the Texas Annexation, **(b)** the Mexican Cession, **(c)** the Oregon Territory. (You may need to look at a map of the present-day United States.)

Questions to Think About

1. After the War of 1812 many Americans argued that it was the destiny of the United States to acquire Florida and the land westward to the Pacific. **(a)** Why did they feel that way? **(b)** How did Spaniards, Mexicans, British, and Canadians probably feel about it?
2. Several generals (among them William Henry Harrison, Andrew Jackson, and Zachary Taylor) have become Presidents of the United States. Why? What qualities might a general have that would make him a good President? Explain your answer.
3. **(a)** Why did the frontier in about 1850 jump from the area just west of the Mississippi to the Pacific coast? **(b)** How would you draw the line of the frontier after that date?

Linking Past and Present

Dallas, Texas. In 1841, a log hut was built on the Trinity River, where Dallas stands today. Soon a village, known as Peter's Colony, grew up. In 1845, the village took the name of Dallas, in honor of George M. Dallas, the Pennsylvania statesman who had just been elected Vice-President of the United States. By 1871 Dallas had been incorporated as a city.

Why did this small village grow into a city so quickly? First, it was located in the famous "black lands" of Texas, a rich agricultural section. On the fertile farms and plantations surrounding Dallas great quantities of cotton were produced. Dallas became the market for this cotton. Railroads were built to move the cotton, and factories were started to make cotton gins. Other businesses followed. Later on, oil was discovered nearby. Even more wealth now flowed through the city, and Dallas grew big and rich and important.

Seattle, Washington. Founded in the 1850's, Seattle grew from a settlement of twenty-one people to become one of the leading cities of the Pacific Northwest. How can this be explained? We must consider Seattle's favorable location as a great port for ocean-going ships. At first the city depended mostly on lumber from the huge forests nearby, and this industry is still important. In 1884, however, the Northern Pacific Railroad reached Seattle and connected the city with eastern trade. Then, when gold was discovered in Canada's Yukon Territory, Seattle became, almost overnight, a teeming city where gold seekers bought their supplies and booked passage for the gold fields. Many of them came back to Seattle to spend the gold they had found. When the Panama Canal was dug, it opened Seattle to easy and inexpensive trade with our eastern ports and with Europe. Since Seattle faces the Pacific, its trade with Asia became important too.

402

● Have students compare Dallas and Seattle to Chicago (p. 368). Discuss the factors that led to the growth of each city.

Discuss the reason for incomplete symbols in pictographs. Tell students to use the information shown in the circle graphs on p. 329 to construct pictographs.

GAINING SKILL

Reading Pictographs

In the late 1840's, thousands of people streamed across the mountains or sailed around Cape Horn to get to California and dig for gold. Never before in American history had the population of a territory increased so fast. Even after the excitement of the gold rush, California's population continued to grow.

The graph below shows how California's population increased during the first thirty years of statehood. This kind of graph is called a pictograph. Pictographs use picture symbols to stand for numbers. To read the graph, make sure you understand what number each picture symbol stands for. The following questions will help you understand the pictograph on this page.

1. What period of years does the pictograph cover?
2. How many people does each symbol stand for in this pictograph?
3. In what year shown on this pictograph was California's population the largest?
4. In what year was California's population less than 100,000?
5. In what year was the population more than 500,000 but less than 600,000?
6. During which decade did California's population more than triple?
7. What was the approximate population in 1860?
8. The following table gives population figures for the state of Texas.

Year	Population
1850	213,000
1860	604,000
1870	819,000
1880	1,592,000

Make a pictograph to show this information. Let each symbol in your pictograph stand for 200,000 people.

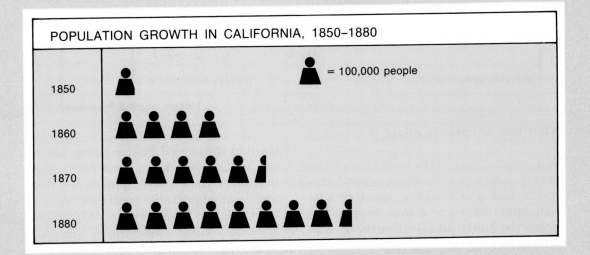

POPULATION GROWTH IN CALIFORNIA, 1850–1880

= 100,000 people

1850

1860

1870

1880

403

Vocabulary preview: states' rights, fugitive, popular sovereignty

The North and the South Break Apart

1820–1861 .See pp. T38–T39 for chapter teaching strategies.

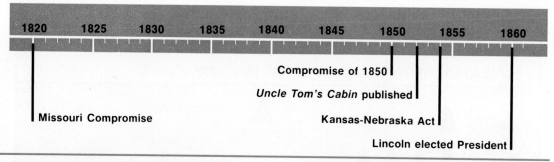

| 1820 | 1825 | 1830 | 1835 | 1840 | 1845 | 1850 | 1855 | 1860 |

Compromise of 1850

Uncle Tom's Cabin published

Missouri Compromise

Kansas-Nebraska Act

Lincoln elected President

What this chapter is about —

Of all wars, those between people of the same country are the most tragic. Between 1861 and 1865 our country was torn apart by such a war, fought between the North and the South. It was called the Civil War.

As you know, different ways of living had developed in the North and in the South. Because of those differences, people in the two sections often disagreed on important questions such as the tariff and foreign trade. When questions like these came up in Congress, debate often became heated.

The differences between North and South grew into a tragic division during the 1850's. In Kansas, the argument over slavery exploded into fighting between northern and southern settlers.

Disagreements are natural in a country as large as the United States, and usually it is possible to settle them peacefully. But by the 1850's, the disagreement over slavery sharply split the North and South. States in the North had given up slavery by the early 1800's. But the southern states had held onto slavery because cotton planters felt they needed slaves to work their fields. Even the slavery issue might in time have been worked out peacefully had the country not been rapidly expanding. Again and again, the North and the South argued over the question of permitting slavery in the new western lands. For several years these arguments were settled by compromises. But finally the quarrel became so bitter that compromise was no longer possible, and our country moved steadily toward war.

The following questions will help you to understand the events that led up to the Civil War:

1. How did the North and the South try to settle their differences?
2. How did the two sections move closer to conflict?
3. What events led to war?

1 How Did the North and the South Try to Settle Their Differences?

In the previous chapter you learned how the United States gained more and more land, until it stretched across the plains and mountains to the Pacific coast. People from both the North and the South moved into these new lands. Naturally they took with them the ways of living and thinking to which they were accustomed. As additional settlements were started, new states were sure to be formed. Both the North and the South realized how important the votes of the Westerners in Congress would be. Would these votes add to the strength of the North or the South? Would the Westerners favor slavery or oppose it? Both sections needed the votes of the new western states.

SLAVERY IS AN ISSUE IN THE LOUISIANA TERRITORY

The admission of Missouri starts a conflict over slavery. The first territory to be added to the United States was the Louisiana Purchase, and the first state to be formed from this territory was Louisiana. There was no question about slavery there. Louisiana was clearly in the lower South, and had allowed slavery since its early days. So Louisiana was admitted to the Union as a slave state. But in 1819, when Missouri asked to become a state, an angry dispute concerning slavery broke out between the North and the South. Missouri, too, was a part of the Louisiana Purchase. But it lay much farther north than the state of Louisiana.

Many slave-owners had settled in Missouri. When Missouri asked permission to become a state, its people adopted a rule that would allow slavery in the new state. But when Missouri's request to enter the Union came before Congress, a northern representative demanded that Congress admit Missouri only if slavery were banned there.

405

Review the ways in which Northerners and Southerners lived. (See Chapters 14 and 15.)

This angered white Southerners. They feared that if slavery were banned in Missouri, it might be forbidden in other states to be carved out of the Louisiana Purchase. Why, they asked, should Northerners without slaves be allowed to go West to settle and form states when southern slave-owners were forbidden to do so?

The Missouri Compromise settles the quarrel. When the dispute was at fever pitch, Maine asked to be admitted to the Union as a separate state. (It was then a part of Massachusetts.) The people of Maine did not want slavery. At once people began to say, "Here is a chance to settle the quarrel over Missouri." In 1820 Congress reached a settlement which is called the Missouri Compromise or the Compromise of 1820.

Under this compromise, (1) Missouri came into the Union as a slave state and (2) Maine as a free state. (3) To settle the question of slavery in the rest of the Louisiana Purchase, a dividing line was agreed upon. This line was a continuation of the southern boundary of Missouri and ran westward across the entire Louisiana Purchase. (See the first map on page 407.) In the future, all states to be made out of the Louisiana Purchase were to be free states if they lay north of that line. If they lay south of the line, they would be permitted to have slavery.

This compromise seemed to settle the argument. The South received what it had asked — slavery in Missouri. The North could count on the votes of Maine in Congress to balance those of Missouri. Both sides were relieved that Congress had passed a law settling the question of slavery within the Louisiana Purchase. The North was especially satisfied, for Congress had taken the position that it had a right to decide about slavery in territories still to become states.

The quarrel leaves a feeling of uneasiness. Even though the quarrel had ended in compromise, many people still felt disturbed. Looking into the future, they feared that new quarrels would arise over slavery, and that these might be even more dangerous than the one which had just been settled. Thomas Jefferson expressed this fear when he wrote: "This momentous question, like a fire bell in the night, awakened and ★ filled me with terror." He added that in "the gloomiest hour of the Revolutionary War" he had not been so afraid for his country.

THE NORTH AND THE SOUTH ARGUE OVER STATES' RIGHTS

The argument over admitting Missouri to the Union had made white Southerners aware of a threat to their way of living. Cotton was wearing out the soil of the South, and Southerners feared that a day might come when they would need new land on which to grow cotton. They were also troubled (as you read in Chapter 17) by high tariff laws, which raised prices on many articles. The South bought quantities of manufactured goods from England, which in turn bought much of the South's cotton. Therefore, high tariff duties seemed to threaten the prosperity of the South. Southerners were loyal to the Union, but they began to ask: "How can we live peaceably in the Union and yet be assured of conditions necessary to our way of life?"

The idea of states' rights grows in the South. It seemed to southern leaders that there was a way to stay in the Union and at the same time protect southern interests. The Constitution, you remember, divides the powers of government between the United States and the individual states. The United States government has only those powers that are listed in the Constitution. All other powers belong to the states. White Southerners believed they could protect their way of living by insisting

406

that the United States government keep its hands off all matters over which the Constitution had not given it definite authority. This idea was the basis for what is known as the principle of **states' rights.**

Southerners defend states' rights. John C. Calhoun of South Carolina became the South's foremost defender of states' rights. You read earlier that he wrote a strong protest against the high tariff law of 1828. In that protest Calhoun declared that Congress did not have the right to set tariff duties so high that one section of the country would suffer. Many Southerners agreed when he protested that the tariff was "unconstitutional, oppressive, and unjust."

One of the most famous debates in the United States Senate took place in 1830 over the question of states' rights. The debate went on for nearly two weeks. Because Calhoun was then Vice-President, he could not take part in the debate. But Senator Robert Y. Hayne, also of South Carolina, spoke eloquently for the South. He argued that in adopting the Constitution the states had surrendered only certain powers to the government of the United States. Any state, he declared, had the right to take steps against a law passed by Congress if the state believed that the law violated the Constitution.

Daniel Webster speaks for a strong Union. Senator Daniel Webster of Massachusetts replied to Senator Hayne's speech. Webster was a short man, but his large head and his eyes, "that seemed to glow like dull coals," gave him a majestic appearance. On days when he intended to make a long

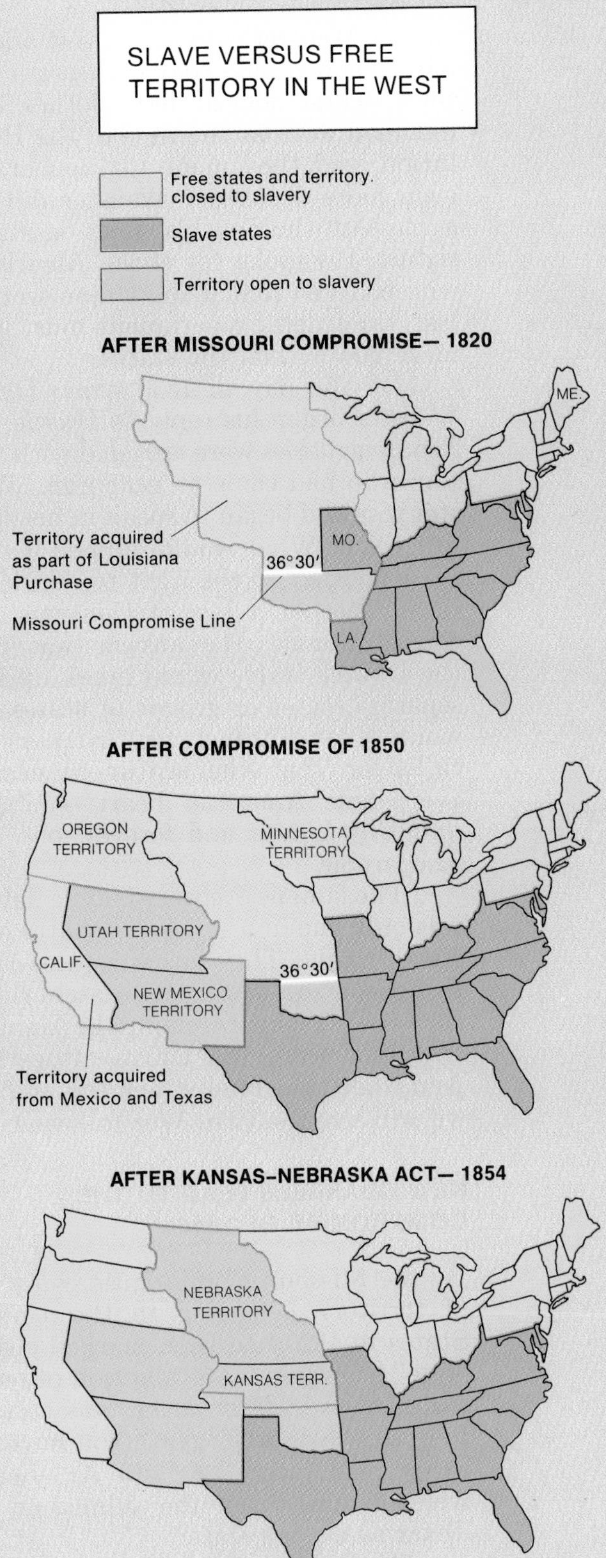

SLAVE VERSUS FREE TERRITORY IN THE WEST

Free states and territory, closed to slavery

Slave states

Territory open to slavery

AFTER MISSOURI COMPROMISE— 1820

Territory acquired as part of Louisiana Purchase

36°30'

Missouri Compromise Line

ME.

MO.

LA.

AFTER COMPROMISE OF 1850

OREGON TERRITORY

MINNESOTA TERRITORY

UTAH TERRITORY

CALIF.

36°30'

NEW MEXICO TERRITORY

Territory acquired from Mexico and Texas

AFTER KANSAS–NEBRASKA ACT— 1854

NEBRASKA TERRITORY

KANSAS TERR.

MAP STUDY See Teacher's Key.
Three steps in the dispute over slavery in the territories are shown here. (a) In each case, what kind of line surrounds the territory that was affected? (b) What different arrangements were made for the Kansas and Nebraska areas in the Missouri Compromise and Kansas-Nebraska Act?

speech, Webster wore a tan vest and an old-fashioned blue coat with brass buttons. These looked like clothes that men had worn at the time of the Revolution, and they made his appearance even more dramatic. Webster did not agree with the South's views on states' rights. He spoke for those Americans who believed that if the Union were to last, the federal government must have more power than the states.

On the day in 1830 when Daniel Webster began his reply to Hayne, the Senate galleries were crowded with visitors who had come to hear him. Webster rose and began to speak in his deep, full voice. What would happen if each state insisted on the right to decide for itself whether a law of Congress was constitutional? His answer was that the United States would break up into separate states or groups of states. In words that thrilled his listeners he called for "that other sentiment, dear to every true American heart — Liberty *and* Union, now and forever, one and inseparable."

The famous Webster-Hayne debate was only one in a series of debates over states' rights. The southern states came to believe so strongly in states' rights that they began to claim the right to withdraw from the Union altogether. And when they finally took this step, as we will see, the Civil War followed.

NEW QUARRELS LEAD TO THE COMPROMISE OF 1850

By the Missouri Compromise every bit of territory belonging to the United States in 1820 had been marked either "free" or "slave." The addition of territories after 1820, however, was certain to open the debate again. You have already read (page 384) how Americans were divided over the admission of Texas as a slave state.

The Mexican War brings a new quarrel over slavery. When the Mexican

War broke out in 1846, it became clear that the United States might win vast new territories. At once there arose the question: "Are the new lands to be slave or free?" The war had hardly begun when a representative from Pennsylvania named David Wilmot suggested an answer to the question. Wilmot hated slavery. He proposed that Congress agree beforehand that no slavery "*shall ever exist in any part*" of any territory which might be secured from Mexico. This proposal was called the Wilmot Proviso. It came up in Congress over and over again but was always defeated. Northern representatives who disliked slavery voted for it; southern congressmen voted against it.

Southerners become alarmed. After the Mexican War ended in 1848, the debate started by Wilmot became more intense. In 1848 there were thirty states in the Union, fifteen of them free states and fifteen of them slave. The North and South each had, as a result, the same number of senators in Congress. But the situation was different in the House of Representatives. Population was growing faster in the North than in the South, and the number of northern representatives was rapidly increasing. The table below shows the steady growth of northern power in the House from 1800 to 1850. Notice that it shows the number of members from North and South and also the *percentage* of members from the South.

Year	Members from free states	Members from slave states	Percentage of southern members
1800	76	65	46
1810	96	79	45
1820	123	90	42
1830	141	99	41
1840	135	88	39.5
1850	142	90	38.8

408

Clay, Calhoun, and Webster

First elected to Congress in the early 1800's, these three men spent 40 years in public service during which they became leading spokesmen for the three different sections of the county—West, South, and North.

Daniel Webster of Massachusetts was Representative, Senator, and twice Secretary of State.

Henry Clay of Kentucky served as Representative, Speaker of the House, Senator, and Secretary of State.

John C. Calhoun of South Carolina was Secretary of War and State and Vice-President, as well as Representative and Senator.

Three old statesmen met in the Senate for the last time to debate the Compromise of 1850. From left to right, white frames mark Webster, Clay, and Calhoun.

409

Jefferson Davis of Mississippi defended the rights of the South and slavery. This picture was taken in 1845, just after his marriage to Varina Howell.

Southerners knew that they were losing voting strength in the House. They also feared that one day a northern President might be elected who would oppose slavery in the territories. If territories entered the Union as free states, the South would then be outnumbered in the Senate too. Southerners were determined, therefore, to do everything possible to prevent new territories from entering the Union as free states.

California wants to become a state. The dispute over what to do about slavery in the lands obtained from Mexico came to a head after the discovery of gold in California. As you read in Chapter 18, the discovery of gold caused many people to rush to California. These people formed a government of their own and asked to be admitted as a free state. To white Southerners this was an outrage. They insisted that California should not be closed to slavery. Northerners insisted that it should be.

If slavery in California was to be discussed in Congress, slavery in the rest of the new territories would have to be discussed also. And if another compromise could not be agreed on, the country might split in two. The outlook was indeed serious.

Great leaders represent the states in Congress. The Congress that faced these difficult problems had many great men in it. Among them were three who had become famous. They had entered Congress about 40 years before and were coming to the end of their careers. There was *Daniel Webster* of Massachusetts, orator and statesman. Although he disliked slavery, he wanted more than anything else to keep the country united. There was *Henry Clay* of Kentucky, known as the "Great Compromiser." Clay was very skillful at finding ways of keeping peace when people disagreed. In 1820 he had helped work out the Missouri Compromise. Now, 30 years later, Clay was to make his last effort to bring about a compromise between the North and the South. And there was *John C. Calhoun* of South Carolina, champion of states' rights. Although he was now in poor health, Calhoun was determined that South Carolina and slavery should have their say. He opposed a compromise.

There were young leaders in Congress too, whose names would be famous in the years to come. One of them, *Stephen A. Douglas* from Illinois, believed the people in the territories should settle the question of slavery for themselves. Another was *William H. Seward* of New York. Seward declared that God's law made all people free, and that God's law was "a higher law" than the Constitution of the United States. Brilliant young Southerners were also speaking out in Congress. Among them

410

Have students prepare written or oral reports on these leaders. (See the feature on p. 409.)

were *Jefferson Davis* of Mississippi and *Alexander H. Stephens* of Georgia. When the South later formed its own government, these two men became its President and Vice-President.

Congress passes the Compromise of 1850. After long discussions, Congress agreed on a settlement, known as the Compromise of 1850. This compromise dealt with the question of slavery in the new land won from Mexico and with some other things as well. The important parts of the Compromise of 1850 were as follows:

(1) California was admitted to the Union as a free state.

(2) The rest of the territory obtained from Mexico was divided into the New Mexico Territory and Utah Territory. (See the second map on page 407.) The question of slavery was left to the people who settled there. In other words, the people there were to decide for themselves whether slavery should be permitted.

(3) Slaves were not to be bought or sold in the District of Columbia.

(4) To make it harder for slaves to win their freedom by escaping from slave states into free states, a strict Fugitive Slave Law was passed. (A **fugitive** is a person who has run away.) This law required people in the free states to help catch escaped slaves.

Congress hoped by this compromise to settle the slavery question forever. The members wanted no more angry debates which might prove dangerous to the nation. Americans sighed with relief. Surely, they thought, the dispute over slavery could now be forgotten.

▶ **CHECK UP**   See Teacher's Key.

1. **(a)** What dispute broke out when Missouri requested admission to the Union as a state? **(b)** How was the dispute settled?
2. **(a)** What is meant by "states' rights"? **(b)** Why did the South favor this point of view? **(c)** How did Webster argue against it?
3. **(a)** Why did the Mexican War lead to a new quarrel over slavery? **(b)** Why did the South want to keep a balance between the number of slave states and free states? **(c)** How did California's request for statehood add to the dispute between the North and the South?
4. How did the the Compromise of 1850 deal with the dispute over slavery in the territories?

2 How Did the Two Sections Move Closer to Conflict?

Americans who thought the Compromise of 1850 would settle the slavery question and end the quarreling between North and South were too hopeful. Certain events in the next ten years were to make the quarrels more frequent, more angry, and more bitter.

***Uncle Tom's Cabin* inflames opinion in the North.** Harriet Beecher Stowe was a New England woman who opposed slavery. In 1852, angered by the Fugitive Slave Law, she wrote a book called *Uncle Tom's Cabin*. Its description of the suffering of enslaved people and the cruelties of their owners was accepted in the North as an accurate picture of life in the South. The book's dramatic story touched the hearts of the hundreds of thousands of Northerners who read it. In fact, *Uncle Tom's Cabin* influenced Northerners against ★ slavery as nothing else had. Abraham

411

★ See p. T38 for a strategy calling for students to examine the impact of *Uncle Tom's Cabin*.

135,000 SETS, 270,000 VOLUMES SOLD.

UNCLE TOM'S CABIN

FOR SALE HERE.

AN EDITION FOR THE MILLION, COMPLETE IN 1 Vol. PRICE 37 1-2 CENTS.
" " IN GERMAN, IN 1 Vol. PRICE 50 CENTS.
" " IN 2 Vols. CLOTH, 6 PLATES, PRICE $1.50.
SUPERB ILLUSTRATED EDITION, IN 1 Vol. WITH 153 ENGRAVINGS,
PRICES FROM $2.50 TO $5.00.

The Greatest Book of the Age.

The publication of *Uncle Tom's Cabin* made the quarrel between the North and South even more bitter. This advertisement shows a scene from the story.

Lincoln in later years is said to have greeted Mrs. Stowe as "the little woman who wrote the book that made this great war." In the South, however, *Uncle Tom's Cabin* aroused a storm of protest and increased the bitter feeling against abolitionists.

Fugitive slaves are helped by the Underground Railroad. In spite of the Fugitive Slave Law, Northerners continued to help black people who had escaped from slavery. One means they used was the Underground Railroad. This was really not a railroad at all but a way of helping escaped slaves to reach places where they would be safe. The slaves who reached the North were sheltered by abolitionists. People called conductors took the slaves by night from one house or station to another, each farther north than the last. Finally the slaves reached Canada and freedom. Only a small percentage of the total number of slaves escaped in this way, but the Underground Railroad further inflamed feeling between the North and the South.

Serious quarrels develop as the slavery question is reopened. Differences between the North and the South continued to grow increasingly serious. It was a series of events beginning in 1854, however, that brought the two sections near the breaking point. If it were possible for us to sit and watch a telecast of some of these important events, here are the scenes we might see:

Scene 1: The Kansas-Nebraska Act reopens the slavery quarrel (1854). We see the Senate Chamber of the Capitol in Washington. The senators are discussing a proposed law. This law would set up two new governments, one in Kansas Territory and one in Nebraska Territory. (See the third map on page 407.) If this bill is passed, the people of these territories are to decide *for themselves* whether slavery shall be permitted there. A northern senator is making a speech, using words like these:

"Gentlemen, look at the map. Kansas is north of the Missouri Compromise line. By the Missouri Compromise, slavery was not to be permitted north of that line. Shall we now permit slavery there? No! The people of the North will not stand for it!"

And a southern senator replies:

"The Missouri Compromise did say that slavery was not to be permitted in this territory. But this proposed law will definitely put an end to the Missouri Compromise. Wherever the United States flag goes, slavery may go. This is as it should be. Slaves are property. It is our right to take our slave property anywhere into the West, just as you of the North may take your property there. The people of the South will insist on this right."

The Senate and the House agreed to pass the law. The Missouri Compromise was now dead. The Kansas-

412

● Review the term *abolitionist*, introduced on p. 325.

People in America's Story

scout, and spy. After the war she helped raise money for black schools. She also established a home for elderly blacks in Auburn, New York.

HARRIET TUBMAN

Herself a runaway slave, Harriet Tubman helped more than 300 slaves escape to freedom on the Underground Railroad.

The slaves in this picture have arrived at a station on the Underground Railroad, a farm in Indiana.

Harriet Tubman became the most famous leader of the Underground Railroad. She risked her own safety nineteen times by returning to the South to guide runaway slaves.

In 1978 the United States Postal Service issued this stamp to honor Harriet Tubman.

413

Nebraska Act took its place. The people in the territories of Kansas and Nebraska could decide for themselves whether to have slavery or not.

Scene 2: Violence breaks out over slavery in Kansas (1854–1857). We see a tall, bearded man standing against the night sky. He is looking down at five dying men. Someone asks, "Why did you shoot them, John Brown?" He replies: "Men opposed to slavery have been killed, so men who favor slavery must also die."

The place is Kansas, which is now open to freedom or slavery. Settlers from the North and the South have been moving in. The settlers from the South say, "We will bring our slaves to Kansas. We will even fight to keep them, if we have to." The people from the North say, "We will allow no slaves in Kansas. We will fight to keep them out, if we have to."

● John Brown's murder of the pro-slavery men was only one of many scenes of violence during the settlement of Kansas. Earlier, flames had destroyed the village of Lawrence which antislavery settlers had built. Bands of men on horseback began to roam the roads. These were proslavery and antislavery forces, fighting to win control of Kansas.

Violence in Kansas finally died down, but the struggle for Kansas went on. Because of their greater numbers, the antislavery settlers finally won, and in 1861 Kansas entered the Union as a free state.

Scene 3: The Republican Party is born (1854). We see people holding an outdoor meeting in a Wisconsin town. "We cannot vote for the old parties, the Whigs and the Democrats, any longer," one of them is saying. The others cheer.

The speaker continues: "The great question today is: Shall there be slavery or freedom in the new territories? The old parties cannot agree on the answer to this question. Congress has just passed the Kansas-Nebraska Act, which says that the people of the territories may decide whether or not to allow slavery. But we who are meeting here believe that *it is both the right and the duty of Congress to forbid slavery in the territories.* We are strong and we will become stronger. Let us form a new party and call ourselves Republicans. Let us fight to keep slavery out of the territories!" In other towns throughout the North, scenes like this are taking place. "No slavery in the territories! Join the Republicans!" ★

The new party gained many members. In the election of 1856, the Republicans won in two thirds of the northern states with John C. Frémont, soldier and explorer, as their candidate. But there were almost no Republicans in the South. So the Democrats in the North and the South were strong enough to elect their candidate, James Buchanan, as President. In spite of their defeat, the Republicans were not down-hearted. They knew they had made a good start and hoped to get a Republican President elected in 1860.

Scene 4: The Missouri Compromise is declared unconstitutional in the Dred Scott Case (1857). We see a small, quiet room where the Supreme Court of the United States is meeting. On the raised platform behind their long carved desk the judges, dressed in black robes, sit solemnly. They are the highest court in the land. They have the power to explain the meaning of the United States Constitution and to decide whether a law of Congress violates the Constitution.

The judges have been considering the case of a black man named Dred Scott. Scott had been a slave in the South, but his owner had taken him to territory north of the Missouri Compromise line. The Missouri Compromise had declared that in this territory there could be no slavery and no slaves. Therefore, Dred Scott claimed to be a

414

In 1858 Abraham Lincoln ran for the Senate against Stephen Douglas. Douglas won the election, but Lincoln gained fame from a series of debates held by the two candidates.

free man. He had asked the Supreme Court to order his owner to free him.

A judge is slowly reading what the Supreme Court has decided. Dred Scott is not free. Slaves, says the judge, do not have the rights of citizens. Under the Constitution, he goes on, Congress has no right to forbid slavery in any part of the territories. Therefore, the Missouri Compromise is unconstitutional.

In the Kansas-Nebraska Act, Congress had declared the Missouri Compromise dead, but had suggested that the voters in a territory could decide the question of slavery for themselves. Now, in the Dred Scott decision, the United States Supreme Court had declared that *slavery could not be kept out of the territories.*

Southerners were naturally delighted with the Court's decision, but Northerners were astounded. Republicans protested vigorously that the Supreme Court was favoring the South.

Scene 5: A great debate takes place in Illinois (1858). We see an open square in a little Illinois town. On a wooden platform two men stand before a crowd that fills the square. What a contrast the two men make! One is much taller than the other. In fact, if the tall one were to stretch his arm straight out from the shoulder, the short one could walk right under it. The tall one is so carelessly dressed that his coat sleeves do not reach to his wrists nor his trousers to his shoes. The short one is the opposite — carefully dressed in the height of fashion. The tall one is awkward, and his face is lined and sad. The short one is confident and graceful.

The tall man is Abraham Lincoln — Republican; the short one is Stephen A. Douglas — Democrat. Each hopes to be elected United States senator from Illinois. To let the people know how they will vote in the Senate, they are debating the question of slavery in the territories. In spite of the Dred Scott decision, Douglas says he believes that the people of a territory should decide for themselves whether to have slavery or not. (This idea is known as

415

● Discuss: How did this decision affect the status of the Compromise of 1850.

popular sovereignty.) No wonder Senator Douglas believes in popular sovereignty, for he himself had written the Kansas-Nebraska Act.

Lincoln says that slavery is wrong. He declares that Congress has the right to get rid of slavery in the land that belongs to all the people of the United States — that is, in the territories, but not in the states. The Republicans, he continues, think slavery is wrong. For this reason they wish to limit slavery to the states where it already exists and prevent its spread to the territories.

But in the back of Lincoln's mind was the fear that a conflict between the North and the South could not be avoided. In an earlier speech he had warned the American people, "A house divided against itself cannot stand. I believe this government cannot endure permanently half slave and half free." ●

Stephen Douglas won the election. But Abraham Lincoln won fame for making the issues clear.

Scene 6: John Brown attacks the arsenal at Harpers Ferry, Virginia (1859). In the village of Harpers Ferry on the Potomac River, we see a federal arsenal (a building where weapons are stored). Rifle shots ring out. Soldiers rush to the door and capture the building. Inside they find John Brown and a handful of men, most of them dead or wounded. This is the same John Brown we saw in Kansas.

John Brown's raid at Harpers Ferry alarmed the nation. After his capture Brown was tried for treason and found guilty. Here, he leaves the courthouse after being sentenced to death.

Brown and a few followers had come to Virginia with the idea of freeing people from slavery. After seizing the arsenal at Harpers Ferry in order to get arms, he had cried to nearby slaves: "We are here to set you free! Seize arms and defend your freedom!" But not a single slave followed him. John Brown is tried for treason, found guilty, and hanged.

Although some abolitionists said Brown was a "saint," many Northerners considered his act the deed of a madman. But white Southerners were filled with dread. They feared that northern abolitionists were working to bring about a black uprising and to free the slaves by force. "What will happen next?" the Southerners wondered.

▶ **CHECK UP**   See Teacher's Key.

1. **(a)** What effect did *Uncle Tom's Cabin* have on the slavery dispute? **(b)** What was the Underground Railroad?
2. **(a)** How did the Kansas-Nebraska Act reopen the slavery quarrel? **(b)** What happened in Kansas as a result of the dispute? **(c)** Why was the Republican Party formed?
3. Why did the Dred Scott decision alarm the North?
4. Describe the views of Lincoln and of Douglas on each of the following: **(a)** the Missouri Compromise, **(b)** the Kansas-Nebraska Act, **(c)** the Dred Scott decision, **(d)** slavery in the states where it already existed.
5. How did John Brown's raid at Harpers Ferry add to the dispute over slavery?

3 What Events Led to War?

A FATEFUL ELECTION TAKES PLACE

By 1860 the country was alert and tense, as though awaiting the climax of the fateful events of the past years. A presidential election was to be held that year. The chief issue would be the question of slavery. What would be the outcome?

Lincoln is elected President. In the 1860 election there were four political parties, not two or three as there had been before. The old Democratic Party split in two. One part, the southern Democratic Party, wanted to elect John C. Breckinridge of Kentucky. It believed in states' rights and insisted that slavery should be protected in the territories. The northern Democratic Party believed that the best answer to the slavery question was Stephen A. Douglas's idea of popular sovereignty (letting the people in the territories decide for

themselves). The northern Democrats chose Senator Douglas as their presidential candidate.

A third party was the Constitutional Union Party. The people who belonged to this party mainly wanted to find some peaceful way of holding the Union together. They hoped for another compromise over slavery. For President they supported John Bell of Tennessee.

Finally, there were the Republicans. They demanded what they had demanded in 1854, that slavery be kept out of the territories. But the Republican Party also tried to gain support in the North and West by favoring (1) a tariff, (2) free land for settlers in the West, and (3) the construction of a railroad to the Pacific. As their candidate for President the Republicans named the lawyer from Illinois, Abraham Lincoln.

417

● See p. T38 for a strategy that asks students to consider the events described in Section 2 from both northern and southern perspectives.

● See p. T38 for a strategy that asks students to make use of the election map on p. 423 in interpreting the results of the 1860 election.

When one party is split, as the Democrats were in 1860, it usually ● loses. So it was in 1860. The Republicans won the election, even though in most of the southern states their candidate had no place on the ballot. Abraham Lincoln would become President in 1861.

★ **Who was Abraham Lincoln?** The man who had won the election of 1860 was one of the most remarkable persons in our history. Brought up in the hard life of the frontier, he lacked the advantages that many of our Presidents have enjoyed. As a poor man, he had to turn his hand to various ways of making a living. Before he became a lawyer, he farmed, split rails, worked on a flatboat on the Mississippi, and tended store. Since Lincoln had few chances to go to school, he educated himself in spare moments during the day and by firelight in the evening. Even his physical characteristics — unusual height, awkward movements, and high-pitched voice — were against him.

In spite of these handicaps, people liked and respected "Abe" Lincoln. His honesty, clear thinking, friendliness, sense of humor, and trust in the common people were qualities that made him popular. Lincoln served several terms in the Illinois legislature. In 1846, he was elected to Congress where he served in the House of Representatives for two years.

When his term in Congress was over, Lincoln returned to his work as a lawyer. He felt he was through with politics. But his deep feelings on the matter of slavery forced him back into public life. Although he hated slavery, Lincoln was not an abolitionist. He did not propose interfering with slavery in the states where it existed. But he firmly believed that slavery should not exist in the *territories* belonging to the United States. His beliefs led him to seek election to the Senate and to take part in the debates with Douglas (pages 415-416).

Although Lincoln was well known in the West, he was little more than a name in the East. He was invited to speak at the Cooper Union Hall in New York City early in 1860. Many people came out of curiosity to see and hear this man from the West who was becoming an important figure in the Republican Party. At first, Lincoln must have seemed plain and "countrified" to the New Yorkers. But when he began to speak, they forgot the awkward appearance of the tall, lanky man. His manner was dignified and convincing. His arguments against slavery in the territories were logical and clearly worded. He closed with these words: "Let us have faith that right makes might; and in that faith let us to the end dare to do our duty as we understand it." The whole audience then rose to its feet in a thunder of applause.

This was the man who in the fall of 1860 was elected the sixteenth President of the United States.

WAR COMES AT LAST

The southern states secede. The southern states had declared that if Lincoln were elected President, they would no longer want to be part of the United States. It was true that the South still had power in Congress and in the Supreme Court. But a Northerner, a Republican, had been elected President. White Southerners no longer felt safe. They feared not only for slavery but also for their way of life, which depended on slavery.

Even before Lincoln was sworn in as President, southern states began to carry out their threat to withdraw, or secede, from the Union. First went South Carolina, soon followed by Mississippi, Florida, and Alabama. Georgia was next, and then Louisiana and

418

★ See p. T38 for a strategy calling for students to put together a bulletin board display featuring Abraham Lincoln.

Secession vs. Union

"It was the *states* that formed the Union and a state can *leave* the Union. For us, the Union no longer exists!"

"No! The Union was set up for keeps! You're part of one country now, and you can't walk out on us, no matter how much you want to!"

Texas. These seven states had seceded by February 1, 1861. President Buchanan, who was nearing the end of his term, took no steps to stop the seceding states. He said, "I have no power to interfere."

The Confederate States of America are established. In February, the seven states that had seceded sent representatives to Montgomery, Alabama, to form a new government. These men drew up a constitution for a new nation, the Confederate States of America or, as it was often called, the Confederacy. The constitution was much like that of the United States. It stated, however, that the Congress of the Confederacy could not interfere with slavery. It also provided that no tariffs could be levied on imports. The President was to serve six years, instead of four, and he could not be re-elected.

Jefferson Davis is elected President of the Confederate States. Jefferson
● Davis of Mississippi was elected President of the Confederate States, and Alexander H. Stephens of Georgia was chosen to be Vice-President. Jefferson Davis was born one year earlier than Abraham Lincoln, and in the same state — Kentucky. But Lincoln's parents had taken him to Indiana and Illinois, while the Davis family had moved to Mississippi. Davis's father was a planter who owned a large plantation and many slaves. Jefferson Davis was a graduate of the United States Military Academy at West Point. He had a distinguished record as an officer in the Mexican War. He had also served in the House of Representatives and in the Senate, and as Secretary of War. In the Senate he strongly defended the rights of the South.

Jefferson Davis was a man of commanding appearance and intelligence. On his shoulders lay the difficult task of helping the seven states of the Confederacy become an independent nation.

Lincoln hopes for peace. When Abraham Lincoln became President of the United States on March 4, 1861, he faced a very difficult problem. What should he do about the seceded states?

419

● Remind students of the picture of Jefferson Davis on p. 410.

In early 1861 men in both the North and South volunteered for service. These Union troops received a warm welcome in New York City.

Lincoln did not want war. As he took the oath of office, he said, "Suppose you go to war, you cannot fight always; and when, after much loss on both sides, and no gain on either, you cease fighting, the [same] old questions . . . are again upon you." Slavery in the South was in no danger, for Lincoln promised that he had no intention of interfering with slavery in the states where it existed. He went on to say, "In your hands, my dissatisfied fellow countrymen, and not in mine, is the momentous issue of civil war. The government will
● not assail you." (*Assail* means "attack.") Lincoln, however, made it clear that he had taken a solemn oath to "preserve, protect, and defend" the United States government. Finally he
420 pleaded with the people of the whole country to unite once again. Solemnly he said: "We are not enemies, but friends. We must not be enemies. . . . "

Thus Lincoln, with "faith in what he believed was right," took upon his shoulders the responsibility of preserving the Union. Yet, in spite of what he had said, the country remained divided. United States forts in the South had been seized by the Confederacy; the laws of the United States were not being obeyed. Lincoln had to act quickly if he hoped to save the Union.

War begins. The harbor of Charleston, South Carolina, was broad and quiet. Warm in the spring sun, the city lay at the western end of the harbor. In the harbor was an island, and on this island was Fort Sumter. Fort Sumter was occupied by soldiers of the United States Army.

Confederate leaders demanded that these soldiers leave the fort. But the commander of Fort Sumter refused.

See p. T39 for a strategy that asks students to construct time lines showing key events discussed in Section 3.

Soon the Confederate leaders learned that Lincoln had ordered ships to take food and other supplies to Sumter. They suspected that reinforcements might also be landed. The days and nights seemed to grow longer. People were tense.

It is now 4:30 in the morning of April 12, 1861, the quiet hour before the dawn. Suddenly a flash of flame is seen and a deep "Boom!" shatters the silence. From all around the harbor Confederate cannon begin to fire at Fort Sumter. Peace and quiet no longer reign in Charleston Harbor — nor anywhere else in the United States. War has begun!

▶ **CHECK UP**   See Teacher's Key.

1. **(a)** What political parties put up presidential candidates in the election of 1860? **(b)** Who was the candidate of each party? **(c)** What was the stand of each party on the slavery question? **(d)** What party won the election of 1860? Why?
2. **(a)** How did the southern states feel about the results of the election? **(b)** What action did they take? **(c)** How was a new government organized in the South?
3. **(a)** What were President Lincoln's views on slavery and the division of the Union? **(b)** How did the Civil War break out?

CHECK UP ON CHAPTER 19   See Teacher's Key.

Words to Know

1. fugitive
2. arsenal
3. treason
4. interfere
5. secede
6. compromise
7. proslavery
8. unconstitutional
9. states' rights
10. popular sovereignty
11. Underground Railroad

Places to Locate

1. Nebraska Territory
2. Kansas Territory
3. Missouri
4. Missouri Compromise line

Facts to Remember

1. **(a)** Why did the question of slavery in the territories become such an important issue? **(b)** How did Congress try to settle that question in the Missouri Compromise? **(c)** In the Kansas-Nebraska Act? **(d)** In the Compromise of 1850?
2. Identify each of the following persons by telling what part he or she took in the events described in this chapter:

(a) Daniel Webster, **(b)** John C. Calhoun, **(c)** Stephen A. Douglas, **(d)** John Brown, **(e)** Harriet Beecher Stowe, **(f)** Dred Scott, **(g)** Jefferson Davis, **(h)** Abraham Lincoln.
3. **(a)** Why was the Republican Party formed? **(b)** What successes did it have in the election of 1856? **(c)** In the election of 1860?
4. **(a)** What states joined together in the Confederate States of America? **(b)** How was the Confederate constitution different from the Constitution of the United States?

Skills to Practice

1. The table below shows Missouri's population from 1840 to 1860. Use this information to make a pictograph. Let each symbol in the pictograph stand for 100,000 people.

Year	Population
1840	384,000
1850	682,000
1860	1,182,000

421

Skills to Practice (cont.)

2. Use the maps on page 407 to answer these questions. **(a)** Why does the first map *not* show any territory west of the Louisiana Purchase? **(b)** What states had entered the Union between the time of the Missouri Compromise and the Compromise of 1850? (It will help you to look at the list of states, showing their dates of admission, in the back of the book.) **(c)** How did the Kansas-Nebraska Act affect slavery in Kansas and Nebraska?

Questions to Think About

1. When slavery was ended in the British West Indies, the British government gave people who had owned slaves money to make up for their financial loss. Could such a policy have been followed in this country? Give reasons for your answer.

2. Most Americans really hoped that the Compromise of 1820 and then the Compromise of 1850 would settle the slavery question at the time each of those compromises was worked out. Why did efforts to find a permanent settlement of the slavery question fail?

3. Why did reading *Uncle Tom's Cabin* make people feel even more strongly about the slavery issue than they had before they read the book? How can a book have such a strong effect on the way people feel about a controversial subject?

Linking Past and Present

Lincoln country. Little did the parents of Abraham Lincoln dream that the farm where he was born in 1809 would one day be made a national park in his honor. Today, not only his birthplace (near Hodgenville, Kentucky) but almost every place where Lincoln lived is preserved as a memorial. The farm in Indiana where he grew to adulthood is now part of the Lincoln State Park. A stone wall shows the location of the log cabin home; the grave of Lincoln's mother, who died there, is marked by a simple stone. In 1830, the family moved to southeastern Illinois, where their old home and the graves of Lincoln's father and stepmother can be seen. New Salem, Illinois, where Lincoln lived after leaving home in 1831, has been rebuilt. Today it looks like the town he knew, with its log cabins, the tavern, the store he worked in, and the original barrel-maker's shop where he used to study law at night.

In Springfield, Illinois, Lincoln's home after 1837, there are many memorials. The house where he lived with his family has been preserved. Furnished with some of the Lincoln family furniture, it looks much as it did well over a century ago. In Springfield you can also see the final resting place of Abraham Lincoln — a beautiful marble tomb at Oak Ridge Cemetery where Lincoln, his wife, and three of their sons are buried.

Citizenship restored. Several southern states pay tribute to Jefferson Davis by celebrating his birthday, June 3, as a legal holiday. They remember his dignity and devotion to principle when he served as president of the Confederate States.

Like other Confederate officials, Jefferson Davis had his United States citizenship taken away after the Civil War. Imprisoned for two years on a charge of treason, he was finally released without having been brought to trial. He spent his last years writing his memoirs. He also made frequent appearances at Confederate reunions.

Just before his death in 1889, an unsuccessful attempt was made in Congress to restore Jefferson Davis's citizenship. Many years later, in 1979, Congress finally acted. It passed a bill restoring citizenship to Davis. As President Jimmy Carter signed the bill into law, he said that it "officially reunites our people following the tragic conflict between the states."

● Have students use state maps to locate the places where Lincoln lived.

GAINING SKILL

Reading Maps: Election Results

The presidential election of 1860 was bitterly contested. The following table shows the results of that election.

Candidate	Popular vote	Electoral vote
Lincoln	1,866,352	180
Douglas	1,375,157	12
Breckinridge	847,953	72
Bell	589,581	39

A table provides you with one way to study the results of an election. Another way is to look at an election map, showing the electoral count by states. As you know, the President is not chosen directly by the voters. Instead, the voters in each state select a group of electors. The electors then vote for the President.

The map below tells the story of the 1860 election. The key helps you see which candidate won the electoral votes of each state. Now use the map and the table to answer the following questions.

1. How many candidates ran for President in 1860?
2. What state had the largest number of electoral votes?
3. How many states and electoral votes did John Bell win?
4. Which candidate won Iowa's electoral votes? Does that mean that every voter in Iowa favored that candidate?
5. What state's electoral votes were split? (You should understand that it is very rare for such a split to take place.)
6. What candidate received the fewest electoral votes? Where did he rank in the popular vote?
7. Which candidate won the election? Did he have the largest number of popular votes? Did he have a *majority* (more than half) of the popular votes? A majority of the electoral votes?

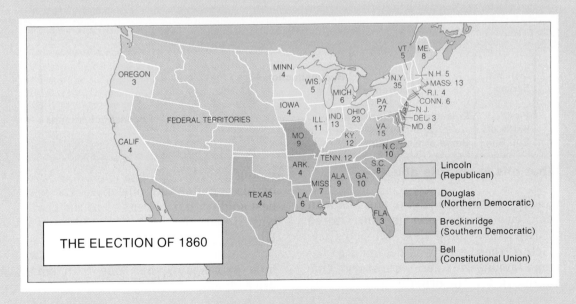

THE ELECTION OF 1860

Vocabulary preview: border state, strategy, emancipate, reconstruction, black codes, tenant farmer, sharecropper

The North and the South Fight a War and Are Reunited

1861–1877   See pp. T39–T40 for chapter teaching strategies.

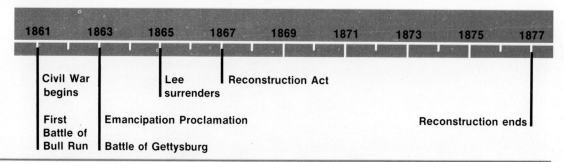

What this chapter is about —

One day toward the end of the Mexican War, two officers met in the United States Army camp near Mexico City. Each of these men was destined to become famous in American history. One was a colonel; the other was an "untidy young captain." The colonel, described by his commanding officer as "the very best soldier that I ever saw in the field," was Robert E. Lee; the captain was Ulysses S. Grant.

Seventeen years later, these two men met again, this time in a small brick house near Appomattox Court

House, Virginia. The years had brought many changes. Once brother officers, they now faced each other as enemies. Grant wore the blue of the United States Army, but Lee was dressed in the gray uniform of the Confederate States of America. Grant had become Lieutenant-General Grant, Commander-in-Chief of the United States Army. Lee was General-in-Chief of all the Confederate armies.

The meeting in the brick house marked the end of a bloody war between the two sections of our country. This war grew out of the clash between the North and the South described in Chap-

ter 19. In this chapter you will read about the major campaigns of the Civil War and learn how victory was won by the North. You will find out how the war affected both the North and the South and what happened to Lincoln's plans for making the United States once more "one nation, indivisible." In order to understand the Civil War and its outcome, keep in mind these questions:

1. How was the nation divided, and what advantages did each side have?
2. How did four years of fighting bring victory to the North?
3. How did the war affect the lives of people in the North and the South?
4. How did Abraham Lincoln plan to unite the divided nation?
5. What happened in the South after the war?

1 How Was the Nation Divided, and What Advantages Did Each Side Have?

War divides the nation. When the Confederates fired upon Fort Sumter, the nation was too deeply divided to be united again by peaceful means. The North and the South had steadily been drifting further and further apart. But now that shots had been fired, Americans faced one question above all others: Will the United States remain one nation or become two? Either the Confederate States of America would win the war and become an independent nation, or the United States would win the war and compel the seceding states to rejoin the Union.

The war divided not only the nation but neighborhoods and even families. Many Northerners went South to fight for the Confederacy; many Southerners fought for the Union. Especially in the **border states** — those at the

dividing line between North and South ● — neighbors marched off to fight on opposite sides. What was even sadder, the war often separated members of the same family. Three brothers of Mary Todd Lincoln, wife of the President of the United States, died for the Confederacy. Close relatives of the wife of the President of the Confederacy fought for the Union. The sons of a high-ranking officer in the Union navy wore Confederate gray. The same story was repeated many times throughout the nation.

What were the sections fighting for? Men went to war for different reasons. Most people, in both the North and the South, adopted the cause favored by their friends and neighbors. Many white people in the South believed in slavery and fought to preserve it. Many

425

● Have students study the map on p. 427. Ask: What states made up the Union? What states joined the Confederacy?

Southerners also felt sure that their way of life, based on the growing of cotton, could not survive in the same nation with the trading and manufacturing states of the North. These Southerners fought for the right to secede from the Union.

On the other hand, some Northerners fought because they hated slavery and hoped the war would put an end to it. Many Northerners believed there was no question so difficult that it could not be settled satisfactorily under a democratic government. They felt deeply that the Union should be stronger than any one state or group of states. They fought to preserve the government established under the Constitution.

The remaining slave states choose sides. When fighting broke out, the slave states that had not yet seceded were forced to decide whether to join the North or the South. Four more states sided with the Confederacy and seceded soon after the firing on Fort Sumter. These were Virginia, Arkansas,

Tennessee, and North Carolina. But the people living in the northwestern part of Virginia refused to join the rest of that state in seceding. They broke away and formed the state of West Virginia, which entered the Union in 1863. The four slave states nearest the North — Missouri, Kentucky, Maryland, and Delaware — remained in the Union. Thus, as the war began, the North had 23 states; the South, 11 states. (See map on the next page.)

What were the advantages of each side? In the end, a war is usually won by the side having the most people, resources, and supplies. Let us compare the North and the South.

The North had certain advantages. (1) More than twice as many people lived in the North as in the South — 22 million in the North and 9 million in the South. Of the 9 million people in the South, two out of every five were blacks, most of whom were slaves. Slaves were not expected to fight. They were expected, however, to do the work at home and thus release white men to join the army. (2) Not only did the North have more people, but it had more resources and supplies. Most of the factories that could make guns, ammunition, uniforms, and the thousands of articles needed by fighting forces were in the

GRAPH STUDY   See Teacher's Key.
(a) In what resources shown on this graph did the North have an advantage over the South?
(b) How did cotton production give the South an advantage?

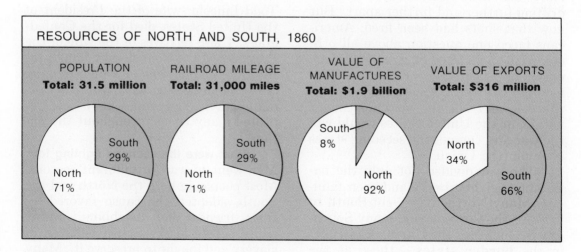

RESOURCES OF NORTH AND SOUTH, 1860

POPULATION
Total: 31.5 million
South 29%
North 71%

RAILROAD MILEAGE
Total: 31,000 miles
South 29%
North 71%

VALUE OF MANUFACTURES
Total: $1.9 billion
South 8%
North 92%

VALUE OF EXPORTS
Total: $316 million
North 34%
South 66%

● See p. T39 for a strategy in which students compare the advantages of the North with those of the South.

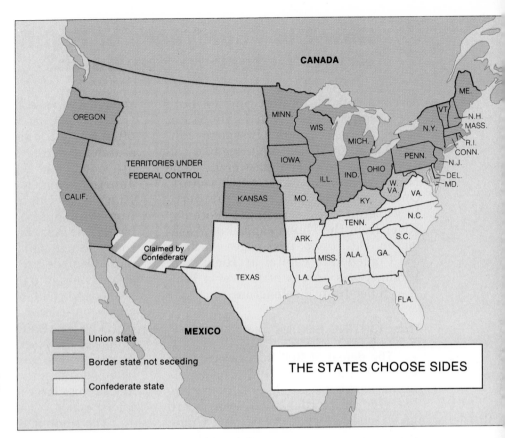

CANADA

OREGON

TERRITORIES UNDER
FEDERAL CONTROL

CALIF.

MINN.

WIS.

MICH.

IOWA

ILL. IND. OHIO

W. VA.

KANSAS MO. KY. VA.

ME.

VT

N.H.

MASS.

N.Y.

PENN.

R.I.

CONN.

N.J.

DEL.

MD.

N.C.

TENN.

ARK. S.C.

MISS. ALA. GA.

TEXAS LA.

FLA.

MEXICO

Union state

Border state not seceding

Confederate state

THE STATES CHOOSE SIDES

Claimed by
Confederacy

See Teacher's Key.

MAP STUDY
(a) What states made
up the Confederacy?
(b) What border states
chose to remain in the
Union? (West Virginia
became a state in
1863.)

North. The North had more railroads
to move goods and more men to do
the fighting. It also had more shipping.
(3) Furthermore, the United States government, its army, and its navy were
already established and working. The
South had to build these things as it
went along.

On the other hand, the South possessed certain advantages over the
North. (1) For one thing, the South was
fighting for the most part on its own
• soil. People fight harder when they are
defending their homes than when they
are invading enemy territory. Also,
they know the territory much better
than the invaders possibly could. (2) In
addition, the South had many outstanding military leaders who had resigned from the United States Army to
fight for the Confederacy. Among these
men was Robert E. Lee. Although Lee

belonged to an old southern family, he
did not believe in slavery and had already freed his slaves. Lee was also
against secession and opposed to the
war. But he could not bring himself to
bear arms against his beloved state, Virginia. When that state seceded, therefore, Lee chose to serve with the Confederacy. Thus the South gained a
brilliant general.

▶ **CHECK UP**   See Teacher's Key.

1. **(a)** In the conflict between the North
and the South, what was the North
fighting for? **(b)** What was the South
fighting for? **(c)** What states joined the
Confederacy? **(d)** What slave states
remained in the Union?
2. **(a)** What were the advantages of the
North? **(b)** Of the South?

427

• Remind students that Americans had enjoyed this
advantage in the Revolutionary War.

● Have students locate these cities on the map on the next page.

2 How Did Four Years of Fighting Bring Victory to the North?

After the attack on Fort Sumter, both the Union and the Confederate States began to raise armies. President Lincoln called for 75,000 volunteers, a call which was speedily answered. The North wanted to win a quick victory. One reason was that Confederate territory began just across the Potomac River from the Union capital of Washington, D.C. (map, next page). In fact, the Confederate capital at Richmond, Virginia, was only a little over a hundred miles from Washington.

THE FIGHTING BEGINS

The defeat at Bull Run awakens the North. In the spring of 1861, the people of the North began to call for action. The cry "On to Richmond!" was heard on all sides. Although the new Union army had many untrained recruits, Union troops were ordered south to capture Richmond if possible.

The Union forces crossed the Potomac into Virginia early in the summer. The advance into enemy territory was a curious sight. The army was accompanied by many people from Washington who wanted to see the Union troops win a victory. There were congressmen, newspaper reporters, and citizens eager to see an exciting event. The troops, not used to military discipline, often fell out of line to pick berries and search for water. Meanwhile, Confederate troops had assembled at Manassas Junction, on a small stream called Bull Run. Near this point, about 30 miles from Washington, the two armies met in battle. At first the Confederates seemed to be losing, but they held firm until more Confederate troops arrived. After a few hours of fighting, the Union lines broke, and the Union army retreated in great confusion to Washington.

The Battle of Bull Run shocked the people of the North and encouraged the people of the South. The leaders of both sides, however, realized that they had to raise large armies and prepare for a long war.

The North and South make plans for ★ **winning the war.** Well-trained troops and plenty of supplies are not enough to win a war. A clear-cut plan for carrying on the war is also necessary. Such planning is called **strategy.**

The strategy of the South was simple. (1) The South planned to hold out until the people of the North grew tired of the war. The Northerners might then say, "If the Confederates want a separate country, let them have it. It's too difficult to force them to return to the Union." (2) Whenever possible, of course, southern forces would invade the North, hoping to win an important victory. (3) Southern leaders counted on help from abroad, especially from Great Britain. They planned to exchange cotton for war supplies, such as guns, ammunition, and medical supplies. Because English textile factories needed a steady supply of cotton from the South, the Confederates expected Britain to take their side in the war.

FIELD GUN FIRING

428

★ See p. T39 for a strategy calling for students to discuss the northern and southern war plans.

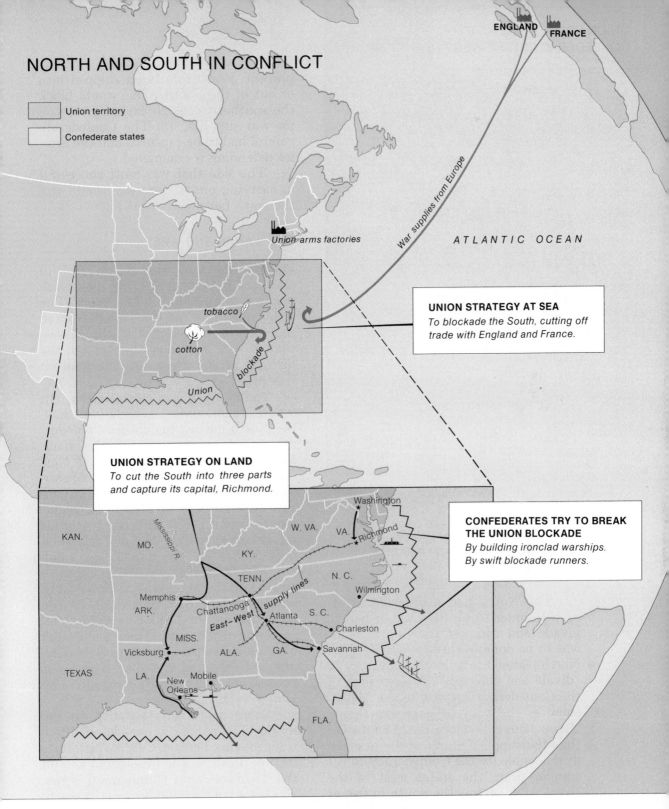

NORTH AND SOUTH IN CONFLICT

Union territory

Confederate states

ENGLAND   FRANCE

War supplies from Europe

Union arms factories

ATLANTIC OCEAN

tobacco

cotton

blockade

Union

UNION STRATEGY AT SEA
To blockade the South, cutting off trade with England and France.

UNION STRATEGY ON LAND
To cut the South into three parts and capture its capital, Richmond.

CONFEDERATES TRY TO BREAK THE UNION BLOCKADE
By building ironclad warships. By swift blockade runners.

Washington

KAN.

MO.

W. VA.

VA.   Richmond

Mississippi R.

KY.

TENN.

N. C.

Wilmington

Memphis

ARK.

Chattanooga

East-West supply lines

Atlanta

S. C.

Charleston

MISS.

Vicksburg

ALA.

GA.

Savannah

TEXAS

LA.

New Orleans

Mobile

FLA.

MAP STUDY   Since the South lacked industry, its most important supply line extended all the way to the factories of Europe. (a) How did the Union plan to break that supply line? (b) What river did the Union leaders want to gain control of as part of their land strategy?

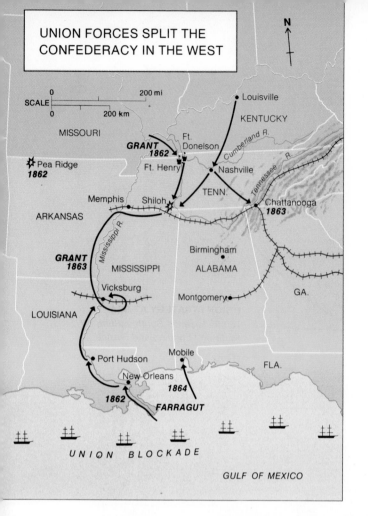

UNION FORCES SPLIT THE CONFEDERACY IN THE WEST

SCALE

0 — 200 mi
0 — 200 km

N

MISSOURI

KENTUCKY

Louisville

GRANT 1862

Ft. Donelson

Ft. Henry

Cumberland R.

Nashville

Tennessee R.

✸ Pea Ridge 1862

Memphis

Shiloh

TENN.

Chattanooga 1863

ARKANSAS

Mississippi R.

GRANT 1863

MISSISSIPPI

Birmingham

ALABAMA

GA.

Vicksburg

Montgomery

LOUISIANA

Port Hudson

Mobile

New Orleans

FLA.

1864

1862

FARRAGUT

GULF OF MEXICO

U N I O N   B L O C K A D E

MAP STUDY   See Teacher's Key.
By winning control of the Mississippi, Union forces split the Confederacy. How did the navy aid Union plans?

The North had a different strategy. In order to win the war, it had to invade and conquer the South. This was to be done in three ways: (1) The ● North planned to follow the strategy of "divide and conquer." A large part of the Confederacy lay west of the Mississippi, as the map on page 429 shows. Union plans called for gaining control of the Mississippi. This move would make it impossible for the Confederacy to get supplies from the states west of the river. After cutting the South in two at the Mississippi, the North would try to cut the eastern part of the Confederacy into smaller pieces. (2) The North also planned a blockade of southern ports, to

430

prevent goods from being shipped into or out of the South. This would block the southern plan to exchange cotton for war supplies. (3) The Confederate capital had to be captured and the armies defending it conquered.

The side that was most successful in carrying out its strategy would win the war. Let us see what happened.

THE WAR IN THE WEST

For months after the Battle of Bull Run, the important fighting took place not in the East, but in the West. The army and navy of the Union worked together to win control of the Mississippi River. To follow the story of the fighting in the West, use the map on this page.

Farragut captures New Orleans. In order to gain control of the Mississippi, the North needed to capture Confederate cities and forts along the river. Most important was the city of New Orleans near the mouth of the Mississippi. The man who was ordered to capture New Orleans was David Farragut, a navy captain. Farragut had begun his naval career in the War of 1812 when only a boy. He was now 60 years old.

In the spring of 1862, Farragut started up the Mississippi with a fleet of wooden ships. In a bold dash, he ran past the fire of Confederate forts on each side of the river. Then he defeated a Confederate fleet guarding New Orleans and captured the city. The lower Mississippi was now controlled by Union forces.

Grant gains early victories for the North. Meanwhile, other Union forces were moving against Confederate forts farther north on the Mississippi and on the Tennessee and Cumberland rivers. The leader of these forces was Ulysses S. Grant. Grant, a West Point graduate, had fought in the Mexican War, but he had not made a name for himself as had Robert E. Lee and other officers. After

● After students have read this section, have them explain how the North carried out each part of its strategy.

Tell students that Robert E. Lee once said *duty* was the best word in the English language.

People in America's Story

Lee's father had served as a cavalry officer in the Revolution. Discuss how this might have affected the difficult choice Lee faced when fighting broke out in 1861.

ROBERT E. LEE

An honor student at West Point, Robert E. Lee later chose loyalty to Virginia over command of the Union army.

Lee's home, Arlington, overlooks the Potomac River in Arlington National Cemetery.

A college president after the war, Lee helped other ex-Confederates adjust to peace.

Lee commanded the Confederate army during the Civil War. Known for his dignity and calm, even in times of danger, he was respected by all as the South's greatest leader.

431

Many soldiers, never expecting the war to drag on for four long years, brought their families with them to camp.

that war, he had resigned from the army. The Civil War gave Grant a chance to re-enter the army and to prove his ability as an officer. A modest man, he was willing to accept advice; yet he was also able to make wise and quick decisions. Above all, Grant had a will of iron. He refused to turn back once he had decided on a course of action.

Early in 1862, Grant attacked Fort Henry and Fort Donelson in western Tennessee. With the help of navy gunboats, the Union forces captured both forts. When the commander of Fort Donelson asked the terms of surrender, Grant replied, "Immediate and unconditional surrender." From then on, he
● was nicknamed "Unconditional Surrender" Grant. Meanwhile, farther west, a Union victory at Pea Ridge, Arkansas, drove Confederate forces out of southern Missouri and northern Arkansas.

After the capture of the two forts in Tennessee, Grant's armies moved south-

ward. The Confederate forces made a surprise attack at Shiloh (SHY-loh) in southern Tennessee. In the battle that followed, the Confederate side at first seemed to be winning. But when fresh Union soldiers arrived, Grant forced the outnumbered Confederate troops to retreat.

The capture of Vicksburg gives the North control of the Mississippi. By 1863, the Union forces controlled all the Mississippi except the 250-mile strip between Vicksburg and Port Hudson (map, page 430). General Grant's chief problem now was to capture Vicksburg. The city stood on high bluffs on the east bank of the river, with swampy ground surrounding it. The forts were in an excellent position to shell attacking forces. When Grant found he could not take Vicksburg by direct attack, he prepared for a long siege. With Union gunboats guarding the river side and Grant's forces on the land side, no supplies could reach the town. On July 4, 1863, the Confederate commander surrendered Vicksburg on Grant's terms. A short time later Port Hudson also surrendered.

432

The Union forces now had control of the Mississippi. Lincoln announced, "The Father of Waters again goes unvexed to the sea." One part of the North's strategy had succeeded. The Confederacy had been cut in two.

THE WAR ON THE SEA

The northern navy cuts off southern shipping. The second part of the Union strategy, you remember, was to blockade southern ports. When the war started, the Union navy had only 90 ships. Vessels of every kind, however, were hastily prepared for blockade duty. Soon Union ships were guarding important Confederate ports from Virginia to Texas.

Of course, the blockade was not complete. Because the southern coastline was over 3,000 miles long, the Union navy could not seal off every port. In an attempt to break the strangle hold on its shipping, the South used blockade-runners built in Great Britain. Under cover of night these ships could slip into southern ports with badly needed ammunition, guns, and other supplies. But

The battle between the *Monitor* (left) and the *Merrimack* (right) was the first clash between ironclad ships.

in spite of all attempts to break the blockade, the South's shipping was slowly strangled. Southern people found it almost impossible to get tea, coffee, and matches. Cotton could not be exported, and countless bales piled up on the wharves.

To make the blockade even tighter, the Union army and navy took steps to capture southern ports. By the end of the war, all Confederate ports except Charleston, South Carolina, and Wilmington, North Carolina, were in Union hands. David Farragut added to his fame by taking the great port of Mobile, Alabama. More than any other plan used by the North, the Union blockade ● helped to defeat the South.

Ironclad ships are used. The first battle ever fought between armored ships took place during the Civil War. Before this time, the navy's ships had all been built of wood. Early in the war, however, the Confederates remodeled the wooden ship *Merrimack,* renamed it *Virginia,* and covered its sides with iron plates. (This kind of ship was called an ironclad.) The *Merrimack* was armed with ten guns. In March, 1862, it attacked Union ships blockading the Virginia coast. Shells that were fired from the Union vessels had no effect on the

433

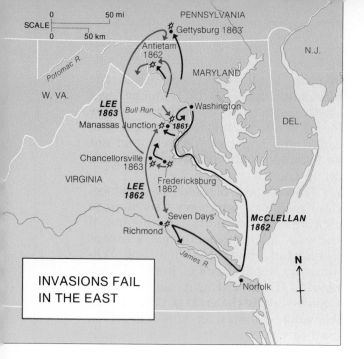

SCALE

0 | 50 mi
0 | 50 km

PENNSYLVANIA

Gettysburg 1863

Antietam
1862

MARYLAND

N.J.

Potomac R.

W. VA.

LEE
1863   Bull Run

Manassas Junction   1861

Washington

DEL.

Chancellorsville
1863

VIRGINIA   LEE
1862   Fredericksburg
1862

Seven Days'

McCLELLAN
1862

Richmond

James R.

Norfolk

N

INVASIONS FAIL
IN THE EAST

MAP STUDY   See Teacher's Key.
Until Gettysburg the Confederate armies won
most of the battles in the East. With what part
of the Union strategy were these battles
concerned?

strange-looking *Merrimack*. It destroyed two ships, ran another one
aground, and then withdrew. Its crew
planned to return to destroy the remaining Union ships.

On the next day, however, the *Merrimack* was challenged by an ironclad
ship that the Union navy had secretly
been building. The Union vessel, the
Monitor, had been designed by a Swed-
ish-American inventor, John Ericsson.
This ship was smaller than the *Merrimack* and had a low, flat iron deck. In a
large revolving turret two powerful guns
were mounted. According to one observer, the *Monitor* looked like a "tin
can on a shingle."

In the battle that followed, neither
ironclad ship was able to damage the
other in any serious way. Finally, they
both gave up the battle. Although the
battle between the *Monitor* and the
Merrimack ended in a draw, it is impor-
• tant in naval history. These ironclads
proved that wooden warships were a
434   thing of the past.

THE WAR IN THE EAST

So far you have read how Union forces
gained control of the Mississippi and
blockaded the southern coast. Meanwhile, other Union forces in the East
had been trying to capture the Confederate capital at Richmond.

**McClellan's attack on Richmond
fails.** After the Union defeat at Bull
Run (page 428), General George B.
McClellan took charge of reorganizing
and drilling the new troops. In a few
months the army was a well-disciplined
and well-equipped body of 100,000 soldiers. But McClellan was too cautious
in attacking the enemy. He did not
move against the Confederate army at
Richmond until Lincoln ordered him to
do so in the spring of 1862. McClellan's
army traveled by water and landed on
the James Peninsula in order to attack
Richmond from the east (map, this
page). The advance up the peninsula
against Richmond was so slow, however,
that the Confederates decided to attack
instead. General Lee sent for General
Thomas "Stonewall" Jackson to join in
the campaign. Jackson had gained his
nickname while holding "like a stone
wall" against the Union troops in the
first Battle of Bull Run. Together Lee
and Jackson forced the Union army to
retreat in the famous Seven Days' Battles. So the second Union attempt to
capture Richmond failed.

**Further defeats discourage the
North.** During the months that followed, the Confederates won battle
after battle in the East. Another advance by Union forces against Richmond ended in defeat at the second Battle of Bull Run. Lee then led his
gray-clad soldiers across the Potomac
into Maryland. He was met at Antietam
(an-TEE-tum) Creek by Union troops.
After a bloody battle, Lee turned back
into Virginia. But he was able to stop
the Union advances that followed by
winning brilliant victories at Freder-

icksburg and Chancellorsville. In the latter battle, Stonewall Jackson was accidentally shot by his own men and died soon afterward. When Lee heard this news, he said sadly, "I have lost my right arm."

These were discouraging days for the North. Robert E. Lee had outfought Union forces much larger than his own. Lincoln had tried several generals after McClellan's failures, but had not been able to find one who could match Lee's military skill. The President himself was harshly criticized. Many people blamed him for the failures of the army. Only Lincoln's determination to save the Union kept him going in those dark days.

Confederate forces invade Pennsylvania. After his victory at Chancellorsville, General Lee decided to invade the North a second time. He hoped to strike a blow that would end the war. As he swung north through Maryland

The Union victory at Gettysburg marked a turning point in the war. The battle was won when Union troops forced back attacking Confederates led by General Pickett.

and into Pennsylvania, watchful Union armies also marched north, keeping between Lee and the city of Washington.

On June 27, 1863, General Lee and his officers stood looking at a map. As he pointed to the village of Gettysburg in Pennsylvania, the Confederate leader declared, "Hereabouts we shall probably meet the enemy and fight a great battle, and if God gives us the victory, the war will be over, and we shall achieve the recognition of our independence."

The Battle of Gettysburg stops the Confederate advance. On July 1, the two armies met and the Battle of Gettysburg began. Under their newly appointed commander, General George Meade, the Union forces took their position on a series of hills and ridges near Gettysburg. The Confederates occupied a ridge opposite them. Through two and a half days the bitter fighting continued. At noon on July 3, there was a sudden silence on the battlefield. General Lee was preparing to make a bold and desperate attack on the northern position. Then about 15,000 brave Confederates, commanded by General

• *The Gettysburg Address*

Four score and seven years ago our fathers brought forth on this continent, a new nation, conceived in liberty, and dedicated to the proposition that all men are created equal.

Now we are engaged in a great civil war, testing whether that nation or any nation so conceived and so dedicated, can long endure. We are met on a great battlefield of that war. We have come to dedicate a portion of that field, as a final resting place for those who here gave their lives that that nation might live. It is altogether fitting and proper that we should do this.

But, in a larger sense, we cannot dedicate — we cannot consecrate — we cannot hallow — this ground. The brave men, living and dead, who struggled here, have consecrated it, far above our poor power to add or detract. The world will little note, nor long remember what we say here, but it can never forget what they did here. It is for us the living, rather, to be dedicated here to the unfinished work which they who fought here have thus far so nobly advanced. It is rather for us to be here dedicated to the great task remaining before us — that from these honored dead we take increased devotion to that cause for which they gave the last full measure of devotion — that we here highly resolve that these dead shall not have died in vain — that this nation, under God, shall have a new birth of freedom — and that government of the people, by the people, for the people, shall not perish from the earth.

George Pickett, advanced across a field against the Union forces on Cemetery Ridge. In perfect order they charged through the murderous Union fire and flung themselves at the Union lines. A handful of men succeeded in planting the Confederate flag high on the hill. But they were forced back. Cannon and musket fire had been so deadly that three fourths of the attackers were killed or wounded. The brave charge had failed. The battle was lost. The next day Lee turned back toward the south.

The President speaks at Gettysburg.
Soon after the Battle of Gettysburg, seventeen acres of the battlefield were set aside as a cemetery for the soldiers who had died there. President Lincoln was asked to dedicate the cemetery by making "a few appropriate remarks." Lincoln's "remarks" at Gettysburg on November 19, 1863, have always been remembered because they say so much in so few words and say it so well. His Gettysburg Address, which appears above, is one of the great documents in our history. It expresses the ideals that we Americans must always keep before us if our nation is to endure.

Gettysburg marks the turning point of the war. The news of the victory at Gettysburg caused great rejoicing in the North. On its heels came word of Grant's success in the West on July 4 — the surrender of Vicksburg (page 432). Grant's victory had cut the Confederacy in two, and the Union success at Gettysburg had hurled back the Confederate invasion of the North. These Union triumphs marked the turning point in the war. In America and abroad, people understood the importance of these victories. Although the South might fight on, it was not likely to win.

General Grant takes command of all the Union armies. During 1862 and 1863, Union forces had carried on bitter and bloody campaigns in Tennessee. Their goal was to capture the important city of Chattanooga in the southeastern part of the state. After the surrender of Vicksburg, General Grant took command of these forces. He defeated Confederate forces at Chattanooga in the late fall of 1863. The Confederates had to retreat toward Atlanta, Georgia (map, page 438). Impressed by Grant's ability in the West, Lincoln gave him command of the Union armies. At last Lincoln had found a general who might be able to lead the North to final victory.

Grant began to make plans that he hoped would end the war: (1) The lower South was to be cut off from the rest of the Confederacy. To accomplish this, Grant ordered General William T. Sherman, who had aided in the capture of

About 180,000 black Americans joined the Union army during the Civil War. Many blacks also served as sailors on Union ships.

Chattanooga, to slash through the Confederacy to Atlanta. (2) Grant himself was to attack Lee in Virginia. No matter what the cost, he would capture Richmond.

Sherman divides the South by marching to the sea. In May, 1864, General Sherman set out from Chattanooga with an army of 100,000 men. Although Confederate troops fought them every step of the way, Sherman's army slowly but surely advanced. In September, Sherman captured Atlanta. (Trace his advance on the map, page 438.)

Shortly afterward, Sherman took a bold step to divide the South still further. With 60,000 men, he struck out for Savannah, Georgia, over 200 miles away on the Atlantic coast. Many southern people never forgave General Sherman for the frightful destruction carried out on this march "from Atlanta to the sea." Between Atlanta and Savannah he and his men left behind them a black and desolate strip of land 60 miles wide. To deprive southern forces of food and supplies, they burned houses and barns, towns and crops. They tore up railroads

437

and killed farm animals as they went along. Late in December, 1864, Sherman telegraphed President Lincoln, "I beg to present you, as a Christmas gift, the city of Savannah." The Confederacy had been divided again.

The end comes. Meanwhile, General Grant was furiously attacking General Lee's armies in Virginia. The fighting began in a thickly wooded section northwest of Richmond, called the Wilderness. Grant was unable to break through Lee's lines, but he kept hammering at them in spite of heavy losses among his own troops. Step by step the armies moved east and then south in a half circle around Richmond. At last, hard-pressed by the enemy, Lee aban-

doned Richmond to march southwest toward the mountains. But Union armies blocked his way. Lee said sadly, "There is nothing for me to do but go and see General Grant, and I would rather die a thousand deaths." At the village of Appomattox (ap-puh-MATtox) Court House on April 9, 1865, this gallant officer surrendered his armies to General Grant.

Grant treated Lee with the respect due a valiant soldier. The two generals began to talk over army experiences during the Mexican War. Then Lee asked Grant for the terms of surrender. Grant allowed the Confederate officers to keep their swords and pistols. He also let the soldiers keep their horses,

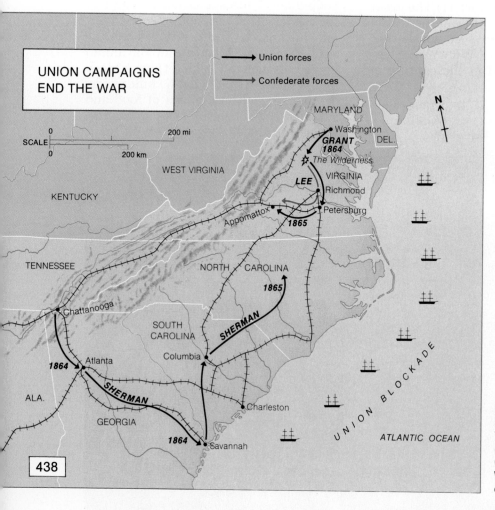

UNION CAMPAIGNS END THE WAR

→ Union forces
→ Confederate forces

438

See Teacher's Key.

MAP STUDY
Two major Union campaigns brought the Civil War to an end. What did each of those campaigns accomplish?

● See p. T39 for a strategy calling for students to write a report on a Civil War battle.

which, he said, would be needed for spring plowing. Learning that Lee's men were hungry, Grant sent food to them. He forbade his soldiers to fire their guns in celebration of the victory, saying, "The war is over."

About two weeks later in North Carolina, the last important Confederate army surrendered to General Sherman, who had marched north from Savannah to join Grant. The South had fought gallantly. Now the tragic war was over. After four long years, the Stars and Stripes again flew over "one nation, indivisible."

On April 9, 1865, Lee signed the terms of surrender to Grant in this Virginia farmhouse. The war was over.

CHECK UP   See Teacher's Key.

1. **(a)** What effect did the Battle of Bull Run have on the North? **(b)** On the South?
2. **(a)** How did the Confederates hope to win the war? **(b)** What was the Union plan? **(c)** How did the Union carry out each part of its plan?
3. Why did the battles of Gettysburg and Vicksburg mark the turning point in the war?
4. **(a)** What were Grant's plans for ending the war? **(b)** How did the war end?

3 How Did the War Affect the Lives of People in the North and the South?

In time of war, many men are called upon to fight, but those who remain at home also have a job to do. People at home must produce food and supplies for the fighting forces. Every kind of transportation is needed to move troops and supplies. Money must be raised to pay the costs of war. Hours of work are long and every person who can work is called on to help.

The South carries on during the war.

★ The people of the South felt the hardships of the war more keenly than the people of the North. Every white man who could fight went into the army. This meant that the work of the South was done for the most part by the slaves and the white women. But as the war went on, slaves began to leave the plantations. Then, too, because of the blockade, the South could not get goods that it usually bought from the North or from foreign countries — clothes, machinery, medicines, and many household items. The white women of the South faced these difficult conditions bravely. They took care of the farms and plantations, worked in hospitals, and collected money to buy clothing and bandages for the soldiers.

As time went on, southern farms, plantations, and buildings became rundown. Roads were not repaired, and railroad tracks were damaged. Railroad cars and locomotives wore out and could not be replaced. It became diffi-

439

★ See p. T40 for a strategy asking students to compare and contrast the effects of the war on Northerners and Southerners.

cult to transport food and supplies to the armies. Many regions were ruined by invading armies and battles. Homes were burned, cities were shelled, the countryside was stripped of crops and farm animals. War's destruction spread through the South. Thousands of families mourned loved ones lost in battle.

The North prospers during the war. Northern families also felt the grief brought by losses in the war. For several reasons, however, the hardships caused by the war were much less severe in the North than in the South. Very little fighting took place on northern soil. Because of its greater population, the North found it easier to carry on at home. The North also had more railroads and factories of every kind than did the South. Old industries worked at top speed, and new industries sprang up to make the clothes, food, blankets, tents, guns, and ammunition needed by the army.

Thousands of northern women replaced the factory hands who went off to war. But the boom in northern industry opened up more jobs than there were workers to fill them. With the increased demand for workers, wages went up. So did prices. High prices brought greater profits to industrialists, shopkeepers, and others who had something to sell. In spite of great losses and grief, therefore, many people in the North prospered during the war.

North and South issue paper money. Both North and South needed money to meet the costs of the war. And in the North as well as the South, the government issued paper money to pay its bills. But many people feared that these paper dollars might never bring their full worth in gold and silver. In the dark days of 1864, when it seemed the war would never end, the paper dollar in the North was worth only about 40 cents. Since it took more paper dollars to pay for goods, prices went higher and higher. The South was much worse off. To carry on the war, it was forced to issue even greater quantities of paper

Women in both the North and South took jobs in factories to replace men who went off to war. This picture shows women making bullets.

money. The value of southern money went down much faster than that of northern money. Toward the end of the war, southern money was worth only about three cents on the dollar. These conditions created great hardships for most Southerners.

▶ **CHECK UP**   See Teacher's Key.

1. **(a)** How did the war affect life in the South? **(b)** In the North?
2. **(a)** Why did both sections issue paper money? **(b)** What was the effect on prices and the value of money?

4 How Did Abraham Lincoln Plan to Unite the Divided Nation?

Even while the war was being fought, Abraham Lincoln struggled with the problem of how peace would be restored after long and bitter fighting. Late at night, when the White House stood silent in the darkened city, Lincoln brooded over what would happen when the guns at last stopped firing.

Lincoln proclaims the freedom of slaves in the Confederate states. From the outset, Lincoln believed that preservation of the Union was the basic war aim of the North. By focusing on this aim rather than on any other, he could enlist broad support for waging the war. But many people thought the chief purpose of the war should be to free the slaves. Despite their urging, Lincoln continued to make clear the purpose of the war as he saw it:

> My paramount object in this struggle is to save the Union. . . . If I could save the Union without freeing any slave, I would do it; if I could save it by freeing all the slaves, I would do it; and if I could save it by freeing some and leaving others alone, I would also do that. What I do about slavery and the colored race, I do because I believe it helps to save this Union.

Nevertheless, when Lincoln wrote these words, he had already decided to take a step toward ending slavery. He realized that freeing the slaves in the Confederacy would be a serious blow to the South. So in the autumn of 1862, he announced that on January 1, 1863, in all parts of the country still fighting the United States, "all persons held as slaves . . . shall be then, thenceforward, and forever free." This statement is known as the Emancipation Proclamation.[1] (To **emancipate** means to free.) Now the people of this country and of Europe understood that the war was being fought not only to save the Union but to free the slaves. Since the people of England did not believe in slavery, their sympathy for the South began to cool. The Proclamation also made it possible for blacks to join the Union army. By the end of the war, some 180,000 black soldiers had served in the Union forces. ★

Lincoln plans for peace. As Lincoln looked ahead to the end of the war, he saw other problems that would have to be solved. When the Union won the war, as he was sure it would, confusion and disorder would spread through the South. On the day the war ended, the Confederate government would collapse. There would be no President, no Congress, no state governments, no police force, no money in the defeated

---

[1]The Emancipation Proclamation did not apply to slaves in the slave states that had remained in the Union. Slavery in those areas was abolished when the Thirteenth Amendment was added to the Constitution in 1865.

★ Mention that some 200,000 black civilians worked for the Union army in a variety of occupations.

People in America's Story

ABRAHAM LINCOLN

Born to a frontier family in Kentucky, Abraham Lincoln rose from humble beginnings to become one of our nation's greatest Presidents.

Determined to save the Union at all costs, Lincoln had little time for relaxation during the war years. This picture shows him sharing a rare moment with his wife Mary and sons Robert (in uniform) and Tad.

Lincoln's understanding and fairness, often expressed in noble words during the war between the North and the South, helped America survive as one nation. His famous speech at Gettysburg (above) will always be remembered for its declaration that "government of the people, by the people, for the people, shall not perish from the earth."

● See p. T40 for a strategy that asks students to identify the main points of Lincoln's plan to unite the country.

states. Lincoln decided to take steps to meet this situation. He wanted to make it possible for the seceded states to re-build the South and to re-enter the Union. Lincoln proposed this plan: In any southern state, as soon as ten per-cent of the persons who had voted in 1860 wished to establish a government loyal to the Union, they could do so.

Lincoln hoped that all Americans would forget the war as soon as possi-ble. He wanted the country to devote all its strength to the building of a new and better nation. When Lincoln took the oath of office as President for the second time, in March of 1865, he ex-pressed this thought in memorable words:

> Fondly do we hope — fervently do we pray — that this mighty scourge of war may speedily pass away. . . .
>
> With malice toward none; with char-ity for all; with firmness in the right, as God gives us to see the right, let us strive on to finish the work we are in; to bind up the nation's wounds; to care for him who shall have borne the battle and for his widow, and his orphan — to do all which may achieve and cherish a just and lasting peace among ourselves, and with all nations.

Lincoln is assassinated. President Lincoln did not live to put his plans into effect. In the middle of April, 1865, the long struggle was drawing to a close and Lincoln felt the need of relaxation. On the evening of April 14, he and Mrs. Lin-coln arranged to go to Ford's Theater in Washington with two guests. Arriving at the theater, they were shown to the box reserved for them.

In an alley outside the theater a man was restlessly pacing back and forth. His name was John Wilkes Booth. Booth, a Virginian, was desper-ate over the defeat of the South. He believed that if Lincoln were not Presi-dent, the South would be better off. Booth had decided to kill Lincoln and

had urged friends to kill other impor-tant government officials. Since Booth was an actor and had often performed in Ford's Theater, he was familiar with the building.

As the audience watched the play, John Wilkes Booth crept through the theater to the door of Lincoln's box. Suddenly he threw open the door, stepped into the box, and shot Lincoln in the back of the head. Then he leaped over the railing and half jumped, half fell, to the stage. As he fell, he shouted a Latin phrase that means, "Thus be it ever to tyrants!" He got to his feet, limped across the stage to the back door of the theater, mounted his horse, and rode away. Booth was killed a few days later by soldiers who were sent to cap-ture him.

The wounded President was carried to a house across the street from the theater. There, shortly after seven o'clock the next morning, he died. Thus ★ ended the life of a great American. Abraham Lincoln had done his work well; the Union had been preserved. It remained for others to "bind up the na-tion's wounds."

Throughout the North, Lincoln was deeply mourned. Even the people of the South began to realize that this great and kindhearted man had been their friend. Jefferson Davis himself said, "Next to the defeat of the Confed-eracy, the heaviest blow that fell upon the South was the assassination of Lin-coln."

▶ **CHECK UP**   See Teacher's Key.

1. **(a)** Why did Lincoln issue the Emanci-pation Proclamation? **(b)** What slaves were affected by this Proclamation? **(c)** What effect did the Proclamation have in Europe?

2. What was Lincoln's plan for helping the Confederate states return to the Union?

443

★ Point out that Lincoln died just six days after Lee's surrender to Grant (p. 438).

5 What Happened in the South After the War?

War leaves its mark on the South. At the end of the war much of the South lay in ruins. Weeds grew in the fields, houses and barns had been burned down, bridges were broken, and two thirds of the railroad lines were destroyed. Southern cities had been especially hard hit. A newspaper reporter
● told what he saw in Charleston, South Carolina:

> A city of ruins, of desolation, of vacant houses, of widowed women, of rotting wharves, of deserted warehouses, of weed-wild gardens, of miles of grass-grown streets, of acres of pitiful and voiceless barrenness — that is Charleston.

Problems must be solved. All over the South men and women were asking what was to become of their region, for there were many problems to be solved.

(1) Southerners knew that somehow they must rebuild the South, repair the destruction brought by war, and return to peacetime living.

(2) Another important problem had to do with the relation of the seceded states to the national government. How were they to be returned to the Union? Would they be treated generously or would they be punished as defeated enemies?

(3) There was also the question of setting up state governments. Would those who had fought against the Union be allowed to vote and hold office? If not, who would run the state governments?

(4) One of the most serious problems was the situation of the freed slaves. When slavery came to an end, most black people were without homes or work. What was their future to be?

During the war, in parts of the South occupied by Union forces, black and white teachers set up schools to help freed slaves learn to read and write. The first of these schools was set up in 1861 by Mary S. Peake, a free black from Virginia. Then, late in the war, Congress established the Freedmen's Bureau to carry on the work of education. The Bureau also supplied food, clothing, fuel, and hospital care to a large number of white and black Southerners. In addition it tried to protect freed slaves from violence and to defend their right to own property. Would the Freedmen's Bureau continue its work, or would it be turned over to the southern states?

CONGRESS TAKES CHARGE OF RECONSTRUCTION

President Johnson's plans are defeated. After Lincoln's death, the heavy duties of the presidency fell upon Andrew Johnson. The former Vice-President intended to carry out Lincoln's generous plans for restoring the seceded states to the Union. But the Republican Congress was not willing to leave the **reconstruction** (rebuilding) ★ of the South in the hands of President Johnson — a Democrat and a Southerner.

When Congress met in December, 1865, newly elected members from the southern states were waiting to take their seats in the two houses. Among them were many men who had held high positions in the Confederacy. Northern senators and congressmen refused to seat the southern delegations.

Congress takes control of reconstruction policy. There were many reasons why Congress demanded a part in

444

★ See p. T40 for a strategy calling for students to examine Congress's plan for reconstruction.

The Freedmen's Bureau was formed to help freed slaves. The women in this Freedmen's Bureau school are sewing clothes for the poor.

working out plans for reconstruction. For one thing, by the end of 1865 it was clear that the former slave states were determined to deny freed slaves the rights of free citizens. They adopted **black codes.** These were laws that made it difficult for black people to own property, earn a living, and get an education. None of the states had given blacks the vote.

The Thirteenth Amendment, which abolished slavery, had gone into effect in December, 1865. Then, a few months later, Congress approved the Fourteenth Amendment, which would become part of the Constitution when enough states ratified it. This amend-

ment declared that "all persons born or naturalized in the United States . . . are citizens. . . ." Black Americans, therefore, were made citizens.

Another section of the Fourteenth Amendment provided that in determining representation, blacks would be counted the same as whites. Thus the South would soon gain more seats in the House. Republicans feared that their party would lose control of Congress unless a Republican Party, supported by black voters, could be built in the

Following the war, many people in the South lacked food, clothing, and shelter. Everyone, black and white, had to start life over again.

South. Therefore they added still another section to the amendment. It said that a state's representation in Congress would be reduced if it refused to let black men vote. The amendment also said that former government officials who had taken sides against the Union could not hold office again until pardoned by Congress.

Congress passes the Reconstruction Act. When only one of the Confederate states — Tennessee — approved the Fourteenth Amendment, Congress decided to use harsher methods. It passed the Reconstruction Act of 1867. Under this act the governments of the other ten Confederate states were swept away, and these states were divided into five military districts. Each district was placed under army rule. Soldiers were to keep order while new state governments more to Congress's liking were formed. In forming these new govern-

ments, Congress ruled that southern whites who had fought against the Union would not be allowed to vote. Black men, however, would be guaranteed the right to vote and to hold office. The southern states were not to be admitted to the Union until (1) new state constitutions had been approved by Congress and (2) the new state governments had accepted the Fourteenth Amendment.

The Fifteenth Amendment is added to the Constitution. Congress also passed the Fifteenth Amendment for the purpose of protecting black rights still further. It stated that no citizen should be kept from voting because of his race or color or the fact that he had once been a slave. The Fifteenth Amendment, approved by the required number of states, was added to the Constitution in 1870.

New state governments are set up. Congressional reconstruction brought great change to the South. For the first time, black voters took part in elections that set up new governments in the ten occupied states. These new governments were called carpetbag governments. The name carpetbagger was given to Northerners who moved South to help carry out Congress's plan of reconstruction. Many were sincerely interested in helping the South, but others saw a chance to get rich quickly. They earned their name from the fact that they traveled to the South with all their belongings hastily packed in old-fashioned traveling bags called carpetbags. Carpetbaggers were not the only white people who took part in the reconstruction governments. They were joined by "scalawags," white southerners who had remained loyal to the Union or who thought the best plan now was to cooperate with the North. Finally, a number of black men were also elected to office. The black officeholders tried to strengthen the political and civil rights of freed blacks.

The first black members of Congress were elected from southern states during reconstruction. Among them were Senator Hiram H. Revels of Mississippi (far left in this picture).

It was the carpetbag governments that wrote new state constitutions and laws and carried out the provisions of the Reconstruction Act. By 1870, all the southern states had been admitted once more to the Union. The new state legislatures established public schools for both whites and blacks. Voting laws were liberalized and the rights of women enlarged. The courts and the county governments were improved. The legislatures also voted large sums of money for buildings, schools, roads, and railroads. Many of these things were badly needed in the war-torn South. Some of the money approved for such purposes was spent unwisely, however. The carpetbag legislatures voted heavy taxes, moreover, to raise the money they wanted to spend. The heavy taxes fell chiefly on the southern whites who owned property. Many had to sell their lands because they could not pay the taxes.

Southern whites strike back. Few southern whites liked the reconstruction governments. Gradually, secret societies were formed to force blacks out of office. The Ku Klux Klan was the most active of these societies. Its purpose was to frighten blacks so that they would not vote. Clad in ghostly white hoods and robes, Klan members rode silently around the countryside in the dead of night, beating, and sometimes killing, blacks and their white friends. The Ku Klux Klan was so active that Congress ordered federal soldiers to break it up.

SOUTHERN WHITES REGAIN CONTROL OF STATE GOVERNMENTS

Reconstruction ends in the South. In time, white people in the South regained control of local governments. Men who had been mere boys during the war reached the age of 21. Since they had not fought against the United States, they were permitted to vote and hold office. Also, in 1872, Congress passed a law restoring the right to vote to all but a few ex-Confederates. Rule by reconstruction governments gradually ended, and southern whites regained control of their states. Soldiers were withdrawn from the last of the ● southern states in 1877.

White Southerners felt that blacks should be prevented from voting. So they found ways to get around the Fifteenth Amendment. They passed laws requiring that all voters must have lived for many years in one place, or must pay a tax (called a poll tax) in order to be eligible to vote. Some states required voters to be able to read and to explain the federal Constitution. These laws were all used to deprive black men of the right to vote.

447

● Mention that the withdrawal of federal troops was part of a compromise plan that enabled Rutherford B. Hayes to become President (p. 586).

Our Presidents

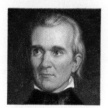

JAMES K. POLK   1845–1849

Democrat from Tennessee. Nominated as a compromise candidate, and not a favorite in the race, Polk became the first "dark horse" to be elected President. Polk favored expansion. During his administration the Mexican War was fought and the boundary dispute with Great Britain over the Oregon Territory was settled. Polk's nomination and his inauguration were the first to be reported by telegraph.

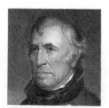

ZACHARY TAYLOR   1849–1850

Whig from Louisiana. "Old Rough and Ready" had served in the army for over 40 years when the Whigs nominated him for the presidency. A popular hero in the Mexican War, Taylor had never held public office before his election and was inexperienced in politics. As President, Taylor took a firm stand in the slavery dispute, threatening to lead an army himself against any attempted secession.

MILLARD FILLMORE   1850–1853

Whig from New York. Distinguished in appearance, Fillmore was a New York legislator and a congressman before he was elected Vice-President. Becoming President at Taylor's death, Fillmore's most important action was to support the Compromise of 1850 — a measure which he mistakenly believed would end the differences between the North and South. Fillmore was the last Whig to serve as President.

FRANKLIN PIERCE   1853–1857

Democrat from New Hampshire. A compromise candidate who didn't want the presidency and made no campaign speeches, Pierce nevertheless won the election by a sweeping majority. The death of their young son just before the family moved to Washington cast a shadow over the Pierces, and there was little entertaining in the White House. Because he favored the South on the slavery issue, Pierce lost northern support.

JAMES BUCHANAN   1857–1861

Democrat from Pennsylvania. "Old Buck" was our only bachelor President. Buchanan had served as a representative, senator, Secretary of State under Polk, and ambassador to Russia and Great Britain before becoming President. Cautious in nature, he took no action when southern states seceded from the Union. Buchanan believed that although the states had no constitutional right to secede, the federal government had no constitutional right to stop them.

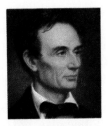

ABRAHAM LINCOLN   1861–1865

Republican from Illinois. One of our greatest Presidents, Lincoln had served in the Illinois legislature and for one term in the House of Representatives before winning the 1860 presidential election. A grave-looking man with a keen sense of humor, Lincoln was widely admired for his expressive words and writings. The first President to be assassinated, his death deprived the country of the firm leadership that had held the Union together through the war years.

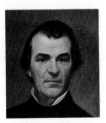

ANDREW JOHNSON   1865–1869

From Tennessee. A self-educated man of intelligence, honesty, and courage, Johnson had risen from humble beginnings to high public office. Though a southern Democrat, he had opposed secession in the Senate and became Lincoln's second-term Vice-President. When Lincoln died, Johnson inherited the task of restoring the South to the Union. Disagreements with Congress led to Johnson's impeachment, but he was acquitted and completed his term of office.

The South becomes solidly Democratic. Most white Southerners found it hard to forgive Congress for its policy of reconstruction. The Southerners blamed the Republicans in Congress for their troubles and became strong supporters of the Democratic Party. In election after election the southern states voted overwhelmingly for Democratic candidates. When people spoke of the "Solid South," they meant that the South could usually be counted on to vote solidly for the Democratic Party. This continued until well into the twentieth century.

A NEW SOUTH DEVELOPS

In time the South, aided by northern capital, repaired the damages caused by war. Cities were rebuilt, railroads repaired, business and trade expanded. Still other changes took place in the South following the Civil War.

Large plantations begin to disappear. One change was the breakdown of the old plantation system. Plantation owners had neither the money nor the slave labor to work their lands as they had before the war. Also, most of the freed blacks did not want to remain on large plantations and toil for wages. Instead, they hoped to start a new life. Because plantation owners lacked workers and because taxes were so high, many were forced to sell much of their land. Most of this land was sold in lots of a few acres. As a result, the number of large plantations in the South grew smaller, while the number of separate farms increased.

Sharecropping becomes common. Instead of selling land, many plantation owners rented their land to **tenant farmers.** Some tenants paid rent in cash or in crops worth the amount of their rent. But many tenants were poor whites or blacks who could furnish nothing but their labor. They became **sharecroppers.** The landlord provided them with food, seed, tools, and a cabin. In return, the sharecroppers gave the landowner a share of the crops raised on their plots of land. Many sharecroppers barely made a living from their share of the crops. They were often in debt to the landowner, especially when harvests were bad.

● Have students prepare written or oral reports about George Washington Carver.

New crops are raised in the South.
Changes also took place in the crops grown in the South. Cotton remained the chief crop. Large quantities of tobacco, rice, and sugar also continued to be raised. But, as transportation improved, farmers found they could make good profits from fruits and vegetables that were suited to the southern soil and climate. Many southern farmers were influenced by the work of George ● Washington Carver. Born of slave parents, Carver won international fame for agricultural research. He developed products from such crops as peanuts, pecans, and sweet potatoes and convinced southern farmers that these crops, rather than cotton, could provide them with a good income.

After the Civil War ended, the South started to rebuild. New factories got under way and business and trade began to grow. Atlanta, a bustling manufacturing center, held a number of fairs to attract investment in business and industry. This picture shows the 1895 fair.

Industry gets a start in the South.
Before the war, most Southerners made their living from farming. After the war, farming was still the chief occupation, but people became more interested in business and industry. The South was rich in natural resources that had never been developed because cotton-growing with slave labor had seemed more profitable. For example, there were great stretches of forest that would yield quantities of lumber. Beneath southern soil there were large deposits of coal, iron, and oil — all needed in industry. Plentiful cotton and a large supply of workers encouraged the building of mills to manufacture cloth.

The South that developed after the war, therefore, was very different from the old "land of cotton." A network of roads and railroad lines began to cover the South. The region became a leading supplier of lumber for the nation, and quantities of coal and iron were mined there. Birmingham, Alabama, became a

thriving steel and industrial center, earning the name "Pittsburgh of the South." Oil wells and refineries dotted such states as Texas, Louisiana, and Arkansas. Factory towns grew up in many regions, drawing large numbers of workers into the manufacture of cotton cloth, tobacco, and cottonseed products. Ports such as New Orleans, Houston, Galveston, Mobile, and Norfolk became important centers of trade and commerce.

With the passing of years, much of the bitterness caused by the war and reconstruction faded from people's memories. In spite of the problems of the reconstruction period, the people of the South gradually returned to loyal support of the Union. Today Southerners and Northerners — Americans all — are united in their allegiance to our country.

▶ **CHECK UP**   See Teacher's Key.

1. What problems faced the South after the war?
2. **(a)** How did President Johnson hope to bring the southern states back into the Union? **(b)** What position did the Republican Congress take on working out plans for reconstruction?
3. **(a)** What was the purpose of the Fourteenth Amendment? **(b)** Of the Reconstruction Act of 1867? **(c)** Of the Fifteenth Amendment? **(d)** How were new state governments organized and the southern states restored to the Union?
4. **(a)** How did southern whites regain control of the state governments? **(b)** What was meant by the term "Solid South"?
5. **(a)** What effect did the war have on the plantation system? **(b)** What kinds of industry developed in the South after the war?

CHECK UP ON CHAPTER 20   See Teacher's Key.

Words to Know

1. siege
2. strategy
3. emancipate
4. blockade
5. document
6. sharecropper
7. scalawag
8. unconditional
9. reconstruction
10. black codes
11. carpetbagger
12. border state
13. tenant farmer

Places to Locate

1. Chattanooga
2. Richmond
3. Atlanta
4. New Orleans
5. Savannah
6. Washington, D.C.
7. Vicksburg
8. Gettysburg

Facts to Remember

1. How was each of these leaders important to the Confederacy? **(a)** Jefferson Davis **(b)** Robert E. Lee **(c)** Stonewall Jackson
2. **(a)** What took place in the battle between the *Monitor* and the *Merri-* *mack*? **(b)** Why was this battle important in naval history?
3. What contribution did each of the following military leaders make to the northern cause? **(a)** U. S. Grant **(b)** William Sherman **(c)** George McClellan
4. **(a)** In what state did the last major campaign of the war take place? **(b)** Give the date of the surrender of Lee to Grant and the town where it took place.
5. **(a)** How did the war affect the lives of women in the South? **(b)** How did it affect the slaves? **(c)** How was northern industry affected?
6. **(a)** What was the Emancipation Proclamation? **(b)** How was it different from the Thirteenth Amendment?
7. Tell where Abraham Lincoln's assassination took place, the date, and who was responsible.
8. Identify each of the following: **(a)** Freedmen's Bureau, **(b)** Fourteenth

451

Facts to Remember (cont.)

Amendment, **(c)** Reconstruction Act, **(d)** Fifteenth Amendment.

Skills to Practice

1. Arrange the following events in the order in which they took place.
   a. Battle of Gettysburg
   b. Final surrender of Confederate forces
   c. Battle of Bull Run
   d. Assassination of Lincoln
   e. Union army's march across Georgia
2. Use the map on page 430 to complete these statements:
   a. As part of the plan to divide the Confederacy, Union forces led by General Grant attacked Forts ____?____ and ____?____ in western Tennessee.
   b. After a long siege, Grant forced the town of ____?____, Mississippi, to surrender in July, 1863.

c. Two important southern ports taken by Union naval forces commanded by David Farragut were ____?____ and ____?____.

Questions to Think About

1. Some historians believe that the South lost the war when Great Britain failed to recognize the Confederacy as an independent country. **(a)** What is the basis for that idea? **(b)** How did Britain's decision affect the South?
2. **(a)** Why did Lincoln say that war solves no problems? **(b)** What problems were not solved by the Civil War? **(c)** What would have been the result if President Lincoln had made no effort to stop the seceding states?
3. The work of black Americans was important to both sides in the Civil War. **(a)** How did blacks contribute to the southern war effort? **(b)** To the northern war effort?

Linking Past and Present

Pictures of war. Photographers, using both still and motion picture cameras, have given us a full pictorial record of recent wars. But at the time of the Civil War, photography was still very new. Cameras were large, difficult to handle, and costly to operate. Some photographs of the war remain, however, chiefly those taken by Mathew Brady and his assistants. (The photograph on page 432 is a Brady picture.) Most of our pictorial record of the war comes from artists such as A. R. Waud, Winslow Homer, and Thomas Nast. These men would watch a battle, then try to draw an accurate picture of it. Their sketches were cut into wooden blocks and printed in newspapers. Many of these old photographs and sketches are reprinted in books and magazines today. They represent a valuable record of our country's past.

Virginia battlefields. Virginia was the scene of much heavy fighting during the Civil

War. This is not surprising when you remember that Richmond, Virginia, the Confederate capital, was not far across the Potomac from Washington, D.C. Today, many battlefields, monuments, and other reminders of the war can be seen in Virginia. At Manassas, visitors can see the old stone tavern and a log cabin that survived the battles of Bull Run, and a statue of Stonewall Jackson, who turned back the Union troops. In the wooded Wilderness region, trenches dug by the opposing armies still remain, grim reminders of the battles once fought there. A national military park now preserves the battlefields of Fredericksburg, Chancellorsville, Spotsylvania Court House, and the Wilderness. The old earthworks, trenches, and cannon sites there remind us of events long past. At Appomattox Court House, the brick house where General Lee surrendered to General Grant is still standing. A stone slab commemorates the historic meeting.

● Have students prepare written or oral reports about Mathew Brady.

For answers see Teacher's Key.

Suggest that students use this method of test preparation as they study or review later chapters.

GAINING SKILL

Studying for Tests

You can get good results on the tests you take in history class — and in your other classes — if you learn to study efficiently. It is very important to keep up with your regular assignments. Preparing for a test will be much easier if you do. The material will be familiar, and all you will need to do is review it carefully.

When you review, look for the main ideas first. In this book, each section in a chapter begins with a heading in large type. The heading asks a question. Try to answer that question without looking at the information in the section. Jot down the answers that come to mind. Now read quickly through the section. Did you leave out anything important?

Once you have reviewed the main ideas, look for important facts and details. (Don't forget to look at the maps and graphs, in addition to the written information.) In a chapter like this one, which has many dates and battles, you may find it helpful to make a simple list. You might list the major battles of the Civil War in chronological order in one column. Put the date of each battle beside it in a second column. Then in a third column, write down which side won and why the battle was important. Cover two of the columns with another sheet of paper, and read down the uncovered column. Can you remember the date when you see the name of the battle? Can you remember the name of the battle when you read its results? You can use the same method to help you remember presidential elections or other important events.

When you are ready to take a test, remember to read all the directions carefully. Read each question carefully too. Do not feel you must rush, but don't spend a lot of time on one question. If you can't answer a question, go on to the next one. That way, you will be sure to get credit for all the ones you *can* answer. When you have tried to answer all the questions, go back to the ones you skipped and work on them again.

Try to plan your time during a test so that you can check your paper when you finish. Be sure your answers are clearly written.

Now answer the following questions. They will give you practice in reviewing and in taking tests.

1. Look back at the first section of this chapter (pages 425–427). Write five sentences about the main ideas in that section. Make some of your statements true and some false. Exchange papers with a partner. Mark your partner's true statements *T* and the false statements *F*.

2. After looking at Section 2 (pages 428–439), write three questions on important facts and details in that section. Exchange papers with a partner. Then see if you are able to answer your partner's questions.

3. Read Section 5 (pages 444–451) and write two questions that take several sentences to answer. (Write out the answers you expect on another sheet of paper.) Exchange papers and answer your partner's questions.

UNDERSTANDING UNIT 6

SUMMARY OF IMPORTANT IDEAS

Unit 6 has told how the United States expanded and how the North and South fought a bitter war.

1. From 1803 to 1853 the United States, through purchase, annexation, treaty, and conquest, expanded beyond the boundaries of 1783 until it reached the Pacific.

　a. Among the reasons for this expansion were (1) a desire to control the inland waterways and to acquire cheap and fertile land, and (2) fear that European countries might become powerful in North America.

　b. The areas obtained by the United States included (1) the Louisiana Purchase, (2) Florida, (3) Texas, (4) the Mexican Cession, (5) the Oregon region, and (6) the Gadsden Purchase.

　c. The new lands were explored and settled. Just west of the Mississippi River, a number of new states were carved out of the Louisiana Purchase and admitted to the Union. Traveling by wagon train, pioneers followed the Santa Fe Trail to the Southwest or the Oregon Trail to the interior of the country and on to the west coast. With the discovery of gold in California, the population on the Pacific coast increased greatly.

2. A bitter quarrel developed between the North and the South over slavery in the new territories.

　a. For a time, compromises like the Missouri Compromise and the Compromise of 1850 checked the quarrel over slavery.

　b. Finally, further compromise was rejected. Leaders in the South opposed any limitations on slavery in the territories (1) because the soil in the Old South was wearing out and new land was needed for growing cotton, and (2) because Southerners believed that their way of life would be destroyed by the North unless a balance between free and slave states was maintained in the Union. In the North the great majority of people were opposed to the extension of slavery into the territories.

　c. The victory in 1860 of the Republican Party (which believed that Congress had the power to pass laws prohibiting slavery in the territories) led to the secession of the southern states and to war.

3. The Civil War (1861–1865) caused great destruction in the South and led to great changes in both the North and South.

　a. The North had the advantages of a larger population and greater industrial resources; the South had the advantages of fighting in defense of its own soil and of brilliant military leadership.

　b. After bitter fighting, the northern plan of blockade and of dividing the South resulted in victory. Thus, the Union was saved. In the North, the war greatly increased the national debt, but industry also grew stronger. In the South, property damage was great and Confederate money became worthless. Slavery was ended, though ways were found to deprive blacks of their rights.

　c. Following the assassination of Lincoln, Congress enacted its own plan for reconstructing the South. This policy was deeply resented by white Southerners.

　d. Important changes took place in the

South after the war. Small farms multiplied, new crops were introduced, and industry became increasingly important.

UNIT REVIEW   See Teacher's Key.

1. How and why did the United States acquire each of the following territories? **(a)** Louisiana Purchase **(b)** Florida **(c)** Texas **(d)** Oregon Territory **(e)** Mexican Cession **(f)** Gadsden Purchase

2. Tell how each of the following contributed to the settlement of the West: **(a)** the Lewis and Clark expedition, **(b)** travel by steamboat, **(c)** the Oregon Trail, **(d)** Stephen F. Austin, **(e)** the Santa Fe Trail, **(f)** the discovery of gold in California, **(g)** the quarrel over slavery, **(h)** the fur trade.

3. **(a)** Why did southern leaders feel that slavery must expand into the new territories? **(b)** Why did they reject popular sovereignty? **(c)** Why did they favor states' rights? **(d)** Why did the victory of the Republican Party in 1860 lead to the secession of the southern states?

4. **(a)** What were some of the advantages of each section in the Civil War? **(b)** Why did the North win the war? **(c)** How was each of the sections affected by the war?

5. **(a)** What was Lincoln's plan for reconstruction of the South? **(b)** Why did Congress develop another plan after his assassination? **(c)** What were the results?

6. What changes in ways of living took place in the South after the war?

THINGS TO DO

The items marked with an asterisk (*) are for the whole class.

*1. Make new cards for your game "Can You Identify?" using items in Chapters 18, 19, and 20.

*2. On an outline map show the original territory of the United States in 1783 and each new piece of territory added to the United States up through 1853. Be sure to mark the dates on each new territory.

*3. Memorize the Gettysburg Address (page 436). Look up the meaning of the words you do not know so that you will understand it better.

*4. The Thirteenth, Fourteenth, and Fifteenth Amendments were passed as a result of the Civil War. With the help of your teacher make a simple outline showing the main ideas of each of these amendments.

5. Prepare a "Who's Who" of the leaders of the North and South during the war. Write a paragraph about each one.

6. Write or tape an imaginary letter by **(a)** an American living in Texas when Texas was annexed; **(b)** a Southerner telling of the changes in the South during the war or reconstruction; **(c)** a northern soldier at the Battle of Bull Run.

7. Study and prepare to read to the class one of these poems: **(a)** *O Captain! My Captain!* by Walt Whitman; **(b)** *Lincoln, the Man of the People* by Edwin Markham; **(c)** *Abraham Lincoln Walks at Midnight* by Vachel Lindsay.

Left to right: McCormick reaper; Brooklyn Bridge; lathe operator; Stanley steamer.

UNIT **7**

Modern America Takes Shape

1860–1940   See p. T41 for a unit preview strategy. See pp. T58–T71 for lists of useful books and audiovisual aids.

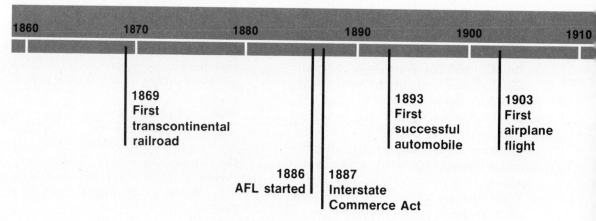

1860	1870	1880	1890	1900	1910

1869
First
transcontinental
railroad

1893
First
successful
automobile

1903
First
airplane
flight

1886
AFL started

1887
Interstate
Commerce Act

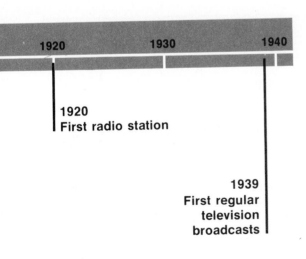

1920

1930

1940

1920
First radio station

1939
First regular
television
broadcasts

In Unit 6 you read how it took a bitter war to preserve the Union. Unit 7 tells the story of our country's progress in the years after the Civil War. In Chapter 21 you will learn how ranchers, miners, and farmers moved into the West. For the Indians of the West, this settlement meant the end to a centuries-old way of life. Chapter 22 tells how the United States became the world's leading industrial nation. Industrial growth brought many benefits but also created new problems. Chapter 23 describes some of those problems and the steps that were taken to meet them. In Chapter 24 you will learn what happened when new machines and new methods were applied to farming.

CHAPTER **21**

Vocabulary preview: public lands, transcontinental, reservation, prospector, long drive, open range

The Last Frontier in the West Is Settled

1860–1940   See pp. T41–T42 for chapter teaching strategies.

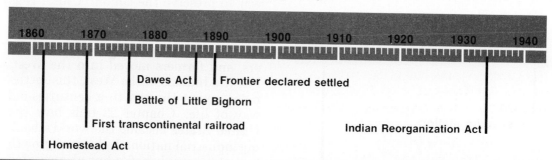

| 1860 | 1870 | 1880 | 1890 | 1900 | 1910 | 1920 | 1930 | 1940 |

Dawes Act

Battle of Little Bighorn

First transcontinental railroad

Frontier declared settled

Indian Reorganization Act

Homestead Act

What this chapter is about —

From the very start of American history, as you have learned in earlier chapters, adventurous pioneers had moved westward. For the most part, this advance came in waves, each wave pushing the frontier farther west. First,

pioneers claimed land and started homes in the territory between the Atlantic coast and the Appalachians. Then, in the early 1800's, settlers poured through the mountains and into the rich valley of the Ohio River. Next, the frontier reached the Mississippi and beyond. In the middle 1800's, lured by

● See p. T41 for a strategy calling for students to find
out more about the Homestead Act.

◀ A train heading west across the plains
symbolizes the advance of pioneer settlements
into the homelands of the western Indians.

the promise of gold and rich farmland, pioneers made their way by land or sea to California and Oregon. There still remained in the West, however, a vast territory. It stretched roughly from the present state of Minnesota south to Texas and westward beyond the Rocky Mountains. This territory was the last American frontier.

For a number of Indian tribes this region was not a frontier but their homeland, where their ancestors had lived for many centuries. But in the years following the Civil War, pioneers streamed into the open spaces between the Mississippi River and the Rocky Mountains. So many pioneers settled in the western region that by 1890 the Indians had been forced to change their ways of living and the frontier had disappeared.

In this chapter you will read how miners, ranchers, and farmers moved into the West and forced the Indians from their lands. The following questions will help you understand what happened:

1. Why did people move into the region beyond the Mississippi?
2. What happened to the Indians who tried to keep their lands?
3. How did miners, ranchers, and farmers settle the last frontier?

1 Why Did People Move into the Region Beyond the Mississippi?

The Homestead Act aids western settlement. In the 1860's, two events encouraged Americans to settle west of the Mississippi. The first was the Homestead Act, passed by Congress in 1862. It had to do with **public lands,** that is, the lands that belonged to the national government. Before this time, the United States had sold public lands to pioneers for as little as $1.25 an acre (page 342). But even this low price kept many poor families from settling in the West. The Homestead Act made public lands easier to get. By this act any head of a family could become the owner of a farm or homestead of 160 acres. The only requirement was that the homesteader live on it and work the land for five years.

Coming at the time it did, the Homestead Act had very important results. At the end of the Civil War, large numbers of soldiers were discharged from military service. These soldiers had given up jobs to go to war. They had led exciting and dangerous lives in battle. Many of them wished to strike out on some bold new venture rather than return to their homes and their former way of living. The Homestead Act made a new start possible.

Black Americans took part in the westward movement too. Once federal troops were withdrawn from the South (page 447), many former slaves feared that their rights would no longer be protected. As a result, thousands of blacks joined the "Exodus of 1879," migrating to Kansas and Oklahoma in search of a better chance in life.

A transcontinental railroad is built. A second important event followed close on the heels of the Homestead Act. This was the building of the first **transcontinental** (cross-country) railroad line. For years some people had

459

★ See p. T41 for a strategy calling for students to discuss the effects of the
transcontinental railroads on western settlement.

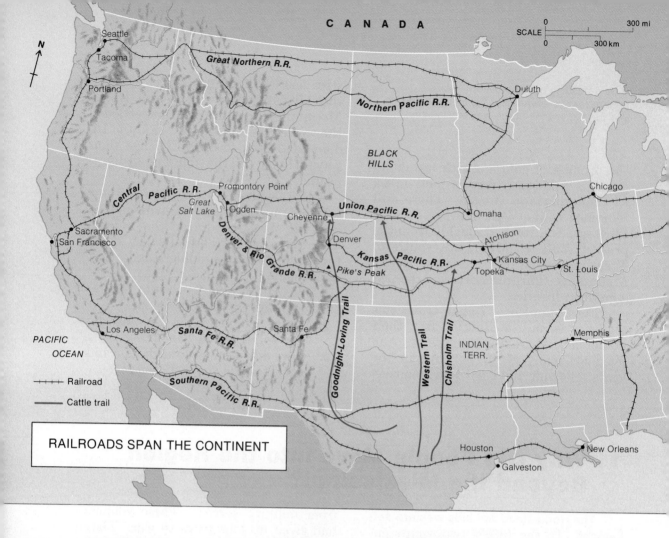

CANADA

Seattle
Tacoma
Portland

Great Northern R.R.

Northern Pacific R.R.

Duluth

BLACK
HILLS

Chicago

Central Pacific R.R.
Promontory Point
Great
Salt Lake
Ogden

Denver & Rio Grande R.R.

Sacramento
San Francisco

Cheyenne

Denver

Union Pacific R.R.

Omaha

Atchison

Kansas City

St. Louis

Pike's Peak

Kansas Pacific R.R.

Topeka

Los Angeles

Santa Fe R.R.

Santa Fe

Memphis

PACIFIC
OCEAN

INDIAN
TERR.

Goodnight-Loving Trail
Western Trail
Chisholm Trail

+++ Railroad

Cattle trail

Southern Pacific R.R.

RAILROADS SPAN THE CONTINENT

Houston

New Orleans

Galveston

N

SCALE
0   300 mi
0   300 km

MAP STUDY   See Teacher's Key.
Railroads speeded up the movement of pioneers
into the West. (a) What railroads linked the
Middle West with the Pacific coast? (b) Why did
cattle trails run north and south?

dreamed of linking the East and West
by railroad. In 1862, these dreams developed into plans. Two companies, the
Union Pacific and the Central Pacific,
were organized to build a railroad between the Middle West and the Pacific
coast. The Union Pacific was to push
westward from Omaha, Nebraska, while
the Central Pacific would build eastward from Sacramento, California.
Somewhere in the huge region the two
railroads would meet. The United
States government took steps to encourage this plan. It offered to lend
generous amounts of money to the rail-

road builders and to give them large
tracts of land on each side of the railroad for every mile of track laid. Thus,
the railroad company which laid the
longest stretch of track would receive
the most land and money.

A race started between the two railroads. Thousands of Chinese and Irish
workers were hired to lay track across
broad prairies and through narrow
mountain passes. At the height of the
race nearly 20,000 men toiled and
sweated. They suffered from scorching
heat and blinding snowstorms, but mile
by mile the two roads crept closer together. On May 10, 1869, two locomotives — *Number 119* of the Union Pacific and *Jupiter* of the Central
Pacific — "touched noses" at Promontory Point near Ogden, Utah. The race
had been won by the Union Pacific.

Because it crossed level country for much of the way, the Union Pacific had succeeded in laying 1,086 miles of track. The Central Pacific, which had to cross the western mountains, had laid only 689 miles of track. There was great rejoicing as Governor Leland Stanford of California drove a golden spike into the final railroad tie. Telegraph wires flashed the news all over the country. The dream of spanning the continent had come true.

The transcontinental railroad brings settlers to the West. Traveling by railroad, an increasing number of people crossed the open spaces of the West. They sent back news of what they had seen to friends and relatives in the East, many of whom joined the westward stream of pioneers. People who wished to set up homes in the West found the task of moving their families and belongings much easier, safer, and more comfortable after the transcontinental railroad was built. The railroad also made it easier for western farmers to send their crops to market, and cattle could be shipped directly to meat-packing centers. By 1884, three more railroads — the Northern Pacific, the Southern Pacific, and the Santa Fe — had lines stretching to the Pacific coast. The railroads sold land given them by the government to settlers at low prices. Towns grew up along all the railroad lines.

Thousands of Chinese men came to America to help build the western railroads. In this photo Chinese workers haul dirt to fill in a trestle supporting a track through mountains.

461

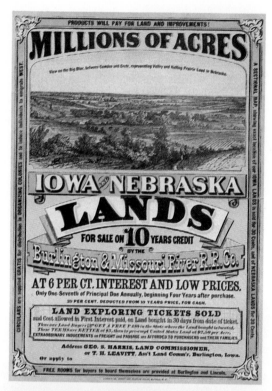

The owners of railroad companies, eager to see the West settled, used advertisements to attract settlers to the Great Plains. What railroad used this advertisement?

Because of the transcontinental railroads as well as the Homestead Act, a mighty wave of settlers moved west during the 1870's and 1880's. Not only Americans but people from Europe joined the throng of pioneers in search of land and new homes. Among them were members of a religious group called Mennonites who came from Russia. They brought with them a special kind of wheat that thrived in the dry weather of the Great Plains. Other farmers came from Germany, and even more from the Scandinavian countries of Norway, Sweden, and Denmark. These eager settlers pushed the frontier farther and farther west.

▶ **CHECK UP** See Teacher's Key.

1. **(a)** What was the Homestead Act? **(b)** Why did it encourage settlement of the West?
2. **(a)** Why was a transcontinental railroad built? **(b)** How did the government encourage its construction? **(c)** Why did railroads attract settlers to the West?

2 What Happened to the Indians Who Tried to Keep Their Lands?

The Indians fight the settlers' advance. When European explorers first landed on America's shores, they found the Indians here before them. As you read in Chapter 2, the Indians had been living in America for many centuries before the Europeans arrived. Naturally they looked upon the land as theirs and theirs alone. But, as the white settlers moved westward, the Indians were pushed out of their homes and hunting grounds. The Indians did not yield easily, however. They bitterly opposed each advance by the pioneers and some-

462

times made war to try to keep their land.

One Indian chief, speaking in 1805, explained his people's side of the story ● in this way:

Brother: Listen to what we say. There was a time when our forefathers owned this great island [by which he meant the whole continent]. Their [lands] extended from the rising to the setting sun. . . . But an evil day came upon us. Your forefathers crossed the great water and landed on this island. Their

● See p. T41 for a strategy calling for students to use primary sources in studying the difficulties faced by Indians during the 1800's.

numbers were small. They found friends and not enemies. They told us they had fled from their own country for fear of wicked men, and had come here to enjoy their religion. They asked for a small [area of land]. We took pity on them, granted their request; and they sat down amongst us. We gave them corn and meat; they gave us poison [rum and whiskey] in return.

The white people, Brother, had now found our country. Tidings were carried back, and more came amongst us. Yet we did not fear them. We took them to be friends. They called us brothers. We believed them and gave them a larger [area of land]. At length their numbers had greatly increased. They wanted more land; they wanted our country. Our eyes were opened, and our minds became uneasy. Wars took place. . . .

Brother: Our [lands] were once large and yours were small. You have now become a great people, and we have scarcely a place left to spread our blankets. You have got our country, but are not satisfied. . . .

In the many battles between white settlers and Indians, the Indians sometimes won. Usually, however, the settlers were victorious, and slowly but surely they pushed the Indians farther inland. Then, in the years following the War of 1812, the United States government followed a policy of removing all ● the eastern Indians to lands west of the Mississippi River. As you have read (page 354), some Indians moved west voluntarily. But many left their homes only when forced by soldiers to do so. The eastern Indians were mostly resettled west and south of the point where the Missouri River bends northward.

The western Indians valued their traditional ways of living. This painting shows a prairie Indian camp before the time when great numbers of white settlers moved west.

This painting is a reminder of the importance of the buffalo to the western Indians' way of life.

Life on the plains is hard for the eastern Indians. Most eastern Indians had been farmers. The new lands west of the Mississippi did not produce good crops, and water and wood were scarce. Furthermore, trouble arose between the eastern Indians and the Indian peoples who had long made their homes on the plains. The western Indians wanted to keep their hunting grounds over which great herds of buffalo roamed. The huge, shaggy creatures furnished an abundant supply of food for the western tribes, and from their hides the Indians made clothing and coverings for tepees or wigwams. Tools were made from buffalo bones.

White settlers invade the Indian lands beyond the Mississippi. Indian claims to the lands in the West did not stop the westward surge of pioneers. By the mid-1800's white settlers were again pushing into Indian lands.

(1) The pioneers who followed the Oregon Trail passed through the heart of the Indian country. Many forty-niners also crossed the Great Plains on their way to California. But a few groups of white people gave up their plans to go all the way to the west coast. Instead, they settled along the Santa Fe and Oregon Trails in the present states of Kansas and Nebraska.

(2) In 1847 a religious group called the Mormons set out to find a place where they could follow their own beliefs and practices. Under the leadership of Brigham Young, they braved many dangers in crossing Indian country. At last the Mormons reached the valley of the Great Salt Lake (in what is now Utah). There they built their homes. In time the Mormon settlements grew and prospered.

(3) Trappers roamed the northern forests in search of furs. Hunters entered the Indian lands and killed buffalo by the thousands to get the skins, which were highly valued in the East.

(4) The Homestead Act and the

464

● Have students turn to "Linking Past and Present" (p. 476) to read how sea gulls saved the first Mormon settlements from disaster.

People in America's Story

CHIEF JOSEPH

A Nez Perce leader, Chief Joseph became known for his valiant attempt to lead his people to safety in Canada.

After fighting broke out between the Nez Perce and U.S. troops, Chief Joseph (right) ordered a retreat to Canada. He brilliantly fought off pursuing forces, but after a march of some 1,300 miles he and his people were forced to surrender (below) just 30 miles from Canada.

Chief Joseph survived the Indian wars and, in fact, eleven years after his surrender met with a military officer who had led troops against the Nez Perce. But he died in 1904, still in exile from his homeland.

465

building of the transcontinental railroads encouraged large groups of settlers to move west of the Mississippi.

The Indians resolve to defend their homeland and hunting grounds. As more and more settlers moved west, the western Indians became desperate. In many cases, settlers took lands that had been granted to the Indians by solemn treaty. Even worse, the Indians faced the loss of their homes and their means of making a living. Fast-growing white settlements cut down the areas in which the Indians could roam freely, and the buffalo were being killed off at a tremendous rate. William F. Cody, better known as "Buffalo Bill," killed more than 4,000 animals in less than two years to provide food for the workers building railroads across the West. Many white hunters slaughtered the animals merely for sport, leaving them where they fell. The buffalo herds grew smaller and smaller, and that meant starvation for the Indians. They took up arms in a desperate attempt to save their lands and their way of life.

Indian attacks grow into wars. At first, bands of Indian warriors struck at wagon trains and stagecoaches. Then they attacked trains, farms, settlements, and trading posts. Naturally the white settlers fought back. To keep the Indians in check, the federal government built army posts in the Indian country. But the attacks continued and finally grew into a series of wars.

The Indian wars were an unhappy chapter in American history. Large numbers of people were killed. Families were broken up, homes destroyed, and men, women, and children slaughtered on both sides. There seemed to be no way of preventing these wars, since each side felt that it was in the right. The Indians were fighting for their lives, their lands, and their way of living. They could point to a long history of broken promises and treaties on the part of white settlers and government

agents. The white people, on the other hand, felt there would be no peace until the power of the Indian tribes was completely broken.

Government troops break the resistance of the Indians. Because each side believed so strongly in its cause, the Indian wars went on for many years. Some of the fiercest fighting took place between United States forces and Sioux (SOO) tribes. In 1862 an Indian war broke out in Minnesota. Led by a chief named Little Crow, the Santee Sioux killed more than 700 settlers before they were defeated and forced onto new lands in the Dakota Territory. But the discovery of gold in the Black Hills brought miners into that area during the mid-1870's. When the Sioux began to gather under Crazy Horse and Sitting Bull, federal troops were sent to round them up. Among the officers leading these troops was Colonel George A. Custer. In June, 1876, on the banks of the Little Bighorn River, Custer and over 200 of his men were killed in an unsuccessful attack on Sitting Bull's camp. The Sioux were short of ammunition and food, however, and had to surrender in the fall.

Other tribes also waged a bitter fight. In 1877 Chief Joseph led the Nez Perce (PURSS) in a brilliant campaign ● against well-equipped army forces. His small band of men, women, and children traveled some 1,300 miles across Oregon, Idaho, and Montana, as they tried to make their way to Canada. Finally, just 30 miles from the Canadian border, Chief Joseph could hold out no longer. He surrendered, saying,

I am tired of fighting. Our chiefs are killed. . . . The little children are freezing to death. My people, some of them, have run away to the hills and have no blankets, no food. . . . Hear me, my chiefs, I am tired; my heart is sick and sad. From where the sun now stands, I will fight no more forever.

● The name *Nez Perce* (meaning ''pierced nose'') was given to this group of Indians by a French interpreter in 1805.

INDIAN RESERVATIONS WEST
OF THE MISSISSIPPI, 1890

Reservation

SCALE
0 — 300 mi
0 — 300 km

MAP STUDY   See Teacher's Key.
By 1890 western Indians had been moved onto reservations. (a) In what state was the Battle of Little Bighorn fought? (b) Where did the Battle of Wounded Knee take place?

The last Indian wars were fought against the Apache in New Mexico. When the Apache leader, Geronimo, was captured in 1886, Indian warfare came to an end. There was still one final tragedy, however. In 1890 some Sioux Indians began to follow a leader who promised them that the performance of certain dances would lead to the return of their lands. The "Ghost Dances" alarmed settlers in South Dakota. Fearing renewed warfare, they called in the army for protection. On December 29, 1890, a fight broke out at Wounded Knee, and more than 200 unarmed Sioux were killed.

The United States government settles the Indians on reservations. In the late 1860's, the government began to place the Indians on **reservations.** The reservations were areas set aside for the different Indian tribes. At about the same time the government stopped treating the Indian tribes as separate nations and making treaties with them. A Bureau of Indian Affairs was established within the Department of the Interior. The Commissioner of Indian Affairs in Washington was now responsible for all the government officials and agents who dealt with the Indians.

The government promised to protect the Indians who lived on reservations and to furnish them with food and

467

other supplies. But the reservation system did not work very well. The defeated Indians felt hemmed in and longed for the freedom of the plains. In addition, many of the white government agents cheated the Indians living on the reservations and treated them with contempt.

The attitude of white people toward Indians changes. Meanwhile, more and more Americans began to take a different view of Indian affairs. Investigations made by the government showed that white people had been to blame as often as Indians for trouble between the two. The old frontier attitude began to change. A best-selling book by Helen Hunt Jackson called *A Century of Dishonor* told how some white people had cheated the Indians and treated them cruelly. More people began to take an interest in the problems that Indians faced.

The government changes its Indian policy. In 1887 Congress passed the Dawes Act, which set up an entirely new Indian policy. The Dawes Act tried to encourage Indians to become farmers. Many Americans felt that if Indians took up farming, all their problems would go away. The Dawes Act divided up the reservations and offered

a piece of land to any Indian who would farm it. The act also authorized the government to sell land and use the profits for setting up schools to educate Indian children.

The Dawes Act was not a success. Few Indians wanted to become farmers. Moreover, the land they were given was often not good for farming. By the 1930's the policies of the Dawes Act were abandoned and new reforms were begun. The Indian Reorganization Act (1934) provided for tribal self-government. It also made federal credit available for tribal businesses and gave Indians help in making the best use of their lands.

▶ **CHECK UP**   See Teacher's Key.

1. **(a)** Why did the Indians resist the western advance of white settlers? **(b)** Name the leaders who united Indian tribes in their efforts to stop white settlements. **(c)** What was the result of the Indian wars?
2. **(a)** What was the reservation system? **(b)** Why did that system not work well? **(c)** How did the Dawes Act change the federal government's Indian policy?

3 How Did Miners, Ranchers, and Farmers Settle the Last Frontier?

In 1890, a United States government ★ report announced that the frontier had disappeared. This statement did not mean that the area between the Mississippi River and the west coast was thickly settled with prosperous farms and busy cities and towns. What it did mean was that pioneers had pushed into most parts of the West and that the ef-

forts of the Indian tribes to halt white settlement had failed.

The West had not yet become what it is today, however. In building up the West, miners, cattle ranchers, and farmers all played an important part. They led lives of hardship and danger, of heartbreaking failure, and of high adventure.

★ Tell students that this report came from the Census Bureau.

Helena, Montana, got its start in the 1860's when prospectors made a lucky find. During its first few years Helena was called Last Chance Gulch.

PROSPECTORS OPEN UP THE ROCKY MOUNTAIN COUNTRY

The story of the miners comes first. It goes back to the time when gold was discovered in California (Chapter 18). When the first gold seekers rushed west to make fortunes in California, there seemed to be plenty of gold. They needed only to sift it out of the soil in creek and river beds, or dig it close to the earth's surface. As these fortune seekers swelled into the thousands, however, the "easy" gold was soon exhausted. Only those with money to use expensive machinery could afford to mine gold deep down in the earth. But if easy gold had been found in the hilly country of California, might it not also be discovered in the Rocky Mountain region? Many people who had looked for gold in California turned back to the rugged mountain country. Still others stopped in these mountains on their way to the west coast. They wandered here and there, drawn by rumors of rich veins of precious ore. These people were called **prospectors.**

Gold and silver are found in the Rockies. The hopes of many prospectors were rewarded during the 1850's and 1860's. Rich deposits of silver were found in what is now Nevada. About the same time gold was discovered in Colorado, especially in the neighborhood of Pike's Peak. Fortune seekers headed for Colorado in wagons bearing the sign "Pike's Peak or Bust." The

469

Spanish ranching traditions were established in the Southwest long before that region became part of the United States. Here a cowboy or *vaquero* (vah-KAIR-oh) lassos a corralled wild horse. Wild horses, called *mustangs,* were captured on the plains and trained for riding.

luckier ones struck gold. Others were disappointed. They changed their signs to "Busted, by Gosh!" and moved to other spots. Still later, silver was found in what are now the states of Idaho and Montana. Gold was also discovered in Wyoming, Arizona, New Mexico, and in the Black Hills of South Dakota.

The mining rush causes the mountain states to grow rapidly. Wherever adventurers swarmed in search of gold, towns sprang up almost overnight. These early mining towns were far different from American towns of today. Visitors found the streets filled with choking dust, deep ruts, or oozing mud. The few buildings were crudely built and ugly.

Wild and noisy crowds roamed through the streets, intent on just one thing — finding a fortune quickly.

Today, except for a few ghost towns, there is little left in the mountain regions of the West to remind us of those early reckless days. How did this change take place? As the rich "strikes" of gold and silver were exhausted, prospectors moved on to other places. Law-abiding citizens formed groups to bring ● the outlaws and bandits of the Wild West to justice. Mining became a business, run by big companies. With expensive machinery, miners tunneled deeper and deeper into the mountain sides to bring forth not only gold and silver but copper, coal, lead, and zinc. Many pioneers who had failed to "strike it rich" settled down, following a trade or farming the soil. The mountain regions would have been settled sooner or later. But the mining rush of the 1850's

470

and 1860's speeded up the organization of such states as Nevada (1864), Colorado (1876), Montana (1889), Idaho (1890), and Wyoming (1890).

CATTLE RAISING SPREADS ACROSS THE WESTERN PLAINS

Just as mining helped to settle the mountain regions of the Far West, so cattle raising helped to develop the western plains. When the Spaniards had settled Mexico and, later, parts of what is now our Southwest, they brought with them cattle and horses. Allowed to roam the open spaces, the cattle developed in time into half-wild animals with a huge spread of horns. The horses used to herd the cattle were wiry broncos, small but swift. When American settlers spread into Texas, New Mexico, and California, many of them took up cattle raising. Because transportation to the East was difficult, however, cattle raising did not promise big profits.

Cattle raising begins to boom. Then, after the Civil War, cattle raising developed into a major industry. When railroads began crossing the prairies, ranchers found that they could drive their steers to railroad points in Kansas and Nebraska. Each year Texas ranchers would collect huge herds of cattle and start them northward on what was called the **long drive.** Often a herd numbered 2,000 or 3,000 cattle. Grazing leisurely across the prairies, the steers finally reached the "cow towns" along the railroad. Imagine the excitement and noise when the herds thundered into corrals on the outskirts of town! From there they were loaded on railroad cars bound for Kansas City or Chicago.

The success of the long drive encouraged the growth of cattle raising throughout the West. The killing of the buffalo herds had made available great stretches of grass-covered prairie extending north from Texas. Ranchers discovered that the prairie grass was good food for their cattle. Before long, cattle were grazing on the **open range**

On the long drives cowboys took great herds of cattle north to cow towns. The cattle were then shipped eastward to meat-packing plants.

471

● See p. T41 for a strategy calling for students to put together a bulletin board display highlighting cattle raising on the plains.

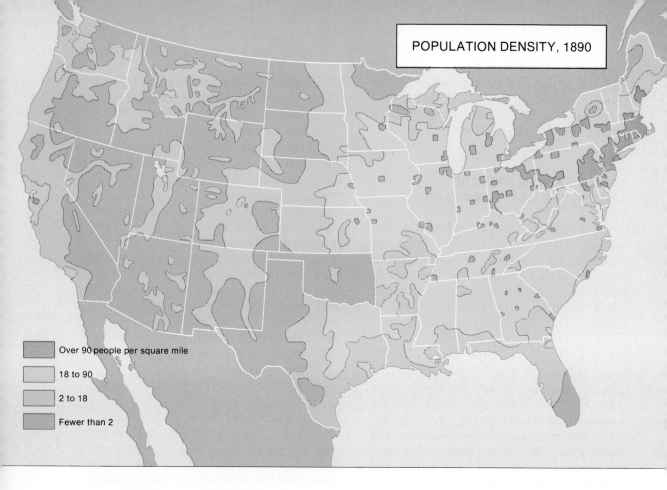

POPULATION DENSITY, 1890

Over 90 people per square mile

18 to 90

2 to 18

Fewer than 2

MAP STUDY See Teacher's Key.
By 1890 pioneers had settled in all western states. Which western states had areas with more than 90 people per square mile? (To review reading maps like this, see page 313.)

(the wide, open spaces of unfenced land belonging to the government). Sometimes cattle were driven as far north as Wyoming or Montana for grazing.

The American cowboy becomes part of the western scene. The long drive would have been impossible without the cowboy. It was his job to protect the cattle from Indians and wild animals and to keep them from straying away. At roundups the young cattle were branded with the marks of their owners, and the steers belonging to various ranches were sorted out. All these activities meant hard work but a free and happy life for the cowboy. The well-known costume of the cowboy was not worn for show. Each part had a use.

Here is a description of what the cowboy wore and why he wore it:

The heavy woolen shirt, loose and open at the neck, was the common wear at all seasons of the year excepting winter. . . . The cowboy's boots were of fine leather and fitted tightly, with light narrow soles, extremely small and high heels. . . . If we rode beside him and watched his seat in the big cow saddle, we found that his high and narrow heels prevented the slipping forward of the foot in the stirrup, into which he jammed his feet nearly full length. If there was a fall, the cowboy's foot never hung in the stirrup. . . .

The cowboy's hat was one of the typical and striking features of his costumes. It was a heavy, wide, white felt hat with a heavy leather band buckled about it. . . . The brim flapped a little and, in time, was turned up and perhaps held fast to the crown by a thong. . . .

472

● See "Skills to Practice" (p. 475) for an assignment based on this description.

He could depend upon his hat in all weathers. In the rain it was an umbrella; in the sun, a shield; in the winter he could tie it down about his ears with a handkerchief.

Loosely thrown about the cowboy's shirt collar was a silk kerchief. It was tied in a hard knot in front, and though it could scarcely be said to be devoted to the uses of a neck scarf, yet it was a great comfort to the back of the neck when one was riding in a hot wind. It was sure to be of some bright color, usually red.

A peculiar and distinctive feature of the cowboy's costume was his "chaps." The chaps were two very wide and full-length trouser-legs made of heavy calf-skin and connected by a narrow belt or strap. They were cut away entirely at front and back so that they covered only the thigh and lower legs and did not heat the body as a complete leather garment would. They were intended solely as a protection against the branches, thorns, briers, and the like, but they were prized in cold or wet weather. Sometimes there was seen, more often on the southern range, a cowboy wearing chaps made of skins tanned with the hair on; for the cowboy of the Southwest early learned that goatskin left with the hair on would turn the cactus thorns better than any other material. . . .

Dressed in this costume and equipped with revolver, lasso, whip, and spurs, the cowboy made a striking figure as he herded cattle or rode into town.

The days of the open range were limited. Cattle raising on the open range did not last many years. There were several reasons.

(1) Before long, the open country was overstocked with cattle and good grazing lands became scarce. In the foothills of the Rockies, sheep farmers took over many feeding grounds formerly used by the cattle raisers. Sheep chew the grass so close to the ground that they leave little for cattle. Bitter fights took place between ranchers and sheepherders for possession of the range.

(2) Farmers came in great numbers from the East to stake out homesteads on the range. To protect their crops from roving cattle, the farmers fenced in their property with barbed wire. The cattle raisers fought the homesteaders in every way they could, but the amount of grazing land open to cattle grew smaller and smaller.

(3) The introduction of the windmill made it possible to pump water which was deep in the ground. The cattle ranchers had built their houses and other buildings near springs and streams. But with windmills, farmers no longer had to settle only along rivers and creeks, and the open range was broken up still more.

As a result of these changes, cattle raising by 1885 mostly took place on fenced-in ranches. Cowboys still work on cattle ranches today, but the colorful cowboy of the 1870's vanished with the open range.

HOMESTEADERS FARM THE PLAINS

Both the miner and the cowboy, who helped to open the unsettled West, were restless figures, often on the move. But wherever the farmers took up land, they came to stay.

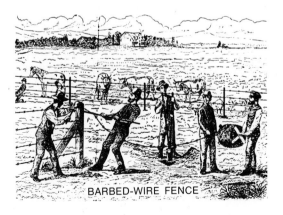

BARBED-WIRE FENCE

473

● Have students read more about barbed wire in "Linking Past and Present" (p. 476).

Pioneer families on the Great Plains lived in houses built of prairie sod (soil matted with grassroots). Much hard work was put into establishing such homesteads.

The last frontier is settled. In 1889, the government opened up to settlers much of the old Indian Territory in what is now Oklahoma. A great land rush then took place. Some 100,000 eager settlers lined up. When a signal was given at noon one spring day, they rushed across the boundary in a wild scramble to stake out desirable homesteads. In the next few years more Indian lands were added to the Oklahoma Territory, and in 1907, it became a state. Other western states which entered the Union as a result of the settling of the last frontier were North Dakota (1889), South Dakota (1889), Utah (1896), and New Mexico and Arizona (1912).

The pioneers endure hardships. Pioneer life on the plains was far from easy. The early farmers had to face dangers and hardships. Blizzards in winter might destroy their livestock, and many pioneers themselves were frozen to death. In summer, farmers might have to stand by helplessly while crops withered for lack of water. At other times, floods might sweep away a family's home and farm. Moreover, many farmers discovered to their sorrow that much of the West was not fertile or was too dry for regular farming.

In spite of the hardships, the early farmers developed a deep attachment to their land and their way of life. One pioneer woman had this to say about farming on the plains:

It might seem a cheerless life, but there were many compensations: the thrill of conquering a new country; the wonderful atmosphere; the attraction of the prairie, which simply gets into your blood and makes you dissatisfied away from it; the low-lying hills and the unobstructed view of the horizon; and the fleecy clouds driven by the never-failing winds.

● Students could read about pioneer living in the series of "Little House" books by Laura Ingalls Wilder.

● See p. T42 for a strategy asking students to prepare reports on one of the following: ranchers, farmers, homesteaders, or prospectors.

● **The old West disappears.** The miners, the cowboys, and the farmers not only filled in the West but brought to a close an important chapter in our country's history. As the frontier vanished, the reckless and independent way of living which had so great an influence on American life began to disappear also. As travel became speedier and communication improved, differences between the East and the West began to disappear. Although some of the old frontier customs lingered on, "the West" no longer meant a completely different way of life.

▶ **CHECK UP** See Teacher's Key.

1. **(a)** How did the discovery of gold and silver help to settle the Rocky Mountain area? **(b)** What was life like in a mining town?
2. **(a)** What two events made cattle raising boom on the western plains? **(b)** What was the life of the cowboy like? **(c)** Why did cattle raising on the open range come to an end?
3. **(a)** What was the last territory opened for settlement? **(b)** What challenges did homesteaders face in farming the plains?

CHECK UP ON CHAPTER 21

See Teacher's Key.

Words to Know

1. long drive
2. public lands
3. bronco
4. open range
5. roundup
6. homestead
7. cow town
8. reservation
9. prospector
10. transcontinental

Places to Locate

1. Omaha
2. Ogden, Utah
3. Sacramento
4. Black Hills
5. Little Bighorn River
6. Great Salt Lake
7. Wounded Knee

Facts to Remember

1. Name two events that led large numbers of Americans to move to the western part of the country in the 1860's.
2. Identify each of the following: **(a)** William F. Cody, **(b)** George A. Custer.
3. **(a)** Why did the western Indians feel threatened by the rapid increase of white settlement in their region? **(b)** What was the result of the clash between the Indians and the settlers?
4. **(a)** What differences were there in the ways the miners, the cattle ranchers, and the farmers lived? **(b)** How did each play a part in the settlement of the West?

5. **(a)** What states entered the Union after 1864 as a result of the mining rush? **(b)** What states entered the Union as a result of the settling of the last frontier?

Skills to Practice

1. Find the transcontinental railroads on the map on page 460. Name the cities between which each railroad ran.
2. Use the primary sources you have read in this chapter to answer these questions:
   a. According to the Indian chief quoted on pages 462-463, what was the Indians' attitude toward the first Europeans who came to America? What reasons does he give for the change in that attitude?
   b. On page 466 Chief Joseph explains why he will surrender. What reasons does he give?
   c. Use the quoted passage on pages 472-473 to explain the purpose of the following parts of the cowboys' clothes: (1) high heels, (2) hat, (3) kerchief, (4) chaps.
   d. What reasons are given by the pioneer woman quoted on page 474 for her love of life on the plains?

Questions to Think About

1. It has been said that the settlement of the Great Plains was made possible by **(a)** the killing of the buffalo, **(b)** the transcontinental railroads, and **(c)** the windmill. What was the significance of each of these developments? Why was each important to settlers?

2. With the disappearance of the western frontier, many Americans believed there was no longer any opportunity to live adventurous lives. Is that true? Are there other "frontiers" to be conquered?

3. Why has western life been so popular as a subject for American songs, stories, television series, and motion pictures?

 # Linking Past and Present

Saved by sea gulls. People in Utah have a special reason for thinking of sea gulls with fondness. They recall that gulls saved the first Mormon pioneers from disaster.

Mormon settlers arrived in the Great Salt Lake region in 1847. They immediately set about planting winter wheat and fruit trees, followed by vegetable gardens in the spring of 1848. These all did well, until one day in June when swarms of grasshoppers moved in to settle like blankets on the fields. The settlers looked on helplessly as the hungry grasshoppers started to devour the young plants. But just when it seemed that the crops would be lost, the skies filled with sea gulls. The gulls ate the insects, and the crops were saved.

Since that day the sea gull has been remembered with gratitude. Moreover, by common agreement it is the official state bird of Utah.

"Don't fence me in." A simple invention helped farming to become established on the western plains. This was the barbed wire fence, so common today that we hardly notice it. East of the Mississippi there had been plenty of timber to make rail fences around a farmer's fields. But farmers who settled on the prairies of the West found little timber there for fences. Then, in 1873, J. F. Glidden of Illinois patented an inexpensive wire fence. With their lands enclosed by barbed wire, farmers could grow crops without danger of having them trampled by wandering cattle or sheep. At first, western cattle and sheep ranchers resented the fencing in of the land, and they had many battles with the farmers. The western cowboys, used to riding the open range with nothing in their way, were especially annoyed. In time, however, ranchers learned that they could raise better animals if they knew where their herds were and could control them. The roaming cowboy was "fenced in," but western farming and cattle raising profited from the invention of the wire fence.

Buffalo still roam. Fertile farms and great ranches now cover much of the land where herds of buffalo once grazed. But if you know where to look, you can still see buffalo ★ roaming over the western grasslands. These herds are carefully fenced in and protected by the United States government. At one time fifty million or more of the shaggy beasts grazed on the grasslands of the West. Then, as Americans pushed westward, vast numbers of buffalo were killed for their meat and hides and often merely for sport. This slaughter went on until the late 1800's, when Americans finally realized that the buffalo had almost disappeared. In 1894 the national government passed a law prohibiting the killing of these animals. By that time there were only a few hundred wild buffalo left in the United States. In the early 1900's, the government set aside land where the buffalo would be protected. Since then the herds have increased to several thousand, and fortunately the American buffalo is no longer in danger of dying out.

476

● Have students find out the official state bird of their own state.

★ Have students prepare reports about buffalo and illustrate their reports with drawings.

For answers see Teacher's Key.

Have students find out about an early photographic process called *daguerreotype*. Mention that many photographs taken in the 1800's were daguerreotypes.

GAINING SKILL

Using Historic Photographs

Until the 1800's, the only way to show how a person or a place looked was to make a painting or a drawing. By the middle of the 1800's, however, people were able to take photographs. During the Civil War, for instance, Americans were able to see photographs of battle scenes for the first time.

Photographs can tell us a good deal about how people lived, worked, and dressed. For that reason, historians often use photographs as primary sources. As you study the remaining chapters of this book, notice how photographs help to tell America's story.

Now use the photograph below to answer the following questions.

1. This picture was taken in 1887 in the Dakota Territory. What work did the men in the picture do?

2. Describe the landscape in this part of the Dakotas.

3. Compare the clothing worn by these men with the description on pages 472–473. What items do you see in the picture that match the written account? Does the photograph match the picture you formed in your mind from reading the description? If not, explain how your idea was different.

4. Compare this photograph with the painting of the *vaquero* on page 470. How does the clothing differ? How are the saddles and bridles on the horses different? Which type of clothing was probably more typical for a cowboy: that shown in the photograph or that shown in the painting? Explain your answer.

477

Vocabulary preview: mass production, division of labor, standard parts, assembly line, partnership, corporation, share of stock, stockholder, dividend

CHAPTER **22**

The United States Becomes a Great Industrial Nation

1865–1940   See pp. T42–T43 for chapter teaching strategies.

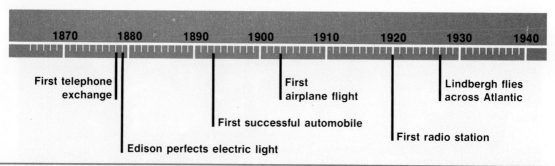

| 1870 | 1880 | 1890 | 1900 | 1910 | 1920 | 1930 | 1940 |

First telephone exchange

First airplane flight

Lindbergh flies across Atlantic

First successful automobile

First radio station

Edison perfects electric light

What this chapter is about —

At the same time that miners, ranchers, and farmers were moving into the West, other Americans were pioneering in business and manufacturing. In so doing they helped make the United States the world's leading industrial nation. From a rural, agricultural republic, this country became a land of growing cities and rapidly expanding industry.

In earlier chapters you learned how American industry got its start. In the years following the Civil War, new sources of power were discovered. In-

◀ In the years after the Civil War the United States was transformed into an industrial giant. The development of a huge iron and steel industry was an important part of that growth.

ventors perfected new machines and scientists worked out new ideas. Bold business leaders backed new ventures which laid the foundation for our great industrial nation.

Advances in transportation and communications went hand in hand with the dramatic industrial growth. The construction of more railroads and the building of a network of telegraph and telephone lines changed ways of living and of doing business.

This chapter will describe the growth of industry in the United States. As you read, be on the lookout for answers to the following questions:

1. What conditions made the United States a leading industrial nation?
2. How did mass production and the growth of corporations aid industry?
3. How did improved communication and transportation affect American life?
4. How did business leaders contribute to the growth of industry?

1 What Conditions Made the United States a Leading Industrial Nation?

The growth of industry in the United States began, you recall, when the Industrial Revolution reached this country from England in the late 1700's (Chapter 14). You remember that machines, run by water power, had been invented to produce many of the articles that had been made by hand in colonial days. Factories were built, particularly in the Northeast, and workers from nearby farms, as well as newcomers from Europe, flocked to take jobs in the mill towns.

By the middle of the 1800's, steam power had begun to take the place of water power for running machines. New inventions, more factories, and the spreading network of railroads — all these helped manufacturing to continue to grow. And, as you read in Chapter 20, the demand for war materials of all kinds during the Civil War further stepped up the rate of production.

The Industrial Revolution gathers speed. When the Civil War ended, the United States was still far behind England as an industrial nation. Only 35 years later, however, this country led the world in the value of its manufactured goods.

No longer was manufacturing limited chiefly to the Northeast. Factories had multiplied in the South, and wherever railroads were built in the fast-growing West, industry quickly developed. Because the use of machines increased so rapidly after 1900, the first half of the twentieth century is often ★ called the Machine Age. You have only to look around you to realize the enormous quantity of goods now produced by machines in America. Machines make our homes comfortable, provide swift means of travel, and save us from much back-breaking labor.

Why did our country become a great industrial power? There are several answers to this question. Let us see what they are.

The United States is blessed with rich natural resources. When the first European settlers came to North America, they found abundant natural resources. During the colonial years the

479

Rich mineral resources contributed to our country's industrial growth. Mining also provided jobs for thousands of workers. Iron ore for the steel industry was mined at Iron Mask Mine, Minnesota (above) in the 1880's.

settlers chiefly made use of the rich soil and the products of the forests. When manufacturing became important, however, our country turned out to be a rich treasure house of materials needed in industry. In mineral wealth, for example, the United States was far more fortunate than most countries. Below the ground were huge supplies of coal. Coal was tremendously important in the iron and steel industry, and in running the machines in our factories. In addition, coal was widely used for heating homes and other buildings.

Our country also possessed great quantities of iron ore from which steel is made. Though ore was found in many places, the chief iron ore fields were located around the western end of Lake Superior. The United States was also blessed with generous quantities of copper, lead, and bauxite (from which aluminum is made). In fact, the United States lacked only a few important minerals, such as manganese (for hardening steel), tin, nickel, and platinum. When petroleum (oil) became important in

industry, our country was found to have the greatest reserves of this precious fluid then known in the world.

Not all of America's natural riches were below the ground. Our vast forests supplied the timber needed in industry. In addition, America's rich soil made it possible for farmers to produce the food crops needed to feed a rapidly growing population.

There are many hands to do America's work. The United States was also fortunate in having a large supply of skilled workers for our industries. Since 1860, the number of people in the United States has grown from about 31 million to over 230 million. This growth resulted largely from the numbers of people who came to America from other countries. Many Europeans left their homes to come to the United States. Other people came from Mexico and the Caribbean, as well as from China and Japan.

Few of these Americans-to-be were wealthy. They came to this country to make a new start in life. Almost all were used to hard work. Their hands supplied the labor that was needed in factories and mines to turn raw materials into manufactured articles.

Foreign money helps the United States to develop its industries. Large amounts of raw materials and many willing hands, however, were not enough to develop the giant industries of our country. Factories and machines cost money. In 1865 there were few Americans who had enough money to make large investments in industry. Fortunately, however, there were wealthy Europeans who were eager to put their money into American industry in the hope of making profits. By 1910, over six billion dollars of foreign money, most of it English, was invested in American mines, factories, and business concerns. These large investments had much to do with the rapid growth of our
● industries.

Inventions aid the growth of industry. Americans have always shown a talent for invention. In an earlier chap-

ter you learned that Eli Whitney's invention of the cotton gin caused cotton growing to boom. In a similar way, Elias Howe's sewing machine paved the way for the making of clothes in factories (page 298). After 1865, American inventions played an even more important part in helping the United States to become a mighty industrial giant. Those inventions made it possible to enlarge existing industries and create new ones.

Thomas A. Edison — inventor. No one person illustrates the American inventive spirit better than Thomas Alva Edison. He was born in 1847 in Ohio. Even as a young boy, he had a keen and restless mind and showed an interest in science. Tom became a newsboy on a train and did so well that he soon had other boys working for him. Much of his spare time was spent reading in the public library and working in a small laboratory at home.

As a young man, Edison held a variety of jobs but kept up his interest in science and especially in electricity. In 1868 he patented his first invention. From then until his death in 1931, his active mind and great energy produced

GRAPH STUDY See Teacher's Key.
About how many people lived in the United States in 1860? In 1940?

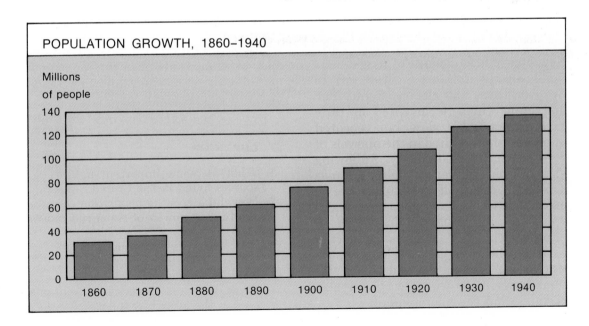

POPULATION GROWTH, 1860–1940

Millions of people

● See p. T42 for a strategy calling for students to examine why our country became a leading industrial nation.

Thomas Edison's invention of the light bulb in 1879 marked the end of a year of steady work. He and his assistants gave all their time to perfecting an invention which they knew would be of tremendous usefulness.

a steady stream of inventions. His genius lay in his knack of putting scientific ideas to practical use rather than in the discovery of new scientific truths. He held more than 1,200 patents on inventions, and his laboratory at Menlo Park, New Jersey, was a place of magic.

Probably Edison's greatest gift to the world was the electric light. The first bulb, which he invented in 1879, gave only a feeble glow, but repeated improvements resulted in the marvels of lighting which we now enjoy. Following his work on the electric light, Thomas Edison devoted half a century more to inventions which have shaped our modern world. Whether by invention or improvement, his name is connected with the phonograph, the telegraph, the stock ticker, generators and power stations, electric street railways, motion pictures, and the microphone.

Rich natural resources, foreign investments, and the skill, hard work, and inventiveness of the American people — all played a part in making the United States a great industrial nation. Just as important, however, were new manufacturing methods and new kinds of business organizations.

▶ **CHECK UP**   See Teacher's Key.

1. What are some important natural resources found in the United States?
2. How did a growing population contribute to the growth of American industry?
3. Why was the investment of foreign money important to the growth of American industry?
4. What part did American inventions play in the growth of industry?

482

● See p. T43 for a strategy calling for students to prepare reports on the life and achievements of Thomas Edison.

2 How Did Mass Production and the Growth of Corporations Aid Industry?

New manufacturing methods lead to mass production. The United States could never have become the industrial giant it is today if a method had not been discovered of producing vast quantities of goods to sell at low prices. This new system was called **mass production.** What steps made mass production possible?

1. *Division of labor.* Before the Industrial Revolution, a single skilled worker usually did every task in changing raw material into a finished product. One shoemaker, for example, would do all the work required to make a pair of shoes out of a piece of leather. When machines came into use, a change took place. The labor of making an article was divided among several workers. Each worker was limited to doing just one or two things. For example, a punch-press operator, punching holes in a metal part, repeated the same operation over and over hundreds of times a day. A welder fastened two pieces of metal together, nothing more. This **division of labor** speeded up production and lowered costs because each worker soon became very skilled in his or her particular task.

2. *Standard parts.* Production was also greatly aided by the use of **standard parts.** Eli Whitney did much to develop this idea. After he invented the cotton gin, he became interested in manufacturing guns. He decided to use standard or interchangeable parts in his guns. In other words, all triggers or gun barrels manufactured for a certain model of gun were to be made exactly the same in shape and measurements. If the parts were identical, reasoned Whitney, guns could be put together faster and more efficiently. Or, if a cer-tain part were damaged, another one, exactly like it, could be substituted. Thus the gun could be repaired easily.

3. *The assembly line.* The most important step in the development of mass production came with the **assembly line** in the 1900's. It was first used in an important way in 1913 by Henry Ford in the making of cars. The assembly line combines on a large scale the use of standard parts and division of labor. An automobile factory, for instance, has a long conveyor belt (a slowly moving track) with many workers stationed at different points beside it. The motor is assembled part by part,

Above you see an assembly line from a Ford plant in 1914. Each worker performed a specific task as the conveyor belt moved along.

483

● Have students read about Ford's Greenfield Village in ''Linking Past and Present'' (p. 498).

the frame of the automobile is added, and other parts are attached. When the end of the line is reached, the car is complete — motor, body, wheels, and all. Each worker does a single task as the automobile-to-be passes on the conveyor belt. In this way the time needed to make a car is greatly reduced.

Mass production methods spread. Division of labor, standard parts, and the assembly line all play a part in mass
● production. Through mass production methods, Ford employees were able to turn out thousands of cars each day, and the price of automobiles was greatly reduced. Ford's methods spread not only throughout the automobile industry but into many other kinds of manufacturing.

AMERICAN INDUSTRY CREATES A MARKET FOR ITS PRODUCTS

You have been reading how new methods of production swelled the output of

American factories. At the same time, businesses began to find new markets for their products and new ways of selling them.

New markets are found. As the population of the United States grew by leaps and bounds, there were more people eager to buy goods. And because mass production made it possible to produce greater quantities of goods at lower prices, people could buy more and more. Newer forms of transportation also opened up new markets. The growth of the nation's railroads helped manufacturers to sell their products throughout the country, rather than only in a small area near their factories.

Modern selling methods develop. Before the growth of big businesses, every community had small general stores where people bought the few things they needed. But after the Civil War ended in 1865, merchants discovered new and more effective ways to sell their goods. They began to discover the power of advertising to make customers want more of their products. They also developed new kinds of stores:

(1) One was the specialty store. The old general store sold cloth, grocer-

In the years after the Civil War specialty stores began to appear, offering customers a wider choice in a particular line of goods. What was sold in the store shown here?

● See p. T43 for a strategy asking students to identify the new kinds of stores which emerged during the late 1800's and to compare them with today's stores.

ies, hardware, meat, and about everything else. Now stores began to specialize in selling clothes, or hardware, or groceries. These stores could carry a larger stock of their particular line of goods.

(2) In large cities, department stores began to appear. Here, in different departments, customers could find almost anything they might need. Through careful management and buying in large quantities, a department store could reduce the cost of its goods and thus attract a larger number of customers. Pioneers in this kind of selling included John Wanamaker, who established a store in Philadelphia in 1875, and Marshall Field, who started his famous store in Chicago in 1881.

(3) Chain stores, that is, a number of stores under the same management, also began to develop in the late 1800's. The chain stores, like the department stores, were able to sell goods at low prices because of large-scale buying and skillful management. Pioneers in chain-store selling included the Great Atlantic and Pacific Tea Company (1859) and F. W. Woolworth Company (1879).

(4) Still another form of mass selling brought low-priced goods to the people of small villages and farms. This was the mail-order house. Companies like Montgomery Ward (1872) and Sears Roebuck (1884) sent out catalogs showing pictures of products and directions for buying the products by mail. On farms throughout America, the arrival of the rural mail carrier with the mail-order catalogs was one of the most exciting events of the year.

A NEW FORM OF BUSINESS ORGANIZATION AIDS THE GROWTH OF INDUSTRY

In early times, most businesses in the United States were easy to run. Not much money or equipment was needed to start them, and they employed only a handful of workers. They were owned and managed by a single person or by several persons known as a **partnership.** As more and more goods were manufactured and sold, these simpler forms of business ownership became less satisfactory. Railroads and factories with expensive machinery cost huge sums. Neither an individual nor a partnership could afford to start such a business or carry on all the duties of managing it. Gradually a new kind of organization, known as the **corporation,** came into use.

A corporation has many owners. ★ These owners provide the money needed to start and carry on the business. When a corporation is formed, **shares of stock** are offered for sale. The persons who buy these shares of stock are called **stockholders.** The stockholders are the actual owners of a corporation. They usually choose a board of directors to manage the corporation's affairs. The stockholders also have the right to vote on all important matters. If the corporation fails, they lose only the money they have invested in it. If it succeeds, the stockholders receive a share of the profits. The money they get is called **dividends.**

There are many advantages to organizing a large business as a corporation. By selling many shares of stock, huge sums of money can be collected to carry on giant industries. Also, stockholders are free at any time to sell their stock to someone else. Thus a corporation continues year after year, whereas a business owned by a single person may stop or be seriously upset by his or her death.

After 1865, the number of corporations in the United States multiplied rapidly. They grew quickly because they could buy large quantities of raw materials more cheaply and could operate more efficiently.

485

★ Remind students that trading companies had financed colonies in the 1600's (p. 99). Have students compare trading companies with corporations.

▶ **CHECK UP** See Teacher's Key.

1. **(a)** What is mass production? **(b)** How did the division of labor, the use of standard parts, and the assembly line help in the development of mass production?

2. **(a)** What new ways of selling their goods did merchants discover in the late 1800's? **(b)** What new kinds of stores were developed?

3. **(a)** What is a corporation? **(b)** What are the advantages of organizing a large business as a corporation?

3 How Did Improved Communication and Transportation Affect American Life?

If Americans living a hundred years ago could have looked into the future, they probably would have been most startled by modern methods of travel and communication. They would stare in wonder at the speeding cars and trucks on our multi-lane highways and at sleek jet planes roaring into the sky headed for distant places. In fact, many of the marvels we take for granted today were developed in this century. Talking movies and color movies, for example, date from the 1920's and 1930's. Television, for its part, began regular broadcasting in 1939 but came into common use only in the late 1940's.

INSTANT COMMUNICATION LINKS AMERICA AND THE WORLD

The world is made smaller by telegraph and cable. The telegraph, as you read in Chapter 14, came into use in the 1840's. Telegraph lines spread rapidly, and new inventions made it possible to send several messages over the same wire at the same time. Then people began to think that telegraph lines could be used to link the United States with other parts of the world.

An American named Cyrus Field developed a plan to lay a line across the bed of the Atlantic Ocean. This cable, as it was called, was reeled out from two ships starting in mid-ocean, one sailing toward the British Isles and the other toward the United States. Field had many disappointments, for the heavy cable broke again and again. Once he succeeded in laying a cable only to have the wires burn out after a month's use. Finally, in 1866, after several attempts, the cable was successfully laid, connecting America and Europe. Important messages no longer had to go by ship but could be flashed in a few moments ● across thousands of miles of ocean.

Alexander Graham Bell, inventor of the telephone, was also known for his development of new ways of educating deaf children.

486

In addition to speeding communication, the invention of the telephone created new job opportunities for women.

In time, additional cables were laid across the Atlantic, and the United States was also linked by cable with other parts of the world. Cables were used by newspapers, by business people, by government officials, and by people who wanted to send personal messages.

The human voice is transmitted by wire. Soon after the Civil War ended in 1865, a young Scotsman named Alexander Graham Bell came to America to teach people who were deaf. Bell became interested in sending the actual sound of the human voice over a wire charged with electricity. He worked for many years on this problem, and finally, on March 16, 1876, spoke into a telephone and was heard by an assistant in another room.

Later that year, Bell showed his telephone, a strange cone-like instrument, at a great exhibition in Philadelphia. Most visitors at the exhibition thought the invention was an interesting toy, but Bell was determined to develop it into a useful machine. Shortly afterward, Bell and his assistant were able to talk over a wire strung a distance of two miles between Boston and Cambridge, Massachusetts. Two years later, in 1878, the first telephone exchange in the United States was set up at New Haven, Connecticut. Alexander Bell had succeeded in his dream of making a machine to transmit the human voice.

The telephone becomes important in American life. Strange as the early instruments were, they were forerunners of the modern telephone. Constant improvements were worked out and service was expanded. Each year the number of telephone lines increased, and more instruments were placed in homes and in business offices. By the early 1900's, the telephone had become an important part of American life. It was no longer a luxury but a necessity to large numbers of people. Long-distance calls were made possible, and in 1915 New York and San Francisco were linked by telephone. When dial telephones came into use, calls could be made without the help of the operator. People in many areas could even dial

487

To attract passengers, railroad companies advertised the comfort and convenience of travel by train.

can homes several years later. The story of radio, however, dates back to the 1890's. Guglielmo Marconi (goo-LYELL-moh mahr-KOH-nih), an Italian inventor, discovered a way to send "wireless" messages through the air by means of electric waves. Before long, he was able to communicate by wireless between Newfoundland and Great Britain. For some time wireless messages were in code, like telegraph messages. The invention was highly useful, especially to ships at sea. Soon, however, scientists turned their efforts toward sending music and the human voice through the air. The result was the radio we know today.

RAILROADS TIE THE NATION TOGETHER WITH BANDS OF STEEL

Railroad building increases. While new inventions were changing methods of communication, travel also was being made easier. You read in Chapter 14 about the early railroads. After peace was restored between the North and the South in 1865, there was a great burst of railroad construction. The southern railroads, damaged during the war, were rebuilt and extended. The North and Midwest were crisscrossed with an ever-increasing number of railroad lines.

Because the United States was growing rapidly, the need for railroads was greater than ever. New villages and towns were clamoring for railroad service. American farms were producing more food and American factories were manufacturing more goods. But building railroads was expensive. The roadbed had to be prepared, tracks had to be laid, stations had to be built, and locomotives and cars had to be bought. Nevertheless, some business leaders saw a chance to become rich by operating railroads. To provide the money, companies were formed and people were persuaded to invest money. Many of the new railroads paid large profits to

calls to distant cities. Today we can talk by telephone to almost any place in the world with greater ease and clearness than people a century ago could shout to their neighbors only a hundred feet away.

Radio serves America and the world. It is difficult for us today to imagine a world without radio. The first American broadcasting station, KDKA in Pittsburgh, was built in 1920, and receiving sets became common in Ameri-

488

the builders and to the people who had invested in them.

Eastern railroads are joined into systems. The early railroad lines were short, linking two or three important cities. There were few connecting lines. This meant delay and inconvenience in moving goods and passengers over long distances. Freight had to be unloaded from cars on one line and hauled to cars on another line. On a long trip goods might have to be loaded and unloaded several times. For example, in the early days of railroads, freight between New York and Chicago had to be moved from one line to another nineteen times!

The man who first joined several short lines into one main line was Cornelius Vanderbilt, a former ship captain. By buying and uniting many of the short lines in New York State, Vanderbilt developed the great New York Central System, which soon extended far beyond New York State. In much the same way, railroads in Pennsylvania were united to form the Pennsylvania Railroad. The Baltimore and Ohio was another important early railroad system. These also extended farther west.

Railroad travel becomes safer and more comfortable. As time went on, Americans were able not only to ride greater distances but to travel with more safety and comfort. Wrecks and breakdowns were reduced when George Westinghouse invented air brakes, and when Andrew J. Beard introduced the ● use of automatic couplers for railroad cars. The use of signals that required trains to halt until the track ahead was clear also cut down accidents. Steel instead of iron was used in making locomotives, cars, and rails. Smoother roadbeds and better springs, as well as new methods of lighting and heating, increased riding comfort. In time the Pullman Company built comfortable day coaches, sleeping cars, and dining cars. In large cities huge stations were erected to provide services for travelers.

Railroads face competition from new forms of transportation. During the late 1800's and early 1900's the railroads were America's most important means of transportation. The railroad companies continued to make improvements. The huge, puffing steam locomotives were replaced by electric or oil-burning engines, and railroads increased their carrying capacity. They made a great contribution to the nation's war effort in both World Wars. In time, however, good roads and the automobile and the growing popularity of airplane transpor-

See Teacher's Key.

MAP STUDY
Four standard time zones were established for the United States in 1883 to make railroad schedules easier to follow. Before, towns and cities had set their own time, based on the sun. How many hours' difference is there between the Eastern and Pacific time zones?

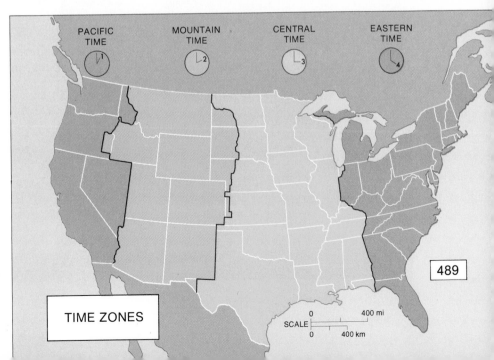

PACIFIC TIME · MOUNTAIN TIME · CENTRAL TIME · EASTERN TIME

TIME ZONES

SCALE 0 — 400 mi / 0 — 400 km

489

● Have students read more about early cars in "Linking Past and Present" (p. 498).

tation cut into railroad passenger business. Moreover, trucks carried more and more of the nation's freight.

THE AUTOMOBILE PUTS AMERICA ON WHEELS

The "horseless carriage" replaces the horse and buggy. It is not possible to fix a single date for the invention of the automobile. For years inventors in America and Europe tried to make a "horseless carriage" — a vehicle that could be driven under its own power. Some of these carriages were driven by steam. Others, which proved more successful, were powered by a new invention — the gasoline engine. Among the American experimenters in the 1890's were George Selden, Charles Duryea, Elwood Haynes, Alexander Winton, ● and Henry Ford.

By the early 1900's automobiles were no longer an unusual sight. Going for a drive in the family car became an American custom.

Soon after 1900, automobiles began to appear on the roads. At first they startled people and caused a good deal of trouble. Every breakdown, and there were many of them, was greeted with shouts of "Get a horse!" from curious and amused bystanders. Drivers had to know how to repair their own cars, since no service stations lined the highways to furnish gasoline, patch tires, or take care of breakdowns. Roads were poor and so dusty in dry weather that passengers wore coats called "dusters" to keep their clothes clean, as well as goggles to protect their eyes. A steady stream of inventions, however, soon made possible the production of better cars at a lower cost. No longer was the automobile a plaything but an accepted part of American living.

Goodyear's experiments in rubber make automobile tires possible. Countless inventions and developments made the modern automobile possible. Special steel, chromium, and other metals were developed for parts and fixtures.

Electrical systems were perfected to light and heat cars and to keep motors running smoothly. High-powered gasoline was developed. One of the greatest needs was for an elastic tire that would make driving safe and comfortable.

We can thank a Connecticut inventor named Charles Goodyear for the discovery that led to the easy-riding tires on our automobiles today. Although Goodyear died in 1860, long before automobiles were invented, he developed a remarkable process for hardening rubber. Before that time, rubber was not useful because it was affected by changes in temperature. It became brittle in cold weather and sticky in the summertime.

Charles Goodyear spent his life experimenting with raw rubber to overcome these faults. His experiments kept him poor, and he borrowed money from friends in order to carry on his work. Once he even sold his furniture to get money; another time he sold his children's schoolbooks. He made rubber shoes and wore them; he made and wore a rubber coat which caused people in the streets to laugh at him. In spite of every difficulty, Goodyear kept on experimenting. He learned that sulfur added to the rubber would prevent stickiness. One day when he dropped some rubber on his stove, he accidentally discovered that heat would harden and improve rubber. Goodyear tried various degrees of heat until he finally produced rubber that was not affected by changes in temperature. This process, known as vulcanizing, became especially valuable for tires when automobiles came into use. It led to the growth of the rubber industry.

THE AIRPLANE SPEEDS TRAVEL

The Wright brothers invent an airplane. The railroad and the automobile did not end the search for swifter transportation. For centuries people had dreamed of flying through the air. By the late 1800's balloons had been used for years, and inventors in England, Germany, and America began trying to build flying machines. It was not until the gasoline engine was invented that modern airplanes became possible.

Samuel Langley, an American scientist, watched birds swoop and turn gracefully in the air. He asked himself: Why can't people fly as well as birds? Langley made several types of flying machines, but none of them was practical. After several attempts to launch his machines failed, Langley gave up his efforts. The honor of building the first airplane actually to fly went to two young mechanics named Wilbur and Orville Wright. They had grown up in Dayton, Ohio, and had been interested in flying since childhood. In December, 1903, an airplane they built made a successful flight at Kitty Hawk, North Carolina. On the fourth trial Wilbur Wright flew it for 59 seconds over a distance of 852 feet. At last the dream of flying had been realized!

Pioneers of aviation prove flying is practical. Many years were to pass before most people took seriously the efforts to perfect a flying machine. After all, they thought, there were plenty of ways for people to be killed or injured on the ground without risking their lives in the air. Now that speedy travel was possible by train and automobile, what was the use of trying to fly? Attempts to improve the airplane, however, continued. In the First World War, airplanes were used for scouting and fighting. During the 1920's many airfields were built, and regular schedules for flying the mail were established.

A number of dramatic flights did much to draw people's attention to the possibilities of air transport. In May, 1927, a young pilot named Charles Lindbergh flew alone from New York to Paris in a nonstop flight which took a little more than 30 hours. Four years

491

Stories of the many flights of Charles and Anne Lindbergh familiarized Americans with air travel.

IMPROVEMENTS IN TRAVEL AND COMMUNICATION AID THE GROWTH OF INDUSTRY

It is easy to see how new forms of transportation and communication affected the daily life of the average American. But why were the changes in travel and communication so important to the growth of American industry? To manufacture cars, for example, a big automobile company in Detroit had to order steel from Pittsburgh or Chicago, rubber from Akron, electrical items from Toledo. Assembly plants — factories where cars are assembled, or put together — were located all over the country.

The people who ran the automobile company needed quick delivery of materials. Fast freight trains and giant trucks provided it. Typewriters and other office machines enabled the company's employees to keep records and communicate with customers and other businesses. If they were in a hurry, they could talk with customers or other business offices by long-distance telephone. Often the company's managers had to visit their plants and offices of the companies that supplied materials. Airplanes and cars made travel to other cities fast and easy. Without this great web of transportation and communication, our industries would have found it difficult to operate.

Improvements in transportation and communication also created vast new industries. Think for a moment of all the raw materials needed to build railroads, automobiles, airplanes, telephones, and radios. Think of the huge factories and the machinery required to make finished parts out of the raw materials. Think of the army of trained workers that assemble the parts; operate trains, trucks, and airplanes; and repair and service cars, telephones, and television sets. When you add up all the people who take part in the building and

later, Wiley Post and Harold Gatty astonished everyone by flying around the world in eight days. The first woman to fly the Atlantic alone was Amelia Earhart, and three years later, in 1935, she flew alone from Honolulu to California. Her career ended tragically in 1937 when her plane disappeared on a flight across the Pacific. The flights of these pioneers of aviation do not seem unusual to us today, but they blazed the trail for our modern airplanes.

The airplane brings great changes in travel. Air travel became more common in the 1930's. But it was during World War II that aviation made amazing progress. Huge factories turned out thousands of fighters and bombers. New types of military planes were developed, each bigger and faster than the one before. For instance, airplanes powered by jet engines came into use.

492

● See p. T43 for a strategy calling for students to discuss how new forms of communication and transportation affected ways of living in the late 1800's.

operating of modern means of travel and communication, you have included a large portion of all American workers.

> **CHECK UP**   See Teacher's Key.

1. How did the telegraph, the cable, the telephone, and the radio improve communication?
2. (a) Why was there an increased need for railroads in the late 1800's? (b) Why were the railroads joined into a few great systems?
3. (a) How did the automobile become an important part of American life? (b) Why is rubber important in modern transportation? (c) What developments made possible the growth of airplane travel?
4. How did better transportation and communication aid the growth of industry?

4 How Did Business Leaders Contribute to the Growth of Industry?

We have seen that certain things encouraged the growth of American industry after 1865 — rich natural resources, mass production of goods, swifter transportation and communication, and the growth of corporations. During the closing years of the 1800's, the forward march of industry was also aided by the activities of a small number of business leaders. Often a single one of these leaders, by his boldness and vision, founded and managed a giant company and built up a huge fortune. Let us read about the careers of three of the most successful "captains of industry."

James J. Hill — railroad builder. One of the most interesting figures in the building of the American railroad industry was James J. Hill. He was born in 1838, in a log cabin on a frontier farm in Canada. On such a farm there was hard work to be done, and young James had his full share of daily chores. After the death of his father, he decided to strike out for himself. Shipping on a lake freighter, he came to the United States. A variety of jobs led him to St. Paul, Minnesota. There he worked for a steamboat company and a railroad.

Until he was about 40 years old, Hill had done nothing out of the ordinary. He had great ideas, but no one took them seriously. One of these ideas was to develop the northwestern part of the country. Hill had traveled through this sparsely settled area on foot and by wagon and dog sled. In 1878 he persuaded a small group of men to take over the railroad for which he worked, and Hill was appointed general manager. The railroad was in poor condition and the outlook not too promising. Yet from this modest beginning, Hill built a railroad empire spanning more than half a continent.

The secret of Hill's success lay in his understanding that the Northwest had to have many prosperous farms if his railroads were to succeed. He arranged for would-be settlers to be taken on trips to view the country. He imported fine cattle and horses from Europe to encourage cattle raising. He also helped farmers to get seed and farm machinery on reasonable terms. He arranged for hundreds of young people to be sent to schools where they learned scientific farming.

By 1893, the Great Northern railway system, under Hill's direction, spanned the country between St. Paul, Minnesota, and Seattle, Washington. In later years, James J. Hill controlled most of the railroad lines in the North-

493

west, totaling about 20,000 miles of track.

Andrew Carnegie — maker of steel. America owes its progress as an industrial nation in large part to its ability to produce tremendous quantities of steel. Railway rails and cars, automobiles, all sorts of machinery, and huge buildings are only a few of the things which are made from steel. For centuries, steel was known to have qualities of strength and toughness not found in iron. But steel was too expensive to be widely used. Impurities had to be removed from iron to make steel, and no cheap method of removing these impurities was known. Then, in the 1850's, an Englishman, Henry Bessemer, and an American, William Kelly, each discovered a startling fact. Working on the same problem separately, they found that a blast of air directed at melted iron would remove its impurities. This new process of making steel was so cheap and easy that steel could be produced in large quantities and at low cost.

The rapid growth of the steel industry in the United States, however, was largely brought about by a man who was not a steelmaker by trade. Andrew Carnegie, a poor Scottish boy, was brought to America by his parents in 1848, when he was thirteen years old. Young Andrew started work in a Pennsylvania cotton mill where his pay was only a dollar and twenty cents a week. Later he worked in the telegraph office of a railroad company. Then he became secretary to a railroad official. By hard work and shrewd common sense, Carnegie advanced rapidly in the business world. From railroading he went into bridge building. Since steel played an important part in both these industries, he became interested in it.

Carnegie was daring as well as shrewd. He finally decided to risk his entire future in producing steel by the new air-blast method discovered by

Kelly and Bessemer. Carnegie was tremendously successful. By 1900, the Carnegie Steel Company, with headquarters in Pittsburgh, Pennsylvania, was the leading producer of steel in this country. To keep his huge blast furnaces and steel mills working at full speed, Carnegie bought vast deposits of iron ore in the region of the upper Great Lakes. He also controlled a fleet of vessels on the Great Lakes and a railroad which carried the ore from Lake Erie to the blast furnaces in Pittsburgh.

In 1901, Andrew Carnegie decided to retire. He sold out his steel business, which kept on growing as the United States Steel Corporation. It was the country's largest producer of steel. Carnegie is remembered today not only for his business success but for the generous gifts he made from his tremendous fortune. Many towns and cities in the United States have public libraries built with funds left by Carnegie. When asked why he gave away so much of his money, he said, "I started life as a poor man, and I wish to end it that way." Carnegie was by no means a poor man when he died; yet he gave away 350 million dollars!

John D. Rockefeller — founder of Standard Oil. While steelmaking was being revolutionized by Andrew Carnegie, another great modern American industry was getting its start. Petroleum, or oil as we commonly call it, lay in great quantities below the earth in Pennsylvania. In some places it seeped through the rock and formed a scum on the surface of creeks. Farmers sometimes skimmed off the oil to grease their wagons, and a few shrewd people even bottled it and sold it as medicine. But no one understood the real value of petroleum until a scientist, Benjamin Silliman, tested it. He found that it could be refined and used for lighting homes and buildings.

In 1859, the first oil well was drilled at Titusville, Pennsylvania. The news

494

People in America's Story

telegrapher for the Pennsylvania Railroad, he
rose to division manager. Later, by promoting
a railroad sleeper car he started the Carnegie
fortune and went into business for himself.

ANDREW CARNEGIE

A daring businessman, Andrew Carnegie organized and expanded the steel
industry to meet the nation's demand for high-quality, low-cost steel.

Realizing that low-cost steel would find a
ready market in industrial America, Andrew
Carnegie made a fortune.

In 1901 Carnegie retired, believing that rich
people should spend their later years
distributing their wealth.

The development of the
Bessemer process,
shown here in a
Pennsylvania plant,
meant that steel could
be made cheaper and
better than ever before.

495

The drilling of oil wells in Pennsylvania in 1859 marked the beginning of the American oil industry.

overnight, wells were drilled and oil derricks dotted the landscape. Western Pennsylvania became the center of a new industry. Towns and cities sprang up like magic, and refineries for producing kerosene began to appear.

About this time, John D. Rockefeller, a 23-year-old merchant in Cleveland, became interested in oil. His ambition was to get control of the entire oil-refining business. Starting with a single oil refinery, Rockefeller and his partners branched out until in the 1880's they controlled 90 percent of all the oil-refining plants in the country. But Rockefeller did not stop there. He bought factories to make barrels; he got control of most of the pipe lines which carried oil from the wells; he built warehouses to store the kerosene. Rockefeller also organized a vast selling force to market his product throughout the country. By the 1900's, Rockefeller and his Standard Oil Company controlled almost all the nation's oil business.

Rockefeller was able to gain a monopoly in oil because of his company's financial power. In the early years, instead of spending all the profits, he put back as much money into the business as he could spare. He advised his partners to do the same. "Take out what you've got to have to live on," he said, "but leave the rest in. Don't buy new clothes and fast horses; let your wife wear her last year's bonnet." As a result of this thrift, Rockefeller had the money with which to buy out rival refineries. In fact, a number of people who tried to get ahead in the oil industry were forced to sell out to Rockefeller. If they refused, Rockefeller would set the price of his kerosene so low that his rivals could not make a profit and so were driven out of business. The money which Rockefeller had put aside carried him along even though he was selling at a loss. This "cut-throat competition" was common in the days when American industry was growing big.

that oil wells could be successfully drilled had much the same effect as the discovery of gold in California. Here was a chance to make a huge fortune! All over the country people would want to use coal oil (kerosene) for lighting in place of candles and whale-oil lamps. Prospectors, therefore, flocked by the thousands to Pennsylvania. Almost

● See p. T43 for a strategy calling for students to examine the achievements of business leaders during the late 1800's.

John D. Rockefeller, shown here as a young man, brought order and efficiency to the American oil industry.

Although the use of electric lights cut down the demand for kerosene in the United States, the oil industry continued to grow. The invention of the gasoline engine created a tremendous demand for petroleum products. Also, oil became an important fuel for heating homes and other buildings.

What Hill, Carnegie, and Rockefeller did to promote American industry is only a part of the story. Other business leaders who had worked their way up ● from humble beginnings helped to advance industry and achieved fame and fortune as well. Sometimes they used selfish and ruthless methods which our laws today do not permit. Nevertheless, present-day American industry owes much to their boldness, energy, and ability.

▶ **CHECK UP**   See Teacher's Key.

1. By what means did James J. Hill develop a great railroad system in the Northwest?
2. What contributions did Andrew Carnegie make in the development of the American steel industry?
3. How did John D. Rockefeller develop the oil industry?

CHECK UP ON CHAPTER 22   See Teacher's Key.

Words to Know

1. mineral
2. dividend
3. cable
4. partnership
5. stockholder
6. investment
7. corporation
8. division of labor
9. share of stock
10. standard parts
11. assembly line
12. natural resources
13. mass production

Facts to Remember

1. Name four conditions that made it possible for American industry to become large and profitable in the years after the Civil War.

2. What new manufacturing methods were important in the development of the mass production of goods?

3. **(a)** How do corporations get the money they need to carry on their business? **(b)** Who are the owners of a corporation? **(c)** Who manages the business of a corporation?

4. For what invention is each of the following people best-known? **(a)** Cyrus Field **(b)** Alexander Graham Bell

497

Facts to Remember (cont.)

(c) Charles Goodyear (d) Andrew J. Beard (e) The Wright brothers (f) Thomas Edison

5. Describe the main achievement of each of the following: (a) Charles Lindbergh, (b) Amelia Earhart, (c) James J. Hill, (d) Andrew Carnegie, (e) John D. Rockefeller.

Skills to Practice

1. Make a time line with the title "Great American Inventions." *Either* start your time line with Robert Fulton's steamboat (1807) *or* use only the inventions described in Chapter 22. Show the inventions in their correct time order.
2. Study the picture of the early automobile on page 490. Name three ways in which that automobile differs from cars today.

Questions to Think About

1. (a) Could the United States have become a great industrial nation without its abundance of natural resources? Explain. (b) Why is it important that natural resources be wisely used?
2. Why do inventions and industrial progress go hand in hand? In answering this question, use the development of the automobile as an example.
3. (a) What are the advantages of mass production? (b) Are there any disadvantages? Explain.
4. (a) How did cars and airplanes change American ways of living? (b) Are more recent inventions likely to affect our ways of living?

Linking Past and Present

● **The horseless carriage.** A forerunner of our modern cars was simply a buggy moved by a one-cylinder engine. The "horseless carriage" of 1896 could make about twelve miles an hour if it didn't break down! President Theodore Roosevelt was a man of great courage, but when he rode in a car in 1902, he had a horse and buggy follow along in case of accident. The early automobiles were considered so dangerous that the state of Tennessee passed a law about their use. The law required people to publish a warning in the newspaper a week ahead of time if they intended to drive a car anywhere!

Greenfield Village. To preserve a part of our country's past, Henry Ford created a typical village of the 1800's outside his home town of Dearborn, Michigan. To make his town true to life, he moved entire buildings to Greenfield Village — an old schoolhouse, a shoemaker's shop, a silk mill, the house in which Noah Webster wrote his famous dictionary, and many others. Ford also built a museum and filled it with original models of inventions and machines which had helped America to become a great industrial nation. Among these were several of Thomas Edison's original inventions, which Ford had collected and put into working order. Ford, who was a friend and great admirer of the inventor, also had Edison's old laboratory rebuilt in Greenfield Village.

Bicycle beginnings. The "ancestor" of our modern bicycle was introduced in America in 1876. It was a strange-looking contraption. The front wheel was about five feet in diameter, with pedals on its axle. The rear wheel was only about 18 inches high. The rider, perched high on a seat above the front wheel, needed a good sense of balance! Soon, new inventions, such as equal-sized wheels, inflatable tires, and a sprocket chain connecting the pedals and the rear wheel, made riding easier; and the bicycle quickly became popular. In the days before the automobile, nearly everyone in the United States used a bicycle for business and pleasure.

GAINING SKILL

Reading Line Graphs

As the United States grew, so did the need for good transportation. On foot and on horseback, by boat and by wagon, by train and eventually in automobiles, people traveled across the country. Improvements in transportation meant that goods could be moved more quickly too. The ability to move goods quickly was essential to the growth of industry.

The graph on this page gives you information about two kinds of transportation. This kind of graph is called a line graph. It is set up in the same way as a bar graph (page 267). Use the information on the graph to answer the following questions.

1. What is the subject of the graph? (Read the title.) What period of time does the graph cover?

2. What do the horizontal axis and the vertical axis on this graph show?

3. What two kinds of transportation are shown on the graph?

4. What was the first year in which there were more than 200,000 miles of surfaced roads in the United States?

5. In what decade did surfaced roads increase most rapidly? (a) 1860–1870 (b) 1910–1920 (c) 1930–1940

6. In what year was railroad mileage at its highest point?

7. In 1940, was the mileage of surfaced roads (a) about the same as the miles of railroad track in use, (b) about double the miles of railroad track, (c) about five times as great as the miles of railroad track?

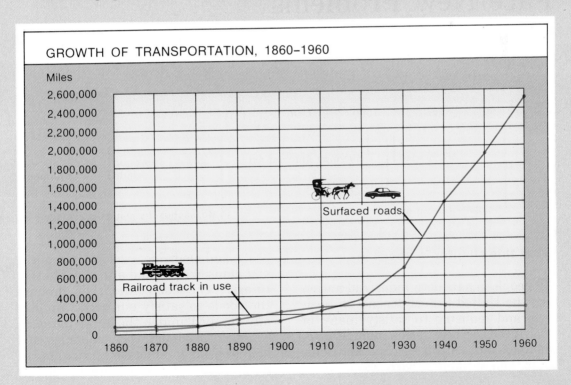

GROWTH OF TRANSPORTATION, 1860–1960

499

CHAPTER **23** *Vocabulary preview:* depression, recession, trust, collective bargaining, arbitration, strike

Business and Industry Face New Problems

1865–1940   See p. T44 for chapter teaching strategies.

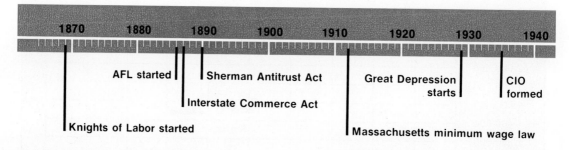

| 1870 | 1880 | 1890 | 1900 | 1910 | 1920 | 1930 | 1940 |

AFL started | Sherman Antitrust Act

Interstate Commerce Act

Great Depression starts | CIO formed

Knights of Labor started

Massachusetts minimum wage law

What this chapter is about —

All people in a modern industrial nation like the United States depend on business and industry to satisfy many of their needs. These needs include food, shelter, and clothing; cars and bus, train, and airplane service; soap, tooth-paste, and medicine; books, newspapers, and amusements; and a thousand other things. The companies that produce the goods to satisfy our needs are usually lumped under the term *industry*. On the other hand, the companies that help to bring products or services to the people who need them are commonly

500

◀ The rapid growth of American industry after the Civil War brought great changes to the lives of working men and women.

called *businesses*. These include wholesale and retail stores, banks, restaurants, gas stations, and so on. As you can see, business and industry work hand in hand to supply the needs of modern communities.

The rapid growth of industry and business that took place after 1865 made it possible to satisfy the needs of people throughout the country. In large part, ● Americans owed their high standard of living to new inventions, new machines, and new means of manufacturing and transportation.

But the growth of industry and business also brought to the American people many problems that their ancestors did not have to face. Among those problems were unemployment and economic depressions. To understand such problems and the efforts that were made to solve them, look for answers to the following questions:

1. What problems did industrialization bring?
2. How did labor and business try to improve working conditions?
3. What role did government take in regulating business and labor?

1 What Problems Did Industrialization Bring?

In Chapter 22 you read how the United States became the world's leading industrial nation. This chapter will point out some of the problems brought about by rapid industrialization. In the following pages we will read about Mr. Charles Jackson, an American businessman of the 1890's. Mr. Jackson is not a ★ real person, but his story will help us understand how the growth of industry affected the American people.

New machinery tempts Mr. Jackson to increase production. Mr. Jackson is president of the Jackson Manufacturing Company, which makes furniture of steel and wood. Mr. Jackson is sitting in his office looking at the production figures for his company. He has just ordered some new machinery. At present his factory can produce 25 chairs each day. With the new machinery, however, Mr. Jackson's company will be able to make 100 chairs a day. Mr. Jackson is pleased for two reasons: (1) The amount of human labor needed to make each chair will be reduced by the use of machinery. Since he will have to pay less money for labor per chair, he hopes to be able to make a larger profit than before. (2) Mr. Jackson's profits will also be greatly increased because his company will be making four times as many chairs each day.

Mr. Jackson now writes letters to the companies from which he buys his steel and wood. "I will need," he writes, "to start buying larger quantities of your products." He explains the exact amounts. When these letters reach the steel and wood companies, they too are pleased at the chance to sell more of their products and to make larger profits. The steel company orders more iron and coal. It is just as though the steel company said to the mining company, "Get more workers! Dig more coal and iron!" The lumber company sends orders to the loggers in the woods, and to the sawmills, to provide it with larger amounts of wood.

★ Point out the key understanding of this story: that industrialization has had both positive and negative effects.

Industrial growth greatly increased the demand for raw materials. How did factories make use of lumber from giant trees like these?

Increased production uses up natural resources. Meanwhile, other factory owners, like Mr. Jackson, are using new machinery and turning out more and more products. The miners and loggers, therefore, can sell all the ore and wood they can produce. They dig and cut more than ever before with bigger crews and better tools. They dig where the deposits of ore are richest and the digging is easiest, and they cut where they can get the most wood with the least work. They must provide huge quantities of ore and wood so that Mr. Jackson's factory and thousands of other factories will have the raw materials they need.

This is what happened to America's natural resources after the Civil War. Everywhere orders were pouring in.

Everywhere people acted on this idea: "Hurry up! Provide the materials quickly!" So people dug into the stores of iron ore that could never be replaced. They mined coal and cut down trees with little concern for the needs of their children and grandchildren. In this way, America's natural resources were carelessly used. In recent years more thought has been given to using our natural resources wisely. Even so, the United States now imports from other parts of the world large quantities of raw materials, such as iron ore and oil.

Mr. Jackson expands his business too far. We return again to the story of Mr. Jackson. Finding, as he expected, that his new machinery turns out more chairs each day and increases his profits, he decides to buy even more machines.

502

So he orders the machines. He orders more steel and wood. He hires more workers to run the new machines and increase his output of chairs. To be sure, he does not have the money to pay cash for all he buys. "But," he thinks, "what does it matter? With prices so high and profits so large, I can borrow the money and pay it back out of my profits later on."

Other manufacturers have the same idea. They enlarge their factories. They buy more materials, hire more workers, make more goods. Like Mr. Jackson, they also borrow money. But after a while the creditors (the people who lend money) become alarmed because so much money has been borrowed. The bank where Mr. Jackson borrows his money is concerned. The officers of the bank wonder, "What will we do, if Mr. Jackson, who owes us so much money, doesn't find enough buyers for his products? How will he be able to repay the bank?"

Thoroughly worried, the bank decides to cut down on the amount of money it lends. The bankers get in touch with the firms to whom the bank has lent money and ask that the loans be paid back. So Mr. Jackson, who owes the bank money, pays his debt. But this takes so much of Mr. Jackson's money that he can buy no more machinery and must spend less for materials and cut down the wages paid to his workers. He therefore tells the steel company and the lumber company not to send the materials he has ordered. With fewer materials, he has to go through his factory saying to workers something like this: "I'm sorry, but after this Saturday we won't have any work for you. I'll call you back to the factory the minute there's work for you to do."

Fear sweeps the country. All around the country sweeps a feeling of fear. Just as Mr. Jackson cuts down his orders for steel and wood, the steel and lumber companies, in turn, are forced to reduce their orders for raw materials. Out goes the word to the loggers and the miners: "Less ore. Less coal. Fewer logs." "I'm sorry, no more work." And the workers go home and tell their families, "I'm sorry, but the boss says no work after Saturday. Better not buy those new shoes you wanted. And we'll have to buy less at the grocery store." And so it goes in countless communities throughout the nation. The shoemaker, the grocer, and other merchants have less business. They begin to cut down, to order less, to fire their helpers. Many businesses fail because they cannot sell their products. Many families are hungry because people have lost their jobs.

America enjoys booms and suffers depressions. This chain of events has been repeated many times in American history. First there has been a time of confidence and growth of business, then a period of fear and falling-off in business. The first kind of period is called a boom, and the time of fear is called a panic. The period of falling business ★ and rising unemployment which follows a panic is usually called a **depression.** You read in Chapter 17 about the panic and hard times during the presidency of Martin Van Buren.

When most Americans were farmers, panics and depressions did not bring hardship to as many people as they did in later years. Living on farms, people could take care of most of their needs even if the nation's business was poor. As business and industry grew, however, an ever-increasing number of Americans made their living in business and manufacturing. Factory and office workers depend on the money they earn to buy what they need. They don't actually make or grow what they and their families need to eat, wear, and use. Thus, after the nation became industrialized, more people suffered during periods of panic and depression.

There were a number of depressions in the period of industrial growth after

503

★ Review the meaning of the term *panic*, introduced on p. 365.

the Civil War. Three of these were especially severe. They followed the panics of 1873, 1893, and 1929. In each case the story was much the same. Business expanded rapidly, wages were high, prices rose. People invested their savings in the hope of making big profits. In the years before 1873 and 1893, they lent money for the building of new railroads. Before 1929, they invested heavily in stocks and bonds. In each case, when the bubble of good times broke, panic and suffering followed. The depression that started in 1929 was the worst the United States had ever known. Business did not get back to normal for about ten years. Then, during World War II, business increased greatly in order to supply the needs of our military forces. During the 1950's a new term, **recession,** came into use to describe a business decline that was not as long or as serious as a depression.

Mr. Jackson plans a monopoly. Let us turn once more to the story of Mr. Jackson to understand another problem faced by industry and business. One day, as Mr. Jackson is thinking about his business, he jumps suddenly to his feet. "I've got a great idea!" he says.

"This will make me rich. Why didn't I think of it before? I'll try to get control of all the manufacturing of chairs in the United States. Of course, I'll need a great deal of money because I'll have to buy out many other furniture factories. I may even have to sell chairs so cheaply that some other manufacturers can't afford to stay in business. But when I control all chair manufacturing, every person who wants to buy chairs will be forced to buy them from me. Then, when there are no other chairs for people to buy, I can ask almost any price I like. People will have no choice but to pay it."

The number of monopolies increases after 1865. Actually, neither our imaginary Mr. Jackson nor anyone else ever controlled all the manufacture of chairs in the United States. But some forms of business or industry have been controlled, or practically controlled, by one company or a small group of companies. You have already read how John D. Rockefeller gained control of most of the oil refining in the country (Chapter 22). To control a product, as you know, is to have a monopoly of it. When a group of corporations with common in-

504

The rapid growth of monopolies and trusts alarmed some Americans. This cartoon criticized the government for being unable or unwilling to regulate the power of the trusts.

● Remind students of the monopoly Italian merchants had on Asian trade during the 1400's (pp. 35–36).

In the days before industrial expansion most manufactured products were made in small workshops. Owners knew their employees well and often worked alongside them.

terests has a monopoly of a product, the group is called a **trust.** After 1865, powerful trusts at one time or another held monopolies of steel, tobacco, sugar, beef, and other products.

What are the benefits and evils of monopolies? In general, trusts or monopolies are huge organizations. Large business organizations have certain advantages: (1) They can buy raw materials in large quantities. (2) They can hire scientists and engineers to develop new products and experts to make their factories more efficient. (3) They can afford to purchase expensive machinery. (4) They can develop ways to use waste materials that might otherwise be thrown away. These advantages can mean more products at lower prices for the public.

Monopolies, on the other hand, may bring serious problems: (1) There is a temptation for monopolies to keep their prices high in order to make larger profits. When this happens, the public does not receive the benefit of lower costs. (2) Monopolies also work a hardship on small businesses, which cannot compete successfully with them. (3) New ideas may be discouraged if a monopoly controls all the business in a particular field. Thus new processes and improved products may be kept off the market. Later in this chapter you will learn how the government took steps to prevent harmful monopolies.

▶ **CHECK UP**   See Teacher's Key.

1. **(a)** Why does new machinery tempt manufacturers to increase production? **(b)** How does increased production affect companies that sell raw materials? **(c)** What are some unfortunate results of overproduction?

2. **(a)** What is a depression? **(b)** Why were the effects of depressions more severe in the period after the Civil War?

3. **(a)** What is a monopoly? **(b)** What are the advantages of monopolies? **(c)** What problems may they create?

505

● See p. T44 for a strategy calling for students to compare the positive and negative aspects of monopolies.

2 How Did Labor and Business Try to Improve Working Conditions?

So far, we have considered three problems brought about by the growth of industry and business: (1) Natural resources were carelessly used. (2) The country experienced periods of boom and depression. (3) Some of the giant business concerns tried to establish monopolies. These three problems affected all American citizens. There were other problems, however, which more directly affected industrial workers themselves.

WORKERS UNITE TO IMPROVE CONDITIONS

You have already learned how the use of machinery and the growth of factories changed conditions for many workers. Operating a machine usually means doing the same thing over and over again. The work is likely to be less interesting than handwork, where the worker has a variety of tasks to do. In addition, carrying out only one or two steps at a machine requires less skill than many kinds of handwork. As a result, workers can more easily be replaced and their jobs are less secure. The use of machines may also have an effect on wages. To illustrate these points, let us turn once more to Mr. Jackson's factory in the 1890's.

Mr. Jackson keeps his labor costs down. Mr. Jackson likes the people who work in his factory. At the same time, the wages he pays them are an important part of the cost of making chairs. Mr. Jackson, therefore, offers them the lowest wages they will accept and still continue to work for him. He also wants the workers to do as much work as possible in return for their wages. For this reason they must work hard for many hours each day.

The workers, on their part, respect Mr. Jackson. Now that the factory is larger and has more employees, however, they see less of Mr. Jackson than in the old days. The workers have a feeling that Mr. Jackson is not as interested in them as he was when the factory was smaller. They also believe that they have to work too many hours and that their wages are too low.

Dissatisfied workers join together to win better conditions. Like Mr. Jackson, most factory owners in the 1890's paid workers as little as possible. The sunup-to-sundown working day of an earlier time had disappeared, but the ten-hour day was standard. In many factories, also, little attention was paid to the health and safety of the employees. Accidents often injured workers severely and left them permanently disabled, with no way of earning a living. Such conditions seemed unfair to workers. And in times of depression when they lost their jobs, they felt bitter. "It's not right," they said. "After we have worked hard and faithfully for our employer in good times, we should not be fired as soon as business falls off."

What could one single worker in the mines, the mills, or the factories do to get higher wages or better working conditions? There was actually very little a few individuals could do. Their bosses might simply fire them and hire other people in their place. But if a great number of workers were to join together and demand changes, they might succeed in improving their wages and working conditions. Employers could not replace large numbers of workers as easily as they could fill one worker's job. As the old saying goes, "In union there is strength." This idea led to the formation of labor unions.

● Discuss whether the conditions described here are still present in some occupations.

The Knights of Labor was the first big union in this country. Black and white members worked together for labor reforms.

Some labor unions were formed as early as the 1830's (Chapter 14), but these early attempts were not lasting. Most people at that time were farmers, and the number of industrial workers who were affected by low pay or poor conditions was small. Also, most early unions were local; they did not have members throughout the country.

The Knights of Labor is organized. When business and industry began to expand after the Civil War, more and more workers felt the need to band together for better conditions. In 1869, a Philadelphia tailor, named Uriah S. Stephens, founded a union known as the Knights of Labor. The Knights of Labor was a single big union open to all workers — men and women, blacks and whites. Its members included both those who did tasks that required long training and those who did unskilled work.

At first the Knights of Labor grew slowly. After the union had succeeded in getting a number of employers to treat their workers better, however, hundreds of thousands joined. But the Knights of Labor was not always wisely led. And it was difficult for so many different kinds of people, in so many different kinds of jobs, to work together well in a single union. The Knights of Labor, therefore, lost power rapidly. By the 1890's it had practically disappeared.

The American Federation of Labor is started. In a shop in New York City worked a young cigarmaker named

507

● See p. T44 for a strategy calling for students to compare and contrast the labor organizations of the late 1800's.

Samuel Gompers. When he was a boy, he and his parents had come from England to seek a new life in America. As his nimble fingers flew at his task, Gompers thought and talked about the problems of working people. Instead of a big general union like the Knights of Labor, Gompers believed there should be a separate union for skilled workers in each trade or craft — a carpenters' union, a hatmakers' union, or a steamfitters' union. Skilled workers are those who have special training and experience. Therefore, they are harder to replace than unskilled workers. Gompers believed that employers would have to listen to the requests of large groups of skilled workers.

● In 1886, the American Federation of Labor was organized. It was based on many of Gompers' ideas. Local unions of skilled workers were formed in many trades. The local unions of each trade or craft were then joined in state and national groups. Gompers was the first president of the American Federation of Labor, and held the office for almost 40 years.

The CIO is based on a new idea. For a long time the American Federation of Labor (commonly called the AFL) was the chief labor organization in the country. Its membership numbered in the millions. Then, in the 1930's, another strong labor organization developed. This was the Congress of Industrial Organizations, or CIO.

Why did the CIO grow up as a rival ★ of the AFL? As you know, the AFL was made up of unions of skilled workers. This meant that there were large numbers of unskilled workers who did not belong to the AFL. The CIO, on the other hand, was based on the idea of industrial unions. An industrial union takes into its membership all the workers, skilled and unskilled, in a particular industry. The CIO recruited most of its members from mass-production industries that employed large numbers of workers, such as the steel, rubber, and automobile industries. Unlike many unions at that time, the CIO welcomed black and women members. The leader

The union membership card below is from the 1870's. What kinds of workers belonged to this union?

508

★ Tell students that the AFL and CIO merged in 1955.

People in America's Story

SAMUEL GOMPERS

Samuel Gompers devoted his life to establishing the right of workers to organize and bargain with employers for better working conditions.

Nationwide unions were Gompers's goal as first president of the American Federation of Labor. He worked tirelessly to organize skilled workers of every craft into unions of their own.

Like his father, Gompers started work as a cigarmaker. There he became familiar with the views and problems of his fellow workers. With this knowledge, he took the lead in organizing a labor union among the cigarmakers of America.

509

in starting the CIO was John L. Lewis, powerful head of the United Mine Workers.

LABOR UNIONS TRY TO WIN BETTER WORKING CONDITIONS

Unions use arbitration and strikes to gain their ends. When union leaders representing a group of workers ask an employer for higher wages, shorter hours of work, or better conditions, the employer may refuse to grant the request. The union can then try to persuade the employer that its request is fair and should be granted. Often when representatives of the union and the employer sit down together to discuss terms, they are able to reach an agreement. This is called **collective bargaining.**

If the union and the employer cannot agree, the union may take its demand before a board of fair-minded persons. When the members of the board have studied all sides of the question, they try to reach a decision which both the employer and the union will accept. This method of settling labor disputes is called **arbitration.**

If no agreement can be reached, however, is there anything the union workers can do to get their employer to grant their request? Naturally employers need workers if they are to carry on their business. So if other methods fail, the workers can refuse to work. When many workers all refuse at the same time to do their jobs, this action is called a **strike.** The strike is the strongest weapon working men and women have. Some strikes have been small and unimportant; others have been widespread and costly. Let us follow the story of one early strike.

A railroad strike is called in 1877. After the Panic of 1873 (page 504), jobs were hard to get, and workers' families were suffering. The railroad companies believed that people would take work at any wages, no matter how low, rather than be idle and hungry. In the summer of 1877, therefore, the railroad companies east of the Mississippi announced that the wages of all railroad workers would be cut 10 percent. The workers went out on strike.

This was the first big strike ever held in the United States. It was also one of the most bitter. When the strike began, trains could not run for lack of workers to operate them. But the railroad companies were as determined to break the strike as the strikers were to stop the trains. In city after city — Baltimore, Pittsburgh, Reading, Buffalo, Columbus, Chicago, and St. Louis — fierce riots took place. In Pittsburgh, for example, 26 people were killed and many more wounded.

In the end this strike failed. The strikers had to have wages to live, so they could not stay off the job forever. When federal troops were finally called in to restore order, the railroad workers unhappily accepted the lowered wages and went back to work. But such a failure only made workers feel more convinced than ever that they needed powerful unions to get improvements in working conditions.

Unions continue their battle for better conditions. After the railroad strike of 1877, there were many long and bitter strikes. In 1886 a struggle for an eight-hour work day was marked by the "Haymarket riot." A bomb exploded in Haymarket Square, Chicago, killing and wounding many people. Another strike in the steel mills at Homestead, Pennsylvania, in 1892 caused the loss of a number of lives. Twenty-six men were killed in a coal mine strike at Herrin, Illinois, in 1922. Strikes in the steel and automobile industries in the depression days of the 1930's caused much bitterness.

Often unions tried to make strikes more effective by organizing picket lines; that is, the strikers would form

● See p. T44 for a strategy calling for students to examine the 1877 railroad strike and the Haymarket riot.

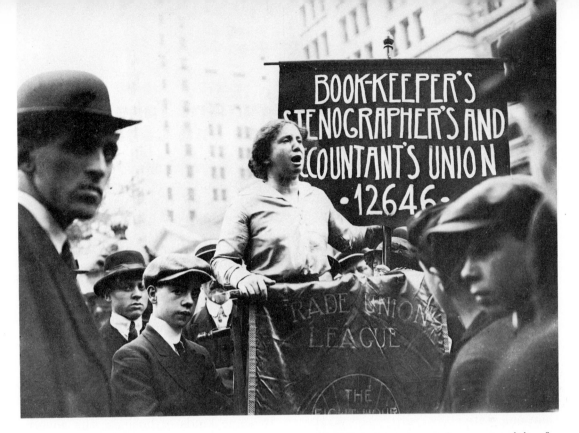

Union officials held open-air rallies in the late 1800's and early 1900's to gain public support. They also hoped to get laws passed that would protect the right to form unions.

lines around the shop or factory against which they were striking. The pickets would urge other workers or customers not to cross the picket line to enter the shop or factory. When employers hired strikebreakers to cross the picket lines, fighting often broke out. Sometimes, too, employers called in police to break strikes.

EMPLOYERS IMPROVE WORKING CONDITIONS

Although labor unions did much for their members, better conditions were also brought about by employers. More and more employers came to realize that contented workers do more and better work than those who are worried or dissatisfied. Such employers listened carefully to requests for better wages and shorter working hours and to suggestions for improvements. They pro-

vided lunchrooms and opportunities for sports and recreation on the factory grounds. They safeguarded the health of their workers by employing nurses and doctors and by providing ventilation and good lighting. Safety fixtures attached to the machinery helped to prevent accidents. Some companies enabled their workers to buy shares of stock and thus become part owners of the company and share in its profits. In addition, many companies began to provide paid vacation time, health insurance, and pension plans for their employees.

▶ **CHECK UP**   See Teacher's Key.

1. **(a)** How did machines make the jobs of factory workers less secure? **(b)** What working conditions made workers dissatisfied?
2. **(a)** Why did workers form unions? **(b)** What groups were included in the Knights of Labor? **(c)** How did the AFL and CIO differ in organization?
3. **(a)** What methods did unions use to win their demands? **(b)** How did employers improve working conditions?

511

● Tell students that the improvements mentioned here are part of what workers and employers today call *fringe benefits*.

● See p. T44 for a strategy calling for students to examine the antitrust legislation
passed by Congress in the late 1800's and early 1900's.

3 What Role Did Government Take in Regulating Business and Labor?

When the rapid growth of business and industry brought about certain problems, both the national and state governments took action. Let us examine some of the steps that were taken.

Harmful monopolies are outlawed. One of the problems, as we have seen (page 505), was the forming of monopolies. To prevent groups of corporations or trusts from setting up harmful monopolies, Congress in 1890 passed the Sherman Antitrust Act. The Sherman Act made it illegal for big businesses to set up monopolies. This meant that no trust could control the sale of oil or sugar or beef or other products in more than one state.

For a number of years, however, the government did not strictly enforce the Sherman Act. Even when the government did try to break up monopolies, the attempts were not always successful. Often the companies that the government accused of being monopolies took their cases to court and won. Congress in later years, therefore, passed other laws to break up monopolies. The Clayton Act (1914) clearly stated what kinds of business combinations were unlawful.

The government regulates some monopolies. It should be remembered that monopolies are not harmful just because they are big. Rather they are harmful when they try to get unfair advantages as a result of their bigness. In some kinds of business the government recognizes that it would be unwise to forbid monopolies. Electric service, for example, is more efficient if it is provided by a single business organization rather than by a number of small, separate companies. Instead of forbidding monopolies in such cases, Congress decided to control them. In 1887, Con-

Until state governments passed laws regulating the number of hours they could work, children like these coal sorters worked as many as twelve hours a day.

512

gress passed the Interstate Commerce Act to regulate the rates that railroads could charge when hauling freight between states. Later, it also approved laws regulating telephone, telegraph, and radio companies. In such cases, monopolies are not broken up but are required to furnish good service at fair rates to the public.

The states pass labor laws. The government also passed laws to protect workers. Most of the early labor laws were passed not by the national government but by various states. State laws provided the following kinds of regulations:

(1) *Child labor.* It takes less strength to run a factory machine than it does to do hard physical labor. Factory owners, therefore, hired children to do adult work. But people in many states pointed out that it seemed harmful and dangerous for children to work ten or twelve hours a day, as adults did in most industries. So state laws were passed limiting the number of hours a child could work.

(2) *Working conditions.* Workers often had to do their jobs under dangerous or unhealthy conditions. Many factories were poorly lighted, badly heated, or unsanitary. Other factories had bad air or materials that could injure a worker's health. Laws were passed to protect working men and women from such harmful conditions.

(3) *Accidents.* Even though working conditions were improved, accidents could not always be prevented. Therefore, many states passed employers' liability or workers' compensation laws. ● Such laws required the employer to pay the worker for injuries suffered on the job.

(4) *Minimum wages.* When wages were so low that a man or woman could not earn a decent living, the states passed laws fixing the lowest wages that could be paid. In other words, employers could not pay wages that were lower than a certain level. Such laws were called minimum wage laws. (*Minimum* means "smallest.") Massachusetts led the way with a minimum wage law in 1912, and other states soon followed.

In these ways, legislation improved the situation of the working man and woman. Although state governments took the first steps, the federal government later played a major role in protecting the rights and interests of workers (Chapter 30).

▶ **CHECK UP**   See Teacher's Key.

1. **(a)** What was the purpose of the Sherman Antitrust Act? **(b)** The Clayton Act? **(c)** The Interstate Commerce Act?
2. What kinds of laws did state governments pass to protect workers?

CHECK UP ON CHAPTER 23   See Teacher's Key.

Words to Know

1. profit
2. boom
3. panic
4. depression
5. recession
6. monopoly
7. trust
8. labor union
9. strike
10. picket line
11. minimum wage
12. arbitration
13. collective bargaining

Facts to Remember

1. **(a)** When manufacturers cut down their production, what effect does that have on the businesses that supply them with raw materials? **(b)** What is the effect on the people who work for the manufacturers or for the suppliers of raw materials?

2. **(a)** What are the advantages to a company of having a monopoly of a certain kind of business? **(b)** What disadvantages might there be for other businesses or for customers?

3. **(a)** What kinds of problems did the increased use of machines create for factory workers? **(b)** Why were labor unions formed?

4. What kind of membership did each of the following unions have? **(a)** Knights of Labor **(b)** AFL **(c)** CIO

5. **(a)** What methods did labor unions use in disputes with employers? **(b)** What is the difference between collective bargaining and arbitration?

Skills to Practice

1. Following are two policies connected with problems that you read about in this chapter. Decide which of the two groups given in each item probably favored the policy and which group probably opposed it. Also give the reasons for your answers.
   a. *Laws to make monopolies illegal*: (1) managers of large corporations; (2) owners of small businesses.
   b. *Laws regulating rates charged by railroads*: (1) railroad companies; (2) farmers.

Questions to Think About

1. **(a)** How have machines helped workers? **(b)** Why have workers sometimes opposed the use of new machines?

2. **(a)** Have big corporations helped the industrial growth of the United States? **(b)** Could this growth have taken place if there had been only small companies? Explain.

3. Can disputes between workers and employers also affect the general public? Explain.

4. Do booms and depressions affect people who work in agriculture as well as those who work in industry? Explain.

Linking Past and Present

Wall Street once had a wall. The story of Wall Street — the famous street in New York City — goes back to the days when the Dutch came to North America. In the 1620's, you remember, the Dutch started the town of New Amsterdam on Manhattan Island. Later, a hot-tempered governor named Peter Stuyvesant built a wall at the lower end of Manhattan to keep out the Indians and also the English. The narrow street along the wall was known as Wall Street. But the wall did little good against the English, for in 1664 New Amsterdam surrendered to them and became the city of New York. As New York City grew, Wall Street became important. By 1870, it was a busy trading center for stocks and bonds.

Today Wall Street is the heart of one of the greatest financial districts in the world. The New York Stock Exchange is located in this financial district. So too are the main offices of huge industrial corporations, banking concerns, investment houses, and other companies and businesses. The expression ''Wall Street'' is often used to refer to big bankers and powerful financial interests, whether they actually have offices on Wall Street or not.

Labor Day. Labor Day is an important American holiday. In 1882, the Knights of Labor established the first Labor Day to honor American workers. The idea of a holiday for working men and women became popular, and in 1894, Congress made Labor Day an official national holiday. Ever since then, Americans have enjoyed a day of leisure on the first Monday of every September.

● Discuss the way in which metaphor is used in this sentence. Why is Wall Street ''the heart'' of one of the world's greatest financial districts?

For answers see Teacher's Key.

Have students make posters or drawings to illustrate
the points of view expressed in the passages quoted
on this page.

GAINING SKILL

Comparing Points of View

As industry grew in the United States, so
did labor unions. By 1900, unions had been
formed in such trades as mining, steel-mak-
ing, printing, carpentry, and hat-making, to
name just a few. Americans held strong
opinions about unions. The quotations that
follow show two different points of view.
The first is from a speech given in 1903 by
David Parry, president of the National Association of Manufacturers.

> Organized labor knows but one law, and
> that is the law of physical force. . . .
> All its purposes are accomplished either
> by actual force or the threat of force. It
> does not place its reliance in reason and
> justice, but in strikes [and] boy-
> cotts. . . . It is, in all essential features,
> a mob power. . . . The stronger it
> grows, the greater a menace it be-
> comes to . . . free government. . . .
>
> It denies to the individual the right of
> being his own judge as to the length of
> time he shall work and as to how much
> he shall do within the time. . . .

A different viewpoint was expressed in a
1911 magazine article by Clarence Darrow,
a famous lawyer who frequently defended
labor leaders in court. Read what Darrow
said and then answer the questions.

> The labor unions have made it a busi-
> ness to organize workingmen for
> shorter hours, better conditions, safer
> tools, and a larger share of the common
> production than [they] could individu-
> ally obtain. . . .
>
> The individual laborer today is help-
> less to make any terms with an em-
> ployer. Imagine one of the 40,000 work-

> men of a great railroad system making
> a demand for shorter hours and better
> wages. He would be met by the an-
> swer: "If you don't like the terms, you
> can find another job." . . . A complete
> organization of workmen would have
> the same power with the railroad com-
> pany that the railroad company has
> with the workmen. And in this way
> only can a real contract be made.

1. According to Parry, how do unions
   achieve their goals? How does he think
   unions threaten the freedom of individual workers?
2. What, from Darrow's point of view, are
   the aims of unions? Why does he think
   it necessary for workers to bargain as a
   group, rather than individually?
3. Compare the views of Parry and Darrow.
   How are their opinions about unions
   different? Find sentences or phrases
   that reveal the two men's points of
   view.

515

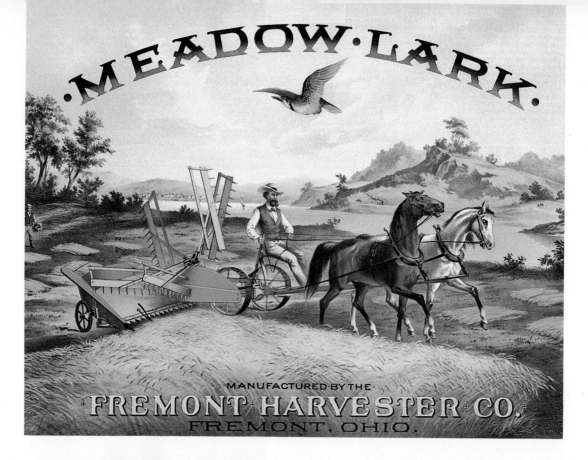

MEADOW·LARK·

MANUFACTURED·BY·THE·
FREMONT·HARVESTER·CO.
FREMONT, OHIO.

CHAPTER **24**

Vocabulary preview: money crop, irrigation, supply and demand, bloc, cooperative, conservation, precipitation

New Forces Affect American Farming

1865–1940   See pp. T45–T46 for chapter teaching strategies.

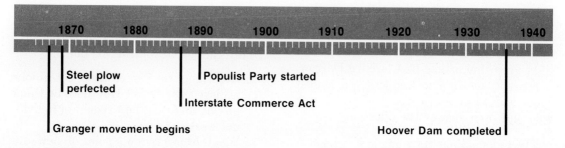

| 1870 | 1880 | 1890 | 1900 | 1910 | 1920 | 1930 | 1940 |

Steel plow perfected

Populist Party started

Interstate Commerce Act

Granger movement begins

Hoover Dam completed

What this chapter is about —

Farming is important to every nation, large or small. A country that cannot produce enough food for its people has to depend on other nations for its food supply. An American statesman, William Jennings Bryan, once expressed the importance of farming in these words:

The great cities rest upon our broad and fertile prairies. Burn down your cities and leave our farms, and your cities will spring up again as if by magic; but destroy our farms, and the grass

◀ New machinery, like the "Meadowlark" harvester shown in this advertisement, helped American farmers raise more crops.

will grow in the streets of every city in the country.

From its early days, our country has been more fortunate than many nations. Because there were tremendous areas of fertile soil in this country, farmers were able to provide enough food for our rapidly growing population. Even before the Civil War, changes had taken place in the size of farms, in the crops raised on them, and in the tools and methods used by farmers. In the years after 1865, however, new machinery and improved methods ● of raising and marketing crops affected farming to a much greater extent.

This chapter will tell how the lives of American farmers changed in the years after the Civil War and what new problems they faced. In order to understand those changes and problems, we will answer the following questions:

1. How did new machines and new methods change farm production?
2. How did changes in farming bring new problems?
3. How did farmers try to overcome their problems?

1 How Did New Machines and New Methods Change Farm Production?

To understand better the great changes that took place on America's farms after 1865, let us first get a picture of farming in the 1840's.

Small farms provide a living. In the South, as you know, there were large plantations where cotton and other crops were raised to be sold abroad (Chapter 15). Most American farms in the 1840's, however, were small. Except for special occasions, when neighbors lent a helping hand, farm families did all their own work. Most farmers had only a few simple tools. These included a plow, a scythe, a wooden "cradle" for harvesting grain, and a few others. For plowing and hauling, the farmer used horses, mules, or oxen.

A farm was not a means of *earning a living* in the sense in which we use these words today. Nowadays most people who work are paid wages and buy what they need with the money they receive. But the small farms of the 1840's brought little money to the farmers. Instead, the farm *provided a liv-* ★ *ing.* Farm families raised most of their own food, as well as most of the materials from which they made their clothes. They sold a few hogs and cattle and some wheat or corn or oats. With the small amount of cash they received, they bought the few things they could not raise or make at home.

Some improvement in farm tools takes place. It would be wrong, however, to think that farmers in the 1840's produced their crops in exactly the same way as their parents and grandparents had. Certain improvements in farm tools had already taken place. An iron tip and iron sides had been added to the wooden plow of colonial days. A few plows with blades entirely of iron had been made. Some new plows also had a slightly different shape. With them the farmers could easily cut a straight, deep furrow in the soil. In addition, plows were manufactured with parts that could be replaced if they were broken.

517

Before improvements in machinery took place, farmers spent long hours in the fields cutting grain by hand.

There were other improved farm machines as well as some new ones. A horse-drawn hayrake, which could do the work of eight or ten people, came into use in the 1820's. Some machines for planting seeds had also been developed. One very important invention speeded up the harvesting of grain. Farmers in earlier times had not planted large fields of grain because cutting the grain by hand was very slow. In the 1830's, a Virginian named Cyrus McCormick patented a successful reaper. Pulled by horses, it swept the grain stalks against a cutter and dropped them in large bundles. Workers followed the reaper and tied up these bundles, making what are called sheaves. Still another step was the development of a thresher. This machine could separate the grain from the husks much faster than it could be done by hand.

Many advances in farm machinery take place after 1865. After the Civil War, far-reaching improvements in farm tools and machinery completely changed farming. In 1869, James Oliver

perfected a plow made of steel, a metal that is much stronger and tougher than iron. Machines called planters were developed that would cut the furrows, break up the clods of earth, and plant the grain in several rows at a time. New seeders could sow the seed, cover it with earth, and spread fertilizer on the soil all at the same time.

Even more striking changes took place in reapers. By about 1860, there were reapers in use that not only cut the wheat but even tied it into sheaves automatically. Finally, there was a giant machine called a combine that cut, threshed, and cleaned wheat, and then dumped it into a wagon. When this machine began its work, there was a field of waving grain; when the combine had finished, the grain was ready for the market.

New sources of power aid farmers. After 1865 farmers' tasks were lightened not only by new machines but also by new kinds of power to run them. At first, farm machines were pulled by horses. Later, some machines were driven by steam power. Soon after 1920,

518

● Discuss how mass production (Chapter 22) would have affected the producing and selling of farm machinery.

● See p. T45 for a strategy calling for students to put together a bulletin board display featuring farming in the late 1800's and early 1900's.

tractors, powered first by a gasoline and later by a diesel engine, pulled the plow or the seeder or the combine. Farmers also found many different uses for electrical power (although power lines did not reach all farm areas until long after electricity was available in the cities and towns). In addition, the rapid growth of industry made it possible to manufacture new and better farm machines at a lower cost. Although the purchase of farm machines still required a large investment of money, more farmers were able to buy them. Not only did the farmer have less work to do by hand, but machines did the work faster.

IMPROVEMENTS IN FARM MACHINERY BRING CHANGES

Greater production is possible. Besides making the work easier, the new farm machinery permitted farmers to do many times the work they had formerly done. A hard worker, using an old-fashioned scythe, could cut perhaps an acre and a half of grain in a day. Using a reaper, the worker could cut ten or twelve acres in the same time. To produce a bushel of wheat in 1840 took a little more than three hours of human labor; in 1894, it took only ten minutes. Much the same was true with corn. In 1840, about four hours and a half of human labor were required to produce a bushel of corn; by 1894, only about forty minutes were needed.

Farms grow larger. With the new machinery, a farm family could take care of a small farm and have time to spare. Because the new machinery was expensive, however, few farmers could afford to buy machines and let them stand idle much of the time. If farmers could plant larger crops, they could make greater use of their equipment. They could also earn larger profits and thus more easily pay for their new tools and machines. Farmers who could afford to do so, therefore, decided to buy more land, and the size of farms grew.

Farming becomes a business. As farmers increased the size of their farms ● and bought expensive machinery, many of them found an advantage in devoting

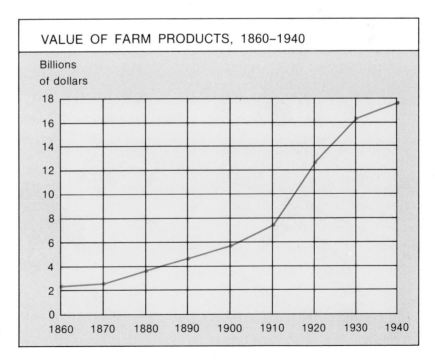

VALUE OF FARM PRODUCTS, 1860–1940

Billions of dollars

See Teacher's Key.

GRAPH STUDY
This graph shows the value in dollars of crops and other farm products every ten years from 1860 to 1940. What was the value of farm products in 1860? In 1920?

519

all their land and time to raising a single crop, such as wheat or cotton. This single crop, which they sold for cash, was called a **money crop.** With the cash they received from the money crop they bought whatever they needed. Sometimes they even bought food that formerly they would have grown on their own farms. So farming became more and more a means of *earning* a living rather than of *providing* a living. In ● fact, farming became a business, and the farmers became business managers who depended on their profits for a living.

FARMERS DEVELOP WESTERN LANDS

In the years following the Civil War, farmers who bought new machinery wondered how they might get enough land to use the machinery profitably. It was only natural that some of them should turn their thoughts to the vast lands west of the Mississippi. As you

Mormon settlers built canals to bring water from mountain streams to their dry croplands. This efficient irrigation system helped their community succeed.

learned in Chapter 21, they moved to those lands in such numbers that by 1890 the frontier had disappeared.

Some western lands lack sufficient rainfall. Where there was ample rainfall, the corn and wheat lands of the Great Plains produced fine crops. But many farmers were disappointed as they went farther west. In much of the western part of our country, there are years when there is too little rainfall to grow ★ farm crops. Sometimes the pioneers arrived in years when the rainfall was heavier than usual, and they were misled by the greenness of the land. When normal dry years followed, their crops wilted and died.

Dry lands become fertile farms. There was rich soil in many of these regions; all that was needed was water. Just as skillful Americans had invented new farm machinery, so others conquered the problem of growing crops in dry ground. This was largely done by **irrigation.** To irrigate means to bring water to a field through canals or pipes. Ditches carry the water into the fields where it runs between the rows of plants or trees.

520

The Shasta Dam was built on the Sacramento River in 1945. Its reservoir, extending for 35 miles, supplies water for northern California.

Irrigation was not new. For centuries the Hopi Indians of Arizona and New Mexico had been successful in irrigating dry lands. Spaniards who settled in the Southwest had built dams and reservoirs to store water. The Mormon settlers in Utah (page 464) also had irrigated their lands. These methods were followed by later settlers. Farmers, of course, had to pay the cost of irrigation, but many were willing to do so rather than have to depend on uncertain rainfall.

In order to provide the water for irrigating large areas, the national government built dams and reservoirs to collect and store water. Some of those
● dams are marvels of construction. Hoover Dam, on the Arizona–Nevada border, stores waters of the Colorado River to irrigate vast regions of the Southwest. Grand Coulee Dam on the Columbia River furnishes water for large sections of the Northwest. Fort Peck Dam and other dams on the Missouri River store up water for lands in Nebraska, the Dakotas, and Montana. In many western states, former desert lands now bloom with fruit trees and other crops.

Farmers also developed a process known as dry farming. This method makes the best use of small amounts of rainfall. The soil is plowed deep before planting. After each rain it is cultivated in order to keep the soil loose. Loose soil not only holds the rain but prevents the moisture below from evaporating. Usually farmers let half their land lie idle each year, so that each crop they plant will have two years' supply of moisture.

▶ **CHECK UP**   See Teacher's Key.

1. **(a)** Why was farming in the 1840's a way of "providing" a living rather than "earning" a living? **(b)** What improvements had been made in farm tools by about 1860?
2. What new farm machines and methods came into use in the years after the Civil War?
3. **(a)** How did new machinery make greater production possible? **(b)** Why did farms grow larger? **(c)** Why did farming come to be considered a business?
4. What methods of farming were developed in areas of little rainfall?

521

● Have students read about one or more of these dams in library books and prepare written or oral reports.

2 How Did Changes in Farming Bring New Problems?

Even under the best of conditions farming can be discouraging. Nature, which the farmer depends on for a successful harvest, can often be cruel. You have just read of the need for irrigation or dry farming on western lands where there was not enough rain. But sometimes there is too much rain and a crop is washed out. Whole crops can also be destroyed by frost, hail, tornadoes, dust storms, or insects. In short, farmers must carry on a continual battle, often against forces that they cannot control.

Price changes seriously affect the farmer. Other difficulties began to concern the American farmer in the late 1800's. Many of the difficulties had to do with the problem of prices. Farmers of the 1840's had not been greatly troubled by prices because their small farms provided for most of their needs. For their children and grandchildren, however, the story was quite different. As modern farmers, they grew a money

crop. If the price of that crop was high, they received a good income. If the price was low, they felt the pinch of hard times.

How are prices determined? Prices go up or down for several reasons. But probably nothing is more important in setting prices than what is known as the rule of **supply and demand.** You have no doubt seen how this rule works. When fresh strawberries first appear in summer, for example, the price is high because they are still scarce and people want them. When the berries become plentiful, the price drops. In other words, when the demand is great for something that is in short supply, prices are high. But when the supply becomes greater, prices are low.

Farmers face low prices and high costs. Now let us see how this rule of supply and demand affected American farmers in the late 1800's. Because farmers were producing huge crops of

★ Why Farmers Organized to Protect Their Interests

"We already have enough grain. We'll buy yours only at a lower price."

"It'll cost you more to ship your grain to market this year. The railroad has raised the rates again."

★ Have students identify the problems shown in the first three drawings. Ask: What does the fourth drawing show?

See p. T45 for a strategy calling for students to examine the problems faced by farmers in the late 1800's and early 1900's.

wheat, oats, barley, corn, and cotton, the price of each product went down. Since more and more farmers were depending on money crops, lower prices caused hardship. At the same time, as you have learned, there had been a great rush to buy farmland. In other words, the supply of good farmland became smaller as the demand for it increased. The *price* of land, therefore, rose steadily. To make matters worse, most farmers had not been able to pay cash for their farms. They had been forced to borrow money and pay high interest rates on it. Nor had most farmers paid cash for their expensive farm machinery. So, on the one hand, farmers owed large amounts of money, while, on the other hand, they received less and less cash from their crops as prices fell. Farmers who could not meet the payments on their debts were in danger of losing their machinery and their farms.

Transportation costs rise. You might think that low prices, added to heavy debts for land and machinery, would make enough problems for farmers in the late 1800's. But they had other troubles too. Trucks had not yet come into use, so farmers depended almost entirely on the railroads to carry their crops to market. A field of grain is a beautiful sight, but the grain is worth nothing until it reaches the buyers who want it. No matter how much money the railroads asked for shipping crops, therefore, a farmer *had* to pay for that service. Farmers, particularly in the West, believed that the railroads charged higher freight rates than were necessary. Many farmers who sold their crops at low prices and had to pay high shipping costs found they had little or nothing to show for their year's labor.

The farmer tries producing larger crops. Facing all these troubles, the farmer probably thought something like this: "It's easy to see what I should do about falling prices. If the selling price of a bushel of wheat or corn is $1.50, I get $150 for 100 bushels. If the price falls to $1, I'll get only $100 for my 100 bushels. To make up for the lowered price, I'll plan to raise 150 bushels." American farmers everywhere had the same thought. The result was that they produced larger crops than ever. But the more they produced, the bigger the

"You should have bought new equipment last year. Prices are on the way up."

"If we get together, we can elect Joe to Congress where maybe he can do something about our problems!"

523

supply became and the bigger the supply became, the lower the price fell. This happened not only in the United States but in other countries too. Thus the idea of producing more and more not only failed to increase farm incomes but made prices of farm products drop even lower.

Intense production ruins the soil. The idea of producing larger crops had another unfortunate result. It wore out the soil. The soil is somewhat like a human being. People can work hard and steadily for a long period of time, but then they need change and refreshment. If they try to work too long without resting, they wear themselves out and may even become ill. It is the same with the soil. If farmers use the soil over and over again for the same crop, and if they fail to add fertilizer or to care for the soil in other ways, the earth simply wears out. Finally there comes a
● time when the soil cannot produce anything worthwhile.

Many American farmers had been in the habit of treating the land carelessly. When the first European settlers landed in America, a wide continent stretched before them. Few people worried when land began to wear out. There always was more to the west. Even after nearly all the land was settled, farmers still acted as though they could get all they could from a piece of land and then move on to another. They cut down trees and plowed up the native grasses, thus making it easy for the soil to erode (ih-ROHD), or wash away, after heavy rains. The results of such careless use of the soil were tragic. At one time experts estimated that at least a hundred million acres of American soil had been worn out or destroyed by erosion.

▶ **CHECK UP**   See Teacher's Key.

1. **(a)** What is the rule of supply and demand? **(b)** How did this rule affect American farmers in the late 1800's?
2. **(a)** How did high transportation costs affect the farmers? **(b)** Why did the production of larger crops only make the farmers' problem worse?
3. What practices ruined large areas of farmland?

3 How Did Farmers Try to Overcome Their Problems?

THE FARMERS ORGANIZE

Debt, high interest on loans, high railroad rates, falling prices, worn-out land — what a collection of difficult problems! Thousands of farmers, all worried by their own troubles, felt that such problems were too big for farmers to solve by themselves. But if they joined together, might they not overcome some of those troubles?

The Grange is started. One man who firmly believed that farmers should get together to work out their problems was Oliver H. Kelley. In 1867, he and a few friends started an organization ★ known as the National Grange of the Patrons of Husbandry. It is commonly called the Grange. At first, few farmers showed interest in the Grange, but Kelley was not discouraged. He traveled about the country, talking to farmers and urging them to form local branches of the Grange. During the 1870's the Grange spread to many states. It was especially strong in the Midwest — in Indiana, Illinois, Wisconsin, Minnesota, and Iowa.

The first national organization for farmers was called the Grange. The Grange poster above gives different views of farm life in the 1870's.

525

● See p. T45 for a strategy that asks students to identify how the Grange and government aided farmers in the late 1800's and early 1900's.

What could the Grange do to help its members? It could teach them to plan their work better. It could teach them that better prices could be obtained by marketing their crops in groups rather than as individuals. It could point out that in many cases farmers should not depend on a single money crop. The Grange could show them how, as a united group, they could better fight the high freight rates charged by the railroads. Also, as a group, they could demand lower interest rates from the banks on loans for farms and farm machinery. All these things the Grange did, and more. At the Grange meetings, men, women, and children from isolated farms were brought together for friendly visits and good times.

The farmer turns to politics for help. The Grange, and other organizations like it, convinced farmers that they could gain greater power by uniting in groups. "But," thought many farmers, "another way to protect ourselves is to get laws passed that will get us what we want." Soon after 1870, therefore, farmers in several states formed political groups. They voted for governors and members of state legislatures who were interested in farm problems, and they helped to elect many such candidates. As a result, the legislatures of several states passed laws that required railroads to charge lower freight rates for shipping farm products.

Most railroads, however, ran through more than one state. In 1886 the United States Supreme Court decided that interstate railroad rates were a matter for the national government rather than the states to control. Farmers then brought pressure on members of Congress to take action on railroad rates. In 1887, as you have learned, Congress passed the Interstate Commerce Act (page 513). This law said railroads could not charge unreasonable railroad rates or follow other practices, many of which had been harmful to the farmers. It established a committee of five members called the Interstate Commerce Commission. People who had complaints against the railroads could bring them to this commission. In 1906, the commission was given power to set the rates charged by railroads.

Farmers organize new political parties. Many farmers also joined national political parties that promised to help ● their cause. One was called the National Greenback Party. Its members wanted to keep in use large amounts of

In the 1870's the Grange became active in politics. Members held meetings to support elected officials who favored laws helpful to farmers.

526

Western and southern farmers formed the Populist Party in the 1890's. In the 1896 presidential election the Populists supported Democratic candidate William Jennings Bryan.

the paper money issued by the government during the Civil War (page 440). These bills were called greenbacks because they were printed with green ink. The western farmers supported the Greenback Party because they believed that if there were more money, farm prices would rise, making it easier for them to pay their debts. The Greenback Party, however, did not win enough supporters to carry out its program.

Many farmers also supported the Populist ("people's") Party, which appeared about 1890. The Populists promised to coin large quantities of silver dollars and to carry out reforms favorable to the farmers. The Populists succeeded in electing several members to Congress, and in 1896 some Populist ideas were taken over by the Democratic Party. In the election that year, many farmers, especially in the West and the South, enthusiastically supported William Jennings Bryan, the Democratic candidate for President.

Bryan sympathized with the western farmers and spoke eloquently of their problems. His stirring speeches won him the title "the silver-tongued orator of the West." The presidential campaign of 1896 was one of the most exciting in American history. In the end, however, Bryan was defeated by the Republican candidate, William McKinley of Ohio.

Trouble hits the farmer in the 1920's. In the early 1900's, the future looked a little brighter to the farmer. European nations were beginning to buy more farm products (such as beef and wheat) from the United States. So Americans received higher prices for their products. Then, when World War I broke out in Europe in 1914, the demand for American farm products increased enormously. To grow larger crops, American farmers borrowed money and bought more land and machinery. But at the end of the war the demand for American farm products dropped off. European farmers returned to their farms, and the European countries began to buy more wheat from Argentina and Canada.

Once more American farmers found themselves in trouble. Their huge crops were more than the United States needed. Farm prices dropped to less than one third of what they had been during the war. Farmers could not pay their taxes or their debts. During the 1920's, many farmers lost their farms because they were unable to pay even the interest on their debts.

The farmer again seeks a remedy in politics. In addition to the Grange, several new farm organizations had grown up in the early 1900's. The Farmers' Union, which started in Texas, became a national organization. The American Farm Bureau Federation grew rapidly and had over two million members by 1920. These groups favored laws helpful to the farmer. Still another, the Non-Partisan League, worked actively for state laws to benefit the farmer.

527

Members of Congress from the farm states tended to vote together in a group called the farm bloc. (A **bloc** is a group of persons, or states, that work together for a common interest.) The farm bloc had enough votes in Congress to pass laws to help farmers. One law enabled farmers who borrowed money on their land to have a longer time to pay it back. Another law made it legal for farmers to organize in large groups called **cooperatives.** These cooperatives could get better prices for crops than an individual farmer could.

THE GOVERNMENT TRIES TO HELP

You have just read about a few laws that were passed to help farmers. Actually the government had long been interested in the farmers' problems and in a number of ways tried to help solve them.

Improvements in agricultural equipment continued to benefit American farmers. This picture shows how a sprinkler system, powered by a gasoline engine, moves across a field, spreading water in the form of mist.

The government helps the farmer to raise better crops. Here are a few of the many things the national government did to assist American farmers:

(1) *Agricultural colleges.* In 1862, Congress passed the Morrill Act, which provided federal land grants to the states. The land was to be sold and the money used to set up colleges and universities that would teach agriculture and engineering. As a result, agricultural schools were established in every state in the Union. These colleges and universities did much to make farming scientific.

(2) *The Department of Agriculture.* Another aid to the farmer was the

528

See p. T45 for a strategy calling for students to find out about government assistance to farmers and to prepare reports.

United States Department of Agriculture. The work of this Department, which was first organized in 1862, was of great value to farmers. Its many bureaus carried on research dealing with farm problems of all kinds. The Department's scientists studied how to develop better plants and animals, and how to find more uses for crops. Another of its concerns was the wise use, or **conservation,** of land. The Department of Agriculture also published bulletins on an endless number of topics of interest to the farmer.

(3) *Aid to states*. In addition to helping the farmer through the services of the Department of Agriculture, the national government cooperated with the states in encouraging agricultural education. In most states this work was carried on at the state colleges or universities of agriculture. Also, the government made funds available to send experts called county agents to work directly with the farmers. These agents gave advice on all kinds of farm problems.

(4) *Farm loans*. The national government also made it easier for farmers to borrow money to pay for their land or to buy seed and machinery. Government agencies helped farmers get loans at fair rates of interest.

The ups and downs of prices remain a problem. The kinds of government services just described helped American farmers to increase and improve their crops. Nevertheless, farmers still had a hard time getting a fair price for their money crops. Farm prices rose and fell because of conditions over which farmers had no control. As you remember, farmers had a hard time in the years following World War I. During the depression of the 1930's, conditions went from bad to worse. Prices dropped still further, and more and more farmers began to say that the federal government should set a minimum price for farm products. There were sharp differences of opinion on that subject. In Chapter 30 you will read how Congress tackled the problem of farm prices.

▶ **CHECK UP** See Teacher's Key.

1. **(a)** Why did farmers organize the Grange? **(b)** Why did they turn to political parties? **(c)** What political parties did they join?
2. **(a)** What problems did farmers face in the 1920's? **(b)** How did they try to solve those problems?
3. How did each of the following help American farmers? **(a)** State agricultural colleges and universities **(b)** The Department of Agriculture **(c)** County agents **(d)** Government farm loans

CHECK UP ON CHAPTER 24   See Teacher's Key.

Words to Know

1. scythe
2. thresher
3. combine
4. money crop
5. irrigation
6. erode
7. conservation
8. freight rate
9. dry farming
10. bloc
11. cooperative
12. supply and demand

Facts to Remember

1. **(a)** What improvements were made in farm equipment between colonial times and 1865? **(b)** After 1865? **(c)** What effect did the use of improved machinery have on ways of farming?
2. How did western farmers deal with the problem of too little rainfall?

529

Facts to Remember (cont.)

3. Explain how each of the following organizations sought to deal with the problems faced by American farmers. **(a)** National Grange **(b)** Greenback Party **(c)** Populist Party **(d)** Non-Partisan League
4. What was the Interstate Commerce Act, and why was it important to farmers?

Skills to Practice

1. Look back at the pictures in the chapter you have just read (pages 516–529). Find a picture that contains evidence of the accuracy of each of the following statements.
   a. Irrigation is essential to the production of crops in some parts of the United States.
   b. After the Civil War, new machinery made greater farm production possible.
   c. Many farmers of the 1890's joined political organizations as a way of seeking solutions to economic problems.
   d. New political leaders gained national attention by winning the support of American farmers.

2. Read again the paragraph on page 522 that tells how the rule of supply and demand works. Using what you read, decide whether each of the following statements is true or false. If a statement is false, tell how you would change it to make it true.
   a. When a product such as a seasonal fruit or vegetable is hard to get, customers will be more willing to pay a high price for it.
   b. As the supply of a product becomes more plentiful in the market, the price generally goes up.
   c. When the suppliers of a product are able to meet the demand for it, the price is likely to go down.

Questions to Think About

1. Explain how the rule of supply and demand affects prices. Give some examples.
2. Most American farmers probably still think of farming as a way of life as well as a way of earning their living. Explain why that is so.
3. Is it possible for American farmers to have hard times when American men and women who work in business and industry are prosperous? Give reasons for your answer.

Linking Past and Present

Young farmers in America. Many young people in this country and in Canada belong to a 4-H Club. (The 4 H's stand for *head, heart, hands,* and *health.*) These clubs began just before the First World War. They are directed by the United States Department of Agriculture and by the land-grant colleges, and their aim is to train better farmers and better citizens. In 4-H Clubs, farm boys or girls compete to see who can raise the finest cows or pigs or grow the best corn or wheat. Members also study good citizenship and carry on community service projects.

The United States Office of Education also plays an important part in helping to train good farmers. It directs an organization called Future Farmers of America. The FFA cooperates with high schools in setting up courses in agriculture. These courses teach young farmers how to raise better animals and crops, repair farm machinery, and so on. The members of Future Farmers of America often meet for good times too. But the chief goal of the 4-H Clubs and the FFA is to help young Americans become well-informed, efficient farmers.

● Have students read more about 4-H Clubs and Future Farmers of America and report back to class. What benefits do these organizations offer young Americans?

For answers see Teacher's Key.

Ask students to watch for news reports of unusual weather patterns in the United States or throughout the world. Discuss the effects of extreme weather on agriculture.

GAINING SKILL

Reading Maps: Yearly Precipitation

When farmers moved west of the Mississippi River, they quickly learned that much of the region was quite different from the eastern part of the nation. West of the 100th meridian (100° west longitude), trees were scarce, grass was short, and there was very little rain. To grow most crops, farmers had to irrigate their fields or use dry farming methods.

One way to see quickly how the region west of the 100th meridian differed from the eastern part of the nation is to look at a precipitation map. (**Precipitation** includes both rainfall and snowfall, since each is a source of moisture.) On the map below you can see that some parts of the United States get much more precipitation than others.

Use the map to answer the following questions.

1. In an average year, how much precipitation can a farmer in Iowa expect? A farmer in North Carolina? A farmer in Nevada?
2. Where does the map show areas that have over 60 inches of precipitation every year?
3. Through what states does the 100th meridian run?
4. In an average year, how much precipitation can a farmer in eastern Nebraska expect? In western Nebraska?
5. What is the average yearly precipitation in most of the area west of the 100th meridian?

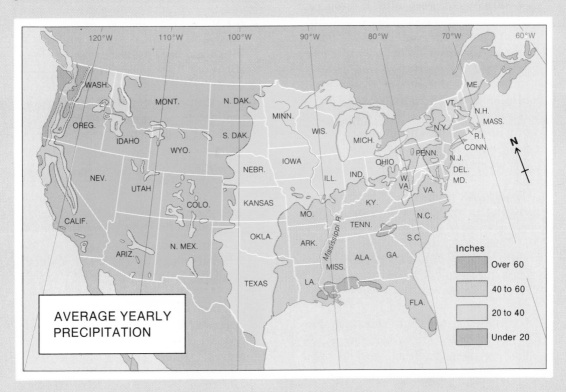

AVERAGE YEARLY PRECIPITATION

Inches
- Over 60
- 40 to 60
- 20 to 40
- Under 20

531

UNDERSTANDING UNIT 7

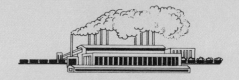

SUMMARY OF IMPORTANT IDEAS

In Unit 7 you have read how American farming and industry developed in the years after the Civil War.

1. After 1865, farming and industry expanded rapidly.

   a. The Homestead Act and the transcontinental railroad encouraged settlers to move to the Great Plains and Rocky Mountain region. Although the Indians fought bitterly against the advancing settlers, the region was opened to mining, ranching, and farming.

   b. The growth of industry was made possible by our great natural resources, a large labor supply, foreign investments, inventions, and improved methods for the mass production of goods. Improved transportation and communication knit the country together and also promoted industrial expansion by speeding up production and selling.

   c. The invention and increased use of farm machinery, as well as improved transportation, revolutionized agriculture.

2. The growth of industry and increased agricultural production were accompanied by a number of problems.

   a. Business tended to follow a "boom, panic, and depression" pattern. The "ups and downs" of business caused suffering to employers and employees and also to the general public.

   b. To further their interests, manufacturers tended to create monopolies. To improve their condition, workers organized unions. The government sought to regulate business, industry, and labor in the public interest.

   c. Farming, like manufacturing, tended to follow a boom and depression pattern. Among the problems of the farmer were debt, high interest rates, overproduction and falling prices, and worn-out land.

   d. To meet these problems farmers formed such organizations as the Grange and also turned to politics. Farmers received much help from the government as well as from agricultural colleges.

UNIT REVIEW   See Teacher's Key.

1. (a) Why did settlers in large numbers move to the Great Plains and Rocky Mountain region after the Civil War? (b) What were the results?

2. (a) How did improved communication and transportation lead to increased production in agriculture and industry? (b) What other factors help to explain the great expansion of American industry after 1865?

3. (a) How did farming change after the Civil War? (b) Why did these changes take place?

4. (a) Why did agriculture and industry tend to follow a "boom, panic, and depression" pattern? (b) What problems developed as a result?

5. (a) How did manufacturers, workers, and farmers try to protect their special interests? (b) How did the government try to help these groups and also the general public?

532

THINGS TO DO

Projects, marked with an asterisk (*) are for the whole class. The others are to be used as your teacher directs.

*1. Start a new set of drill cards for your game "Can You Identify?" A quick drill at the beginning of the class period is a good way to learn the important names, dates, and events you should know.

*2. Make a map of the last frontier in the United States showing the following: the Great Plains region; Rocky Mountain region; Pacific Northwest and Pacific Southwest; the route of the transcontinental railroad; the cattle country and the long drive; the wheat lands; the mining territory.

*3. Make a time line showing important inventions that helped make the United States the greatest manufacturing nation in the world.

4. Make a pictorial map of the United States showing important manufacturing cities and the articles manufactured there. You may draw illustrations or paste in small pictures from magazines or newspapers.

5. Write a newspaper article on one of these events: (a) the completion of the transcontinental railroad, (b) the completion of the transatlantic cable, (c) the Wright brothers' flight, (d) the invention of the telephone or the wireless, (e) Charles Lindbergh's historic flight to Paris.

6. Write and present to the class an imaginary dialogue (conversation) between: (a) an Indian and a white settler on the Great Plains, (b) a woman born in 1850 and her granddaughter born in 1900, (c) James J. Hill and John D. Rockefeller, (d) a sheepherder and a rancher.

7. Write a page or two in a diary that might have been written by: (a) Charles Goodyear, (b) a girl whose family owned one of the first automobiles, (c) a worker in a factory in the late 1800's, (d) a cowboy in the days of the open range.

8. Select a committee to prepare a report to the class on the Indians of North America. Let each member of the committee choose one of the following topics: (a) where the Indians came from and what clothing they wore; (b) the most important tribes and the regions in which they lived; (c) food, homes, and handicrafts of the Indians; (d) religion, music, and amusements of the Indians.

9. Find pictures in books or magazines that show how farm methods and machinery have changed in modern times.

10. Find out more about the main achievements of one of the following: (a) Charles Lindbergh, (b) Amelia Earhart, (c) James J. Hill, (d) Andrew Carnegie, (e) John D. Rockefeller, (f) Samuel Gompers, (g) John L. Lewis.

UNIT **8**

Left to right: baseball players, 1870's; immigrants entering New York harbor; suffrage stamp; American street scene, early 1900's.

New Conditions Bring Changes in American Life

1865–1965 See p. T47 for a unit preview strategy. See pp. T58–T71 for lists of useful books and audiovisual aids.

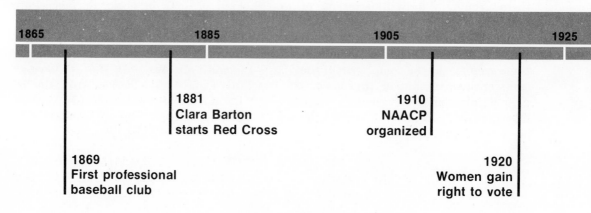

1865		1885		1905		1925

1881
Clara Barton
starts Red Cross

1910
NAACP
organized

1869
First professional
baseball club

1920
Women gain
right to vote

534

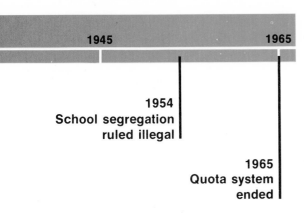

1945   1965

1954
School segregation
ruled illegal

1965
Quota system
ended

In earlier units you have followed the march of our young nation's progress. But what is a nation? A nation is made up of people who have the will to make a great dream come true. This unit, then, is about the American people in the century after the Civil War. Chapter 25 describes the effects of industrialization. You will find that our population grew rapidly as millions of people came to this country in search of a better life. Meanwhile, ways of living in cities and towns and on farms changed. Chapter 26 tells how the dream of America as a land of opportunity came closer to reality. It also describes changes that were taking place in education, in literature and the arts, and in the use of leisure time.

535

Vocabulary preview: immigrant, quota, rural, urban, tenement house, suburb, metropolitan area, megalopolis

Industrialization Changes Life in Cities and on Farms

1865–1965   See pp. T47–T48 for chapter teaching strategies.

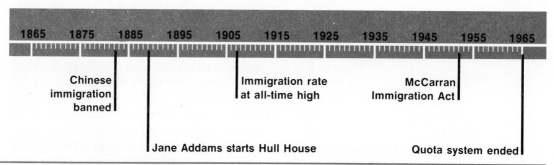

| 1865 | 1875 | 1885 | 1895 | 1905 | 1915 | 1925 | 1935 | 1945 | 1955 | 1965 |

Chinese immigration banned

Immigration rate at all-time high

McCarran Immigration Act

Jane Addams starts Hull House

Quota system ended

What this chapter is about —

It was not until August, 1956, that death came to the last veteran of the Union army. This Civil War veteran, Albert Woolson, had been born in 1847 and lived to be 109 years old. Astonishing as it may seem, Mr. Woolson's life spanned more than half the history of the United States!

Think of the changes that this man saw in our ways of living. When he was born, there were only 29 states in the Union. The population of the United States was about 23 million, and the largest city in the country had only

536

500,000 inhabitants. At the time of Mr. Woolson's birth there were no electric lights, no telephones, and, of course, no radio or television. The invention of the automobile was about 45 years in the future. The first college football game would not be played for 22 years. Basketball would not even be invented until Mr. Woolson was about 50 years old. The list of changes could go on and on.

In this chapter you will read about some of those changes that took place during Albert Woolson's lifetime. You will learn how the growth of industry brought large numbers of men, women, and children to our shores. In addition, you will see how industrialization caused striking changes in the way Americans lived in cities, on farms, and in towns. As you read about the effects of industrialization, look for answers to the following questions:

1. How did the growth of industry encourage immigration?
2. Why did cities grow so rapidly in the century after the Civil War?
3. How did ways of living change in the cities?
4. How did ways of living change on farms and in small towns?

1 How Did the Growth of Industry Encourage Immigration?

The United States is a nation of immigrants. The dream of America as a "land of the second chance" has played an important part in the growth of the United States. People of other countries have long felt, in the words of the American poet William Cullen Bryant,

> There's freedom at thy gates, and rest
> For Earth's downtrodden and
> oppressed,
> A shelter for the hunted head,
> For the starved laborer toil and
> bread.

Drawn by this dream, immigrants from many lands have come in search of freedom, homes, and jobs. (**Immigrants** are people who move from one country to settle permanently in another.)

At first the stream of immigrants to America was small. During the 1600's and 1700's, it took great courage to cross the Atlantic and establish a new home in America. As settlements were started along the Atlantic coast, more people set out for the English colonies from their homes in Europe. Still, the number of newcomers to America's eastern shores remained small for two hundred years after the first English settlements. Most of these early immigrants were farmers. But others were merchants, craftworkers, laborers, lawyers, and so on.

Because the thirteen colonies were under British control, most of the immigrants who came in the 1600's were of British stock, that is, from England, Scotland, or Wales. Then in the 1700's sizable numbers of Scotch-Irish (page 128) and Germans came to the English colonies as well. As we read earlier, many of the Scotch-Irish headed for the frontier. They pushed their way inland in Pennsylvania, Virginia, the Carolinas, and even beyond the mountains into Kentucky and Tennessee. Many Germans settled in southern Pennsylva-

537

See p. T47 for a strategy calling for students to examine why immigrants came to the United States.

nia. Known as Pennsylvania Dutch, they built sturdy stone houses and great barns on their fertile and prosperous farms (page 114).

We should remember, however, that there were some people who did not come to America as willing immigrants. For a long time Africans were brought to America against their will. Instead of coming in search of freedom and better living conditions, they were seized by slave traders in Africa and sold into slavery in America. There were others too who were not immigrants at all, but who found themselves living in the United States when their homelands were taken over by this country. These included the people who lived in the lands acquired from Mexico after the Mexican War.

The growth of industry attracts more immigrants. No one knows exactly how many people came to what is now the United States. In fact, no attempt was made to count immigrants until 1820. Since that time, however, more than 48 million men, women, and children have come to our shores. (See the graph on this page.)

Why did the small stream of immigrants in the early 1800's broaden into a mighty flood during the late 1800's and early 1900's? The answer is that a growing America offered great opportunities. During these years, for one thing, many immigrants came to America because it was easy to obtain land for farming. As the frontier moved ever westward, new groups of families, many of them immigrants, established farms on lands which had formerly been forest or endless prairie.

Even more important in bringing immigrants to our shores was the growth of industry. You remember how factories and mills spread throughout the Northeast during the first half of the 1800's (Chapter 14). Many workers were needed to operate the factory machines. Others were needed to ship and sell manufactured goods. The building and running of railroads also opened up more jobs. After 1865, the number of workers needed in industry grew even faster. Workers by the millions were needed to dig in the mines, construct buildings and bridges, build and operate machines, and transport goods from factories to the people who would use or sell them.

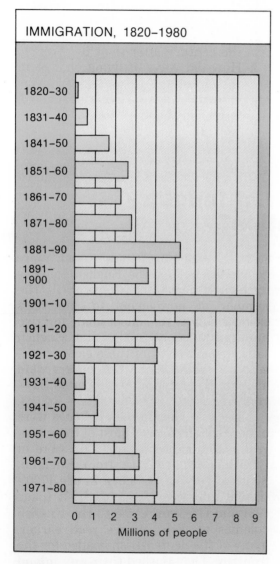

IMMIGRATION, 1820–1980

Millions of people

GRAPH STUDY   See Teacher's Key.
The number of immigrants during ten-year periods from 1820 to 1980 is shown on this graph. In which period did immigration reach a peak?

538

See p. T47 for a strategy asking students to use the graph on this page to study patterns of immigration.

Large numbers of people came to the United States from Ireland in the early 1800's. Here, Irish immigrants arrive at New York City.

Immigrants come from northern and western Europe. People from many lands swelled the growing tide of immigration. Until the 1890's, these waves of newcomers came chiefly from northern and western Europe.

Irish immigration. From 1820 until 1850, more people came to the United States from Ireland than from any other country. Many Irish left their homeland to escape harsh British rule. Also, great numbers left Ireland in the 1840's after crop failures led to hunger and even starvation.

For the most part, Irish immigrants settled in America's cities. Many of them took jobs in industry and as police officers and fire fighters. Others rose to positions of influence and leadership in local, state, and national government. Thousands of Irish workers helped to build canals and railroads, thus playing a valuable part in the growth of modern America.

German immigration. The next great wave of immigrants came from Germany. Political unrest and the failure of a revolution in the late 1840's caused many Germans to seek freedom in America. Thousands of other Germans came to earn a better living. From 1850 to 1890, Germany led all countries in the number of immigrants that came to America. For the most part, the newcomers from Germany moved to the Middle West. Great numbers became farmers and helped to develop new states in that region. Others gave such cities as Milwaukee, St. Louis, and Cincinnati a background of German customs and ways of living.

Scandinavian immigration. While the German immigration was still at its height, large numbers of immigrants came from the Scandinavian countries — Sweden, Norway, and Denmark. The Scandinavian immigration reached its peak in the 1880's. Like many of the Germans, the Scandinavians were skilled farmers. Many established farms in the prairie lands of Minnesota, the Dakotas, Illinois, Wisconsin, and Iowa.

The sources of immigration shift to eastern and southern Europe. From about 1890 to the 1920's, most immigrants to the United States came not from northern and western Europe, but

539

● Have students study the world map in the atlas and note the countries that make up northern and western Europe.

Many Scandinavian immigrants settled in the Middle West. This family lived in Madison, Wisconsin, in the 1870's.

from southern and eastern Europe. Newcomers poured into the United States from Italy, Russia, Poland, Austria-Hungary, and the Balkan countries. It was during these same years that the rate of immigration reached an all-time high.

People came to the United States from southern and eastern Europe for the same reasons as earlier immigrants. They came to seek a better chance for themselves and their children in a country that offered real opportunities. But there were additional reasons for the great flood of immigrants from that region. By the late 1800's many countries in southern and eastern Europe were overcrowded. Governments therefore changed old policies that had made it difficult for people to leave their homes. Now they encouraged people to go to America. In addition, cheaper transportation became available. Steamship lines scheduled regular trips between the United States and ports in the Mediterranean and Baltic seas, making it easier for people to come to this country.

Many of the immigrants from southern and eastern Europe found jobs in mines and factories. Thus they settled in industrial cities and communities. Other immigrants entered business in the large cities and so aided in the commercial growth of our country.

The Jews in America. Many of the newer immigrants were Jews who came from eastern Europe. They did not come from a particular country, since for hundreds of years the Jewish people had been scattered in many countries. They were held together by their belief in the same religion, Judaism.

Because of persecution from time to time in one country or another, Jews have come to America since the 1600's. Some Jews sought religious freedom in colonial Rhode Island. During the Revolutionary War, Haym Salomon, a Jewish banker of Philadelphia, raised large sums of money (much of which came from his own fortune) to aid the fight for

Have students study the world map in the atlas and note the countries that make up eastern and southern Europe.

independence. Jewish immigrants came in larger numbers in the late 1800's. More than two million Jews, many fleeing from Russia, came to the United States from 1870 to 1900. Many found jobs in cities as tailors, garment workers, and laborers. Some became doctors, lawyers, scientists, or business leaders. Still others enriched America's art, literature, music, and theater.

Immigrants come from other regions. Europeans were not the only people to leave their homes and move to America. Asian immigrants, mostly from China, began coming to this country in the days of the California gold rush (page 393). Chinese workers also helped build the transcontinental railroads in the 1860's (page 460). Gradually, most immigrants from Asia settled in large cities.

During the late 1800's immigrants began arriving in the United States from French-speaking Canada. Many found work in New England textile mills. There were also immigrants from Mexico, the West Indies, and other Latin American countries. Some took jobs as farm workers, and others settled in this country's cities. Their numbers increased greatly in the early 1900's.

Immigrants face problems. Life was difficult for the millions of immigrants who came to our shores. Most of the newcomers had little or no knowledge of English. Yet in order to get work, buy food and clothing, and find their way from one place to another, they needed to know at least a few words of English. Newcomers also had to get used to customs that seemed strange to them. It was only natural that many chose to live near earlier immigrants from their own country. Then they were able not only to speak the language they knew best but to share customs and memories of the old country. Whole sections of cities and towns, therefore, were settled by people of a single nationality, who formed a distinct community.

Most immigrants had little or no money when they arrived in America. Finding work, moreover, was difficult unless the newcomers had special skills. Often they had no choice but to accept the hardest and lowest-paying jobs.

Between 1890 and 1920 most immigrants came from southern and eastern Europe. Like immigrants before them, they sought the opportunity to start a new life.

Newcomers worked hard to adjust to life in America. This school in San Francisco held classes for Chinese immigrants who wanted to study their new country's history. Italian immigrants learned English from the book shown at the right.

Immigrants become less welcome. In its earlier years, the United States generally welcomed immigrants. But
● not all people were friendly to immigrants. By the closing years of the 1800's, many Americans began to wonder if unlimited immigration was wise. This feeling grew stronger as the number of immigrants increased. Could such great numbers of immigrants be taught American ways? Were they a threat to our customs and traditions? In raising these questions, some Americans pointed to the foreign settlements in the large cities. Here, they stated, was proof that immigrants were not learning our ways of living. Those who opposed the flood of newcomers also argued that many immigrants worked for low pay. Because of this, they said, immigrants were the cause of low wages for all American workers.

Limits are placed on the number of immigrants. As a result of these fears, people began to say that immigration should be restricted. Even as early as 1882 a law had been passed forbidding the immigration of Chinese workers. Californians, in particular, objected to letting in Chinese, as well as Japanese, because they worked for low wages. From time to time other laws were passed to limit immigration. In 1917, for example, a law barred immigrants

542

● Tell students that this fear of foreigners is called *xenophobia.*

● See p. T47 for a strategy asking students to put together a bulletin board display featuring the growth of cities.

who could not read. Then, from 1921 to 1924, a series of new laws limiting immigration was passed. The number of immigrants to be admitted from each country was known as a **quota** (KWOH-tuh). Quotas were based on the number of persons of each nationality living in the United States. The quotas set for countries in southern and eastern Europe were much smaller than those set for northern and western Europe.

After World War II, millions of Europeans uprooted by the war sought new homes. As a result, the United States admitted more than 400,000 displaced Europeans between 1948 and 1952. Most of these people were counted as part of future quotas for their countries. A new immigration law, the McCarran Act, was passed in 1952. It continued the quota system, though it lifted the ban against immigration from Asian countries. The McCarran Act limited quota immigration to about 155,000 persons per year.

The quota system is dropped. Many people felt that the quota system put unfair restrictions on would-be immigrants from southern and eastern Europe. Efforts to repeal this system were successful in 1965 when Congress adopted a new immigration law. Total immigration from countries outside the Western Hemisphere was set at 170,000 annually, and no more than 20,000 immigrants were to come from any one country each year. The law provided, however, that members of families of American citizens might enter without being counted as part of the total immigration figure. The new law also set a ceiling of 120,000 immigrants a year from other countries of the Western Hemisphere. Previously immigration from these countries had been unlimited.

▶ **CHECK UP**   See Teacher's Key.

1. During the 1600's and 1700's from what European countries did most immigrants to America come?
2. **(a)** Why did the number of immigrants to America increase greatly in the late 1800's and early 1900's? **(b)** Where did many of the immigrants in those years come from?
3. **(a)** What problems have immigrants faced in this country? **(b)** Why did some Americans want to restrict immigration? **(c)** How was immigration limited?

2 Why Did Cities Grow So Rapidly in the Century After the Civil War?

The beginnings of many American cities stretch far back in our history. Cities
● grew at a rapid rate after 1865, however, both in size and number, as the United States became an industrial nation.

Each community has its own special history, but in some ways the
★ growth of all cities and towns has been much the same. The following description will show you how one city might have grown.

A village is settled on a river. In the late 1700's a pioneer family stepped from the deep woods and stood upon the banks of a stream. They were looking for a place to build their home. After exploring the surrounding country for a few days, they decided to build their cabin near the river.

Soon other pioneer families came, and a village grew up. In addition to the homes of the settlers, the village had a

★ Have students read about the growth of several American cities in "Linking Past and Present" (p. 554).

Seattle, located on the east shore of Puget Sound, is the largest city in the Pacific Northwest. Compare the view of the city today with the picture taken in 1884 (above).

blacksmith shop, a schoolhouse, a general store, and other shops. There was a mill to grind flour, its huge water wheel turned by the flow of water from the river. A sawmill also was set up.

Steamboats and a canal help the village grow. In about 1825 a canal was dug to connect the settlement with another, larger river which ran into the Atlantic Ocean. On this larger river were ports where big ships could load and unload their cargoes. The villagers spoke of the steamboats which moved easily up and down the large river. "Why not on our river?" they asked. Before long, steamboats were busily puffing along between the tree-shaded banks of this river. As commerce moved up and down the river, much of it was unloaded at the wharves of the village

for shipment on the canal. Warehouses were built. More and more people took part in trade.

The village becomes a city. Fifteen years after the canal was opened, workers started laying tracks for a railroad which was to run through the town. Soon their work was finished, and then they moved on to extend the track farther and farther west. Every man, woman, and child in town gathered at the railroad station to watch the first train come puffing out of the east and rumble to a stop at the new station. Before long, however, railroads had reached the town from other directions, and trains were a common sight.

So many families came to live in the town that it could now be called a city. Factories and mills had been es-

● See p. T47 for a strategy calling for students to construct a table using the statistics in this paragraph.

tablished because the city was a center of transportation. Hundreds of workers had jobs in the factories and mills. Because the city was a junction where several railroad lines crossed, large yards were developed for handling freight, assembling trains, and making repairs. Many people worked in these railroad yards. The number of factories continued to grow because for each new one there were advantages in having the others close by. As the number of workers increased, the city got bigger and bigger.

American cities increase in size and number. The growth of the city we have described above is just an example of what took place all over the United States. This was especially true during the century after the Civil War. Why did cities grow more rapidly during that period than ever before? There were four main reasons: (1) the growth of population; (2) the growth of industry; (3) the movement of people from farm areas to the cities; and (4) the development of new methods of construction and of transportation and communication.

The nation's population grows. Only about forty million people lived in the United States in 1870. By 1960 we had almost 180 million. Today we have more than 230 million. What caused this increase in the number of Americans? In part it came from the birth of new citizens. In part, also, it resulted from the huge numbers of immigrants who came from abroad. (See the graph on page 538.) As you have already read, many of these new Americans settled in cities.

The growth of industry affects cities. Spurred by the needs of the Union army during the Civil War, many northern business leaders built new factories and new warehouses. As industry grew, railroads reached more cities and the number of factories and business offices multiplied. It was natural that the people who worked in factories and shops should live in the cities where their jobs were located. Early each morning the city streets were filled with crowds of people hurrying to the day's work. In the evening, city traffic flowed just as strongly from factories to homes.

Farm people move to cities. New job opportunities in industry drew more and more of our nation's growing population to cities. You have already read about new inventions and new methods of farming that enabled farmers to raise larger crops with less labor (Chapter 24). As a result, fewer farm workers were needed to grow food to supply the nation. People from farm areas, therefore, flocked to cities to find jobs.

See Teacher's Key.

MAP STUDY

In 1880, nineteen cities had a population of 100,000 or more.
(a) Were most of these cities located in the eastern or western half of the country?
(b) Which cities had a population of 500,000 or more?

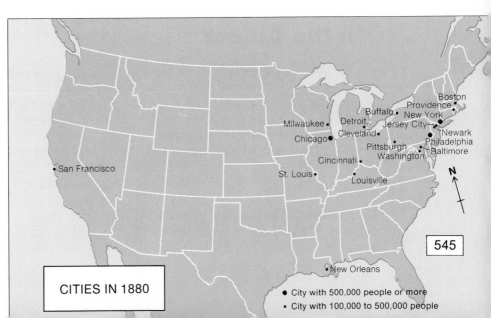

CITIES IN 1880

- City with 500,000 people or more
- City with 100,000 to 500,000 people

545

New inventions make possible the growth of cities. Cities could not have grown without the development of new ways of doing things after 1865. One of the most familiar features of our cities, for example, is their tall buildings — their "skyscrapers." Such buildings could not have been erected before iron and steel came into widespread use as building materials. To take another example, nobody would want to walk to the upper floors of a skyscraper. Tall buildings, therefore, require elevators. In 1857 an elevator with safety features was installed in a building in New York City. Fifteen years later an improved elevator was invented, and taller buildings became more practical.

As cities grew ever larger, improved transportation was also needed. American inventiveness supplied the answer. Cities had "elevated railroads," with small steam locomotives pulling cars on tracks raised above the streets. Soon electricity replaced steam power. No longer did the elevated railroads shower sparks on the people below and pour smoke into the windows of nearby buildings. Another important development was the telephone, invented in the 1870's. City dwellers could now communicate directly with each other, instead of depending on hired messengers.

The United States becomes a nation of city dwellers. For many years, our country had been a nation of farmers and of dwellers in small towns. In other words, the United States was still mostly **rural.** As late as 1880, only about two people out of every ten lived in cities or in towns of over 2,500 people. But during the late 1800's, the **urban** population (people living in cities) was growing fast. By 1920, five out of every ten Americans lived in communities of more than 2,500 people. Now more than seven out of ten people live in such communities. In addition, business and industry have spread from the Northeast to all parts of the nation.

▶ **CHECK UP**   See Teacher's Key.

1. **(a)** How did a typical town come to be started? **(b)** What kinds of developments helped it grow?
2. How did each of the following stimulate the growth of cities? **(a)** Immigration **(b)** The growth of industry **(c)** Improved methods of farming **(d)** New inventions
3. When did the United States become an urban nation?

3   How Did Ways of Living Change in the Cities?

Cities have changed enormously since the 1880's. To get an idea of how they have changed, let us visit a city of 1880 and a modern city. Our visit to the city of the 1880's will be made with an imaginary couple, John and Alice Osgood.

A CITY IN THE 1880'S

The visitors go to the city by train. The Osgoods decided one day to travel by train to a large city several hundred miles from their home. Since the journey was to be a long one, they reserved space on a sleeping car. Pullman sleeping cars, with seats that could be made into beds at night, were large, comfortable, and brightly lighted. ★

During their long journey, the Osgoods had a choice of ways to get their meals. The train stopped at stations for twenty minutes at breakfast, lunch, and dinner time. At these stops they could rush into the station restau-

As this picture of New York's Broadway shows, city streets in the 1880's were filled with all sorts of horse-drawn vehicles.

rant and eat a hurried meal. Or, if they chose, they could have their meals, elegantly prepared and served, in a dining car on the train.

At last the Osgoods reached the city. They got out of the train in a large station. It was one of the showplaces of the city, with high ceilings and decorated stone walls. The Osgoods made their way out of the railroad station and rode in a horse-drawn cab to a hotel.

The country visitors tour the city. To John and Alice Osgood this city of 100,000 looked tremendous. Today a city of that size does not seem large. But in 1880 only nineteen cities in the country had as many as 100,000 people. Only three of those cities had populations of more than half a million — New York, Philadelphia, and Chicago.

The Osgoods enjoyed seeing so many high buildings. The tallest were a dozen stories high! They also noticed that the streets were filled with horse-drawn vehicles of every sort. These included wagons, carts, and streetcars (the electric streetcar had not yet been invented).

Above the vehicles and the people was a maze of wires. In 1880 these were mostly telegraph wires. If the Osgoods had delayed their visit for a few years, they would have seen electric and tele-phone wires too. The poles then sprouted new crossbars, and the wires threatened to blot out the sun. Indeed, in a few years some cities began to require that wires be placed underground. If New York had been the city visited by the Osgoods, they would have seen something else overhead. The elevated railroad, or the "El" as it was called, had been built in 1869.

Many people live in slum areas. As they walked about the city, John and Alice Osgood noticed that in some parts of the city there were single-family houses. In other sections, however, there were dingy **tenement houses** (large buildings, often in run-down condition, which housed many families). The crowded tenement sections of many cities had become slums, where people lived in poverty.

When John and Alice Osgood returned home after a week of sightseeing, they agreed that the city had many exciting things. But they had learned that there was an unhappy side to city life as well.

Americans fight slum conditions. Fortunately there were men and women in the United States who were determined to do something about slum conditions. One of these persons was Jacob Riis (REES). Riis had come to America

547

● See pp. T47–T48 for a strategy asking students to find out more about their community.

from Denmark when he was 21 years old. While getting his start in this new land, Riis lived in the slums of New York City. He became a newspaper reporter and wrote several books to draw the public's attention to the problems existing in large cities.

Another person concerned about slum conditions was Jane Addams. Brought up in a comfortable midwestern home, Miss Addams was deeply troubled when she first saw the slums of Chicago. She made up her mind to do what she could to improve conditions among the poor. In an old mansion in the heart of Chicago's tenement district Jane Addams established Hull House in 1889. Here she helped the families of the neighborhood. Mothers who had jobs or were sick could leave their children in nurseries where they would be sure of good care. Nourishing food was provided for the underfed children of the neighborhood. Inexpensive rooms in good surroundings were found for working women who needed a decent place to live.

The example of Jane Addams inspired other people to action. They banded together to improve conditions in other cities. They organized houses like Hull House. They formed boys' and girls' clubs to furnish wholesome activities — bowling, swimming, hiking, team sports, and study groups.

THE MODERN AMERICAN CITY

● How different are our modern cities from the one visited by the Osgoods in 1880! The most obvious difference, of course, is that today's cities are much larger. By 1980 there were six cities in the United States of more than one million people. Another sixteen cities had between half a million and a million inhabitants. All together, 169 cities had populations of more than 100,000.

Suburbs develop near cities. Another difference is that our cities have

spread into the regions around them. The fast-growing cities of the late 1800's were noisy, crowded, smoky, dirty. Would it be possible, wondered some city dwellers, to work in an office in the city, yet live in the green and quiet country nearby? In the mid-1800's a dozen people, at the end of the business day, boarded a train from New York City to Greenwich, Connecticut. When the train slowed before crossing a bridge near their homes, they jumped to the ground. In the mornings they rode back to the city on the train.

From this small beginning has grown the **suburb,** so familiar in the United States today. Suburban communities have grown up around all our large cities. From the suburbs large numbers of people go to jobs in the city each morning and return to their homes each night. In earlier days they went by train and then by electric railways. Later they began to travel by bus and automobile.

Cars became, in fact, a problem for modern cities. Countless miles of broad, smooth streets were needed to handle the millions of cars that Americans drove. Great express highways were built to let the cars enter and leave cities quickly. Often buildings were torn down to make way for the new roads and parking areas. Now, every morning and evening, highways crowded with cars on their way to and from the city are a common sight.

Cities provide necessary services. The smaller cities of earlier days did not require many of the services we take for ★ granted nowadays. As cities grew larger, however, they needed ample supplies of pure water, good sewage systems, and well-paved streets. They needed regular garbage-collection systems. They needed police and fire-fighting forces. Some of these services were slow in coming. But come they did. Water, for example, often is piped from lakes and streams far from the city.

548

★ Have students read more about occupations in "Thinking About Careers" (p. 718). Ask students to collect pictures of people employed in public-service occupations.

People in America's Story

she wrote and lectured on a wide variety of topics, worked to reform child-labor laws, and was a leader in the women's suffrage movement.

JANE ADDAMS

A leader in the movement to improve life in the cities, Jane Addams combined her concern for people with great administrative ability.

Many Hull House programs were aimed at helping the children of families in need.

Cooking classes for young people (below) were just one of the many programs offered at Hull House. Jane Addams contributed energy and new ideas to other movements besides urban reform. But the example set by Hull House was her greatest success.

The rapid growth of American cities created a need for large, professional police forces to keep order and protect life and property.

● Remind students of the meaning of the prefix *sub*. (Under or near.)

This service provides not only drinking water but water for bathing, cleaning, fighting fires, and industry.

Buildings grow taller. Many of our modern cities have tall, soaring skylines, quite different from earlier cities. When the Osgoods paid their visit to the city in 1880, large buildings were made of stone and brick. The use of these materials placed a limit on the height of buildings. Thus, the Monadnock Building in Chicago, erected in the early 1890's, had walls fifteen feet thick at the base to support the weight of its sixteen stories.

As more businesses crowded into big cities, land became scarce and expensive. As you read on page 546, the only way to find the space for more businesses was to erect taller buildings. When new building materials — first iron and then steel — came into use, the buildings could go up and up without thick walls. Now we have skyscrapers more than 100 stories high.

Means of transportation and lighting change. Visitors to the city nowadays might make their journey, like the Osgoods, by train. But they can also travel by airplane. Or they can take a bus or drive to the city in their own car. Once they arrive, they are caught up in the swarming automobile traffic. An elevated railroad — electric now, of course — may still exist. They may find, in addition, subways in the larger cities. In most cities, buses have replaced streetcars.

The streets of our cities are bright with electric lights. Shops keep their display windows lighted until late in the evening. Advertising signs stare or blink at the passer-by. Until the neon tube was invented in the 1920's, all the lights were white. Now you see electric signs in red, green, blue, and other colors.

Urban areas continue to spread. A final way in which our cities differ from those of the 1880's is that modern American cities have grown into **metropolitan areas.** A metropolitan area refers

Firefighting forces were another service that cities needed.

550

to the area covered by a central city and its surrounding suburbs. In a metropolitan area people who live in the suburbs depend on the central city for jobs, stores, and services. The suburbs, in turn, provide housing for many people who work in the city's offices, stores, and factories.

By the mid-1900's some metropolitan areas had spread so far that they began to blend with neighboring cities. It was hard to see where one metropolitan area stopped and another began. When several cities form a single urban area, that area is called a **megalopolis** (meg-uh-LOP-uh-lis). The largest megalopolis in this country extends from Boston, Massachusetts to Washington, D.C. The California coast has a megalopolis running from San Francisco through Los Angeles to San Diego. A third such area, located on the southern shore of Lake Michigan, includes Milwaukee, Chicago, and northwest ● Indiana.

▶ **CHECK UP**   See Teacher's Key.

1. **(a)** Describe a typical American city of 1880. **(b)** What are slums?
2. Why did suburbs develop around modern cities?
3. **(a)** What services do modern cities provide? **(b)** How have transportation and lighting been improved in American cities? **(c)** How have cities dealt with the problems of traffic?
4. **(a)** What is a metropolitan area? **(b)** A megalopolis?

4 How Did Ways of Living Change on Farms and in Small Towns?

Just as new inventions altered life in the cities, they also changed ways of living on the farms. We learned in Chapter 24 how new machines and methods affected working conditions on America's farms. But how did industrialization change the daily living of farm families? We can get an idea of the differences by comparing farm life in the 1880's with farm life in more recent times.

An Iowa farm in the 1880's. It is night over the wide lands of Iowa. In the darkness each farmhouse, set far from its neighbors, seems as lonely as a ship at sea. Inside the Jones farmhouse, John Jones is reading a farmers' news-
★ paper by the light of a kerosene lamp. He is tired from a long day of hard work, aided only by horses and the few machines they pull.

Martha Jones sits near him, bending over a pile of clothes that need mending. She too has had a long day.

Cooking the family's meals on a wood-burning stove is not a simple task. Moreover, this was her day to do the wash, a weekly chore that meant pumping water by hand, heating the water on the stove, and scrubbing the clothes in wooden tubs. She knows that tomorrow she will have a long day of ironing.

The children have finished their work for the day too. They have fed the cows and chickens, rubbed down the horses, and cut kindling wood. Now they are studying the lessons they must have ready for school in the morning.

The Jones family does not often see other people. To visit friends means hitching the horses to the wagon and setting out for a slow drive over rough roads. They do meet their neighbors at church on Sunday. Now and again they drive to the small town nearby. There at the general store they trade farm produce for the articles they need. At   551

Rectangular fields give a checkerboard look to this farm scene. The people on these farms live much like the people on the Iowa farm described below.

times the family attends a meeting of the Grange. The family also goes to hear speeches at big political gatherings when an election is near.

An Iowa farm in modern America. Now it is another evening in Iowa many years later. Al Jones, great-grandson of John Jones, sits with his wife Beth and their children in their comfortable living room. Electric lamps light the room, and two teenagers are viewing their favorite television program. At the moment their father is reading a farm bulletin that describes a new formula for feeding cattle. Their mother is on the telephone, calling members of a committee that is planning the program for the next PTA meeting at the regional high school. She has time for such activities because central heating, hot and cold running water, and electric appliances have made housework easier. In fact, Beth Jones also has time to work with her husband in the management of their farm.

Farm life is no longer as lonely as it once was. The telephone brings the Jones family into close contact with their neighbors. Shopping in Des Moines or Chicago is no problem because of the family car. Next Saturday the whole family will drive to a nearby city for a football game.

As you read in the last chapter, running a farm in modern America is really a business. For that reason, Beth and Al Jones need much more information and more machinery than the Joneses of 1880 did. The radio and television bring them the daily weather forecast and market report. Trucks, tractors, combines, and other machinery make it easier for them to run a farm of 480 acres than it was for their great-grandparents to farm 160 acres. It is true that Al and Beth Jones have problems that never troubled farmers in the past. They must keep careful records in order to prepare their federal and state income tax reports. They must keep well informed about international events that might affect crop prices. And now they have a new problem, one that even their parents would not have had to contend with. Some of their neighbors have just sold their farms to a developer who is planning to build new houses for people who work in town but want to live in the country. Al and Beth are wondering what that will mean for farming in their area.

The small town sees many changes. Like the city and the farm, the small town has changed a great deal in this century. To understand what kinds of changes these were, let us make an

552

imaginary visit to such a town. We will visit young Lisbeth Brown and her
● mother. They are reading a journal that Lisbeth's great-grandmother wrote about her childhood in Waterville, the town where the Browns still live.

"I moved to Waterville when I was a girl," her great-grandmother had written. "The town was very small in those days. It hasn't grown much since then, though it has grown some. But the
★ greatest changes are in our comforts and conveniences.

"When I was young, we had harder work to do. Each house stood by itself, in the midst of its own lawn. We had to draw water by pumping it from the well, with a hand pump. Only a few of us had central heating in our homes; in many houses there were only stoves and fireplaces. Even if we had central heat, we had to shovel coal into the furnaces by hand. Our light came from kerosene lamps. What a chore cleaning those lamps used to be!

"None of the streets were paved in those early days. They were dusty in summer and muddy in spring and fall. The sidewalks were made of wood. We had only a few gas lamps to light our way if we walked anywhere after dark. In the country outside of town it was

dark as dark could be. As for amusements, we made them ourselves. We got together for parties and sang or played games. When a circus or other show came to town, we had great times. And the Fourth of July was always a special day, with parades and picnics."

Mrs. Brown put down the journal.
"Life was different for grandmother, wasn't it Lisbeth?" she asked. "Today we have television and radio, and we see and hear the same things the people in big cities do. We get around more by car and in planes. In my grandmother's day people could not travel far except by train. There are other changes too. At one time, some young people were leaving our town for good. They believed there were more opportunities elsewhere. In recent years, however, our town has been getting bigger. People have been moving here from cities. I wonder where you will choose to live, Lisbeth, when you grow up."

▶ **CHECK UP**   See Teacher's Key.

1. What are some ways in which inventions have changed life on American farms?
2. How has life in small towns changed?

CHECK UP ON CHAPTER 25   See Teacher's Key.

Words to Know

1. immigrant
2. urban
3. refugee
4. quota
5. rural
6. suburb
7. central city
8. tenement house
9. metropolitan area
10. megalopolis

Facts to Remember

1. (a) From what countries or continents did most immigrants to America come in the 1700's? (b) In the first half of the 1800's? (c) In the period from 1890 to the 1920's?

2. (a) What kinds of problems have immigrants faced during their first years in this country? (b) What advantage did immigrants from England have over other newcomers?

3. (a) Name three trends that caused cities to grow fast in the late 1800's. (b) Why were skyscrapers and elevators important in the growth of cities?

4. Identify (a) Jacob Riis and (b) Jane Addams. Who were they and why was their work important?

5. (a) Name three ways in which modern farm life is different from farm life in

553

★ See p. T48 for a strategy calling for students to discuss the changes on farms and in small towns during the past century.

the 1880's. **(b)** Name three ways in which life in America's small towns has changed since then.

Skills to Practice

1. Look at the pictures in this chapter and read their captions. Which picture or caption gives evidence of the truth of each of the following statements?
   a. Many large American cities grew up on the banks of rivers or shores of oceans.
   b. By the late 1800's some American cities had elevated railway systems.
   c. Schools taught immigrants American ways.
2. Arrange the following events or developments in the order in which they happened. Start with the earliest event or development.
   a. For a period of forty years, the great majority of immigrants are from Germany.
   b. The United States acquires land from Mexico, thus adding many Spanish-speaking people to its population.
   c. Congress passes a law that ends the quota system.
   d. For about a century, most immigrants are from England, Scotland, and Wales.
   e. Congress passes laws that set limits on immigration by establishing a quota system.

Questions to Think About

1. Why do some people prefer to live in suburbs or towns while other people prefer to live in cities? Compare the advantages and disadvantages of living in each kind of area.
2. City governments today are expected to provide certain kinds of services, such as the piping of clean water into homes, office buildings, and public places. **(a)** What are other examples of "necessary" city services? **(b)** Why is it difficult for individuals to provide those services for themselves?

Linking Past and Present

Where do cities grow? Why do cities grow up in one place rather than in another? One reason is that certain locations are ideal for the growth of industry. *Pittsburgh, Pennsylvania,* became the first great steel center because it was near all the needed raw materials. Before the discovery of high-grade iron ore around Lake Superior, iron ore was mined near Pittsburgh. Water and rail transportation were good, and immigrants from Europe furnished plenty of labor.

Pittsburgh remains a center of industry today. Meanwhile, other great cities have grown up in more recent years. In the South, *Atlanta, Georgia,* has become one of our largest cities. With its excellent air, rail, and trucking connections, Atlanta serves as the trade and transportation center for the entire southeastern part of this country. Hundreds of industries have moved to Atlanta to benefit from the city's ideal location.

Atlanta's favorable climate has been another factor in its growth. So too has climate made *Phoenix, Arizona,* one of the fastest growing cities in the United States. From 1945 to 1980 Phoenix jumped from 99th to 9th in size among American cities. A big reason for its growth was its annual average temperature of 70°. Starting in the 1950's, the widespread use of air conditioning attracted industry and large numbers of retired people to Phoenix.

Orlando, Florida, is another city that has benefited from a mild climate. Citrus farming had always been important around Orlando. Then, during the 1970's several entertainment parks were built in the Orlando area, contributing to a boom in tourism. Many people moved to Orlando to work in the businesses and industries that were attracted by the advantages of Orlando's favorable climate.

● Have students find out the average temperature of their community.

GAINING SKILL

Reading Tables

In 1880, twice as many Americans lived on farms or in small towns as in cities. Over the next hundred years that situation changed. The urban population increased more rapidly than the rural population as new cities were started and old cities grew. Now, three out of four Americans live in urban areas.

While American cities are generally larger today than they were a century ago, they have not all grown at the same rate. The largest cities of 1880 are not necessarily the largest cities of today.

One way to organize population figures is to put them in a table. A table makes it easy to find information quickly and to make comparisons. In a table, information is arranged in columns (going down) and in rows (going across).

The tables on this page show the ten largest cities of the United States in 1880 and in 1980. Use the tables to answer the following questions.

1. What was the population of St. Louis in 1880?
2. What was the seventh largest city in the United States in 1880? In 1980?
3. What cities from the top ten in 1880 were still on the list in 1980?
4. How many more people lived in Chicago in 1980 than in 1880?
5. How many people lived in the three largest cities in 1880? (Add the three figures to find out.) In 1980?
6. Look at the map on page 545. In 1880, how many of the ten largest cities were located west of the Mississippi? In 1980, how many were?

Cities, 1880	Population
New York	1,773,000
Philadelphia	847,000
Chicago	503,000
Boston	363,000
St. Louis	351,000
Baltimore	332,000
Cincinnati	255,000
San Francisco	234,000
New Orleans	216,000
Washington, D.C.	178,000

Cities, 1980	Population
New York	7,071,000
Chicago	3,005,000
Los Angeles	2,967,000
Philadelphia	1,688,000
Houston	1,594,000
Detroit	1,203,000
Dallas	904,000
San Diego	876,000
Phoenix	790,000
Baltimore	787,000

America Provides More Opportunities for More People

1865–1965 See pp. T48–T49 for chapter teaching strategies.

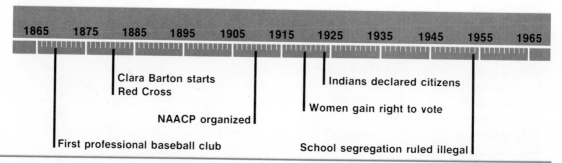

| 1865 | 1875 | 1885 | 1895 | 1905 | 1915 | 1925 | 1935 | 1945 | 1955 | 1965 |

Clara Barton starts
Red Cross

Indians declared citizens

NAACP organized

Women gain right to vote

First professional baseball club

School segregation ruled illegal

What this chapter is about —

In 1981 almost 10,000 people took the oath of American citizenship in a single huge ceremony held in Los Angeles. It was the largest ceremony of this kind that had ever taken place. Like hundreds of thousands of people before them, the new citizens had come to the United States in search of a better life.

Throughout America's history, as we have seen, this country has provided people with opportunities. As a result, the story of our country has been one of growth and change. In some cases that growth and change has been easy to

◀ People continue to come to this country in search of greater opportunities. Here, new Americans take the oath of citizenship.

measure. We can say, for example, that in 1860 there were 33 states, while in 1960 there were 50. We know too that during this hundred-year period the population of the United States grew from 31 million to almost 180 million.

Other examples of growth and change can only be described in more general terms. We can say that in the years after the Civil War the United States changed from a rural country to an industrialized, urban country. We can also talk about the effects of industrialization on most people of the na-

tion. For example, we know that after 1900 the increased use of machines reduced the length of the working day for most Americans. As a result, people had greater opportunities for education, recreation, and enjoyment of literature, music, and art. In general terms, therefore, we can say that in the years after the Civil War opportunities expanded for most Americans.

In this chapter we will take a closer look at the following questions:

1. How did minority groups gain greater opportunities?
2. How did American women seek greater rights?
3. How have opportunities for education and use of leisure time increased?

1 How Did Minority Groups Gain Greater Opportunities?

What is a minority group? Anywhere in the world, people like to think that the way they look and act is the way others should look and act. When they meet people who are "different," they may think of them as outsiders. They may find it hard to treat those "others" as part of the accepted group. After England had established colonies along the Atlantic seacoast, for example, the settlers of those colonies were often unfriendly to people who came from such countries as Germany or Ireland. Much later, when immigrants arrived in America from eastern and southern Europe, they too were treated with suspicion. Their languages, religions, and ways of living seemed strange to the majority of Americans. (**Majority** means over half the population.)

A **minority group** is a group that has a different race, language, religion, or national origin from that of the ma-

jority of Americans. As you read in Chapter 25, many of the immigrants who came to the United States in the late 1800's had different religions, languages, races, or national origins from those of most people who were already here. Of course, members of minority groups had been living in America long before the late 1800's. Black Americans have been present in this country from early colonial days. American Indians, though they are a minority group today, were, as you know, the original settlers of the Western Hemisphere.

The rights of minorities are important. Under our representative form of government, decisions are made by the majority. Nevertheless, Americans recognize the need to guarantee the rights of minorities. From the beginning of our history, Americans have tried to solve the problem of finding a balance between the rights of minorities and the

557

● See p. T48 for a strategy calling for students to put together a bulletin board display featuring contributions made by members of minority groups.

● See p. T48 for a strategy calling for students to examine how the Constitution protects citizens' rights.

decisions of the majority. One solution
● was to add the Bill of Rights to our Constitution. The Bill of Rights gives people the right, for example, to choose their own religion. Still other amendments were later added to the Constitution for the purpose of protecting minority rights. As Thomas Jefferson said when the Constitution was adopted, there are some rights that must be protected "against every government on earth."

In spite of these constitutional protections, people of minority groups have often been prevented from playing a full part in American life. For one thing, they have sometimes encountered **prejudice** — an unreasonable and unfriendly attitude from the majority group. Furthermore, prejudice has often led to **discrimination** — actions that deny people their rights.

BLACK AMERICANS FIGHT DISCRIMINATION

To see how minority groups have had to overcome the effects of prejudice and discrimination, let us look at the situation of black Americans in the years following the Civil War. This period was a time of raised hopes for blacks, but it was soon followed by great disappointment.

Discrimination takes many forms. During the period of reconstruction, blacks took part in the rebuilding of the South. But when the last federal troops were removed from southern states in 1877, laws were passed to curtail the rights of black citizens. Most southern blacks were prevented by state and local regulations from voting (page 447). Also, by 1890 most southern states required blacks to use separate schools, hospitals, railroads, and streetcars. It was against the law for them to use the same public facilities as whites. ★ Through state laws, **segregation** (the separation of one group from another)

came into being throughout the South. And, in a bitter defeat for black Americans, the Supreme Court ruled in 1896 that segregation was legal. In *Plessy v. Ferguson* the court upheld a Louisiana law requiring separate railroad cars for blacks and whites, so long as equal service was provided. For over fifty years "separate-but-equal" laws were used throughout the South to segregate the races. Rarely were the facilities provided for black citizens equal to those for whites.

Many southern blacks moved north in the early 1900's, hoping to find a freer life and more economic opportunities. In the North, blacks had legal and political rights that were denied them in the South. And many black workers were able to find jobs in northern industry. Even so, black people found that most

Black Southerners who moved north had a hard time finding good jobs. By 1911, blacks were able to join the New York City police force.

558

★ Tell students that segregation laws were commonly called *Jim Crow laws*.

Black leaders of the late 1800's and early 1900's debated the tactics of fighting discrimination. Booker T. Washington believed that vocational training was the best way for blacks to improve their position.

white people in the North shared the same prejudices that were widespread in the South. In the early 1900's black workers found it almost impossible to join unions. In addition, during times of economic trouble, black workers were almost always the first to be fired. Furthermore, few blacks could move into neighborhoods with good housing. Northern cities were strictly segregated, and black people usually had to live in the worst parts of town.

Black Americans overcome obstacles. What could blacks do to fight discrimination? The best-known black leader of the late 1800's and early 1900's was Booker T. Washington. He argued that the best way for blacks to succeed in life was by learning useful skills that would help them become good farmers, mechanics, and industrial workers. In 1881 Washington started Tuskegee (tus-KEE-ghee) Institute in Alabama to put his ideas into practice.

Not all black leaders agreed with Booker T. Washington. Some wanted immediate equality and opportunities for black Americans. One such leader was W. E. B. Du Bois (doo-BOYS), for many years a professor at Atlanta University. Another was Ida Wells-Barnet, a black newspaperwoman from Tennessee. Du Bois and Ida Wells-Barnet were among sixty prominent Americans who formed an organization in 1910 called the National Association for the Advancement of Colored People (NAACP). The purpose of this organization was to help blacks secure legal equality. Another organization, the National Urban League, was started in 1911 to help southern blacks who had moved to northern cities.

Over the years NAACP lawyers took the fight against discrimination to the courts. Progress was slow until 1954, when the Supreme Court decided a case called *Brown v. Board of Education of Topeka*. The Court ruled that in education the doctrine of "separate but equal" was unconstitutional. It went on to say that school systems should make a "prompt and reasonable start" to end segregation.

559

● The type of segregation blacks encountered in the South was *de jure* (by law). They encountered *de facto* (in actual fact) segregation in the North.

Barbara Jordan of Texas was the first black woman from a southern state to serve in Congress.

Black leaders were quick to follow up on the Supreme Court decision. Plans were made for ending other types of discrimination. As you will read in Chapter 32, the decade of the 1960's finally saw black Americans gain full legal rights.

Black citizens contribute to American life. Despite great odds, black Americans have made striking achievements. Blacks are active in every aspect of American life and culture. In government, to take one example, the 1960's saw the appointment of the first black Supreme Court Justice, Thurgood Marshall. Black mayors have served in such major cities as Los Angeles, Atlanta, Detroit, Newark, and New Orleans. ● Black members of Congress in recent years have included Representatives Shirley Chisholm and Barbara Jordan. A number of black ambassadors represent the United States abroad, while black Cabinet members have served the Presidents of both major parties. Government is just one field in which black Americans fully participate. The life of the nation has been greatly enriched by the contributions of black business leaders, athletic performers, scientists, educators, and other professional people.

OTHER GROUPS SEEK GREATER OPPORTUNITY

Throughout our history, other minority groups besides blacks have sought opportunity in this country. Many of them have also had to overcome discrimination of various kinds.

Hispanic Americans. In recent years Hispanic Americans have become the fastest growing minority group in the United States. The term *Hispanic* (his-PAN-ic) refers to people whose parents or ancestors came from countries where Spanish was spoken. People from many countries are, therefore, Hispanic Americans. Their ancestral origin may be Spain or one of the Latin American countries. They may be Cuban refugees who have fled from their homeland since Fidel Castro came to power in 1959. Or they may be the descendants of people who settled what is now the Southwest years before the *Mayflower* landed at Plymouth. Most, however, are members of the two largest Hispanic groups living in the United States today — Mexican Americans and Puerto Ricans.

Mexican Americans. As many as ten million people of Mexican origin live in the United States. Some are descendants of the original Spanish settlers of the Southwest. Others came to this country later, to find work in the mines and on the ranches and railroads of the Southwest, or to work in California's orchards and vegetable fields.

From the beginning Mexican Americans faced discrimination from English-speaking Americans. Many were forced to work for low wages and to live in poor housing in segregated

560

neighborhoods called *barrios* (BAH-ryohz). Some were even the victims of violence. In 1943 there were riots between servicemen and young Mexican Americans in Los Angeles.

Today Mexican Americans live in all regions of the country. Many work in business, politics, service occupations, and the professions, while others continue to make their living as farm workers. Strikes organized by farm workers in the 1960's and 1970's brought nationwide attention to their living and working conditions. Whether city dwellers or farm workers, Mexican Americans play an important part in the economic and cultural life of the United States.

Puerto Ricans. As you will learn in Chapter 28, Puerto Rico has had a special relationship with the United States since 1898. In fact, the island of Puerto Rico is part of the United States, and the Puerto Rican people are American citizens. Over the years, hundreds of thousands of Puerto Ricans have moved to American cities on the mainland in search of jobs. There they have entered all walks of life.

Like other minority groups, Puerto Ricans have sometimes encountered discrimination when looking for good jobs and housing. For that reason many have turned to politics as a way to improve conditions. In 1970, for example, Herman Badillo (bah-DEEL-yoh), a

Hispanic Americans have found opportunities in important fields of work. Left, a Mexican American fire captain in Houston. The nation's cultural life is also enriched by the contributions of Hispanic Americans. Every year the Puerto Rican people of New York City hold a parade (below) to honor their heritage.

New Yorker born in Puerto Rico, became the first Puerto Rican member of Congress. Puerto Rican leaders have also joined with other Hispanic groups to persuade cities with large Spanish-speaking populations to print official publications both in English and in Spanish.

Asian Americans. China, Japan, the Philippines, Korea, and Vietnam are some of the Asian countries from which people have come to the United States. As you read in Chapter 25, people have been coming to this country from Asia since the mid-1800's when workers were needed in California's mines and on the transcontinental railroads.

Life was hard for the first Asians who came to this country. Prejudice against people from China and Japan was strong. In the 1870's anti-Chinese riots broke out in California and in 1882 Congress banned further immigration from China (page 542). Later this law was extended to include people from

Japan and other Asian countries. Another example of anti-Asian discrimination came during World War II when this country was at war with Japan. Thousands of loyal Japanese Americans were forced to sell their homes and businesses and move to special camps. But that day is past. Today many Asian Americans are successful in business, the professions, and other occupations. Political figures of Asian descent have ● served in Congress as well.

American Indians. No group of people in America has suffered discrimination in the same way that the Indians have. The Indians were the first Americans. The land was theirs long before Europeans ever knew the American continents existed. When white people started coming to America, they took away the Indians' lands. Time and again white settlers broke treaties they had made with Indian tribes. The Indians fought back in a desperate effort to keep their homelands. By the late 1880's, however, the Indians had been forced onto reservations.

Today well over one million Indians live in this country, about half of them

Indian tribal councils like the one below now have the opportunity to take a greater role in managing reservation life.

on reservations. They are all citizens, by the terms of a law passed in 1924.

Different approaches towards solving the problems facing the Indians have been tried. During the 1950's Congress reversed the policies of the Indian Reorganization Act (page 468) and proposed shifting all federal ties with Indians to the states. An attempt was made to encourage Indians to leave reservations and find jobs in cities. For many Indians, this policy proved to be a failure. Since the 1960's, therefore, Congress has returned to the idea of encouraging Indians to develop tribal life on the reservations. It provides government support for housing, job training, and economic development. One goal of this policy is to give Indians greater control over their own affairs.

Meanwhile, in recent years some Indian tribes have gone to the courts to claim lands that they believe were unfairly taken from them, or to obtain payment for oil or minerals lying beneath their lands. They have been granted sizable cash settlements in some instances. Congress, for its part, has set up an Indian Claims Commission to decide whether injustices have been done in particular cases.

▶ **CHECK UP**   See Teacher's Key.

1. **(a)** Why have members of minority groups sometimes faced problems? **(b)** How have Americans tried to protect the rights of minority groups?
2. **(a)** What problems did southern blacks face in the years following the Civil War? **(b)** What problems did northern blacks face? **(c)** What steps did black people take to fight discrimination? **(d)** What contributions have black citizens made to American life?
3. What obstacles did each of the following groups have to overcome? **(a)** Hispanic Americans **(b)** Asian Americans **(c)** American Indians

2 How Did American Women Seek Greater Rights?

The 1830's and 1840's marked the beginning of a movement in America to win for women full rights and opportunities. In Chapter 17 you read about a declaration of women's rights that was adopted by the Seneca Falls convention in 1848. That declaration urged that women be granted "all the rights and privileges which belong to them as citizens of the United States." For many years little progress was made in achieving that goal, but a start had been made.

New opportunities appear in the late 1800's. American women had taken an active part in the abolitionist movement before the Civil War. After 1865, women took an increasing interest in such public issues as improving living conditions and health standards. Women like Jane Addams (page 548) worked to improve the lives of poor people in the cities. Clara Barton, who had helped nurse sick and wounded soldiers during the war, organized the American Red Cross in 1881. She was its able and energetic leader for many years.

For other women, opportunity ● meant taking jobs in business and industry. There were, of course, large numbers of working women in the years before the Civil War. You have already read about women factory workers (page 300). Women also worked as teachers, nurses, servants, laundresses,

563

● See p. T49 for a strategy calling for students to examine changes which led to new opportunities for women.

Clara Barton, who started the American Red Cross, began her nursing during the Civil War.

and cleaners. But with the growth of industry after the Civil War, more and more opportunities for work outside the home were opened to women. For one thing, great numbers of department stores were established in the late 1800's. These stores soon started hiring women as salespeople. Saleswomen worked long hours and their pay was low. Many women preferred such jobs, however, to working in factories or as servants.

Inventions also played a part in creating new opportunities for women. By 1880, typewriters were widely used, and business offices began to hire women as typists and secretaries. The telephone also created new kinds of jobs. By the early 1900's over 90 percent of the people who operated telephone switchboards in this country were women.

Wages for women were much lower than those paid to men. As early as 1866 Congress set the salaries of women clerks working for the government at $900 a year, while men received from $1,200 to $1,800 for the same work. At the end of the century, men working in manufacturing received an average of $587 a year, and women $314. Black women could count on only about half what white women received.

Throughout these years, teaching and nursing remained the chief professions for women. The number of schools grew steadily, and more schools, of course, required more teachers. Elementary schools existed in most northern communities by the end of the Civil War and about two thirds of their teachers were women. The number of high schools increased rapidly after 1865 (although the entire country had only 800 in 1880) and so more teachers were needed. No education had been provided for black children in the days of slavery, but after 1865 a new force of teachers was needed. This created a new field of work for black women.

The first American schools of nursing opened in 1873. Linda Richards was the first graduate of the New England Hospital for Women and Children, located in Boston. She later became a teacher in nursing schools in New York and Boston, and even in Japan. The census of 1870 reported that the nation had 1,154 trained nurses, and within ten years there were about three times as many. Nursing became almost entirely a women's profession.

● Have students prepare written or oral reports on the women mentioned in this paragraph.

★ See p. T49 for a strategy asking students to do additional reading on the suffrage movement.

Although they met strong resistance, women began to enter professions that once had been closed to them. In 1849 Elizabeth Blackwell became the first woman to graduate from a medical school. Four years later Dr. Blackwell started a hospital for women and children in New York City. Arabella Mansfield, the nation's first woman lawyer, was licensed to practice in Iowa in 1869. Maria Mitchell, who taught herself astronomy, gained fame in 1847 when she discovered a comet. She later taught astronomy at Vassar College.

Women gain opportunities for higher education. Having an equal chance to gain an education was important to women. Progress in this field had been made earlier when, in 1833, Oberlin College in Ohio had accepted women students. Three years later Wesleyan College, in Macon, Georgia, became the first college established for women.

In spite of these gains, at the end of the Civil War almost all colleges in the United States were still closed to women. It was only in the next few decades that changes in higher education began to offer women significant opportunities. Many men's colleges began to accept women students, and by 1879 about 3,500 women were studying at colleges and other institutions of higher learning. They were about one third of all the students enrolled. Meanwhile, the number of colleges for women continued to increase; by 1901 there were more than 120 women's colleges in the country. Because of these greater opportunities more women were able to enter such professions as law and medicine.

Women gain the right to vote. Ever since the 1840's the question of women's **suffrage** (voting rights) had been debated in this country. At first most people — both men and women — agreed that political decisions should be made by men only. As women became more active in community life, however, more people began to think there was no reason to deny women the right to vote.

In the years after the Civil War educated women looking for jobs often found work as school teachers. Compare this Kansas classroom of the late 1800's with your own school.

565

People in America's Story

ELIZABETH CADY STANTON

A forceful and eloquent speaker, Elizabeth Cady Stanton was one of the earliest leaders of the women's suffrage movement.

The parent of seven children, Elizabeth Cady Stanton once said that motherhood required "more knowledge than any other department in human affairs."

The campaign for women's suffrage went on for many years. Women wore buttons and marched in parades to draw attention to their cause. Finally, in 1920 the effort begun by leaders like Elizabeth Cady Stanton resulted in passage of the Nineteenth Amendment.

VOTES FOR WOMEN
PATRIOTISM

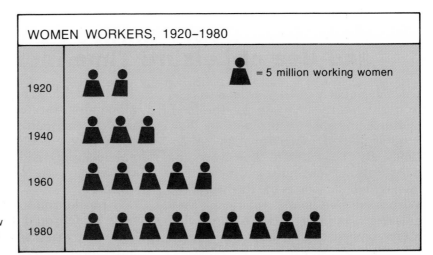

WOMEN WORKERS, 1920–1980

1920

1940

1960

1980

= 5 million working women

See Teacher's Key.

GRAPH STUDY

The number of women workers has grown rapidly in this country since 1920. About how many women held jobs in 1920? In 1980?

Susan B. Anthony and Elizabeth Cady Stanton were leaders of the National Woman Suffrage Association. They carried on a campaign to win equal rights for women, sometimes in the face of scorn and fierce opposition. The first victory for women's suffrage came in 1869. In that year Wyoming Territory granted women over 21 the right to vote. When Wyoming asked to become a state, in 1889, it insisted that women's suffrage be included in its constitution. The state legislature informed Congress, "We may stay out of the Union a hundred years, but we will come in with our women." Congress
● finally agreed, and the next year Wyoming entered the Union, calling itself the Equality State.

By 1900, three other western states — Colorado, Utah, and Idaho — had joined Wyoming in granting women the right to vote. But leaders of the suffrage movement had to fight long and hard to win the vote for all American women. These leaders wrote newspaper articles and gave lectures. They paraded in front of the White House, hoping to win public attention to their cause. The suffrage movement was given a big boost during World War I (Chapter 29). Women took over many jobs held by men who joined the Ameri-

can armies in Europe. By the end of the war, it was generally agreed that American women had made an important contribution to the war effort. Finally, in 1920, the Nineteenth Amendment was added to the Constitution. It stated that citizens should not be denied the right to vote "on account of sex." Women in all parts of the country voted in the presidential election of 1920.

Women have expanded their participation in the nation's political life in the years since 1920. They have voted, served on juries, and held public office. Jeannette Rankin, a Republican from Montana, was the first woman to sit in Congress. Starting with Frances Perkins, Secretary of Labor during the 1930's, a number of women have served in the Cabinet. Women also serve as governors, ambassadors, judges, and ★ mayors of cities.

▶ **CHECK UP**   See Teacher's Key.

1. **(a)** How did the growth of industry lead to greater opportunities for women? **(b)** How were more women able to gain an education?
2. **(a)** How did women gain the right to vote? **(b)** What part have women played in the nation's political life since 1920?

567

3 How Have Opportunities For Education and Use of Leisure Time Increased?

During our early history, people worked from sunrise to sunset to get the food, clothing, and shelter they needed. Few Americans had much time for education. By the 1900's, however, the greater use of machines and new kinds of power had shortened the workday. With more free hours, Americans were able to give more attention to improving themselves through education.

EDUCATION

More young people attend schools. By the mid-1800's, interest in education was much greater than in colonial days. Many communities had public elementary schools paid for by taxes, and a few public high schools had been opened (page 361). Still, school terms were short and boys and girls were not required to attend school. Many of those who did go to school dropped out after completing a few grades, in order to go to work.

This situation changed following the Civil War. More Americans began to see education as providing a chance to get ahead in life. By the end of the 1800's, over thirty states required attendance at school. Millions of children completed elementary school, and high school enrollments grew. In 1870 there had been fewer than 7 million students enrolled in public schools; by 1920 there were more than 21 million.

Colleges and professional schools expand. The number of college students also increased. Most early American colleges were private; that is, they were built and supported by funds from individuals or from churches. But in the late 1800's many colleges and universities were established and supported by states or, in some cases, by cities.

The Morrill Act (page 528) provided money for state colleges which specialized in agriculture and engineering. More people could afford to attend the public-supported colleges and universities since little or no tuition was required.

In addition to colleges and universities, professional schools were established to meet special needs. As you have already read, the first American schools of nursing were established in 1873 to train young women for that profession (page 564). Schools of law, medicine, architecture, engineering, and social work were also set up in the late 1800's.

Public libraries increase. Public libraries played an important part in the spread of educational opportunities. Some libraries had been established in colonial times, but few were open to the public until after the Civil War. The generous gifts of Andrew Carnegie (page 494) made possible the building of public libraries in communities all across the country. Today the "Carnegie Library" is still an important center of culture in many towns and cities in the ★ United States.

RECREATION

In early times, as we have seen, Americans had few opportunities for amusements and play. Most amusements were simple and took place in the home. Some people frowned on those who spent much time on sports or other play. But as changes took place in American life, this feeling tended to disappear. As more time became available for recreation, Americans developed a keen interest in sports and other kinds of entertainment.

Baseball becomes the national sport. Most Americans consider baseball the national sport. It began in the early 1800's with such games as "one o'cat" and "rounders." The following description of "rounders" shows how different that early game was from baseball today:

We used to dig a hole in the ground for the home position and place four stones in a circle, or nearly so, for the bases and, choosing up sides, we went in for a lively time at what was the parent game of baseball. When the ball tosser, or "feeder," sent a ball to the bat, and it was hit into the field, the player running round the bases at once became the target of the fielders. Their efforts, if the ball was not caught, were directed at hitting him with the ball, in which case he was out. Failing to do this, they would try and toss the ball into the hole at "home."

About 1840, rules were proposed which led to baseball as we know it today. The diamond-shaped playing field came into use and players were limited to nine on each side. The Knickerbocker Baseball Club of New York City was perhaps the first group to play under the new rules. The Knickerbockers wore uniforms of blue trousers, white shirts, and straw hats.

In the late 1800's, baseball grew rapidly. Baseball clubs were formed in many cities. The first paid professional

Baseball began in the mid-1800's and grew rapidly in popularity. By the late 1800's people flocked to large stadiums like this one to enjoy games played by professional teams.

baseball team, known as the Cincinnati Red Stockings, appeared in 1869. By 1900, two major leagues, the National and the American Leagues, had been formed. Three years later, the first World Series was played between the champions of the two leagues. Today baseball is played on Little League fields throughout the country as well as in schools and colleges. Millions of people follow the progress of the major league teams. Baseball's greatest players over the years have included Honus Wagner, Ty Cobb, Cy Young, Lou Gehrig, Babe Ruth, Joe DiMaggio, Ted Williams, Stan Musial, Roberto Clemente, Willie Mays, and Hank Aaron.

Football wins great popularity. Another favorite American sport is football. The American game had its beginnings in the English game of rugby. In the early days, as played by American schoolboys and college students, it was largely a game of kicking the ball. The first real college game of football was played between Princeton and Rutgers

FOOTBALL—ABOUT 1880

569

New York's Times Square, with its bright lights and theater signs, was the capital of America's entertainment world in the 1920's.

in 1869. Football spread rapidly to other colleges.

Today football is played all over the country. Modern rules make it a much different game from that of former days. Schools and colleges now share the spotlight with professional football teams.

Basketball catches up with baseball and football in popularity. Basketball was not played until the 1890's. Dr. James Naismith of Springfield (Massachusetts) YMCA College wanted a sport for his students to play in winter. He worked out the rules for a new game to be played indoors and gave it the name basketball. At first, players tried to score points by tossing a ball into peach baskets, set up at each end of a hall. The referee had to climb a stepladder to remove the ball after each "basket" had been made. (This problem was soon solved by cutting a hole in the bottom of the peach basket.) Because basketball required little equipment, it quickly became popular. Today professional, college, and high school basketball games attract much interest.

The movies entertain the American public. Motion pictures became another form of amusement for the American people. Pioneered in America by Thomas Edison, early motion pictures were very different from those we see today. The film flickered and was dim. The motions of the actors were quick and jerky; and their facial expressions as they showed fear, joy, or sadness would seem rather silly to us. But the movies improved rapidly. In 1915, the success of *Birth of a Nation* encouraged the building of silent-movie theaters in cities and towns throughout the country. A second landmark took place in 1927 when Al Jolson's *The Jazz Singer* successfully introduced motion pictures with sound. Then during the 1930's, pictures in color added to the enjoyment of movie-goers. In those years as many as 100 million people would go to the movies each week. The widespread popularity of television after World War II, however, reduced the number of movie-goers. But through the years,

BASKETBALL—ABOUT 1905

570

● See p. T49 for a strategy calling for students to prepare posters on national parks.

★ Remind students of earlier authors, such as Irving and Cooper, who had written about America (p. 363).

"going to the movies" has continued to be the favorite recreation of millions of Americans.

Vacations become part of American life. Vacations are another example of new uses Americans found for their leisure time. In the late 1800's only well-to-do families left home for a vacation. They went to expensive hotels in the mountains or at the seashore. Some families stayed at a farmhouse or had their own camps or cottages.

The situation changed completely when employers began to give workers paid vacation time. More families nowadays can afford to take vacation trips. Moreover, they have cars to take them where they want to go. They may go to a nearby lake or a seashore resort, or they may visit relatives who live in a different part of the country. Or they may visit one of the scores of national parks that are scattered all across the nation. The Grand Canyon in Arizona is such a park; so are Yellowstone, Yosemite (yoh-SEM-uh-tee), and many others.

Yosemite has long been a favorite American vacation place. This painting shows visitors at Yosemite in 1874.

READING AND LITERATURE

In the years after the Civil War great changes took place in American reading and literature. For one thing, the spread of education meant that more people were able to enjoy reading. At the same time that the audience for literature was growing larger, writers turned more and more to writing about America itself. In their books they portrayed America — its people, its regions, and ways of life that seem typically American.

Some writers specialize in "local color." In the last half of the 1800's, there grew up a group of authors known as the "local color" writers. These authors wrote about the sections of the country which they knew well. Perhaps the best known of the "local color" writers was Bret Harte, who wrote vivid tales, such as *The Luck of Roaring Camp,* about the mining camps of California. Another popular author, Sarah Orne Jewett, told about life in her native New England.

America produces great storytellers. The greatest American writer of stories and novels in the last half of the 1800's — and one of the greatest authors in

571

all American literature — was Mark Twain. Twain, whose real name was Samuel Langhorne Clemens, painted an unforgettable picture of life along the Mississippi. *The Adventures of Tom Sawyer, Adventures of Huckleberry Finn,* and *Life on the Mississippi* are favorite stories of Americans of all ages. Another writer of this time, Jack London, wrote exciting stories of the sea and the frozen northland in Alaska and Canada. O. Henry (his real name was William Sydney Porter) won fame in the field of the short story by giving his stories unexpected or surprise endings.

Writers describe life in the West and in the South. Also important in the new American literature were writers who told about the West and the South. Among the many authors who wrote realistically about pioneers was Willa Cather. In her novels *My Antonia* and *O Pioneers!* she described the life and people of the western prairies. Another such writer was Hamlin Garland, whose short stories and novels provide a true picture of pioneer life in Wisconsin and Iowa.

The South also inspired American authors. Ellen Glasgow of Virginia wrote stories about the changes that took place in southern society after the Civil War. Joel Chandler Harris based his "Uncle Remus" stories on folktales brought from Africa by slaves.

Books are published especially for young people. Some authors wrote books for young people. Louisa May Alcott's *Little Women* became a lasting favorite. Laura Ingalls Wilder was the author of *Little House on the Prairie* and *The Long Winter*, stories about life on the Dakota prairies. Marjorie Kinnan Rawlings's *The Yearling* told about a boy growing up in rural Florida. In 1900 one of this country's most popular children's books was published. It was *The Wizard of Oz* by L. Frank Baum.

Novelists of the 1920's and 1930's deal with new ways of life. Many writers pointed out problems on the American scene that they felt needed attention. This was especially true during the 1920's and 1930's when authors such as John Dos Passos criticized economic conditions in this country. Other novelists showed how Americans in different walks of life reacted to the changes of the modern age. For example, Sinclair Lewis, winner of the Nobel Prize in literature, vividly described in his novels the people of a small midwestern town, the life of a typical American businessman, a doctor, and so on.

Americans are proud of famous playwrights and poets. America has had poets and playwrights as well as writers of fiction. Eugene O'Neill, America's best-known dramatist, wrote one-act plays of the sea as well as full-length dramas. One of his plays, *Ah Wilderness!,* describes with sympathy the problems of a teen-age boy.

Walt Whitman is one of the world's great poets. Whitman was stirred by America's past and looked forward with great hope to its future. Through all his poems shines a strong faith in the American people. Other great American poets include Emily Dickinson, Paul Laurence Dunbar, Carl Sandburg, and Robert Frost.

Newspapers and magazines change to meet new conditions. In the years after 1865, newspapers underwent many changes and reached larger and larger numbers of people. With the aid of the telephone, cable, and radio, they were able to print up-to-the-minute information from all over the world. News services such as the Associated Press and the United Press were formed to gather the latest news. Popular features (including sports pages and comic strips) and the use of pictures increased the number of readers. Columnists, who interpret or comment on the news,

572

Known for his paintings of western life, Frederic Remington was also a fine sculptor, as shown by this statue of a bronco-buster.

American art portrays American life. Interest in all forms of art increased following the Civil War. In those years wealthy men and women brought some of the world's finest paintings and art objects to our country. Eventually, most of these private collections found their way into museums, where now they can be viewed with pleasure by millions of Americans. The Metropolitan Museum of Art in New York City, started in 1870, is one of the world's largest museums.

Among America's famous sculptors were Daniel Chester French and Augustus Saint-Gaudens. French's statue of Lincoln in the Lincoln Memorial, Washington, D.C., and of the minuteman at Concord, Massachusetts, have stirred the hearts of millions of people. Saint-Gaudens's statues and memorials are found in Boston, New York, Philadelphia, and many other cities.

There have been many fine American painters. Three well-known artists of the late 1800's were Frederic Remington, Mary Cassatt (kuh-SAT), and James McNeill Whistler. Remington painted exciting scenes of life in the Far West. Cassatt dealt with the theme of mothers and their children in her paintings. Whistler's portrait of his mother is one of the most famous paintings in the world.

Three twentieth-century artists were especially noted for their paintings of the American scene. They are Thomas Benton, John Steuart Curry, and Grant Wood, all from the Middle West. Benton lived as a boy in Missouri, in the same surroundings as Mark Twain's famous characters Huck Finn and Tom Sawyer. The color and vigor of American life are dramatized in his paintings. Curry was a farm boy who grew up to paint the people and the plains of his native Kansas. Grant

began writing articles that appeared in papers from coast to coast. Another change that took place was the growth of the newspaper chain — that is, a group of newspapers owned and controlled by the same company.

Magazines were also becoming more popular. One publisher who developed a magazine read by millions across the nation was Edward Bok. Bok, who came from Holland as a small boy in 1870, became the editor of the *Ladies' Home Journal.* In the 1900's publishers began offering the American public a greater variety of magazines. By mid-century, these included (1) "digests," which reprinted shortened articles from other magazines and papers; (2) news magazines, which printed articles about current events; and (3) picture magazines, which featured high-interest photographs. Magazines were also published that had special appeal to blacks, women, or other groups.

Mary Cassatt has long been regarded as one of America's finest artists. This Cassatt painting is entitled *Young Mother Sewing.*

Wood, sometimes called America's "Painter of the Soil," pictured in exact and clear details his scenes of Iowa farms and farm people.

MUSIC

America develops music of its own. Music has always been a part of American life. As men and women struggled to build America, they sang at their work. Spirituals, sailors' tunes, cowboy songs, canal and river songs, songs of pioneers, ballads — all these became the folk music of America. In the 1800's, a favorite way of spending the evenings was for a group to gather around an organ or a piano and sing. Old and young went to community "sings." The songs of Stephen Foster, such as *My Old Kentucky Home* and *Old Folks at Home,* were favorites.

After the Civil War, American music became more varied. John Philip Sousa (SOO-zuh), who won fame as a bandmaster, composed a number of popular march tunes. Edward Mac-Dowell became a leading composer of serious music. He wrote hauntingly lovely music on American subjects. In the field of light opera the name of Victor Herbert stands out. An immigrant from Ireland, Herbert composed nearly 40 light operas, some of whose catchy tunes are still sung and played. By the late 1800's, opportunities to enjoy good music expanded as most large cities started symphony orchestras.

New forms of music become popular. In the early 1900's, a new kind of music appeared. Ragtime, as it was called, was distinctly American and expressed the vigor and fast movement of modern life. First played by black

Americans, ragtime soon became popular all over the country. After World War I, ragtime was followed by jazz. George Gershwin later borrowed the rhythm of jazz in composing music for symphony orchestras. His *Rhapsody in Blue* and the opera *Porgy and Bess* are still popular, not only in the United States but in many other countries too. Among America's great jazz performers have been trumpeter Louis Armstrong and singer Ella Fitzgerald.

Many of our best-loved songs have been written for musical comedies, which combine music and dancing with a story. A famous team, Richard Rodgers and Oscar Hammerstein II, produced a number of great musical comedy hits: *Oklahoma!*, *South Pacific,* and *The King and I.* Musical comedies continue to be a popular form of entertainment in this country.

● In reading about America's achievements in literature, art, and music, we have come across the names of many famous Americans. Famous names also stand out in other fields of activity — government service, business and industry, engineering, sports, and so on. We honor these people for their part in making life in America richer and fuller.

Proud as we are, however, of the famous names in our country's story, we must not forget that ordinary Americans have been key figures in building America. By their work and faith in liberty and democracy, Americans from many lands, of all races, and of different religions have made this country what it is today.

▶ **CHECK UP** See Teacher's Key.

1. **(a)** How did education change in the years after the Civil War at the high school level? **(b)** At the college level? **(c)** At the professional level?
2. How did baseball, football, and basketball become popular sports in America?
3. **(a)** What is a "local color" writer? **(b)** Who have been some of American's great story tellers? **(c)** What authors have written about the West? **(d)** About the South? **(e)** Name some outstanding American poets.
4. How did newspapers and magazines change to meet new conditions?
5. **(a)** What contributions did Americans make in art? **(b)** In music?

CHECK UP ON CHAPTER 26   See Teacher's Key.

Words to Know

1. majority
2. minority group
3. prejudice
4. discrimination
5. segregation
6. barrio
7. suffrage
8. columnist
9. Hispanic
10. mainland

Facts to Remember

1. **(a)** What are the largest minority groups living in the United States today? **(b)** How did the people of each of those minority groups come to this country?

2. Explain the importance of each of the following Supreme Court decisions: **(a)** *Plessy v. Ferguson,* **(b)** *Brown v. Board of Education of Topeka.*
3. **(a)** What new developments in business and industry led to greater opportunities for women in the late 1800's? **(b)** How did women gain the vote?
4. Tell how each of the following persons contributed to American life: **(a)** Clara Barton, **(b)** Maria Mitchell, **(c)** James Naismith, **(d)** Mark Twain, **(e)** Joe DiMaggio, **(f)** Robert Frost, **(g)** Frederic Remington, **(h)** George Gershwin, **(i)** Louis Armstrong.

575

● See p. T49 for a strategy suggesting that students sample works mentioned in pages 571–575.

Facts to Remember (cont.)

5. **(a)** How did enrollment figures show the growth of education between 1870 and 1920? **(b)** How did opportunities for college education expand?
6. **(a)** Tell how baseball developed into the sport we know today. **(b)** When was football started? **(c)** How was basketball started?
7. **(a)** Name six famous American writers and give the title of one book or story written by each. **(b)** Name three famous American artists. **(c)** Name three important people in the history of American music.

Skills to Practice

1. On a sheet of paper make a list of outstanding women in American history. Mark three columns on your paper and give each column a heading. Use the headings *Name, Time Period,* and *Achievement.* Look back through the book for names of women to include. The index at the end of the book will also be helpful.

Questions to Think About

1. Read again the paragraphs on pages 557–558 concerning the protection of rights of minority groups. Why is it important in a nation like ours that minority citizens' rights be protected?
2. Most people in the United States believe that education should be available to all citizens. Why?
3. Is there a difference between "spectator sports" and "participation sports"? Explain. What can people gain from each?
4. In what different ways did opportunities expand for most Americans in the years after the Civil War? Sum up in two or three sentences what you learned from reading this chapter.

 # Linking Past and Present

The Lady of Liberty. To all Americans, as well as to people all over the world, the Statue of Liberty in New York Harbor is a symbol of the United States of America and ● the freedom for which it stands.

The statue is a colossal bronze figure of a woman, 150 feet tall. In her left hand is a tablet with the inscription, "July 4, 1776." With her right hand she holds a lighted torch, symbolizing the light of liberty. Thousands of people visit the statue every year. Those who wish may climb 168 steps from the feet of the statue to its head.

The statue was presented by the people of France to the people of the United States on July 4, 1884 as a symbol of the liberty that citizens enjoy under a free form of government. It also symbolizes the long friendship between the French and American people, a friendship that began when Lafayette and his French soldiers came to the aid of the Patriots in our War of Independence.

Woman's Building. On May 1, 1893, a great world's fair opened in Chicago. Among the many displays was a special Woman's Building which featured exhibits from every state and from forty countries honoring the achievements of women. The building was designed and decorated by women, and women organized the exhibits. It was unusual at that time for women to be completely in charge of such an undertaking. On view at the Woman's Building were pottery, stained glass, and textiles, as well as an exhibit on American women of science. Among the popular lecturers at the Woman's Building was May French Sheldon, a woman who had explored East Africa.

Today few people remember the 1893 Woman's Building. But at the time it had great importance. Many women who visited the fair were encouraged to take a greater interest in public affairs. As a result, they became active in women's clubs and in the movement for women's suffrage.

576

● Have students use library sources to find a copy of the poem inscribed on the base of the statue.

GAINING SKILL

Distinguishing Fact from Opinion

You may have heard the saying, "The facts speak for themselves." Sometimes a simple list of facts does provide all the information you need. But discussions on most topics usually include statements of both fact and opinion. Statements of fact can be checked for accuracy and completeness. Statements of opinion are based on personal beliefs.

When you are reading an article or listening to a speech, it is important to separate fact from opinion. In some cases, you may want to check the facts before deciding whether you agree with the opinions of the writer or speaker.

In the speech quoted below, Susan B. Anthony used facts to support her opinions on women's suffrage. Read the speech and then answer the questions that follow.

It is said that women do not need the ballot for their protection because they are supported by men. Statistics show that there are 3,000,000 women in this nation supporting themselves. In the crowded cities of the East they are compelled to work in shops, stores, and factories for [low pay]. In New York alone, there are over 50,000 of these women receiving less than fifty cents a day. Women wage-earners in different occupations have organized themselves into trades unions, from time to time, and made their strikes to get justice at the hands of their employers just as men have done, but I have yet to learn of a successful strike of any body of women. The best organized one I ever knew was that of the collar laundry women of the city of Troy, N.Y. [But that strike failed because newspaper editors and politicians did not take the women seriously.] If those collar laundry women had been voters, they would have held, in that little city of Troy, the "balance of political power." . . .

My friends, the condition of those collar laundry women . . . represents the utter helplessness of disfranchisement [lack of voting rights]. The question with you, as men, is not whether you want your wives and daughters to vote, nor with you, as women, whether you yourselves want to vote; but whether you will help put this power of the ballot into the hands of the 3,000,000 wage-earning women, so that they may be able to compel politicians to legislate in their favor and employers to grant them justice. . . .

1. Does the first sentence in the quotation represent Susan B. Anthony's opinion or an opinion she disagrees with?
2. Which of her statements in the first paragraph are facts — statements that could be checked for accuracy?
3. According to this speech, how would the vote help working women? Is that conclusion a fact or an opinion?

577

UNDERSTANDING UNIT 8

SUMMARY OF IMPORTANT IDEAS

1. After 1820, millions of people immigrated to the United States.

a. Among the reasons that immigrants had for coming to America were the desire for greater freedom and the hope of earning a better living. Whether they settled on farms or in towns and cities, immigrants made great contributions to American life.

b. Before the 1890's the majority of immigrants came from the countries of northern and western Europe. From 1890 to 1920 immigrants came chiefly from southern and eastern Europe.

c. Other countries from which immigrants have come to the United States included China, Japan, Canada, Mexico, and a number of other Latin American nations.

d. In the late 1800's and early 1900's some Americans urged that immigration be limited. As a result, legislation placed restrictions on immigration. Immigration acts passed in the 1920's established a quota system.

e. In 1965 a new law repealed the quota system. It set the ceiling on total immigration from outside the Western Hemisphere at 170,000 and on immigration from within the Western Hemisphere at 120,000.

2. With the growth of industry following the Civil War, American cities expanded rapidly in both number and size.

a. Job opportunities in industry attracted immigrants and reduced the percentage of Americans living in rural areas.

b. As urban population grew, cities began to provide essential services, such as clean water supplies, and to build tall buildings and new systems of transportation and lighting.

c. Crowded urban sections, where great numbers of poor people had to live in rundown housing, attracted the attention of reformers like Jane Addams.

d. Another effect of urbanization was the growth of suburban residential areas around large cities. Most large cities today are metropolitan areas, each one consisting of a central city and the surrounding suburbs.

3. Industrialization also affected American farms and small towns in the years after the Civil War. New inventions and household conveniences made life easier for rural and town people.

4. To gain the opportunity to participate fully in American society, minority groups had to overcome the effects of discrimination.

a. For black Americans in the South, discrimination took the form of laws requiring segregation. In the North, blacks had to deal with economic injustices and residential segregation.

b. Efforts by black Americans to overcome obstacles included the formation of such organizations as the NAACP and the undertaking of legal actions.

c. Other minority groups that sought greater opportunities included Hispanic Americans, Asian Americans, and American Indians.

5. In the years after the Civil War, American women increased their participation in many aspects of the nation's life.

a. Industrialization and expanded educational opportunities opened up new fields of employment to women.

b. After years of effort women won the suffrage campaign with the addition of the Nineteenth Amendment to the Constitution in 1920.

6. Another effect of industrialization was that more Americans had increased time for education, self-improvement, and leisure.

a. Education on all levels became available to more people.

b. Both newspapers and magazines changed to meet new conditions. Books became readily available through purchase or library loan. Radio and, later, television brought news of the world and entertainment into the home. Movies and sports events attracted millions.

c. Distinctly American types of literature, art, and music developed.

UNIT REVIEW   See Teacher's Key.

1. **(a)** For what reasons have immigrants come to this country? **(b)** From what countries did the largest numbers of immigrants come in the years after the Civil War? **(c)** Where did they tend to settle? **(d)** Why was immigration restricted after World War I?

2. **(a)** Why did the percentage of the population living in cities increase rapidly after about 1880? **(b)** What were some problems resulting from the crowding of large numbers of people into American cities?

3. **(a)** How did life on farms and in small towns change in the years after the Civil War? **(b)** Why did these changes come about?

4. **(a)** How did women gain increased rights? **(b)** Why did they become more active in work outside the home?

5. **(a)** What is discrimination? **(b)** Why was it a problem for black Americans? **(c)** How did they overcome the effects of discrimination? **(d)** How have other minority groups in this country overcome the effects of discrimination?

6. How did education change in the years after 1865?

7. **(a)** What new games or sports were developed in the United States? **(b)** What contributions did Americans make to music? To art? To literature?

THINGS TO DO

The "things to do" which are marked with an asterisk (*) are for the whole class. The others are to be used as your teacher directs.

*1. Add to the drill cards the new names, words, and dates you have learned about in Unit 8.

2. Prepare a report to the class on one of these outstanding black Americans: Marian Anderson, Ralph Bunche, Jackie Robinson, Booker T. Washington, George Washington Carver, Mary McLeod Bethune.

3. If you read poetry well, select and read to the class some of the poems of Walt Whitman, Carl Sandburg, or Robert Frost.

4. Make models or draw pictures to show different stages of the growth of the city whose story is told on pages 543–545. The models or pictures could show the city as a village, how it looked after the canal was built, and how it looked as an industrial city.

5. Find some pictures of paintings by one of the American artists mentioned in the text and show them to the class.

6. Tell the class about the life and work of one of the following: Willa Cather, Mark Twain, Augustus Saint-Gaudens, George Gershwin, Louis Armstrong, Jacob Riis, John Philip Sousa, Paul Laurence Dunbar, Jane Addams.

UNIT **9**

Left to right: Theodore Roosevelt and the Rough Riders; American warships off the coast of Cuba, 1898; World War I poster.

The United States Widens Its Horizons

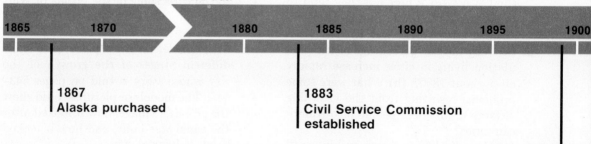

1865–1920   See p. T50 for a unit preview strategy. See pp. T58–T71 for lists of useful books and audiovisual aids.

1865	1870	1880	1885	1890	1895	1900

1867
Alaska purchased

1883
Civil Service Commission established

1898
Spanish-American War

1898
Hawaii annexed

KEEP HIM FREE

BUY
WAR SAVINGS STAMPS
ISSUED BY THE UNITED STATES TREASURY DEPT.

W.S.S.
WAR SAVINGS STAMPS
ISSUED BY THE
UNITED STATES
GOVERNMENT

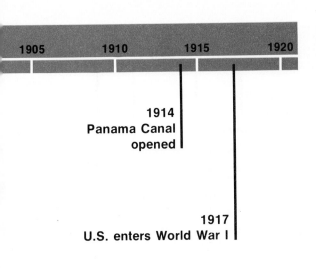

1905   1910   1915   1920

1914
Panama Canal
opened

1917
U.S. enters World War I

In Units 7 and 8 you read about many changes that affected the American way of life after the Civil War. Unit 9 will describe the growing importance of our country in the world. In Chapter 27 you will read about some of our Presidents from 1865 to 1920 and the steps they took to meet important problems. Chapter 28 will point out how the United States became interested in affairs beyond our borders and how we gained new possessions. By the early 1900's the United States had embarked on new foreign policies, particularly in Latin America and East Asia. In Chapter 29 you will read about these events and about World War I and the peace treaty that followed.

581

Vocabulary preview: third party, impeach, direct primary, referendum, initiative, recall, income tax, flow chart

American Leaders Face New Issues

1865–1920   See p. T50 for chapter teaching strategies.

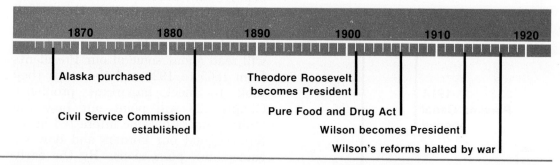

1870   1880   1890   1900   1910   1920

Alaska purchased

Theodore Roosevelt
becomes President

Civil Service Commission
established

Pure Food and Drug Act

Wilson becomes President

Wilson's reforms halted by war

What this chapter is about —

Whenever you have a new teacher, a new president of your club, a new captain of your team — even when you make New Year's resolutions on December 31 — a feeling of change is in the air. You decide to begin again, to do old things in a different way, and to do them better. You say to yourself, "This is a chance for a new start. This time I'll avoid old mistakes; this time I'll do the job right!"

The same thing happens in history. Every now and then there comes a time when people feel there is a chance to

582

make a new start. In the United States such a time often comes when a new President is elected. People say, "What does the President intend to do? What plan does the new administration have for the country? How will that plan work?"

This chapter is concerned with the Presidents and the national government from the 1860's to 1920. We will not try to tell everything that all of those Presidents did during those years. (You will find brief sketches of the Presidents of this period on pages 587–588.) We will find that some Presidents were unwilling or unable to make any important changes. But we will tell about a few of the occasions when the country had a new President who felt we should work together to make a "fresh start." These Presidents believed it was time for the United States to clear up certain problems that were troubling the American people.

For the important parts of the story, look for answers to these questions:

1. How did the Presidents of the late 1800's deal with changing needs?
2. What problems did President Theodore Roosevelt try to solve?
3. What reforms did President Wilson undertake?

1 How Did the Presidents of the Late 1800's Deal with Changing Needs?

It is easy for us today to look back and realize that after 1865 the United States was entering a new era. Growing use of machines and new methods of manufacturing enabled the United States to become a leading industrial nation. New machines and improved methods of farming made it possible for fewer farmers to raise larger crops than ever before. Trade with other nations increased. As the population of the United States soared, our cities increased in size and number. These and other developments not only changed the face of America but created new problems.

PRESIDENTS JOHNSON AND GRANT DO LITTLE TO MEET NEW PROBLEMS

Political parties fail to deal with serious problems. For a number of years after the Civil War, political parties looked backward instead of forward. The Republicans were in control of the government in Washington from 1861 to 1885. In election after election they reminded the American people that the Republican Party had saved the Union. In other words, Republican candidates asked the voters to elect them because of their party's record during the Civil War rather than for what they might do about new problems. Both Republicans and Democrats showed more interest in gaining political power than in carrying out the wishes of the people.

Because the two national parties were slow to respond to public needs, people who strongly favored reforms sometimes organized new political parties. Several of these **third parties** were formed in the late 1800's. One was the Prohibition Party, which was formed by people who wanted to forbid, or prohibit, the manufacture and sale of

583

liquor. The National Equal Rights Party was another party that had a special purpose. It wanted to get equal voting and property rights for women. This party even put up a candidate for President in the 1884 election. She was a lawyer from Washington, D.C., named Belva Lockwood. Third parties like these did not get many votes in elections, but they did make their causes known to the people. One third party even succeeded in getting a major party to adopt its reform programs. This happened in the 1890's when farmers of the West and South organized the Populist Party (page 527). In the election of 1896 the Democratic Party adopted the chief reforms of the Populist program.

Presidents Andrew Johnson and Grant have troubled terms of office. Neither of the first two Presidents who followed Abraham Lincoln in office undertook important reforms. In the election of 1864, Andrew Johnson had been named by the Republicans as their candidate for Vice-President. Johnson was a Democrat from Tennessee who was fiercely loyal to the Union. The Republicans had nominated him in hopes that he would bring southern votes to their side. When Lincoln was killed, Johnson became President. During most of his term of office, Johnson and leading Republicans in Congress carried on a quarrel that grew out of their conflicting plans for readmitting the southern states (page 444). In fact, Johnson was the only one of our Presidents to be **impeached** (accused of misconduct) by the House of Representatives. He was found not guilty by a close vote in the Senate.

Ulysses S. Grant, our next President, had been the leading northern general during the Civil War. He was elected for two terms. As President, Grant was honest and upright, but he was inexperienced in politics and unable to tell good advice from bad. As a result, Grant's eight years in the White House were clouded by public scandals and problems left by the war.

THE UNITED STATES BUYS ALASKA

One very important event during Andrew Johnson's presidency added new territory to the United States. After the nation had reached the Pacific coast in the 1840's, there was little interest in adding more territory. But a few Americans had other ideas. One such person was William H. Seward.

Secretary of State Seward believes in expansion. Seward became Secretary of State in 1861, under President Lincoln. In 1867, during President Johnson's administration, he still held that position. Seward was a slender, white-haired man with stooped shoulders and a habit of slouching. As Secretary of State, he had charge of all the dealings of our government with the other countries of the world. Seward knew how the United States, with giant strides, had marched westward across the continent. "But why stop at the water's edge?" he thought. "Having advanced to the shoreline of the Pacific, why not go even farther?"

Alaska is purchased. One day in March, 1867, the Russian representative to the United States called at Seward's office and began to talk about Alaska. (Alaska, as you read on page 397, had been claimed for Russia by Vitus Bering in the 1700's.) This vast region, complained the Russian official, was much too far from Russia's main center of population. Furthermore, Alaska was expensive to protect and to develop. Did that mean, asked Seward, that Russia would consider selling Alaska to the United States? The Russian official said he believed Russia would sell. Seward felt that such an opportunity might never come again. Acting quickly, he persuaded the Senate to approve the necessary treaty and sealed the bargain. The price for Alaska was set at

584

In the early 1830's Russian settlers built a fort on Norton Sound in Alaska. By the time this picture was painted in 1843, a small settlement had grown up around the fort.

$7,200,000. This was less than two cents an acre for a region of half a million square miles.

Many Americans joked about • Seward's purchase of Alaska. They called Alaska "Seward's Folly" and "Seward's Icebox." But Seward was a wiser man than they realized. The fur seals which were caught in the waters near Alaska were very valuable. Later, gold was discovered in Alaska and plentiful supplies of oil, natural gas, and other resources also were found. No longer does anyone speak of Alaska as "Seward's Folly." Alaska has paid for itself many times over. For many years a territory of the United States, Alaska was admitted to the Union as the forty-ninth state in 1959.

Americans lose interest in further expansion. Seward's dreams of expansion did not end with Alaska. In 1867, the same year that Alaska was purchased, the United States took possession of the Midway Islands, far out in the Pacific Ocean northwest of Hawaii (map, page 605). But here William H. Seward had to stop. Although he dreamed of obtaining more land, the Senate would not approve his plans for further expansion. Americans were still too wrapped up in affairs at home to

look very far beyond their shores. Thirty years were to pass before the United States again acquired any important amount of territory.

PRESIDENTS HAYES AND CLEVELAND UNDERTAKE REFORMS

Hayes is named President by an Electoral Commission. On March 4, 1877, Rutherford B. Hayes, a Republican from Ohio, took office as President under unusual conditions. Many Americans, perhaps half the nation, did not believe that he had a right to his high position. Some newspapers even hinted that he had gained his election through trickery. How could this have happened?

During the presidential election of 1876, an exciting race had developed between Hayes and the Democratic candidate, Samuel J. Tilden. A dispute arose over the election returns. Three of the southern states still under reconstruction governments had sent two sets of electoral votes to Congress. The "carpetbag" governments had sent in Republican votes. Local Democrats, protesting that the state elections were unfair, had sent in Democratic electoral votes. Which votes would be counted?

585

• See p. T50 for a strategy asking students to compare the purchases of Louisiana and Alaska.

"Another such victory and I am undone," says the wounded Republican elephant in this cartoon published after the election of 1876 left the Republican Party victorious but battered.

To settle the dispute, Congress appointed a special Electoral Commission. This Commission decided to count the states' votes that favored Hayes. Many Americans did not agree with the Commission's decision, but Hayes was declared the winner and he became President.

Hayes removes federal troops from the South. In spite of this unfortunate beginning, President Hayes undertook several important changes. Before the Electoral Commission had given its decision on the election, federal troops had been withdrawn from Florida, one of the three southern states where election returns had been disputed. President Hayes now ordered the removal of troops from the other two states (South Carolina and Louisiana) that still had reconstruction governments.

Hayes begins the fight for civil service reform. President Hayes also undertook an important change in the method of appointing people to government jobs. Ever since the days of President Andrew Jackson (Chapter 17), the spoils system had been widely used. New Presidents had removed large numbers of government officials to make room for their own friends and supporters. As a result, many government offices had been held by people who had neither the ability nor the experience to carry out their duties efficiently.

President Hayes thought that using public office as a way of rewarding political supporters was wrong. Hayes believed that appointment to public office should depend on ability and experience. One way of filling government positions is to have people take examinations, with the jobs going to those who make the highest scores. Government employees who get their positions in that way are said to be under the **merit system.** The movement to establish the merit system was called civil service reform.

Although many members of his own party opposed him, President Hayes was determined to fight for civil service reform. When he entered the White House, Hayes did not replace large numbers of officeholders with his own friends or supporters. He chose Carl Schurz, who had come from Germany as a young man, to be a member of his Cabinet. A tireless worker for good government, Schurz is remembered as one of the most enthusiastic supporters of the merit system.

Civil service reforms are adopted. These beginnings were small, but they aroused interest throughout the country. Then a dramatic event occurred.

This decision was called the Compromise of 1877. Have students find out the main points of that compromise and report back to class.

Our Presidents

ULYSSES S. GRANT   1869–1877

Republican from Illinois. Grant had retired from the army after serving in the Mexican War but returned to serve as an officer in the Civil War. He eventually became general of all the Union forces. Though well-meaning himself, Grant's administration was marred by scandals involving dishonest government officials. Later, he failed in business but spent his last months writing his life story to pay his debts.

RUTHERFORD B. HAYES   1877–1881

Republican from Ohio. Hayes was an officer in the Union army when elected to Congress. In Congress, and later as governor of Ohio, he earned a reputation for complete honesty. As President, Hayes encouraged civil service reform and tried to restore friendship between the North and the South by withdrawing the last federal troops from southern states. Hayes had the first telephone installed in the White House.

JAMES A. GARFIELD   1881

Republican from Ohio. In his youth, Garfield had worked as a canal boy to support his widowed mother and to put himself through college. He later served as president of Hiram College in Ohio, as the youngest brigadier general in the Union army, and in Congress. In 1880 he was nominated as a compromise candidate for President. Four months after his inauguration he was shot by a disappointed office-seeker.

CHESTER A. ARTHUR   1881–1885

Republican from New York. A tall, courtly gentleman, he dressed so stylishly that he was called "Elegant Arthur." His association with political bosses won him the nomination for Vice-President. After Garfield's death, however, Arthur proved to be an honest, efficient President who put duty to his country first. His endorsement of civil service reform cost him the support of the bosses and chances of renomination.

GROVER CLEVELAND   1885–1889   1893–1897

Democrat from New York. A stout, stubbornly honest man, Cleveland had taught school, studied law, and been a sheriff, a mayor, and governor of New York. As President, he tried to lower the tariff. Though Cleveland won the popular vote in the election of 1888, he lost the electoral vote. In 1892, however, he won easily and returned to the presidency. His second term was plagued by a severe economic depression.

Our Presidents

BENJAMIN HARRISON   1889–1893

Republican from Indiana. Benjamin Harrison was the only President whose grandfather — William Henry Harrison — had also been President. A cautious man, Harrison tried to maintain a "middle-of-the-road" policy to please various groups. A program to build a two-ocean navy was begun during his term. The Harrisons were the first family to have electric lights in the White House.

WILLIAM McKINLEY   1897–1901

Republican from Ohio. McKinley had been a soldier, lawyer, congressman, and governor of Ohio. His presidency was marked by booming business and by the growing activity of the United States in world affairs, including the short war with Spain, which brought overseas territories under American control. McKinley was assassinated six months after his second term in office began.

THEODORE ROOSEVELT   1901–1909

Republican from New York. Big-game hunter and author of over thirty books, "Teddy" (or "TR") became President at McKinley's death. He started the air force in 1909 by purchasing a plane from the Wright brothers. For helping to end the Russo-Japanese War, he became the first President to receive the Nobel Peace Prize. He was also the first President to ride in an automobile.

WILLIAM HOWARD TAFT   1909–1913

Republican from Ohio. Taft was over six feet tall and weighed at one time more than 300 pounds. A judge for nearly twenty years and the first governor of the Philippine Islands, this friendly man was Secretary of War under Theodore Roosevelt but later became his rival for the presidency. Taft was named Chief Justice of the United States in 1921, the only President who has held that position.

WOODROW WILSON   1913–1921

Democrat from New Jersey. President of Princeton University, Wilson had been a college professor and historian but had never held political office until elected governor of New Jersey. Within two years he was elected President. A strong executive, he led Congress in lowering tariffs and passing the Federal Reserve Act. At the end of World War I Wilson's peace proposals made him the second President to win the Nobel Peace Prize.

President Garfield, who succeeded Hayes in 1881, was shot by a disappointed office-seeker. That assassination helped people see the need for the merit system in selecting persons for government jobs. In 1883, Congress created a Civil Service Commission. This commission established a system of examinations for people seeking government jobs. When there was a vacancy, it was filled by naming one of the three persons who had scored highest on the examination for that position. At first only about one in every seven federal workers was placed under the merit system. But later Presidents extended it to cover about 90 percent of all government jobs. Many states and local governments also use the merit system in selecting employees.

Cleveland becomes President. March 4, 1885, marked still another unusual inauguration day. For the first time in 25 years, there was a Democratic President in the White House. The new President, Grover Cleveland, had risen from poverty to high office through hard work, honesty, and courage. He had been a sheriff, then mayor of Buffalo, and finally governor of New York State. Even when it might cost him popularity, he did not hesitate to say no. For Grover Cleveland a public office was a public trust, not an opportunity to reward political supporters.

Cleveland works for reforms. During Grover Cleveland's first term of office, several important laws were passed, including the Interstate Commerce Act to regulate railroad rates (page 513). Cleveland also worked hard to lower the tariff.

After the Civil War, tariffs on goods imported from foreign countries had been kept at high levels to protect American industry. President Cleveland found that these high taxes were earning the government more money than it was spending. Cleveland felt that American industries had become so strong that high tariff duties were no longer needed to protect them from foreign competition. He also argued that high tariff duties raised the prices of many goods, thereby increasing the cost of living for the average American. Under pressure from President Cleveland, a bill to reduce the tariff was introduced into Congress. Although the bill failed to pass, President Cleveland did not lose heart. He kept up his fight to lower the tariff.

Cleveland returns to the White House. President Cleveland was defeated in his attempt at re-election. But four years later, in 1892, he was again elected President. Thus he has the distinction of being the only President who has served a second term in office after having once left the presidency. During Cleveland's second term, the country went through a severe depression. Many of his policies were not popular at the time. But in later years it became clear that Cleveland had done his duty as he saw it, and had worked for what he thought were the best interests of the American people.

▶ **CHECK UP**   See Teacher's Key.

1. **(a)** Why were political parties slow to deal with the new problems that arose in American life in the second half of the 1800's? **(b)** Why was little accomplished during the administrations of Presidents Johnson and Grant?
2. How did the United States acquire Alaska?
3. **(a)** What is civil service reform? **(b)** Why was it needed? **(c)** How did President Hayes try to improve the merit system? **(d)** What improvements were introduced by the Civil Service Commission?
4. **(a)** What reforms did President Cleveland favor? **(b)** Why did he want to lower the tariff?

589

● Mention that under the 1883 Pendleton Act, Congress stipulated that people appointed by the merit system could not be removed for political reasons.

● See p. T50 for a strategy calling for students to put together a bulletin board display featuring Theodore Roosevelt.

2 What Problems Did President Theodore Roosevelt Try to Solve?

A frail boy becomes a vigorous man. In a comfortable house in a fashionable district of New York City, a worried man paced the floor with a baby boy in his arms. Although it was night, the baby could not sleep. Fighting for breath, he struggled with terrible coughing spells. The same thing happened night after night. Sometimes the father would call for a carriage and take the baby for a drive through the streets. It didn't matter where they went, so long as a breeze made it easier for the boy to breathe.

Father and son were both named Theodore Roosevelt. Theodore, Jr., continued to be in ill health until he was well into his teens. Then, as his health began to improve, young Theodore grew more active physically and became interested in sports. While at Harvard College, he took up boxing. Still later he lived on a ranch in the Dakota Bad Lands, where he fished and hunted and came to love outdoor life.

● Over the years, Roosevelt developed into a vigorous man. He became, in fact, a bundle of energy. He moved quickly, talked fast, and laughed loudly. He seemed to burst into rooms, not enter them. He seemed to shout, not talk. He seemed to run, not walk.

Roosevelt chooses a career of public service. Very soon after his graduation from college, Roosevelt turned his great energy to the field of government. Elected to the New York state legislature, he later served on the United States Civil Service Commission. As president of the Police Board of New York City, Roosevelt spurred on the police in their fight against crime. Then, in the spring of 1897, he was appointed Assistant Secretary of the Navy.

When the United States declared war on Spain in April, 1898 (Chapter 28), Roosevelt resigned at once to form a cavalry regiment which became known as the "Rough Riders." This was a group of hard-riding, quick-shooting volunteers that included western cowboys as well as fashionable "gentlemen riders." Roosevelt's war record made him a popular hero, and he was elected governor of New York. Soon afterward he was nominated for the vice-presidency by the Republican Party. Many people believed that Theodore Roosevelt made a mistake in accepting this nomination, since a Vice-President in those days did not have great responsi-

Theodore Roosevelt, shown here with his family, was one of this nation's most popular Presidents. A man of great energy, he fought for reforms that he hoped would benefit the American people.

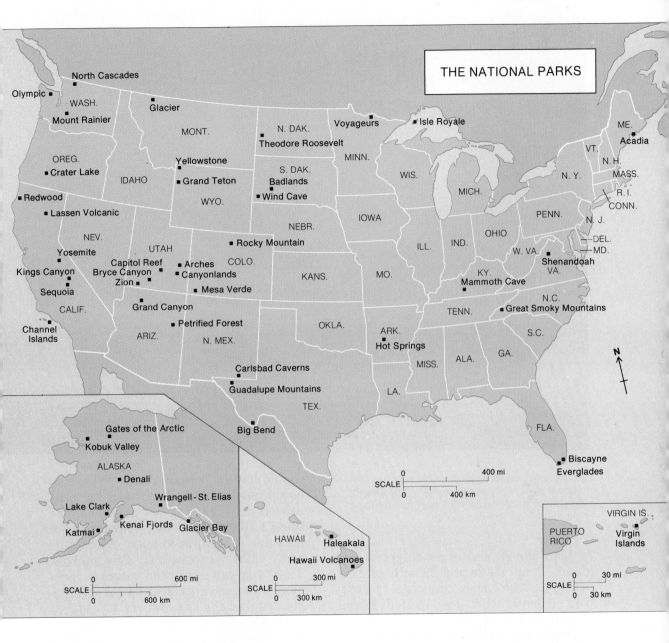

THE NATIONAL PARKS

North Cascades
Olympic
WASH.
Mount Rainier
Glacier
MONT.
N. DAK.
Theodore Roosevelt
Voyageurs
Isle Royale
ME.
Acadia
VT.
N. H.
OREG.
Crater Lake
IDAHO
Yellowstone
Grand Teton
WYO.
MINN.
S. DAK.
Badlands
Wind Cave
WIS.
MICH.
N. Y.
MASS.
R. I.
CONN.
Redwood
Lassen Volcanic
NEV.
Yosemite
Kings Canyon
Sequoia
CALIF.
UTAH
Capitol Reef
Bryce Canyon
Zion
Arches
Canyonlands
Mesa Verde
COLO.
NEBR.
IOWA
Rocky Mountain
KANS.
MO.
ILL.
IND.
OHIO
W. VA.
PENN.
N. J.
DEL.
MD.
Shenandoah
VA.
KY.
Mammoth Cave
N.C.
Great Smoky Mountains
S.C.
Grand Canyon
Petrified Forest
ARIZ.
N. MEX.
OKLA.
ARK.
Hot Springs
TENN.
MISS.
ALA.
GA.
Channel
Islands
Carlsbad Caverns
Guadalupe Mountains
TEX.
LA.
N

FLA.
Biscayne
Everglades

Gates of the Arctic
Kobuk Valley
ALASKA
Denali
Lake Clark
Wrangell - St. Elias
Katmai
Kenai Fjords
Glacier Bay
Big Bend

SCALE
0   400 mi
0   400 km

HAWAII
Haleakala
Hawaii Volcanoes

SCALE
0   300 mi
0   300 km

SCALE
0   600 mi
0   600 km

VIRGIN IS.
PUERTO
RICO
Virgin
Islands

SCALE
0   30 mi
0   30 km

MAP STUDY   See Teacher's Key.
During Theodore Roosevelt's presidency
Americans became more concerned about
preserving the great outdoors. As a result the
national park system grew larger. What state
has the most parks today?

bilities. Roosevelt himself once said
that he would rather be almost anything than Vice-President.

The Republicans won the election
of 1900. William McKinley was elected

to a second term as President and Theodore Roosevelt became Vice-President.
But soon thereafter President McKinley was shot and killed by an assassin.
Theodore Roosevelt thus became President of the United States when he was
not quite 43, the youngest person ever ●
to hold that high office.

**President Roosevelt takes an active
part in foreign affairs.**   As President,
Theodore Roosevelt was quick-witted,   591

Yellowstone, established in 1872, was the first national park. This scene, called "The Grand Canyon of the Yellowstone," was painted by American artist Thomas Moran.

well informed, and eager to get things done. Chapters 28 and 29 will tell how he dealt with other countries. Roosevelt believed that the United States should be strong. He built up a powerful navy and sent it around the world to impress other countries with our strength. Long before he became President, he had said in a speech, "Speak softly and carry a big stick, and you will go far." His attitude toward foreign affairs became widely known as the *big stick policy*.

Roosevelt tackles problems in American life. Theodore Roosevelt was equally active in affairs at home. He believed that the American people

should have a "square deal." Where he found conditions in American life that needed correcting, he set out to change them. His efforts were supported by millions of reform-minded Americans who called themselves Progressives. The Progressives wanted voters to have more influence in political affairs. They also wanted the government to concern itself with the well-being of all citizens. The Progressives were encouraged by several steps taken by Roosevelt during his presidency.

(1) *Trusts and monopolies.* One problem, in Roosevelt's opinion, was the wealth and power held in those days by the big business monopolies called trusts. These trusts not only controlled a large share of American business but also had a strong influence in politics. They spent money to elect government officials likely to be friendly to them.

Roosevelt believed that in a democratic country it was wrong for huge business monopolies to have such power. He set out to break them up. The Sherman Antitrust Law (page 512) had already been passed, but a law is of no use unless it is enforced. Former Presidents had done very little to stop monopolies. Under Roosevelt, however, the government went to court against several great trusts to compel them to obey the Sherman Law. Because of his fight against these trusts, Roosevelt was given the nickname of "trust-buster."

(2) *Conservation.* Theodore Roosevelt was greatly troubled by the careless use of much of the nation's natural wealth — its forests, soil, water power, and coal and other minerals (page 480). Experts who had studied this problem predicted that in a few years most of our natural resources might be entirely used up. Roosevelt decided to take measures to save or conserve these resources. Laws were passed to set aside millions of acres as national forests and parks. Other laws encouraged the building of dams to make use of water power and to provide irrigation for dry western lands. Roosevelt also supported laws to conserve mineral resources. At a conference in 1908 he called together important national leaders to study conservation problems. His efforts made people aware of the need to use natural resources wisely.

(3) *Protection from harmful products.* The President also wanted to prevent the sale of certain harmful products. In 1906 Congress passed a law that allowed government officials to inspect meat sold in interstate trade. By the terms of this law, meat that passed inspection was to be given a government stamp. Another law, the Pure Food and Drug Act, prohibited the manufacture and sale of impure or dishonestly labeled foods and drugs. Roosevelt said, "No man may poison the people for his private profit."

(4) *Better government.* Theodore Roosevelt was interested in still another problem. Many Americans in the early 1900's, including Roosevelt, believed that the people should have more of a chance to participate in government. They felt that too many representatives and government officials listened only to special interest groups who put pressure on them to favor or oppose certain matters.

Several reforms were suggested, especially in western states. One was called the **direct primary.** It let members of a political party nominate candidates themselves, instead of having the candidates selected by party leaders at a convention. Another, called the **referendum,** said that a bill passed by a state legislature must be submitted to the voters for their approval before it went into effect. A third reform, the

593

● See p. T50 for a strategy that calls for students to examine the Pure Food and Drug Act.

In 1904 Roosevelt easily won election as President in his own right. A campaign button (above) reminded voters of Roosevelt's war record.

initiative, let citizens suggest new laws. Still another, the **recall,** allowed the voters to remove from office an official whose services they believed to be unsatisfactory.

President Theodore Roosevelt approved of these efforts to give people a more direct voice in their government. He did what he could to help these reforms. Neither in his day nor since have any of these measures been put into practice by the national government in Washington. But most states have adopted the direct primary, and a large number of them permit the use of the referendum, the initiative, and the recall.

How successful was Theodore Roosevelt? There is no doubt that Theodore Roosevelt succeeded in many things. He made America's influence felt in world affairs. Later Presidents carried on and expanded his plans to conserve our natural resources. But in some ways Theodore Roosevelt may

594

remind us of a person racing against a car. Although the person runs hard and fast, the car leaves the runner farther and farther behind. For example, Roosevelt sought to break up powerful business groups. Yet because of the nation's rapid industrial growth, there were more monopolies at the end of his presidency than when he took office. Nevertheless, by his vigorous actions and stirring speeches, Roosevelt awakened the American people and helped them to understand better the problems their nation faced.

▶ **CHECK UP**   See Teacher's Key.

1. Describe Theodore Roosevelt's career before he became President.
2. **(a)** What were Theodore Roosevelt's views on monopolies? On conservation? On the sale of harmful products? On reforms in government? **(b)** How successful was he in carrying out these ideas?

3 What Reforms Did President Wilson Undertake?

When the election of 1908 drew near, Theodore Roosevelt had completed nearly two terms in the White House. Although he had declared he would not run for re-election, he was still popular with the voters. He recommended that the next President be William Howard Taft, a Republican from Ohio who had held several government offices and who had been Roosevelt's Secretary of War. ● With Roosevelt's support, Taft was elected President in 1908.

The Democrats win the 1912 election. In many ways President Taft continued the work begun by Roosevelt. Under Taft, for example, the government carried forward the regulation of trusts and monopolies. But Taft did not go fast enough or far enough in his reforms to please Roosevelt. Before long, in fact, Theodore Roosevelt became convinced that Taft was not carrying on the policies that he, Roosevelt, favored. The split between the two friends became so deep that Roosevelt decided to seek the Republican presidential nomination for himself in 1912. Failing to win it, he ran for President as the candidate of a new third party called the Progressive Party. Although the Republican Party renominated Taft, many Republicans voted for Roosevelt. The Democrats, who were united, won the election. (See map, page 596.)

Woodrow Wilson becomes President. The man whom the Democrats had elected was Woodrow Wilson. Like Theodore Roosevelt, Wilson wanted to solve the important problems facing the country. But in many ways he was different from Roosevelt. Roosevelt, the soldier and outdoor man, believed in action; Wilson, on the other hand, was a thinker whose most effective weapons were words. Roosevelt was almost boy-ish in his enthusiasms and sudden changes of mood. Wilson's manner was calm and composed.

Woodrow Wilson, a scholar and ★ teacher almost all his life, had been president of Princeton University. His only political experience was one term as governor of New Jersey. Nevertheless, he intended to be a strong President, offering an ambitious program which he called a "New Freedom" for the American people.

Wilson puts through important reforms. Woodrow Wilson went to Congress in person to read his important messages, a thing no President had done since John Adams. When he took the oath of office as President, and when he sent messages to Congress, Wilson spoke in favor of a number of reforms backed by the Progressives.

(1) *The tariff.* President Wilson asked Congress to lower the tariff duties on many articles so that trade could flow freely between the United States and other nations. He believed that foreign countries could not buy our goods unless they could also sell their own goods in this country. President Cleveland, you remember, had fought for a lower tariff but had not been successful. In fact, tariff laws passed in the 1890's and early 1900's had actually *increased* tariff duties. But Congress now followed Wilson's wishes and passed the Underwood Tariff Law, lowering tariff rates.

(2) *Banking reforms.* President Wilson also asked for changes in the banking system. During panics, many banks had been forced to close their doors when large numbers of people tried to withdraw their savings. Wilson wanted to set up a banking system that would make it possible for banks to get

595

★ See p. T50 for a strategy calling for students to write reports on the life of Woodrow Wilson.

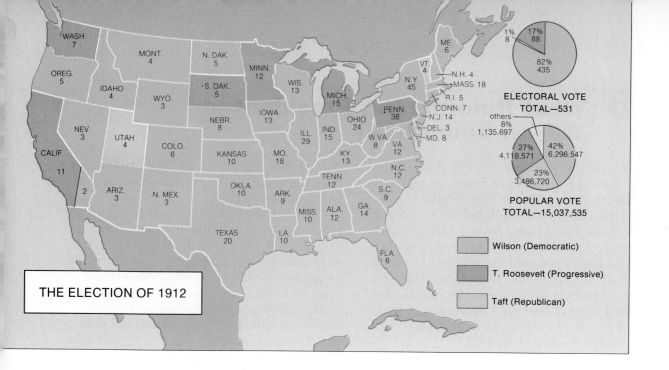

WASH. 7
OREG. 5
IDAHO 4
MONT. 4
N. DAK. 5
MINN. 12
WIS. 13
MICH. 15
N.Y. 45
VT. 4
ME. 6
N.H. 4
MASS. 18
R.I. 5
CONN. 7
N.J. 14
DEL. 3
MD. 8
NEV. 3
UTAH 4
WYO. 3
S. DAK. 5
IOWA 13
NEBR. 8
ILL. 29
IND. 15
OHIO 24
PENN. 38
W.VA. 8
VA. 12
CALIF. 11
2
ARIZ. 3
N. MEX. 3
COLO. 6
KANSAS 10
MO. 18
KY. 13
TENN. 12
N.C. 12
S.C. 9
OKLA. 10
ARK. 9
MISS. 10
ALA. 12
GA. 14
TEXAS 20
LA. 10
FLA. 6

1% 8   17% 88
82% 435

ELECTORAL VOTE
TOTAL—531

others 8% 1,135,697
27% 4,118,571
42% 6,296,547
23% 3,486,720

POPULAR VOTE
TOTAL—15,037,535

Wilson (Democratic)

T. Roosevelt (Progressive)

Taft (Republican)

THE ELECTION OF 1912

MAP STUDY   See Teacher's Key.
This map shows the results of the 1912 election. (To review how to read an election map, look back at page 423.) (a) How many electoral votes did the winner receive? (b) How many popular votes did he receive? (c) What was the combined popular vote of all the other candidates?

the money needed to meet such emergencies. Congress therefore passed the Federal Reserve Act. This act set up a central bank in each of twelve major regions of the country, all under the control of the Federal Reserve Board. The Federal Reserve Banks had broad powers to regulate the supply of money and to help local banks.

(3) *The income tax.* For a number of years many people had favored a new form of taxation — a tax on a person's wages or income. Their argument for an **income tax** was that people with large incomes are able to pay a higher tax than people with small incomes. Congress had tried to pass an income tax law in 1894, but the Supreme Court had declared it unconstitutional. In 1913, however, just before Wilson took office, the Sixteenth Amendment was added to the Constitution, permitting Congress to levy such a tax. At President Wil-

son's request, a new tax law was passed, and we have had a federal income tax ever since.

(4) *Business and monopolies.* Woodrow Wilson, like Theodore Roosevelt, believed that powerful monopolies were dangerous. He urged Congress, therefore, to pass laws to control such monopolies. One of these was the Clayton Act, which listed things that big corporations should not do (page 512). Another law set up a government bureau, the Federal Trade Commission, with power to find out facts about business and to prevent companies from building monopolies.

(5) *Farmers and workers.* Under Wilson's guidance, arrangements were made so that farmers could borrow money more easily and for longer periods of time. Nor were workers in industry forgotten. A law was passed to reduce the regular working day on interstate railroads to eight hours. Meanwhile, a number of individual states passed laws to prevent employees from hiring children and, so far as possible, to require safe and healthful working conditions.

War halts reform at home. We will never know how far-reaching President

596

Wilson's New Freedom program might have been, because it was interrupted by the First World War (Chapter 29). That conflict, which broke out in Europe just a little over a year after Wilson took office, demanded more and more of the President's attention. At last, in 1917, when the United States entered the war, Woodrow Wilson had to turn from his program of reforms at home to the problems created by a great war abroad.

When World War I ended, President Wilson continued to give his attention to world problems. He went to Europe to help write a peace treaty and to push plans for a world peace organization. On his return to the United States, Wilson wore himself out trying to interest Congress and the nation in his plans. In 1921, he ended his second term a sick and disappointed man. He died three years later. Although he failed to achieve his dream of a peaceful world, Wilson is recognized today as one of our great Americans.

Between 1865 and 1920, Woodrow Wilson was the only President who had to face the crushing burden of a world war and of trying to make a world-wide peace. But you will learn in the remaining chapters of this book that foreign affairs brought increasing responsibilities to all our Presidents after the late 1800's.

Woodrow Wilson's first wife, Ellen, died in 1914. Two years later the widowed President married Edith Bolling Galt (above).

▶ **CHECK UP**   See Teacher's Key.

1. Why was Woodrow Wilson elected President in 1912?
2. What were Wilson's ideas on each of the following, and what action was taken in each case? **(a)** The tariff **(b)** Banking reforms **(c)** The income tax **(d)** Monopolies **(e)** Farm aid and labor laws
3. Why did reforms receive little attention during President Wilson's second term in office?

CHECK UP ON CHAPTER 27   See Teacher's Key.

Words to Know

1. impeach
2. prohibit
3. recall
4. initiative
5. referendum
6. income tax
7. conservation
8. merit system
9. direct primary
10. third party
11. big stick policy

Facts to Remember

1. Name the Presidents in order from Andrew Johnson through Woodrow Wilson. (You will need to look at the list of Presidents in the back of this book.) Identify the political party to which each belonged.

● See p. T50 for a strategy calling for students to examine the achievements of two great Americans: Theodore Roosevelt and Woodrow Wilson.

Facts to Remember (cont.)

2. Identify each of the following: **(a)** Belva Lockwood, **(b)** Carl Schurz, **(c)** William H. Seward, **(d)** Samuel J. Tilden.
3. **(a)** What actions did Theodore Roosevelt take to oppose trusts? **(b)** To conserve natural resources?
4. Identify each of the following laws enacted during Woodrow Wilson's administration: **(a)** Underwood Tariff Law, **(b)** Federal Reserve Act, **(c)** Sixteenth Amendment, **(d)** Clayton Act.

Skills to Practice

1. Name the "third party" that campaigned for the viewpoint expressed in each of the following statements.
   a. "It is not fair to deny the vote to half the people of this country."
   b. "The national government should give more attention to the needs of farmers."
   c. "Many problems will be solved if the drinking of alcohol is made illegal."
   d. "We need an active man back in the White House."
2. Using the map on page 591, identify the state in which each of the following national parks is located: **(a)** Acadia, **(b)** Big Bend, **(c)** Yosemite, **(d)** Denali.

Questions to Think About

1. Explain why a high tariff on foreign goods may prevent other countries from buying goods in this country.
2. **(a)** Why have third political parties sometimes been organized? **(b)** How successful have these third parties been in achieving their goals?
3. **(a)** Why have many people favored civil service reform? **(b)** Why have some people opposed it?

Linking Past and Present

How old have our Presidents been?
According to the Constitution, an individual must be at least 35 years old to be eligible for the office of President. The ages of our Presidents, at the time each *first* took office, have ranged from 42 to 69 years. Twenty-three were in their fifties when they became President; nine were in their sixties; and seven were in their forties. The oldest man to take office was Ronald Reagan, who was 69 years old when inaugurated. Theodore Roosevelt was only 42 when he succeeded to the presidency after the death of President McKinley. But since Roosevelt had not been elected to the office, the honor of being the youngest man to be *elected* President goes to John F. Kennedy.

Our national parks. Various parts of our country have been set aside by the national government as parks for Americans to visit and enjoy. These areas have been left in their natural state as much as possible. They include some of the most beautiful and unusual sights to be found anywhere — snow-capped mountains, rock formations, deep river gorges, geysers, and glaciers, as well as all kinds of wild life. Yellowstone National Park was the first to be established, in 1872. Here visitors can see steaming geysers, volcanoes that spout mud, and other wonders of nature. Sequoia National Park, with its ancient redwoods, and Yosemite, with its magnificent cliffs and waterfalls, were established in 1890. Not all the parks are in the fifty states; one is the Virgin Islands National Park, on the American island of St. John. Its chief attractions are white sandy beaches and beautiful Caribbean scenery.

It was Theodore Roosevelt who did most to preserve our natural heritage. Working with Gifford Pinchot of the Forestry Service, he reserved great stretches of western land for national parks. Since 1916, our parks have been in the care of the National Park Service, a bureau of the Department of the Interior.

GAINING SKILL

Reading Flow Charts

The Constitution gives Congress the power to make laws. But making federal laws is a complicated process with many steps. Of all the bills that are introduced in Congress every year, only about one in ten completes all the required steps and goes on to become a law.

The chart on this page shows the steps a bill, or proposed law, usually goes through to become a law. This kind of chart is called a **flow chart** because it shows the steps in the order they take place.

Study the flow chart. Make sure that you follow the arrows as you observe the steps bills usually take before they become law. Then answer the following questions.

1. Where are most bills first introduced?
2. After a bill is introduced, what groups have the first chance to talk about it?
3. What happens to a bill if the Senate and the House of Representatives pass different versions of it?
4. After both houses of Congress pass a bill, what is the next step?

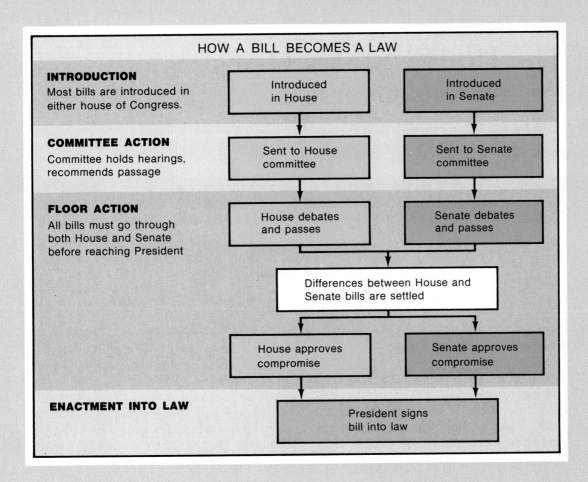

HOW A BILL BECOMES A LAW

INTRODUCTION
Most bills are introduced in either house of Congress.

Introduced in House — Introduced in Senate

COMMITTEE ACTION
Committee holds hearings, recommends passage

Sent to House committee — Sent to Senate committee

FLOOR ACTION
All bills must go through both House and Senate before reaching President

House debates and passes — Senate debates and passes

Differences between House and Senate bills are settled

House approves compromise — Senate approves compromise

ENACTMENT INTO LAW

President signs bill into law

599

The United States Gains Possessions Overseas

1865–1920   See p. T51 for chapter teaching strategies.

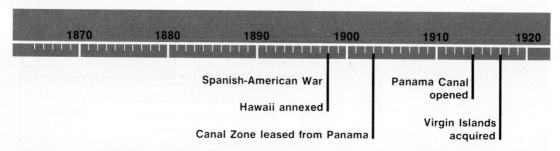

| 1870 | 1880 | 1890 | 1900 | 1910 | 1920 |

Spanish-American War

Hawaii annexed

Canal Zone leased from Panama

Panama Canal opened

Virgin Islands acquired

What this chapter is about —

Throughout their lives the activities and interests of people change. As children their time is occupied by school work, sports, hobbies, and perhaps part-time jobs. As young people they may marry and seek full-time employ-ment. They then become interested in better job opportunities and in providing for their families. They may begin to take part in community affairs, join a neighborhood club, become active in local government, or give time to help a church. By the time they are fifty years old, their interests and activities are

600

◄ Victories in the Spanish-American War made the United States a world power. In 1898, Commodore Dewey defeated the Spanish at Manila Bay.

natural for a country grown large and powerful, led the United States to acquire territory outside its borders.

In this chapter we will learn how the United States began to look beyond its own boundaries. As you read, look for answers to these questions:

1. Why did Americans begin to take a greater interest in world affairs?
2. How did the United States gain islands in the Pacific and Caribbean?
3. How did the United States handle problems in lands freed from Spain?
4. What led to the building of the Panama Canal?
5. How did the nation gain more island possessions?

entirely different from those they had at the age of fifteen.

Nations, like people, grow and change. A small, weak nation acts one way, but a big, powerful country acts another way. Thus when the United States was young, it was interested in starting new settlements, in expanding westward across the continent, in creating and enlarging industries. But the time came when the United States began to take a greater interest in world affairs. This interest, which was only

1 Why Did Americans Begin to Take a Greater Interest in World Affairs?

What is foreign policy? When a nation follows a certain plan of action toward other nations over a period of time, such a plan is called the nation's **foreign policy.** Early in the 1800's, for example, the United States decided that it did not want European nations to interfere in the Western Hemisphere. The United States, therefore, announced the Monroe Doctrine (page 282). A century later, the United States decided to act together with other countries in North and South America for the common good. With this purpose, it adopted the Good Neighbor Policy (page 651). These are examples of foreign policy.

The United States had little interest in foreign affairs before the late 1800's. For a while after 1865, the United States was not much concerned with foreign policy. Americans were too busy with things close at home. The Civil War was over. Great open spaces attracted people seeking land of their own. Rail-

roads had to be built, mines had to be dug, farms had to be established. How well Americans succeeded in these tasks between 1860 and 1890 is shown by a few significant facts. In 1860, for example, only 31 million people lived in the United States, most of them east of the Mississippi. In 1890, thirty years later, the American population had doubled to 63 million. In 1860, there were about 30,000 miles of railroad track in the United States, but no railroad yet crossed the continent. By 1890, there were over 165,000 miles of track, and several railroads connected the Pacific coast and the Middle West. In 1890, American farmers produced twice as much corn, and more than twice as much wheat and cotton, as in 1860. The value of goods manufactured in the United States in 1890 was five times as great as in 1860.

Growth like this calls for much hard work. The job at hand was big

601

● See p. T51 for a strategy asking students to examine how the need for new markets affected American foreign policy in the late 1800's and early 1900's.

enough for most Americans. What need did they have to think of distant lands?

Americans look for new markets. After a time, however, the very success of their work at home led Americans to look beyond their country. The American farmer, for example, grew more cotton and wheat and produced more ham and bacon than other Americans could buy and use. The American miner likewise dug more copper and more coal than could be sold in the United States. The American logger and sawmill owner produced more lumber than was required in this country. And the American manufacturer made more than people could buy. This extra supply of goods is called a **surplus.**

Because these producers could not sell their surplus goods in this country, ● they had to look abroad for new markets. American business leaders also found that at times they had more money than they could invest at home. They, too, began to look to other countries for chances to put their money to good use. In countries that lacked money to develop their own resources, business people and bankers could invest in mining, industry, or business and often make large profits. One American, thinking of all these things, remarked, "Whether they will or no, Americans must now begin to look outward."

Trade increases the interest of this country in world affairs. As Americans increased their foreign trade or invested their money abroad, they became more interested in the affairs of other countries. Business leaders are always concerned about countries where they sell or buy. If a business makes money, the managers of that business naturally want to increase their profits by widening their markets or by finding ways to invest more money. On the other hand, if a business loses money, its managers want to know why. Perhaps conditions in a foreign country are upset or its government is unfriendly or weak. Business leaders cannot do much by themselves to change such conditions. So they may ask the aid of their own government. The United States on several occasions took a hand in the affairs of foreign countries in order to protect the interests of American businesses.

Thus, with the growth of American trade came a growth of interest in other parts of the globe. Beginning slowly at first, this interest increased as the years went by.

▶ **CHECK UP**   See Teacher's Key.

1. **(a)** What is a nation's foreign policy? **(b)** Why did Americans take little interest in foreign affairs before the late 1800's?
2. Why did the growth of American industry and agriculture lead Americans to seek new markets?
3. How did overseas trade cause Americans to become interested in the affairs of other countries?

2 How Did the United States Gain Islands in the Pacific and Caribbean?

In 1867 Secretary of State William Seward, with dreams of gaining more land for this country, persuaded the Senate that the United States should buy Alaska from Russia (page 584). For some thirty years after that time, few Americans cared about further expansion. Then, in the late 1890's, Americans became interested in the Pacific and the Caribbean.

★ Have students read more about Alaska in "Linking Past and Present" (p. 616).

THE UNITED STATES ANNEXES HAWAII

In the Pacific Ocean, more than 2,000 miles southwest of San Francisco, lies a group of islands topped by jagged mountains. These islands, called Hawaii, have an area about the size of New Jersey. The first inhabitants of Hawaii were Polynesians (PAHL-uh-NEE-zhunz) from other Pacific islands. Paddling giant canoes, they made their way to Hawaii over 1,000 years ago.

Americans settle in Hawaii. In the late 1700's, Yankee sailors from whaling ships and trading vessels began to stop at these islands for water and supplies. Then American missionaries, traders, and storekeepers settled in Hawaii. Peoples of other countries also went there to live — Chinese, Japanese, British, and Germans. But the Americans gained control of most of the land and business.

American involvement in Hawaii grows. Because Americans had settled in Hawaii, the American government began to take a keen interest in these

Hawaii's ideal climate and rich soil attracted American settlers to the islands. This picture shows what Honolulu, the capital of Hawaii, looked like in 1883.

islands. The United States made an agreement with the ruler of Hawaii (1) that no part of the islands should be given to any foreign country and (2) that only Americans would be able to use Pearl Harbor, the best harbor in the islands.

The Americans who lived in Hawaii, however, wanted even closer ties with the United States. Most of them made their living by growing sugar cane, and most of the huge sugar crop was sold in the United States. The prosperity of Americans in Hawaii, therefore, depended on maintaining good trade relations between the United States and Hawaii.

The American sugar growers in Hawaii hoped for an even stronger connection between the islands and the United States. "Why," they asked each other, "shouldn't Hawaii become a part of the United States? Then there would always be a sure market for our sugar." This idea gained more and more support. Finally, a revolution, led by American sugar planters, broke out in 1893. The ruler of Hawaii, Queen Liliuokalani (lee-LEE-oo-oh-kah-LAH-nee), was forced to give up her throne. ● But when those taking part in the revolution asked that Hawaii be made a part

● Mention that Queen Liliuokalani reigned from 1891 to 1893.

Queen Liliuokalani, the last ruler of Hawaii, was overthrown in 1893 by American settlers who wanted the islands to become a possession of the United States.

of the United States, their request was refused. President Grover Cleveland objected because he did not believe that the uprising was supported by the Hawaiian people themselves. He disapproved of the part played by Americans in the revolution. He was especially disturbed because marines from an American warship had taken part in the uprising against the queen.

Disappointed by the failure of their plan, the leaders of the revolution declared Hawaii to be a republic. After William McKinley became President, however, Congress voted in 1898 to annex Hawaii. It was organized as an American territory, and American citizenship was given to all citizens of the

islands. Under American rule, Hawaii prospered, exporting sugar and pineapples to the mainland and in turn buying large amounts of manufactured goods.

More than once, the Hawaiians voted to become a state in the Union. In 1959 Congress accepted their petition, and Hawaii became our fiftieth state.

WAR WITH SPAIN BRINGS THE UNITED STATES NEW TERRITORIES

The annexation of Hawaii did not seem as important to most Americans as events taking place about the same time on the island of Cuba. About 90 miles south of Key West (Florida), Cuba had been under Spanish rule ever since Christopher Columbus landed there in 1492. When the rest of Spanish America revolted and won independence (Chapter 10), Cuba and Puerto Rico, another Caribbean island, remained loyal to Spain.

Cuba revolts against Spain. In the late 1800's, however, the Cubans became restless under Spanish rule. Several times they rebelled and tried to win their independence. Each time the soldiers of Spain overpowered them. In 1895 they tried again. In a village of eastern Cuba, a small group of men unfurled a flag with five bars and a single star. Standing under this flag, they declared Cuba an independent country.

When Spain refused to give Cuba its freedom, rebellion flamed from one end of the island to the other. Spanish troops marched against the Cubans, seeking to stamp out the uprising. But the Cubans avoided open battle. They carried out surprise attacks on the Spanish soldiers, doing what damage they could and dashing away. They burned supplies and fields of sugar cane, the island's chief crop. The Spanish forces fought back, hoping to trap enough Cubans in one place to put an end to the revolt.

604

● See p. T51 for a strategy calling for students to put together a bulletin board display featuring Hawaii.

AMERICA ADVANCES ACROSS THE PACIFIC

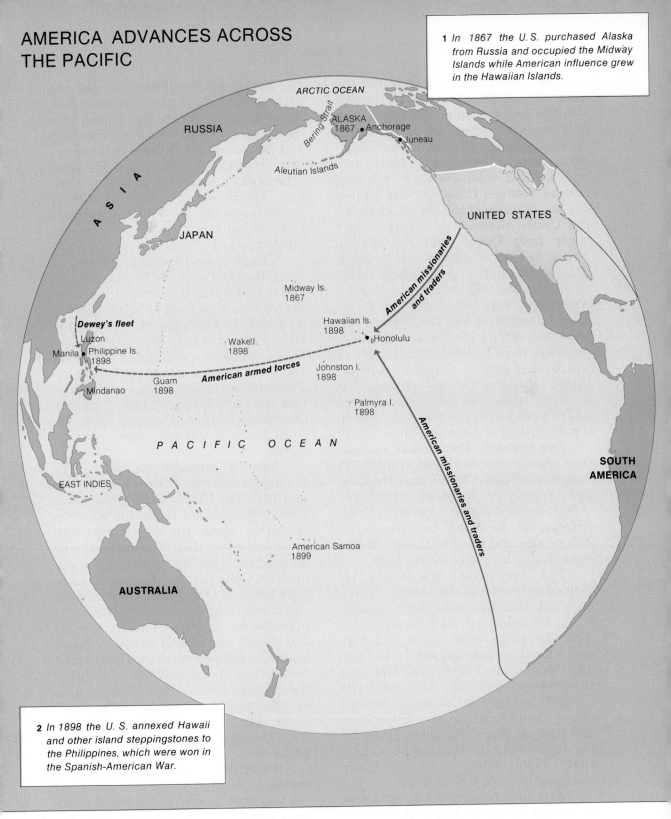

1 *In 1867 the U.S. purchased Alaska from Russia and occupied the Midway Islands while American influence grew in the Hawaiian Islands.*

ARCTIC OCEAN

RUSSIA

ASIA

ALASKA
1867
Anchorage
Juneau

Bering Strait

Aleutian Islands

JAPAN

UNITED STATES

Midway Is.
1867

American missionaries and traders

Dewey's fleet
Luzon
Manila • Philippine Is.
1898

Hawaiian Is.
1898
Honolulu

Wake I.
1898

American armed forces

Guam
1898

Mindanao

Johnston I.
1898

Palmyra I.
1898

American missionaries and traders

PACIFIC OCEAN

EAST INDIES

American Samoa
1899

SOUTH
AMERICA

AUSTRALIA

2 *In 1898 the U.S. annexed Hawaii and other island steppingstones to the Philippines, which were won in the Spanish-American War.*

MAP STUDY On this map you see how American influence moved westward across the Pacific. (a) When was Alaska purchased? (b) What other American possessions are shown and when was each acquired? (c) What routes did American missionaries and traders take to Hawaii?

605

See Teacher's Key.

The American people favor the Cubans. The United States watched the struggle between Cuba and Spain with deep concern. Americans had invested great sums of money in Cuban sugar plantations, mines, and other businesses. Also, extensive trade was carried on between Cuba and the United States. Because of the revolt, however, the United States was unable to buy sugar from Cuba. And the United States in turn could not export meat, flour, and manufactured goods to Cuba.

There was still another reason why Americans were interested in Cuba. They remembered how the thirteen colonies had revolted and won their independence from England. The people of the United States, therefore, sympathized with the Cubans' struggle for freedom. American newspapers were full of news about the revolt, and were highly critical of Spanish policy.

The battleship *Maine* blows up. As the Cuban revolt continued, the United States government feared that the lives and property of American citizens in Cuba were in danger. To protect these citizens, an American battleship, the *Maine,* steamed into the harbor of Havana, Cuba, late in January, 1898.

For three weeks the *Maine* remained at anchor in the harbor. Then, on a hot, still night, the ship's captain sat in his cabin writing a letter to his wife. Suddenly there was a dull roar and a terrible explosion shook the city. The *Maine* had blown up! The ship sank immediately, and soon only the tangled wreckage of its masts showed above the surface. Of the 350 officers and men on board, 260 were killed by the explosion or drowned in the sinking ship. Eight others were so badly wounded that they later died.

War comes between the United States and Spain. Nobody knows for certain who or what caused the explosion on the *Maine.* It would have been foolish of the Spaniards to blow up the ship, for the last thing Spain wanted was war with the United States. Nevertheless, in 1898, angry Americans blamed the Spaniards for the destruction of the ship and the loss of life. Everywhere the cry was "Remember the *Maine*!" Americans said, "Spain must be taught a lesson! The people of Cuba, and of other Spanish colonies as well, must be freed from the control of the Spanish government!"

Congress was in a fighting mood. It voted that Cuba should be independent and that the armed forces of the United States should be used to help Cuba win its freedom. Congress also voted that after Cuba became free, the United States would "leave the government and control of the island to its people." This announcement was meant to show that the United States had no intention of selfishly grabbing Cuba for itself. On April 25, 1898, war with Spain was declared.

America prepares for war. The Spanish navy was both weak and ill-prepared; the United States Navy was more powerful and ready for war. On the other hand, the entire American army had fewer than 30,000 officers and men, while Spain had about 80,000 soldiers in Cuba alone. Immediate steps were taken to strengthen the American army and prepare it for battle. The plan was for American forces to invade and occupy the islands owned by Spain in the Caribbean Sea. As for the United States Navy, it was ordered to blockade the Cuban coast so that no more men and supplies from Spain could reach Cuba. The navy would also seek to destroy the enemy's ships, wherever they might be.

Dewey destroys the Spanish fleet at Manila. The first important battle of the war took place thousands of miles from Cuba. War had hardly been declared when Commodore George Dewey with several American warships set sail from a port in China. His goal was the

606

See p. T51 for a strategy calling for students to do additional research on the war between the United States and Spain.

Both black and white troops took part in the famous battle at San Juan Hill.

Philippine Islands (map, page 605), then owned by Spain. On the morning of May 1, 1898, Dewey boldly attacked a Spanish squadron of ships in Manila Bay in the Philippines. Back and forth steamed the American warships, firing until the Spanish vessels were destroyed.

In spite of Dewey's victory, the Philippine Islands could not be conquered until American soldiers arrived to defeat the Spanish land forces. Dewey blockaded the capital city of Manila, but it took many months to send an army all the way from the United States. In August, 1898, after an attack by American soldiers and Filipino patriots who were eager to win freedom from Spain, Manila surrendered.

Swift victories are won in Cuba. Meanwhile, American forces had been winning victories in the Spanish islands in the Caribbean Sea. Late in June a force of American soldiers landed in Cuba. In the campaign that followed, these soldiers fought under serious handicaps. When they left the United States, they wore heavy woolen uni-

forms totally wrong for the stifling Cuban heat. Much of the food sent with them turned out to be spoiled. Furthermore, there was little protection from malaria and yellow fever, diseases which flourished in the warm climate. More American soldiers in Cuba actually died from disease than were killed on the battlefields. Nevertheless, the American army advanced against the city of Santiago (map, page 612).

One of the famous battles of the war occurred just outside Santiago. The American army unit known as the Rough Riders, together with several units of black troops, stormed and captured San Juan (sahn HWAHN) Hill. The Rough Riders, as we have seen, were volunteers commanded by Colonel Leonard Wood and Lieutenant Colonel Theodore Roosevelt (page 590). After the Americans had seized San Juan Hill, as well as other hills surrounding the city, Santiago could not be defended and it later surrendered.

Meanwhile, an American naval squadron in Cuban waters won nearly as complete a victory as Dewey had at Manila. A few Spanish ships had

607

● Have students look back at the picture of Roosevelt as a Rough Rider on p. 580.

crossed the Atlantic early in the war. But they had been bottled up in the harbor of Santiago by American vessels. One July morning the Spanish ships made a dash for freedom. The ● American fleet attacked and destroyed every enemy ship.

After the surrender of Santiago, American forces landed on the island of Puerto Rico. Within a short time they had occupied most of that island.

Peace brings new territories to the United States. Having suffered such losses, the Spanish government sought an end to the conflict. On August 12, 1898, less than four months after Congress had declared war, the United States and Spain agreed to end the fighting. But several questions needed to be answered. What was to be done with Cuba? With Puerto Rico? With the Philippines?

The American people could not agree about what to do with the islands. Some believed that the United States should not take any responsibility for lands outside our mainland boundaries. These persons also felt that a democracy should not force its rule on foreign peoples. Others believed that Americans had a duty toward the people they had freed from Spain. In the end, ownership of Puerto Rico in the Caribbean Sea, and Guam (GWAHM) and the Philippines in the Pacific, was transferred to the United States. (Find these islands on the maps on pages 605 and 612.) In return for the Philippines, however, the United States paid Spain $20 million. In addition, Spain agreed to give independence to Cuba.

▶ **CHECK UP**   See Teacher's Key.

1. **(a)** Why did Americans become interested in Hawaii? **(b)** How did the United States acquire Hawaii?
2. **(a)** Why did the Cubans revolt against Spain? **(b)** Why was the United States concerned? **(c)** What event led to war between Spain and the United States?
3. **(a)** What was the American plan for action against Spain? **(b)** What were the results of the fighting?
4. What territories did the United States acquire in the peace settlement?

3 How Did the United States Handle Problems in Lands Freed from Spain?

The United States gives a helping hand to Cuba. Although the Spanish-American War freed Cuba, the newly independent country faced many problems. There was no organized government. Many Cubans were homeless, poorly clothed, and starving. Disease, especially yellow fever, was widespread. American troops, therefore, remained in Cuba to lend a helping hand.

Yellow fever is conquered in Cuba. The Americans also helped Cuba to stamp out yellow fever. For many centuries yellow fever had been a dreaded disease in tropical countries, but no one knew what caused it. A Cuban doctor, Carlos Finlay, believed that yellow fever was carried by mosquitoes which bred in swamps and in stagnant water. But he had not been able to prove his theory. One sure test was to allow healthy humans to be bitten by mosquitoes that had previously bitten yellow fever victims. A number of soldiers volunteered to risk their lives in this experiment. As a result, Major Walter Reed and other army doctors were able to make an important discovery. They proved beyond a doubt that yellow fever was carried by a certain kind of mosquito.

The remedy for yellow fever, then, was to wipe out all mosquitoes wherever they were found. Swamps were drained, and oil was spread over pools of stagnant water to destroy the young mosquitoes. In three months Major William C. Gorgas, in charge of health conditions in Cuba, was able to rid Havana of yellow fever.

Cubans resent American controls. The United States also helped Cuba establish a government. Cubans adopted a constitution and elected a president and a legislature. In 1902, American soldiers were withdrawn from the island, but the United States kept some control over Cuba. A special treaty allowed the United States to maintain naval bases there. It also gave our country the right to intervene in Cuban affairs if the lives and property of American citizens or the freedom of Cuba were threatened. Under this treaty American forces returned to Cuba more than once when revolutions broke out. Cubans, however, resented American interference. It reminded them that Cuba was not completely independent.

The Philippines and Puerto Rico present problems. The United States also faced difficult problems in the Philippine Islands and Puerto Rico. Unlike earlier additions to American territory (such as Florida, Louisiana, California, and Oregon), these islands were separated from the mainland by oceans. They were inhabited by peoples unfamiliar with American speech, customs, or form of government. What was the future of these former Spanish possessions to be? Were they to remain American colonies? Were they to become independent? Few Americans felt certain about these matters. The "march of the flag" outside our borders had brought heavy responsibilities to the United States. Many people wondered if we had undertaken too much.

The United States governs the Philippines. The Philippines had special

William Howard Taft (center), named the first governor of the Philippines in 1901, later became our twenty-seventh President.

problems of its own. On its many islands lived people of many different languages and cultures. Most of the Filipinos resented American control. They had expected that the United States would give them freedom. After the surrender of the Spanish, Filipino troops fought for their independence against American forces. Fighting took many lives on both sides before the conflict ended.

After order had been restored, the United States tried to improve conditions in the Philippines. A bureau of health was set up. To provide education, teachers were trained. By the 1930's, more than 7,000 schools had been established. Local government was organized in towns and villages. Good roads were built. To provide farms for poor people, the government bought great tracts of land which were divided into small plots. Modern ways of farming and better tools were introduced.

Growing trade also helped the Philippines. Americans bought great quantities of Philippine sugar, hemp, and

609

See p. T51 for a strategy calling for students to examine the consequences of this "march of the flag."

In 1952 Puerto Rico became a self-governing commonwealth under the protection of the United States. What does this picture tell you about life today in San Juan, Puerto Rico's capital?

tobacco. After 1909, these products entered the United States free of tariff duties.

The Filipinos seek independence. As conditions in the islands improved, the United States gave the Filipinos a greater share in their own government. Beginning in 1907, they elected members to their own Philippine Assembly. In 1916, Congress approved a constitution for the Philippine Islands. This constitution provided for a senate and a house of representatives to be elected by the Filipinos. Laws made by the Philippine legislature, however, could be vetoed by the American governor-general. Except for the governor-general and a few other officials, government positions were to be held by Filipinos. The United States also promised to withdraw its control from the islands as soon as a stable government was established.

Many Filipinos were not satisfied with greater self-government under American control. Believing they were already capable of governing themselves, they asked for immediate independence. In 1934 Congress responded to these demands by granting the Philippines self-government. The country was to remain under American protection for ten years, after which it would become completely independent. World War II delayed these plans, but on July 4, 1946, the independent Philippine Republic was born.

Puerto Rico comes under American rule. After the United States took over Puerto Rico, conditions were improved on that island. The way was made clear for Puerto Rican products to enter the United States without tariff duties. As a result, sugar, tobacco, and banana production boomed. The United States built roads, improved health conditions, and increased the number of schools.

In spite of these improvements, Puerto Rico still had serious problems. Although trade with the United States brought more wealth to Puerto Rico, very little of it reached the ordinary person. There was much unemployment and poverty.

Then, the Puerto Ricans started a program called Operation Bootstrap, ● which encouraged the establishment of manufacturing on the island and attracted investments from the United States. Many new factories were set up, creating thousands of jobs and adding greatly to the island's income. In addition, Puerto Rico's tropical scenery attracted many vacationers, and so the tourist trade became an important source of income.

In spite of these hopeful developments, unemployment led thousands of Puerto Ricans to move to the mainland

● Mention that Operation Bootstrap began in the 1940's.

in the years after World War II. By the 1970's about a third of all Puerto Ricans — more than one and a half million people — were living on the American mainland. Of these about half had settled in New York City. Many also lived in Philadelphia, Chicago, Miami, Los Angeles, and San Francisco.

Puerto Rico is a free commonwealth. Puerto Ricans have been American citizens since 1917 and for many years have elected representatives to make their own laws. In 1952 Puerto Rico became a commonwealth, or free republic, under United States military protection. As a commonwealth, Puerto Rico has certain advantages. Puerto Ricans pay no federal income tax on money earned in Puerto Rico. They also enjoy free trade with the United States and unrestricted migration to the mainland. Moreover, the people of Puerto Rico are free to decide what their rela-

tions with the United States will be. Some people, for example, say the island should become the fifty-first state; others favor independence. But in election after election Puerto Rico's voters have chosen to keep the island's commonwealth status.

▶ **CHECK UP** See Teacher's Key.

1. **(a)** How did Americans help Cuba after 1898? **(b)** What sort of control did the United States keep in Cuba? **(c)** How did the Cubans feel about this control?
2. **(a)** How did the United States try to improve conditions in the Philippines? **(b)** By what steps did the Philippines become independent?
3. **(a)** How did conditions improve in Puerto Rico after 1898? **(b)** Why was Operation Bootstrap started? **(c)** What advantages does Puerto Rico enjoy as a commonwealth?

4 What Led to the Building of the Panama Canal?

At the beginning of the 1900's, United States territory stretched not only from the Atlantic to the Pacific but halfway across the world. Yet there was no shortcut by which our navy and merchant ships could reach the Pacific coast from the Atlantic coast. They had to travel south the full length of South America, around Cape Horn and north again, a trip of about 12,000 miles. To protect our possessions in the Pacific and to help American commerce, it became important to shorten this long trip. A glance at the map on page 612 will show you that the narrowest place between the North and South American continents is the Isthmus of Panama. Why not build a canal across the Isthmus?

The United States decides to dig a canal. The idea of building a canal across Panama was not a new one. During the 1800's, France and England as well as the United States had considered such a canal. But in 1898 the United States government became fully aware of how necessary a canal was for the defense of our coasts. When the Spanish-American War broke out in that year, the *Oregon,* a battleship of the United States Navy, was in the Pacific. Ordered to Cuba, the *Oregon* made the long trip around South America and did not arrive until the short war was almost over! The government was convinced that a canal must be built and that the United States must build it.

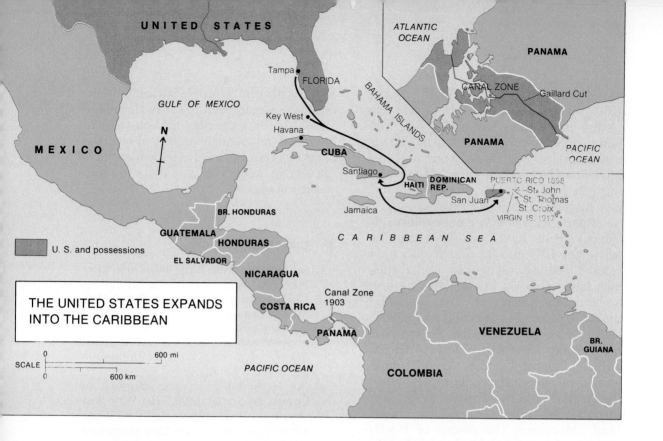

THE UNITED STATES EXPANDS INTO THE CARIBBEAN

U. S. and possessions

MAP STUDY See Teacher's Key.
The arrows show American campaigns during the Spanish-American War. Dates tell when territories came under American control. (a) When was the Panama Canal Zone acquired? (b) In what direction do ships entering the Panama Canal from the Caribbean Sea travel?

For many years the United States had had an agreement with Great Britain that neither country should control by itself a canal route across Central America. In 1901 our government made a new treaty with Great Britain. This agreement stated that the United States alone could build and control a canal if ships of all nations were allowed to use it.

The next step was to decide where to build the canal. Two routes were considered — one across Nicaragua, the other across Panama. The shorter route across Panama was finally recommended, although it meant cutting through mountains in the interior. A French company had already tried to build a canal through the Isthmus of Panama. But the company failed. The diseases of malaria and yellow fever took the lives of some 40,000 workers and the company ran out of money. The United States bought the property rights of this French company.

The United States secures land for the canal. The next step was to make arrangements for the right to build the canal across Panama. At that time Panama was a part of the Republic of Colombia in South America. Colombia refused to give the United States permission to dig a canal in Panama. But the people of Panama were eager to have the canal built. They did not want the United States to choose the Nicaraguan route. In 1903, with the encouragement of the American President, Theodore Roosevelt, Panama revolted from Colombia and set up an independent republic. American warships off the coast of Panama prevented Colombian troops from landing to stop the revolt. Also, the United States hastily made an agreement with the new Republic of Panama. For a down payment of

612

● See p. T51 for a strategy asking students to use the picture on page 613 in discussing the building of the Panama Canal.

● Have students prepare written or oral reports that describe how yellow fever was conquered.

$10,000,000 and rent of $250,000 a year, its government leased to the United States a strip of land ten miles wide.

Disease is conquered in Panama. Our government had not forgotten the reason for the French failure in Panama. Colonel William Gorgas, the man who had ended yellow fever in Cuba, was sent to Panama. In the ten-mile-wide strip called the Canal Zone, Colonel Gorgas drained swamps and ponds to keep the deadly mosquitoes from breeding. Not only the Zone, but much of Panama surrounding it, was freed of mosquitoes. Deaths from malaria and
● yellow fever became rare. After two years, work began on the canal.

The "Big Ditch" is dug. Colonel George Goethals (GOH-thalz), of the United States Army Engineers, was given the tremendous task of building the canal. Because of mountains in the interior, it was decided to build a canal which would be 85 feet above sea level in the middle of the Isthmus. Locks were to be built to raise and lower ships, and rivers were to be dammed to create a waterway in the interior. For seven years, using huge steam shovels and other powerful machinery, workers blasted and dug and dredged. The most difficult task was cutting a channel, eight or nine miles long, through mountains of solid rock.

In August, 1914, the great engineering feat was at last completed. In faraway Washington, President Wilson pushed a switch that released the dammed-up waters and filled the "Big Ditch." Soon ships were passing from one ocean to the other. These ships could now travel from the east coast of our country to the west coast at a saving of 7,000 miles! Many ports in other parts of the world were also brought closer together.

Control of the Canal Zone is set up. The Canal Zone, 10 miles wide and about 40 miles long, was controlled by the American government. Thousands of Americans lived there, most having some connection with the canal — workers, engineers, or members of the armed forces. As time went on, however, the people and government of Panama asked for more authority over the Zone and operation of the canal. After

Thousands of workers, using huge machinery, moved earth and mountains to dig the Panama Canal. This picture shows work on one section of the canal in 1907.

long negotiations, both countries agreed in 1978 to a treaty that would turn the canal over to Panama at the end of 1999. Another treaty guaranteed the neutrality of the canal after that. Many Americans have been unhappy with these treaties. They have said that since the United States built the canal, our country should continue to own and operate it.

▶ **CHECK UP** See Teacher's Key.

1. **(a)** Why did the United States want to build a canal across Central America? **(b)** How did the United States acquire the right to build the canal in Panama?
2. **(a)** What problems were overcome in building the canal? **(b)** How was the Canal Zone governed? **(c)** How will that change in 1999?

5 How Did the Nation Gain More Island Possessions?

The story of American overseas possessions would not be complete without mentioning the other islands in the Pacific Ocean and the Caribbean Sea that the United States acquired. As you read about these islands, locate them on the maps on pages 605 and 612.

The United States bought the Virgin Islands from Denmark in 1917. Below, part of the Virgin Islands National Park on St. John Island.

Wake, Midway, and Guam become American possessions. You read in Chapter 27 that our government acquired the Midway Islands, so named because they lie halfway between America and Asia. When the first cable was laid across the Pacific, it went by way of the main island, Midway. About 2,000 miles straight west of Honolulu lies Wake Island, three square miles in area. In 1898, the United States Navy

614

● See p. T51 for a strategy that asks students to identify and locate the islands acquired by the United States in the late 1800's and early 1900's.

took possession of it. Midway and Wake, both of which are barren coral islands, are used as stopping points for planes winging their way across the Pacific.

Guam, ceded to us by Spain, is the largest of the Pacific island group called the Marianas. It was first important as a naval station. Later, a government radio station was set up there. Guam also became a stop on air routes to Asia. For many years Guam was governed by an American naval officer. Then, in 1950, the people of Guam became United States citizens. They elect their own governor and legislature, and send a nonvoting representative to Congress. Because Guam is so far from the United States, it is six hours earlier there than it is in California. The people of Guam like to say that their island is "the place where America's day begins."

American Samoa and the Virgin Islands are other dependencies. On the ocean route between San Francisco and Australia lie the Samoan (sah-MOH-un) Islands. Rivalry with Great Britain and Germany, who were also interested in Samoa, led the United States to take possession of five of the islands in 1899. The first popularly elected governor of

American Samoa took office in 1978. In addition, the Samoans have their own legislature.

The last territory acquired by the United States was in the Caribbean. In 1917, we paid $25 million to Denmark for three small islands in the Virgin Islands group. These islands were considered necessary for the defense of the Panama Canal. For several years they were governed by a naval officer. Today the people of the Virgin Islands elect their own governor as well as members of their own legislature. The residents of the Virgin Islands have been citizens of the United States since 1927.

By the early 1900's, then, the island ● possessions of the United States stretched from the nearby Caribbean Sea to remote areas of the Pacific. In accepting responsibility for these islands and their peoples, the United States took another step toward the role of world leader.

▶ **CHECK UP**   See Teacher's Key.

1. **(a)** What islands did the United States acquire in the Pacific? **(b)** In the Caribbean?
2. How are these islands governed?

CHECK UP ON CHAPTER 28   See Teacher's Key.

Words to Know

1. isthmus
2. canal lock
3. yellow fever
4. surplus
5. mainland
6. commonwealth
7. foreign policy

Places to Locate

1. Hawaii
2. Cuba
3. Havana
4. Guam
5. Puerto Rico
6. Philippines
7. Manila
8. Caribbean Sea
9. Wake Island
10. American Samoa
11. Midway Islands
12. Virgin Islands
13. Panama
14. Canal Zone

Facts to Remember

1. What things happened in this country in the late 1800's that made business leaders and the government take a greater interest in world affairs?
2. **(a)** What groups of Americans settled in Hawaii in the 1800's? **(b)** What events led to Hawaii's becoming an American possession?
3. **(a)** Why did the United States declare war against Spain in 1898? **(b)** Where did the fighting take place? **(c)** What was the outcome of the war?
4. **(a)** How did the United States acquire

615

Facts to Remember (cont.)

the Panama Canal Zone? **(b)** What problems had to be solved in building the canal?

Skills to Practice

1. Choose the correct answer in each of the following statements. Use the maps on pages 605 and 612 to find the answers.
   a. Puerto Rico is (east, west) of Cuba.
   b. The Virgin Islands include an island named (San Juan, St. Thomas).
   c. Mexico is (east, west) of the Caribbean Sea.
   d. Guam is (east, west) of the Philippines.
   e. The United States acquired Alaska (before, after) it acquired American Samoa.
   f. Alaska is (northeast, northwest) of the first 48 states.
   g. Commodore Dewey won an important victory at (Manila, Honolulu).

2. Make a chart listing the overseas territories that the United States has owned. Include those that are no longer United States territories. List the territories at the left side of the chart. Along the top of the chart write the following headings for columns to be filled in: Location; Date Acquired; From What Country; How Acquired (war or purchase, for example); Present Status.

Questions to Think About

1. Why was it hard for the United States government and people to decide what to do about the lands acquired from Spain after the Spanish-American War?
2. **(a)** What was the importance of the Panama Canal when it was opened in 1914? **(b)** Is it still important today? Explain.
3. Why did the people of Cuba and of the Philippines strongly want independence rather than American rule?

Linking Past and Present

The United States Naval Academy. Much of the Spanish-American War was fought at sea. The conflict demonstrated to the American public the importance of the United States Naval Academy.

Secretary of the Navy George Bancroft had started the Naval Academy at Annapolis, Maryland, in 1845 as a place to educate and train young men to become officers in the United States Navy and Marine Corps. The school was small in its early days, with only eighty students, called midshipmen, in the first class. The Spanish-American War stimulated American interest and pride in the navy, however. New buildings were constructed at the school and the course of study was greatly expanded. The academy grew in size so that enrollment today stands at over 4,000 midshipmen. Women were first admitted in 1976. Four years later, fifty-five women midshipmen were graduated.

How cold is Alaska? Probably no one in 1867 ever dreamed that the Alaskan "icebox" would become a state of the Union. Oddly enough, there may be some people today who still think of Alaska as an icebox. There are of course vast frozen areas in the Arctic region to the north. But in central and southern Alaska, temperatures are not so cold. One reason is that the coastal region is warmed by an ocean stream called the Japan Current.

The interior of Alaska is warm and often hot during the short summer, and in the winter it is no colder than some of the states just south of Canada. It is true that the winters are long and the summer season is short, lasting only about two months. But during these summer months the sun shines up to nineteen hours a day. The long hours ★ of sunshine produce fine crops of vegetables, fruits, and flowers.

★ Tell students that these crops are grown in a soil known as *loess* (soil made up of particles of sand and clay deposited by wind).

For answers see Teacher's Key.

Have students bring news stories to class. Ask them to identify the facts in those stories.

GAINING SKILL

Evaluating Information

Americans get their information about public affairs through reading newspapers and magazines, listening to radio and television reports, and taking part in discussions. But people often disagree on public issues. It is not unusual to hear or read reports that give different opinions on the same issue. How can you evaluate the information given in such reports? (To *evaluate* a report is to judge its truth and fairness.) Applying the following questions to what you read and hear will help you do that.

(1) *Is the report a first-hand report*? If the reporter did not actually observe what he or she describes, the report might include errors. Stories have a way of "growing" as they are told and retold.

(2) *Is the report accurate*? Some people are better qualified than others to report on certain situations. In a foreign country, for instance, a person who does not understand the language and customs will have difficulty in reporting accurately on what is happening.

(3) *Is the source trustworthy*? Some sources of information and some persons develop a reputation for being trustworthy; others do not. An account may be untrustworthy because the reporter is careless. Or a reporter might be influenced by emotions such as fear, anger, or excitement.

(4) *Is the report a statement of fact or of opinion*? Since statements of both fact and opinion appear in almost all reports, you must try to distinguish between them. Also, you should be aware that a reporter sometimes selects facts to support a particular point of view.

Now use what you have learned to evaluate the information shown below on the front page of the New York *Journal*. Study the *Journal* and answer these questions.

1. What statements of fact can you identify in the paper's reports? What statements are opinions?
2. What words reveal strong feelings about the sinking of the *Maine*?
3. How could reports such as this one have affected relations between the United States and Spain?

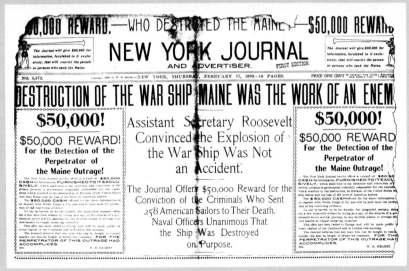

This issue of the *New York Journal* appeared on February 17, 1898, two days after the *Maine* was sunk.

617

CHAPTER **29**

Vocabulary preview: international law, draft, armistice, reparations, isolationism

The United States Plays a Larger Part in World Affairs

1865–1920   See p. T52 for chapter teaching strategies.

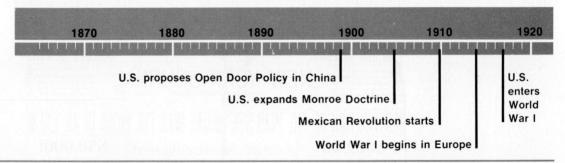

U.S. proposes Open Door Policy in China

U.S. expands Monroe Doctrine

Mexican Revolution starts

World War I begins in Europe

U.S. enters World War I

What this chapter is about —

The course of history does not always move in a straight line. Nations, like people, change their plans and policies. A plan or policy that seems wise and desirable at one time may seem less attractive, or even dangerous, at another

time. The affairs of a nation, it should be remembered, are more complicated than those of individual people. People can make their own decisions — to take a new job, for example, or to buy a new car. In a democracy like the United States, however, millions of voters have opinions on issues that affect the whole

618

world affairs. At times Americans took a vigorous and important part in world events. At other times they favored a less active part. For example, after a period of neutrality from 1914 to 1917, the United States entered World War I.

As you read how the foreign policy of the United States developed and changed, look for answers to these questions:

1. How did American foreign policy develop in the early 1900's?
2. What part did the United States play in World War I?
3. Why did efforts to establish a lasting peace fail?

nation. When the country is faced by a problem, there is much debate on the subject before government leaders finally decide what course to follow.

This chapter will tell about a period when the United States had some difficulty in making up its mind. In the early 1900's, our nation was growing larger and stronger. But it still could not quite decide what part to play in

1 How Did American Foreign Policy Develop in the Early 1900's?

You read in the last chapter how the Spanish-American War marked a turning point in America's relations with the rest of the world. As a result of the war, the United States had possessions and important interests in the far Pacific area as well as in the Western Hemisphere. As Theodore Roosevelt said, it was no longer a question whether we would take part in world affairs, but "whether we should play that part well or ill." Even so, Americans still disagreed on the question of how active a part the United States should play in world affairs. Many Americans felt that overseas responsibilities were troublesome and expensive. When government leaders urged that the United States adopt an active foreign policy, they could expect a good deal of opposition. But our country could not ignore what was going on in the rest of the world. It continued, therefore, to develop new policies in its relations with other countries.

THE UNITED STATES DEVELOPS THE OPEN DOOR POLICY

Trade brings the United States in contact with China. Suppose a piece of string is tied tightly around a world globe so that it runs through Washington, D.C., and through the North and South Poles. On the side of the globe opposite Washington, this string will pass through Chungking, an important city in China.

Half a world away! We might suppose that people on opposite sides of the world would have no interest in each other. This is far from true. Very early in American history, Yankee ships made their way to China and began a brisk trade between the two countries (Chapter 14). At one time the speediest ships in the world were the China clippers that sailed between American and Chinese ports. One of the earliest airplanes to fly regularly across the Pacific Ocean was named the *China Clipper* after

619

● Have students use library sources to find pictures of clipper ships.

those sailing ships. For 150 years, until after World War II, the United States and China were generally on friendly terms.

European powers and Japan help themselves to parts of China. China was a united country long before the European nations were formed. Over many hundreds of years, the Chinese had developed their own art and literature and their own way of living. The Chinese people had not, however, gone through the same kind of Industrial Revolution that Europe and the United States had experienced. As a result, although China had many millions of people, it was not able to defend itself against stronger nations. In the 1800's, therefore, when certain European countries wanted to gain more trade and colonies in Asia, they were able to seize parts of China.

Great Britain, for example, forced China to give up Hong Kong and to permit English people to live and trade in

American troops joined with the forces of other nations in putting an end to the Boxer Rebellion in China.

five other Chinese cities. France gained trading rights in southern China. It also seized and ruled Indochina, on China's southern border. Russia forced China to give it special privileges in Manchuria and Port Arthur. (Locate these places on the map on the next page.) In the 1890's, Japan made war on China and forced it to give up territory.

The Chinese strike back in the Boxer Rebellion. Patriotic Chinese became angry. Why, they asked, should our country be handed out bit by bit to foreigners? Why should so many foreigners come to live and make money in China? Patriotic Chinese formed secret societies known by such names as "Great Sword Society," the "Plum-Blossom Fists," and the "Fists of Public Harmony." Because the members of these Chinese societies practiced gymnastics, foreigners called them "boxers." In their secret meetings the "boxers" talked of the great day when foreigners would be driven out of China.

Sooner or later, such angry feelings were bound to result in trouble. In 1900, Chinese people rioted in the city of Peking. They killed some foreigners

620

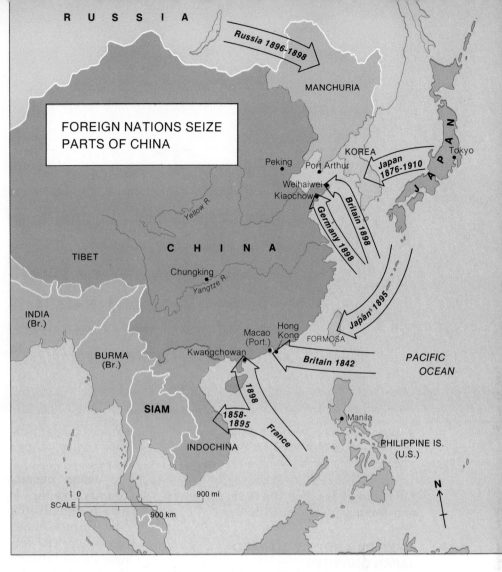

MAP STUDY

In the late 1800's several nations competed for trade and colonies in China. The arrows on this map point to places seized by those nations. (a) What nation acquired rights in Hong Kong? (b) In Port Arthur? (c) What areas did Japan acquire?

See Teacher's Key.

FOREIGN NATIONS SEIZE PARTS OF CHINA

RUSSIA

Russia 1896-1898

MANCHURIA

KOREA

Tokyo

Peking

Port Arthur

Japan 1876-1910

Weihaiwei

Britain 1898

Kiaochow

Germany 1898

Yellow R.

C H I N A

TIBET

Chungking

Yangtze R.

Japan 1895

INDIA (Br.)

Hong Kong

FORMOSA

Macao (Port.)

BURMA (Br.)

Kwangchowan

Britain 1842

PACIFIC OCEAN

1898

SIAM

1858-1895

France

Manila

INDOCHINA

PHILIPPINE IS. (U.S.)

0   900 mi
SCALE
0   900 km

N

and destroyed foreign-owned property. Embassies and foreign business houses in Peking were surrounded. This outbreak of violence became known as the Boxer Rebellion.

European countries, Japan, and the United States sent soldiers to stop the rioting in Peking and restore order. The Chinese government was forced to pay large sums of money for the damages suffered by foreigners and the trouble which the rioting had caused. The European powers and Japan kept their shares of this money, but the United States later returned more than half of its share. The money returned was used to send Chinese students to American schools and colleges.

The Open Door Policy urges fair play for China. In 1899, just a year before the Boxer Rebellion, the United States had shown its interest in China in another way. John Hay, the American Secretary of State, asked the other leading powers to declare that the people of all nations should be treated alike when they lived and traded in China. None were to seek special favors. Since Hay's idea meant that the door of China should be open to all, it was called the Open Door Policy. The United States ● hoped that this policy would benefit all who sought trade in China and also protect China's independence.

In time, other nations halfheartedly agreed to Hay's idea. The Open

621

● See p. T52 for a strategy asking students to examine how this policy and a new interpretation of the Monroe Doctrine affected American involvement in world affairs.

A Japanese artist painted this picture to show the arrival of Commodore Matthew Perry and other American officers in Tokyo.

Door Policy became the basis of American foreign policy in China.

AMERICAN POLICY TOWARD JAPAN CHANGES

Perry opens Japan to the world. The year 1854 was an important date in the history of Japan. For hundreds of years Japan had little to do with foreigners. It would not allow any foreigners (except a few Dutch ships) to enter its ports to carry on trade. Japan was almost completely shut off from the rest of the world.

Then, in 1854, Commodore Matthew C. Perry (a brother of Oliver H. Perry, the naval hero of the War of 1812) visited Japan with part of the United States fleet. The Japanese government was impressed by the strength of the American navy. It agreed to Perry's demand that Japan make a treaty with the United States, allowing Americans to trade in its ports. As a result of this treaty, Japan was opened to the world.

Japan becomes a strong, modern country. Before Perry's visit, the Japanese people lived in much the same way that Europeans had lived in the Middle Ages (pages 27–28). But when the Japanese came into contact with the rest of the world, they decided to make Japan a modern industrial country. In less than fifty years Japan became one of the world's great powers and a strong commercial and industrial nation.

Theodore Roosevelt helps settle Japan's war with Russia. For many years after Perry's visit, the United States and Japan were on friendly terms. Japan, to be sure, had been one of the countries that had "helped themselves" to parts of China. But Japan seemed to accept the Open Door Policy and joined the United States and the other foreign powers in putting down the Boxer Rebellion.

During the early 1900's, Russia was the country that seemed the most eager to expand into Chinese territory. Rus-

● See p. T52 for a strategy that calls for students to answer research questions about Perry's visit to Japan.

sia appeared to be trying to get a stronger grip on Manchuria, China's large northern territory. But Japan did not want any other country to get special rights in Manchuria. Manchuria was rich in iron and other minerals which Japan lacked and which it needed to build up its industry. So, in 1904, Japan went to war against Russia. Americans generally sympathized with Japan, much the smaller of the two nations.

To the surprise of many, Japan won victory after victory over Russia, both on land and at sea. When President Theodore Roosevelt offered his help in bringing the war to a close, Russia was glad to accept. As a result of Roosevelt's efforts, delegates from Russia and Japan met at Portsmouth, New Hampshire, and agreed on a treaty of peace ending the war. By the terms of the treaty, Japan was awarded the special rights which Russia had previously held in Manchuria. The treaty also recognized that Japan had special interests in Korea (map, page 621). But the Japanese were disappointed. They had hoped their victories would bring them even greater gains.

The United States and Japan become less friendly. With the end of the Russian-Japanese War, a change took place in relations between Japan and the United States. The Japanese, on the one hand, felt that President Roosevelt had favored Russia in the peace settlement. The Japanese also resented the restrictions placed on Japanese immigration into this country (pages 542–543). Many Americans, on the other hand, feared that a strong Japan would try to take over the Philippines.

Japan fails to support the Open Door Policy. The most important reason for unfriendliness between Japan and the United States grew out of Japan's attitude toward China. Japan seemed intent on controlling China and "shutting the door" on the rest of the world.

Japan openly took over Korea in 1910. Many Japanese spoke of a "Monroe Doctrine" for Asia, which would exclude Americans and Europeans. Then, during World War I, Japan made harsh demands on China. These were withdrawn only when the United States and other countries strongly objected.

THE UNITED STATES USES THE MONROE DOCTRINE

Every nation tries to protect certain vital interests such as its independence, its security, and its foreign trade. The United States believed that the Monroe Doctrine helped to protect its vital interests. The Doctrine had declared that European nations should not interfere with the governments of countries in the Americas (page 283). On two important occasions between 1860 and 1900 the United States used the Monroe Doctrine to protect its interests and those of other countries in the Western ● Hemisphere.

France feels the force of the Monroe Doctrine. Although Napoleon had sold Louisiana to the United States (page 275), France had never quite given up the hope of regaining an empire in the Western Hemisphere. During the American Civil War, Napoleon III of France (the nephew of the great Napoleon) planned to set up a government in Mexico under French control. He believed that the United States would be too busy with the war to object. Using debts owed to France by Mexico as an excuse, Napoleon III sent an army to invade Mexico in 1861. The invasion was successful, and Napoleon made an Austrian archduke, Maximilian, Emperor of Mexico.

Aided by French soldiers and Mexicans who approved the scheme, Maximilian ruled Mexico for a few years. As soon as the Civil War came to a close, however, the United States government showed that it meant to enforce the

Monroe Doctrine. Since Napoleon III did not want war with the United States, he began to withdraw his troops from Mexico. The Mexicans then rose in revolt against the helpless Maximilian. In 1867 they put him to death and regained control of their country.

The United States uses the Monroe Doctrine against Great Britain. In 1895 the Monroe Doctrine met another serious challenge. The cause was a quarrel between Venezuela and Great Britain. Great Britain owned the colony of British Guiana (ghee-AH-nuh) on the coast of South America just east of Venezuela (map, page 612). Exactly where British Guiana ended and Venezuela began had never been settled. When Great Britain suggested a boundary cutting deeper into Venezuela than had ever been thought of before, the United States became concerned. The Monroe Doctrine forbade the establishment of new colonies in the Americas, but did it also apply to making a colony larger? Believing that it did, President Cleveland demanded that Great Britain agree to arbitrate the dispute. Great Britain, however, felt that the United States had no right to interfere. For a time it seemed that there might be war between Britain and the United States. But the British government finally agreed to arbitration. As it turned out, Britain received a large part of the disputed land. Nevertheless, the United States had made it clear to the world that the Monroe Doctrine could not be ignored.

Latin Americans grow suspicious of the Monroe Doctrine. At first, the countries of Latin America were glad to accept the protection offered by the Doctrine. They knew they could not hold their own against European nations that might want to gain territory in the Americas. As time went on, however, the countries of Latin America came to look at their powerful neighbor to the north with suspicion. They saw the United States annex Mexican territory as a result of the Mexican War (page 388). They saw it make Puerto Rico an American possession, interfere in Cuban affairs, and obtain the Panama Canal Zone. What if the United States should look to the south for more territory? In the early 1900's certain events made it seem that their fears were coming true.

Theodore Roosevelt expands the Monroe Doctrine. At this time, most of the republics of Central America and those in the Caribbean Sea suffered from bad government. They had piled up big debts and had borrowed much money from European countries. Soon after 1900, conditions became desperate in several of these countries. There were frequent revolts. Furthermore, European governments were demanding the repayment of their loans. They were even threatening to send warships to collect the money.

Theodore Roosevelt was President of the United States at this time. He reminded Congress that the Monroe Doctrine forbade European nations to interfere in this hemisphere. He declared that the United States should step in and manage the affairs of any Latin American country that could not keep order or pay its debts.

The United States "polices" Latin America. In 1905, the United States did step in to straighten out the tangled affairs of the Dominican Republic. American officials took charge of its money affairs and arranged for the payment of its debts. Under United States control, conditions in the little country improved greatly, but the people of the Dominican Republic did not like our interference. The United States also took over control of finances in the republic of Haiti. To maintain order, United States marines were sent to Haiti in 1915 and stayed there for nineteen years. The Haitians naturally resented the presence of foreign soldiers. Even earlier, in 1912, the United States

● Review the meaning of the term *arbitration*, introduced on p. 510.

★ Mention that Roosevelt's interpretation of the Monroe Doctrine became known as the *Roosevelt Corollary*.

had begun to "police" Nicaragua in Central America.

The actions of the United States cause resentment. To many people, especially Latin Americans, the United States seemed to be depriving these small republics of their independence. They began to ask, "Does the United States intend to use its Monroe Doctrine as an excuse to gain control of all Latin America?" Latin American newspapers wrote bitterly about the actions of the United States. Authors of books and magazine articles compared the United States to a huge octopus reaching out to seize the Latin American republics in its tentacles.

A revolution takes place in Mexico. Meanwhile, trouble broke out in Mexico. For almost 35 years (1877–1911) Mexico had been under the rule of a harsh dictator named Porfirio Díaz (DEE-ahs). Díaz had allowed foreign businesses to obtain large tracts of land, to build railroads, and to develop Mexico's rich oil wells. In return, the Mexican government received a share of the large profits made by the foreign companies. While foreign businesses and a few Mexican politicians grew rich, conditions among the common people of Mexico grew no better.

At last the Mexican people rose in revolt. From 1910 to 1920, all Mexico was a bloody battlefield. First, the people fought to get rid of Díaz. Then they took part in the struggles that developed between rival leaders fighting each other for power. Finally, a new constitution was put into effect in Mexico. It provided for a president who could serve one term only and a congress to be elected by the people. Rights to oil and mineral resources were to belong to the nation. The government was also given the power to buy land from large landowners and divide it among the small farmers and agricultural workers. These changes did not come at once, but over the years the Mexicans gained

General John J. Pershing led the American expedition that crossed into Mexico in pursuit of Pancho Villa.

many of the things for which they had fought.

The United States sends troops to Mexico. What did the United States have to do with the Mexican Revolution? During the revolution, as you can imagine, Mexico was in a state of great confusion. Its government was not strong enough to protect the property and the lives of Americans and other foreigners who lived there. Through our representative in Mexico, the United States tried to bring about the establishment of an orderly government. This action was resented by the Mexicans as interference with their affairs. Then an unfortunate incident occurred.

One of the revolutionary leaders was a man named Pancho Villa (VEE-yuh). In 1916, he seized eighteen Americans from a train and killed them. Two months later, Villa's men crossed the border and killed seventeen more Americans in a town in New Mexico. American soldiers under General John J. Pershing were sent into Mexico to catch

625

and punish Villa and his men. The American troops had several skirmishes with Villa, but he escaped into the mountains. In 1917, our soldiers returned home. The United States at that time was about to enter World War I and the American troops in Mexico might soon be needed in Europe. But the withdrawal of American forces did not end the bitterness felt by Mexicans toward the United States.

THE UNITED STATES SUPPORTS PLANS FOR WORLD PEACE

You have already read about several important changes in our country's foreign policy that occurred in 1898 and the years that followed: (1) The United States acquired possessions outside the North American continent. (2) It supported the Open Door Policy in East Asia. (3) It broadened the Monroe Doctrine in its relations with the countries of Latin America.

The Hague Court is formed. Still another policy that the United States followed after 1898 was to support plans for keeping peace among nations. Down through the years different plans had been suggested as ways of keeping peace. In 1899, many governments sent representatives to a meeting at The Hague (HAYG), a city in Holland. Another meeting was held at The Hague in 1907. At these meetings plans were drawn up for a court that would settle disputes between nations. The quarreling nations could select judges, from a list made beforehand, to act as umpires. These judges would listen carefully to both sides of the quarrel and then make their decision.

The United States took a leading part in the meetings at The Hague. It sent representatives to assist in making plans. Andrew Carnegie gave the money to erect a building at The Hague where the judges in such disputes would meet. The United States also was the first country to use this method of avoiding war. It referred an old dispute with Mexico to the Hague Court for settlement.

World peace is difficult to enforce. Unhappily the hopes for peace aroused by the meetings at The Hague were soon dashed. In a world of many nations each nation considered itself the equal of every other. Each country insisted upon the right to act as it saw fit, without outside interference. Nations might agree to observe a set of rules or customs (called **international law**). They might agree to submit disputes to an umpire like the Hague Court. But when a quarrel developed, there was no way of forcing nations to keep their promises or to settle their differences peacefully. The outbreak of fighting in Europe in 1914 made this fact painfully clear.

▶ **CHECK UP**   See Teacher's Key.

1. **(a)** Why did the European powers and Japan seize parts of China in the late 1800's? **(b)** How did the Chinese strike back? **(c)** What were the results? **(d)** What was the Open Door Policy?
2. **(a)** What happened to Japan after it was opened to trade with the rest of the world? **(b)** Why did Japan and Russia go to war? **(c)** How was the war ended?
3. **(a)** Why did Japan and the United States become less friendly? **(b)** What was Japan's attitude toward the Open Door Policy?
4. **(a)** Why were Latin Americans suspicious of the Monroe Doctrine? **(b)** What new meaning did Theodore Roosevelt give to the Monroe Doctrine? **(c)** Where was the Doctrine applied in Latin America?
5. **(a)** Why did a revolution break out in Mexico in 1910? **(b)** What action was taken by the United States in Mexico?
6. **(a)** What was the Hague Court? **(b)** Why was it formed? **(c)** Why are quarrels between nations very hard to settle?

626

2 What Part Did the United States Play in World War I?

World War I begins. On a night early in August, 1914, the citizens of a Belgian village on the border of Germany awoke with a feeling of fear. Into the village rode the advance guard of the German army. Soon, long columns of infantry followed, and there could be heard the rumble and thunder of guns. The citizens knew what all this meant — Germany had invaded neutral Belgium to strike quickly at France. Once more war had come to Europe. It was to be the worst war the world had known up to that time.

What were the causes of World War I? The real causes of the conflict lay in the jealousies and rivalry for power among the leading European countries. For a number of years, there had been two rival groups of nations in Europe. All that was needed was a spark to set off the explosion of war. That spark came from a quarrel between Austria-Hungary and Serbia.[1] When a Serbian

---

[1]Serbia today is part of Yugoslavia. Austria and Hungary are now separate nations.

sympathizer murdered the archduke ● who was heir to the Austro-Hungarian throne, the Austrian government declared war on Serbia.

The different nations in the two groups soon sprang into action. Russia, which considered itself the protector of several small countries in the Balkan ★ Peninsula, went to Serbia's aid. France and Great Britain had an understanding with Russia and so could be expected to take its side. Germany, on the other hand, had promised support to Austria-Hungary and, therefore, declared war on Russia and France.

One by one the countries of Europe took sides. Soon the war was under way. On one side were the Central Powers, including Germany, Austria-Hungary, Bulgaria, and Turkey. On the other side were the Allies, including France, Great Britain, Russia, Belgium, and later Italy.

Before World War I ended, 27 nations took part in it, and their combined armies made up a total of 65 million men. It was indeed a "world war."

AIR, SEA, AND LAND WEAPONS—WORLD WAR I

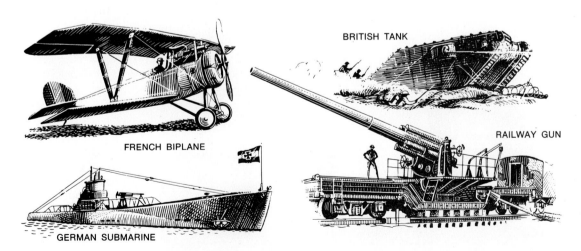

FRENCH BIPLANE

BRITISH TANK

RAILWAY GUN

GERMAN SUBMARINE

627

★ Have students locate the Balkan Peninsula on the map (p. 629).

THE UNITED STATES
TRIES TO REMAIN AT PEACE

President Wilson urges neutrality. Americans were shocked at the way European nations rushed into war. Yet Europe and its quarrels seemed far away. Americans remembered how George Washington had warned them to keep out of the quarrels of Europe. Now they listened to President Woodrow Wilson. As soon as World War I began, he advised them to be "neutral in fact as well as in name . . . impartial in thought as well as in action." "Good," they thought. "The United States will not have to fight in this war. We will stay neutral."

The United States finds it hard not to take sides. Through 1914, through 1915 and 1916, war continued to rage. Slowly, first in one way and then in another, America was drawn closer to the conflict in Europe. (1) It appeared to most Americans that Austria and Germany were chiefly responsible for the war. (2) Also, most of the war news that reached the United States came through the Allies and was favorable to the Allied cause. This fact helped to strengthen the belief that the Allies were right and the Central Powers wrong. (3) Then, too, there was an enormous demand for American goods of all kinds. Because the British navy was blockading Germany, Americans found it easier to trade with the Allies. American shipping was a tremendous help to the Allies. The United States was naturally more sympathetic toward the nations buying American goods. (4) Probably Americans were influenced most of all by the submarine warfare carried on by Germany.

The Germans start submarine warfare. In response to the British blockade of the Central Powers, Germany sent large numbers of submarines, called U-boats, to roam the seas and sink the ships of any nation that traded with Britain. Sometimes Germany issued orders limiting the actions of its U-boat commanders. At other times Germany ordered its submarines to attack ships without warning. The neutral rights of American vessels, and of United States citizens on other vessels, were often disregarded. American ships were sunk; American lives were lost. Our government protested strongly to Germany, but the sinkings continued. In the view of German leaders, cutting Britain's supply lines was essential to Germany's war effort.

The Germans sink the *Lusitania*. May 7, 1915, was a clear day, and off the coast of southern Ireland the sea was calm. In the early afternoon, a large steamship was making its way past a landmark on the coast known as the "Old Head of Kinsale." The ship was one of the largest and fastest in the

Torpedoed ships sank very quickly. Here a German U-boat crew watches a British ship go down in the Atlantic.

N

NORWAY

SWEDEN

BALTIC SEA

DENMARK

British blockade

NORTH SEA

German submarines

IRELAND

Liverpool

GREAT BRITAIN

London

NETH.
Hague

BELGIUM

PRUSSIA

• Warsaw

RUSSIA

GERMANY

• Berlin

Supplies and troops from U.S.

LUX.
Argonne Forest
St. Mihiel

Line of trench warfare July, 1918

Paris
Marne R.

ATLANTIC OCEAN

FRANCE

SWITZERLAND

• Vienna

AUSTRIA-HUNGARY

BLACK SEA

RUMANIA

BULGARIA

MONTENEGRO

SERBIA

BALKAN PENINSULA

PORTUGAL

SPAIN

ITALY

• Rome

ALBANIA

TURKEY

GREECE

MEDITERRANEAN SEA

THE UNITED STATES ENTERS WORLD WAR I

Allies

Central Powers

Neutral nations

SCALE

0 — 300 mi

0 — 300 km

See Teacher's Key.

MAP STUDY
In 1917 the United States entered World War I on the side of the Allies. (a) Which nations were the Central Powers? (b) Which Allied nations were invaded by the forces of the Central Powers? (c) Why was Germany unable to invade Great Britain?

world at that time — the British *Lusitania,* bound for Liverpool from New York. Steaming proudly through familiar waters near the end of its voyage, the ship headed toward St. George's Channel, between Ireland and Britain. The *Lusitania's* moves, however, were watched by the German submarine *U-20.* Without any warning, the *U-20* fired a single torpedo at the huge liner. There was one explosion, then another,

and fire broke out in the *Lusitania.* The ship slowed down and tilted sharply. In eighteen minutes it sank. Of nearly two thousand passengers and crew members, 1,198 died. Among those lost were 128 Americans.

After this sinking, the United States issued strong warnings to the German government that the lives of American citizens must not be put in danger. For a time, Germany limited its submarine warfare. But early in 1917, U-boats again began to sink ships without warning. Altogether, submarine warfare cost 209 American lives on the high seas between 1914 and April, 1917.

Must the United States enter the war? President Wilson realized how

629

horrible war was. He knew full well the serious responsibility he carried as President. For two and a half years he had kept the United States out of war. Yet there were times when President Wilson wondered whether this country should enter the war against Germany.

In April, 1917, soon after German U-boats had sunk several American ships, Wilson prepared a message to Congress saying that the United States must go to war. But on the night before he delivered this fateful message to Congress, he walked restlessly in the White House. Thinking of the awful results of war, he said to a friend, "What else can I do? Is there anything else I can do?" "No," replied his friend, "Germany has forced the war upon the United States." Sadly the President spoke of things destroyed in war: not only lives and money, but the spirit of good will and perhaps even freedom itself.

● When, on the next day, President Wilson asked Congress to declare war on Germany, his words showed how carefully he had weighed his decision:

> It is a fearful thing to lead this great peaceful people into war, into the most terrible and disastrous of all wars, civilization itself seeming to be in the balance. But the right is more precious than peace, and we shall fight for the things which we have always carried nearest our hearts — for democracy, for the right of those who submit to authority to have a voice in their own government, for the rights and liberties of small nations.

On April 6, 1917, Congress declared war.

THE UNITED STATES PLAYS A VALIANT PART IN WORLD WAR I

America prepares for war. Once war had been declared, the United States bent all its efforts to the tasks that lay ahead. Congress at once passed a **draft** law. This law required all men between

Government posters urged citizens to support the American war effort in World War I. What was the message of this poster?

the ages of 21 and 31 to register for possible call to military duty. Later the age limits were extended to 18 through 44. Before the war ended, well over four million men wore the uniform of the armed forces of the United States. Women were not drafted, but many volunteered to serve as military nurses.

The draftees could not be trained and sent into battle overnight. They needed food and clothing and shelter. They had to have weapons and ammunition. Far greater supplies were needed than in any earlier war. Locomotives, freight cars, railroad tracks, and trucks, together with weapons and supplies, had to be shipped to France for the army's use.

To provide all these things, America's factories and shipyards increased their production. Farmers worked into the night. The railroads strained to move supplies and men to the points where they were needed. As industries expanded, they hired new workers from minority groups such as blacks and Mexican Americans. Also, many

630

● See p. T52 for a strategy calling for students to examine President Wilson's Declaration of War to Congress.

● See p. T52 for a strategy asking students to work on projects relating to World War I.

women for the first time took jobs in industry, replacing men who had left to enter military service. People saved light and heat, observed meatless days, and lent money to the government by buying Liberty Bonds. Throughout the nation citizens did what they could to help win the war.

While the country was working at top speed to supply the needs of its armed forces, the army itself was preparing for its grim task in France. General John J. Pershing was placed in command. Pershing said he would need three million soldiers, of whom at least one million must be ready to fight in France by the spring of 1918. The American navy had already swung into action. Its ships swept the seas for mines and tracked down German U-boats. The navy also escorted the ships carrying soldiers and supplies across the Atlantic.

Both sides use trench warfare in France. At the opening of the war in 1914, the Germans had high hopes for a quick victory. They planned to defeat the French army, capture Paris, and force France out of the war. But this plan failed. The French massed their strength along the Marne River near Paris and halted the onrushing enemy (map, page 629).

Since neither side had been able to win a clear-cut victory, both the Allies and the Germans dug deep trenches which the soldiers used for protection. In a few months the trenches extended for miles, like a gash in the earth. They ran from a point on the North Sea coast of Belgium across northern France and southward to the boundary of Switzerland. From these trenches the opposing armies thundered and smashed at each other from 1914 to 1917. Sometimes one side made gains, sometimes the other. But neither side could win the war.

The Allies suffer discouraging setbacks. Toward the end of 1917, however, the fortunes of war so favored the Central Powers that it seemed they might soon win. Crushing defeats at the hands of the German army and a revolution within its own borders forced Russia to quit the war. German troops which had been stationed on the Russian front could now be moved to France to prepare for the winning blow. On the Italian front, German and Austrian forces had smashed the Italian army and sent it reeling back. In the spring, the Germans surely would make a supreme effort to overwhelm the exhausted British and French forces. Only the United States, pouring in its fresh troops, could be expected to hold

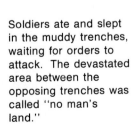

Soldiers ate and slept in the muddy trenches, waiting for orders to attack. The devastated area between the opposing trenches was called "no man's land."

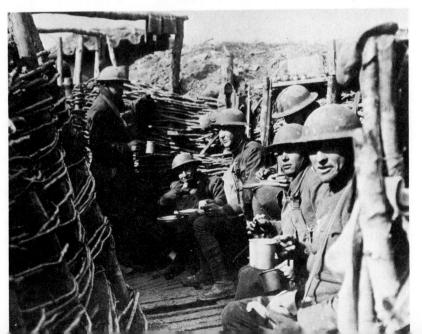

back the German advance. The Allied leaders wondered, "Will American troops appear in time?"

The tide of war finally turns against the Germans. In March, 1918, the German infantry moved forward in a great attack. On and on the Germans swept, pushing back the Allied lines. At one point they were only 50 miles from Paris. But hundreds of thousands of American soldiers (affectionately called doughboys) had arrived to back up the battle-weary French and British troops. The Allies slowed down the German advance and finally, in mid-July, brought the German attack to a standstill. The American troops, fresh and confident of victory, had helped turn the tide of war against the Germans. The chancellor (prime minister) of Germany said: "On the 18th [of July] even the most optimistic among us knew that all was lost. The history of the world was played out in three days."

The war is won. Without allowing the Germans to rest, the Allies began a counterattack all along the line, pushing back the enemy more and more rapidly. American troops took their position at the eastern end of the long battle line. They fought valiantly at St. Mihiel (SAN mee-YELL) and in the Argonne Forest (map, page 629). On November 11, 1918, the Germans finally gave up and signed an **armistice** (an agreement to stop fighting). The war was over.

▶ **CHECK UP**   See Teacher's Key.

1. **(a)** What conditions in Europe led to the outbreak of World War I? **(b)** What groups of powers opposed each other in the war?
2. **(a)** Why did the United States find it hard to remain neutral? **(b)** Why did this country finally enter the war?
3. **(a)** What part did the United States play in winning the war? **(b)** How did the Allies finally turn back the German advance?

3   Why Did Efforts to Establish a Lasting Peace Fail?

The Allies had won World War I but at a frightful cost. Thirty-seven million people were killed, wounded, or missing. Three hundred *billion* dollars' worth of property had been used up. Much land had been laid waste. An enormous amount of energy had been spent in destruction which in peacetime might have been put to useful purposes. Little wonder, then, that people everywhere looked forward with hope to plans for peace. They said, "Can't we build a peace that will last? Can't we save our children and our children's children from other terrible wars?"

The victorious Allies disagree over terms of peace. The peace was made at a meeting of representatives from the victorious Allied countries at Versailles (vehr-SIGH), just outside Paris, in 1919. President Woodrow Wilson himself represented the United States at the conference. Great Britain sent its Prime Minister, David Lloyd George; France, its Premier, Georges Clemenceau (kleh-mahn-SOH); and Italy, its Prime Minister, Vittorio Orlando. The last three came from countries worn out by the war and full of hatred for their enemies. In the discussion of how much Germany should pay for war damages, where boundary lines should be drawn, or how other questions should be settled, the leaders of Great Britain,

● Have students read in "Linking Past and Present" (p. 636) how Americans honor those who died for this country.

France, and Italy insisted upon extremely severe terms for Germany.

President Wilson, on the other hand, came from a country 3,000 miles away from the fighting. The United States had entered the war late and finished still fresh and strong. It wanted no territorial gains. In Wilson's words, its chief aims were to "make the world safe for democracy" and to make the war "a war to end wars."

Wilson proposes a peace based on his Fourteen Points. Even while the fighting still raged, President Wilson had stated plainly the kind of world the United States was fighting for. He listed Fourteen Points as a basis for a better world. The chief items in the Fourteen Points were these: (1) Agreements among nations should be open and public. (2) There should be freedom of the seas "alike in peace and war." (3) Trade barriers between nations should be broken down. (4) Nations should reduce their armies and navies. (5) Colonial claims should be settled as fairly as possible. (6) Nations should have the right to self-determination (the right to govern themselves). (7) "A general association of nations" should be set up to promise independence and safety "to great and small nations alike."

The Treaty of Versailles is written. President Wilson's peace plans did not win the support of the other members of the "Big Four" at the peace table. Lloyd George, Clemenceau, and Orlando were more eager to get advantages for their own countries than to help make a better world. Very reluctantly, Wilson was forced to give up most of his Fourteen Points. On one point, however, President Wilson refused to give in. He insisted that the peace treaty should set up an association of nations — called the League of Nations — to help keep peace.

The Versailles Treaty (1919) and other peace treaties signed with the de-

President Wilson stopped in Belgium on his way to the peace conference at Versailles. The man in uniform was the Belgian king.

feated countries included the following points: (1) Germany was held responsible for starting the war; hence, it would have to pay for the losses and damage. (2) Germany was stripped of a huge quantity of supplies, and it also had to pay a large sum of money, called **reparations.** (3) Germany was disarmed and its colonies and some territory in Europe were taken over by other countries. (4) Several new nations were formed in Europe out of land taken from the defeated countries and Russia. The boundaries of these new nations were planned with the idea of including most of the people of a national group within one country. Among these countries were Poland and Czechoslovakia. (See map, page 634.) (5) Woodrow Wilson's dream, a League of Nations, was made a reality.

The League of Nations is formed. ● The League of Nations, which was provided for in the Treaty of Versailles, included an assembly. All member nations were to have a voice in this body. There was also a council in which the leading powers had seats and to which the smaller nations elected representatives. In addition, there was a World

633

● See p. T52 for a strategy calling for students to examine the League of Nations.

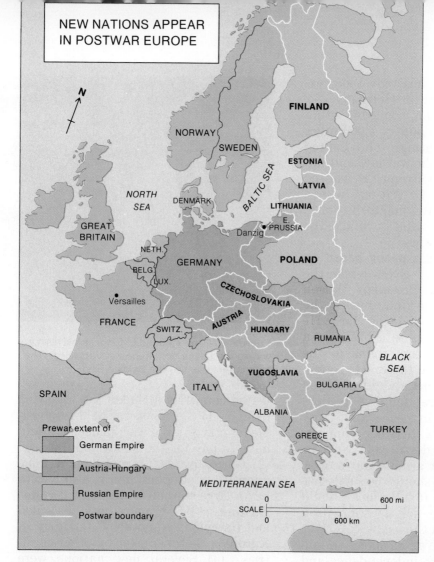

NEW NATIONS APPEAR IN POSTWAR EUROPE

N

FINLAND
NORWAY
SWEDEN
ESTONIA
LATVIA
NORTH SEA
DENMARK
BALTIC SEA
LITHUANIA
E. PRUSSIA
Danzig
GREAT BRITAIN
NETH.
GERMANY
POLAND
BELG.
LUX.
Versailles
CZECHOSLOVAKIA
FRANCE
SWITZ.
AUSTRIA
HUNGARY
RUMANIA
BLACK SEA
SPAIN
ITALY
YUGOSLAVIA
BULGARIA
ALBANIA
TURKEY
GREECE

Prewar extent of
German Empire
Austria-Hungary
Russian Empire
Postwar boundary

MEDITERRANEAN SEA

SCALE
0   600 mi
0   600 km

See Teacher's Key.

MAP STUDY
In 1919 new nations were formed in eastern Europe from lands that had been part of Austria-Hungary, Russia, and Germany. Which countries gave up land to form Poland?

Court, which was organized by the League in 1921. This court could decide certain disputes between nations.

The countries which joined the League of Nations agreed that its purpose was to promote cooperation among nations and bring about international peace. If a country attacked another country and continued fighting in spite of the League's orders, the members could take action against it. They could stop lending money to such a nation or cut off trade with it. The League might even ask its members to use force against a warring country.

The United States rejects the League of Nations. President Wilson returned to the United States feeling sure that the League of Nations provided a way to preserve peace. But our Constitution requires that treaties such as the one drawn up at Versailles must be approved by the United States Senate. Some senators were angry because President Wilson had ignored them in working out the peace treaty. Others were tired of Europe and its troubles. They thought Wilson had made a mistake in insisting on the League of Nations. Might not the League draw the United States into new European quarrels?

Many senators also did not believe that the United States should become a leader in the effort to keep peace in the world. They wanted the government to stay out of the League and out of foreign difficulties. This attitude came to be known as **isolationism** (and the people who supported it were called isolationists). Large numbers of Americans were isolationists after World War I.

When some senators proposed putting restrictions on American membership in the League, Wilson decided he must appeal to the people of the United States for their support of the peace treaty and the League. He began a speaking tour. In glowing words he explained to the public what the League meant to him and what benefits it might bring to the world. But one night as Wilson's train sped through the countryside from Colorado to Kansas, he became seriously ill. Although he remained in office until the end of his term, President Wilson never recovered.

In spite of Wilson's efforts, many Americans were not ready to accept responsibility in affairs outside the Ameri-

cas. The United States, therefore, did not join the League of Nations or approve the Treaty of Versailles. Instead, it made a separate peace with Germany in 1921. The League was set up without the United States, but, as we will learn, this new association of nations was not strong enough to carry out Wilson's dream of a peaceful world.

▶ **CHECK UP**   See Teacher's Key.

1. **(a)** What countries had most to say about the peace treaty? **(b)** Why did their leaders at Versailles disagree? **(c)** What were the Fourteen Points? **(d)** What did they provide?
2. What were the chief points of the final peace treaties?
3. **(a)** What was the League of Nations? **(b)** How was it supposed to reduce the chance of war? **(c)** Why did the United States not join the League?

CHECK UP ON CHAPTER 29   See Teacher's Key.

Words to Know

1. embassy
2. draft
3. policy
4. neutrality
5. armistice
6. counterattack
7. reparations
8. isolationism
9. trench warfare
10. international law

Places to Locate

1. Peking
2. Japan
3. Manchuria
4. Italy
5. Belgium
6. Serbia
7. France
8. Mediterranean Sea
9. Balkan Peninsula
10. Argonne Forest
11. Poland
12. Czechoslovakia

Facts to Remember

1. **(a)** How did powerful nations take advantage of China's weakness in the late 1800's? **(b)** What was the Boxer Rebel-

lion? **(c)** What was the policy of the United States toward China?
2. **(a)** How did Japan change during the period 1850–1900? **(b)** Describe relations between Japan and the United States after Japan's war with Russia.
3. **(a)** How did Theodore Roosevelt use the Monroe Doctrine in dealing with Latin American countries? **(b)** How did Latin American people feel about Roosevelt's policy?
4. **(a)** How did World War I start in Europe? **(b)** Which nations were the Central Powers? **(c)** Which were the Allies?
5. **(a)** Why did the United States find it hard to stay neutral in World War I? **(b)** When did it enter the war, and on what side?
6. **(a)** How did the United States get men for its armed forces? **(b)** Who was John J. Pershing? **(c)** How did other Americans help in the war effort?
7. Identify the following: **(a)** Fourteen   635

Facts to Remember (cont.)

Points, **(b)** League of Nations, **(c)** World Court.

Skills to Practice

1. Look back at the words of the German chancellor on page 632. **(a)** What does the word *optimistic* mean? **(b)** What people did the chancellor mean when he spoke of "us"? **(c)** What do the words *played out* in his statement mean? **(d)** In your own words tell what his last sentence meant.
2. Arrange the following events in the order in which they happened. Start with the earliest event.
   a. Beginning of World War I in Europe.
   b. U.S. enters World War I.
   c. Russian-Japanese War is fought.
   d. Sinking of the *Lusitania*.
   e. Versailles Treaty signed.
   f. Armistice ends fighting in World War I.

Questions to Think About

1. **(a)** Why did the United States favor the Open Door Policy in China? **(b)** Why did Japan oppose it?
2. **(a)** What does *foreign policy* mean? **(b)** What does *international law* mean? **(c)** Is it possible for a nation's foreign policy to disagree with international law? Explain.
3. Were the terms of the Versailles Peace Treaty closer to what Woodrow Wilson wanted or to what the leaders of the European allies wanted? Explain.

Linking Past and Present

The Unknown Soldier. On a marble terrace in Arlington National Cemetery in Washington, D.C., stands the Tomb of the Unknown Soldier. Inside the simple and dignified tomb lies the body of an American soldier killed in World War I. This Unknown Soldier was buried in Arlington on November 11, 1921 — the third anniversary of the armistice ending World War I. The inscription on the tomb reads: "Here rests in honored glory an American soldier known but to God." By honoring the Unknown Soldier, our nation honors all the men and women who have fought and died for their country.

The Nobel Peace Prize. Every year the Nobel Peace Prize is awarded to the person who is judged to have contributed most toward world peace. Several Americans have received this prize, including two of our Presidents. Theodore Roosevelt received it in 1906 for helping to end the Russian-Japanese War and for supporting the Hague Court. In 1919, the peace prize was given to Woodrow Wilson for his part in establishing the League of Nations. The money for the prize comes from a fund left by Alfred Nobel, a Swedish chemist and inventor who died in 1896. Other American winners of the Nobel Peace Prize have included Jane Addams, Ralph Bunche, George C. Marshall, Martin Luther King, Jr., and Norman Borlaug.

Khaki uniforms. The "doughboys" of World War I, like American soldiers of more recent years, wore uniforms of khaki — a dull yellow-brown color. American soldiers first wore uniforms of this color in the Spanish-American War. The first troops that had been sent to the Philippines and Cuba had sweltered in the regulation dark blue uniforms. So the United States Army began to use uniforms of khaki cloth, which was lighter and cooler. But the change was made chiefly because of a lesson learned by the British army in India many years before. The British soldiers in bright red or white uniforms were easy targets in battle. On one occasion British troops under heavy fire rolled in muddy pools to make their uniforms less conspicuous. So British troops were soon issued khaki uniforms. The word "khaki" comes from a Persian word *khak* meaning "earth."

636

Have students look in newspapers and news magazines for examples of political cartoons. Encourage them to find a range of styles and viewpoints.

GAINING SKILL

Reading Political Cartoons

You may have seen political cartoons in newspapers or magazines. Like an editorial, a political cartoon expresses an opinion or a point of view. A cartoon may make us laugh at our mistakes, or it may point out a problem that needs attention. Cartoons often express support or disapproval for political leaders.

Both cartoons on this page show Theodore Roosevelt when he was President. Look at the two cartoons carefully. Then answer the following questions.

1. In the cartoon on the left, what is Roosevelt doing? How does the cartoonist use size to suggest Roosevelt's importance?

2. What detail in the cartoon on the left indicates that the canal will become very important to world transportation?

3. Which of the following phrases best describes the way Roosevelt is shown in the second cartoon? **(a)** An effective military leader of world-wide importance **(b)** A gallant Rough Rider **(c)** A warlike person who doesn't accomplish very much

4. Which of these cartoonists was probably a supporter of President Roosevelt's policies? Which of these cartoonists was probably opposed to President Roosevelt's policies?

UNDERSTANDING UNIT 9

SUMMARY OF IMPORTANT IDEAS

In this unit you have read about the American Presidents from 1865 to 1920 and how the United States became more active in foreign affairs during that period.

1. Demands for change after the Civil War led, in time, to reforms.

a. Federal legislation established the merit system, curbed trusts and monopolies, and provided for the conservation of natural resources. Later, the tariff was cut and the Federal Reserve banking system adopted. Laws also cut the working day to eight hours for interstate railroad workers and made it easier for farmers to borrow money.

b. An amendment to the Constitution provided for a federal income tax.

c. Some states adopted the direct primary, initiative, referendum, and recall.

2. The growth of American farming and industry after 1865 caused the United States to seek new markets. Commercial expansion in turn led to a more active interest in world affairs.

a. The United States obtained territories by purchase (Alaska), annexation (Hawaii), and war with Spain (the Philippines, Puerto Rico, and Guam). The United States helped the islands freed from Spain, and maintained for a time the right to intervene in Cuba.

b. To aid commerce and to protect our possessions, the United States needed a shorter water route between the east and the west coasts. This need was met when the United States built the Panama Canal.

3. The basis of American foreign policy was the Monroe Doctrine for the Western Hemisphere and the Open Door for eastern Asia.

a. The Monroe Doctrine was used in forcing the French to leave Mexico and in the Venezuelan boundary dispute with Great Britain.

b. In the early 1900's the Latin American republics came to fear that the United States meant to use the Monroe Doctrine, and especially Theodore Roosevelt's broad interpretation of the Doctrine, to extend its influence over the Western Hemisphere.

c. The Boxer Rebellion broke out in China as a protest against the European powers and Japan, who had forced China to give up land and rights. In proposing the Open Door Policy, the United States urged that trade with China should be open to all.

d. In the mid-1850's the United States opened Japan to Western influence, but later opposed Japan's efforts to expand at the expense of China.

4. In the early 1900's the United States supported plans for maintaining peace among nations. When World War I broke out in Europe, this country at first sought to remain neutral.

a. German submarine policy, and the threat to this country implied in a German victory, finally caused the United States to enter the war.

b. The arrival of American forces in Europe helped turn the tide, leading to an Allied victory in 1918.

c. President Wilson was able to make the League of Nations a part of the peace settlement. The United States, however, failed to join the League and returned to a policy of isolation after the war.

1. What reforms were favored by each of the following? **(a)** Hayes **(b)** Cleveland **(c)** Theodore Roosevelt **(d)** Wilson

2. **(a)** Why did the United States become interested in overseas territories in the late 1800's? **(b)** What possessions did the United States acquire? **(c)** Explain how and why in each case.

3. **(a)** Why did the United States become interested in a canal connecting the Atlantic and the Pacific? **(b)** Why was the Panama route favored? **(c)** How was it obtained?

4. **(a)** Why did the United States go to war with Spain? **(b)** What efforts were made to help the people in the islands freed from Spain?

5. **(a)** What is the Monroe Doctrine? **(b)** Give examples of how and when it was applied. **(c)** How did Latin American countries feel about intervention by the United States in Cuba, Haiti, Nicaragua, and Mexico? Why?

6. **(a)** What was the Open Door Policy? **(b)** Why did the United States favor this policy? **(c)** What countries did not agree with it? Why?

7. **(a)** Why did the United States try to remain neutral in World War I? **(b)** Why did it finally go to war in 1917? **(c)** Why did Wilson urge the establishment of the League of Nations? **(d)** Why did this country fail to join it?

THINGS TO DO

The "things to do" marked with an asterisk (*) are for the whole class. Select from the others as your teacher directs.

*1. Start a new set of cards for Unit 9. A class quiz two or three times a week with these cards will help you remember the important dates, events, and people.

2. Draw a cartoon to show one of the following: **(a)** the sinking of the *Maine*; **(b)** the Open Door Policy; **(c)** the Good Neighbor Policy; **(d)** the Boxer Rebellion; **(e)** the Senate vote against the League of Nations.

3. Present to the class some statistics on the Panama Canal, such as the cost of passage through the canal, the number of ships a day, etc. Consult an almanac or encyclopedia for information. Also show on a globe or world map how the canal shortens the distance between some of the world's important ports. Use examples such as New York to San Francisco, New Orleans to Yokohama, Japan, etc.

4. Read and report to the class on one of the following topics: **(a)** the conquest of yellow fever; **(b)** the building and opening of the Panama Canal; **(c)** the resources of Alaska; **(d)** Operation Bootstrap.

5. Write or tape an account of one of these events as it might have appeared in a newspaper of the time: **(a)** the purchase of Alaska from Russia; **(b)** the Battle of Manila Bay or Santiago; **(c)** Villa's raid in New Mexico; **(d)** the sinking of the *Lusitania*; **(e)** the American declaration of war against Germany, April 6, 1917.

6. Write a newspaper editorial taking a stand for or against one of these questions of the day: **(a)** the annexation of Hawaii; **(b)** war with Spain; **(c)** United States interference in Haiti and the Dominican Republic; **(d)** the Open Door Policy; **(e)** the United States and the League of Nations.

7. Find out what songs were popular during World War I. Tell the class a little about each song and organize a group to sing them.

UNIT **10**

Left to right: flag raising at Iwo Jima; Dallas skyline; civil rights march, Washington, D.C.; 1960's space shot.

The United States Becomes a World Leader

1920–1985

See p. T53 for a unit preview strategy. See pp. T58–T71 for lists of useful books and audiovisual aids.

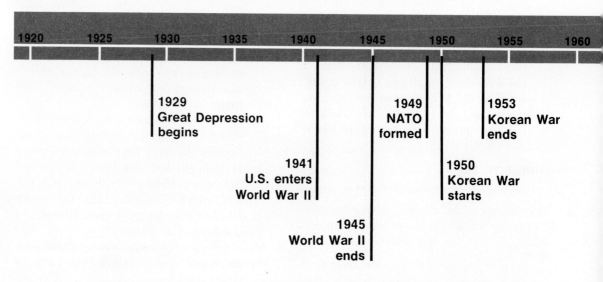

1920	1925	1930	1935	1940	1945	1950	1955	1960

1929
Great Depression
begins

1941
U.S. enters
World War II

1945
World War II
ends

1949
NATO
formed

1950
Korean War
starts

1953
Korean War
ends

640

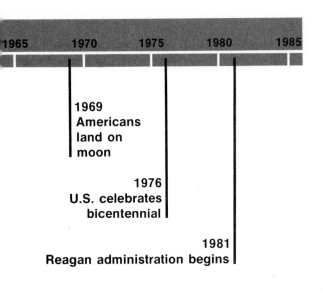

1965   1970   1975   1980   1985

1969
Americans
land on
moon

1976
U.S. celebrates
bicentennial

1981
Reagan administration begins

Unit 9 carried our story through World War I. In this final unit we bring the story up to recent times. The years since 1920 have been a time of remarkable experiences for the American people. We have seen changes in ways of living and working and traveling, and we have even begun the exploration of space. But there have also been periods of war and economic trouble. In Chapter 30 you will read about the depression of the 1930's and the events of World War II. Chapter 31 tells how our country met challenges at home and abroad in the years after that war ended. In Chapter 32 you will learn about our most recent Presidents and about new developments that affect the way Americans live today.

CHAPTER **30**

Vocabulary preview: prohibit, disarmament, capitalism, free enterprise system, dictator, appeasement, inflation, public opinion.

Our Country Faces Problems at Home and Abroad

1920–1945   See pp. T53–T54 for chapter teaching strategies.

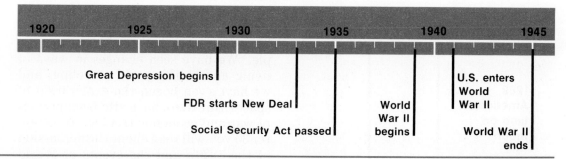

1920   1925   1930   1935   1940   1945

Great Depression begins

FDR starts New Deal

Social Security Act passed

World War II begins

U.S. enters World War II

World War II ends

What this chapter is about —

In 1789, George Washington became the first President of the United States. At that time our country was small and had little influence in world affairs. Yet as leader of this new republic, Washington realized that he would have to face serious problems. As he left his Mount Vernon home to take up his new duties, he knew that he was leaving "a peaceful abode for an ocean of difficulties."

All our Presidents since Washington have carried heavy burdens, and many have had to make agonizing decisions. This has been especially true

642

◄ When aggressor nations in Europe and Asia destroyed hopes for peace in the 1930's, Americans prepared for another global conflict.

In this chapter you will learn how Presidents who were in office during these difficult times dealt with problems at home and abroad. As you read, look for answers to the following questions:

1. What goals did Presidents Harding, Coolidge, and Hoover seek?
2. What changes took place during the New Deal?
3. What events after World War I destroyed hopes for world peace?
4. How did the United States and its allies gain victory in World War II?

since the end of World War I. During the 1920's most Americans hoped to return to the kind of life they had known before the war broke out. But during the 1930's, the United States was plunged into the worst depression in its history. Then in the early 1940's our country entered World War II.

1 What Goals Did Presidents Harding, Coolidge, and Hoover Seek?

You have already read how Presidents Theodore Roosevelt and Woodrow Wilson both believed that the great problems of their day called for reforms (Chapter 27). Then came World War I, and the American people, led by President Wilson, turned their full attention to winning the war.

Warren G. Harding is elected President. By the time of the 1920 election, the nation's mood had changed. People wanted to forget everything connected with war — the death and destruction, the heavy taxes, the strain and the worry. Warren G. Harding, a senator from Ohio, was elected President on the Republican ticket. Harding was a friendly, folksy person, who fully agreed with most Americans that the nation should "get back to normal." So the United States under Harding turned its back on reform at home and membership in the League of Nations abroad.

Calvin Coolidge becomes President. Before his term was completed, President Harding died. He was succeeded by the Vice-President, Calvin Coolidge of Massachusetts. Then, in 1924, Coolidge was elected President in his own right. A shrewd man who never wasted words, he was quite a different kind of person from Harding. Yet Coolidge, like Harding, believed that Americans should be left alone to go about their lives without government interference. President Coolidge lowered taxes and cut down government expenses. Meanwhile, Congress passed several laws to help business, and a higher tariff, which had been put into effect under Harding, was continued.

During President Coolidge's administration, the country as a whole enjoyed prosperity. Business activity and profits increased, and the incomes of many people rose. The Coolidge years were often referred to as the "Golden Twenties."

Herbert Hoover takes office. In 1928, Herbert Hoover was elected President, the third Republican to be chosen since World War I. Hoover had been an engineer and was known for his great organizing ability. During World War I, he had won fame as food administrator in the United States and as director of war

643

● See p. T53 for a strategy that asks students to consider factors influencing the national mood in the 1920's.

Our Presidents

WARREN G. HARDING   1921–1923

Republican from Ohio. A handsome, successful businessman, newspaper owner, and senator, Harding's platform called for a "return to normalcy" — that is, a return to peaceful times and the enjoyment of life. His election as President was the first to be broadcast over the radio. The Washington Disarmament Conference was held during his administration. Harding died two years after taking office.

CALVIN COOLIDGE   1923–1929

Republican from Massachusetts. As Governor of Massachusetts, Coolidge became famous for his handling of a Boston police strike in 1919. Elected Vice-President in 1920, he became President at Harding's death. He was a quiet man of few words who believed in working hard, spending little, and limiting the powers of the federal government. During his administration, the country enjoyed a period of prosperity.

HERBERT HOOVER   1929–1933

Republican from California. A successful mining engineer, Hoover was also known as a great humanitarian for his organization of food relief projects in Europe after World War I. He later served as Secretary of Commerce. Because he was President at the time, Hoover was blamed for the depression that started in 1929. In later years, he gave valuable service in reorganizing the executive branch of government.

FRANKLIN D. ROOSEVELT   1933–1945

Democrat from New York. Roosevelt had served as a New York state senator, Assistant Secretary of the Navy, and Governor of New York. The only President to serve more than two terms, "FDR" led the country through its worst depression and greatest war. In office he introduced the "New Deal" program and made wide use of radio and news conferences. He was the first President to travel by plane while in office. Roosevelt died in 1945, at the beginning of his fourth term.

relief in Belgium. Later, he had served as Secretary of Commerce under Presidents Harding and Coolidge.

Hoover won the election on a pledge to continue the prosperity which the country had enjoyed under the preceding Republican Presidents. Popular with business leaders, he believed firmly in leaving people and business free from government controls. But Hoover was no mere follower of Coolidge and Harding; he had ideas of his own. During his administration Hoover Dam was begun on the Colorado River, to provide electric power and water for irrigation. Hoover also made an important goodwill visit to Latin America. If prosperity had continued, Hoover's term in office might have been remembered for its important achievements.

The Hoover years are overshadowed by a depression. Hoover had been in the White House for less than a year, however, when he was faced with the worst depression the country had ever known (page 504). Factories stood idle, their empty windows staring blankly at passers-by. Farmers had trouble selling their crops, even at very low prices. In the cities, millions of Americans could not find work. Men and women stood in long lines to apply for the few jobs that were offered. The unlucky ones formed other lines to get food and clothing from organizations that helped needy people. Month after month, for one year, a second year, a third year, the situation grew worse.

    ●   The Great Depression, as it came to be called, was not President Hoover's fault, of course. It was the result of world-wide conditions beyond the power of any one person or country to prevent. Yet the President in office usually receives the credit when things go well with the country and the blame when things go wrong. President Hoover was the first President to use the power of the national government to try to stop a depression. But many people believed that he was not doing enough.

A Cabinet member under Presidents Harding and Coolidge, Herbert Hoover himself became President after winning the election of 1928.

When the election of 1932 came along, the voters wanted a change. Franklin D. Roosevelt, a Democrat who was a distant cousin of Theodore Roosevelt, was elected President.

▶ **CHECK UP**   See Teacher's Key.

1. **(a)** What did President Harding think the country needed after World War I? **(b)** What role did President Coolidge favor for the national government?
2. **(a)** What were some accomplishments of President Hoover's administration? **(b)** What great problem developed during his term?

2 What Changes Took Place During the New Deal?

Franklin D. Roosevelt was born in New York State, the child of a wealthy family. After graduation from college, he studied law. He became interested in politics and served for two years in the New York legislature. In World War I he was Assistant Secretary of the Navy. Although he failed to be elected Vice-President in 1920, he later served two terms as Governor of New York.

645

● See p. T53 for a strategy asking students to put together a bulletin board display featuring American life during the Great Depression.

In 1921, while vacationing in Canada, Roosevelt suffered a severe attack of polio. The doctors said his legs were so badly paralyzed that he might never walk again. But Roosevelt refused to give up. With the encouragement of his
● wife, Eleanor, he triumphed over the disease. Although permanently disabled, he returned to play an active part in public life.

Roosevelt tries to end the Depression. When Franklin D. Roosevelt became President, the American people were fearful of the future. Millions of Americans had lost their jobs, their homes, and their farms. Banks all over the country had closed their doors as panicky depositors tried to withdraw their savings.

In his inaugural address Roosevelt spoke directly to the American people, trying to restore their confidence. "The only thing we have to fear," he said, "is fear itself." Roosevelt was determined to use the power of the United States government to end the Depression. He also wanted to protect Americans against the effects of depressions in the future. As the new President expressed it, the country needed a change — a
★ "New Deal."

No sooner had he taken office than Roosevelt began planning ways to relieve urgent problems. The day after his inauguration, for example, he closed the nation's banks for four days. Government inspectors checked the banks and allowed only those that seemed safe and reliable to reopen.

In the early days of the New Deal, Congress passed a long list of laws at the request of President Roosevelt.

Agriculture. American farmers had been especially hard hit by the Depression. Prices of farm products were so low that many farmers could not pay the costs of production. Beginning in 1933, Congress passed a series of laws to aid American farmers. Government organizations lent money to farmers. Laws encouraged farmers to grow smaller crops so that prices would be higher and farmers would get larger profits. The government also tried to protect the farmer by establishing minimum prices for basic crops such as wheat, corn, and cotton. These prices were usually based on the prices of the things the farmer had to buy. If the prices of the things that farmers bought went up, then the minimum prices for their crops were raised accordingly.

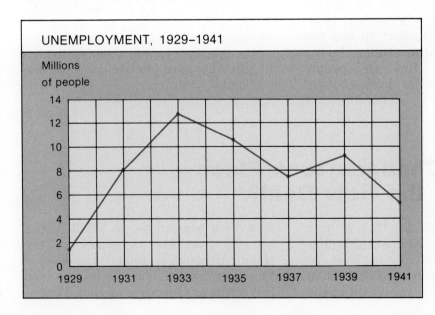

UNEMPLOYMENT, 1929–1941

Millions of people

See Teacher's Key.

GRAPH STUDY
During the Great Depression millions of workers could not find jobs. In what year was unemployment at its high point?

★ See p. T53 for a strategy that calls for students to identify programs of the New Deal.

People in America's Story

Roosevelt. Both men traced their family
history back to a Dutch landowner who
settled in New York during the 1640's.

FRANKLIN D. ROOSEVELT

The only President elected four times, Franklin Roosevelt led the nation
during the challenging years of the Great Depression and World War II.

A courageous man, Franklin Roosevelt refused
to give up his career when crippled by polio.
In this decision he was aided by his wife
Eleanor (shown above in a 1908 photo with
two of their children). His re-election as
governor of New York in 1930 (left) made him
the leading contender for the 1932 Democratic
presidential nomination.

The Civilian Conservation Corps provided jobs and training for men between the ages of 18 and 25. This corpsman is learning engineering.

Unemployment. The government tried to find work for jobless Americans. Much of this work was on such projects as roads, dams, parks, and public buildings. A Civilian Conservation Corps (CCC) was organized to give work to thousands of young men who could not get jobs. They lived in camps and worked at such tasks as clearing forests and planting trees. But on the public works projects, less useful work was sometimes arranged quickly, just to give the unemployed something to do. The government spent huge amounts of money to provide jobs. Other large sums supplied food and clothing and shelter to the families of people who could not find work.

Business and banking. Congress passed laws approving loans of government money to businesses, so that mines, mills, and stores could provide jobs. At the same time, laws were passed to regulate and control industry and business. The New Deal did not stop there. Because many Americans had lost their savings when banks failed, banking laws were passed to insure people's savings.

The New Deal adopts labor laws. Many of the laws of the 1930's had to do with workers. President Roosevelt believed that workers should have the right to join labor unions and to bargain collectively (in groups) with employers. In 1935, Congress passed the National Labor Relations Act (more commonly called the Wagner Act) which stated that the government would protect those rights. Congress also gave the National Labor Relations Board the power to keep employers "from engaging in any unfair labor practices."

Another part of Roosevelt's labor program had to do with wages and working hours. The President believed that the country would be more prosperous if wages were increased and working hours reduced so that more workers could be given jobs. To meet those goals, Congress passed the Wages and Hours Act in 1938. This law regulated the hours of work and minimum wages to be paid to workers who made goods sold in interstate trade.

The Social Security Act is passed. One of the most important laws passed under President Roosevelt was the Social Security Act (1935). For years workers had been asking, "What will happen to me and my family when I am too old to work? I haven't been able to save much money for retirement. How will we live?" Other workers wondered how they would support themselves if they lost their jobs. These problems became much more serious with the high unemployment of the Depression years.

Congress passed the Social Security Act in the belief that people should be protected against unemployment as

648

well as poverty in old age. This act provides for the payment of certain amounts of money over a period of time to workers who are out of a job. Also, when workers retire they are paid a monthly sum as long as they live. In order to get the money for these benefits, a certain percentage is taken out of workers' wages, with employers contributing an equal amount. The states work with the federal government in the handling of unemployment payments. Old-age insurance, however, is the responsibility of the federal government.

The New Deal seeks to use natural resources wisely. Like Theodore Roosevelt, Franklin D. Roosevelt was interested in the conservation of natural resources. Many of the laws passed to help the farmer included plans for conserving the soil. The CCC, which provided work for many young men, also helped to protect our forests. The building of dams like Grand Coulee in Washington state not only created more jobs but made possible flood control and the irrigation of large sections of land.

An important project started under the New Deal was the Tennessee Valley Authority (TVA). The TVA was a long-range plan to control floods in a region covering parts of seven southern states. The TVA built a network of dams for that purpose, and supplied
● cheap electric power for the Tennessee Valley.

Prohibition is ended. An important step taken during the early days of the New Deal was to end the ban on liquor. You have already read (Chapter 17) about the beginnings of the temperance movement. Throughout the late 1800's and early 1900's reformers had sought to forbid or **prohibit** the manufacture and sale of intoxicating drinks. Through churches, clubs, and organizations like the Women's Christian Temperance Union (WCTU) and the Anti-Saloon League, prohibitionists took up the fight against the use of liquor.

As a result of these efforts, the Eighteenth Amendment was added to the Constitution in 1919. It banned the manufacture, transportation, and sale of intoxicating liquor within the United States. But prohibition, as it was called, proved to be difficult to enforce. Beer, wine, whiskey, and gin were manufactured illegally, sometimes for sale to others, but often by ordinary citizens for their own use. Liquor was also smuggled in from other countries and distributed by lawbreakers known as "bootleggers." In 1933 national prohibition was brought to an end by the Twenty-First Amendment to the Constitution. Control of the sale and manufacture of liquor was returned to the states. ★

The New Deal increases the cost and the power of the federal government. To carry out the many New Deal reforms, new government agencies were created. These agencies or boards hired thousands of workers and spent large sums of money. The government departments in Washington greatly expanded in size. Many Americans criticized the New

Newspaper cartoonists often criticized the New Deal. What does this cartoon say about the effect of New Deal programs?

649

President Roosevelt had an air of confidence that helped to restore the morale of the American people. Here he is shown in a 1933 photo greeting admirers in Warm Springs, Georgia.

Deal for spending so much money and piling up a huge debt. These people also believed that the government was interfering too much with business. They said, for example, that the TVA was creating unfair competition for private power companies. The critics pointed out, moreover, that the New Deal had not put an end to the high unemployment and hard times of the Depression. They also accused President Roosevelt of building up an army of government workers to keep the Democrats in power. In fact, most of the criticism of the New Deal was directed against Roosevelt himself. The President had strong admirers and supporters, however. Roosevelt was re-elected in 1936, carrying every state except Maine and Vermont. Later he was elected a third and then a fourth time, thus becoming the only President in our history to be elected for more than two terms.[1]

---

[1]The Twenty-Second Amendment was added to the Constitution in 1951. It says no future President may serve more than two terms.

Roosevelt takes his place in history. ●
Franklin D. Roosevelt died in 1945, just a few months after he was elected for a fourth term as President. Well before that, world events had brought his New Deal to a close, just as World War I had ended Woodrow Wilson's New Freedom reforms. But before seeing how that happened, we must turn back to the years after World War I. We must look at what happened in Europe and Asia to see how hopes for world peace were destroyed.

▶ **CHECK UP**   See Teacher's Key.

1. **(a)** How did President Franklin Roosevelt try to help farmers? **(b)** What did he do to find work for the unemployed? **(c)** To stimulate business and regulate banks?

2. **(a)** What laws were passed during the 1930's to protect workers? **(b)** How did the New Deal plan to protect natural resources?

3. How did the New Deal affect the cost and the power of the federal government?

● See p. T53 for a strategy calling for students to write reports on the life of Franklin D. Roosevelt.

3 What Events After World War I Destroyed Hopes for World Peace?

The United States was the only great power to come out of World War I stronger than ever before. President Wilson's stirring words and his efforts to create the League of Nations (page 633) had given promise of a better, peaceful world. It was only natural, therefore, that many countries looked to the United States for leadership. After World War I, however, most Americans wanted to return to their own interests and activities. They thought other countries should solve their problems without the involvement of the United States.

The United States takes part in peace efforts. It would be a mistake, however, to think that our country showed no interest in working for a peaceful world during the 1920's and 1930's. Americans served as judges on the World Court. The United States, although not a member of the League of Nations, took part in the League's efforts to control the international drug trade and to improve world labor conditions.

Nations agree to reduce their navies. The United States was also a leader in the effort to cut down the size of armed forces. In 1921 several world powers were invited to meet in Washington, D.C., to discuss **disarmament** (the reduction of armed forces). At the Washington Conference, Secretary of State Charles Evans Hughes declared that our government would reduce its navy if other countries would do the same. As a result of the conference, the United States, Great Britain, Japan, France, and Italy agreed to limit the number of their largest warships.

At a conference in London in 1930 another agreement was made to limit the size of navies. Within a few years, however, all the plans to reduce arma-

ments were abandoned. As you will learn, Germany disregarded the Versailles Treaty and began rebuilding its army and navy. Other nations felt they must have large armed forces in case war broke out. Nations again began to rearm.

Relations with Latin America improve. Meanwhile, the United States set about improving relations with its neighbors to the south. You have already read how the United States, starting with the administration of Theodore Roosevelt, began taking an active hand in the affairs of some Latin American nations. Under Presidents Coolidge and Hoover the situation began to change. In 1924 Calvin Coolidge withdrew marines that had been sent to the Dominican Republic eight years earlier. He also named an ambassador to Mexico, Dwight W. Morrow, whose friendly attitude did much to improve relations between the two countries. Later, Herbert Hoover made a good-will visit to eleven Latin American republics.

When Franklin D. Roosevelt became President in 1933, he announced that the United States would not interfere in Latin American affairs. Instead it would follow the "policy of the good neighbor — the neighbor who . . . respects himself and, because he does so, respects the rights of others." Roosevelt soon put the Good Neighbor Policy into effect. In 1934 the United States signed a treaty giving up the right to interfere in Cuban affairs (page 609).

NEW GOVERNMENTS ARE FORMED

After World War I, many European nations needed rebuilding. But would they be restored just as they were before, or rebuilt along different lines?

● Have students reread the terms of the Versailles Treaty (p. 633).

The people of some countries wanted to return to the conditions that had existed before World War I began. These people wished only to live out their lives in peace and quiet. But in other nations people were bitter and unhappy. When the people of a nation are dissatisfied, they are likely to follow leaders who promise them better conditions. They may even be persuaded to change the form of government of their country. In three important countries — Russia, Germany, and Italy — World War I brought such changes.

Russia establishes a new government and way of life. The change in Russia came first and was the greatest change of all. In 1917, while World War I was still going on (page 631), the Russian people revolted. They overthrew their government and imprisoned their ruler. Later in 1917, a small party called the Bolshevists used armed force to seize power. The Bolshevists established a Communist dictatorship and forced their way of life on all the Russian people. The official name of the country was changed to the Union of Soviet Socialist Republics. It is often referred to as the USSR or the Soviet Union.

The Communists did not stop with taking over the government. They also made great changes in the ways the Russian people earned their living. In the United States, as you know, the land, the mines, and other natural resources are privately owned. Individual persons or groups of persons own and operate the factories and the stores and other forms of businesses. This system of private ownership is called **capitalism** or the **free enterprise system.**

The Communists did away with private ownership in the Soviet Union. The Soviet government owns and operates large farms and factories, railroads and mines, stores and newspapers. The people work for the government. This system is called *communism,* because the Soviet government claims that all the factories, businesses, and property are owned *in common* by the people. But as it has worked out, everything in the Soviet Union is actually controlled by a small group, the leaders of the government, who are also the leaders of the Communist Party. The people of the Soviet Union are not free to own and operate businesses or to select their own jobs. Nor do the Soviet people have the freedoms — such as freedom of speech and the press — that mean so much to Americans and the people of other free nations. The Soviet leaders call their system a "people's republic" and claim that they have a "democratic system," but it is not what we think of as democracy. There are elections but the people can vote only for candidates of the Communist Party.

A new government is formed in Italy. The Communist leaders boldly proclaimed that their seizure of power in Russia was only the first step in a revolution that would spread around the world. Because of the fear that this might actually happen, people in other countries listened to leaders who promised to save them from communism. In Italy, a man named Benito Mussolini (moos-oh-LEE-nih) used this fear to make himself all-powerful. He convinced the Italian people that communism might spread to Italy and that he was the man who could save them from it.

In 1922 Mussolini seized control of the Italian government for himself and his followers, who were called Fascists (FASH-ists). Mussolini thus became dictator of Italy. (A **dictator** is a ruler who has complete control over a country.) Italians who actively opposed Mussolini were driven out of the country, thrown into prison, or killed. The Italian people were repeatedly told that under the Fascists their country would become a great world power. Mussolini spent huge sums of money on building up Italy's army, navy, and air force.

● Have students compare the free enterprise system with communism. Point out the absence of individual freedom under communism.

Germany is taken over by the Nazis. Germany was another country where discontent brought change. At the end of World War I, the Germans set up a republic with a constitution, a president, and a congress. Unfortunately, many Germans disliked the new republic. They blamed it for signing the hated Treaty of Versailles. As you learned in Chapter 29, the Treaty of Versailles had held Germany responsible for starting World War I and had reduced that nation's power, wealth, and territory. In spite of these difficul-

In the years after World War I, dictators rose to power in Germany and Italy. Adolf Hitler (below) put an end to democratic government in Germany and prepared for war.

ties, the new German government might have succeeded if hard times had not hit Germany. In the years following the war many Germans could not find jobs and there was much poverty. During the world-wide depression of the early 1930's, conditions went from bad to ● worse.

Taking advantage of widespread discontent, a dictator came to power in Germany in 1933. The German dictator was Adolf Hitler, and his followers were called Nazis (NAH-tsihz). Hitler promised to make Germany a great nation again and to recover the land it had lost. To carry out his ambitions, Hitler began to rearm Germany and set its factories to making war materials.

Under Hitler, Germany once more became a powerful country. But this gain was achieved at heavy cost. Under the Nazi government, people were no longer free. Anyone who disagreed with Hitler lived in fear of the Nazi secret police. The Nazis imprisoned, tortured, killed, or drove from the country anyone who dared speak out against them. They were especially cruel to Jews, whom they blamed for all of Germany's troubles. By the time World War II ended in 1945, the Nazis had killed some six million European Jews. This mass murder became known as the Holocaust (HOH-luh-kawst).

AMBITIOUS NATIONS ATTACK THE WEAK

To be rich and powerful, a nation must have many men and women to do its work. It also needs mines and factories and farms and forests. If all these are not found within its borders, an ambitious nation may be tempted to seize the land of neighboring countries. If a nation wants to grow in this way, it can always find excuses for seizing land. If necessary, a quarrel can be started as an excuse to take over territory belonging to another nation.

653

Japan seeks to control China. There were a number of "land-hungry" countries after World War I. The first of these to cause trouble was Japan. As explained in Chapter 29, Japan was eager to gain power over China. Already Japan had acquired the island of Formosa, a number of small Pacific islands, and Korea on the mainland of Asia. Then, late in 1931, the Japanese army marched into Manchuria, a section of northern China. In a short time Japan made Manchuria into a Japanese-controlled state. Even that was not enough. In 1937, Japanese troops launched a full-scale attack on China.

Italy and Germany seize land. Germany and Italy were also eager to ex-

pand. Germany had lost its colonies and some land in Europe under the Treaty of Versailles. Italy, though one of the victorious Allies, had received less in the treaty than it had demanded. So the ambitious dictators of these two countries, tempted by Japan's success in China, set out to grab what they wanted.

Mussolini, for example, was eager to expand Italy's empire in Africa. In 1935, he sent Italian troops into the African kingdom of Ethiopia. After a few months, the ruler of that kingdom was driven from his throne. Ethiopia became part of the Italian empire.

Germany made conquests nearer to home. By the terms of the Versailles

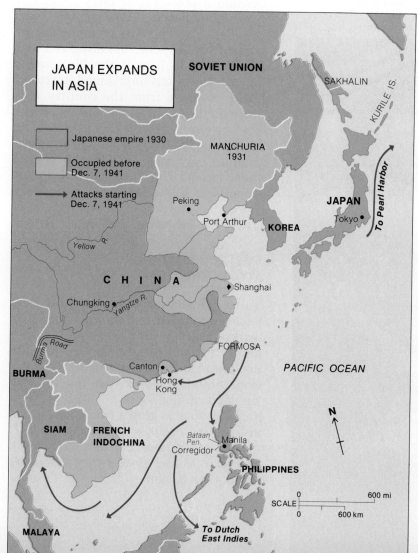

See Teacher's Key.

MAP STUDY
Japan had acquired Korea and Formosa by 1930. What other areas had Japan occupied by December 7, 1941?

654

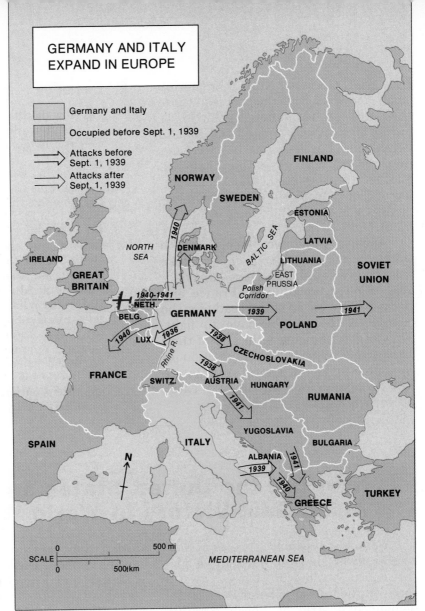

GERMANY AND ITALY EXPAND IN EUROPE

Germany and Italy

Occupied before Sept. 1, 1939

Attacks before Sept. 1, 1939

Attacks after Sept. 1, 1939

See Teacher's Key.

MAP STUDY
By 1939 Germany and Italy had seized several countries in Europe. (a) What country did Italy conquer? (b) What two countries east of Germany did Hitler take over before September, 1939?

Treaty, Germany was supposed to have only a small army. Moreover, no troops were to be permitted in a certain area along the Rhine River between Germany and France. But Hitler ignored these rules. In 1936, he sent German troops into that area.

What next? South and east of Germany were two small nations, Austria and Czechoslovakia. In both of these countries, there were some people who thought they would be better off as a part of Germany. Hitler made the interests of these people an excuse for sending his army into Austria and Czechoslovakia. It was soon clear that he had similar plans for Poland.

Why did other nations permit these conquests? Small countries like Ethiopia, Austria, and Czechoslovakia could not defend themselves against nations as strong as Italy and Germany. But what were the other European powers doing while Italy and Germany swallowed up one small country after another?

Perhaps Great Britain, France, and the Soviet Union could have prevented

Italy and Germany from conquering small countries. But the people of those three nations had suffered great losses during World War I and did not want to fight again. Furthermore they were not prepared for war. So rather than risk another war, they stood aside. This policy of giving in to the demands of the dictators became known as **appeasement** (uh-PEEZ-ment).

Another world war looms. With Germany and Italy determined to take what they wanted, war seemed unavoidable. Slowly, unwillingly, France and Great Britain began to get ready for the day when they might have to fight. They began to increase the size of their armies and to step up production of warships, guns, airplanes, and tanks. But they had a long way to go to catch up with Germany and Italy.

▶ **CHECK UP**   See Teacher's Key.

1. **(a)** How did the United States show its interest in world peace after World War I? **(b)** Why did peace efforts prove useless?

2. **(a)** How did our Latin American policy change during the 1920's and 1930's? **(b)** How was that policy put into effect under Franklin D. Roosevelt?

3. **(a)** What kind of government was established in the Soviet Union after World War I? **(b)** How was the Russian way of life affected by this change? **(c)** How did Mussolini come to power in Italy? **(d)** What kind of rule did Hitler set up in Germany?

4. **(a)** What attacks did Japan make against China in the 1930's? **(b)** What territorial gains were made by Italy? **(c)** By Germany? **(d)** What attitude did other nations take toward these conquests? Why?

4 How Did the United States and Its Allies Gain Victory in World War II?

World War II begins. It was in September, 1939, that the destructive conflict called World War II began in Europe. In the late summer of 1939, Hitler demanded a strip of Polish territory that separated East Prussia from the rest of Germany. Meanwhile, Germany and the Soviet Union signed a neutrality agreement. (The two countries also secretly agreed to divide Poland.) Hitler was free to act. When his demand for Polish territory was refused, he ordered the German invasion of Poland. This time, however, Hitler did not go unchallenged. There was no appeasement as there had been in the case of Czechoslovakia. Great Britain and France came to Poland's assistance and declared war on Germany on September 3, 1939. But the German forces attacked Poland swiftly and fiercely in what they called a *blitzkrieg* (lightning war). Poland was overcome before the British and French could furnish any real aid.

The war spreads over western Europe. For a few months after the conquest of Poland there was little real fighting. But in the spring of 1940, the Nazis unleashed an all-out attack. Norway and Denmark were easily overrun. Then the German blitzkrieg turned south. In a lightning campaign, the Netherlands, Belgium, and finally France were forced to surrender to Hitler's forces. German troops rushed to cut off the retreating British army before it could escape across the English Channel. By a frantic effort, however, some 338,000 British and French soldiers were ferried across the Channel from the French port of Dunkirk in

656

● See p. T53 for a strategy that asks students to examine the events that drew the world into war again.

Hitler ordered his army to invade Poland on September 1, 1939, without a declaration of war. The Polish defenders had no chance against the well-equipped German forces.

ships, tugboats, yachts, and other vessels sent from England.

For a time it seemed that Great Britain might be the next to fall. The valiant British, led by their new prime minister, Winston Churchill, prepared to resist an invasion. The Germans, however, chose to attack by air. Wave after wave of German airplanes bombed Britain, but the British Royal Air Force outfought Hitler's bombers. During most of the war the British people endured frightful air attacks, but their island country was not invaded.

Hitler attacks on other fronts. Elsewhere in Europe, however, the German armies met with great success. Most of the countries of eastern Europe were forced to join the Nazis or were conquered and enslaved. In 1941, in spite of the agreement that he had signed with the Soviet government, Hitler launched a full-scale attack against Russia. Though the Soviet forces fought fiercely, German armies occupied western Russia. The battle line extended from near Leningrad in the north to near Stalingrad on the Volga River before the German advances could be halted. German forces also pushed into North Africa. Meanwhile, on the seas German submarine attacks sank many

ships carrying food and supplies to Britain. (Look at the map on page 661 to see how much territory was conquered by Germany and Italy in Europe.)

Italy and Japan join Germany. Before the war had begun, Mussolini and Hitler had formed an alliance, and their countries became known as the Axis Powers. Then, when the defeat of France seemed certain, Italy entered the war on Germany's side. Late in 1940 Japan also joined the Axis. The Japanese made plans for further expansion in Asia.

Japan conquers more territory. After 1937 the Chinese had continued to fight to halt the Japanese invasion. Japan rapidly took over many of the cities and the best farmland in China. But the Chinese leader, Chiang Kai-shek (chee-AHNG KYE-SHEK), refused to give in. Under his leadership, thousands of Chinese made their way into the mountainous interior region of their country. From mountain strongholds the Chinese launched raids behind the Japanese lines, destroying railroads and supply depots controlled by the Japanese.

Instead of completing their conquest of China, Japanese leaders turned their eyes to Southeast Asia. Why not

657

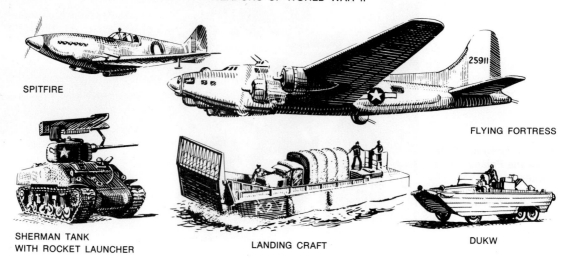

WEAPONS OF WORLD WAR II

SPITFIRE

FLYING FORTRESS

SHERMAN TANK
WITH ROCKET LAUNCHER

LANDING CRAFT

DUKW

take over French Indochina, Siam, the Malay Peninsula, the Dutch East Indies, the Philippines, and, for that matter, Australia? (Locate these countries on the map on page 664.) And why not go west to Burma — and even beyond, to seize the wealth of India? (India was a British possession at that time.) Great Britain was besieged in Europe. France was defeated. Only the United States stood in the way.

The United States hopes to keep out of the war. What had the United States been doing while war raged in other parts of the world? When Japan seized Manchuria, our Secretary of State, Henry L. Stimson, strongly objected. The United States, he declared, would not recognize any "situation, treaty, or agreement which may be brought about" by war. Again and again President Roosevelt appealed to Hitler and Mussolini not to disturb the peace of Europe.

Meanwhile, Congress passed neutrality laws stating that we would not take sides in foreign wars. These laws forbade Americans to lend money or to send military supplies to nations at war. Americans were not allowed to travel on any ships belonging to warring countries. The idea behind these neutrality laws was, of course, to keep our country from being drawn into another world war. Americans at this time believed strongly that the United States should keep out of World War II.

American sympathy grows for nations fighting the Axis. Just as in the early years of World War I, Americans found it more and more difficult to keep neutral. As German victories continued, the threat of war approached our own shores. What if Hitler succeeded in conquering all of Europe? Would he be content to stop there or would he try to extend his power to the Americas?

As German conquests spread, moreover, freedom and liberty disappeared. Because Hilter and his followers considered the Germans to be a "master race," defeated peoples everywhere were forced to labor in the fields and factories for their conquerors. It seemed that unless the Nazis were checked, human freedom would be destroyed throughout the world. Americans, therefore, felt increasing friendship for the people fighting the Axis nations.

The United States takes a stronger stand against the Axis. During 1940 and

● Mention that by 1940 Americans were sending war supplies to Allied nations. In early 1941 Roosevelt called the United States "the arsenal of democracy."

● Students can read more about Pearl Harbor in "Linking Past and Present" (p. 666).

1941, as Americans became less strictly neutral, our government took steps to strengthen the army and navy. Congress also passed a law permitting countries at war to buy weapons in America; later it passed the Lend-Lease Act. This act allowed the President to sell or lend war materials to any nation whose defense was considered essential to America's safety. In addition, the production of war materials was speeded up.

Meanwhile, our relations with Japan grew steadily worse. Japanese leaders insisted that their goal was to help other Asian peoples. Our government, however, believed that Japan's main purpose was to enlarge its empire at the expense of weaker nations. The United States insisted upon protecting American rights in Asia. Our government also gave aid to China and broke off a long-standing trade agreement with Japan. To achieve its goals, Japan decided that the United States must be crushed. While carrying on negotiations to iron out differences with the United States, Japan prepared for a surprise attack in the Pacific.

War! The blow fell on December 7, 1941. Without warning, waves of Japanese bombers attacked the great American base at Pearl Harbor in Hawaii. Many airplanes were destroyed on the ground by the attacking bombers. Five battleships were sunk or disabled, and fourteen other vessels were badly damaged. Nearly 2,500 American soldiers, sailors, and civilians were killed. The Japanese attack shocked and angered the entire nation.

On December 8, President Franklin D. Roosevelt asked Congress for an immediate declaration of war against Japan. Congress approved the President's request and declared war that same day. Britain also declared war against Japan. A few days later, Germany and Italy declared war against the United States. The United States thus joined Britain, the Soviet Union, and China, who were known as the Allies, against the Axis Powers.

The American nation goes "all out" for victory. Once war had been declared, the American people turned all their efforts toward victory. Men between 18 and 45 were called into military service.

Over fifteen million American men served in the armed forces during the Second World War. This photo shows young Americans of Japanese descent lined up at an army induction center in Denver.

659

● See p. T54 for a strategy that calls for students to examine how the war affected the lives of Americans.

At top strength, the armed forces included over fifteen million men and women. Among them were over one million black Americans.

To provide needed war materials, mines and factories began hiring new workers. In 1941 discrimination in hiring was ended in defense industries, thus making it possible for hundreds of thousands of black and Hispanic Americans to help in the war effort. Factories also turned to the disabled to replace workers who had left for the armed services. Eighty percent of the nation's industries hired disabled workers. And as they had done in previous wars, American women contributed to the national effort by taking jobs in factories, stores, and government offices. By 1943 some two million women were working in war plants.

Business and labor pulled together to meet the demands of war, and American production became the marvel of the world. Meanwhile, American farmers were outdoing themselves to produce the food needed by this country and its allies. To help pay the costs of war, high taxes were levied. Boys and girls, as well as men and women, bought billions of dollars' worth of war bonds.

The war brings great changes in American life. ● Americans quickly adjusted to war conditions. Civilians learned what to do in case enemy airplanes ever attacked American cities. Because enormous quantities of food were needed for our forces overseas, as well as for our allies, many peacetime goods disappeared entirely from stores. Meat, fats, coffee, sugar, gasoline, and fuel oil were so scarce that people were permitted to buy them only in small quantities. To prevent **inflation** (a continuing rise in prices), the government set limits or "ceilings" on the prices of food, clothing, and other things, and also on rents.

People did all sorts of extra or unusual jobs during the war. They served

On the home front thousands of Americans took on new jobs to help the war effort. The women below worked on an aircraft assembly line.

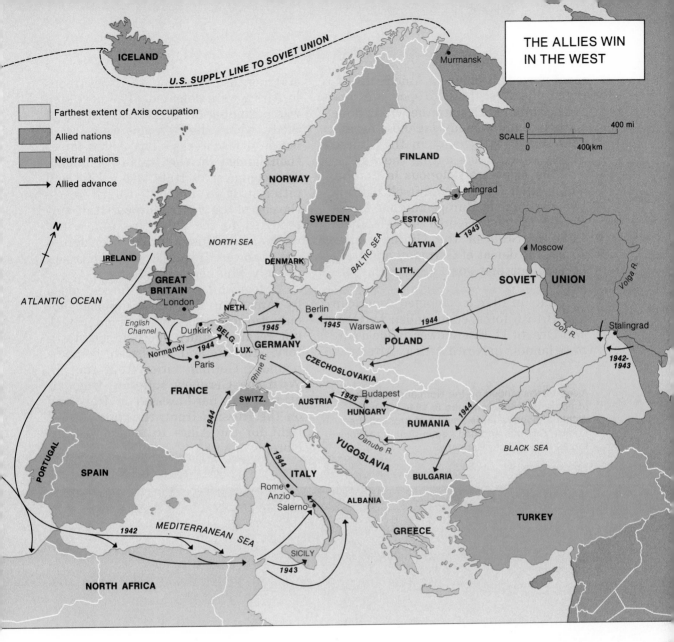

THE ALLIES WIN IN THE WEST

Farthest extent of Axis occupation

Allied nations

Neutral nations

Allied advance

U.S. SUPPLY LINE TO SOVIET UNION

ICELAND

Murmansk

NORWAY

FINLAND

SWEDEN

Leningrad

NORTH SEA

ESTONIA

DENMARK

LATVIA

Moscow

BALTIC SEA

LITH.

IRELAND

SOVIET UNION

Volga R.

ATLANTIC OCEAN

GREAT BRITAIN

London

NETH.

Berlin

1945 Warsaw

1944

Don R.

Stalingrad

English Channel

Dunkirk

BELG.

1945

1944

Normandy

LUX.

GERMANY

POLAND

1942-1943

Paris

CZECHOSLOVAKIA

FRANCE

Rhine R.

SWITZ.

AUSTRIA

1945 Budapest

HUNGARY

1944

RUMANIA

BLACK SEA

PORTUGAL

SPAIN

1944

YUGOSLAVIA

Danube R.

ITALY

Rome

Anzio

Salerno

ALBANIA

BULGARIA

TURKEY

MEDITERRANEAN SEA

1942

SICILY

GREECE

1943

NORTH AFRICA

N

SCALE

0   400 mi

0   400 km

MAP STUDY See Teacher's Key.
This map shows how much territory in Europe
the Axis armies held at one time. (a) In what
part of Europe did the western Allies make their
first invasion? (b) What European countries
remained neutral throughout the war?

as airplane spotters and air-raid war-
dens. They assisted in hospitals and in
the entertainment of troops. After Dr.
Charles Drew found a way to preserve
blood, millions of Americans became
blood donors to save the lives of the

wounded. Boys and girls harvested
crops, helped collect rubber, scrap
metal, and paper, or took jobs after
school. To release more men for actual
fighting, women enlisted in the WAC
(army), the WAVES (navy), the SPARS
(Coast Guard), and the Marine Corps.

Japanese Americans are relocated.
After the attack on Pearl Harbor,
Americans felt extremely bitter toward
the Japanese. Such emotion worked
great hardship on many loyal Americans of Japanese ancestry. The govern-

661

ment moved all Japanese Americans living on the West Coast to special camps farther inland. Despite the wrong done to their families, many Japanese Americans served with honor in the United States armed forces during the war.

The Allies are victorious in Europe. The United States found itself fighting two wars, one in Europe and one in the Pacific. Under George C. Marshall, Chief of Staff of the United States Army, the defeat of Germany and Italy became our first goal. (See map, page 661.)

Late in 1942, a combined American and British force, commanded by General Dwight D. Eisenhower, made a surprise landing in North Africa. After several months of fighting, the Nazi troops in Africa were defeated. The next step was a landing on the Italian island of Sicily, where the Germans were forced out in a few weeks. The Allied forces then landed on the Italian mainland. The conquest of Italy was a long and bitter struggle that lasted until nearly the end of the war in Europe. Italy surrendered to the Allies in 1943, a few weeks after Mussolini had been forced out of power. It was the German troops in Italy who kept on fighting.

Meanwhile, Russian forces, aided by American lend-lease supplies, not only turned back the German attack but regained much of their lost territory. British and American bombers pounded German cities from the air. With the Germans suffering from air attacks and hard-pressed in Italy and on the Russian front, the time seemed right for the Allies to invade western Europe.

Allied troops landed on the Normandy beaches of northern France on June 6, 1944 (D-Day). Within a month a million men had crossed the English Channel and had begun pushing Hitler's forces back toward Germany.

On June 6, 1944, a great force of Americans, Canadians, and British landed on beaches in Normandy, in northern France. Naval guns bombarded the coast, and squadrons of planes gave protection in the air as the soldiers scrambled ashore. The landings were successful, and by August, France had been freed from Nazi control. The Americans and British then pushed on against Germany. After bitter fighting, they succeeded in crossing the Rhine River. With Nazi armies being cut to pieces by Allied drives from the east and the west, and with round-the-clock bombing of its cities and factories, the Nazi cause was hopeless. On May 8, 1945, Germany surrendered and the war in Europe was over.

Adolf Hitler committed suicide in April, 1945, just before the Russians entered Berlin. The Italian dictator, Mussolini, had been captured and killed by some of his own countrymen a few weeks earlier.

The United States fights a bitter war with Japan. In the Pacific the task of defeating Japan fell mainly on the United States. At first the war went badly. Soon after Pearl Harbor, the Japanese launched an invasion of the Philippine Islands. American and Filipino troops fought bravely, but they were forced to surrender in June, 1942.

The Japanese were equally successful in other parts of Asia. They had already occupied French Indochina and now captured the British colony of Hong Kong. Advancing overland, Japanese soldiers occupied the Malay Peninsula and took the British stronghold at Singapore. The Dutch Empire in the East Indies also fell to Japanese attacks. Japanese forces then pushed on through Burma and broke the Allied supply line to China over the Burma Road. Worn out by war, the Chinese fell back still farther before enemy attacks. The Japanese also seized Pacific islands as far north as the Aleutians, off

When news of Germany's surrender reached the United States, happy crowds of people jammed city streets in celebration.

the coast of Alaska. (See map, page 664.)

American forces push back the Japanese. Slowly but surely, however, the tide turned. The American navy won two smashing victories. The Battle of ● the Coral Sea (May, 1942) blocked an invasion of Australia; the Battle of Midway (June, 1942) saved Hawaii. General Douglas MacArthur, chief of the Allied forces in the Pacific area, made plans to recapture lost ground. Beginning with 663

● Tell students that these two battles were mainly fought by airplanes based on aircraft carriers of the two opposing forces.

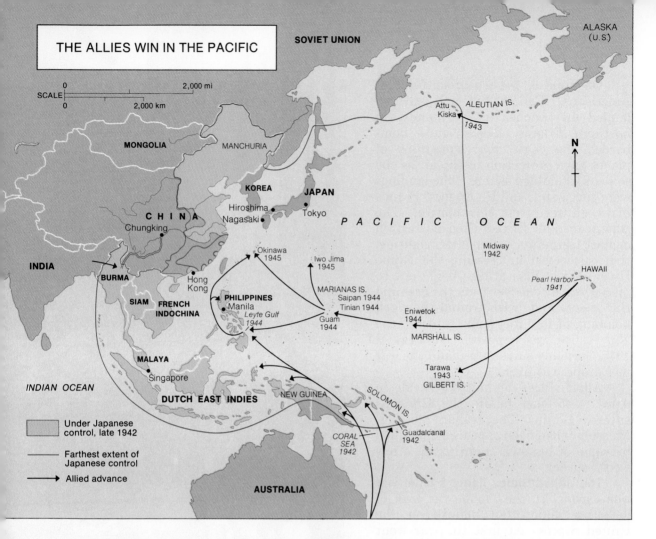

THE ALLIES WIN IN THE PACIFIC

Guadalcanal, American marines and soldiers, supported by the navy, began to capture important bases. They seized some islands and leapfrogged others, pushing ever closer to Japan. Some of the island attacks — Guadalcanal, Iwo Jima (EE-woh JEE-muh), and Okinawa — were among the most costly battles of the Pacific war.

In October, 1944, American forces, led by General MacArthur, returned to the Philippines and in a few months regained control of the islands. One of the greatest naval battles of history, in which the Japanese lost a large part of their fleet, took place in the Gulf of Leyte (LAY-tay).

● **World War II ends.** These successes, as well as others on the mainland of Asia, dashed Japan's hopes of empire. But Japan itself still had to be con-

MAP STUDY   See Teacher's Key.
By mid-1942 Japan controlled a wide area of the Pacific. Allied sea, air, and land forces closed in on Japan by "island hopping" across the Pacific. The dates show when important battles were fought. (a) When was the Battle of the Coral Sea fought? (b) What islands south of Japan did the Allied forces capture in 1945?

quered. American bombers, based on huge carriers and Pacific islands, began hammering at Japanese cities. Allied plans for invading Japan, however, never had to be used.

In 1939 Albert Einstein, a famous scientist who had left Germany to settle in this country, urged the United States to begin work on a bomb that would make use of atomic energy. Many scientists heeded this call and worked at top speed to develop such a bomb. Cut

664

● See p. T54 for a strategy that asks students to report on various aspects of World War II.

off from the world in specially built towns with laboratories, factories, and living quarters, these scientists carried on their research. At last their efforts were successful.

On August 6, 1945, the first atomic bomb used against an enemy was dropped on the Japanese city of Hiroshima (hear-uh-SHEE-muh), causing frightful loss of life and property. Two days later, a second atomic bomb practically wiped out the city of Nagasaki (nah-guh-SAH-kee). Faced with utter destruction, the Japanese government on August 14 agreed to surrender. On September 2 the peace terms were signed.

As Americans either celebrated wildly or quietly offered prayers of thanksgiving, World War II came to an end — the most destructive war in history. It is estimated that 22 million people had been killed and over 34 million wounded.

▶ CHECK UP   See Teacher's Key.

1. **(a)** Why did war break out in Europe in 1939? **(b)** What nations were conquered by Nazi Germany? **(c)** How was Great Britain able to hold out? **(d)** Against what other countries did Germany launch attacks?
2. **(a)** How successful had Japan been in its war against China? **(b)** What other areas did Japan seek to conquer?
3. **(a)** What did the United States do to keep out of the war? **(b)** Why did this country's attitude change? **(c)** How did the United States become involved in the war? **(d)** In what ways did Americans take part in the war effort?
4. **(a)** Describe the Allied campaigns in North Africa and Italy. **(b)** Tell how the Allies landed in France and pressed on into Germany.
5. **(a)** What was the extent of the Japanese conquests? **(b)** How did American forces in the Pacific push back the Japanese? **(c)** What event brought about Japan's surrender?

CHECK UP ON CHAPTER 30   See Teacher's Key.

Words to Know

1. prohibit
2. disarmament
3. unemployment
4. agency
5. neutrality laws
6. capitalism
7. inflation
8. besiege
9. communism
10. dictator
11. appeasement
12. free enterprise system

Places to Locate

1. Germany
2. Italy
3. Sicily
4. Japan
5. Manchuria
6. English Channel
7. Czechoslovakia
8. Burma
9. Poland
10. Leningrad
11. Pearl Harbor
12. North Africa
13. East Indies
14. Soviet Union
15. Stalingrad
16. Coral Sea
17. Midway
18. Guadalcanal
19. Okinawa
20. Hiroshima

Facts to Remember

1. Name the Presidents in order from Warren Harding through Franklin D. Roosevelt. Identify the political party to which each belonged.
2. **(a)** What serious problem became the nation's chief concern in the early and middle 1930's? **(b)** How did it affect the American people?
3. **(a)** What was the New Deal? **(b)** What was its aim in general? **(c)** What kinds of steps were taken to meet that aim? **(d)** Why was the New Deal criticized?
4. What was the Good Neighbor Policy?
5. Identify each of the following persons: **(a)** Adolf Hitler, **(b)** Benito Mussolini, **(c)** Chiang Kai-shek, **(d)** Winston Churchill, **(e)** Dwight D. Eisenhower, **(f)** Douglas MacArthur.
6. **(a)** What steps led to the Allied victory over Germany in 1945? **(b)** What new weapon led to the surrender of Japan?

Skills to Practice

1. Following is a list of New Deal laws and programs. In each case tell what groups of Americans were probably *most* in favor of the law or program. In answering, name such groups as unemployed workers, farmers, business managers, older citizens, and so on. Give reasons for your answer in each case.
   a. Government price supports for crops
   b. Civilian Conservation Corps
   c. Government insurance of bank deposits
   d. Wages and Hours Act
   e. Social Security Act
2. Arrange the following events in the order in which they happened. Start with the earliest event.
   a. Germany invades Poland.
   b. F. D. Roosevelt becomes President.
   c. World War II ends.
   d. Battle of Midway is fought.
   e. Allied forces land in German-occupied France.
   f. Japanese attack Pearl Harbor.

Questions to Think About

1. Explain why Presidents are usually given credit for prosperous times and are blamed for hard times.
2. Franklin D. Roosevelt was elected President four times. The Twenty-Second Amendment now prevents anyone from being elected President more than twice. What might be some arguments in support of such a limitation? What might be some of the arguments against it?
3. Compare the Communist system in the Soviet Union with the American government and economic system. Base your comparison on ownership of property, personal freedoms, and political rights.

Linking Past and Present

Remember Pearl Harbor! Beneath the waters of Pearl Harbor in Hawaii lies the rusting hulk of the U. S. battleship *Arizona,* a sad reminder of a disastrous day in American history. During the Japanese attack on December 7, 1941, the *Arizona* was hit by bombs. The ship blew up and sank, carrying with it a crew of a thousand men. Many years have passed, but the *Arizona* is not forgotten. A white concrete-steel structure now spans the hulk of the sunken ship, which is clearly visible just below the surface of the water. The ship has become a national memorial to all the men who lost their lives in the historic attack on Pearl Harbor.

"Sighted sub — sank same." At crucial times in our history, heroic Americans have made short, dramatic reports on some important victory or event, such as Commodore Perry's "We have met the enemy and they are ours" in the War of 1812 (page 280). The story goes, too, that when American troops arrived in France in World War I, General Pershing, their commander, said "Lafayette, we are here." In this way he expressed our country's gratitude to the young Frenchman who had fought in our Revolutionary War.

Out of World War II came another short and dramatic report. After the United States entered the war, the Germans sent packs of submarines to prey on our Atlantic coast shipping. Many a ship was torpedoed and many a crew left to drown. The Army and Navy sent out planes and boats of all kinds to spot the deadly submarines. On a January day in 1942, an aviation machinist's mate named Donald Mason was flying a Navy bomber over the Atlantic. Suddenly the periscope of a German sub was sighted below. After dropping two depth bombs on the target, the crew of the plane watched closely. They saw a submarine rise to the surface, turn on its side, and plunge into the ocean. Only an oil slick was left to tell the tale. Mason radioed back the news in four short words: "Sighted sub — sank same."

666

● Tell students that Pearl Harbor is located on the southern coast of the island of Oahu (see map, p. 680).

GAINING SKILL

Understanding Public Opinion Polls

You have already learned that in reading an article or listening to a speech, it is important to distinguish between statements of fact and statements of opinion (page 577). Statements of opinion are based on personal beliefs or attitudes.

In our representative form of government the opinions of citizens are of great importance. When they make their opinions known to their elected officials, citizens play a part in helping government run smoothly. But how can elected officials learn what the American public is thinking? How can they measure **public opinion**? One way, of course, is for officials to meet and talk with citizens. Another way is for them to read the many letters they receive every day. Third, officials can study the results of public opinion polls.

The first professional opinion polls were taken in the 1930's. Selected numbers of people were asked their opinions on certain questions. The results of the polls showed what large sections of the American public were thinking.

The polls on this page were taken in the late 1930's, when people feared an outbreak of war in Europe. Did Americans think that the United States might soon be fighting in Europe? Study the polls to find out. Then answer the questions that follow.

1. In what year was the first poll taken? In that year, what percentage of Americans thought the United States could stay out of a European war? In what region did a majority of people think this country could *not* stay out of a war?

2. In what year was the second poll taken? In that year, how had the opinion of the majority of the American public changed? In what regions did most people believe that the United States would be drawn into a war?

October 2, 1938

European War

If England and France go to war against Germany, do you think the United States can stay out?

Yes 57%
No 43

By Region

	Yes	No
New England	46%	54%
Middle Atlantic	61	39
East Central	60	40
West Central	57	43
South	60	40
West	51	49

August 20, 1939

European War

If England and France have a war with Germany and Italy, do you think the United States will be drawn in?

Yes 76%
No 24

By Region

	Yes	No
New England	69%	31%
Middle Atlantic	74	26
East Central	78	22
West Central	78	22
South	75	25
West	75	25

667

CHAPTER **31** *Vocabulary preview:* right-to-work laws, cold war, arms race, affluent

The Postwar Years Bring Change

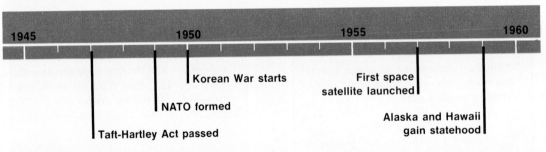

1945–1960   See pp. T54-T55 for chapter teaching strategies.

| 1945 | 1950 | 1955 | 1960 |

Korean War starts

First space
satellite launched

NATO formed

Alaska and Hawaii
gain statehood

Taft-Hartley Act passed

What this chapter is about —

On April 12, 1945, Vice-President Harry Truman was suddenly called to the White House. When he arrived, Eleanor Roosevelt told him that the President had died. "Is there anything I can do for you?" Truman asked. Mrs. Roo-

sevelt answered, "Is there anything *we* can do for *you*?" That evening Truman was sworn in as President.

The next day Truman told a group of reporters, "Boys, if you ever pray, pray for me now. I don't know whether you fellows ever had a load of hay fall on you, but when they told me yesterday

● See p. T54 for a strategy calling for students to prepare written reports on the life of Harry S. Truman.

◀ The building of new suburban communities throughout the country was evidence of the prosperity of the 1950's.

what had happened, I felt like the moon, the stars, and all the planets had fallen on me."

Harry Truman recognized the challenge he now faced. For more than twelve years President Roosevelt had headed the nation. Suddenly there was a new President. How successful would he be in leading the nation to victory in Europe and in the Pacific and in guiding America through its adjustment to peacetime living?

There were many other problems that President Truman and his succes-sor, President Eisenhower, would have to face, especially in our country's relations with other nations. As World War II came to an end, people hoped that countries would work together to create a new and better world. In this chapter you will learn why that hope did not work out. You will also learn what steps the United States took to keep its defenses strong in the 1940's and 1950's.

As you read, look for answers to these questions:

1. How did President Truman deal with postwar conditions at home?
2. Why did the cold war develop after World War II?
3. How did President Eisenhower meet the problems of the cold war?
4. What changes took place at home during the Eisenhower years?

1 How Did President Truman Deal with Postwar Conditions at Home?

● When Harry S. Truman entered the White House, he was the seventh Vice-President to succeed to the highest office in the land because of the death of a President. A native of Missouri, Harry Truman had seen action as an artillery captain in World War I. He was elected to the United States Senate in 1934 as a Democrat, and was re-elected six years later. Nominated for the vice-presidency in 1944, Truman had actually held that office for only three months when he was called to lead the nation.

The nation adjusts to peacetime. The new President's first task was to end World War II quickly. The complete defeat of Germany came just a month after Truman took office, and Japan surrendered in August, 1945 (page 665). Next, the Truman administration had to struggle with challenges that came about when Americans changed back to peacetime living. In 1945 and 1946, millions of veterans came home and were discharged from the armed forces. A law passed by Congress ★ in 1944 eased the return of these veterans to civilian life. Under the GI Bill of Rights the federal government paid expenses for men and women who wanted to attend college. Money was also lent to veterans for building homes and starting businesses.

As the veterans returned home, industries shifted from producing war materials to making goods for peacetime use. But the public demanded more goods than industries could produce. Americans had been unable to buy many things during the war. They had, therefore, saved their money. Now that the war was over they wanted to buy everything at once. With so much demand for too few goods, and with wartime price controls no longer in effect, inflation became a serious problem. To

669

★ See p. T54 for a strategy that asks students to examine how the federal government assisted Americans in their adjustment to peacetime.

meet the increased cost of living, labor unions demanded higher wages and there were frequent strikes.

Congress passes the Taft-Hartley Act. By 1946 many Americans were concerned by the great number of
● strikes. Senator Robert Taft of Ohio and other leaders in Congress felt that the Wagner Act (page 648) had given unfair advantages to labor unions. They urged new legislation to protect the rights of employers and to prevent strikes that could interfere with the delivery of essential goods and services. Under Taft's leadership, Congress passed a new labor law in 1947. The Taft-Hartley Act placed limits on certain union activities. Among other things, it (1) outlawed the closed shop, which had forbidden the hiring of non-union workers; (2) required a 60-day "cooling off" period before a union could strike; and (3) provided that both employers and unions might sue each other for breaking a contract. The Taft-Hartley Act also said that states had the

Harry Truman became President in 1945 when Franklin Roosevelt died. Here Truman is shown with his wife Bess and daughter Margaret.

right to pass **right-to-work laws.** Such laws allow workers to get and keep jobs without joining a labor union.

President Truman opposed the Taft-Hartley Act. But Congress, believing that this act restored the balance between labor and business, overrode the President's veto and the Taft-Hartley Act became law in 1947.

Truman proposes new reforms. At the same time that President Truman was dealing with labor problems, he backed new reforms. Among them were steps to end discrimination against black Americans. Earlier, during World War II, President Roosevelt had ordered defense industries to end discrimination in the hiring of workers. In the postwar years, other racial barriers began to fall. In 1948 President Truman banned discrimination in the hiring of federal employees. He also took steps to end segregation in the nation's armed forces.

Truman wins the 1948 election. As the 1948 presidential election approached, Truman's chances looked very slim. The Democratic Party was split. Many southern Democrats were angry because of the President's support of policies to end discrimination. They formed a States' Rights Party and nominated their own candidate for the presidency. Other dissatisfied Democrats organized a new Progressive Party. The Progressive candidate for President called for sweeping reforms and friendly relations with the Soviet Union. Meanwhile, the Republicans were united behind Governor Thomas Dewey of New York. Almost every newspaper writer and public opinion poll predicted that Dewey would win. President Truman refused to be discouraged, though, and carried on a vigorous campaign. Speaking in all parts of the country, he blamed the Republican-controlled Congress for the nation's problems. When the votes were counted, President Truman surprised

As troops returned home at the end of World War II, the American economy began to convert to peacetime production.

the political experts by winning the election.

Truman asks for Fair Deal legislation. The President believed his victory proved that the people wanted the measures he had favored. Greatly encouraged, he asked Congress to approve further reforms in a program that he called the Fair Deal. These included government financing of housing, broader Social Security coverage, and a plan for health insurance. Congress did pass some of the laws Truman wanted, but on many issues Democrats in Congress sided with the Republicans.

Partly for that reason, President Truman could not get Congress to approve very much of his Fair Deal program.

▶ **CHECK UP**   See Teacher's Key.

1. What problems did President Truman face after the end of World War II?
2. **(a)** What was the Taft-Hartley Act? **(b)** Why did Congress pass this law? **(c)** What position did President Truman take?
3. **(a)** What were the results of the election of 1948? **(b)** What was the Fair Deal?

2 Why Did the Cold War Develop After World War II?

During World War II there had been encouraging signs that after the conflict nations might work together for a free and peaceful world. One example was the meeting of President Roosevelt and Prime Minister Churchill of Great Britain on a ship off the coast of Newfoundland in August, 1941. In a statement known as the Atlantic Charter, the two leaders summarized the aims of their countries for a better world. The Atlantic Charter pledged that all peoples should have the right to choose their own forms of government. It stated

that the United States and Britain desired no changes of territory without the approval of the people living in that territory. Roosevelt and Churchill also promised to work for a fairer division of world trade and natural resources.

The President and the Prime Minister held several other important conferences during the war. On two occasions — at Tehran (teh-RAHN) in Iran and at Yalta in the Soviet Union — they were joined by Soviet Premier Joseph Stalin (STAH-lin). At these meetings, the leaders naturally spent

671

● Point out that Truman's Fair Deal program was an extension of Roosevelt's New Deal (p. 646).

Our Presidents

HARRY S. TRUMAN   1945–1953

Democrat from Missouri. Captain of artillery in World War I, Truman rose through local politics to become a United States senator. As Vice-President he became President at Roosevelt's death and continued the New Deal approach in his Fair Deal program. During his administration, World War II ended, the United States adopted plans for aiding the recovery of Europe, and American troops fought in the Korean War.

DWIGHT D. EISENHOWER   1953–1961

Republican. Born in Texas and raised in Kansas, Eisenhower was a soldier for most of his life. During World War II General Eisenhower commanded the Allied forces in the invasion of Europe. Later, he served as Chief of Staff of the Army, as president of Columbia University, and as NATO commander in Europe. A highly popular leader, Eisenhower was Chief Executive during a time of general prosperity.

much of their time making plans to win the war. But they also gave thought to the problems of peace after victory.

The United Nations gets under way. World leaders agreed on one thing. A new start should be made on forming an organization of nations, in which all countries would work together for world peace. In April, 1945, representatives of 46 nations gathered at San Francisco to complete plans for such an organization. In two months they wrote a charter for the United Nations (called the UN).

How is the United Nations organized? The charter set up several groups or bodies to carry out the purposes of the United Nations. Chief among these bodies are the General Assembly, the Security Council, and the Secretariat.

Every member nation has a seat in the General Assembly and each of these countries, large or small, has one vote. The Assembly may discuss any subject which comes under the charter.

The goal of the Security Council is to keep the world at peace. Five countries — the United States, Great Britain, the Soviet Union, China, and France — are permanent members of the Council. Ten other members are elected by the Assembly to serve two-year terms. The Security Council has the right to use troops against an aggressor country. Before any such action can be taken, however, all five permanent members must agree to it. Thus, any of these nations can veto decisions of the Council.

The Secretariat carries out the day-to-day work of the UN. Its employees handle correspondence, gather information, and publish reports. The head of the Secretariat, called the secretary-general, is elected by the General Assembly. The headquarters of the United Nations is a group of buildings near the East River in New York City. More than 150 nations are now members of the organization.

World peace is threatened by the cold war. The true and lasting peace that the world longed for in the late 1940's was not achieved. Instead, after World War II, there was only an uneasy peace. Again and again, trouble in one part of the world or another threatened to start a new war. This period of uneasy peace was called the **cold war.**

The world splits into two opposing groups of nations. The great barrier to real peace grew out of a split of nations into two opposing groups after 1945. The United States led one of these groups; the Soviet Union led the other. Gone was the spirit of cooperation that had existed during the Second World War. The Soviet Union refused to with-

draw its armies from eastern Germany or to help work out a final peace treaty with Germany. In the United Nations, the Soviet Union would not work with its former allies. Again and again in the Security Council, Soviet delegates vetoed proposals by the United States and other nations.

Communists take over Eastern Europe. During World War II, when Hitler's forces swept eastward, the Soviet Union had suffered enormous losses. Soviet troops, however, not only turned back the invaders but helped to conquer Germany. At the close of the war, the Soviet Union took control of the European countries through which its armies had advanced. (See map, this page.) Between these occupied countries and Western Europe the Soviets dropped an "iron curtain." In other words, they ● took steps to stop the exchange of goods and ideas. The people behind the iron curtain lost their freedom and the right to govern themselves. The countries of Eastern Europe that were dominated by the Soviet Union became known as the satellite nations.

MAP STUDY   See Teacher's Key.
After World War II the Soviet Union took control of most nations in Eastern Europe. To resist the Communist challenge, the United States and western European nations formed NATO. What European nations became NATO members?

EUROPE AFTER WORLD WAR II

NATO countries in Europe

Communist countries

FINLAND
NORWAY
SWEDEN
NORTH SEA
Moscow ●
IRELAND
GREAT BRITAIN
DENMARK
London
NETH.
Berlin
E. GERMANY
POLAND
SOVIET UNION
ATLANTIC OCEAN
W. GERMANY
BELG.
Paris
LUX.
CZECHOSLOVAKIA
FRANCE
SWITZ.
AUSTRIA
HUNGARY
CASPIAN SEA
YUGOSLAVIA
RUMANIA
BLACK SEA
PORTUGAL
ITALY
Rome
BULGARIA
SPAIN
ALBANIA
TURKEY
GREECE
MEDITERRANEAN SEA

673

0   400 mi
SCALE
0   400 km

THE KOREAN WAR

CHINA

Yalu River

Farthest advance
of UN forces,
November 1950

SOVIET
UNION

NORTH KOREA

• Pyongyang

SEA OF JAPAN

Truce line, July 1953

38th parallel

Panmunjom
• Seoul
Inchon •

YELLOW SEA

SOUTH KOREA

N

• Pusan

JAPAN

SCALE
0 _____ 200 mi
0 _____ 200 km

MAP STUDY   See Teacher's Key.
A UN army was formed to help South Korea
resist the North Korean attack in 1950. Find the
line that shows the farthest advance of the UN
forces. What country lay a short distance north
of that line?

**Communists come to power in
China.** Perhaps the greatest victory for
communism occurred in China. While
the war with Japan was still going on, a
bitter struggle began between the Chinese Nationalist government of Chiang
Kai-shek (page 657) and the Chinese
Communists. In 1949 Chiang Kai-shek
674   and his supporters were forced to take

★ Mention that the United States gave about 13 billion
dollars in aid.

refuge on the island of Formosa. The
Chinese Communists won control of
China.

The United States aids other coun- ●
tries. Because of the Communist gains
in Europe and in Asia, the United
States began after World War II to help
nations that found themselves in danger. Early in 1947, President Truman
asked Congress to vote large sums of
money to help Greece and Turkey resist
communism. This idea of aiding nations that opposed communism was
called the Truman Doctrine.

Later in that same year, Secretary
of State George C. Marshall announced
that the United States would give
"friendly aid" to European nations to
help them recover from the damage of
war. This aid was offered to the Soviet
Union and the Communist countries of
Eastern Europe too, but they refused
it. The Western European countries
accepted the American offer. Under the
Marshall Plan the United States provided huge sums of money to enable the ★
farms and factories of Europe to operate
effectively once more. The Marshall
Plan had remarkable results. It was responsible for helping Western Europe to
become prosperous again in a very short
time.

The United States begins to build alli-
ances. As bad feelings between the
Communists and the Western powers
grew stronger, the United States began
to form alliances with other nations.
The first alliance made after World War
II was in the region nearest the United
States. In 1947, the United States
signed the Rio Pact with nineteen Latin
American countries. The treaty said
that all these nations should act together against an armed attack on any
one of them.

The North Atlantic nations make an
alliance. Many of the nations of the
non-Communist world lie on one side or
the other of the Atlantic Ocean. In 1949
these countries formed the North At-

● See p. T55 for a strategy that asks students to examine American involvement in
world affairs during the Truman administration.

● See p. T55 for a strategy calling for students to examine characteristics of the cold war period.

lantic Treaty Organization, commonly called NATO. This organization was made up originally of Great Britain, France, Belgium, the Netherlands, Luxembourg, the United States, Canada, Norway, Denmark, Iceland, Italy, and Portugal. Greece, Turkey, and West Germany joined later. The members of NATO declared that they supported the United Nations and wished to settle all disputes by peaceful means. But they also said that an attack on any one of them should be considered an attack on all. They would unite, they declared, to resist such an attack. Each nation contributed to the armed forces of NATO, and each had representatives on the Council of NATO.

● **The cold war turns hot.** The greatest challenge faced by President Truman as a leader of the non-Communist world was the war which broke out in Korea in 1950. After World War II, Korea was divided at the 38th parallel of latitude (map, page 674). The northern half was placed under Soviet control and the southern half under the supervision of the United States. The United States helped to establish the Republic of Korea in the southern half and then withdrew American soldiers. The Soviet Union withdrew its soldiers from North Korea after a Communist government had been organized there.

Fighting breaks out in Korea. Suddenly, on June 25, 1950, North Korean forces invaded South Korea. At once
★ the Security Council of the United Nations asked the North Koreans to stop fighting. The Security Council also asked members of the UN to help South Korea resist the attack and restore peace. President Truman immediately announced that the United States would support the UN. He ordered General Douglas MacArthur to send troops to Korea. MacArthur was commander of the American forces that had remained in Japan after the end of World War II.

In 1950 President Truman met with General Douglas MacArthur, commander of the UN forces in Korea. The two leaders later disagreed over war policy, and Truman fired MacArthur.

Fighting raged up and down the Korean peninsula. Although the United States provided most of the supplies and South Korea supplied most of the troops, other UN members sent soldiers or ships and planes.

In November, 1950, as the UN army approached the Chinese border, large numbers of soldiers from Communist China joined the North Korean forces. The greatly outnumbered UN troops retreated into South Korea. Yet, even after China's entry into the war, the UN troops drove the Communist forces back to the 38th parallel.

A truce fails to bring permanent peace. After a year of fighting, officers from each side in the Korean War met to discuss a cease-fire. For more than two years these meetings dragged on. At last, in 1953, a truce was signed. But today troops continue to guard both sides of the boundary between North and South Korea.

675

★ Tell students that the Soviet Union was absent from the United Nations the day the Security Council voted to take action against North Korea.

1. **(a)** What was the Atlantic Charter? **(b)** Why was the United Nations formed? **(c)** What are the three chief bodies of the United Nations?
2. **(a)** How did the cold war divide the world? **(b)** How did the Soviet Union extend communism into Eastern Europe? **(c)** Where else in the world did communism become a threat?
3. **(a)** How did the United States oppose communism through the Truman Doctrine? **(b)** Through the Marshall Plan?
4. What alliances did the United States form with other countries for the defense of the non-Communist world?
5. **(a)** What led to the outbreak of war in Korea? **(b)** How did the United Nations meet this threat to world peace? **(c)** What part did China play in the conflict?

3 How Did President Eisenhower Meet the Problems of the Cold War?

In 1952, while fighting was still going on in Korea, the American people elected a new President. Dwight D. Eisenhower had been the commander of Allied forces in Europe during World War II. A warm, friendly man, he was well-known to the American people for his wartime service. He promised to end the war in Korea, to take a strong stand against communism, and to reduce the power of the federal government. Eisenhower won the presidency by a landslide, becoming the first Republican to occupy the White House in twenty years.

A crisis arises in the Middle East. The shift of power in Washington brought no change in the tensions of the cold war. During much of President Eisenhower's term of office the Middle East was the chief danger spot for world peace. After World War II the state of Israel had been established as a Jewish homeland. But Arab countries in the Middle East refused to accept Israel's right to exist and threatened to destroy the new nation. This situation gave the Soviet Union an opportunity to increase its influence in the Middle East by offering aid to Israel's Arab neighbors.

A crisis developed in 1956 when Egypt took over the Suez Canal (map, page 696) and closed the waterway to Israeli shipping. This led, in 1957, to a war in which Britain and France sided with Israel and attacked Egypt. Both the United States and the Soviet Union called for an end to the fighting. In time, the UN was able to establish a cease-fire and Israel, Britain, and

Dwight and Mamie Eisenhower were a highly popular President and First Lady.

676

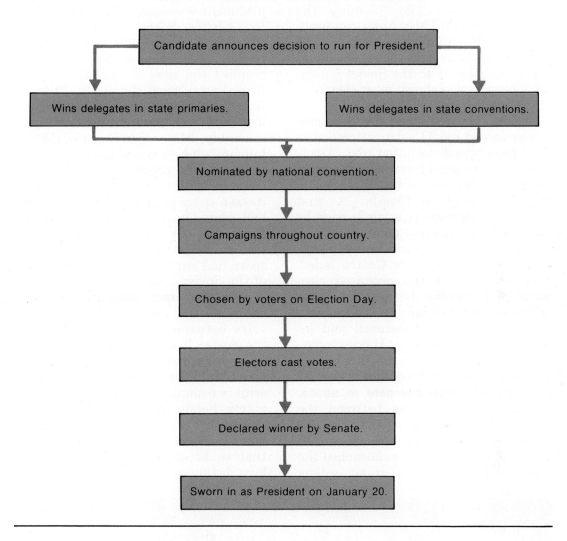

HOW A CANDIDATE BECOMES PRESIDENT

Candidate announces decision to run for President.

Wins delegates in state primaries.

Wins delegates in state conventions.

Nominated by national convention.

Campaigns throughout country.

Chosen by voters on Election Day.

Electors cast votes.

Declared winner by Senate.

Sworn in as President on January 20.

This flow chart shows steps a candidate must take to reach the presidency. By what two ways can a candidate win support from delegates?

France reluctantly withdrew their forces from Egypt.

The United States was still suspicious of what the Soviet Union might be planning in the Middle East. As a result, Congress gave President Eisenhower authority to use American armed forces if they were requested by any Middle Eastern countries to check Communist aggression. Under this act the President sent American marines into Lebanon in 1958 to protect that country's independence.

The cold war affects Latin America. The ties of friendship between the United States and its southern neighbors were severely tested during the 1950's. Communist groups sought to take advantage of discontent and the desire for a higher standard of living among Latin Americans. Whenever possible, Communists tried to stir up

● See p. T55 for a strategy calling for students to put together a bulletin board display featuring American achievements in space.

feelings against the "Yanquis," as people of the United States were called by Latin Americans. By blaming the United States for Latin American problems, the Communists hoped to convince Latin Americans that they should form closer ties with the Soviet Union. This purpose was shown most clearly in Cuba.

Early in 1959, a revolutionary leader named Fidel Castro succeeded in overthrowing a dictator in Cuba. Americans took a special interest in this startling news because of Cuba's location, just 90 miles from Florida. At first Americans supported Castro because he promised the Cubans a democratic government. As time went on, however, American sympathy for Castro faded. Castro postponed the promised elections and steadily became friendlier with the Soviet Union. In his speeches Castro constantly threatened and insulted the United States. Having a government so unfriendly to the United States in Cuba alarmed Americans.

East and West compete in space. Meanwhile, competition between the United States and the Soviet Union also led toward the exploration of space. In October, 1957, the Soviets launched the first space satellite, a small sphere called Sputnik, which circled the earth for three months. This great accomplishment was soon followed by others. In 1959 the Soviet Union announced that it had hit the moon with one space rocket, and with another had photographed the side of the moon always turned away from the earth. Then, on April 12, 1961, the Soviet Union launched the world's first manned spaceship. Major Yuri Gagarin, the first human being to travel in space, circled the earth and returned safely.

The United States soon launched its own space program. Early in 1958 it had orbited its first small earth satellite, Explorer I. By the end of the 1960's, as you will see, American achievements in space had equaled and surpassed those of the Soviet Union.

An arms race develops. Through the 1950's there was another form of rivalry between the United States and the Soviet Union. This was the **arms race,** a contest to see which country could build the greatest supply of powerful weapons. Both countries built atomic bombs as well as an even more powerful weapon — the hydrogen bomb. Missiles were also developed that could carry the deadly weapons long distances.

COMMUNIST PARTY ORGANIZATION U.S.A-FEB. 9, 1950

During the early 1950's Senator Joseph McCarthy (left) gained power by charging that Communists were present in many areas of American life. When he accused the Army of allowing Communists on military bases, however, the Senate censured him and his influence rapidly declined.

Hopes for better relations between East and West are dashed. For a time during the late 1950's the cold war seemed to ease. Following Stalin's death, Nikita Khrushchev (kroosh-CHOFF) became the new Soviet leader. Khrushchev appeared willing to improve relations with non-Communist nations. Groups of Soviet and American citizens even visited each other's countries. Khrushchev himself came to the United States in 1959. Plans were made for President Eisenhower to make a return visit to the Soviet Union and for a meeting of top world leaders to be held in Paris in 1960. But just before the Paris meeting, an American spy
● plane was shot down over the Soviet Union. The Soviet government was fu-

rious that American planes had been spying on Soviet territory. Premier Khrushchev refused to meet with the Western leaders. As President Eisenhower's term in office came to a close, world tensions seemed worse than ever.

▶ **CHECK UP** See Teacher's Key.

1. What events in the Middle East threatened world peace during President Eisenhower's term in office?
2. **(a)** What problem did the United States face in its relations with Latin America during the 1950's? **(b)** Why did Cuba present a special problem?
3. Why did American-Soviet relations reach a low point at the end of Dwight D. Eisenhower's presidency?

4 What Changes Took Place at Home During the Eisenhower Years?

The Eisenhower presidency was a time of prosperity for many Americans. More people than ever were working and earning good money. Inflation was not the problem it had been just after World War II.

A prosperous society undergoes many changes. The new prosperity showed itself in many ways. During the 1950's, for instance, many Americans were able to afford new cars. As a result, Congress approved a vast road-building program in 1956. It called for the construction of over 40,000 miles of four-lane highways. As the roads were built, people found it easier to live in suburbs outside the big cities and drive to work. Spacious new shopping centers (or malls) were built in the suburbs so that people could shop close to home. Americans also began moving to the south and west.

Americans in the 1950's were not only buying new cars. They were also

buying new homes, freezers, washers and dryers, television sets, expensive cameras, and boats. As most Americans shared in the new prosperity, people began to say that the United States had become an **affluent** (AFF-loo-ent) or wealthy society.

The Supreme Court rules on the schools. Perhaps the most important event of President Eisenhower's administration was a decision of the Supreme Court. On May 17, 1954, all nine members of the Court agreed in a decision called *Brown v. Board of Education of Topeka* that state laws requiring separate public schools for black children were unconstitutional (page 559). Some states quickly changed their laws to carry out the Court's decision. Other states proceeded slowly. A few states took no action at all.

Black Americans fight discrimina- ★ **tion.** Spurred by the 1954 Court decision, black Americans began a drive to

679

HAWAII

KAUAI

NIIHAU

OAHU
Honolulu
★
Pearl Harbor

MOLOKAI

LANAI   MAUI

KAHOOLAWE
(uninhabited)

N

PACIFIC OCEAN

20°N

Mauna Kea ▲
HAWAII   ● Hilo
Mauna Loa

SCALE
0 ————————— 150 mi
0 ————————— 150 km

Southernmost point
of United States

MAP STUDY   See Teacher's Key.
Hawaii and Alaska became states during
President Eisenhower's last year in office.
Which of the Hawaiian islands is farthest west?

end other kinds of segregation. One December day in 1955, a black woman named Rosa Parks boarded a bus in Montgomery, Alabama. She sat at the back of the bus, as a local law required blacks to do. As the bus filled up, there were more white passengers than there were seats in the white section toward the front of the bus. The driver ordered Mrs. Parks to give up her seat to a white passenger. She refused to move and was arrested.

The arrest of Mrs. Parks caused blacks to boycott the buses in Montgomery. They refused to ride the buses until they were promised the same treatment as white passengers. A leader in the Montgomery bus boycott was Dr. Martin Luther King, Jr., a young Baptist minister. King declared that blacks should seek equal treatment but should not use force or violence to reach that goal.

The Montgomery boycott lasted for months. Finally the Supreme Court settled the issue, declaring that it was

170°E   180°   170°W   160°W   150°W   140°W   130°W   120°W

SCALE
0 ————— 400 mi
0 ————— 400 km

ARCTIC OCEAN

Prudhoe Bay
70°N

Barrow

SOVIET UNION

BROOKS RANGE

Arctic Circle

N

CANADA

Bering Strait

Nome

Yukon River

Fairbanks

60°N

Mt. McKinley ▲

ALASKA RANGE

Valdez

Bethel

Anchorage

BERING SEA

Seward

Juneau
★

GULF OF ALASKA

Sitka

Ketchikan ●

Kodiak

ALASKA PEN.

——— Alaska pipeline
(built 1974-1977)

680

ALEUTIAN   ISLANDS

PACIFIC OCEAN

50°N

ALASKA

See Teacher's Key.

MAP STUDY
(a) What country shares a border with Alaska? (b) What country lies across the Bering Strait from Alaska? (c) Between which two locations was the Alaska pipeline built?

unconstitutional for a city to have a seg-regated bus system. Black leaders were encouraged by this victory. Boycotts were started against restaurants, movie theaters, and stores that were segre-gated. Since most businesses did not want to lose customers, they began to serve black people.

President Eisenhower is re-elected. In spite of two serious illnesses during his first term, President Eisenhower decided to run for re-election in 1956. The election showed that the President was still popular with the American people. He won 457 electoral votes, while Adlai Stevenson, his Democratic opponent, received only 74.

Labor reform becomes an important issue. A major piece of legislation passed during President Eisenhower's second term had to do with labor. The American people had become disturbed by evidence that some labor leaders had misused their power. After long debate, Congress passed the Landrum-Griffin Act (1959), the first important labor law since the Taft-Hartley Act. The aim of the new law was to safeguard the rights of union members in such matters as union elections and dues. It also said racketeers, convicts, and members of the Communist Party could not hold union offices.

Alaska and Hawaii become states. President Eisenhower's second term in office saw the admission of two more states to the Union. It was the first time new states had been admitted since Arizona and New Mexico joined the Union in 1912. On January 3, 1959, Ei-

Rosa Parks's refusal to move to the back of a city bus led to the historic Montgomery, Alabama, boycott in 1955.

senhower signed a proclamation an-nouncing the admission of Alaska. Two months later, Hawaii was admitted. The nation's new 50-star flag was offi-cially raised on July 4, 1960.

▶ **CHECK UP**   See Teacher's Key.

1. Why did people say in the 1950's that the United States had become an afflu-ent society?
2. **(a)** What was the importance of the 1954 Supreme Court decision on school segregation? **(b)** In what other ways did black Americans seek an end to seg-regation?
3. **(a)** What was the outcome of the elec-tion of 1956? **(b)** What were the high-lights of the second Eisenhower admin-istration?

CHECK UP ON CHAPTER 31   See Teacher's Key.

Words to Know

1. affluent
2. cold war
3. arms race
4. right-to-work laws
5. iron curtain

Places to Locate

1. North Korea
2. South Korea
3. 38th parallel
4. West Germany
5. Soviet Union
6. China

Facts to Remember

1. **(a)** What problems faced the nation during the period of adjustment to peacetime after 1945? **(b)** What was the outcome of the 1948 election?
2. **(a)** What was the Taft-Hartley Act? **(b)** The Landrum-Griffin Act?
3. **(a)** What were the two opposing sides in the cold war? **(b)** What alliances did the United States form in the late 1940's?
4. **(a)** What opposing forces fought each other in the Korean War? **(b)** How was that war ended?
5. In what parts of the world did trouble spots arise during President Eisenhower's years in office?
6. **(a)** How were the Soviet Union and the United States rivals in space? **(b)** In the development of atomic weapons?
7. Tell what changes took place during the Eisenhower years in connection with each of the following: **(a)** highway construction, **(b)** discrimination laws, **(c)** number of states.

Skills to Practice

1. Use the maps on page 680 to answer the following questions: **(a)** Name the following places in Alaska: (1) the state capital, (2) five other towns or cities, (3) two mountain ranges. **(b)** Name the following places in Hawaii: (1) the state capital and one other city, (2) the five largest islands, (3) two mountain peaks.
2. Decide whether the following statements are *facts* or whether they are *opinions* that cannot be proved or disproved:
   a. President Truman should not have sought re-election in 1948.
   b. The United Nations was organized in April, 1945.
   c. Military leaders make good Presidents.
   d. The country of Israel was established after World War II.

Questions to Think About

1. Why did President Truman have less success with his Fair Deal program than President Franklin D. Roosevelt had with the New Deal?
2. Why did the United States form alliances with other nations in the late 1940's even though there was no war going on? What was the purpose of those alliances?
3. Why were the building of a new highway system, the spread of suburban areas, and the increased buying of household appliances all evidence of a growing prosperity in the mid-1950's? How were these developments all connected with each other?

Linking Past and Present

The St. Lawrence Seaway. Ever since the days of European exploration of North America, people had dreamed of connecting the St. Lawrence River with the Great Lakes. If that were done, ocean-going vessels could travel from the Atlantic far into the interior of the continent. During Dwight Eisenhower's presidency that dream came true. In 1959 the St. Lawrence Seaway was opened.

The United States and Canada had begun work on the joint project five years earlier. Giant locks were built to carry ships around rapids and to raise and lower them as they passed from one body of water to another. Canals were also built as part of the Seaway.

On June 26, 1959, President Eisenhower and Queen Elizabeth formally dedicated the St. Lawrence Seaway in a ceremony near Montreal. Since then the Seaway has proved to be a big success. Every year thousands of ocean-going vessels travel inland from the Atlantic to Chicago and other Great Lakes ports. Trade and industry in both Canada and the United States have benefited greatly from this cooperative project.

682

● Mention that another part of the cooperative project involved the operation of a huge hydroelectric plant.

GAINING SKILL

Exploring Local History

Some American communities were first settled in the early 1600's. Others have been started much more recently. But in any community, old or young, interesting records can be found that will give people a better understanding of the past.

You and your classmates can use local information to put together a history of your community. You should consider the following topics when doing your research:

1. Indians who lived in the area
2. When later settlers arrived
3. How settlers lived
   a. Their food, clothing, tools, shelter, furniture
   b. Their churches, schools, libraries, amusements
   c. Their plan of government
   d. Their means of communication and transportation
   e. Their most important ways of earning a living
   f. Interesting and exciting adventures of early settlers

Where can you look for information? Here are some sources that may help you in your investigation:

1. Written sources
   a. State, county, and local histories; biographies of leaders
   b. Old newspapers, anniversary editions of newspapers, official records, maps
   c. Letters, diaries, account books
   d. Markers, tombstones
2. Oral sources
   a. Interviews with older residents in the community
   b. Old songs

3. Pictorial sources
   a. Paintings
   b. Photographs
   c. Slides
   d. Movies
4. Buildings and things used by people in the past
   a. Town hall, meeting houses, churches, schools
   b. Old houses
   c. Old mills, stores, factories
   d. Old furniture, clothing, tools
   e. Museum displays

The following questions will help you explore the history of your own community.
1. For which of the following topics would interviews be a good source of firsthand information about your community?
   a. How the Civil War affected your community
   b. How World War II affected your community
   c. How ways of making a living have changed since 1950
   d. What the population of your community was in 1950 and what it is today
2. Suppose you wanted to know about political attitudes in the community during the administrations of Truman and Eisenhower. Suggest two sources from those listed on this page that might be helpful.
3. Suppose you found a large collection of old photographs of your community. Briefly explain what kinds of information you might gain from the pictures on each of the following topics: (1) housing, (2) businesses, (3) transportation.

683

CHAPTER **32**

Vocabulary preview: civil rights movement, détente, bicentennial, technology, computer, sunbelt, trend

Americans Face the Challenge of a Modern World

1960–1985   See pp. T56-T57 for chapter teaching strategies.

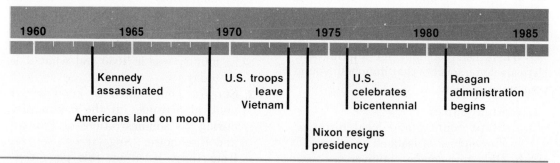

1960	1965	1970	1975	1980	1985

Kennedy assassinated

Americans land on moon

U.S. troops leave Vietnam

Nixon resigns presidency

U.S. celebrates bicentennial

Reagan administration begins

What this chapter is about —

In 1981, President Ronald Reagan spoke at a ceremony marking the two-hundredth anniversary of the British surrender at Yorktown, Virginia. "We have come to this field to celebrate the triumph of an idea," he said. "Our revolution was won by and for all who cherish the timeless and universal rights of man." President Reagan went on to say the following: "The surrender at Yorktown was and is the affirmation that freedom will eventually triumph over tyranny. The beacon of freedom shines here for all."

684

◀ The United States reaffirmed its leadership in space exploration with the successful launch of the space shuttle *Columbia* in 1981.

In your study of American history you have learned that great changes have taken place in our country since the days of exploration and colonization. You found out how the United States won its independence from Great Britain. You learned, moreover, how the nation grew in size and became a modern, industrial giant. But while you were reading about changes, you also found out about some of our nation's long-lasting beliefs and traditions. You learned of the American people's deep

respect for the Constitution and our republican form of government. You learned too how this nation, in President Reagan's words, has been a "beacon of freedom" for people around the world.

In this final chapter you will read about events of recent years and about the challenges Americans have faced. As you read, look for answers to these questions:

1. What were the important issues of the Kennedy–Johnson years?
2. What challenges did the nation face during the Nixon administration?
3. How have Americans met the challenges of recent years?

1 What Were the Important Issues of the Kennedy–Johnson Years?

JOHN F. KENNEDY IS ELECTED PRESIDENT

Under the terms of the Twenty-Second Amendment (page 650), Dwight Eisenhower was not eligible for a third term as President. In his place, the Republicans chose Vice-President Richard Nixon as their candidate for President
● in 1960. When the Democrats held their convention, they nominated Senator John F. Kennedy of Massachusetts for President and Senator Lyndon B. Johnson of Texas for Vice-President.

Kennedy wins the election. For the first time in a presidential campaign the two candidates appeared together on television to debate important issues. Because of his two terms as Vice-President, Nixon was better known than Kennedy. But Kennedy's appearances in the four debates made him as familiar to the voters as his opponent.

The election itself was one of the closest in our history; Kennedy received

only about 118,000 more popular votes than Nixon. His margin in the electoral college, however, was 303 to 219. At the age of 43, Senator Kennedy was the youngest man ever to be elected President of the United States. He was also the first Catholic to become President.

Congress reacts to the President's domestic program. John Kennedy brought to the presidency a feeling of energy and enthusiasm. Seeking to "get the country moving again," Kennedy offered a domestic program that he called the New Frontier. He asked Congress to pass laws that would provide job training, aid to public schools and cities, a cut in income taxes, and medical insurance for the elderly. But, although the Democrats had a majority in both the House and Senate, Congress did not pass very much New Frontier legislation. ★

Black Americans ask that they be treated the same as other citizens. Much of President Kennedy's time during his

685

★ See p. T56 for a strategy asking students to examine phrases (such as the "New Frontier") that sum up the goals of certain Presidents.

Confident and energetic, John Kennedy was the youngest candidate to win election to the presidency.

three years in office was claimed by the movement of black Americans to gain equal treatment under the law. This effort was called the **civil rights movement.**

Black Americans had been encouraged by the Supreme Court school decision of 1954 (page 559) and by the victory in the Montgomery bus boycott (page 680). By the early 1960's they were seeking to overcome other inequalities. In parts of the country there were customs and laws that denied blacks their rights. Black Americans were barred from using certain hotels, lunch counters, waiting rooms, beaches, and other public places. Progress in carrying out the Supreme Court decision against separate schools for blacks and whites had been slow. In addition, blacks in many parts of the South were still prevented from voting. Not only in the South but also in other sections of the country, black Americans faced restrictions in the jobs they could get and the places where they could live.

Black Americans make political gains. People who took part in the civil rights movement used several methods to draw attention to their cause. There were protest marches, including a huge gathering in Washington, D.C. in 1963. Boycotts, "freedom rides," "sit-ins,"

and picketing were also used. Blacks were joined in many of their protests by white supporters. Demonstrations took place not only in the South but in northern and western cities as well.

The civil rights movement made gains through the ratification of two amendments to the Constitution. Early in President Kennedy's administration, the Twenty-Third Amendment made it possible for residents of the District of Columbia, most of whom were black, to vote in presidential elections. Then, in 1962, Congress approved the Twenty-Fourth Amendment, which became part of the Constitution in 1964. This amendment said that no voter could be required to pay poll taxes (page 447) in order to vote. ●

The President is shot. President Kennedy proposed a number of civil rights laws, but before Congress acted on them a terrible event took place. On November 22, 1963, John Kennedy was in Dallas, Texas. As his car passed through the streets, shots were fired. Kennedy slumped into the arms of his wife, Jacqueline, who was riding beside him, and died almost at once. A man named Lee Harvey Oswald was arrested by the Dallas police. Two days later, as police were moving Oswald to a different jail, he too was shot and killed.

686

● Mention that the measures proposed by President Johnson were a part of his "Great Society" program.

LYNDON JOHNSON BECOMES PRESIDENT

Two hours after the assassination of President Kennedy, Vice-President Lyndon B. Johnson took the oath of office as President. A native of Texas, Johnson had worked for many years in government. After serving several terms in the House of Representatives, he was elected to the Senate in 1948. As a senator, he served for six years as the Democratic majority leader.

Lyndon Johnson wins the 1964 election. During his first year in office, President Johnson carried out policies that the late President Kennedy had started. In the summer of 1964, the Democratic Party nominated Johnson for the presidency in his own right. The Republicans chose Barry Goldwater, senator from Arizona, as their candidate in the presidential election. President Johnson won the election by a huge margin, receiving over fifteen million more votes than the Republican candidate.

President Johnson proposes new
● **measures.** As a former Senate leader, President Johnson used his influence to win the passage of many new laws. A number of these new laws were part of what Johnson called a War on Poverty. A former school teacher, President Johnson believed that lack of education and training caused poverty. To meet this problem, he succeeded in persuading Congress to pass the Economic Opportunity Act of 1964. Its purpose was to help young people who were not in school and who were unemployed by training them for jobs. In addition, Congress passed laws under which the federal government would give financial aid to schools and colleges.

Congress passed other important legislation during the Johnson years. In 1965, for example, it passed Medicare, a program that provided medical insurance for people over 65. When Medicare

went into effect, it covered nineteen million Americans.

Congress also approved the Twenty-Fifth Amendment to the Constitution. By this amendment, the President could appoint a new Vice-President whenever there was a vacancy in that office. The amendment also made clear how the duties of the presidency could be taken over by the Vice-President if ever a President, because of illness or for some other reason, could not carry out those duties. After ratification by the states, the Twenty-Fifth Amendment became law in 1967.

New civil rights laws are passed. During Lyndon Johnson's years as President, Congress passed three civil rights laws. The Civil Rights Act of 1964 protected the right of all qualified citizens to vote, and it forbade employers to discriminate in hiring. It also required that *all* persons be allowed to use such

Lyndon Johnson became President after John Kennedy's assassination. He went on to win the 1964 presidential election by a wide margin.

687

Soon after he took office, President Kennedy announced the formation of the Peace Corps. Under this plan, Americans volunteered to serve overseas, living and working with people in poor countries. Here, Peace Corps volunteers run a child nutrition program in Peru.

public places as hotels and motels, restaurants, lunch counters, stores, theaters, parks, and sports arenas.

In 1965 President Johnson proposed a new civil rights bill that would make it easier for black citizens to register to vote. The Voting Rights Act of 1965 said states could not ask voters to pass reading tests. Such tests had often been used unfairly to keep blacks from voting.

Three years later, Congress passed the Civil Rights Act of 1968. This bill banned discrimination in the selling and renting of houses and apartments.

The civil rights movement continues. By the mid-1960's there were disagreements among black leaders over the direction the civil rights movement should take. Many blacks believed that progress toward equal rights was too slow. During these years the slogan "black power" came into use. Different people gave different meanings to this phrase. To some black people, it meant that they themselves should lead efforts to secure better education, decent housing, and equal job opportunities. One way to reach this goal, they said, was for black people to use political and economic pressure. But a small number went further in their interpretation of black power. They claimed that more forceful methods were needed to achieve equality and freedom. Moreover, to some people the final goal of black power was the complete separation of the races.

Assassinations again shock the nation. Americans were stunned in the spring of 1968 when two more national leaders were assassinated. In April, Martin Luther King, Jr. (page 680) was shot by a sniper while standing on the balcony of a motel in Memphis, Tennessee. The shooting was followed by a wave of rioting, burning, and looting in a number of cities. Two months after Dr. King's death, Senator Robert F. Kennedy, the brother of the murdered President Kennedy, was shot at a victory celebration in Los Angeles. He had been campaigning for the Democratic nomination in the 1968 presidential race and had just won the California Democratic primary. Kennedy had been an active supporter of equal rights for minority groups.

● Have students prepare written or oral reports on Martin Luther King, Jr., or Robert F. Kennedy.

People in America's Story

MARTIN LUTHER KING, JR.

A leader in the civil rights movement, Martin Luther King, Jr., appealed for nonviolent opposition to discrimination and won the support of millions of Americans, both black and white.

In his efforts to win fair treatment for black people, Martin Luther King, Jr., led several peaceful marches. In the picture below, Dr. King (center) leads marchers in a voting rights demonstration in Alabama. One of Dr. King's greatest successes came in 1963 when he made an eloquent plea for racial justice before a crowd of more than 200,000 people in Washington, D.C. (right).

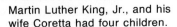
Martin Luther King, Jr., and his wife Coretta had four children.

● See p. T56 for a strategy that asks students to examine how President Kennedy's actions reflected principles established by the Monroe Doctrine.

RELATIONS WITH OTHER NATIONS

Throughout the 1960's American Presidents faced serious international problems. From the very start of President Kennedy's administration, Communist forces in Southeast Asia (map, page 692) threatened to take over Laos and South Vietnam. There were other problems too — in Berlin and in Cuba.

The Berlin Wall is built. After World War II the city of Berlin, which lies deep within East Germany, was divided into four zones. West Berlin was occupied by forces of the United States, Great Britain, and France. East Berlin was in the Soviet zone. Many times during the cold war, the Soviet Union threatened to take over West Berlin. At one time, in the late 1940's, the Soviet Union blockaded West Berlin. All highway, river, and rail traffic to the city was stopped for almost a year. In response, American airplanes loaded with supplies and food were sent to West Berlin. The American airlift saved West Berlin, and the Soviet Union finally ended its blockade.

In the years after the Berlin airlift, West Germany became a strong, prosperous country. Communist East Germany was not so prosperous. By 1960, thousands of people were leaving East Germany every week. Most passed easily from East Berlin to West Berlin. The Soviet premier, Nikita Khrushchev (page 679), wanted to stop the East Germans from fleeing to the West. He also wanted to make East and West Berlin into one city under Communist rule.

In 1961 East Germany, with Soviet support, built a wall between East and West Berlin. When it was finished, the wall did keep people from leaving East Germany. But the Soviet Union had not gained control of West Berlin.

President Kennedy faces the Cuban missile crisis. The most serious threat to world peace in the early 1960's took place very close to the shores of the United States. After the revolution in 1959 which brought Fidel Castro to power (page 678), Cuba and the Soviet Union established friendly relations. The United States did not want a government in Cuba that favored communism. As a result, several plans had been made during the last days of the Eisenhower administration to overthrow Castro. One plan called for the invasion of Cuba by some anti-Castro Cubans who had come to the United States. One of John Kennedy's first decisions as President was to approve the invasion plan. But when the anti-Castro forces landed at the Bay of Pigs on the southern coast of Cuba in April, 1961, they were easily defeated. The Bay of Pigs incident added to the tension between Cuba and the United States.

In the fall of 1962, an even more dangerous crisis developed. President Kennedy reported to the nation that the Soviet Union was supplying Cuba with nuclear (NOO-klee-er) missiles. Calling these missiles a threat to the United States, the President told the Soviet Union to remove them from the island. He also announced an embargo on all Soviet military supplies being shipped to Cuba and ordered American ships to use force if necessary to keep such supplies from reaching Cuba.

After a few tense days, Premier Khrushchev agreed to remove the missiles from Cuba. In return, the United States promised not to invade Cuba. War had been avoided.

The test-ban treaty is signed. The missile crisis was followed by one of the few bright spots in the cold war picture during the 1960's. As you have read (page 664), atomic weapons were developed during World War II. In the years that followed, the United States and the Soviet Union set off on an arms race (page 678) to develop even more power-

690

ful means of destruction. President Kennedy hoped to reach an agreement with the Soviet Union to control nuclear weapons. In 1963 the United States, Britain, and the Soviet Union held a conference in Moscow. The three nations agreed not to carry out nuclear ● tests in the atmosphere, in space, or under water. They would test bombs only by setting them off underground. Soon more than one hundred nations had signed the test-ban treaty.

International problems demand President Johnson's attention. Following the assassination of President Kennedy, Lyndon Johnson worked hard to get Congress to pass reform legislation. As time went on, however, President Johnson had to give more and more attention to international problems. In 1965, for instance, there was danger of a civil war in the Dominican Republic. In a move that was not popular in Latin America, President Johnson sent American troops to restore peace in that island nation.

There was further action in the Middle East as well, though this did not directly involve Americans. Fighting broke out between Israel and its Arab neighbors in June, 1967. The war lasted ★ for only a short time, but it left the situation in the Middle East more tense than before.

The Vietnam War grows more serious. The most difficult foreign policy problem facing the Johnson administration was in Vietnam, a country in Southeast Asia (map, page 692). An international conference had separated North and South Vietnam in 1954. North Vietnam had a Communist government and had support from China and the Soviet Union; South Vietnam had an anti-Communist government. North Vietnam began to help the Viet Cong in an effort to overthrow the government of South Vietnam. (The Viet Cong were South Vietnamese Commu-

American involvement in Southeast Asia grew during the 1960's. By the end of the decade over half a million American soldiers were stationed in South Vietnam.

nists.) To help defend itself, South Vietnam asked for military aid from the United States and from other non-Communist nations.

During the late 1950's and early 1960's the United States sent military advisers to help the South Vietnamese government. As the situation worsened, American military assistance to South Vietnam grew. At the end of 1964 there were 23,000 American troops in South Vietnam. Four years later the total had grown to half a million. By then the United States was fighting an all-out war.

As the fighting continued, many Americans became deeply troubled by the war in Vietnam. Some said that this

691

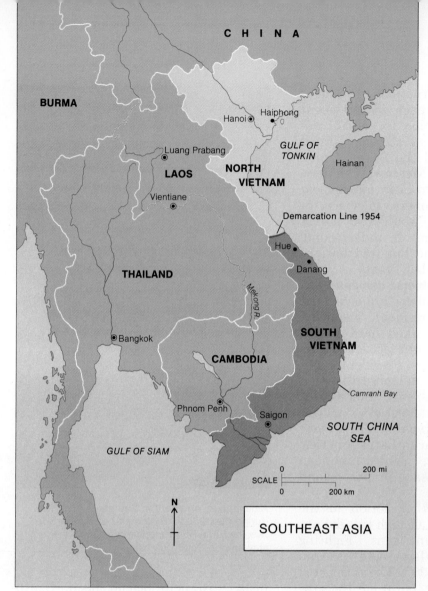

CHINA

BURMA

Hanoi ⊙   Haiphong ●

GULF OF TONKIN

Hainan

Luang Prabang ⊙

LAOS

NORTH VIETNAM

Vientiane ⊙

Demarcation Line 1954

Hue ●

THAILAND

Danang ●

Mekong R.

Bangkok ⊙

SOUTH VIETNAM

CAMBODIA

Camranh Bay

Phnom Penh ⊙

Saigon ⊙

GULF OF SIAM

SOUTH CHINA SEA

SCALE
0   200 mi
0   200 km

N

SOUTHEAST ASIA

See Teacher's Key.

MAP STUDY
This map shows the countries of Southeast Asia at the time of the Vietnam War. (Vietnam is now one country and Saigon is called Ho Chi Minh City.) What line divided Vietnam in 1954?

country should be doing more to win the war. Others said that it was wrong for the United States to be fighting in Vietnam. More and more people began to say that the United States should get out of Vietnam.

Peace talks begin. In the spring of 1968 President Johnson surprised the nation. In a television speech he announced that he would not run for another term in the White House. President Johnson also said that the United States would soon start peace talks in Paris with representatives of the North Vietnamese government and the Viet Cong.

▶ **CHECK UP**   See Teacher's Key.

1. **(a)** What were the results of the 1960 election? **(b)** What did President Kennedy call his domestic program?
2. **(a)** What conditions caused the civil rights movement to gain strength in the 1960's? **(b)** What success did this movement have?
3. **(a)** What were the results of the 1964 election? **(b)** What legislation did Congress enact during President Johnson's administration?
4. **(a)** What international problems developed during President Kennedy's years in office? **(b)** During the Johnson administration?

692

● Point out that Congress has the power to declare war. Congress never officially declared war against North Vietnam.

2 What Challenges Did the Nation Face During the Nixon Administration?

When President Johnson announced his plan to retire in 1968, the Democratic Party chose Vice-President Hubert Humphrey to run for President and Senator Edmund Muskie of Maine to be his running mate. The Republicans nominated Richard Nixon, their unsuccessful presidential candidate from eight years before. Governor Spiro Agnew of Maryland became the Republican vice-presidential candidate. A third presidential candidate was George Wallace, former governor of Alabama.

The popular vote on election day in 1968 was close. But in the electoral vote, Nixon had a clear majority. By winning 301 out of 538 electoral votes, Richard Nixon was elected President.

THE WAR IN SOUTHEAST ASIA

Americans debate the war issue. As the Nixon administration began, inflation and racial unrest troubled the nation. But perhaps the greatest problem was the wave of protests directed against the Vietnam War. Many people questioned whether the war could ever be successfully ended. The cost of the war in deaths, injuries, and destruction of property mounted higher and higher.

The nation was deeply divided in its feelings over the war issue. Not all citizens opposed the war. Many Americans organized marches to support the President's war policy and to urge that the nation fight on to win a military victory in Vietnam.

Meanwhile, the peace talks in Paris (page 692) got under way in 1969. The meetings went on for months, and seemed at times to make no progress. But in spite of that disappointment, the United States began cutting back its forces in Southeast Asia. By 1972 just 140,000 American troops remained in Vietnam.

The war ends. Early in 1973 an agreement between the United States and North Vietnam was finally reached. It called for a cease-fire, withdrawal of all United States troops from Vietnam, and the release of prisoners by both sides.

Within sixty days, as agreed, the last United States troops left Vietnam. The cease-fire between North and South Vietnam soon fell apart, and fighting began again between the forces of those two countries. Then in 1975 the South Vietnamese were defeated. North and South Vietnam became a single nation under a Communist government. Communist governments were also established in neighboring Laos and Cambodia (map, page 692).

America ends the draft. Early in 1973 the United States government had announced the end of the military draft. Since large numbers of American military forces were being withdrawn from Vietnam, the need for further inductions into the armed services had ended. Moreover, military planners believed that volunteers, rather than draftees, would be more effective in our modern, highly technical armed forces.

SPACE EXPLORATION

Throughout the 1960's the United States made great progress in its space program (page 678). Unmanned spacecraft entered the atmosphere of the planet Venus and sent valuable scientific information back to earth. Satellites orbited earth and transmitted live television programs between the conti-

Astronauts Neil Armstrong and Edwin Aldrin stepped onto the moon's surface in 1969. Here, Aldrin salutes after planting the American flag in front of the lunar landing ship.

nents. Other space vehicles sent back photographs of the moon and the planet Mars.

Then, on July 20, 1969, the centuries-old dream of exploring the moon became a reality. The historic moment arrived during the flight of Apollo II, which had gone into orbit around the moon with three astronauts aboard. While Michael Collins continued to pilot Apollo II in moon orbit, his two companions, Neil Armstrong and Edwin Aldrin, Jr., set the lunar landing ship down on the moon's surface. As millions of people watched on television, Neil Armstrong stepped from the ship, placed his foot on the surface of the moon, and spoke these words: "That's one small step for a man, one giant leap ● for mankind."

Other giant leaps were to follow. From 1969 until the end of 1972, five more Apollo missions landed American astronauts at different locations on the moon. Samples of moon dust and rock were gathered and brought back to earth for scientific study. In 1971 an unmanned Mariner vehicle completed a journey across 247 million miles and went into orbit around the planet Mars. It thus became the first spacecraft to orbit another planet. Late in 1974 a Pioneer spacecraft, after a voyage of 260 million miles, sent back to earth pictures of the planet Jupiter.

The series of Apollo missions was followed in 1975 by a project in which American and Soviet astronauts circled earth together. But by the late 1970's there were fewer space flights. Congress had cut down the amount of money budgeted for space exploration.

CHANGES IN FOREIGN POLICY

President Nixon visits China. Even before the war in Vietnam ended, President Nixon was looking for a way to reduce world tensions. His chief adviser on foreign affairs, Henry Kissinger, made a secret visit to China in 1971 and held a series of talks with Premier Chou En-lai (joh-en-LIE). The world soon learned of Kissinger's visit when the President announced that he too would

694

● Remind students that *mankind* in this statement means "humanity" and includes both men and women.

● Have students compare the aims of détente with American foreign policy during the cold war period (p. 673).

meet personally with the Chinese leader. The aim was to seek better relations between the two countries. The United States had had no official contacts with China since 1949, when Communists took over that huge nation (page 674).

President and Mrs. Nixon arrived in the Chinese capital in February, 1972, and were greeted by Premier Chou En-lai. Later the President conferred with Communist Party Chairman Mao Tse-tung (MAH-oh tsuh-TOONG). These meetings signaled the beginning of better relations with China.

The President meets with Soviet leaders. President Nixon began to use a new word to describe his policy for bringing peace to the world. He called
● his policy **détente** (day-TAHNT), a French word that means the relaxing of tensions.

As part of his détente policy, President Nixon followed up his China trip by traveling to the Soviet Union a few months later. The President's visit resulted in an agreement on the need to limit nuclear weapons. The two superpowers also agreed to hold more discussions on the arms race. These meetings were named the Strategic Arms Limitation Talks (called "SALT" for short).

President Nixon is re-elected. Richard Nixon's visits to China and the Soviet Union pleased most Americans. They looked forward to a new period of international trade and cooperation. American farmers were particularly happy with agreements that permitted big grain sales to the Soviet Union. In 1972 the President was re-elected by an overwhelming vote. Nixon won 49 of the states, while his Democratic opponent, Senator George McGovern of South Dakota, carried only Massachusetts and the District of Columbia.

The Middle East flares up again. In October, 1973, the uneasy peace between Israel and its Arab neighbors broke down. This time Egypt and Syria launched a surprise attack on the Israeli forces. A few days later, the Israelis counterattacked. They drove the Syrians back to within a few miles of Damascus, the Syrian capital city, and crossed to the Egyptian side of the Suez Canal.

During this October War, the Soviet Union gave help to the Arabs while Israel received supplies from the United

As part of his détente policy, President Nixon visited China in 1972. While in Peking, President and Mrs. Nixon were entertained by Premier Chou En-lai (far left in picture).

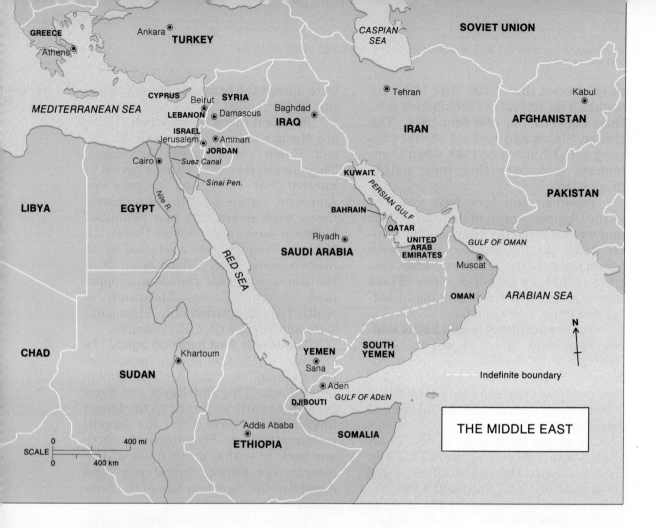

GREECE
Athens
Ankara • TURKEY
CASPIAN SEA
SOVIET UNION
MEDITERRANEAN SEA
CYPRUS
Beirut
LEBANON • Damascus
SYRIA
Baghdad •
IRAQ
Tehran •
Kabul •
AFGHANISTAN
ISRAEL
Jerusalem • • Amman
JORDAN
Cairo • Suez Canal
Sinai Pen.
KUWAIT
IRAN
PAKISTAN
LIBYA
EGYPT
Nile R.
BAHRAIN
PERSIAN GULF
QATAR
UNITED ARAB EMIRATES
Riyadh •
SAUDI ARABIA
GULF OF OMAN
Muscat •
OMAN
ARABIAN SEA
RED SEA
CHAD
Khartoum •
SUDAN
YEMEN
Sana •
SOUTH YEMEN
N
Aden •
DJIBOUTI
GULF OF ADEN
Indefinite boundary
SCALE
0   400 mi
0   400 km
Addis Ababa •
ETHIOPIA
SOMALIA
THE MIDDLE EAST

MAP STUDY   See Teacher's Key.
Rich oil reserves make the Middle East a region of great importance. Name the strategic waterway that is found in that region, linking the Mediterranean Sea and the Red Sea.

States. The chance that the two superpowers might come into direct conflict made the situation dangerous. But, as in the past, a cease-fire was worked out.

The nation faces a shortage of oil. The October War caused a fuel crisis in the United States. For years this country had had more than enough fuel to power its industries, heat its homes, and run its transportation systems. The United States had large deposits of coal and oil. Few people ever worried that the nation might someday run out of fuel. But by the early 1970's the demand for oil had grown larger than the

actual supply. One response to the problem was to build a pipeline across Alaska to move oil quickly from oil fields in that state to the rest of the country (map, page 680). Even so, the United States had to buy more and more of its oil from other countries, many of them in the Middle East. At the time of the October War, some Arab nations cut off oil shipments to the United States. They did this to try to stop our country from helping Israel.

The oil embargo soon ended, but it made Americans see the danger of depending on other nations for such an important source of energy as oil. To meet the immediate problem President Nixon asked Congress to pass laws reducing auto speeds to 55 miles an hour and limiting outdoor lighting. Meanwhile, plans were made for the nation's future energy needs. Oil companies not ●

696

● See p. T56 for a strategy calling for students to examine how Americans have conserved existing energy sources and developed new ones.

only stepped up production, but also increased their search for new oil fields. The American people, for their part, began looking for ways of conserving energy. Other energy sources also began to be developed. One of these energy sources was nuclear power. Another was the heat of the earth itself, which can be tapped through shafts sunk deep in the ground. (Hot springs and geysers are natural examples of this.) Scientists also began looking for ways of capturing the huge amounts of energy given off by the sun.

CHANGES AT HOME

The Nixon years were a time when the American people were greatly concerned with foreign policy questions. At the same time, however, changes at home were bringing new challenges to the American way of life.

Young people win the right to vote. During the Nixon years, Americans were more aware than ever of the role of young people in the United States. Young men and women, for example, took the lead in protesting the war in Vietnam. To be sure, there were more young Americans than ever before. Following World War II so many children had been born that people talked about a baby boom. Now these young people were about to take on adult responsibilities. Reflecting the importance of young people in our society, the ● Twenty-Sixth Amendment to the Constitution was ratified in 1971. The amendment lowered the voting age to 18 for all federal, state, and local elections. Before that time, only four states — Georgia, Kentucky, Alaska, and Hawaii — allowed people under 21 to vote. The amendment was adopted largely because of a growing feeling that young people, many of whom had served in Vietnam, were old enough to vote.

Americans take steps to stop pollution. By 1970 almost three fourths of the people of the United States lived in cities or in suburbs. When large numbers of people live close together, there is sure to be an effect on air, water, and land. Over the years, factories, power plants, trash burners, automobiles, trucks, buses, and airplanes filled the air with smoke and fumes. Industries and cities poured wastes and sewage into rivers, lakes, and oceans. Outside the cities, thousands of acres of land were used as trash dumps. And the use of chemical pesticides in agriculture often proved harmful to fish and animal life.

As Americans became more aware of pollution problems, local, state, and federal governments began to pass strict laws. Industries took steps to control smoke, fumes, and waste material. Cities built better sewage treatment systems. Automobile manufacturers developed more effective exhaust-control devices for cars, trucks, and buses. And the use of certain chemicals in agriculture was forbidden.

A CRISIS IN WASHINGTON

During President Nixon's second term the nation was shaken by crises that affected the highest officials in the land. The first person involved in a crisis was Spiro Agnew, Vice-President since 1969. In 1973 Agnew resigned after he ★ was accused of illegally accepting money from business friends while in office. Following the procedure outlined in the Twenty-Fifth Amendment (page 687), President Nixon nominated Congressman Gerald R. Ford of Michigan to be Vice-President. Congress gave its approval of the appointment, and Gerald Ford became Vice-President on December 6, 1973.

The nation learns about the Watergate break-in. An even more serious political scandal was known as Watergate. During the presidential election campaign in 1972, five men were arrested as they broke into the headquar-

697

Our Presidents

JOHN F. KENNEDY   1961–1963

Democrat from Massachusetts. A Navy PT boat commander during World War II, Kennedy began his political career as a representative and became a senator in 1953. As President, he proposed New Frontier legislation to solve national problems. In foreign affairs, Kennedy called for the removal of nuclear missiles from Cuba and secured a test-ban treaty with the Soviet Union. President Kennedy was assassinated in 1963.

LYNDON B. JOHNSON   1963–1969

Democrat from Texas. Johnson's 24 years in Congress, first as representative and later as senator, covered the administrations of three Presidents. Elected Vice-President in 1961, he was sworn in as President after the assassination of John Kennedy in 1963. After election as President in his own right in 1964, Johnson secured passage of important civil rights legislation, undertook a War on Poverty, and strengthened American military efforts in Vietnam.

RICHARD M. NIXON   1969–1974

Republican. Born in California, Nixon served that state as a representative and as a senator before being elected Vice-President in 1952 and again in 1956. Elected President in 1968, he withdrew American troops from Vietnam and promoted international cooperation. Nixon was re-elected in 1972, but his administration was shaken by the Watergate affair, and in 1974 he became the first President to resign from office.

GERALD R. FORD   1974–1977

Republican from Michigan. Born in Nebraska, Ford served in the Navy during World War II and then entered law practice in Michigan. He was elected to Congress from Michigan in 1948, and served as House Minority Leader from 1965 to 1973. Following the resignation of Spiro Agnew, he was appointed Vice-President in December, 1973. When Richard Nixon resigned in August, 1974, Ford became President.

ters of the Democratic National Committee, located in the Watergate office building in Washington. One of the men worked for President Nixon's re-election campaign.

During the investigations that followed, it became clear that close aides and advisers of the President himself had planned and then tried to cover up the Watergate break-in. Evidence emerged that to hide their guilt these men had committed perjury (telling lies under oath) and had obstructed justice (interfered with the investigation of a

● Review the meaning of the term *impeach,* introduced on p. 584.

JIMMY CARTER 1977–1981

Democrat from Georgia. Governor of Georgia from 1971 to 1975, Jimmy Carter was a newcomer to national politics before his election as President in 1976. During his administration, Carter supported human rights and helped bring about a peace agreement between Israel and Egypt. Other challenges included seeking the release of American hostages in Iran and reducing inflation at home.

RONALD REAGAN 1981–

Republican from California. Born in Illinois, Ronald Reagan moved to California in the late 1930's and became a successful motion-picture and television actor. Reagan served as governor of California from 1967 to 1975 and gained nationwide attention for his support of conservative causes. Elected President in 1980, Reagan took steps to reduce government spending and strengthen the nation's economy. He appointed the first woman to the Supreme Court.

crime). Cases of illegal wiretapping, destroying evidence, and seeking illegal campaign gifts also came to light. By the summer of 1974 over thirty persons, including four former Cabinet members, had been charged with serious offenses. Over a dozen of these people confessed or were convicted.

Richard Nixon resigns. Throughout the Watergate investigations, the President claimed that he had not been involved in any of the illegal activities. Others now challenged this claim. Under our system of government, when a President is accused of serious wrongdoing, Congress may bring impeachment proceedings against him. In early 1974, the Judiciary Committee of the House of Representatives began to debate whether President Nixon should be
● impeached.

Much of the discussion in the Committee had to do with the President's tapes. Beginning in his first term, President Nixon had made tape recordings of conversations in his offices and on his telephones. He had done this to make a historical record of his administration. When the existence of the tapes became known, Congress tried to get recordings of certain conversations. After first claiming that no one but himself had a right to the tapes, the President yielded to public pressure and turned over many of them to Congress. He continued to hold back other tapes. A majority of the House Judiciary Committee felt that these tapes and other evidence, taken together, showed that the President had known about certain illegal activities. They recommended that he be impeached.

Gerald Ford was sworn in as President after Richard Nixon left office. Mrs. Betty Ford watched as Chief Justice Warren Burger administered the oath of office.

● Point out that this ruling made clear that no President is above the "law of the land."

American communities from coast to coast held celebrations in 1976 to mark the nation's bicentennial. New York City celebrated with a giant fireworks display.

Meanwhile, the Supreme Court
● had made an important ruling that affected the case. By an 8 to 0 majority the Court said that the President must hand over the tapes he had held back. One of these tapes showed that President Nixon had known of the Watergate cover-up a few days after it began. Further, it showed that he had acted to block the government's investigation of the crime.

President Nixon had little support in Congress. His impeachment and removal now a certainty, the President resigned his office on August 9, 1974.

Gerald Ford becomes President. On that same day, Gerald Ford was sworn in as President. He was the first person in American history to become Chief Executive without being elected President or Vice-President.

One of the new President's first acts was to grant Richard Nixon a pardon. That meant the former President could never be tried for any crimes he might

have committed. Many Americans disagreed with Ford's decision. Others, however, agreed that the nation should be spared any further trouble over Watergate.

Gradually the country turned its attention away from Watergate. By the end of Ford's term in office, Americans looked back on his presidency as a healing time for the nation. Most Americans admired Gerald Ford's openness and honesty. They felt he had restored trust in the nation's highest office.

The nation celebrates two centuries of independence. During President Ford's last year in office the American people had a chance to show their pride in the nation. In 1976 the United States was two hundred years old. Throughout the nation **bicentennial** celebrations were held. (*Bicentennial* means "two-hundredth.") The American flag flew proudly as people in communities all over the country joined together in celebration.

★ See p. T56 for a strategy calling for students to put together a bulletin board display featuring bicentennial themes.

1. **(a)** What was the outcome of the 1968 election? **(b)** What problems did President Nixon face at home?
2. **(a)** How did the Vietnam War come to an end? **(b)** What change took place in the draft in 1973?
3. What was America's greatest achievement in space exploration?
4. What great change did President Nixon bring about in the foreign policy of our country?
5. How did the Twenty-Sixth Amendment increase the number of voters?
6. Why did many Americans become concerned with controlling pollution?
7. **(a)** What events led to President Nixon's resignation? **(b)** Who followed Nixon as President?

3 How Have Americans Met the Challenges of Recent Years?

MODERN ADVANCES AFFECT WAYS OF LIVING

So far in this chapter you have read about the Presidents who held office from 1960 through the nation's two-hundredth birthday celebration in 1976. Before reading about the most recent Presidents, let's take time to ex-amine some of the forces that have made dramatic changes in American life in recent decades.

Science and technology. Two hundred years ago "science" meant little to the average American. In fact, science was not even taught in schools, and few people thought of science as something that affected their lives. As time went

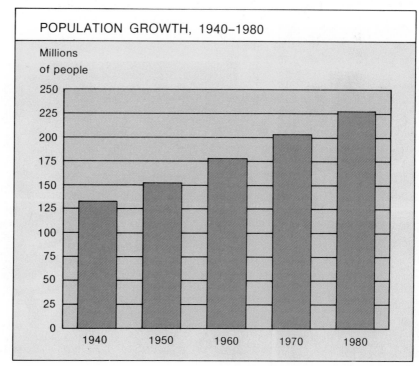

POPULATION GROWTH, 1940–1980

GRAPH STUDY
See Teacher's Key.
When the 1980 census was taken, the population of the United States had just passed the 225 million mark. According to the graph, what was the first year in which there were more than 200 million Americans? More than 175 million Americans? More than 150 million Americans?

● See p. T57 for a strategy that asks students to examine technological changes which have affected American ways of living.

on, however, science and technology began to change American life. (**Technology** is the application of scientific knowledge, especially in business and industry.)

You have already learned about the advances made in farming, industry, travel, and communication in the years after the Civil War. In recent years, developments in technology have had an even wider influence upon our ways of living. Just one example is the great variety of electrical appliances that American families use in their homes. Chemical research has shown the way to new products and to the making of old products from new sources. Plastics and other materials produced in laboratories are used for such everyday goods as camera film, raincoats, dishes, garden hose, and upholstery materials. Synthetic (or artificial) fibers such as nylon, acrylic, and polyester are widely used.

Scientific progress has had a dramatic effect on the length of people's lives. Two hundred years ago the average American lived about 35 years. By the 1980's Americans could expect to live into their 70's. A number of advances in medical science made the longer life span possible. Surgical operations that were once considered very risky are now performed almost every day. Medicines called antibiotics have conquered diseases that in past years killed great numbers of people. Inoculations have also contributed to the ending of epidemics of contagious diseases. Meanwhile, doctors and scientists have made great advances in the treatment of cancer and heart diseases, and research on the causes of those illnesses continues.

The computer revolution. In the late 1700's and early 1800's, during the days of the Industrial Revolution (Chapter 14), Americans began experimenting with new machines that could produce goods in great quantities. The Industrial Revolution, as you know, changed life in America. Today we are

Computers affect millions of Americans. Students learn to use computers to help solve problems, while skilled workers are trained to operate computers.

living through another kind of "revolution." The use of high-speed automatic machines known as **computers** promises to affect our lives as dramatically as the Industrial Revolution affected earlier Americans.

One of the first machines to signal the beginning of the computer age was called ENIAC. Built in 1946, this computer filled a huge room and had 19,000 vacuum tubes. By the mid-1950's, smaller computers had been invented. The introduction of the transistor (which replaced the larger and more expensive tubes) played an important part in this development. Research in the exploration of space played a part too, as new kinds of computers were invented to speed up space projects.

After the computer revolution got under way, improvements came faster and faster, and more and more people found jobs in designing or manufacturing computer systems. Other people were trained to write the programs, or instructions, that tell the computer what to do. Today small-size computers (called microcomputers) have been developed for use in homes, schools, and offices. You yourself have probably used hand-sized calculators. They too are a kind of computer.

What are some of the tasks computers do for us? They count, sort, remember, and select information — all faster than if the task were done by hundreds of workers. For instance, when someone reserves a seat for an airplane flight, a computer makes a record of that information. Computers keep track of library books, handle credit-card bills, and read the prices of goods at supermarket checkout counters. Today almost all business offices, banks, factories, hospitals, and school systems use computers in their daily operations.

As the computer revolution continues, even more complicated machines will be invented. Robots, for example, are being developed for use in factories

No development in technology has had a greater impact on American life than television. Here a television broadcast director selects the best camera shots at a professional basketball game.

to perform repetitious or dangerous jobs. Perhaps one day there will even be robots to help with housework!

Transportation and communication. Years ago it took days or even weeks to travel distances that do not seem far to us today. As you have read in earlier chapters, great changes took place in transportation. First railroads, then cars, and finally airplanes made travel much easier and more convenient.

Today Americans are served by a number of modern transportation networks. For instance, the road construction program that was started during the Eisenhower administration (page 679) resulted in a vast network of superhighways. Because so many good roads are available, millions of Americans own cars. They depend on them for all kinds of transportation needs — driving to work, shopping, visiting friends, and so forth.

Meanwhile, other transportation networks have become essential. Our airline system allows people to travel quickly and easily to distant cities in this country and abroad. Great num-

703

bers of people depend on mass-transit systems (subways, commuter trains, and buses) for transportation in metropolitan areas. Mass-transit systems are especially important today because they can move large numbers of people at a low cost in energy.

One of the great revolutions in American life has been in communication. In Chapter 22 you read about the invention of the telephone and the radio. The greatest change in communication in recent decades has been brought about by television. Television was invented before World War II, but sets for private use did not become available until after 1945. By the early 1980's, more than 120 million television sets were in use in the United States. Television brings into our homes news reports, sports events, a variety of entertainment, educational programs, and coverage of special events. Communication satellites allow us to see live broadcasts from all over the world. Television has, moreover, become a vital part of

the nation's economy. The making, selling, and repairing of sets, as well as the preparing and producing of programs and advertising, have created giant industries, employing great numbers of workers.

Shifts in population. Much of what you have read in this book has been the story of restless Americans on the move, settling one region after another and contributing to this country's remarkable growth. Today no Americans set off in covered wagons to start new lives on the frontier. But information gained from the 1980 census shows that they continue to be a people on the move. ●

For decades Americans had been moving into big cities and the surrounding suburbs. Most of those big cities were in the North and East. But in recent years there has been a change in that pattern. The 1980 census showed that Americans have moved in great numbers to the **sunbelt** region. The sunbelt is the part of the country that stretches from the southeastern Atlantic coast to southern California. People have been attracted to sunbelt areas by the warm climate and expanding job opportunities. As a result of this movement, cities like San Diego, Phoenix,

GRAPH STUDY   See Teacher's Key.

These graphs show the nation's population by region. Which regions have grown the fastest in recent decades? Which regions now have smaller percentages of the nation's population?

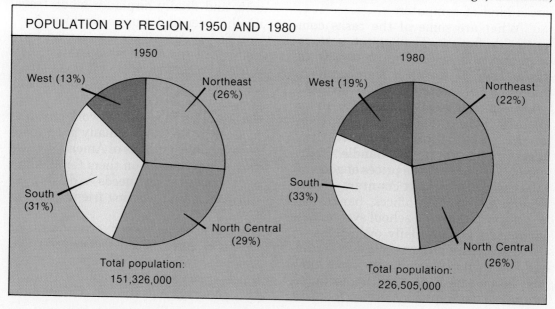

POPULATION BY REGION, 1950 AND 1980

1950

West (13%)   Northeast (26%)

South (31%)

North Central (29%)

Total population: 151,326,000

1980

West (19%)   Northeast (22%)

South (33%)

North Central (26%)

Total population: 226,505,000

San Antonio, Dallas, Houston, and Orlando have grown tremendously.

As people have moved to the sunbelt, the population of some big northern cities has declined. The suburbs and small towns surrounding those cities have continued to grow, however, so that most metropolitan areas have actually gained population. Perhaps the most remarkable change revealed in the 1980 census was that for the first time since 1820, rural areas and small towns were growing faster than metropolitan areas. Many Americans enjoy the open spaces of the countryside. At the same time, new industrial plants are being built in rural areas.

Changes in the work force. As you know, the United States was once a farming nation. Then, after the Civil War, industry grew rapidly. By 1900, millions of jobs had been created in mills and factories, and most Americans were employed in non-agricultural work. Today, fewer than 4 percent of American workers make their living on farms.

In recent decades the biggest change in employment has been in the growth of service occupations. Workers in those fields provide services, rather than produce goods. They are teachers, salespeople, lawyers, researchers, restaurant and hotel workers, computer operators, office managers, repair workers, government workers, and so on. Well over half the total number of America's jobholders are now service workers.

The role of women in the work force has also changed. In 1950 about 30 percent of American women held jobs. By the early 1980's that figure had risen to around 50 percent. As more and more women entered the job force, they found they were often paid less than men for doing the same work. Moreover, they had fewer opportunities for promotion to management jobs. Women succeeded in getting laws passed that would ensure them of having an equal opportunity in employment. Meanwhile, as more women became active in the nation's economic life, they also played a greater role in politics. Women were elected as governors and mayors, as well as senators and representatives.

OUR RECENT PRESIDENTS

Let us now return to the story of our ★ more recent Presidents. Gerald Ford served as President for two years after replacing Richard Nixon. In 1976 President Ford decided to try for a full term in his own right. Defeating a challenge from Ronald Reagan, former governor of California, Ford won the Republican presidential nomination.

The Democrats regain the White House. The Democratic national convention named Jimmy Carter as its presidential candidate in 1976. A former naval officer, Carter was a

Jimmy Carter, shown with his wife Rosalynn, was the first President from the Deep South since Zachary Taylor in 1848.

705

farmer and businessman who had served as governor of Georgia. He had been almost unknown to the country when he set out to run for President. But his success in state primaries had proved his ability to win votes.

By Election Day pollsters said the contest between Ford and Carter was "too close to call." The results were close, but Carter won a majority of the 80 million votes cast. Moreover, Carter's total of 297 electoral votes to Ford's 241 gave the Democratic candidate a clear victory. The Democrats also kept their control of Congress. Thus, for the first time in eight years, the country had a presidency and a Congress controlled by the same party.

Jimmy Carter takes office. Early in 1977, Jimmy Carter became the first President from the Deep South since before the Civil War. He took office with hopes of improving the nation's economy. But in 1978, inflation became a serious problem. One cause of inflation was the rapid rise in oil prices. As you have learned (page 696), during the 1970's the United States began to buy oil from other countries. Many of those countries belonged to the Organization of Petroleum Exporting Countries, or
● OPEC. The OPEC members raised their oil prices again and again.

President Carter proposed a national energy program, to reduce our need for OPEC oil. The program aimed at cutting oil imports. It also encouraged some industries to use coal instead of oil or natural gas.

The President supports human rights. During his first year in office, Jimmy Carter offered a new direction in foreign policy. He stated his strong support for human rights. He criticized countries that denied freedom of speech and of press, that did not allow fair trials, and that treated prisoners cruelly. The United States, Carter said, should stop aid to countries that did not respect human rights.

After being held for 444 days by their Iranian captors, the American hostages were welcomed home to freedom by a grateful nation.

President Carter set other foreign policy goals too. One was to reach an agreement with Panama on the Panama Canal. As you have read (page 614), the United States signed a treaty in 1978 promising to give Panama control of the canal in 1999.

President Carter also worked hard to reduce tension in the Middle East (page 695). He helped Israel and Egypt reach a peace agreement early in 1979.

The United States faces new challenges overseas. In 1979 the nation's attention shifted to Iran, another country in the Middle East. In November, a mob attacked the United States embassy in Tehran, Iran's capital city, and seized Americans who worked there. The Iranians threatened to hold the Americans hostage until their nation's former ruler, then in a New York hospital, was returned to Iran for trial. The United States refused to meet this demand. (Later the Iranian ruler took up residence in Egypt where he died, still in exile.) After an attempt to rescue the hostages failed, President Carter said he would try to gain their release through negotiation.

Meanwhile, there was trouble late in 1979 when large numbers of Soviet troops were sent into Afghanistan. The United States protested this invasion of a neutral country. It showed its displeasure by leading a boycott of the 1980 Olympic Games, held in Moscow.

Americans vote in 1980. As Americans watched events in Iran and Afghanistan with concern, they set about choosing candidates for President. Jimmy Carter won renomination. Ronald Reagan, former governor of California, was nominated by the Republican Party.

There was a third major candidate in 1980. Congressman John B. Anderson of Illinois ran as an independent. Anderson appealed to voters who had difficulty choosing between Reagan and Carter.

As the campaign began, Reagan appeared to have a big lead over the other candidates. Many voters liked his promises to strengthen the nation's military forces, to reduce taxes, and to cut waste in government. Despite hard campaigning, President Carter was not able to turn back the growing conservative mood of the country. On election day the voters gave Ronald Reagan 44 million votes to Jimmy Carter's 35 million. With victories in 44 states for a total of 489 electoral votes, Ronald Reagan won an overwhelming victory. So great was his triumph that the Republicans were also able to gain control of the Senate for the first time since 1954.

The hostages win their freedom. Throughout the election campaign, the Carter administration had continued its efforts to get the American hostages in Iran released. In the final days of President Carter's term of office an agreement was finally worked out. On January 20, 1981, after more than a year in captivity, the hostages were freed.

The Reagan administration begins. Soon after he was sworn in as President, Ronald Reagan began planning to fulfill his campaign promises. One of his first steps was to propose a reduction in taxes while at the same time making big cuts in government spending.

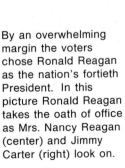

By an overwhelming margin the voters chose Ronald Reagan as the nation's fortieth President. In this picture Ronald Reagan takes the oath of office as Mrs. Nancy Reagan (center) and Jimmy Carter (right) look on.

● Have students review the meaning of the term *recession*, introduced on p. 504.

As Congress debated Ronald Reagan's plan, the nation learned the shocking news of an attempt to kill the new President. While leaving a Washington, D.C., hotel in March, 1981, the President was struck by a would-be assassin's bullet. Fortunately, President Reagan soon made a full recovery.

Meanwhile, the debate in Congress over Reagan's budget cuts was short-lived. Given the President's wide margin of victory in the 1980 election and his popularity with the American people, Congress agreed to the tax-cut plan. In the months that followed, however, the United States economy entered a recession. Congress became increasingly concerned about further cuts in spending.

In foreign affairs, President Reagan announced changes in policies started by earlier administrations. For one thing he was critical of foreign policy that was based solely on a country's support for human rights (page 706). He also made changes in the policy of détente. In response to the growing military strength of the Soviet Union, he got Congress's approval for big increases in defense spending. The United States did, however, resume talks with the Soviet Union on reducing nuclear weapons in Europe.

President Reagan gave his backing to the plan Jimmy Carter had worked out to bring peace to the Middle East (page 706). But the success of that plan was put in question when the president of Egypt was assassinated in 1981. President Anwar Sadat, who had been one of America's greatest friends in the Middle East, was killed by rebellious soldiers while reviewing a military procession.

Reagan makes a historic apointment. Early in his administration President Reagan carried out one of his campaign promises — that of naming a woman to serve on the Supreme Court. He appointed Sandra Day O'Connor, a former Arizona state senator and judge, to the Court. After confirmation by the Senate, Mrs. O'Connor became the first woman member of the Supreme Court. ★

The space-shuttle program gets under way. During President Reagan's first year in office the nation took pride in yet another triumph of American technology. At Cape Canaveral, Florida, a powerful rocket launched the space shuttle *Columbia* into orbit. Then the *Columbia* orbited earth for three days like a spacecraft. Finally, for its return to earth it landed like an airplane at Edwards Air Force Base in California. Millions of Americans watched as the astronauts who piloted *Columbia* made a perfect landing. A new era in space exploration seemed to have begun, as future plans called for the spacecraft to shuttle back and forth between earth and space stations circling the globe.

President Reagan named Sandra Day O'Connor, shown here with Chief Justice Warren Burger, to serve on the Supreme Court.

★ Mention that Sandra Day O'Connor was the 102nd justice to be appointed to the Supreme Court.

During Ronald Reagan's presidency, the Communist government in Poland limited labor union activity and placed the country under military rule. Thousands of Americans demonstrated against the restrictions of freedom in Poland.

You have now read what this book has to tell you about America's story. But remember that the story is not over. It will go on for years to come — and you are part of that continuing story. America's greatness lies in its people;

and you and your classmates and millions of other young Americans are the citizens of tomorrow. When you have completed your review of this chapter and of Unit 10, go on to read about your part in the future of the nation, as told in "America Faces the Future," beginning on page 714.

▶ **CHECK UP** See Teacher's Key.

1. How has American life been affected by **(a)** medical advances, **(b)** the computer revolution, **(c)** improvements in transportation and communication?
2. What information gained from the 1980 census supports the statement that Americans are still a people on the move?
3. **(a)** How have the kinds of work that people do changed in recent years? **(b)** How has the role of women in the work force changed?
4. **(a)** Why did the cost of energy become a problem during Jimmy Carter's presidency? **(b)** What were some of President Carter's goals in foreign policy?
5. **(a)** What new directions did Ronald Reagan offer in economic policy? **(b)** In foreign policy? **(c)** What historic apointment did President Reagan make?

CHECK UP ON CHAPTER 32 See Teacher's Key.

Words to Know

1. détente
2. solar energy
3. baby boom
4. pollution
5. bicentennial
6. computer
7. sunbelt
8. space shuttle
9. technology
10. test-ban treaty
11. civil rights movement

Places to Locate

1. South Vietnam
2. North Vietnam
3. China
4. Iran
5. Egypt
6. Israel
7. Suez Canal

Facts to Remember

1. Name the Presidents in order from John Kennedy through Ronald Reagan. To which political party did each belong?
2. **(a)** What was President Kennedy's New Frontier program? **(b)** Describe President's Johnson's War on Poverty.
3. **(a)** What advances did black Americans make during the 1960's in gaining voting rights? **(b)** In ending discrimination? **(c)** What role did Martin Luther King, Jr., play in these efforts?

709

● Tell students that the hammer and sickle on this sign are symbols of communism.

4. Of what country was each of the following a leader? **(a)** Nikita Khrushchev **(b)** Fidel Castro **(c)** Chou En-lai **(d)** Anwar Sadat
5. **(a)** What changes did President Nixon's policy of détente bring in America's relations with China and the Soviet Union? **(b)** How did Presidents after Nixon continue détente?
6. Identify each of the following persons: **(a)** Barry Goldwater, **(b)** Hubert Humphrey, **(c)** George Wallace, **(d)** Neil Armstrong, **(e)** Sandra Day O'Connor.

Skills to Practice

1. Arrange the following events in the order in which they happened.
   a. Nixon visits China.
   b. Congress passes Medicare.
   c. Reagan is elected President.
   d. Anti-Castro forces land at Bay of Pigs.
   e. American embassy workers are held hostage in Iran.
2. Choose the correct answer in each of the following statements. Use the maps on pages 692 and 696 to find the answers.

a. China is (north, south) of Vietnam.
b. The capital of Thailand is (Hanoi, Bangkok).
c. Saigon is about (150, 300) miles from Phnom Penh.
d. The Suez Canal is located in (Saudi Arabia, Egypt).
e. Iran is (east, west) of Iraq.
f. Lebanon is (smaller, larger) in size than Syria.

Questions to Think About

1. What did Ronald Reagan mean when he called the United States a "beacon of freedom"?
2. What was unusual about the way Gerald Ford became President?
3. Why did Americans become concerned about pollution? What steps were taken to end pollution?
4. What changes has television brought to American life?
5. Explain why population in the sunbelt region has grown so rapidly in recent years.
6. This chapter has told about many important events in recent American history. Choose two or three of those events and tell why each was important.

Linking Past and Present

The center of population. In the first few chapters of this book you read about the early explorers of North America. One of them, Hernando De Soto (page 82), journeyed through the South and West of what is now the United States. Today the name of a small town in Missouri reminds us of the past as well as the present. According to the 1980 census, De Soto, Missouri, is the nation's center of population.

Every ten years the Census Bureau locates the center of population — that point where the United States would balance if it were perfectly flat and if each American on it

weighed the same. At the time of the first census, in 1790, the center of population was 23 miles east of Baltimore. This reflected the fact that most Americans lived along the Atlantic coast at that time. Over the years, as more Americans went west, the center of population moved west too. Then, in 1950, the center began to turn a little to the south. By 1980 the center had moved across the Mississippi River to De Soto, in eastern Missouri. The new center of population tells us that for the first time in the nation's history, the majority of Americans live in the South and West.

● Have students use current almanacs to find the centers of population between the years 1790 and 1980.

GAINING SKILL

Analyzing Trends

Suppose you kept track of the number of green cars you saw every day for several months. On some days the number would be high and on others it would be low. At the end of six months, you probably would not be able to see any pattern in the numbers. But suppose instead you kept track of the temperature each day. Although there would be day-to-day changes, over a period of six months you would probably see a pattern developing. Depending on the time of year you started, you could see the temperature gradually grow warmer or colder. You would see a **trend** in the temperature. A trend is a change in a particular direction.

Arranging information on a graph helps to make a trend clear. The graph may reveal a trend that explains past events. Or it may show a trend that enables you to predict future developments. The graphs on this page provide information about several trends. Use the graphs to answer the following questions.

1. What does the line graph show? What period does it cover?
2. About how many seventeen-year-olds were there in the United States in 1930? About how many of them finished high school?
3. What trend does the graph show for the number of seventeen-year-olds enrolled in high school from 1950 to 1980?
4. In 1980, about how many seventeen-year-olds finished high school?
5. Which has grown faster since 1930: the number of seventeen-year-olds or the number of high school graduates?
6. What trend does the bar graph show? How does this trend help to explain the trend shown on the line graph?

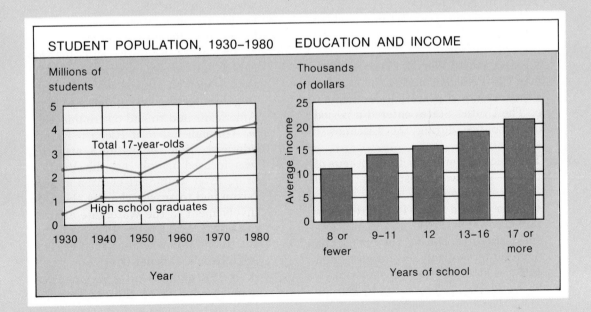

STUDENT POPULATION, 1930–1980

EDUCATION AND INCOME

UNDERSTANDING UNIT 10

SUMMARY OF IMPORTANT IDEAS

In Unit 10 you have read about our country's part in international affairs from 1920 to the present. You have also read about the Presidents who have guided the country during that period, and you have studied important changes in American life.

1. In the years after World War I our country's domestic policies passed through a series of stages.

    a. From 1920 to 1929 the emphasis was on little government interference in business.

    b. In the early 1930's many people were hard hit by the Great Depression. In response, President Franklin D. Roosevelt offered a reform program that he called the New Deal.

    c. The wartime period from 1941 to 1945 was one of full employment and peak production.

    d. After World War II, Harry S. Truman was President during the nation's adjustment to a peacetime economy.

    e. The United States entered a period of prosperity during the Eisenhower administration.

2. The peaceful world which the League of Nations was intended to ensure after World War I did not come about.

    a. After World War I, dictatorships gained power in the Soviet Union, Italy, and Germany. During the 1930's the Axis powers — Italy, Germany, and Japan — attacked weaker countries.

    b. World War II broke out in Europe when Germany invaded Poland in 1939. The United States remained neutral until the Japanese attack on Pearl Harbor brought our country into the war in December, 1941.

3. World War II was followed by a cold war which divided much of the world.

    a. When World War II ended in 1945, the nations allied against the Axis powers formed the United Nations. The UN had to deal with a world split by differences between Communist and non-Communist countries.

    b. The cold war at times became a shooting war, as in Korea and Vietnam.

    c. The policy of détente, put into effect by President Nixon, led to a lessening of cold-war tensions in the early 1970's.

    d. The Soviet Union's invasion of Afghanistan in 1979 hurt relations with the United States. Nevertheless, the two superpowers started talks in 1981 to try to halt the spread of nuclear weapons in Europe.

4. Presidents since 1960 have faced the challenges of a changing America.

    a. Presidents Kennedy and Johnson called for reform programs. Under their leadership, legislation was passed to guarantee the voting rights of black Americans and to end discrimination.

    b. Through much of Richard Nixon's administration the nation's attention was focused mainly on the Vietnam War. After winning re-election in 1972, Nixon had to answer charges about his involvement in the Watergate affair.

    c. Gerald Ford became President after the threat of impeachment led to Richard Nixon's resignation.

    d. In 1979 Jimmy Carter became President. Carter faced the challenges of high energy prices and of securing the release of American hostages in Iran.

e. Ronald Reagan won the 1980 presidential election. One of his goals was to reduce government spending.

5. Modern advances influence the ways in which Americans live.

    a. Science and technology have had a dramatic effect on American life. Medical advances have lengthened the average life span. Modern technology has led to the computer revolution.

    b. Improvements in transportation have made the automobile an important part of American life. Far-reaching changes in communication have been brought about by the widespread use of television.

    c. Technological advances have changed the ways Americans work. By the early part of this century, millions of jobs had been created in mills and factories. In more recent decades, the biggest change in employment has been in the growth of service occupations.

UNIT REVIEW   See Teacher's Key.

1. **(a)** Why did Japan, Italy, and Germany seek to expand their territories after World War I? **(b)** What were the results? **(c)** What was the attitude of the United States? **(d)** Why did this country take part in World War II?

2. **(a)** What is the United Nations? **(b)** Why was it formed? **(c)** How is it organized?

3. **(a)** Of what importance to the civil rights movement was the *Brown* decision? **(b)** The Montgomery bus strike? **(c)** The Twenty-Third and Twenty-Fourth Amendments? **(d)** The Civil Rights Act of 1964? **(e)** The Voting Rights Act of 1965? **(f)** The Civil Rights Act of 1968?

4. **(a)** What was the outcome of the Korean War? **(b)** The Cuban missile crisis? **(c)** The Vietnam War? **(d)** The hostage crisis in Iran?

5. Explain the circumstances by which each of the following became President: **(a)** Harry Truman, **(b)** Lyndon Johnson, **(c)** Gerald Ford.

THINGS TO DO

The items marked with an asterisk (*) are for the whole class.

*1. Start a new set of cards for Unit 10. A class quiz two or three times a week with these cards will help you remember the important dates, events, and people of Chapters 30, 31, and 32.

*2. Make a map showing the Latin American countries and their capital cities. Then show by arrows what products are exchanged in trade between Latin America and the United States. Consult a geography book or atlas for information.

3. Write a report on one of the following: Douglas MacArthur, George Marshall, Rosa Parks, Robert Kennedy, Martin Luther King, Jr., Sandra Day O'Connor.

4. Find out how the nation's bicentennial was celebrated in your community and report on it to the class.

5. Look through magazines for pictures that show different ways in which people use computers. Use the pictures (or copy them in drawings) to make a scrapbook or to assemble a bulletin board display that will show the effect of computers on people's lives.

6. Write an account of one of these events as it might have appeared in a newspaper of the time: **(a)** the attack on Pearl Harbor; **(b)** the first space flight by an American astronaut; **(c)** the release of the Iranian hostages; **(d)** Ronald Reagan's election as President.

America Faces the Future

The Gateway Arch rises above the Mississippi River in St. Louis.

The purpose of *This Is America's Story* has been to give you a better understanding of our nation's history and its remarkable record of achievement. Has this achievement been just a matter of good luck? The answer to that question is clearly "No!" Of course, America's open spaces and rich natural resources have played an important part in its history. For many years, moreover, the Atlantic and Pacific oceans kept us separated from troubles elsewhere in the world and helped to protect us from attack. But, to get a full understanding of our nation's achievement, we must look beyond abundant natural resources and favorable geographic conditions.

OUR AMERICAN HERITAGE

This nation was built on the principles of liberty and self-government. The English colonists brought with them a heritage of rights which has flourished in America. The colonists prized their liberty so much that they were willing to fight for its preservation. As a result of their efforts and those of later generations of Americans, we today are guaranteed many rights, such as freedom of speech and worship, the right to assemble in groups and to petition the government, and

714

Ask: When did colonists fight to preserve their liberty? (American Revolution.)

the right to a fair trial. Moreover, because of the efforts of earlier Americans, we live under a government based on the will of the majority of citizens, expressed through elected representatives.

Our nation has also grown great because of its leaders and its people. Remarkable leaders like Washington and Lincoln have come forward in times of national crisis to serve our country in battle or in government affairs. Still other leaders have made possible our progress in industry, science and invention, and education. But the United States has also benefited from the hard work and loyalty of
● countless other men and women who have made use of the opportunities offered by our free way of life.

As you learned during your study of America's history, there were periods in our history when some groups of people were denied liberty and freedom of opportunity. Ownership of property or membership in a particular church was once a requirement for voting. For a long time women were not allowed to vote. Again and again Indians were forced to give up their land. For nearly two centuries black people were brought to the United States against their will and sold into bondage. And hundreds of thousands of European and Asian immigrants labored for long hours at jobs that were scorned by "old settlers." Nevertheless, the promise of a better life has shone brightly in the United States. Pursuing this goal as individuals, the American people have also shown the ability to work together to achieve common purposes.

Principles of liberty and self-government, dedicated leaders, and devoted citizens — these constitute our American heritage. A nation without a sound heritage rarely reaches greatness. Nor can a nation which does not guard its heritage remain great.

The Jefferson Memorial, in Washington, D.C., honors Thomas Jefferson, our third President and the author of the Declaration of Independence.

715

AMERICA IN A CHANGING WORLD

Each generation of Americans has faced changes and new challenges. Ours is no exception. Changes are all around us. They affect the food we eat, the places where we live, the clothes we wear, the kinds of transportation and communication we use, the work we do, and the way we spend our leisure time.

Such changes often result in greater convenience and a fuller life; they may also raise new problems and challenges. Our striking industrial growth, for example, used up many natural resources and increased air and water pollution. As millions of Americans began to live in urban areas, it became more difficult to provide good housing, schools, and essential services. A continuing challenge is to maintain a high level of employment and to ensure that all Americans share in the promise of equal opportunities.

MEETING THE CHALLENGE OF THE FUTURE

● How can the United States meet the challenges of the future? There are several things our nation can do.

It is important that the United States uphold its belief in the freedom of the individual. Preserving the ideals of liberty is important not only for our nation's future but also for other nations. Throughout the world other nations take notice of the success of our free government and way of life in meeting today's problems. Whenever any American citizen is denied his or her rights, this nation's enemies declare that our way of life is a failure. Americans should always be alert to see that every citizen's rights are protected and that our way of life is defended.

Special classes, like this one in Chicago, prepare individuals for American citizenship.

716

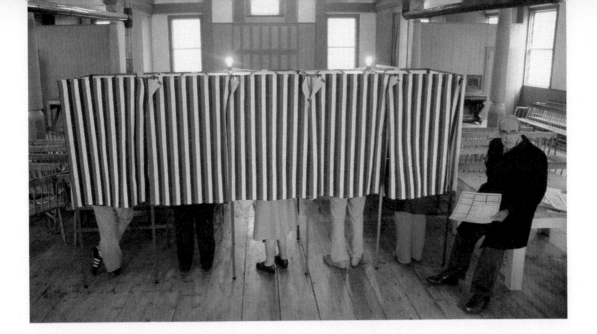

So far we have mentioned the steps which Americans as a nation can take to meet the challenge of the future. But what can we as *individuals* do? Often you hear someone say: "I am only one of millions of Americans. What can I do?"

There are several possible answers. First, each one of us, young people in school as well as adults, can take full advantage of our opportunities to become well informed. Such opportunities do not exist in nations that do not have free governments. In the United States, however, information is readily available. All Americans can keep informed about the problems that face their country and the world.

Citizens can do even more if they read widely and listen carefully. If they are convinced that the government should take some action, they can talk about it with friends. They can join organizations which will voice their opinions. They can also write to their representatives and senators. All too often people neglect the power of public opinion. They merely grumble and do nothing. They forget that the free individual must be a responsible citizen.

Adult citizens can exercise their right to vote. They can choose local and state officials. They can also vote for members of Congress and for President and Vice-President. If government officials fail to keep their promises, voters can refuse to support them in the next election. In America, citizens control their government through representatives chosen in free elections.

We recognize that our government is not perfect; our way of life sometimes falls short of what it ought to be. But conditions can be improved if each individual does his or her full share. Years ago, when the Constitutional Convention had finished its work, Benjamin Franklin was asked, "What have you given us?" This wise leader replied: "A republic, if you can keep it." Franklin knew that if liberty and self-government were to endure, citizens must accept responsibilities. This truth applies just as much in the world of today as it did when the United States was created.

Election Day is a time for citizens to exercise their right to vote. Here, voters in Strafford, Vermont, cast their ballots.

See p. T57 for a strategy asking students to examine ways citizens are responsible for "keeping the republic."

● See p. T57 for a strategy calling for students to put together a bulletin board display featuring careers in present-day America.

Thinking About Careers

During the past school year you have learned how Americans in different periods of our history earned a living. You have read about farmers, merchants, factory and construction workers, engineers, miners, steelworkers, business leaders, and many others. All helped to make our nation what it is today.

WAYS OF EARNING A LIVING CHANGE

You have also seen that ways of making a living changed as our country developed. For example, a century ago driving a stagecoach was one way of earning money, but no one made a living piloting an airplane. A blacksmith made shoes for horses, but no one sold gasoline. A bookkeeper kept handwritten records of sales, but no one used a computer. Throughout our history, changes in technology have created new jobs and caused other kinds of work to change or even disappear.

Ways of making a living were also affected by where people lived. Early in our history most Americans lived on farms. But, as towns and cities grew, new jobs appeared. There was work for city planners, street cleaners, traffic officers, firefighters, and many others. As hospitals, banks, museums, and schools were established, still other jobs appeared.

WHAT CAREER WILL YOU CHOOSE?

It is easy to see why career opportunities (ways of earning a living) changed as our country grew. Today Americans can earn a living in many different ways. Have you thought about what you want to do when you finish school?

One way to start thinking about earning a living is to determine what kinds of things you like to do. The questions that follow will help you take a look at your interests and skills.

What kinds of things do you like to do?

Would you rather work indoors or outdoors?

Do you like to work with words?

Do you like to work with your hands?

Do you like to work alone or with other people?

Do you like to figure out how something works?

How many years are you willing to spend being trained for a career?

HOW CAN YOU LEARN MORE ABOUT CAREERS?

Some people choose careers that provide services. Other people earn their living by using resources to make needed products. The *Dictionary of Occupational Titles,* published by the United States Department of Labor, classifies ways of making a living by job areas. Look at the broad categories of ★ jobs listed below and choose one or two job areas you'd like to explore.

Business and Office Work
Communication
Construction
Consumer Education
Entertainment
Farming
Health Services
Manufacturing
Transportation

How can you find out more about these job areas? You might begin by asking your school counselor or adviser for help. Libraries usually have books and magazines that tell about jobs. Finally, people who work in the job areas that interest you may be a good source of career education.

The way you choose to earn your living is important not only to you but also to our nation. To meet the challenges of the future, our country needs skillful citizens.

★ Discuss the occupations within each of the broad categories. (For example, *health services* could include doctors, dentists, nurses, x-ray technicians, and so on.)

Glossary

For a class game, have students prepare flashcards, each featuring the boldface word on one side and the glossary definition on the other.

On pages 719-723 you will find important words and terms used in this book. Remember that many words have more than one meaning. The definitions given here are the ones that will be most helpful to you in reading this book.

abolish (uh-BOL-ish): to put an end to.

abolitionist (AB-uh-LISH-un-ist): a person who worked in the movement to end slavery.

affluent (AFF-loo-ent): wealthy.

allies: countries that have friendly relations with one another.

amend: to change by adding to.

amendment: an addition, especially to a constitution.

annex: to add to a larger area.

appeasement (uh-PEEZ-ment): the policy of giving in to the demands of dictators in order to avoid war.

apprentice (uh-PREN-tiss): a person who works for a skilled master in order to learn a trade.

arbitration (AR-buh-TRAY-shun): a process for settling labor disputes by asking a board of fair-minded persons to propose a solution agreeable to both the union and the employer.

armistice (AR-miss-tiss): an agreement to stop fighting.

arms race: the competition between nations to build the greatest supply of weapons.

assembly line: an arrangement by which industrial products are put together as they pass from worker to worker, usually on a conveyor belt.

bicentennial (by-sen-TEN-ee-el): the two-hundredth anniversary of our nation's independence.

black codes: laws passed by southern states after the Civil War to deny freed slaves their rights.

bloc: a group of persons, or states, that work together for a common interest.

blockade: the use of naval forces to cut off shipping.

border state: one of the states along the line that divided North and South during the Civil War.

boycott: the refusal by an organized group to do further business with a person or country until certain practices are changed.

Cabinet: the official advisers of the President.

capitalism: the free enterprise system, in which natural resources, factories, and businesses are privately owned.

census: a count of the population.

century: a period of one hundred years.

charter: a document from a ruler or government granting certain rights.

checks and balances: the system of limiting the power of the three branches of government by having each branch check the others.

chronological: arranged in order of occurrence, from earliest to most recent.

civil rights movement: the effort of black Americans to gain equal treatment under the law.

cold war: the uneasy peace after World War II when bitter rivalry developed between the United States and the Soviet Union.

collective bargaining: discussions between a union and an employer to determine such things as employees' wages, hours, and working conditions.

compromise (KOM-pruh-mize): a settlement of differences reached when each side gives way a little in its demands.

computer: a high-speed, automatic machine that can count, sort, remember, and select information.

conquistador (kohn-keess-tah-DOHR): one of the Spanish conquerors of Mexico and Peru.

conservation: the wise use of land or other natural resources.

constitution: a written plan of government.

convention: a formal meeting of people who share a common interest or purpose.

cooperative: an organization formed by farmers to get better prices for their products.

719

corporation: a business owned by people who buy shares of stock.

decade (DEK-ayd): a period of ten years.

democracy: a form of government in which the great majority of the people can vote for candidates of their choice.

depression: a period of falling business and rising unemployment.

détente (day-TAHNT): a policy calling for the relaxing of tensions between nations.

diagram: a drawing that shows how something works or how it is organized.

dictator: a ruler who has complete control over a country.

direct primary: an election in which the members of a political party rather than party leaders choose the party's candidates for public office.

disarmament: the reduction of armed forces.

discrimination (dis-KRIM-uh-NAY-shun): actions, based on prejudice, that deny people their rights.

dividend (DIV-uh-dend): the share of a corporation's profits paid to a stockholder.

division of labor: a production method in which each worker does only one task in making a product.

draft: a call to military service.

duty: a tax on goods brought in from another country.

elector: a person chosen by a state to cast one of its votes in a presidential election.

emancipate (ee-MAN-suh-payt): to free.

embargo: a government order to end trade with a certain country.

equator (ee-KWAY-ter): the imaginary east-west line that divides the Northern Hemisphere from the Southern Hemisphere; 0° latitude.

executive (eg-ZEK-yoo-tiv): the branch of government headed by the President. It is responsible for putting the laws into effect and seeing that they are obeyed.

expansionist (ex-PAN-shun-ist): a person who wanted to add territory to the United States.

factory system: the method of bringing workers together to produce goods by machinery in factories.

federal government: the central government under which states with power to control their local affairs are united in a federal system of government.

federal system: a system of government in which separate states are united under a strong central government.

flow chart: a chart that shows the steps of a process in the order they take place.

foreign policy: a nation's plan for dealing with other countries over a period of time.

forty-niner: one of the people who rushed to California for gold in 1849.

free enterprise system: the system of private ownership and operation of farms, factories, and other businesses; capitalism.

frontier: the region just beyond or at the edge of a settled area.

fugitive (FYOO-juh-tiv): a person who has run away from the law.

geographical conditions: the temperature, rainfall, soil, and land surface of a region.

graph: a drawing that shows the meaning of a given set of figures.

grid: a set of crisscross lines on a map or globe, used to help people locate places.

House of Representatives: the house of Congress that has representation from each state according to its population.

immigrant: a person who moves from one country to settle permanently in another.

impeach: to accuse a public official of misconduct in a proper court of justice.

impress: to take sailors from American ships and force them to serve in the British navy, as the British did in the early 1800's.

income tax: a tax on a person's wages or other income.

indentured servant: a colonist who, in exchange for passage to America, worked for a definite number of years without pay and then was freed.

Industrial Revolution: the change brought about by the large-scale use of machines to produce goods, beginning in the late 1700's.

inflation (in-FLAY-shun): a continuing rise in prices.

initiative: a political reform that lets citizens suggest new laws.

international law: a set of rules or customs that nations are expected to follow in their relations with one another.

irrigation (ear-uh-GAY-shun): the watering of fields by means of canals or pipes.

isolationism (eye-soh-LAY-shun-izm): the policy of a government that tries to stay out of foreign difficulties.

isthmus (ISS-mus): a narrow strip of land that connects two larger masses of land.

joint occupation: the agreement between Great Britain and the United States that both countries would settle the Oregon Country.

judicial (joo-DISH-ul): the branch of government that makes decisions in legal cases and on the constitutionality of laws.

judicial review: the power of courts to declare laws unconstitutional.

jury: a group of citizens called to hear the facts and decide the outcome of a case brought before a court of law.

labor union: a group of workers who join together to protect their rights and interests.

latitude: distance north or south of the equator.

legislative: the branch of government that makes the laws.

legislature: a body of representatives elected to make laws.

long drive: the yearly herding of cattle from Texas to railroad towns farther north.

longitude (LON-juh-tood): distance east or west of the prime meridian.

majority: more than half of a given group.

mass production: the manufacture of great quantities of goods through use of division of labor, standard parts, and assembly lines.

megalopolis (meg-uh-LOP-uh-lis): a large region made up of several large cities and their suburban areas.

merit system: an examination system for filling government positions with qualified men and women.

mesa: a steep hill with a flat top.

metropolitan area: an area consisting of a central city and its suburbs.

militia (muh-LISH-uh): local military forces.

minority group: a group that is different in race, language, religion, or national origin from the larger population.

mission: a frontier settlement, founded by Spanish or French priests. It usually included a church, a village, a fort, and farmland.

money crop: a single crop raised for cash sale.

monopoly (muh-NOP-uh-lee): the control of all business in a certain product or service.

neutral (NYOO-trul): not favoring either side, as in a war.

nullify (NULL-uh-fy): to declare that a law need not be obeyed.

open range: the unfenced, government-owned lands where western ranchers grazed their cattle.

overseer: a person hired by a plantation owner to supervise slaves who worked in the fields.

panic: a great fear that sweeps through a nation as people become alarmed about severe financial problems.

partnership: an agreement by two or more people to own and manage a business.

patent: a government document that grants an inventor the sole right to build and sell his or her invention.

plain: a flat or rolling stretch of land with very few trees.

plantation: a large farm, worked by laborers who live on the same property.

plantation system: the system of growing one crop on large tracts of land with slave labor.

popular sovereignty (SOV-uh-rin-tee): the principle that the people who lived in a territory should decide for themselves whether to have slavery.

721

population: the total number of people in an area.

population density: the average number of people in a given area.

precipitation: water that reaches the ground as rain or snow.

prejudice: an unreasonable and unfriendly attitude toward a particular group.

primary source: a first-hand account, or a picture or document dating from the time an event occurred.

prime meridian (muh-RID-ee-un): the imaginary north-west line that divides the Eastern Hemisphere from the Western Hemisphere; 0° longitude.

privateer (pry-vuh-TEER): a ship privately owned but armed in wartime for capturing enemy vessels.

prohibit (proh-HIB-it): to forbid.

proprietary colony: an English colony established on land granted to a noble by the monarch.

proprietor (proh-PRY-uh-ter): a noble who was granted a colony in America.

prospector: a person who explores for gold or other valuable minerals.

public lands: lands that are owned by the federal government.

public opinion: the thoughts and feelings of the American people about current issues.

quota (KWOH-tuh): a limit set on the number of immigrants to be admitted from any one country.

ratify: to make legal by officially approving.

recall: a political reform that allows voters to remove an official from office.

recession (ree-SESS-shun): a business decline that is not as long or as serious as a depression.

reconstruction: rebuilding.

referendum (ref-er-EN-dum): a political reform that requires voters' approval of a law before it can be put into effect.

reform: to change conditions that are thought to be wrong or unfair.

reparations (rep-uh-RAY-shunz): money paid by a defeated nation for war damages.

repeal: to end a law in an official way.

representative government: a government in which officials and lawmakers are chosen by the citizens.

republic: a form of government controlled by the people through the representatives and officials they elect.

reservation: an area set aside by the United States government for the use of an Indian tribe.

responsible government: the form of government demanded in the early 1800's by Canadians, whereby legislative bodies and officials would answer to the people rather than to Great Britain.

revolution: a change or upheaval in society.

right-to-work laws: state laws that allow workers to get and keep jobs without joining a labor union.

rural: of land in the country as opposed to the city or suburbs.

scale: distance in miles or kilometers shown on a map as inches or centimeters.

secede (see-SEED): to withdraw formally from membership in an alliance or organization.

secession (suh-SESH-un): the withdrawal of a state from the Union.

secondary source: an account of an event written at a later time by someone who was not an eyewitness.

segregation: the separation of one group from another.

Senate: the house of Congress made up of two members from each state.

separation of powers: the division of the government into three branches, each with its own powers.

sharecropper: a farm tenant who pays the landlord a share of the crops instead of rent money.

share of stock: one of many equal parts in the ownership of a corporation.

slave codes: strict laws passed by southern states before the Civil War to keep control over slaves.

spoils system: the practice of giving government jobs to friends and supporters after an election victory.

standard parts: parts designed and produced to fit all identical manufactured items.

states' rights: the principle that upholds the powers of the states as opposed to the powers of the federal government.

stockholder: a person who owns stock in a corporation.

strategy: an overall plan for carrying on a war.

strike: the refusal of employees to work.

suburb: a residential community near a large city.

suffrage (SUF-rij): voting rights.

sunbelt: the part of the United States that stretches from the southeastern Atlantic coast to southern California.

supply and demand: the general rule that prices rise when demand for a product is high and supply is low, and that prices fall when supplies increase.

surplus: an amount over and above what is needed or used.

survey (SUR-vay): to measure land to determine its exact boundaries.

table: information arranged in columns.

tariff: a tax on imported goods.

technology: the application of scientific knowledge, especially in business and industry.

tenant farmer: a renter of farmland who pays the landlord either in cash or in crops worth the amount of the rent.

tenement house: a large building, often in run-down condition, that houses many families.

territory: land not yet made into states.

third party: a political party formed by groups whose interests have been neglected by the two major parties.

town meeting: a meeting at which all the voters of a town or village decide local issues.

transcontinental: cross-country, coast-to-coast.

treaty: a formal agreement between two or more countries.

trend: a change in a particular direction.

trust: a group of corporations that has a monopoly of a product.

turnpike: a road which people pay to use.

unconstitutional: contrary to the Constitution.

urban: of the city or city life.

veto (VEE-toh): to refuse to approve.

viceroy: a governor of a Spanish colony.

vigilante (vij-uh-LAN-tee): a member of a citizens' group formed to keep order.

writs of assistance: legal papers that allowed British officers to enter and search any colonist's house or building.

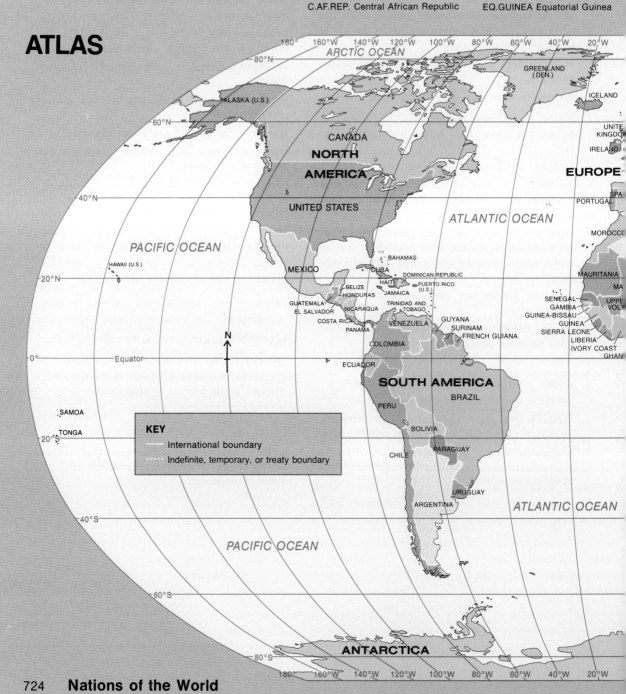

ATLAS

ARCTIC OCEAN

GREENLAND (DEN.)

ICELAND

ALASKA (U.S.)

CANADA

NORTH AMERICA

UNITED STATES

UNITE KINGDO

IRELAND

EUROPE

SPA

PORTUGAL

ATLANTIC OCEAN

MOROCCO

PACIFIC OCEAN

HAWAII (U.S.)

MEXICO

BAHAMAS

CUBA

DOMINICAN REPUBLIC

HAITI

PUERTO RICO (U.S.)

MAURITANIA

MA

BELIZE
HONDURAS

JAMAICA

GUATEMALA
EL SALVADOR   NICARAGUA

TRINIDAD AND TOBAGO

SENEGAL
GAMBIA
GUINEA-BISSAU
GUINEA

UPPE
VOL

COSTA RICA

PANAMA

VENEZUELA

GUYANA

SURINAM

FRENCH GUIANA

SIERRA LEONE
LIBERIA
IVORY COAST

GHAN

N

COLOMBIA

ECUADOR

SOUTH AMERICA

BRAZIL

SAMOA

TONGA

PERU

BOLIVIA

KEY

International boundary

Indefinite, temporary, or treaty boundary

PARAGUAY

CHILE

URUGUAY

ARGENTINA

ATLANTIC OCEAN

PACIFIC OCEAN

ANTARCTICA

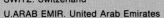

HUNG. Hungary
NETH. Netherlands
SWITZ. Switzerland
U.ARAB EMIR. United Arab Emirates

W.GER. West Germany
YEMEN (P.D.R.) People's Democratic Republic of Yemen
YUGO. Yugoslavia

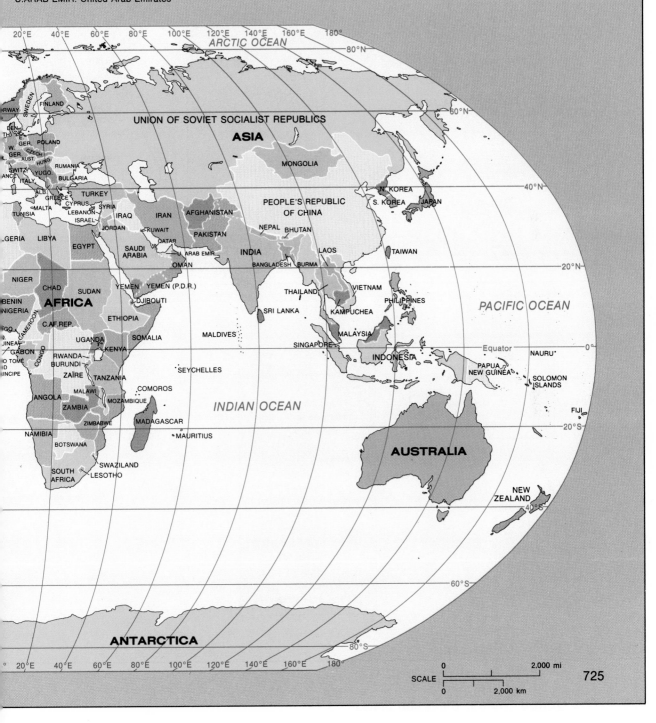

725

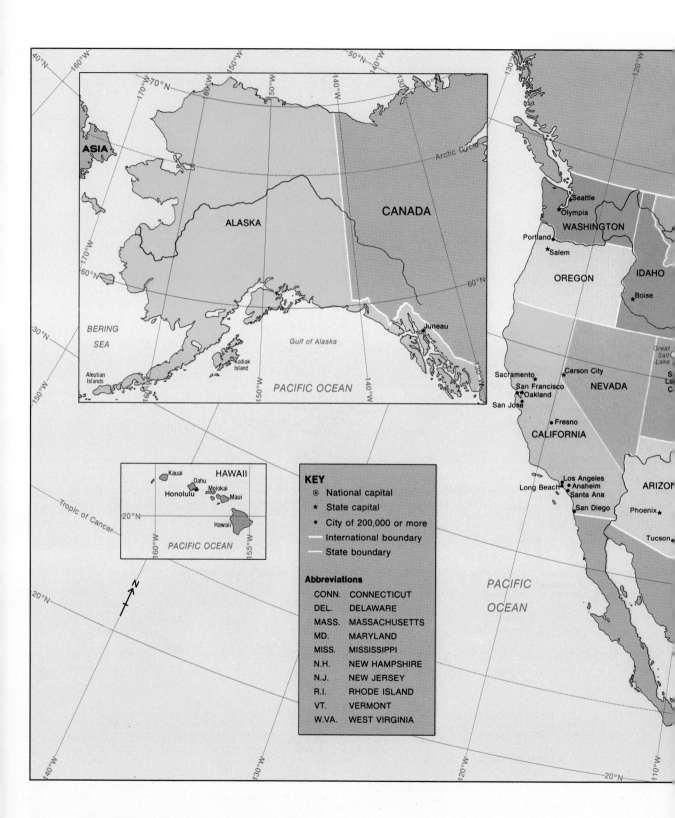

KEY

- ◎ National capital
- ★ State capital
- • City of 200,000 or more
- —— International boundary
- —— State boundary

Abbreviations

CONN.	CONNECTICUT
DEL.	DELAWARE
MASS.	MASSACHUSETTS
MD.	MARYLAND
MISS.	MISSISSIPPI
N.H.	NEW HAMPSHIRE
N.J.	NEW JERSEY
R.I.	RHODE ISLAND
VT.	VERMONT
W.VA.	WEST VIRGINIA

The United States: *Cities and States*

Hudson Bay

CANADA

Helena ★

MONTANA

NORTH DAKOTA
Bismarck ●

MINNESOTA

MICHIGAN

Lake Superior

Lake Huron

MAINE

Augusta ★

WYOMING

SOUTH DAKOTA
Pierre ●

Minneapolis ● St. Paul ★

WISCONSIN

Madison ★

Lansing ●

Lake Michigan

Lake Ontario

Lake Erie

Montpelier ★ N.H.
VT. ★ Concord
NEW YORK
Albany ★ MASS.
Rochester ● Boston ●
Buffalo ● Hartford ● Providence ●
R.I.
CONN.

NEBRASKA

Cheyenne ★

IOWA

Des Moines ★

Milwaukee ●
Chicago ●

Detroit ●
Toledo ●

Cleveland ●
Akron ●

Jersey City ●
New York ●
Newark ●
Trenton ★
N.J.
Philadelphia ●

Omaha ●
Lincoln ●

ILLINOIS

INDIANA

OHIO

PENNSYLVANIA

Pittsburgh ●

Harrisburg ★

TAH

UTAH

COLORADO

Denver ★

Colorado Springs ●

KANSAS

Topeka ★

Kansas City ●

Springfield ●

Indianapolis ★

Columbus ★
Dayton ●
Cincinnati ●

W.VA.

Charleston ●

Baltimore ●
Washington, D.C. ⊙
MD.
Annapolis ★
Dover ★
DEL.

Santa Fe ★

Albuquerque ●

NEW MEXICO

El Paso ●

Wichita ●

MISSOURI

Jefferson City ★

St. Louis ●

Louisville ●

Frankfort ★
Lexington ●

KENTUCKY

Richmond ●

VIRGINIA

Norfolk ●
Virginia Beach ●

ATLANTIC OCEAN

Oklahoma City ★
Tulsa ●

ARKANSAS

OKLAHOMA

Little Rock ★

Memphis ●

Nashville ●

TENNESSEE

Charlotte ●

NORTH CAROLINA

Raleigh ★

SOUTH CAROLINA

Columbia ★

Fort Worth ● Dallas ●

Shreveport ●

Jackson ★

Birmingham ●

MISS.

ALABAMA

Montgomery ★

Atlanta ★

GEORGIA

TEXAS

Austin ★

San Antonio ●

Houston ●

Baton Rouge ●

LOUISIANA

New Orleans ●

Mobile ●

Tallahassee ★

Jacksonville ●

FLORIDA

St. Petersburg ●

Tampa ●

Miami ●

BAHAMAS

Corpus Christi ●

MEXICO

Gulf of Mexico

Tropic of Cancer

CUBA

50°N

40°N

30°N

20°N

110°W

100°W

90°W

80°W

70°W

0   300 mi
SCALE
0   300 km

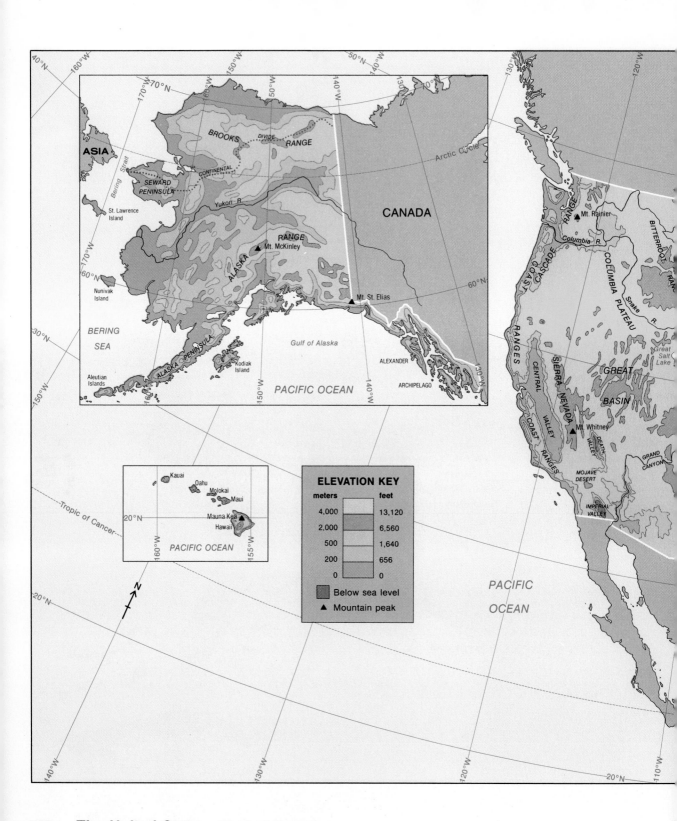

ELEVATION KEY

meters		feet
4,000		13,120
2,000		6,560
500		1,640
200		656
0		0

Below sea level

▲ Mountain peak

728 **The United States:** *Physical Features*

HUDSON BAY

CANADA

Missouri R.

ROCKY

CONTINENTAL

DIVIDE

BLACK
HILLS

GREAT

PLAINS

MESABI
RANGE

Lake Superior

Mississippi R.

Lake Michigan

Lake Huron

MOUNTAINS

Platte R.

Missouri R.

INTERIOR

PLAINS

Lake Erie

Lake Ontario

St. Lawrence R.

GREEN
MTS.

WHITE
MTS.

ADIRONDACK
MTS.

CATSKILL
MTS.

CAPE
COD

Colorado R.

Mt. Elbert

Pikes Peak

Ohio R.

CUMBERLAND PLATEAU

APPALACHIAN

Long Island

40°N

COLORADO

PLATEAU

MOUNTAINS

Arkansas R.

OZARK PLATEAU

BLUE RIDGE MTS.

ATLANTIC

OCEAN

CAPE
HATTERAS

LLANO

ESTACADO

Red R.

OUACHITA MTS.

Mississippi R.

ATLANTIC COASTAL PLAIN

70°W

EDWARDS

PLATEAU

Rio Grande

GULF

COASTAL

PLAIN

30°N

MISSISSIPPI
DELTA

CAPE
CANAVERAL

EVERGLADES

BAHAMAS

MEXICO

Gulf of Mexico

FLORIDA KEYS

Tropic of Cancer

CUBA

20°N

SCALE

0   300 mi

0   300 km

729

The Constitution of the United States

● Starting on this page, you will find the complete text of the United States Constitution. The actual text of the Constitution appears in the column that is printed on a color background on each page. In the other column you will find explanations of each part of the Constitution.

Headings and subheadings have been added to the Constitution to help you identify its different parts. Those parts of the original document that are no longer in effect are printed in slanted type.

PREAMBLE

We the people of the United States, in order to form a more perfect union, establish justice, insure domestic tranquillity, provide for the common defense, promote the general welfare, and secure the blessings of liberty to ourselves and our posterity, do ordain and establish this Constitution for the United States of America.

PREAMBLE

The Preamble states the purposes for which the Constitution was written: (1) to form a union of states that will benefit all, (2) to make laws and establish courts that are fair, (3) to maintain peace within the country, (4) to defend the nation against attack, (5) to help the people lead happy and useful lives, and (6) to make sure that this nation's people and their descendants remain free.

The opening words of the Preamble make clear that it is the people themselves who have the power to establish a government or change it.

Article I

SECTION 1

All legislative powers herein granted shall be vested in a Congress of the United States, which shall consist of a Senate and House of Representatives.

SECTION 2

a. The House of Representatives shall be composed of members chosen every second year by the people of the several

Article I

Legislative Branch

SECTION 1

The Congress of the United States

All national laws must be made by Congress. But Congress can make no laws except those permitted under the Constitution. Congress is made up of two houses — the Senate and the House of Representatives.

SECTION 2

The House of Representatives

a. **Election and term of members.** Members of the House of Representatives are elected in each state every two years. Any person

states, and the electors in each state shall have the qualifications requisite for electors of the most numerous branch of the state legislature.

b. No person shall be a representative who shall not have attained to the age of twenty-five years, and been seven years a citizen of the United States, and who shall not, when elected, be an inhabitant of that state in which he shall be chosen.

c. Representatives *and direct taxes* shall be apportioned among the several states which may be included within this Union, according to their respective numbers, *which shall be determined by adding to the whole number of free persons, including those bound to service for a term of years, and excluding Indians not taxed, three fifths of all other persons.* The actual enumeration shall be made within three years after the first meeting of the Congress of the United States, and within every subsequent term of ten years, in such manner as they shall by law direct. The number of representatives shall not exceed one for every thirty thousand, but each state shall have at least one representative; *and until such enumeration shall be made, the State of New Hampshire shall be entitled to choose three; Massachusetts, eight; Rhode Island and Providence Plantations, one; Connecticut, five; New York, six; New Jersey, four; Pennsylvania, eight; Delaware, one; Maryland, six; Virginia, ten; North Carolina, five; South Carolina, five; and Georgia, three.*

d. When vacancies happen in the representation from any state, the executive authority thereof shall issue writs of election to fill such vacancies.

e. The House of Representatives shall choose their Speaker and other officers; and shall have the sole power of impeachment.

who has the right to vote for representatives to the larger house of the state legislature has the right to vote for the state's representatives in the House of Representatives. This is the only qualification for voting listed in the original Constitution. It made sure that the House would be elected by the people themselves.

b. Qualification of members. A representative must be at least 25 years old, a United States citizen for at least seven years, and a resident of the state from which he or she is elected.

c. Apportionment of representatives and of direct taxes. The number of representatives each state has is determined by the state's population. Direct taxes are to be collected from the states according to the number of people living in each state. (Amendment 16 made the income tax an exception to this rule.) A direct tax is one paid to the government by the person who is taxed. Since there now are no slaves or indentured servants in the United States and Indians are citizens, all the people of a state are counted in determining the number of representatives a state shall have. Congress decides how the population is to be counted, but a census must be taken every ten years. The House of Representatives cannot have more than one member for every 30,000 persons in the nation. But each state is entitled to one representative, no matter how small its population. In 1910 Congress limited the number of representatives to 435.

d. Filling vacancies. When a state does not have all the representatives to which it is entitled — for example, when a representative resigns or dies — the governor of that state must call a special election to fill the vacancy.

e. Officers; impeachment. The House of Representatives elects its presiding officer (the Speaker) and other officers such as the chaplain and the sergeant at arms. Only the House has the right to impeach, that is, to bring charges of misdeeds in office against an official of the United States.

a. The Senate of the United States shall be composed of two senators from each state, chosen *by the legislature thereof,* for six years; and each senator shall have one vote.

b. Immediately after they shall be assembled in consequence of the first election, they shall be divided as equally as may be into three classes. *The seats of the senators of the first class shall be vacated at the expiration of the second year, of the second class at the expiration of the fourth year, and of the third class at the expiration of the sixth year,* so that one third may be chosen every second year; *and if vacancies happen by resignation, or otherwise, during the recess of the legislature of any state, the executive thereof may make temporary appointments until the next meeting of the legislature, which shall then fill such vacancies.*

c. No person shall be a senator who shall not have attained to the age of thirty years, and been nine years a citizen of the United States, and who shall not, when elected, be an inhabitant of that state for which he shall be chosen.

d. The Vice-President of the United States shall be President of the Senate, but shall have no vote, unless they be equally divided.

e. The Senate shall choose their own officers, and also a President pro tempore, in the absence of the Vice-President, or when he shall exercise the office of President of the United States.

f. The Senate shall have the sole power to try all impeachments. When sitting for that purpose, they shall be on oath or affirmation. When the President of the United States is tried, the Chief Justice shall preside; and no person shall be convicted without the concurrence of two thirds of the members present.

SECTION 3
The Senate

a. Number and election of members. The Senate is made up of two senators from each state. Senators are no longer chosen by the legislatures of their states. Amendment 17 states that they are to be elected by the people. A senator serves a six-year term.

b. Choosing senators. Senators were divided into three groups so that their terms would not all end at the same time. Today all senators are elected for six-year terms, but only one third are elected in any election year. The provision for filling vacancies in the Senate was changed by Amendment 17.

c. Qualifications of members. A senator must be at least thirty years old, a United States citizen for nine years, and a resident of the state from which he or she is elected.

d. President of Senate. The Vice-President of the United States serves as the president of the Senate, but cannot vote except in case of a tie. This is the only duty that the Constitution assigns to the Vice-President. In recent years the Vice-President has been given more responsibilities by the President.

e. Other officers. The Senate chooses its other officers, including a President pro tempore. *Pro tempore* means "for the time being." The President pro tempore presides in the Senate when the Vice-President is absent or when the Vice-President is serving as President of the United States.

f. Trials of impeachment. The Senate tries the case when a federal official is impeached by the House of Representatives. The senators must formally declare that they will be honest and just. If the President of the United States is tried, the Chief Justice presides over the Senate. Two thirds of the sen-

g. Judgment in cases of impeachment shall not exceed further than to removal from office, and disqualification to hold and enjoy any office of honor, trust, or profit under the United States; but the party convicted shall nevertheless be liable and subject to indictment, trial, judgment, and punishment, according to law.

SECTION 4

a. The times, places, and manner of holding elections for senators and representatives shall be prescribed in each state by the legislature thereof; but the Congress may at any time by law make or alter such regulations, *except as to the places of choosing senators.*

b. The Congress shall assemble at least once in every year, *and such meeting shall be on the first Monday in December, unless they shall by law appoint a different day.*

SECTION 5

a. Each house shall be the judge of the elections, returns, and qualifications of its own members, and a majority of each shall constitute a quorum to do business; but a smaller number may adjourn from day to day, and may be authorized to compel the attendance of absent members, in such manner, and under such penalties as each house may provide.

b. Each house may determine the rules of its proceedings, punish its members for disorderly behavior, and with the concurrence of two thirds, expel a member.

ators present must agree that the charge is true for the impeached person to be found guilty.

g. Punishment. If the Senate finds an impeached official guilty, it may only punish that official by keeping him or her from ever holding a government job again. Once out of office, however, the former official may be tried in a regular court and, if found guilty, punished like any other person.

SECTION 4
Elections and Meetings of Congress

a. Method of holding elections. The legislature of each state has the right to determine how, when, and where senators and representatives are elected, but Congress may pass election laws which the states must follow. For example, a federal law requires that secret ballots be used. Congressional elections are held on the Tuesday following the first Monday in November of even-numbered years.

b. Meeting of Congress. Congress must meet at least once a year. Amendment 20 made January 3 the day for beginning a regular session of Congress.

SECTION 5
Organization and Rules of Each House

a. Organization. Each house of Congress has the right to decide whether its members are qualified and fairly elected. Either house may by a majority vote refuse to seat a newly elected member. A *quorum* is the number of members which must be present for official business to be carried on. The Constitution states that a majority — half the members plus one — is a quorum in either the Senate or the House. When fewer than a quorum are present, that house may adjourn until the next day and may use penalties to force absent members to attend.

b. Rules. Each house of Congress has the right to make rules to follow in its work. Over the years many rules have grown up concerning the duties of officers and committees and the procedures used in conducting business. Each house may punish its

c. Each house shall keep a journal of its proceedings, and from time to time publish the same, excepting such parts as may in their judgment require secrecy; and the yeas and nays of the members of either house on any question shall, at the desire of one fifth of those present, be entered on the journal.

d. Neither house, during the session of Congress, shall without the consent of the other adjourn for more than three days, nor to any other place than that in which the two houses shall be sitting.

SECTION 6

a. The senators and representatives shall receive a compensation for their services, to be ascertained by law, and paid out of the Treasury of the United States. They shall in all cases, except treason, felony, and breach of the peace, be privileged from arrest during their attendance at the session of their respective houses and in going to and returning from the same; and for any speech or debate in either house, they shall not be questioned in any other place.

b. No senator or representative shall, during the time for which he was elected, be appointed to any civil office under the authority of the United States which shall have been created, or the emoluments whereof shall have been increased during such time; and no person holding any office under the United States shall be a member of either house during his continuance in office.

members for wrongdoing or even expel them by a two-thirds vote.

c. Journal. Each house of Congress must keep a record of what goes on at its meetings and must publish the record. The *Congressional Record* is issued daily during sessions of Congress. Parts of the record that the members of Congress believe should be kept secret may be withheld. How members of either house vote on a question may be entered in the record if one fifth of those present in that house wish this to be done.

d. Adjournment. When Congress is meeting, neither house may stop work for more than three days without the consent of the other house. Neither house is allowed to hold its sessions in another city without the consent of the other house.

SECTION 6
Privileges and Restrictions

a. Pay and privileges of members. Senators and representatives are paid out of the United States Treasury. Their salary is determined by laws passed by Congress. At the present time the salary is $60,662 annually, plus allowances for travel, office staff, stationery, and other expenses. Members of Congress also enjoy the *franking privilege,* that is, the right to send free any mail stamped with their name. Members of Congress may not be arrested at meetings of Congress or while going to or from such meetings unless they are suspected of treason, other serious crimes, or disturbing the peace. They may not be punished for anything they say in Congress, except by the house of which they are a member.

b. Holding other offices prohibited. Until after their terms have ended, senators or representatives may not hold offices created by the Congress of which they are members. The same restriction applies to jobs for which Congress has voted increased pay. No person may be a member of Congress without first giving up any other federal office he or she may hold.

SECTION 7

a. All bills for raising revenue shall originate in the House of Representatives; but the Senate may propose or concur with amendments as on other bills.

b. Every bill which shall have passed the House of Representatives and the Senate shall, before it become a law, be presented to the President of the United States; if he approves he shall sign it, but if not he shall return it, with his objections, to that house in which it shall have originated, who shall enter the objections at large on their journal, and proceed to reconsider it. If after such reconsideration two thirds of that house shall agree to pass the bill, it shall be sent, together with the objections, to the other house, by which it shall likewise be reconsidered, and if approved by two thirds of that house, it shall become a law. But in all such cases the votes of both houses shall be determined by yeas and nays, and the names of the persons voting for and against the bill shall be entered on the journal of each house respectively. If any bill shall not be returned by the President within ten days (Sundays excepted) after it shall have been presented to him, the same shall be a law, in like manner as if he had signed it, unless the Congress by their adjournment prevent its return, in which case it shall not be a law.

c. Every order, resolution, or vote to which the concurrence of the Senate and House of Representatives may be necessary (except on a question of adjournment) shall be presented to the President of the United States; and before the same shall take effect, shall be approved by him, or being disapproved by him, shall be repassed by two thirds of the Senate and House of Representatives, according to the rules and limitations prescribed in the case of a bill.

SECTION 7
Method of Passing Laws

a. Revenue bills. Bills for raising money for the federal government must start in the House of Representatives, but the Senate may make changes in such bills. Actually, the Senate has as much influence over revenue bills as does the House.

b. How bills become laws. A bill (except one for raising revenue) may start in either the Senate or the House of Representatives. However, exactly the same bill must be passed by a majority vote in both houses of Congress. Differences are usually ironed out in a conference committee made up of members of both houses. When both the Senate and House have voted in favor of the bill, it is sent to the President. The President can then do one of two things: sign the bill or veto it. If the bill is vetoed, it must then be discussed again in Congress. If two thirds of both houses of Congress vote for the bill after reconsidering it, the bill becomes law without the President's signing it. In such cases, the vote of each member of Congress is recorded.

The President has ten days (not counting Sundays) to study any bill. If the President keeps a bill more than ten days without signing or vetoing it and Congress continues to meet, the bill becomes a law. But if Congress adjourns before the ten-day period ends, the bill is dead. This is known as a "pocket veto."

c. Approval or disapproval by the President. Other acts which require approval of both houses of Congress take effect only if they are signed by the President or passed over a presidential veto by a two-thirds vote of both houses. However, a vote to adjourn Congress requires only a majority vote of both houses.

SECTION 8

The Congress shall have power

a. To lay and collect taxes, duties, imposts, and excises; to pay the debts and provide for the common defense and general welfare of the United States; but all duties, imposts, and excises shall be uniform throughout the United States;

b. To borrow money on the credit of the United States;

c. To regulate commerce with foreign nations, and among the several states, and with the Indian tribes;

d. To establish a uniform rule of naturalization, and uniform laws on the subject of bankruptcies throughout the United States;

e. To coin money, regulate the value thereof and of foreign coin, and fix the standard of weights and measures;

f. To provide for the punishment of counterfeiting the securities and current coin of the United States;

g. To establish post offices and post roads;

h. To promote the progress of science and useful arts by securing for limited times to authors and inventors the exclusive right to their respective writings and discoveries;

i. To constitute tribunals inferior to the Supreme Court;

SECTION 8

Powers Granted to Congress

a. Congress may pass laws for collecting various kinds of taxes. All federal taxes must be the same in all parts of the nation.

b. Congress has the power to borrow money that the federal government may need and to promise to repay this money. Borrowing is generally done by issuing government bonds or certificates of indebtedness that are bought by people or organizations.

c. Congress has the power to pass laws concerning trade between this country and foreign countries and between one state and another state.

d. Congress has the power to make laws determining how citizens of other countries may become citizens of the United States. Congress also makes laws to protect those to whom a person or organization owes debts that cannot be paid. Such bankruptcy laws must be the same throughout the country.

e. Congress controls the minting of money and decides how much each coin is worth. And it may determine the value of foreign coins used in the United States. Congress also sets up standards for measuring weight and distance.

f. Congress passes laws punishing people who make counterfeit money and government bonds.

g. Congress provides for a postal system and may build and maintain roads over which the mail is carried.

h. Congress encourages art, science, and invention by passing laws which protect artists and inventors. Copyright laws make it illegal for a person to use the work of an artist, musician, or author without permission. In the same way, patent laws protect inventors and those who discover new methods and procedures in business, industry, and transportation.

i. Congress has the power to establish federal courts other than the Supreme Court.

j. To define and punish piracies and felonies committed on the high seas and offenses against the laws of nations;

k. To declare war, grant letters of marque and reprisal, and make rules concerning captures on land and water;

l. To raise and support armies, but no appropriation of money to that use shall be for a longer term than two years;

m. To provide and maintain a navy;

n. To make rules for the government and regulation of land and naval forces;

o. To provide for calling forth the militia to execute the laws of the Union, suppress insurrections, and repel invasions;

p. To provide for organizing, arming, and disciplining the militia, and for governing such part of them as may be employed in the service of the United States, reserving to the states respectively the appointment of the officers and the authority of training the militia, according to the discipline prescribed by Congress;

q. To exercise exclusive legislation in all cases whatsoever over such district (not exceeding ten miles square) as may, by cession of particular states and the acceptance of Congress, become the seat of the government of the United States, and to exercise like authority over all places purchased by the consent of the legislature of the state in which the same shall be for the erection of forts, magazines, arsenals, dock-yards, and other needful buildings;

j. Congress may specify what acts committed on American ships are crimes because they violate United States laws or international laws. The accused will stand trial in a federal court when the ship returns to port.

k. Congress alone has the power to declare war. *Letters of marque and reprisal* are government licenses authorizing the holders to fit out armed ships for use in capturing enemy merchant ships. This power to commission privateers to prey upon enemy commerce was used extensively in the War of 1812. The practice is no longer followed.

l. Congress may create an army for the United States. But Congress may not vote the money to support the armed forces for more than two years in advance.

m. Congress may create a navy for the United States and vote the money necessary to operate it.

n. Congress may make rules for our armed forces. While on active duty, members of the armed forces are under military law and regulation rather than civil law.

o. Congress may determine when and how the militia, the citizen soldiers of the various states, may be called into the service of the national government. The militia may be used to enforce law, to put an end to rebellion, and to drive back an invasion of the country.

p. Congress provides for organizing, arming, and disciplining the militia. The states appoint the officers and train the militia under the regulations set up by Congress. When called out by the national government, however, the militia is part of the national armed forces.

q. Congress has the power to make laws for the District of Columbia. Because it contains the national capital, the District of Columbia is not under the control of any state. Congress also makes laws regulating the use of all other property belonging to the national government — forts, arsenals, etc.

r. To make all laws which shall be necessary and proper for carrying into execution the foregoing powers, and all other powers vested by this Constitution in the government of the United States, or in any department or officer thereof.

SECTION 9

a. *The migration or importation of such persons as any of the states now existing shall think proper to admit shall not be prohibited by the Congress prior to the year one thousand eight hundred and eight, but a tax or duty may be imposed on such importation, not exceeding ten dollars for each person.*
b. The privilege of the writ of habeas corpus shall not be suspended, unless when in cases of rebellion or invasion the public safety may require it.

c. No bill of attainder or ex post facto law shall be passed.

d. No capitation or other direct tax shall be laid, unless in proportion to the census or enumeration herein before directed to be taken.
e. No tax or duty shall be laid on articles exported from any state.

f. No preference shall be given by any regulation of commerce or revenue to the ports of one state over those of another; nor shall vessels bound to or from one state be obliged to enter, clear, or pay duties in another.
g. No money shall be drawn from the treasury, but in consequence of appropriations made by law; and a regular statement

r. Congress also has the power to pass all laws needed to carry out the responsibilities assigned it by the Constitution. This is the so-called "elastic clause." It can be stretched to meet the changing needs of the nation. It is the basis for much legislation not authorized in any other provision of the Constitution. The taxing power and the commerce clause, in particular, have led to legislation that the authors of the Constitution did not foresee.

SECTION 9
Powers Denied to the Federal Government

a. In 1808 Congress prohibited further importation of slaves.

b. Congress may not take away a person's right to the writ of habeas corpus except in time of great national danger. (A *writ of habeas corpus* is a court order directing that a prisoner be given a hearing so that the court can decide whether that person should be held and charged with a crime or released.)
c. Congress may not pass a bill of attainder. (A *bill of attainder* is a legislative act which condemns a person without a trial in court.) Neither can Congress pass an *ex post facto* law. Such a law makes an act a crime after the act has been committed.
d. Congress may not levy a direct tax that is not in proportion to population. Amendment 16 provides an exception in the case of the income tax.
e. Congress may not tax goods sent from one state to another or goods sent to other countries.
f. In laws concerning commerce, Congress may not favor one port over other ports. Congress must not tax goods being sent by water from one state to another state.

g. Money can be paid out of the Treasury only if Congress has voted the appropriation. (An *appropriation* is money granted

and account of the receipts and expenditures of all public money shall be published from time to time.

h. No title of nobility shall be granted by the United States; and no person holding any office of profit or trust under them shall, without the consent of Congress, accept of any present, emolument, office, or title, of any kind whatever, from any king, prince, or foreign state.

SECTION 10

a. No state shall enter into any treaty, alliance, or confederation; grant letters of marque and reprisal; coin money; emit bills of credit; make any thing but gold and silver coin a tender in payment of debts; pass any bill of attainder, ex post facto law, or law impairing the obligation of contracts; or grant any title of nobility.

b. No state shall, without the consent of the Congress, lay any imposts or duties on imports or exports, except what may be absolutely necessary for executing its inspection laws; and the net produce of all duties and imposts, laid by any state on imports or exports, shall be for the use of the treasury of the United States; and all such laws shall be subject to the revision and control of the Congress.

c. No state shall, without the consent of Congress, lay any duty of tonnage; keep troops or ships of war in time of peace; enter into any agreement or compact with another state or with a foreign power; or engage in war, unless actually invaded or in such imminent danger as will not admit of delay.

for a given purpose.) An account of money received and money spent must be published from time to time.

h. The United States may not grant a title of nobility. Federal officials may not accept titles, gifts, or honors from any foreign ruler or government unless Congress gives its permission.

SECTION 10

Powers Denied to the States

a. States may not make treaties, enter into agreements with foreign countries, or grant their citizens the right to make war. States cannot issue their own money or declare that any money other than that of the United States can be used as legal money.

The states as well as the national government are forbidden to punish people without giving them a trial, to pass laws that would punish people for acts that were not against the law at the time they were committed, and to grant titles of nobility. State governments must not pass any laws that would make contracts or other legal agreements less binding on the people who agreed to them.

b. States may not tax goods leaving or entering their territory. However, they may charge fees to cover the costs of inspection. Any profit from such inspection fees must be turned over to the United States Treasury. Congress has the power to change the inspection laws of a state.

c. Unless Congress gives permission, a state may not tax ships entering its ports, keep an army or navy — except the militia — in time of peace, make treaties with other states or foreign countries, or make war except when it is invaded.

Article II

SECTION 1

a. The executive power shall be vested in a President of the United States of America. He shall hold his office during the term of four years, and, together with the Vice-President chosen for the same term, be elected as follows:

b. Each state shall appoint, in such manner as the legislature thereof may direct, a number of electors, equal to the whole number of senators and representatives to which the state may be entitled in the Congress; but no senator or representative, or person holding an office of trust or profit under the United States, shall be appointed an elector.

The electors shall meet in their respective states and vote by ballot for two persons, of whom one at least shall not be an inhabitant of the same state with themselves. And they shall make a list of all the persons voted for and of the number of votes for each; which list they shall sign and certify, and transmit sealed to the seat of government of the United States, directed to the President of the Senate. The President of the Senate shall, in the presence of the Senate and House of Representatives, open all the certificates, and the votes shall then be counted. The person having the greatest number of votes shall be the President, if such number be a majority of the whole number of electors appointed; and if there be more than one who have such majority, and have an equal number of votes, then the House of Representatives shall immediately choose by ballot one of them for President; and if no person have a majority, then from the five highest on the list the said house shall in like manner choose the President. But in choosing the President the votes shall be taken by states, the representation from each state having one vote; a quorum for this purpose shall consist of a member or members from two thirds of the states, and a majority of all

Article II

Executive Branch

SECTION 1

President and Vice-President

a. Term of office. The President of the United States enforces or executes the nation's laws and is elected, as is the Vice-President, for a four-year term.

b. Electors. The President and Vice-President are elected by electors chosen by the states according to rules established by the legislatures. Each state has as many electors as it has senators and representatives in Congress. No senator or representative or other person holding a federal job may be an elector. Today electors usually are important party members whose votes are pledged to a given candidate.

Original election method. This clause did not work well in practice and was changed by Amendment 12.

the states shall be necessary to a choice. In every case, after the choice of the President, the person having the greatest number of votes of the electors shall be the Vice-President. But if there should remain two or more who have equal votes, the Senate shall choose from them by ballot the Vice-President.

c. The Congress may determine the time of choosing the electors, and the day on which they shall give their votes; which day shall be the same throughout the United States.

d. No person except a natural-born citizen, *or a citizen of the United States, at the time of the adoption of this Constitution,* shall be eligible to the office of President; neither shall any person be eligible to that office who shall not have attained the age of thirty-five years, and been fourteen years a resident within the United States.

e. In case of the removal of the President from office or of his death, resignation, or inability to discharge the powers and duties of the said office, the same shall devolve on the Vice-President; and the Congress may by law provide for the case of removal, death, resignation, or inability, both of the President and Vice-President, declaring what officer shall then act as President; and such officer shall act accordingly, until the disability be removed or a President shall be elected.

f. The President shall, at stated times, receive for his services a compensation, which shall neither be increased nor diminished during the period for which he shall have been elected, and he shall not receive within that period any other emolument from the United States, or any of them.

g. Before he enter on the execution of his office, he shall take the following oath or affirmation: "I do solemnly swear (or affirm) that I will faithfully execute the office of President of the United States, and will to the best of my ability, preserve, protect, and defend the Constitution of the United States."

c. Time of elections. Congress determines when electors are chosen and when they vote. The day is the same throughout the United States. The popular vote for electors takes place on the Tuesday after the first Monday of November in each "leap year." In mid-December the electors meet in their state capitals and cast their electoral votes.

d. Qualifications for President. To be President, a person must be a citizen of the United States by birth, at least 35 years old, and a resident of the United States for at least 14 years.

e. Vacancy. If the presidency becomes vacant, the Vice-President becomes the President of the United States. If neither the President nor the Vice-President is able to serve, Congress has the right to decide what government official shall act as President. Amendment 25 practically assures that there always will be a Vice-President to succeed to the presidency.

f. The President's salary. The President is paid a salary fixed by Congress. That salary may not be increased or decreased during the term of office. The President may not receive any other salary from the United States or from one of the states. The salary of the President is now $200,000 a year, plus additional amounts for expenses.

g. Oath of office. In taking the oath of office, the President promises to preserve, protect, and defend the Constitution of the United States.

SECTION 2

a. The President shall be Commander-in-Chief of the Army and Navy of the United States, and of the militia of the several states, when called into the actual service of the United States. He may require the opinion, in writing, of the principal officer in each of the executive departments, upon any subject relating to the duties of their respective offices, and he shall have power to grant reprieves and pardons for offenses against the United States, except in cases of impeachment.

b. He shall have power, by and with the advice and consent of the Senate, to make treaties, provided two thirds of the senators present concur; and he shall nominate and, by and with the advice and consent of the Senate, shall appoint ambassadors, other public ministers and consuls, judges of the Supreme Court, and all other officers of the United States, whose appointments are not herein otherwise provided for, and which shall be established by law; but the Congress may by law vest the appointment of such inferior officers as they think proper in the President alone, in the courts of law, or in the heads of departments.

c. The President shall have power to fill up all vacancies that may happen during the recess of the Senate, by granting commissions which shall expire at the end of their next session.

SECTION 3

He shall from time to time give to the Congress information of the state of the Union,

SECTION 2
Powers of the President

a. Military powers; reprieves and pardons. The President is Commander-in-Chief of the armed forces and of the militia when it is called out by the national government. As Commander-in-Chief, the President has great power, especially in time of war. The President may ask the heads of the executive departments for advice and for reports on the work of the various departments. No provision is made in the Constitution for the Cabinet or for Cabinet meetings. But the existence of executive departments is implied here. The President may pardon persons convicted of crimes against the federal government or delay the punishment of such persons, except in cases of impeachment.

b. Treaties and appointments. The President may make treaties, but all treaties must be approved in the Senate by a two-thirds vote of the senators present. The President may also appoint important government officials. Such appointments must be approved in the Senate by a majority of the senators present. Congress may, however, pass laws giving the President, the courts, or the heads of departments power to appoint less important officials without the consent of the Senate.

c. Filling vacancies. If the Senate is not meeting, the President may make temporary appointments to fill vacancies. These appointments end at the close of the next session of Congress unless the Senate approves them. Congress, with the approval of the President, has given the Office of Personnel Management responsibility for determining the fitness of job applicants and for ranking them on civil service lists from which appointments to many federal positions are made.

SECTION 3
Duties of the President

The President must report to Congress from time to time on conditions within the

and recommend to their consideration such measures as he shall judge necessary and expedient; he may, on extraordinary occasions, convene both houses, or either of them, and in case of disagreement between them with respect to the time of adjournment he may adjourn them to such time as he shall think proper; he shall receive ambassadors and other public ministers; he shall take care that the laws be faithfully executed, and shall commission all the officers of the United States.

SECTION 4

The President, Vice-President and all civil officers of the United States shall be removed from office on impeachment for, and conviction of, treason, bribery, or other high crimes and misdemeanors.

Article III

SECTION 1

The judicial power of the United States shall be vested in one Supreme Court and in such inferior courts as the Congress may from time to time ordain and establish. The judges, both of the Supreme and inferior courts, shall hold their offices during good behavior and shall, at stated times, receive for their services a compensation which shall not be diminished during their continuance in office.

SECTION 2

a. The judicial power shall extend to all cases, in law and equity, arising under this Constitution, the laws of the United States, and treaties made, or which shall be made, under their authority; to all cases affecting ambassadors, other public ministers, and

United States. The President may also suggest that Congress act to pass certain laws or to solve problems facing the nation. The President may call a special session of Congress if a situation arises which requires action by Congress when that body is not in regular session. In case the Senate and House cannot agree when to end a session, the President may adjourn Congress. The President receives representatives of foreign nations, sees that the laws of the nation are enforced, and commissions officers in the armed services.

SECTION 4
Impeachment

The President, Vice-President, and other important government officials may be removed from office if impeached and found guilty of treason, bribery, or other serious crimes.

Article III
Judicial Branch

SECTION 1
The Federal Courts

The powers to interpret the laws of the United States belongs to the Supreme Court and the other federal courts established by Congress. District courts and courts of appeal are now part of the regular court system. Federal judges are appointed by the President with the approval of the Senate. They hold office as long as they live, unless they retire, resign, or are impeached and found guilty. Judges are paid salaries which cannot be lowered during their terms of service.

SECTION 2
Jurisdiction of the Federal Courts

a. Federal courts in general. Federal courts may try cases concerning (1) the Constitution and federal laws and treaties, (2) representatives of foreign nations, (3) laws governing ships and sailors, (4) disputes between the United States and a person or

consuls; to all cases of admiralty and maritime jurisdiction; to controversies to which the United States shall be a party; to controversies between two or more states; *between a state and citizens of another state;* between citizens of different states; between citizens of the same state claiming lands under grants of different states, and between a state, or the citizens thereof, and foreign states, citizens, or subjects.

b. In all cases affecting ambassadors, other public ministers, and consuls, and those in which a state shall be a party, the Supreme Court shall have original jurisdiction. In all the other cases before mentioned, the Supreme Court shall have appellate jurisdiction, both as to law and fact, with such exceptions and under such regulations as the Congress shall make.

c. The trial of all crimes, except in cases of impeachment, shall be by jury; and such trial shall be held in the state where the said crimes shall have been committed; but when not committed within any state, the trial shall be at such place or places as the Congress may by law have directed.

SECTION 3

a. Treason against the United States shall consist only in levying war against them or in adhering to their enemies, giving them aid and comfort. No person shall be convicted of treason unless on the testimony of two witnesses to the same overt act, or on confession in open court.

b. The Congress shall have power to declare the punishment of treason, but no attainder of treason shall work corruption of blood, or forfeiture except during the life of the person attainted.

Article IV

SECTION 1

Full faith and credit shall be given in each state to the public acts, records, and judi-

another government, (5) disputes between states, (6) disputes between citizens of different states, (7) disputes in which citizens of the same state claim lands granted by different states, and (8) disputes between a state or its citizen and a foreign state or its citizens.

b. Supreme Court. Any case involving a representative of a foreign country or one of the states is first tried in the Supreme Court. Any other case is first tried in a lower court. But the Supreme Court may hear a case from a lower court on appeal. Since the Supreme Court is the highest court in the land, its decision cannot be appealed.

c. Rules respecting trials. Except in cases of impeachment, the accused has a right to a trial by jury in the state in which the crime was committed. If the crime did not take place within a state, a law passed by Congress determines where the trial is to be held.

SECTION 3
Treason

a. Definition of treason. A citizen who makes war on the United States or aids this country's enemies is guilty of treason. To be judged guilty of treason, one must confess in court or be convicted by the testimony of two or more persons.

b. Punishment for treason. Congress decides what the punishment for treason will be. But the family or descendants of a guilty person may not be punished.

Article IV
The States and the Federal Government

SECTION 1
State Records

The records and court decisions of one state must be accepted in all states. Congress has the power to see that this is done.

cial proceedings of every other state. And the Congress may by general laws prescribe the manner in which such acts, records, and proceedings shall be proved, and the effect thereof.

SECTION 2

a. The citizens of each state shall be entitled to all privileges and immunities of citizens in the several states.

b. A person charged in any state with treason, felony, or other crime who shall flee from justice and be found in another state shall, on demand of the executive authority of the state from which he fled, be delivered up, to be removed to the state having jurisdiction of the crime.

c. *No person held to service or labor in one state, under the laws thereof, escaping into another shall, in consequence of any law or regulation therein, be discharged from such service or labor, but shall be delivered upon claim of the party to whom such service or labor may be due.*

SECTION 3

a. New states may be admitted by the Congress into this Union; but no new state shall be formed or erected within the jurisdiction of any other state; nor any state be formed by the junction of two or more states, or parts of states, without the consent of the legislatures of the states concerned, as well as of the Congress.

b. The Congress shall have power to dispose of and make all needful rules and regulations respecting the territory or other property belonging to the United States; and nothing in this Constitution shall be so construed as to prejudice any claims of the United States, or of any particular state.

SECTION 2
Privileges and Immunities of Citizens

a. **Privileges.** The citizens of all states have in a given state the rights and privileges granted to the citizens of that state. For example, a citizen of Oregon going into California would be entitled to all the privileges of citizens of California.

b. **Extradition.** If the governor makes the request, a person charged with a crime in one state may be returned from another state to stand trial. Such action is called *extradition.* A request for extradition may be denied, however.

c. **Fugitive workers.** This clause referred to slaves. Amendment 13 abolished slavery.

SECTION 3
New States and Territories

a. **Admission of new states.** Congress has the power to add new states to the Union. However, no state can have some of its territory taken away without its consent as well as the consent of Congress.

b. **National territory.** Congress has the power to make rules and regulations concerning the property and the territory of the United States.

The United States shall guarantee to every state in this Union a republican form of government, and shall protect each of them against invasion; and on application of the legislature, or of the executive (when the legislature cannot be convened), against domestic violence.

Article V

The Congress, whenever two thirds of both houses shall deem it necessary, shall propose amendments to this Constitution, or, on the application of the legislatures of two thirds of the several states, shall call a convention for proposing amendments, which, in either case, shall be valid to all intents and purposes, as part of this Constitution, when ratified by the legislatures of three fourths of the several states or by conventions in three fourths thereof, as the one or the other mode of ratification may be proposed by the Congress; provided that *no amendments which may be made prior to the year one thousand eight hundred and eight shall in any manner affect the first and fourth clauses in the ninth section of the first article; and that* no state, without its consent, shall be deprived of its equal suffrage in the Senate.

Article VI

a. All debts contracted and engagements entered into, before the adoption of this Constitution, shall be as valid against the United States under this Constitution as under the Confederation.
b. This Constitution, and the laws of the United States which shall be made in pursuance thereof, and all treaties made, or which shall be made, under the authority of the United States, shall be the supreme law of the land; and the judges in every state

SECTION 4
Guarantees to the States

It is the duty of the federal government to see that each state (1) has a republican form of government, (2) is protected from invasion, and (3) receives help to put down riots and other disorders when such help is requested by the legislature or the governor of the state.

Article V
Amending the Constitution

The Constitution may be changed by amendment. An amendment may be proposed by a two-thirds vote of both houses of Congress or by a convention called at the request of the legislatures of two thirds of the states. Proposed amendments must be approved by the legislatures of three fourths of the states or by conventions called in three fourths of the states. When an amendment is approved, it becomes part of the Constitution. However, no amendment may take away equal state representation in the Senate.

Article VI
Supremacy of Federal Laws

a. Public debt. The framers of the Constitution agreed that the United States would be responsible for all debts contracted by the Confederation government.

b. Supremacy of the Constitution. The Constitution and the laws and treaties of the United States are the supreme law of the nation. If state law is in conflict with national law, it is the national law that must be obeyed.

shall be bound thereby, anything in the Constitution or laws of any state to the contrary notwithstanding.

c. The senators and representatives before mentioned, and the members of the several state legislatures, and all executive and judicial officers, both of the United States and of the several states, shall be bound by oath or affirmation to support this Constitution; but no religious test shall ever be required as a qualification to any office or public trust under the United States.

c. Oath of office; no religious test. All government officials, federal and state, must take an oath to support the Constitution. But no religious test can ever be required for an official to hold office.

Article VII

The ratification of the conventions of nine states shall be sufficient for the establishment of this Constitution between the states so ratifying the same.

Article VII
Ratification of the Constitution

The Constitution went into effect when nine states voted to accept it.

AMENDMENTS

Amendment 1

Congress shall make no law respecting an establishment of religion or prohibiting the free exercise thereof; or abridging the freedom of speech, or of the press; or the right of the people peaceably to assemble, and to petition the government for a redress of grievances.

AMENDMENTS

Amendment 1
Freedom of Religion, Speech, Press, Assembly, and Petition (1791)

Congress must not pass laws that stop people from worshiping as they see fit. Congress cannot stop people from speaking, writing, or printing anything they want to, except that they must not slander or libel others nor urge violent overthrow of the government. Congress must not take away the people's right to meet together for any lawful purposes provided they do not interfere with the rights of others. And Congress must not take away the people's right to ask the government to correct grievances or abuses.

Amendment 2

A well-regulated militia being necessary to the security of a free state, the right of the people to keep and bear arms shall not be infringed.

Amendment 2
Right to Bear Arms (1791)

The federal government cannot deny states the right to enlist citizens in the militia and to provide them with training in the use of weapons.

Amendment 3

No soldier shall, in time of peace, be quartered in any house without the consent of the owner, nor in time of war, but in a manner to be prescribed by law.

Amendment 4

The right of the people to be secure in their persons, houses, papers, and effects, against unreasonable searches and seizures, shall not be violated, and no warrants shall issue but upon probable cause, supported by oath or affirmation and particularly describing the place to be searched and the persons or things to be seized.

Amendment 5

No person shall be held to answer for a capital or otherwise infamous crime, unless on a presentment or indictment of a grand jury, except in cases arising in the land or naval forces, or in the militia, when in actual service in time of war or public danger; nor shall any person be subject for the same offense to be twice put in jeopardy of life or limb; nor shall be compelled in any criminal case to be a witness against himself, nor be deprived of life, liberty, or property, without due process of law; nor shall private property be taken for public use without just compensation.

Amendment 6

In all criminal prosecutions, the accused shall enjoy the right to a speedy and public trial by an impartial jury of the state and district wherein the crime shall have been committed, which districts shall have been previously ascertained by law, and to be informed of the nature and cause of the accusation; to be confronted with the witnesses against him; to have compulsory process for obtaining witnesses in his favor; and to have the assistance of counsel for his defense.

Amendment 3
Quartering of Soldiers (1791)

In time of peace the government may not force people to have soldiers live in their homes. In wartime people cannot be compelled to do this without passage of a law.

Amendment 4
Search and Seizure (1791)

The government may not search a home or arrest a person without good cause and then only after the official who makes the search or arrest has obtained a *warrant* — an official order from a judge. Judges may not issue warrants unless they believe such action is necessary to enforce the law.

Amendment 5
Rights of Accused Persons (1791)

No person may be tried in a federal court for a serious crime unless a grand jury decides that the person ought to be tried. (But members of the armed forces may be tried in military court under military law.) People who have been tried for a crime and judged innocent cannot be tried again for the same crime. Neither can they be forced to give evidence against themselves. And no person may be executed, imprisoned, or fined except as punishment after a fair trial. A person's private property may not be taken for public use without a fair price being paid for it.

Amendment 6
Jury Trial in Criminal Cases (1791)

A person accused of a crime is entitled to a prompt public trial before an impartial jury. The trial is held in the district where the crime took place. The accused must be told what the charge is. The accused must be present when witnesses give their testimony. The government must help the accused bring into court friendly witnesses. The accused must be provided a lawyer.

Amendment 7

In suits at common law, where the value in controversy shall exceed twenty dollars, the right of trial by jury shall be preserved, and no fact tried by a jury shall be otherwise re-examined in any court of the United States than according to the rules of common law.

Amendment 8

Excessive bail shall not be required, nor excessive fines imposed, nor cruel and unusual punishments inflicted.

Amendment 9

The enumeration in the Constitution of certain rights shall not be construed to deny or disparage others retained by the people.

Amendment 10

The powers not delegated to the United States by the Constitution, nor prohibited by it to the states, are reserved to the states respectively, or to the people.

Amendment 11

The judicial power of the United States shall not be construed to extend to any suit in law or equity commenced or prosecuted against one of the United States by citizens of another state or by citizens or subjects of any foreign state.

Amendment 12

The electors shall meet in their respective states and vote by ballot for President and Vice-President, one of whom, at least, shall

Amendment 7
Rules of Common Law (1791)

If a lawsuit involves property or settlement worth more than twenty dollars, the case may be tried before a jury.

Amendment 8
Protection from Excessive Penalties (1791)

Persons accused of crimes may in most cases be released from jail by posting a bond that they will not run away. This is called "being out on bail." Bail, fines, and punishments must be reasonable.

Amendment 9
Other Rights of the People (1791)

Since it was impossible to list in the Constitution all the rights of the people, the listing of certain rights does not mean that people do not have other rights.

Amendment 10
Powers Kept by States and the People (1791)

The powers which the Constitution does not give to the United States and does not deny to the states belong to the states and to the people.

Amendment 11
Suits Against a State (1798)

No federal court may try a case in which a state is being sued by a citizen of another state or of a foreign country. Amendment 11 changes a provision of Article III, Section 2, Clause "a."

Amendment 12
Election of President and Vice-President (1804)

Amendment 12 describes the present-day procedure in the electoral college. The most important change made by this amendment

not be an inhabitant of the same state with themselves; they shall name in their ballots the person voted for as President, and in distinct ballots the person voted for as Vice-President, and they shall make distinct lists of all persons voted for as President, and of all persons voted for as Vice-President, and of the number of votes for each, which lists they shall sign and certify, and transmit sealed to the seat of the government of the United States, directed to the President of the Senate; the President of the Senate shall, in the presence of the Senate and House of Representatives, open all the certificates and the votes shall then be counted; the person having the greatest number of votes for President shall be the President, if such number be a majority of the whole number of electors appointed; and if no person have such majority, then from the persons having the highest numbers not exceeding three on the list of those voted for as President, the House of Representatives shall choose immediately, by ballot, the President. But in choosing the President, the votes shall be taken by states, the representation from each state having one vote; a quorum for this purpose shall consist of a member or members from two thirds of the states, and a majority of all the states shall be necessary to a choice. And if the House of Representatives shall not choose a President whenever the right of choice shall devolve upon them, *before the fourth day of March next following,* then the Vice-President shall act as President, as in the case of the death or other constitutional disability of the President. The person having the greatest number of votes as Vice-President shall be the Vice-President, if such number be a majority of the whole number of electors appointed, and if no person have a majority, then from the two highest numbers on the list, the Senate shall choose the Vice-President; a quorum for the purpose shall consist of two thirds of the whole number of senators, and a majority of the whole number shall be necessary to a choice. But no person constitutionally ineligible to the office of President shall be eligible to that of Vice-President of the United States.

was that the presidential electors would vote for President and Vice-President on separate ballots. In 1800, when only one ballot was used, Thomas Jefferson and Aaron Burr received the same number of votes, and the election had to be decided by the House of Representatives. To guard against this possibility in the future, Amendment 12 calls for separate ballots.

The electors meet in their state capitals and cast their separate ballots for President and Vice-President. They send them to the President of the Senate, showing the votes for each candidate. They are opened, and the electoral votes for President are counted in the presence of both houses. The candidate having a majority is declared elected. If no candidate for President receives a majority, the election goes to the House. The members of the House then vote for one of the three highest candidates. Each state casts one vote. A quorum consists of at least one member from two thirds of the states. The candidate who receives a majority of the votes of the states is elected President. If the House fails to elect a President, the Vice-President acts as President.

The electoral votes for Vice-President are also counted in the presence of both houses. The candidate having a majority is declared elected. If no candidate for Vice-President receives a majority, the Senate chooses a Vice-President from the two highest candidates. For this purpose, a quorum consists of two thirds of the total membership of the Senate. A majority of the whole number of the Senate is necessary to elect a Vice-President. No person can be Vice-President who does not meet the qualifications for President.

Amendment 13

Section 1. Neither slavery nor involuntary servitude, except as a punishment for crime whereof the party shall have been duly convicted, shall exist within the United States or any place subject to their jurisdiction.

Section 2. Congress shall have the power to enforce this article by appropriate legislation.

Amendment 14

Section 1. All persons born or naturalized in the United States, and subject to the jurisdiction thereof, are citizens of the United States and of the state wherein they reside. No state shall make or enforce any law which shall abridge the privileges or immunities of citizens of the United States; nor shall any state deprive any person of life, liberty, or property, without due process of law; nor deny to any person within its jurisdiction the equal protection of the laws.

Section 2. Representatives shall be apportioned among the several states according to their respective numbers, counting the whole number of persons in each state, *excluding Indians not taxed.* But when the right to vote at any election for the choice of electors for President and Vice-President of the United States, representatives in Congress, the executive and judicial officers of a state, or the members of the legislature thereof, is denied to any of the male inhabitants of such state, being twenty-one years of age and citizens of the United States, or in any way abridged, except for participation in rebellion, or other crime, the basis of representation therein shall be reduced in the proportion which the number of such male citizens shall bear to the whole number of male citizens twenty-one years of age in such state.

Amendment 13

Slavery Abolished (1865)

SECTION 1

Abolition of Slavery

Slavery cannot exist in the United States or its territories. No one may be forced to work, except as punishment for committing a crime.

SECTION 2

Enforcement

Congress may pass whatever laws are necessary to enforce Amendment 13. Many amendments include such an *enabling act.*

Amendment 14

Civil Rights Guaranteed (1868)

SECTION 1

Definition of Citizenship

All persons born or naturalized in the United States and subject to this country's laws are citizens of the United States and of the state in which they live. No state may take away the rights of citizens or take any person's life, liberty, or property except according to law. All state laws must apply equally to everyone in the state.

SECTION 2

Apportionment of Representatives

In counting population to determine a state's representation, all people in the state are counted. But if the right to vote is denied to any male inhabitants of a state who are entitled to vote, that state's representation can be reduced accordingly. This section abolished the provision in Article I, Section 2, Clause "c" which said that only three fifths of the slaves should be counted as population.

Section 3. No person shall be a senator or representative in Congress, or elector of President and Vice-President, or hold any office, civil or military, under the United States, or under any state, who, having previously taken an oath as a member of Congress, or as an officer of the United States, or as a member of any state legislature, or as an executive or judicial officer of any state, to support the Constitution of the United States, shall have engaged in insurrection or rebellion against the same, or given aid or comfort to the enemies thereof. But Congress may by vote of two thirds of each house remove such disability.

Section 4. The validity of the public debt of the United States, authorized by law, including debts incurred for payment of pensions and bounties for services in suppressing insurrection or rebellion, shall not be questioned. But neither the United States nor any state shall assume or pay any debt or obligation incurred in aid of insurrection or rebellion against the United States, or any claim for the loss or emancipation of any slave; but all such debts, obligations, and claims shall be held illegal and void.

Section 5. The Congress shall have power to enforce by appropriate legislation the provisions of this article.

Amendment 15

Section 1. The right of citizens of the United States to vote shall not be denied or abridged by the United States or by any state on account of race, color, or previous condition of servitude.

Section 2. The Congress shall have power to enforce this article by appropriate legislation.

Amendment 16

The Congress shall have power to lay and collect taxes on incomes, from whatever source derived, without apportionment among the several states and without regard to any census or enumeration.

SECTION 3
Restrictions on Public Office

Persons who hold appointed or elective offices or commissions in the armed forces which required an oath to support the Constitution of the United States violate that oath by taking up arms against the United States. They cannot hold any office which would again require them to take such an oath. Congress may abolish this rule by a two-thirds vote of each house. This provision was designed to bar leaders of the Confederacy from holding federal offices.

SECTION 4
Public Debt of the United States Valid; Confederate Debt Void

All debts contracted by the United States are to be paid. But neither the United States nor any state government is to pay the debts of the Confederacy. Neither is any payment to be made as compensation for slaves who were set free.

Amendment 15
Right to Vote (1870)

Citizens may not be kept from voting because of their race or color or because they were once slaves.

Amendment 16
Income Tax (1913)

Congress may tax incomes. The total amount in federal income tax paid by people in the various states does not have to be determined by the number of people who live in the states.

Amendment 17

a. The Senate of the United States shall be composed of two senators from each state, elected by the people thereof, for six years; and each senator shall have one vote. The electors in each state shall have the qualifications requisite for electors of the most numerous branch of the state legislatures.

b. When vacancies happen in the representation of any state in the Senate, the executive authority of such state shall issue writs of election to fill such vacancies: provided that the legislature of any state may empower the executive thereof to make temporary appointments until the people fill the vacancies by election as the legislature may direct.

c. This amendment shall not be so construed as to affect the election or term of any senator chosen before it becomes valid as part of the Constitution.

Amendment 18

Section 1. *After one year from the ratification of this article the manufacture, sale, or transportation of intoxicating liquors within, the importation thereof into, or the exportation thereof from the United States and all territory subject to the jurisdiction thereof for beverage purposes is hereby prohibited.*

Section 2. *The Congress and the several states shall have concurrent power to enforce this article by appropriate legislation.*

Section 3. *This article shall be inoperative unless it shall have been ratified as an amendment to the Constitution by the legislatures of the several states, as provided in the Constitution, within seven years from the date of the submission hereof to the states by the Congress.*

Amendment 19

Section 1. The right of citizens of the United States to vote shall not be denied or abridged by the United States or by any state on account of sex.

Amendment 17
Direct Election of Senators (1913)

a. Election by the people. The original Constitution provided that senators were to be elected by the state legislatures. Amendment 17 changed that to election by popular vote. Anyone qualified to vote for a state representative can vote for United States senators.

b. Vacancies. If a vacancy occurs in the United States Senate, the governor of the state affected may call a special election to fill the vacancy. The state legislature, however, may permit the governor to appoint someone to fill the vacancy until an election is held.

c. Not retroactive. Senators chosen by state legislatures before Amendment 17 was added to the Contitution could complete their terms.

Amendment 18
Prohibition (1919)

Amendment 18 forbade the manufacture, sale, or shipment of intoxicating beverages within the United States. The importation or exportation of such beverages was also forbidden. Amendment 18 was repealed by Amendment 21.

Amendment 19
Women's Voting Rights (1920)

No citizen may be denied the right to vote because she is a woman.

Section 2. The Congress shall have power to enforce this article by appropriate legislation.

Amendment 20

Section 1. The terms of the President and Vice-President shall end at noon on the 20th day of January, and the terms of senators and representatives at noon on the 3rd day of January, of the years in which such terms would have ended if this article had not been ratified; and the terms of their successors shall then begin.

Section 2. The Congress shall assemble at least once in every year, and such meeting shall begin at noon on the 3rd day of January, unless they shall by law appoint a different day.

Section 3. If, at the time fixed for the beginning of the term of the President, the President-elect shall have died, the Vice-President-elect shall become President. If a President shall not have been chosen before the time fixed for the beginning of his term, or if the President-elect shall have failed to qualify, then the Vice-President-elect shall act as President until a President shall have qualified; and the Congress may by law provide for the case wherein neither a President-elect nor a Vice-President-elect shall have qualified, declaring who shall then act as President, or the manner in which one who is to act shall be selected, and such person shall act accordingly until a President or a Vice-President shall have qualified.

Section 4. The Congress may by law provide for the case of the death of any of the persons from whom the House of Representatives may choose a President whenever the right of choice shall have devolved upon them, and for the case of the death of any of the persons from whom the Senate may choose a Vice-President whenever the right of choice shall have devolved upon them.

Amendment 20

Terms of Office (1933)

SECTION 1

Terms of President, Vice-President, and Congress

The terms of the President and Vice-President end at noon on January 20 following a presidential election. The terms of one third of the senators and of all representatives end at noon on January 3 in years ending in odd numbers. The new terms begin when the old terms end.

SECTION 2

Sessions of Congress

Congress meets at least once a year. The regular session begins on January 3 unless Congress sets a different day.

SECTION 3

Presidential Succession

If the President-elect dies before being sworn in, the Vice-President-elect becomes President. If the President-elect has not been chosen or does not qualify for office, the Vice-President-elect acts as President until a President is chosen or qualifies. If neither the President-elect nor Vice-President-elect qualifies to hold office, Congress decides who shall act as President until a President or Vice-President is chosen or qualifies.

SECTION 4

Choice of President by the House

In cases in which the election is thrown into Congress because no candidate for either President or Vice-President receives a majority of the electoral votes, Congress may make a law to decide what to do if one of the candidates dies.

Section 5. Sections 1 and 2 shall take effect on the fifteenth day of October following the ratification of this article.

Section 6. *This article shall be inoperative unless it shall have been ratified as an amendment to the Constitution by the legislatures of three fourths of the several states within seven years from the date of its submission.*

Amendment 21

Section 1. The eighteenth article of amendment to the Constitution of the United States is hereby repealed.

Section 2. The transportation or importation into any state, territory, or possession of the United States for delivery or use therein of intoxicating liquors, in violation of the laws thereof, is hereby prohibited.

Section 3. *This article shall be inoperative unless it shall have been ratified as an amendment to the Constitution by conventions in the several states, as provided in the Constitution, within seven years from the date of the submission hereof to the states by the Congress.*

Amendment 22

Section 1. No person shall be elected to the office of the President more than twice, and no person who has held the office of President, or acted as President, for more than two years of a term to which some other person was elected President shall be elected to the office of the President more than once. But this article shall not apply to any person holding the office of President when this article was proposed

SECTION 5
Date Effective

Section 5 set the date on which the first two sections of Amendment 20 were to take effect after the amendment had been approved by the states.

SECTION 6
Limited Time for Ratification

To become a part of the Constitution, Amendment 20 had to be approved within seven years.

Amendment 21
Repeal of Prohibition (1933)

SECTION 1
Repeal of Amendment 18

Amendment 21 repeals the Eighteenth Amendment.

SECTION 2
States Protected

Intoxicating liquors may not be transported or imported into any state or territory of the United States if the laws of that state or territory prohibit the sale of liquor.

SECTION 3
Limited Time for Ratification

Section 3 set a time limit of seven years for approval of Amendment 21.

Amendment 22
Two-Term Limitation on Presidency (1951)

SECTION 1
Definition of Limitation

No person may be elected President more than twice. A person who has served more than two years in the place of an elected President may be elected President only once. This limitation did not apply to President Truman, who was in office when Amendment 22 was proposed. Before this

by the Congress, and shall not prevent any person who may be holding the office of President, or acting as President, during the term within which this article becomes operative from holding the office of President, or acting as President during the remainder of such term.

Section 2. *This article shall be inoperative unless it shall have been ratified as an amendment to the Constitution by the legislatures of three fourths of the several states within seven years from the date of its submission to the states by the Congress.*

amendment was added, the Constitution placed no limit on the number of terms a President might serve. Presidents Washington and Jefferson, however, decided against a third term. This practice had been observed until 1940, when Franklin D. Roosevelt was elected for a third term.

SECTION 2
Limited Time for Ratification

Section 2 called for the approval of Amendment 22 within seven years.

Amendment 23

Section 1. The District constituting the seat of government of the United States shall appoint, in such manner as the Congress may direct:

A number of electors of President and Vice-President equal to the whole number of senators and representatives in Congress to which the District would be entitled if it were a state, but in no event more than the least populous state; they shall be in addition to those appointed by the states, but they shall be considered, for the purposes of the election of President and Vice-President, to be electors appointed by a state; and they shall meet in the District and perform such duties as provided by the twelfth article of amendment.

Section 2. The Congress shall have power to enforce this article by appropriate legislation.

Amendment 23
Voting in the District of Columbia (1961)

People who live in the District of Columbia may vote in presidential elections. They may choose as many electors as does the state with the smallest population. Before this amendment was adopted, residents of the District of Columbia had not voted for President and Vice-President because the Constitution provided that only states should choose presidential electors.

Amendment 24

Section 1. The right of citizens of the United States to vote in any primary or other election for President or Vice-President, for electors for President or Vice-President, or for senator or representative in Congress, shall not be denied or abridged by the United States or any state by reason of failure to pay any poll tax or other tax.

Amendment 24
Poll Tax Prohibited (1964)

Citizens may not be prevented from voting in a national election because they have not paid a state poll tax or other tax.

Section 2. The Congress shall have power to enforce this article by appropriate legislation.

Amendment 25

Section 1. In case of the removal of the President from office or of his death or resignation, the Vice-President shall become President.

Section 2. Whenever there is a vacancy in the office of the Vice-President, the President shall nominate a Vice-President who shall take office upon confirmation by a majority vote of both Houses of Congress.

Section 3. Whenever the President transmits to the President pro tempore of the Senate and the Speaker of the House of Representatives his written declaration that he is unable to discharge the powers and duties of his office, and until he transmits to them a written declaration to the contrary, such powers and duties shall be discharged by the Vice-President as Acting President.

Section 4. Whenever the Vice-President and a majority of either the principal officers of the executive departments or of such other body as Congress may by law provide, transmit to the President pro tempore of the Senate and the Speaker of the House of Representatives their written declaration that the President is unable to discharge the powers and duties of his office, the Vice-President shall immediately assume the powers and duties of the office as Acting President.

Thereafter, when the President transmits to the President pro tempore of the Senate and the Speaker of the House of Representatives his written declaration that no inability exists, he shall resume the powers and duties of his office unless the Vice-President and a majority of either the principal officers of the executive department or of such other body as Congress may by

Amendment 25
Presidential Disability (1967)

SECTION 1
Accession of the Vice-President

If the President dies or resigns, the Vice-President becomes President.

SECTION 2
Replacing the Vice-President

When there is a vacancy in the office of Vice-President, the President may appoint a person to be Vice-President. The appointment must be approved by a majority vote in both houses of Congress.

SECTION 3
Vice-President as Acting President

A President who is ill or unable to carry out official duties may assign those duties to the Vice-President by notifying the Speaker of the House and the President pro tempore of the Senate. The Vice-President then acts as President until the President is again able to serve.

SECTION 4
Determining Presidential Disability

If the President is ill or unable for other reasons to carry out official duties and is unable or unwilling to assign those duties to the Vice-President, the Vice-President and a majority of the Cabinet must notify the Speaker of the House and the President pro tempore of the Senate. The Vice-President then acts as President. The President cannot again assume official duties unless the Vice-President and a majority of the Cabinet agree that he is fit to do so. If the Vice-President and a majority of the Cabinet do not believe that the President is fit, Congress must meet and make a decision within 21 days. If two thirds of both houses of Congress feel that the President is unable to carry out the duties of his office, the Vice-President continues to act as President.

757

law provide, transmit within four days to the President pro tempore of the Senate and the Speaker of the House of Representatives their written declaration that the President is unable to discharge the powers and duties of his office. Thereupon, Congress shall decide the issue, assembling within forty-eight hours for that purpose, if not in session. If the Congress, within twenty-one days after receipt of the latter written declaration, or, if Congress is not in session, within twenty-one days after Congress is required to assemble, determines by two-thirds vote of both Houses that the President is unable to discharge the powers and duties of his office, the Vice-President shall continue to discharge the same as Acting President; otherwise, the President shall resume the powers and duties of his office.

Amendment 26

Section 1. The right of citizens of the United States who are eighteen years of age or older to vote shall not be denied or abridged by the United States or by any state on account of age.
Section 2. The Congress shall have power to enforce this article by appropriate legislation.

Otherwise, the President again takes over the duties of the presidency.

Amendment 26

Voting Age (1971)

The right to vote may not be denied because of age to any citizen who is eighteen or older.

The States

See p. T57 for a strategy asking students to use this table and the pictures of state flags in preparing a bulletin board display.

	State Name	Date of Admission	Population (1980 census)	Number of Representatives	Capital
1	Delaware	1787	595,225	1	Dover
2	Pennsylvania	1787	11,866,728	23	Harrisburg
3	New Jersey	1787	7,364,158	14	Trenton
4	Georgia	1788	5,464,265	10	Atlanta
5	Connecticut	1788	3,107,576	6	Hartford
6	Massachusetts	1788	5,737,037	11	Boston
7	Maryland	1788	4,216,446	8	Annapolis
8	South Carolina	1788	3,119,208	6	Columbia
9	New Hampshire	1788	920,610	2	Concord
10	Virginia	1788	5,346,279	10	Richmond
11	New York	1788	17,557,288	34	Albany
12	North Carolina	1789	5,874,429	11	Raleigh
13	Rhode Island	1790	947,154	2	Providence
14	Vermont	1791	511,456	1	Montpelier
15	Kentucky	1792	3,661,433	7	Frankfort
16	Tennessee	1796	4,590,750	9	Nashville
17	Ohio	1803	10,797,419	21	Columbus
18	Louisiana	1812	4,203,972	8	Baton Rouge
19	Indiana	1816	5,490,179	10	Indianapolis
20	Mississippi	1817	2,520,638	5	Jackson
21	Illinois	1818	11,418,461	22	Springfield
22	Alabama	1819	3,890,061	7	Montgomery
23	Maine	1820	1,124,660	2	Augusta
24	Missouri	1821	4,917,444	9	Jefferson City
25	Arkansas	1836	2,285,513	4	Little Rock
26	Michigan	1837	9,258,344	18	Lansing
27	Florida	1845	9,739,992	19	Tallahassee
28	Texas	1845	14,228,383	27	Austin
29	Iowa	1846	2,913,387	6	Des Moines
30	Wisconsin	1848	4,705,335	9	Madison
31	California	1850	23,668,562	45	Sacramento
32	Minnesota	1858	4,077,148	8	St. Paul
33	Oregon	1859	2,632,663	5	Salem
34	Kansas	1861	2,363,208	5	Topeka
35	West Virginia	1863	1,949,644	4	Charleston
36	Nevada	1864	799,184	2	Carson City
37	Nebraska	1867	1,570,006	3	Lincoln
38	Colorado	1876	2,888,834	6	Denver
39	North Dakota	1889	652,695	1	Bismarck
40	South Dakota	1889	690,178	1	Pierre
41	Montana	1889	786,690	2	Helena
42	Washington	1889	4,130,163	8	Olympia
43	Idaho	1890	943,935	2	Boise
44	Wyoming	1890	470,816	1	Cheyenne
45	Utah	1896	1,461,037	3	Salt Lake City
46	Oklahoma	1907	3,025,266	6	Oklahoma City
47	New Mexico	1912	1,299,968	3	Santa Fe
48	Arizona	1912	2,717,866	5	Phoenix
49	Alaska	1959	400,481	1	Juneau
50	Hawaii	1959	965,000	2	Honolulu
	District of Columbia		637,651	1 (non-voting)	
			226,504,825	435	

759

Flags of the Nation and the States

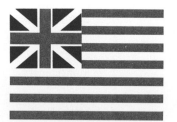

The Grand Union Flag

The First Stars and Stripes

The Flag of 1818

Above you see flags that have flown over our country. Patriot forces fought under the Grand Union flag during the first days of the Revolution. In 1777 Congress approved a new flag, with thirteen stripes and thirteen stars. After independence was won, an additional stripe and star were added each time a state entered the Union. In 1818 Congress decided to set the number of stripes at thirteen and to add a star for each new state. That practice has been followed ever since.

Alaska

Arizona

Florida

Georgia

Kansas

Kentucky

Minnesota

Mississippi

New Jersey

New Mexico

Oregon

Pennsylvania

Utah

Vermont

Have students prepare written or oral reports on the
history of their state flag.

Alabama

Arkansas

California

Colorado

Connecticut

Delaware

Hawaii

Idaho

Illinois

Indiana

Iowa

Louisiana

Maine

Maryland

Massachusetts

Michigan

Missouri

Montana

Nebraska

Nevada

New Hampshire

New York

North Carolina

North Dakota

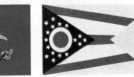

Ohio

Oklahoma

Rhode Island

South Carolina

South Dakota

Tennessee

Texas

Virginia

Washington

West Virginia

Wisconsin

Wyoming

The Presidents

See p. T57 for a strategy calling for students to list the Vice-Presidents and answer research questions.

	President	Dates	Years in Office	Party	Elected From
1	George Washington	1732–1799	1789–1797	None	Virginia
2	John Adams	1735–1826	1797–1801	Federalist	Massachusetts
3	Thomas Jefferson	1743–1826	1801–1809	Democratic–Republican	Virginia
4	James Madison	1751–1836	1809–1817	Democratic–Republican	Virginia
5	James Monroe	1758–1831	1817–1825	Democratic–Republican	Virginia
6	John Quincy Adams	1767–1848	1825–1829	National–Republican	Massachusetts
7	Andrew Jackson	1767–1845	1829–1837	Democratic	Tennessee
8	Martin Van Buren	1782–1862	1837–1841	Democratic	New York
9	William H. Harrison	1773–1841	1841	Whig	Ohio
10	John Tyler	1790–1862	1841–1845	Whig	Virginia
11	James K. Polk	1795–1849	1845–1849	Democratic	Tennessee
12	Zachary Taylor	1784–1850	1849–1850	Whig	Louisiana
13	Millard Fillmore	1800–1874	1850–1853	Whig	New York
14	Franklin Pierce	1804–1869	1853–1857	Democratic	New Hampshire
15	James Buchanan	1791–1868	1857–1861	Democratic	Pennsylvania
16	Abraham Lincoln	1809–1865	1861–1865	Republican	Illinois
17	Andrew Johnson	1808–1875	1865–1869	Republican	Tennessee
18	Ulysses S. Grant	1822–1885	1869–1877	Republican	Illinois
19	Rutherford B. Hayes	1822–1893	1877–1881	Republican	Ohio
20	James A. Garfield	1831–1881	1881	Republican	Ohio
21	Chester A. Arthur	1830–1886	1881–1885	Republican	New York
22	Grover Cleveland	1837–1908	1885–1889	Democratic	New York
23	Benjamin Harrison	1833–1901	1889–1893	Republican	Indiana
24	Grover Cleveland	1837–1908	1893–1897	Democratic	New York
25	William McKinley	1843–1901	1897–1901	Republican	Ohio
26	Theodore Roosevelt	1858–1919	1901–1909	Republican	New York
27	William H. Taft	1857–1930	1909–1913	Republican	Ohio
28	Woodrow Wilson	1856–1924	1913–1921	Democratic	New Jersey
29	Warren G. Harding	1865–1923	1921–1923	Republican	Ohio
30	Calvin Coolidge	1872–1933	1923–1929	Republican	Massachusetts
31	Herbert Hoover	1874–1964	1929–1933	Republican	California
32	Franklin D. Roosevelt	1882–1945	1933–1945	Democratic	New York
33	Harry S. Truman	1884–1972	1945–1953	Democratic	Missouri
34	Dwight D. Eisenhower	1890–1969	1953–1961	Republican	New York
35	John F. Kennedy	1917–1963	1961–1963	Democratic	Massachusetts
36	Lyndon B. Johnson	1908–1973	1963–1969	Democratic	Texas
37	Richard M. Nixon	1913–	1969–1974	Republican	New York
38	Gerald R. Ford	1913–	1974–1977	Republican	Michigan
39	Jimmy Carter	1924–	1977–1981	Democratic	Georgia
40	Ronald Reagan	1911–	1981–	Republican	California

Important Dates in American History

1000 Vikings cross Atlantic.
1095 Pope calls for Crusades.
1215 Magna Charta.
1275 Marco Polo reaches China on Asian travels (1271–1295).
1418 Portuguese explore African coast.
1450 Printing begins in Europe about this time.
1487 Dias reaches southern tip of Africa.
1492 Columbus lands in the Bahamas.
1493 Line of Demarcation.
1497 Cabot reaches North America.
1498 Da Gama reaches India.
1500 Cabral reaches Brazil.
1513 Balboa reaches Pacific Ocean.
Ponce de León explores Florida.
1519 Cortés lands in Mexico; conquers Aztec capital (1521).
1519–1522 Magellan's crew sails around world.
1524 Verrazano explores North American coast.
1532 Pizarro begins conquest of Peru.
1534 Cartier explores St. Lawrence River.
1540–1542 Coronado explores Southwest.
1541 De Soto reaches Mississippi River.
1551 University of Mexico started.
1565 Spanish start St. Augustine.
1576 Frobisher explores North American coast.
1577–1580 Drake sails around the world.
1585 "Lost Colony" started on Roanoke Island.
1588 Spanish Armada defeated.
1603 Champlain's first voyage to America.
1607 English start Jamestown.
1608 Champlain starts Quebec.
1609 Santa Fe settled.

1610 Hudson explores Hudson Bay.
1619 Virginia House of Burgesses established.
First blacks arrive in Jamestown.
1620 Pilgrims start Plymouth; draw up Mayflower Compact.
1625 Dutch start New Amsterdam.
1630 Puritans settle Boston.
1636 Roger Williams starts Rhode Island.
Connecticut settlements are begun.
Harvard College started.
1647 Massachusetts school law.
1649 Toleration Act in Maryland.
1660–1663 Navigation Acts passed.
1664 English capture New Amsterdam.
1670 Charles Town (Charleston), South Carolina, started.
1673 Marquette and Joliet explore Mississippi River.
1682 Pennsylvania started by Penn and Quakers.
La Salle reaches mouth of Mississippi River.
1689 English Bill of Rights.
1689–1763 English and French fight for North America.
1691 Plymouth and Massachusetts Bay Colony unite.
1693 College of William and Mary started.
1733 Georgia started.
1754 Albany Plan of Union.
1754–1763 French and Indian War.
1755 Braddock defeated.
1759 Battle of Quebec.
1763 Peace of Paris.
France is driven out of North America.
1763 Proclamation of 1763.
Pontiac's War.
1765 Stamp Act passed.
Stamp Act Congress.
Colonial boycott.

1766 Stamp Act repealed.
1767 Townshend Acts passed.
1769 Spanish build first mission in California.
First settlement in Tennessee.
1770 Boston Massacre.
1773 Boston Tea Party.
1774 Intolerable Acts.
First Continental Congress meets.
First settlement in Kentucky.
1775 Boonesborough settled.
1775–1783 Revolutionary War.
1775 Battles of Lexington and Concord.
Second Continental Congress meets.
Ethan Allen captures Crown Point and Ticonderoga.
Battle of Bunker Hill.
1776 Tom Paine's *Common Sense*.
British troops leave Boston.
Declaration of Independence.
Battle of Trenton.
1777 Battle of Princeton.
Battle of Saratoga; Burgoyne surrenders.
1777–1778 Washington at Valley Forge.
1778 Treaty of alliance with France.
1779 George Rogers Clark captures Vincennes.
Bonhomme Richard defeats *Serapis*.
1780 Battles of Kings Mountain and Cowpens.
1781 Cornwallis surrenders at Yorktown.
1783 Treaty of Paris; thirteen states win independence.
1781 Articles of Confederation go into effect.
1783 Loyalists sail for Halifax.
1784 *Empress of China* opens trade with China.
1785 Land Ordinance in Northwest Territory.

763

1787 Northwest Ordinance.
Constitution drafted.
1788 Marietta, Ohio, first town in Northwest Territory, started.
Constitution ratified.
1789 George Washington becomes President.
First Congress meets.
Supreme Court established.
French Revolution begins.
1790 Slater starts U.S. factory system.
1791 Vermont becomes a state.
Bill of Rights added to Constitution.
Quebec divided into Upper and Lower Canada.
1792 Kentucky becomes a state.
1793 Whitney invents cotton gin.
1794 Whiskey Rebellion.
Battle of Fallen Timbers.
1795 Jay's Treaty approved.
1796 Tennessee becomes a state.
1797 John Adams becomes President.
XYZ Affair.
1798 Sedition Act.
1801 Thomas Jefferson becomes President.
American fleet sent to fight Barbary pirates.
1803 Ohio becomes a state.
Fort Dearborn (Chicago) built.
Louisiana Purchase.
Marbury v. Madison decision.
1804 Lewis and Clark explore Louisiana Territory.
Republic of Haiti established.
1806 Pike explores more of Louisiana Territory.
1807 Embargo Act.
Fulton's steamboat is successful.
1809 James Madison becomes President.
1810 Father Hidalgo starts Mexican revolt against Spain.

Miranda starts Venezuelan revolt against Spain.
1811 National Road is begun.
Battle of Tippecanoe.
1812 Louisiana becomes a state.
1812–1814 War of 1812.
1814 Francis Scott Key writes "The Star-Spangled Banner."
Hartford Convention.
Treaty of Ghent.
1815 Jackson defeats British at New Orleans.
1816 Congress approves a protective tariff.
Indiana becomes a state.
1817 James Monroe becomes President.
Mississippi becomes a state.
1818 Illinois becomes a state.
1819 Spain cedes Florida to U.S.
Alabama becomes a state.
1820 Missouri Compromise.
Maine becomes a state.
Land law makes public lands cheaper.
1821 First public high school (Boston).
Missouri becomes a state.
Mexico and Peru proclaim independence from Spain.
Bolívar's victory frees Venezuela.
1822 Austin leads American colonists into Texas.
Brazil proclaims independence from Portugal.
1823 Monroe Doctrine proclaimed.
1824 Battle of Ayacucho. All Spanish colonies in South America are liberated.
1825 John Quincy Adams becomes President.
Erie Canal completed.
1829 Andrew Jackson becomes President.
1830 Cooper's locomotive makes successful run.
Webster-Hayne debate.
Congress passes Indian Removal Act.

1831 McCormick reaper invented.
Nat Turner leads slave revolt.
First issue of *The Liberator*.
1832 South Carolina nullifies protective tariff.
Jackson vetoes Bank Bill.
1833 Compromise tariff.
New York *Sun* begins first penny daily newspaper.
Oberlin accepts women students.
1834 Whig Party formed.
1836 Texas declares independence from Mexico; Battles at Alamo, San Jacinto.
Arkansas becomes a state.
First women's college opens.
1837 Martin Van Buren becomes President.
Panic of 1837.
Michigan becomes a state.
1838 Lord Durham's report recommends responsible government for Canada.
Cherokee forced west.
1841 William Henry Harrison becomes President.
John Tyler becomes President on Harrison's death (April).
1844 Morse telegraph successful.
1845 James K. Polk becomes President.
Florida and Texas become states.
Howe perfects sewing machine.
1846 Oregon divided between Britain and U.S.
Iowa becomes a state.
Canada gains responsible government.
1846–1848 Mexican War.
1847 Mormons settle in Utah.
Douglass publishes *The North Star*.
1848 Gold discovered in California.

Mexican Cession.
Women's Rights Convention at Seneca Falls.
Wisconsin becomes a state.

1849 Zachary Taylor becomes President.
California gold rush.

1850 Millard Fillmore becomes President on Taylor's death (July).
Compromise of 1850.
California becomes a state.
Cotton production passes two million bales.

1852 *Uncle Tom's Cabin* published.
First railroad from East reaches Chicago.

1853 Franklin Pierce becomes President.
Gadsden Purchase.

1854 Perry persuades Japan to make trade treaty with U.S.
Kansas-Nebraska Act.
Republican Party started.

1856 Bessemer process for making steel.

1857 James Buchanan becomes President.
Dred Scott decision.
First elevator in New York City.

1858 Lincoln-Douglas debates.
Minnesota becomes a state.

1859 John Brown attacks Harpers Ferry.
First oil well drilled in Pennsylvania.
Oregon becomes a state.

1860 South Carolina secedes.
Pony Express established.

1861 Abraham Lincoln becomes President.
Kansas becomes a state.
Confederacy is formed.

1861– 1865 Civil War.
1861 Fort Sumter fired upon.
First Battle of Bull Run.
1862 *Monitor* fights *Merrimack.*
Farragut captures New Orleans for North.

Battles of Shiloh, Seven Days, Fredericksburg.
1863 Emancipation Proclamation.
Battle of Chancellorsville.
Battle of Gettysburg.
Surrender of Vicksburg.
Gettysburg Address.
1864 Sherman captures Atlanta and Savannah.
1865 Lee surrenders to Grant at Appomattox Court House.

1862 Homestead Act passed.
Morrill Act paves way for land-grant colleges.

1863 West Virginia, a part of Virginia, becomes a separate state.

1864 Nevada becomes a state.

1865 Andrew Johnson becomes President on Lincoln's assassination (April).
Thirteenth Amendment abolishes slavery.

1866 Atlantic cable successfully laid.

1867 Nebraska becomes a state.
First Reconstruction Act.
Alaska bought from Russia.
Midway Islands acquired.
Grange movement starts.

1868 Fourteenth Amendment defines American citizenship.

1869 Ulysses S. Grant becomes President.
First transcontinental railroad completed.
Knights of Labor founded.
First professional baseball club.
Steel plow perfected.

1870 Fifteenth Amendment states voters' rights.

1873 First American schools of nursing opened.

1876 Bell invents telephone.
Custer's force wiped out by Sioux Indians.
Colorado becomes a state.

1877 Rutherford B. Hayes becomes President.
Chief Joseph surrenders.
Last Union troops withdrawn from South.
Railroad strike.

1878 First telephone exchange.

1879 Edison invents electric light.

1881 James A. Garfield becomes President.
Chester A. Arthur becomes President on Garfield's death (September).
American Red Cross established.

1882 Chinese immigration restricted.

1883 Civil Service Commission established.

1885 Grover Cleveland becomes President.

1886 AFL (American Federation of Labor) formed.

1887 Interstate Commerce Act.
Dawes Act provides land and citizenship for Indians.

1889 Benjamin Harrison becomes President.
Jane Addams establishes Hull House.
North Dakota, South Dakota, Montana, Washington become states.

1890 Disappearance of frontier announced.
Sherman Antitrust Law.
Idaho and Wyoming become states.
Populist Party started.

1893 Grover Cleveland becomes President for second time.
First successful automobile.

1896 *Plessy v. Ferguson* decision.
Utah becomes a state.

1897 William McKinley becomes President.

1898 Spanish-American War: U.S. acquires Philippines, Puerto Rico, Guam; frees Cuba.
U.S. annexes Hawaii; acquires Wake Island.

1899 Open Door Policy proposed.
First Hague Peace Conference.
U.S. acquires American Samoa.

1900 Boxer Rebellion.

1901 Theodore Roosevelt becomes President on McKinley's assassination (September).

1903 U.S. leases Canal Zone in Panama.
Wright brothers make first successful airplane flight.

1905 U.S. expands Monroe Doctrine.

1906 Pure Food and Drug Act.

1907 Second Hague Peace Conference.
Immigration rate at all-time high.
Oklahoma becomes a state.

1908 National Conservation Conference.

1909 William H. Taft becomes President.

1910 Mexican Revolution starts.
NAACP (National Association of Colored People) formed.

1912 New Mexico and Arizona become states.
Massachusetts minimum wage law.

1913 Woodrow Wilson becomes President.
Sixteenth Amendment makes income tax legal.
Seventeenth Amendment provides for election of senators by voters.
Federal Reserve Act.

1914 Panama Canal opened.
Federal Trade Commission formed.
Clayton Act.

1914–1918 World War I.
1915 *Lusitania* sunk.
1917 U.S. enters the war.
1918 Battles of St. Mihiel, Argonne.
Armistice, on November 11, 1918, ends World War I.

1917 Virgin Islands purchased from Denmark.
Communists seize power in Russia.

1919 Eighteenth Amendment establishes prohibition.
Treaty of Versailles.

1919–1920 U.S. rejects League of Nations.

1920 League of Nations formed.
Nineteenth Amendment gives all women the vote.
First American radio broadcasting station.
Half of U.S. population counted as urban.

1921 Warren G. Harding becomes President.
Washington Arms Conference.
World Court organized.

1922 Mussolini seizes power in Italy.

1923 Calvin Coolidge becomes President on Harding's death (August).

1924 All Indians made citizens.

1927 Lindbergh flies non-stop from New York to Paris.
The Jazz Singer—first talking movie.

1929 Herbert Hoover becomes President.
Great Depression begins.

1931 Japan invades Manchuria.

1932 Amelia Earhart flies the Atlantic alone.

1933 Franklin D. Roosevelt becomes President.
Hitler seizes power in Germany.
Twentieth Amendment provides that presidential and congressional terms begin earlier.
Roosevelt pledges Good Neighbor policy.
Tennessee Valley Authority.
Twenty-First Amendment repeals prohibition.

1934 U.S. Marines leave Latin America.
U.S. gives up right of interference in Cuba.

Indian Reorganization Act.

1935 CIO (Congress of Industrial Organizations) formed.
Wagner Act.
Social Security Act.
Italy attacks Ethiopia.

1936 Hoover Dam completed.

1937 Japanese invade China.

1938–1939 Germany occupies Austria and Czechoslovakia.

1939 First regular television broadcasts.

1939–1945 World War II.
1939 Germany invades Poland.
1940 Nazis conquer Norway, Denmark, Belgium, Holland, France.
1941 Lend-Lease Act.
Germany attacks Russia.
Atlantic Charter.
Pearl Harbor attacked by Japan—U.S. enters war.
1942 American troops in Philippines forced to surrender. U.S. victories at Coral Sea, Midway, Guadalcanal.
Allies land in North Africa.
1943 Allies land in Sicily and Italy.
1944 Allied invasion at Saipan, Guam, Leyte.
1945 Battles of Iwo Jima and Okinawa.
UN formed.
Germany surrenders.
Atomic bombs force Japan to surrender.

1944 GI Bill of Rights.

1945 Harry S. Truman becomes President on Roosevelt's death (April).

1946 Philippine independence.

1947 Truman Doctrine announced.
Marshall Plan.
Taft-Hartley Act.

1949 NATO created.
Communists come to power in China.

1950 UN intervention in Korea.

1951 Twenty-Second Amendment puts two-term limit on presidency.
1952 McCarran Immigration Act.
Puerto Rico becomes self-governing commonwealth.
1953 Dwight D. Eisenhower becomes President.
Korean truce signed.
1954 Supreme Court decision on school segregation.
1955 AFL-CIO merger.
1956 Suez Canal crisis.
1957 Soviet Union launches first Sputnik.
1958 U.S. launches its first satellite.
1959 Alaska and Hawaii become states.
Castro leads Cuban revolt.
Landrum-Griffin Act.
1960 Summit meeting canceled over U-2 incident.
1961 John F. Kennedy becomes President.
Peace Corps formed.
Twenty-Third Amendment allows D.C. residents to vote for President.

Berlin Wall built.
First men in space.
1962 U.S. quarantines Cuba.
First U.S. manned orbital space flight.
1963 Civil rights demonstrations.
Test-ban treaty.
1963 Lyndon Johnson becomes President on Kennedy's assassination (November).
1964 Twenty-Fourth Amendment abolishes poll tax.
Civil Rights Act.
1965 Increased American involvement in Vietnam.
Medicare and Voting Rights Act passed.
Immigration quota system ended.
1967 Twenty-Fifth Amendment establishes procedures in case of presidential disability.
Arab-Israeli war.
1968 Martin Luther King, Jr. and Robert F. Kennedy assassinated.
1969 Richard M. Nixon becomes President.
American astronauts land on the moon.

1971 Twenty-Sixth Amendment lowers the voting age to 18 years.
1972 President Nixon visits China and Soviet Union.
1973 Vietnam War ends.
Military draft ended.
Arab-Israeli War resumes.
Gerald R. Ford replaces Spiro T. Agnew as Vice-President.
1974 Gerald R. Ford becomes President on resignation of Richard M. Nixon (August).
1976 U.S. celebrates two-hundredth birthday.
1977 Jimmy Carter becomes President.
1978 Agreement reached with Panama over Panama Canal.
1981 Ronald Reagan becomes President.
American hostages released by Iran.
First woman appointed to Supreme Court.

Acknowledgments

Text Credits

Grateful acknowledgment is made to authors, publishers, and other copyright holders for permission to reprint (and in some selections to adapt slightly) copyright material listed below.

Page 33: From *The Travels of Marco Polo,* translated by W. Marsden (1811), revised by T. Wright (1854), Everyman's Library Edition. Reprinted by permission of E. P. Dutton & Co., Inc. **Page 42:** From *The Journal of Christopher Columbus,* translated by Clements R. Markham. The Hakluyt Society, London, 1960. Reprinted by permission of The Hakluyt Society, c/o The British Library. **Page 74:** From "The Spanish Conquerors," by I. B. Richman, Volume 2, The Yale Chronicles of America series, copyright United States Publishers Association, Inc. **Pages 105-106:** From *History of Plimouth Plantation* by William Bradford. **Page 124:** From *The Life of George Mason* by Kate Rowland, 1892, G. P. Putnam's Sons. **Page 177:** *A Retrospect of the Boston Tea Party with a Memoir of George R. T. Hewes,* 1834. **Pages 177-178:** "An Ancient Prophecy," by Philip Freneau. **Pages 181-182:** "Paul Revere's Ride," by Henry Wadsworth Longfellow. **Page 182:** "Concord Hymn," by Ralph Waldo Emerson. **Page 185:** From *Familiar Letters of John Adams and His Wife Abigail Adams, during the Revolution* by Charles Francis Adams (New York: Hurd and Houghton), 1876. **Page 210:** From *Military Journal during the American Revolutionary War, from 1775 to 1783* by James Thacher, 1854. **Page 251:** Speech by Benjamin Franklin at the Constitutional Convention, 1787. **Page 280:** "The Star-Spangled Banner," by Francis Scott Key. **Page 292:** From *Two Years Before the Mast* by Richard Henry Dana, 1840, E. P. Dutton & Co., Inc. **Page 298:** From *America Visited* by Edith I. Coombs (New York: The Book League of America). **Pages 306-307:** From *Leading American Inventors* by George Iles. Holt, Rinehart & Winston, 1912. **Pages 307-308:** From "Oliver Evans and His Inventions," by Coleman Sellers, *Journal of the Franklin Institute* (July, 1886: Vol. CXXII). **Pages 308-309:** From *American Notes* by Charles Dickens, 1842. **Page 315:** From "Correspondence of Eli Whitney," edited by M. B. Hammond, *The American Historical Review,* Vol. III, 1897-98. **Page 340:** From *Recollections of Life in Ohio from 1813 to 1840* by William Cooper Howells. Published by Robert Clarke, Cincinnati, 1895. **Page 341:** From *Domestic Manners of the Americans* by Frances Trollope, 1832. **Page 345:** From *The United States: The History of a Republic* by Richard Hofstadter, William Miller, and Daniel Aaron, p. 123. Copyright ©1957. Reprinted by permission of Prentice-Hall, Inc., Englewood Cliffs, N.J. **Page 345:** From *American History Told by Contemporaries,* Vol. III, edited by Albert Bushnell Hart (New York: The Macmillan Company), 1901. **Pages 374-375:** Speech by Major Davezac at the New Jersey State Democratic Convention, 1844. **Pages 390-391:** From *Sutter of California* by Julian Dana, Macmillan Publishing Company, Inc., 1934. **Pages 395-396:** From *Roughing It* by Mark Twain. Reprinted by permission of Harper & Row, Publishers, Inc. **Pages 462-463:** From *The Life and Times of Red-Jacket, or Sa-Go-Ye-Wat-Ha; Being the Sequel to the History of the Six Nations* by William L. Stone, 1841. **Pages 472-473:** From *The Story of the Cowboy* by Emerson Hough. Copyright ©1930, D. Appleton Company, 1958, Clara Hough. Reprinted by permission of Hawthorn Properties (Elsevier-Dutton Publishing Co., Inc.). **Page 474:** From *Pioneer Women: Voices from the Kansas Frontier* by Joanne L. Stratton. Copyright ©1981. Reprinted by permission of Simon & Schuster, Inc. **Page 515:** Speech by David Parry, from *Proceedings of the Eighth Annual Convention of the National Association of Manufacturers of the United States of America Held at New Orleans, La., April 14, 15, and 16, 1903,* Indianapolis, 1903: "Annual Report of the President." **Page 515:** From "Why Men Fight for the Closed Shop," by Clarence Darrow. *American Magazine,* September, 1911. Reprinted from *Annals of America,* ©1968 by Encyclopedia Britannica. **Page 569:** From *The Game of Baseball.* George Munro and Son, 1868. **Page 577:** From *The Life and Work of Susan B. Anthony* by Ida Husted Harper, Vol. II (Indianapolis: The Hollenbeck Press), 1908. **Page 667:** From *The Gallup Poll, 1935-1971, Volume I* by Dr. George H. Gallup. Copyright ©1972 by American Institute for Public Opinion. Reprinted by permission of Random House, Inc.

Art Credits

Cover: Concept and photograph by Skolos/Wedell & Raynor.

Frontispiece: Museum of the City of New York.

Maps: All maps pages 29-696 by Dick Sanderson. All maps pages 724-729 by Donnelley Cartographic Services (pages 724-725, Robinson Projection).

Time lines, graphs, and diagrams by I² Graphics, except pages 149, 285, 369, 599 by Mark Mulhall.

Illustrations on pages 68, 150, 232, 286, 370, 454, 532, 578 and 638 by John V. Morris. Page 712 by Mark Mulhall.

Issue Cartoons by Bill Ogden.

The following abbreviations are used for a few sources from which many illustrations were obtained:

HPS — Historical Pictures Service, Inc., Chicago.
NPG — National Portrait Gallery, Smithsonian Institution, Washington, D.C.
UPI — United Press International.
WHHA — ©White House Historical Association, photograph by The National Geographic Society.

5 "Washington at Verplank's Point, New York, 1782, Reviewing the French Troops after the Victory at Yorktown," by John Trumball, courtesy of the Henry Francis du Pont Winterthur Museum (detail). 6 "First Landing of Christopher Columbus" (detail) by Frederick Kemmelmeyer, National Gallery of Art, Washington, gift of Edgar William and Bernice Chrysler Garbisch. 7 "The Battle of Bunker's Hill" (detail) by John Trumbull, ©Yale University Art Gallery. 8 Marshall Johnson, "U.S.S. Constitution" (detail), Peabody Museum of Salem, photo by Mark Sexton. 9 ©Jay Lurie Photography. 10 ©Bill Weems/Woodfin Camp and Associates. 11, 12 Library of Congress. 13 Chuck O'Rear/West Light. 20 John Colwell/Grant Heilman. 21 Tim Kilby/Uniphoto. 22 ©David Cupp 1980/Woodfin Camp and Associates. 23 G. Brimacombe/The Image Bank.

24-25 (clockwise from left) The Granger Collection, New York; National Maritime Museum/Michael Holford; courtesy of the United States Naval Academy Museum; reproduced by permission of the Huntington Library, San Marino, CA. 26 Rare Book and Manuscripts Division, New York Public Library/Astor, Lenox and Tilden Foundations. 28 The Granger Collection, New York. 31 HPS. 38 The British Museum/photo: Michael Holford. 39 The Granger Collection, New York. 41 Christian Krohg: "Leif Eiriksson Discovers America," Nasjonalgalleriet, Oslo. 44 (clockwise from top left)

Brogi/Alinari/EPA; from *The Journal of Christopher Columbus,* published by Clarkson N. Potter, Inc.; The Granger Collection, New York. 48 "Chief of the Taensa Indians Receiving La Salle, March, 1682" (detail), George Catlin/National Gallery of Art, Washington: Paul Mellon Collection. 51 The Thomas Gilcrease Institute of American History and Art, Tulsa, Ok. 58 Courtesy of The Power Authority of the State of New York. 61 "Father Marquette and the Indians" (detail), 1869, by William Lamprecht, Marquette University Art Collection.

70-71 (left to right) The Granger Collection, New York; ©Terence Spencer/Colorific!; The National Park Service; Confederation Life Collection. 72 Stokes Collection, New York Public Library/Astor, Lenox and Tilden Foundations. 74 The Bettmann Archive. 76 Pete Turner/Image Bank. 79 (top) Courtesy of American Museum of Natural History; (bottom) American Museum of Natural History/Lee Boltin. 80 Evans from Shostal Associates. 81 Courtesy of Remington Art Museum, Ogdensburg, N.Y. 82 ©David Barr/Arizona Department of Library, Archives and Public Records. 84 (clockwise from top left) Courtesy of the Edward E. Ayer Collection, The Newbury Library, Chicago, Il.; Ted Mahieu/Image Bank; The Granger Collection, New York. 88 Christian Delbert/Picture Cube. 90 Detail from painting by Tom Leas, Dallas Museum of Fine Arts, gift of Life Magazine, 1960. 92 Mansell Collection. 96 Courtesy of the Pilgrim Society, Plymouth, Ma. 100, 102 Colonial Williamsburg photograph. 103 The Virginia State Library. 104 The Granger Collection, New York. 107 Courtesy of The New-York Historical Society, New York City. 109 HPS. 112 Stokes Collection, New York Public Library/Astor, Lenox and Tilden Foundations. 114 Historical Society of Pennsylvania. 118 Print Collection, New York Public Library/Astor, Lenox and Tilden Foundations. 120 Colonial Williamsburg photograph. 121 New York State Historical Association, Cooperstown. 122 Gift of Joseph W., William B., and Edward H. R. Revere/courtesy Museum of Fine Arts, Boston. 125 Collection of Carolina Art Association/Gibbes Art Gallery. 128 The Abby Aldrich Rockefeller Folk Art Center. 131 The Brooklyn Museum, Dick S. Ramsay Fund. 135, 136 Stokes Collection, New York Public Library/Astor, Lenox and Tilden Foundations. 138-139 Courtesy of The Power Authority of the State of New York. 141 Courtesy of the Fruitlands Museums, Harvard, Ma. 144 Culver Pictures. 145 Metropolitan Toronto Library. 146 Picture Division, Public Archives of Canada, Ottawa.

152 (left) Courtesy of Kennedy Galleries, Inc., N.Y.; (right) "The Spirit of '76" (detail) by Archibald M. Willard, Board of Selectmen, Abbot Hall, Marblehead, Ma. 153 The Metropolitan Museum of Art, gift of John Stewart Kennedy, 1897 (detail). 154 Virginia State Library. 157 ©W. Hubbell, 1979/Woodfin Camp and Associates. 159 James Holland/Stock Boston. 161 The New-York Historical Society, New York City. 162 National Park Service. 164-165 Stokes Collection, New York Public Library/Astor, Lenox and Tilden Foundations. 168 ©1974, American Heritage Publishing Co., Inc., by Don Troiani. 171, 172 HPS. 175 (clockwise from top) Franklin Institute of Boston; John Hancock Life Insurance Company; U.S. Post Office. 176 Courtesy of The Bostonian Society. 177 The Harry T. Peters Collection, Museum of the City of New York. 179 Library of Congress. 180 Patrick Henry Memorial Foundation. 181 John Hancock Life Insurance Company. 186 Delaware Art Museum, Howard Pyle Collection (detail). 188 The Joseph Dixon Crucible Company Collection. 189 National Park Service. 192 Historical Society of Pennsylvania. 198 New York State Historical Association, Cooperstown. 199 (clockwise from top left) Washington/Custis/Lee Collection Washington and Lee University (detail); "The Washington Family" (detail) by Edward Savage, National Gallery of Art, Washington, Andrew W. Mellon Collection; Collection of The Valley Forge Historical Society. 200 HPS. 202 Emmet Collection, New York Public Library/Astor, Lenox and Tilden Foundations. 204 National Archives. 207 HPS. 210 ©Jim Anderson, 1981/Woodfin Camp and Associates. 214 ¡BOLIVAR LIBERTADOR! (detail) by Tito Salas, courtesy of Geomundo. 216 HPS. 217 Picture Division, Public Archives of Canada, Ottawa, Negative #C2001. 220 Picture Division, Public Archives of Canada, Ottawa, Negative #C-396. 222 HPS. 223 Hamilton Wright, N.Y. 226 The Bettmann Archive. 228 ©Loren McIntyre.

234 (left) The Metropolitan Museum of Art, "The American Star" (detail) by F. Kemmelmeyer; (right) Louisiana State Museum. 235 "Salute to General Washington In New York Harbor" (detail) by L. M. Cooke, National Gallery of Art, Washington, gift of Edgar William and Bernice Chrysler Garbisch. 236 Index of American Design, National Gallery of Art, Washington. 243 Keystone Mast Collection, California Museum of Photography, University of California, Riverside. 245 National Geographic Society, courtesy U.S. Capitol Historical Society. 247 The State of New Hampshire. 251 The Metropolitan Museum of Art, "Benjamin Franklin" (detail) by J. S. Duplessis. 252 Library of Congress. 255 The Bettmann Archive. 259 Historical Paintings Collection — The Continental Insurance Companies. 261 (clockwise from top) Historical Society of Pennsylvania; courtesy The United States Coast Guard; The Metropolitan Museum of Art, gift of Henry G. Marquand, 1881 (detail). 264 (top to bottom) NPG; WHHA; WHHA; NPG; James Monroe Museum (Fredricksburg, Va). 268 The Metropolitan Museum of Art, gift of Edgar William and Bernice Chrysler Garbisch, 1968 (detail). 271 The Bettmann Archive. 272 New York Public Library/Astor, Lenox and Tilden Foundations. 275 The Bettmann Archive. 277 (clockwise from top) The Bettmann Archive; courtesy of The New-York Historical Society, New York City; Thomas Jefferson Memorial Foundation. 278 The Bettmann Archive. 281 Stokes Collection, New York Public Library/Astor, Lenox and Tilden Foundations. 283 Library of Congress.

288-289 (left to right) The Harry T. Peters Collection, Museum of the City of New York; Chicago Historical Society; Chicago Historical Society; courtesy of Kennedy Galleries, Inc., N.Y. 290 J. P. Newell: Lazell Perkins and Co., in the Collection of the Corcoran Gallery of Art, Museum Purchase, Mary E. Maxwell Fund (detail). 294 Courtesy of The Mariners Museum of Newport News, Va. 295 Peabody Museum of Salem/photo by Mark Sexton. 297 Smithsonian Institution, photo #P64260-A (detail). 301 Barfoot for Dartan "Progress of Cotton (#6 — Spinning)" (detail) Yale University Art Gallery, The Mabel Brady Garvan Collection. 304 New York State Historical Association, Cooperstown. 306 The Harry T. Peters Collection, Museum of the City of New York. 308-309 The Metropolitan Museum of Art, "The 9:45 Accomodation . . ." (detail) by Edward Lamson Henry. 314 Los Angeles County Museum of Art, acquisition made possible through Museum Trustees: Robert O. Anderson, R. Stanton Avery, B. Gerald Canton, Edward W. Carter, Justin Dart, Charles E. Ducommun, Mrs. F. Daniel Frost, Julian Ganz, Jr., Dr. Armand Hammer, Harry Lenart, Dr. Franklin Murphy, Mrs. Joan Palevsky, Richard E. Sherwood, Maynard J. Toll and Hal B. Wallis (detail). 316 "Eli Whitney" (detail) by Samuel F. B. Morse, Yale University Art Gallery, gift of George Hoadley, 1801. 318 Library of Congress. 320 Knox College, Galesburg, Il./Mississippi River Collection. 321 "The Wedding" (detail) by E. L. Henry, Clapp Collection, Fitchburg Art Museum, Fitchburg, Ma. 322 The Brooklyn Museum, gift of Miss Gwendlyn O. L. Conkling. 323 Courtesy of the San Antonio Museum Association, San Antonio, Tx. 325 Bradley Smith. 326 HPS. 330 Collection of Miss Amelia Peabody/courtesy of Time-Life Books, Inc. 332 Transylvania University Library. 337 Stokes Collection, New York Public Library/Astor, Lenox and Tilden Foundations. 338 Delaware

Art Museum (detail). **339** The Granger Collection, New York. **341** Public Buildings Service, photo #121-PS-1832 in the National Archives. **342** Kentucky Library, Western Kentucky University. **346** Architect of the Capitol/James R. Dunlop Inc. **348** Library of Congress. **352** NPG. **353** (clockwise from top right) The Bettmann Archive; Collection of The Hermitage/Roloc Color Slides; "General Andrew Jackson" (detail) by Thomas Sully, in the collection of the Corcoran Gallery of Art, gift of William Wilson Corcoran. **356** Courtesy of The Henry Francis du Pont Winterthur Museum (detail). **358** Life Magazine/J. R. Eyerman. **359** The Sophia Smith Collection (Women's Archive), Smith College, Northampton, Ma. **360** Karolik Collection/Museum of Fine Arts, Boston. **364** (top to bottom) WHHA; The Metropolitan Museum of Art, Harris Brisbane Dick Fund, 1964 (detail); WHHA; NPG; NPG. **366** Indiana Historical Society.

372-373 (left to right) Library of Congress; West Point Museum Collections, United States Military Academy; National Park Service; The Museum of the Confederacy, Brockenbrough Library. **374** Private Collection/Time-Life Books, Inc. **376** Montana Historical Society, Helena, Mt. **380** ©Steve Proehl/Photo Researchers, Inc. **381** Courtesy of the San Antonio Museum Association, San Antonio, Tx. **382** The Granger Collection, New York. **383** (clockwise from top left) The Bettmann Archive; Texas Highway Department; courtesy of the R. W. Norton Art Gallery, Shreveport, La (detail). **387** Courtesy Amon Carter Museum, Fort Worth. **389** William H. Meyers, "Battle of the Plains" (detail), courtesy of Franklin D. Roosevelt Library. **390-391** Karolik Collection/Museum of Fine Arts, Boston. **393** State Historical Society of Wisconsin. **395** Tucson Museum of Art/Scott Garber. **396** The Thomas Gilcrease Institute of American History and Art, Tulsa, Ok. **397** Museum of Fine Arts, Houston, The Hogg Brothers Collection. **398-399** Amon Carter Museum, Fort Worth, Tx. **404** Anne S. K. Brown Military Collection, Brown University Library. **409** (portraits) NPG; (bottom) H. S. Newman/courtesy Time-Life Books, Inc. **410** The Granger Collection, New York. **412** Courtesy of The New-York Historical Society, New York City. **413** (top left) Cincinnati Art Museum; (others) Library of Congress. **415** Courtesy of the Illinois State Historical Library. **416** The Metropolitan Museum of Art, gift of Mr. and Mrs. Carl Stoeckel, 1897 (detail). **420** The Seventh Regiment Fund. **424** New York Public Library/Astor, Lenox and Tilden Foundations. **431** (clockwise from top left) Uniphoto/Robert M. Anderson; National Archives; courtesy United States Naval Academy Museum. **432** Library of Congress. **433** Collection of Oliver Jensen. **435, 437** Chicago Historical Society. **439** National Park Service, Department of the Interior. **440** Culver Pictures. **442** (clockwise from top left) Courtesy of the New-York Historical Society, New York City; Library of Congress; "Lincoln at Gettysburg" (detail) by Fletcher Cransom, Forest Lawn Museum, Glendale, California. **445** Culver Pictures. **446** The Metropolitan Museum of Art, "The Cabbage Patch" (detail) by Thomas Anschutz. **447** Library of Congress. **448** (top to bottom) WHHA; WHHA; WHHA; NPG; NPG. **449** (top) "Abraham Lincoln" (detail) by George Peter Alexander Healy, in the collection of the Corcoran Gallery of Art. **449** (bottom) Andrew Johnson National Site. **450** Atlanta Historical Society.

456-457 (left to right) State Historical Society of Wisconsin; Museum of the City of New York; "The Turret Lathe Operator" (detail) by Grant Wood, 1925, Cedar Rapids Art Center, Cedar Rapids, Iowa, courtesy of Associated American Artists; ©1968 by Henry Austin Clark, Jr. **458** The Harry T. Peters Collection, Museum of the City of New York. **461** Courtesy of Southern Pacific Company. **462** Library of Congress. **463** Gift of Mrs. Blanche F. Hooker, courtesy of the Detroit Institute of Arts. **464** American Museum of Natural History. **465** (clockwise from top left) The Thomas Gilcrease Institute of American History and Art, Tulsa, Ok.; NPG; Smithsonian Institu-

tion, photo #43.201. **469** Montana Historical Society, Helena, Mt. **470** The Thomas Gilcrease Institute of American History and Art, Tulsa, Ok. **471** Courtesy of the Buffalo Bill Historical Center, Cody, Wy. **474** Solomon D. Butcher Collection, Nebraska State Historical Society. **477** Library of Congress. **478** The Metropolitan Museum of Art, "Forging the Shaft: A Welding Heat" (detail) by John F. Weir. **480** (left) Amon Carter Museum, Fort Worth; (right) The Denver Art Museum. **482** General Electric Lamp Division. **483** Henry Ford Museum, The Edison Institute. **484** Courtesy of The New-York Historical Society, New York City. **486** HPS. **487** AT&T. **488** Library of Congress. **490** Culver Pictures. **492** Brown Brothers. **495** (top left) NPG; (bottom left) Bethlehem Steel Corporation. **496** New York Public Library/Astor, Lenox and Tilden Foundations. **497** Rockefeller Archive Center. **502** Library of Congress. **505** Private Collection. **507** Culver Pictures. **508** Public Affairs Press. **509** (clockwise from top left) Harper's Weekly, December 25, 1886; Tamiment Collection, Elmer Holmes Bobst Library, New York University; Brown Brothers. **511** Brown Brothers. **512** Department of Labor. **515** Brown Brothers. **516** International Harvester. **518** G. E. Anderson/Heritage Prints Collection Library. **520** Utah State Historical Society. **521** Harald Sund. **525** Library of Congress. **526** New York Public Library/Astor, Lenox and Tilden Foundations. **527** Brown Brothers. **528** Grant Heilman Photography.

534-535 (left to right) "Baseball Players Practicing" (detail) by Thomas Eakins, Rhode Island School of Design Museum; The Granger Collection, New York; The Sophia Smith Collection (Women's Archive), Smith College, Northampton, Ma.; Parrish Art Museum, Littlejohn Collection/photo: Richard P. Meyer. **536, 539** Museum of the City of New York. **540** State Historical Society of Wisconsin. **541** (both) International Museum of Photography at the George Eastman House. **542** (top) Photoworld; (bottom) reproduced by permission of the American Museum in Britain, Bath. **544** (top) Amon Carter Museum, Fort Worth, Tx.; (bottom) ©Jay Lurie Photography. **547** Courtesy The New-York Historical Society, New York City. **549** (all) University of Illinois Library at Chicago Circle Campus, Jane Addams Memorial Collection. **550** (top) Library brary of Congress; (bottom) The Metropolitan Museum of Art, The Jefferson P. Burdick Collection (detail). **552** Charlton Photos/Webb-Ag. **556** Brett/Liaison. **558** Brown Brothers. **559** Culver Pictures. **560** Lawrence Fried/Image Bank. **561** (left) Owen Franken/Stock Boston; (right) ©Jason Lauré/Woodfin Camp and Associates. **562** John Running/Stock, Boston. **564** Bradley Smith. **565** Kansas State Historical Society. **566** (clockwise from top left) New York Public Library/Astor, Lenox and Tilden Foundations; The Bettmann Archive; The Sophia Smith Collection (Women's Archive), Smith College, Northampton, Ma. **569** Library of Congress. **570** Courtesy of The New-York Historical Society, New York City. **571** California Historical Society, San Francisco. **573** The Thomas Gilcrease Institute, Tulsa, Ok. **574** The Metropolitan Museum of Art, bequest of Mrs. H. O. Havemeyer, 1929, The H. O. Havemeyer Collection (detail). **577** Culver Pictures.

580-581 (all) Library of Congress. **582** Courtesy of Kennedy Galleries, Inc., N.Y. **585** Hudson's Bay Company. **586** Harper's Weekly, March 24, 1877. **587** (top to bottom) Chicago Historical Society; WHHA; NPG; NPG; WHHA. **588** (top to bottom) WHHA; Eugene Matie/National Portrait Gallery, Smithsonian, Washington, D.C.; WHHA; NPG; NPG. **590** The Bettmann Archive. **592-593** National Museum of American Art (formerly the National Collection of Fine Arts), Smithsonian Institution, lent by Department of the Interior, National Park Service. **594** (left) The Bettmann Archive; (right) Theodore Roosevelt Collection/Harvard College Library. **597** Culver Pictures. **600** Chicago Historical Society. **603** Peabody Museum of Salem/photo by Mark Sexton. **604** The Granger Collection, New York. **607** Chicago Historical Society. **609** Library of Congress. **610** ©Luis Villota/The Stock Market.

613 National Archives photo #185-G-2046. **614** Richard Steedman/The Stock Market. **617** The New York *Journal*. **618** Courtesy United States Naval Academy Museum. **620** Library of Congress. **622** Milt and Joan Mann. **625** Brown Brothers. **628** Erich Lessing/Magnum. **630** Library of Congress. **631** The Granger Collection, New York. **633** Keystone Press Agency. **637** (right) ©*Punch*/Rothco.

640-641 (left to right) U.S. Marine Corps, Art Collection History and Museums Division, HQMC; Shelly Katz/Black Star; Robert Kelly/Life Magazine, ©Time Inc.; NASA. **642** U.S. Army. **644** (top to bottom) WHHA; Division for Historic Preservation, Vt.; NPG; NPG. **645** Brown Brothers. **647** (clockwise from left) UPI; Franklin Delano Roosevelt Library; The Little White House, Franklin D. Roosevelt Warm Springs Memorial Commission, Warm Springs, Ga. **648** National Archives photo #35-G-262. **650** UPI. **653** Library of Congress. **657** Katherine Young Photography. **659** Wide World. **660** (left) National Archives, Exhibit #168; (right) Library of Congress. **662** Library of Congress. **663** UPI. **668** ©Tom Tracy/Black Star. **670** Wide World Photos. **671** F. Henle/Photo Researchers, Inc. **672** (both) WHHA. **675** UPI. **676** ©1961, Burt Glinn/Magnum. **678** UPI photo 1059-460. **681** UPI from JO/Files. **684** NASA. **686** George Tames/*The New York Times*. **687** Fred Ward/Black Star. **688** Sergio Larrain/Magnum. **689** (clockwise from left) Bob Adelman/Magnum; UPI; Dan Weiner/Magnum. **691** ©Jim Pickerell, 1981. **694** Pictorial Parade, Inc./NASA. **695** Magnum. **698** (top) ©Bachrach; (remainder) UPI. **699** (top to bottom) UPI; White House, Washington; UPI. **700** J. P. Laffont/Sygma. **702** (left) ©Freda Leinwand/Monkmeyer Press; (right) ©Gerald Brimacombe/Image Bank. **703** ©Jay Lurie Photography. **705** Uniphoto. **706** Melloul/Sygma, Paris. **707** Bill Fitzpatrick, The White House. **708** UPI. **709** John Sotomayor/*The New York Times*.

714 ©Jim Pickerell. **715** ©Robert M. Anderson/Uniphoto. **716** Roger A. Clark, Jr./Photo Researchers. **717** Richard Howard. **760-761** Early U.S. flags by Rusty Brough, state flags courtesy of *The Texas Star*, Texaco, Inc.

Index

Fourteenth Amendment, 445–446, 751

Fox Indians, *m* 50, 354, *m* 354

Fox River, 62, *m* 62

France, explorations by, 57–58, *m* 59, 59–60, *m* 62, 62–63; claims in America, 63, 64, *m* 64, *m* 67; pirates of, 91; American colonies of, 137–140, *m* 143, 155; conflicts with Britain, 140–147, *m* 143, *p* 144, *p* 146, 197, 275; and American Revolution, 197, *m* 205, 208, 209–210; settlers in Haiti, 222, *m* 225; U.S. relations with, 269, 270, 272–273, 275, 276; end of treaty of alliance with, 273; sells Louisiana territory to U.S., 275, 375; and Panama Canal, 611, 612; and China, 620; and Mexico, 623–624; in World War I, 627, *m* 629, 631, 632; and Versailles Treaty, 632–633; and naval limitation, 651; and policy of appeasement, 655–656; in World War II, *m* 655, 655–656, 658, *m* 661, 663; and UN, 672; after World War II, *m* 673; in NATO, 675; in Suez crisis, 676–677; Berlin zone of, 690

Franklin, Benjamin, 216; picture story, *p* 175; in Revolution, *p* 192, 197; at Constitutional Convention, 242–243, *p* 245, 246, 251; quoted, 251; portrait, *p* 251

Frederick, King of Prussia, 197

Fredericksburg, Md., *m* 434, 434–435

Freedmen's Bureau, 444, *p* 445

Freedom, sought by settlers, 92–99, *p* 98–99; growing spirit of, 157, 164; individual, and factory system, 301; problems of, with abolition of slavery, 325; in Northwest Territory, 336; restricted in Soviet Union, 652; Nazi threat to, 658

Freedom of the press, 166

Freedom of religion, in colonies, 98–99, 105, 106, 109, 110, 128, 540; denied by Puritans, 106–107

Freedom rides, 686

Free enterprise system, 652

Free trade, 610, 611

Frémont, John C., 387, 414

French, Daniel Chester, 573

French and Indian War, 142–147, *m* 143, *m* 146, 238

French Canadians, 218, 219, 398

French Indochina, *m* 654, 658, 663, *m* 664

Frobisher, Martin, 58–59, *m* 60, 64, 93

Frobisher Bay, *m* 60

Frontier, life on, 129–132, *p* 132, 340–341; British try to close, *m* 170; Revolution on, 206, 208; pushed west, 331–332, 333, 462, 538; Vermont as part of, 339; disappearance of, 468, 475, 520; last, settlement of, 474; immigrants head for, 537. *See also* West

Frost, Robert, 572

Fugitive Slave Law, 411

Fulton, Robert, 306–307; quoted, 306–307

Fur trade, in New Netherland, 113; on colonial frontier, 129, 131; in New France, 138–139; China and, 292; in late 1700's, 331; in 1800's, 378, 398, 399, 464; in Alaska, 585

Future Farmers of America, 530

Gadsden Purchase, *m* 388, 389

Gagarin, Yuri, 678

Gage, Thomas, 178, 180, 187

Gallaudet, Thomas H., 359

Galveston, Texas, 451, *m* 460

Galvez, Bernardo de, 197

Gama, Vasco da, *m* 37, 38, 39

Gao, *m* 37, 38

Garfield, James A., 589; portrait, *p* 587

Garland, Hamlin, 572

Garrison, William Lloyd, 357–358

Gas, natural, 706

Gasoline, 491

Gasoline engine, 490, 491, 519

Gatty, Harold, 492

Gehrig, Lou, 569

Genesee Road, *m* 303

Genêt, "Citizen" Edmond, 270

Genoa, *m* 29, 31, *m* 32, 35, 36, 39

George II, King of England, 111

George III, King of England, 173, 178, 179, 189, 211

Georgia, colonial, *m* 108, 111, 158–159; in Revolution, 208; ratifies Constitution, 248; cotton and rice grown in, 317, 318, *m* 319; runaway slaves from, 379; secedes, 418; in Civil War, 437–438, *m* 438; first women's college established in, 565; voting age in, 697; *m* 727; flag, *p* 760

Germantown, Battle of, *m* 201, 203

Germany, immigrants from, 114, 128, 462, 537–538, 539; revolution in, 539; and World War I, 627, 628–630, *m* 629, 631–632, *m* 634; and Versailles Treaty, 633, 651, 653, 654–655; U.S. makes separate peace with, 635; under Hitler, 653; aggressions of, 654–655, *m* 655; and World War II, 656–657, 658, 659, *m* 661, 662, 663, 669, 673

Geronimo, 467

Gershwin, George, 575

Gettysburg, Battle of, *m* 434, *p* 435, 435–436

Gettysburg Address, 436; text of, 436

Ghent, *m* 279; Treaty of, 281

Ghost Dances, 467

Ghost towns, 394, 470

Gibbs, Jonathan, 362

GI Bill of Rights, 669

Gila River, *m* 385, *m* 392

Gilbert Islands, *m* 664

Glasgow, Ellen, 572

Glidden, J. F., 476

Goethals, George, 613

Gold, in California, 389–393, *p* 390–391, 469; in Black Hills, 466, 470; in Rocky Mountains, 469–471; in Alaska, 585

Gold Bug, The (Poe), 363

Golden Hind (ship), *p* 70, 91–92

Goldwater, Barry, 687

Goliad, Tex., 384, *m* 385

Gompers, Samuel, 508; picture story, *p* 509

Good Neighbor Policy, 601, 651

Goodnight-Loving Trail, *m* 460

Goodyear, Charles, 491

Gorgas, William C., 609, 613

Government, of English colonies, 104, 105, 155–156, 158–160, *c* 167; of Upper and Lower Canada, 218, 219, 220; of states, 237, 446–447; under Articles of Confederation, 238–241, *c* 254; under Constitution, 253–257, *c* 254, *c* 257; encourages manufacturing, 299–300; in Northwest Territory, 334–336, *p* 342; and states' rights, 406–407; in South after Civil War, 446–447, 585; encourages railroad building, 460; policy toward Indians, 463, 466, 467–468; aid to farmers by, 526, 528–529, 596, 646; and merit system, 586, 589; and reforms of early 1900's, 593–594; and business interests, 602, 650; efforts to end depression, 645, 646–648; increased cost and power of, 649–650; and loans to veterans, 669

Governors, colonial, 138, 158–159; of Canada, 218; of Northwest, 334; women as, 567; of Philippines, 610; of Guam and American Samoa, 615

Grand Canyon, *m* 83, 571, *m* 591, *m* 728

Grand Coulee Dam, 521, 649

Grange, 524–526, *p* 525, *p* 526

Grant, Ulysses S., in Civil War, 424–425, 430–432, 436, 438–439, *p* 439; as President, 584; portrait, *p* 587

Graphs, reading, 267, 329, 403, 499, 711

Gray, Robert, 292, 397

Great Britain, relations with Canada, 215, 219–220; U.S. disputes with, 269, 270–272; and War of 1812, 275–282; Industrial Revolution in, 296; American trade with, 299, 300, 365; and Oregon claim, 397, 399, 400–401; and South, in Civil War, 428; wireless communication with, 488; and Panama Canal, 611, 612; seizes Hong Kong, 620; Monroe Doctrine used against, 624; in World War I, 627,

779

419–420; quoted, 418, 420, 436, 441, 443; and problem of seceded states, 419–420; in Civil War, 428, 433, 434, 435, 437; gives Gettysburg Address, 436; issues Emancipation Proclamation, 441; plans for peace, 441–443; picture story, *p* 442; re-elected President, 443; assassinated, 443; portrait, *p* 449

Lincoln, Mary Todd, 425, *p* 442, 443

Lincoln Memorial, *p* 10, *p* 373, 573

Lindbergh, Ann Morrow, *p* 492

Lindbergh, Charles, 491, *p* 492

Line of Demarcation, *m* 56, 57, 91

Liquor, forbidden in Maine, 360; and temperance movement, 649

Lisbon, Portugal, *m* 37, 39

Literature, in early 1800's, 363; about America, 571–572

Lithuania, *m* 634, *m* 661

Little Bighorn, Battle of, 466, *m* 467

Little Crow, Chief, 466

Little House on the Prairie (Wilder), 572

Little Women (Alcott), 572

Livingstone, Robert, 274

Lloyd George, David, 632, 633

Local history, exploring, 683

Lockwood, Belva, 584

Log cabin, *p* 132

London, England, 651, *m* 661

London, Jack, 572

London Company, 103, 104

Lone Star Republic, 384

Long drive, 471, 472

Longfellow, Henry Wadsworth, 363; quoted, 181–182

Long hunters, 331

Long Island, 201, *m* 201

Longitude, 34; lines of, 47, *m* 47

Long Winter, The (Wilder), 572

Looms, power, 296

Los Angeles, *m* 385, *m* 392, 394, *m* 460; name of, 94; as part of megalopolis, 551; black mayor of, 560; Puerto Ricans in, 611

Louis XIV, King of France, 140

Louisbourg, 142, *m* 143, 145, *p* 145

Louisiana, French settlers in, 148; name of, 250; sugar cane grown in, 318; becomes state, 318, 339, 378, 379, 405; secedes, 418; in Civil War, *m* 430; federal troops removed from, 586; *m* 727; flag, *p* 761

Louisiana Purchase, *m* 274, 274–275, *m* 388

Louisiana Territory, acquired by U.S., 375, *m* 377; explored by Lewis and Clark, and by Pike, *p* 376, 376–377, *m* 377; settlers in, 378; issue of slavery in, 405–406

Louisville, Ky., *m* 303, *m* 545

L'Ouverture, Toussaint, 222, *p* 222

Lowell, Francis, 297

Lowell, Mass., 298

Lower California, 82, *m* 83

Lower Canada, 218, *m* 218, 219, 220

Loyalists, in Revolution, 196, 201; go to Canada, 216–217, *p* 217, 218, *m* 218

Luck of Roaring Camp, The (Harte), 571

Lumber industry, 402, 450, 502

Lusitania, 628–629

Luxembourg, *m* 673, 675

MacArthur, Douglas, in World War II, 663, 664; in Korean War, 675, *p* 675

McCarran Act, 543

McCarthy, Joseph, *p* 678

McClellan, George B., 434

McCormick, Cyrus, 518

MacDowell, Edward, 574

McGovern, George, 695

Machines, goods produced by, 479; office, 492, 564; and increased production, 501; working conditions changed by, 506; farm, 518–519, 552. *See also* Factories; Manufacturing

McKay, Donald, 295

McKinley, William, 527, 591, 604; portrait, *p* 588

McLoughlin, John, 399

Madison, Dolley, 280

Madison, James, at Constitutional Convention, 242; and *Federalist*, 248; as President, 265, 276; portrait, *p* 264

Magazines, 573

Magellan, Ferdinand, 54–56, *m* 55, *m* 57, 64

Magna Charta, 156

Mail service, colonial, 312; by stagecoach and Pony Express, 394–396; by airplane, 491

Mail-order houses, 485

Maine, *m* 108, 339, 360, 406, *m* 727; flag, *p* 761

Maine (ship), 606

Majority, defined, 557

Malaya, *m* 654, 658, 663, *m* 664

Mali, 37, *m* 37, 38

Manassas Junction, 428, *m* 434

Manchuria, *m* 621; Russia controls, 620, 623; seized by Japan, 654; *m* 654, 658

Mandan Indians, *m* 50, 376

Manhattan Island, 113

Manila, *m* 605, 607, *m* 654, *m* 664

Manitoba, *m* 231

Mann, Horace, 361

Manor, 27–28, *p* 28

Mansfield, Arabella, 565

Manufacturing, colonial, 162; and War of 1812, 282; growth of, 296–298, 365, 479, 601; government encourages, 299–300; and steam power, 305; and mineral resources, 480; and mass production, 483–

484; new markets for, 484–485; in Puerto Rico, 610. *See also* Factories; Industry

Mao Tse-tung, 695

Maps, reading, 47, 67, 95, 231, 313, 423, 531

Marbury v. Madison, 263

Marconi, Guglielmo, 488

Mardi gras, 148

Marianas Islands, 615, *m* 664

Marietta, Ohio, *m* 335, 337

Mariner spacecraft, 694

Marines, sent to Haiti, 624; withdrawn from Dominican Republic, 651; in World War II, 661, 664; sent to Lebanon, 677

Marion, Francis, *m* 205, 208

Marketing, 484–485, 602

Marne River, *m* 629, 631

Marquette, Jacques, *p* 61, 61–62, *m* 62, 64, 139

Mars, orbited by spacecraft, 694

Marshall, George C., 636, 662, 674

Marshall, James, 390–391

Marshall, John, 263

Marshall, Thurgood, 560

Marshall Islands, *m* 664

Marshall Plan, 674

Maryland, colonial, *m* 108, 110, 158; Annapolis Convention in, 241; ratifies Constitution, 248; name of, 250; in Civil War, 426, *m* 434; *m* 727; flag, *p* 761

Mason, Donald, 666

Mason and Dixon's Line, *m* 319, 324

Massachusetts, colonial, 105–107, *m* 108, 121–122, 155–156, 158–159; resistance to Britain in, 174–177, 180–183; British punishment of, 178; ratifies Constitution, 248; name of, 250; textile industry in, 296, 297, 298; western land claims of, *m* 239; minimum wage law in, 513; *m* 727; flag, *p* 761

Massachusetts Bay Company, 106

Mass selling, 485

Mass-transit systems, 703–704

Maximilian, Emperor of Mexico, 623–624

Mayas, *m* 77

Mayflower (Pilgrim ship), *p* 96, 105

Mayflower (flatboat), 337

Mayflower II, 116

Mayflower Compact, 105

Mays, Willie, 569

Meade, George, 435

Meat, inspection of, 593

Medicare, 687

Medicine, advances in, 360, 702

Mediterranean Sea, *m* 29, 294

Megalopolis, 551

Memphis, *m* 310, *m* 429, *m* 430, *m* 460, 668

Menlo Park, 482

Mennonites, 462

Merit system, 586, 589

785